Fodor's 20th Edition

Eastern and Central Europe

The Guide
for All Budgets

Completely
Updated

Where to Stay, Eat,
and Explore

On and Off
the Beaten Path

When to Go,
What to Pack

Maps, Travel Tips,
and Web Sites

Fodor's Travel Publications • New York, Toronto, London, Sydney, Auckland
www.fodors.com

Fodor's Eastern and Central Europe

EDITORS: Deborah Kaufman, Douglas Stallings

Editorial Contributors: Andrew Anderson, Maria Nickolova Anderson, Joyce Dalton, Lisa Dunford, Jane Foster, Satu Hummasti, Raymond Johnston, Tomáš Kleisner, Betsy Maury, Saša Petriskova, Julie Tomasz, Dorota Wąsik, Scott Alexander Young, Slawomir Zurek
Maps: David Lindroth, *cartographer*; Rebecca Baer and Robert Blake, *map editors*
Design: Fabrizio La Rocca, *creative director*; Guido Caroti, *art director*; Jolie Novak, *senior picture editor*; Melanie Marin, *photo editor*
Cover Design: Pentagram
Production/Manufacturing: Robert B. Shields
Cover Photo (Old Town Square, Prague): David Hanson/Stone/Getty Images

Copyright

Twentieth Edition

ISBN 1–4000–1094–2

ISSN 1074–1216

Important Tip

Although all prices, opening times, and other details in this book are based on information supplied to us at press time, changes occur all the time in the travel world, and Fodor's cannot accept responsibility for facts that become outdated or for inadvertent errors or omissions. So **always confirm information when it matters,** especially if you're making a detour to visit a specific place.

Special Sales

Fodor's Travel Publications are available at special discounts for bulk purchases for sales promotions or premiums. Special editions, including personalized covers, excerpts of existing guides, and corporate imprints, can be created in large quantities for special needs. For more information, contact your local bookseller or write to Special Markets, Fodor's Travel Publications, 1745 Broadway, New York, NY 10019. Inquiries from Canada should be directed to your local Canadian bookseller or sent to Random House of Canada, Ltd., Marketing Department, 2775 Matheson Boulevard East, Mississauga, Ontario L4W 4P7. Inquiries from the United Kingdom should be sent to Fodor's Travel Publications, 20 Vauxhall Bridge Road, London SW1V 2SA, England.

PRINTED IN THE UNITED STATES OF AMERICA

10 9 8 7 6 5 4 3 2 1

CONTENTS

ON THE ROAD WITH FODOR'S

A trip takes you out of yourself. Concerns of life at home completely disappear, driven away by more immediate thoughts—about, say, what marvels will beguile the next day, or where you'll have dinner. That's where Fodor's comes in. We make sure that you know all your options, so that you don't miss something that's around the next bend just because you didn't know it was there. Mindful that the best memories of your trip might have nothing to do with what you came to Eastern and Central Europe to see, we guide you to sights large and small all over the region. You might set out to see Prague Castle but back at home you find yourself unable to forget the sunset over Lake Bled in Slovenia or that beautiful church in Gdańsk. With Fodor's at your side, serendipitous discoveries are never far away.

Andrew Anderson and Maria Nickolova Anderson, who updated our Bulgaria chapter, live in Roussé and Sofia. Andrew, who is from London, saw Bulgaria for the first time on a bicycle trip from London to Istanbul in 1996. He later came back to work for the United Nations and spent four years restoring historic buildings. He now works in real estate. Maria, who was born in Russia, returned to her father's homeland as a child. She is presently studying law in Sofia and has published stories in the Bulgarian magazine *PS*.

Romania updater **Joyce Dalton,** a New Jersey–based travel writer and photographer, contributes to numerous trade and consumer publications. She fell under the spell of Romania's mountains and traditional villages in 1988, and although her travels have taken her to some 150 countries on six continents, it's Romania that draws her back again and again. She owns land in the traditional Maramureş region and hopes to construct a house, complete with hand-carved Maramureş gate.

Slovakia updater **Lisa Dunford** is a freelance travel writer and editor who spent several years living and working in Bratislava. She returns to Slovakia as often as possible, though she now calls Texas home. Lisa

has been an editor on several Fodor's Gold Guides, including *Brazil, 2nd edition; Japan, 16th edition;* and *Australia 2003.*

Jane Foster, who put together this edition's new Croatia chapter, is a freelance writer from the Yorkshire Dales, U.K. She studied for a degree in architecture before moving to Rome in 1990, where travel, art, and culture became her main interests. In 1996 she made a brief visit to Croatia and was immediately captivated by the countries of the former Yugoslavia. She now lives in Split, Dalmatia, and has traveled extensively through Slovenia, Croatia, and Bosnia-Herzegovina, rating the Adriatic coast, "where the mountains reach the sea," the most stunningly beautiful region in Europe. She writes for a number of American and European travel publications, focusing primarily on Slovenia, Croatia, and Italy.

Born and raised in New York City, **Raymond Johnston,** our updater for the Czech Republic, worked for on-line publications in the early days of the Internet before moving to Prague in 1996. After a stint teaching English, he returned to journalism and has written about Czech culture, film production, and travel for numerous publications including *The Prague Post,* where he is the editor of the entertainment section. His hobby of visiting castles and ruins has taken him all over Central Europe.

Tomáš Kleisner was born in Prague when it was still under Communist control. He studied art history at Charles University and now works in the National Museum in Prague. He has contributed to other travel guides on his native city and updated Smart Travel Tips for this book.

Betsy Maury, a former senior editor with the U.S. publisher Bantam Doubleday Dell, spent four years in Slovenia before settling in Budapest, where she now lives with her husband and works as a freelance writer. She updated the Slovenia chapter for our guide.

Saša Petriskova, who also worked on the Slovakia chapter, is the mother of two beautiful and challenging children and a native of the country, where she resides with her family in Bratislava. Previously Saša has worked for Slovak Radio, as a tour guide, and for the U.S. Agency for International Development.

Cracovian by birth, education, and choice, **Dorota Wąsik,** who updated sections of the Poland chapter on Kraków, Małopolska, and Eastern Poland, has been studying and teaching the history of her city for nearly three decades. She's traveled her country far and wide, working as a guide and filmmaker. Although she's seen the world, all roads take her back to Kraków. She's published two guidebooks to her city, *Living in Kraków* and *Visible Cities Kraków,* as well as numerous articles on art, architecture, and travel.

Hungary updater **Scott Alexander Young** is now back in the U.K. after quite a few years all over Central and Eastern Europe, where he lived in Budapest and Kraków. Though originally he took the attitude that writing assignments in Central and Eastern Europe would lead to "better things," he is in the process of reinventing his life in the West.

Slawomir Zurek, who updated the Warsaw and Western Poland sections of our Poland chapter, works in a public relations agency in Warsaw. He used to work in a number of marketing firms in London, where he also began doing freelance work for *Newsweek* and *People.* Now he is also a correspondent for *People* in Poland.

You can rest assured that you're in good hands—and that no property mentioned in the book has paid to be included. Each has been selected strictly on its merits, as the best of its type in its price range.

How to Use This Book

Up front is **Smart Travel Tips A to Z,** arranged alphabetically by topic and loaded with tips, Web sites, and contact information. **Destination: Eastern and Central Europe** helps get you in the mood for your trip. Subsequent chapters in *Fodor's Eastern and Central Europe* are arranged regionally. All city chapters begin with exploring information, with a section for each neighborhood (each recommending a good tour and listing sights alphabeti-

cally). All regional chapters are divided geographically; within each area, towns are covered in logical geographical order, and attractive stretches of road between them are indicated by the designation **En Route.** To help you decide what you'll have time to visit, all chapters begin with our writers' favorite itineraries. (Mix itineraries from several chapters, and you can put together a really exceptional trip.) The **A to Z** section that ends every chapter lists additional resources. At the end of the book you'll find some suggestions for **Further Reading,** followed by **Vocabularies** for all the languages spoken in the region.

Icons and Symbols

★	Our special recommendations
✕	Restaurant
🏠	Lodging establishment
✕🏠	Lodging establishment whose restaurant warrants a special trip
🛆	Campgrounds
🐤	Good for kids (rubber duck)
☞	Sends you to another section of the guide for more information
✉	Address
☎	Telephone number
☉	Opening and closing times
💷	Admission prices (those we give apply to adults; substantially reduced fees are almost always available for children, students, and senior citizens)

Numbers in white and black circles ③ ❸ that appear on the maps, in the margins, and within the tours correspond to one another.

For hotels, you can assume that all rooms have private baths, phones, TVs, and air-conditioning unless otherwise noted and that all hotels operate on the European Plan (with no meals) if we don't specify another meal plan. We always list a property's facilities but not whether you'll be charged extra to use them, so when pricing accommodations, do ask what's included. For restaurants, it's always a good idea to book ahead; we mention reservations only when they're essential or are not accepted. All restaurants we list are open daily for lunch and dinner unless stated otherwise; dress is mentioned only when men are required to wear a jacket or a jacket and tie. Look for an overview of local dining-out habits in **Smart Travel Tips A to Z** and in the **Pleasures and Pastimes** section that follows each chapter introduction.

Don't Forget to Write

Your experiences—positive and negative—matter to us. If we have missed or misstated something, we want to hear about it. We follow up on all suggestions. Contact the Eastern and Central Europe editor at editors@fodors.com or c/o Fodor's at 1745 Broadway, New York, NY 10019. And have a fabulous trip!

Karen Cure
Editorial Director

Eastern and Central Europe

ESSENTIAL INFORMATION

AIR TRAVEL

BOOKING

When you book **look for nonstop flights** and **remember that "direct" flights stop at least once.** Try to avoid connecting flights, which require a change of plane. Two airlines may operate a connecting flight jointly, so ask if your airline operates every segment of the trip; you may find that the carrier you prefer flies you only part of the way. To find more booking tips and to check prices and make on-line flight reservations, log on to www.fodors.com.

CARRIERS

Many U.S. airlines have a European co-carrier that provides connecting service to Eastern and Central Europe from a gateway in Europe. The major European airlines listed here offer service from North America, with connecting service to Eastern and Central Europe from the country's capital. Several of the national airlines of the countries in Eastern and Central Europe offer nonstop service from the U.S.; others offer only connecting service from within Europe. There is no direct air service between North America and Croatia, Slovakia, or Slovenia. Slovak Airlines offers service only between Moscow and Bratislava and is not listed here.

➤ MAJOR U.S. AND EUROPEAN AIRLINES: **Air France** (☎ 800/237–2747 in the U.S; 0845/084–5111 in the U.K.; WEB www.airfrance.com). **Alitalia** (☎ 800/223–5730 in the U.S.; 0870/544–8259 in the U.K.; WEB www.alitaliausa.com in the U.S.; www.alitalia.co.uk in the U.K.). **American** (☎ 800/433–7300 in the U.S.; 0845/778–9789 in the U.K.; WEB www.aa.com). **Austrian Airlines** (☎ 800/843–0002 in the U.S.; 0845/601–0948 in the U.K.; WEB www.austrianair.com in the U.S.; www.austrianairlines.co.uk in the U.K.). **British Airways** (☎ 800/

247–9297 in the U.S.; 0845/733–3777 in the U.K.; WEB www.britishairways.com). **Continental** (☎ 800/231–0856 in the U.S.; 0800/776–464 in the U.K.; WEB www.continental.com). **Delta** (☎ 800/241–4141 in the U.S.; 0800/414–767 in the U.K.; WEB www.delta.com). **Finnair** (☎ 800/950–5000 in the U.S.; 0870/241–4411 in the U.K.; WEB www.finnair.com). **KLM Royal Dutch Airlines** (☎ 800/225–2525 in the U.S.; 0870/507–4074 in the U.K.; WEB www.klm.com). **Lufthansa** (☎ 800/645–3880 in the U.S.; 0845/773–7747 in the U.K.; WEB www.lufthansa.com). **Northwest** (☎ 800/447–4747 in the U.S.; 0870/507–4074 in the U.K.; WEB www.nwa.com). **SAS Scandinavian Airlines** (☎ 800/221–2350 in the U.S.; 0845/6072–7727 in the U.K.; WEB www.scandinavian.net). **Swiss International Airlines** (☎ 877/359–7947 in the U.S.; 0845/601–0956 in the U.K.; WEB www.swiss.com). **United** (☎ 800/538–2929 in the U.S.; 0845/844–4777 in the U.K.; WEB www.ual.com).

➤ NATIONAL AIRLINES WITH SERVICE FROM BOTH THE U.S. AND EUROPE: Czech Republic: **Czech Airlines** (CSA; ☎ 212/765–6022 in the U.S.; 020/7255–1898 in the U.K.; WEB www.csa.cz). Hungary: **Malév Hungarian Airlines** (☎ 212/757–6480 or 800/223–6884 in the U.S.; 020/7439–0577 in the U.K.; WEB www.malev.hu). Poland: **LOT Polish Airlines** (☎ 800/223–0593 in the U.S.; 0845/601–0949 or 020/7580–5037 in the U.K.; WEB www.lot.com). Romania: **Tarom Romanian Airlines** (☎ 212/560–0840 in the U.S.; 020/7224–3693 in the U.K.).

➤ NATIONAL AIRLINES WITH SERVICE ONLY WITHIN EUROPE: Croatia: **Croatia Airlines** (☎ 020/8563–0022 in the U.K.; 2/413–776 in Croatia; WEB www.croatiaairlines.hr). Slovenia: **Adria Airways** (☎ 020/7734–4630 in the U.K.; 01/436–9720 in Slovenia; WEB www.adria.si).

CHECK-IN AND BOARDING

Always **ask your carrier about its check-in policy.** Plan to arrive at the airport about 2 hours before your scheduled departure time for domestic flights and 2½ to 3 hours before international flights.

Assuming that not everyone with a ticket will show up, airlines routinely overbook planes. When everyone does, airlines ask for volunteers to give up their seats. In return, these volunteers usually get a certificate for a free flight and are rebooked on the next flight out. If there are not enough volunteers, the airline must choose who will be denied boarding. The first to get bumped are passengers who checked in late and those flying on discounted tickets, so **get to the gate and check in as early as possible,** especially during peak periods.

Always **bring a government-issued photo ID to the airport;** even when it's not required, a passport is best.

CUTTING COSTS

The least expensive airfares to Eastern and Central Europe are priced for round-trip travel and must usually be purchased in advance. Airlines generally allow you to change your return date for a fee; most low-fare tickets, however, are nonrefundable. It's smart to **call a number of airlines and check the Internet;** when you are quoted a good price, **book it on the spot**—the same fare may not be available the next day. Always **check different routings** and look into using alternate airports. Also, price off-peak flights, which may be significantly less expensive than others. Travel agents, especially low-fare specialists (☞ Discounts and Deals, *below*), are helpful.

Consolidators are another good source. They buy tickets for scheduled international flights at reduced rates from the airlines, then sell them at prices that beat the best fare available directly from the airlines. Sometimes you can even get your money back if you need to return the ticket. Carefully read the fine print detailing penalties for changes and cancellations, purchase the ticket with a credit card, and **confirm your consolidator reservation with the airline.**

➤ CONSOLIDATORS: **Cheap Tickets** (☎ 800/377–1000 or 888/922–8849, WEB www.cheaptickets.com). **Discount Airline Ticket Service** (☎ 800/576–1600). **Unitravel** (☎ 800/325–2222, WEB www.unitravel.com). **Up & Away Travel** (☎ 212/889–2345, WEB www.upandaway.com). **World Travel Network** (☎ 800/409–6753).

ENJOYING THE FLIGHT

State your seat preference when purchasing your ticket, and then repeat it when you confirm and when you check in. For more legroom, you can request one of the few emergency-aisle seats at check-in, if you are capable of lifting at least 50 pounds—a Federal Aviation Administration requirement of passengers in these seats. Seats behind a bulkhead also offer more legroom, but they don't have under-seat storage. Don't sit in the row in front of the emergency aisle or in front of a bulkhead, where seats may not recline.

Ask the airline whether a snack or meal is served on the flight. If you have dietary concerns, **request special meals when booking.** These can be vegetarian, low-cholesterol, or kosher, for example. It's a good idea to pack some healthy snacks and a small (plastic) bottle of water in your carry-on bag. On long flights, try to maintain a normal routine, to help fight jet lag. At night, **get some sleep.** By day, **eat light meals, drink water** (not alcohol), and **move around the cabin** to stretch your legs. For additional jet-lag tips consult *Fodor's FYI: Travel Fit & Healthy* (available at bookstores everywhere).

Smoking policies vary from carrier to carrier. Many airlines prohibit smoking on all of their international flights; others allow smoking only on certain routes or certain departures. Ask your carrier about its policy.

FLYING TIMES

Travel time to Central Europe can vary greatly depending on whether or not you can get a nonstop flight. A nonstop flight from NYC to Prague takes 8 hours; connecting flights to Sofia can make that trip last more than 14 hours. The only three non-stop flights from New York are to Prague (8 hours), Budapest (9 hours), and Warsaw (9 hours). There are two direct flights from Chicago: to Warsaw (9 hours) and Dubrovnik (15 hours). Most trips from the U.S. require a change at Frankfurt, London, Paris, Prague, Zurich, Amsterdam, or Vienna and can take up to 15 hours. Direct flights from London to all Central European capitals take between 2 and 3½ hours. From Sydney you will have to fly first of all to London or Amsterdam (23 hours).

HOW TO COMPLAIN

If your baggage goes astray or your flight goes awry, complain right away. Most carriers require that you **file a claim immediately.** The Aviation Consumer Protection Division of the Department of Transportation publishes *Fly-Rights,* which discusses airlines and consumer issues and is available on-line. At PassengerRights.com, a Web site, you can compose a letter of complaint and distribute it electronically.

➤ AIRLINE COMPLAINTS: **Aviation Consumer Protection Division** (✉ U.S. Department of Transportation, Room 4107, C-75, Washington, DC 20590, ☎ 202/366–2220, 𝕎𝔼𝔹 www.dot.gov/airconsumer). **Federal Aviation Administration Consumer Hotline** (☎ 800/322–7873).

RECONFIRMING

Check the status of your flight before you leave for the airport. You can do this on your carrier's Web site, by linking to a flight-status checker (many Web booking services offer these), or by calling your carrier or travel agent. Always confirm international flights at least 72 hours ahead of the scheduled departure time.

AIRPORTS

For more in-depth airport information, and for the best way to get between the airport and your destination, *see* ☞ Airports *in the* A to Z section at the end of each country chapter, or in the A to Z section of the city you are flying into.

➤ BULGARIA: **Sofia Airport** (☎ 02/937–2213 domestic flight informa-tion; 02/937–2211 international flight information).

➤ CROATIA: **Dubrovnik Airport** (☎ 20/773–333). **Split Airport** (☎ 21/203–555). **Zagreb Airport** (☎ 01/4562–222).

➤ CZECH REPUBLIC: Prague's **Ruzyně Airport** (☎ 02/2011–1111). **Brno Airport** (☎ 05/455–21111). **Karlovy Vary Airport** (☎ 017/333–1102).

➤ HUNGARY: Budapest's **Ferihegy Repülőtér** (☎ 1/296–9696 same-day flight information; 1/296–8000 arrivals; 1/296–7000 departures; 1/296–8108 lost and found).

➤ POLAND: **Warszawa Okęcie** (☎ 022/650–30–00). **Gdańsk-Rębiechowo** (☎ 058/348–1111). **Kraków-Balice** (☎ 012/285–5120). **Poznań-Ławica** (☎ 061/868–15–11). **Szczecin-Goleniów** (☎ 091/418–27–08). **Wrocław-Strachowice** (☎ 071/358–12–03). **Rzeszów-Jasionka** (☎ 017/852–00–81).

➤ ROMANIA: Bucharest's **Otopeni Airport** (☎ 01/201–3304). **Baneasa Airport** (☎ 01/232–0020).

➤ SLOVAKIA: Bratislava's **M. R. Štefánik Airport** (☎ 07/4857–33–53). **Košice Airport** (☎ 055/622–1093).

➤ SLOVENIA: Ljubljana's **Brnik Airport** (☎ 04/206–1981); **Maribor Airport** (☎ 02/629–1175); **Portorož Airport** (☎ O5/672–2525).

BIKE TRAVEL

The prevalence of bicycles varies greatly from country to country within Eastern and Central Europe. While, for instance, bike touring and mountain biking are gaining popularity in the Czech Republic, in Romania recreational cycling is uncommon and on some roads can be dangerous. Most major cities have some sort of bike rental available, and in less populated areas it's sometimes possible to arrange rentals through informal sources; your hotel is often a good resource for finding rentals. For more information, *see* Pleasures and Pastimes *and* Outdoor Activities and Sports *in* individual country chapters.

BIKES IN FLIGHT

Most airlines accommodate bikes as luggage, provided they are dismantled and boxed; check with individual airlines about packing requirements. Airlines sell bike boxes, which are often free at bike shops, for about $15 (bike bags start at $100). International travelers often can substitute a bike for a piece of checked luggage at no charge; otherwise, the cost is about $100. Domestic and Canadian airlines charge $40–$80 each way.

BOAT AND FERRY TRAVEL

Ferries offer a pleasant and cheap mode of transportation to Eastern and Central Europe, although you have to be fairly close to your destination already to hop a Europe-bound ferry or hydrofoil. Flying into the appropriate hub, however, is an option. Water bookings connect Copenhagen, Denmark, to Świnoujście and Gdańsk, Poland. A hydrofoil shuttles visitors from Vienna to Bratislava, Slovakia, or Budapest, Hungary. Ferries also operate on Lake Balaton in Hungary. There is ferry service between Venice and the Slovenian coast. For further country-specific information, *see* Boat and Ferry Travel *in* the A to Z section *for* Bulgaria (Chapter 2), Hungary (Chapter 5), Poland (Chapter 6), Romania (Chapter 7), Slovakia (Chapter 8), and Slovenia (Chapter 9).

Traveling by boat or ferry is a possibility up and down the coast in Croatia. Cabins must be booked in advance, but regular seats are readily available. Ferries between Ancona, Trieste, Bari, and Venice in Italy and Croatia operate daily. Journeys along the Croatian coast are more expensive than buses but more comfortable.

➤ FERRY LINES: Bulgaria: **Balkantourist** (✉ 1, bul. Vitosha, Sofia, ☎ 02/980–2324). Croatia: **Jadrolinija** (☎ 51/666–111). **SEM Marina** (☎ 21/338–292 in Split, 02/4851–9688 in Milan; 071/204–090 in Ancona). Hungary: **MAHART Tours** (✉ District V, Belgrád rakpart, Budapest, ☎ 1/484–4025; 1/484–4010 information). Poland: **Orbis** (✉ Hotel Helvelius, ul. Heweliusa 22, Gdańsk, ☎ 058/321–0000). **Polish Baltic Shipping Co.** (✉ ul. Przemysłowa 1, Gdańsk, ☎ 058/343–1887). **Stena Line** (☎ 058/660–9200). Slovakia: **Slovenská plavba** (☎ 07/5296–35–22; 07/5293–22–26 reservations).

Slovenia: **Kompas Turizem** (☎ 01/200–6111).

BUS TRAVEL

In some countries, especially where trains are largely local (and stop seemingly every 100 ft), buses are actually speedier than rail travel. Comfort and fares vary drastically by nation. *See* Bus Travel *in* the A to Z section at the end of each country chapter.

Unless you latch on to a real deal on airfare, a bus ticket from London's Victoria Terminal on Eurolines is probably the cheapest transit from the United Kingdom to Eastern and Central Europe, with regularly scheduled service to Budapest, Kraków, Prague, and Warsaw.

FROM THE U.K.

Eurolines (☎ 01582/404–511 in the U.K., 🌐 www.eurolines.com).

BUSINESS HOURS

For country-specific opening and closing times and business hours, *see* Business Hours *in* the A to Z section at the end of each country chapter.

CAMERAS
AND PHOTOGRAPHY

In general, people are pleased to be photographed, but ask first. Never photograph Gypsies, however colorful their attire, without explicit permission and payment clearly agreed upon. Photographing anything military, assuming you'd want to, is usually prohibited. The *Kodak Guide to Shooting Great Travel Pictures* (available at bookstores everywhere) is loaded with tips.

➤ PHOTO HELP: **Kodak Information Center** (☎ 800/242–2424, 🌐 www.kodak.com).

EQUIPMENT PRECAUTIONS

Don't pack film and equipment in checked luggage, where it is much more susceptible to damage. X-ray machines used to view checked luggage are becoming much more powerful and therefore are much more likely to ruin your film. Try to **ask for hand inspection of film,** which becomes clouded after repeated exposure to airport X-ray machines, and

keep videotapes and computer disks away from metal detectors. Always **keep film, tape, and computer disks out of the sun.** Carry an extra supply of batteries, and **be prepared to turn on your camera, camcorder, or laptop** to prove to airport security personnel that the device is real.

FILM AND DEVELOPING

Major brands of film are available throughout the region, and 24-hour developing is the rule rather than the exception in large and medium-size cities. The variable is cost—prices fluctuate widely from place to place.

VIDEOS

Due to differing television systems, VHS tapes bought in Central and Eastern Europe (which use the SECAM standard) are not compatible with U.S. machines (which use the NTSC standard).

CAR RENTAL

Major rental agencies are represented throughout the region, but **don't overlook local firms;** they can offer bargains, but watch for hidden insurance conditions. It can sometimes be impossible to get an automatic transmission in the region. Rates and regulations vary widely from country to country. For more information, *see* the A to Z sections *in* individual country chapters.

➤ MAJOR AGENCIES: **Alamo** (☎ 800/522–9696; WEB www.alamo.com). **Avis** (☎ 800/331–1084; 800/879–2847 in Canada; 0870/606–0100 in the U.K.; 02/9353–9000 in Australia; 09/526–2847 in New Zealand; WEB www.avis.com). **Budget** (☎ 800/527–0700; 0870/156–5656 in the U.K.; WEB www.budget.com). **Dollar** (☎ 800/800–6000; 0124/622–0111 in the U.K., where it's affiliated with Sixt; 02/9223–1444 in Australia; WEB www.dollar.com). **Hertz** (☎ 800/654–3001; 800/263–0600 in Canada; 020/8897–2072 in the U.K.; 02/9669–2444 in Australia; 09/256–8690 in New Zealand; WEB www.hertz.com). **National Car Rental** (☎ 800/227–7368; 020/8680–4800 in the U.K.; WEB www.nationalcar.com).

CUTTING COSTS

For a good deal, **book through a travel agent who will shop around.**

Do **look into wholesalers,** companies that do not own fleets but rent in bulk from those that do and often offer better rates than traditional car-rental operations. Prices are best during off-peak periods. Rentals booked through wholesalers often must be paid for before you leave home.

➤ WHOLESALERS: **Auto Europe** (☎ 888/223–5555, FAX 207/842–2222, WEB www.autoeurope.com). **Destination Europe Resources** (DER; ✉ 9501 W. Devon Ave., Rosemont, IL 60018, ☎ 800/782–2424, WEB www.der.com). **Europe by Car** (☎ 212/581–3040 or 800/223–1516, FAX 212/246–1458, WEB www.europebycar.com). **Kemwel** (☎ 800/678–0678 or 800/576–1590, FAX 207/842–2124, WEB www.kemwel.com).

INSURANCE

When driving a rented car you are generally responsible for any damage to or loss of the vehicle. Collision policies that car-rental companies sell for European rentals typically do not cover stolen vehicles. Before you rent—and purchase collision or theft coverage—see what coverage you already have under the terms of your personal auto-insurance policy and credit cards. Collision-damage waivers must be purchased in all countries in Central and Eastern Europe, so car rentals are liable to be more expensive than in the West. It is advised to check that any advertised prices apply to visitors and not only locals. Most countries require that you will have held your driver's license for at least a year before you can rent a car.

REQUIREMENTS AND RESTRICTIONS

In most Eastern and Central European countries, visitors need an International Driver's Permit; U.S. and Canadian citizens can obtain one from the American or Canadian Automobile Association, respectively. In some countries, such as Hungary, many car rental agencies will accept an international license, but the formal permit is technically required. If you intend to drive across a border, ask about **restrictions on driving into other countries.** The minimum age required for renting is usually 21 or older, and some companies also have maximum ages; be sure to inquire when making your arrangements.

SURCHARGES

Before you pick up a car in one city and leave it in another, **ask about drop-off charges or one-way service fees,** which can be substantial. Note, too, that some rental agencies charge extra if you return the car before the time specified in your contract. To avoid a hefty refueling fee, **fill the tank just before you turn in the car,** but be aware that gas stations near the rental outlet may overcharge. It's almost never a deal to buy the tank of gas in the car when you rent it; the understanding is that you'll return it empty, but some fuel usually remains.

CAR TRAVEL

The positive side of driving is an itinerary free from the constraints of bus and train schedules and lots of trunk room for extra baggage. The negatives are many, however, not the least of which are shabbily maintained secondary roads, the risk of theft and vandalism, and difficulty finding gas. Crowded roads and fast and/or careless drivers add to the danger element, particularly in Poland. However, car travel does make it much easier to get to out-of-the-way monasteries and other sights not easily accessible by public transportation. Good road maps are usually available.

A word of caution: if you have drunk any alcohol whatsoever, do not drive. Penalties are substantial, and the blood-alcohol limit is practically zero. (In the Czech Republic and Hungary, it *is* zero.)

AUTO CLUBS

➤ IN EASTERN AND CENTRAL EUROPE: Croatia: **Hrvatski Autoklub** (☎ 1/464–0800, WEB www.hak.hr). Czech Republic: **Autoturist** (✉ 4, Na Strži 9, Prague, ☎ 02/6110–4333, WEB www.autoturist.cz). Hungary: **Hungarian Automobile Club** (✉ District II, Rómer Flóris u. 4/A, Budapest, ☎ 1/345–1800, WEB www.autoklub.hu). Poland: **Polish Motoring Association** (PZMot; ☎ 022/629–83–36, WEB www.pzm.pl). Romania: **Automobil Clubul Roman** (✉ 27 Tache Ionescu,

Sector 1, Bucurest, ☎ 1/315–5510, WEB www.acr.ro). Slovakia: **Narodny automotoklub** (✉ Exnarova 59, Bratislava, ☎ 2/4341–3915, WEB www.namk.sk). Slovenia: **Automobile Association of Slovenia** (✉ Dunajska 128, Ljubljana, ☎ 01/530–5300, WEB www.amzs.si).

EMERGENCY SERVICES

In case of a breakdown, your best friend is the telephone. Try contacting your **rental agency** or the appropriate national breakdown service.

➤ CONTACTS: **Bulgaria** (☎ 146). **Croatia** (☎ 987). Czech Republic: **ABA** (☎ 124; 0124 in rural areas). **ÚAMK** (☎ 123; 0123 in rural areas). **Hungary** (Hungarian Automobile Club; ☎ 1/345–1755). **Poland** (☎ 9637). **Romania** (Romanian Auto Club; ☎ 1/222–2222 in Bucharest). **Slovakia** (☎ 018/154 or 018/123). **Slovenia** (Automobile Association of Slovenia; ☎ 1987).

GASOLINE

Gas stations are easy to come by on major thoroughfares and near large cities. Many are open around the clock, particularly in the Czech Republic and Hungary. At least two grades of gasoline are sold in Eastern and Central European countries, usually 90–93 octane (regular) and 94–98 octane (super). Lead-free gasoline is now available in most gas stations.

For additional country-specific information relating to roads, gasoline, and insurance, *see* Car Travel *in the* A to Z section at the end of each country chapter.

ROAD CONDITIONS

Eastern and Central Europe's main roads are built to a fairly high standard. There are now quite substantial stretches of highway on main routes, and a lot of rebuilding is being done.

ROAD MAPS

In Bulgaria, maps are plentiful at street kiosks in Sofia, and you can also find them at the Ministry of Trade and Tourism National Advertising Center across from the Sheraton. Outside the capital, the many Shell gas stations along the highway usually offer a good selection of road maps.

In Croatia try the tourist information services or gas stations and main bookstores.

In the Czech Republic, the ubiquitous 24-hour gas stations often sell road maps, or try a bookstore, such as Jan Kanzelsberger bookshop, which has a good selection of hiking maps and auto atlases.

In Hungary, good maps are sold at most large gas stations. In Budapest, the Globe Térképbolt has an excellent supply of domestic and foreign maps.

In Poland, check at large bookshops for driving maps; major hotels will also supply them, and all the modern gas stations have them. Esso driving maps are available at Esso gas stations and sometimes elsewhere.

For maps of Romania check bookstores, travel agencies, and sidewalk vendors. They may also be obtained from the Romanian Tourism Promotion Office in your home country.

In Slovakia, road maps are available at most gas stations. In Bratislava, the most convenient place selling road maps is Academia Bookstore.

In Slovenia road maps are available from larger bookshops and gas stations throughout the country. The Slovenian Tourist Board offers a comprehensive tourist map, free of charge.

➤ CONTACTS: **Academia Bookstore** (✉ Štúrova 9, Bratislava, Slovakia, ☎ 07/5296–87–72). **Bulgarian Ministry of Trade and Tourism National Advertising Center** (✉ 1, ul. Sveta Sofia, Sofia, Bulgaria, across from the Sheraton, ☎ 02/987–9778). **Globe Térképbolt** (Globe Map Store; ✉ District VI, Bajcsy-Zsilinszky út 37, Budapest, Hungary, ☎ 1/312–6001). **Jan Kanzelsberger bookshop** (✉ Václavské nám. 42, Prague, Czech Republic, ☎ 02/2421–7335).

RULES OF THE ROAD

Throughout Eastern and Central Europe, driving is on the right and the same basic rules of the road practiced in the United States and the rest of Europe apply. For further information *see* Car Travel *in* the A to Z section at the end of each country chapter.

CHILDREN IN EASTERN AND CENTRAL EUROPE

Be sure to plan ahead and **involve your youngsters** as you outline your trip. When packing, include things to keep them busy en route. On sightseeing days try to schedule activities of special interest to your children. If you are renting a car, don't forget to **arrange for a car seat** when you reserve. For general advice about traveling with children, consult *Fodor's FYI: Travel with Your Baby* (available in bookstores everywhere).

FLYING

If your children are two or older, **ask about children's airfares.** As a general rule, infants under two not occupying a seat fly at greatly reduced fares or even for free. When booking, **confirm carry-on allowances** if you're traveling with infants. In general, for babies charged 10% of the adult fare you are allowed one carry-on bag and a collapsible stroller; if the flight is full, the stroller may have to be checked or you may be limited to less.

Experts agree that it's a good idea to use safety seats aloft for children weighing less than 40 pounds. Airlines set their own policies: U.S. carriers usually require that the child be ticketed, even if he or she is young enough to ride free, since the seats must be strapped into regular seats. Do **check your airline's policy about using safety seats during takeoff and landing.** Safety seats are not allowed everywhere in the plane, so get your seat assignments as early as possible.

When reserving, **request children's meals or a freestanding bassinet** (not available at all airlines) if you need them. But note that bulkhead seats, where you must sit to use the bassinet, may lack an overhead bin or storage space on the floor.

LODGING

Most hotels in Eastern and Central Europe allow children under a certain age to stay in their parents' room at no extra charge, but others charge for them as extra adults; be sure to **find out the cutoff age for children's discounts.** Some spa hotels don't allow children under 12.

The Accor group, which owns the Novotel, Mercure, Ibis, and Sofitel chains, has hotels all over Eastern and Central Europe and allows up to two children under 12 to stay free in their parents' room. The same policy theoretically holds for hotels in Sofia and Plovdiv in Bulgaria, but you will have to ask or even bargain. For Novotel branches in Poland, the cutoff age is 16. The Budapest Hilton has an unusual policy allowing children of any age—even middle-aged adults—to stay for free in their parents' room. In Bratislava, Slovakia, there are a few hotels with discounts; the Danube Hotel allows kids under 3 to stay free in their parents' room, and gives a 50% discount for children between 3 and 10. The Perugia Hotel will add a children's bed in the parents' room, charging an additional $30 for the entire stay.

Young visitors to the Czech Republic will enjoy staying at one of Prague's picturesque floating "botels." For further information contact the Czech Tourist Authority. Prague's luxurious Palace and Savoy hotels, managed by Vienna International, allow children under 12 to stay free in their parents' room.

➤ BEST CHOICES: **Accor Hotels** (WEB www.accorhotels.com). **Budapest Hilton** (☎ 1/488–6600 in Budapest, WEB www.hilton.com).

SIGHTS AND ATTRACTIONS

Places that are especially appealing to children are indicated by a rubber duckie icon (🦆) in the margins throughout the book.

COMPUTERS ON THE ROAD

Bring an adapter for your laptop plug. Adapters are inexpensive, and some models have several plugs suitable for different systems throughout the world. Some hotels lend adapters to guests for use during their stay.

At the airport, **be prepared to turn on your laptop** to prove to security personnel that the device is real. Security X-ray machines can be damaging to a laptop, and **keep computer disks away from metal detectors.**

CONSUMER PROTECTION

Whenever buying travel services for a trip to Eastern and Central Europe, **pay with a major credit card** when you can, so you can cancel payment or get reimbursed if there's a problem. But be aware that credit cards are not as widely accepted in the region as they are in Western Europe and the United States—many hotels and restaurants operate on a cash-only basis. If you're doing business with a travel-services company for the first time, **contact your local Better Business Bureau and the attorney general's offices** in your own state and the company's home state, as well. Have any complaints been filed? Finally, if you're buying a package or tour, always **consider travel insurance** that includes default coverage (☞ Insurance, *below*).

➤ BBBs: **Council of Better Business Bureaus** (✉ 4200 Wilson Blvd., Suite 800, Arlington, VA 22203, ☎ 703/276–0100, FAX 703/525–8277, WEB www.bbb.org).

CUSTOMS AND DUTIES

When shopping abroad, **keep receipts** for all purchases. Upon reentering the country, **be ready to show customs officials what you've bought.** If you feel a duty is incorrect, appeal the assessment. If you object to the way your clearance was handled, note the inspector's badge number. In either case, first ask to see a supervisor. If the problem isn't resolved, write to the appropriate authorities, beginning with the port director at your point of entry.

IN AUSTRALIA

Australian residents who are 18 or older may bring home A$400 worth of souvenirs and gifts (including jewelry), 250 cigarettes or 250 grams of tobacco, and 1,125 ml of alcohol (including wine, beer, and spirits). Residents under 18 may bring back A$200 worth of goods. Prohibited items include meat products. Seeds, plants, and fruits need to be declared upon arrival.

➤ INFORMATION: **Australian Customs Service** (Regional Director, ✉ Box 8, Sydney, NSW 2001; ☎ 02/9213–2000 or 1300/363263; 1800/020504 quarantine-inquiry line; FAX 02/9213–4043; WEB www.customs.gov.au).

IN CANADA

Canadian residents who have been out of Canada for at least seven days may bring in C$750 worth of goods duty-free. If you've been away fewer than seven days but more than 48 hours, the duty-free allowance drops to C$200. If your trip lasts 24 to 48 hours, the allowance is C$50. You may not pool allowances with family members. Goods claimed under the C$750 exemption may follow you by mail; those claimed under the lesser exemptions must accompany you. Alcohol and tobacco products may be included in the seven-day and 48-hour exemptions but not in the 24-hour exemption. If you meet the age requirements of the province or territory through which you reenter Canada, you may bring in, duty-free, 1.5 liters of wine *or* 1.14 liters (40 imperial ounces) of liquor *or* 24 12-ounce cans or bottles of beer or ale. If you are 19 or older you may bring in, duty-free, 200 cigarettes and 50 cigars. Check ahead of time with the Canada Customs and Revenue Agency or the Department of Agriculture for policies regarding meat products, seeds, plants, and fruits.

You may send an unlimited number of gifts (only one gift per recipient, however) worth up to C$60 each duty-free to Canada. Label the package UNSOLICITED GIFT—VALUE UNDER $60. Alcohol and tobacco are excluded.

➤ INFORMATION: **Canada Customs and Revenue Agency** (✉ 2265 St. Laurent Blvd. S, Ottawa, Ontario K1G 4K3, ☎ 204/983–3500, 506/636–5064, 800/461–9999, WEB www.ccra-adrc.gc.ca/).

IN EASTERN AND CENTRAL EUROPE

You may import duty-free into Slovakia, Hungary, Poland, or Bulgaria 250 cigarettes or the equivalent in tobacco, 1 liter of spirits, and 2 liters of wine (in Poland, 1 liter of spirits and 2 liters of wine). In addition to the above, you are permitted to import into Hungary gifts valued up to 30,500 Ft; into Poland, gifts valued at up to €70; into Slovakia, gifts valued at up to 1,000 Sk (approximately

$30). In Croatia visitors will not pay duty on quantities of food and drink "appropriate to their needs for length of their stay." There is no duty on personal belongings and other items less than 300 Kn in value. You may import duty-free into the Czech Republic tobacco products equivalent to 200 cigarettes, 100 cigarillos, 250 grams of tobacco, or 50 cigars; 1 liter of spirits, 2 liters of wine, and personal medicines, as well as gifts and personal items valued at up to 6,000 Kč (3,000 Kč for visitors under 15) (about $170/$85). On arrival in Romania, you may bring in a personal computer and printer, two cameras, 10 rolls of film, one small video camera and VCR, 10 videocassette tapes, one typewriter, binoculars, one radio/tape recorder, one small television set, one bicycle, one child's stroller, 200 cigarettes, 2 liters of liquor, and 4 liters of wine or beer. Gifts are permitted, though you may be charged duty on some electronic goods. Cash in excess of $10,000 should be declared on arrival. Arriving in Slovenia, personal items are not subject to any toll, but duty-free restrictions are 200 cigarettes or 50 cigars, 1 liter of wine, and 0.75 liter of spirits.

If you are bringing into any of these countries any valuables or foreign-made equipment from home, such as cameras, it's wise to carry the original receipts with you or register the items with U.S. Customs before you leave (Form 4457). Otherwise you could end up paying duty upon your return. When traveling to Bulgaria, you should declare video cameras, personal computers, and expensive jewelry upon arrival. Be aware that leaving the country without expensive items declared upon entering can present a huge hassle with airport police.

IN NEW ZEALAND

All homeward-bound residents may bring back NZ$700 worth of souvenirs and gifts; passengers may not pool their allowances, and children can claim only the concession on goods intended for their own use. For those 17 or older, the duty-free allowance also includes 4.5 liters of wine or beer; one 1,125-ml bottle of spirits; and either 200 cigarettes, 250 grams of tobacco, 50 cigars, *or* a combination of the three up to 250 grams. Meat products, seeds, plants, and fruits must be declared upon arrival to the Agricultural Services Department.

➤ INFORMATION: **New Zealand Customs** (Head office: ✉ The Customhouse, 17–21 Whitmore St., [Box 2218, Wellington], ☎ 09/300–5399 or 0800/428–786, WEB www.customs.govt.nz).

IN THE U.K.

From countries outside the European Union, including those in Eastern and Central Europe, you may bring home, duty-free, 200 cigarettes or 50 cigars; 1 liter of spirits or 2 liters of fortified or sparkling wine or liqueurs; 2 liters of still table wine; 60 ml of perfume; 250 ml of toilet water; plus £145 worth of other goods, including gifts and souvenirs. Prohibited items include meat products, seeds, plants, and fruits.

➤ INFORMATION: **HM Customs and Excise** (✉ Portcullis House, 21 Cowbridge Rd. E, Cardiff CF11 9SS, ☎ 029/2038–6423 or 0845/010–9000, WEB www.hmce.gov.uk).

IN THE U.S.

U.S. residents who have been out of the country for at least 48 hours may bring home, for personal use, $800 worth of foreign goods duty-free, as long as they haven't used the $800 allowance or any part of it in the past 30 days. This exemption may include 1 liter of alcohol (for travelers 21 and older), 200 cigarettes, and 100 non-Cuban cigars. Family members from the same household who are traveling together may pool their $800 personal exemptions. For fewer than 48 hours, the duty-free allowance drops to $200, which may include 50 cigarettes, 10 non-Cuban cigars, and 150 ml of alcohol (or perfume containing alcohol). The $200 allowance cannot be combined with other individuals' exemptions, and if you exceed it, the full value of all the goods will be taxed. Antiques, which the U.S. Customs Service defines as objects more than 100 years old, enter duty-free, as do original works of art done

entirely by hand, including paintings, drawings, and sculptures.

You may also send packages home duty-free, with a limit of one parcel per addressee per day (except alcohol or tobacco products or perfume worth more than $5). You can mail up to $200 worth of goods for personal use; label the package PERSONAL USE and attach a list of its contents and their retail value. If the package contains your used personal belongings, mark it PERSONAL GOODS RETURNED to avoid paying duties. You may send up to $100 worth of goods as a gift; mark the package UNSOLICITED GIFT. Mailed items do not affect your duty-free allowance on your return.

➤ INFORMATION: **U.S. Customs Service** (for inquiries, ✉ 1300 Pennsylvania Ave. NW, Washington, DC 20229, ☎ 202/354–1000, WEB www.customs.gov; for complaints, ✉ Customer Satisfaction Unit, 1300 Pennsylvania Ave. NW, Room 5.5A, Washington, DC 20229; for registration of equipment, ✉ Office of Passenger Programs, 1300 Pennsylvania Ave. NW, Room 5.4D, Washington, DC 20229, ☎ 202/927–0530).

DINING

For country-specific dining information, *see* Dining *in* Pleasures and Pastimes at the beginning of each country chapter. Additional city-specific dining information may also be found at the start of a city's dining listings. The restaurants we list are the cream of the crop in each price category.

MEALTIMES

Unless otherwise noted, the restaurants listed in this guide are open daily for lunch and dinner.

RESERVATIONS AND DRESS

Reservations are always a good idea; we mention them only when they're essential or not accepted. Book as far ahead as you can, and reconfirm as soon as you arrive. (Large parties should always call ahead to check the reservations policy.) We mention dress only when men are required to wear a jacket or a jacket and tie.

DISABILITIES
ACCESSIBILITY

Provisions for travelers with disabilities in Eastern and Central Europe are extremely limited; probably the best solution is to travel with a companion who can help you. While many hotels, especially large American or international chains, offer some wheelchair-accessible rooms, special facilities at museums and restaurants and on public transportation are difficult to find. In Poland wheelchairs are available at all airports, and most trains have special seats designated for people with disabilities, but it is wise to notify ahead. In Slovenia a law was passed in 1997 requiring all public buildings and infrastructure, including hotels, to be made fully accessible to people with disabilities.

➤ LOCAL RESOURCES: Bulgaria: **Center for Independent Living** (✉ Buzludja 43, Sofia 1463, ☎ 02/954–9892, cil@aster.net). Croatia: **Hrvatska udruga paraplegičara** (Croatian Association of Paraplegics; ✉ Park prijateljstva 1, Zagreb, ☎ 01/3831–195, WEB www.hupt.hr). Czech Republic: **Sdružení zdravotně postižených** (Association of Disabled Persons; ✉ Karlínské nám. 12, Prague 8, ☎ 02/2481–5914, WEB www.czechia.com/szdp). Hungary: **Mozgáskorlátozottak Egyesületeinek Országos Szövetsége** (National Association of People with Mobility Impairments, or MEOSZ; ✉ San Marco u. 76, Budapest 1032, ☎ 1/388–5529, WEB www.meoszinfo.hu). Slovakia: **Slovenský zväz telesne postihnutých** (Slovak Association of People with Mobility Impairments; ✉ Ševčenkova 19, Bratislava, ☎ 02/6381–4469; must arrange for an English-language interpreter in advance). Slovenia: **Slovenian Union of People with Mobility Impairments** (✉ Stihova 14, Ljubljana, ☎ 01/432–7138).

LODGING

Most hotels take few or no measures to accommodate travelers with disabilities. Your best bets are newer hotels and international chains.

RESERVATIONS

When discussing accessibility with an operator or reservations agent, **ask hard questions.** Are there any stairs, inside *or* out? Are there grab bars next to the toilet *and* in the shower/tub? How wide is the doorway to the room? To the bathroom? For the most extensive facilities meeting the latest legal specifications, **opt for newer accommodations.** If you reserve through a toll-free number, consider also calling the hotel's local number to confirm the information from the central reservations office. Get confirmation in writing when you can.

SIGHTS AND ATTRACTIONS

Most tourist attractions in the region pose significant problems. Many are historic structures without ramps or other means to improve accessibility. Streets are often cobblestone, and potholes are common.

TRANSPORTATION

A few Czech trains are equipped with carriages for travelers using wheelchairs. Some stations on the Prague metro have elevators, and there are two lines of accessible buses, but the system is light-years from being barrier-free. Elsewhere in the region, public transportation is difficult, if not impossible, for many travelers with disabilities.

TRAVEL AGENCIES

In the United States, the Americans with Disabilities Act requires that travel firms serve the needs of all travelers. Some agencies specialize in working with people with disabilities.

➤ TRAVELERS WITH MOBILITY PROBLEMS: **Access Adventures** (✉ 206 Chestnut Ridge Rd., Scottsville, NY 14624, ☎ 716/889–9096, dltravel@prodigy.net), run by a former physical-rehabilitation counselor. **Flying Wheels Travel** (✉ 143 W. Bridge St. [Box 382, Owatonna, MN 55060], ☎ 507/451–5005, FAX 507/451–1685, WEB www.flyingwheelstravel.com).

DISCOUNTS AND DEALS

Be a smart shopper and **compare all your options** before making decisions. A plane ticket bought with a promotional coupon from travel clubs, coupon books, and direct-mail offers

Smart Travel Tips A to Z

or purchased on the Internet may not be cheaper than the least expensive fare from a discount ticket agency. And always keep in mind that what you get is just as important as what you save.

In Budapest, the Budapest Card entitles holders to unlimited travel on public transportation; free admission to many museums and sights; and discounts on various services from participating businesses. The cost (at this writing) is 2,800 Ft. for two days, 3,400 Ft. for three days; one card is valid for an adult plus one child under 14. It is available at many tourist offices along with a similar pass called the Hungary Card, which gives discounts to museums, sights, and service in the entire country.

DISCOUNT RESERVATIONS

To save money, **look into discount reservations services** with Web sites and toll-free numbers, which use their buying power to get a better price on hotels, airline tickets, even car rentals. When booking a room, always **call the hotel's local toll-free number** (if one is available) rather than the central reservations number—you'll often get a better price. Always ask about special packages or corporate rates.

When shopping for the best deal on hotels and car rentals, **look for guaranteed exchange rates,** which protect you against a falling dollar. With your rate locked in, you won't pay more, even if the price goes up in the local currency.

➤ AIRLINE TICKETS: ☎ 800/FLY–ASAP.

➤ HOTEL ROOMS: **Hotel Reservations Network** (☎ 800/964–6835, WEB www.hoteldiscount.com). **International Marketing & Travel Concepts** (☎ 800/790–4682, WEB www.imtc-travel.com). **Steigenberger Reservation Service** (☎ 800/223–5652, WEB www.srs-worldhotels.com). **Travel Interlink** (☎ 800/888–5898, WEB www.travelinterlink.com). **Turbotrip.com** (☎ 800/473–7829, WEB www.turbotrip.com).

PACKAGE DEALS

Don't confuse packages and guided tours. When you buy a package, you travel on your own, just as though you had planned the trip yourself. Fly-drive packages, which combine airfare and car rental, are often a good deal. If you **buy a rail-drive pass,** you may save on train tickets and car rentals. All Eurail- and Europass holders get a discount on Eurostar fares through the Channel Tunnel.

ECOTOURISM

In the Czech Republic, the most active organization promoting ecotourism is Greenways. Ecotourism—often just another word for rural B&Bs—is slowly gathering pace in mountainous such as the south Bohemian Šumava and in the flatter, bike-friendly country of south Moravia. In Poland there are plenty of eco- and agrotourist destinations, which are increasingly popular spots for Dutch and German tourists. For more information on ecotourism in Poland contact Polska Federacja Turystyki Wiejskiej. Romania offers wonderful opportunities for hiking through the beautiful countryside and in the forested mountains. Animals such as bears, chamois, and boar still inhabit the forests, but as yet, there is no organized program for ecotourism.

➤ CONTACTS: **Greenways** (WEB www.pragueviennagreenways.org). **Polska Federacja Turystyki Wiejskiej** (✉ ul. Wspólna 30, Warsaw, ☎ 052/398–1434, WEB www.agroturystyka.pl).

ELECTRICITY

To use electric-powered equipment purchased in the U.S. or Canada, **bring a converter and adapter.** The electrical current in Eastern and Central Europe is 220 volts, 50 cycles alternating current (AC); wall outlets generally take plugs with two round prongs.

If your appliances are dual-voltage, you'll need only an adapter. Don't use 110-volt outlets marked FOR SHAVERS ONLY for high-wattage appliances such as blow-dryers. Most laptops operate equally well on 110 and 220 volts and so require only an adapter.

EMBASSIES

For Australian, Canadian, U.S., and U.K. embassy and consulate contact information, *see* the A to Z section for the first-listed city *in* each country chapter. There are no New Zealand embassies or consulates in the region.

EMERGENCIES

For country-specific emergency numbers, *see* Emergencies *in* the A to Z section at the end of each country chapter. For medical emergency contacts, *see also* Health, *below.*

ENGLISH-LANGUAGE MEDIA

The largest cities in the region have English-language weekly newspapers that cover current events and culture. Prague in particular is remarkably rich in English-language publishing of all kinds, from general-interest newspapers to poetry chapbooks, reflecting the city's large, relatively stable community of English-speaking expatriates. *In Your Pocket* guides are available in many cities in Eastern and Central Europe.

In the broadcast media, BBC World Service and CNN are widely available.

GAY AND LESBIAN TRAVEL

Throughout Eastern and Central Europe, gay and lesbian resources are thin on the ground, if not underground. While the level of tolerance varies, the region is generally conservative; strongly Catholic countries are the least accepting.

Though gays and lesbians are gaining acceptance in Bulgaria, there are no national organizations. Social steps toward acceptance are quite new; the first openly gay disco opened in Sofia in 1997. In general, attitudes toward homosexuality throughout the Bulgarian interior are hostile, while at the more cosmopolitan Black Sea coast resorts people tend to be more open-minded.

In Croatia although homosexuality is generally tolerated, open displays of affection can meet with hostile reactions especially in the less urban parts of the country.

The Czech Republic is one of the most liberal countries in the region. Prague fosters a growing gay and lesbian scene. You could try visiting one of the gathering places, such as Gejzeer Club.

Hungary is relatively open-minded, though even in Budapest, the gay population keeps a fairly low profile. Some of Budapest's thermal baths are popular meeting places, as are the city's several gay bars and clubs, which you can find listed in English-language newspapers and the monthly magazine *Mások,* which is available only in Hungarian.

Gay and lesbian organization is a relatively new thing in Poland, and clubs and meeting points change addresses frequently. One of the longest-standing gay organizations is Lambda.

Until the late 1990s, homosexuality was illegal in Romania. Though greater acceptance exists today, especially among the young and better educated, it remains basically a closed topic.

In Slovakia resources are limited; the Ganymedes hot line operates on Tuesday and Thursday from 6 to 8 PM.

In Slovenia homosexuality is widely tolerated. Gays and lesbians are united in several associations and clubs, with the main center at the student-run nightclub K4. K4 has a gay night every Sunday 10 PM–4 AM.

➤ RESOURCES AND ORGANIZATIONS: **Bulgaria** (WEB www.gay.bg). **Croatia** (WEB www.gay-croatia.com). **Czech Republic** (WEB www.gayguide.net/ europe/czech/prague). **Hungary** (WEB www.gayguide.net/europe/hungary/ budapest). **Poland** (Lambda; ✉ ul. Czerniakowska 178/16, Warsaw, ☎ 022/628–52–22). **Romania** (WEB www.rogay.com). **Slovakia** (Ganymedes Hotline; ☎ 0905/618291). **Slovenia** (K4; ✉ Kersnikova 4, Ljubljana, ☎ 01/131–7010, WEB www. klubk4.org).

➤ GAY- AND LESBIAN-FRIENDLY TRAVEL AGENCIES: **Different Roads Travel** (✉ 8383 Wilshire Blvd., Suite 902, Beverly Hills, CA 90211, ☎ 323/ 651–5557 or 800/429–8747, FAX 323/ 651–3678, lgernert@tzell.com). **Kennedy Travel** (✉ 314 Jericho Turnpike, Floral Park, NY 11001, ☎ 516/352–4888 or 800/237– 7433, FAX 516/354–8849, WEB www. kennedytravel.com). **Now, Voyager** (✉ 4406 18th St., San Francisco, CA

94114, ☎ 415/626–1169 or 800/
255–6951, FAX 415/626–8626,
WEB www.nowvoyager.com). **Skylink
Travel and Tour** (✉ 1006 Mendocino
Ave., Santa Rosa, CA 95401, ☎ 707/
546–9888 or 800/225–5759, FAX 707/
546–9891, WEB www.skylinktravel.
com), serving lesbian travelers.

HEALTH

You may gain weight, but there are
few other serious health hazards for
the traveler in Eastern and Central
Europe. Tap water may taste bad but
is generally drinkable (though see the
precautions below); when it runs
rusty out of the tap or the aroma of
chlorine is overpowering, it might
help to have some iodine tablets or
bottled water handy. Tap water isn't
considered safe in Romania's Danube
Delta. Throughout the country,
bottled water is inexpensive and
widely available; it might be a better
choice, especially for children, as
there is a history of tap water with
heavy lead content. In Bulgaria and
Poland, faulty plumbing, especially in
cities, ruins the water quality. Buy
bottled water, particularly if staying
in an older home or a hotel.

Vegetarians and those on special diets
may have a problem with the heavy
local cuisine, which is based largely
on pork and beef. To prevent your
vitamin intake from dropping to
danger levels, buy fresh fruits and
vegetables at seasonal street markets—regular grocery stores often
don't sell them. In Romania, unrefrig-
erated milk sold in outdoor markets
or in villages may not be pasteurized
and can make Westerners sick. In
Bulgaria, mayonnaise-based fillings
are very common in "sandvitchee"—
the ubiquitous toasted sandwiches
sold at many street kiosks; avoid
them.

No vaccinations are required for
entry into any of the Eastern and
Central European countries covered
in this book, but selective vaccinations are recommended. Those traveling in forested areas of most Eastern
and Central European countries
should consider vaccinating themselves against Central European, or
tick-borne, encephalitis. Tick-borne
Lyme disease is also a risk in the

Czech Republic. If you plan to travel
for an extended period of time in
rural Bulgaria, it is a good idea to
consider vaccinations for hepatitis A
and B, spread through food and
water. Schedule vaccinations well in
advance of departure because some
require several doses, and others may
cause uncomfortable side effects.

To avoid problems clearing customs,
diabetic travelers carrying needles and
syringes should have on hand a letter
from their physician confirming their
need for insulin injections.

OVER-THE-COUNTER
REMEDIES

Pharmacies throughout the region
carry a variety of nonprescription as
well as prescription drugs. For recommended pharmacies, *see* the A to Z
sections *in* each country chapter.

HOLIDAYS

For country-specific holidays, *see*
National Holidays in the A to Z
section at the end of each country
chapter.

INSURANCE

The most useful travel-insurance plan
is a comprehensive policy that includes coverage for trip cancellation
and interruption, default, trip delay,
and medical expenses (with a waiver
for pre-existing conditions).

Without insurance you will lose all or
most of your money if you cancel
your trip, regardless of the reason.
Default insurance covers you if your
tour operator, airline, or cruise line
goes out of business. Trip-delay
covers expenses that arise because of
bad weather or mechanical delays.
Study the fine print when comparing
policies.

If you're traveling internationally, a
key component of travel insurance is
coverage for medical bills incurred if
you get sick on the road. Such expenses are not generally covered by
Medicare or private policies. U.K.
residents can buy a travel-insurance
policy valid for most vacations taken
during the year in which it's purchased (but check pre-existing-condi-
tion coverage).British and Australian
citizens need extra medical coverage
when traveling overseas.

Always **buy travel policies directly from the insurance company**; if you buy them from a cruise line, airline, or tour operator that goes out of business you probably will not be covered for the agency or operator's default, a major risk. Before making any purchase, **review your existing health and home-owner's policies** to find what they cover away from home.

➤ TRAVEL INSURERS: In the U.S.: **Access America** (⊠ 6600 W. Broad St., Richmond, VA 23230, ☎ 800/284–8300, FAX 804/673–1491 or 800/346–9265, WEB www.accessamerica.com). **Travel Guard International** (⊠ 1145 Clark St., Stevens Point, WI 54481, ☎ 715/345–0505 or 800/826–1300, FAX 800/955–8785, WEB www.travelguard.com).

➤ INSURANCE INFORMATION: In the U.K.: **Association of British Insurers** (⊠ 51 Gresham St., London EC2V 7HQ, ☎ 020/7600–3333, FAX 020/7696–8999, WEB www.abi.org.uk). In Canada: **RBC Travel Insurance** (⊠ 6880 Financial Dr., Mississauga, Ontario L5N 7Y5, ☎ 905/791–8700 or 800/668–4342, FAX 905/813–4704, WEB www.rbcinsurance.com). In Australia: **Insurance Council of Australia** (⊠ Level 3, 56 Pitt St., Sydney, NSW 2000, ☎ 02/9253–5100, FAX 02/9253–5111, WEB www.ica.com.au). In New Zealand: **Insurance Council of New Zealand** (⊠ Level 7, 111–115 Customhouse Quay, [Box 474, Wellington], ☎ 04/472–5230, FAX 04/473–3011, WEB www.icnz.org.nz).

LANGUAGE

For country-specific information about language issues, *see* Language *in* the A to Z section at the end of each country chapter.

LODGING

If your experience of Eastern and Central European hotels is limited to capital cities such as Prague and Budapest, you may be pleasantly surprised. There are baroque mansions turned guest houses and elegant high-rise resorts, not to mention bed-and-breakfast inns presided over by matronly babushkas. Many facilities throughout the region are being upgraded.

Outside major cities, hotels and inns are more rustic than elegant. Standards of service generally do not suffer, but in most rural areas the definition of "luxury" includes little more than a television and a private bathroom. In some instances, you may have no choice but to stay in one of the cement high-rise hotels that scar skylines from Poland to the Czech Republic. Huge, impersonal concrete hotels are part of the Communist legacy, and it may take a few more years to exorcise or "beautify" these ubiquitous monsters. However, even in Bulgaria, where changes are very slow, new, luxurious hotels can be found in most regions of the country, if you're willing to pay Western prices.

In rural Eastern and Central Europe, you may have difficulty parting with more than $25–$30 per night for lodgings. Reservations are vital if you plan to visit Prague, Budapest, Warsaw, or most other major cities during the summer season. Reservations are a good idea but aren't imperative if you plan to strike out into the countryside.

For country-specific lodging information, *see* Lodging *in* Pleasures and Pastimes at the beginning of each country chapter. Additional city-specific lodging information may also be found at the start of a city's lodging listings. The lodgings we list are the cream of the crop in each price category. We always list the facilities that are available, but we don't specify whether they cost extra; when pricing accommodations, always ask what's included and what costs extra. Properties are assigned price categories based on the range from their least-expensive standard double room at high season (excluding holidays) to the most expensive. Properties marked ✕🏨 are lodging establishments whose restaurants warrant a special trip.

Assume that hotels operate on the **European Plan** (EP, with no meals) unless we specify that they use the **Breakfast Plan** (BP, with a full breakfast), **Modified American Plan** (MAP, with breakfast and dinner), or the **Full American Plan** (FAP, with all meals).

APARTMENT AND VILLA RENTALS

If you want a home base that's roomy enough for a family and comes with cooking facilities, **consider a furnished rental.** These can save you money, especially if you're traveling with a group. Home-exchange directories sometimes list rentals as well as exchanges.

If you are looking for a private room in Prague, try APT-Rent. Rental apartments are common in Hungary. In Budapest, the best bet is to go through an agency; in the rest of the country, either check with a local tourist information office or, especially in smaller cities, simply walk around until you see a sign outside a house reading *apartman.*

If you are looking for a private room in Warsaw, try Syrena. In Poland outside Warsaw look to the local tourist information for assistance.

➤ INTERNATIONAL AGENTS: **Hideaways International** (✉ 767 Islington St., Portsmouth, NH 03801, ☎ 603/430–4433 or 800/843–4433, FAX 603/430–4444, WEB www.hideaways. com; membership $129). **Interhome** (✉ 1990 N.E. 163rd St., Suite 110, North Miami Beach, FL 33162, ☎ 305/940–2299 or 800/882–6864, FAX 305/940–2911, WEB www. interhome.com). **Villas International** (✉ 4340 Redwood Hwy., Suite D309, San Rafael, CA 94903, ☎ 415/499–9490 or 800/221–2260, FAX 415/499–9491, WEB www.villasintl.com).

➤ LOCAL AGENTS: Hungary: In Budapest, **Amadeus Apartments** (✉ District IX, Üllői út 197, H-1091, ☎ 06/309–422–893, WEB www.amadeus.hu). **TRIBUS Welcome Hotel Service** (✉ District V, Apáczai Csere János u. 1, ☎ 1/318–5776, WEB www.tribus.hu); Czech Republic: In Prague, **APT-Rent** (✉ Ostrovni 7, ☎ 02/2499–0900, WEB www.apartments.cz). Croatia: **Broker** (✉ 21 000 Split, ☎ 021/547–004, WEB www.croatia-tourism.com). Poland: In Warsaw, **Syrena** (✉ ul. Krucza 17, ☎ 022/628–75–40, · WEB www.syrena.com.pl).

BED-AND-BREAKFASTS

Although B&Bs of the traditional English variety aren't prevalent in the region, there are numerous variations on the concept available, including comfortable and elaborately decorated facilities in Hungary and agrotourism (essentially rural home stays) in Romania. For further information, *see* B&B Reservation Agencies *in* the A to Z sections of the individual country chapters.

CAMPING

For information on camping facilities in Croatia, contact the Croatian Camping Union.

For information on camping in the Czech Republic, contact the Czech Tourist Authority (☞ Visitor Information, *below*). The Prague Information Service can supply a map of the dozen or so campgrounds in and around Prague.

For Hungary, campground information, reservations, and an informative map listing all campgrounds can be obtained from travel agencies and Tourinform (☞ Visitor Information *in* the Hungary A to Z section of Chapter 5). You may also contact the Hungarian Camping and Caravanning Club.

There are more than 500 official campsites in Poland. Check *Campingi w Polsce,* which is available in major bookstores, for details.

More than 100 campsites exist in Romania; conditions vary. Many are in mountain, seaside, and spa areas.

For information on camping facilities in Slovakia, contact Satur or Tatratour travel agencies (☞ Visitor Information *in* Bratislava A to Z, of Chapter 8).

➤ CONTACTS: **Croatian Camping Union** (✉ Pionirska 1, Poreč, HR-52440, ☎ 52/451–324, FAX 52/451–279, WEB www.camping.hr). **Hungarian Camping and Caravanning Club** (✉ VIII, Mária u. 34, Budapest, ☎ 1/267–5255 or 1/267–5256).

HOME EXCHANGES

If you would like to exchange your home for someone else's, **join a home-exchange organization,** which will send you its updated listings of available exchanges for a year and will include your own listing in at least one of them. It's up to you to make specific arrangements.

➤ EXCHANGE CLUBS: **HomeLink International** (✉ Box 47747, Tampa, FL 33647, ☎ 813/975–9825 or 800/638–3841, FAX 813/910–8144, WEB www.homelink.org; $106 per year). **Intervac U.S.** (✉ 30 Corte San Fernando, Tiburon, CA 94920, ☎ 800/756–4663, FAX 415/435–7440, WEB www.intervacus.com; $90 yearly fee for a listing, on-line access, and a catalog; $50 without catalog).

HOSTELS

No matter what your age, you can **save on lodging costs by staying at hostels.** In some 4,500 locations in more than 70 countries around the world, Hostelling International (HI), the umbrella group for a number of national youth-hostel associations, offers single-sex, dorm-style beds and, at many hostels, rooms for couples and family accommodations. Membership in any HI national hostel association, open to travelers of all ages, allows you to stay in HI-affiliated hostels at member rates; one-year membership is about $25 for adults (C$35 for a two-year minimum membership in Canada, £13 in the U.K., A$52 in Australia, and NZ$40 in New Zealand); hostels run about $10–$30 per night. Members have priority if the hostel is full; they're also eligible for discounts around the world, even on rail and bus travel in some countries.

In Hungary, most hostels are geared toward the college crowd. Among several good ones in Budapest are the friendly, Internet-equipped Back Pack Guesthouse, where rates range from 1,300 Ft. (8- to 10-bed rooms) to 1,900 Ft. (2-bed rooms), and the Sirály Youth Hostel, situated in the relative peace, quiet, and clean air of an island-park on the Danube, where the per-person rate in 12-bed rooms is 1,400 Ft. For further information, consult the free annual accommodations directory published by Tourinform (☞ Visitor Information *in* the Hungary A to Z section of Chapter 5) or the listings in *Budapest In Your Pocket,* available at newsstands or visit the Web site Backpackers.hu.

The Croatian YHA runs summer hostels in Zagreb and Pula. Although the hostels are open only to members, the cost of membership is relatively small and varies according to age: the younger you are, the cheaper it is.

All but one or two Czech hostels are located in two towns: Prague and Český Krumlov. They tend to be either backpacker-happy, party-all-night places or affiliated with sports clubs or colleges. Most accommodation services in Prague book hostel rooms. The Prague representative of Hostelling International is KMC Travel Service. A relatively well run Prague hostel, with six local sites and affiliates in Český Krumlov, Budapest, and Berlin, is Travellers' Hostel.

Hostels in Slovakia are only run in university dormitories during summer vacation, July to September. For general orientation, contact Satur or Bratislavská Informačná Služba (☞ Visitor Information *in* the Bratislava A to Z section *in* Chapter 8).

➤ LOCAL CONTACTS: **Back Pack Guesthouse** (✉ District XI, Takács Menyhért u. 33, Budapest, ☎ 1/385–8946, WEB www.backpackbudapest.hu). **Backpackers.hu** (WEB www.backpackers.hu). **Croatian YHA** (✉ Dežmanova 9, Zagreb, ☎ 01/4847–953, FAX 01/4841–269). The Prague representative of Hostelling International is **KMC Travel Service** (✉ Karolíny Světlé 30, Prague, ☎ 02/2222–1328). **Sirály Youth Hostel** (✉ District XIII, Margit-sziget [Margaret Island], Budapest, ☎ 1/329–3952). A relatively well run Prague hostel, with six local sites and affiliates in Budapest and Berlin, is **Travellers' Hostel** (✉ Dlouhá 33, Český Krumlov, ☎ 02/2482–6662, WEB www.travellers.cz).

➤ ORGANIZATIONS: **Hostelling International—American Youth Hostels** (✉ 733 15th St. NW, Suite 840, Washington, DC 20005, ☎ 202/783–6161, FAX 202/783–6171, WEB www.hiayh.org). **Hostelling International—Canada** (✉ 400–205 Catherine St., Ottawa, Ontario K2P 1C3, ☎ 613/237–7884 or 800/663–5777, FAX 613/237–7868, WEB www.hihostels.ca). **Youth Hostel Association of England and Wales** (✉ Trevelyan House, Dimple Rd., Matlock, Derbyshire DE4 3YH, U.K., ☎ 0870/870–8808, FAX 0169/592–702, WEB www.yha.

org.uk). **Youth Hostel Association Australia** (✉ 10 Mallett St., Camperdown, NSW 2050, ☎ 02/9565–1699, FAX 02/9565–1325, WEB www.yha.com.au). **Youth Hostels Association of New Zealand** (✉ Level 3, 193 Cashel St. [Box 436, Christchurch], ☎ 03/379–9970, FAX 03/365–4476, WEB www.yha.org.nz).

HOTELS

Throughout the past decade the quality of hotels in Eastern and Central Europe has improved notably. Many formerly state-run hotels were privatized, much to their benefit—a transition process that is still on-going in some countries. International hotel chains have established a strong presence in the region; while they may not be strong on local character, they do provide a reliably high standard of quality.

Hotels listed throughout the book have private bath unless otherwise noted.

➤ TOLL-FREE NUMBERS: **Best Western** (☎ 800/528–1234, WEB www.bestwestern.com). **Choice** (☎ 800/424–6423, WEB www.choicehotels.com). **Days Inn** (☎ 800/325–2525, WEB www.daysinn.com). **Four Seasons** (☎ 800/332–3442, WEB www.fourseasons.com). **Hilton** (☎ 800/445–8667, WEB www.hilton.com). **Holiday Inn** (☎ 800/465–4329, WEB www..sixcontinentshotels.com). **Hyatt Hotels & Resorts** (☎ 800/233–1234, WEB www.hyatt.com). **Inter-Continental** (☎ 800/327–0200, WEB www.intercontinental.com). **Marriott** (☎ 888/236–2427, WEB www.marriott.com). **Le Meridien** (☎ 800/543–4300, WEB www.lemeridien-hotels.com). **Radisson** (☎ 800/333–3333, WEB www.radisson.com). **Renaissance Hotels & Resorts** (☎ 888/236–2427, WEB www.marriott.com). **Sheraton** (☎ 800/325–3535, WEB www.starwood.com/sheraton).

MAIL AND SHIPPING

For country-specific mail information, *see* Mail *in* the A to Z section at the end of each country chapter.

MONEY MATTERS

For country-specific money information, *see* Money and Expenses *in* the A to Z section at the end of each country chapter.

Prices throughout this guide are given for adults. Substantially reduced fees are almost always available for children, students, and senior citizens. For information on taxes, *see* Taxes, *below.*

ATMS

ATMs are common in large and midsize cities and more often than not are part of the Cirrus and Plus networks; outside of urban areas, machines are scarce and you should plan to carry enough cash to meet your needs.

CREDIT CARDS

Credit cards are accepted in places that cater regularly to foreign tourists and business travelers: hotels, restaurants, and shops, particularly in major urban centers. When you leave the beaten path, be prepared to pay cash. Always inquire about credit card policies when booking hotel rooms. Visa and EuroCard/MasterCard are the most commonly accepted credit cards in the region.

It's smart to **write down (and keep separate) the number of each credit card you're carrying** along with the international service phone number that usually appears on the back of the card.

Throughout this guide, the following abbreviations are used: **AE,** American Express; **DC,** Diners Club; **MC,** MasterCard; and **V,** Visa.

CURRENCY EXCHANGE

For the most favorable rates, **change money through banks.** Although ATM transaction fees may be higher abroad than at home, ATM rates are excellent because they are based on wholesale rates offered only by major banks. You won't do as well at exchange booths in airports or rail and bus stations, in hotels, in restaurants, or in stores. Romania is an exception; exchange bureaus have the best rates, especially in Bucharest and other large cities. To avoid lines at airport exchange booths, **get a bit of local currency before you leave home.**

➤ EXCHANGE SERVICES: **International Currency Express** (☎ 888/278–6628 orders). **Thomas Cook Currency Services** (☎ 800/287–7362 orders and retail locations, WEB www.us.thomascook.com).

TRAVELER'S CHECKS

Do you need traveler's checks? It depends on where you're headed. If you're going to rural areas and small towns, go with cash; traveler's checks are best used in cities. However, traveler's checks are virtually useless in Bulgaria, and in Romania are accepted only at large hotels, banks, and selected exchange offices. Lost or stolen checks can usually be replaced within 24 hours. To ensure a speedy refund, buy your own traveler's checks—don't let someone else pay for them: irregularities like this can cause delays. The person who bought the checks should make the call to request a refund.

PACKING

Don't worry about packing lots of formal clothing. Fashion was all but nonexistent under 40 years of Communist rule, although residents of Budapest, Prague, and even Bucharest and Sofia—catching up with their counterparts in other European capitals—are considerably more fashionably dressed than even a few years ago. Still, Western dress of virtually any kind is considered stylish: a sports jacket for men and a dress or pants for women are appropriate for an evening out. Everywhere else, you'll feel comfortable in casual pants or jeans.

Eastern and Central Europe enjoy all the extremes of an inland climate, so plan accordingly. In the higher elevations winter can last until April, and even in summer the evenings will be on the cool side.

Many areas are best seen on foot, so take a pair of sturdy walking shoes and be prepared to use them. High heels will present considerable problems on the cobblestone streets of Prague, Sofia, Warsaw, and towns in Hungary, or the potholed streets in Romania. If you plan to visit the mountains, make sure your shoes have good traction and ankle support, as some trails can be quite challenging.

Some items that you take for granted at home are occasionally unavailable or of questionable quality in Eastern and Central Europe, though the situation has been steadily improving. Toiletries and personal-hygiene products have become relatively easy to find, but it's always a good idea to bring necessities when traveling in rural areas. If you're heading to Bulgaria, make sure you have a flashlight with you at all times. Streetlights are rare, even in city centers, and often interior hallways are unlit.

In your carry-on luggage, **pack an extra pair of eyeglasses or contact lenses and enough of any medication** you take to last a few days longer than the entire trip. You may also ask your doctor to write a spare prescription using the drug's generic name, since brand names may vary from country to country. In luggage to be checked, **never pack prescription drugs or valuables.** And don't forget to carry with you the addresses of offices that handle refunds of lost traveler's checks. Check *Fodor's How to Pack* (available in bookstores everywhere) for more tips.

To avoid customs and security delays, carry medications in their original packaging. Don't pack any sharp objects in your carry-on luggage, including knives of any size or material, scissors, manicure tools, and corkscrews, or anything else that might arouse suspicion.

CHECKING LUGGAGE

You are allowed one carry-on bag and one personal article, such as a purse or a laptop computer. Make sure that everything you carry aboard will fit under your seat or in the overhead bin. Get to the gate early, so you can board as soon as possible, before the overhead bins fill up.

If you are flying internationally, note that baggage allowances may be determined not by piece but by weight—generally 88 pounds (40 kilograms) in first class, 66 pounds (30 kilograms) in business class, and 44 pounds (20 kilograms) in economy.

Airline liability for baggage is limited to $2,500 per person on flights within the United States. On international flights it amounts to $9.07 per pound or $20 per kilogram for checked baggage (roughly $640 per 70-pound bag) and $400 per passenger for unchecked baggage. You can buy additional coverage at check-in for about $10 per $1,000 of coverage, but it excludes a rather extensive list of items, shown on your airline ticket.

Before departure, **itemize your bags' contents** and their worth, and label the bags with your name, address, and phone number. (If you use your home address, cover it so potential thieves can't see it readily.) Inside each bag, **pack a copy of your itinerary.** At check-in, **make sure that each bag is correctly tagged** with the destination airport's three-letter code. If your bags arrive damaged or fail to arrive at all, file a written report with the airline before leaving the airport.

PASSPORTS AND VISAS

When traveling internationally, **carry your passport** even if you don't need one (it's always the best form of ID) and **make two photocopies of the data page** (one for someone at home and another for you, carried separately from your passport). If you lose your passport, promptly call the nearest embassy or consulate and the local police.

U.S. passport applications for children under age 14 require consent from both parents or legal guardians; both parents must appear together to sign the application. If only one parent appears, he or she must submit a written statement from the other parent authorizing passport issuance for the child. A parent with sole authority must present evidence of it when applying; acceptable documentation includes the child's certified birth certificate listing only the applying parent, a court order specifically permitting this parent's travel with the child, or a death certificate for the nonapplying parent. Application forms and instructions are available on the Web site of the U.S. State Department's Bureau of Consular Affairs (www.travel.state.gov).

ENTERING EASTERN AND CENTRAL EUROPE

See the A to Z section at the end of each country chapter for specific entrance requirements.

PASSPORT OFFICES

The best time to apply for a passport or to renew is in fall and winter. Before any trip, check your passport's expiration date, and, if necessary, renew it as soon as possible.

➤ AUSTRALIAN CITIZENS: **Australian State Passport Office** (☎ 131–232, WEB www.passports.gov.au).

➤ CANADIAN CITIZENS: **Passport Office** (to mail in applications: ✉ Department of Foreign Affairs and International Trade, Ottawa, Ontario K1A 0G3; ☎ 800/567–6868 in Canada; 819/994–3500; WEB www. dfait-maeci.gc.ca/passport).

➤ NEW ZEALAND CITIZENS: **New Zealand Passport Office** (☎ 0800/ 22–5050 or 04/474–8100, WEB www. passports.govt.nz).

➤ U.K. CITIZENS: **London Passport Office** (☎ 0870/521–0410, WEB www. passport.gov.uk).

➤ U.S. CITIZENS: **National Passport Information Center** (☎ 900/225– 5674, 35¢ per minute for automated service or $1.05 per minute for operator service, WEB www.travel.state.gov).

REST ROOMS

Public rest rooms are more common, and cleaner, than they used to be in the Czech Republic. You nearly always have to pay 2 Kč–10 Kč to the attendant. Restaurant and bar toilets are generally for customers only, but, as prices are low, this isn't a significant burden.

While the rest rooms at Budapest's Ferihegy Airport may sparkle and smell of soap, don't expect the same of those at Hungarian train and bus stations—which, by the way, usually have attendants on hand who collect a fee of about 40 Ft. Especially outside Budapest, public rest rooms are often run-down and sometimes rank. Pay the attendant on the way in; you will receive toilet tissue in exchange. Since public rest rooms are generally few and far between, you will sometimes find yourself entering cafés, bars, or restaurants primarily to use their toilets; when doing so, unless it happens to be a bustling fast-food place, you should probably order a little something.

In Poland, public washrooms generally have an attendant who will charge zł 1 for use. This usually ensures that the facilities are clean. There are plenty of hotels, pubs, and fast-food restaurants with rest rooms that can be used.

Public rest rooms are clean in major hotels and restaurants in Romania. Another safe bet is McDonald's. Otherwise, cleanliness and the supply of toilet paper and paper towels are hit and miss. Toilets in trains and train stations are only for the most desperate.

In Slovakia, toilets in restaurants and bars are generally well kept. Other public rest rooms are rare.

SAFETY

Crime rates are still relatively low in Eastern and Central Europe, but travelers should beware of pickpockets in crowded areas, especially on public transportation, at railway stations, and in big hotels. In general, always keep your valuables with you—in open bars and restaurants, purses hung on or placed next to chairs are easy targets. Make sure your wallet is safe in a buttoned pocket, or watch your handbag.

Keep a sharp eye out for pickpockets in Bulgaria and be very careful with your passport. (The black market price for an American or Canadian passport is around $1,000, which is almost the average yearly salary.) Ironically, you are required by Bulgarian law to carry your passport on your person at all times. In urban areas, you should also watch out for packs of stray dogs.

In Croatia the exceptional danger from land mines has been greatly reduced by government programs; however, care should be taken when in East Slavonia, the former area of conflict, and all deserted and unreconstructed areas should be considered still potentially hazardous. Nevertheless even here the main roads are guaranteed to be safe.

In the Czech Republic, except for widely scattered attacks against people of color, violent crime against tourists is extremely rare. Pickpocketing and bill-padding are the most common complaints.

In Hungary, pickpocketing and car theft are the main concerns. While a typical rental car is less likely to be stolen, expensive German makes such as Audi, BMW, and Mercedes are hot targets for car thieves.

Crime rates have been rising in major cities in Poland; besides watching out for the omnipresent pickpockets, you should observe the usual urban rules of caution: be extra attentive and stick to well-lit, well-trafficked areas at night.

In Romania, the streets are generally safe, but pickpocketing and scams are on the rise in cities, especially on trains and buses and in stations.

In Slovakia, car theft and pickpocketing at crowded areas and stores are the main concern.

Slovenia claims to have one of the lowest crime rates in Europe.

LOCAL SCAMS

To avoid potential trouble in the Czech Republic: ask taxi drivers what the approximate fare will be before getting in, and ask for a receipt (*paragon*); carefully look over restaurant bills; be extremely wary of handing your passport to anyone who accosts you with a demand for ID; and never exchange money on the street.

A notorious scam in some Romanian cities involves men flashing fake police badges and accusing you of exchanging currency illegally. Do not hand over your passport or money; instead, offer to accompany them (on foot) to your hotel or a police station. If you spot a uniformed policeman, summon him. On trains and buses, groups sometimes cause distractions, then make off with your valuables.

In Slovakia, ask taxi drivers about the expected fare before getting in. Asking for a receipt (*potvrdenka*) might also discourage a driver from charging you enormous fare, or it could be used when complaining about a fare to a taxi dispatcher.

WOMEN IN EASTERN AND CENTRAL EUROPE

Don't wear a money belt or a waist pack, both of which peg you as a tourist. If you carry a purse, choose one with a zipper and a thick strap that you can drape across your body; adjust the length so that the purse sits in front of you at or above hip level. Store only enough money in the purse to cover casual spending. Distribute the rest of your cash and any valuables (including credit cards and your passport) between a deep front pocket, an inside jacket or vest pocket, and a hidden money pouch. Do not reach for the money pouch once in public. It isn't wise for a woman to go alone to a bar or nightclub or to wander the streets late at night. When traveling by train at night, seek out compartments that are well populated.

SENIOR-CITIZEN TRAVEL

To qualify for age-related discounts, **mention your senior-citizen status up front** when booking hotel reservations (not when checking out) and before you're seated in restaurants (not when paying the bill). Be sure to have identification on hand. When renting a car, ask about promotional car-rental discounts, which can be cheaper than senior-citizen rates.

➤ EDUCATIONAL PROGRAMS: **Elderhostel** (✉ 11 Ave. de Lafayette, Boston, MA 02111-1746, ☎ 877/426–8056, FAX 877/426–2166, WEB www.elderhostel.org). **Interhostel** (✉ University of New Hampshire, 6 Garrison Ave., Durham, NH 03824, ☎ 603/862–1147 or 800/733–9753, FAX 603/862–1113, WEB www.learn.unh.edu).

STUDENTS IN EASTERN AND CENTRAL EUROPE

For country-specific student and youth travel information, *see* Student and Youth Travel *in* the A to Z section at the end of each country chapter.

➤ IDs AND SERVICES: **STA Travel** (☎ 212/627–3111 or 800/781–4040, FAX 212/627–3387, WEB www.sta.com). **Travel Cuts** (✉ 187 College St., Toronto, Ontario M5T 1P7, ☎ 416/979–2406 or 888/838–2887, FAX 416/979–8167, WEB www.travelcuts.com).

TAXES

Most Eastern and Central European countries have some form of value-added tax (VAT); rebate rules vary by country and seem to be in an ongoing state of evolution. Check with tourism offices (☞ Visitor Information, *below*) for current regulations. One thing you can depend on—you'll need to present your receipts on departure.

TELEPHONES

For additional country-specific telephone information, *see* Telephones *in* the A to Z section at the end of each country chapter.

AREA AND COUNTRY CODES

Country and select city codes are as follows: Bulgaria (359), Sofia (2); Croatia (385), Dubrovnik (20), Split (21), Zagreb (1); Czech Republic (420), Prague (2); Hungary (36), Budapest (1); Poland (48), Warsaw (22); Romania (40), Bucharest (1); Slovakia (421), Bratislava (7); Slovenia (386), Ljubljana (1).

When dialing an Eastern or Central European number from abroad, drop the initial 0 from the local area code. The country code for the United States and Canada is 1, 61 for Australia, 64 for New Zealand, and 44 for the U.K.

LONG-DISTANCE SERVICES

AT&T, MCI, and Sprint access codes make calling long distance relatively convenient, but you may find the local access number blocked in many hotel rooms. First ask the hotel operator to connect you. If the hotel operator balks, ask for an international operator, or dial the international operator yourself. One way to improve your odds of getting connected to your long-distance carrier is to travel with more than one company's calling card (a hotel may block Sprint, for example, but not MCI). If all else fails, call from a pay phone.

➤ ACCESS CODES: **AT&T Direct** (☎ 008000010 in Bulgaria; 0800220111 in Croatia; 0042000101 in the Czech Republic; 0042100101 in Slovakia; 0080001111 in Hungary; 008001111111 in Poland; 01/800–4288 in Romania; 800/435–0812 for

other areas). **MCI WorldPhone**
(☎ 008000001 in Bulgaria;
08000122222 in Croatia;
0042000112 in the Czech Republic;
0680001411 in Hungary;
008001112122 in Poland; 01/800–
1800 in Romania; 0018814220042
in Slovakia; 080–8808 in Slovenia).
Sprint International Access (☎
008001010 in Bulgaria; 0800220113
in Croatia; 0042087187 in the Czech
Republic; 0680001877 in Hungary;
008001113115 in Poland; 01/800–
0877 in Romania; 0018818249242 in
Slovakia; 800/877–4646 for other
areas).

TIME

Croatia, the Czech Republic, Hungary, Poland, Slovakia, and Slovenia
are on Central European Time (CET),
one hour ahead of Greenwich Mean
Time and six hours ahead of the
Eastern time zone of the United States.
Bulgaria and Romania are two hours
ahead of Greenwich Mean Time.

TIPPING

For country-specific tipping guide-
lines, *see* the A to Z section at the end
of each chapter.

TOURS AND PACKAGES

Because everything is prearranged on
a prepackaged tour or independent
vacation, you'll spend less time planning—and often get it all at a good
price.

BOOKING WITH AN AGENT

Travel agents are excellent resources.
But it's a good idea to collect brochures from several agencies, as some
agents' suggestions may be influenced
by relationships with tour and package firms that reward them for volume sales. If you have a special
interest, **find an agent with expertise
in that area**; the American Society of
Travel Agents (ASTA; ☞ Travel
Agencies, *below*) has a database of
specialists worldwide.

Make sure your travel agent knows
the accommodations and other services of the place being recommended. Ask about the hotel's
location, room size, beds, and
whether it has a pool, room service,
or programs for children, if you care
about these. Has your agent been

there in person or sent others whom
you can contact?

Do some homework on your own,
too: local tourism boards can provide
information about lesser-known and
small-niche operators, some of which
may sell only direct.

Each year consumers are stranded or
lose their money when tour operators—even large ones with excellent
reputations—go out of business. So
check out the operator. Ask several
travel agents about its reputation, and
try to **book with a company that has a
consumer-protection program.** (Look
for information in the company's
brochure.) In the United States, members of the National Tour Association
and the United States Tour Operators
Association are required to set aside
funds to cover your payments and
travel arrangements in the event that
the company defaults. It's also a good
idea to choose a company that partici-
pates in the American Society of
Travel Agents' Tour Operator Program (TOP); ASTA will act as media-
tor in any disputes between you and
your tour operator.

Remember that the more your package or tour includes the better you
can predict the ultimate cost of your
vacation. Make sure you know exactly what is covered, and **beware of
hidden costs.** Are taxes, tips, and
transfers included? Entertainment and
excursions? These can add up.

➤ TOUR-OPERATOR RECOMMENDA-
TIONS: **American Society of Travel
Agents** (☞ Travel Agencies, *below*).
National Tour Association (NTA;
✉ 546 E. Main St., Lexington, KY
40508, ☎ 859/226–4444 or 800/
682–8886, WEB www.ntaonline.com).
**United States Tour Operators Associ-
ation** (USTOA; ✉ 275 Madison Ave.,
Suite 2014, New York, NY 10016, ☎
212/599–6599 or 800/468–7862, FAX
212/599–6744, WEB www.ustoa.com).

TRAIN TRAVEL

Although standards have improved, on
the whole they are far short of what is
acceptable in the West. Trains are very
busy, and it is rare to find one running
less than full or almost so. All seven
countries operate their own dining,
buffet, and refreshment services.

Always crowded, they tend to open and close at the whim of the staff. In Bulgaria and Hungary, couchette cars are second-class only and can be little more than a hard bunk without springs and adequate bed linen. In Romania, there are first-class couchettes (though they are comparable to second- or third-class compartments in Western Europe); these have room for two people and are relatively safe and clean. First-class couchettes are also available on Czech and Slovak trains, and there are two types of second-class couchettes. The cheaper have six hard beds per compartment; the slightly more expensive have three beds and a sink and are sex-segregated. Some of the most comfortable trains are the express trains in Croatia, the Czech Republic, Hungary, Poland, Slovakia, and Slovenia—they're normally less crowded and more comfortable. (You should make a reservation.)

Although trains in Eastern and Central Europe can mean hours of sitting on a hard seat in a smoky car, traveling by rail is very inexpensive. Rail networks in all the Eastern and Central European countries are very extensive, though trains can be infuriatingly slow. You'll invariably enjoy interesting and friendly traveling company, however; most Eastern and Central Europeans are eager to hear about the West and to discuss the enormous changes in their own countries.

For information about fares and schedules and other country-specific train information, *see* Train Travel *in* the A to Z section at the end of each country chapter.

CUTTING COSTS

To save money, **look into rail passes.** But be aware that if you don't plan to cover many miles you may come out ahead by buying individual tickets.

You can use the European East Pass on the national rail networks of Austria, the Czech Republic, Hungary, Poland, and Slovakia. The pass covers five days of unlimited first-class travel within a one-month period for $199. Additional travel days may be purchased.

You can also combine the East Pass with a national rail pass. The Bulgar-ian Flexipass costs $70 for three days of unlimited first-class travel within a one-month period. A pass for the Czech Republic costs $69 for 5 days of train travel within a 15-day period—far more than you'd spend on individual tickets. The Hungarian Flexipass costs $64 for five days of unlimited first-class train travel within a 15-day period or $80 for 10 days within a one-month period.

The Balkan Flexipass covers first-class train travel through Bulgaria and Romania, as well as Greece, Macedonia, Turkey, and Yugoslavia; there are passes for 5, 10, or 15 travel days in a one-month period for $152, $264, and $317, respectively.

Hungary is one of 17 countries in which you can **use Eurailpasses,** which provide unlimited first-class rail travel in all of the participating countries for the duration of the pass. If you plan to rack up the miles, get a standard pass. These are available for 15 days ($554), 21 days ($718), one month ($890), two months ($1,260), and three months ($1,558).

In addition to standard Eurailpasses, **ask about special rail-pass plans.** Among these are the Eurail Youthpass (for those under age 26), the Eurail Saverpass (which gives a discount for two or more people traveling together), a Eurail Flexipass (which allows a certain number of travel days within a set period), the Euraildrive Pass and the Europass Drive (which combines travel by train and rental car). Whichever pass you choose, remember that you must **purchase your pass before you leave** for Europe.

Many travelers assume that rail passes guarantee them seats on the trains they wish to ride. Not so. You need to **book seats ahead even if you are using a rail pass;** seat reservations are required on some European trains, particularly high-speed trains, and are a good idea on trains that may be crowded—particularly in summer on popular routes. You will also need a reservation if you purchase sleeping accommodations.

➤ INFORMATION AND PASSES: **Rail Europe** (⊠ 500 Mamaroneck Ave., Harrison, NY 10528, ☎ 914/682–

5172 or 800/438–7245, FAX 800/432–1329; ⊠ 2087 Dundas E, Suite 106, Mississauga, Ontario L4X 1M2, ☎ 800/361–7245, FAX 905/602–4198, WEB www.raileurope.com). **DER Travel Services** (⊠ 9501 W. Devon Ave., Rosemont, IL 60018, ☎ 800/782–2424, FAX 800/282–7474 information; 800/860–9944 brochures; WEB www.dertravel.com). **CIT Tours Corp** (⊠ 15 W. 44th St., 10th floor, New York, NY 10036, ☎ 212/730–2400; 800/248–7245 in the U.S.; 800/387–0711; 800/361–7799 in Canada; WEB www.cit-tours.com).

FROM THE U.K.

There are no direct trains from London. You can take a direct train from Paris to Warsaw or via Frankfurt to Prague (daily) or from Berlin to Warsaw or via Dresden to Prague (5 times a day). Vienna is a good starting point for Prague, Brno, or Bratislava. There are three trains a day to Prague from Vienna's Südbahnhof (South Station) via Brno (5 hours). Bratislava can be reached from Vienna by a 67-minute shuttle service, which runs every two hours during the day. You should check out times and routes before leaving. Sofia has service to Bucharest, Budapest, and Vienna, but for travelers without the necessary visas, it can be a long, out-of-the-way journey to skirt Serbia.

TRAVEL AGENCIES

A good travel agent puts your needs first. Look for an agency that has been in business at least five years, emphasizes customer service, and has someone on staff who specializes in your destination. In addition, **make sure the agency belongs to a professional trade organization.** The American Society of Travel Agents (ASTA)—the largest and most influential in the field, with more than 24,000 members in some 140 countries—maintains and enforces a strict code of ethics and will step in to help mediate any agent-client disputes involving ASTA members if necessary. ASTA (whose motto is "Without a travel agent, you're on your own") also maintains a Web site that includes a directory of agents. (If a travel agency is also acting as your tour operator, *see* Buyer Beware *in* Tours and Packages, *above*.)

▶ LOCAL AGENT REFERRALS: **American Society of Travel Agents** (ASTA; ⊠ 1101 King St., Suite 200, Alexandria, VA 22314, ☎ 800/965–2782 24-hr hot line, FAX 703/739–3268, WEB www.astanet.com). **Association of British Travel Agents** (⊠ 68–71 Newman St., London W1T 3AH, ☎ 020/7637–2444, FAX 020/7637–0713, WEB www.abtanet.com). **Association of Canadian Travel Agents** (⊠ 130 Albert St., Suite 1705, Ottawa, Ontario K1P 5G4, ☎ 613/237–3657, FAX 613/237–7052, WEB www.acta.ca). **Australian Federation of Travel Agents** (⊠ Level 3, 309 Pitt St., Sydney, NSW 2000, ☎ 02/9264–3299, FAX 02/9264–1085, WEB www.afta.com.au). **Travel Agents' Association of New Zealand** (⊠ Level 5, Tourism and Travel House, 79 Boulcott St. [Box 1888, Wellington 6001], ☎ 04/499–0104, FAX 04/499–0827, WEB www.taanz.org.nz).

VISITOR INFORMATION

▶ BULGARIA: **Balkan Holidays** (⊠ 19 Conduit St., London, W1S 2BH, ☎ 020/7543–5555 or 0845/130–1114, FAX 020/7543–5577, WEB www.balkanholidays.co.uk).

▶ CROATIA: **Croatian National Tourist Office** (in the U.S.: ⊠ 350 5th Ave., Suite 4003, New York, NY 10118, ☎ 212/279–8672 or 212/279–8674, FAX 212/279–8683; in the U.K.: ⊠ 2, Lanchesters, 162–164 Fulham Palace Rd., London W6 9ER, ☎ 020/8563–7979, FAX 020/8563–2616, WEB www.croatia.hr).

▶ CZECH REPUBLIC: **Czech Tourist Authority** (in the U.S.: ⊠ 1109–1111 Madison Ave., New York, NY 10028, ☎ 212/288–0830, FAX 212/288–0971, www.czechcenter.com; in Canada: ⊠ Czech Airlines office, Simpson Tower, 401 Bay St., Suite 1510, Toronto, Ontario M5H 2YA, ☎ 416/363–3174, FAX 416/363–0239; in the U.K.: ⊠ 95 Great Portland St., London W1N 5RA, ☎ 020/7291–9925, FAX 020/7436–8300, WEB www.czechcentre.org.uk).

▶ HUNGARY: In the U.S. and Canada: **Hungarian National Tourist Office** (⊠ 150 E. 58th St., New York, NY 10155, ☎ 212/355–0240, FAX 212/207–4103, WEB www.gotohungary.com). In Canada: **Hungarian Consulate General Office** (⊠

121 Bloor St. E, Suite 1115, Toronto M4W3M5, Ontario, ☎ 416/923–8981, FAX 416/923–2732). In the U.K.: **Hungarian National Tourist Board** (✉ c/o Embassy of the Republic of Hungary, Commercial Section, 46 Eaton Pl., London, SW1X 8AL, ☎ 020/7823–1032 or 020/7823–1055, FAX 020/7823–1459, htlondon@hungarytourism.hu).

➤ POLAND: **Polish National Tourist Office** (in the U.S. and Canada: ✉ 275 Madison Ave., Suite 1711, New York, NY 10016, ☎ 212/338–9412, FAX 212/338–9283; in the U.K.: ✉ Remo House, 1st floor, 310–312 Regent St., London W1R 5AJ, ☎ 020/7580–8811, FAX 020/7580–8866, WEB www.polandtour.org).

➤ ROMANIA: **Romanian National Tourist Office** (in the U.S. and Canada: ✉ 14 E. 38th St., 12th floor, New York, NY 10016, ☎ 212/545–8484, FAX 212/251–0429; in the U.K.: ✉ 22 New Cavendish St., London W1M 7LH, ☎ 020/7224–3692, FAX 020/7935–6435).

➤ SLOVAKIA: In the U.S.: **Slovak Information Center** (✉ 406 E. 67th St., New York, NY 10021, ☎ 212/737–3971, FAX 212/737–3454). In Canada: **Slovak Culture and Information Center** (✉ 12 Birch Ave., Toronto, Ontario M4V 1C8, ☎ 416/925–0008, FAX 416/925–0009, WEB www.slovak.com/scic). In the U.K.: **Czech and Slovak Tourist Centre** (✉ 16 Frognal Parade, Finchley Rd., London NW3 5HG, ☎ 0207/7794–3263, FAX 020/7794–3265, WEB www.czechtravel.co.uk).

➤ SLOVENIA: In the U.S.: **Slovenian Tourist Office** (✉ 345 E. 12th St., New York, NY 10003, ☎ 212/358–9686, FAX 212/358–9025, WEB www.sloveniatravel.com). In the U.K.: **Slovenian Tourist Office** (✉ 49 Conduit St., London W1R 9FB, ☎ 020/7287–7133, FAX 020/7287–5476).

➤ U.S. GOVERNMENT ADVISORIES: **U.S. Department of State** (✉ Overseas Citizens Services Office, Room 4811, 2201 C St. NW, Washington, DC 20520, ☎ 202/647–5225 interactive hot line; 888/407–4747; WEB www.travel.state.gov); enclose a business-size SASE.

WEB SITES

Do check out the World Wide Web when planning your trip. You'll find everything from weather forecasts to virtual tours of famous cities. Be sure to **visit Fodors.com** (www.fodors.com), a complete travel-planning site. You can research prices and book plane tickets, hotel rooms, rental cars, vacation packages, and more. In addition, you can post your pressing questions in the "Travel Talk" section. Other planning tools include a currency converter and weather reports, and there are loads of links to travel resources.

➤ SUGGESTED WEB SITES: Bulgaria: **National Information and Advertising Centre** (WEB www.bulgariatravel.org). Croatia: **Croatian National Tourist Board** (WEB www.htz.hr). Czech Republic: **Czech Tourist Authority** (WEB www.visitczechia.cz). Hungary: **Live Budapest** (www.livebudapest.com). Poland: **Poland National Tourist Office** (www.polandtour.org). Romania: **Romania Tourist Promotion Office** (WEB www.romaniatravel.org). Slovakia: **Slovakia.Org** (WEB www.slovakia.org). Slovenia: **Slovenia Tourism Board** (www.slovenia-tourism.si).

WHEN TO GO

The tourist season generally runs from April or May through October; spring and fall combine good weather with a more bearable level of tourism. The ski season lasts from mid-December through March. Outside the mountain resorts you will encounter few other visitors; you'll have the opportunity to see the region covered in snow, but many of the sights are closed, and it can get very, very cold. If you're not a skier, try visiting the Giant Mountain of Bohemia, the High Tatras in Slovakia and Poland, and the Romanian Carpathians in late spring or fall; the colors are dazzling, and you'll have the hotels and restaurants pretty much to yourself. Bear in mind that many attractions are closed from November through March.

Prague and Budapest are beautiful year-round, but avoid midsummer (especially July and August) and the Christmas and Easter holidays, when the two cities are choked with visitors. Warsaw, too, suffers a heavy influx of tourists during the summer season, though not on quite the same grand scale. Lake Balaton in Hungary becomes a mob scene in July and August. In Slovenia, the Adriatic coast is terribly busy through mid-summer: Better to visit in June or September, or head for the mountain lakes of Triglav National Park instead. In Bulgaria, the best summer destinations are the gorgeous Black Sea fishing villages, or the medieval mountain towns in the interior, where cool breezes and sports opportunities make for a refreshing, if rugged, summer holiday. At the opposite end of the spectrum, Bucharest and Sofia are rarely crowded, even at the height of summer. In July and August, however, the weather in these capitals sometimes borders on stifling. Croatia enjoys a Mediterranean climate on its coast, and the mountains provide protection from extremes. Spring comes early, and fall is long and pleasant.

For additional country-specific information, *see* When to Tour following the Great Itineraries at the beginning of each country chapter.

CLIMATE

The following are the average daily maximum and minimum temperatures for major cities in the region.

➤ FORECASTS: **Weather Channel Connection** (☎ 900/932–8437), 95¢ per minute from a Touch-Tone phone.

BRATISLAVA

Jan.	36F	2C	May	70F	21C	Sept.	72F	22C
	27	− 3		52	11		54	12
Feb.	39F	4C	June	75F	24C	Oct.	59F	15C
	28	− 2		57	14		45	7
Mar.	48F	9C	July	79F	26C	Nov.	46F	8C
	34	1		61	16		37	3
Apr.	61F	16C	Aug.	79F	26C	Dec.	39F	4C
	43	6		61	16		32	0

BUCHAREST

Jan.	34F	1C	May	74F	23C	Sept.	78F	25C
	19	− 7		51	10		52	11
Feb.	38F	4C	June	81F	27C	Oct.	65F	18C
	23	− 5		57	14		43	6
Mar.	50F	10C	July	86F	30C	Nov.	49F	10C
	30	− 1		60	16		35	2
Apr.	64F	18C	Aug.	85F	30C	Dec.	39F	4C
	41	5		59	15		26	− 3

BUDAPEST

Jan.	34F	1C	May	72F	22C	Sept.	73F	23C
	25	− 4		52	11		54	12
Feb.	39F	4C	June	79F	26C	Oct.	61F	16C
	28	− 2		59	15		45	7
Mar.	50F	10C	July	82F	28C	Nov.	46F	8C
	36	2		61	16		37	3
Apr.	63F	17C	Aug.	81F	27C	Dec.	39F	4C
	25	− 4		61	16		30	− 1

LJUBLJANA

Jan.	36F	2C	May	68F	20C	Sept.	71F	22C
	25	− 4		48	9		51	11
Feb.	41F	5C	June	75F	24C	Oct.	59F	15C
	25	− 4		54	12		43	6
Mar.	50F	10C	July	80F	27C	Nov.	47F	8C
	32	0		57	14		36	2
Apr.	60F	15C	Aug.	78F	26C	Dec.	39F	4C
	40	4		57	14		30	− 1

PRAGUE

Jan.	36F	2C	May	66F	19C	Sept.	68F	20C
	25	– 4		46	8		50	10
Feb.	37F	3C	June	72F	22C	Oct.	55F	13C
	27	– 3		52	11		41	5
Mar.	46F	8C	July	75F	24C	Nov.	46F	8C
	32	0		55	13		36	2
Apr.	58F	14C	Aug.	73F	23C	Dec.	37F	3C
	39	4		55	13		28	– 2

SOFIA

Jan.	35F	2C	May	69F	21C	Sept.	70F	22C
	25	– 4		50	10		52	11
Feb.	39F	4C	June	76F	24C	Oct.	63F	17C
	27	– 3		56	14		46	8
Mar.	50F	10C	July	81F	27C	Nov.	48F	9C
	33	1		60	16		37	3
Apr.	60F	16C	Aug.	79F	26C	Dec.	38F	4C
	42	5		59	15		28	– 2

SPLIT

Jan.	50F	10C	May	76F	24C	Sept.	76F	24C
	41	5		61	16		63	17
Feb.	54F	12C	June	81F	27C	Oct.	63F	17C
	43	6		64	18		52	11
Mar.	59F	15C	July	86F	30C	Nov.	55F	13C
	45	7		68	20		48	9
Apr.	68F	20C	Aug.	81F	27C	Dec.	50F	10C
	50	10		64	18		41	5

WARSAW

Jan.	32F	0C	May	68F	20C	Sept.	66F	19C
	21	– 6		48	9		50	10
Feb.	32F	0C	June	73F	23C	Oct.	55F	13C
	21	– 6		54	12		41	5
Mar.	43F	6C	July	75F	24C	Nov.	43F	6C
	28	– 2		59	15		34	1
Apr.	54F	12C	Aug.	73F	23C	Dec.	36F	2C
	37	3		57	14		27	– 3

FESTIVALS AND SEASONAL EVENTS

BULGARIA

For exact dates of annual events or other information, check with any local tourist agency. These agencies generally have an English-speaking staff member on hand who will have the most up-to-date information.

➤ DEC.–JAN.: **Sofia International New Year's Music Festival** is a winter version of the summer Music Days. Parties on New Year's Eve turn almost every *mehana* (folk restaurant) in the mountain towns of Bansko, Pamporovo, and Borovets into must-see Bulgarian folk spectacles.

➤ MAR.: The **March Music Days Festival** in Roussé brings together musicians, conductors, and orchestras from all over the world. Some of the finest pieces of classical music are performed by internationally known artists throughout the month.

➤ MAY–JUNE: **Sofia Music Days,** focusing on classical and contemporary orchestral repertoire, attract internationally recognized musicians, conductors, orchestras, and choruses. Concerts are held at the Bulgaria Concert Hall and the National Palace of Culture. The **Albena Chess Festival and International Masters' Tournament** is held annually at the Black Sea resort of Albena. The **Rose Festival** in the Valley of the Roses is held in the town of Kazanlak. Dancers and singers perform after the predawn gathering of rosebuds by "rose maidens." In Stara Zagora, in May, you can spend a week learning to appreciate Bulgarian stagecraft during the **Festival of Opera and Ballet,** or in the first weekend of June, check out the newly instituted **Festival of Folk Arts.** At the end of June Plovdiv hosts the **International Chamber Music Festival,** when many intimate concerts are held in the small churches of the Old Town.

➤ JUNE–JULY: **Varna Summer International Music Festival** is held in Varna and Golden Sands. A variant of **Sofia Music Days,** focusing on modern and international music, continues through the end of July in the capital. On June 16, the border town of Roussé holds a folk festival called **Golden Rebec,** featuring singing, crafts, and feasts with a slight Romanian influence.

➤ JUNE–AUG.: The **International Windsurfing Regatta** takes place at the Black Sea resorts of Golden Sands, Sunny Beach, and Sozopol.

➤ AUG.: **Rozhen Sings National Fair,** held in Rozhen near the mountain resort Pamporovo, features Bulgarian folk singers, dancers, and revelers outfitted in traditional costumes. A similar gathering can be found at the end of the month on the Black Sea in the city of Burgas. The historic village of **Koprivshtitsa** also hosts a folk music festival over an early August weekend. Plovdiv also has a **Folk Festival** held on the last weekend in August. The most popular August event is the **Golden Orpheus,** an international festival of Bulgarian pop music. It has been drawing crowds to Sunny Beach, or Slanchev Bryag, during the last week in August, for the last 30 years.

➤ SEPT.: Probably the most famous and popular festival in all of Bulgaria, the **Apollonia Festival of the Arts** in Sozopol, includes art exhibitions, theater, poetry readings, and street events. At the end of the month, the cosmopolitan crowds move to Varna for the **Golden Rose International Film Festival.** Though the event has taken place annually for more than 40 years, it has only recently begun to feature some of the best and brightest filmmakers in Eastern Europe and farther abroad.

➤ OCT.: Roussé attracts jazz lovers to its **International Jazz Forum,** with concerts in the larger performance venues as well as a tight schedule of back-to-back jazz in bars and clubs.

➤ NOV.: **Kinomania,** roughly translated as Film Fever, turns Sofia's National Palace of Culture into a giant film complex for three weeks. With the newest and best Bulgarian and international films of the year playing all day long in all 15 theaters, it is a movie-lover's extravaganza.

CROATIA

For exact dates and further information about the following events, check the Croatian National Tourist Board Web site, www.croatia.hr.

➤ FEB.: Rijeka stages **Karneval,** the second-biggest Carnival celebration in Europe after Venice.

➤ JULY: The Roman Arena in Pula makes a stunning venue for the five-day **Pula Film Festival.** Around the same time, the five-day **International Folklore Festival** in Zagreb attracts folklore groups from Eastern Europe and beyond, staging music and dance in traditional costume.

➤ JULY–AUG.: Croatia's largest and most prestigious cultural event, the **Dubrovnik Summer Festival,** draws international artists and musicians and features drama, ballet, concerts, and opera, all performed on open-air stages within the city fortifications. Similarly, the **Split Summer Festival** hosts opera, theater, and dance events at open-air venues within the walls of Diocletian's Roman Palace. In the capital, **Zagreb Summer Evenings** sees a range of concerts performed by internationally renowned musicians at various venues around the city. In Porec, the **Jazz Concerts** in the Porec Lapidarium attracts local and foreign musicians, and cover the jazz spectrum from classical to ethno.

➤ JULY–SEPT.: In Porec, the **Concert Season** in the Basilica of St Euphrasius features eminent musicians from Croatia and abroad, with sacral and secular music from all periods played inside the magnificent 6th-century basilica.

➤ SEPT.–OCT.: The **Varaždin Baroque Evenings** see eminent soloists and orchestras from Croatia and abroad perform Baroque music recitals in the city's most beautiful churches.

➤ NOV.: In Zagorje, **Martinje (St Martin's Day)** sees the blessing of the season's new wine, accompanied by a hearty feast and endless toasts.

CZECH REPUBLIC

➤ DEC.: **Christmas Fairs and Programs** take place in most towns and cities; among those particularly worth catching are **Christmas in Valašsko,** in Rožnov pod Radhoštěm, and the **Arrival of Lady Winter Festival,** in Prachatice.

➤ JAN.: Prague hosts the **FebioFest International Film, Television and Video Festival.**

➤ MAR.: The Czech Republic's **Alpine Skiing Championships** take place in Špindlerův Mlýn; Prague holds **St. Matthew's Fair,** an annual children's fair at the Výstaviště exhibition grounds. Prague is also the site of **Days of European Film.**

➤ APR.: Eastertime brings two festivals of sacred music to Prague, **Musica Ecumenica** and **Musica Sacra Praga.** Brno puts on an **Easter Spiritual Music Festival.** English-language and world authors appear at the **Prague Writers' Festival.**

➤ MAY: There are events both athletic and artistic in Prague; there's the **Prague Spring International Music Festival** as well as the **Prague Marathon.** An **International Children's Film Festival** is held in Zlín, while the **Janáček's May Music Festival** begins in Ostrava. For music in a Bohemian spa town, head to the **Karlovy Vary International Jazz Festival.**

➤ JUNE: The international dance festival **Tanec Praha** hits the capital. There's an **International Folklore Festival** in the Moravian town Strážnice, and world-record attempts and other weirdness grace the **Town of Records Festival** in Pelhřimov. The long-running **Smetana's Litomyšl** festival brings opera lovers to the composer's birthplace; and the equally venerable **Kmoch's Kolín** lures brass-band enthusiasts to central Bohemia.

➤ JULY: Karlovy Vary has its own **International Film Festival. Chrudim Puppeteering** is a puppet theater festival; Jindřichův Hradec puts on a folk music festival, **Folk Rose.** The **Dvořák's Nelahozeves** concert series gets started in that composer's home village.

➤ AUG.: This is a great month for music of all kinds. Prague's **Verdi Festival** is staged at the State Opera, while Český Krumlov has an **International Music Festival** and Strakonice hosts the **International Bagpipe Festival.** For something more musically ornate, visit the **Baroque Opera Festival** in Valtice.

➤ SEPT.: You'll need to book a hotel room well in advance for Brno's **International Engineering Fair.** Prague holds several arts festivals, preeminently the **Prague Autumn International Music Festival.** It's also the season for wine festivals, such as the **Pálava Vintage Celebrations** in Mikulov and the **Mělník Vintage Celebrations.**

➤ OCT.: The capital continues its run of cultural events, including an **International Jazz Festival** and the **Dance Theater Festival.** Out in eastern Bohemia, the **Velká Pardubická Steeplechase** is considered one of Europe's toughest racing events, and Hradec Králové holds its **Jazz Goes to Town Festival.**

➤ NOV.: Prague stokes the cultural fires against the approach of winter with the **Czech Press Photo Exhibition** and **Musica Iudaica,** a festival of Jewish music.

HUNGARY

For contact information about most of these festivals, inquire at the Budapest Tourinform office or the local visitor information center.

➤ MID-MAR.–EARLY APR.: The season's first and biggest arts festival, the **Budapest Spring Festival,** showcases Hungary's best opera, music, theater, fine arts, and dance, as well as visiting foreign artists. Other towns—including Kecskemét, Szentendre, and Pécs—also participate. This includes, for example, the **Debrecen Jazz Festival,** which features local and international ensembles.

➤ MAY: The **Balaton Festival** in Keszthely features high-caliber classical concerts and other festivities held in venues around town and outdoors on Kossuth Lajos utca.

➤ JUNE: Kőszeg's biggest cultural event, held early in the month, is the annual **East West Folk Festival**—a weekend of open-air international folk music and dance performances. Szombathely's gala **Savaria International Dance Competition** (one day in early June) features a full day of elegant ballroom dancing by competing pairs from around the world. The monthlong **Sopron Festival Weeks,** beginning in mid-June, brings music, dance, and theater performances and art exhibits to churches and venues around town.

➤ LATE JUNE–EARLY JULY: The **World Music Festival** in Budapest, held in early July, has several days of world music concerts by local and international artists. The **International Puppet Festival** draws puppeteers from Hungary and abroad to Sárospatak, July 1–4 every two years, in even-numbered years.

➤ LATE JUNE–LATE AUG.: The **Szentendre Summer Days** festival, which begins in late June and goes right through the third week in August, offers open-air theater performances and jazz and classical concerts.

➤ JULY: The **Visegrád International Palace Games** includes medieval jousting tournaments and festivities. Late in the month, Balatonfüred's **Anna Ball** is a traditional ball and beauty contest. In Vác the last weekend in July, the **Váci Világi Vígalom** (Vác World Jamboree) festival is held, with folk dancing, music, crafts fairs, and other festivities.

Every two years in early or mid-July (even-numbered years), Kecskemét hosts a giant children's festival, **Európa Jövője Gyermektalálkozó** (Future of Europe Children's Convention), during which children's groups from some 25 countries put on colorful folk-dance and singing performances. Debrecen's biannual **Béla Bartók International Choral Festival,** early in the month (in even-numbered years) is an international choir competition.

➤ JULY–AUG.: Equestrian fans will not want to miss the **Hortobágy International Horse Show,** held in Máta annually for three or four days between early July and mid-August. Established in the 1930s, the annual **Szegedi Szabadtéri Napok** (Open-Air Days) offers a gala series of dramas, operas, operettas, classical concerts, and folk-dance performances by Hungarian and international artists. Tickets are always a hot commodity; plan far ahead. From around the last week in July and the first in August, the **Festival Weeks in Baroque Eger** presents classical concerts, dance, and other arts programs.

➤ AUG.: Toward mid-month, Budapest hosts a **Formula 1** car race, while the weeklong **BudaFest** opera and ballet festival takes place mid-month at the opera house after the opera season ends. **St. Stephen's Day** (August 20) is a major national holiday. Two highlights are the fireworks in Budapest and Debrecen's **Flower Carnival,** which features a festive parade of flower-covered floats and carriages. Held annually around August 20, **Hortobágy Bridge Fair** brings horse shows, a folk-art fair, ox roasts, and festive crowds to the plot beneath the famous Nine-Arch Bridge. The weeklong **Jewish Summer Festival,** held in late August and early September, features cantors, classical concerts, a kosher cabaret, films, and theater and dance performances, in Budapest and sometimes elsewhere.

Every two years Esztergom hosts the **Nemzetközi Gitár Fesztivál** (International Guitar Festival), during which renowned classical guitarists from around the world hold master classes and workshops for participants. The festival runs for two weeks early in the month in odd-numbered years.

➤ SEPT.: The **Eger Harvest Festival** early in the month celebrates the grape harvest with a traditional parade and wine tastings.

➤ EARLY OCT.: Tokaj's annual **Szüreti Hét** (Harvest Week) celebrates the autumn grape harvest with a parade, street ball, folk-art markets, and a plethora of wine-tasting opportunities from the local vintners' stands set up on and around the main square.

POLAND

➤ DEC.: **St. Nicholas Day** (December 6) is prevalent in the south; children receive gifts and dress as mummers. Kraków's **Christmas Crèche Competition** displays handmade nativity crèches.

➤ JAN.: Warsaw holds a Polish theater festival, **Warsawskie Spotkania Teatralne.**

➤ MAR.–APR.: All over Poland, you'll find **Easter Celebrations.** On Good Friday, symbolic "God's graves" are dressed and displayed in churches. Everyone celebrates at Ressurrection Masses on Saturday night. In Kalwaria Zebrzydowska, 30 km southwest of Kraków, a famous Passion Play has been enacted since the 17th century. Church fairs abound on Easter Monday.

➤ MAY: Spring starts off with plenty of music; there's a **Chamber Music Festival** in Łańcut, an **International Jazz Festival "Jazz on the Oder"** in Wrocław, and the **International Festival of Music** in Częstochowa. The **Warsaw International Book Fair** is Central and Eastern Europe's largest fair of books, magazines, and manuscripts.

➤ MAY–JUNE: The **International Festival of Short Feature Films** (Kraków) presents hundreds of short, video, documentary, animated, and experimental films.

➤ JUNE: Kraków has a **Festival of Jewish Culture.** The **International Oratorios and Cantata Festival "Wratislavia Cantans"** is staged in Wrocław. Kraków's and Warsaw's **Midsummer Ceremonies** (June 23) include throwing candlelit wreaths into the Vistula; the capital also has Sunday morning and afternoon **Open-air Chopin Concerts** at the Chopin Memorial in Łazienki Park and **Chopin Concerts** at Żelazowa Wola (these run until October) and the **Warsaw Summer Jazz Days Festival.** Kazimierz Dolny's summer **Cultural Festival** has folk music, dance, film, and other cultural events.

➤ JUNE–JULY: Warsaw offers a **Mozart Festival.** There are two **International Festivals of Organ, Choir, and Chamber Music,** one in Gdańsk–Oliwa, the other in Kamien Pomorski, near Szczecin. Poznań's **International Theater Festival** offers performances in various outdoor venues.

➤ JULY: The **Music of Karol Szymanowski** is celebrated in Zakopane, the village where the Polish composer lived during the 1920s.

➤ AUG.: Artisans, folk dancers, and musicians take over the streets of Gdańsk for the **Dominican Fair and Festival,** the annual commemoration of St. Dominic. The **International Festival of Highland Folklore** in Zakopane celebrates highland cultures with folk-art and costume exhibits, poetry competitions, and musical concerts. The **International Country Music Festival** in Mrągowo features local and foreign performers. Other August festivals include the **International Song Festival** (Sopot), **International Festival of Choir Songs** (Międzyzdroje), **International Chopin Festival** (Duszniki Zdrój), and **Knights and Crossbow Tournament for the Sword of Jan III Sobieski** (Gniew).

➤ SEPT.: **Wratislavia Cantans** in Wrocław features oratorio and cantata music. The **"Warsaw Autumn" Festival of Contemporary Music** showcases symphony and chamber concerts, opera, ballet, and electronic-music performances. Krynica presents the **Jan Kiepura Festival of Opera Songs,** and during the last week of September, the archaeological site of **Biskupin** has a festival, including historic reenactments.

➤ OCT.: **Warsaw's Jazz Jamboree** is the oldest jazz festival in Europe. Kraków hosts its own **Jazz Festival.**

➤ NOV.: Thousands of candles are placed on graves in cemeteries on **All Saints' Day** (November 1).

ROMANIA

➤ JULY: In times past, young men chose brides at **Târgu de Fete** (Maidens' Fair). Now, folk songs, dances, and traditional dress characterize this event atop Mount Găina.

➤ AUG.: **Hora la Prislop,** staged at the Prislop Pass between Maramureş and Moldavia, attracts costume-clad participants from several counties for traditional dance, music, and food.

➤ DEC.: In Sighetu Marmației, the **Festivalul Datinilor de Iarnă** (Winter Festival) re-creates old Christmas–New Year's customs with a multitude of traditionally garbed villagers, masked demons, folk dance, and music.

SLOVAKIA

In addition to hosting the events noted below, many villages also have annual folklore festivals, usually on a weekend in late summer or early fall, which are often filled with singing, dancing, and drinking. For more information, look for the English-language annual events calendar put out by the Slovak Ministry of Economy, available in travel agencies and tourist information centers, or check the weekly *Slovak Spectator*, available at newsstands.

➤ DEC.: **Christmas at the Castle** is in Bojnice. Visiting children are presented with Christmas gifts by local historical characters.

➤ MAR.: Bardejov has a **Musical Spring** performance series; Liptovský Mikuláš has a **Folk Song Festival.**

➤ APR.: The **International Festival of Ghosts and Phantoms** is held every year at the end of April in the striking castle in Bojnice.

➤ MAY: **Košice Musical Spring** takes place in May.

➤ JUNE: An **International Folklore Festival** is held in Košice.

➤ JULY: **Folklore Festival Východná** takes place in Eastern Slovakia.

➤ SEPT.: A **Vintage Festival** takes place in Pezinok, near Bratislava.

➤ OCT.: The **Bratislava Jazz Festival** attracts national and international musicians to venues throughout the capital late in the month.

SLOVENIA

For exact dates and further information about the following events and festivals, contact the Slovenian Tourist Board.

➤ FEB.: **Kurentovanje** in Ptuj is the largest and most spectacular of numerous Carnival celebrations throughout the country.

➤ MAR.: The **World Cup Ski-jump Championship** is held at Planica, Kranjska Gora.

➤ JUNE: **Lent Festival** in Maribor, featuring music and dance events through June and July, opens with the traditional *Rafters' Baptism* on the River Drava. **Druga Godba,** a one-week festival of alternative and world music, takes place in Ljubljana.

➤ JULY–AUG.: The **International Jazz Festival** is held in Ljubljana in July, followed by the **International Summer Festival,** running through July and August, incorporating a range of events from classical music recitals to street theater. The **Primorski Summer Festival** of open-air theater and dance is staged in the coastal towns of Piran, Koper, Portorož, and Izola. **Piran Musical Evenings** are held in the cloisters of the Minorite Monastery in Piran, every Friday through July and August. The **Lace-making Festival** is held in Idrija in August, lasting one week.

➤ SEPT.: The **Kravji Bal** (Cow Ball) in Bohinj marks the end of summer and the return of herdsmen and their cows from the mountain pastures to the valleys. The **Maritime Baptism** celebrates the initiation of new students to the Portorož Maritime Academy.

➤ OCT.: The **Ceremonial Grape Harvest** on October 1 marks the gathering of grapes from Slovenia's oldest vineyard, in Maribor.

➤ NOV.: **St. Martin's Day,** on November 11, sees festivities throughout the country, culminating with the traditional blessing of the season's young wine.

1 DESTINATION: EASTERN AND CENTRAL EUROPE

What a Difference a Decade Makes

What's Where

Fodor's Choice

WHAT A DIFFERENCE A DECADE MAKES

DIVERSITY HAND IN HAND with unity—today, as for centuries past, this paradox underlies the special character of Eastern and Central Europe. The region is so diverse that it might seem to have no unifying features at all. From the Baltic to the Black Sea, from the European heartland to the Asian frontier, it presents a historical and ethnic crazy quilt that can both attract and confound you.

But what a difference a decade makes. Not very long ago, most outsiders would have lumped all the region's countries into a single pile of unlikely compatriots under the Soviet umbrella. The Soviet empire, however, was only the last in a string of imperial overlords that have molded this part of Europe for two millennia. Rome, Byzantium, Ottoman Turkey, Austria-Hungary, and Nazi Germany all left their indelible marks. In the short span of time since the epochal year of 1989, the states of the region have each been free, as hardly ever before in their long histories, to find their own paths. The results have been successful in some cases, as with Poland, Hungary, and the Czech Republic, new NATO members who are knocking on the European Union's door. At this writing, Bulgaria, Romania, Slovakia, and Slovenia are also EU candidates and almost assured of a NATO invitation, too. Elsewhere, long-suppressed tensions in Bosnia and Kosovo exploded into Europe's worst conflict since World War II. With the conflict there resolved, the United Nations is now trying to restore order in the ravaged region and to prevent further eruptions of violence.

Where countries have chosen the road of peaceful development, travel today is far more comfortable than it used to be. Surly service and grim, cell-like accommodations are becoming little more than bad memories, at least in the more prosperous western half of the region. Here, trains and buses are far more comfortable, the phones work, and ATMs have sprung up everywhere. You'll still find a sense of exoticism farther east, in the lands shaped by Ottoman Muslim and Orthodox Christian influences. Change here is happening with dizzying speed, largely because of launching from a much lower platform. Data from Bulgaria, for example, indicate that the Internet there reached fewer than 1,000 people in 1995. By 2000 the soaring figure had already passed 300,000. At this writing, it is estimated that 25% of Bulgarians (around two million) use the Internet daily.

In every country of the region, local peoples have forged their own cultures while drawing freely on the contributions of other groups sharing the same territory. Ancient Greeks, Romans, Thracians, and Dacians left their footprints in Bulgaria and Romania. In Central Europe, from Bohemia to Transylvania, from Poland to Slovenia, the touch of German and Austrian culture is found everywhere, in Gothic churches, in baroque manors, in institutions and customs. Jewish communities maintain a tenuous hold, though one that in many places may not survive the current generation. Another group, stateless as the Jews once were, still ekes a living in every country of the region: the much-reviled Roma, or Gypsies, who are only just beginning to nurture a sense of themselves as a distinct people.

In the 1930s, also a period of great social change in these lands, the Austrian novelist Joseph Roth wrote his masterly elegy for Austria-Hungary, *The Radetzky March*. In Central Europe before the First World War, Roth mused, "Anything that grew took its time growing, and anything that perished took a long time to be forgotten. But everything that had once existed left its traces."

Three empires may have fallen since the period Roth was recalling, but today, throughout this fascinating land, the traces are still there to find and follow.

— Ky Krauthamer

WHAT'S WHERE
Bulgaria
The southernmost frontier of Eastern and Central Europe, Bulgaria borders Greece and Turkey to the south and the Black Sea

to the east; to the west are Serbia and Montenegro, and Macedonia, territories of the former Yugoslavia. Covering approximately 111,000 square km (43,000 square mi), Bulgaria has a population of about 8 million. **Sofia,** the bustling, cosmopolitan capital, sits on the Sofia Plain in western Bulgaria and is surrounded by rugged mountain ranges. The wooded and mountainous interior is sprinkled with attractive "museum" villages and ancient towns. In the **Balkan Range** in the north is the old Bulgarian capital of **Veliko Târnovo.** South of there, in the foothills of the Balkan Range, you'll find the verdant Valley of Roses, and beyond that **Plovdiv,** the country's second-largest city and reputed intellectual center. South of Plovdiv are the **Rhodope Mountains,** whose villages and monasteries keep alive many of Bulgaria's folk traditions. South of Sofia are the **Pirin** and **Rila** mountains, the highest range of mountains between the Alps and the Caucasus and home to two national parks and well-established ski resorts. The sunny, sandy beaches of Bulgaria's **Black Sea coast** attract visitors from all over Europe; the historic port city of **Varna** makes a good base for exploring the region.

Croatia

Presiding over the eastern shore of the Adriatic Sea, Croatia borders Slovenia and Hungary to the north; to the south and east lie the Balkan states of the Union of Serbia and Montenegro, and Bosnia and Herzegovina. Covering 56,600 square km (21,853 square mi) and with a population of approximately 4,400,000, the area that is now Croatia was once the meeting point of three great empires: Venice, Austro-Hungary, and the Ottomans Turks. The capital, **Zagreb,** in the north, was for centuries a Hapsburg stronghold and has retained its Mitteleuropean identity up to the present day. In contrast, **Istria,** a large peninsula in the northwest, spent half a millennium under Venetian rule, and the popular coastal resort towns of Porec and Rovinj bear witness to that era. On the southern tip of the peninsula, the region's main administrative center and port is Pula, while the inland area is home to romantic hill towns amid undulating vineyards. Neighboring **Kvarner** curves around a deep bay and the busy port of Rijeka. Nearby Opatija is a sedate 19th-century holiday resort, while the island of Rab offers wonderful beaches, several reserved for nudist bathing. In the south, **Dalmatia** is a narrow coastal strip along the Adriatic coast backed by the rugged Dinaric Alps. In central Dalmatia, Split is renowned for its magnificent Roman palace, while a short ferry ride away lie the unspoiled islands of Brac, Hvar, and Vis. In the south, Dubrovnik, enclosed within 13th-century fortifications, has been called the "Pearl of the Adriatic." From here, you can visit the islands of Korcula and Mljet.

Czech Republic

Planted firmly in the heart of Central Europe—Prague is some 320 km (200 mi) north*west* of Vienna—the Czech Republic is culturally and historically more closely linked to Western, particularly Germanic, culture than any of its former Eastern-bloc brethren. Encompassing some 79,000 square km (30,500 square mi), the Czech Republic is made up of the regions of Bohemia in the west (sharing long borders with Germany and Austria) and Moravia in the east. Moravia's White Carpathian Mountains (Bílé Karpaty) form the border with the young Slovak Republic, which broke its 74-year-old union with the Czechs in 1993 to establish itself as an independent nation. With a population of more than 10 million, the Czech Republic is one of the most densely populated countries of Eastern and Central Europe.

The capital city of **Prague** sits on the Vltava (Moldau) River, roughly in the middle of Bohemian territory. A stunning city of human dimensions, Prague offers the traveler a lesson in almost all the chief architectural styles of Western European history; relatively unscathed by major wars, most of Prague's buildings are remarkably well preserved. **Southern Bohemia** is dotted with stunning medieval towns, several of which played important roles in the Hussite religious wars of the 15th century. The two most notable towns are Tábor and Český Krumlov. **Western Bohemia,** especially the far western hills near the German border, remains justly famous for its mineral springs and spa towns, in particular Karlovy Vary, Mariánské Lázně, and Františkovy Lázně. **Northern Bohemia,** with its rolling hills and the not-so-giant **Krkonoše** (Giant Mountains), is a hiker's and camper's delight.

The wine country in the south of **Moravia,** dotted with attractive towns such as Znojmo, rises gently toward the extensive forested hills in the north and east, where bear and, some say, wolves roam. The country's second city, **Brno,** offers its own array of historical and cultural attractions.

Hungary

Sandwiched between Slovakia and Romania, Hungary was the Austro-Hungarian Empire's eastern frontier. Measuring approximately 93,000 square km (36,000 square mi), with a population of more than 10 million, it is the geographical link between the Slavic regions of Central Europe and the Black Sea region's amalgam of Orthodox and Islamic cultures. The heart of the nation is **Budapest,** in the northwest on the Danube, just 1½ hours from Bratislava in Slovakia and under three hours from Vienna. Just north of Budapest, the Danube River forms a gentle, heart-shape curve along which lie the romantic and historic towns of the region called the **Danube Bend.** Southwest of Budapest are the vineyards, quaint villages, and popular, developed summer resorts around **Lake Balaton,** the largest lake in Central Europe. The more rural and gently mountainous stretch of **northern Hungary** also includes the handsome, vibrant town of Eger and the famous wine village of Tokaj; the contrastingly flat and dry expanses of the Great Plain, in the east, are known for traditions of horsemanship and agriculture and anchored by the interesting and lively cities of Kecskemét and Debrecen. The verdant, rolling countryside of **Transdanubia** stretches west of the Danube to the borders of Austria, Slovenia, and Croatia; in the northern hills nestle the beautifully restored towns of Sopron and Kőszeg and, in the south, the dynamic, beautiful city of Pécs.

Poland

The northernmost country in Central Europe, Poland has a long coastline on the Baltic Sea. A vast nation of 312,677 square km (119,755 square mi), Poland is made up primarily of a great plain in the north and central region and a small but dramatic stretch of mountainous territory to the south (on its border with Slovakia and the Czech Republic). **Warsaw,** just to the east of the country's center, has rebuilt itself several times over the course of its tumultuous history and since the end of communism has been changing faster than any other city or region in Poland.

Travelers interested in art and architecture shouldn't miss **Kraków** in the south and the historic small towns of the surrounding region known as Little Poland. Outdoors enthusiasts will want to move on to the west and south, to the **Podhale** region and the **Tatra Mountains.** Many of the natural wonders and recreational areas of these two regions are within two hours' drive of downtown Kraków.

Gdańsk and the north offer wide-open vistas, long stretches of coast, great lakes dotting large stretches of forest, and historic cities and castles rising up from the plain. This is a great area for enjoying water sports, hiking, and camping. **Lublin** and the east offer a trip back into the traditional way of life of rural Central Europe: small towns whose great age was in the Renaissance but that have slept since, vast palaces of the nobility, and gently varied countryside where the tractor has not yet replaced the horse.

Apart from the far southwest and a few park areas around **Poznań** and **Wrocław,** the countryside of western Poland is flat and somewhat monotonous—lots of dairy farms and hay fields. Poznań and Wrocław have fine historic centers and a thriving cultural life.

Romania

Generally considered one of the most beautiful countries on the continent, Romania is bordered by Bulgaria, the Black Sea, the Republic of Moldova, Ukraine, Hungary, and Serbia. Its 238,000 square km (92,000 square mi) encompass cities with intact medieval districts and villages where traditional culture thrives. From **Bucharest,** the capital, you can explore the province of **Transylvania,** where cities such as Braşov, Sighişoara, and Sibiu have preserved their historic core. In the northwest, **Maramureş** county transports you back to the past with hand-carved wooden gates, tiny wooden churches, and villagers in traditional dress.

Bucovina, in the province of Moldavia to the northeast, has five 15th- and 16th-century monasteries whose exterior walls are covered, ground to eaves, with glorious frescoes. UNESCO has conferred World Heritage Monument status on them.

Bucovina also claims lovely villages where colorful traditional houses are common and festivals keep old customs alive.

In the east, the **Black Sea** coast claims a string of hotels where sea and sand offer a respite from sightseeing. Roman ruins, wineries, and the port city of **Constanţa** all merit a look. The prime attraction is the **Danube Delta,** Europe's largest wetland and home to 300-plus bird species.

Slovakia

Deep-rooted traditions and folklore continue to flourish in the heart of the largely agrarian Slovak countryside. After ending a 74-year union with the Czech Republic in 1993, Slovakia's road to a free-market economy was a bit bumpy at first, but because of recent improvements, European Union membership no longer seems inaccessible. **Bratislava,** the capital, lies on the Danube in the southwestern corner of the country, just a few miles away from both the Austrian and Hungarian borders. Its small Old Town is charming and contains several buildings and churches of note (especially to those interested in the history of the Austro-Hungarian Empire), but Slovakia's real assets lie to the north and east. **Central Slovakia,** a hilly region crossed by hiking trails, is rich in folklore and medieval history. The **High Tatra Mountains** attract skiers, campers, and mountaineers from all across Europe; they are a meeting ground for tourists from east and west. And relatively undiscovered **eastern Slovakia** lures travelers with its country lanes—watch out for herds of sheep and gaggles of geese—fairy-talelike villages, castles, and wooden churches.

Slovenia

Geographically, politically, and culturally, Slovenia lies in a fascinating corner of Europe: here the former Yugoslavia meets the former Soviet bloc meets the gradually expanding European Union.

Covering a territory of just 20,300 square km (7,900 square mi), Slovenia has a population of 2 million, 90% of whom are Slovene; the remaining 10% is made up primarily of Italians, Hungarians, and natives of the other former Yugoslav republics.

The refined yet progressive capital, **Ljubljana,** lies in the center of the country. In less than three hours you can reach the border with Italy to the west, Austria to the north, Hungary to the northeast, Croatia to the southeast, and the Adriatic coast to the southwest.

The greatest draw for tourists, and the pride of Slovenes, lies northeast of Ljubljana. The beautiful **Triglav National Park** and the **Soča Valley** offer a dramatic alpine landscape, perfect for skiing in winter and hiking, biking, and water sports in summer. In contrast, the **Adriatic Coast and Karst region,** southeast of the capital, provide sea and sunshine, plus intriguing underground caves.

East of Ljubljana the River Krka forms the **Krka Valley,** winding its way through gently undulating farmland dotted with lonely monasteries and medieval castles. Northeast of the capital lies the country's second largest city, Maribor. The region of **Maribor, Ptuj, and the Haloze Hills** produces some of the finest Slovenian wines.

FODOR'S CHOICE

Dining

Bulgaria

Nad Aleyata, Zad Shkafut, Sofia. You can dine among diplomats in this old brick house; the menu shares the clientele's international bent. $$–$$$$

Rotisserie National, Sofia. Come here for a fine meal and old-fashioned elegance, all at pleasantly affordable prices. The Bulgarian and Continental menu emphasizes seasonal specialties. $$–$$$$

Croatia

Vela Nera, Pula. At this restaurant, often considered Croatia's top spot, creative fish, lobster, steak, and truffle specialties are served on a large terrace, overlooking the yacht harbor. $$$–$$$$

Adio Mare, Korcula. The menu at this renowned eatery hasn't changed since it opened in 1974: traditional Dalmatian seafood and meat dishes, prepared over burning coals. Dinner here is unforgettable. $$–$$$$

Macondo, Hvar. Visitors in the know come here for carefully prepared, fresh seafood, served at tables on a narrow, cobbled side street. In the winter you eat before a log fire in the cozy dining room. *$$–$$$$*

Czech Republic

Café Savoy, Prague. Homemade ravioli and fresh seafood are served in surprising tasty combinations in this very grand café that was reborn in 2001. *$$–$$$$*

V Zátiší, Prague. In one of the city's oldest and calmest squares—the restaurant's name means "still life"—this refined dining room offers tantalizing international specialties and wonderful service. *$$–$$$$*

Kavárna Slavia, Prague. To lap up some of the artistic scene, come to this art deco café; the views of the Prague Castle and the National Theater aren't too shabby, either. *$*

Hungary

Gundel, Budapest. Established at the turn of the 20th century, Budapest's most famous restaurant continues its legacy of old-world grandeur and elegant cuisine. *$$$–$$$$*

Aranysárkány, Szentendre. Its small size and turbulent open kitchen give this restaurant a decidedly convivial atmosphere. *$–$$$*

Hortobágyi Csárda, Hortobágy. A favorite of wayfarers since it opened in 1699, the Great Plain's legendary old inn consistently serves excellent traditional fare. *$$*

Baraka, Budapest. A welcome addition to the serious dining scene and a bargain to boot, this gleaming restaurant is on a quiet side street near all the action downtown. *$–$$*

Poland

Belvedere, Warsaw. It doesn't get much more romantic than this: exquisitely prepared Polish cuisine in an elegant candlelit orangerie in Warsaw's serene Łazienki Park. *$$$–$$$$*

Copernicus, Kraków. At the foot of Wawel Hill, Kraków's best restaurant serves food that is both imaginative yet traditionally Polish. *$$$–$$$$*

Pod Łososiem, Gdańsk. This historic Old Town inn is named for its strong suit: fish (though there's also fowl on the menu). *$$–$$$$*

Romania

Casa Vernescu, Bucharest. If you're going to splurge, this elegant French restaurant housed in a 19th-century mansion is the place to do it. *$$$$*

Club Contele Dracula, Bucharest. Tasty Romanian dishes are served amid a decor that's faithful to the Dracula novel and its inspiration, Prince Vlad Ţepeş. *$–$$*

Coliba Haiducilor, Poina Braşov. Decor, music, waiters' costumes, and the menu are traditionally Romanian at this popular spot, whose name means "Outlaws' Hut." *$–$$*

Slovakia

Restaurant Koliba, Starý Smokovec. This charming, rustic spot on the slopes of the Tatra Mountains serves up grilled specialties to the accompaniment of Gypsy folk music. *$$–$$$*

Modrá Hviezda, Bratislava. Eat homey Slovak specialties by candlelight in this winecellar restaurant. *$$*

Slovenská reštauracia, Poprad. The very best of eastern Slovakian comfort food is served in a cheery village-style atmosphere. *$–$$*

Slovenia

AS, Ljubljana. This excellent fish restaurant has old-fashioned ambience but takes a modern approach to good food and wine. *$$$–$$$$*

Pri sv. Florijanu, Ljubljana. On one of Llubljana's most charming streets in the Old Town, this restaurant sets a new standard for innovative Slovenian cuisine. *$$$–$$$$*

Gostilna Lectar, Radovljica. One of Slovenia's best-known restaurants, Gostlina Lectar serves local dishes by candlelight, not far from the sublime Lake Bled. *$$$*

Ribič, Portorož. A perfect place for a summer evening—take a table in the garden and indulge in locally caught fresh fish. *$$–$$$*

Lodging

Bulgaria

Grand Hotel Varna, Sveti Konstantin. The best hotel on Bulgaria's Black Sea coast, the Varna offers its guests spa services in addition to lodging. *$$$$*

Radisson SAS Grand Hotel, Sofia. This is one of the latest and most successful improvements in the Bulgarian hotel business. Its perfect location near the Bulgarian Parliament is coupled with first-class service. *$$$$*

Croatia

Villa Angelo d'Oro, Rovinj. In the heart of the Old Town, this beautifully restored 16th-century residence is furnished with antiques. There's a glorious roof terrace and such luxuries as a hot tub and sauna. *$$$$*

Villa Orsula, Dubrovnik. This exclusive 1930s villa is perched on a hillside above the sea, offering magnificent views of the city. A lovely terraced garden leads down to a private beach. *$$$$*

Czech Republic

Růže, Český Krumlov. Some rooms in this refurbished monastery on a hill facing Krumlov Castle afford stunning views of the loveliest of Bohemian towns. *$$$$*

Grandhotel Pupp, Karlovy Vary. Expansive and redolent of a more refined era, the Pupp is the undoubted queen of this gracious spa town. *$$$–$$$$*

Dům U Červeného Iva, Prague. Spare decor sets off beautiful antiques and painted-beam ceilings in this polished baroque building. *$$$*

Pension 189 Karel Bican, Tábor. This picturesque family-run guest house dates from the 14th century but has all the modern conveniences you've come to expect in the 21st. *$$*

Hungary

Hotel Palota, Miskolc-Lillafüred. This turreted castle in a magical setting in the forested hills of northern Hungary provides comfortable lodging and a perfect base for walking and fishing. *$$$$*

Danubius Hotel Gellért, Budapest. This grand 1918 Art Nouveau hotel on the Danube at the foot of Gellért Hill is the pride of Budapest. Housing an extensive, elegant complex of marble bathing facilities fed by ancient curative springs, it is also one of Europe's most famous Old World spas. *$$$–$$$$*

Kastély Hotel, Tihany. A neo-baroque mansion that once belonged to Archduke József Hapsburg, the hotel is quietly elegant; rooms have soaring ceilings, and the best have balconies overlooking Lake Balaton. *$$$–$$$$*

Kulturinov, Budapest. Set on one of historic Castle Hill's most famous cobblestone squares, this neo-baroque castle provides budget accommodations in a priceless location. *$*

Poland

Le Royal Méridien Bristol, Warsaw. Warsaw's only truly legendary hotel, the Bristol has emerged from a decade of extensive refurbishing and is once again pampering guests with luxurious service. *$$$$*

Sheraton Warsaw Hotel and Towers, Warsaw. This American-run hotel has much to recommend it: outstanding service, the best health club in the city, and a great location near parks and downtown Warsaw. *$$$$*

Grand Orbis Hotel, Sopot. This legendary late-19th-century luxury hotel fronts directly onto Sopot Beach and stands in its own gorgeous gardens. *$$$*

Pod Różą, Kraków. One of Kraków's oldest hotels, this property has bright, modern guest rooms and a prime location. *$$$*

Romania

Athenée Palace Hilton, Bucharest. This Bucharest landmark, dating to 1914, retains its shine with attractive rooms and a grand lobby. *$$$$*

Tirol, Poiana Brașov. Opened in 1999, this small hotel offers attractive rooms, each furnished differently; a fireplace in the lobby; and a mountain-view restaurant. *$$$$*

Slovakia

Radisson SAS Carlton Hotel, Bratislava. The historic integrity and the original luxury of this 1837 hotel have been retained in a modern renovation. *$$$$*

Grandhotel Praha, Tatranská Lomnica. This multiturreted mansion in the foothills of the Tatras has retained the elegance and gentility of an earlier age. *$$–$$$*

Arkada Hotel, Levoča. The bright and comfortable rooms in this boutique hotel belie the building's 13th-century origins. *$$*

Slovenia

Grand Hotel Toplice, Bled. With a central, lakeside location, this elegant hotel is the place to stay if you want to take in stunning views of Lake Bled. *$$$*

Hotel Hvala, Kobarid. The management of this family-run hotel treats its guests like old friends and feeds them like royalty. *$$*

Hotel Tartini, Piran. Take a front room overlooking the delightful oval-shape piazza, Trg Tartini: you couldn't hope to wake up in a nicer place. *$$*

Kendov Dvorec, Spodnje Idrija. This beautifully restored 14th-century manor house has antique furniture and traditional cuisine to match. *$$*

Castles and Churches

Bulgaria

Hram-pametnik Alexander Nevski (Alexander Nevski Memorial Cathedral), Sofia. A modern, neo-Byzantine structure with glittering interlocking domes, this memorial to Bulgaria's Russian neighbor-liberators can hold some 5,000 worshipers; the Crypt Museum has an outstanding collection of icons and religious artifacts.

Croatia

Dvor Trakošcan (Trakošcan Castle), Trakošcan. This 19th-century, neo-Gothic fairy-tale castle is perched on a hilltop amid beautifully landscaped grounds, overlooking a small lake.

Eufrazijeva Basilica (St. Euphrasius Basilica), Porec. The interior of this magnificent 6th-century Byzantine church is decorated with stunning golden mosaics, rightly earning it a place on the UNESCO's list of World Heritage Sites.

Katedrala Sveti Lovrijenac (Cathedral of St Lawrence), Trogir. A perfect example of the massiveness and power of Romanesque architecture, the most striking detail is the main portal, decorated with minutely carved stonework during the 13th century.

Czech Republic

Chrám svaté Barbory (St. Barbara's Cathedral), Kutná Hora. Arguably the best example of the Gothic impulse in Bohemia, St. Barbara's Cathedral lifts the spirit and gives the town of Kutná Hora its unmistakable skyline.

Chrám svatého Vita (St. Vitus's Cathedral), Prague. Soaring above the castle walls and dominating the city at its feet, St. Vitus's is among the most memorable churches in Europe. Its stained-glass windows are particularly brilliant.

Španělská synagóga (Spanish Synagogue), Prague. The interior of this florid 19th-century Moorish temple has been restored to its original splendor.

Kostel Panny Marie před Týnem (Church of the Virgin Mary Before Týn, Old Town Square), Prague. The exterior of this soaring church, with its twin gold-tip, jet-black spires, is a sterling example of Prague Gothic.

Vranov Castle, Vranov, Moravia. You'll admire or wince at this multicolor mix of Gothic, Renaissance, and baroque styles; the eclectic effect always sparks an opinion.

Hungary

Bazilika (Cathedral), Esztergom. The imposing neoclassical dome of Hungary's largest church looming over the village and river below is one of the Danube Bend's best sights.

Eszterházy Palace, Fertőd. Known as the Hungarian Versailles, this yellow, 18th-century baroque palace near Sopron in northern Transdanubia was a residence of the noble Eszterházy family.

Fellegvár (Citadel), Visegrád. This 13th-century hilltop fortress was once the seat of Hungarian kings. The hike up will reward you with gorgeous, panoramic views of the Danube Bend.

Festetics Kastély (Festetics Palace), Keszthely. A tremendous library, lush park, and distinctive tower make this one of the finest baroque complexes in Hungary.

Mátyás Templom (Matthias Church), Budapest. Castle Hill's soaring Gothic church is colorfully ornate inside with lavishly frescoed Byzantine pillars.

Nagy Zsinagóga (Great Synagogue), Budapest. This giant Byzantine-Moorish beauty (Europe's largest synagogue) underwent a massive restoration four decades after being ravaged by Hungarian and German Nazis during World War II.

Pécs Bazilika (Pécs Basilica), Pécs. This four-spire cathedral is one of Europe's most mag-

nificent, its breathtaking interior resplendent with shimmering frescoes and
ornate statuary.

**Szent István Bazilika (St. Stephen's Basil-
ica), Budapest.** Inside this massive neo-Renaissance beauty, the capital's biggest
church, is a rich collection of mosaics and
statuary, as well as the mummified right
hand of Hungary's first king and patron
saint, St. Stephen.

Poland

**Klasztor Paulinów (Pauline Monastery),
Częstochowa.** The 14th-century church in
this monastic complex holds Poland's
holiest religious image, the famous Black
Madonna of Częstochowa, a destination
for pilgrims from around the world.

**Kościół Mariacki (Church of Our Lady),
Kraków.** This church on Kraków's central marketplace has a magnificent wooden
altarpiece with more than 200 carved figures, works of the 15th-century master Wit
Stwosz.

**Kościół Najświętszej Marii Panny (St.
Mary's Church), Gdańsk.** Climbing up the
tower of the largest church in Poland results in breathtaking views.

Łańcut Palace, Łańcut. This aristocratic residence is truly grandiose; there are extensive gardens, an impressive art collection,
and even a small, private theater.

**Pałac Wilanów (Wilanów Palace), War-
saw.** A baroque gem on the outskirts of
the capital, this palace was home to several Polish kings and queens; when you
get tired of royal portraits and gilt, explore
the Romantic gardens with their pagodas,
summerhouses, and bridges overlooking
a lake.

Zamek, Lublin. The castle dates from the
late 14th century, though much was rebuilt in the 19th century. Be sure to see
the Byzantine-style murals in the Kaplica
Trójcy świętego (Chapel of the Holy Trinity).

Zamek Królewski (Royal Castle), Kraków.
Stroll the courtyards and chambers of
Kraków's 14th-century Royal Castle to get
a compact lesson in the trials and tribulations of Polish history and to view fine
collections of artwork, arms and armor,
and tapestries.

Zamek w Malborku (Malbork Castle).
This huge, redbrick castle was one of the
most powerful strongholds in medieval Europe, serving as the residence for the
Grand Master of the Teutonic Order. The
museum contains beautiful examples of
amber.

Romania

Biserica din Deal and **Biserica din Șjes, Ieud,
Maramureș.** Ieud's two churches—one
on a hill, the other along the road—ex-
emplify Maramureș's wooden church architecture. The upper church has lovely
interior frescoes.

**Biserica Stavropoleos (Stavropoleos Church),
Bucharest.** Inside this Orthodox church are
superb examples of Romanian folk-style
carvings and a richly ornate iconostasis.

Peleș Castle, Sinaia. This 19th-century
castle, summer home of Romania's former royalty, is ornately decorated and
features the heavy carved-wood furnishings typical of German Renaissance style.

Voroneț Monastery, Bucovina. The most
famous of Bucovina's "painted monasteries," Voroneț has exterior walls that are
covered with vivid frescoes depicting
scenes from the Bible. The unusually penetrating shade of blue that predominates
is known to art historians and artists as
Voroneț blue.

Slovakia

Bojnice hrad, Bojnice. Visible from miles
around, this fairy-tale castle is a great
way to explore medieval life on a candlelight
tour.

**Dóm svätej Alžbety (Cathedral of St. Eliz-
abeth), Košice.** Inside this 15th-century
Gothic cathedral—the largest in Slovakia—
stands a monumental piece of wood carving, the 35-ft Altar of the Holy Elizabeth.

**Kostol svätého Jakuba (St. Jacob's Church),
Levoča.** This is the most impressive memorial to Gothic art in Eastern Europe; front
and center on the main altar is wood-
carver Pavol of Levoča's breathtaking
masterpiece, *The Last Supper*.

Wooden churches of eastern Slovakia.
Even the nails are made of wood in these
handsome Byzantine structures; religious
paintings and icons line the interior walls
of many.

Slovenia

**Cerkev sveti Trojice (Church of the Holy Trin-
ity), Hrastovlje.** Up on a hill above the Adri-

atic, the interior walls of this tiny church are decorated with an intriguing cycle of 15th-century frescoes.

Pleterje Samostan (Pleterje Monastery), Šentjernej. You can't go inside the monastery, but you can visit the beautiful Gothic church and watch an enlightening audiovisual presentation about the way the monks live.

Museums

Bulgaria

Natzionalen Archeologicheski Musei (National Archaeological Museum), Boyana. In the former presidential residence, this collection is devoted to the various peoples who have inhabited Bulgarian territory over the centuries.

Natzionalen Istoricheski Musei (National History Museum), Sofia. Considered the city's most important museum, it houses priceless Thracian treasures, Roman mosaics, and enameled jewelry from the First Bulgarian Kingdom.

Croatia

Meštrovic Atelier, Zagreb. The former home and studio of Ivan Meštrovic, Croatia's greatest 20th-century sculptor, has been turned into a memorial museum with a permanent exhibition of his sculptures and drawings.

Galerija Meštrovic (Meštrovic Gallery), Split. Designed by Meštrovic as a summer retreat, this modern villa is surrounded by extensive gardens overlooking the sea. Some 200 of the artist's sculptural works can be seen here, both indoors and out.

Czech Republic

Malá Pevnost (Small Fortress), Terezín. The grounds and buildings of the most notorious Nazi concentration camp on Czech territory have been preserved as a testament to the horrific legacy of the Holocaust.

Národní galerie (National Gallery), Prague. Spread among a half dozen branches around the city, the National Gallery's collections span most major periods of European art, from medieval and baroque masters to a vast constructivist gallery of modern and contemporary works.

Židovské muzeum v Praze (Prague Jewish Museum), Prague. In this collection of

several must-see sights and exhibits, standouts include the Starý Židovský hřbitov (Old Jewish Cemetery) and several historic synagogues, including the Staranová synagóga (Old-New Synagogue).

Hungary

Néprajzi Múzeum (Museum of Ethnography), Budapest. A majestic 1890s structure across from the Parliament building—the lavish marble entrance hall alone is worth a visit—houses an impressive exhibit on Hungary's folk traditions.

Szépművészeti Múzeum (Museum of Fine Arts), Budapest. Hungary's best collection of fine art includes esteemed works by Dutch and Spanish old masters, as well as exhibits on major Hungarian artists.

Zsolnay Múzeum (Zsolnay Museum), Pécs. Pécs's oldest surviving building houses an extensive collection of the world-famous Zsolnay family's exquisite porcelain art.

Poland

Czartoryski Collection, Kraków. Part of the National Museum's holdings, housed in Municipal Arsenal, this is one of the best art collections in Poland; among its highlights are works by Leonardo, Raphael, and Rembrandt.

Muzeum Narodowe (National Museum), Warsaw. This is a remarkable collection of contemporary Polish and European paintings and ceramics, as well as Gothic icons and works from antiquity.

Oświęcim (Auschwitz-Birkenau), near Kraków. A million Jews, Gypsies, and others were killed by the Nazis at this concentration camp, which more than any other has come to be seen as the epicenter of the moral collapse of the West; it has been preserved as a museum.

Romania

Muzeul Brukenthal (Brukenthal Museum), Sibiu. This baroque palace houses a fine collection of Romanian and Western art, plus close to 300,000 books.

Muzeul Satului (Village Museum), Bucharest. This fascinating open-air museum exhibits some 300 village homes and other structures from around the country.

Muzeul Țăranului Român (Peasant Museum), Bucharest. You can catch an evocative glimpse of Romanian peasantry through these beautifully displayed costumes, icons, carpets, and other items of rural life.

Slovakia

Múzeum židovskej kultúry (Museum of Jewish Culture in Slovakia), Bratislava. Housed in a mid-17th-century Renaissance mansion, this exhibition covers the history of Jews in Slovakia from the time of the Great Moravian Empire to the present.

Šariš (Icon Museum), Bardejov. The myth of St. George and the dragon is one of the favorite themes in this captivating collection of Greek Catholic and Orthodox artwork from the region's churches.

Múzeum moderného umenia rodiny Warholovcov (Warhol Family Museum of Modern Art), Medzilaborce. In this tiny town, view original Andy Warhol silk screens, including two from the famous Campbell's Soup series, as well as portraits of Lenin and singer Billie Holiday.

Slovenia

Kobariški muzej (Kobarid Museum), Kobarid. This award-winning museum records the tragic battles fought in the Soča Valley during World War I, which were immortalized by Ernest Hemingway in *A Farewell to Arms*.

Muzej Novejše Zgodovine (Museum of Modern History), Ljubljana. A recent installation, "Slovenes in the 20th century," gives an even-handed account of political events since the fall of the Austro-Hungarian Empire in 1918.

Vinska Klet (Wine Cellars), Ptuj. At the home of Slovenia's oldest vintage wines, a tour of the underground cellars is followed by a wine-tasting session.

Towns and Villages

Bulgaria

Koprivshtitsa, inland Bulgaria. Situated among mountain pastures and pine forests in the Sredna Gora Range, Koprivshtitsa is a showcase of the Bulgarian Renaissance style, where buildings are covered in brightly painted designs and ornate carvings.

Croatia

Dubrovnik, south Dalmatia. Terra-cotta rooftops and baroque churches nestle within magnificent 13th-century walls, making this former independent republic one of Europe's most stunningly beautiful coastal cities.

Hvar Town, central Dalmatia. A favorite destination among the yachting fraternity, Hvar remains completely at ease with its age-old beauty: medieval stone houses are built around a natural harbor and backed by a hilltop fortress.

Rovinj, Istria. Winding, cobbled streets lead up to a hilltop church on this former island, while colorful Venetian-style facades rim the pretty harbor below.

Czech Republic

Český Krumlov, Bohemia. The repainted Renaissance facades and the new shops and pensions that now crowd the lanes have banished much of Krumlov's charming old decay, but the hard-earned dignity of the houses and the sweet melancholy of the streetscapes abide in this lovely southern Bohemian town.

Mariánské Lázně, Bohemia. In this genteel spa town, you can take the waters while strolling under gracious colonnades.

Telč, Moravia. The perfectly preserved town square, clustered with superb examples of Gothic, Renaissance, and baroque architecture, is almost preternaturally perfect.

Hungary

Pécs, Transdanubia. This vibrant, cultured city's numerous museums—among the best in the country—glorious basilica, and picturesque location in the Mecsek Hills make it one of Hungary's lesser-known gems.

Szentendre, the Danube Bend. A tremendously popular day-trip destination from Budapest, this quaint town offers cobblestone streets for strolling and numerous art galleries for browsing and buying.

Szigliget, Lake Balaton. A tranquil, attractive little village on the lakeshore, Szigliget is a collection of traditional thatch-roof houses clustered together on narrow streets at the base of a hill crowned by a 13th-century fortress; the views of the lake from the ruins are exceptional.

Poland

Kazimierz Dolny, eastern Poland. Perched on a steep, hilly bank above the Vistula

River, Kazimierz Dolny is a cluster of whitewashed facades and red-tile roofs; known in an earlier incarnation as the "Pearl of the Polish Renaissance," the town is something of an artists' colony.

Toruń, western Poland. One of the few cities to come through World War II unscathed, Toruń is a lovely blend of medieval, baroque, Gothic, and Renaissance buildings.

Zamość, eastern Poland. The main square of this fortified town is a graceful, arcaded plaza punctuated by a baroque town hall.

Romania

Bârsana, Maramureş. This Iza Valley village has some of the most ornately carved gates in the country, while its church claims the tallest steeple.

Sighişoara, Transylvania. The birthplace of Vlad Ţepeş, the real-life inspiration for Dracula, Sighişaora's cobble streets, clock tower, and medieval citadel are among the best preserved in Europe.

Slovakia

Bardejov, eastern Slovakia. The colorful merchant buildings of the old town square are just one of the attractions, which include a spa and a village museum.

Levoča, eastern Slovakia. The medieval capital of the Spiš region seems frozen in time; between the 14th and 17th centuries it flourished as an important center of trade, crafts, and art.

Slovenia

Bovec, the Soča Valley. This town in the foothills of the Julian Alps is the best starting point for exploring the scenic Soča River valley. Rafting, kayaking, and hiking excursions can be arranged easily by one of the town's many outdoor outfitters.

Piran, the Adriatic coast. An architect's dream, the Old Town of Piran has at its center an oval piazza, Trg Tartini, which opens onto the harbor. The surrounding facades are pure Venice, and the scene is presided over by a hilltop cathedral.

2 · BULGARIA

At the crossroads of Europe and Asia,
once ruled by the Turks, the "Jewel of the
Balkans" is an exotic and initially puzzling
mix of cultures, where Eastern mysticism
and mosques coexist with Slavic traditions
and the remnants of a Communist past.
Mountains crowned by rugged hilltop
monasteries, peaceful farmland villages
dotting the fertile Danube plains, and
a coastline strewn with miles of golden
beaches and tranquil waterfront towns give
undiscovered Bulgaria its intoxicating allure.

Updated by
Andrew
Anderson
and Maria
Nickolova
Anderson

ULGARIA, A LAND OF MOUNTAINS AND SEASCAPES, of rustic unspoiled beauty and proud hospitality, lies in the eastern half of the Balkan Peninsula. From the end of World War II up until the collapse of communism, it was the closest ally of the Soviet Union. "The forgotten corner of Europe," as locals still sometimes call it, Bulgaria during the Cold War period presented a mysterious and even sinister image to Western travelers. When this period ended in 1989 with the overthrow of Communist Party head Todor Zhivkov, Bulgaria opened its doors to the West, readopted its traditions and religion, and embraced the opportunity to present its unique character to the rest of the world. Politically and economically, Bulgaria has struggled and suffered. Many Bulgarians believed the "miracle" of democracy and capitalism would bring stability and prosperity overnight. Instead, upheaval dashed the people's dreams. Since 1989, the government has changed hands seven times, primarily between parties composed of the former communist leaders. Uniquely in Eastern Europe, the former king has since returned and, to the surprise of all political observers at the time, has succeeded in being elected prime minister.

The winter of 1996 was the lowest point for Bulgaria. Massive unemployment, hyperinflation, rampant corruption, and growing breadlines turned into anger. The people of Bulgaria took to the streets, surrounded the parliament building where members of the BSP (Bulgarian Socialist Party) were barricaded inside, and demanded new elections. Finally the Socialists agreed to hold elections, and in April 1997 the people voted the new Union of Democratic Forces (UDF) into power. This was the first time since the end of WWII that the country had not been under Socialist rule. The new government had a tremendous task before it and for the next five years succeeded in bringing order out of near chaos. It succeeded in making Bulgaria a contender for membership in the European Union, reducing the influence of the Mafia, and kick-starting a stagnant economy. Despite a stable government, levels of disillusionment remained high, especially from the majority who were not benefiting from the newfound wealth. The return of the former king, Simeon II, who had been exiled by the Communists as a child in 1946, provided an alternative to either the Socialists or UDF party. In June 2001 Simeon's party won the elections by a landslide, and the former king was voted prime minister, as Simeon Saxe-Coburg-Gotha. Just to confuse outside observers even further, the presidential elections later that year saw the former leader of BSP Georgi Pavanov elected president. Thus, a former monarch and former communist now lead the country into its next phase of development. Bulgarians realize that meaningful reform will take years to implement, but integration into the EU remains the top priority across all shades of the political spectrum.

Having survived the recent turmoil, Bulgaria is once again a relatively peaceful destination in the Balkans. Courting EU and NATO membership, it studiously avoided involvement in the Kosovo conflict, even though Serbia is a mere 80 km (50 mi) from Sofia and errant NATO missiles landed within its borders. Visitors will find Bulgarians exuberantly welcoming, especially to Western tourists and the coveted hard currency they carry into the country. With gorgeous countryside, low prices, friendly people, thriving nightlife, and an eclectic and hearty cuisine, Bulgaria will not remain undiscovered for long. For adventurous souls who don't mind dealing with a few rough edges (and wrestling with Cyrillic), Bulgaria provides not only an extraordinary vacation destination but a chance to see history in the making.

Founded in 681 by the Bulgars, a Turkic tribe from Central Asia, Bulgaria was a crossroads of civilization even before that date. Archaeological finds in Varna, on the Black Sea coast, give proof of civilization from as early as 4600 BC. Bulgaria was part of the Byzantine Empire from AD 1018 to 1185 and was occupied by the Turks from 1396 until 1878. Today, Bulgaria remains a dizzying blend of cultures, with its Eastern-influenced architecture, Turkish fast food, Greek ruins, Soviet monuments, and European outdoor cafés. Five hundred years of Muslim occupation and nearly half a century of Communist rule did not wipe out Christianity, and many lovely, icon-filled churches dot the countryside. The country's 120 monasteries, with their icons and frescoes, chronicle the development of Bulgarian cultural and national identity.

The capital, Sofia, is picturesquely situated in a valley near Mt. Vitosha. Culturally and historically rich, the city has good hotels, a wide variety of restaurants, excellent ballet and opera, and a vibrant Mediterranean-style nightlife with scores of bars and discos. The interior landscape of the country offers magnificent scenic beauty, with tranquil forested ridges, spectacular valleys, and rural communities where folklore is a colorful part of village life. Veliko Turnovo, just north of the Balkan Range in the center of the country, was the capital from the 12th to the 14th century and is well worth a visit for its medieval ramparts and vernacular architecture. Plovdiv, a university town and the intellectual center of the country, lies southeast of Sofia and has a picturesque Old Town as well as one of the best-preserved Roman amphitheaters in the world.

The Black Sea coast along the country's eastern border has secluded coves and old fishing villages, as well as wide stretches of sandy beaches that have been developed into self-contained resorts. Varna was once the summer beach playground for the entire Eastern Bloc but now draws a wider array of visitors. A thriving city in the winter as well, it is among the most important ports on the Black Sea.

Pleasures and Pastimes

Architecture

Old Bulgarian architecture is best seen in the country's towns and villages, with cobble streets, stone-vaulted bridges, and wooden houses. Within the solid walls of typical houses in small mountain towns such as Bansko are delicate rooms with carved ceilings and colorful handmade rugs. Koprivstitsa and the Old Town of Plovdiv are known for their excellent examples of National Revival architecture, a 19th-century style that helped reestablish Bulgarian artistic identity after the Turkish occupation. These houses are colorfully painted, often with ornately carved wooden ceilings and second stories that extend out over the first, supported by wooden pillars.

Churches, Monasteries, and Icon Paintings

Most Bulgarian churches and monasteries are from the National Revival period (18th and early 19th centuries), a time of vigorous cultural activity and increased awareness of a national identity. The famous Rila Monastery is included on the UNESCO list of World Heritage Sites. The Bachkovo and Troyan monasteries are both known for their splendid murals and icons, painted by Zahari Zograph and other great National Revival artists.

The tradition of Bulgarian icons goes back to the 9th century, when the Bulgarians converted to Christianity. During and after the National Revival period, many icon-painting schools were formed. The schools of Bansko, Samokov, and Troyan produced icons for the newly built churches and private homes. The biggest collections of icons are displayed in the Crypt Museum of Alexander Nevski Memorial Cathedral in Sofia and in the Museum of Art and History in Varna.

Dining

Balkan cooking revolves around lamb, pork, sheep's-milk cheese, eggplant, and other vegetables. Typical Bulgarian dishes include wonderful *shopska salata* (tomato, cucumber, and feta cheese salad), *sarmi* (vine leaves stuffed with meat and rice), and *kiufté* (grilled meatballs). Bulgaria invented *kiselo mlyako* (yogurt); excellent *tarator* (cold yogurt soups) are served in summer. Syrupy baklava and *palachinki* (crepes stuffed with chocolate or nuts and honey) are the favored desserts.

The national drink is *rakia* (brandy), either *slivova* (made from plums) or *grosdova* (made from grapes). Many Bulgarians make their own—or know someone who does—and claim this is the best of drinks. Cold rakia is typically taken with the salad course. Bulgarian wines are usually full-bodied, dry, and inexpensive. Reds from Melnik, Roussé, Suhindol, and Sliven regions and whites from the Black Sea area are worth requesting. Coffee is strong and is often drunk along with a cold beverage, such as cola.

Visitors have a choice between the familiar Western-style, sometimes uninspired hotel dining and the more adventurous outing to a local restaurant or café, where the menu may only be offered in Cyrillic. In larger cities, international cuisine is easy to find, but in smaller towns the best bets are the small restaurants called *mehana*, which serve national dishes and local specialties. Dinner out in a mehana is considered a recreational experience. Bulgarians share tables with strangers (feel free to do this yourself—it's perfectly acceptable) and linger for hours over the smallest of salads while drinking rakia, smoking, and listening to loud music. (Restaurant turnover is practically unheard of—don't bother waiting if all the tables are full.) Calmer atmospheres are easily found in restaurants featuring more Continental cuisine. If cigarette smoke bothers you, choose one of the many places with outdoor seating.

CATEGORY	COST*
$$$$	over 24 leva
$$$	16 leva–24 leva
$$	8 leva–16 leva
$	under 8 leva

per person for a main course at dinner

Hiking and Walking

Mt. Vitosha and the mountains of the Rila, Pirin, and Rhodope ranges are good for walking. Nature lovers will appreciate Vitosha for its beautiful moraines, Rila and Pirin for their clear blue lakes, and the Rhodopes for their green slopes and rare plants. The Balkan Range, which crosses the entire country, has splendid rocks and caves. Two of the most interesting caves are Ledenika and Magura, with their veritable sculptures of stalactites and stalagmites. Ledenika is about 200 km (124 mi) northeast of Sofia, while Magura is approximately 250 km (155 mi) north of the capital.

Lodging

Bulgaria offers a wide choice of accommodations, from hotels to apartment rentals, rooms in private homes, and campsites. Since the changes in 1989, the country has been witnessing a time of incessant and speedy development in the sphere of private business. The result is a rich market for lodging all over the place. Until recently, Balkantourist and Interhotels owned most hotels used by Western visitors. At this writing, nearly all of them had been privatized. The major towns and especially the capital, Sofia, are quite capable of satisfying the demands of those traveling for pleasure or on business.

Though many of the newly opened hotels could not survive the severe competition and had to close down, numerous others still appear and flourish, introducing new facilities and levels of comfort and luxury. Along the Black Sea Coast, construction work is at its peak. In the most-visited resorts you might encounter half-finished buildings standing next to modern, splendid, brand-new hotels in Mediterranean style, with swimming pools, bars, restaurants, and tennis courts.

In the small, historic towns, despite growing numbers of small hotels, rooms in private homes are still the most common type of lodging and one of the best ways to experience the real Bulgaria. The hosts are extremely friendly and welcoming, and the prices are lower than elsewhere, though you should not expect all the facilities of a hotel. It is not a problem to find a tourist agency or travelers' information desk in the towns and villages that are frequent tourist destinations. But in major cities, it's highly recommended to make your reservations in advance.

Hotel rates are most often quoted in U.S. dollars or euros, but your bill can be paid in either one of these currencies or leva, the Bulgarian currency. Credit cards are frequently—but not always—accepted.

CATEGORY	SOFIA*	OTHER AREAS*
$$$$	over $200	over $75
$$$	$140–$200	$55–$75
$$	$100–$140	$30–$55
$	under $100	under $30

All prices are for two people in a double room with breakfast.

Music

You can hear Bulgarian folk music at numerous festivals around the country, including the festival held in May in Koprivshtitsa and the late-September event held near Pamporovo, just south of Plovdiv. Bulgarian folk dances are performed by dancers in brightly colored costumes, which differ according to the region of the country they are from. Rhodope mountain music is eerie and beautiful, unfamiliar to most foreigners.

Spa Resorts

There are hundreds of mineral springs in Bulgaria. Their healing properties were well known to the ancient Romans. The spa hotels in the resorts of Sandanski and Velingrad provide various treatments, including manual therapy, acupuncture, phytobalneology, phytotherapy, and slimming cures. (Sandanski is a half hour from the Greek border crossing at Kulata; Velingrad is southeast of Sofia in the Rhodopes.) The Black Sea hydrotherapy centers in Sveti Konstantin, Albena, and Pomorie are famous for their healing mud. The mineral springs along the northern Black Sea coast turn the sea resorts into year-round spas.

Exploring Bulgaria

Bordered by Romania to the north (the Danube River forms the border), Serbia and Montenegro and the former Yugoslav Republic of Macedonia to the west, Greece and Turkey to the south, and the Black Sea to the east, Bulgaria is in the southeastern corner of Europe in the heart of the Balkan Peninsula. Geographically, Bulgaria can be divided into two basic regions: the Inland and the Black Sea's Golden Coast. Inland you'll find one of Bulgaria's two chief attractions, its towering mountains, and on the Black Sea you'll find the other, its glittering seacoast.

Great Itineraries

Bulgaria may be small, but its nature and landscapes are strikingly diverse. If you have more than a week to tour the country, you'll be able to see most of it. If you have less than a week, you'll still get to see some major sights and get an impression of the country and its people. If two or three days are all you have, you'll have to choose between the mountains and the sea.

IF YOU HAVE 3 DAYS

Begin in ⊡ **Sofia** and spend the day in the central part of the city—be sure to visit the magnificent Hram-pametnik Alexander Nevski (Alexander Nevski Memorial Cathedral) and some of the new art galleries. On the second day, head for ⊡ **Plovdiv.** Spend the morning walking around in Plovdiv's Old Town and have coffee on the terrace overlooking the magnificent Rimski Amfiteatur (Roman Amphitheater). On the third day, pass through the town of Karlovo to ⊡ **Koprivshtitsa,** where you can see some of the finest examples of typical old Bulgarian architecture. Or, instead of heading toward Koprivshtitsa, you can go to ⊡ **Borovec,** the oldest and biggest mountain resort in Bulgaria, at the foot of Vrah Musala, the highest peak on the Balkan Peninsula.

IF YOU HAVE 5 DAYS

Spend a day in **Sofia,** and from there travel to ⊡ **Rilski Manastir** (Rila Monastery), founded in the 10th century. Spend the night here, either in the local hotel or in one of the sparse monks' rooms in the compound, and leave the next morning for ⊡ **Bansko,** a museum town with charming National Revival houses. The third day, go hiking in the Pirin Mountains, and the next, visit the tiny village of **Melnik,** famous for its architecture, sandstone formations, lively taverns, and red-wine tasting in ancient caves. From Melnik, before going back to Sofia, you can visit the Rozhenski Manastir (Rozhen Monastery), most of it decorated by unknown painters.

When to Tour

Summers here are warm, and winters are crisp and cold. If you're looking for sun, head to Bulgaria in July or August. Although this is Bulgaria's "high season," the only places you'll find crowds are the Black Sea coast and Sofia. Even when the temperature climbs in summer, the Black Sea breezes and the cooler mountain air prevent the heat from being overpowering. Don't limit yourself to summer for a visit to Bulgaria, though—the coastal areas get considerable sunshine year-round. The inland areas, however, are wet during most of March and April.

SOFIA

Exploring Sofia

Bulgaria's bustling capital sprawls on the high Sofia Plain, ringed by mountain ranges: the Balkan Range to the north; the Lyulin Mountains to the west; part of the Sredna Gora Mountains to the southeast; and, to the southwest, Mt. Vitosha—the city's summer and winter playground—which rises to more than 7,600 ft. The area has been inhabited for about 7,000 years, but the first impression is of haphazard and thoughtless modern urban development. Driving in, don't be daunted by the surreal expanse of outwardly grim Socialist-era block housing. The city center is of a more human scale, with spacious parks, open-air cafés, and broad streets filled with an incongruous mix of pedestrians, expensive Western cars, and archaic farmers' wagons. As recently as the 1870s Sofia was part of the Ottoman Empire, and one mosque still remains. Most of the city, however, was planned after 1880, and

Sofia

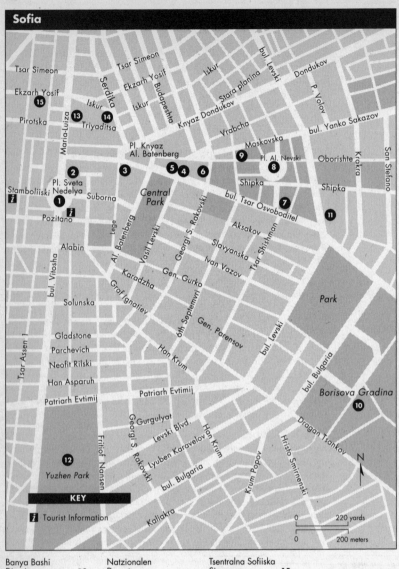

Tsar Simeon
Ekzarh Yosif
Pirotska
Stamboliiski
Pl. Sveta Nedelya
Pozitano
Alabin
bul. Vitosha
Solunska
Gladstone
Parchevich
Neofit Rilski
Han Asparuh
Patriarh Evtimij
Tsar Assen 1
Yuzhen Park

Tsar Simeon
Serdika
Iskur
Maria-Luiza
Triyaditsa
Ekzarh Yosif
Iskur
Budapeshta
Pl. Knyaz
Al. Batenberg
Suborna
Central
Park
lege
Al. Batenberg
Vasil Levski
Karadzha
Graf Ignatiev
6th Septemvri
Han Krum
Patriarh Evtimij
Gurgulyat
Georgi S. Rakovski
Levski Blvd.
Lyuben Karavelov
Fritiof Nansen
bul. Bulgaria
Kaltakra

Iskur
Knyaz Dondukov
Pl. Knyaz
Al. Batenberg
Georgi S. Rakovski
Gen. Gurko
Ivan Vazov
Gen. Porensov
Han Krum
Krum Popov

Stara planina
Vrabcha
Moskovska
Pl. Al. Nevski
Shipka
bul. Tsar Osvoboditel
Aksakov
Slavyanska
Tsar Shishman
bul. Levski
Dragan Tsankov
Hristo Smirnenski

bul. Levski
Dondukov
P. Volov
bul. Yanko Sakazov
Oborishte
Krakra
San Stefano
Shipka
Park
bul. Bulgaria
Borisova Gradina

N

KEY

i Tourist Information

```
0                    220 yards
0                    200 meters
```

Banya Bashi
Djamiya **13**

Borisova
Gradina **10**

Hram-pametnik
Alexander
Nevski **8**

Narodno
Subranie **7**

Natzionalen
Archeologicheski
Musei **3**

Natzionalen
Dvoretz na
Kulturata **12**

Natzionalen
Etnografski
Muzei **4**

Natzionalna
Hudozhestvena
Galeria **5**

Rotonda Sveti
Georgi **2**

Sofiiski Universitet . .**11**

Tsentralna Sofiiska
Sinagoga **15**

Tsentralnata
Banya **14**

Tzarkva Sveta
Nedelya **1**

Tzarkva Sveta
Sofia **9**

Tzarkva Sveti
Nikolai **6**

following the destruction of World War II, many of the main buildings were rebuilt in the Socialist style.

Numbers in the text correspond to numbers in the margin and on the Sofia map.

A Good Walk

Begin your tour in the heart of Sofia at the crowded and lively ploshtad Sveta Nedelya (St. Nedelya Square), named after the church, **Tzarkva Sveta Nedelya** ①, that dominates its south side. On the north side of ploshtad Sveta Nedelya is the **Rotonda Sveti Georgi** ②, the oldest archaeological monument in Sofia. Heading east from here, you'll enter ploshtad Alexander Batenberg and see the huge Partiynien Dom, the former headquarters of the Bulgarian Communist Party—its architecture is reminiscent of the country's recent Communist history.

Near the southwestern corner of the square is the **Natzionalen Archeologicheski Musei** ③. Follow the yellow-brick road east to the faded green former royal palace, which today houses the **Natzionalen Etnografski Musei** ④ and the **Natzionalna Hudozhestvena Galeria** ⑤. Pause for a moment to regard the broad expanse of yellow brick in front of the royal palace and the pleasant Central Park to the south. Consider that in 1999 one of the city's landmarks, the somber and squat mausoleum of Communist leader Georgi Dimitrov, was wiped off the map, a symbolically charged gesture financed by private donors. One block away on the left side of the street is **Tzarkva Sveti Nikolai** ⑥. From this church, walk down bulevard Tsar Osvoboditel, with its monument to the Russians, the Tsar Osvoboditel (Tsar Liberator), topped by the equestrian statue of Russia's czar Alexander II. It stands in front of the **Narodno Subranie** ⑦, where during the January 1997 uprising protesters lobbed stones from the plaza through the windows at members of Parliament barricaded inside. Behind it, just beyond ulitsa Shipka, you'll be confronted by the shining **Hram-pametnik Alexander Nevski** ⑧, where you can pause to browse through the outdoor antiques and icons market. Here you should also take a look at the extensive collection of icons in the basement Crypt Museum. Across the square from the memorial church is a much older church, **Tzarkva Sveta Sofia** ⑨. Return to bulevard Tsar Osvoboditel through ploshtad Alexander Nevski. If you continue east, just before you reach **Borisova Gradina** ⑩, you will see the imposing building and the moss-covered domes of **Sofiiski Universitet** ⑪.

From the park, walk south past the big sports stadium until you come to bulevard Dragan Tsankov. Next, turn down ulitsa Graf Ignatiev and head west to the monument of Patriarh Evtimij, a 14th-century Christian patriarch; always crowded, it's the most popular meeting point in the city. Take the boulevard of the same name until you reach the **Natzionalen Dvoretz na Kulturata** ⑫, where young couples meet and stroll, children skateboard, and the elderly sit on park benches enjoying the spectacle.

Next, walk along bulevard Vitosha, the main shopping street in Sofia, back to ploshtad St. Nedelya, and then follow bulevard Knyaginya Maria-Luiza toward the train station. On the right is the Tsentralen Universalen Magazin (Central Department Store), an expensive four-story mall. Just beyond this big store are the **Banya Bashi Djamiya** ⑬ and the **Tsentralnata Banya** ⑭, the latter closed for ongoing renovations. Across the boulevard is the Tsentralni Hali (Central Market Hall), built in 1907 and restored in 2000. Just west of the Central Market Hall is the **Tsentralna Sofiiska Sinagoga** ⑮, with gleaming Moorish domes and the largest chandelier in the Balkans. Turning left on ulitsa

Ekzarh Yosif and walking west toward ulitsa Stefan Stambolov will immerse you in the crowds coming and going from the Zhenski Pazaar, the most fascinating outdoor bazaar in the city. With hordes of villagers hawking produce, pirated CDs, clothes, and homemade goods, this area is sensory overload and the perfect end to a full and fascinating day.

Timing

This walking tour covers 5 or 6 km (3 or 4 mi) and will take about four hours to complete. You can also combine a tour of Sofia with a short walk on Mt. Vitosha. To do this, you'll need six to seven hours. It's best to head for Vitosha during the week, when it's much less crowded than on weekends. Vitosha is usually covered with snow from December to March. There are ski lifts on the mountain, and rental skis are available.

Sights to See

⑬ **Banya Bashi Djamiya** (Banya Bashi Mosque). A legacy of Turkish domination, this 16th-century mosque is one of the most noteworthy sights in Sofia, with its imposing dome and elegant minaret. Built in 1576 by the Turkish architect Sinan, the mosque was named for its proximity to mineral baths (*banya* means baths). The interior is closed to the non-Islamic public, and the fence around it is festooned with vendors. ⊠ *Bul. Maria-Luiza, across from Central Market Hall, Center.*

👆 ⑩ **Borisova Gradina** (Boris's Garden). Though it's neglected to a certain extent, littered with garbage, and inhabited by stray dogs, you can imagine what the park was like before Bulgaria's recent depression. An empty lake, a dry fountain, and statues to Communist victory over Fascism are surrounded by dense, overgrown woods—still a favorite spot for strolling. In summer, ice cream vendors, children riding around in battery-operated minicars or skateboarding, a cool outdoor disco, and a surprisingly pristine public pool with children's water slides bring life to the park. ⊠ *Bul. Bulgaria between bul. Tsar Osvoboditel and bul. Dragan Tsankov, Center.*

★ ⑧ **Hram-pametnik Alexander Nevski** (Alexander Nevski Memorial Cathedral). You may recognize this neo-Byzantine structure with glittering interlocking domes from the pictures of it that appear on almost every piece of tourist literature. It was built by the Bulgarian people at the beginning of the 20th century as a mark of gratitude to their Russian liberators. Inside are alabaster and onyx, Italian marble and Venetian mosaics, magnificent frescoes, and space for a congregation of 5,000. There's a fine collection of icons and religious artifacts in the Crypt Museum, representing Byzantine influence, Ottoman rule, and the National Revival period. On Sunday morning you can attend a service to hear the superb choir. In the area near and around the church are many ladies selling lace tablecloths. ⊠ *Pl. Alexander Nevski, Center,* ☎ *02/987–76–97.* ⬚ *5 leva.* ☉ *Wed.–Mon. 10:30–6:30.*

❼ **Narodno Subranie** (National Assembly). During the January 1997 uprising, CNN made this building famous by repeatedly broadcasting clips of protesters smashing and climbing through the windows and dragging members of the Socialist parliament out into the plaza in a demand for new elections. Topped by the Bulgarian national flag, the blocky building is adorned with an inscription reading UNITY MAKES STRENGTH, referring to the unification of the country in 1885, a few years after the defeat of the Turks. ⊠ *Bul. Tsar Osvoboditel at pl. Narodno Subranie, Center.*

★ ❸ **Natzionalen Archeologicheski Musei** (National Archaeological Museum). This museum is housed in the former Great Mosque. Recent renovations make the 15th-century building as fascinating as its contents, which illustrate the cultural history of the country up through the 19th century. ⊠ *Pl. Alexander Batenberg, behind the Sheraton hotel, Center,* ☎ *02/988–24–06.* ☐ *Free.* ☉ *Tues.–Sun. 10–4.*

⑫ **Natzionalen Dvoretz na Kulturata** (National Palace of Culture, or NDK). This modern building contains the largest multipurpose Congress Center in southeastern Europe, designed and equipped to hold both conferences and cultural activities. Press conferences of newly elected presidents, international concerts, and trade exhibitions usually take place here. In the underpass you'll find a tourist information office, shops, restaurants, discos, and an Internet café. ⊠ *Pl. Bulgaria, 1, Center,* ☎ *02/916–62–760.*

NEED A BREAK? For Italian ice cream with fruits, chocolate, nuts, pancakes, and syrups combined with architectural skill, and a range of coffees to please every taste, try **Jimmy's** (⊠ ul. Angel Kunchev, 11, Center). It's open daily from 7 AM.

❹ **Natzionalen Etnografski Musei** (National Ethnographical Museum). Collections of costumes, handicrafts, and tools exhibited here in the former palace of the Bulgarian czar illustrate rural life through the 19th century. ⊠ *Pl. Alexander Batenberg, 1, Center,* ☎ *02/987–41–91,* WEB *hs41.iccs.bas.bg.* ☐ *3 leva, guided tour 5 leva.* ☉ *Tues.–Sat. 10–4.*

❺ **Natzionalna Hudozhestvena Galeria** (National Art Gallery). Here, in the west wing of the former royal palace, are paintings by the best Bulgarian artists as well as representative works—notably prints—from the various European schools. ⊠ *Pl. Alexander Batenberg, Center,* ☎ *02/ 980–00–93.* ☐ *3 leva, guided tour 9 leva; free Sun.* ☉ *Daily 10:30–6.*

❷ **Rotonda Sveti Georgi** (Rotunda of St. George). These ancient remains of what is billed as the oldest public building in Bulgaria are in the courtyard behind the Sheraton hotel. The rotunda was built in the 4th century as a Roman temple, destroyed by the Huns, rebuilt by Justinian, and turned into a mosque by the Turks before being restored as a church. Restoration has revealed medieval frescoes. ⊠ *Off pl. St. Nedelya, Center.* ☐ *Free.* ☉ *Daily 8–6.*

⑮ **Tsentralna Sofiiska Sinagoga** (Central Sofia Synagogue). After decades of disrepair, the Moorish turrets and gilt domes of this 1909 synagogue have been beautifully restored. It is now one of the most spectacular buildings in downtown Sofia. ⊠ *Ul. Ekzarh Yosif and bul. Washington, Center.* ☐ *Free.* ☉ *Weekdays 9–5, Sat. 9–1.*

⑭ **Tsentralnata Banya** (Central Baths). For years, this splendid building, once an Ottoman bathhouse, was left to disintegrate. Renovations began in 1997; at this writing the baths were not yet open to the public, but visitors can taste the hot mineral water at the spring in the adjacent park. ⊠ *Ul. Serdika at ul. Triyaditsa, Center.*

❶ **Tzarkva Sveta Nedelya** (St. Nedelya Church). This impressive church was constructed from 1856 to 1863 and later altered by a Russian architect. In 1925 it was destroyed by terrorist action; it was rebuilt in 1931. Today it's open to visitors, and services are held each Sunday. You may even get a peek at a bride—this is one of the most popular wedding spots in the city. ⊠ *Pl. Sveta Nedelya, Center.* ☐ *Free.* ☉ *Daily 7–7.*

❾ **Tzarkva Sveta Sofia** (Church of St. Sofia). One of the oldest churches in the city, it dates to the 6th century, though excavations have uncovered the remains of even older structures on the site. Because of its great age and its simplicity, the church provides a dramatic contrast to the showy Alexander Nevski Memorial Cathedral nearby. While the church undergoes seemingly endless renovation, it's open to visitors, and services are held daily at 9:30 AM. ⊠ *Ul. Moskovska, Center.* ⊠ *Free.* ☉ *Daily 9–1 and 2–5.*

⓫ Sofiiski Universitet Sv. Kliment Ochridski (Sofia University St. Kliment Ohridskik). The best and most respected university in Bulgaria was built in 1888, just after the liberation from the Ottoman rule, with the financial aid of brothers Georgievi, merchants and passionate supporters of Bulgarian culture and spirit. Stone, wood, marble, and stained glass make Alma Mater one of the most impressive architectural sites of the capital. ⊠ *Bul. Tzar Osvoboditel, 15, Center,* ☎ *02/9871–045,* FAX *02/946–02–55,* WEB *www.uni-sofia.bg.*

❻ Tzarkva Sveti Nikolai (Church of St. Nicholas). This small and very ornate Russian church—it has five gold-plate domes and a green spire—was erected between 1912 and 1914. Inside, mosaics depict favored Russian saints and czars. It's commonly called (surprise) the Russian Church. ⊠ *Bul. Tsar Osvoboditel, Center.* ⊠ *Free.* ☉ *Daily 9–1 and 2–5.*

Dining

Near the influences of Western Europe and the Mediterranean as well as the Middle East, Sofia is a crossroads for culinary influences, with exotic foods ranging from spicy Indian curries to Turkish *döner kebaps* (meat roasted on a spit). New restaurants and cafés offering high-quality, inexpensive cuisines from around the world are springing up everywhere. Still, for those willing to brave cigarette smoke and crowded seating for some local color, the most authentic and enjoyable experience is to be had in a *mehana* (tavern), where the music is loud and Bulgarians relax for hours over rakia and traditional meals such as grilled pork sausages and french fries smothered in *cyrene,* a delicious variant of feta cheese.

$$–$$$$ ✕ **Kushtatas Chasovnika.** Next door to the British embassy, the "House with the Clock" is always an interesting place to go. Because the restaurant offers a rotating menu of different European cuisines, you may be served by waiters dressed in Scottish kilts or Spanish folk costumes while sitting in the patio's well-kept garden. Live guitar and piano music in the evenings, intriguing seafood specialities, English-language menus, and a service up to Western standards all make this a place to try. ⊠ *Ul. Moskovska, 15, Center,* ☎ *02/987–56–56. Reservations essential. DC, MC, V.*

$$–$$$$ ✕ **Nad Aleyata, Zad Shkafa.** In English "Beyond the Alley, Behind the Cupboard," this small, upscale restaurant occupies an old Jewish house and serves innovative Bulgarian and European cuisine. Popular with local diplomats and visiting officials, the restaurant has a large selection of salads and an excellent wine list; the staff is accustomed to serving foreigners. There's a quiet patio for warm-weather dining, and in the afternoons theater performances take place upstairs in the "attic." You'll also find what many consider to be the nicest toilets in town. ⊠ *Ul. Budapeshta, 31, Center,* ☎ *02/983–55–45 or 02/980–90–67. Reservations essential. DC, MC, V.*

$$–$$$$ ✕ **Rotisserie National.** This subterranean restaurant just off Vitosha ★ serves both Bulgarian and Continental cuisine; seasonal game dishes are a particular strength. There's a bit of a pretentious air here—sorbet between courses, the menu in French, jackets required—and the food may not always meet the high standards to which they aspire. But the costumed waitstaff is attentive, if unhurried, and Sofiantsi come here for the experience and the excellent value. ⊠ *Corner of Hristo*

Belchev and Neofit Rilski, 40, Center, ☎ *02/980–17–17. Jacket required. No credit cards.*

$$–$$$ ✕ **La Province.** Although the front gate covered with tar and feathers gives this restaurant a creative-looking exterior, the interior is nothing special. But that shouldn't deter you from coming to enjoy the great food. Chicken livers in cream sauce is a real experience, together with a fresh large salad as a starter. A friendly staff, fast service, and a no-smoking room are some of the other advantages of this homey restaurant. But don't be surprised if the TV shows a soccer match at a low volume. ✉ *Ul. San Stefano, 3, Center,* ☎ *02/43–52–57. Closed Sun. No lunch Sat. No credit cards.*

$–$$$ ✕ **Da Vidi.** You might prefer this restaurant if you are looking for a
★ truly elegant place. The interior is stylishly simple and a bit Japanese; the food (European) is a pleasant surprise. Da Vidi is proud of its beef in coffee sauce and broullé Napoléon emperial. You will be never left unattended, and the staff is well prepared to serve to foreigners. Private and cozy, this restaurant is one of the pleasant establishments in Sofia worthy of recommendation. ✉ *Ul. Han Asparuh, 36, Center,* ☎ *02/980–67–46. Jacket required. No credit cards.*

$–$$ ✕ **Bel Ami.** This Serbian restaurant, cozy and unpretentious, is the place that you may choose if you are ready for a wild Balkan night. The real party starts at about 10 PM with live Serbian, Greek, and Bulgarian music. The chef prepares the food in front of your eyes, standing behind a huge glass wall. Meats are cooked on charcoals, in the typical regional style. The English-speaking staff and menus in English, as well as the proximity to popular night clubs, make this a welcoming place for foreigners. ✉ *Ul. 6 septemvri, 22, Center,* ☎ *02/988–22–80. No credit cards.*

$–$$ ✕ **Flannagan's.** Though called an Irish pub, this large restaurant serves what is more traditionally considered English cuisine. You can have an English breakfast (called Irish on the menu) or a proper meal, or you could just go for a beer in the evening. Situated on the ground floor of the Radisson hotel, it offers a view of the whole square in front of Narodno Subranie. Half of the patrons are British or American, though MPs and journalists also frequent the place as well as Bulgarians who crave the international society and English cuisine. ✉ *Radisson hotel, pl. Narodno Subranie, 4, Center,* ☎ *02/933–47–40 or 02/987–37–37. DC, MC, V.*

Lodging

The following hotels maintain a high standard of cleanliness and are open year-round unless otherwise stated. Those on the higher end of the price range are comparable to luxury hotels in Western Europe, while those at the lower end might be redolent of Bulgaria's Communist past. Still, most of the lower-end hotels are undergoing gradual renovation, so many offer rooms on several refurbished floors while the rest of the hotel remains unrenovated. You may find rates set in leva, U.S. dollars, or euros, depending on the policy of each hotel. On occasion, prices are given in U.S. dollars but payment is required in leva.

$$$$ 🏨 **Radisson SAS Grand Hotel.** Directly on Narodno Subranie Square and
★ facing the Alexander Nevski Memorial Cathedral, this hotel is in the very heart of Sofia. Its proximity to the airport, the railway station, the national theater, museums, and some of the best nightclubs of the capital makes it a good choice for business or leisure. The staff is fluent in English and very responsive. ✉ *Pl. Narodno Subranie, 4, Center, 1000,* ☎ *02/933–43–34,* FAX *02/933–43–35,* WEB *www.radissonsas.com. 136 rooms. 2 restaurants, cafeteria, cable TV, gym, massage, sauna, bar, lobby lounge, pub, casino, nightclub, dry cleaning, Internet, business services,*

meeting rooms, car rental, travel services; no-smoking rooms. AE, DC, MC, V. BP.

$$$–$$$$ 🏨 **Downtown Hotel.** This brand-new hotel has pleasant, generously proportioned rooms, which are luxuriously furnished. The location in the very center of the city makes it easy to get to and from the airport as well as rail and bus connections. Children up to six stay free in their parents' room. ✉ *Bul. Vasi Levski, 27, Center, 1040,* ☎ *02/930–52–00,* FAX *02/930–53–00,* WEB *www.hotel-downtown.net. 62 rooms. Restaurant, minibars, cable TV, gym, hair salon, massage, sauna, lobby lounge, dry cleaning, Internet, business services, meeting room, car rental, travel services; no-smoking floor. AE, DC, MC, V. BP.*

$$$–$$$$ 🏨 **Hilton Sofia.** This eight-story business hotel, which opened in 2000, is centrally located and Sofia's premier business hotel. Well up to Western standards of service and comfort, the hotel has all the facilities you would expect, including a multilingual staff and full business center. ✉ *Bul. Bulgaria, 1, Ivan Vazov, 1421,* ☎ *02/933–50–00,* FAX *02/933–51–11,* WEB *www.hilton.com. 245 rooms. Restaurant, in-room data ports, in-room safes, minibars, cable TV, pool, gym, massage, sauna, bar, dry cleaning, laundry service, Internet, business services, meeting rooms, car rental, travel services; no-smoking rooms. AE, DC, MC, V. BP.*

$$$–$$$$ 🏨 **Hotel Kempinski Zografski.** The large rooms at this luxurious hotel
    ★   have views of Mt. Vitosha. With audiovisual and simultaneous-translation facilities available, it is a prime option for business conferences. The hotel also has the most expensive restaurant in the entire country, Sakura, Bulgaria's one and only spot for sushi; there's also a highly rated Italian restaurant, Parma. ✉ *Bul. James Bourchier, 100, Lozenets, 1407,* ☎ *02/62–518 or 02/62–51–300,* FAX *02/68–12–25 or 02/96–25–232,* WEB *www.kempinski.bg. 431 rooms. 5 restaurants, minibars, cable TV, pool, health club, bar, casino, shops, dry cleaning, Internet, business services, meeting rooms, car rental, travel services. AE, DC, MC, V. BP.*

$$–$$$$ 🏨 **Castle Hotel Hrankov.** This luxury hotel is 10 km (6 mi) from the
    ★   Sofia city center in the suburban Dragalavci district, at the foot of Mt. Vitosha. It has high-quality accommodations and extensive fitness facilities; in addition, the hotel provides shuttles to the ski slopes and helps with renting skis. It's not an authentic castle (it opened in 1996), but the turrets, gardens, and nighttime lighting make it a good facsimile. ✉ *Krusheva, 53, Gradina, Dragalevtsi, 1415,* ☎ *02/932–72–00,* FAX *02/932–73–27,* WEB *www.hrankov-bg.com. 65 rooms. 2 restaurants, café, minibars, cable TV, tennis court, 2 pools, gym, squash, bar, casino, nightclub, dry cleaning, Internet, business services, meeting rooms, car rental, travel services. AE, DC, MC, V. BP.*

$$–$$$$ 🏨 **Sheraton Sofia Hotel Balkan.** This first-class hotel, part of the Sheraton Luxury Collection, has a central location in the city center, which is its greatest asset. The massive structure is made of stone; the rooms are comfortable and richly decorated, with large bathrooms. The hotel offers free pickup from the airport upon request seven days a week. ✉ *Pl. St. Nedelya, 5, Center, 1000,* ☎ *02/981–65–41,* FAX *02/980–64–64.* WEB *www.sheraton.com. 188 rooms. 3 restaurants, café, minibars, cable TV, gym, health club, hair salon, massage, 3 bars, lobby lounge, casino, night club, shop, dry cleaning, Internet, business services, meeting rooms, airport shuttle, car rental, travel services. AE, DC, MC, V. BP.*

$$–$$$ 🏨 **Gloria Palace.** Polished stone and glass interiors, though a bit sterile, promise a cool relief from the hot Bulgarian summer. The hotel is comfortably located on one of Sofia's major boulevards but well isolated from street noise. And you can easily pop out to the little park just around the corner, behind the old mosk Banya Bashi Djamiya, where people come to fill bottles with water from the spa and Gypsies hold amusing performances. ✉ *Bul. Maria Luiza, 20, Center, 1000,* ☎ *02/*

980–78–95, FAX *02/980–78–94. 30 rooms. Restaurant, café, minibars, cable TV, hair salon, nightclub, shop, Internet, car rental, travel services. AE, MC, V. BP.*

$$ ☒ **Hotel Maria Luiza.** This cozy, upscale bed-and-breakfast is in a historical building in the city center. Rooms are bright and comfortable, and the excellent downtown location affords views of Banya Bashi Mosque and the Central Baths. The friendly staff also helps makes staying here a pleasure. ☒ *Bul. Maria Luiza, 29, Center, 1000,* ☎ *02/9–10–44,* FAX *02/980–33–55. 20 rooms. Restaurant, café, cable TV, bar, lobby lounge, business services, travel services. AE, DC, MC, V. BP.*

$ ☒ **Grand Hotel Bulgaria.** Though centrally located, this small hotel is quiet and old-fashioned. The interior, with its marble staircase, arched windows, low wooden beds, and lace curtains in the guest rooms, is charming. At this writing a renovation was under way—some floors having been completed, with others still in progress. The staff, however, sometimes seem to lack direction. ☒ *Bul. Tsar Osvoboditel, 4, Center, 1000,* ☎ *02/987–19–77 or 02/988–44–77,* FAX *02/988–41–77. 92 rooms. Restaurant, café, cable TV, lobby lounge, shop, Internet, business services, meeting room, car rental, travel services. DC, MC, V. BP.*

Nightlife and the Arts

Nightlife

Like the residents of neighboring Greece, Bulgarians love all-hours Mediterranean-style dance clubs. New nightspots are opening up every week, so consult the English-language *Sofia City Guide,* which is available at tourist agencies and at major hotel reception desks, to find out about current hot spots. If you're looking to go out, gravitate to one of the city's nightlife districts, such as on ulitsa Tsar Shishman near bulevard Graf Ignatiev, and see what strikes your fancy. Things don't get going at clubs or live music venues until about 11 PM, though the beer halls currently en vogue are busy from the early evening on.

BARS AND NIGHTCLUBS

Bibliotekata (☒ Basement of National Library, enter on ul. Oborishte, ☎ 02/943–3978) is a labyrinth of chambers with karaoke, two dance floors, and several bars, the largest of which has a tiny stage where live bands play. Trendy beer gardens such as **Bohemi** (☒ bul. Vasil Levski, 55, ☎ 02/987–73–25) are popping up throughout the city; this *biraria* not far from Sofia University has a couple of floors, sequestered corner tables, and a patio. Bulgarian staples are served. **J.J. Murphy's** (☒ ul. Karnigradska, 6, ☎ 02/980–2870) is a genuine Irish pub popular with Bulgarians and the ex-pat community alike. **Mojito** (☒ ul. Ivan Vazov, 12, ☎ no phone) is a small club with different music every night; it's popular with young actors who stay and dance until dawn. For live music, **Swingin' Hall** (☒ bul. Dragan Tsankov, 8, ☎ 02/963–0696), one of the first "Western" clubs to open in the city, is still a popular spot.

DISCOS

One of the city's most chic and expensive discos, **Chervilo** (☒ bul. Tsar Osvoboditel, 5, just off ploshtad Narodno Subranie, ☎ 02/981–66–33), or "Lipstick," draws Sofia's well-to-do twenty- and thirtysomethings. When taking a cab, just tell the driver the disco's name. In the smaller room, Sofia's best DJs take turns playing acid jazz and house music, and in the larger room, crowds dance to Euro-techno. Next door to Chervilo in the venerable Military Club is **Vsi Svetii** (☒ bul. Tsar Osvoboditel, 7, ☎ no phone), or "All Saints," which is a tony restaurant serving Bulgarian food in nouvelle-size servings by day and dance club by night. **Neo** (☒ ul. Neofit Rilski, 70, just off bul. Graf Ignatiev) is a vast pop and soul disco decorated in metal, with a huge TV screen and a round bar in the middle of the dance floor. Next door to Neo is the arty, 24-hour bistro **Ugo,** where you can stay or take your food to go, but try the wine. **Scream** (⊠ ul. Pirotska, 5, behind the Sinagoga) is an enormous disco on two levels in a massive ex-administrative building; the music is pop, soul, and rap.

The Arts
MUSIC AND DANCE
The standard of music in Bulgaria is high, whether it takes the form of operatic, symphonic, or folk. To experience some of the real Bulgarian folk art in dancing and singing go to see **Natsionalen Ansambul za Narodni Tantsi y Pesni.** Balkantourist arranges outings (*see* Visitor Information *in* Sofia Essentials). **Bulgaria Hall** (⊠ ul. Aksakov, 1, ☎ 02/98–401) is a fine-sounding intimate venue for top-rate performances by the Sofia Philharmonic and the New Symphony Orchestra. Consult the "Cultural Diary" column of the English-language *Sofia Echo,* available at many city-center newsstands or hotel reception desks, or the *Sofia City Guide* monthly arts supplement for symphony, opera, ballet, and other events listings. The box office is open daily 10–1:30 and 3:30–6:30. You don't need to understand Bulgarian to enjoy a performance at the **Kuklen Teatur** (Central Puppet Theater; ⊠ ul. Gen. Gurko, 14, ☎ 02/988–54–16). **Sofiska Durjhavna Opera** (Sofia National Opera and Ballet; ⊠ ul. Vrabcha, 1, ☎ 02/987–1549; box office: ⊠ bul. Dondukov, 30, ☎ 02/987–13–66) has excellent performances; stop by the box office to find out what's playing. While the quality of the dance is often high, ask at the box office if the performance is with an orchestra, since some performances are accompanied by recorded music.

FILM
Sofia seems to have a movie theater on nearly every street. Most of them show recent foreign films in their original languages with Bulgarian subtitles. You can find comfortable seating and good sound systems, cafés, and air-conditioning in the summer. **F/X Cinema** (⊠ ul. Angel Kanchev, 5, ☎ 02/981–2717) has a DTS sound system and is air-conditioned. **Kino Pozitano** (⊠ corner of ul. Kniaz Boris and ul. Pozitano, west from Sv. Nedelq Church, ☎ 02/87–07–07) has two screens with DTS sound, air-conditioning, and a café. **Levski** (⊠ bul. Yanko Sakuzov, 30, walk east from the Levski monument, ☎ 02/467–171) has a DTS sound system, air-conditioning, and a café. **Mir** (⊠ ul. Denkogloo, 6, ☎ 02/986–11–35), with two screens, has DTS sound, air-conditioning, and a café. The **Multiplex United New Cinema** (⊠ Pl. Bulgaria, 1, in the subway of National Palace of Culture, ☎ 02/951–51–01) has three screens with DTS sound, plus an Internet café.

Shopping
Gift and Souvenir Shops
The shop at the **National Ethnographic Museum** (⊠ Pl. Alexander Batenberg, 1, Center) sells genuine crafts, including a selection of carpets, as well as cheap imitations. Prices may not be competitive, but it is one-stop shopping. For recordings of Bulgarian music, go to the basement labyrinth market underneath the **National Palace of Culture** (⊠ Pl. Bulgaria, 1, Center).

Markets
The quintessential shopping excursion in Sofia is to its outdoor produce and crafts markets. A little less touristy and slightly less pricey are the stalls in the underpass that runs beneath bulevard Vitosha, just north of ploshtad Sveta Nedelya at ulitsa Trapezitsa, between the Sheraton

and Central Department Store; here the shopkeepers sell handmade lace, knitted sweaters and caps, and a variety of both new and old jewelry. One of the most popular crafts and souvenir-stall markets is **Nevski Pazaar,** just west of the Nevski Cathedral, where you can find everything from antique Greek coins to original icon paintings and old Soviet whiskey flasks. The most exotic and entertaining of Sofia's markets is the **Zhenski Pazaar** (Women's Market; ⊠ ul. Stefan Stambolov, between ul. Tsar Simeon and bul. Slivnitsa), named for the swarms of women from neighboring villages who commute daily to hawk everything from homemade brooms and lace to produce and used electronic equipment. With all the sights and sounds of bartering—sometimes a little overwhelming—the Zhenski Pazaar can give you a feel of the Middle East. Be wary of pickpockets.

Shopping Malls
Tsentralni Hali (Central Market Halls; ⊠ bul. Maria-Luiza) specializes in food, with more than 100 different pavilion shops offering all kinds of fresh food. These shops are on three levels, with an indoor bar, a little area for children, and a change bureau; stalls are open daily 7 AM–midnight. What used to be Sofia's monolithic state-run department store, **Tsentralen Universalen Magazin** (Central Department Store; ⊠ bul. Knyaginya Maria-Luiza, 2), reopened in April 2000 as a mixed retail and office space—the closest thing Sofia has to a Western-style shopping mall. It still goes by the old name, or TSUM for short.

Sofia Essentials

AIR TRAVEL
There is twice-weekly nonstop service from New York to Sofia on Balkan Airlines (also called Balkanair). This is the only direct service from North America to Bulgaria. Balkan Airlines also flies to Sofia from Budapest, Prague, and Warsaw. Most European airlines offer connecting service from North America through their European hubs. In the summer season several airlines offer direct flights to the Black Sea airports at Varna and Bourgas.

➤ AIRLINES: **Air France** (⊠ ul. Saborna, 2, Center, ☎ 02/980–61–50 or 02/981–78–30; ⊠ Sofia International Airport, ☎ 02/937–32–07). **Alitalia** (⊠ ul. Graf Ignatiev, 40, Center, ☎ 02/981–67–02; ⊠ Sofia International Airport, ☎ 02/7932–23–28). **Austrian Airlines** (⊠ bul. Vitosha, 41, Center, ☎ 02/981–24–24; ⊠ Sofia International Airport, ☎ 02/937–31–31). **Balkan Airlines** (⊠ ul. Alabin, 16, Center, ☎ 02/987–47–36). **British Airways** (⊠ ul. Alabin, 56, Center, ☎ 02/981–70–00); ⊠ Sofia International Airport, ☎ 02/937–31–11). **Lufthansa** (⊠ ul. Saborna, 9, Center, ☎ 02/980–41–41; ⊠ Sofia International Airport, ☎ 02/937–31–42). **Swiss** (⊠ ul. Angel Kanchev, 1, Center, ☎ 02/980– 44–59, ⊠ Sofia International Airport, ☎ 02/988–26–30).

AIRPORTS AND TRANSFERS
Most international flights to Bulgaria arrive at Sofia International Airport, which is 10 km (6 mi) from the city center.
➤ AIRPORTS: **Sofia International Airport** (☎ 02/79–80–35 or 02/72–06–72 international flight information; 02/72–24–14 or 02/79–32–21–16 domestic flight information; WEB www.sofia-airport.bg).

AIRPORT TRANSFERS
Bus 84 serves the airport and travels the route in about 25 minutes, but it is crowded and impractical if you have a lot of luggage. A taxi will take about 15 minutes for the trip into the city. The fare for taxis taken from the airport taxi stand can vary from $15 to $20 (dollars are normally accepted as well as leva) for the ride into Sofia. A much

more affordable option (if you have local currency and know where you're going) is to pick up a taxi from outside the airport departures hall, which has just dropped someone off and will get you to the center of town for around 12 leva ($6), far less than the taxis waiting outside the arrivals hall charge. Be sure to agree on the fare before starting off, however.

BED-AND-BREAKFAST RESERVATION AGENCIES
Staying in private homes is becoming a popular alternative to hotels as a means of cutting costs and having increased contact with Bulgarians. Some private homes offer bed-and-breakfast or bed only; some provide full board. Agencies that can help you arrange accommodations include Balkantour and Sofia Tour. You can also contact the National Information and Advertising Center or Balkantourist offices (see ☞ Visitor Information).
➤ CONTACTS: **Balkantour** (⊠ bul. Stamboliiski, 27, Center, ☎ 02/987–72–33). **Sofia Tours** (⊠ bul. Slivnitsa, Sveta Troitsa, Sofia, ☎ 02/920–14–96, FAX 02/25–89–77).

BUS TRAVEL
Some Bulgarian tourist agencies have regular round-trip bus service from Sofia to Victoria Coach Station in London. Alma Tour-BG bus service leaves London on Friday night, stops in Amsterdam the following morning, and reaches Sofia Monday morning. There is regular bus service from Sofia to most major European cities. Contact Group Travel, the best private bus company in the country; it has comfortable, modern, air-conditioned buses serving all parts of Bulgaria, as well as destinations throughout Eastern and Western Europe.
➤ CONTACTS: **Alma Tour-BG** (⊠ bul. V. Levski, 83, Sofia, ☎ 02/981–40–52). **Group Travel** (⊠ Tsentralna Avtogara, bul. Maria Luiza, 131, Sofia, ☎ 02/9310–679 or 02/32–01–22).

BUS AND TRAM TRAVEL WITHIN SOFIA
Buses, trolleys, and trams run quite frequently—between every 5 and 20 minutes. Buy a ticket (a single fare is 40 stotinki) from kiosks and newspaper stands near the tram or trolley car stop and punch it into the machine as you board. You can also pay the driver. Persons traveling with baggage or large backpacks are required by law to have both a ticket for themselves *and* a ticket for their baggage. If you or your bag is caught without a ticket, an on-the-spot fine of 2 leva will be issued. Trams and trolleys tend to get crowded, so keep an eye on your belongings and be alert at all times. There is also a fleet of privately run "Marsh-route" taxis (white or blue mini-buses) that will stop when you hail them down. They serve parts of the city not covered by public bus routes; pay the driver as you board (1 leva flat fare).

CAR RENTALS
Rental car prices vary widely in Bulgaria. The major companies, such as Hertz and Avis, generally charge upwards of $60 a day for mid-range rentals. Smaller, local companies can charge less, but you may find yourself behind the wheel of an old Russian Moskvich. Many cars have air-conditioning, but it is almost impossible to rent a car with automatic transmission. Car rental prices are comparable whether you make arrangements before your trip or on arrival. It's a good idea to take out collision, or Casco, insurance; the cost should be around $5 a day.

Both Avis and Hertz have offices at the airport. You can hire a car and driver through Balkantour. Litex Travel is a travel agency that can rent a car for you as well as provide any tourist information you might need.

➤ CONTACTS: **Avis** (✉ Sheraton hotel, Pl. St. Nedelya, 5, Center, ☎ 02/988–81–67; ✉ Sofia International Airport, ☎ 02/73–80–23). **Balkantour** (✉ bul. Stamboliiski, 27, Center, ☎ 02/987–72–33). **Hertz** (✉ Sofia International Airport, ☎ 02/945–92–17). **Litex Travel** (✉ Radisson hotel, Pl. Narodno Subranie, 4, Center, ☎ 02/988–98–55).

CAR TRAVEL

If you're staying in or near the city center, there's really no need for a car. Besides, driving in Sofia is not enjoyable—traffic is heavy and potholes abound. Parking is also difficult in the city center. All hotels that have parking charge a sometimes substantial fee; garages are similarly expensive.

EMBASSIES AND CONSULATES

All embassies and consulates are in Sofia (*See* ☞ A to Z at the end of this chapter for addresses).

EMERGENCIES

If you need a doctor, there is a clinic in Sofia specifically for foreign citizens. Also, Dr. Dimitrov is a dentist who was trained in the U.S. and often works with foreigners.

➤ CONTACTS: **Ambulance** (☎ 150). **Clinic for Foreign Citizens** (✉ ul. Eugeni Pavlovski, 1, Mladost I, ☎ 02/75–361). **Dentist** (Dr. Dimitrov; ✉ ul. San Stefano, 18, Center, ☎ 02/43–10–43). **Fire** (☎ 160). **Pirogov Emergency Hospital** (☎ 02/5–15–31). **Police** (☎ 166). **Pharmacy information** (☎ 178).

GUIDED TOURS

Balkantourist organizes all kinds of tours, from guided Sofia orientation tours to various evening tours, such as a night out to eat local food or to watch folk dances. Odysseia-In offers a broad range of adventure and outdoor recreation tours with experienced guides, including skiing–snowboarding, rafting, mountain biking, and hiking.

➤ CONTACTS: **Balkantourist** (✉ bul. Vitosha, 1, Center, ☎ 02/987–51–92). **Odysseia-In** (✉ bul. Alexander Stamboliiski, 20V, Center, ☎ 02/981–05–60, WEB www.uniquebulgaria.com).

TAXIS

All registered taxi cabs must be yellow and should have an operating meter; rates are between 35 and 56 stotinki per 1 km (½ mi) and are displayed on the windows. To tip, round out the fare 5%–10%. The most reliable way to get a taxi is to order it by phone; if you hail one on the street, make sure it is a company taxi with a phone number listed on the door. Inex Taxi is one of the best and newest companies. Okay Supertrans is reputable, as is Yes Taxi, which will charge you the going rate for a fast ride. Taxi-S-Express is a good bargain, but its cars are somewhat out of date.

➤ TAXI COMPANIES: **Inex Taxi** (☎ 91919). **Okay Supertrans** (☎ 973–21–21). **Taxi–S–Express** (☎ 91–280). **Yes Taxi** (☎ 91119 or 91009).

TRAIN TRAVEL

The Tsentralna Gara (Central Station) is at the northern edge of the city. Apart from the station, tickets are sold downtown, in the underpass of the Natzionalen Dvoretz na Kulturata (National Palace of Culture). Rila International Travel Agency sells train tickets.

➤ CONTACTS: **Natzionalen Dvoretz na Kulturata** (National Palace of Culture; ✉ Pl. Bulgaria, 1, Center, ☎ 02/65–71–85 international trains; 02/65–84–02 domestic trains). **Rila International Travel Agency** (✉ ul. Gen. Gurko, 5, Center, ☎ 02/987–07–77 or 02/987–59–35). **Tsentralna Gara** (Central Station; ✉ bul. Maria Luiza, 112, ☎ 02/931–11–11 or 02/932–33–33).

VISITOR INFORMATION

Two English-language publications, *Sofia Echo* and the *Sofia City Guide*, are available at the Sofia airport news kiosk, hotels lobbies, and kiosks throughout the city center, and on-line as well. The former reviews restaurants and clubs, while the latter has detailed information on everything from hotels and shops to exchange rates and driving law requirements.

Balkantourist, formerly the state-run tourism organization, is now a private travel agency but in many places in the country still functions as an information office, with locations in most major hotels. Green Travel Agency is locally much advertised and has proven to be a good consultant. A perfect central location and a great variety of services are provided by Litex Travel, which is in the Radisson hotel. A central source of information is the National Information and Advertising Center, conveniently located at the intersection of boulevards Stamboliiski and Vitosha. Wagonlit Travel stands on a street occupied by several other travel agencies.

➤ CONTACTS: **Balkantourist** (✉ bul. Vitosha, 1, ☎ 02/987–51–92). **Green Travel Agency** (✉ ul. Patriarh Evtimii, 25, ☎ 02/981–42–74). **Litex Travel** (✉ Pl. Narodno Subranie, 4, ☎ 02/988–98–55 or 02/988–98–56). **National Information and Advertising Center** (✉ ul. Sveta Sofia, 1, ☎ 02/987–97–78). *Sofia City Guide* (WEB www.sofiacityguide.com). *Sofia Echo* (WEB www.online.bg/sofiaecho). **Wagonlit Travel** (✉ ul. Legue, 10, ☎ 02/980–81–26).

SIDE TRIPS FROM SOFIA

Boyana

10 km (6 mi) south of the city center. Hire a taxi or take Tram 19 from ulitsa Graf Ignatiev in central Sofia to the southwestern part of Sofia, where you can catch Bus 63 or 64. The trip takes less than an hour.

At the foot of Mt. Vitosha, this settlement was a medieval fortress near the beginning of the 11th century. Today it is one of Sofia's wealthiest residential neighborhoods. The tiny, medieval **Tzarkvata Boyana** (Boyana Church) is one of Bulgaria's most precious monuments. Dating back to the 13th century, it is a historical treasure on UNESCO's World Heritage list. Unfortunately at this writing it was closed for at least a decade's restoration, but a replica, complete with copies of the exquisite 13th-century frescoes, is open to visitors. This is usually a tour destination, but if you're coming by car, follow ulitsa Alexander Pushkin uphill until you can turn uphill again onto ulitsa Sveti Kaloian, which branches out to ulitsa Brezovitsa. This will take you to ulitsa Boyansko Ezero, where you'll have to hike up the mountain to the church from the trail head. ✉ *Boyansko Ezero.* 🎟 *10 leva.* ☉ *June–Aug., Thurs.–Sun. 9–1 and 2–5; Sept.–May, weekends 10–1 and 2–5.*

In 2000 the **Natzionalen Istoricheski Musei** (National History Museum), considered one of Bulgaria's most important museums, was transplanted from central Sofia's Courts of Justice to the former president's residence in Boyana. In this new home you'll find priceless Thracian treasures, Roman mosaics, enamel jewelry from the First Bulgarian Kingdom, and glowing religious art that survived the years of Ottoman oppression. The collection vividly illustrates the art history of Bulgaria. To get here, take Bus 63 or 111, trolley bus 2, or Marsh-route bus 21. ✉ *Residence Boyana, Palace No. 1,* ☎ *02/955–42–80.* 🎟 *10 leva, guided tour 20 leva.* ☉ *Daily 9:30–6.*

OFF THE
BEATEN PATH

PERNIK – Less than half an hour by car southwest of Sofia is this coal-mining town, and though it has (difficult-to-find) hilltop ruins of a medieval fortress and a mining museum, the principal attraction is the *kukeri*, or mummers, festival in early February. The kukeri rites are intended to ward off evil spirits and promote fertility. Groups of men, analogous to Mardi Gras krewes, don elaborate masks and parade through the streets, making as much noise as possible. Many Bulgarian villages have kukeri events of one form or another, but Pernik has an international reputation. Sofia-based tour companies can provide information about kukeri events throughout the country.

Dragalevci

Take a taxi or Tram 19 from ulitsa Graf Ignatievto in central Sofia to the last stop, and switch to the Dragalevci Bus 64. You can also take Bus 66 or 93 from Hladilnika.

Picturesquely sprawled across the lower part of Mt. Vitosha, this was a slow-paced village just a few years ago. Today, it has been built up with modern homes and absorbed by the city, making it more or less a quiet suburb of Sofia.

In the woods above Dragalevci is the nearby **Dragalevski Manastir** (Dragalevci Monastery). It's currently a convent, but you can visit the 14th-century church with its outdoor frescoes. Hike to the church from the Dragalevci bus stop (about 1½ km [1 mi]), or take Bus 64 or 93 from the Hladilnika bus station. ⊠ *Dragalevci.* ⊘ *Thurs.–Sun. 10–6.*

A **chairlift** ride or two will give you stunning views of the area. The lift on ulitsa Panorama in Dragalevci takes you up to the Aleko resort. From the terminus, walk over to the next chairlift to head farther up to the top of Malak Rezen. There are well-marked walking and ski trails in the area. ⊠ *Ul. Panorama.* ▤ *5 leva.* ⊘ *Daily 8–5.*

Dining

$–$$　✕ **Vodenicharski Mehani.** Appropriately enough, the Miller's Tavern is made up of three old mills linked together. A folklore show and a menu of Bulgarian specialties give it a tourist-friendly but authentic atmosphere. Try the *gyuveché* (potatoes, tomatoes, peas, and onions baked in an earthenware pot). ⊠ *Ul. Panorama, at southern end of town next to chairlift,* ☎ 02/967–10–21 or 02/967–10–01. *No credit cards.*

$　✕ **Chichovtsi.** This unassuming pizza place at the top of the main square in Dragalevci has a cozy fireplace in winter and patio seating in summer. It's almost always busy with hordes of weekend Mt. Vitosha pilgrims. Try a "golyam" Zagorka (a big, frosty beer) and any of the tasty pizzas—but be aware that they may not conform to your expectations; pickles are a topping option, and mayonnaise and ketchup come on the side. ⊠ *Pl. Dragalevci,* ☎ 02/967–17–70. *No credit cards.*

THE BLACK SEA GOLDEN COAST

The Black Sea, contrary to its name, is a brilliant blue and is warm and calm most of the time. Its sunny, sandy beaches are backed by the easternmost slopes of the Balkan range and by the Strandja Mountains. Although the traditional tourist centers tend to be huge, state-built complexes with a somewhat lean feel, some have modern amenities that attract German, British, and Eastern European tourists year after year. Many of the formerly state-owned resort complexes have been privatized and are

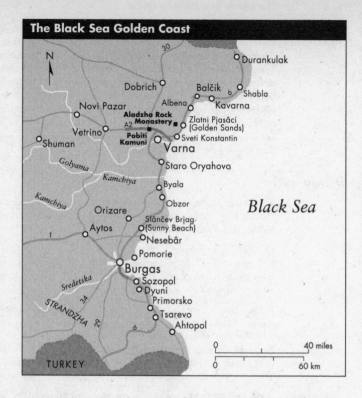

The Black Sea Golden Coast

N

Durankulak

Dobrich

Balčik

Shabla

Albena

Kavarna

Novi Pazar

Aladzha Rock
Monastery

A2

Zlatni Pjasâci
(Golden Sands)

Vetrino

Pobiti
Kamuni

Sveti Konstantin

Shuman

Varna

Golyama

Staro Oryahovo

Kamchiya

Byala

Kamchiya

Obzor

Black Sea

Orizare

Slânčev Brjag
(Sunny Beach)

Aytos

Nesebâr

Pomorie

Burgas

Sozopol

Dyuni

Primorsko

Tsarevo

Ahtopol

STRANDZHA

Sredetska

TURKEY

0   40 miles

0   60 km

renovated or in the process of renovation, while the less desirable properties are in various stages of decay. Resort complexes in the Varna region tend to remain open year-round, unlike those on the southern coast, where many places shut down for the winter. In fishing villages with traditional taverns, Roman and Byzantine ruins, and peaceful swimming coves, new small, private hotels offer a welcome, affordable alternative to the resorts.

Begin your exploration of the southern Black Sea coast, famous for its sheltered bays and cliffs, in the industrial port of Burgas. From Burgas, you can visit the fishing villages of Nesebâr (with Sunny Beach), Sozopol, and Djuni. Coastal towns south of Sozopol have experienced a building boom in recent years, with small hotels popping up in Kiten, Primorsko, and Ahtopol.

Varna

470 km (282 mi) east of Sofia.

The ancient city of Varna, named Odyssos by the Greeks, became a major Roman trading center and is now an important shipbuilding and industrial city. With its beaches and tourism, Varna has a cosmopolitan flair, cultivated with events such as a yearly film festival held in August. Though it is the third-largest city in Bulgaria, its older parts still possess a small-town charm. With wide tree-lined boulevards, numerous gardens and parks, and a beachfront boardwalk, Varna is easily accessible to pedestrians. Running north from the Varna cathedral is ulitsa Vladislav Varnenchik, with shops, movie theaters, and eateries. Another important shopping street is bulevard Osmi Primorski Polk, especially the northeastern end. Bulevard Knyaz Boris I is another of Varna's shopping streets, where you can buy handcrafted souvenirs.

★ The **Natsionalen Arheologicheski Musei** (National Archaeological Museum) is one of the great—if lesser-known—museums of Europe. The splendid collection includes the world's oldest gold treasures, from the Varna necropolis of the 4th millennium BC, discovered in 1972, as well as Thracian, Greek, and Roman treasures and richly painted icons. ⊠ *Bul. Maria Luisa, 41,* ☏ *052/23–70–57.* 🎟 *2 leva.* ⊙ *Tues.–Sat. 10–5.*

The imposing **Tsentralnata Tzarkva** (Cathedral of the Assumption) was built during the period 1880–1886. Take a look inside at the lavish murals. ⊠ *Bul. Maria Luiza, at pl. Metropolit Simeon.* 🎟 *Free.* ⊙ *Daily 7–6.*

Opposite the cathedral, in the Gradska Gradina (City Gardens), is the 19th-century **Starata Chasovnikova Kula** (Old Clock Tower; ⊠ bul. Maria Luiza). In the very city center on the south side of the City Gardens stands **Natsionlen Teatur Stoyan Buchvarov** (Stoyan Buchvarov National Theater; ⊠ Pl. Nezavisimost), a magnificent baroque building. The theater was founded in 1921 and showcased some of Bulgaria's greatest actors. You can see what remains of the **Rimskata Stena** (Roman Fortress Wall; ⊠ corner of bul. Knyaz Boris I and ul. Shipka) of the original Greek city, Odyssos.

If you walk south along ulitsa Odessos to ulitsa Han Krum you will find the remains of the **Roman Thermae.** These public baths dating from the 2nd to the 3rd century AD are among the largest and most substantial Roman ruins in Bulgaria. ⊠ *Ul. Han Krum, 1.* 🎟 *2 leva.*

If you follow bulevard Primorski with the sea on your right, you will reach the **Voennomorski Musei** (Naval Museum), with its displays of the early days of navigation on the Black Sea and the Danube. ⊠ *Corner of Graf Ignatiev and bul. Primorski, just inside park entrance,* ☏ *052/63–20–18.* 🎟 *2 leva, guided tour 12 leva.* ⊙ *Tues.–Sat. 10–6.*

☾ From the extensive and luxuriant **Morska Gradina** (Seaside Gardens), you can catch a great view over the bay. There are restaurants, an open-air theater, and a fascinating astronomy complex with a natural science museum, an observatory, and a planetarium. ⊠ *Off Graf Ignatiev, inside Primorski Park, just outside entrance to municipal beach.*

OFF THE
BEATEN PATH

POBITI KAMMANI – If you plan to drive from Sofia to Varna, allow time to see the so-called "Stone Forest" just off the Sofia–Varna road between Devnya and Varna, about 20 km (13 mi) west of Varna. The unexpected groups of sandstone pillars are thought to have been formed when the area was the bed of the Lutsian Sea.

Dining and Lodging

$$–$$$ ✕ **Paraklisa.** Half-hidden behind an old chapel and surrounded by a green hedge, this is one of the coziest and most timeless little restaurants in town. A rich menu available in English describes in detail all the traditional Bulgarian dishes. Friendly waitresses wearing carnations behind their ears, wine from the best regions in the country, and a genuinely homey feeling guarantee a perfect evening. ⊠ *Bul. Primorski, 47,* ☏ *052/22–34–95. No credit cards.*

$–$$ ✕ **Bistro Europe.** Standing on the busiest point of the main street, this restaurant is one of the best combinations of location and delicious food. You can have a seat outside under the trees and order a large portion of fresh mussels—still a rarity even here on the sea coast—that the owner himself brings every day from a small village nearby. The Italian and French specialties are following original recipes—another rarity in the country. For dessert the friendly, English-speaking waitresses will offer you a rich list of ice creams with fruits and syrups. ⊠ *Bul. Slivnitsa, 11,* ☏ *052/60–39–50. No credit cards.*

$$–$$$ ✕⬚ **Villa Sagona.** Built in the beginning of the 20th century as a mer-
★ chant's family villa is cozy and homey. Book a room with a balcony
to get a view of the sea. You can take your food either in your room
or in the dining room, where the old piano and record player of the
original owners still stand. You needn't be a Villa Sagona guest to try
the exquisite Bulgarian cuisine of the restaurant, and a taxi back to
your hotel will be called for you. The manager will give you any kind
of tourist information you may need. ⊠ *Villa N37, ul. Nikola, 8, Morska
Gradina 9005,* ☎ *052/30–37–83, 052/30–37–84, or 088–536–916,* Ⅸ
*052/30–23–39. 9 rooms. Restaurant, café, minibars, cable TV, tennis
court, pool, lobby lounge, dry cleaning, Internet, car rental, travel services, some pets allowed. No credit cards. BP.*

$$–$$$$ ⬚ **Černo Moré.** Two of the best things about this 22-floor hotel, on
the city's main drag leading to the beach, are the panoramic view and
perfect location. Apart from the fifth floor, which was renovated in 2000,
the rest of the hotel still preserves its outdated and somewhat gloomy
appearance and furnishings. ⊠ *Bul. Slivnitza, 33, 9000,* ☎ *052/23–
21–15 or 052/25–30–91. 200 rooms. 3 restaurants, café, some mini-
bars, cable TV, gym, bar, casino, nightclub, some pets allowed. AE,
DC, MC, V. BP.*

Sveti Konstantin

8 km (5 mi) north along the coast from Varna.

Sveti Konstantin, Bulgaria's oldest Black Sea resort, is small and inti-
mate, spreading through a wooded park near a series of sandy coves.

Dining and Lodging

$$ ✕ **Korab–Restorant Sirius** (Ship–Restaurant Sirius). This real World War
I–era *korab* (ship) is now an attractive restaurant with a grand view.
Take a table at the top deck and enjoy the sunset and the meal. ⊠ *Sveti
Konstantin,* ☎ *052/36–19–32 or 052/36–20–07. No credit cards.*

$$$$ ⬚ **Grand Hotel Varna.** This Swedish-built hotel has a reputation for
★ being the best on the coast. It is only 150 yards from the beach and
offers a wide range of hydrotherapeutic treatments featuring the area's
natural warm mineral springs. Yearly upgrades enable the Grand to
keep pace with brand-new hotels, but the luxury comes at a cost: it is
no longer an inexpensive secret. ⊠ *Sveti Konstantin 9006* ☎ *052/36–
14–91,* Ⅸ *052/36–19–20.* ⅦⅢ *www.vega.bg/~ghv. 325 rooms. 3 restaurants, café, minibars, cable TV, 2 tennis courts, 3 pools (1 indoor), health
club, sauna, spa, 6 bars, casino, nightclub, bowling, squash, dry cleaning, Internet, business services, meeting rooms, car rental, travel services; no-smoking rooms. AE, DC, MC, V. BP*

$$–$$$ ⬚ **Čajka.** Čajka means "seagull" in Bulgarian, and this hotel has a bird's-
eye view of the entire resort from its perch above the northern end of
the beach. You can have a TV in your room on request, but there is a
fee. ⊠ *Sveti Konstantin 9005,* ☎ *052/36–12–57. 102 rooms. Restaurant, café, minibars, pool, travel services, some pets allowed. No credit
cards. BP*

Zlatni Pjasâci

8 km (5 mi) north of Sveti Konstantin.

In contrast to the sedate atmosphere of Sveti Konstantin, Zlatni Pjasâci
(Golden Sands) is lively, with extensive leisure-time amenities, mineral-
spring medical centers, and sports and entertainment facilities. Just over
4 km (2½ mi) inland from Zlatni Pjasâci is **Aladja Manastir** (Aladja
Rock Monastery; ⊠ Zlatni Pjasâci), one of Bulgaria's oldest, dating
from around the 9th or 10th century. The monastery is cut out of the

cliff face and accessible to visitors by sturdy iron stairways. To get there, take a taxi from the entrance of Zlatni Pjasâci Resort; it costs 2 leva and is open daily 10–6.

Albena

10 km (6 mi) north of Zlatni Pjasâci.

Albena, a 1970s resort, is between Balčik and Golden Sands. It is well known for its long, wide beach, clean water, and good campsites.

Dining and Lodging

$$–$$$$ ✕ **Hashové.** This open-air restaurant offering traditional Bulgarian appearance and cuisine is right on the beach. In the evenings live entertainment includes a folk orchestra and fire-walkers; a lamb is cooked on a spit in front of your eyes. The bar is open all day long, and the staff is used to Western standards of service. ⊠ *Albena,* ☎ *0579/629–77. No credit cards.*

$$$$ ▥ **Dobrudja Hotel.** Albena's most luxurious hotel is large and comfortable, with a mineral-water health spa, where you can relax in healing mud, enjoy a massage, or indulge in a curative bath. ⊠ *Albena 9620,* ☎ *0579/620–20,* ℻ *0579/622–16. 284 rooms. 2 restaurants, café, mini-bars, cable TV, 2 pools (1 indoor), children's pool, health club, spa, bar, lobby lounge, casino, nightclub, dry cleaning, Internet, business services, meeting rooms, car rental, travel services, some pets allowed. DC, MC, V. BP.*

Balčik

35 km (22 mi) north of Sveti Konstantin, 8 km (5 mi) north of Albena.

Part of Romania until just before World War II, Balčik is now a relaxed haven for Bulgaria's writers, artists, and scientists. On its white cliffs are crescent-shape tiers of vacation homes. Among Balčik's many summer retreats is **Dvoretsa Balčik** (Balčik Palace), once the grand summer getaway for Romania's Queen Marie and her six children. Surrounding the palace are the beautiful **Botanicheska Gradina v Balčik** (Botanical Gardens), dotted with curious buildings, terraces overlooking the sea, and a small Byzantine-style **church** where the late Marie's heart was encased in a jewel-encrusted box. Her remains were returned to Romania when Bulgaria reclaimed the region. ⊠ *Balčik.* ▨ *4 leva.* ⊙ *Gardens and palace daily 8–8, church Tues.–Sun. 9–5.*

Slâncev Brjag

95 km (60 mi) south of Varna, 140 km (87 mi) south of Balčik.

The enormous Slâncev Brjag (Sunny Beach) is especially popular with families because of its safe beaches, gentle tides, and playgrounds for children. During the summer there are kindergartens for young vacationers, children's concerts, even a children's disco. Slâncev Brjag has come a long way since the early 1990s. Still, a big part of it is in a process of renovation, while the rest is covered with numerous new and luxuriant hotels with pools, fountains, and Greek pillars.

Dining and Lodging

$$ ✕ **Hanska Šatra.** In the coastal hills behind the sea, this combination restaurant and nightclub has been built to resemble the tents of the Bulgarian rulers of old. It has entertainment well into the night and a magnificent view to half of the southern sea coast. ⊠ *5 km (3 mi) west of Slâncev Brjag,* ☎ *0554/228–11. No credit cards. Reservations essential.*

$ ✗ **Ribarska Hiza.** This lively beachside restaurant specializes in fish and has music until 1 AM. ✉ *Ul. Slanchev Brjag, 4, at northern end of Slânčev Brjag,* ☎ *0554/221–86. No credit cards.*

$$$$ ▥ **Čajka.** The Čajka offers one of the best locations—it's directly across from the best stretch of beach. Renovated in 2002, it has been turned into an imposing and expensive mixture of ancient Greek-style marble lounge and corridors and comfortable, colorful modern rooms. It has a Pizza Castle (really looks like a castle) in its garden and a transparent elevator. ✉ *Ul. Slânčev Brjag, 8, 8240,* ☎ *0554/223–08. 415 rooms. Restaurant, café, minibars, some microwaves, cable TV, 2 pools, massage, bar, pub, laundry service, travel services, some pets allowed. No credit cards. BP.*

$$$$ ▥ **Grand Hotel Sunny Beach.** In the center of the resort, this large, pink hotel is just a short stroll from the beach. Built in 2001, it is modern, comfortable, and calm. ✉ *Slânčev Brjag 8240,* ☎ *0554/280–00,* ℻ *0554/25–24 or 0554/29–21. 192 rooms. Restaurant, café, minibars, cable TV, pool, hair salon, massage, bar, shop, laundry, meeting room, car rental, travel services, some pets allowed (fee). No credit cards. BP.*

$$–$$$ ▥ **Globus.** Once considered the best hotel in the resort area, Globus has a central location that helps make up for its fading, dingy rooms. The larger apartments with seaside terraces are preferred. There is a cash machine in the lounge. ✉ *Ul. Slânčev Brjag, 22, 8240,* ☎ *0554/ 22–45 or 0554/20–18,* ℻ *0554/222–45 or 0554/220–18. 110 rooms. Restaurant, bar, 2 cafés, some minibars, cable TV, pool, gym, massage, sauna, car rental, travel service. No credit cards. BP.*

Nesebâr

5 km (3 mi) south of Slânčev Brjag (Sunny Beach) and accessible by regular excursion buses.

Just 10 minutes south of Slânčev Brjag (Sunny Beach) is a painter's and poet's retreat. Founded by the Greeks in about 500 BC on a rocky peninsula reached by a narrow causeway, this ancient settlement exudes an aura of its past. Among its vine-covered houses are beautiful Byzantine ruins, richly decorated medieval churches, and crumbling Ottoman bathhouses. Quaint—though not undiscovered—Nesebâr is densely packed with outdoor markets, galleries, and seaside cafés, where fried seafood is served in heaping portions. Small hotels, both on the peninsula and the mainland, have popped up in recent years, offering a welcome alternative to the dated resorts nearby. If you want to stay in the Old Town, make your reservations well in advance.

Lodging

$–$$$ ▥ **Monte Cristo.** This small, stylish hotel tucked between National Revival homes and the ruins of Byzantine churches is pricey by Bulgarian standards, but the location and quality of the facilities are worth it. It's also one of the few Nesebâr hotels open year-round. It's popular, and reservations are difficult to come by during high season. Ask for a room on the upper floors to avoid the thudding music of the restaurant-bar. ✉ *Ul. Venera, 2, 8230,* ☎ *0554/420–55,* ℻ *0554/455–55. 5 rooms, 4 suites. Restaurant, café, minibars, cable TV, car rental. MC, V. BP.*

$–$$ ▥ **Mistral Hotel.** On the mainland, a short walk north of the causeway leading to the Old Town, are several small hotels and restaurants that were built in the late 1990s. Mistral is one of the better of the hotels. It's pleasant, affordable, and busy all year. The proprietor is a good source for information about the region. ✉ *Ul. Khan Krum, 22, 8230,* ☎ *0554/425–93,* ℻ *0554/429–33. 18 rooms, 2 suites. Restaurant, gym, sauna, some pets allowed. No credit cards. BP.*

Burgas

38 km (24 mi) south of Nesebâr.

The next place of any size south along the coast from Nesebâr is the city of Burgas. Bulgaria's second main port on the Black Sea, Burgas is industrial and chaotic, with heavy traffic, chemical plants, a massive state-owned oil refinery, and huge ships anchored off shore. Despite the noise, construction, and pollution, Burgas can provide a pleasant stay, with its long Primorska Gradina (Seaside Park), expansive beach, and pedestrian alleyways winding through a lively city center.

Lodging

$$$–$$$$ ⊞ **Bulgaria.** This high-rise Interhotel is in the center of town. While the rooms aren't exactly upbeat—dark green, brown, and black predominate—it has its own nightclub with a floor show. ⊠ *Ul. Aleksandrovska, 21 8000,* ☎ *056/84–28–20 or 056/84–26–10,* ⅎⁿ *056/84–72–91. 200 rooms. Restaurant, hair salon, laundry service, nightclub. MC, V.*

Sozopol

32 km (20 mi) south of Burgas.

Built on and around numerous Byzantine ruins, this fishing port was once Apollonia, the oldest of the Greek colonies in Bulgaria. With narrow, cobbled streets leading down to the harbor, it is now a popular haunt for Bulgarian and, increasingly, foreign writers and artists, who find private accommodations with locals in rustic Black Sea–style houses. As romantic, historic, and quaint as Nesebâr, Sozopol is more well known, and from August to September its tiny streets can barely contain the crowds that arrive for the **Apollonia Arts Festival.** To see the quieter side of the village, come in the off-season, when you will be one of few tourists. Sozopol is a good base for exploring the coast south to the Turkish border, where unspoiled rivers pour out of the forested Strandja Mountains.

Dining and Lodging

$ ✕ **Mehana Sozopol.** This touristy spot on a street with several mehani and bars serves typical Bulgarian and seasonal fish dishes. During the summer there are folk music and patio dining. Replenish yourself with a few cups of sturdy red wine and a *sirene po shopski* (white cheese baked with tomato, herbs, and egg) after touring the cobbled streets. ⊠ *Ul. Apollonia,* ☎ *05514/23–84. No credit cards.*

$ ⊞ **Kavaler.** You'll find this small, year-round hotel on a quiet street off the main drag in the new part of town, but it's a short walk from the beach and the Old Town. It's very clean, with pleasant service, but the desk clerks keep random hours—look for help in the busy restaurant. The two apartments on the top floor have terraces with sweeping views. ⊠ *Ul. Yani Popov, 21,* ☎ *05514/36–46, 12 rooms, 2 suites. Restaurant, refrigerators, cable TV. No credit cards.*

The Black Sea Golden Coast Essentials

AIR TRAVEL

During the summer season, there are direct international flights from many European cities to Varna and Burgas. Although these are normally booked as part of a holiday package, flight-only options are also available. A major tour company offering these Bulgaria packages is Balkan Holidays in the U.K. There are also daily 50-minute flights from Sofia and Plovdiv to Varna and Burgas on Balkan Airlines.

➤ CONTACTS: **Balkan Holidays** (☎ 0500/245–165, WEB www. balkanholidays.co.uk). **Balkan Airlines** (☎ 02/981–51–70 in Sofia).

BOAT TRAVEL

A regular boat service travels the Varna–Sveti Konstantin–Golden Sands–Albena–Balčik route. Travel arrangements are made through Balkantourist.

BUS TRAVEL

Buses make frequent runs up and down the coast and are inexpensive. Buy your ticket in advance from the kiosks near the bus stops.

GUIDED TOURS

A wide range of trips can be arranged from all resorts. There are bus excursions to Sofia; a one-day bus and boat trip along the Danube; and a three-day bus tour of Bulgaria departing from Zlatni Pjasâci (Golden Sands), Sveti Konstantin, and Albena. All tours are run by Balkantourist (☞ Visitor Information, *below*). Yacht cruises are organized by Yacht–Port Nerssebar.

➤ CONTACTS: **Yacht–Port Nerssebar** (☎ 088–269–172).

TRAIN TRAVEL

It's a six- to eight-hour train ride from Sofia to Varna or Burgas.

VISITOR INFORMATION

Balkantourist Albena (✉ Main Administration Building, Albena, ☎ 0579/627–21 or 0579/621–52). **Balkantourist Burgas** (✉ Hotel Primorets, ul. Knyaz Batenberg, 1, Burgas, ☎ 056/84–31–37). **Balkantourist Slânčev Brjag** (✉ Main Administration Bldg., Slânčev Brjag, ☎ 0554/224–69). **Balkantourist Varna** (✉ ul. Moussala, 3, Varna, ☎ 052/35–55–24). **Balkan Tourist Zlatni Pjasâci** (✉ Main Administration Bldg., Zlatni Pjasâci, ☎ 052/35–56–83).

INLAND BULGARIA

Inland Bulgaria is less well known to tourists than the capital and the coast. Adventurous travelers willing to put up with rustic hotel facilities and unreliable transportation will be rewarded with unjaded hospitality and scenic beauty. Wooded and mountainous, the interior is dotted with attractive "museum" villages (entire settlements listed for preservation because of their historical value) and ancient ruins. The region's folk culture, often pagan in nature, is a strong survivor from the past, not a tourist-inspired re-creation, and spending a few nights in a secluded mountain village can feel like journeying into medieval times. The foothills of the Balkan range, marked Stara Planina (Old Mountains) on most maps, lie parallel to the lower Sredna Gora Mountains, with the verdant Valley of Roses between them. In the Balkan range is the ancient capital of Veliko Târnovo; north of Târnovo, on the River Danube, lies the town of Roussé, an old Roman port. South of the Sredna Gora stretches the fertile Thracian Plain and Bulgaria's second-largest and most progressive city, Plovdiv. To the south, in the Rila Mountains, is Borovec, first of the mountain resorts.

Koprivshtitsa

★ *105 km (65 mi) east of Sofia, reached by a minor road south from the Sofia–Kazanlak expressway.*

One of Bulgaria's showplace villages, Koprivshtitsa is set amid mountain pastures and pine forests, about 3,000 ft up in the Sredna Gora

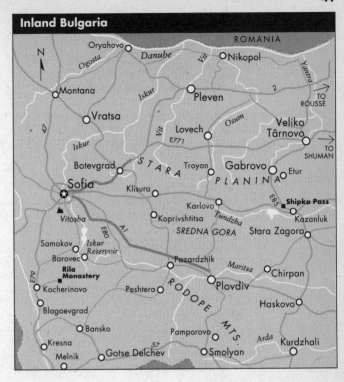

Inland Bulgaria

range. Founded in the 14th century, it became a prosperous trading center with close ties to Venice during the National Revival period 400 years later. The architecture of this period, also called the Bulgarian Renaissance, features carved woodwork on broad verandas and overhanging eaves, brilliant colors, and courtyards with studded wooden gates. Throughout the centuries, artists, poets, and wealthy merchants have made their homes here; many of the historic houses once inhabited by Ottoman landowners are open to visitors. The town has been well preserved and is revered by Bulgarians as a symbol of freedom, for it was here in April 1876 that the first shots were fired in the rebellion that led to the end of Turkish occupation.

Dining and Lodging

$–$$ ✕▦ **Traianova Kushta.** This charming inn uphill from the town square offers rustic rooms furnished in the traditional National Revival style, with woven rugs and low beds. One room has a fireplace; all have shared baths. An intimate restaurant offers traditional Bulgarian dishes, but no breakfast is included in the rates. All payment for rooms and meals is in leva. ✉ *Ul. Generilo 5, 2090,* ☎ *07184/22–50. 6 rooms with shared bath. Restaurant, cable TV; no a/c, no room phones. No credit cards.*

$ ✕▦ **Family Hotel Kalina.** This small hotel is in the central part of the town, surrounded by a beautiful garden. It offers a laundry service; for recreation, you can play table tennis or chess. An advantage is that all rooms have private baths, telephones, and TVs. Food is served in the restaurant of the hotel, though breakfast is not included in the rates. All payment for rooms and meals is in leva. ✉ *Ul. Liuben Karavelov, 35,* ☎ *07184/20–32 or 07184/27–03. 6 rooms. Restaurant, cable TV; no a/c. No credit cards.*

Troyan

At the village of Karnare, 17 km (11 mi) east of Klisura, take the wind-ing scenic road north over the Balkan range to Troyan, 93 km (58 mi) northeast of Koprivshtitsa.

The **Troyan Monastir** (Troyan Monastery), built during the 1600s, is in the heart of the mountains. The church was painstakingly remod-eled during the 19th century, and its icons, wood carvings, and fres-coes are classic examples of National Revival art. Although there are no phones and no regular hours, you should be able to find someone to open the gate in the daytime. ⊠ *Troyan.*

Veliko Târnovo

Travel north on the mountain road from Troyan until it meets Hwy. E772, where you turn right for Veliko Târnovo, 82 km (50 mi) north-east of Karnare; 240 km (144 mi) northeast of Sofia.

From the 12th to the 14th century, Veliko Târnovo was the capital of the Second Bulgarian Kingdom and was often referred to at that time as the second Constantinople. Damaged by Ottoman attacks and again by an earthquake in 1913, it has been reconstructed and is now a mu-seum city with panoramic vistas of steep mountain slopes through which the idyllic River Jantra runs its jagged course. The town warrants one or two days of exploration. Try to begin at a vantage point above the town to get a sense of its layout, and be sure to visit the three impor-tant churches on Tsaravec and Trapezitsa hills, all of which are open daily from June to September and Tuesday through Sunday from Oc-tober to May.

Tsarevec (Carevec on some maps), protected by a river loop, is the hill where medieval czars and patriarchs had their palaces. Steep paths pro-vide opportunities to view the extensive ruins of the Patriarchate and the royal palace. On summer nights, a spectacular sound-and-light show presented here can be seen from the surrounding pubs. **Tzarkvata Cheteridesette Machenika** (Church of the Forty Martyrs) is a 13th-cen-tury structure with frescoes of the Târnovo school and two inscribed columns, one dating from the 9th century. The **Tserkvata Sveti Dimi-tar** (Church of St. Dimitrius), from the 12th century, is built on the spot where the Second Bulgarian Kingdom was proclaimed in 1185.

The 14th-century **Tzarkvata Sveti Peter y Pavel** (Church of Sts. Peter and Paul; Trapezitsa) has vigorous murals both inside and out.

In the Old Town, **Samovodene Street,** lined with restored crafts work-shops, is a good place to find souvenirs, Turkish candy, or a charming café.

Dining and Lodging

$ ✕ **The City Pub.** If you've come to Veliko Târnovo, you can't miss this British pub. Being one of the most popular places in town, it is fre-quented by locals and visitors alike. You can eat or drink here at any time of the day and night, and it is always lively. Christmas and foot-ball championships days have witnessed dancing on tables and singing. It shares toilets with the neighboring dance club, so you can slip next door without paying the entrance fee. Enjoy it. ⊠ *Ul. Hristo Botev, 15,* ☎ *062/637–824. No credit cards.*

$–$$ ✕⊞ **Hotel–Mehana Gurko.** Homey and modern, this hotel overlooks the river and has a great view. The rooms are clean and very comfortable, with tubs. On the ground floor is the restaurant, which offers a good example of traditional Bulgarian cuisine. Reserve a table in advance.

✉ *Ul. Gurko, 33,* ☎ *062/62–78–38,* FAX *062/62–78–38. 11 rooms. Restaurant, minibars, cable TV. No credit cards.*

$$$$ 🏨 **Veliko Târnovo.** In the historic heart of town, this modern Interhotel has good facilities. They may not have much personality, but the rooms are modern, with Western-style showers in the bathrooms. ✉ *Ul. Al. Penchev, 2,* ☎ *062/60–10–00 or 062/62–15–95. 201 rooms. 4 restaurants, café, cable TV, indoor pool, health club, bar, nightclub, meeting rooms, travel services. DC, MC, V. BP.*

$$$–$$$$ 🏨 **Hotel Millennium.** Being modern and centrally located, this hotel is a popular and cheaper alternative for foreign tourists than the Veliko Târnovo. Its advantages are the smart rooms and clean, contemporary decor. ✉ *Ul. Tsanko Tserkovski, 20,* ☎ *062/616–01,* FAX *062/616–01. 16 rooms. Restaurant, cable TV, massage, sauna, lobby lounge. No credit cards. BP.*

OFF THE
BEATEN PATH

A BULGARIAN HOMESTAY – Are you a traveler rather than a tourist? Spend a night with a local family. Uri and Mimi Mihailovi provide bed-and-breakfast (and a glass or two of home-made rakia) about 20 km (12 mi) outside Veliko Târnovo. You'll find forest views and great hospitality in a genuine no-frills setting for 20 leva per person per night, including breakfast. Ask Uri to take you on a local walking tour or to take you fishing. ✉ *Mahala Siarovtsy,* ☎ *062/60–12–45.*

En Route If you leave Veliko Târnovo by E85 and head south toward Plovdiv, you'll go through the Shipka Pass, with its mighty monument on the peak to the 200,000 Russian soldiers and Bulgarian volunteers who died during the Russian-Turkish Wars. Continuing along N6, between the towns of Karlovo and Kazanluk, is the area called the Valley of Roses, hotbed of the flower industry. While most of the crop is harvested in early June, several fields of roses are left for the benefit of passing tourists.

Roussé

110 km (65 mi) northeast of Veliko Tûrnovo, along E85; 305 km (182 mi) northeast of Sofia, along A2 and then E83.

Regrettably, Roussé is one of Bulgaria's least-visited towns, primarily due to its distance from any other major tourist spots. But the town and the surrounding area are rich in historical sites—from Roman castles to medieval monasteries to world-class nature reserves. Consider flying to nearby Bucharest, Romania—only 35 mi away—and crossing by the bridge with neighboring Romania (☞ Bucharest A to Z *in* Chapter 7).

Since the Romans built an important castle here as part of a line of fortifications along the Danube, which formed the northern edge of the Roman Empire, Roussé has been a major military and commercial center. Under the Ottoman Empire, it was a key trading post with Christian Europe. After the 1878 liberation from Ottoman rule, Italian and Austrian architects created the historic center, which you can still see today. The **March Music Festival** brings musicians from all over to the city's many venues. In summer, the town square is the site of numerous outdoor concerts, beer festivals, and constant street entertainment. The historic center, laid out in squares and connected with pedestrian-only streets, is well signposted in English.

Ploshtad na Svobodata (Freedom Square) is the town's central square, surrounded by open cafés and lush greenery, and connects with the main street Alexandrovska, favorite of the townsfolk for their daily stroll.

On the west end of ulitsa Alexandrovska stands the **Dvoretsa Batenberg** (Batenberg Palace), newly renovated to be used for the city's **Istoricheski Muzei** (Historical Museum). The palace was built as a residence in the 1880s for Prince Batenberg, the first Bulgarian monarch after the Liberation. At this writing the museum had not yet opened, so admission prices and hours were not set. ✉ *Ul. Alexandrovska.*

Northeast of the Batenberg Palace is the **Sexaginta Prista,** the ruins of a Roman fort on a landscaped riverwalk. ✉ *Ul. Slavianska (enter from river end of street),* ☎ *no phone.* ☜ *2 leva.* ☺ *Weekdays 10–5.*

Roussé was the childhood home of Elias Canetti, who won the Nobel Prize in literature. His boyhood home is now the **Kushtata na Elias Canetti** (Canetti's House). His books include *Tongues Set Free,* which recounts his childhood in Roussé. ✉ *Ul. Slavianska.*

If you prefer a good walk along the Danube, follow the **Pridunavski Bulevard** (Danube Boulevard) eastward until you reach a large staircase leading down to the riverbank. Stop for a drink or a bite to eat on one of the restaurant-boats that sometimes make two-hour cruises to the Dunav Most (the border bridge with Romania) and back.

Dining and Lodging

$–$$$ ✕ **Chiflika.** This popular, traditional-style restaurant on two levels has nightly live folk music and a dance floor, so it's definitely not a quiet place for dinner. However, it is recommended. Order the *Meshana skara Vulchi glad* (mixed grill, also known as "wolf's hunger") or *Pileshka kavarma* (a thick stew of meat, onions, and vegetables). Food is served on heated, wrought-iron platters and in clay pots. Try the wine from Roussé region. ✉ *Ul. Otets Paisiy, 10,* ☎ *082/82–82–22. No credit cards.*

$$–$$$$ ☷ **Danube Plaza Hotel.** Since its renovation in 2000, this hotel—perfectly located on the main square—has been the best choice in town. The modern rooms are comfortable and well furnished; a garden restaurant offers excellent local and Continental cuisine. The hotel's tourist office can assist in all travel arrangements, including local sightseeing and direct transfers to the Bucharest Airport. ✉ *Pl. Svoboda, 5,* ☎ *082/82–29–29,* FAX *082/82–29–52,* WEB *www.danubeplaza.com. 78 rooms. 2 restaurants, café, minibars, cable TV, massage, lobby lounge, dry cleaning, laundry service, meeting rooms, travel services, some pets allowed. DC, MC, V.*

OFF THE   **SKALEN MANASTIR V IVANOVO –** The world-famous rock monasteries of
BEATEN PATH   Ivanovo, both of which are on UNESCO's list of World Heritage Sites, are a network of small churches perched in cliff faces of the Lom River, a tributary of the Danube. Located 21 km (8 mi) southwest of Roussé, the monastery was founded in the 5th or 6th century AD and was a center of religion and art in the Middle Ages. Its setting within the **Roussenski Lom Nature Park** makes it worth a whole day's exploration for hikers and those in search of a bit of untouched nature. It's possible to book private accommodations in the park office in Ivanovo. Hours for the rock monasteries are erratic, and they are often closed during lunch. ✉ *Ivanovo,* ☎ *082/27–23–97.* ☜ *Free.* ☺ *Usually Wed.–Sun. 10–5.*

TRAKIJS KA GROBNITSA V SVESHTARI – The Thracian tombs, dating from the 3rd century BC are about 50 km (33 mi) from Roussé near the village of Sveshtari. The tombs themselves appear throughout the fields, visible as house-size earth mounds, built for the rich and powerful of a Thracian civilization long since gone. Some are open to the public. From inside, the tombs are richly decorated with impressive murals. The most famous has 10 statues of women, supposedly goddesses. They can be visited on a day trip from Roussé or en route to the Black Sea. ⊠ *Sveshtari*. 🖼 *2 leva*. ⊙ *Weekdays 9–4*.

Plovdiv

174 km (104 mi) southeast of Sofia, 197 km (123 mi) southwest of Veliko Târnovo.

Plovdiv may be the quintessential Bulgarian city, with colorful, well-kept National Revival buildings, progressive nightlife, and stunning ruins. Bulgaria's second-largest city is not only one of the oldest settlements in Europe, but it's a major industrial and cultural center—it was a "Cultural Capital" of Europe in 1999. The breathtaking, lantern-lit Stariya grad (Old Town) lies on the hillier southern side of the Maritsa River. Plovdiv hosts several large annual trade fairs, including a wine fair in early February and two large industrial fairs in early May and late September. They are open to the public, but be aware that they fill area hotels; if you can get a room the price will be double the norm.

The **Natsionalen Etnografski Muzei** (National Ethnographic Museum) is in the much-photographed former home of a Greek merchant. It is an elegant example of the National Revival style, which made its first impact in Plovdiv; the museum is filled with artifacts from that fertile period. ⊠ *Ul. Chomakov, 2*, ☎ *032/62–42–61*. 🖼 *2 leva*. ⊙ *Tues.–Sun. 9–noon and 2–5.*

Below the medieval gateway of Hisar Kapiya, the **Georgiadieva Kushta** (Georgiadi House) is a grandiose example of National Revival–style architecture, with its overhanging upper story, carved pillars, and intricate, painted floral decoration. It has a small museum dedicated to the 1876 uprising against the Turks. ⊠ *Ul. Starinna, 1.* 🖼 *2 leva.* ⊙ *Wed.–Sun. 9:30–12:30 and 2–5.*

Steep, narrow **Strumna Street** is lined with workshops and boutiques, some reached through little courtyards. Beyond the jewelry and leather vendors in ploshtad Stamboliiski are the remains of a **Rimski stadion** (Roman stadium; ⊠ ul. Saborna and ul. Knyaz Alexander I) that dates from the 2nd century.

★ The old **Kapana District** (⊠ northwest of Pl. Stamboliiski) has narrow, winding streets and restored shops and cafés. The exquisite hilltop **Rimski amfiteatur** (Roman amphitheater; ⊠ ul. Tsar Ivailo), only discovered and excavated in 1981, has been sensitively renovated and is open for exploration. In summer, this timeless setting is frequently used for dramatic and musical performances. Admission is 2 leva, and it is usually open daily 10:30–5:30.

NEED A BREAK?	At the self-serve **Rhetora** (⊠ ul. T. Samodoumov, 8A, ☎ 032/62–20–93) the coffee is instant and the pastries shipped in, but the mediocrity of the snacks is far outweighed by the absolute beauty of the setting (and the dirt-cheap prices)—you can sip a drink while looking out over the Roman ruins.

The **Natsionalen Archeologicheski Muzei** (National Archaeological Museum) has a wealth of ancient Thracian artifacts from Plovdiv and the surrounding area. ⊠ *Pl. Suedinenie, 1*, ☎ *032/63–17–60*. 🖼 *1½ leva.* ⊙ *Tues.–Sun. 9–12:30 and 2–5:30.*

Dining and Lodging

$$–$$$$ ✕ **Apolonia.** A spacious patio and several dining rooms in an Old Town National Revival–style house make an exceptional setting for a leisurely meal. The food is better than average Bulgarian fare, the service is friendly,

and there's an English-language menu available. There is often piano music or karaoke as well as Internet service. Reservations are recommended. ⊠ *Ul. Vasil Kanchev, 1,* ☎ *032/63–26–99. No credit cards.*

$$ ✕ **Alafrangite.** This classic Old Town mehana—with shared tables, folk music, and heavy food—is set in a restored 19th-century house with carved wooden ceilings and a vine-covered courtyard. A house specialty is *kiopolu* (vegetable puree of baked eggplant, peppers, and tomatoes). ⊠ *Ul. Nektariev, 17,* ☎ *032/26–95–95. No credit cards.*

$ ✕ **Cuchura.** This favorite of artists and students offers Bulgarian standards. It's located just outside of the Old Town, where prices drop and the quality must satisfy the locals. ⊠ *Ul. Otets Paisii, 12A,* ☎ *032/ 62–34–09. No credit cards.*

$$$$ 🏨 **Hotel Hebrus.** This small, pricey hotel in the Old Town is open year-round. The newly renovated rooms, furnished with antique replicas and goose-down duvets, showcase the painted walls and richly carved ceilings characteristic of fine Old Town homes. ⊠ *Ul. K. Stoilov, 51A, 4000,* ☎ *032/26–02–25. 6 rooms. Restaurant, café, minibars, cable TV, sauna, dry cleaning, laundry, Internet, meeting room, travel services. MC, V.*

$$$$ 🏨 **Novotel Plovdiv.** The modern, well-equipped Novotel lies across the river from the new part of town, near the fairgrounds. There are large beds (for Bulgaria), big windows, and up-to-date bathrooms. ⊠ *Ul. Zlatyu Boyadzhiev, 2, 4000,* ☎ *032/93–44–44 or 032/93–49–99,* 🌐 *www.novotel.com. 328 rooms. 2 restaurants, café, minibars, cable TV, tennis court, pool, gym, hair salon, massage, sauna, nightclub, shops, dry cleaning, laundry, Internet, business services, meeting rooms. AE, DC, MC, V.*

Borovec

Travel west along the E80 Sofia Rd. At Dolna Banja, turn off to Borovec, about 4,300 ft up the northern slopes of the Rila Mountains; 109 km (68 mi) from Plovdiv.

This is an excellent walking center and winter sports resort, well equipped with hotels, taverns, and ski schools. A winding mountain road leads to Sofia, 70 km (44 mi) from here, past Lake Iskar, the largest lake in the country. For information on resorts, hotels, and winter sports facilities, contact the National Information and Advertising Center (☞ Visitor Information *in* Bulgaria A to Z).

En Route On the road between Borovec and Sofia is the **Rilski Manastir** (Rila Monastery), founded in the 10th century by St. Ivan of Rila, a prophet and healer. Cut across to E79, travel south to Kočerinovo, and turn east to follow the steep forested valley past the village of Rila. The monastery has suffered so frequently from fire that most of it is now a grand National Revival reconstruction, although a rugged 14th-century tower has survived. The atmosphere carries a strong sense of the past—monks are still in residence, although some of the monks' cells are now guest rooms. You can see 14 small chapels with frescoes from the 15th and 17th centuries, a lavishly carved altarpiece in the new Assumption Church, the sarcophagus of Ivan of Rila, icons, and ancient manuscripts—a reminder that the monastery was a stronghold of art and learning during the centuries of Ottoman rule. Sofia's Balkantourist office can make arrangements for overnight stays.

Bansko

150 km (93 mi) south of Sofia via Blagoevgrad.

The houses in this small, picturesque town at the foot of the Pirin Mountains may seem inaccessible with their lattice windows and heavy gates, designed to fend off Ottoman invaders, but the rooms inside these "fortresses" are delicate and beautiful, with carved ceilings and hand-made rugs. Generally, these homes are not open as museums, but by planning an overnight stay, or even politely asking, you may be able to see some interiors. Tourism is booming in Bansko, with numerous plans in the works for expanding facilities. The **Tzarkvata Sveta Troitsa** (Holy Trinity Church), built in 1835, along with the tower and the town clock, is part of the architectural complex in the center of the town. ✉ *Pl. Vuzrazhdane, 2.*

Dining and Lodging

Privately owned bed-and-breakfasts can be found on almost every street, and the Vrah Vihren mountain is covered with sprawling ski resorts. The former offer small rooms and home-cooked meals, while the latter are usually comfortable but lack charm. Reservations are necessary at the height of ski season (March) and around New Year's.

$ ✕ **Dedo Pene.** A string of cowbells clangs as you open the heavy wooden door of this traditional *krutchma* (tavern). A waitress will pour you a glass of homemade red wine before you've hung your coat on the rack. The walls are adorned with furs, stuffed bobcats, and hand-woven rugs. This pagan tavern exudes authenticity (along with the aroma of uncured hides) and serves up hearty medieval meat dishes. ✉ *Southeast corner of Tsentralnia Ploshtad,* ☎ *07443/50–71 or 07443/22–23. No credit cards.*

$$ 🛏 **Pirin Hotel.** This popular hotel is large and modern, but the plain wooden furniture and wool blankets give it a state-owned feel. In the winter you can rent skis from the hotel, and you get free transport to the slopes. ✉ *Ul. Tsar Simeon, 68,* ☎ *07443/25–36,* ⅢⅩ *07443/42–44. 55 rooms, 7 suites. 2 restaurants, café, minibars, cable TV, indoor pool, gym, massage, sauna, billiards, ski shop, nightclub, video game room, Internet, meeting room, travel services; no a/c in some rooms. DC, MC, V.*

Melnik

From Sandanski, head south down E79 about 8 km (5 mi); Melnik is east of E79.

"The village that slept for a century from drinking too much wine," according to local legend, Melnik is famous for its grape orchards, its wine aged in deep cellars, and its archaic ambience. Just north of the Greek border, this area was an important Byzantine stronghold from the 12th through 14th centuries. It developed rapidly again during the 1700s due to wine and tobacco trade but declined by the end of the following century. Today Melnik retains houses of the National Revival period and is populated by fewer than 400 permanent residents. Bulgarians and foreigners alike are charmed by the village's old-fashioned taverns, fire-warmed guest rooms, and cobblestone streets unmarred by electrical and phone wires. There's even a cave behind the village where you can taste wine straight from the barrel.

Rozhenski Manastir (Rozhen Monastery), rising above Melnik, dates to the 12th century but was rebuilt in the 16th century after being ravaged by fire. Within its walls is a church dating from 1600. To reach it, you can either hike up the footpath for about 6 km (3 mi) or take the bus that goes through Melnik roughly every hour (no fixed schedule) and get off at the first stop. A caretaker is normally around and will let you in; while there's no admission charge, it's a nice gesture to buy a few candles in the church. ✉ *Rozhen.*

Inland Bulgaria Essentials

AIR TRAVEL

No airports serve inland Bulgaria, but Roussé is fairly convenient to the airport in Bucharest, Romania, just 35 mi away. It's possible to get a taxi from Bucharest to Roussé for about $100. For airport and air-line information, *see* Air Travel *in* Bucharest A to Z *in* Chapter 7.

BUS TRAVEL

Although there are usually public buses between most towns, private bus companies are much more reliable. In every town there is a bus station where you can get a ticket and travel to almost all parts of the country. Book tickets through a local travel agency or purchase them at the bus station.

CAR TRAVEL

Though expensive by Western standards and accompanied by its own set of problems (poor road conditions, absence of road signs), the best way to see Bulgaria's interior is to rent a car. It is advisable to drive only during daylight hours. If you don't care to do the driving, you can hire a driver through one of the tour guide companies.

TRAIN TRAVEL

You can get direct trains from Sofia to most cities inland, including Russe (7 hrs), Plovdiv (3 hrs), and Veliko Turnovo (5 hrs). Less important destinations may not be reachable by train. The central station at Gorna Oriahovitsa, 10 km (6 mi) from Veliko Turnovo, offers the best interchange for smaller train lines in all directions. Direct trains also operate from Sofia to Istanbul, Bucharest, and from there to other Eastern European destinations. If you are going a long distance, it's better to take an overnight train and reserve a sleeping compartment.

VISITOR INFORMATION

The Pirin Tourism Forum provides information on Bansko, ski resorts, the Pirin Mountains, and the historical Gotse Delchev region. Dunav Tours can give you information about Roussé.

➤ CONTACTS: **Balkantourist Plovdiv** (✉ bul. Bulgaria, 106, Plovdiv, ☎ 032/63–21–80). **Balkantourist Veliko Târnovo** (✉ ul. Al. Penchev, 2, Veliko Târnovo, ☎ 062/633–975). **Koprivshtitsa Tourist Information** (✉ Pl. Dvadeseti April, Koprivshtitsa, ☎ FAX 07184/21–91). **Pirin Tourism Forum** (✉ Blagoevgrad, Varosha, Pirin [office is next to church], ☎ 073/367–95 or 073/814–58, FAX 073/354–58, WEB www.pirin-tourism.bg). **Roussé Tourist Information Center** (✉ ul. Aleksandrovska, 61, Roussé [opposite McDonald's], ☎ 082/82–47–04 or 082/23–59–60). **Veliko Târnovo Tourist Information Center** (✉ ul. Hristo Botev, 5, Veliko Târnovo, ☎ 062/22–148).

BULGARIA A TO Z

AIR TRAVEL

There are twice-weekly direct flights from New York (JFK) to Sofia on Balkan Airlines (also known as Balkanair). There are daily direct flights from major European airports, also to Sofia (☞ *Air Travel* in *Sofia Essentials*). During the summer season, there are direct flights from some major European airports directly to Varna or Burgas; Balkan Airlines also flies from Sofia to Varna and Burgas (☞ *Air Travel* in *Black Sea Golden Coast Essentials*). A word of caution: don't pack valuables in your suitcase when flying into and out of Sofia, as expensive items have a way of disappearing in customs and you may not realize the loss until you unpack.

BOAT AND FERRY TRAVEL

Modern luxury vessels once regularly cruised the Danube from Germany and Austria to Roussé in Bulgaria. However, the 1999 bombing of bridges over the Danube at Novi Sad, Yugoslavia, effectively blocked all river traffic. Services have now begun again more sporadically. Dunav Tours in Roussé handles bookings of cruises on the Danube. You can cruise between Black Sea resorts, as well as to Romania and Turkey. For information, consult the National Information and Advertising Center (☞ *Visitor Information, below).*

➤ CONTACTS: **Dunav Tours Roussé**(⊠ Pl. Han Kubrat, 5, Roussé, ☎ 082/224–268 or 082/225–250, WEB www.dunavtours.bg).

BUS TRAVEL

There is regular international coach service to Sofia. For more information, *see* Bus Travel *in* Sofia Essentials. For bus trips between major Bulgarian cities you can choose among the numerous companies offering transport services. Group Travel is well established and reliable, offering service to cities all over Bulgaria. Etap Adress owns buses in very good condition, with facilities. It has offices in more than 25 cities. For a small jaunt between towns, the sometimes unpleasant public buses may be the only way to go.

➤ BUS LINES: **Etap Adress** (⊠ Tsentralna Avtogara, ul. Belogradchik, 1, Sofia, ☎ 02/931–15–62; 02/931–04–94 in Sofia). **Group Travel** (⊠ Tsentralna Avtogara, bul. Maria Luiza, 131, Sofia, ☎ 02/9810–679; 02/32–01–22 in Sofia).

BUSINESS HOURS

Banks are open weekdays 8:30–4:30. Museums are usually open 9–6:30 but are often closed Monday or Tuesday. Shops are open Monday–Saturday 9–7; some shops are open on Sunday. A handful of *denonoshtni magazini* (day and night minimarkets) are open around the clock in city centers.

CAR RENTALS

You can rent a car from one of the major agencies either in Sofia or at the airport (☞ Car Rentals *in* Sofia Essentials). If you plan to leave the country during your rental period, you must also have documentation from the rental company that proves the car is indeed rented.

CAR TRAVEL

If you plan on driving into Bulgaria, be aware that border guards will stamp your passport to register that you and the vehicle have entered the country. You must leave the country with that same vehicle unless the car is deposited to a special customs compound, a difficult procedure that is not recommended. If you have rented a car in Bulgaria and drive outside the border for a few days, make sure that when you cross back into Bulgaria the border guards realize the car is rented, or *pod naem* (pronounced poad nai-em). Otherwise, airport border guards may give you trouble—people have been known to miss flights—when you try leave the country without the car that is registered in your passport.

Gas stations are spaced at regular intervals on main roads but may be few and far between off the beaten track. All are marked on Balkantourist's free driving map. Hotels, most tourist offices, and sidewalk book vendors also sell maps. Before buying a map, make sure that the names on it are in the Roman alphabet and not in Cyrillic.

If you have car trouble, contact the main office of the Bulgarian Automobile Touring Association (SBA); there are English-speaking staff.

➤ CONTACTS: **Bulgarian Automobile Touring Association** (⊠ ul. Pozitano, 3, Center, Sofia, ☎ 02/980–33–08).

In cities, roads might be poor, with lots of potholes. Main roads between towns, however, are generally well engineered, although some routes are narrow for the volume of traffic they have to carry. A large-scale expressway construction program is under way to link Bulgaria's main cities and towns. Completed stretches run from Kalotina—on the Serbian border—to Sofia and from Sofia to Plovdiv.

RULES OF THE ROAD
In the bigger cities, trams, buses, and cars fight for the right of way without any clear rules, so drive defensively. Drive on the right, as in the United States. The speed limit is 50 kph or 60 kph (31 mph or 36 mph) in built-up areas and 80 kph (50 mph) elsewhere, except on highways, where it is 120 kph (70 mph). You are required to carry a first-aid kit, fire extinguisher, and breakdown triangle in the vehicle. Front seat belts must be worn. The drunk-driving laws are strict—it is illegal to drive after you have had more than one drink. If pulled over by the police for any reason, be prepared for an on-site fine (i.e., a *bribe*) of a subjective amount determined by the officer. Your identity card or passport and driving license must always be with you.

NAMES OF STREETS
In Bulgaria the street names are set in the reverse order to Western Europe and the United States. The first part is the abbreviation for the word street/square/boulevard (ulitsa/ploshtad/bulevard); then comes the name of the street, and finally the number. Addresses in this chapter are given in this format.

CUSTOMS AND DUTIES
You may import duty-free into Bulgaria 250 grams of tobacco products, plus 1 liter of hard liquor and 2 liters of wine. Items intended for personal use during your stay are also duty-free. Currency that exceeds 5,000 leva must be declared when entering or leaving the country. Travelers are advised to declare items of greater value—cameras, tape recorders, etc.—so there will be no problems with Bulgarian customs officials on departure. But beware: if you declare an item, such as a computer, when entering the country, you *cannot* leave the country without it. After declaring something, if you lose it or are robbed, you may be detained for hours of questioning at police headquarters. It is prohibited to take works of art, church icons, and coins of particular historical or cultural value out of the country.

EMBASSIES AND CONSULATES
Canadians, Australians, and New Zealanders are on their own in terms of diplomatic representation; they're normally referred to the British or American embassy.
➤ CONTACTS: **U.K. Embassy** (✉ ul. Moskovska, 9, Center, Sofia, ☎ 02/933–92–22). **U.S. Consulate** (✉ ul. Kapitan Andreev, 1, Center, Sofia, ☎ 02/963–2022). **U.S. Embassy** (✉ ul. Suborna, 1, Center, Sofia, ☎ 02/937–51–00).

EMERGENCIES
Ambulance (☎ 150). **Emergency Roadside Assistance** (☎ 146 or 048–146). **Fire** (☎ 160). **Police** (☎ 166).

HOLIDAYS
January 1 (New Year's Day); March 3 (Bulgaria National Day); May 1 (Labour Day); May 6 (Day of Bulgarian Army); late April to mid-May (Orthodox Easter Sunday and Monday); May 24 (Bulgarian Culture Day); September 6 (Unification Day); September 22 (Bulgarian

Independence Day); November 1 (Day of the Leaders of the Bulgarian Revival); December 24–26 (Christmas).

LANGUAGE
The official language of the country, Bulgarian, is written in Cyrillic and is very close to Old Church Slavonic, the root of all Slavic languages. In some resorts, railway stations, and airports, names and directions are spelled out in the Roman alphabet. English is spoken in major hotels and restaurants but is unlikely to be heard in smaller towns. It is essential to remember that in Bulgaria a nod of the head means "no" and a shake of the head means "yes." But there are people who are adopting the Western way, so you have to be careful.

MAIL AND SHIPPING
Letters weighing up to 10 grams to North America cost 86 stotinki; to the U.K., 70 stotinki. Rates change constantly with inflation, so ask for the current price at the post office before sending mail. It generally takes around two weeks for mail to reach Western Europe and the United States.
➤ CONTACTS: **DHL International** (✉ bul. Tsar Osvoboditel, 8, Center, Sofia, ☎ 02/969–33–60). **Sofia Central Post Office** (✉ ul. Gen. Gurko, 6, Center, Sofia 1000). **United Parcel Service** (✉ ul. Graf Ignatiev, 13A, Center, Sofia, ☎ 02/986–31–87 or 02/986–39–38, WEB www.ups–bg.com).

MONEY MATTERS
Bulgaria is still a true cash economy. To avoid getting stuck without cash, be sure to bring crisp, clean, unmarked, and untorn bills of hard currency with you to exchange at the many change bureaus. ATMs are found in most towns, and the number is growing; most will accept cards from the U.S. and U.K. if you have a four-digit PIN (personal identification number).

When changing money in a exchange office, always ask in advance how much you will get, as some of the offices use little tricks to make profit.

CREDIT CARDS
The major international credit cards are accepted in a few of the larger stores and in upscale hotels and restaurants. Even in these establishments, the list of cards accepted may not always be correctly posted. Before you book a room or place an order, check to see whether you can pay with your card.

CURRENCY
The unit of currency in Bulgaria is the lev (plural leva), also abbreviated BGL. There are bills of 1, 2, 5, 10, 20, and 50 leva. One hundred stotinki equal one lev. Although prices might sometimes be quoted in dollars, all goods and services (except the expensive hotels, some restaurants, and international airline tickets) must be paid for in leva. It is illegal to import or export large amounts of Bulgarian currency.

CURRENCY EXCHANGE
You may import any amount of foreign currency and exchange it at banks, hotels, airports, border posts, and the plentiful private exchange offices (which offer the best rates and no commission). Due to the recent phenomenon of counterfeiting, only new, clean bills will be accepted. Changing traveler's checks is always problematic. Though changing them is theoretically possible at a few select locations, such as the airport and some major hotels, commissions are exorbitant. In small towns, traveler's checks are worthless.

The lev is now pegged to the euro. The value of the lev continues to fluctuate, however, and the exchange rate and price information quoted here may be outdated quickly. At this writing, the rate quoted by the Bulgarian State Bank was 2.12 leva to the U.S. dollar, 1.38 leva to the Canadian dollar, and 3.09 leva to British pound.

TAXES

Bulgaria has a value-added tax (VAT) of 18%.

PASSPORTS AND VISAS

All visitors need a valid passport. Americans, Canadians, and citizens of the U.K. do not need visas when traveling as tourists in Bulgaria for 30 days or less but are required to pay a border tax upon entering the country. Entry with a car is subject to a $10 entrance fee. Other tourists, traveling independently, can also travel without a visa for up to one month. Many package tours are exempt from the visa requirements.

TELEPHONES

Phone numbers in Bulgaria can be anywhere from four to eight digits, depending on whether it is an old line or a new digital one.

COUNTRY CODE

For international calls to Bulgaria, the country code is 359. The area code for Sofia is 2 from outside Bulgaria and 02 from within the country.

INTERNATIONAL CALLS

Calls to the United States can be made from the two types of calling-card phones, *Mobika* and *Bulfon,* by using a local calling card to reach the international operator and then a long-distance calling card to reach the United States. They can also be made from your hotel, for a surcharge, or placed from a post office. In Sofia, direct-dial calls to the United States can also be made from the international phone office (½ block west of the main post office).
➤ CONTACTS: **AT&T USA Direct** (☎ 00–800–0010).

LOCAL CALLS

Local calls can be made from your hotel, from pay phones (with a token costing 8 stotinki), or from calling-card phones. Card-operated phones come in two varieties: *Mobika* (which are blue) and *Bulfon* (which are orange). Cards can be bought at newsstands and post offices.

TIPPING

Tipping is expected especially by waiters, taxi drivers, and barbers, who usually get about 10%.

TOURS

Odysseia-In offers a broad range of adventure and outdoor recreation tours with experienced guides, including skiing/snowboarding, kayaking, mountain biking, and hiking. SunShineTours offers special-interest tours for all ages.
➤ CONTACTS: **Odysseia-In** (✉ bul. Alexander Stamboliiski, 20V, Center, Sofia, ☎ 02/981–05–60, WEB www.uniquebulgaria.com). **SunShineTours** (✉ ul. Shipchenski prohod, 47, Redouta, Sofia, ☎ 02/971–28–25, WEB www.sunshinetours.net).

TRAIN TRAVEL

Most international trains arrive at Sofia's Tsentralna Gara (☞ Train Travel *in* Sofia Essentials). You can book tickets for just about any destination in Europe, though certain routes are covered infrequently. Be careful not to book a ticket for a train that passes though a country you don't have a visa for, such as Serbia, because you will be uncere-moniously booted off the train at the border.

Within Bulgaria, trains cost about the same as buses but are often over-crowded, smoky, and slow. There are three classifications of trains: *ex-presni* (express), *burzi* (fast), and *puticheski* (slow). If possible, always take the fastest train and pay a few dollars more for a seat reservation in first class (or else you may find yourself standing in the smoke-filled aisle for hours). Timetables are posted in every station listing *pristi-gashti* (arrivals) and *zaminavashti* (departures).

From Sofia there are six main routes—to Varna and Burgas on the Black Sea coast (overnight trains between Sofia and Black Sea resorts have first- and second-class sleeping cars and second-class *couchettes,* which are cheaper but less comfortable); to Plovdiv and on to the Turkish bor-der; to Dragoman and the Serbian border; to Kulata and the Greek border; and to Roussé on the Romanian border.

RAIL PASSES

Bulgaria is not included in the Eurail network, but it is included in the Balkan Flexipass, sold through Rail Europe in the United States. A Bul-garia-only Flexipass is also available, as is a student version. However, train tickets are still so cheap that you should estimate your costs to decide if a pass is practical or necessary.
➤ CONTACTS: **Rail Europe** (☎ 914/682–2999 or 800/848–7245, WEB www.raileurope.com).

VISITOR INFORMATION
The Bulgaria National Information and Advertising Center is the of-ficial tourist assistance office. Staff members speak English. The Sveta Sofia office is conveniently located off bulevard Vitosha across from the Sheraton. Balkantourist, formerly the state-run tourism organiza-tion, is now a private travel agency but in many places in the country still functions as an information office, with locations in most major hotels.

Regional not-for-profit tourism promotion forums, offering informa-tion on accommodations, sights, and activities, include the Black Sea Tourism Association, the Tourist Agency-Resort Bureau (connected to the National Social Security Institute), and the Stara Planina Associa-tion, which specializes in the Central Balkan Mountains region.
➤ CONTACTS: **Balkantourist** (✉ bul. Vitosha, 1, Center, Sofia, ☎ 02/987–51–92). **Black Sea Tourism Association** (✉ ul. Vdin, 20, 2nd floor, Varna, ☎ 052/24–21–92). **Bulgaria National Information and Ad-vertising Center** (✉ Ministry of Economy, ul. Sveta Sofia, 1, Center, Sofia, ☎ 02/987–97-78, WEB www.bulgariatravel.org). **Stara Planina As-sociation** (✉ ul. Rajcho Karolev, 4, Gabrovo 5300, ☎ 066/291–61 or 066/284–83). **Tourist Agency–Resort Bureau** (✉ ul. Shejnovo, 24, Burgas, ☎ 056/84–34–83).

3 · CROATIA

With 1,778 km (1,111 mi) of coastline and more than a thousand islands (66 of which are inhabited), Croatia is one of Europe's most beautiful yet undiscovered seaside destinations. Backed by undulating green hills to the north and dramatic mountains to the south, the emerald-blue waters are presided over by a series of finely preserved, walled medieval towns, packed with Venetian monuments. In contrast, the capital, Zagreb, owes much of its cultural wealth to the centuries spent under Austro-Hungarian control.

By Jane Foster

CROATIA'S CALM BLUE SEA, majestic mountains, and lovingly preserved historical buildings belie a checkered past. Like its Balkan neighbors, the country has a history shadowed by conflict and political strife.

The region's earliest inhabitants were the Illyrians, and two principal tribes, the Delmata and the Histri, gave their names to Dalmatia and Istria, respectively. The Greeks arrived in the 4th century BC, setting up various colonies along the coast, notably Issa on the island of Vis and Pharos on Hvar. In the 2nd century BC, feeling threatened by the Illyrians, the Greeks called for Roman assistance, and a period of Roman expansion began.

The Romans set up military outposts and administration centers, the most important being Pola (Pula) in Istria and Salona (Solin) in Dalmatia, while inland Croatia became the Roman province of Pannonia. In 395 Roman territory was divided into the western and eastern empires, a decisive event in Balkan history, as this same border was later to divide Catholics and Orthodox, Croats and Serbs. The 7th century saw the arrival of Slavic tribes, among them the Croats. Relations with the Latin-speaking Roman population were initially fraught, but with time the two groups assimilated.

In 910, the Croatian leader Tomislav united Dalmatia and Pannonia and with the Pope's consent took the title of king. When the Christian church split between Rome and Constantinople in 1054, Croatian royalty sided with Rome. In 1091, King Zvonimir died without heirs, and the Croatian crown was ceded to Hungary. Thus from the late 11th century to the mid-19th century, much of inland Croatia was governed by a local *ban* (viceroy), answerable to the Hapsburgs.

Meanwhile the coast, Istria, and Dalmatia (excluding Dubrovnik, which remained an independent republic) came under the rule of Venice. Lying on the trade route to the Orient, port towns such as Split, Hvar, and Korčula flourished, and many of the regions' finest buildings date from this period.

However, by the 16th century the threat of a third Balkan presence, the Ottoman Turks, was looming on the horizon. The Venetian port towns enclosed themselves within sturdy fortifications against attack from the sea, while the Hapsburgs, fearing Turkish expansion overland, created the Vojna Krajina (Military Frontier) and employed mercenaries to guard this buffer zone between Austria and the Turkish-occupied territory to the southeast. These recruits were predominantly Orthodox Christians fleeing the Turks in Serbia, and they enjoyed a certain autonomy until the Vojna Krajina was united with the rest of Croatia in the late 19th century. The creation of the Krajina explains the presence of the Serb communities within Croatia that became a major force during the war of the 1990s.

Venice fell in 1797, and by the 19th century all of Croatia was under Austria-Hungary. A pan-Slavic movement was born, calling for Croats and Serbs to unite, and with the demise of the Hapsburgs at the end of WWI, Croatia became part of the Kingdom of the Serbs, Croats, and Slovenes. However, Croatian nationalists soon objected to being ruled by Serbian royalty, and when the country was renamed Yugoslavia (Land of the Southern Slavs) in 1929, Ante Pavelić founded the Ustaše Croatian Liberation Movement. In 1934, Croatian and Macedonian extremists assassinated the Yugoslav king Alexander.

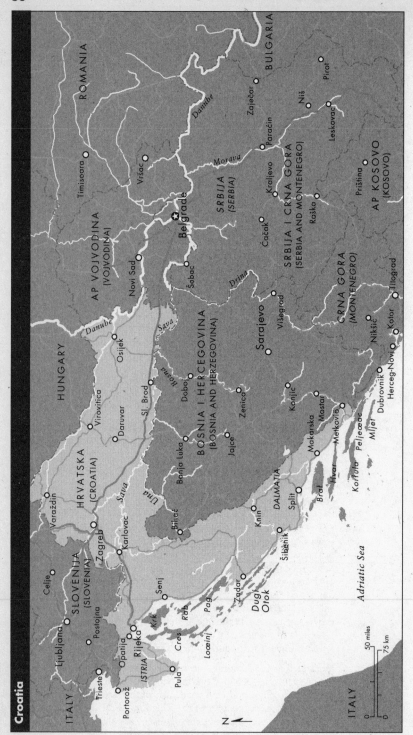

ITALY

HUNGARY

ROMANIA

BULGARIA

SLOVENIJA
(SLOVENIA)

HRVATSKA
(CROATIA)

AP VOJVODINA
(VOJVODINA)

SRBIJA
(SERBIA)

SRBIJA I CRNA GORA
(SERBIA AND MONTENEGRO)

AP KOSOVO
(KOSOVO)

CRNA GORA
(MONTENEGRO)

BOSNIA I HERCEGOVINA
(BOSNIA AND HERZEGOVINA)

DALMATIA

ISTRIA

ITALY

Adriatic Sea

Ljubljana
Celje
Postojna
Trieste
Portorož
Opatija
Rijeka
Pula
Cres
Lošinj
Krk
Senj
Rab
Pag
Zadar
Dugi
Otok
Varaždin
Zagreb
Karlovac
Virovitica
Daruvar
Sl. Brod
Osijek
Novi Sad
Belgrade
Timisoara
Vršac
Šabac
Bihać
Banja Luka
Doboj
Jajce
Zenica
Sarajevo
Šibenik
Split
Knin
Brač
Hvar
Korčula
Pelješac
Mljet
Makarska
Metković
Konjic
Mostar
Dubrovnik
Herceg-Novi
Nikšić
Kotor
Titograd
Višegrad
Čačak
Kraljevo
Raška
Priština
Paraćin
Zaječar
Niš
Leskovac
Pirot

Danube
Danube
Sava
Sava
Drava
Bosna
Una
Morava
Drina

N

50 miles
75 km
0
0

After Germany declared war on Yugoslavia in 1941, Paveliča set up the Independent State of Croatia (NDH), notorious for the mass murder of Jews, Serbs, and Gypsies in the concentration camps within its borders. Out of retaliation, Josip Broz Tito founded the Partizan movement, aimed at pushing Fascist forces out of Yugoslavia. When the war ended, Tito created the Socialist Federal Republic of Yugoslavia with Croatia as one of six constituent republics. The Tito years saw a period of peace and prosperity, and during the 1960s Croatia became a popular international tourist destination.

But following Tito's death in 1980, an economic crisis set in, and relations between Croatia and the Serb-dominated Yugoslav government deteriorated. In 1989 Franjo Tudjman founded the Croatian Democratic Union (HDZ), calling for an independent Croatia, while in Serbia the nationalist leader Slobodan Milošević rose to power. The events that followed led to civil war.

In 1991, incited by Belgrade media reports that Croatia was returning to the days of the Ustaše, Croatian Serbs proclaimed the Republic of Serbian Krajina, arguing that if Croatia took autonomy from Belgrade, they would demand autonomy from Zagreb. Thanks to backing from the Serb-dominated federal Yugoslav People's Army (JNA), by the end of the year Krajina, which represented nearly one-third of Croatia, was under Serb control.

In January 1992, Croatia was recognized by the European Union, and United Nations peacekeeping troops were sent in to oversee a ceasefire. After a period of relative calm, Croat forces crossed UN lines in May 1995 and took back a Serb-held enclave in western Slavonia. Encouraged by their success, they launched the surprise *Oluja* (Operation Storm) that August, overrunning the Krajina and causing 200,000 Serbs to flee the country.

Meanwhile, there was evidence of growing corruption within the HDZ, and Croatia faced increasing international isolation for failing to respect human rights. President Tudjman's death in December 1999 saw the demise of his party. In January 2000, a new center-left alliance was voted into power, with Ivica Račan as prime minister and Stjepan Mesić as president. Mesić immediately announced that all refugees who had fled Croatia should be allowed to return to their homes, and his victory was widely welcomed in the West.

After almost 10 years of political and economic isolation, Croatia is now back on the map as a desirable holiday destination. While Croats themselves continue to struggle against problems of severe unemployment, low wages, and high living costs, foreign visitors can expect more than comfortable accommodations, excellent restaurants serving fresh seasonal produce, and a truly stunning coastline, still as beautiful as it ever was.

Pleasures and Pastimes

Beaches

With crystal-clear, emerald-blue waters, the coast and islands are a haven for beach goers, the water being warm enough to swim from mid-May to late September. Most beaches are of pebble (not sand), so if you have sensitive feet you'll need to invest in a pair of water shoes or flip-flops. Away from the larger, more commercial beaches (equipped with showers, beach chairs, and umbrellas), you'll probably find a number of small, secluded coves where you can escape the crowds. Naturism has a long tradition in Croatia. Naked bathing first became popular in Istria and Dalmatia in the 1930s and has carried on to this day. *Nudističke Plaže*

(Nudist Beaches) tend to be isolated and are marked "FKK" (from the German, *Freie Kunst und Kultur*).

Dining

Formal dining takes place in a *restoran* (restaurant), while lighter meals accompanied by a plentiful supply of local wine are served in a more rustic *konoba* (tavern). Classic starters are *pršut* (cured ham) and *paški sir* (sheep's-milk cheese from the island of Pag), *juha* (soup), or *salata od hobotnice* (octopus salad).

In Dalmatia, the menu tends to quite basic, featuring *rižot* (risotto) followed by fresh fish prepared *na žaru* (barbecue-style) served with *blitva sa krumpirom* (Swiss chard and potatoes in olive oil and garlic). In Istria, the choice is wider and more refined: besides fish and seafood, the specialties are *tartufi* (truffles) served with either pasta (the local variation is *fuži*) or steak; the salads are exceptionally colorful, containing mixed leaves such as *rukola* (rocket) and radicchio.

Wherever you go, fish are priced by weight (Kn/kg) rather than by portion and can be divided into two categories: Class I, which encompasses quality white fish like *zubatac* (dentrix), *šampier* (John Dory), and *orada* (gilthead bream); and the cheaper Class II blue fish, including *skuše* (mackerel) and *srdele* (sardines).

Inland, meat dishes are more popular. Balkan favorites such as *janjetina* (spit-roast lamb), *kobasica* (sausage), *gulaš* (goulash), and *čevapčiči* (kebabs) are widespread, while the Zagreb area is noted for *purica* (roast turkey).

Popular desserts are *palačinke* (pancakes) and baklava (just like in Greece).

CATEGORY	COST*
$$$$	over 80 Kn
$$$	60 Kn–80 Kn
$$	35 Kn–60 Kn
$	under 35 Kn

*per person for a main course at dinner

Lodging

Croatia offers a wide choice of lodgings: hotels, apartments, rooms in private homes, campsites, and agrotourism (working farms offering accommodation). Hotel prices tend to be on a par with those in Western Europe. While you can find some excellent low-season offers, prices skyrocket through July and August with an influx of German and Italian visitors.

Tourism started here in the late 1800s under the Hapsburgs, and along the coast you'll find a number of grand hotels built for the Central European aristocracy of the time. The second stage of tourist development took place between the 1960s and 1980s in Tito's Yugoslavia. The resulting Socialist-era hotels tend to be vast, modern structures slightly lacking in soul but endowed with truly excellent sport and recreation facilities. During the war years of the 1990s, some hotels were used to house refugees. Most of these establishments have since been fully refurbished, but in certain areas (notably Split) several are still closed or undergoing renovation. In addition, a number of small, luxurious private hotels have popped up, notably in Istria.

Along the coast, tourist agencies can help you find rooms in private homes. Standards are high, en-suite bathrooms and self-catering facilities being the norm. Host families are generally friendly and hospitable, and many visitors find a place they like, then return year after year.

Agrotourism is a great option for families with kids. The idea has already taken off in Istria and will probably soon develop in other parts of the country, too. If you stay on a farm, you can expect pleasant rural surroundings, delicious home cooking, and a warm family welcome.

CATEGORY	COST*
$$$$	over 1200 Kn
$$$	800 Kn–1200 Kn
$$	550 Kn–800 Kn
$	under 550 Kn

All prices are for two people in a double room with breakfast.

Sailing

With an indented coastline abounding in natural harbors, countless islands, emerald-blue seas, and unspoiled nature, Croatia is a sailor's dream destination. The main company for nautical tourism is Adriatic Croatia International (ACI), which runs 21 fully equipped marinas, extending from Umag in the north to Dubrovnik in the south. There are 75 registered charter companies dealing with more than 14,000 yachts and motorboats. To rent a yacht without a skipper, you need to have a license plus two years' sailing experience.

Scuba-Diving

Along the mainland coast and on the islands you'll find numerous scuba-diving centers offering diving tuition, rental equipment, and organized diving expeditions to wrecks, caves, and reefs. To dive to the depth of 59 ft, you need to have a diving license (valid for one year) issued by the Croatian Divers' Association through recognized scuba-diving centers.

Wine and Spirits

Croatia produces some excellent wines, which have finally gained recognition abroad. The best Istrian wines are the white *Malvazija* and the red *Teran,* both of which are similar to the wines of the same names from neighboring Slovenia. Dalmatian wines have a higher alcohol content, thanks to the southwest-facing slopes, which take full advantage of the sun. The best reds are the full-bodied *Dingač,* from Pelješac peninsula, and *Plavac,* from the islands of Hvar and Vis. Among whites, *Pošip Čara,* from Hvar, and *Grk,* from Korčula, are equally respectable. The national spirit, as in Slovenia, is *rakija,* a potent brew made from a grape base, which is distilled and flavored with herbs.

Exploring Croatia

Along the eastern shore of the Adriatic, Croatia is Eastern and Central Europe's prime seaside destination. While the capital, Zagreb, lies inland, all the other main attractions are found along the coast, from the regions of Istria and Kvarner in the north to Dalmatia in the south.

Great Itineraries

The sea and islands are undoubtedly Croatia's most alluring feature. The ancient cities of Split and Dubrovnik are the main centers on the coast, offering regular ferry connections to neighboring islands. The capital, Zagreb, provides good air, road, and rail links to other countries included in this book.

IF YOU HAVE 3 DAYS
With just three days at your disposal, concentrate on Dalmatia. Fly into ⊞ **Split** to explore Diocletian's palace. The following morning, take a boat to one of the nearby islands, either ⊞ **Hvar** or ⊞ **Korčula**. Devote your final day to the walled city of ⊞ **Dubrovnik.**

With five days, expand the above itinerary to begin with the capital, ⊡ **Zagreb.** The following morning, transfer to Rijeka and spend the day in **Opatija.** Take the overnight coastal ferry from Rijeka to Dalmatia, and spend your final three days following the three-day itinerary.

If you have a couple of extra days, it would be best to do the same tour at a more leisurely pace. Another day in one of the islands as well as Dubrovnik would be most welcome.

When to Tour

During peak season (July and August) the coast is crowded and expensive. You'll need to book a place to stay well in advance, and some people will find the temperatures unbearably hot. On the plus side, all restaurants, beach-side bars, and sports facilities will be open, and you'll find a wide range of open-air cultural events and a vibrant nightlife. For a more peaceful holiday by the sea, try to tour in early summer (June) or late summer (September), when the water is still warm enough to swim in but the resorts are not too busy. The inland areas are particularly attractive in autumn, when the trees take on golden and russet hues and the grape harvest is in full swing.

ZAGREB

The capital of Croatia, Zagreb, with a population of roughly 1 million, is situated at the extreme edge of the Pannonian Plain, between the north bank of the Sava River and the southern slopes of Mt. Medvednica. Its early years are shrouded in mystery, though there are indications of a neolithic settlement on this site. The Romans are said to have established a municipality of sorts, destroyed around AD 600, when Croatian tribes moved in.

Like so many other notable European cities, Zagreb started out as a strategic crossroads along an international river route, which was followed much later by north–south and east–west passage by road and then rail. For much of its history the city also served as a bastion on a defensive frontier, pounded for half a millennium by thundering hordes of invaders, among them Hungarians, Mongols, and Turks.

From the late Middle Ages until the 19th century, Zagreb was composed of two adjoining but separate towns situated on the high ground (Gornji Grad), one town secular, the other religious. In 1242 the secular town, named Gradec (Fortress), was burned to the ground in a wave of destruction by the Tartars, after which it locked itself up behind protective walls and towers. It is from this time that the real Zagreb (Behind the Hill) began to evolve; it was accorded the status of a free royal city in the same year by the Hungarian king Bela IV. In the 15th century, the ecclesiastical center, named Kaptol (Chapter House), also enclosed itself in defensive walls in response to the threat of a Turkish invasion.

When Zagreb became the capital of Croatia in 1557, the country's parliament began meeting alternately in Gradec and at the Bishop's Palace in Kaptol. When Kaptol and Gradec were finally put under a single city administration in 1850, urban development accelerated. The railway reached Zagreb in 1862, linking the city to Vienna, Trieste, and the Adriatic. It was at this time that Donji Grad (Lower Town) came into being. Lying between Gornji Grad and the main train station, it was designed to accommodate new public buildings—the National Theater, the university, and various museums. Built in grandiose style and interspersed by wide tree-lined boulevards, parks, and gardens, it makes a fitting monument to the Hapsburg era.

The Tito years brought a period of increasing industrialization coupled with urban expansion, as the new high-rise residential suburb of Novi Zagreb was constructed south of the Sava. In 1991, the city escaped the war of independence relatively unscathed, but for an attempted rocket attack on the Croatian Parliament building in Gradec. Zagreb did, however, suffer severe economic hardship as the country's industries collapsed, post-Communist corruption set in, and an influx of refugees—mainly Croats from Herzegovina—arrived in search of a better life.

Since 2000, public morale has picked up considerably: trendy street cafés are thriving, a number of smart new stores have opened, and the public gardens are once again carefully tended. However, underlying this apparent affluence, unemployment remains a major problem.

Exploring Zagreb

The city is clearly divided into two distinct districts: **Gornji Grad** (Upper Town) and **Donji Grad** (Lower Town). While hilltop Gornji Grad is made up of winding cobbled streets and terra-cotta rooftops sheltering the cathedral and the Croatian Parliament building, Donji Grad is where you'll find the city's most important 19th-century cultural institutions, including the National Theater, the university, and a number of museums, all in an organized grid.

Numbers in the text correspond to numbers in the margin and on the Zagreb map.

Gornji Grad (Upper Town)

The romantic hilltop area of Gornji Grad dates back to medieval times and is undoubtedly the loveliest part of Zagreb.

A GOOD WALK

Begin your walk from the main square, **Trg Bana Jelačića** ①, a vast paved area flanked by busy cafés. Traffic-free—except for the constant coming and going of some half-dozen tram lines—this is the focal point of the city's pedestrian activity. From here, wide steps lead up to **Dolac** ②, the central market, also known as the "Belly of Zagreb." From Dolac, take a narrow side street to the right to arrive in front of the **Katedrala Svetog Stjepana** ③, where a gilded statue of the Virgin, protected by four angels, stands on a high stone column. From the cathedral, Kaptol's main wide street (also Kaptol) runs uphill past tile-roofed antique houses. Take the first turn left; then turn right to pass through a doorway into a walled public garden and descend a short flight of steps to arrive on **Tkalčićeva** ④. Turn left and walk down Tkalčićeva; then turn right into a narrow passage known as Krvavi Most (Bloody Bridge), the scene of bloody armed combat between the warring factions of Gradec and Kaptol during the Middle Ages. This brings you to Radićeva, where you should turn right and walk uphill; then take the first left onto Kamenita, to arrive at the delightful **Kamenita Vrata** ⑤.

Follow Kamenita to Markov Trg, dominated by much-photographed **Crkva Svetog Marka** ⑥. The building on the east of the square is the Sabor (Croatian Parliament). Leave Markov Trg by Mletačka, which brings you to the **Meštrović Atelier** ⑦, displaying a fine collection of works by Ivan Meštrović, Croatia's most prominent 20th-century sculptor. Continue to the end of Mletačka; then turn right onto Demetrova to reach Opatička, home to the **Muzej Grada Zagreba** ⑧. Now retrace your steps to Markov Trg, cross the square, and take Ćir-

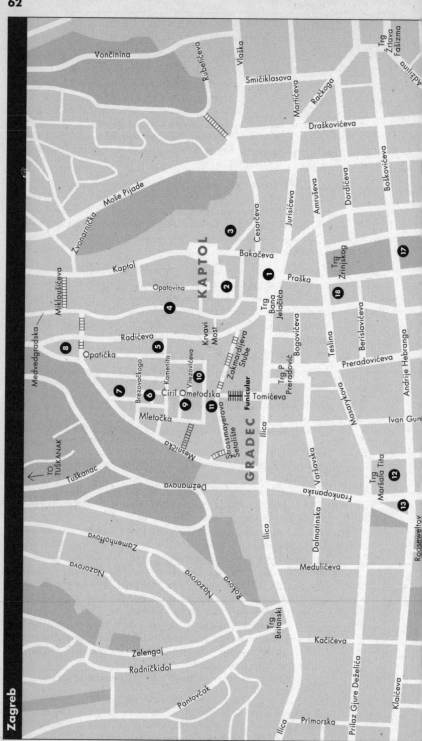

Zagreb

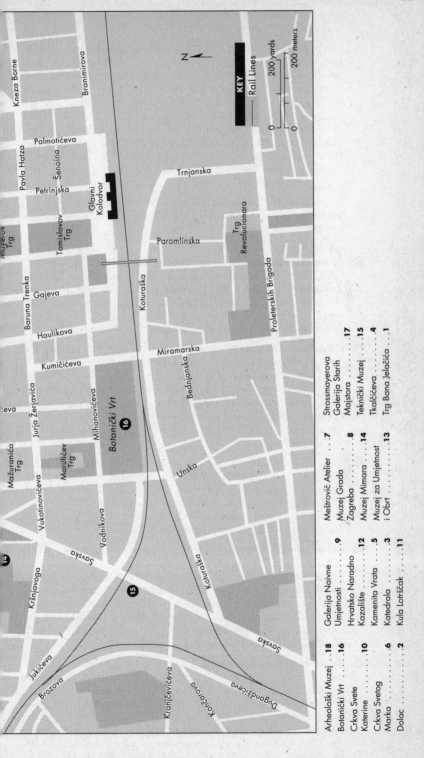

ilometodska to arrive at the **Galerija Naivne Umjetnosti** ⑨ for an introduction to Croatian naïve art.

East of Ćirilometodska stands **Crkva Svete Katerine** ⑩, considered by many to be Croatia's most beautiful baroque church. Close by, **Kula Lotršćak** ⑪ offers a dramatic panorama across the city to Novi Zagreb on the far side of the River Sava, while below the tower Strossmayer Šetalište (Strossmayer Promenade) follows the line of Gradec's former south-facing wall and affords more stunning rooftop views. At the foot of the tower stands a *uspinjaca* (funicular railway), dating back to 1891 and connecting Gornji Grad to Ilica, Zagreb's main shopping street. Either ride down or take the steps; then turn left on Ilica to return to Trg Bana Jelačića, the original starting point.

TIMING

This tour is best done in the morning, when stalls at the open-air market are heaving with a colorful array of fruits and vegetables and you are more likely to find the church doors open.

SIGHTS TO SEE

⑩ **Crkva Svete Katerine** (St. Catherine's Church). Built for the Jesuit order between 1620 and 1632, this church was modeled on Giacomo da Vignola's Il Gesu in Rome. Inside, the vaults are decorated with pink and white stucco and 18th-century illusionist paintings, while the altars are the work of Francesco Robba and 17th-century Croatian artists. ✉ *Katerinin Trg, Gornji Grad.* 🎫 *Free.* ⊙ *Daily 8–8.*

❻ **Crkva Svetog Marka** (St. Mark's Church). The original building was erected in the 13th century and was once the parish church of Gradec. The baroque bell tower was added in the 17th century, while the steeply pitched roof—decorated in brilliant, multicolored tiles arranged to depict the coats of arms of Zagreb on the right and the Kingdom of Croatia, Dalmatia, and Slavonia on the left—was added during reconstruction in the 19th century. ✉ *Markov Trg, Gornji Grad.* 🎫 *Free.* ⊙ *Daily 8–8.*

❷ **Dolac** (Market). Farmers from the surrounding countryside set up their stalls here daily, though the market is at its busiest on Friday and Saturday mornings. On the upper level, brightly colored umbrellas shade fresh fruit and vegetables on an open-air piazza, while dairy products and meats are sold in an indoor market below. ✉ *Trg Bana Jelačića, Gornji Grad.* ⊙ *Weekdays 7–4, weekends 7–noon.*

❾ **Galerija Naivne Umjetnosti** (Gallery of Naïve Art). This unusual school of painting dates back to the 1930s and features the work of untutored peasant artists, primarily from the village of Hlebine in Slavonia. Canvases by the highly esteemed Ivan Generalić dominate here, though there are also several works by other noted members of the movement, plus a section devoted to foreigners working along similar lines. ✉ *Ćirilometodska 3, Gornji Grad,* ☎ *01/485–1911,* WEB *www.hmnu.org.* 🎫 *10 Kn.* ⊙ *Tues.–Fri. 10–6, weekends 10–1.*

❺ **Kamenita Vrata** (Stone Gate). The original 13th-century city walls had four gates, of which only Kamenita Vrata remains. Deep inside the dark passageway, locals stop to pray before a small shrine adorned with flickering candles. In 1731 a devastating fire consumed all the wooden elements of the gate, except for a painting of the Virgin and Child, which was found in the ashes, remarkably undamaged. Kamenita Vrata has since become a pilgrimage site, as can be seen from the numerous stone plaques saying *hvala* (thank you). ✉ *Kamenita, Gornji Grad.*

❸ **Katedrala Marijina uznesenja i Svetog Stjepana** (Cathedral of the Assumption of the Blessed Virgin and St. Stephen). Built on the site of a former 12th-century cathedral destroyed by the Tartars in 1242, the present structure was constructed between the 13th and 16th centuries. The neo-Gothic facade was added by architect Herman Bolle following the earthquake of 1880, its twin steeples being the identifying feature of the city's skyline. The interior is high and bare, the main point of interest being the north wall, which bears an inscription of the 10 Commandments in 12th-century Glagolithic script. ✉ *Kaptol 31, Gornji Grad.* ☒ *Free.* ☉ *Daily 8–8.*

⓫ **Kula Lotršćak** (Lotršćak Tower). Formerly the entrance to the fortified medieval Gradec, Kula Lotršćak now houses an art gallery. Each day at noon, a small canon is fired from the top of the tower, in memory of the times when it was used to warn off the possibility of an Ottoman attack. ✉ *Strossmayer Šetalište, Gornji Grad,* ☎ *01/485–1768.* ☒ *10 Kn.* ☉ *Tues.–Sun. 11–8.*

★ ❼ **Meštrović Atelier** (Meštrović Atelier). This 17th-century building, with its interior courtyard, served as home and studio to Ivan Meštrović from 1922 until his emigration to the United States in 1942. The building was extensively remodeled according to plans devised by the artist and was turned into a memorial museum with a permanent exhibition of his sculptures and drawings after his death in 1962. (There is a larger collection of his works in the Meštrović Gallery in Split.) ✉ *Mletačka 8, Gornji Grad,* ☎ *01/485–1123.* ☒ *15 Kn.* ☉ *Tues.–Fri. 9–2, Sat. 10–6.*

❽ **Muzej Grada Zagreba** (Zagreb City Museum). Well worth a visit for anyone interested in urban design, this museum traces the city's most important historical, economic, political, social, and cultural events from medieval times up to the present day. Exhibits include detailed scale models of how the city has evolved, as well as sections devoted to the old trade guilds, domestic life, and sacral art. ✉ *Opatička 20, Gornji Grad,* ☎ *01/485–1364,* ⎗ *www.mdc.hr/mgz.* ☒ *15 Kn.* ☉ *Tues.–Fri. 10–6, weekends 10–1.*

❹ **Tkalčićeva.** This street was once a channel forming the boundary between Kaptol and Gradec, then known as Potok (the brook). Today it is a pretty pedestrian zone lined with 19th-century town houses, many of which have been converted into popular café-bars at street level. ✉ *Tkalčićeva north of Krvavi Most, Gornji Grad.*

NEED A BREAK? For morning coffee or an early evening aperitif, stop at **Sunčani Sat** (✉ Tkalčićeva 27). Take a comfy wicker chair on the open-air summer terrace and enjoy watching the comings and goings of Zagreb café life.

❶ **Trg Bana Jelačića** (Ban Jelačić Square). Buildings lining the square date from 1827 onward and include several fine examples of Viennese Secessionist architecture. The centerpiece is an equestrian statue of Ban Jelačić, the first Croatian viceroy, erected in 1866. After the Second World War the Communist government ordered the dismantling and removal of the statue, but it was put back in place in 1991. ✉ *Between Ilica to the west, Praška to the south, and Jurišićeva to the east.*

Donji Grad (Lower Town)

Donji Grad came into being during the late 19th century. The urban plan, which follows a grid pattern, was drawn up by Milan Lenuci and combines a succession of squares and parks laid out in a "U" shape (known as the Green Horseshoe), all overlooked by the city's main public buildings and cultural institutions.

A GOOD WALK

Leave Trg Bana Jelačića, which is right on the border between the upper and lower town, on Gajeva Street, passing the Hotel Dubrovnik; then turn right onto Bogovićeva to arrive at Preradovićev Trg, better known to locals as Cvijetni Trg (Flower Square) in tribute to the flower sellers who used to set up their stalls here. At the far end of the square stands the Orthodox church, still attended by Zagreb's now depleted Serb community. Leave the square by Preradovićeva, and then take the first right onto Masarykova to reach the vast green Trg Maršala Tita, the first of a series of three squares that make up one side of Lenuci's so-called Green Horseshoe. The dominant building here is the monumental neo-baroque **Hrvatsko Narodno Kazalište** ⑫. Close by, on the western side of the square, the **Muzej za Umjetnost i Obrt** ⑬ displays an impressive collection devoted to Croatian arts and crafts. Proceed to the next square, Mažuranića Trg; then cross the busy Savska Cesta to reach Roosevelt Trg, where you will find the renowned **Muzej Mimara** ⑭. South from here, farther down Savska Cesta, lies the **Teknički Muzej** ⑮.

Retrace your steps a little way up Savska Cesta, and then take the second street on the right, Vodnikova, which in turn becomes Mihanovićeva and runs between the south side of Marulićev Trg and the **Botanički Vrt** ⑯, a carefully tended garden offering respite from the bustle of city life. Proceed along Mihanovićeva to arrive at Tomislavov Trg, overlooked by the *glavni kolodvor* (main railway station) and presided over by an equestrian statue of King Tomislav, the first king of the medieval state of Croatia. At the north end of the square stands the Umjetnički Paviljon (Art Pavilion), a 19th-century domed structure hosting temporary exhibitions. You are now on the second series of three adjoining squares that complete the Green Horseshoe. Continue to Strossmayerov Trg, home to the impressive **Strossmayerova Galerija Starih Majstora** ⑰, where you can view a fine collection of old-master paintings. Overlooking the next square, Trg Zrinjskog, stands the **Arheološki Muzej** ⑱. Complete the walk by returning to Trg Bana Jelačića, the original starting point of the tour, via Praška.

TIMING

This walk can be done in either the morning or the afternoon, but if you plan to visit some of the museums listed, you should check opening times (which vary from day to day) before setting out.

SIGHTS TO SEE

⑱ **Arheološki Muzej** (Archaeological Museum). Museum exhibits focus on prehistoric times to the Tartar invasion. Pride of place is taken by the Vučedol Dove, a three-legged ceramic vessel in the form of a bird, dating back to the 4th millennium BC, and a piece of linen bearing the longest known text in ancient Etruscan writing. ⊠ *Trg Zrinjskog, Donji Grad,* ☎ *01/487–3101,* ₩ᴱᴮ *www.amz.hr.* ☞ *15 Kn.* ☉ *Tues.– Fri. 10–5, weekends 10–1.*

⑯ **Botanički Vrt** (Botanical Garden). Founded in 1889 as research grounds for the faculty of botany at Zagreb University, the garden includes an arboretum with English-style landscaping, a small artificial lake, and an ornamental Japanese bridge. ⊠ *Marulićeva Trg 9a, Donji Grad.* ☞ *Free.* ☉ *Tues.–Sun. dawn–dusk.*

⑫ **Hrvatsko Narodno Kazalište** (Croatian National Theatre). The building dates from 1895, designed by the Viennese firm Hellmer and Fellner, as part of the preparations for a state visit by Emperor Franz Josef. In front of the theater presides the Meštrović's Zdenac Života (Fountain of Life), dating back to 1912. The only way to see the inside of the theater is to attend a performance. ⊠ *Trg Maršala Tita 15, Donji Grad,* ☎ *01/482–8532,* WEB *www.hnk.hr.*

⓮ **Muzej Mimara** (Mimara Museum). This vast private collection, including paintings, sculpture, ceramics, textiles, and rugs, was donated by Ante Topić-Mimara (1898–1987), a Croatian who spent many years abroad where he made his fortune, supposedly as a merchant. On display are canvases attributed to such old masters as Raphael, Rembrandt, and Rubens, as well as more modern works by the likes of Manet, Degas, and Renoir, and ancient artifacts including Egyptian glassware and Chinese porcelain. ⊠ *Rooseveltov trg 4, Donji Grad,* ☎ *01/482–8100.* ☞ *15 Kn.* ☉ *Tues.–Wed. and Fri.–Sun. 10–5, Thurs. 10–7.*

⓭ **Muzej za Umjetnost i Obrt** (Arts and Crafts Museum). Designed in 1888 by Herman Bolle, the architect responsible for the Katedrala Marijina uznesenja i Svetog Stjepana facade, this pleasant museum traces the development of the applied arts from the baroque period up to the 20th century. Exhibits are displayed in chronological order, and while furniture design predominates, there are also sections devoted to sacral art, clocks, and clothing. ⊠ *Trg Maršala Tita 10, Donji Grad,* ☎ *01/ 482–6922,* WEB *www.muo.hr.* ☞ *15 Kn.* ☉ *Tues.–Fri. 10–6, weekends 10–1.*

⓱ **Strossmayerova Galerija Starih Majstora** (Strossmayor Gallery of Old Masters). Now under the custody of the Croatian Academy of Sciences and Arts, this impressive gallery was founded in 1884 by Bishop Strossmayer and later expanded to include many private donations. Works by Venetian Renaissance and baroque artists, such as Bellini and Carpaccio, predominate, but there are also masterpieces by Dutch painters Brueghel and Van Dyck, as well as a delightful Mary Magdalene by El Greco. ⊠ *Trg Zrinjskog 11, Donji Grad,* ☎ *01/489–5111,* WEB *www.mdc.hr/strossmayer.* ☞ *15 Kn.* ☉ *Tues. 10–1 and 5–7, Wed.– Sun. 10–1.*

NEED A BREAK?   The green expanse of Strossmayerov Trg with its majestic trees and carefully tended flower beds makes an ideal stopping place for weary feet. The café terrace at the **Palace Hotel** (⊠ Strossmayerov Trg 10) offers outdoor seating overlooking this leafy square, plus Viennese coffee and a range of tempting cakes and pastries.

⓯ **Teknički Muzej** (Technical Museum). This museum is guaranteed to appeal to children and civil engineers alike; try to see it in the afternoon, when a series of guided visits are on offer. The highlight here is the demonstration of some of Nikola Tesla's inventions, which takes place daily at 3:30, but there's also the tour of a lifelike reconstruction of a coal mine at 3 and a planetarium visit at 4. ⊠ *Savska Cesta 18, Donji Grad,* ☎ *01/484–4050,* WEB *www.mdc.hr/tehnick.* ☞ *15 Kn.* ☉ *Tues.–Fri. 9– 5, weekends 9–1.*

Dining

Traditional Zagrebian cuisine is based on roast meats with heavy side dishes such as *zagorski štrukli* (baked cheese dumplings). However, there are now a number of excellent fish restaurants in the capital, mainly owned and run by natives of Dalmatia.

$$$$ ✕ **A G Matoš Klub.** A unique first-floor view down onto the main square, coupled with a stylish modern interior and subtle lighting, makes this a memorable spot for dinner. Start with beef carpaccio, followed by veal medallions with truffle sauce and roast potatoes, or fillet of sole in wine and chives with asparagus. The entrance is rather obscure: pass through the arcade behind the Znanje bookshop, and then take the stairs next to a kiosk selling cakes and pastries. ⊠ *Gajeva 2, Donji Grad,* ☎ *01/487–2544. AE, DC, MC, V.*

$$$$ ✕ **Paviljon.** This chic restaurant occupies the ground floor of the charming 19th-century Art Pavilion, close to the train station. The Italian-inspired menu includes dishes such as tagliatelli with prosciutto and asparagus as well as crispy roast duck on red cabbage with figs. The wine list is equally impressive, with a choice of Croatian, Italian, and French vintages. ⊠ *Tomislavov Trg 22, Donji Grad,* ☎ *01/481–3066. AE, DC, MC, V. Closed Sun.*

$$$–$$$$ ✕ **Dubravkin Put.** Amid the greenery of Tuškanac Park, just 10 minutes from the center, this prestigious fish restaurant specializes in dishes from the Dubrovnik area, with the house favorite being *brodet* (fish stew prepared with fresh herbs). The dining room is light and airy, with a wooden floor, plants, and colorful abstract canvases by the Croatian artist Edo Murtić. Throughout summer there's outdoor seating on an ample, leafy terrace. ⊠ *Dubravkin put 2, Gornji Grad,* ☎ *01/483–4975. AE, DC, MC, V.*

$$–$$$$ ✕ **Murter.** Occupying the vaulted brick cellar of a charming old building behind the cathedral, this highly regarded restaurant is renowned for Dalmatian fish dishes such as octopus with new potatoes. There's an open-plan kitchen, so you can watch the cooks while they work. ⊠ *Kaptol 27, Gornji Grad,* ☎ *01/481–7745. AE, DC, MC, V. Closed Aug. and Sun.*

$$–$$$ ✕ **Atlantic Caffè Restaurant.** One of the first restaurants to open among the myriad thriving cafés that line Tkalčićeva, Atlantic boasts a stylish interior with warm terra-cotta walls hung with enormous gilt-framed mirrors. You might begin with spaghetti carbonara, followed by *pureći stek u gorgonzola* (turkey breast with Gorgonzola), rounded off with tiramisu. ⊠ *Tkalčićeva 65, Gornji Grad,* ☎ *01/481–3848. AE, DC, MC, V.*

$$–$$$ ✕ **Baltazar.** Behind the cathedral, Baltazar is best known for classic Balkan dishes such as *ražnjići* (mixed barbecued meats), *čevapčiči* (kebabs), and *zapečeni grah* (oven-baked beans). In summer, there are tables in the vine-covered courtyard. ⊠ *Nova Ves 4, Gornji Grad,* ☎ *01/466–6824. AE, DC, MC, V. Closed Sun.*

$$–$$$ ✕ **Pod Gričkim Topom.** This small, informal restaurant, perched on the hillside close to the funicular station in Gornji Grad (Upper Town), affords stunning views over the city rooftops. Dalmatian cooking predominates, with dishes such as *lignje na žaru* (barbecued squid) and *crni rižot* (cuttlefish-ink risotto) appreciated by locals and visitors alike. ⊠ *Zakmardijeve stube 5, Gornji Grad,* ☎ *01/483–3607. AE, DC, MC, V.*

$$–$$$ ✕ **Stari Fijaker.** An old-fashioned restaurant with vaulted ceilings, wood-paneled walls, and crisp white table linens, Stari Fijaker lies just off Ilica, a five-minute walk from the main square. The menu features carefully presented traditional Croatian dishes such as *pečena teletina* (roast veal), *zagorski štrukli* (baked cheese dumplings), and *punjene paprike* (stuffed peppers). ⊠ *Mesnička 6, Donji Grad,* ☎ *01/483–3829. AE, DC, MC, V.*

$–$$$ ✕ **Medvedgrad Pivnica.** Best known for its excellent beers, which are brewed on the premises, Medvedgrad also serves up generous portions of roast meats, goulash, and beans and sausage, accompanied by a range of salads. The location is close to the Cibona stadium. To get here, take either Tram 4 from the train station or Tram 17 from the main square. ⊠ *Savska 56, Donji Grad,* ☎ *01/617–7110, AE, DC, MC, V.*

$–$$ ✕ **Boban.** Close to Hotel Dubrovnik, Boban comprises a street-level bar and a restaurant specializing in pasta dishes in a large vaulted cellar space below. The owner, Zvonimir Boban, was captain of the Croatian national football team during the 1998 World Cup. This place is extremely popular with locals, so be prepared to line up for a table, since reservations are not accepted. ⊠ *Gajeva 9, Donji Grad,* ☎ *01/ 481–1549. AE, DC, MC, V.*

Lodging

Zagreb offers a good choice of large, expensive hotels geared up to business travelers, but less in the way of tourist accommodations. The establishments listed here are quite central and reasonably priced.

$$$$ 🏨 **Opera Zagreb.** This colossal 17-story modern structure lies between the Mimara Museum and the Botanical Garden. Rooms are furnished with quality reproduction antiques and coordinated fabrics. There are first-rate sports and business facilities, and a hotel limousine is available for transfers to and from the airport. ⊠ *Kršnjavoga 1, Donji Grad, 10000,* ☎ *01/489–2000,* FAX *01/489–2001,* WEB *www.opera-zagreb.com. 369 rooms, 36 suites. 2 restaurants, room service, cable TV with movies, minibars, indoor pool, gym, hair salon, massage, sauna, bar, lounge, Internet, business services, meeting rooms, car rental. AE, DC, MC, V. BP.*

$$$$ 🏨 **Sheraton.** A 10-minute walk from the city center, this modern six-story hotel opened in 1995. Rooms are furnished in classical style with en-suite marble bathrooms. There are excellent sports, business, and entertainment facilities. ⊠ *Kneza Borne 2, Donji Grad, 10000,* ☎ *01/ 455–3535,* FAX *01/455–3035,* WEB *www.sheraton.com/zagreb. 312 rooms, 11 suites. 2 restaurants, room service, cable TV with movies, in-room data ports, minibars, some kitchenettes, some refrigerators, indoor pool, gym, sauna, bar, piano bar, casino, nightclub, baby-sitting, Internet, business services, convention center, meeting rooms, car rental, some pets allowed. AE, DC, MC, V. BP.*

$$$$ 🏨 **Hotel Esplanade.** This prestigious hotel, lying opposite the train station, was originally built for travelers on the Orient Express and first opened its doors in 1925. The high-ceilinged rooms are spacious, comfortable, and well equipped, making it popular with business travelers and tourists alike. ⊠ *Mihanovićeva 1, Donji Grad, 10000,* ☎ *01/ 456–6666,* FAX *01/457–7907,* WEB *www.esplanade.hr. 171 rooms, 8 suites. 2 restaurants, room service, cable TV, minibars, some in-room safes, massage, sauna, casino, Internet, business services, convention center, meeting rooms. AE, DC, MC, V. BP.*

$$$ 🏨 **Hotel Dubrovnik.** Claiming the most central location in the city, just off Trg Bana Jelačića, Hotel Dubrovnik is popular with business travelers and tourists alike. The garish mirrored-glass facade conceals basic but comfortable rooms and facilities. ⊠ *Gajeva 1, Donji Grad, 10000,* ☎ *01/487–3555,* FAX *01/481–8447,* WEB *www.tel.hr/hotel-dubrovnik. 268 rooms, 8 suites. Restaurant, café, room service, cable TV, minibars, some refrigerators, bar, business services, meeting rooms. AE, DC, MC, V. BP.*

$$$ 🏨 **Palace Hotel Zagreb.** Built in 1891 as the Schlessinger Palace and converted in 1907 to become the city's first hotel, the Palace Hotel offers romantic, old-fashioned comfort but few extras. Overlooking a green square, between the train station and the city center, it's best known by locals for the street-level Viennese-style café. ⊠ *Strossmayerov Trg 10, Donji Grad, 10000,* ☎ *01/481–4611,* FAX *01/481–1358,* WEB *www. palace.hr. 125 rooms, 5 suites. Restaurant, café, room service, cable TV, minibars, laundry service, casino, meeting rooms. AE, DC, MC, V. BP.*

$$ 🏨 **Hotel Central.** Lying in a narrow side street between the train station and the main square, the Central is convenient rather than romantic. Rooms are simply furnished in shades of blue, and the staff are friendly and efficient. ⊠ *Branimirova 3, Donji Grad, 10000,* ☎ *01/484–1122,*

FAX *01/484–1304,* WEB *www.hotel-central.hr. 79 rooms, 4 suites. Cable TV, in-room data ports, minibars, bar. AE, DC, MC, V. BP.*

$$ ⬛ **Vila Tina.** This delightful family-run hotel lies out of the center, in a peaceful side street close to Maksimir Park. Each room is individually and tastefully furnished and has extras such as fresh fruit and flowers. There's a good restaurant with a summer garden and a beautiful indoor pool. ⊠ *Bukovačka cesta 213, Donji Grad, 10000,* ☎ *01/244–5138,* FAX *01/244–5204,* WEB *www.vilatina.com. 16 rooms. Restaurant, cable TV, minibars, indoor pool, sauna. AE, DC, MC, V. BP.*

$ ⬛ **Hotel Sliško.** This small, friendly hotel lies just a 5-minute walk from the bus station and a 15-minute walk from the center. Rooms are smart and functional, and there's a bar and breakfast room. Its normally fully booked during trade fairs, so check for dates in advance. ⊠ *Supilova 13, Donji Grad, 10000,* ☎ FAX *01/618–4777,* WEB *www. slisko.hr. 12 rooms. Restaurant, bar. AE, DC, MC, V. BP.*

Nightlife and the Arts

Finally climbing out of the economic depression caused by the war, Zagreb now has an entertainment scene that is picking up. Bars, clubs, and cinemas are predominantly frequented by the city's student population, while the concert hall and theater remain the domain of the older generation. For information about what's on, pick up a free copy of either the monthly *Events and Performances,* published by the city tourist board, or the bimonthly English-language guide, *In Your Pocket, Zagreb.*

Nightlife

BARS AND NIGHTCLUBS

BP Jazz Club (⊠ Teslina 7, Donji Grad, ☎ 01/481–4444, WEB www. bpclub.hr), the capital's top venue for live jazz, is a smoky basement bar. **Bulldog** (⊠ Bogovićeva 6, Donji Grad, ☎ 01/481–7393) is a popular split-level café-bar with a large summer terrace. **Old Pharmacy** (⊠ Andrije Hebranga 11a, Donji Grad, ☎ 01/455–4367), a peaceful pub with CNN on television and a selection of English-language newspapers, also has a non-smoking side room. **Pivnica Medvedgrad** (⊠ Savska 56, Donji Grad, ☎ 01/617–7110) is a beer hall and microbrewery serving the best ale in town.

DISCOS

Aquarius (⊠ Aleja mira bb, Jarun, ☎ 01/364–0231, WEB www. aquarius.hr) is Zagreb's top club for dance, especially for disco and techno music. It overlooks Lake Jarun, 4 km (2½ mi) from the city center. **Saloon** (⊠ Tuškanac 1a, Gornji Grad, ☎ 01/483–4903) is the city's most glamorous club, where you can rub shoulders with the stars and dance to commercial disco and Croatian music.

The Arts

Broadway Tkalča (⊠ Nova Ves 17, Gornji Grad, ☎ 01/486–0241) is Croatia's first multiscreen cinema, in the Centar Kaptol shopping complex, behind the cathedral. Most foreign films (including those from the United States) are shown in their original language with Croatian subtitles. The **Hrvatsko Narodno Kazalište** (Croatian National Theater; ⊠ Trg Maršala Tita 15, Donji Grad, ☎ 01/482–8532, WEB www.hnk.hr), a beautiful 19th-century building, hosts classical and contemporary dramas, opera, and ballet performances. **Komedija** (⊠ Kaptol 9, Gornji Grad, ☎ 01/481–4566, WEB www.komedija.hr) is a small theater specializing in operettas and Croatian musicals, close to the cathedral. **Koncertna Dvorana Vatroslav Lisinski** (Vatroslav Lisinski Concert Hall; ⊠ Stjepana Radića 4, Donji Grad, ☎ 01/612–1166, WEB www.lisinski.hr), a large, modern complex with two auditoriums, is Zagreb's top venue for orchestral and classical music concerts.

Shopping

The number of Croats who take shopping buses to Italy and Austria illustrates that this is hardly a great place for acquisitions. Clothes and household goods are still mainly imported as the country's manufacturing industries struggle to recover from the after-effects of the war.

The capital's new shopping center, **Centar Kaptol** (✉ Nova Ves 11, Gornji Grad), shows that things are, however, looking up. Stores include Marks & Spencer, Kenzo, and Max & Co. The center is open Monday–Saturday 9–9, with late-night shopping until 11 on Thursday. For an authentic Croatian shopping experience, visit the **Dolac** open-air market (✉ Trg Bana Jelačića, Gornji Grad), where besides fresh fruit and vegetables there are also a number of arts-and-crafts stalls. It's open weekdays 7–4 and weekends 7–noon.

Ties may not be the most original of gifts, but few people know that the tie originated in Croatia. During the 17th century, Croatian mercenaries who fought in France sported narrow, silk neck scarfs, which soon became known to the French as *cravat* (from the Croatian *hrvat*). At **Croata** (✉ Kaptol 13, Gornji Grad, ☎ 01/481–4600, WEB www. croata.hr) you can buy "original Croatian ties" in presentation boxes, accompanied by a brief history of the tie. Housed in a tastefully arranged, vaulted brick cellar, **Vinoteka Bornstein** (✉ Kaptol 19, Gornji Grad, ☎ 01/481–2363) stocks a wide range of quality Croatian wines, olive oils, and truffle products.

Zagreb Essentials

AIR TRAVEL
There are no flights between the United States and Zagreb. However, the national carrier, Croatia Airlines, flies to Zagreb from Amsterdam, Brussels, Frankfurt, London, Paris, and Vienna, where connections can be made to and from U.S. flights, and major European carriers also have flights to Zagreb from their European bases. Zagreb is also a destination from most carriers in other Eastern and Central European countries. Croatia Airlines operates at least three flights daily to Split (45 mins) and two flights daily to Dubrovnik (50 mins). Through summer, there is also daily service to Prague (1 hr, 30 mins) and flights several times a week to Warsaw (1 hr, 40 mins).

CARRIERS
➤ AIRLINES AND CONTACTS: **Adria** (☎ 01/481–0011). **Air France** (☎ 01/456–2220). **Austrian Airways** (☎ 01/626–5900). **British Airways** (☎ 01/456–2506). **Croatia Airlines** (☎ 01/481–9633). **CŠA** (☎ 01/ 487–3301). **LOT** (☎ 01/483–7500). **Lufthansa** (☎ 01/456–2159). **Malev** (☎ 01/483–6935).

AIRPORTS AND TRANSFERS
Zagreb Airport (ZAG) is in Pleso, 17 km (10 mi) southeast of the city. ➤ AIRPORT INFORMATION: **Zagreb Pleso Airport** (☎ 01/626–5222 general information; 01/456–2229 lost and found; WEB www.tel.hr/ zagreb-airport).

AIRPORT TRANSFERS
A regular shuttle bus runs from the airport to the main bus station every 30 minutes from 7 AM to 8 PM and from the main bus station to the airport from 6 AM to 7:30 PM. A one-way ticket costs 25 Kn, and the trip takes 25 minutes. By taxi, expect to pay 150 Kn–200 Kn to make the same journey; the trip will take about 20 minutes.
➤ CONTACTS: **Airport bus** (☎ 01/615–7992).

BUS TRAVEL

Regular coach service to destinations all over mainland Croatia departs from the capital. The traveling time is 6 hours from Zagreb to Split, 10½ hours from Zagreb to Dubrovnik. There are also daily international bus lines to Slovenia (Ljubljana), Hungary (Barcs and Nagykanisza), Yugoslavia (Belgrade), Austria (Graz), Germany (Munich, Stuttgart, Frankfurt, Dortmund, Cologne, and Dusseldorf), and Switzerland (Zurich). Timetable information is available from the main bus station, a 20-minute walk from the center.

➤ BUS INFORMATION: **Zagreb Bus Station** (✉ avenija M Držićabb, Donji Grad, ☎ 060/313–333, WEB www.akz.hr).

BUS AND TRAM TRAVEL WITHIN ZAGREB

An extensive network of city buses and trams runs day (4 AM–11:45 PM) and night (11:35 PM–3:45 AM). Tickets cost 6 Kn if you buy them from a street kiosk, or 7 Kn from the driver. A full-day ticket costs 16 Kn. After you board the bus or tram, you must validate your ticket with a time stamp; tickets are good for 1½ hours. If you are caught without a valid ticket, you will be fined 150 Kn.

➤ BUS INFORMATION: **ZET** (Zagreb Transport Authority; ☎ 01/660–0442, WEB www.zet.hr).

CAR RENTALS

A small car (e.g., Fiat Uno) costs 335 Kn per day or 2,010 Kn per week. A slightly larger car (e.g., Fiat Punto) costs 439 Kn per day or 2,634 Kn per week. A large car (e.g., Opal Astral Automatic) costs 794 Kn per day or 4,764 Kn per week. These prices include CDW (collision damage waiver) and TP (theft protection) but not PAI (personal accident insurance) and allow for unlimited mileage. If you drive one-way (say, from Zagreb to Dubrovnik), there is an additional drop-off charge, but it depends on the type of car and the number of days you are renting.

➤ AGENCIES: **Avis** (✉ Hotel Opera, Kršnjavoja 1, Donji Grad, ☎ 01/483–6006, WEB www.avis.hr; ✉ Zagreb Airport, Pleso, ☎ 01/626–5840). **Budget** (✉ Praška 5, Donji Grad, ☎ 01/480–5687, WEB www.budget.hr; ✉ Zagreb Airport, Pleso, ☎ 01/626–5854). **Hertz** (✉ Mažuranićev Trg 2, Donji Grad, ☎ 01/484–7222, WEB www.hertz.hr; ✉ Zagreb Airport, Pleso, ☎ 01/456–2635). **Sixt** (✉ Roosevelt trg 4, Donji Grad, ☎ 01/482–8385, WEB www.sixt.hr; ✉ Zagreb Airport, Pleso, ☎ 01/621–9900).

CAR TRAVEL

While staying in the capital you are certainly better off without a car, though if you wish to visit the nearby hills of Zagorje, a vehicle is almost essential. When it comes to moving on, you will find that Rijeka in the Kvarner region to the west is well connected to Zagreb by train and bus, as are Split in Dalmatia to the south. However, a car makes your travel plans more flexible.

EMBASSIES AND CONSULATES

All embassies are in Zagreb. *See* the A to Z section at the end of this chapter for addresses.

EMERGENCIES

➤ AMBULANCE: **Ambulance** (☎ 94).
➤ DOCTORS AND DENTISTS: **Hitno Ponoč** (Hospital) (✉ Draškovićeva 19, Donji Grad, ☎ 01/461–0011).
➤ FIRE: **Fire Emergencies** (☎ 93).
➤ PHARMACIES: **24-hour Pharmacy** (✉ Ilica 43, Donji Grad, ☎ 01/484–8450; ✉ Ilica 301, Donji Grad, ☎ 01/377–4423).
➤ POLICE: **Police Emergencies** (☎ 92).

TAXIS

You can find taxis ranks in front of the bus and train stations, near the main square, and in front of the larger hotels. It is also possible to order a radio taxi. All drivers are bound by law to run a meter, which should start at 25 Kn and increase 7 Kn per kilometer. Each piece of luggage incurs a further 5 Kn. The night tariff operates from 10 PM to 5 AM and implies a 20% markup.

➤ CONTACTS: **Radio Taxi** (☎ 01/668–2505 or ☎ 01/668–2558, 🖪 www.radio-taksi-zagreb.hr).

TOURS

The Tourist Information Center close to the train station, organizes amusing and informative guided tours of the city.

➤ CONTACTS: **Zagreb Tourist Information** (✉ Trg Nikole Šubića Zrinskoga 14, Donji Grad, ☎ 01/492–1645).

TRAIN TRAVEL

The main train station lies in Donji Grad, a 10-minute walk from the center. There are daily international lines to and from Budapest (Hungary), Belgrade (Yugoslavia), Munich (Germany), Vienna (Austria), and Venice (Italy).

From Zagreb, there are four trains daily to Split in Dalmatia (8 hrs) and five trains daily to Rijeka in Kvarner (3 hrs, 30 min).

➤ TRAIN STATIONS: **Zagreb Train Station** (✉ Trg Kralja Tomislava, Donji Grad, ☎ 060/333–444 domestic train information; 01/481–1892 international train information; 🖪 www.hznet.hr).

VISITOR INFORMATION

Zagreb's main Tourist Information Center overlooks the main square. It's open weekdays 8:30 AM–8 PM, Saturday 9–5, and Sunday 10–2. A smaller office is close to the train station and open Monday, Wednesday, and Friday 9–5 and Tuesday and Thursday 9–6.

➤ CONTACTS: **Zagreb Tourist Information** (✉ Trg Bana Jelačića 11, Donji Grad, ☎ 01/481–4051, 🖪 www.zagreb-touristinfo.hr; ✉ Trg Nikole Šubića Zrinskoga 14, Donji Grad, ☎ 01/492–1645).

SIDE TRIPS FROM ZAGREB

A favorite excursion to the outskirts of Zagreb is to the heights of Sljeme and its observatory. Northwest of Zagreb, beyond the Medvednica hills, lies a pastoral region known as Zagorje. The scenery is calm and enchanting: red-brick villages, such as Kumrovec, are animated with ducks and chickens, and the hillsides are inlaid with vineyards and orchards. Medieval hilltop castles, including Veliki Tabor and Dvor Trakoščan, survey the surrounding valleys. To the northeast of Zagreb is the charming medieval town of Varaždin.

Numbers in the margins refer to numbers on the Side Trips from Zagreb map.

Sljeme

❶ *5 km (3 mi) north of Zagreb by cable car.*

A favorite excursion to the outskirts of Zagreb is to the heights of Sljeme, the peak of **Mt. Medvednica**, at 3,390 ft. You can reach it taking Tram 14 (direction Mihaljevac), all the way to the terminal stop, where you should change to Tram 15 (direction Dolje), also to its terminal stop. From there a cable car operates hourly from 8 to 8 for the 20-minute journey to the top of the mountain for breath-taking views over the surrounding countryside. It's an ideal place for picnicking, but you may

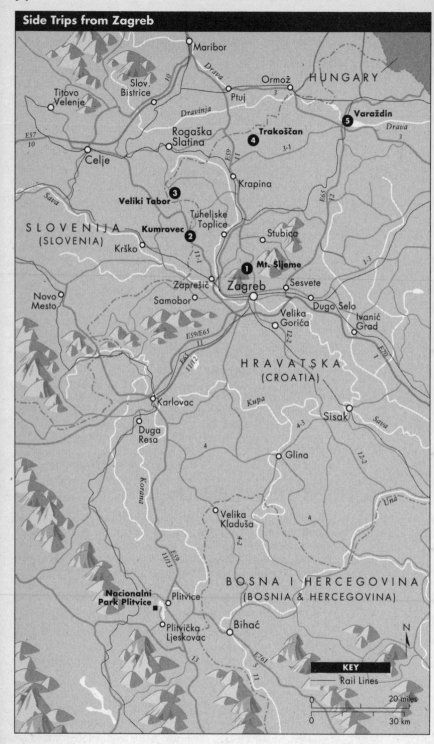

Side Trips from Zagreb

HUNGARY

Maribor

Drava

Ormož

Slov. Bistrice

Titovo Velenje

Ptuj

Dravinja

Varaždin

Drava

Trakošćan

④

⑤

Rogaška Slatina

3-1

E57 10

Celje

Sava

E59 11

Krapina

Veliki Tabor

③

E65 12

SLOVENIJA
(SLOVENIA)

Kumrovec

②

Tuheljske Toplice

Stubica

Krško

11-1

1-3

Mt. Sljeme

①

Sesvete

Novo Mesto

Zaprešić

Samobor

Zagreb

Dugo Selo

Ivanić Grad

Velika Gorića

12-2

E70 1

E59/E65 11

E65 11/12

HRAVATSKA
(CROATIA)

Karlovac

Kupa

Sisak

Sava

Duga Resa

4-3

12-2

Korana

Glina

Una

4

Velika Kladuša

4-2

4

E59 11/13

BOSNA I HERCEGOVINA
(BOSNIA & HERCEGOVINA)

Nacionalni Park Plitvice

Plitvice

Bihać

N

Plitvička Ljeskovac

13

E761 5 11

KEY

Rail Lines

0   20 miles

0   30 km

wish to save your appetite for dinner at one of the excellent restaurants on the road home. The round-trip cable-car ticket costs 15 Kn. ✉ *Dolje.*

Dining

$$–$$$ ✕ **Stari Puntijar.** On the road between Zagreb and Sljeme, Stari Puntijar is renowned for game and traditional 19th-century Zagreb dishes such as *podolac* (ox medallions in cream and saffron), *orehnjaca* (walnut loaf), and *makovnjaca* (poppy-seed cake). The wine list is excellent. ✉ *Gračanka Cesta 65, Medveščak, Zagreb,* ☎ *01/467–5500. AE, DC, MC, V.*

Kumrovec

❷ *40 km (25 mi) northwest of Zagreb.*

The late president Josip Broz Tito was born here in 1892, and his childhood home has been turned into a small memorial museum. In the courtyard of his birthplace stands an imposing bronze likeness of him by Antun Augustinčić. The old quarter of Kumrovec, known as **Kumrovec Staro Selo** (Kumrovec Old Village), is an open-air museum with beautifully restored thatched cottages and wooden farm buildings, orchards, and a stream giving a lifelike reconstruction of 19th-century rural life. On weekends craftsmen, including a blacksmith, a candlemaker, and others, demonstrate their skills. ✉ *Kumrovec,* ☎ *049/553–131.* 🎟 *10 Kn.* ☉ *May–Sept., daily 8–6; Oct.–Apr., daily 9–3.*

Veliki Tabor

❸ *15 km (9 mi) north of Kumrovec.*

On a lofty hilltop stands the fortress of Veliki Tabor. The main pentagonal core of the building dates back to the 12th century, while the side towers added in 15th century as protection against Turks. ✉ *Desinić,* ☎ *049/343–052,* WEB *www.veliki-tabor.hr.* 🎟 *20 Kn.* ☉ *Daily 10–6.*

Dining

$–$$ ✕ **Grešna Gorica.** Visiting this rustic tavern is like stepping into a
★ friend's home. All the produce is supplied by local farmers, and the menu features typical Zagorje dishes, including *zagorski štrukli* (baked cheese dumplings) and *pura s mlincima* (turkey with savory pastries). The garden affords great views down onto Veliki Tabor fortress. ✉ *Desinić,* ☎ *049/343–001. No credit cards.*

Trakošćan

❹ *36 km (22½ mi) northeast of Veliki Tabor.*

★ The romantic white hilltop **Dvor Trakošćan** (Trakošćan Castle) is set amid beautifully landscaped grounds, overlooking a small lake. It took on its present neo-Gothic appearance during the 19th century, though there has been a building here since the 13th century. Inside, the wood-paneled rooms are filled with period furnishings and family portraits, giving you some idea of how the wealthy local aristocracy once lived. ✉ *Trakošćan,* ☎ *042/796–422,* WEB *www.trakoscan.net.* 🎟 *20 Kn.* ☉ *May–Sept., daily 9–6; Oct.–Apr., daily 9–3.*

Varaždin

❺ *70 km (48 mi) northeast of Zagreb.*

Situated on a plain near the River Drava, Varaždin is the most harmonious and beautiful medieval town in this corner of the continent.

It is adorned by extraordinary churches and the baroque palaces of the aristocratic families that once lived here. The well-preserved castle, now a historic museum, is in a park surrounded by grassy ramparts close to the town center. Nearby is an unusual cemetery with immense hedges trimmed and shaped around ornate memorials. Each autumn, the **Varaždin Baroque Evenings** hosts a program of classical music concerts, now considered one of the most important cultural events in north Croatia.

Varaždin's main attraction is the impressive **Stari Grad** (Castle), surrounded by fortifications and a moat, serving as the seat of the county prefect from the 12th century up until 1925. You enter through a 16th-century tower gatehouse with a wooden drawbridge to arrive in the internal courtyard with three levels of open-arched galleries. Indoors, there's an extensive display of antique furniture, with pieces laid out in chronological order and each room representing a specific period. ⊠ *Strossmayerovo Šetalište 7*, ☎ *042/210–399*, WEB *www.varazdin.hr.* 🎫 *15 Kn.* ☉ *Oct.–Apr., Tues.–Fri. 10–3, weekends 10–1.*

Dining

$$–$$$ ✕ **Restoran Zlatna Guska.** In a vaulted brick cellar in the center of town, this is a great place to stop for either a quick lunch or a relaxed dinner over a bottle of local wine. The chicken-and-mushroom-filled pancakes are delicious, while vegetarians might opt for the vegetable medallions with grilled cheese. ⊠ *Habdelića 4*, ☎ *042/213–393. AE, DC, MC, V.*

OFF THE
BEATEN PATH
NACIONALNI PARK PLITVIČLA JEZERA – On the road from Zagreb to Split (E71), you pass Plitvice Lakes National Park, a UNESCO World Heritage Site and haven of lakes and waterfalls set amid dense forests. Croatia's top inland tourist destination, this 8,000-acre park is home to 16 beautiful emerald lakes connected by a series of cascading waterfalls, stretching 8 km (5 mi) in length. A series of wooden bridges and waterside paths leads through the park. ⊠ *Velika Poljana, 128 km (79 mi) southwest of Zagreb,* ☎ *053/75–015,* WEB *www.np-plitvice.tel.hr/ np-plitvice.* 🎫 *60 Kn.* ☉ *May–Sept., daily 8–7; Oct.–Apr., daily 9–4.*

ISTRIA

The Istrian peninsula lies in the northwest corner of the country, bordering Slovenia. There's a sizable Italian minority here, and Italian influence is apparent in the architecture, the cuisine, and the local dialect.

The region's principal city and port, Pula, is on the tip of the peninsula and is best known for its remarkably preserved 1,900-year-old Roman amphitheater. Close by, the beautifully nurtured island retreat of Brijuni National Park can be visited in a day. Towns along the west coast have an unmistakable Venetian flavor left by more than 500 years of Venetian occupation (1238–1797). Poreč and Rovinj, Croatia's two most popular seaside resorts, are both endowed with graceful campanili, loggias, and reliefs of the winged lion of St. Mark, patron saint of Venice.

If you're in Istria during autumn, a side trip to the romantic hill towns of Motovun and Grožnjan is recommended. This inland area is particularly rich in truffles and mushrooms, and from mid-September to late-October these local delicacies are celebrated with a series of gastronomic festivals.

Numbers in the margins correspond to numbers on the Istria and Kvarner map.

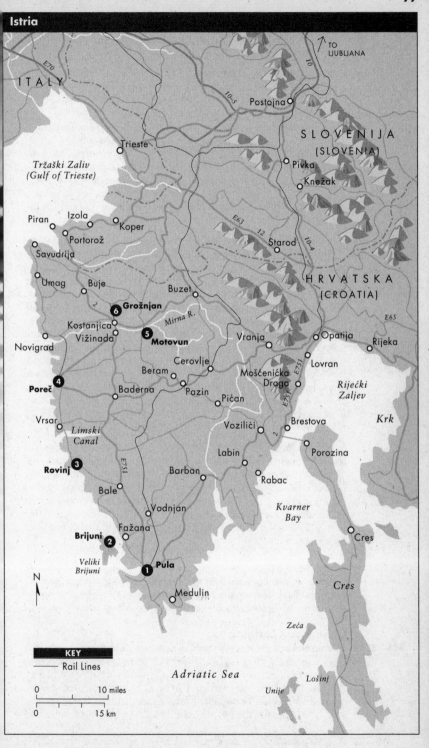

Istria

TO
LJUBLJANA

ITALY

Trieste

Tržaški Zaliv
(Gulf of Trieste)

Postojna

SLOVENIJA
(SLOVENIA)

Pivka

Knežak

Piran   Izola

Portorož   Koper

Savudrija

Umag   Buje

Buzet

Starod

HRVATSKA
(CROATIA)

❻ Grožnjan

Kostanjica

Vižinada

❺ Motovun

Mirna R.

Vranja

Opatija

Rijeka

Novigrad

Beram

Cerovlje

Moščenička
Draga

Lovran

Riječki
Zaljev

Krk

❹ Poreč

Baderna

Pazin

Pićan

Vrsar

Limski
Canal

Vozilići

Brestova

❸ Rovinj

Labin

Porozina

Bale

Barban

Rabac

Vodnjan

Kvarner
Bay

Fažana

Brijuni ❷

Cres

❶ Pula

Veliki
Brijuni

N

Medulin

Cres

Zeća

KEY

—— Rail Lines

Adriatic Sea

Lošinj

Unije

0   10 miles

0   15 km

Pula

❶   *292 km (182½ mi) southwest of Zagreb.*

Today an industrial port town and Istria's chief administrative center, Pula was founded by the Romans in 177 BC. Remains from its ancient past have survived up to the present day: as you drive in on the coastal route, the monumental Arena, an enormous Roman amphitheater, blocks out the sky on your left. Under Venetian rule (1331–1797), Pula was sadly neglected. Many structures from the Roman era were pulled down, and stones and columns were carted off across the sea to Italy to be used for new buildings there. Pula's second great period of development took place in the late 19th century, under the Hapsburgs, when it served as the chief base for the Imperial Austrian Navy. Today it's more of a working city than a tourist destination, but there are a few outstandingly good restaurants and a number of pleasant family-run hotels.

★   Designed to accommodate 22,000 spectators, the **Arena** (Roman Amphitheater) is the sixth-largest building of its type in the world (after the Colosseum in Rome and similar arenas in Verona, Catania, Capua, and Arles). Construction was completed in the 1st century AD, and the Romans staged gladiator games here until such blood-thirsty sports were forbidden during the 5th century. During the 16th century the Venetians planned to move the Arena stone by stone to Venice, where it was to be reconstructed in its original form. Fortunately the plan failed, and it has remained more or less intact, except for the original tiers of stone seats and numerous columns that were hauled away for other buildings. Today it is used for summer concerts (recent musicians include Sting, James Brown, and Jose Carreras), opera performances, and the annual film festival. The underground halls house a museum with large wooden oil presses and amphoras. ✉ *Amfiteaterska ul..* ☎ *16 Kn.* ☉ *May–Sept., daily 8–8; Oct.–Apr., daily 9–5.*

Still Pula's most important public meeting place after 2,000 years, the ancient Roman **Forum** is today a vast paved piazza ringed with cafés. There were once three temples here, of which only one remains: the perfectly preserved **Augustov Hram** (Temple of Augustus), built in the 1st century AD on the north side of the square. Next to it stands the **Gradska Palača** (Town Hall), erected during the 13th century using part of the Roman Temple of Diana as the back wall. The Renaissance arcade was added later.

NEED A BREAK?	Stop at the chic but unpretentious **Café Cvajner** (✉ Forum 2) for morning coffee or an evening aperitif. Inside, pieces of contemporary art and minimalist furniture are played off against frescoes uncovered during restoration, while outdoor tables offer great views over Forum Square.

Dining and Lodging

$$$–$$$$ ✗ **Vela Nera.** Several times voted the best restaurant in Croatia, Vela
★   Nera is located 3 km (2 mi) from the city center at Medulin, overlooking a yachting marina. Favorite dishes include pasta with lobster and truffles, fish baked in a salt crust, and an ever-changing range of creative seafood specialties. The quality of the wines matches that of the cuisine. ✉ *Pješčana Uvala bb, Medulin,* ☎ *052/219–209. AE, DC, MC, V.*

$$–$$$ ✗▦ **Valsabbion.** This delightful family-run hotel and restaurant is 3 km (2 mi) from the city center, overlooking the sea. Rooms are furnished in pine with cheerful colored linens, fresh fruit, and flowers. There's a small swimming pool on the top floor and a range of beauty treatments and aerobics courses. The highly acclaimed restaurant was

one of the first in Croatia to specialize in "slow food." The menu changes daily depending on available produce, but you can expect goodies such as frogfish in vine leaves or tagliatelli with aromatic herbs and pine nuts. ⊠ *Pješčana Uvala IX/26, Medulin, 52100,* ☎ FAX *052/218–033,* WEB *www.valsabbion.com. 10 rooms. Restaurant, room service, cable TV, minibars, in-room safes, indoor pool, aerobics, health club, sauna, spa. AE, DC, MC, V.*

$$–$$$ ✕⊞ **Hotel and Restaurant Scaletta.** Ideally situated close to the Arena,
★   this small family-run hotel occupies a tastefully refurbished old town house. The interior is decorated in cheerful yellows and greens, with simple modern furniture and spanking-fresh bathrooms. The hotel restaurant offers a small but select menu with exquisite dishes such as filet mignon in bread crumbs with dates and croquettes, while the Scaletta Pavilion, across the road, serves pizza, grilled meats, and fish dishes. ⊠ *Flavijevska 26, 52100,* ☎ *052/541–025,* FAX *052/541–026,* WEB *www.hotel-scaletta.com. 12 rooms. Restaurant, pizzeria, minibars, in-room safes. AE, DC, MC, V. BP.*

$$ ⊞ **Hotel Riviera.** Located between the train station and the Arena but also close to the sea, this slightly run-down hotel was opened in the early 20th century when Istria was a part of Austria-Hungary. The grandiose yellow exterior conceals basic but reasonably comfortable rooms and a restaurant. ⊠ *Splitska 1, 52100,* ☎ *052/211–166,* FAX *052/219–117. 89 rooms. Restaurant, bar, some pets allowed. AE, DC, MC, V. BP.*

Brijuni

➋ *Ferry from Fažana, which is 15 km (9 mi) northwest of Pula.*

The Brijuni archipelago is made up of 14 islands and islets. Under Austria-Hungary, Brijuni was a vacation haven for Vienna's nobility and high society. Archduke Franz Ferdinand summered here, as did such literary lights as Thomas Mann and Arthur Schnitzler. From 1949 to 1979, the largest island, Veliki Brijuni, was the official summer residence of Marshal Josip Broz Tito, Yugoslavia's "president for life." Here he retreated to work, rest, and pursue his hobbies. World leaders, film and opera stars, artists, and writers were frequent guests, and together with Nasser of Egypt and Nehru of India, Tito forged the "Brioni Declaration" uniting the so-called non-aligned nations (countries adhering to neither NATO nor the Warsaw Pact). The archipelago was designated a national park in 1983 and opened to the public. Before visiting, you need to call Brijuni National Park to make a reservation. To get here, take the National Park ferry (8 boats a day from April to October, 4 boats a day from November to March) from Fažana, which takes about 15 minutes.

The first view of **Nacionalni Park Brijuna** (Brijuni National Park) is of a low-lying island with a dense canopy of evergreens over blue waters. Ashore, a **tourist train** takes visitors past villas in the seaside forest and relics from the Roman and Byzantine eras. The network of roads on this 6½-km (4-mi) long island was laid down by the Romans, and stretches of original Roman stonework remain. Rows of cypresses shade herds of deer, and peacocks strut along pathways. The train stops at the **Safari Park,** a piece of Africa transplanted to the Adriatic, its zebras, antelopes, llamas, and elephants all gifts from visitors from faraway lands. In the **museum,** an archaeological exhibition traces life on Brijuni through the centuries while a photography exhibition, "Tito on Brijuni," focuses on Tito and his guests. ⊠ *Veliki Brijun,* ☎ *052/525–888,* WEB *www.np-brijuni.hr.* ☜ *160 Kn.*

Rovinj

3   *35 km (22 mi) northwest of Pula.*

In a fantastic setting, with centuries-old red-roofed houses clustered around the hill of a former island, Rovinj is crowned by the monumental baroque Crkva Sv Eufemije (Church of St. Euphemia), which has a typical Venetian bell tower topped by a gleaming bronze figure of St. Euphemia. Far below, a wide harbor crowded with pleasure boats is rimmed with bright awnings and colorful café umbrellas. Artists, writers, musicians, and actors have long gravitated to this pretty place to carve out apartments in historic houses. Throughout the summer, the winding cobbled streets are crowded with vacationers from nearby resort developments. South of the harbor lies the beautiful landscaped park of Zlatni Rt, planted with avenues of cedars, oaks, and cypresses and offering numerous secluded coves for bathing.

Inside the 18th-century baroque **Crkva Sv Eufemije** (Church of St. Euphemia), the remains of the saint are said to lie within a 6th-century sarcophagus, which according to legend floated out to sea from Constantinople and was washed ashore in Rovinj in AD 800. ⊠ *Grisia.* 🎫 *Free.* ☉ *Daily 10–noon and 4–7.*

The **Akvarij** (Aquarium) displays tanks of Adriatic marine fauna and flora. It opened in 1891, making it one of the oldest institutions of its type in Europe. It's housed within the Ruđer Bošković Institute's Centre for Maritime Research. ⊠ *obala G. Paliage 5,* ☎ *052/804–700.* 🎫 *10 Kn.* ☉ *May–Sept., daily 9–9; Oct.–Apr., by appointment only.*

Dining and Lodging

$$$ ✕ **Enoteca Al Gastaldo.** Walls lined with wine bottles and candlelight create a warm and intimate atmosphere in this sophisticated eatery, hidden away in the Old Town a couple of blocks back from the harbor. Indulge in spaghetti with either truffles or crab, fresh fish prepared over an open fire, and a colorful rocket and radicchio salad. Round off with a glass of local *rakija.*⊠ *Iza Kasarne 14,* ☎ *052/814–109. AE, DC.*

$$ ✕ **Veli Jože.** This extremely popular *konoba* lies close to the seafront, at the foot of the Old Town. Specialties include *bakalar in bianco* (dried cod in white wine with onion and potatoes), *fuži* (pasta) with goulash, and roast lamb with potatoes. The house wine is excellent. ⊠ *Sv Križa 1,* ☎ *052/816–337. AE, DC, MC, V.*

$$$$ 🏨 **Villa Angelo d'Oro.** This enchanting hotel opened in 2001 and has
★ already gained an excellent reputation. In a beautifully restored 16th-century building, rooms are individually furnished with antiques and quality fabrics. Breakfast is served on a glorious garden roof terrace, and there's a high-class restaurant on the ground floor. The hotel boat and yacht are at the guests' disposal. It lies in the heart of the Old Town, one block in from the seafront.⊠ *V Švalbe 38–42, 52210,* ☎ *052/840–502,* 🖷 *052/840–111,* 🌐 *www.rovinj.at. 20 rooms. Restaurant, room service, cable TV, minibars, hot tub, sauna. AE, DC, MC, V. BP.*

$–$$ 🏨 **Hotel Rovinj.** Located on the tip of the peninsula, below the Church of St. Euphemia, this large, white modern hotel is constructed in a series a terraces looking out to sea. Facilities are minimal and rooms are spare, but the views are wonderful. ⊠ *Svetog Križa 59, 52210,* ☎ *052/811–288,* 🖷 *052/840–757,* 🌐 *www.ipc.hr/hotel-rovinj. 68 rooms. Restaurant, bar, minibars. AE, MC, V. BP.*

Poreč

4   *45 km (28 mi) northwest of Pula.*

A pretty, tile-roofed town on a peninsula jutting out to sea, Poreč was founded as a Roman castrum (fort) in the 2nd century BC. Within the historic center, the network of streets still follow the original urban lay-out, and Dekumanova, the Roman decumanus (the main traverse street), has maintained its character as the principal thoroughfare. Today it is a worn flagstone passage lined with Romanesque and Gothic mansions and patrician palaces, some of which host cafés and restaurants. Close by lies the magnificent UNESCO-listed Eufrazijeva Basilica (St. Euphrasius Basilica), Istria's prime attraction and one of the coast's major artistic showpieces. Although the town itself is small, Poreč has an ample capacity for overnight stays, thanks to the vast hotel complexes of Plava and Zelena Lagun, situated along the pine-rimmed shoreline, a short distance from the center.

★ The magnificent **Eufrazijeva Basilica** (St. Euphrasius Basilica) is among the most perfectly preserved early Christian churches in Europe and one of the most important monuments of Byzantine art on the Adriatic. It was built by Bishop Euphrasius in the middle of the 6th century and consists of a delightful atrium, a church decorated with stunning mosaics, an octagonal baptistery, a 16th-century bell tower, and the bishop's residence. The church interior is dominated by biblical mosaics above, behind, and around the main apse. In the apsidal semi-dome the Virgin holding the Christ child is seated in a celestial sphere on a golden throne, flanked by angels in flowing white robes. On the right side there are three martyrs, the patrons of Poreč; the mosaic on the left shows Bishop Euphrasius holding a model of the church, slightly askew. High above the main apse, just below the beamed ceiling, Christ holds an open book in his hands while apostles approach on both sides. Other luminous, shimmeringly intense mosaics portray further ecclesiastical themes. ⊠ *Eufrazijeva.* 🕾 *Free.* ⊙ *Daily 7–7.*

Dining and Lodging

$$–$$$ ✕ **Dvi Murve.** Lying on the edge of town in a suburb, this highly acclaimed restaurant was founded in 1973. Favorite dishes include fish baked in a salt crust and beefsteak *dvi murve* (with a cream, mushroom, and ham sauce). The interior is decorated in the style of a traditional Istrian *konoba,* and outside there's a large summer terrace shaded by two mulberry trees, after which the restaurant is named. ⊠ *Grožnjanska 17, Vranići,* 🕾 *052/434–115. AE, D.*

$$–$$$ ✕ **Peterokutna Kula.** A 15th-century pentagonal tower in the heart of the Old Town has been cleverly renovated to accommodate this sophisticated restaurant on a series of levels and terraces. House specialties include spaghetti with lobster and steak with truffles. Finish your meal with a glass of *šlivovica* (plum rakija). ⊠ *Decumanus 1,* 🕾 *052/451–378. No credit cards.*

$$$ 🏨 **Hotel Laguna Galijot.** This large, modern hotel sits on a small peninsula surrounded by pines in the Plava Laguna resort complex, 2 km (1 mi) south of the Old Town. Most rooms have balconies and sea views. Its excellent sports facilities make it ideal for families on a longer stay and those in search of an active holiday. ⊠ *Plava Laguna, 52440,* 🕾 *052/451–877,* 🖷 *052/452–399,* 🖳 *www.plavalaguna.hr. 103 rooms. Restaurant, grill, café, cable TV, minibars, tennis court, pool, dive shop, boating, water-skiing, bicycles, bar, some pets allowed, parking (fee). AE, DC, MC, V. Closed Oct.–Apr. BP.*

$$ 🏨 **Hotel Neptun.** On the seafront promenade, where Poreč's oldest hotels are found, the Neptune was renovated in 2000 to provide smart, functional accommodations right in the center of town. ⊠ *obala M Tita 15, 52440,* 🕾 *052/400—800,* 🖷 *052/431–351,* 🖳 *www.riviera.hr. 145 rooms. Restaurant, room service, cable TV, minibars. AE, DC, MC, V. BP.*

Motovun

⑤ *30 km (19 mi) east of Poreč.*

A day exploring the undulating green countryside and medieval hill-towns of inland Istria makes a pleasant contrast to life on the coast. Motovun is probably the best preserved of all the Istrian hill towns, with a double ring of defensive walls as well as towers and town gates. A walk around the ramparts offers views across the oak forests and vineyards of the Mirna Valley, while just outside the walls stands a church built according to plans by Palladio.

Dining and Lodging

$$–$$$ ✕ **Restaurant Mcotič.** If you love truffles, either with pasta or steak, this is the place to eat. Unquestionably an acquired taste, these earthy delicacies are gathered each autumn in the nearby Mirna Valley. Mcotoč has a large summer terrace and lies on the edge of new Motovun, at the foot of the old hill town. ⊠ *Zadrugarska 19, Motovun,* ☎ *052/ 681–758. AE, DC, MC, V.*

$ 🏨 **Hotel Kaštel.** Just outside the Motovun town walls, this peaceful old-fashioned hotel makes an ideal retreat if you prefer green hills to sea and islands. Out front there's a small garden and pretty summer terrace. ⊠ *Šetalište V. Nazora 8, Motovun 52424,* ☎ *052/681–735,* FAX *052/681–652,* WEB *www.hotel-kastel-motovun.hr. 29 rooms. Restaurant, café, minibars, some pets allowed. AE, DC, MC, V. BP.*

Grožnjan

⑥ *10 km (7 mi) east of Motovun.*

Grožnjan is another of the attractive hill towns near Poreč, with a Renaissance loggia adjoining the town gate. Since the 1960s the settlement has attracted artists and musicians. Galleries display paintings and sculpture, and an international federation of young musicians meets for summer courses, presenting concerts beneath the stars through July and August.

Istria Essentials

BOAT AND FERRY TRAVEL

In summer, the Italian company Adriatica runs a catamaran service from Trieste and Grado (in Italy) to Rovinj and Brijuni. In Rovinj, tickets for the catamaran are available from Eurostar Travel. The Adriatica agent in Trieste is Samer & Co.

➤ BOAT CONTACTS: **Adriatica** (WEB www.adriatica.it). **Eurostar Travel** (⊠ obala P. Budičina 1, Rovinj, ☎ 052/813–144). **Samer & Co.** (⊠ Piazza dell'Unita d'Italia 7, Trieste, Italy, ☎ 0039–040/6702–7211).

BUS TRAVEL

There are also domestic connections all over mainland Croatia to and from Pula, Poreč, and Rovinj. International buses offer daily connections to Italy (Trieste) and Slovenia (Ljubljana, Koper, Piran, and Portorož). Timetables are available in the Pula Bus Station.

➤ BUS INFORMATION: **Pula Bus Station** (⊠ Trg 1 Istarske Brigade, Pula, ☎ 052/500–040).

CAR TRAVEL

While visiting Pula, Rovinj, and Poreč a car is not really necessary: all three towns are served by good bus connections, and having your own vehicle only causes parking problems. However, you may wish to hire a car to move onto other regions of the country. Major agencies have offices in Pula.

➤ CAR RENTAL AGENCIES: **Avis** (✉ S Dobrića 1, Pula, ☎ 052/223–739).
Budget (✉ ACI marina, Riva 1, Pula, ☎ 052/218–252). **Hertz** (✉ Hotel
Histria, Verudela bb, Pula, ☎ 052/210–868).

EMERGENCIES
➤ AMBULANCE: **Ambulance** (☎ 94).
➤ DOCTORS AND DENTISTS: **Hitno Ponoč** (Casualty; ✉ M. Gioseffija
2, Poreč, ☎ 052/431–154; ✉ Zagrebaćka 30, Pula, ☎ 052/214–433;
✉ Istarska ul. bb, Rovinj, ☎ 052/813–004).
➤ FIRE: **Fire Emergencies** (☎ 93).
➤ PHARMACIES: **24-hr Pharmacy** (✉ Giardini 15, Pula, ☎ 052/222–
551).
➤ POLICE: **Police Emergencies** (☎ 92).

TRAIN TRAVEL
Istria is not connected to the rest of Croatia by rail. However, there is
a line running north from Pula to Slovenia.
➤ TRAIN INFORMATION: Pula Train Station (✉ Kolodvorksa bb, Pula,
☎ 052/541–733).

VISITOR INFORMATION
➤ CONTACTS: **Brijuni Tourist Information** (✉ Fažana, ☎ 052/525–888,
WEB www.np-brijuni.hr). **Grožnjan Tourist Information** (✉ Umberto
Gorjan 3, Grožnjan, ☎ 052/776–131). **Istria Tourist Information** (WEB
www.istria.com). **Motovun Tourist Information** (✉ Šetalište V. Nazora
1, Motovun, ☎ 052/681–642). **Poreč Tourist Information** (✉ Za-
grebačka 9, Poreč, ☎ 052/451–293, WEB www.istria.com/porec). **Pula
Tourist Information** (✉ Forum 3, Pula, ☎ 052/19–197, WEB www.
istria.com/pula). **Rovinj Tourist Information** (✉ obala P. Budičina 12,
Rovinj, ☎ 052/811–566, WEB www.istria.com/rovinj).

KVARNER

Separating the Istrian peninsula from Dalmatia to the south, the
Kvarner Gulf is a large, deep bay backed by mountains. The principal
city, Rijeka, is a busy port with good road and rail connections to Zagreb. Gentile Opatija was founded by the Hapsburgs in the mid-19th
century as Croatia's first seaside resort, while Rab is probably the region's most beautiful island, not to mention the birthplace of nudist
bathing on the Adriatic.

Numbers in the margins correspond to numbers on the Kvarner map.

Rijeka

❶ *182 km (114 mi) west of Zagreb.*

While Rijeka goes back to the days of Imperial Rome, the modern city
evolved under the rule of Austria-Hungary. The historic core retains
vestiges of the old Hapsburg monarchy from the time when Rijeka served
as Budapest's outlet to the Adriatic. During the 1960s, under Yugoslavia, the suburbs expanded rapidly. Rijeka (Fiume in Italian) was
the country's largest port, with a huge shipyard, massive dry-dock facilities, refineries, and other heavy industries offering large-scale em-
ployment. Since the break-up of Yugoslavia, Rijeka's role as a shipping
town has declined significantly, though it remains Croatia's largest port.

From here, a coastal ferry runs south to Zadar, Split, Hvar, Korčula,
and Dubrovnik. This is also the start of the Jadranska Magistrala (the
coastal highway), which follows the coast high above the seaside on
the scenic route south all the way to the Montenegro border. More of
a transit town than a holiday destination, Rijeka doesn't have much

Kvarner

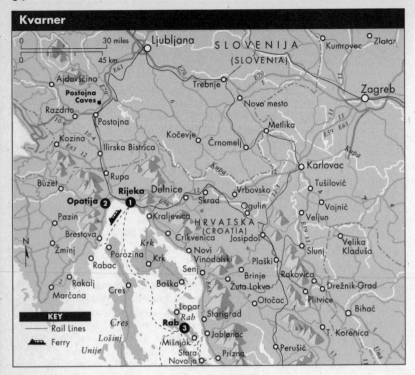

of interest apart from the hilltop fortress of Trsat. Most visitors stay in the nearby seaside resort of Opatija.

The medieval **Trsat Castle** was built on the foundations of a prehistoric fort. In the early 1800s it was bought by an Austrian general of Irish descent, who converted it into a kind of pre-Disneyland confection, including a Greek temple with Doric columns. Today it hosts a popular café, offering some stunning views of the Kvarner Bay; throughout the summer, open-air theater performances and concerts take place here. Across the street, the pilgrimage church of **Sveta Marija** (St. Mary) was constructed in 1453 to commemorate the Miracle of Trsat, when angels carrying the humble house of the Virgin Mary are said to have landed here. Although the angels later moved the house to Loreto in Italy, Trsat has remained a place of pilgrimage. The pilgrimage path up to Trsat begins in the city center, close to Titov Trg, at a bridge across the Rječina. It passes through a stone gateway, then makes a long, steep climb up 538 steps. Local bus 1 will get you here, too. ⊠ *Frankopanski trg.* 🕾 *10 Kn.* ☉ *Apr.–Oct., Tues.–Sun. 9 AM–11 PM; Feb.–Mar. and Nov.–Dec., Tues.–Sun. 9 AM–3 PM.*

Dining and Lodging

$$–$$$$ ✕ **Feral.** This excellent seafood restaurant lies on a side road close to the main bus station. House specialties are *crni rižot* (cuttlefish-ink risotto), seafood tagliatelli, and *fuži* with asparagus and scampi. ⊠ *M Gupca 6,* 🕾 *051/212–274. AE, DC, MC, V. Closed Sun.*

$$$$ 🏨 **Hotel Bonavia.** In the city center, one block back from the Korzo, this modern, luxury high-rise hotel reopened in 2000 after extensive renovation. Suited for business travelers and tourists alike, all the comfortable rooms have specially designed furnishings and original oil paintings, lending a definite feeling of luxury. Those on the top two floors have balconies and views of Kvarner Bay. The restaurant has a sophisticated dining room with tables in the garden throughout summer. A limousine and chauffeur are at guests' disposal. ✉ *Dolac 4, 51000,* ☎ *051/357–100,* FAX *051/335–969,* WEB *www.bonavia.hr. 114 rooms, 7 suites. Restaurant, coffee shop, room service, cable TV, minibars, gym, 4 bars, Internet, convention center, car rental, parking (fee). AE, DC, MC, V. BP.*

Opatija

❷ *15 km (9 mi) west of Rijeka.*

The mild climate year-round and resulting subtropical vegetation, frequently sunny skies, and the shelter from cold north winds provided by Mt. Učka give Opatija springlike weather even in January. In summer, fresh sea breezes tend to dispel any oppressive heat, making the city an ideal seaside resort.

In the late 19th century, Opatija (Abbazia in Italian) was among the most elegant and fashionable resorts in Europe. Its history dates from the 1840s, when villas were built for members of minor royalty. In 1882 the start of rail service from Vienna and Budapest, along with an aggressive publicity campaign, put Abbazia on the tourist map as a spa of first magnitude. With the high mineral content of the sea water, iodine in the air, and an annual average of 2,230 hours of sunshine, it qualified as a top-rated climatic health resort and emerged as a favorite wintering place for Central European nobility and high society.

Today Opatija attracts an older, sedate clientele, so there's little in the way of nightlife. The main street, ulica Maršala Tita, runs parallel to the coast for the length of town, and you can go from one end of town to the other on foot in about half an hour, passing numerous terrace cafés along the way. The best seafood restaurants are in the neighboring fishing village of Volosko, a 15-minute walk along the seafront.

★ If you enjoy walking by the sea, set off along the magnificent **Lungomare.** Built in 1889, this 12-km (7½-mi) paved waterfront promenade leads from the fishing village of Volosko, through Opatija—passing in front of old hotels, parks, and gardens and around yacht basins—and all the way past the villages of Ičiči and Ika to Lovran. ✉ *Obalno Šetalište Franza Josefa.*

Opatija's **Botanički Vrt** (Botanical Garden) forms the grounds of Villa Angiolina. During the late 19th century, local sailors brought home seeds from East Asia, India, Australia, and the Americas and discovered that many of the plants thrived here. The vegetation is strikingly lush: palms, cacti, bamboo, camellias, and magnolia, plus neatly kept beds of colorful flowers and sweet-scented shrubs. In summer, the open-air theater hosts evening performances. ✉ *Between Maršala Tita and the seafront.* 🎫 *Free.* ☉ *Tues.–Sun. sunrise–sunset.*

Dining and Lodging

$$$–$$$$ ✕ **Bevanda.** Widely known as the most exclusive restaurant in the area, Bevanda is in the fishing village of Volosko, on the main road above the coast. Its upmarket reputation is built upon upscale decor, impeccable service, great food, and a carefully chosen wine list. There's a good assortment of fresh fish, shellfish, and lobster on the menu, plus a select choice of meat dishes such as the excellent beef stroganoff. ✉ *Maršala Tita 62, Volosko,* ☎ *051/701–411. AE, DC, MC, V. Closed mid-June–mid-July.*

$$–$$$ ✕ **Bevandica.** With tables outside overlooking the fishing harbor in Volosko, a pleasant 15-minute walk along the coast from Opatija, Bevandica is easy-going and inexpensive. Favorites are the spaghetti with

either mussels or scampi, to be followed by the mixed fish platter for two and a crisp side salad.⊠ *Supilova obala 12, Volosko,* ☏ *051/701–357. AE, DC, MC, V.*

$$$ ⛱ **Grand Hotel Kvarner-Amalia.** The former summer residence of European royalty, Opatija's oldest hotel first opened its doors to guests in 1884. More suited to sedentary tourists than business travelers, it's a grand neoclassical-style building with peaceful gardens and a terrace overlooking the sea, close to Villa Angelina. The Crystal Ballroom is used for the annual Miss Croatia contest. ⊠ *Park 1 Maja 4, 51410,* ☏ *051/271–233,* ℻ *051/271–202,* ⓌⒺⒷ *www.liburnia.hr. 86 rooms. Restaurant, café, room service, minibars, outdoor pool, indoor saltwater pool, massage, sauna, beach, bar, convention center, parking (fee). AE, DC, MC, V. BP.*

$$$ ⛱ **Millennium.** On the coastal promenade, this luxury hotel is part old and part new, and rooms are furnished accordingly with either Louis XV–style antiques or modern designer pieces. There's a pleasant café terrace overlooking the sea and outstanding beauty, fitness, and business facilities.⊠ *Maršala Tita 109, 51410,* ☏ *051/202–000,* ℻ *051/271–812,* ⓌⒺⒷ *www.ugohoteli.hr. 83 rooms, 11 suites. Restaurant, café, room service, minibars, indoor-outdoor pool, gym, hot tub, massage, sauna, Turkish bath, bar, shops, Internet, business services, meeting rooms, parking (fee). AE, DC, MC, V.*

Rab

❸   *Jablanac is 100 km (62½ mi) south of Rijeka; then take the ferry 1½ nautical mi to Mišnjak, 9 km (6 mi) from the town of Rab.*

Sitting compact on a narrow peninsula, the well-preserved medieval town of Rab (on the island of the same name) is best known for its distinctive skyline of four elegant bell towers. Closed to traffic, the narrow cobbled streets of the old town, which are lined with Romanesque churches and patrician palaces, can be explored in an hour's leisurely stroll. The urban layout is simple: three longitudinal streets run parallel to the waterfront promenade and are linked together by steep passages traversing the hillside. The lower street is Donja ulica, the middle street Srednja ulica, and the upper street Gornji ulica. On the edge of town, the green expanse of Komrčar Park, laid out in the 19th century, offers avenues lined with pine trees for gentle strolling and access down to the sea. While the old town and its immediate surroundings are Rab's chief treasures, the city is also a gateway to the great stretches of beach that rim the towns of Kampor, Suha Punta, Lopar, and neighboring islands. And there's yet one more draw: Rab has a long tradition of nudism. The first Naturist Holiday Camp opened on Rajska Plaža (Paradise Beach) in 1934, and still today there are numerous nudist beaches to be found.

The tallest and most beautiful of Rab's campaniles, the free-standing **Veli Zvonik** (Great Bell Tower) forms part of the former cathedral complex and dominates the southwest side of the peninsula. Built in the 12th century, it stands 85 ft high. A climb to the top offers breathtaking views over the town and sea. ⊠ *Gornja ul.* ⚏ *5 Kn.* ☼ *Daily 10 AM–1 PM and 5 PM–8 PM.*

Dining and Lodging

$$–$$$ ✕ **Zlatni Zlatag.** In Supertarska Draga, 10 km (6½ mi) from Rab Town, Zlatni Zlatag is frequently mentioned as the best restaurant on the island. Nestled in a small bay and backed by Mediterranean woods, the restaurant and its summer terrace offer wonderful views of the sea. *Škampi i školjke Sv Kristofor* (scampi and shells baked in béchamel sauce) is a favorite offering. ⊠ *Supertarska Draga 379, Supertarska Draga,* ☏ *051/775–150. AE, DC, MC, V. Closed Jan.*

$$–$$$ ✕ **Konoba Rab.** Tucked away in a narrow side street between Srednja ulica and Gornja ulica in Rab Town, this *konoba* is warm and inviting, with exposed-stone walls and rustic furniture. Barbecued fish and meat are the house specialties, along with a good choice of pastas and risottos. ✉ *Kneza Branimira 3,* ☎ *051/725–666. AE, DC, MC, V.*

$$ ⛫ **Hotel Imperial.** On edge of old town amid the greenery of Komrčar Park, this peaceful 1930s resort hotel has excellent sports facilities and a beach. Rooms are modern and comfortable, offering either seaside or parkside views. Rates include half-board; there is a reduction if you take only bed and breakfast. ✉ *Palit bb, 51280,* ☎ *051/724–522,* FAX *051/724–126,* WEB *www.imperial.hr. 134 rooms. Restaurant, café, room service, minibars, miniature golf, 3 tennis courts, gym, sauna, beach, bar. AE, DC, MC, V. Closed Jan.–Mar. MAP.*

$$ ⛫ **Hotel International.** In Rab's town center, this building was carefully designed to fit in with the surrounding medieval architecture. Rooms offer views onto either the harbor or the Old Town, and there are good sports facilities. Guests of the International can also use the facilities at the Hotel Imperial, a 10-minute walk. ✉ *obala K. P. Krešimira IV, 51280,* ☎ *051/724–266,* FAX *051/724–206,* WEB *www.imperial.hr. 130 rooms. Restaurant, café, room service, minibars, indoor saltwater pool, gym, hair salon, billiards, bar, convention center, some pets allowed. AE, DC, MC, V. Closed Nov.–Mar. MAP.*

Kvarner Essentials

BOAT AND FERRY TRAVEL

During high season (July–August), Jadrolinija coastal ferries depart from Rijeka most evenings to arrive in Dubrovnik in early afternoon the following day (journey time approximately 20 hrs), stopping at Zadar, Split, Stari Grad (island of Hvar), Korčula, and Sobra (island of Mljet) en route. During the rest of the year, the service is less frequent.

Ferries run from Jablanica on the mainland to Mišnjak (island of Rab), from which it is a 9-km (6-mi) drive to the town of Rab. The island of Krk, which is north of Rab, is joined to the mainland by a road bridge, and during summer it is possible to take a ferry from Baška (island of Krk) to Lopar (island of Rab).

➤ FERRY INFORMATION: **Jadrolinija** (☎ 051/211–444, WEB www. jadrolinija.hr).

BUS TRAVEL

International buses arrive from and depart daily for Italy (Trieste), Slovenia (Ljubljana and Nova Gorica), and Germany (Dortmund, Frankfurt, Munich, and Stuttgart). It is also possible to reach destinations all over mainland Croatia from Rijeka and Opatija. Timetable information is available from the Rijeka Bus Station.

➤ BUS INFORMATION: **Rijeka Bus Station** (✉ Žabica 1, Rijeka, ☎ 051/211–222).

CAR TRAVEL

A car is useful if you plan to leave the Kvarner region and head for Istria (passing through the Učka Tunnel). However, good train and bus services to Zagreb and a comfortable overnight ferry to Dalmatia mean that a vehicle is not essential for moving on to other areas.

➤ CAR RENTAL AGENCIES: **Avis** (✉ Riva 22, Rijeka, ☎ 051/337–917).

EMERGENCIES

➤ AMBULANCE: **Ambulance** (☎ 94).
➤ DOCTORS AND DENTISTS: **Hitno Ponoč** (Casualty; ✉ Krešimirova 42, Rijeka, ☎ 051/658–111).

➤ FIRE: **Fire Emergencies** (☎ 93).
➤ PHARMACIES: **24-hour Pharmacy** (✉ Jadranski trg 1, Rijeka, ☎ 051/
213–101).
➤ POLICE: **Police Emergencies** (☎ 92).

TRAIN TRAVEL

There are five trains daily from Rijeka to Zagreb (journey time is approximately 3½ hours).
➤ TRAIN INFORMATION: **Rijeka Train Station** (✉ Krešimirova 5, Rijeka,
☎ 051/213–333).

VISITOR INFORMATION

➤ CONTACTS: **Opatija Tourist Information** (✉ Vladimira Nazora 3,
Opatija, ☎ 051/271–710, WEB www.opatija-tourism.hr). **Rab Tourist
Information** (✉ Donja ul. 2, Rab, ☎ 051/724–064, WEB www.
tzg-rab.hr). **Rijeka Tourist Information** (✉ Uzarska 14, Rijeka, ☎ 051/
213–145, WEB www.multilink.hr/tz-rijeka).

SPLIT AND CENTRAL DALMATIA

Central Dalmatia is more mountainous, wild, and unexploited than the northern regions of Istria and Kvarner. Tourist facilities may be less sophisticated, but Dalmatia's magnificent coastal towns and rugged islands offer an unrefined Mediterranean charm all their own. The region's capital is the busy port of Split, with its historic center surrounded by the sturdy walls of an imperial Roman palace. Nearby Trogir is a gem of medieval stone architecture, on a tiny island connected to the mainland by a bridge. The island of Brač has a stunning beach. The most exclusive destination in Central Dalmatia is Hvar, with its charming 16th-century Venetian architecture and a labyrinth of winding cobbled streets. To see Dalmatia at its most authentic, take a ferry ride to Vis, Croatia's most distant inhabited island.

Split

Exploring Split

Some 365 km (228 mi) south of Zagreb, Split's ancient core is so spectacular and unusual that it's more than worth the visit. The heart of the city lies within the walls of Emperor Diocletian's 3rd-century Roman palace. Diocletian, born in the nearby Roman settlement of Salona in AD 245, achieved a brilliant career as a soldier in Rome and became emperor at the age of 40. In 295 he ordered this vast palace to be built in his native Dalmatia, and when it was completed, he stepped down from the throne and retired to his beloved homeland. Upon his death, he was laid to rest in an octagonal mausoleum, around which Split's magnificent cathedral was built.

In 615, when Salona was sacked by barbarian tribes, those fortunate enough to escape found refuge within the stout palace walls and divided up the vast imperial apartments into more modest living quarters. Thus, the palace developed into an urban center, and by the 11th century the settlement had expanded beyond the ancient walls.

Under the rule of Venice (1420–1797), Split—as a gateway to the Balkan interior—became one of the Adriatic's main trading ports, and the city's splendid Renaissance palaces bear witness to the affluence of those times. When the Hapsburgs took control during the 19th century, an overland connection to Central Europe was established by the construction of the Split–Zagreb–Vienna railway line.

After World War II, the Tito years saw a period of rapid urban expansion: industrialization accelerated and the suburbs extended to accommodate high-rise apartment blocks. Today the historic center of Split is included on UNESCO's list of World Heritage Sites.

Numbers in the text correspond to numbers in the margin and on the Split map.

A GOOD WALK

Start your tour on the seafront promenade, obala Hrvatskog Narodnog Preporoda (known to locals as the *Riva*), and enter the vast **Dioklecijanova Palača** ① through the Mjedena Vrata (Bronze Gate) to pass through the dark-vaulted chambers of the Podrum (Underground Hall), lined with stalls selling souvenirs. Climb a steep set of steps to arrive on **Peristil** ②. Directly above the steps stands the **Vestibul** ③, formerly the main entrance from Peristil into Diocletian's private living quarters. To the right of the steps, a 3,500-year-old Egyptian sphinx of black granite guards Split's elegant **Katedrala Sveti Dujam** ④. If you have a head for heights, climb the cathedral's bell tower for a stunning panorama over the city. Opposite the cathedral, a narrow side street leads off the Peristil to arrive at the small, classical **Jupiterov Hram** ⑤.

Now return to Peristil and take Poljana Kraljice Jelene to arrive at Srebrena Vrata (Silver Gate). Within the gate there are several stands selling flowers, and beyond it lies the *pazar,* the colorful open-air fruit and vegetable market, which takes place each morning beside the outer walls. Double back on your tracks to return to Peristil; then turn right down Dioklecijanova, then right again into Papaličeva to visit the **Gradski Muzej** ⑥, housed within the beautiful late-Gothic Palača Papalić. Return to Dioklecijanova and turn right to arrive at **Zlatna Vrata** ⑦. Exit the palace and turn left, follow the outer palace wall through a landscaped garden, and then turn left into Bosanska. Follow Bosanska to arrive on the main square, **Narodni Trg** ⑧, lined with several notable buildings, including the 15th-century Venetian-Gothic Vijećnica, the former town hall, with its loggia and three-pointed arches. At the top end of square, the Zeljezna Vrata (Iron Gate), today topped by a 16th-century clock tower, is the fourth entrance into Diocletian's Palace.

As you face the clock, take the street to your right, Marulićeva, to arrive on Trg Brace Radića (Radić Brothers' Square), invariably referred to as Voćni Trg. In the middle of the square stands Meštrović's statue of Marko Marulić (1450–1524), the first poet to write in the Croatian language. Between the square and the seafront stands the 15th-century Hrvojeva Kula (Hrvoje Tower), part of Venice's defense system against the Turks. Leave Trg Brace Radića by Dobrić, which will lead you to the Ribarnica (a covered fish market) on Kraj Sv Marije, which is well worth a look for the stunning variety of fresh fish and seafood on sale each morning. Close by, Marmontova will bring you back to the seafront.

From here, Split's two most important collections, the **Muzej Hrvatskih Arheološki Spomenika** ⑨ and the **Galerija Meštrović** ⑩, lie west of the center. You can reach them either by taking a pleasant 20-minute stroll along the coast or by catching Bus No. 12, which departs from the bus stop opposite Trg Republike (Republic Square) and will drop you more or less in front of the museums. If you prefer the great outdoors, climb the steep steps that wind their way past the stone cottages of Varoš to arrive on **Marjan** ⑪. From this hilltop vantage point you have magnificent views over the city, sea, and islands.

TIMING

The route described here can be walked in about three hours. However, if you wish to stop at all the various sights en route, you should set aside an entire day, covering the city center in the morning and the museums in the afternoon.

Split

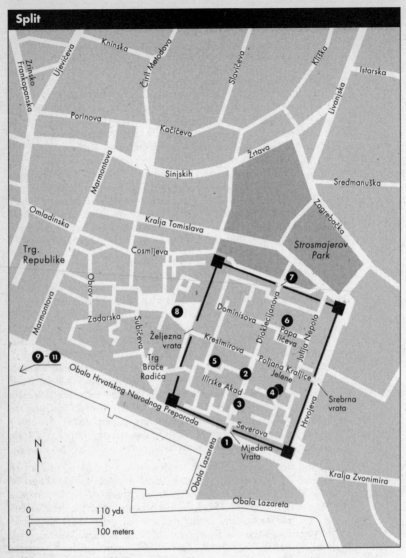

★ ❶ **Dioklecijanova Palača** (Diocletian's Palace). The original palace was a combination of a luxurious villa and a Roman garrison, based on the ground plan of an irregular rectangle. Each of the four walls bore a main gate, the largest and most important being the northern Zlatna Vrata (Golden Gate), opening onto the road to the Roman settlement of Salona. The entrance from the western wall was the Željezna Vrata (Iron Gate), and the entrance through the east wall was the Srebrena Vrata (Silver Gate). The Mjedna Vrata (Bronze Gate) in the south wall faced directly onto the sea, and during Roman times boats would have docked here. ⊠ *obala Hrvatskog Narodnog Preporoda, Grad.*

★ ❿ **Galerija Meštrović** (Meštrović Gallery). A modern villa surrounded by extensive gardens, this building designed by Ivan Meštrovic was his summer residence during the 1920s and '30s. Some 200 of his sculptural works in wood, marble, stone, and bronze are on display, both indoors and out. Entrance to the Galerija Meštrovića is also valid for the nearby **Kaštelet** (⊠ Šetalište Ivana Meštrovića 39), housing a chapel containing a cycle of New Testament bas-relief wood carvings that many consider Meštrović's finest work.⊠ *Šetalište Ivana Meštrovića 46, Meje,* ☎ *021/358–450.* ⊠ *15 Kn.* ☉ *June–Oct., Tues.–Sat. 10–6, Sun. 10–3; Nov.–May, Tues.–Sat. 10–4, Sun. 10–2.*

❻ **Gradski Muzej** (City Museum). Split's city museum is worth a quick look both to witness the collection of medieval weaponry and to see the interior of this splendid 15th-century town house. The dining room, on the first floor, is furnished just as it would have been when the Papalić family owned the house, giving some idea of how the aristocracy of that time lived. ⊠ *Papalićeva 1, Grad,* ☎ *021/341–240.* ⊠ *10 Kn.* ☉ *Nov.–May, Tues.–Fri. 9–4, weekends 10–noon; June–Oct., daily 9–noon and 6–9.*

❺ **Jupiterov Hram** (Jupiter's Temple). This Roman temple was converted into a baptistery during the Middle Ages. The entrance is guarded by the mate (unfortunately damaged) of the black-granite sphinx that stands in front of the cathedral. Inside, beneath the coffered barrel vault and ornamented cornice, the 11th-century baptismal font is adorned with a stone relief showing a medieval Croatian king on his throne. Directly behind it, the bronze statue of St. John the Baptist is the work of Meštrović. You must request a visit to the temple at the cathedral. ⊠ *Kraj Sv Ivana, Grad.* ☉ *By appointment only.*

❹ **Katedrala Sveti Dujam** (Cathedral of St. Dominius). The main body of the cathedral is the 3rd-century octagonal mausoleum designed as a shrine to Emperor Diocletian. During the 7th century, refugees from Salona converted it into an early Christian church, ironically dedicating it to Sv Duje (St. Domnius), after Bishop Domnius of Salona, one of the many Christians martyred during the late emperor's persecution campaign. The cathedral's monumental main door is ornamented with magnificent carved wooden reliefs, the work of Andrija Buvina of Split, portraying 28 scenes from the life of Christ and dated 1214. Inside, the hexagonal Romanesque stone pulpit, with richly carved decoration, is from the 13th century. The high altar, surmounted by a late-Gothic canopy, was executed by Bonino of Milan in 1427. Nearby is the 15th-century canopied Gothic altar of Anastasius by Juraj Dalmatinac. The elegant 200-ft Romanesque-Gothic bell tower was constructed in stages between the 12th and 16th centuries. ⊠ *Peristil, Grad.* ⊠ *Cathedral free, bell tower 5 Kn.* ☉ *Daily 8–noon and 4:30–7.*

⓫ **Marjan** (Marjan Hill). Situated on a hilly peninsula, this much-loved park is planted with pine trees and Mediterranean shrubs and has been a protected nature reserve since 1964. A network of paths crisscrosses the grounds, offering stunning views over the sea and islands. ⊠ *Marjan.*

NEED A
BREAK?
Having reached this point you're undoubtedly in need of refreshment. Take a seat on the **Vidilica** (⊠ Nazorov Prilaz bb, Marjan) café terrace and order a long, cold drink. Then sit back and enjoy the breathtaking view.

❾ **Muzej Hrvatskih Arheološki Spomenika** (Museum of Croatian Archaeological Monuments). This modern building displays early Croatian religious art from the 7th through the 12th centuries. The most interesting exhibits are fine stone carvings decorated with plaitwork design, surprisingly similar to the geometric patterns typical of Celtic art. In the garden you can see several stećci, monolithic stone tombs dating back to the cult of the Bogomils (an anti-imperial sect that developed in the Balkans during the 10th century). ⊠ *Šetalište Ivana Meštrovića, Meje,* ☏ *021/358–420.* ▱ *15 Kn.* ☉ *Tues.–Sat. 9–4, Sun. 9–noon.*

❽ **Narodni Trg** (People's Square). A pedestrianized expanse paved with gleaming white marble, this is contemporary Split's main square. While religious activity has to this day centered on Peristil, Narodni Trg became the focus of civic life during the 14th century. In the 15th century, the Venetians constructed several important public buildings here: the Town Hall (now housing the Ethnographic Museum, presently closed for reconstruction), plus the Rector's Palace and a theater, the latter two sadly demolished by the Hapsburgs in the 19th century. The Austrians, for their part, added a secessionist building at the west end of the square. ⊠ *Grad.*

❷ **Peristil** (Peristyle). From Roman times up to the present day the main public meeting place within the palace walls, this spacious central courtyard is flanked by marble columns topped with Corinthian capitals and richly ornamented cornices linked by arches. There are six columns on both the east and west sides, and four more at the south end, which mark the monumental entrance to the Vestibul. During the Split Summer Festival, Peristil becomes an open-air stage hosting evening opera performances. ⊠ *Grad.*

NEED A
BREAK?
The summer terrace at the **Luxor Café** (⊠ Peristil bb, Grad) makes a perfect place to sit over coffee or a glass of local wine and absorb the 2,000 years of magnificent architecture that surround you.

❸ **Vestibul.** The cupola of this domed space would once have been decorated with marble and mosaics. Today there's only a round hole in the top of the dome, but it produces a stunning effect: the dark interior, the blue sky above, and the tip of the cathedral's bell tower framed in the opening. ⊠ *Peristil, Grad.*

❼ **Zlatna Vrata** (Golden Gate). Formerly the main land entrance into the palace, Zlatna Vrata, on the north side of the palace, is the most monumental of the four gates. Just outside the Zlatna Vrata stands Meštrović's gigantic bronze **statue of Grgur Ninski** (Bishop Gregory of Nin). During the 9th century, the bishop campaigned for the use of the Slav language in the Croatian Church, as opposed to Latin, thus infuriating Rome. This statue was created in 1929 and placed on Peristil to mark the 1,000th anniversary of the Split Synod, then moved here in 1957. Note the big toe on the left foot, which is considered by locals to be a good luck charm and has been worn gold through constant touching. ⊠ *Dioklecijanova, Grad.*

Dining

Split does have some good restaurants, though they're not always easy to find. As in any city of fishermen and sailors, seafood predominates here. In most restaurants, fresh fish is normally prepared over a charcoal fire and served with *blitva sa krumpirom* (Swiss chard and potato with garlic and olive oil). For a cheaper option, bare in mind that the pizza in Split is almost as good as (and sometimes even better than) that in Italy. Last but not least, compliment your meal with a bottle of Dalmatian wine.

$$$–$$$$ ✕ **Restaurant Boban.** Founded in 1973, this highly regarded fish restaurant has a slightly kitschy interior with black and silver chrome furnishings and violet table linens. However, there's a leafy summer terrace and good choice of carefully prepared seafood dishes, barbecued fish and meat, and an excellent wine list. You'll find it just off Spiničićeva, a couple of blocks back from Zenta Bay. ✉ *Hektorovićeva 49, Firule,* ☎ *021/543–300. AE, DC, MC, V.*

$$$–$$$$ ✕ **Šumica.** The first thing you'll notice upon arrival at Šumica, which is in a pine forest overlooking Bačvice Bay, is the number of black BMWs in the parking lot. The atmosphere in the dining room, which tends to be overly formal, is more than compensated for by the fresh sea breezes on the summer terrace. The house specialty is tagliatelli with salmon and scampi. ✉ *Put Firula 6, Bačvice,* ☎ *021/389–895. AE, DC, MC, V.*

$$–$$$ ✕ **Kod Jose.** This typical Dalmatian *konoba* is relaxed and romantic, with exposed stone walls and heavy wooden furniture set off by candlelight. The waiters are wonderfully discreet and the *rižot frutta di mare* (seafood risotto) delicious. You'll find it just outside the palace walls, a five-minute walk from Zlatna Vrata (Golden Gate). ✉ *Sredmanuška 4, Manuš,* ☎ *021/347–397. AE, DC, MC, V.*

$$–$$$ ✕ **Konoba Varoš.** The dining-room walls are hung with seascapes and fishing nets while the waiters wear traditional Dalmatian waistcoats. The place can seem a little dour at lunchtime but mellows when the candles are lit during the evening. The fresh fish and *pržene lignje* (fried squid) are excellent, and there's also a reasonable choice of Croatian meat dishes. It lies a five-minute walk west of the center, at the bottom of Varoš. ✉ *Ban Mladenova 7, Varoš,* ☎ *021/396–138. AE, DC, MC, V.*

$–$$$ ✕ **Adriana.** Overlooking the seafront promenade, Adriana is a perfect spot for people-watching day and night. It can get a little rowdy, with loud music and large groups, but the food is remarkably good, with good grilled meat dishes such as *čevapčići* (kebabs), *pohani sir* (fried cheese), salads, and pizzas. ✉ *obala Hrvatskog Narodnog preporoda 6, Grad,* ☎ *021/344–079. AE, DC, MC, V.*

$–$$$ ✕ **Bilo Idro.** At the entrance to the ACI marina, close to the gardens of Sveti Stipan, Bilo Idro doubles as a restaurant and pizzeria. The cheerful interior is minimalist, with simple furnishings, colorful modern paintings, and fresh flower arrangements, while the summer terrace offers a perfect vantage point for watching yachts sail in and out of port. ✉ *Uvala Baluni 1, Zvončac,* ☎ *021/398–575. AE, DC, MC, V.*

$ ✕ **Pizzeria Galija.** In the city center, close to the fish market, this pizzeria is where locals flock in droves. And it serves the best pizzas in town. The restaurant is bustling and informal, with heavy wooden tables and benches; draft beer and wine are sold by the glass. The owner, Željko Jerkov, is a retired Olympic gold medal–winning basketball player. ✉ *Tončićeva 12, Grad,* ☎ *021/347–932. No credit cards.*

Lodging

Split has often been overlooked as a sightseeing destination and considered a mere transit point to the islands. As a result, it suffers from a shortage of good places to stay. What's more, during the 1990s many hotels were used to house refugees, and some still need to be refurbished. However, several establishments are pleasant, fairly central, and reasonably priced.

$$$ 🏨 **Hotel Park.** Now offering the best accommodation in town, Hotel Park reopened in 2001 after extensive renovation work. The building dates back to 1921 and lies 10 minutes east of the city walls, overlooking Bačvice Bay. The rooms are modern and smartly furnished, while a pleasant terrace with palms offers views over the sea. ⊠ *Hatzeov Perivoj 3, Bačvice, 21000,* ☎ *021/406–400,* FAX *021/406–401,* WEB *www.hotelpark-split.hr. 54 rooms, 3 suites. Restaurant, room service, minibars, aerobics, massage, sauna, bar, laundry service, Internet, meeting rooms. AE, DC, MC, V. BP.*

$$$ 🏨 **Hotel Split.** A 25-minute trek east of the center, Hotel Split is a white modernist building overlooking the sea. The rooms are well equipped with modern furnishings, a comfortable work desk, and decorated in blues and whites. There are excellent sports and business facilities. ⊠ *Put Trstenika 19, Trstenik, 21000,* ☎ *021/303–111,* FAX *021/303–011,* WEB *www.hotelsplit.hr. 135 rooms, 8 suites. Restaurant, room service, cable TV, minibars, pool, gym, massage, sauna, beach, bar, laundry service, business center, meeting rooms, car rental. AE, DC, MC, V. BP.*

$$ 🏨 **Hotel Consul.** Situated in a peaceful residential side street set back from the sea, Hotel Consul became popular with international humanitarian aid workers during the late 1990s. It is now popular with business travelers and vacationers in search of peace and quiet. This is one of the few hotels in town not overlooking the sea. The rooms are modern and comfortable, the management professional, and there's a pretty terrace out front. ⊠ *Trščanska 34, Manuš 21000,* ☎ *021/486–080,* FAX *021/486–079,* WEB *www.hotel-consul.net. 17 rooms, 3 suites. Restaurant, room service, cable TV, minibars. AE, DC, MC, V. BP.*

$$ 🏨 **Hotel Marjan.** Although it was once considered the best hotel in town, today only the lower level of this modernist structure is in use, while the main tower stands derelict. Despite the sad exterior, rooms are comfortable and the staff extremely helpful. You'll find it west of the old town, a five-minute walk from the ACI marina. ⊠ *obala Kneza Branimira 8, Zvončac, 21000,* ☎ *021/399–211,* FAX *020/342–930,* WEB *www.hotel-marjan.com. 106 rooms, 5 suites. Restaurant, café, room service, minibars, bar, convention center, meeting rooms, car rental. AE, DC, MC, V.*

$ 🏨 **Hotel Jadran.** This small 1970s-style hotel lies close to the ACI marina and the gardens of Sveti Stipan, overlooking Zvončac Bay. A pleasant 15-minute walk along the seafront brings you to the city center. ⊠ *Sustipanjska put 23, Zvončac, 21000,* ☎ *021/398–622,* FAX *021/398–586. 20 rooms. Café, pool, bar. AE, DC, MC, V.*

Nightlife and the Arts

Split is much more lively at night during the summer season, when bars stay open late, discos hold open-air parties by the sea, and the Split Summer Festival offers a respectable program of opera and classical music concerts.

Nightlife

Through summer, many bars have extended licenses and stay open until 2 AM. In August, rock musicians from Croatia and the other countries of the former Yugoslavia perform open-air concerts. There's no particular source of information about what's on, but you'll see posters around town if anything special is planned.

Jazz (✉ Poljana Grgur Ninski, Grad, ☎ no phone) is probably the most renowned bar in the Old Town, hidden away on a small piazza, with outdoor tables and an artsy intellectual clientele. Overlooking a small harbor behind the ACI marina, **Jungle** (✉ Uvala Zvončac, Zvončac, ☎ no phone) is a popular summer meeting point thanks to its plentiful outdoor seating, funky music, and late-night hours. One of several hip summer bars overlooking Bačvice Bay, **Tropic Club Equador** (✉ Kupalište Bačvice bb, Bačvice, ☎ 021/323–574) serves excellent cocktails to a background of Caribbean music and fake palms.

At **Metropolis** (✉ Matice Hrvatska 1, Trstenik, ☎ 021/305–110) a program of theme nights and special performances attracts a mixed crowd of all ages. Commercial techno music predominates, with a smattering of rock and pop. Croatian singers perform at **Shakespeare** (✉ Cvjetna 1, Trstenik, ☎ 020/519–492) on weekends, backed up by a selection of commercial techno and disco dance music played by DJs.

The Arts

Kino Bačvice (✉ Put Firula bb, Bačvice) is an open-air summer cinema in the pine woods above Bačvice Bay. Predominantly English-language films are shown in original version with subtitles. Running from mid-July to mid-August, the **Split Summer Festival** (✉ Trg Gaje Bulata 1, Grad, ☎ 021/585–999, WEB www.hnk-split.hr) includes a variety of open-air opera, classical music concerts, and theatrical performances, the highlight being *Aïda* on Peristil.

Outdoor Activities and Sports

Beaches

The best beach is **Uvala Bačvica** (Bačvice Bay), where you will find showers, beach chairs, and umbrellas to rent, plus numerous cafés and bars offering refreshments.

Sailing

The 360-berth **ACI marina** (✉ uvala Baluni bb, Zvončac, ☎ 021/398–548) is southwest of the city center. It stays open all year and is a base for many charter companies organizing sailing on the Adriatic.

Shopping

Dalmatian women—and those from Split in particular—are renowned for their elegant sense of style. Despite a poor local economy, you'll find countless exclusive little boutiques selling ladies' clothes and shoes imported from Italy. However, the city's most memorable shopping venue remains the *pazar*, the colorful open-air market held each morning just outside the palace walls. When looking for gifts, bear in mind that Dalmatia produces some excellent wines, which you can buy either in Split or while visiting the islands.

Croata (✉ Mihovilova Širina 7, Grad, ☎ 021/346–336), overlooking Trg Brace Radića, close to the seafront, specializes in "original Croatian ties" in presentation boxes. **Vinoteka Bouquet** (✉ obala Hrvatskog Narodnog Preporoda 3, Grad, ☎ 021/348–031) is a small shop selling a select choice of Croatian regional wines, plus some truffle products and olive oils.

Split and Central Dalmatia Essentials

AIR TRAVEL

CARRIERS

The national carrier, Croatia Airlines, operates at least three flights daily from Zagreb (45 mins) and one flight a week to Dubrovnik (35 mins). Through summer, it also flies daily from Ljubljana (50 mins) and several times a week from Prague (2 hrs). Also, Adria, ČSA, Lufthansa, and Austrian Airlines all fly to Split. Since Austrian Airlines has an office only in Zagreb, the Croatia Airlines office handles inquiries regarding Austrian Airlines flights to Split during the summer season.

➤ AIRLINES AND CONTACTS: **Adria Airways** (✉ obala kneza Domagoja bb, Gradska Luka, Split, ☎ 021/338–445). **ČSA** (✉ Split Airport, Kaštela, ☎ 021/203–107). **Croatia Airlines** (✉ obala hrvatskog narodnog preporoda 9, Grad, Split, ☎ 021/362–997). **Lufthansa** (✉ obala Lazareta 3, Gradska Luka, Split, ☎ 021/345–183).

AIRPORTS AND TRANSFERS

Split is served by Split Airport (SPU) at Kaštela, 25 km (16 mi) northwest of the city center.

➤ AIRPORT INFORMATION: **Split Airport** (✉ Kaštela, ☎ 021/203–171 general information; 021/203–218 lost and found; WEB www.split-airport.tel.hr).

AIRPORT TRANSFERS

You can take an airport bus to obala Lazereta, near the Split Bus Station. For your return, the airport bus leaves Split 90 minutes before each flight. A one-way ticket costs 30 Kn. Journey time is 40 minutes.

➤ CONTACTS: **Airport bus** (☎ 021/203–305).

BOAT AND FERRY TRAVEL

From June to September, Jadrolinija, SEM, and Adriatica all run regular services to Ancona (Italy), departing 9 PM from Split and arriving in Ancona at 7 AM the following day. The same vessels depart at 9 PM from Ancona to arrive in Split at 7 AM. Journey time is approximately 10 hours either direction. Through winter these services are reduced slightly.

From June to September, the Italian company SNAV runs Croazia Jet, a daily catamaran service between Ancona (Italy) and Split, departing at 5 PM for Split and arriving in Ancona at 9 PM. The same vessel departs at 11 AM from Ancona to arrive in Split at 3 PM. The journey time is four hours either direction.

Ferries to Dubrovnik and Rijeka: during high season (July–Aug.), Jadrolinija coastal ferries depart from Rijeka most evenings to arrive in Split early morning the following day (journey time is approximately 12 hours) and then continue down the coast to Dubrovnik (journey time is approximately 8 hours), stopping at Stari Grad (island of Hvar), Korčula, and Sobra (island of Mljet) en route. During the rest of the year the service is less frequent.

Jadrolinija runs daily ferries to Supetar (island of Brač), Stari Grad (island of Hvar), and Vis from Split.

Jadrolinija runs a daily catamaran to Hvar Town (island of Hvar), which then continues to Vela Luka (island of Korčula). A separate service runs to Bol (island of Brač) and then continues to Jelsa (island of Hvar).

➤ BOAT AND FERRY INFORMATION: **Adriatica** (☎ 021/338–335, WEB www.adriatica.it). **Jadrolinija** (☎ 021/338–333, WEB www.jadrolinija.hr). **SEM** (☎ 021/338–92, WEB www.sem-marina.hr). **SNAV** (☎ 021/343–055, WEB www.snavali.com).

BUS TRAVEL

International buses arrive daily from Italy (Trieste), Slovenia (Ljubljana), and Germany (Munich and Stuttgart). There is a bus once a week from Vienna (Austria). It is possible to reach Split from travel destinations all over mainland Croatia. Timetable information is available from the Split Bus Station.

➤ BUS INFORMATION: **Split Bus Station** (⊠ obala Kneza Domogoja, Split, ☎ 021/338–483).

CAR TRAVEL

While visiting Split and the nearby islands of Brač, Hvar, and Vis, you are certainly better off without a car. However, you may wish to hire a vehicle to drive south if you are moving on to Dubrovnik or if you are driving north to Zagreb, rather than use public transport.

➤ CAR RENTAL AGENCIES: **Avis** (⊠ Hotel Marjan, obala K Branimira, Split, ☎ 021/342–976; ⊠ Split Airport, Kaštela, ☎ 021/895–320). **Budget** (⊠ Hotel Marjan, obala K Branimira, Kaštela, ☎ 021/345–700; Split Airport, Kaštela, ☎ 021/203–151). **Hertz** (⊠ Tomića Stine 9, Split, ☎ 021/360–455; ⊠ Split Airport, Kaštela, ☎ 021/895–230). **Mack** (⊠ Hotel Split, Put Trstenik 19, Split, ☎ 021/303–008, WEB www.mack-concord.hr).

EMERGENCIES

➤ AMBULANCE: **Ambulance** (☎ 94).

➤ DOCTORS AND DENTISTS: **Hitno Ponoč** (Casualty; ⊠ Spinčićeva 1, Split, ☎ 021/556–111).

➤ FIRE: **Fire Emergencies** (☎ 93).

➤ PHARMACIES: **Dobri** (⊠ Gundulićeva 52, Split, ☎ 021/341–190). **Lučac** (⊠ Pupačićeva 4, Split, ☎ 021/533–188).

➤ POLICE: **Police Emergencies** (☎ 92).

TAXIS

In Split, the main taxi rank lies at the end of the *Riva* (obala hrvatskog preporoda) in front of the *pazar* (open-air market).

➤ CONTACTS: **Radio Taxi** (☎ 970).

TOURS

In Split, the Tourist Information Center organizes informative and amusing guided tours of the city.

➤ CONTACTS: **Tourist Information Center** (⊠ Peristil bb, Split, ☎ 021/342–606).

TRAIN TRAVEL

There is one day train and three night trains (with sleeping cars) daily between Split and Zagreb (journey time approximately 8 hrs).

➤ TRAIN INFORMATION: **Split Train Station** (⊠ obala Kneza Domogoja, Split, ☎ 060/333–444).

VISITOR INFORMATION

➤ CONTACTS: **Bol Tourist Information Center** (⊠ Porat bolskih pomoraca bb, Bol, ☎ 021/635–638, WEB www.bol.hr). **Hvar Town Tourist Information Center** (⊠ Trg Sv Stjepana 16, Hvar, ☎ 021/741–059, WEB www.hvar.hr). **Split Tourist Information Center** (⊠ Trg Republike 2, Split, ☎ 021/355–088, WEB www.visitsplit.com). **Trogir Tourist Information Center** (⊠ obala Bana Berislavića 12, Trogir, ☎ 021/881–412). **Vis Tourist Information Center** (⊠ Šetalište Stare Isse 5, Vis, ☎ 021/711–144).

SIDE TRIPS FROM SPLIT

Numbers in the margin correspond to numbers on the Southern Dalmatia map.

Trogir

❶ *27 km (17 mi) west of Split*

On a small island no more than a few city blocks in length, the beautifully preserved medieval town of Trogir is connected to the mainland by one bridge and tied to the outlying island of Čiovo by a second. The settlement dates back to the 3rd century BC when it was colonized by the Greeks, who named it Tragurion. It later flourished as a Roman port. With the fall of the Western Roman Empire, it became part of Byzantium and then followed the shifting allegiances of the Adriatic. In 1420 the Venetians moved in and stayed until 1797.

Today it is a UNESCO World Heritage Site and survives principally from tourism. You can explore the city in about an hour. A labyrinth of narrow, cobbled streets centers on Narodni Trg, the main square, where the most notable buildings are located: the 15th-century loggia and clock tower, the Venetian-Gothic Čipko Palace, and the splendid *katedrala* (cathedral), with its elegant bell tower. The south-facing seafront promenade is lined with cafés, ice cream parlors, and restaurants, and there are also a couple of small hotels that offer a reasonable alternative to accommodations in Split.

★ The remarkable **Katedrala Sveti Lovrijenac** (Cathedral of St. Lawrence), completed in 1250, is a perfect example of the massiveness and power of Romanesque architecture. The most striking detail is the main (west) portal, adorned with superb Romanesque sculpture by the Croatian master Radovan. The great door, flanked by a pair of imperious lions that form pedestals for figures of Adam and Eve, is framed by a fascinating series illustrating the daily life of peasants in a kind of Middle Ages comic strip. In the dimly lit Romanesque interior, the 15th-century chapel of Sveti Ivan Orsini (St. John Orsini) of Trogir features statues of saints and apostles in niches facing the sarcophagus, on which lies the figure of St. John. The bell tower, built in successive stages—the first two stories Gothic, the third Renaissance—offers stunning views across the ancient rooftops. ⊠ *Trg Ivana Pavla II.* 🖾 *Free.* ☉ *Daily 8–noon and 4:30–7.*

Dining and Lodging

$–$$$ ✕🖾 **Hotel Restaurant Fontana.** On the seafront overlooking the Trogir Channel, this old building has been tastefully refurbished to form a small hotel. The same management runs the highly esteemed adjoining restaurant and pizzeria with a large waterside terrace. Fresh fish and seafood top the menu, while pizza makes a cheap alternative. ⊠ *Obrov 1, 21220,* ☎ *021/885–744,* 🖾 *021/885–755. 13 rooms, 1 suite. Restaurant, pizzeria, room service, minibars, bar, meeting room. AE, DC, MC, V. BP.*

Brač

❷ *9 nautical mi south of Split by ferry*

Close at hand and well connected to Split by ferry and catamaran services, the island of Brač can be visited in an easy day trip. With extensive tourist development along the coast and a stark wild interior, the island is best known as a prime windsurfing spot. To get there, either catch an early morning Jadrolinija ferry from Split to Supetar (9

Southern Dalmatia

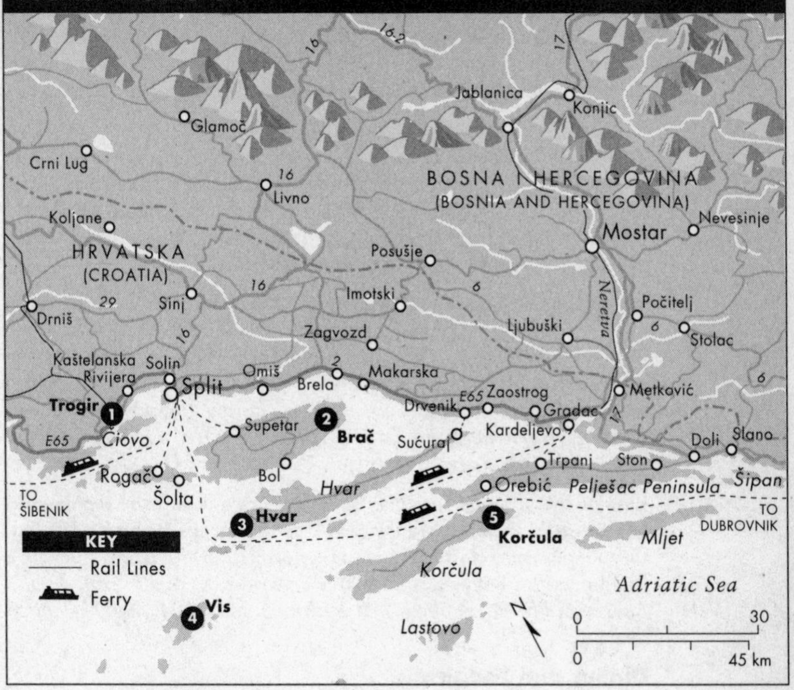

nautical mi) and then take a bus across the island to the south coast or join an organized day trip from Split direct to Bol (24 nautical mi) by catamaran.

★ A spectacular beach, **Zlatni Rt** (Golden Cape), in the south-coast fishing village of Bol, is the main attraction on Brač. A tree-lined coastal promenade leads from the village of Bol to an extraordinary geographical cape composed of tiny pebbles, which juts out ¾ km (⅓ mi) to sea, moving and changing shape slightly from season to season depending on the winds. This is Croatia's prime site for windsurfing and an ideal beach for kids, as the water is shallow and the sea bed easy on their feet. ✉ *Bol, 2 km (1 mi) west of town center.*

Outdoor Activities and Sports

Windsurfing and scuba-diving training are available from **Big Blue** in Bol. The group also hires out equipment to experienced surfers and divers (✉ Podan Glavice 2, Bol, ☎ 021/635–614, WEB www.big-blue-sport.hr).

Hvar

❸ *Hvar Town is 23 nautical mi south of Split by ferry.*

The island of Hvar bills itself as the "sunniest island in the Adriatic." Not only does it have the figures to back up this claim—an annual average of 2,724 hours of sunshine with a maximum of two foggy days a year—but it also makes visitors a sporting proposition, offering them a money-back guarantee if it snows (which has been known to happen).

Hvar is also the name of the capital, near the island's western tip. The little town rises like an amphitheater from its harbor, backed by a hilltop fortress and protected from the open sea by a scattering of small islands known as Pakleni Otoci. Along the palm-lined quay, a string of cafés and restaurants is shaded by colorful awnings and umbrellas. A few steps away, the magnificent main square, Trg Sveti Stjepan, the largest piazza in Dalmatia, is backed by the 16th-century Katedrala Sveti Stjepan (Cathedral of St. Stephen). Other notable sights include the kazalište (Theater) and the Franjevački Samostan (Franciscan Monastery).

To reach Hvar Town, take an early morning Jadrolinija ferry from Split to Stari Grad (23 nautical mi) and then catch a local bus across the island. Through summer, there is also a regular catamaran service direct from Split to Hvar Town (23 nautical mi). If you plan to stay overnight, be sure to book well in advance.

On the upper floor of the Arsenal, the **Kazalište** (Theater) opened in 1612, making it the oldest institution of its kind in Croatia and one of the first in Europe. The Arsenal building, where Venetian ships en route to the Orient once docked for repairs, dates back to the 13th century but was reconstructed after damage during a Turkish invasion in 1571. ⊠ *Trg Sv Stjepana.* 🎟 *10 Kn.* ☉ *May–Oct., daily 9–noon and 7–9; Nov.–Apr., daily 10–noon.*

East of town, along the quay past the Arsenal, lies the **Franjevački Samostan** (Franciscan Monastery). Within its walls, a pretty 15th-century Renaissance cloister leads to the former refectory, now housing a small museum with several notable artworks. ⊠ *obala Ivana Lučića Lavčevića bb,* ☎ *no phone.* 🎟 *10 Kn.* ☉ *May–Oct., daily 10–noon and 5–7.*

Dining and Lodging

$$–$$$$ ★ ✕ **Macondo.** This superb fish restaurant lies hidden away on a narrow, cobbled street between the main square and the fortress—to find it, follow the signs from Trg Sv Stjepana. The dining room is simply furnished with wooden tables, discreet modern art, and a large open fire. The food and service are practically faultless: begin with the delicate scampi pâté, followed by a mixed seafood platter, and round off with a glass of homemade *orahovica* (walnut rakija). ⊠ *Hvar, 1 block north of Trg Sv Stjepana,* ☎ *021/742–850. AE, DC, MC, V. Closed Jan.*

$$–$$$$ ✕ **Hanibal.** The interior of this restaurant overlooking the main square is incongruously hip: exposed stone walls, pine beams, and a catwalk-style entrance. The menu offers traditional Dalmatian dishes with a creative twist. Try the *hvarska gregada* (local fish stew with aromatic herbs and potatoes) or the grilled salmon with dill. ⊠ *Trg Sv Stjepana 12,* ☎ *021/742–760. AE, DC, MC, V.*

$$$ 🏨 **Amfora.** A colossal white, modern structure overlooking its own bay with a pebble beach, the Amfora is backed by pine woods and lies a pleasant 10-minute walk along the coastal path from the center of town. All rooms have balconies, and there are excellent sports and recreation facilities, making this an ideal choice for families on longer stays. ⊠ *Hvar, 21450,* ☎ *021/741–202,* ℻ *021/741–711,* 🌐 *www.suncanihvar.hr. 300 rooms. Restaurant, café, room service, cable TV, minibars, 6 tennis courts, indoor pool, gym, hair salon, massage, sauna, beach, dive shop, windsurfing, boccie, bowling, bar, Internet, convention center. AE, DC, MC, V. Closed Nov.–Mar. BP.*

$$$ 🏨 **Palace.** Commanding a prime site on the edge of the main square and overlooking the harbor, the Palace remains open year-round, offering much lower prices during low season. A former Venetian loggia is incorporated into the hotel and used as an elegant salon. The indoor pool has heated sea water, and the upper-level restaurant terrace affords splendid views out to sea. ⊠ *Trg Sv Stjepana, 21450,* ☎ *021/741–966,* ℻ *021/742–420,* 🌐 *www.suncanihvar.hr. 76 rooms. Restaurant, café, indoor pool, massage, sauna, bar, Internet. AE, DC, MC, V.*

Vis

❹ *34 nautical mi southwest of Split by ferry.*

Closed to foreigners until 1989, the distant island of Vis is relatively wild and unexploited. To get here from Split, you need to take a 2½-hour Jadrolinija ferry ride to arrive in Vis Town. Built around a wide harbor, the town is popular with yachters, who appreciate its rugged nature, unpretentious fish restaurants, and excellent locally produced wine. The pretty fishing village of Komiža is 11 km (7 mi) from Vis Town. From here, you're just a 40-minute boat ride away from the Modra Spilja (Blue Cave), often compared to the Blue Grotto on Italy's Capri.

Through summer, regular organized excursions from both Vis Town and Komiža take visitors into the **Modra Spilja** (Blue Cave) by boat. Hidden away on the small island of Biševo (5 nautical mi southwest of Komiža), the cave is 78 ft long and 39 ft wide. Sunlight enters through the water, reflects off the seabed, and casts the interior in a fantastic shade of blue. If you're lucky, you'll have time for a quick swim. Ask at the tourist information office for details.

Dining and Lodging

$$–$$$$ ✕ **Villa Kaliopa.** With tables set under the trees in the romantic walled
★ garden of a 16th-century villa, dinner at this restaurant in Vis Town is an unforgettable experience. The menu changes daily depending on what fresh fish and shellfish have come in. Your server will bring a platter to the table so you can choose your own fish before it's cooked. ⊠ *V Nazora 32,* ☎ *021/711–755. AE, DC, MC, V. Closed Nov.–Apr.*

$$–$$$ ✕ **Konoba Bako.** Popular with locals and visitors alike, this excellent fish restaurant overlooks a tiny bay in Komiža. Outdoors, tables are set right up to the water's edge, while inside there's a small pool with lobsters and amphoras. The *salata od hobotnice* (octopus salad), *škampi rižot* (scampi risotto), and barbecued fish are all delicious. ⊠ *Gundulićeva 1, Komiža,* ☎ *021/713–008. AE, DC, MC, V.*

$ ⌂ **Hotel Paula.** In Vis Town, east of the ferry quay, this friendly, family-run hotel is hidden away between stone cottages in a quiet, cobbled side street. All the rooms are smartly furnished and modern; downstairs, there's a good fish restaurant with tables on a walled summer terrace. ⊠ *Petra Hektorovića 2, 21480,* ☎ ℻ *021/711–362. 12 rooms. Restaurant, bar. AE, DC, MC, V. Closed Nov.–Mar.*

$ ⌂ **Tamaris.** Overlooking the harbor and seafront promenade in Vis Town, Tamaris occupies a late-19th-century building. The location is perfect, the rooms basic but comfortable, and it stays open all year. ⊠ *Šetalište Apolonija Zanelle 5, 21480,* ☎ ℻ *021/711–350. 27 rooms. Restaurant, bar. AE, DC, MC, V.*

DUBROVNIK AND SOUTHERN DALMATIA

The highlight of southern Dalmatia is undoubtedly the majestic walled city of Dubrovnik, which was once a rich and powerful independent republic. Overlooking the sea and backed by rugged mountains, it's an unforgettable sight and probably Croatia's most photographed city. If you're traveling to Dubrovnik by coastal ferry from either Split or Rijeka, you might choose to stop overnight in Korčula Town, on the island of Korčula, with its fine Gothic and Renaissance stone buildings laying witness to almost 800 years of Venetian rule. In contrast, the island of Mljet offers little in the way of architectural monuments but has preserved its indigenous coniferous forests, which are now contained within Mljet National Park. If you're traveling from central to southern Dalmatia by road, you'll pass through a narrow coastal strip given over to Bosnia, so have your passport at hand for the border checkpoint. The stopover is inconsequential, and you are usually off after a brief passport check. Most Croatian buses have a 20-minute stop here so people can jump off and shop, since many things—notably cigarettes—are much cheaper in Bosnia.

Dubrovnik

Exploring Dubrovnik

Lying 216 km (135 mi) southeast of Split and commanding a splendid location overlooking the Adriatic, Dubrovnik is undoubtedly one of the world's most beautiful fortified cities. Its massive stone ramparts and splendid fortress towers curve around a tiny harbor, enclosing graduated ridges of sun-bleached orange-tile roofs, copper domes, and elegant bell towers.

Early in the 7th century AD, residents of the once Greek and later Roman Epidaurum (now the small town of Cavtat) fled the Avars and Slavs north to build a new settlement on a small rocky island below the slopes of Mt. Srd. Strong walls were built, and as the town grew in importance it was called Laus and then Ragusa. This fortress city had a fleet of the fastest and most seaworthy ships of its time. On the mainland hillside opposite the island, the Slav settlement called Dubrovnik grew up along the fringe of oak forests (called *dubrava*, meaning woodlands). By the 12th century the narrow channel separating the two towns was filled in, and Ragusa and Dubrovnik became one, although the city did not officially take the name Dubrovnik until 1918.

For 450 years—from 1358 to 1808—the city existed as a powerful independent republic, keeping its freedom by paying off would-be aggressors, which included, first, Hungary and later the Ottoman Turks. During the Middle Ages, Ragusa rivaled Venice for sea supremacy, and Ragusan caravans traded goods between Europe and the Middle East by way of Constantinople. By the 16th century, Ragusa had consulates in some 50 foreign ports along with a merchant fleet of 200 ships sailing through the Mediterranean and as far as England, the Netherlands, and eventually the New World.

The chief citizen was the Rector, elected for only a month at a time to share management of the city's business with the Grand Council and the Senate. Most of the military and naval commands were held by members of the nobility, while the increasingly prosperous middle class carried on trade.

In 1667 the city was largely destroyed by several earthquakes and was rebuilt in the baroque style. Dubrovnik lost its independence to Napoleon in 1808, and after his rule ended, control was passed to Austria-Hungary. During the 20th century, as part of Yugoslavia, the city became a popular tourist destination. In 1979 it was listed as a UNESCO World Heritage Site. From November 1991 to May 1992, during the war of independence, the city came under heavy siege. Fortunately, the ancient fortifications stood up well to bombardments, and none of the main monuments were seriously harmed, though the terra-cotta rooftops were devastated. During the 1990s, money poured in from all over world, and today—thanks to careful restoration work—barely any traces of war damage remain.

Numbers in the margins correspond to numbers on the Dubrovnik map.

A GOOD WALK

Start your tour at the main entrance to the old town, **Vrata od Pila** ①. Inside, opening before you is **Placa** ② (also known as Stradun), a street of glistening white paving polished to a high gloss over the centuries. However, before exploring the center, all first-time visitors would benefit by walking a circuit of the **Gradske Zidine** ③, the City Walls, offering unforgettable views over the terra-cotta rooftops and out to sea. To access the walls, climb the steps immediately to your left as you pass through Vrata od Pile. The full circuit (2 km [1 mi]) takes about an hour.

Upon returning to Pile, proceed along Placa, passing the 15th-century Onofrio Fountain, which was once the city's main water supply. On your left stands the **Franjevačka Samostan** ④, worth a quick look in for its pretty cloistered garden. Now continue all the way down Placa, to the far end. On your left stands the 16th-century Palace Sponza, one of the few buildings that survived the 1667 earthquake. To your right lies **Crkva Svetog Vlaha** ⑤, dedicated to the city's patron saint, and behind it the **Knežev Dvor** ⑥, where the citizen holding the one-month term as bishop was obliged to reside.

If you enjoy open-air markets, make a slight detour to Gundulićeva Poljana to see the colorful fruit and vegetable stalls that set up here each morning; then turn left to reach the **Katedrala Velika Gospa** ⑦ on Bunićeva Poljana, noted for its particularly rich treasury. Finish the tour with a visit to the St. John's Fortress complex, lying behind the cathedral, overlooking the sea. Here, time permitting, you can explore the **Pomorski Muzej** ⑧, tracing the history of Dubrovnik on the high seas, and the **Akvarij** ⑨, introducing the underwater life of the Adriatic.

TIMING

Try to make an early morning start on the city walls before temperatures get too hot. Before lunch, time permitting, visit either the Bishop's Palace or the Maritime Museum. During the afternoon you can call at the Franciscan Monastery, saving the Aquarium and the churches for early evening.

SIGHTS TO SEE

❾ Akvarij (Aquarium). This dark, cavernous space houses several small pools and 27 well-lit tanks containing a variety of fish from rays to small sharks and other underwater life such as sponges and sea urchins. Children will the find the octopus, in his glass tank, either very amusing or horribly scary. ✉ *Damjana Jude 2, Stari Grad,* ☎ *020/427–937.* ⌨ *15 Kn.* ◷ *May–Sept., daily 9–8, Oct.–Apr., Mon.–Sat. 9–1.*

❺ Crkva Svetog Vlaha (Church of St. Blaise). This 18th-century Baroque church replaced an earlier one destroyed by fire. Of particular note is the silver statue on the high altar of St. Blaise holding a model of Dubrovnik, which is paraded around town each year on February 3, the Day of St. Blaise. ✉ *Luža, Stari Grad.* ⌨ *Free.* ◷ *Daily 8–noon and 4:30–7.*

NEED A BREAK?
With an ample summer terrace overlooking Luža Square, **Gradska Kavarna** (✉ Placa, Stari Grad) occupies the old Arsenal building and has long rated as Dubrovnik's favorite meeting place for morning coffee or an evening aperitif.

---

❹ Franjevačka Samostan (Franciscan Monastery). The monastery's chief claim to fame is that of founding a pharmacy in 1318, still in existence today and said to be the oldest in Europe. There's also a delightful cloistered garden, framed by Romanesque arcades supported by double columns, each crowned with a set of grotesque figures. In the Treasury a painting shows what Dubrovnik looked like before the disastrous earthquake. ✉ *Placa 2, Stari Grad,* ☎ *020/321–410.* ⌨ *5 Kn.* ◷ *Daily 9–4.*

Dubrovnik

KEY

Ferry

0 — 100 yds

0 — 100 meters

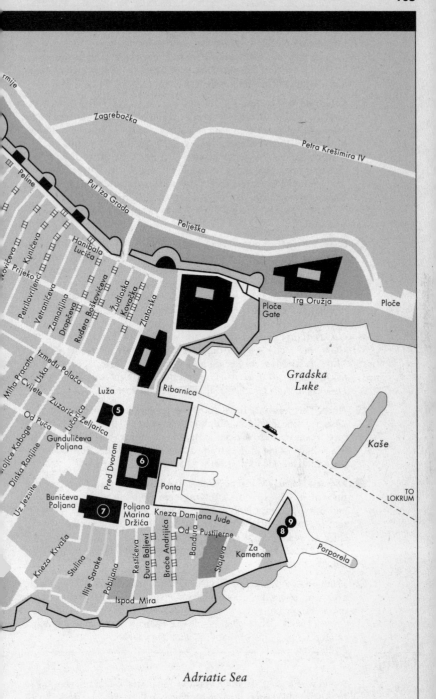

Zagrebačka

Petra Krešimira IV

rmije

Put Iza Grada

Pelline

Peliješka

Hanibala
Lucića

Trg Oružja

Ploče
Gate

Ploče

skovićeva
Prijeko
Kunićeva
Petrilovrijenci
Vetranićeva
Zamanjina
Dropčeva
Rudera Boškovićeva
Žudioska
Kovačka
Zlatarska

Miha Pracata
Uska
Cvijete
Izmedu Polača
Zuzorić
Lučarica
Željarica

Luža
Ribarnica

Gradska
Luke

⑤

Od Puča

Gundulićeva
Poljana

⑥

Pred Dvorom

Kaše

Dinka Ranjine
jojice Kaboge

Ponta

TO
LOKRUM

Uz Jezuite

Bunićeva
Poljana

⑦

Poljana
Marina
Držića

Kneza Damjana Jude

Kneza Krvaša
Stulina
Ilije Sarake
Pobijana

Restićeva
Đura Baljevi
Braće Andrijića
Bandura
Od a Pustijerne
Stajeva
Za
Kamenom

⑨

⑧

Porporela

Ispod Mira

Adriatic Sea

★ ❸ **Gradske Zidine** (City Walls). Most of the original construction took place during the 13th century, though the walls were further reinforced with towers and bastions during the following 400 years. On average they are 80 ft high and up to 10 ft thick on the seaward side, 20 ft on the inland side. ✉ *Placa, Stari Grad.* 🎫 *15 Kn.* 🕒 *May–Sept., daily 9–6:30; Oct.–Apr., daily 9–3.*

❼ **Katedrala Velika Gospa** (Cathedral of Our Lady). The present structure was built in Baroque style after the original was destroyed in the 1667 earthquake. The interior contains a number of notable paintings, including a large polyptych above the main altar depicting the *Assumption of Our Lady,* attributed to Titian. The Treasury displays 138 gold and silver reliquaries, including the skull of St. Blaise in the form of a bejeweled Byzantine crown and also an arm and a leg of the saint, likewise encased in decorated golden plating. ✉ *Bunićeva Poljana, Stari Grad,* ☎ *020/411–715.* 🎫 *Cathedral free, Treasury 5 Kn.* 🕒 *Daily 9–noon and 3–7.*

❻ **Knežev Dvor** (Bishop's Palace). Originally created in the 15th century but reconstructed several times through the following years, this exquisite building with an arcaded loggia and an internal courtyard shows a combination of late-Gothic and early Renaissance styles. On the ground floor there are large rooms where, in the days of the Republic, the Great Council and Senate held their meetings. Over the entrance to the meeting halls a plaque reads: OBLITI PRIVATORUM PUBLICA CURATE (Forget private affairs, and get on with public matters). Upstairs, the rector's living quarters now accommodate the Gradski Muzej (City Museum), containing exhibits that give a picture of life in Dubrovnik from early days until the fall of the Republic. ✉ *Pred Dvorom 3, Stari Grad,* ☎ *020/321–422.* 🎫 *15 Kn.* 🕒 *Daily 9–2.*

❷ **Placa.** This was once the shallow sea channel separating the island of Laus from the mainland. Although it was filled in during the 12th century, it continued to divide the city socially for several centuries, with the nobility living in the area south of Placa and the commoners living on the hillside to the north. ✉ *Stari Grad.*

❽ **Pomorski Muzej** (Maritime Museum). Above the Aquarium, on the first floor of St. John's Fortress, this museum's exhibits illustrate how rich and powerful Dubrovnik became as one of the world's most important sea-faring nations. On display are intricately detailed models of ships as well as engine-room equipment, sailors' uniforms, paintings, and maps. ✉ *Damjana Jude 2, Stari Grad,* ☎ *020/426–465.* 🎫 *15 Kn.* 🕒 *Daily 9–2.*

❶ **Vrata od Pila** (Pile Gate). Built in 1537 and combining a Renaissance arch with a wooden drawbridge on chains, this has always been the main entrance to the city walls. A niche above the portal contains a statue of Sveti Vlah (St. Blaise), the city's patron saint, holding a replica of Dubrovnik in his left hand. ✉ *Pile, Stari Grad.*

Dining

As elsewhere along the coast, seafood dominates restaurant menus. The narrow, cobbled street Prijeko, running parallel to Placa, is packed with touristy restaurants and waiters touting for customers. Less commercial and infinitely more agreeable eateries are scattered throughout the town.

$$$–$$$$ ✕ **Restaurant Atlas Club Nautika.** Probably Dubrovnik's most exclusive restaurant, Nautilus lies close to Pile Gate, just outside the city walls. It occupies the former Nautical Academy building, dating from 1881,

and has two terraces overlooking the sea. A sound choice for business lunches and formal celebrations, the restaurant serves shellfish, lobster, and fresh fish, as well as meat dishes and an excellent wine list. ⊠ *Brsalje 3, Pile,* ☎ *020/442–526. AE, DC, MC, V.*

$$$–$$$$ ✕ **Steak House Domino.** Ideal for those who prefer meat to fish, Domino specializes in steak, though you might sample the oyster starters and round off with a crepe flambé. The dining room is an unusual double-level space with exposed stone walls and a wrought-iron spiral staircase. You'll find it in the Old Town, south of Placa. ⊠ *Od Domina 6, Stari Grad,* ☎ *020/432–832. AE, DC, MC, V.*

$$–$$$$ ✕ **Moby Dick.** One of the many enticing restaurants that line Prijeko, Moby Dick has a sound reputation for good fresh fish and seafood. Dinner at one of the outdoor tables is a memorable event, though you may be rushed if other guests are waiting for a spot. ⊠ *Prijeko 20, Stari Grad,* ☎ *020/321–170. AE, DC, MC, V. Closed Nov.–Mar.*

$$–$$$ ✕ **Marco Polo.** This favorite haunt of actors and musicians during the Summer Festival is in the Old Town, close to Crkva Sv Vlaha. The minuscule dining room is only big enough for four tables, but there's a summer terrace in the courtyard. Choose from a range of excellent seafood dishes, including shellfish, risottos, and fresh fish. ⊠ *Lučarica 6, Stari Grad,* ☎ *020/422–304. AE, DC, MC, V.*

$$–$$$ ✕ **Tovjerna Sesame.** Just outside the city walls, close to Pile Gate, this romantic eatery occupies a candlelit vaulted space with bohemian decor. It's popular with locals, and the menu is adventurous by Dalmatian standards: beef carpaccio with Parmesan, rocket (arugula), and capers; pasta truffle dishes; and a range of beautifully presented, creative salads. It's ideal for a light supper over a good bottle of wine. ⊠ *Dante Alighieria bb, Pile,* ☎ *020/412–910. AE, DC, MC, V.*

$–$$ ✕ **Kamenica.** This restaurant overlooks the morning market in the Old ★ Town and remains popular for its fresh oysters and generous platters of *girice* (small fried fish) and *pržene ligne* (fried squid). It's cheap and cheerful, and if you don't like seafood, you can always get a cheese omelet. ⊠ *Gundulićeva Poljana 8, Stari Grad,* ☎ *no phone. No credit cards. No dinner Nov.–Mar.*

$ ✕ **Mea Culpa.** Within the city walls and open until midnight year-round, Mea Culpa is said to make the best pizza in town. The dining room is a bit cramped, and you may find the music unreasonably loud, but from spring to autumn there are large wooden tables outside on the cobbled street. ⊠ *Za Rokom 3, Stari Grad,* ☎ *020/424–819. No credit cards.*

Lodging

There are no hotels within the city walls. The more exclusive places line the coastal road east of the center, offering stunning views of the Old Town and the sea, while package hotels with cheaper rooms can be found on Lapad peninsula, 3 km (2 mi) west of the center.

$$$$ 🏨 **Hotel Excelsior.** On the coastal road east of the center, this prestigious modern hotel offers well-furnished rooms with balconies overlooking the sea and Old Town. It's slightly lacking in charm, but there are excellent sports and business facilities. ⊠ *Put Frane Supila 12, Ploče 20000,* ☎ *020/414–222,* FAX *020/414–413,* WEB *www.hotel-excelsior.hr. 154 rooms, 18 suites. Restaurant, café, room service, cable TV, in-room fax, some in-room hot tubs, minibars, indoor pool, gym, massage, sauna, bar, Internet, convention center, meeting rooms. AE, DC, MC, V. BP.*

$$$$ 🏨 **Villa Orsula.** Occupying a villa built in 1936, this is now the most ★ exclusive hotel in town. Beautifully furnished rooms offer magnificent views over the Old Town, while a lovely terraced garden leads down to a private beach. Guests have access to recreation facilities at the much larger, neighboring Hotel Argentina, which is under the same management. ⊠ *Put Frana Supila 14, Ploče 20000,* ☎ *020/440–555,* 𝔽𝔸𝕏 *020/423–465,* 𝕎𝔼𝔹 *www.hoteli-argentina.hr. 12 rooms, 3 suites. Restaurant, room service, minibars, tennis court, pool, massage, sauna, beach, bar. AE, DC, MC, V. BP.*

$$$$ 🏨 **Villa Dubrovnik.** A 20-minute walk east of the center, this white modernist structure is built into the rocks, with a series of terraces and a garden coming down to a hideaway cove with a small beach. The rooms are light and airy, and there's a complimentary boat service to and from the Old Town. Airport transfer by private car is available on request. ⊠ *V Bukovaca 6, Ploče 20000,* ☎ *020/422–933,* 𝔽𝔸𝕏 *020/423–465,* 𝕎𝔼𝔹 *www.villa-dubrovnik.hr. 40 rooms. Restaurant, café, room service, cable TV, minibars, beach. AE, DC, MC, V. Closed Nov.–Mar. BP.*

$$–$$$ 🏨 **Grand Hotel Park.** This modern hotel in Lapad is surrounded by a green, leafy park and is close to the sea. Rooms are simple, modern, and comfortable with views of either the sea or gardens; 71 rooms in an annex are more basic. The restaurant offers live music on an open-air terrace through summer, and there's a good range of sports and business facilities. Rates include half-board. ⊠ *Šetalište Kralja Zvonimira 39, Lapad 20000,* ☎ *020/434–444,* 𝔽𝔸𝕏 *020/437–433,* 𝕎𝔼𝔹 *www.grandhotel-park.hr. 156 rooms, 71 annex rooms, 6 suites. Restaurant, café, room service, cable TV, minibars, indoor pool, massage, sauna, bar, convention center, meeting rooms. AE, DC, MC, V. MAP.*

$$–$$$ 🏨 **Hotel Lapad.** Occupying a 19th-century building with a garden and an outdoor pool, Hotel Lapad overlooks Gruž harbor. A boat service to nearby beaches is at guests' disposal. It stays open all year and has good discounts through low season. ⊠ *Lapadska obala 37, Lapad 20000,* ☎ *020/432–922,* 𝔽𝔸𝕏 *020/417–230,* 𝕎𝔼𝔹 *www.hotel-lapad.hr. 193 rooms. Restaurant, café, room service, cable TV in some rooms, minibars, pool, hair salon, bar. AE, DC, MC, V. BP.*

Nightlife and the Arts

Sleepy through winter, Dubrovnik wakes up with a vengeance come summer. Most nightlife takes place under the stars, as bars set up outdoor seating, discos take place by the sea, and even the cinema is open-air. The world-renowned Dubrovnik Summer Festival offers quality theatrical performances and classical music concerts.

An after-dinner drink at an outdoor table in the Old Town makes a romantic way to round of the evening. Those in search of more lively pursuits should visit Lapad peninsula, where a number of popular open-air discos set up through summer.

BARS

Beebap (⊠ Kneza Damjana Jude bb, Stari Grad, ☎ no phone), open daily until 2 AM (and even later in summer) with occasional live concerts, is one of the few bars within the city walls to stay open after midnight all year-round. **Hard Jazz Cafe Troubadour** (⊠ Bunićeva Poljana, Stari Grad, ☎ no phone) is the place to see and be seen. All summer, this small bar has tables outside and hosts occasional live concerts.

DISCOS

Divinae Folie (⊠ Put V Lisinskog, Lapad, ☎ 020/435–677) is an open-air, Italian-run disco, open May–September, where commercial techno predominates.

THE ARTS

Dubrovnik's cultural highlight is the annual **Dubrovnik Summer Festival** (⊠ Poljana P Miličevića 1, Stari Grad, ☎ 020/323–400, 𝕎𝔼𝔹 www.dubrovnik-festival.hr), which runs from early July to late August.

The world-renowned festival includes a variety of open-air classical concerts and theatrical performances, notably Shakespeare's *Hamlet*, at various venues within the city walls. **Kino Slavica** (⊠ Dr. A. Starčevića 42, Pile) is an open-air summer cinema in a walled garden between the Old Town and Lapad. Predominantly English-language films are shown in their original versions with subtitles.

Outdoor Activities and Sports

Beaches

The best beaches lie on the tiny island of **Lokrum,** a short distance south of the Old Town. Through high season boats leave regularly from the Arsenal, ferrying visitors back and forward from morning to early evening.

Sailing

The 450-berth **ACI marina** (⊠ Mokošica, ☎ 020/455–020) is 2 nautical mi from Gruž harbor and 6 km (3½ mi) from the city walls. The marina is open all year, and a number of charter companies are based there.

Shopping

Despite its role as an important tourist destination, Dubrovnik offers little in the way of shopping or souvenir hunting. If you're in search of gifts, your best bet is a bottle of good Dalmatian wine or *rakija*. **Croata** (⊠ Put Frane Supila 12, Ploče, ☎ 020/353–279), a small boutique in the Hotel Excelsior, specializes in "original Croatian ties" in presentation boxes. **Dubrovačka Kuća** (⊠ Svetog Dominika bb, Stari Grad, ☎ 020/322–092), a tastefully decorated wine shop, stocks a fine selection of regional Croatian wines, *rakija*, olive oil, and truffle products; it's close to Ploče Gate.

Dubrovnik and Southern Dalmatia Essentials

AIR TRAVEL

The national carrier, Croatia Airlines, operates at least three flights daily from Zagreb (50 mins) and one flight a week from Split (35 mins). Adria, Lufthansa, ČSA, and Austrian Airlines also have regularly scheduled service to Dubrovnik (*see* ☞ Zagreb Essentials *for* contact information). Since Austrian Airlines has no office in Dubrovnik, the Croatia Airlines office deals with inquiries.
➤ AIRLINES AND CONTACTS: **Croatia Airways** (⊠ Brsalje 9, Pile, Dubrovnik, ☎ 020/413–776).

AIRPORTS AND TRANSFERS

Dubrovnik is served by Dubrovnik Airport (DBV) at Čilipi, 18 km (11 mi) southeast of the city.
➤ AIRPORT INFORMATION: **Dubrovnik Airport** (☎ 020/773–377 general information; 020/773– 328 lost and found; ᴡᴇʙ www. airport-dubrovnik.hr).

AIRPORT TRANSFERS
The airport bus leaves the Dubrovnik Bus Station 90 minutes before each flight and meets all incoming flights. A one-way ticket costs 25 Kn. Journey time is approximately 20 minutes.
➤ CONTACTS: **Airport bus** (☎ 020/773–232). **Dubrovnik Bus Station** (⊠ Put Republike 19, Pile, Dubrovnik, ☎ 020/357–088).

BOAT AND FERRY TRAVEL

From June to September, Jadrolinija run a twice-weekly ferry to and from Bari (Italy). Ferries depart from Bari late in the evening, arriving in Dubrovnik early the next morning, with a similar schedule from Dubrovnik to Bari (journey time approximately 9 hours either direction). After September, the service is reduced to one ferry a week.

During high season (July–August), Jadrolinija coastal ferries depart Rijeka most evenings, arriving in Dubrovnik early the following afternoon. From Dubrovnik, the ferries depart mid-morning to arrive in Rijeka early the following morning (journey time approximately 20 hours in either direction). Coming and going, these ferries stop at Sobra (island of Mljet), Korčula, Stari Grad (island of Hvar), Split, and Zadar. During the rest of the year the service is less frequent.

Jadrolinija run daily ferries to Sobra (island of Mljet). Take the Dubrovnik–Rijeka coastal ferry for Korčula.
➤ BOAT AND FERRY INFORMATION: **Jadrolinija** (☎ 020/418–000, WEB www.jadrolinija.hr).

BUS TRAVEL

There is daily bus service between Dubrovnik and Trieste (Italy) and thrice-weekly service to and from Frankfurt (Germany). There are regular bus routes between Dubrovnik and destinations all over mainland Croatia. Timetable information is available from Dubrovnik Bus Station.
➤ BUS INFORMATION: **Dubrovnik Bus Station** (✉ Put Republike 19, Pile, Dubrovnik, ☎ 020/357–088).

CAR TRAVEL

While visiting Dubrovnik and the nearby islands of Mljet and Korčula, you are certainly better off without a car. However, as the city is not linked to the rest of Croatia by train, you may wish to rent a car if you are driving to or from Split or Zagreb, rather than taking the bus.
➤ CAR RENTAL AGENCIES: **Avis** (✉ V Nazora 9, Pile, Dubrovnik, ☎ 020/422– 043). **Budget** (✉ obala Stjepana Radića 20, Gruž, Dubrovnik, ☎ 020/418–997; ✉ Dubrovnik Airport, Čilipi, ☎ 020/773–290). **Hertz** (✉ F Supila 5, Ploče, ☎ 020/425–000; ✉ Dubrovnik Airport, Čilipi, ☎ 020/771–568). **Mack** (✉ F Supila 3, Ploče, Dubrovnik, ☎ 020/423–747, WEB www.mack-concord.hr).

EMERGENCIES

➤ AMBULANCE: **Ambulance** (☎ 94).
➤ DOCTORS AND DENTISTS: **Hitno Ponoč** (Casualty; ✉ Roka Mišetića bb, Lapad, Dubrovnik,. ☎ 020/431–777).
➤ FIRE: **Fire Emergencies** (☎ 93).
➤ PHARMACIES: **Gruž** (✉ Gruška obala, Gruž, Dubrovnik, ☎ 020/418–900). **Kod Zvonika** (✉ Placa, Stari Grad, Dubrovnik, ☎ 020/428–656).
➤ POLICE: **Police Emergencies** (☎ 92).

TAXIS

In Dubrovnik, there are taxi ranks just outside the city walls at Pile Gate and Ploče Gate, and in front of Gruž harbor.
➤ CONTACTS: **Taxi Station Gruž** (☎ 020/418–112). **Taxi Station Pile** (☎ 020/424–343). **Taxi Station Ploče** (☎ 020/423–164).

TOURS

The Dubrovnik Tourist Office organizes informative and amusing guided tours of the city.
➤ CONTACTS: **Dubrovnik Tourist Office** (✉ ul. Cvijete Zuzorić 1, Stari Grad, Dubrovnik, ☎ 020/426–304).

VISITOR INFORMATION

➤ CONTACTS: **Dubrovnik Tourist Office** (✉ ul. Cvijete Zuzorić 1, Stari Grad, Dubrovnik, ☎ 020/426–304). **Korčula Tourist Office** (✉ obala

Dr Franje Tudjmana bb, Korčula, ☎ 020/715–701). **Mljet Tourist Office** (✉ Polače, ☎ 020/744–086).

SIDE TRIP FROM DUBROVNIK

The number in the margin corresponds to numbers on the Southern Dalmatia map.

Korčula

⑤ *Korčula island is 49 nautical mi northwest of Dubrovnik and 57 nautical mi southeast of Split by ferry.*

At first view, the town of Korčula seems like a much smaller version of Dubrovnik: the same high walls, the circular corner fortresses, and the church tower projecting from within an expanse of red roofs. The main difference lies in the town plan, as narrow side streets run off the main thoroughfare at odd angles to form a herring-bone pattern, preventing cold winter winds from whistling unimpeded through town. The center is small and compact and can be explored in an hour.

For eight centuries Korčula was under Venetian rule, and it shows. Inside the massive gates is a treasure trove of Gothic and Renaissance palaces and courtyards furnished with statuary, as well as a splendid 14th-century **cathedral** built from a wheat-colored stone that turns pale gold in sunlight, amber at sunset. Korčula claims to have been the birthplace of the explorer Marco Polo (1254–1324). Many historians agree that he may have been born here, since the Venetians recruited many sea captains from Dalmatia. However, **Kuća Marca Pola** (Marco Polo House), in the center of town, where he is said to have been born, was constructed hundreds of years after his death. Far more authentic is the Moreška, a colorful sword dance originally performed annually on July 27 but now put on each Thursday evening from May to September just outside the city walls, next to the Land Gate. This traditional war dance commemorates a great battle between the King of the Moors and the Sultan of Turkey for the possession of a beautiful princess. You can reach Korčula by ferry from either Dubrovnik or Split, but Dubrovnik is closer.

Dining and Lodging

$$–$$$$ ✕ **Adio Mare.** A long-standing favorite with locals and visitors alike,
★   Adio Mare occupies a Gothic-Renaissance building in the Old Town close to Kuća Marca Pola. There's a high-ceiling dining room and an open-plan kitchen so you can watch the cooks while they work. Fresh fish and seafood predominate, and the local wine, *pošip,* is excellent. ✉ *Svetog Roka,* ☎ *020/711–253. No credit cards. Closed Oct.–Apr.*

$$ 🏨 **Hotel Korčula.** Built in 1871 under Austria-Hungary, the building was converted to become the island's first hotel in 1912. Exuding old-fashioned charm, it offers discreet service and a delightful seafront café terrace, ideal for watching the sunset over the water. It's the only hotel in the old town; all the others are a short distance east of the center. ✉ *obala Dr Franje Tudmana bb, 20260,* ☎ 𝖥𝖠𝖷 *020/711–078. 20 rooms. Restaurant, café, room service. AE, DC, MC, V. BP.*

CROATIA A TO Z

AIR TRAVEL

CARRIERS

There are no direct air connections between the United States and Croatia, though some U.S.-based airlines offer codeshare flights through their European travel partners. Travelers from the U.S. must fly into a major

European hub such as Amsterdam, Brussels, London, Frankfurt, Prague, Vienna, or Warsaw and then transfer to a flight to Zagreb, Split, or Dubrovnik. Connections are on Croatia Airlines or another European-based carrier. For information on flying into a specific city, *see* the A to Z section for that city.

FLYING TIMES
Flying time from London to Zagreb is 2 hours, 30 minutes; from Prague to Zagreb it is 1 hour, 30 minutes; and from Warsaw it is 1 hour, 40 minutes.

AIRPORTS
Most international flights arrive at Zagreb (ZAG); however, there are also many connecting flights from various European airports to Split (SPU) and Dubrovnik (DBV). For more information on specific airports as well as airport transfers, *see* the A to Z and Essentials sections for those cities.

➤ AIRPORT INFORMATION: **Dubrovnik Airport** (☎ 020/773–377, WEB www.airport-dubrovnik.hr). **Split Airport** (☎ 021/203–171, WEB www.split-airport.tel.hr). **Zagreb Airport** (☎ 01/626–5222, WEB www.tel.hr/zagreb-airport).

BOAT AND FERRY TRAVEL
Several companies run ferries from Italy to Croatia. The most popular route, which is offered by all ferry services, is Ancona to Split. Jadrolinija also runs services from Bari to Dubrovnik and from Ancona to Zadar. From June to September, SNAV runs a daily high-speed catamaran service between Ancona and Split. Jadrolinija and SEM are based in Rijeka and Split, respectively. Adriatica is based in Venice, and SNAV is based in Ancona.

➤ BOAT AND FERRY COMPANIES: **Adriatica** (☎ 39–041/781–861 in Venice, Italy, WEB www.adriatica.it). **Jadrolinija** (☎ 051/666–111, ☎ www.jadrolinija.hr). **SEM** (☎ 021/338–292, WEB www.sem-marina.hr). **SNAV** (☎ 39–071/207–6116 in Ancona, Italy, WEB www.snavali.com).

BUS TRAVEL
There are regular international buses connecting Croatia with Slovenia, Hungary, Italy, Austria, France, Germany, the Slovak Republic, Serbia and Montenegro, and Bosnia and Herzegovina. For information on connections to a specific destination within Croatia, *see* the A to Z or Essential section for that city or region.

BUSINESS HOURS
BANKS
In all the main cities banks are open weekdays 7 AM–7 PM without breaks and on Saturday 7 AM–11 AM. In smaller towns, banks have shorter hours and are often closed during lunchtime.

POST OFFICES
In all the main cities, post offices are open weekdays 7 AM–7 PM without breaks, and on Saturday 7 AM–noon. In smaller towns, post offices are open shorter hours, sometimes only in the morning. During the high tourist season (June–September), post offices are generally open until 9 PM, including Saturday.

SHOPS
In Zagreb, shops and department stores are open weekdays 8 AM–8 PM without breaks, and on Saturday 8 AM–1 PM. Along the coast, most shops are open weekdays 8 AM–1 PM and 5–8 PM, and Saturday 8 AM–1 PM. On the islands hours vary greatly from place to place, but usually at least one general store will be open Monday–Saturday for essentials.

CAR RENTAL

The major agencies have offices in Zagreb, Pula, Rijeka, Split, and Dubrovnik. *See* the individual A to Z and Essentials sections for information on car-rental agencies in specific cities.

CAR TRAVEL

Having a car certainly gives you greater mobility in rural areas on the mainland but causes endless complications if you plan to go island-hopping. In high season, cars wait for hours to board ferries; there is no reservation system, so it's a matter of first-come, first-served. In addition, parking in coastal resorts is very restricted. There are tolls on a number of highways and for passage through the Učka Tunnel between Rijeka and Istria.

GASOLINE

Gas stations are open daily 7 AM–7 PM; from June–September, many stations are open until 10 PM. In the bigger cities and on main international roads some stations offer 24-hour service. All pumps sell Eurosuper 95, Super 98, Normal, and Eurodiesel.

PARKING

The historic centers of walled medieval towns along the coast (Split, Trogir, Hvar, Korčula, and Dubrovnik) are completely closed to traffic, putting heavy pressure on the number of parking spaces outside the fortifications.

ROAD CONDITIONS

The coastal route from Rijeka to Dubrovnik is scenic but tiring and can be notoriously slippery when wet. During winter, driving through the inland regions of Gorski Kotar and Lika is occasionally made hazardous by heavy snow. It's advisable not to take a car to the islands, but if you do decide to drive, remember that the roads are narrow, twisty, and poorly maintained.

RULES OF THE ROAD

Croatians drive on the right and follow rules similar to those in other European countries. Speed limits are 50 kph (30 mph) in urban areas, 80 kph (50 mph) on main roads, and 130 kph (80 mph) on motorways. Seatbelts are compulsory. The permitted blood alcohol limit is 0.5%; drunken driving is punishable and can lead to severe fines.

CUSTOMS AND DUTIES

Duty-free allowances for those entering the country are 200 cigarettes, 1 liter of spirits, and 2 liters of wine.

EMBASSIES AND CONSULATES

All the main foreign embassies are found in Zagreb; the British also have consulates in Split and Dubrovnik.

➤ CONTACTS: **Australian Embassy** (✉ Nova Ves 11, Zagreb, ☏ 01/489–1200). **Canadian Embassy** (✉ Prilaz Gjure Deželića 4, Zagreb, ☏ 01/488–1200). **U.K. Embassy** (✉ Vlaška 121, Zagreb, ☏ 01/455–5310; U.K. Consulate in Dubrovnik, ✉ Petilovrijenci 2, Dubrovnik, ☏ 020/311–466; U.K. Consulate in Split, ✉ obala hrvatskog narodnog preporoda 10, Split, ☏ 021/341–464). **U.S. Embassy** (✉ Hebrangova 2, Zagreb, ☏ 01/661–2200).

EMERGENCIES

There are nationwide numbers to call to summon an ambulance, the fire brigade, and the police.

➤ AMBULANCE: **Ambulance** (☏ 94).
➤ FIRE: **Fire Emergencies** (☏ 93).
➤ POLICE: **Police Emergencies** (☏ 92).

HEALTH

Water is safe for drinking throughout the country. EU countries have reciprocal health-care agreements with Croatia, entitling those nationals to medical consultation for a basic minimum fee. Citizens from outside the EU have to pay in accordance with listed prices. Most doctors speak some English.

LANGUAGE

The country's official language is Croatian, a Slavic language that uses the Latin alphabet. In Istria signs are posted in both Croatian and Italian, and many towns and villages have two names (one Croatian, one Italian), which can be confusing. Throughout the country, English is widely spoken by people working in tourism, though German and Italian are probably more widely spoken.

MAIL AND SHIPPING

Air-mail letters and postcards take about five days to reach other European countries and two weeks to get to Australia, Canada, and the United States. Internet cafés are popping up all over the place and can even be found in small towns on the islands. To send a post card costs 3.5 Kn to Europe, 5 Kn to the United States. A letter costs 5 Kn to Europe, 6.5 Kn to the United States.

MONEY MATTERS

ATMS

ATMs are now found throughout the country, even on the islands.

CREDIT CARDS

Major credit cards are accepted in most shops, hotels, and restaurants.

CURRENCY

The Croatian currency is called the kuna (Kn), which is made up of 100 lipa. The kuna is not yet fully convertible, so you cannot buy the currency outside of Croatia or exchange it once outside the country.

CURRENCY EXCHANGE

You can exchange money and traveler's checks in a *banka* (bank) or *mjenjačnica* (exchange office). Rates for changing currency and traveler's checks are usually about the same.

NATIONAL HOLIDAYS

January 1 (New Year's Day); January 6 (Epiphany); Easter Sunday and Monday; May 1 (May Day); May 30 (National Day); June 22 (Antifascist Day); August 5 (National Thanksgiving Day); August 15 (Assumption), November 1 (All Saints' Day), December 25 and 26 (Christmas).

PASSPORTS AND VISAS

Australian, Canadian, U.S., and U.K. citizens do not need visas to enter the country if they plan to stay for 90 days or less.

SAFETY

Croatia is relatively safe by Western standards, and there are no particular local scams that visitors should be aware of. Violent crime is rare. Be on guard for pickpockets in crowded markets, and don't wander alone down dark streets at night.

TAXES AND SERVICE CHARGES

Foreigners who spend over 500 Kn in one go can reclaim *PDV* (tax) return upon leaving the country. To do this, you need to present the receipts and the goods bought at *carina* (customs) at the airport, ferry port, or border crossing on your way out of the country.

TELEPHONES

You can make calls from the *pošta* (post office), where you enter a kiosk and pay when you have finished, or from a public telephone booth on the street, where magnetic phone cards are necessary.

COUNTRY CODE

The country code for Croatia is 385. When dialing from outside the country, drop the initial "0" from the area code.

INTERNATIONAL CALLS

To make an international call, dial "00," then the appropriate country code (Australia 61; Canada 1; U.S. 1; and U.K. 44).
➤ CONTACTS: **International Directory Assistance** (☎ 902).

LOCAL CALLS

To make a local call, dial the area code (if you are not already in that area) followed by the number you wish to reach.
➤ CONTACTS: **Local Directory Assistance** (☎ 988).

TIPPING

When eating out, if you have enjoyed your meal and are satisfied with the service, it is customary to leave a 10% tip. It is not usual to tip in cafés or bars. Maids and taxi drivers are not usually tipped. Tour guides do receive a tip, especially if they are particularly good.

TRAIN TRAVEL

Zagreb is connected to Rijeka and Split by rail, but there is no line south of Split to Dubrovnik. International services run from Zagreb to the European cities of Ljubljana, Budapest, Belgrade, Vienna, Munich, Berlin, and Venice.
➤ TRAIN INFORMATION: **International Train Information** (☎ 01/481–1892).

RAIL PASSES

The "Zone D" Interail pass is valid for Croatia, but Eurail is not.

VISITOR INFORMATION

See also the A to Z and Essentials sections for specific cities.
➤ BEFORE YOU LEAVE: **Croatian Tourist Board** (✉ 350 5th St., Suite 4003, New York, 10118, ☎ 212/279–8672; ✉ 2 The Lanchesters, 162–164 Fulham Palace Rd., London W6 9ER, ☎ 44/208–563–7979).
➤ IN CROATIA: **Croatian Tourist Board** (✉ Iblerov Trg 10/4, Zagreb, 10000, ☎ 01/455–6455, WEB www.croatia.hr).

4 · THE CZECH REPUBLIC

Since the fall of the Communist regime, the Czech Republic has become a thriving democracy that offers visitors some of Central Europe's most alluring attractions. The "hundred-spired" capital city of Prague—one of the world's best-preserved architectural cityscapes—offers world-class cultural performances and increasingly distinctive dining and shopping. Beyond Prague, medieval castles perch quietly near lost-in-time baroque and Renaissance villages. Pine forests and gentle green mountains beckon outdoor enthusiasts with a multitude of pleasures.

By Mark Baker

Updated by
Raymond
Johnston

A VICTIM OF ENFORCED OBSCURITY throughout much of the 20th century, the Czech Republic, encompassing the provinces of Bohemia and Moravia, is once again in the spotlight. In 1989, in a world where revolution was synonymous with violence and in a country where truth was quashed by the tanks of Eastern-bloc socialism, Václav Havel's sonorous voice proclaimed the victory of the "Velvet Revolution" to enthusiastic crowds on Wenceslas Square and preached the value of "living in truth." Recording the dramatic events of the time, television cameras panned across Prague's glorious skyline and fired the world's imagination with the image of political renewal superimposed on somber Gothic and voluptuous baroque.

Travelers have rediscovered the country, and Bohemians and Moravians have rediscovered the world. The stagnant "normalization" of the last two decades under Communist rule gave way in the 1990s to a new dynamism and international outlook. You now encounter enthusiasm and such conveniences as English-language newspapers and attentive service. Not that the Czech Republic has joined the ranks of "Western" countries—it remains the poor relation compared with its Central European neighbors Germany and Austria, with the average Czech worker's wage standing at around $400 a month. This makes the signs of modernity even more remarkable. Nowadays there are cybercafés and cell phones to help you stay in touch with the outer world. It's all happening fastest in Prague, but the pace of change is accelerating everywhere. In the small towns and villages where so many Czechs still live, however, you may struggle with a creeping sensation of melancholy and neglect—or, putting a positive spin on it, you may enjoy the slower, more relaxed tempo.

The drab remnants of socialist reality are still omnipresent on the back roads of Bohemia and Moravia. But many of the changes made by the Communists were superficial—adding ugliness but leaving the society's core more or less intact. The colors are less jarring, not designed to attract the moneyed eye; the fittings are as they always were, not adapted to the needs of a new world.

The experience of visiting the Czech Republic still involves stepping back in time. Even in Prague, now deluged by tourists two-thirds of the year, the sense of history—stretching back through centuries of wars, empires, and monuments to everyday life—remains uncluttered by the trappings of modernity. The peculiar melancholy of Central Europe still lurks in narrow streets and forgotten corners. Crumbling facades, dilapidated palaces, and treacherous cobbled streets both shock and enchant the visitor used to a world where what remains of history has been spruced up for tourist eyes.

The arrival of designer boutiques, chain restaurants, and shopping malls does mean that the country has lost some of the "feel" it had just a few years ago. Although the dark side of freedom—rising unemployment and corruption—began to hit home in the late 1990s, the Czechs continued to move toward harmonization with Western ways. The country joined the NATO alliance in 1999 and will become a European Union member state, perhaps as early as 2004. Yet the process goes slowly. Economic and social integration into the "common European home," which in the postrevolutionary euphoria seemed possible within a few years, must now be measured in decades.

The strange, old-world, and at times frustratingly bureaucratic atmosphere of the Czech Republic is not all a product of the Communist era. Many of the everyday rituals are actually remnants of the Haps-

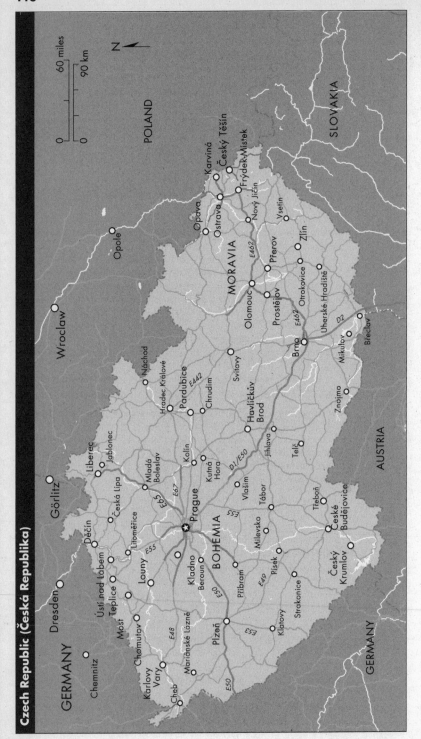

Czech Republic (Česká Republika)

burg Empire and are also to be found, perhaps to a lesser degree, in Vienna and Budapest. The *šatna* (coat room), for example, plays a vivid role in any visit to a restaurant or theater at any time of year other than summer. Coats must be given with a few coins to the attendant, usually an old lady with a sharp eye for ignorant or disobedient tourists.

Outside the capital, for those willing to put up with the inconveniences of shabby hotels and mediocre restaurants, the sense of rediscovering a neglected world is even stronger. And the range is startling, from imperial spas, with their graceful colonnades and dilapidated villas, to the many arcaded town squares, modestly displaying the passing of time with each splendid layer of once-contemporary style. Gothic towers, Renaissance facades, baroque interiors, and aging modern supermarkets merge. Between the man-made sights, you are rewarded with glorious mountain ranges and fertile rolling countryside laced with carp ponds and forests.

The key to enjoying the country is to relax. There is no point in demanding high levels of service or quality. And for the budget-conscious traveler, this is Central Europe at its most beautiful, at prices that are several times lower than those of Austria and Germany.

Pleasures and Pastimes

Bicycling
Czechs are avid cyclists. The flatter areas of southern Bohemia and Moravia are ideal for biking. Outside the larger towns, quiet roads stretch out for miles. The hillier terrain of northern Bohemia makes it popular with mountain-biking enthusiasts. Not many places rent bikes, though. For rental information, inquire at a visitor bureau or at your hotel.

Boating and Sailing
The country's main boating area is the enormous series of dams and reservoirs along the Vltava south of Prague. The most popular reservoir is Slapy, an hour's drive due south of the capital, where it is possible to rent small paddleboats or relax and swim on a hot day. Rowboats are available for rent along Prague's Vltava in summertime.

Castles and Châteaux
More than 2,000 castles, manor houses, and châteaus collectively form a precious and not-to-be-missed part of the country's cultural and historical heritage. Grim ruins glower from craggy hilltops, and fantastical Gothic castles guard ancient trade routes. Hundreds of noble houses—Renaissance, baroque, and Empire—dot the countryside. Their former bourgeois and aristocratic owners were expelled in the anti-German reaction of 1945–1946 or forced out by the Communists. Today, many of their valuable old seats stand in near ruin, and just as many more have been returned to the care of the original owners. Others remain in state hands as museums, homes for the elderly, or conference centers. More sights than ever are now open to the public. Picture galleries, rooms full of historic furniture, exquisite medieval stonework, and baroque chapels—all speak of a vanished way of life whose remnants survive in every town and village of Bohemia and Moravia.

Dining
The quality of restaurant cuisine and service in the Czech Republic remains uneven. The exception is found in the capital, where dozens of restaurants compete for an increasingly discriminating clientele. The traditional dishes—roast pork or duck with dumplings, or broiled meat with sauce—can be light and tasty when well prepared. Grilled

pond trout appears on most menus and is often the best item available. An annoying "cover charge" (20 Kč–50 Kč in expensive places) usually makes its way onto restaurant bills, seemingly to subsidize the salt and pepper shakers. You should discreetly check the bill, since a few unscrupulous proprietors still overcharge foreigners.

Restaurants generally fall into three categories. A *pivnice* or *hospoda* (beer hall) usually offers a simple, inexpensive menu of goulash or pork with dumplings. The atmosphere tends to be friendly and casual, and you can expect to share a table. More attractive, and more expensive, are the *vinárna* (wine cellar) and the *restaurace* (restaurant), which serve a full menu. Wine cellars, some occupying Romanesque basements, can be a real treat.

Ignoring the familiar fast-food outlets that are now a common sight, the quickest and cheapest dining option is the *lahůdky* (snack bar or deli). In larger towns, the *kavárna* (café) and *čajovna* (tea house) are ever more popular—and welcome—additions to the dining scene.

Lunch, usually eaten between noon and 2, is the main meal for Czechs and the best deal. Many restaurants put out a special luncheon menu (*denní lístek*), with more appetizing selections at better prices. If you don't see it, ask your waiter. Dinner is usually served from 5 until 9 or 10, but don't wait too long to eat. Most Czechs eat only a light meal in the evening. Also, restaurant cooks frequently knock off early on slow nights, and the later you arrive, the more likely it is that the kitchen will be closed. In general, dinner menus do not differ substantially from lunch offerings, except the prices are higher.

CATEGORY	PRAGUE*	OTHER AREAS*
$$$$	over 500 Kč	over 400 Kč
$$$	350–500 Kč	250–400 Kč
$$	150–350 Kč	100–250 Kč
$	under 150 Kč	under 100 Kč

per person for a main course at dinner

Hiking

The Czech Republic has 40,000 km (25,000 mi) of well-kept, -marked, and -signposted trails both in the mountainous regions and leading through beautiful countryside from town to town. The most scenic areas are the Beskydy range in northern Moravia and the Krkonoše range (Giant Mountains) in northern Bohemia. The rolling Šumava hills of southern Bohemia are also excellent hiking territory, and the environment there is the purest in the country. You'll find colored markings denoting trails on trees, fences, walls, rocks, and elsewhere. The main paths are marked in red, others in blue and green, while the least important trails are marked in yellow. Hiking maps can be found in almost any bookstore; look for the large-scale *Soubor turistických* maps.

Lodging

The number of hotels and pensions has increased dramatically throughout the Czech Republic, in step with the influx of tourists. Finding a suitable room should pose no problem, although it is highly recommended that you book ahead during the peak tourist season (nationwide, July and August; in Prague, April through October and the Christmas, New Year, and Easter holidays). Hotel prices, in general, remain high. This is especially true in Prague and in the spa towns of western Bohemia. Some Prague hotels reduce rates slightly in July and August, when many European travelers prefer to head for the beaches. Better value can often be found at private pensions and with individual home-owners offering rooms to let. In the outlying towns, the best strategy is to inquire at the local tourist information office or simply fan out around the town and look for room-for-rent signs on houses (usually in German: ZIMMER FREI or PRIVATZIMMER).

Most of the old-fashioned hotels away from the major tourist centers, invariably situated on a town's main square, have been modernized and now provide private bathrooms in most or all rooms and a higher comfort level throughout. Newer hotels, often impersonal concrete boxes, tend to be found on the outskirts of towns; charming, older buildings in the center of town, newly transformed into hotels and pensions, are often the best choice. Bare-bones hostels are a popular means of circumventing Prague's summer lodging crunch; many now stay open all year. In the mountains you can often find little *chaty* (chalets), where pleasant surroundings compensate for a lack of basic amenities. *Autokempink* parks (campsites) generally have a few bungalows.

Czech hotels set their own star ratings, which more or less match the international star system. Often you can book rooms—both at hotels and in private homes—through visitor bureaus. Otherwise, try contacting the hotel directly. Keep in mind that in many hotels, except at the deluxe level, a "double" bed means two singles that can be pushed together. (Single-mattress double beds are generally not available.)

At certain times, such as Easter and during festivals, prices can jump 15%–25%. As a rule, always ask the price before taking a room. Your best bet for lodging in the $ price range will usually be a private room. Unless otherwise noted, breakfast is included in the rate.

As for camping, there are hundreds of sites for tents and trailers throughout the country, but most are open only in summer (May–mid-September), although a number of campsites in and around Prague have year-round operation. You can get a map from the Prague Information Service of all the sites, with addresses, opening times, and facilities. Camping outside official sites is prohibited. Campgrounds generally have hot water and toilets.

CATEGORY	PRAGUE*	OTHER AREAS*
$$$$	over 7,000 Kč	over 3,500 Kč
$$$	5,000–7,000 Kč	2,500–3,500 Kč
$$	2,500–5,000 Kč	1,000–2,500 Kč
$	under 2,500	under 1,000

All prices are for a standard double room during peak season, including breakfast.

Shopping

In Prague, Karlovy Vary, and elsewhere in Bohemia, look for elegant and unusual crystal and porcelain. Bohemia is also renowned for the quality and deep-red color of its garnets; keep an eye out for beautiful garnet rings and brooches. You can also find excellent ceramics, especially in Moravia, as well as other folk artifacts, such as printed textiles, lace, hand-knit sweaters, and painted eggs. There are attractive crafts stores throughout the Czech Republic. In Karlovy Vary buy the strange pipelike drinking mugs used in the spas; vases left to petrify in the mineral-laden water; and Becherovka, a tasty herbal aperitif that makes a nice gift to take home.

Skiing

The two main skiing areas in the Czech Republic are the Giant Mountains in northern Bohemia and, for cross-country skiing especially, the Šumava hills of southern Bohemia. Lifts operate from January through March. In both areas you'll find a number of organizations renting skis—although supplies may be limited and lines may be long.

Wine and Beer

Czechs are reputed to drink more beer per capita than any other people on Earth; small wonder, as many connoisseurs rank Bohemian lager-style beer as the best in the world. This cool, crisp brew was invented in Plzeň in 1842, although Czech beer had already been brewed for centuries prior to that time. Aside from the world-famous Plzeňský Prazdroj (Pilsner Urquell) and milder Budvar (the original Budweiser) brands, some typical beers are the slightly bitter Krušovice; fruity Radegast; and the sweeter, Prague-brewed Staropramen. *Světlé pivo,* or golden beer, is most common, although many pubs also serve *černé* (dark), which is often slightly sweeter than the light variety.

Czechs also produce quite drinkable wines: peppy, fruity whites and mild, versatile reds. Southern Moravia, with comparatively warm summers and rich soil, grows the bulk of the wine harvest. Look for the Mikulov and Znojmo regional designations. Favorite white varietals are Müller-Thurgau, with a fine muscat bouquet and light flavor, and Neuburské, yellow-green in color and with a dry, smoky bouquet. Rulandské bílé, a semidry burgundy-like white, has a flowery bouquet and full-bodied flavor. Belying the notion that northerly climes are more auspicious for white than red grapes, northern Bohemia's scant few hundred acres of vineyards produce reliable reds and the occasional jewel. Frankovka is fiery red and slightly acidic, while the cherry-red Rulandské červené is an excellent, drier choice. Vavřinecké is dark and slightly sweet.

Exploring the Czech Republic

The stunning silhouette of Prague is undeniably one of the country's strongest magnets, but there are plenty of beautiful vistas, spired castles, and peaceful town squares beyond the capital. Bohemia, for centuries its own kingdom, spreads around Prague to the borders of Germany, Austria, and Poland. This region is rich with spa towns in the west, walled towns and castles to the south, and moving reminders of World War II in the north. Moravia, the area east of Prague, is anchored by Brno. This relatively modern city is surrounded by smaller, traditional towns, some tied to the wine trade. To the north a stretch of rural hills leads into Slovakia's more rugged ranges.

Great Itineraries

IF YOU HAVE 3 DAYS

Make ☎ **Prague** your base. This will allow you plenty of time to explore the beauties and wonders of the Old Town and Hradčany and to make a day trip to one of the country's fascinating smaller cities, the splendid spa town of **Karlovy Vary,** nestled in the hills of western Bohemia.

IF YOU HAVE 5 DAYS

Plan to spend three full days exploring Prague. You could easily spend a day each in the Old Town, the Lesser Quarter, and the castle and the other two days visiting the well-preserved medieval mining town of **Kutná Hora** and the unforgettable concentration camp **Terezín.** Or you could spend a day amid the Renaissance charm of **Český Krumlov.**

When to Tour

Prague is beautiful year-round, but in summer and during the Christmas and Easter holidays the city is overrun with tourists. Spring and fall generally combine good weather with a more bearable level of tourism. In winter you'll encounter fewer other visitors and have the opportunity to see Prague breathtakingly covered in snow, but it can get very cold. In much of the rest of Bohemia and Moravia, even in midsummer, the number of visitors is far smaller than in Prague. The Giant Mountains of Bohemia come into their own in winter. January and February generally bring the best skiing—and great difficulty in finding a room. If you're not a skier, try visiting the mountains in late spring (May or June) or fall, when the colors are dazzling and you'll have the hotels and restaurants nearly to yourself. The "off" season keeps shrinking as people discover the pleasures of touring the country in every season. Castles and museums now frequently stay open 9, 10, or even 12 months of the year. In midwinter, however, you may well come across this disappointing notice tacked to the door of a museum or even a hotel: CLOSED FOR TECHNICAL REASONS—which, for those in the proper frame of mind, merely adds to the charm of winter travel.

PRAGUE

It's been more than a decade since November 17, 1989, when Prague's students took to the streets to help bring down the 40-year-old Communist regime, and in that time the city has enjoyed an exhilarating cultural renaissance. Amid Prague's cobblestone streets and gold-tipped spires, new galleries, cafés, and clubs teem with young Czechs (the middle-aged are generally too busy trying to make a living) and members of the city's colony of "expatriates." New shops and, perhaps most noticeably, scads of new restaurants have opened, expanding the city's culinary reach far beyond the traditional roast pork and dumplings. Many have something to learn in the way of presentation and service, but Praguers still marvel at a variety that was unthinkable not so many years ago.

The arts and theater are also thriving in the "new" Prague. Young playwrights, some writing in English, regularly stage their own works. Weekly poetry readings are standing room only. Classical music maintains its famous standards, while rock, jazz, and dance clubs are jammed nightly. The arts of the new era—nonverbal theater, "installation" art, world music—are as trendy in Prague as in any European capital but possess a distinctive Czech flavor.

All of this frenetic activity plays well against a stunning backdrop of towering churches and centuries-old bridges and alleyways. Prague achieved much of its present glory in the 14th century, during the long reign of Charles IV, king of Bohemia and Moravia and Holy Roman Emperor. It was Charles who established a university in the city and laid out the New Town, charting Prague's growth.

During the 15th century, the city's development was hampered by the Hussite Wars, a series of crusades launched by the Holy Roman Empire to subdue the fiercely independent Czech noblemen. The Czechs were eventually defeated in 1620 at the Battle of White Mountain (Bílá Hora) near Prague and were ruled by the Hapsburg family for the next 300 years. Under the Hapsburgs, Prague became a German-speaking city and an important administrative center, but it was forced to play second fiddle to the monarchy's capital, Vienna. Much of the Lesser Quarter, on the left bank of the Vltava, was built up at this time, and there you could find the Austrian nobility and its baroque tastes.

Prague regained its status as a national capital in 1918, with the creation of the modern Czechoslovak state, and quickly asserted itself in the interwar period as a vital cultural center. Although the city escaped World War II essentially intact, Czechoslovakia fell under the political and cultural domination of the Soviet Union until the 1989 popular uprisings. The election of dissident playwright Václav Havel to the post of national president set the stage for the city's renaissance, which

124

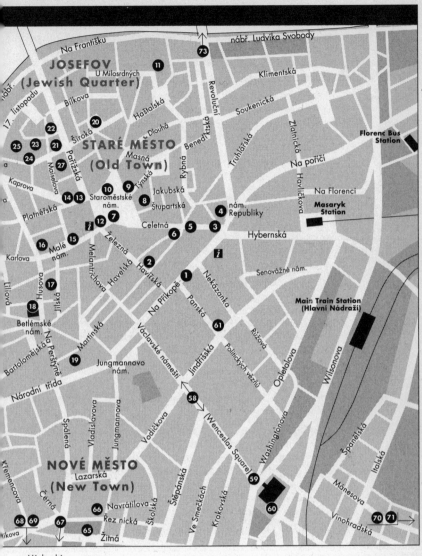

has since proceeded at a dizzying, quite Bohemian rate. Although Prague was beset by massive floods in 2002, most of the tourism infrastructure was only temporarily affected, and things are back to normal now.

Exploring Prague

The spine of the city is the River Vltava (also known by its German name, Moldau), which runs through the city from south to north with a single sharp curve to the east. Prague originally comprised five independent towns, represented today by its main historic districts: Hradčany (Castle Area), Malá Strana (Lesser Quarter), Staré Město (Old Town), Nové Město (New Town), and Josefov (the Jewish Quarter).

Hradčany, the seat of Czech royalty for hundreds of years, has as its center the Pražský hrad (Prague Castle), which overlooks the city from its hilltop west of the Vltava. Steps lead down from Hradčany to the Lesser Quarter, an area dense with ornate mansions built by 17th- and 18th-century nobility.

Karlův most (Charles Bridge) connects the Lesser Quarter with the Old Town. Just a few blocks east of the bridge is the district's focal point, Staroměstské náměstí (Old Town Square). The Old Town is bounded by the curving Vltava and three large commercial avenues: Revoluční to the east, Na Příkopě to the southeast, and Národní třída to the south. North of Old Town Square, the diminutive Jewish Quarter fans out around the wide avenue called Pařížská.

Beyond the Old Town to the south is the New Town, a highly commercial area that includes the city's largest square, Karlovo náměstí (Charles Square). Roughly 1 km (½ mi) farther south is Vyšehrad, an ancient castle high above the river.

On a promontory to the east of Václavské náměstí (Wenceslas Square) stretches Vinohrady, once the favored neighborhood of well-to-do Czechs. Bordering Vinohrady are the crumbling neighborhoods of Žižkov to the north and Nusle to the south. On the west bank of the Vltava lie many older residential neighborhoods and several sprawling parks. About 3 km (2 mi) from the center in every direction, Communist-era housing projects begin their unsightly sprawl.

Numbers in the text correspond to numbers in the margin and on the Prague map.

Staré Město (Old Town)

A GOOD WALK

Ever-hopping Wenceslas Square, convenient to hotels and transportation, is an excellent place to begin a tour of the Old Town, although it actually lies within the New Town. To begin the approach to the Old Town proper, start at the lower end of the square, walk past the tall art deco Koruna complex, and turn right onto the handsome pedestrian zone of **Na Příkopě** ①. Turn left onto Havířská ulice and follow this small alley to the glittering green-and-cream splendor of the 18th-century theater called the **Stavovské divadlo** ②.

Return to Na Příkopě, turn left, and continue to the end of the street. On weekdays between 8 AM and 5 PM, it's well worth taking a peek at the stunning interior of the Živnostenská banka (Merchant's Bank), at No. 20.

Na Příkopě ends abruptly at náměstí Republiky (Republic Square), an important New Town transportation hub (with a metro stop). The severe Depression-era facade of the Česká Národní banka (at Na Příkopě 30) makes the building look more like a fortress than the nation's central bank. Close by stands a stately tower, the **Prašná brána** ③, its festive Gothic spires looming above the square. Adjacent to this dignified building, the **Obecní dům** ④ concert hall looks decidedly decadent.

Walk through the arch at the base of the Prašná brána and down the formal **Celetná ulice** ⑤, the first leg of the so-called Royal Way. Monarchs favored this route primarily because the houses along Celetná were among the city's finest, providing a suitable backdrop to the coronation procession. Baroque influence is even visible in the Cubist department store **Dům U černé Matky Boží** ⑥, now a museum.

Staroměstské náměstí ⑦, at the end of Celetná, is dazzling, thanks partly to the double-spired **Kostel Panny Marie před Týnem** ⑧, which rises over the square from behind a row of patrician houses. To the immediate left of this church, at No. 13, is Dům U Kamenného zvonu (House at the Stone Bell), a baroque town house that has been stripped down to its original Gothic elements.

Next door stands the gorgeous pink-and-ocher **Palác Kinských** ⑨. At this end of the square, you can't help noticing the expressive **Jan Hus monument** ⑩. At this point, you may wish to take a detour to see the National Gallery's Gothic art collection at **Klášter svaté Anežky České** ⑪. Go northeast from the square up Dlouha Street, and then straight along Kozi Street all the way until it ends at U Milosrdných.

Return to Staroměstské náměstí, and just beyond the Jan Hus monument is the Gothic **Staroměstská radnice** ⑫, which, with its impressive 200-ft tower, gives the square its sense of importance. As the hour approaches, join the crowds milling below the tower's 15th-century astronomical clock for a brief but spooky spectacle taken straight from the Middle Ages, every hour on the hour. The square's second church, the baroque **Kostel svatého Mikuláše** ⑬, is not to be confused with the Lesser Quarter's Chrám svatého Mikuláše on the other side of the river.

You'll find the **Franz Kafka Exposition** ⑭ adjoining Kostel svatého Mikuláše on náměstí Franze Kafky, a little square that used to be part of U Radnice Street. Continue along U Radnice proper just a few yards until you come to **Malé náměstí** ⑮, a mini-square with arcades on one side. Look for tiny Karlova ulice, which begins in the southwest corner of the square, and take another quick right to stay on it (watch the signs—this medieval street seems designed to confound the visitor). At the České muzeum výtvarných umění (Czech Museum of Fine Arts), pause and inspect the exotic **Clam-Gallas palác** ⑯, behind you at Husova 20. You'll recognize it easily: look for the Titans in the doorway holding up what must be a very heavy baroque facade. Head the other way down Husova for a glimpse of ecstatic baroque stuffed inside somber Gothic at the **Kostel svatého Jiljí** ⑰, at No. 8.

Continue walking along Husova to Na Perštýně and turn right at tiny Betlémská ulice. The alley opens up onto a quiet square, Betlémské náměstí, and upon the most revered of all Hussite churches in Prague, the **Betlémská kaple** ⑱.

Return to Na Perštýně and continue walking to the right. As you near the back of the buildings of the busy Národní třída (National Boulevard), turn left at Martinská ulice. At the end of the street, the forlorn but majestic church **Kostel svatého Martina ve zdi** ⑲ looks as if it got lost. Walk around the church to the left and through a little archway of apartments onto the bustling Národní třída. To the left, a five-minute walk away, lies Wenceslas Square and the starting point of this walk.

TIMING·

Wenceslas Square and Old Town Square are busy with activity around-the-clock almost all year round. If you're in search of a little peace and quiet, you will find the streets at their most subdued on early week-end mornings or right after a sudden downpour. The streets in this walking tour are reasonably close together and can be covered in a half-day. Remember to be in the Old Town Square just before the hour if you want to see the astronomical clock in action.

SIGHTS TO SEE

⑱ Betlémská kaple (Bethlehem Chapel). The original church was built at the end of the 14th century, and the Czech religious reformer Jan Hus was a regular preacher here from 1402 until his exile in 1412. After the Thirty Years' War the church fell into the hands of the Jesuits and was finally demolished in 1786. Excavations carried out after World War I uncovered the original portal and three windows, and the entire church was reconstructed during the 1950s. Although little remains of the first church, some remnants of Hus's teachings can still be read on the inside walls. ⊠ *Betlémské nám. 5, Staré Město.* 🎟 *30 Kč.* ⊙ *Daily 10–5.*

❺ Celetná ulice. Most of this street's facades indicate the buildings are from the 17th or 18th century, but appearances are deceiving: many of the houses in fact have parts that date back to the 12th century. Be sure to look above the street level storefronts to see the fine examples of baroque detail.

⑯ Clam-Gallas palác (Clam-Gallas Palace). The beige-and-brown palace, the work of Johann Bernhard Fischer von Erlach, the famed Viennese architectural virtuoso of the day, was begun in 1713 and finally finished in 1729. Enter the building for a glimpse of the finely carved staircase, the work of the master himself, and of the Italian frescoes featuring Apollo that surround it. The building now houses the municipal archives and is rarely open to visitors (so walk in as if you have business there). Classical music concerts are sometimes held in the Great Hall in the evening, which is one way to peek inside. ⊠ *Husova 20, Staré Město,* WEB *www.ahmp.cz/eng.* ⊙ *Weekdays 8–4.*

❻ Dům U černé Matky Boží (House of the Black Madonna). In the second decade of the 20th century, young Czech architects boldly applied Cubism's radical reworking of visual space to structures. Adding a decided jolt to the architectural styles along Celetná, this Cubist building, designed by Josef Gočár, is unflinchingly modern yet topped with an almost baroque tile roof. The museum interior was renovated in 2002 to better suit the permanent collection of Cubist art. A café in the basement reopened as well. ⊠ *Celetná 34, Staré Město,* ☎ *224–211–732,* WEB *www.ngprague.cz.* 🎟 *100 Kč.* ⊙ *Tues.–Sun. 10–6.*

⑭ Franz Kafka Exposition. Kafka came into the world on July 3, 1883, in a house next to the Kostel svatého Mikuláše (Church of St. Nicholas). For years the writer was only grudgingly acknowledged by the Communist cultural bureaucrats, reflecting the traditionally ambiguous attitude of the Czech government toward his work. As a German and a Jew, moreover, Kafka could easily be dismissed as standing outside the mainstream of Czech literature. Following the 1989 revolution, however, Kafka's popularity soared, and his works are now widely available in Czech. Though only the portal of the original house remains, inside the building is a fascinating little exhibit (mostly photographs) on Kafka's life, with commentary in English. ⊠ *Nám. Franze Kafky 3, Staré Město.* 🎟 *50 Kč.* ⊙ *Tues.–Fri. 10–6, Sat. 10–5.*

❿ Jan Hus monument. Few memorials have elicited as much controversy as this one, which was dedicated in July 1915, exactly 500 years after

Hus was burned at the stake in Constance, Germany. Some maintain that the monument's Secessionist style (the inscription seems to come right from turn-of-the-20th-century Vienna) clashes with the Gothic and baroque of the square. Others dispute the romantic depiction of Hus, who appears here in flowing garb as tall and bearded. The real Hus, historians maintain, was short and had a baby face. Still, no one can take issue with the influence of this fiery preacher, whose ability to transform doctrinal disputes, both literally and metaphorically, into the language of the common man made him into a religious and national symbol for the Czechs. ⊠ *Staroměstské nám., Staré Město.*

⑪ **Klášter svaté Anežky České** (St. Agnes's Convent). Situated near the river between Pařížská and Revoluční streets, this peaceful complex has Prague's first buildings in the Gothic style, built between the 1230s and the 1280s. The convent now provides a fitting home for the National Gallery's marvelous collection of Czech Gothic art, including altarpieces, portraits, and statues. ⊠ *U Milosrdných 17, Staré Město,* ☎ *224–810–628,* WEB *www.ngprague.cz.* ▦ *100 Kč.* ☉ *Tues.–Sun. 10–6.*

★ ⑧ **Kostel Panny Marie před Týnem** (Church of the Virgin Mary Before Týn). The exterior of the church is one of the best examples of Prague Gothic and is in part the work of Peter Parler, architect of the Charles Bridge and Chrám svatého Víta (St. Vitus's Cathedral). Construction of its twin black-spire towers was begun later, by King Jiří of Poděbrad in 1461, during the heyday of the Hussites. Jiří had a gilded chalice, the symbol of the Hussites, proudly displayed on the front gable between the two towers. Following the defeat of the Czech Protestants by the Catholic Hapsburgs, the chalice was removed and eventually replaced by a Madonna. As a final blow, the chalice was melted down and made into the Madonna's glimmering halo (you still can see it by walking into the center of the square and looking up between the spires). The entrance to the church is through the arcades on Old Town Square, under the house at No. 604.

Much of the interior, including the tall nave, was rebuilt in the baroque style in the 17th century. Some Gothic pieces remain, however: look to the left of the main altar for a beautifully preserved set of early Gothic carvings. The main altar itself was painted by Karel Škréta, a luminary of the Czech baroque. Before leaving the church, look for the grave marker (tucked away to the right of the main altar) of the great Danish astronomer Tycho Brahe, who came to Prague as "Imperial Mathematicus" in 1599 under Rudolf II. As a scientist, Tycho had a place in history that is assured: Johannes Kepler (another resident of the Prague court) used Tycho's observations to formulate his laws of planetary motion. But it is myth that has endeared Tycho to the hearts of Prague residents. The robust Dane, who was apparently fond of duels, lost part of his nose in one (take a closer look at the marker). He quickly had a wax nose fashioned for everyday use but preferred to parade around on holidays and festive occasions sporting a bright silver one. ⊠ *Staroměstské nám., between Celetná and Týnská, Staré Město.*

⑰ **Kostel svatého Jiljí** (Church of St. Giles). This church was an important outpost of Czech Protestantism in the 16th century. The exterior is a powerful example of Gothic architecture, including the buttresses and a characteristic portal. The interior, as in many important Czech churches, is baroque, with a design by Johann Bernhard Fischer von Erlach and sweeping frescoes by Václav Reiner. The interior can be viewed during the day from the vestibule or at the evening concerts held several times a week. ⊠ *Husova 8, Staré Město.*

⑲ **Kostel svatého Martina ve zdi** (Church of St. Martin-in-the-Wall). It was here in 1414 that Holy Communion was first given to the Bohemian laity in the form of both bread and wine, in defiance of the Catholic custom of the time, which dictated that only bread was to be offered to the masses, with wine reserved for the priests and clergy. From then on, the chalice came to symbolize the Hussite movement. The church is open for evening concerts, held several times each week. ⊠ *Martinská ul., Staré Město.*

⑬ **Kostel svatého Mikuláše** (Church of St. Nicholas). Designed in the 18th century by Prague's own master of late baroque, Kilian Ignaz Dientzenhofer, this church is probably less successful in capturing the style's lyric exuberance than its namesake across town, the Chrám svatého Mikuláše. Still, Dientzenhofer utilized the limited space to create a well-balanced structure. The interior is compact, with a beautiful but small chandelier and an enormous black organ that seems to overwhelm the rear of the church. The church hosts almost continuous afternoon and evening tourist concerts. ⊠ *Staroměstské nám., Staré Město.* ☉ *Apr.–Oct., Mon. noon–4, Tues.–Sat. 10–4, Sun. noon–3; Nov.–Mar., Tues., Fri., and Sun. 10–noon; Wed. 10–4.*

⑮ **Malé náměstí** (Small Square). Note the iron fountain dating from around 1560 in the center of the square. The colorfully painted house at No. 3, originally a hardware store, is not as old as it looks, but here and there you can find authentic Gothic portals and Renaissance sgraffiti that betray the square's true age.

❶ **Na Příkopě.** The name means "At the Moat" and harks back to the time when the street was indeed a moat separating the Old Town from the New Town. Today the pedestrian zone Na Příkopě is prime shopping territory. At No. 19 an oversize new building, one of the worst excesses of the 1990s in Prague, houses a Marks & Spencer store. Have a look at the chic, hard-edged black-and-white Černá Růže (Black Rose) arcade at No. 12. A little ways farther at No. 22, the late-18th-century neoclassical facade of Slovanský dům hides a modern mall filled with stores, restaurants, and a cinema multiplex.

❹ **Obecní dům** (Municipal House). The city's Art Nouveau showpiece still fills the role it had when it was completed in 1911: it's a center for concerts, rotating art exhibits, and café society. The mature Art Nouveau style recalls the lengths the Czech middle classes went to at the turn of the 20th century to imitate Paris, then the epitome of style and glamour. Much of the interior bears the work of Art Nouveau master Alfons Mucha, Max Švabinský, and other leading Czech artists. Mucha decorated the Hall of the Lord Mayor upstairs with impressive, magical frescoes depicting Czech history; unfortunately it's not open to the public. The beautiful **Smetanova síň** (Smetana Hall), which hosts concerts by the Prague Symphony Orchestra as well as international players, is on the second floor. The ground-floor café is touristy but lovely with its glimmering chandeliers and exquisite woodwork. There's also a beer hall in the cellar with passable beer, mediocre food, and superbly executed ceramic murals on the walls. ⊠ *Nám. Republiky 5, Staré Město,* ☎ *222–002–100,* WEB *www.obecnidum.cz.* ☉ *Information center and box office daily 10–6.*

NEED A BREAK?   If you prefer subtle elegance, head around the corner from the Obecní dům to the café at the **Hotel Paříž** (⊠ U Obecního domu 1, Staré Město, ☎ 224–222–151), a Jugendstil jewel tucked away on a relatively quiet street.

9 **Palác Kinských** (Kinský Palace). This exuberant building, built in 1765 from Kilian Ignaz Dientzenhofer's design, is considered one of Prague's finest late-baroque structures. With its exaggerated pink overlay and numerous statues, the facade looks extreme when contrasted with the more staid baroque elements of other nearby buildings. (The interior, however, was "modernized" under Communism.) The palace once housed a German school—where Franz Kafka was a student for nine misery-laden years—and presently contains the National Gallery's graphics collection. It was from this building that Communist leader Klement Gottwald, flanked by his Slovak comrade Vladimír Clementis, first addressed the crowds after seizing power in February 1948—an event recounted in the first chapter of Milan Kundera's novel *The Book of Laughter and Forgetting.* ✉ *Staroměstské nám. 12, Staré Město,* ☎ *224–210–758,* WEB *www.ngprague.cz.* ✆ *100 Kč.* ☉ *Tues.–Sun. 10–6.*

3 **Prašná brána** (Powder Tower). Construction of the tower, which replaced one of the city's 13 original gates, was begun by King Vladislav II of Jagiello in 1475. At the time, the kings of Bohemia maintained their royal residence next door, on the site of the current Obecní dům, and the tower was intended to be the grandest gate of all. But Vladislav was Polish and thus heartily disliked by the rebellious Czech citizens of Prague. Nine years after he assumed power, fearing for his life, he moved the royal court across the river to Prague Castle. Work on the tower was abandoned, and the half-finished structure was used for storing gunpowder—hence its odd name—until the end of the 17th century. The oldest part of the tower is the base. The golden spires were not added until the end of the 19th century. Climb to the top for a striking view of the Old Town and Prague Castle in the distance. ✉ *Nám. Republiky, Staré Město.* ✆ *30 Kč.* ☉ *Apr.–Oct., daily 9–6.*

★ **12** **Staroměstská radnice** (Old Town Hall). This is one of Prague's magnets: hundreds of people gravitate to it to see the hour struck by the mechanical figures of the **astronomical clock.** Just before the hour, look to the upper part of the clock, where a skeleton begins by tolling a death knell and turning an hourglass upside down. The Twelve Apostles parade momentarily, and then a cockerel flaps its wings and crows, piercing the air as the hour finally strikes. To the right of the skeleton, the dreaded Turk nods his head, seemingly hinting at another invasion like those of the 16th and 17th centuries. This small spectacle doesn't clue viewers in to the way this 15th-century marvel indicates the time—by the season, the zodiac sign, and the positions of the sun and moon. The calendar under the clock dates from the mid-19th century.

The Old Town Hall served as the center of administration for the Old Town beginning in 1338, when King John of Luxembourg first granted the city council the right to a permanent location. The impressive 200-ft **Town Hall Tower,** where the clock is mounted, was first built in the 14th century and given its current late-Gothic appearance around 1500 by the master Matyáš Rejsek. For a rare view of the Old Town and its maze of crooked streets and alleyways, climb the ramp or ride the elevator to the top of the tower.

If you walk around the hall to the left, you'll see it's actually a series of houses jutting into the square; they were purchased over the years and successively added to the complex. On the other side, jagged stonework reveals where a large, neo-Gothic wing once adjoined the tower until it was destroyed during fighting between townspeople and Nazi troops in May 1945.

Guided tours (most guides speak English, and English texts are on hand) of the Old Town Hall depart from the main desk inside. Previously unseen parts of the tower were opened to the public in 2002, and you can now see the inside of the famous clock. ⊠ *Staroměstské nám., Staré Město.* ⊙ *May–Sept., Tues.–Sun. 9–6, Mon. 11–6; Oct.–Apr., Tues.– Sun. 9–5, Mon. 11–5.* ☞ *Tower 30 Kč, tours 40 Kč.*

★ **❼**   **Staroměstské náměstí** (Old Town Square). There are places that, on first glimpse, stop you dead in your tracks in sheer wonder. Old Town Square is one such place. Long the heart of the Old Town, the square grew to its present proportions when the city's original marketplace was moved away from the river in the 12th century. Its shape and appearance have changed little over the years. During the day the square is festive, as musicians vie for the favor of onlookers and artists display renditions of Prague street scenes. At night, the gaudily lit towers of the Church of the Virgin Mary Before Týn rise ominously over the glowing baroque facades. The crowds thin out, and the ghosts of the square's stormy past return.

During the 15th century the square was the focal point of conflict between Czech Hussites and German Catholics. In 1422 the radical Hussite preacher Jan Želivský was executed here for his part in storming the New Town's town hall three years earlier. In the 1419 uprising, three Catholic consuls and seven German citizens were thrown out the window—the first of Prague's many famous defenestrations. Within a few years, the Hussites had taken over the town, expelled the Germans, and set up their own administration.

Twenty-seven white crosses set flat in the paving stones in the square, at the Old Town Hall's base, mark the spot where 27 Bohemian noblemen were killed by the Hapsburgs in 1621 during the dark days following the defeat of the Czechs at the Battle of White Mountain. The grotesque spectacle, designed to quash any further national or religious opposition, took some five hours to complete, as the men were put to the sword or hanged one by one.

One of the most interesting houses on the Old Town Square juts out into the small extension leading into Malé náměstí. The house, called **U Minuty** (⊠ 3 Staroměstské nám., Staré Město), with its 16th-century Renaissance sgraffiti of biblical and classical motifs, was the home of the young Franz Kafka in the 1890s.

❷   **Stavovské divadlo** (Estates Theater). Built in the 1780s in the classical style, this handsome theater was for many years a beacon of Czech-language culture in a city long dominated by the German variety. It is probably best known as the site of the world premiere of Mozart's opera *Don Giovanni* in October 1787, with the composer himself conducting. Prague audiences were quick to acknowledge Mozart's genius: the opera was an instant hit here, though it flopped nearly everywhere else in Europe. Mozart wrote most of the opera's second act in Prague at the Villa Bertramka, where he was a frequent guest. You must attend a performance here to see inside. ⊠ *Ovocný tř. 1, Staré Město,* ☎ *224–215–001 box office,* ᴡᴇʙ *www.narodni-divadlo.cz.*

Josefov (Jewish Quarter)

Prague's Jews survived centuries of discrimination, but two unrelated events of modern times have left their historic ghetto little more than a collection of museums. Around 1900, city officials decided for hygienic purposes to raze the minuscule neighborhood—it had ceased to be a true ghetto with the political reforms of 1848–49, and by this time the majority of its residents were poor Gentiles—and pave over its crooked streets. Only some of the synagogues, the town hall, and the cemetery survived this early attempt at urban renewal. The second event was the Holocaust. Under Nazi occupation, a staggering percentage of the city's Jews were deported or murdered in concentration camps. Of the 35,000 Jews living in Prague before World War II, only about 1,200 returned to resettle the city after the war. The community is still tiny. Only a scant few Jews, mostly elderly, live in the "ghetto" today.

Treasures and artifacts of the ghetto are now the property of the **Židovské muzeum v Praze** (Prague Jewish Museum), which includes the Old Jewish Cemetery and collections installed in four surviving synagogues and the Ceremony Hall. (The Staronová synagóga, or Old-New Synagogue, a functioning house of worship, technically does not belong to the museum, but the Prague Jewish Community oversees both.) The museum was founded in 1906 but traces the vast majority of its holdings to the Nazis' destruction of 150 Jewish communities in Bohemia and Moravia. Dedicated museum workers, nearly all of whom were to die at Nazi hands, gathered and cataloged the stolen artifacts under German supervision. Exhibitions were even held during the war. A ticket good for all museum sites may be purchased at any of the synagogues but the Old-New Synagogue; single-site tickets apply only at the Old-New Synagogue and during occasional exhibits at the Spanish Synagogue. All museum sites are closed Saturday and Jewish holidays.

A GOOD WALK

To reach the Jewish Quarter, leave Old Town Square via handsome Pařížská ulice, centerpiece of the urban renewal effort, and head north toward the river. The festive atmosphere changes suddenly as you enter the area of the ghetto. The buildings are lower here; the mood is hushed. Take a right on Široká and stroll two blocks down to the recently restored **Španělská synagóga** ㉚. Head back the other way, past Pařížská, turn right on Maiselova, and you'll come to the **Židovská radnice** ㉑, which is now the Jewish Community Center. Adjoining it on Červená is the 16th-century High Synagogue. Across the street, at Červená 2, you see the **Staronová synagóga** ㉒, the oldest surviving synagogue in Prague.

Go west on the little street U starého hřbitova. The main museum ticket office is at the **Klausová synagóga** ㉓ at No. 3A. Separated from the synagogue by the exit gate of the Old Jewish Cemetery is the former building of the Jewish Burial Society, Obřadní síň, which exhibits traditional Jewish funeral objects.

Return to Maiselova and follow it to Široká. Turn right to find the **Pinkasova synagóga** ㉔, a handsome Gothic structure. Here also is the entrance to the Jewish ghetto's most astonishing sight, the **Starý židovský hřbitov** ㉕.

For a small detour, head down Široká street to the **Rudolfinum** ㉖ concert hall and gallery; across the street is the Uměleckoprůmyslové muzeum (Museum of Decorative Arts). Both are notable neo-Renaissance buildings.

Return to Maiselova once more and turn right in the direction of the Old Town. Look in at the displays of Czech Jewish history in the **Maiselova synagóga** ㉗.

TIMING

The Jewish Quarter is one of the most popular areas in Prague, especially in the height of summer, when its tiny streets are jammed to bursting with tourists almost all the time. The best time for a quieter visit is early morning when the museums and cemetery first open. The area itself is very compact, and a fairly thorough tour should only take half a day, but don't go on the Sabbath (Saturday), when all the museums are closed.

SIGHTS TO SEE

㉓ Klausová synagóga (Klausen Synagogue). This baroque former synagogue was built at the end of the 17th century in the place of three small buildings (a synagogue, school, and ritual bath) that were destroyed in a fire that devastated the ghetto in 1689. Inside, displays of Czech Jewish traditions emphasize celebrations and daily life. In the neo-Romanesque **Obřadní síň** (Ceremony Hall), which adjoins the Klausen Synagogue, the focus is on rather grim subjects: Jewish funeral paraphernalia, old gravestones, and medical instruments. Special attention is paid to the activities of the Jewish Burial Society through many fine objects and paintings. ⊠ *U starého hřbitova 3A, Josefov,* ☎ *224–819–456,* WEB *www.jewishmuseum.cz.* 🎟 *Combined ticket to museum sites and Old-New Synagogue 500 Kč; museum sites only, 300 Kč.* ☉ *Apr.–Oct., Sun.–Fri. 9–6; Nov.–Mar., Sun.–Fri. 9–4:30.*

㉗ Maiselova synagóga (Maisel Synagogue). Here, the history of Czech Jews from the 10th to the 18th century is illustrated with the aid of some of the Prague Jewish Museum's most precious objects, including silver Torah shields and pointers, spice boxes, and candelabra; historic tombstones; and fine ceremonial textiles, including some donated by Mordechai Maisel to the synagogue he founded. The richest items come from the late 16th and early 17th century—a prosperous era for Prague's Jews. ⊠ *Maiselova 10, Josefov,* ☎ *224–819–456,* WEB *www.jewishmuseum.cz.* 🎟 *Combined ticket to museum sites and Old-New Synagogue 500 Kč; museum sites only, 300 Kč.* ☉ *Apr.–Oct., Sun.–Fri. 9–6; Nov.–Mar., Sun.–Fri. 9–4:30.*

㉔ Pinkasova synagóga (Pinkas Synagogue). This synagogue has two particularly moving testimonies to the appalling crimes perpetrated against the Jews during World War II. One tribute astounds by sheer numbers: the inside walls are covered with nearly 80,000 names of Bohemian and Moravian Jews murdered by the Nazis. Among them are the names of the paternal grandparents of former U.S. Secretary of State Madeleine Albright, who learned of their fate only in 1997. There is also an exhibition of drawings made by children at the Nazi concentration camp Terezín. The Nazis used the camp for propaganda purposes to demonstrate their "humanity" toward the Jews, and prisoners were given relative freedom to lead "normal" lives. However, transports to death camps in Poland began in earnest in 1944, and many thousands of Terezín prisoners, including many of these children, eventually perished. The entrance to the old Jewish cemetery is through this synagogue. ⊠ *Enter from Široká 3, Josefov,* ☎ *224–819–456,* WEB *www.jewishmuseum.cz.* 🎟 *Combined ticket to museum sites and Old-New Synagogue 500 Kč; museum sites only, 300 Kč.* ☉ *Apr.–Oct., Sun.–Fri. 9–6; Nov.–Mar., Sun.–Fri. 9–4:30.*

㉖ Rudolfinum. Thanks to a thorough makeover and exterior sandblasting, this neo-Renaissance monument designed by Josef Zítek and Josef Schulz presents the cleanest, brightest stonework in the city. Completed in 1884 and named for then–Hapsburg Crown Prince Rudolf, the rather low-slung sandstone building was meant to be a combination concert hall and exhibition gallery. After 1918 it was converted into the parliament of the newly independent Czechoslovakia until German invaders reinstated the concert hall in 1939. Czech writer Jiří Weil's novel *Mendelssohn Is on the Roof* tells of the cruel farce that ensued when officials ordered the removal of the Jewish composer's statue from the roof balustrade. Now the Czech Philharmonic has its home base here. The 1,200-seat **Dvořákova síň** (Dvořák Hall) has superb acoustics (the box office faces 17 listopadu). To see the hall, you must attend a concert.

Behind Dvořák Hall is a set of large exhibition rooms, the **Galerie Rudolfinum** (WEB www.galerierudolfinum.cz), an innovative, state-supported gallery for rotating shows of contemporary art. Four or five large shows are mounted here annually, showcasing excellent Czech work along with international artists such as photographer Cindy Sherman. The gallery is open Tuesday–Sunday 10–6; admission is 100 Kč. ✉ *Nám. Jana Palacha, Josefov,* ☎ *224–893–111 box office; 224–893–205 gallery;* WEB *www.czechphilharmonic.cz.*

★ ⓴ **Španělská synagóga** (Spanish Synagogue). A domed Moorish-style synagogue was built in 1868 on the site of the Altschul, the city's oldest synagogue. Here, the historical exposition that begins in the Maisel Synagogue continues, taking the story up to the post–World War II period. The displays are not that compelling, but the building's painstakingly restored interior definitely is. ✉ *Vězeňská 1, Josefov,* ☎ *224–819–456.* WEB *www.jewishmuseum.cz.* ⌨ *Combined ticket to museum sites and Old-New Synagogue 500 Kč; museum sites only, 300 Kč,* ☎ *224–819– 456.* ☉ *Apr.–Oct., Sun.–Fri. 9–6; Nov.–Mar., Sun.–Fri. 9–4:30.*

★ ⓶⓶ **Staronová synagóga** (Old-New Synagogue, or Altneuschul). Dating from the mid-13th century, this is one of the most important works of early Gothic in Prague. The odd name recalls the legend that the synagogue was built on the site of an ancient Jewish temple and that stones from the temple were used to build the present structure. The oldest part of the synagogue is the entrance, with its vault supported by two pillars. The synagogue has not only survived fires and the razing of the ghetto at the end of the last century but also emerged from the Nazi occupation intact; it is still in active use. As the oldest synagogue in Europe that still serves its original function, it is a living storehouse of Bohemian Jewish life. Note that men are required to cover their heads inside and that during services men and women sit apart. ✉ *Červená 2, Josefov,* ☎ *224–819–456,* WEB *www.jewishmuseum.cz.* ⌨ *Combined ticket to Old-New Synagogue and museum sites 500 Kč; Old-New Synagogue only, 200 Kč.* ☉ *Apr.–Oct., Sun.–Thurs. 9–6; Nov.–Mar., Sun.– Thurs. 9–4:30; closes 2–3 hrs early on Fri.*

★ ⓶⓹ **Starý židovský hřbitov** (Old Jewish Cemetery). This unforgettably melancholy sight not far from the busy city was, from the 15th century to 1787, the final resting place for all Jews living in Prague. The confined space forced graves to be piled one on top of the other. Tilted at crazy angles, the 12,000 visible tombstones are but a fraction of countless thousands more buried below. Walk the path amid the gravestones; the relief symbols you see represent the names and professions of the deceased. The oldest marked grave belongs to the poet Avigdor Kara, who died in 1439; the grave is not accessible from the pathway, but the original tombstone can be seen in the Maisel Synagogue. The best-known marker is that of Jehuda ben Bezalel, the famed Rabbi Loew (died 1609), a chief rabbi of Prague and profound scholar who is credited with creating the mythical Golem. Even today, small scraps of paper bearing wishes are stuffed into the cracks of the rabbi's tomb in the hope he will grant them. Loew's grave lies near the exit. ✉ *Široká 3, Josefov (enter through Pinkasova synagóga),* ☎ *224–819–456,* WEB *www.jewishmuseum.cz.* ⌨ *Combined ticket to museum sites and Old- New Synagogue 500 Kč; museum sites only, 300 Kč.* ☉ *Apr.–Oct., Sun.– Fri. 9–6; Nov.–Mar., Sun.–Fri. 9–4:30.*

⓶⓵ **Židovská radnice** (Jewish Town Hall). The hall was the creation of Mordechai Maisel, an influential Jewish leader at the end of the 16th century. It was restored in the 18th century and given its clock and bell tower at that time. A second clock, with Hebrew numbers, keeps time counterclockwise. Now the Jewish Community Center, the building also houses a kosher restaurant, Shalom. ✉ *Maiselova 18, Josefov,* ☎ *222–319–012.*

Karlův most (Charles Bridge) and Malá Strana (Lesser Quarter)

One of Prague's most exquisite neighborhoods, the Lesser Quarter (or Little Town) was established in 1257 and for years was where the merchants and craftsmen who served the royal court lived. The Lesser Quarter is not for the methodical traveler. Its charm lies in the tiny lanes, the sudden blasts of bombastic architecture, and the soul-stirring views that emerge for a second before disappearing behind the sloping roofs.

A GOOD WALK

Begin your tour on the Old Town side of **Karlův most** ㉘, which you can reach by foot in about 10 minutes from the Old Town Square. Rising above it is the majestic Staroměstská mostecká věž. The climb of 138 steps is worth the effort for the view you get of the Old Town and, across the river, of the Lesser Quarter and Prague Castle.

It's worth pausing to take a closer look at some of the statues as you walk across Karlův most toward the Lesser Quarter. You'll see Kampa Island below you, separated from the mainland by an arm of the Vltava known as Čertovka (Devil's Stream).

By now you are almost at the end of the bridge. In front of you is the striking conjunction of the two Malá Strana bridge towers, one Gothic, the other Romanesque. Together they frame the baroque flamboyance of Chrám svatého Mikuláše in the distance. At night this is an absolutely wondrous sight.

Walk under the gateway of the towers into the little uphill street called Mostecká. You have now entered the Lesser Quarter. Return to Mostecká and follow it up to the rectangular **Malostranské náměstí** ㉙, now the district's traffic hub rather than its heart. In the middle of the square stands **Chrám svatého Mikuláše** ㉚.

Nerudova ulice ㉛ runs up from the square toward Prague Castle. Lined with gorgeous houses (and in recent years an ever-larger number of places to spend money), it's sometimes burdened with the moniker "Prague's most beautiful street." A tiny passageway at No. 13, on the left-hand side as you go up, leads to Tržiště ulice and the **Schönbornský palác** ㉜, once Franz Kafka's home, now the embassy of the United States. Tržiště winds down to the quarter's traffic-plagued main street, Karmelitská, where the famous Infant Jesus of Prague resides in the **Kostel Panny Marie vítězné** ㉝. A few doors away, closer to Tržiště, is a quiet oasis, the **Vrtbovská zahrada** ㉞. Tiny Prokopská ulice leads off of Karmelitská, past the former Church of St. Procopius (now converted, oddly, into an apartment block), and into Maltézské náměstí (Maltese Square), a characteristically noble compound.

A tiny bridge at the cramped square's lower end takes you across the creeklike Čertovka to the island of **Kampa** ㉟ and its broad lawns, cafés, and river views. Winding your way underneath Karlův most and along the street U lužického semináře brings you to a quiet walled garden, **Vojanovy sady** ㊱. To the northwest, hiding off busy Letenská ulice near the Malostranská metro station, is **Zahrada Valdštejnského paláce** ㊲, a more formal garden with an unbeatable view of Prague Castle looming above. A bit farther north is another garden, the baroque **Ledeburská zahrada** ㊳.

TIMING

The area is at its best in the evening, when the softer light brings you into a world of glimmering beauty. The basic walk described here could take as little as half a day—longer if you'd like to explore the area's lovely nooks and crannies.

SIGHTS TO SEE

★ ③⓪ **Chrám svatého Mikuláše** (Church of St. Nicholas). With its dynamic curves, this church is one of the purest and most ambitious examples of high baroque. The celebrated architect Christoph Dientzenhofer began the Jesuit church in 1704 on the site of one of the more active Hussite churches of 15th-century Prague. Work on the building was taken over by his son Kilian Ignaz Dientzenhofer, who built the dome and presbytery. Anselmo Lurago completed the whole in 1755 by adding the bell tower. The juxtaposition of the broad, full-bodied dome with the slender bell tower is one of the many striking architectural contrasts that mark the Prague skyline. Inside, the vast pink-and-green space is impossible to take in with a single glance. Every corner bristles with movement, guiding the eye first to the dramatic statues, then to the hectic frescoes, and on to the shining faux-marble pillars. Many of the statues are the work of Ignaz Platzer, and in fact they constitute his last blaze of success. Platzer's workshop was forced to declare bankruptcy when the centralizing and secularizing reforms of Joseph II toward the end of the 18th century brought an end to the flamboyant baroque era. The tower, with an entrance on the side of the church, is open in summer. ⊠ *Malostranské nám., Malá Strana.* 🎫 *30 Kč.* ☉ *Daily 9–4.*

③⑤ **Kampa.** Prague's largest island is cut off from the "mainland" by the narrow Čertovka streamlet. The name Čertovka, or Devil's Stream, reputedly refers to a cranky old lady who once lived on Maltese Square (given the river's present filthy state, the name is certainly appropriate). The unusually well kept lawns of the **Kampa Gardens** that occupy much of the island are one of the few places in Prague where sitting on the grass is openly tolerated. At night this stretch along the river is especially romantic. The spotlit jewel on Kampa Island is **Museum Kampa,** a remodeled mill house that now displays a private collection of paintings by Czech artist František Kupka and other artists, which opened in 2002. Kampa was heavily damaged during the floods of 2002, but at this writing the Museum Kampa was scheduled to reopen in January 2003. ⊠ *U Sovových mlýnů 2, Malá Strana,* ☎ *257–786–147.* 🎫 *100 Kč.* ☉ *Tues.–Sun. 10–5.*

★ ②⑧ **Karlův most** (Charles Bridge). The view from the foot of the bridge on the Old Town side is nothing short of breathtaking, encompassing the towers and domes of the Lesser Quarter and the soaring spires of St. Vitus's Cathedral to the northwest. This heavenly vision changes subtly in perspective as you walk across the bridge, attended by the host of baroque saints that decorate the bridge's peaceful Gothic stones. At night its drama is spellbinding: St. Vitus's Cathedral lit in a ghostly green, the castle in monumental yellow, and the Church of St. Nicholas in a voluptuous pink, all viewed through the menacing silhouettes of the bowed statues and the Gothic towers. If you do nothing else in Prague, you must visit the Charles Bridge at night. During the day the pedestrian bridge buzzes with activity. Street musicians vie with artisans hawking jewelry, paintings, and glass for the hearts and wallets of the passing multitude. At night the crowds thin out a little, the musicians multiply, and the bridge becomes a long block party—nearly everyone brings a bottle.

When the Přemyslid princes set up residence in Prague in the 10th century, there was a ford across the Vltava at this point—a vital link along one of Europe's major trading routes. After several wooden bridges and the first stone bridge had washed away in floods, Charles IV appointed the 27-year-old German Peter Parler, the architect of St. Vitus's

Cathedral, to build a new structure in 1357. After 1620, following the defeat of Czech Protestants by Catholic Hapsburgs at the Battle of White Mountain, the bridge became a symbol of the Counter-Reformation's vigorous re-Catholicization efforts. The many baroque statues that began to appear in the late 17th century, commissioned by Catholics, eventually came to symbolize the totality of the Austrian (hence Catholic) triumph. The Czech writer Milan Kundera sees the statues from this perspective: "The thousands of saints looking out from all sides, threatening you, following you, hypnotizing you, are the raging hordes of occupiers who invaded Bohemia 350 years ago to tear the people's faith and language from their hearts."

The religious conflict is less obvious nowadays, leaving only the artistic tension between baroque and Gothic that gives the bridge its allure. It's worth pausing to take a closer look at some of the statues as you walk toward the Lesser Quarter. The third on the right, a bronze crucifix from the mid-17th century, is the oldest of all. It is mounted on the location of a wooden cross destroyed in a battle with the Swedes (the golden Hebrew inscription was reputedly financed by a Jew accused of defiling the cross). Eighth on the right, the statue of St. John of Nepomuk, designed by Johann Brokoff in 1683, begins the baroque lineup of saints. On the left-hand side, sticking out from the bridge between the 9th and 10th statues (the latter has a wonderfully expressive vanquished Satan), stands a Roland (Bruncvík) statue. This knightly figure, bearing the coat of arms of the Old Town, was once a reminder that this part of the bridge belonged to the Old Town before Prague became a unified city in 1784.

In the eyes of most art historians, the most valuable statue is the 12th on the left, near the Lesser Quarter end. Mathias Braun's statue of St. Luitgarde depicts the blind saint kissing Christ's wounds. The most compelling grouping, however, is the second from the end on the left, a work of Ferdinand Maxmilian Brokoff (son of Johann) from 1714. Here the saints are incidental; the main attraction is the Turk, his face expressing extreme boredom at guarding the Christians imprisoned in the cage at his side. When the statue was erected, just 31 years after the second Turkish siege of Vienna, it scandalized the Prague public, who smeared it with mud. A half-dozen of the 30 bridge sculptures are 19th-century replacements for originals damaged in wars or sunk in a 1784 flood. All but a couple of the bridge's surviving baroque statues, including St. Luitgarde and the Turk, have been replaced by modern copies. The 17th- and 18th-century originals are in safer quarters, protected from Prague's acidic air. Several, including St. Luitgarde, can be viewed in the Lapidarium museum at the Výstaviště exhibition grounds in Prague 7; a few more occupy a man-made cavern at Vyšehrad.

Staroměstská mostecká věž (Old Town Bridge Tower), at the bridge entrance on the Old Town side, is where Peter Parler, the architect of the Charles Bridge, began his bridge building. The carved facades he designed for the sides of the tower were destroyed by Swedish soldiers in 1648, at the end of the Thirty Years' War. The sculptures facing the Old Town, however, are still intact (although some are recent copies); they depict an old and gout-ridden Charles IV with his son, who later became Wenceslas IV. Above them are two of Bohemia's patron saints, Adalbert of Prague and Sigismund. The top of the tower offers a spectacular view of the city for 30 Kč; it's open daily 10–5 (until 7 in the summer).

㉝ **Kostel Panny Marie vítězné** (Church of Our Lady Victorious). This comfortably ramshackle church on the Lesser Quarter's main street is the unlikely home of one of Prague's best-known religious artifacts, the

Pražské Jezulátko (Infant Jesus of Prague). Originally brought to Prague from Spain in the 16th century, this tiny wax doll is renowned world-wide for showering miracles on anyone willing to kneel before it and pray. Nuns from a nearby convent arrive at dawn each day to change the infant's clothes; pieces of the doll's extensive wardrobe have been sent by believers from around the world. A museum in the church tower displays many of the outfits and a jewel-studded crown. ⊠ *Karmelitská 9A, Malá Strana.* ▩ *Free.* ⊘ *Mon.–Sat. 10–5:30, Sun. 1–5.*

㊳ Ledeburská zahrada (Ledeburg Garden). Rows of steeply banked baroque gardens rise behind the palaces of Valdštejnská ulice. This one makes a pleasant spot for a rest amid shady arbors and niches. The garden, with its frescoes and statuary, was restored with support from a fund headed by Czech president Václav Havel and Charles, Prince of Wales. You can also enter directly from the south gardens of Prague Castle in the summer. ⊠ *Valdštejnské nám. 3, Malá Strana.* ▩ *40 Kč.* ⊘ *Daily 10–6.*

㉙ Malostranské náměstí (Lesser Quarter Square). The arcaded houses on the east and south sides of the square, dating from the 16th and 17th centuries, exhibit a mix of baroque and Renaissance elements. The Czech Parliament resides partly in the gaudy yellow-and-green palace on the square's north side, partly in the street behind the palace, Sněmovní. The huge bulk of the Church of St. Nicholas divides the lower, busier section—buzzing with restaurants, street vendors, clubs, and shops—from the quieter, upper part.

㉛ Nerudova ulice. This steep little street used to be the last leg of the Royal Way walked by the king before his coronation, and it is still the best way to get to Prague Castle. It was named for the 19th-century Czech journalist and poet Jan Neruda (after whom Chilean poet Pablo Neruda renamed himself). Until Joseph II's administrative reforms in the late 18th century, house numbering was unknown in Prague. Each house bore a name, depicted on the facade, and these are particularly promi-nent on Nerudova ulice. House No. 6, **U červeného orla** (At the Red Eagle), proudly displays a faded painting of a red eagle. No. 12 is known as **U tří housliček** (At the Three Fiddles). In the early 18th century, three generations of the Edlinger violin-making family lived here. Joseph II's scheme numbered each house according to its position in its "town" (here the Lesser Quarter) rather than its sequence on the street. The red plates record the original house numbers; the blue ones are the num-bers used in addresses today. To confuse the tourist, many architec-tural guides refer to the old, red-number plates.

Two palaces break the unity of the burghers' houses on Nerudova ulice. Both were designed by the adventurous baroque architect Giovanni San-tini, one of the Italian builders most in demand by wealthy nobles of the early 18th century. The **Morzin Palace,** on the left at No. 5, is now the Romanian Embassy. The fascinating facade, with an allegory of night and day, was created in 1713 and is the work of Ferdinand Brokoff of Charles Bridge statue fame. Across the street at No. 20 is the **Thun-Hohenstein Palace,** now the Italian Embassy. The gateway with two enormous eagles (the emblem of the Kolovrat family, who owned the building at the time) is the work of the other great Charles Bridge statue sculptor, Mathias Braun. Santini himself lived at No. 14, the **Valkoun House.**

The archway at Nerudova 13 hides one of the many winding pas-sageways that give the Lesser Quarter its enchantingly ghostly char-acter at night. Higher up the street at No. 33 is the **Bretfeld Palace,** a rococo house on the corner of Jánský vršek. The relief of St. Nicholas on the facade is the work of Ignaz Platzer, a sculptor known for his classic and rococo work, but the building is valued more for its historical associations than for its architecture: this is where Mozart, his lyricist partner Lorenzo da Ponte, and the aging but still infamous philanderer and music lover Casanova stayed at the time of the world premiere of *Don Giovanni* in 1787.

NEED A BREAK? Nerudova ulice is filled with little restaurants and snack bars and offers something for everyone. **U zeleného čaje** (⊠ Nerudova 19) is a fragrant little tearoom offering herbal and fruit teas as well as light salads and sweets. **U Kocoura** (⊠ Nerudova 2) is a popular local pub.

㉜ Schönbornský palác (Schönborn Palace). Franz Kafka had an apartment in this massive baroque building at the top of Tržiště ulice in mid-1917, after moving from Zlatá ulička, or Golden Lane. The heavily guarded U.S. Embassy now occupies this prime location. If you look through the gates, you can see the beautiful formal gardens rising up to the Petřín hill. They are unfortunately not open to the public but can be glimpsed from the neighboring garden, Vrtbovská zahrada. ⊠ *Tržiště at Vlašská, Malá Strana.*

㊱ Vojanovy sady (Vojan Park). Once the gardens of the Monastery of the Discalced Carmelites, later taken over by the Order of the English Virgins, and now part of the Ministry of Finance, this walled garden, with its weeping willows, fruit trees, and benches, makes another peaceful haven in summer. Exhibitions of modern sculptures are often held here, contrasting sharply with the two baroque chapels and the graceful Ignaz Platzer statue of John of Nepomuk standing on a fish at the entrance. The park is surrounded by the high walls of the old monastery and new Ministry of Finance buildings, with only an occasional glimpse of a tower or spire to remind you that you're in Prague. ⊠ *U lužického semináře, between Letenská ul. and Míšeňská ul., Malá Strana.* ☉ *Nov.–Mar., daily 8–5; Apr.–Oct., daily 8–7.*

★ **㉞ Vrtbovská zahrada** (Vrtba Garden). An unobtrusive door on noisy Karmelitská hides the entranceway to a fascinating oasis that also has one of the best views over the Lesser Quarter. The street door opens onto the intimate courtyard of the Vrtbovský palác (Vrtba Palace), which is now private housing. Two Renaissance wings flank the courtyard; the left one was built in 1575, the right one in 1591. The owner of the latter house was one of the 27 Bohemian nobles executed by the Hapsburgs in 1621 before the Old Town Hall. The house was given as confiscated property to Count Sezima of Vrtba, who bought the neighboring property and turned the buildings into a late-Renaissance palace. The Vrtba Garden, created a century later, reopened in summer 1998 after an excruciatingly long renovation. This is the most elegant of the Lesser Quarter's public gardens, built in five levels rising behind the courtyard in a wave of statuary-bedecked staircases and formal terraces to reach a seashell-decorated pavilion at the top. (The fenced-off garden immediately behind and above belongs to the U.S. Embassy.) The powerful stone figure of Atlas that caps the entranceway in the courtyard and most of the other classically derived statues are from the workshop of Mathias Braun, perhaps the best of the Czech baroque sculptors. ⊠ *Karmelitská 25, Malá Strana.* 🎫 *20 Kč.* ☉ *Apr.–Oct., daily 10–6.*

OFF THE BEATEN PATH **VILLA BERTRAMKA –** Mozart fans won't want to pass up a visit to this villa, where the great composer lived during a couple of his visits to Prague. The small, well-organized W. A. Mozart Museum is packed with memorabilia, including a flyer for a performance of *Don Giovanni* in 1788, only months after the opera's world premiere at the Estates Theater. Also on hand is one of the master's pianos. Take Tram No. 12 from Karmelitská south (or ride metro Line B) to the Anděl metro station; then transfer to Tram No. 4, 7, 9, or 10 and ride to the first stop (Bertramka). A 10-minute walk, following the signs, brings you to the villa. ✉ *Mozartova ul. 169, Smíchov,* ☎ *257–327–732,* WEB *www. bertramka.cz.* 🎫 *90 Kč.* ☉ *Apr.–Oct., daily 9:30–6; Nov.–Mar., daily 9:30–5.*

★ ㊲ **Zahrada Valdštejnského paláce** (Wallenstein Palace Gardens). Albrecht von Wallenstein, onetime owner of the house and gardens, began a meteoric military career in 1622 when the Austrian emperor Ferdinand II retained him to save the empire from the Swedes and Protestants during the Thirty Years' War. Wallenstein, wealthy by marriage, offered to raise 20,000 men at his own cost and lead them personally. Ferdinand II accepted and showered Wallenstein with confiscated land and titles. Wallenstein's first acquisition was this enormous area. Having knocked down 23 houses, a brick factory, and three gardens, in 1623 he began to build his magnificent palace with its idiosyncratic high-walled gardens and superb, vaulted Renaissance *sala terrena* (room opening onto a garden). Walking around the formal paths, you'll come across numerous statues, an unusual fountain with a woman spouting water from her breasts, and a lava-stone grotto along the wall. Most of the palace itself now serves the Czech Senate as meeting chamber and offices. The palace's cavernous former *Jízdárna,* or riding school, now hosts occasional art exhibitions. ✉ *Letenská 10, Malá Strana.* 🎫 *Free.* ☉ *May–Sept., daily 9–7; mid-Mar.–Apr. and Oct., daily 10–6.*

Hradčany (Castle Area)

To the west of Prague Castle is the residential Hradčany (Castle Area), the town that during the early 14th century emerged out of a collection of monasteries and churches. The concentration of history packed into Prague Castle and Hradčany challenges those not versed in the ups and downs of Bohemian kings, religious uprisings, wars, and oppression. The picturesque area surrounding Prague Castle, with its breathtaking vistas of the Old Town and the Lesser Quarter, is ideal for just wandering. But the castle itself, with its convoluted history and architecture, is difficult to appreciate fully without investing a little more time.

A GOOD WALK

Begin on Nerudova ulice, which runs east–west a few hundred yards south of Prague Castle. At the western (upper) end of the street, look for a flight of stone steps guarded by two saintly statues. Take the stairs up to Loretánská ulice, and enjoy panoramic views of the Church of St. Nicholas and the Lesser Quarter. At the top of the steps, turn left and walk a couple hundred yards until you come to a dusty, elongated square named Pohořelec (Scene of Fire), which suffered tragic fires in 1420, 1541, and 1741. Go through the inconspicuous gateway at No. 8 and up the steps, and you'll find yourself in the courtyard of one of the city's richest monasteries, the **Strahovský klášter** ㊴.

Retrace your steps to Loretánské náměstí, the square at the head of Loretánská ulice that is flanked by the feminine curves of the baroque church **Loreta** ㊵. Across the road, the 29 half pillars of the Černínský palác (Černín Palace) now mask the Czech Ministry of Foreign Affairs. At the bottom of Loretánské náměstí, a little lane trails to the left into the area known as **Nový Svět** ㊶; the name means "New World," though the district is as old-world as they come. Turn right onto the street Nový Svět. Around the corner you get a tantalizing view of the cathedral through the trees. Walk down the winding Kanovnická ulice past the Austrian Embassy and the dignified but melancholy Kostel svatého Jana Nepomuckého (Church of St. John of Nepomuk). At the top of the street on the left, the rounded, Renaissance corner house, Martinický palác, catches the eye with its detailed sgraffiti decorations. Martinický palác opens onto **Hradčanské náměstí** ㊷, with its grandiose gathering of Renaissance and baroque palaces. To the left of the bright yellow Arcibiskupský palác (Archbishop's Palace) on the square is an alleyway leading down to the **Národní galerie** ㊸ and its collections of European art. Across the square, the handsome sgraffito sweep of **Schwarzenberský palác** ㊹ beckons; this is the building you saw from the back side at the beginning of the tour.

TIMING

To do justice to the subtle charms of Hradčany, allow at least an hour just for ambling and admiring the passing buildings and views of the city. The Strahovský klášter halls need about a half-hour to take in, more if you tour the small picture gallery there, and the Loreta and its treasures need at least that length of time. The Národní galerie in the Šternberský palác deserves at least a couple of hours. Keep in mind that several places are not open on Monday.

SIGHTS TO SEE

㊷ **Hradčanské náměstí** (Hradčany Square). With its fabulous mixture of baroque and Renaissance housing, topped by the castle itself, the square had a prominent role (disguised, ironically, as Vienna) in the film *Amadeus*, directed by the then-exiled Czech director Miloš Forman. The house at No. 7 was the set for Mozart's residence, where the composer was haunted by the masked figure he thought was his father. Forman used the flamboyant rococo Arcibiskupský palác (Archbishop's Palace), on the left as you face the castle, as the Viennese archbishop's palace. The plush interior, shown off in the film, is open to the public only on Maundy Thursday. No. 11 was home for a brief time after World War II to a little girl named Marie Jana Korbelová, who would grow up to be Madeleine Albright.

㊵ **Loreta** (Loreto Church). The church's seductive lines were a conscious move on the part of Counter-Reformation Jesuits in the 17th century who wanted to build up the cult of Mary and attract the largely Protestant Bohemians back to the church. According to legend, angels had carried Mary's house from Nazareth and dropped it in a patch of laurel trees in Ancona, Italy. Known as *Loreto* (from the Latin for laurel), it immediately became a center of pilgrimage. The Prague Loreto was one of many symbolic reenactments of this scene across Europe, and it worked: pilgrims came in droves. The graceful facade, with its voluptuous tower, was built in 1720 by Kilian Ignaz Dientzenhofer, the architect of the two St. Nicholas churches in Prague. Most spectacular of all is a small exhibition upstairs displaying the religious treasures presented to Mary in thanks for various services, including a monstrance studded with 6,500 diamonds. ⊠ *Loretánské nám. 7, Hradčany.* ☎ *80 Kč.* ☉ *Tues.–Sun. 9–12:15 and 1–4:30.*

★ ㊸ **Národní galerie** (National Gallery). Housed in the 18th-century Šternberský palác (Sternberg Palace), this collection, though impressive, is limited compared to German and Austrian holdings. During the time when Berlin, Dresden, and Vienna were building up superlative old-master galleries, Prague languished, neglected by her Viennese rulers—one reason why the city's museums lag behind. Part of the museum reopened in 2002 after a long renovation, but some floors are still closed.

Works by Rubens and Rembrandt are already back on display, while some other key pieces in the collection are still waiting in the wings. Other branches of the National Gallery are scattered around town. ✉ *Hradčanské nám. 15, Hradčany,* ☎ *220–514–634,* WEB *www. ngprague.cz.* ▨ *60 Kč.* ☉ *Tues.–Sun. 10–6.*

㊶ Nový Svět. This picturesque, winding little alley, with facades from the 17th and 18th centuries, once housed Prague's poorest residents; now many of the homes are used as artists' studios. The last house on the street, No. 1, was the home of the Danish-born astronomer Tycho Brahe. Living so close to the Loreto, so the story goes, Tycho was constantly disturbed during his nightly stargazing by the church bells. He ended up complaining to his patron, Emperor Rudolf II, who instructed the Capuchin monks to finish their services before the first star appeared in the sky.

㊹ Schwarzenberský palác (Schwarzenberg Palace). This boxy palace with its extravagant sgraffito facade is the **Vojenské historické muzeum** (Military History Museum), one of the largest of its kind in Europe. The beautifully decorated exterior is all that is on display while the interior undergoes a long-term renovation. ✉ *Hradčanské nám. 2, Hradčany.*

★ **㊴ Strahovský klášter** (Strahov Monastery). Founded by the Premonstratensian order in 1140, the monastery remained in its hands until 1952, when the Communists suppressed all religious orders and turned the entire complex into the **Památník národního písemnictví** (Museum of National Literature). The major building of interest is the **Strahov Library,** with its collection of early Czech manuscripts, the 10th-century Strahov New Testament, and the collected works of famed Danish astronomer Tycho Brahe. Also of note is the late-18th-century **Philosophical Hall.** Engulfing its ceilings is a startling sky-blue fresco that depicts an unusual cast of characters, including Socrates' nagging wife, Xanthippe; Greek astronomer Thales, with his trusty telescope; and a collection of Greek philosophers mingling with Descartes, Diderot, and Voltaire. Also on the premises is the order's small art gallery, highlighted by late-Gothic altars and paintings from Rudolf II's time. The library and gallery are accessible only on a guided tour; you can arrange for a tour in English with several days' advance notice. ✉ *Strahovské nádvoří 1/132, Hradčany,* ☎ *220–516–671 to arrange tours.* ▨ *Library tour 50 Kč, gallery tour 30 Kč.* ☉ *Gallery Tues.–Sun. 9– noon and 12:30–5; library daily 9–noon and 1–5.*

OFF THE
BEATEN PATH

PETŘÍN – For a superb view of the city—from a mostly undiscovered, tourist-free perch—stroll over from the Strahov Monastery along the paths toward Prague's own miniature version of the Eiffel Tower, which was restored in 2002. You'll find yourself in a hilltop park, laced with footpaths, with several buildings clustered together near the tower—just keep going gradually upward until you reach the tower's base. The tower and its breathtaking view, the mirror maze (*bludiště*) in a small structure near the tower's base, and the seemingly abandoned svatý Vavřinec (St. Lawrence) church are beautifully peaceful and well worth an afternoon's wandering. You can also walk up from Karmelitská ulice or Újezd down in the Lesser Quarter or ride the funicular railway from U lanové dráhy ulice, off Újezd. Regular public-transportation tickets are valid. For the descent, take the funicular or meander on foot down through the stations of the cross on the pathways leading back to the Lesser Quarter.

Pražský Hrad (Prague Castle)

Numbers in the text correspond to numbers in the margin and on the Prague Castle (Pražský hrad) map.

Despite its monolithic presence, the Prague Castle is not a single structure but rather a collection of buildings dating from the 10th to the 20th century, all linked by internal courtyards. The most important structures are **Chrám svatého Víta** (50), clearly visible soaring above the castle walls, and the **Královský palác** (51), the official residence of kings and presidents and still the center of political power in the Czech Republic. The castle is compact and easy to navigate. Be forewarned: in summer, the castle, especially Chrám svatého Víta, is hugely popular. **Zlatá ulička** (55) became so crowded that in 2002 a separate admission fee was imposed for it.

TIMING

The castle is at its mysterious best in early morning and late evening, and it is incomparable when it snows. The cathedral deserves an hour, as does the Královský palác, while you can easily spend an entire day taking in the museums, the views of the city, and the hidden nooks of the castle. Remember that some sights, such as the Lobkovický palác and the National Gallery branch at Klášter svatého Jiří, are not open on Monday.

SIGHTS TO SEE

53 **Bazilika svatého Jiří** (St. George's Basilica). This church was originally built in the 10th century by Prince Vratislav I, the father of Prince (and St.) Wenceslas. It was dedicated to St. George (of dragon fame), who it was believed would be more agreeable to the still largely pagan people. The outside was remodeled during early baroque times, although the striking rusty-red color is in keeping with the look of the Romanesque edifice. The interior looks more or less as it did in the 12th century and is the best-preserved Romanesque relic in the country. The effect is at once barnlike and peaceful, the warm golden yellow of the stone walls and the small arched windows exuding a sense of enduring harmony. The house-shape painted tomb at the front of the church holds the remains of the founder, Vratislav I. Up the steps, in a chapel to the right, is the tomb Peter Parler designed for St. Ludmila, the grandmother of St. Wenceslas. ✉ *Nám. U sv. Jiří, Hradčany,* ☎ *224–373–368 castle information,* WEB *www.hrad.cz.* *Requires 1-day castle ticket (180 Kč).* ⊙ *Apr.–Oct., daily 9–5; Nov.–Mar., daily 9–4.*

★ 50 **Chrám svatého Víta** (St. Vitus's Cathedral). With its graceful, soaring towers, this Gothic cathedral—among the most beautiful in Europe—is the spiritual heart not only of Prague Castle but of the entire country. It has a long and complicated history, beginning in the 10th century and continuing to its completion in 1929. If you want to hear its history in depth, English-speaking guided tours of the cathedral and the Královský palác can be arranged at the information office across from the cathedral entrance.

Once you enter the cathedral, pause to take in the vast but delicate beauty of the Gothic and neo-Gothic interior glowing in the colorful light that filters through the startlingly brilliant stained-glass windows. This western third of the structure, including the facade and the two towers you can see from outside, was not completed until 1929, following the initiative of the Union for the Completion of the Cathedral, set up in the last days of the 19th century. Don't let the neo-Gothic illusion keep you from examining this new section. The six stained-glass windows to your left and right and the large rose window behind are modern masterpieces. Take a good look at the third window up on the

Prague Castle (Pražský hrad)

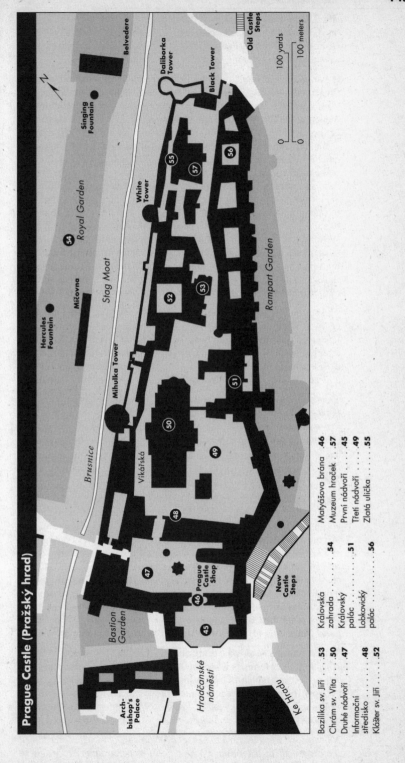

Belvedere

Singing Fountain

Daliborka Tower

Black Tower

Old Castle Steps

Royal Garden

White Tower

Míčovna

Stag Moat

Rampart Garden

Hercules Fountain

Mihulka Tower

Brusnice

Vikářská

New Castle Steps

Bastion Garden

Arch- bishop's Palace

Hradčanské náměstí

Ke Hradu

100 yards
100 meters

left. The familiar Art Nouveau flamboyance, depicting the blessing of Sts. Cyril and Methodius (9th-century missionaries to the Slavs), is the work of the Czech father of the style, Alfons Mucha. He achieved the subtle coloring by painting rather than staining the glass.

If you walk halfway up the right-hand aisle, you will find the **Svatováclavská kaple** (Chapel of St. Wenceslas). With a tomb holding the saint's remains, walls covered in semi-precious stones, and paintings depicting the life of Wenceslas, this square chapel is the ancient heart of the cathedral. Stylistically, it represents a high point of the dense, richly decorated though rather gloomy Gothic favored by Charles IV and his successors. Wenceslas (the "good king" of Christmas-carol fame) was a determined Christian in an era of widespread paganism. Around 925, as prince of Bohemia, he founded a rotunda church dedicated to St. Vitus on this site. But the prince's brother, Boleslav, was impatient to take power, and he ambushed Wenceslas in 929 (or 935 according to some experts) near a church at Stará Boleslav, northeast of Prague. Wenceslas was originally buried in that church, but his grave produced so many miracles that he rapidly became a symbol of piety for the common people, something that greatly irritated the new Prince Boleslav. Boleslav was finally forced to honor his brother by reburying the body in the St. Vitus Rotunda. Shortly afterward, Wenceslas was canonized.

The rotunda was replaced by a Romanesque basilica in the late 11th century. Work was begun on the existing building in 1344. For the first few years the chief architect was the Frenchman Mathias d'Arras, but after his death in 1352 the work was continued by the 22-year-old German architect Peter Parler, who went on to build the Charles Bridge and many other Prague treasures.

The small door in the back of the chapel leads to the **Korunní komora** (Crown Chamber), the repository of the Bohemian crown jewels. It remains locked with seven keys held by seven important people (including the president) and is definitely not open to the public.

A little beyond the Chapel of St. Wenceslas on the same side, stairs lead down to the underground **royal crypt,** interesting primarily for the information it provides about the cathedral's history. As you descend the stairs, you'll see parts of the old Romanesque basilica and portions of the foundations of the rotunda. Moving around into the second room, you'll find a rather eclectic group of royal remains ensconced in new sarcophagi dating from the 1930s. In the center is Charles IV, who died in 1378. Rudolf II, patron of Renaissance Prague, is entombed at the rear in the original tin coffin. To his right is Maria Amalia, the only child of Empress Maria Theresa to reside in Prague. Ascending the wooden steps back into the cathedral, you'll come to the white-marble **Kralovské mausoleum** (Royal Mausoleum), atop which lie stone statues of the first two Hapsburg kings to rule in Bohemia, Ferdinand I and Maximilian II, and of Ferdinand's consort, Anne Jagiello.

The cathedral's **Kralovské oratorium** (Royal Oratory) was used by the kings and their families when attending mass. Built in 1493, the work is a perfect example of late Gothic, laced on the outside with a stone network of gnarled branches very similar in pattern to the ceiling vaulting in the Královský palác. The oratory is connected to the palace by an elevated covered walkway, which you can see from outside.

A few more steps toward the east end, you can't fail to catch sight of the ornate silver **sarcophagus of St. John of Nepomuk.** According to legend, when Nepomuk's body was exhumed in 1721 to be reinterred, the tongue was found to be still intact and pumping with blood. This strange tale served a highly political purpose. The Catholic Church and the Hapsburgs were seeking a new folk hero to replace the Protestant forerunner Jan Hus, whom they despised. The 14th-century priest Nepomuk, killed during a power struggle with King Václav IV, was sainted and reburied a few years later with great ceremony in the 3,700-pound silver tomb, replete with angels and cherubim; the tongue was enshrined in its own reliquary.

The eight chapels around the back of the cathedral are the work of the original architect, Mathias d'Arras. A number of old tombstones, including some badly worn grave markers of medieval royalty, can be seen within, amid furnishings from later periods. Opposite the wooden relief, depicting the looting of the cathedral by Protestants in 1619, is the **Valdštejnská kaple** (Wallenstein Chapel). Since the 19th century, the chapel has housed the Gothic tombstones of its two architects, d'Arras and Peter Parler, who died in 1352 and 1399, respectively. If you look up to the balcony, you can just make out the busts of these two men, designed by Parler's workshop. The other busts around the triforium depict royalty and other VIPs of the time.

The Hussite wars in the 15th century put an end to the first phase of the cathedral's construction. During the short era of illusory peace before the Thirty Years' War, the massive south tower was completed, but lack of money quashed any idea of finishing the building, and the cathedral was closed by a wall built across from the Chapel of St. Wenceslas. Not until the 20th century was the western side of the cathedral, with its two towers, completed in the spirit of Parler's conception.

A key element of the cathedral's teeming, rich exterior decoration is the **Last Judgment mosaic** above the ceremonial entrance, called the Golden Portal, on the south side. The use of mosaic is quite rare in countries north of the Alps; this work, dating from the 1370s, is made of 1 million glass and stone chunks. The once-clouded glass now sparkles again thanks to many years of restoration funded by the Getty Conservation Institute, which was finished in 2001. The central field shows Christ in glory, adored by Charles IV and his consort, Elizabeth of Pomerania, as well as several saints; the risen dead and attendant angels are on the left; and on the right the flames of Hell lick around the figure of Satan. ⊠ *St. Vitus's Cathedral, Hradčany*, ☎ *224–373–368 Castle Information,* 🌐 *www.hrad.cz.* 💳 *Western section free; chapels, crypt, and tower require 1-day castle ticket (180 Kč).* ☉ *Apr.–Oct., daily 9–5; Nov.–Mar., daily 9–4.*

47 **Druhé nádvoří** (Second Courtyard). Empress Maria Theresa's court architect, Nicolò Pacassi, received the imperial approval to remake the castle in the 1760s, as it was badly damaged by Prussian shelling during the Seven Years' War in 1757. The Second Courtyard was the main victim of Pacassi's attempts at imparting classical grandeur to what had been a picturesque collection of Gothic and Renaissance styles. Except for the view of the spires of St. Vitus's Cathedral, the exterior courtyard offers little for the eye to feast upon. This courtyard also houses the rather gaudy **Kaple svatého Kříže** (Chapel of the Holy Cross), with decorations from the 18th and 19th centuries, which now serves as a souvenir and ticket stand.

Built in the late 16th and early 17th century, the Second Courtyard was originally part of a reconstruction program commissioned by Rudolf II, under whom Prague enjoyed a period of unparalleled cultural development. Once the Prague court was established, the emperor gathered around him some of the world's best craftsmen, artists, and scientists, including the brilliant astronomers Johannes Kepler and Tycho Brahe.

Rudolf II amassed a large and famed collection of fine and decorative art, scientific instruments, philosophic and alchemical books, natural wonders, coins, and everything else under the sun. The bulk of the collection was looted by the Swedes during the Thirty Years' War, removed to Vienna when the imperial capital returned there after Rudolf's death, or auctioned off during the 18th century. Artworks that survived the turmoil, for the most part acquired after Rudolf's time, are displayed in the **Obrazárna** (Picture Gallery), on the left side of the courtyard as you face St. Vitus's. In rooms elegantly redecorated by the official castle architect, Bořek Šípek, there are good Renaissance, mannerist, and baroque paintings that hint at the luxurious tastes of Rudolf's court. Across the passageway by the gallery entrance is the **Císařská konírna** (Imperial Stable), where temporary exhibitions are held. The passageway at the northern end of the courtyard forms the northern entrance to the castle and leads out over a luxurious ravine known as the **Jelení příkop** (Stag Moat), which can be entered (from April through October) either here or at the lower end via the metal catwalk off Chotkova ulice, when it isn't closed for sporadic renovations. ✉ *Obrazárna: Second Courtyard, Hradčany,* ☎ *224–373–368 Castle Information,* 🌐 *www.hrad.cz.* 💰 *Courtyard free, Picture Gallery 100 Kč.* 🕐 *Picture Gallery daily 10–6.*

48 **Informační středisko** (Castle Information Office). This is the place to come for entrance tickets, guided tours, headphones for listening to recorded tours in English, tickets to cultural events held at the castle, and money changing. Tickets are valid for one day and allow admission to the older parts of St. Vitus's Cathedral (the 20th-century sections are free), Královský palác, St. George's Basilica (but not the adjacent National Gallery exhibition, which has an additional entry fee), and a medieval bastion called Mihulka with an exhibition on alchemy. Other castle sights—including Golden Lane—require separate tickets, and you purchase these at the door. If you just want to walk through the castle grounds, note that the gates close at midnight April–October and at 11 PM the rest of the year, while the gardens are open April–October only. ✉ *Třetí nádvoří, across from entrance to St. Vitus's Cathedral, Hradčany,* ☎ *224–373–368,* 🌐 *www.hrad.cz.* 💰 *1-day Castle tickets 180 Kč; Golden Lane 40 Kč; combination 1-day and Golden Lane 220 Kč; English-language guided tours 400 Kč for up to 5 people, 60 Kč per additional person (advance booking recommended); grounds and gardens free.* 🕐 *Apr.–Oct., daily 9–5; Nov.–Mar., daily 9–4.*

52 **Klášter svatého Jiří** (St. George's Convent). The first convent in Bohemia was founded here in 973 next to the even older St. George's Basilica. The National Gallery collections of Czech mannerist and baroque art are housed here. The highlights include the voluptuous work of Rudolf II's court painters, the giant baroque religious statuary, and some fine paintings by Karel Škréta and Petr Brandl. ✉ *Nám. U sv. Jiří, Hradčany,* ☎ *257–320–536,* 🌐 *www.ngprague.cz.* 💰 *100 Kč.* 🕐 *Tues.–Sun. 10–6.*

54 **Královská zahrada** (Royal Garden). This peaceful swath of greenery affords an unusually lovely view of St. Vitus's Cathedral and the castle's walls and bastions. Originally laid out in the 16th century, it endured devastation in war, neglect in times of peace, and many redesigns, reaching its present parklike form early in the 20th century. Luckily, its Renaissance treasures survive. One of these is the long, narrow **Míčovna** (Ball Game Hall), built by Bonifaz Wohlmut in 1568, its garden front completely covered by a dense tangle of allegorical sgraffiti.

The **Královský letohrádek** (Royal Summer Palace, also known as the Belvedere), at the garden's eastern end, deserves its usual description as one of the most beautiful Renaissance structures north of the Alps. Italian architects began it; Wohlmut finished it off in the 1560s with a copper roof like an upturned boat's keel riding above the graceful arcades of the ground floor. During the 18th and 19th centuries, military engineers tested artillery in the interior, which had already lost its rich furnishings to Swedish soldiers during their siege of the city in 1648. The Renaissance-style *giardinetto* (little garden) adjoining the summer palace centers on another masterwork, the Italian-designed, Czech-cast Singing Fountain, which resonates to the sound of falling water. ☒ *U Prašného mostu ul. and Mariánské hradby ul. near Chotkovy Park, Hradčany,* ☎ *224–373–368 Castle Information,* WEB *www.hrad.cz.* ☒ *Free.* ☉ *Apr.–Oct., daily 10–5:45.*

⑤ Královský palác (Royal Palace). The palace is an accumulation of the styles and add-ons of many centuries. The best way to grasp its size is from within the **Vladislavský sál** (Vladislav Hall), the largest secular Gothic interior space in Central Europe. The enormous hall was completed in 1493 by Benedikt Ried, who was to late-Bohemian Gothic what Peter Parler was to the earlier version. The room imparts a sense of space and light, softened by the sensuous lines of the vaulted ceilings and brought to a dignified close by the simple oblong form of the early Renaissance windows. In its heyday, the hall was the site of jousting tournaments, festive markets, banquets, and coronations. In more recent times, it has been used to inaugurate presidents, from the Communist Klement Gottwald in 1948 to Václav Havel in 1989, 1993, and 1998.

From the front of the hall, turn right into the rooms of the **Česká kancelář** (Bohemian Chancellery). This wing was built by the same Benedikt Ried only 10 years after the hall was completed, but it shows a much stronger Renaissance influence. Pass through the Renaissance portal into the last chamber of the chancellery. This room was the site of the second defenestration of Prague, in 1618, an event that marked the beginning of the Bohemian rebellion and, ultimately, the Thirty Years' War. This peculiarly Bohemian method of expressing protest (throwing someone out a window) had first been used in 1419 in the New Town Hall, during the lead-up to the Hussite wars. Two hundred years later the same conflict was reexpressed in terms of Hapsburg-backed Catholics versus Bohemian Protestants. Rudolf II had reached an uneasy agreement with the Bohemian nobles, allowing them religious freedom in exchange for financial support. But his next-but-one successor, Ferdinand II, was a rabid opponent of Protestantism and disregarded Rudolf's tolerant "Letter of Majesty." Enraged, the Protestant nobles stormed the castle and chancellery and threw two Catholic officials and their secretary, for good measure, out the window. Legend has it they landed on a mound of horse dung and escaped unharmed, an event the Jesuits interpreted as a miracle. The square window in question is on the left as you enter the room.

At the back of the Vladislav Hall, a staircase leads up to a gallery of the **Kaple všech svatých** (All Saints' Chapel). Little remains of Peter Parler's original work, but the church contains some fine works of art. The large room to the left of the staircase is the **Stará sněmovna** (council chamber), where the Bohemian nobles met with the king in a kind of prototype parliament. The descent from Vladislav Hall toward what remains of the **Romanský palác** (Romanesque Palace) is by way of a wide, shallow set of steps. This **Jezdecké schody** (Riders' Staircase) was the entranceway for knights who came for the jousting tournaments. ☒ *Royal Palace, Třetí nádvoří, Hradčany,* ☎ *224–373–368 Castle Information,* WEB *www.hrad.cz.* ☒ *Requires 1-day Castle ticket (180 Kč).* ☉ *Apr.–Oct., daily 9–5; Nov.–Mar., daily 9–4.*

❺❻ Lobkovický palác (Lobkowicz Palace). From the beginning of the 17th century until the 1940s, this building was the residence of the powerful Catholic Lobkowicz family. It was supposedly to this house that the two defenestrated officials escaped after landing on the dung hill in 1618. During the 1970s the building was restored to its early baroque appearance and now houses the National Museum's permanent exhibition on Czech history. If you want to get a chronological understanding of Czech history from the beginnings of the Great Moravian Empire in the 9th century to the Czech national uprising in 1848, this is the place. Copies of the crown jewels are on display here, but it is the rich collection of illuminated Bibles, old musical instruments, coins, weapons, royal decrees, paintings, and statues that makes the museum well worth visiting. Detailed information on the exhibits is available in English. ✉ *Jiřská ul., Hradčany,* ⟨WEB⟩ *www.nm.cz.* 🖃 *40 Kč.* ⊗ *Tues.–Sun. 9–5.*

❹❻ Matyášova brána (Matthias Gate). Built in 1614, the stone gate once stood alone in front of the moats and bridges that surrounded the castle. Under the Hapsburgs, the gate survived by being grafted as a relief onto the palace building. As you go through it, notice the ceremonial white-marble entrance halls on either side that lead up to President Václav Havel's reception rooms (which are only rarely open to the public).

❺❼ Muzeum hraček (Toy Museum). The building that once belonged to a high royal official called the Supreme Burgrave houses a private collection of modern dolls and other toys, somewhat incongruous to the historical surroundings but fun for those who still love Barbie. Enter at the eastern entrance to the Castle. ✉ *Jiřská ul., Hradčany.* 🖃 *40 Kč.* ⊗ *Daily 9:30–5:30.*

❹❺ První nádvoří (First Courtyard). The main entrance to Prague Castle from Hradčanské náměstí is a little disappointing. Going through the wrought-iron gate, guarded at ground level by Czech soldiers and from above by the ferocious *Battling Titans* (a copy of Ignaz Platzer's original 18th-century work), you'll enter this courtyard, built on the site of old moats and gates that once separated the castle from the surrounding buildings and thus protected the vulnerable western flank. The courtyard is one of the more recent additions to the castle, designed by Maria Theresa's court architect, Nicolò Pacassi, in the 1760s. Today it forms part of the presidential office complex. Pacassi's reconstruction was intended to unify the eclectic collection of buildings that made up the castle, but the effect of his work is somewhat flat.

❹❾ Třetí nádvoří (Third Courtyard). The contrast between the cool, dark interior of St. Vitus's Cathedral and the brightly colored Pacassi facades of the Third Courtyard just outside is startling. The courtyard's clean lines are the work of Slovenian architect Josip Plečnik in the 1930s, but the modern look is a deception. Plečnik's paving was intended to cover an underground world of house foundations, streets, and walls dating from the 9th through 12th centuries and rediscovered when the cathedral was completed. (You can see a few archways through a grating in a wall of the cathedral.) Plečnik added a few eclectic features to catch the eye: a granite obelisk to commemorate the fallen of the First World War, a black-marble pedestal for the Gothic statue of St. George (a copy of the National Gallery's original statue), the inconspicuous entrance to his Bull Staircase leading down to the south garden, and the peculiar golden ball topping the eagle fountain near the eastern end of the courtyard.

❺❺ Zlatá ulička (Golden Lane). An enchanting collection of tiny, ancient, brightly colored houses crouches under the fortification wall looks remarkably like a set for *Snow White and the Seven Dwarfs*. Legend has it that these were the lodgings of the international group of alchemists whom Rudolf II brought to the court to produce gold. The truth is a little less romantic: the houses were built during the 16th century for the castle guards, who supplemented their income by practicing various crafts. By the early 20th century, Golden Lane had become the home of poor artists and writers. Franz Kafka, who lived at No. 22 in 1916 and 1917, described the house on first sight as "so small, so dirty, impossible to live in and lacking everything necessary." But he soon came to love the place. As he wrote to his fiancée: "Life here is something special . . . to close out the world not just by shutting the door to a room or apartment but to the whole house, to step out into the snow of the silent lane." The lane now houses tiny stores selling books, music, and crafts and has become so popular that a separate admission fee is now charged.

Within the walls above Golden Lane, a timber-roof **corridor** (enter between No. 23 and No. 24) is lined with replica suits of armor and weapons (some of it for sale), mock torture chambers, and the like. A shooting range allows you to fire five bolts from a crossbow for 50 Kč. ⊠ *Hradčany*, ☎ *224–373–368*, WEB *www.hrad.cz.* ⊡ *40 Kč; combination 1-day and Golden Lane 220 Kč.* ◔ *Castle and Golden Lane Apr.–Oct., daily 9–5; Nov.–Mar., daily 9–4. Golden Lane Corridor Apr.–Oct., Tues.–Sun. 10–5, Mon. 1–5; Nov.–Mar., Tues.–Sun. 10–4, Mon. 1–4.*

Nové Město (New Town) and Vyšehrad

To this day, Charles IV's building projects are tightly woven into the daily lives of Praguers. His most extensive scheme, the New Town, is still such a lively, vibrant area you may hardly realize that its streets, Gothic churches, and squares were planned as far back as 1348. With Prague fast outstripping its Old Town parameters, Charles IV extended the city's fortifications. A high wall surrounded the newly developed 2½ square km (1½ square mi) area south and east of the Old Town, tripling the walled territory on the Vltava's right bank. The wall extended south to link with the fortifications of the citadel called Vyšehrad. In the mid-19th century, new building in the New Town boomed in a welter of Romantic and neo-Renaissance styles, particularly on Wenceslas Square and avenues such as Vodičkova, Na Poříčí, and Spálená. One of the most important structures was the Národní divadlo (National Theater), meant to symbolize in stone the revival of the Czechs' history, language, and sense of national pride. Both preceding and following Czechoslovak independence in 1918, modernist architecture entered the mix, particularly on the outer fringes of the Old Town and in the New Town. One of modernism's most unexpected products was Cubist architecture, a form unique to Prague, which produced four notable examples at the foot of ancient Vyšehrad.

A GOOD WALK

Václavské náměstí ⑤⑧ is a long, gently sloping boulevard rather than a square in the usual sense. Marked by the **Statue of St. Wenceslas** ⑤⑨, it is bounded at the "top" (actually the southern end) by the **Národní muzeum** ⑥⓪ and at the "foot" (actually the northern end) by the pedestrian shopping areas of Národní třída and Na Příkopě. Today Václavské náměstí has Prague's liveliest street scene. Don't miss the dense maze of arcades tucked away from the street in buildings that line both sides. You'll find an odd assortment of cafés, shops, ice cream parlors, and movie houses, all seemingly unfazed by the passage of time. One eye-catching building on the square is the Hotel Europa, at No. 25, a riot of Art Nouveau that recalls the glamorous world of turn-of-the-20th-century Prague. Work by the Czech artist whose name is synonymous with Art Nouveau is on show just a block off the square, via Jindřišská, at the **Mucha Museum** ⑥.

From the foot of the square, head down 28 října to Jungmannovo náměstí, a small square named for the linguist and patriot Josef Jungmann (1773–1847). In the courtyard off the square at No. 18, have a look at the Kostel Panny Marie Sněžné (Church of the Virgin Mary of the Snows). Building ceased during the Hussite wars, leaving a very high, foreshortened church that never grew into the monumental structure planned by Charles IV. Beyond it lies a quiet sanctuary: the walled Františkánská zahrada (Franciscan Gardens). A busy shopping street, Národní třída, extends from Jungmannovo náměstí about ¾ km (½ mi) to the river and the **Národní divadlo** ⑥. From the theater, follow the embankment, Masarykovo nábřeží, south toward Vyšehrad. Note the Art Nouveau architecture of No. 32, the amazingly eclectic design by Kamil Hilbert at No. 26, and the tile-decorated Hlahol building at No. 16. Opposite, on a narrow island, is a 19th century, yellow-and-white ballroom-restaurant, Žofín.

Straddling an arm of the river at Myslíkova ulice are the modern Galerie Mánes (1928–1930) and its attendant 15th-century water tower, where, from a lookout on the sixth floor, Communist-era secret police used to observe Václav Havel's apartment at Rašínovo nábřeží 78. This building, still part-owned by the president, and the adjoining **Tančící dům** ⑥ are on the far side of a square named Jiráskovo náměstí after the historical novelist Alois Jirásek. From this square, Resslova ulice leads uphill four blocks to a much larger, parklike square, **Karlovo náměstí** ⑥. On the park's northern end is the **Novoměstská radnice** ⑥ (New Town Hall).

If you have the energy to continue on toward Vyšehrad, a convenient place to rejoin the riverfront is Palackého náměstí via Na Moráni street at the southern end of Karlovo náměstí. The square has a (melo)dramatic monument to the 19th-century historian František Palacký, "awakener of the nation," and the view from here of the Benedictine **Klášter Emauzy** ⑥ is lovely. The houses grow less attractive south of here, so you may wish to hop a tram (No. 3, 16, or 17 at the stop on Rašínovo nábřeží) and ride one stop to Výtoň, at the base of the **Vyšehrad** ⑥ citadel. Walk under the railroad bridge on Rašínovo nábřeží to find the closest of four nearby **Cubist buildings** ⑥. Another lies just a minute's walk farther along the embankment; two more are on Neklanova, a couple of minutes' walk "inland" on Vnislavova. To get up to the fortress, make a hard left onto Vratislavova (the street right before Neklanova), an ancient road that runs tortuously up into the heart of Vyšehrad.

It's about 2¼ km (1½ mi) between Národní divadlo and Vyšehrad. Note that Tram No. 17 travels the length of the embankment, if you'd like to make a quicker trip between the two points.

TIMING

You might want to divide the walk into two parts, first taking in the busy New Town between Václavské náměstí and Karlovo náměstí, then doing Vyšehrad and the Cubist houses as a side trip. A leisurely stroll from the Národní divadlo to Vyšehrad may easily absorb two hours, as may an exploration of Karlovo náměstí and the Klášter Emauzy. Vyšehrad is open every day, year-round, and the views are stunning on a clear day or evening, but keep in mind that there is little shade along the river walk on hot afternoons.

SIGHTS TO SEE

⑥ **Cubist buildings.** Born of zealous modernism, Prague's Cubist architecture followed a great Czech tradition in that it fully embraced new ideas while adapting them to existing artistic and social contexts. Between 1912 and 1914, Josef Chochol (1880–1956) designed several of the city's dozen or so Cubist projects. His apartment house **Neklanova 30**, on the corner of Neklanova and Přemyslova, is a masterpiece in dingy concrete. The pyramidal, kaleidoscopic window mouldings and roof cornices are completely novel while making an expressive link to baroque forms; the faceted corner balcony column elegantly alludes to Gothic forerunners. On the same street, at **Neklanova 2**, is another apartment house attributed to Chochol; like the building at Neklanova 30, it uses pyramidal shapes and the suggestion of Gothic columns.

Nearby, Chochol's **villa**, on the embankment at Libušina 3, has an undulating effect created by smoothly articulated forms. The wall and gate around the back of the house use triangular moldings and metal grating to create an effect of controlled energy. The **three-family house**, about 100 yards away from the villa at Rašínovo nábřeží 6–10, was completed slightly earlier, when Chochol's Cubist style was still developing. Here, the design is touched with baroque and neoclassical influence, with a mansard roof and end gables.

㉔ Karlovo náměstí (Charles Square). This square began life as a cattle market, a function chosen by Charles IV when he established the New Town in 1348. The horse market (now Wenceslas Square) quickly overtook it as a livestock-trading center, and an untidy collection of shacks accumulated here until the mid-1800s, when it became a green park named for its patron. ⊠ *Bounded by Řeznická on the north, U Nemocnice on the south, Karlovo nám. on the west, and Vodičkova on the east, Nové Město.*

Just south of Karlovo náměstí is another of Charles IV's gifts to the city, **㉖** the Benedictine **Klášter Emauzy** (Emmaus Monastery). It is often called Na Slovanech, literally "At the Slavs'," in reference to its purpose when established in 1347: the emperor invited Croatian monks here to celebrate mass in Old Slavonic and thus cultivate religion among the Slavs in a city largely controlled by Germans. A faded but substantially complete cycle of biblical scenes by Charles's court artists lines the four cloister walls. The frescoes, and especially the abbey church, suffered heavy damage from a February 14, 1945, raid by Allied bombers that may have mistaken Prague for Dresden, 121 km (75 mi) away. The church lost its spires, and the interior remains a blackened shell. Some years after the war, two curving concrete "spires" were set atop the church. ⊠ *Vyšehradská 49, Vyšehrad (cloister entrance on left at rear of church).* 🏷 *10 Kč.* ☉ *Weekdays 8–6 or earlier depending on daylight.*

㉑ Mucha Museum. For decades it was almost impossible to find an Alfons Mucha original in the homeland of this famous Czech artist, until, in 1998, this private museum opened with nearly 100 works from his long career. What you'd expect to see is here—the theater posters of actress Sarah Bernhardt, the magazine covers, and the luscious, sinuous Art Nouveau designs. There are also paintings, photographs taken in Mucha's studio (one shows Paul Gauguin playing the piano in his underwear), and even Czechoslovak banknotes designed by the artist. ⊠ *Panská 7, Nové Město (1 block off Wenceslas Square, across from Palace Hotel),* ☏ *221–451–335,* WEB *www.mucha.cz.* 🏷 *120 Kč.* ☉ *Daily 10–6.*

㉒ Národní divadlo (National Theater). The idea for a Czech national theater began during the revolutionary decade of the 1840s. In a telling display of national pride, donations to fund the plan poured in from all over the country, from people of every socioeconomic stratum. The cornerstone was laid in 1868, and the "National Theater generation" who built the neo-Renaissance structure became the architectural and artistic establishment for decades to come. Its designer, Josef Zítek (1832–1909), was the leading neo-Renaissance architect in Bohemia. The nearly finished interior was gutted by a fire in 1881, and Zítek's onetime student Josef Schulz (1840–1917) saw the reconstruction through to completion two years later. Statues representing Drama and Opera rise above the riverfront side entrances; two gigantic chariots flank figures of Apollo and the nine Muses above the main facade. The performance space itself is filled with gilding, voluptuous plaster figures and plush upholstery. Next door is the modern (1970s–1980s) Nová scéna (New Stage), where the popular Magic Lantern black-light shows are staged. The Národní divadlo is one of the best places to see a performance; ticket prices start as low as 30 Kč, and you'll have to buy a ticket if you want to see inside because there are no public tours. ⊠ *Národní tř. 2, Nové Město,* ☏ *224–901–448 box office,* WEB *www.narodni-divadlo.cz.*

60 **Národní muzeum** (National Museum). This imposing structure, designed by Prague architect Josef Schulz and built between 1885 and 1890, does not come into its own until it is bathed in nighttime lighting. By day the grandiose edifice seems an inappropriate venue for a musty collection of stones and bones, minerals, and coins. This museum is only for dedicated fans of the genre. ⊠ *Václavské nám. 68, Nové Město,* ☏ *224–497–111,* WEB *www.nm.cz.* ⊡ *80 Kč.* ☉ *May–Sept., daily 10–6; Oct.–Apr., daily 9–5; except for first Tues. of each month, when it is closed.*

65 **Novoměstská radnice** (New Town Hall). At the northern edge of Karlovo náměstí, the New Town Hall has a late-Gothic tower similar to that of the Old Town Hall, as well as three tall Renaissance gables. The first defenestration in Prague occurred here on July 30, 1419, when a mob of townspeople, followers of the martyred religious reformer Jan Hus, hurled Catholic town councillors out the windows. Historical exhibitions and contemporary art shows are held here regularly (admission prices vary), and you can climb the tower for a view of the New Town. ⊠ *Karlovo nám. at Vodičkova, Nové Město.* ⊡ *Tower 20 Kč.* ☉ *Tower May–Sept., Tues.–Sun. 10–6; gallery Tues.–Sun. 10–6.*

59 **Statue of St. Wenceslas.** Josef Václav Myslbek's huge equestrian grouping of St. Wenceslas with other Czech patron saints around him is a traditional meeting place at times of great national peril or rejoicing. In 1939, Praguers gathered to oppose Hitler's takeover of Bohemia and Moravia. It was here also, in 1969, that the student Jan Palach set himself on fire to protest the bloody invasion of his country by the Soviet Union and other Warsaw Pact countries in August of the previous year. The invasion ended the "Prague Spring," a cultural and political movement emphasizing free expression, which was supported by Alexander Dubček, the popular leader at the time. Although Dubček never intended to dismantle Communist authority completely, his political and economic reforms proved too daring for fellow comrades in the rest of Eastern Europe. In the months following the invasion, conservatives loyal to the Soviet Union were installed in all influential positions. The subsequent two decades were a period of cultural stagnation. Hundreds of thousands of Czechs and Slovaks left the country, a few became dissidents, and many more resigned themselves to lives of minimal expectations and small pleasures. ⊠ *Václavské nám., Nové Město.*

63 **Tančící dům** (Dancing House). This whimsical building was partnered into life in 1996 by architect Frank Gehry (of Guggenheim Museum in Bilbao fame) and his Croatian-Czech collaborator Vlado Milunic. A wasp-waisted glass-and-steel tower sways into the main structure as though they were a couple on the dance floor—a "Fred and Ginger" effect that gave the wacky, yet somehow appropriate, building its nickname. The French restaurant La Perle de Prague occupies the top floors, and there is a café at street level. ⊠ *Rašínovo nábř. 80, Nové Město.*

⑱ Václavské náměstí (Wenceslas Square). You may recognize this spot from your television set, for it was here that some 500,000 students and citizens gathered in the heady days of November 1989 to protest the policies of the former Communist regime. The government capitulated after a week of demonstrations, without a shot fired or the loss of a single life, bringing to power the first democratic government in 40 years (under playwright-president Václav Havel). Today this peaceful transfer of power is half-ironically referred to as the "Velvet" or "Gentle" Revolution (*něžná revoluce*). It was only fitting that the 1989 revolution should take place on Wenceslas Square: throughout much of Czech history, the square has served as the focal point for popular discontent. The long "square," which is more like a broad, divided boulevard, was first laid out by Charles IV in 1348 as a horse market at the center of the New Town.

At No. 25, the **Hotel Europa** (⊠ Vaclavske nám. 25) is an Art Nouveau gem, with elegant stained glass and mosaics in the café and restaurant. The terrace is an excellent spot for people-watching. Note in particular the ornate sculpture work of two figures supporting a glass egg on top of the building and the ornate exterior mural. In 1906, when the hotel opened, this was a place for the elite; now the rooms reflect a sense of sadly faded grandeur.

🖐 ⑰ Vyšehrad. Bedřich Smetana's symphonic poem *Vyšehrad* opens with four bardic harp chords that seem to echo the legends surrounding this ancient fortress. Today, the flat-topped bluff standing over the right bank of the Vltava is a green, tree-dotted expanse showing few signs that splendid medieval monuments once made it a landmark to rival Prague Castle.

The historical father of Vyšehrad, the "High Castle," is Vratislav II (ruled 1061–92), a Přemyslid duke who became first king of Bohemia. He made the fortified hilltop his capital, but, under subsequent rulers, it fell into disuse until the 14th century, when Charles IV transformed the site into an ensemble of palaces, the Gothicized main church, battlements, and a massive gatehouse called *Špička,* whose scant remains are on V pevnosti ulice. By the 17th century, royalty had long since departed, and most of the structures they built were crumbling. Vyšehrad was turned into a fortress.

Vyšehrad's place in the modern Czech imagination is largely thanks to the National Revivalists of the 19th century, particularly writer Alois Jirásek (1851–1930), who mined medieval chronicles for legends and facts to glorify the early Czechs. In his rendition, Vyšehrad was the court of the prophetess-ruler Libuše, who had a vision of her husband-to-be, the ploughman Přemysl—father of the Přemyslid line—and of "a city whose glory shall reach the heavens" called Praha. (In truth, the Czechs first came to Vyšehrad around the beginning of the 900s, slightly later than the building of Prague Castle.)

Traces of the citadel's distant past do remain. A heavily restored **Romanesque rotunda,** built by Vratislav II, stands on the east side of the compound. Foundations and a few embossed floor tiles from the late-10th-century **Basilika svatého Vavřince** (St. Lawrence Basilica) are in a structure on Soběslavova Street (if it is locked, you can ask for the key at the refreshment stand just to the left of the basilica entrance; admission is 5 Kč). Part of the medieval fortifications stand next to the surprisingly confined foundation mounds of a medieval palace over-looking a ruined watchtower called Libuše's Bath. A nearby plot of grass hosts a statue of Libuše and her consort Přemysl, one of four large sculpted images of couples from Czech legend by J. V. Myslbek (1848–1922), the sculptor of the St. Wenceslas monument.

The military history of the fortress and the city is covered in a small exposition inside the **Cihelná brána** (Brick Gate). The gate is also the entrance to the **casemates**—a long, dark passageway within the walls that ends at a dank hall used to store several original, pollution-scarred Charles Bridge sculptures. A guided tour into the casemates and the statue storage room starts at the military history exhibit. With its neo-Gothic spires, **Kapitulní kostel svatých Petra a Pavla** (Chapter Church of Sts. Peter and Paul; ✉ K rotundì 10, Vyšehrad, ☎ 224–911–353) dominates the plateau as it has since the 11th century. Next to the church lies the burial ground of the nation's revered cultural figures. Most of the buildings still standing are from the 19th century, but scattered among them are a few older structures and some foundation stones of the medieval palaces. Surrounding the ruins are gargantuan, excellently preserved brick fortifications built from the 17th to the mid-19th century; their broad tops allow strollers to take in sweeping vistas up- and downriver.

A concrete result of the National Revival was the establishment of the **Hřbitov** (cemetery; Vinohradská 294/212, Vyšehrad, ☎ 224–919–815, WEB www.slavin.cz) in the 1860s, adjacent to the Church of Sts. Peter and Paul—it peopled the fortress with the remains of luminaries from the arts and sciences. The grave of Smetana faces the Slavín, a mausoleum for more than 50 honored men and women including Alfons Mucha, sculptor Jan Štursa, inventor František Křižík, and the opera diva Ema Destinnová. All are guarded by a winged genius who hovers above the inscription AČ ZEMŘELI, JEŠTĚ MLUVÍ ("Although they have died, they yet speak"). Antonín Dvořák (1841–1904) rests in the arcade along the north wall of the cemetery. Among the many writers buried here are Jan Neruda, Božena Němcová, Karel Čapek, and the Romantic poet Karel Hynek Mácha, whose grave was visited by students on their momentous November 17, 1989, protest march. ✉ *V Pevnosti 159/5b, Vyšehrad,* ☎ *241–410–348,* WEB *www.praha-vysehrad.cz.* 🔲 *Casemates tour 20 Kč, military exhibit 10 Kč, cemetery free, Church of Sts. Peter and Paul 10 Kč.* ☺ *Grounds daily. Casemates, military history exhibit, and St. Lawrence Basilica Apr.–Oct., daily 9:30–5:30; Nov.–Mar., daily 9:30–4:30. Cemetery Apr.–Oct., daily 8–6; Nov.–Mar., daily 8–4. Church of Sts. Peter and Paul daily 9–noon and 1–5. Metro: Vyšehrad (Line C).*

Vinohrady

From Riegrovy Park and its sweeping view of the city from above the National Museum, the eclectic apartment houses and villas of the elegant residential neighborhood called Vinohrady extend eastward and southward. The pastel-tint ranks of turn-of-the-20th-century apartment houses—many crumbling after years of neglect—are slowly but unstoppably being transformed into upscale flats, slick offices, eternally packed new restaurants, and all manner of shops unthinkable only a half decade ago. Much of the development lies on or near Vinohradská, the main street, which extends from the top of Wenceslas Square to a belt of enormous cemeteries about 3 km (2 mi) eastward. Yet the flavor of daily life persists: smoky old pubs still ply their trade on the quiet side streets; the stately theater, Divadlo na Vinohradech, keeps putting on excellent shows as it has for decades; and on the squares and in the parks nearly everyone still practices Prague's favorite form of outdoor exercise—walking the dog.

69 **Kostel Nejsvětějšího Srdce Páně** (Church of the Most Sacred Heart). If you've had your fill of Romanesque, Gothic, and baroque, this church will give you a look at a startling art deco edifice. Designed in 1927 by Slovenian architect Josip Plečnik (the same architect commissioned to update Prague Castle), the church resembles a luxury ocean liner more than a place of worship. The effect was conscious: during the 1920s and 1930s, the avant-garde imitated mammoth objects of modern technology. Plečnik used many modern elements on the inside. Notice the hanging speakers, seemingly designed to bring the word of God directly to the ears of each worshiper. You may be able to find someone at the back entrance of the church who will let you walk up the long ramp into the fascinating glass clock tower. ⊠ *Nám. Jiřího z Poděbrad, Vinohrady.* ☒ *Free.* ☉ *Daily 10–5. Metro: Jiřího z Poděbrad (Line A).*

70 **Nový židovský hřbitov** (New Jewish Cemetery). Tens of thousands of Czechs find eternal rest in Vinohrady's cemeteries. In this, the newest of the city's half-dozen Jewish burial grounds, you'll find the modest **tombstone of Franz Kafka,** which seems grossly inadequate to Kafka's stature but oddly in proportion to his own modest ambitions. The cemetery is usually open, although guards sometimes inexplicably seal off the grounds. Men may be required to wear a yarmulke (you can buy one here). Turn right at the main cemetery gate and follow the wall for about 100 yards. Kafka's thin, white tombstone lies at the front of section 21. City maps may label the cemetery *Židovské hřbitovy.* ⊠ *Vinohradská at Jana Želivského, Vinohrady.* ☒ *Free.* ☉ *June–Aug., Sun.–Thurs. 9–5, Fri. 9–1; Sept.–May, Sun.–Thurs. 9–4, Fri. 9–1. Metro: Želivského (Line A).*

71 **Pavilon.** This gorgeous, turn-of-the-20th-century, neo-Renaissance, three-story market hall is one of the most attractive sites in Vinohrady. It used to be a major old-style market, a vast space filled with stalls selling all manner of foodstuffs plus the requisite grimy pub. After being spiffed up in the 1990s, it mutated into an upscale shopping mall. Off the tourist track, Pavilion is a good place to watch Praguers—those who can afford its shops' gleaming designer pens and Italian shoes— ostentatiously drinking in *la dolce vita,* cell phones in hand. Walk west two blocks down Vinohradská after exiting the metro. ⊠ *Vinohradská 50, Vinohrady,* ☎ *222–097–111.* ☉ *Mon.–Sat. 8:30 AM–9 PM, Sun. noon–6. Metro: Jiřího z Poděbrad (Line A).*

Letná and Holešovice

From above the Vltava's left bank, the large, grassy plateau called Letná gives you one of the classic views of the Old Town and the many bridges crossing the river. (To get to Letná from the Old Town, take Pařížská Street north, cross the Čechův Bridge, and climb the stairs.) Beer gardens, tennis, and Frisbee attract people of all ages, while amateur soccer players emulate the professionals of Prague's top team, Sparta, which plays in the stadium just across the road. A 10-minute walk from Letná, down into the residential neighborhood of Holešovice, brings you to a massive, gray-blue building whose cool exterior gives no hint of the treasures of Czech and French modern art that line its corridors. Just north along Dukelských hrdinů Street is Stromovka—a royal hunting preserve turned gracious park.

Numbers in the margin correspond to numbers on the Exploring Prague map.

72 **Letenské sady** (Letna Park). Come to this large, shady park for an unforgettable view of Prague's bridges. From the enormous cement pedestal at the center of the park, the largest statue of Stalin in Eastern Europe once beckoned to citizens on the Old Town Square far below. The statue was ripped down in the 1960s, when Stalinism was finally discredited. On sunny Sundays expatriates often meet up here to play ultimate Frisbee. Head east on Milady Horáové street after exiting the metro. ⊠ *Holešovice. Metro: Hradčanská.*

🕖 **Veletržní palác** (Trade Fair Palace). The National Gallery's **Sbírka moderního a soucasného umění** (Collection of Modern and Contemporary Art) has become a keystone in the city's visual-arts scene since its opening in 1995. Touring the vast spaces of this 1920s Constructivist exposition hall and its comprehensive collection of 20th-century Czech art is the best way to see how Czechs surfed the forefront of the avant-garde wave until the cultural freeze following the Communist takeover in 1948. Also on display are works by Western European—mostly French—artists from Delacroix to the present. Especially noteworthy are the early Cubist paintings by Picasso and Braque. The 19th-century Czech art collection of the National Gallery was installed in the palace in the summer of 2000. Watch the papers and posters for information on traveling shows and temporary exhibits. The collection is divided into sections, so be sure to get a ticket for exactly what you want to see. ⊠ *Dukelských hrdinů 47, Holešovice,* ☎ *224–301–111,* WEB *www.ngprague.cz.* 🎫 *One floor 100 Kč, 2 floors 150 Kč, 3 floors 200 Kč, special exhibits 40 Kč.* 🕐 *Tues.–Wed. and Fri.–Sun. 10–6, Thurs. 10–9. Metro: Vltavská (Line C).*

Dining

Dining choices in Prague have increased greatly in the past decade as hundreds of new places have opened to meet the soaring demand from tourists and locals alike. These days, out-and-out rip-offs have almost disappeared, but before paying up at the end of a meal it's a good idea to take a close look at the added cover charge on your bill. Also keep an eye out for a large fee tacked on to a credit card bill. In pubs and neighborhood restaurants, ask if there is a *denní lístek* (daily menu) of cheaper and often fresher selections, but note that many places provide daily menus for the midday meal only. Special local dishes worth making a beeline for include *cibulačka* (onion soup), *kulajda* (potato soup with sour cream), *svíčková* (beef sirloin in cream sauce), and *ovocné knedlíky* (fruit dumplings, often listed under "meatless dishes").

The crush of tourists has placed tremendous strain on the more popular restaurants. The upshot: reservations are an excellent idea, especially for dinner during peak tourist periods. If you don't have reservations, try arriving a little before standard meal times: 11:30 AM for lunch or 5:30 PM for dinner.

For a cheaper and quicker alternative to the sit-down establishments listed below, try a light meal at one of the city's growing number of street stands or fast-food places. Look for stands offering *párky* (hot dogs) or the fattier *klobásy* (grilled sausages served with bread and mustard). Also, chic new cafés and bakeries spring up all the time. For more exotic fare, try the very good vegetarian cooking at **Country Life** (⊠ Melantrichova 15, Staré Město, ☎ 224–213–366). **Vzpomínky na Afriku** (⊠ Rybná at Jakubská, Staré Město, near the Kotva department store) has the widest selection of gourmet coffees in town, served at the single table or to go.

Staré Město (Old Town)

$$$–$$$$ ✕ **Bellevue.** The first choice for visiting dignitaries and businesspeople blessed with expense accounts, Bellevue has creative, freshly prepared cuisine, more nouvelle than Bohemian—and the elegant location

not far from Charles Bridge doesn't hurt. Look for the lamb carpaccio with fresh rosemary, garlic, and extra-virgin olive oil or the wild berries marinated in port and cognac, served with vanilla-and-walnut ice cream. Window seats have stunning views of Prague Castle. The Sunday jazz brunch is a winner, too. ⊠ *Smetanovo nábř. 18, Staré Město,* ☎ 222–221–449. AE, MC, V.

$$–$$$$ ✕ **Allegro.** Some of the best—and most expensive—Italian food in town can be had at the restaurant in the Four Seasons Prague. Don't plan on just dropping in, though; reservations are essential and the dress code bans shorts and sneakers. Jackets are suggested for the evening. In the summer, dining on the terrace, with a spectacular view of the Charles Bridge, makes it worth the extra effort it takes to polish your shoes. The international wine list features selections from the National Wine Bank. ⊠ *Veleslavinova 21, Staré Město, 110 00 Prague 1,* ☎ *221–427–000. Reservations essential. AE, DC MC, V.*

$$–$$$$ ✕ **Jewel of India.** Although generally Asian cooking of any stripe is not Prague's forte, here is a sumptuous spot well worth seeking out for northern Indian tandooris and other moderately spiced specialties, including some delicious vegetarian dishes. ⊠ *Pařížská 20, Staré Město,* ☎ 224–811–010. AE, MC, V. Metro: Staroměstská.

$$–$$$$ ✕ **V Zátiší.** White walls and casual grace accentuate the subtle flavors ★ of smoked salmon, plaice, beef Wellington, and other non-Czech specialties. Here, as at most of the city's better establishments, the wine list has expanded in recent years and now includes most of the great wine-producing regions, though good Moravian vintages are still kept on hand. In behavior unusual for the city, the benign waiters fairly fall over each other to serve diners. ⊠ *Liliová 1 at Betlémské nám., Staré Město,* ☎ 222–222–025. AE, MC, V.

$$$ ✕ **Barock.** Call it chic or call it pretentious, Barock exemplifies the revolution in Prague's dining and social life since those uncool Communists decamped. Thai and Japanese dishes predominate, and there are other Asian choices and international standards. Although eating isn't the main point here—being seen is—the fish dishes and sushi won't let you down. ⊠ *Pařížská 24, Josefov,* ☎ 222–329–221. AE, DC, MC, V.

$–$$ ✕ **Chez Marcel.** At this authentic French bistro on a quiet street you can get a little taste of that *other* riverside capital. French-owned and -operated, Chez Marcel has a smallish but reliable menu listing pâtés, salads, rabbit, and chicken, as well as some of the best steaks in Prague. The specials board usually has some tempting choices, such as salmon, beef daube, or foie gras. ⊠ *Haštalská 12, Staré Město,* ☎ 222–315–676. No credit cards.

$–$$ ✕ **Pizzeria Rugantino.** Bright and spacious, this buzzing pizzeria serves up thin-crust pies; big, healthy salads; and good Italian bread. It can get quite loud when full, which is most nights. ⊠ *Dušní 4, Staré Město,* ☎ 222–318–172. No credit cards. No lunch Sun.

$ ✕ **Kavárna Slavia.** This legendary hangout for the best and brightest ★ in Czech arts—from composer Bedřich Smetana and poet Jaroslav Seifert to then-dissident Václav Havel—reopened after being held hostage in absurd real-estate wrangles for most of the 1990s. Its Art Deco interior is a perfect backdrop for people-watching, and the vistas (the river and Prague Castle on one side, the National Theater on the other) are a compelling reason to linger for hours over a coffee—although it's not the best brew in town. The Slavia is a café to its core, but you can also get a light meal, such as a small salad with Balkan cheese, an open-face sandwich. ⊠ *Smetanovo nábř. 1012/2, Staré Město,* ☎ 224–220–957. AE, MC, V.

Prague Dining and Lodging

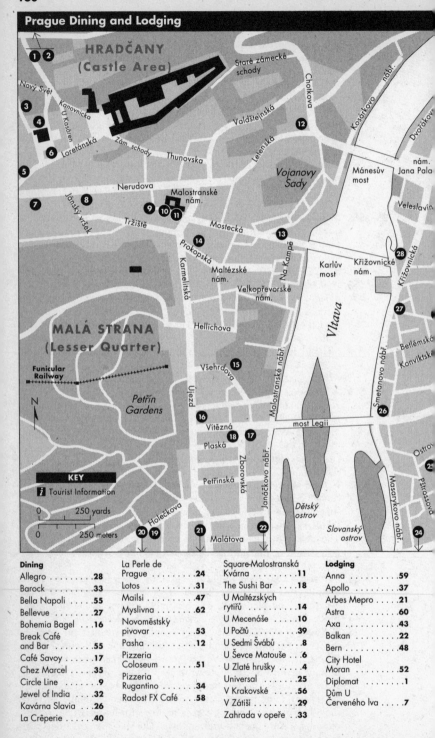

Dining

Allegro **28**
Barock **33**
Bella Napoli **55**
Bellevue **27**
Bohemia Bagel . .**16**
Break Café
and Bar **55**
Café Savoy **17**
Chez Marcel **35**
Circle Line **9**
Jewel of India . . .**32**
Kavárna Slavia . .**26**
La Crêperie **40**

La Perle de
Prague **24**
Lotos **31**
Mailsi **47**
Myslivna **62**
Novoměstský
pivovar **53**
Pasha **12**
Pizzeria
Coloseum **51**
Pizzeria
Rugantino **34**
Radost FX Café . .**58**

Square-Malostranská
Kvárna **11**
The Sushi Bar **18**
U Maltézských
rytířů **14**
U Mecenáše **10**
U Počtů **39**
U Sedmi Švábů . .**8**
U Ševce Matouše . .**6**
U Zlaté hrušky . . .**4**
Universal **25**
V Krakovské **56**
V Zátiší **29**
Zahrada v opeře . .**33**

Lodging

Anna **59**
Apollo **37**
Arbes Mepro **21**
Astra **60**
Axa **43**
Balkan **22**
Bern **48**
City Hotel
Moran **52**
Diplomat **1**
Dům U
Červeného lva **7**

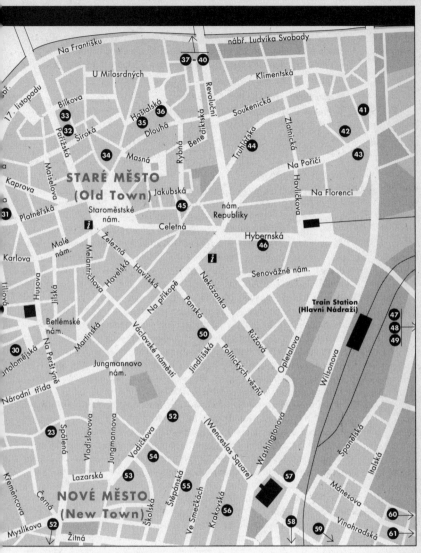

$ ✕ **Lotos.** Banana ragoût with polenta and broccoli strudel are two favorites at what is undoubtedly the best of the city's scant selection of all-vegetarian restaurants. Blond-wood tables and billowing tie-dyed fabric wall-hangings set an informal yet elegant atmosphere. The salads and soups are wonderful. ⊠ *Platnéřská 13, Staré Město,* ☎ *222–322–390. MC, V.*

Malá Strana (Lesser Quarter)

$$$–$$$$ ✕ **Pasha.** This inviting Middle Eastern spot at the foot of Prague Castle hits just the right notes of luxury and easiness. The à la carte menu includes luscious *adana kebab* (skewer of minced lamb), pilaf, and shish kebab. Baklava served with fresh mint tea makes a splendid dessert. ⊠ *U Lužického semináře 23, Malá Strana,* ☎ *257–532–439. AE, MC, V. Closed Mon.*

$$–$$$$ ✕ **Circle Line.** Now moved out of the cellar into two elegant dining rooms, one done up in blue and the other in pink, Circle Line maintains its high standards with such dishes as fallow deer with spaetzle, pike perch, and yellowfin tuna carpaccio. The service can't be faulted. There are creative seasonal specials such as the warm foie gras with cherries, but be sure to save room for the chocolate plate for dessert. Brunch is served daily until 6 PM. ⊠ *Malostranské nám. 12, Malá Strana,* ☎ *257–530–022. AE, MC, V.*

$$–$$$$ ✕ **Café Savoy.** Opened in 1887 as a grand café, the Savoy lasted only
★ a few years before the long, airy room was divided up to be made into shops. In 2001 the grand café was reborn as an upscale restaurant with bright cloth ceiling hangings and a shocking orange facade. Menu items include duck appetizers, homemade ravioli, and fresh seafood, served in a variety of surprising taste combinations and presented with an artistic, nouvelle flair. Lunch specials are a real value. ⊠ *Vítězná 5, Malá Strana,* ☎ *257–329–860. MC, V.*

$$–$$$$ ✕ **Square - Malostranská kvárna.** An older café on this main square has been given an upscale new look that might not please all preservationists. The food, which includes such main courses as grilled skate wing or bucatini and duck ragoût, should put smiles on the faces of those looking for something different at a central location. Outdoor seating in the summer makes this a prime spot for people-watching, but make sure to peek inside at the trendy decor. ⊠ *Malostranské nám,* ☎ *257–532–109. AC, DC, MC, V.*

$$–$$$$ ✕ **The Sushi Bar.** This chic little joint with the wacky whale sculpture floating overhead could have been transported straight from San Francisco. Given Prague's distance from the sea, the selection of sushi and sashimi is excellent. For the same reason, call ahead to check when the fresh seafood is due (it's delivered twice a week), or stick to the broiled salmon or tempura dishes. ⊠ *Zborovská 49, Malá Strana,* ☎ *0603–244–882. DC, MC, V.*

$$–$$$ ✕ **U Maltézských rytířů.** The tongue-twisting name means "At the Knights of Malta," a reference to the Catholic order whose embassy is nearby. The upstairs dining room and bar are cozy, but ask for a table in the deep cellar—then ask the proprietress to regale you with yarns about this ancient house. They've dropped some old favorites from the menu but still offer good steaks, game, and fish. ⊠ *Prokopská 10, Malá Strana,* ☎ *257–533–666. AE, MC, V.*

$$ ✕ **U Mecenáše.** A fetching Renaissance inn from the 17th century, with dark, high-back benches in the front room and cozy, elegant sofas and chairs in back, this is a place to splurge. From the aperitifs to the specialty steaks or beef Wellington and the cognac (swirled lovingly in oversize glasses), the presentation is seamless. ⊠ *Malostranské nám. 10, Malá Strana,* ☎ *257–531–631. AE, MC, V.*

$–$$ ✕ **U Sedmi Švábů.** Medieval decorations and waitresses in peasant dresses serving beer and mead to diners seated at long wooden tables make this medieval-theme restaurant worth a stop. Unusual menu items include millet pancakes with herbs, carp on garlic, and roast pork knuckle for two. Special multicourse "knight's feasts" are also available. Chicken, steaks, and other mundane dishes are available for the less adventuresome. ⊠ *Jánskývršek 14, Malá Strana,* ☎ *257–531–645. AE, MC, V.*

$ ✕ **Bohemia Bagel.** It's not New York, but the friendly, North American–owned Bohemia Bagel still serves up a plentiful assortment of fresh bagels, from raisin-walnut to "supreme," with all kinds of toppings. The thick soups are among the best in Prague for the price, and the bottomless cups of coffee are a further draw. ⊠ *Újezd 16, Malá Strana,* ☎ *257–310–694. No credit cards.*

Hradčany

$$–$$$$ ✕ **U Zlaté hrušky.** At this fetching little rococo house perched on one of Prague's prettiest cobblestone streets, slide into one of the cozy dark-wood booths and let the cheerful staff advise you on wines and specials. Among the regular offerings are a superb leg of venison with pears and millet gnocchi, and an excellent appetizer of foie gras in wine sauce. After dinner, stroll to the castle for an unforgettable panorama. ⊠ *Nový Svět 3, Hradčany,* ☎ *220–514–778. AE, MC, V.*

$–$$ ✕ **U Ševce Matouše.** Steaks are the raison d'être at this former shoe-maker's shop, where a gold shoe still hangs from the ceiling of the arcade outside to guide patrons into the vaulted dining room. Appetizers are hit-and-miss; stick with the dozen or so tenderloins and filet mignons. ⊠ *Loretánské nám. 4, Hradčany,* ☎ *220–514–536. MC, V.*

Nové Město (New Town) and Vyšehrad

$$–$$$$ ✕ **La Perle de Prague.** Delicious Parisian cooking awaits at the top of the curvaceous "Fred and Ginger" building. The interior of the main room is washed with soft tones of lilac and sea green. This room also has smallish windows—typical of architect Frank Gehry's designs—and rather cheesy nude photographs, but the semi-private dining room at the very top has a riveting view over the river. Try the red snapper Provençal, freshwater *candát* (pike perch), or tournedos of beef Béarnaise. Make reservations as early as you can. This is also a good reason to unpack your tie. ⊠ *Rašínovo nábř. 80, Nové Město,* ☎ *221–984–160. AE, DC, MC, V. Closed Sun. No lunch Mon.*

$$–$$$$ ✕ **Bella Napoli.** The decor may make you think you're in Las Vegas, but the food is genuine and the price-to-quality ratio hard to beat. Close your eyes to the alabaster Venus de Milos astride shopping-mall fountains and head straight for the antipasto bar, which will distract you with fresh olives, eggplant, squid, and mozzarella. For your main course, go with any of a dozen superb pasta dishes or splurge with shrimp or chicken parmigiana. ⊠ *V Jámě 8, Nové Město,* ☎ *222–232–933. No credit cards.*

$$–$$$ ✕ **Zahrada v opeře** (Garden in the Opera). Ignore the concrete barri-
★ cades, armored personnel carriers, and machine-gun toting soldiers. They are on hand to protect the adjacent Radio Free Europe head-quarters. The pebbled floor, subdued lighting, and gentle classical music of "the safest garden in the world" make for a romantic setting that contrasts sharply with the security outside. The prices for fresh seafood, steaks, and salads are quite reasonable, and the international wine list offers some surprising selections. ⊠ *Legerova 75, Nové Město,* ☎ *224–239–685. AE, MC, V.*

$–$$ ✕ **Break Café and Bar.** A reasonably priced selection of salads and sand-
★ wiches in the daytime gives way to an international menu in the evening that includes such extremes as Scandinavian gravlax and steak tartare,

the latter according to a recipe from Maxim's. A comfortable, relaxed atmosphere makes this a nice break from the hustle of nearby Wenceslas Square. ⊠ *Štepanská 32, Nové Město*, ☎ *222–231–065. No credit cards.*

$–$$ ✗ **Novoměstský pivovar.** It's easy to lose your way in this crowded microbrewery-restaurant with its maze of rooms, some painted in mock-medieval style, others covered with murals of Prague street scenes. *Vepřové koleno* (pork knuckle) is a favorite dish. The beer is the cloudy, fruity "fermented" style. ⊠ *Vodičkova 20, Nové Město*, ☎ *222–231–662. AE, MC, V.*

$–$$ ✗ **Pizzeria Coloseum.** An early entry in the burgeoning pizza-and-pasta trade, this one has kept its popularity due largely to its position right off Wenceslas Square. Location doesn't have everything to do with it, though; the pizzas have a wonderfully thin, crisp crust, and the pasta with Gorgonzola sauce will have you blessing Italian cows. Steaks and seafood are also on the menu. Long picnic tables make this an ideal spot for an informal lunch or dinner. There's even a salad bar. ⊠ *Vodičkova 32, Nové Město*, ☎ *224–214–914. AE, MC, V.*

$–$$ ✗ **Radost FX Café.** Colorful and campy in design, this lively café is a street-level adjunct to the popular Radost dance club. It's a favorite vegetarian outpost for both Czechs and expatriates. The creative specials of a Mexican or Italian persuasion are tasty, and filling enough to satisfy carnivores. If you suddenly find yourself craving a brownie, this is the place to get a fudge fix. Another plus: it's open until around 3 AM. ⊠ *Bělehradská 120, Nové Město*, ☎ *224–254–776. No credit cards.*

$–$$ ✗ **Universal.** A pioneer in the neighborhood behind the National Theater that's fast becoming a trendy dining ghetto, Universal serves up satisfying French- and Indian-influenced main courses, giant side orders of scalloped potatoes, and luscious lemon tarts or chocolate mousse—all at ridiculously low prices. ⊠ *V Jirchářích 6, Nové Město*, ☎ *224–918–182. No credit cards.*

$ ✗ **V Krakovské.** At this clean, proper pub close to the major tourist sights, the food is traditional and hearty. This is the place to try *svíčková na smetaně* (thinly sliced sirloin beef in cream sauce) paired with an effervescent pilsner beer. ⊠ *Krakovská 20, Nové Město*, ☎ *222–210–204. No credit cards.*

Vinohrady

$–$$ ✗ **Myslivna.** The name means "Hunting Lodge," and the cooks at this neighborhood eatery certainly know their way around venison, quail, and boar. Attentive staff can advise on wines: try Vavřinecké, a hearty red that holds its own with any beast. The roasted pheasant with bacon and the leg of venison with walnuts get high marks. ⊠ *Jagellonská 21, Vinohrady*, ☎ *222–723–252. AE, MC, V.*

Letná and Holešovice

$–$$ ✗ **U Počtů.** This is a charmingly old-fashioned neighborhood restaurant with comparatively skilled service. Garlic soup and chicken livers in wine sauce are flawlessly rendered, and the grilled trout is delicious. ⊠ *Milady Horákové 47, Letná*, ☎ *233–371–419. AE, MC, V.*

$ ✗ **La Crêperie.** Started by a Czech-French couple, this creperie near the Veletržní palác (Trade Fair Palace) serves all manner of crepes, both sweet and savory. (It may take at least three or four to satisfy a hearty appetite.) Make sure to leave room for the dessert crepe with cinnamon-apple puree layered with lemon cream. The wine list offers both French and Hungarian vintages. ⊠ *Janovského 4, Holešovice*, ☎ *220–878–040. No credit cards.*

Žižkov

$–$$$ ✕ **Mailsi.** Funky paintings of Arabian Nights–type scenes in a low-ceil-
★ ing cellar make this Pakistani restaurant casual and cheerful. Chicken
is done especially well here—the *murgh vindaloo* may well be the
spiciest dish in Prague, and the thin-sliced marinated chicken (*murgh
tikka*) appetizer is a favorite. Take Tram 5, 9, or 26 to the Lipanská
stop, and then walk one block uphill. ✉ *Lipanská 1, Žižkov,* ☎ 222–
717–783. *No credit cards.*

Lodging

A slow rise in lodging standards continues, but at all but the most ex-
pensive hotels standards lag behind those of Germany and Austria—
as do prices. In most of the $$$$ and $$$ hotels, you can expect to
find a restaurant and an exchange bureau on or near the premises. Dur-
ing the peak season reservations are absolutely imperative; for the re-
mainder of the year they are highly recommended. Many hotels in Prague
go by a three-season system: the lowest rates are charged from December
through February, excluding Christmas (at some hotels) and New
Year's (at all hotels), when high-season rates are charged; the middle
season includes March, November, and often July and August; and spring
and fall bring the highest rates. Easter sees higher-than-high-season rates,
and some hotels up the price for other holidays and trade fairs. It always pays to ask first. Standard room rates almost always include breakfast. Only the top-end hotels have air-conditioning.

A private room or apartment can be a cheaper and more interesting
alternative to a hotel. You'll find agencies offering such accommodations all over Prague, including at the main train station (Hlavní
nádraží), Holešovice station (Nádraží Holešovice), and at Ruzyně Airport. These bureaus normally are staffed with people who can speak
some English, and most can book rooms in hotels and pensions as well
as private accommodations. Rates for private rooms start at around
$15 per person per night and can go much higher for better-quality
rooms. In general, there is no fee, but you may need to try several bureaus to find the accommodation you want. Ask to see a photo of the
room before accepting it, and be sure to pinpoint its location on a map—
you don't want to wind up in an inconveniently distant location. You
may be approached by (usually) men in the stations hawking rooms,
and while these deals aren't always rip-offs, you should be wary of them.
Prague Information Service arranges lodging from all of its central offices, including the branch in the main train station, which is in the
booth marked TURISTICKÉ INFORMACE on the left side of the main hall
as you exit the station.

The bluntly named **Prague Accommodation Service** (✉ Opatovická 20,
Nové Město, ☎ FAX 233–376–638, WEB www.accommodation-prague-
centre.cz) can help you find a reasonably priced apartment in the center of town for a short stay. **Stop In** (✉ V Holešovičkách 15, Libeň,
☎ FAX 284–680–115, WEB www.stopin.cz) offers private apartments and
rooms, some in the more residential areas.

Staré Město (Old Town)

$$$$ 🏨 **Four Seasons Prague.** A new central building joins together a
baroque house from 1737 and a renovated neoclassical former factory
from 1846 into a large, modern hotel with an unbeatable riverside location. Rooms with a view of the Charles Bridge or the Castle cost more.
Movie stars such as Sean Connery and Owen Wilson made this their
base when they worked in Prague. Breakfast can be included for a little extra. ✉ *Veleslavinova 21, Staré Město, 110 00 Prague 1,* ☎ 221–
427–000, FAX 221–426–977, WEB *www.fourseasons.com/prague.* 142

rooms, 20 suites. Restaurant, cable TV with movies, in-room safe, mini-bars, health club, massage, sauna, bar, concierge, Internet, business services, meeting rooms, parking (fee), some pets allowed (fee), no-smoking rooms. AE, DC MC, V.

$$$$ 🏨 **Grand Hotel Bohemia.** This beautifully refurbished Art Nouveau town palace sits across the street from Obecní dům (Municipal House), near the Prašná brána (Powder Tower). During the Communist era it was a nameless, secure hideaway for ranking foreign party members. Once it was restored to private hands, the hotel was remodeled by its new Austrian owners, who opted for a muted, modern look in the rooms but left the sumptuous Boccaccio ballroom in its faux-rococo glory. In the rooms, sweeping, long drapes frame spectacular views of the Old Town. Each has a trouser press and answering machine. ✉ *Králodvorská 4, Staré Město, 110 00 Prague 1,* ☎ *224–804–111,* FAX *222–329–545,* WEB *www.grandhotelbohemia.cz. 73 rooms, 5 suites. Restaurant, café, in-room fax, in-room safes, minibars, cable TV, bar, meeting rooms, some pets allowed (fee); no-smoking floor. AE, DC, MC, V. BP.*

$$$ 🏨 **Maximilian.** Oversize beds, classic French cherrywood furniture, and thick drapes make for a relaxing stay in this luxurious hotel. A relatively new property (opened in 1995), it's on a peaceful square, well away from traffic, noise, and crowds, yet within easy walking distance to Old Town Square and Pařížská Street. ✉ *Haštalská 14, Staré Město, 110 00 Prague 1,* ☎ *221–806–111,* FAX *221–806–110,* WEB *www.goldentulip.com. 72 rooms. In-room fax, in-room safes, minibars, cable TV, Internet, meeting rooms, some pets allowed (fee), parking (fee); no-smoking rooms. AE, DC, MC, V. BP.*

$ 🏨 **Pension Unitas.** The spartan rooms of this former convent, now operated by the Christian charity Unitas, used to serve as interrogation cells for the Communist secret police. (Václav Havel was once a "guest.") Today conditions are much more comfortable, though it feels much more like a hostel than a pension. There's a common (but clean) bathroom on each floor. You'll need to reserve well in advance, even in the off-season. Note that there is an adjacent three-star hotel, Cloister Inn, using the same location and phone number, so when calling, specify the pension. ✉ *Bartolomějská 9, Staré Město, 110 00 Prague 1,* ☎ *224–211–020,* FAX *224–210–800,* WEB *www.unitas.cz. 40 rooms with shared bath. Restaurant; no a/c, no smoking. No credit cards. BP.*

Malá Strana (Lesser Quarter)

$$$$ 🏨 **U Tří Pštrosů.** The location could not be better: a romantic corner just a stone's throw from the river and within arms' reach of the Charles Bridge. The airy rooms of the centuries-old building still have their original oak-beam ceilings and antique furniture, and many have views over the river. Massive walls keep out the noise of the crowds on the bridge. An excellent in-house restaurant serves traditional Czech dishes to guests and non-guests alike. Rates drop slightly in July and August—probably because there's no air-conditioning, though the building's thick walls help keep it cool. ✉ *Dražického nám. 12, Staré Město, 118 00 Prague 1,* ☎ *257–532–410,* FAX *257–533–217,* WEB *www.utripstrosu.cz. 14 rooms, 4 suites. Restaurant, cable TV, minibar, Internet; no a/c. AE, DC, MC, V. BP.*

$$$ 🏨 **Dům U Červeného lva.** On the Lesser Quarter's main, historic thoroughfare, a five-minute walk from Prague Castle's front gates, the
★ baroque " House at the Red Lion" is an intimate, immaculately kept hotel. Guest rooms have parquet floors, 17th-century painted-beam ceilings, superb antiques, and all-white bathrooms with brass fixtures. The two top-floor rooms can double as a suite. Note that there is no elevator, and the stairs are steep. ✉ *Nerudova 41, Staré Město, 118*

00 Prague 1, ☎ *257–533–832,* FAX *257–532–746,* WEB *www. hotelredlion.com. 5 rooms, 3 suites. 2 restaurants, in-room safes, mini-bars, cable TV, bar, some pets allowed; no a/c. AE, DC, MC, V. BP.*

$$$ ⚏ **Kampa.** This early baroque armory turned hotel is tucked away on
★ an abundantly picturesque street at the southern end of the Lesser Quarter, just off Kampa Island. The bucolic setting and comparatively low rates make it one of the city's better bargains. Note the late-Gothic vaulting in the massive dining room. ⊠ *Všehrdova 16, Staré Město, 118 00 Prague 1,* ☎ *257–320–508 or 257–320–404,* FAX *257–320–262,* WEB *www.bestwestern-ce.com/kampa. 85 rooms. Restaurant, minibars, cable TV; no a/c. AE, MC, V. BP.*

Hradčany

$$$$ ⚏ **Savoy.** A restrained yellow Jugendstil facade conceals one of the city's
★ most luxurious small hotels. Once a budget hotel, the building was gutted and lavishly refurbished in the mid-1990s. A harmonious maroon-and-mahogany color scheme carries through the public spaces and the rooms, some of which are furnished in purely modern style, while others have a rococo look. The Restaurant Hradčany is one of the city's best hotel dining rooms. The biggest disappointment: although Prague Castle is just up the road, none of the rooms have a view of it. ⊠ *Keplerova 6, Hradčany, 118 00 Prague 6,* ☎ *224–302–430,* FAX *224–302–128,* WEB *www.hotel-savoy.cz. 55 rooms, 6 suites. Restaurant, café, in-room safes, minibars, cable TV, sauna, gym, meeting rooms, Internet, some pets allowed (fee); no-smoking floor. AE, DC, MC, V. BP.*

$$$ ⚏ **Romantik Hotel U Raka.** This private guest house, since 1997 a
★ member of the Romantik Hotels & Restaurants organization, has a quiet location on the ancient, winding streets of Nový Svět, just behind the Loreto Church and a 10-minute walk from Prague Castle. One side of the 18th-century building presents a rare example of half-timbering, and the rooms sustain the country feel with heavy furniture reminiscent of a Czech farmhouse. There are only six rooms, but if you can get a reservation (try at least a month in advance), you will have a wonderful base for exploring Prague. ⊠ *Černínská 10/93, Hradčany, 118 00 Prague 1,* ☎ *220–511–100,* FAX *220–510–511,* WEB *www.romantikhotels.com. 5 rooms, 1 suite. Cable TV; no kids under 10. AE, MC, V. BP.*

Nové Město (New Town)

$$$$ ⚏ **Palace.** For the well-heeled, this is Prague's most coveted address—
★ a muted, pistachio-green Art Nouveau building perched on a busy corner only a block from Wenceslas Square. The hotel's spacious, well-appointed rooms, each with a white-marble bathroom, are dressed in velvety pinks and greens cribbed straight from an Alfons Mucha print. The hotel's restaurant is pure Continental, from the classic garnishes to the creamy sauces. Two rooms are set aside for travelers with disabilities. Children 12 and under stay for free. ⊠ *Panská 12, Nové Město, 111 21 Prague 1,* ☎ *224–093–111,* FAX *224–221–240,* WEB *www.hotel-palace.cz. 114 rooms, 10 suites. 2 restaurants, in-room safes, minibars, sauna; no-smoking floors. AE, DC, MC, V. BP.*

$$$ ⚏ **City Hotel Moran.** This renovated 19th-century town house has a bright, inviting lobby and equally bright and clean rooms that are modern, if slightly bland. Some upper-floor rooms have good views of Prague Castle. ⊠ *Na Moráni 15, Nové Město, 120 00 Prague 2,* ☎ *224–915–208,* FAX *224–920–625,* WEB *www.bestwestern-ce.com/moran. 57 rooms. Restaurant, cable TV, Internet, meeting room, some pets allowed; no-smoking floor. AE, DC, MC, V. BP.*

$$$ ⚏ **Elite.** An extensive renovation preserved the 14-century Gothic facade and many interior architectural details of this building while allowing for modern comforts. Rooms are furnished with antiques, and

many have decorated Renaissance-style wooden ceilings and large desks. One of the suites has a mural ceiling. The central garden, with bar service in the daytime, makes a nice refuge from busy nearby Náodní třiADda. ⊠ *Ostrovní 32, Nové Město, 110 00 Prague 1,* ☎ *224–932–250,* FAX *224–930–787,* WEB *www.hotelelite.cz. 77 rooms, 2 suites. Restaurant, room service, cable TV with movies, in-room safes, minibars, hair salon, bar, laundry service, business services, meeting room, some pets allowed (fee), parking (fee). AE, DC, MC, V. BP.*

$$$ 🏨 **Meteor Plaza.** This Best Western hotel offers modern conveniences in a historical building (Empress Maria Theresa's son, Joseph II, stayed here when he was passing through in the 18th century). The baroque building is only five minutes on foot from downtown. Renovations have left most of the rooms with a surprisingly modern look that masks the hotel's history. To get a sense of the hotel's age, visit the original 14th-century wine cellar. Rates drop markedly in midsummer and even more in winter. ⊠ *Hybernská 6, Nové Město, 110 00 Prague 1,* ☎ *224–192–111,* FAX *224–213–005,* WEB *www.hotel-meteor.cz. 90 rooms, 6 suites. Restaurant, minibars, cable TV with movies, gym, parking (fee). AE, DC, MC, V. BP.*

$$ 🏨 **Opera.** Once the lodging of choice for divas performing at the nearby Státní opera (State Theater), the Opera greatly declined under the Communists. The mid-1990s saw the grand fin-de-siècle facade rejuvenated with a perky pink-and-white exterior paint job. This exuberance is strictly on the outside, though, and the rooms are modern and easy on the eyes. ⊠ *Těšnov 13, Nové Město, 110 00 Prague 1,* ☎ *222–315–609,* FAX *222–311–477,* WEB *www.hotel-opera.cz. 64 rooms. Restaurant, minibars, cable TV, bar, meeting room, some pets allowed; no a/c. AE, DC, MC, V. BP.*

$$ 🏨 **Axa.** Funky and functional, this 1932 high-rise was once a mainstay of the budget-hotel crowd. Over the years, the rooms have certainly improved; however, the lobby and public areas are still decidedly tacky, with plastic flowers, lots of mirrors, and glaring lights. There are scores of free weights in Axa's gym, making it one of the best in Prague. ⊠ *Na Poříčí 40, Nové Město, 113 03 Prague 1,* ☎ *224–812–580,* FAX *224–214–489,* WEB *www.vol.cz/axa. 126 rooms, 6 suites. Restaurant, cable TV, indoor pool, hair salon, health club, sauna, meeting room, bar, some pets allowed; no a/c. AE, DC, MC, V. BP.*

$$ 🏨 **Harmony.** This is one of the renovated, formerly state-owned standbys. A stern 1930s facade clashes with the bright 1990s interior, but cheerful receptionists, comfortably casual rooms, and an easy 10-minute walk to the Old Town compensate for the aesthetic flaws. Ask for a room away from the bustle of one of Prague's busiest streets. ⊠ *Na Poříčí 31, Nové Město, 110 00 Prague 1,* ☎ *222–311–229,* FAX *222–310–009. 60 rooms. 2 restaurants, cable TV, meeting rooms, some pets allowed; no a/c. AE, DC, MC, V. BP.*

$–$$ 🏨 **Salvator.** An efficiently run establishment just outside the Old Town, this pension offers more comforts than most in its class, including satellite TV and minibars in most rooms, and a combination breakfast room and bar with a billiard table. Rooms are pristine if plain, with the standard narrow beds; those without private bath also lack TVs but are a good value nonetheless. ⊠ *Truhlářská 10, Nové Město, 110 00 Prague 1,* ☎ *222–312–234,* FAX *222–316–355,* WEB *www.salvator.cz. 28 rooms, 16 with bath; 7 suites. Restaurant, some minibars, cable TV in some rooms, bar, some pets allowed (fee), parking (fee); no a/c, no TV in some rooms. AE, MC, V. BP.*

Vinohrady

$$ ⊡ **Anna.** The bright neoclassical facade and Art Nouveau details have been lovingly restored on this 19th-century building. While the street it's on is quiet, a few minutes' walk will get you to bustling New Town. The suites on the top floors offer a nice view of the historic district. In 2002, the hotel opened an annex, the Dependance Anna, in the central courtyard of the block with 12 less expensive rooms, but you must return to the main hotel for breakfast. ✉ *Budečská 17, Vinohrady, 120 21 Prague 2,* ☎ *222–513–111,* FAX *222–515–158,* WEB *www.hotelanna.cz. 22 rooms, 2 suites, 12 annex rooms. Cable TV, meeting room, Internet, some pets allowed (fee); no a/c. AE, MC, V. BP.*

Smíchov

The name means "mixed neighborhood" because, when the city had walls, Smíchov was on the outside, and all manner of people could live there. While it's still a colorful, working-class area, lots of new construction has made it a shopping and entertainment hub with relatively easy access, by tram, metro, or foot, to the city's historical center.

$$$ ⊡ **Kinsky Garden.** You could walk the mile or so from this hotel to Prague Castle entirely on the tree-lined paths of Petřín, the hilly park that starts across the street. Opened in 1997, the hotel takes its name from a garden established by Count Rudolf Kinsky in 1825 on the southern side of Petřín. The public spaces are not spaces, nor are some rooms, but everything is tasteful and comfortable. Try to get a room on one of the upper floors for a view of the park. The management and restaurant are Italian. ✉ *Holečkova 7, Smíchov, 150 00 Prague 5,* ☎ *257–311–173,* FAX *257–311–184,* WEB *www.hotelkinskygarden.cz. 60 rooms. Restaurant, cable TV with movies, bar, Internet, meeting room, some pets allowed; no-smoking floor. AE, DC, MC, V. BP.*

$$ ⊡ **Arbes Mepro.** Renovations in 2001 redecorated and added fancier furniture and room safes to this conveniently located hotel. The Smíchov neighborhood has several good restaurants (including the U Mikuláše Dačického wine tavern, across the street from the hotel) and nice strolls along the river or up the Petřín hill. The wine cellar serves as a breakfast room and can be booked for group dinners. Trams to the historical center are just a block away, or it's a 10-minute walk to the historic center. ✉ *Viktora Huga 3, Smíchov, 150 00 Prague 5,* ☎ *257–210–410,* FAX *257–215–263,* WEB *www.arbes-mepro.cz. 27 rooms. Cable TV, in-room safes, bar, meeting room; no a/c. AE, MC, V. BP.*

$$ ⊡ **Petr.** Set in a quiet part of Smíchov, just a few minutes' stroll from the Lesser Quarter, this is an excellent value. As a "garni" hotel, it does not have a full-service restaurant, but it does serve breakfast (included in the price). The rooms are simply but adequately furnished. It's a 10-minute walk from the closest metro stop. ✉ *Drtinova 17, Smíchov, 150 00 Prague 5,* ☎ *257–314–068,* FAX *257–314–072,* WEB *www.hotelpetr.cz 37 rooms, 2 suites. Restaurant, cable TV, Internet, some pets allowed (fee); no a/c. AE, MC, V. BP. Metro: Anděl (Line B).*

$ ⊡ **Balkan.** A fresh coat of bright paint on the outside helps this bare-knuckles hotel to stand out from its run-down surroundings. The spartan Balkan is on a busy street not far from the Lesser Quarter and the Národní divadlo (National Theater). Breakfast is available for an additional 85 Kč. ✉ *Svornosti 28, Smíchov, 150 00 Prague 5,* ☎ FAX *25732–7180, 25732–2150, or 25732–5583. 30 rooms. Restaurant, cable TV, sauna, some pets allowed (fee); no a/c. AE, MC, V.*

Žižkov

It's hard to go for more than a block in this densely populated neighborhood without finding a pub or a nightclub. Several places offer live music, making it a center of nightlife. Plus, the restaurants here are generally quite good and a bit cheaper than those in the center. As in all cities, some of the nightlife has a slightly seamy side. It's best to exercise a moderate amount of caution, especially on side streets, and avoid the seedier pubs that offer gambling machines or other dubious attractions.

$$ ⊞ **Olšanka.** The main calling card of this boxy modern hotel is its outstanding 50-meter swimming pool and modern sports center, which includes a pair of tennis courts and aerobics classes. Rooms are clean and, though basic, have the most important hotel amenities. There's also a relaxing sauna with certain nights reserved for men, women, or both. Note that the sports facilities may be closed in August. The neighborhood is nondescript, but the Old Town is only 10 minutes away by direct tram. ⊠ *Táboritská 23, Žižkov, 130 87 Prague 3,* ☎ *267–092–212,* FAX *222–713–315,* WEB *www.hotelolsanka.cz. 200 rooms. Restaurant, cable TV, tennis court, pool, aerobics, health club, bar, Internet, meeting rooms, some pets allowed (fee). AE, MC, V.*

$ ⊞ **Bern.** The cream-colored Bern is a comfortable alternative to staying in the city center. Rooms are on the plain side, with fairly basic, dark-wood furniture. Bathrooms have showers only. Although rather far out, it is situated on several city bus routes into the New and Old Towns; buses run frequently even on evenings and weekends, and the trip takes 10 to 15 minutes. ⊠ *Koněvova 28, Žižkov, 130 00 Prague 3,* ☎ FAX *22258–4420. 26 rooms. Restaurant, cable TV, minibars, bar, some pets allowed. AE, DC, MC, V. BP.*

Eastern Suburbs

$ ⊞ **Apollo.** This is a standard, no-frills, square-box hotel where clean rooms come at a fair price. Its primary flaw is its location: roughly 20 minutes away by metro and tram from the city center. ⊠ *Kubišova 23, Libeň, 182 00 Prague 8,* ☎ *284–680–628. 35 rooms. Restaurant, cable TV; no a/c. MC, V. BP. Metro: Nádraží Holešovice (Line C), then Tram 5, 14, or 17 to Hercovka stop.*

$ ⊞ **Astra.** The location of this modern hotel best serves drivers coming into town from the east, although the nearby metro station makes it easy to reach from the center. The neighborhood is quiet, if ordinary, and the rooms are more comfortable than most in this price range. ⊠ *Mukařovská 1740/18, Stodůlky, 100 00 Prague 10,* ☎ *274–813–595,* FAX *274–810–765,* WEB *www.hotelastra.cz. 43 rooms, 10 suites. Restaurant, cable TV, nightclub, meeting room, some pets allowed, parking (fee); no a/c. AE, DC, MC, V. BP. Metro: Skalka (Line A), then walk south on Na padesátém about 5 mins to Mukařovská.*

$ ⊞ **Pension Louda.** The friendly owners of this family-run guest house
★ go out of their way to make you feel welcome. The large, spotless rooms are an exceptional bargain, and although the place is in the suburbs, the hilltop site offers a stunning view of greater Prague from the south-facing rooms. ⊠ *Kubišova 10, Libeň, 182 00 Prague 8,* ☎ *284–681–491,* FAX *284–681–488. 9 rooms. Gym, sauna; no a/c. No credit cards. BP. Metro: Nádraží Holešovice (Line C), then Tram 5, 14, or 17 to Hercovka stop.*

Western Suburbs

$$–$$$$ ⊞ **Diplomat.** This sprawling complex opened in 1990 and remains popular with business travelers thanks to its location between the airport and downtown. From the hotel, you can easily reach the city center by metro. The modern rooms may not exude much character, but they are tastefully furnished and quite comfortable. You can drive a miniature racing car at the indoor track next door. ⊠ *Evropská 15, Dejvice, 160 00 Prague 6,* ☎ *296–559–111,* FAX *296–559–215,* WEB

*www.diplomatpraha.cz. 369 rooms, 13 suites. 2 restaurants, café, cable
TV with movies, gym, sauna, bar, nightclub, meeting room, Internet,
parking (fee); no-smoking floors. AE, DC, MC, V. BP. Metro: Dejvická
(Line A).*

$ ☎ **Penzion Sprint.** Straightforward rooms, most of which have their
own bathroom (however tiny), make the Sprint a fine choice. This pension is on a quiet residential street, next to a large track and soccer
field in the outskirts of Prague. It's about 20 minutes from the airport.
Tram 18 rumbles directly to the Old Town from the Batérie stop just
two blocks away. ✉ *Cukrovárnická 62, Střešovice, 160 00 Prague 6,*
☎ *233–343–338,* FAX *233–344–871,* WEB *web.telecom.cz/penzionsprint.
21 rooms, 6 with bath. Restaurant, some pets allowed; no a/c. AE, MC,
V. BP.*

Nightlife and the Arts

The fraternal twins of the performing arts and nightlife continue to enjoy
an exhilarating growth spurt in Prague, and the number of concerts,
plays, musicals, and clubs keeps rising. Some venues in the city center
pitch themselves to tourists, but there are dozens of places where you
can join the local crowds for music, dancing, or the rituals of beer and
conversation. For details of cultural and nightlife events, look for the
English-language newspaper the *Prague Post* or one of the multilingual monthly guides available at hotels, tourist offices, and newsstands.

Nightlife

CABARET

For adult stage entertainment (with some nudity) try the **Varieté Praga**
(✉ Vodičkova 30, ☎ 224–215–945).

DISCOS

Dance clubs come and go regularly. **Gejzeer Club** (✉ Vinohradská 40,
Vinorhady, ☎ 02/2251–6036, WEB www.gejzeer.com) is one of the
newer gay discos to emerge on the scene in Prague. **Karlovy Lázně** (✉
Novotného lávka, Staré Město), near the Charles Bridge, is a four-story
dance palace with everything from Czech oldies to ambient chill-out
sounds. A longtime favorite is **Radost FX** (✉ Bělehradská 120, Nové
Město, ☎ 222–513–144), with imported and homegrown DJs playing the latest house, hip-hop, and dance music.

JAZZ CLUBS

Jazz gained notoriety under the Communists as a subtle form of protest,
and the city still has some great jazz clubs, featuring everything from
swing to blues and modern. All listed clubs have a cover charge.
AghaRTA (✉ Krakovská 5, Nové Město, ☎ 222–211–275) presents
jazz acts in an intimate space. Music starts around 9 PM, but come earlier to get a seat. **Jazz Club U staré paní** (✉ Michalská 9, Staré Město,
☎ 224–228–090, WEB www.ustarepani.cz) has a rotating list of tried-
and-true Czech bands. **Jazz Club Železná** (✉ Železná 16, Staré Město,
☎ FAX 224–239–697, WEB www.jazzclub.cz) mixes its jazz acts with world
music. **Reduta** (✉ Národní 20, Nové Město, ☎ 224–912–246) has a
full program of local and international musicians.

PUBS AND BARS

Bars and lounges are not traditional Prague fixtures, but bars catering
to a young crowd have elbowed their way in over the past few years.
Still, most social life of the drinking variety takes place in pubs (*pivnice*
or *hospody*), which are liberally sprinkled throughout the city's neighborhoods. Tourists are welcome to join in the evening ritual of sitting
around large tables and talking, smoking, and drinking beer. Before

venturing in, however, it's best to familiarize yourself with a few points of pub etiquette: always ask if a chair is free before sitting down (*Je tu volno?*). To order a beer (*pivo*), do not wave the waiter down or shout across the room; he will usually assume you want beer—most pubs serve one brand—and bring it over to you without asking. He will also bring subsequent rounds to the table without asking. To refuse, just shake your head or say no thanks (*ne, děkuju*). At the end of the evening, usually around 10:30 or 11, the waiter will come to tally the bill. There are plenty of popular pubs in the city center, all of which can get impossibly crowded.

The oldest brewpub in Europe, **U Fleků** (✉ Křemencova 11, Nové Město, ☎ 224–930–831, WEB www.ufleku.cz) has been open since 1499 and makes a tasty, if overpriced, dark beer. **U Medvídků** (✉ Na Perštýně 7, Staré Město, ☎ 224–211–916, WEB www.umedkidku.cz) was a brewery at least as long ago as the 15th century. Beer is no longer made on the premises; rather, they serve draft Budvar shipped from České Budějovice. **U svatého Tomáše** (✉ Letenská 12, Malá Strana, ☎ 257–320–101) brewed beer for Augustinian monks starting in 1358. Now it serves commercially produced beer in a tourist-friendly, mock-medieval hall in the Lesser Quarter. **U Zlatého Tygra** (✉ Husova 17, Staré Město, ☎ 222–221–111) is famed as one of the three best Prague pubs for Pilsner Urquell, the original and perhaps the greatest of the pilsners. It also used to be a hangout for such raffish types as the writer Bohumil Hrabal, who died in 1997.

The **James Joyce Pub** (✉ Liliová 10, Staré Město, ☎ 224–248–793, WEB www.jamesjoyce.cz) is authentically Irish (it has Irish owners), with Guinness on tap and excellent food of the fish-and-chips persuasion. **U Malého Glena** (✉ Karmelitská 23, Malá Strana, ☎ 257–531–717, WEB www.malyglen.cz) offers a popular bar and a stage for local and expat jazz, blues, and folk music.

ROCK CLUBS

Prague's rock, alternative, and world-music scene is thriving. The younger crowd flocks to **Lucerna Music Bar** (✉ Vodičkova 36, Nové Město, ☎ 224–217–108, WEB www.lucerna.cz) to catch popular Czech rock and funk bands and visiting acts. **Malostranská Beseda** (✉ Malostranské nám. 21, Malá Strana, ☎ 257–532–092) is a dependable bet for sometimes bizarre but always good musical acts from around the country. The cavernous **Palác Akropolis** (✉ Kubelíkova 27, Žižkov, ☎ 299–330–913, WEB www.palacakropolis.cz) has top Czech acts and major international world-music performers; as the name suggests, the space has an Acropolis theme. Hard-rock enthusiasts should check out the **Rock Café** (✉ Národní 20, Nové Město, ☎ 224–914–416, WEB www.rockcafe.cz). For dance tracks, hip locals congregate at **Roxy** (✉ Dlouhá 33, Staré Město, ☎ 224–810–951, WEB www.roxy.cz).

The Arts

Prague's cultural flair is legendary, and performances are sometimes booked far in advance by all sorts of Praguers. The concierge at your hotel may be able to reserve tickets for you. Otherwise, for the cheapest tickets go directly to the theater box office a few days in advance or immediately before a performance. Ticket agencies may charge higher prices than box offices do. American Express offices sell tickets to many concerts. **Bohemia Ticket International** (✉ Na Příkopě 16, Nové Město, ☎ 224–215–031, WEB www.ticketsbti.cz; Malé nám. 13, Staré Město, ☎ 224–227–832) specializes in mostly classical music. **Ticketpro** (✉ Salvátorská 10, Staré Město, ☎ 224–814–020, WEB www.ticketpro.cz), with outlets all over town, accepts major credit cards. Tickets for some club and live music events are handled by **Ticketstream** (✉ Koubkova 8, Nové

Město, ☎ 224–263–049, WEB www.ticketstream.cz), which also has outlets at some hotels and restaurants.

Classical concerts are held all over the city throughout the year. In addition to Prague's two major professional orchestras, classical ensembles are the most common finds, and the standard of performance ranges from adequate to superb, though the programs tend to take few risks. Serious fans of baroque music may have the opportunity to hear works of little-known Bohemian composers at these concerts. Some of the best chamber ensembles are the Martinů Ensemble, the Prague Chamber Philharmonic (also known as the Prague Philharmonia), the Wihan Quartet, the Czech Trio, and the Agon contemporary music group.

Performances are held regularly at many of the city's palaces and churches, including the Garden on the Ramparts below Prague Castle (where the music comes with a view); both Churches of St. Nicholas; the Church of Sts. Simon and Jude on Dušní in the Old Town; the Church of St. James on Malá Štupartská, near Old Town Square; the Zrcadlová kaple (Mirror Chapel) in the Klementinum on Mariánské náměstí in the Old Town; and the Lobkowicz Palace at Prague Castle. If you're an organ-music buff, you'll most likely have your pick of recitals held in Prague's historic halls and churches. Popular programs are offered at the Church of St. Nicholas in the Lesser Quarter and the Church of St. James, where the organ plays amid a complement of baroque statuary.

Dvořák Hall (✉ Rudolfinum, nám. Jana Palacha, Staré Město, ☎ 224–893–111, WEB www.czechphilharmonic.cz) is home to one of Central Europe's best orchestras, the Czech Philharmonic. Frequent guest conductor Sir Charles Mackerras is a leading proponent of modern Czech music. One of the best orchestral venues is the resplendent Art Nouveau **Smetana Hall** (✉ Obecní dům, nám. Republiky 5, Staré Město, ☎ 222–002–100, WEB www.obecnidum.cz), home of the excellent Prague Symphony Orchestra and major venue for the annual Prague Spring music festival. Concerts at the **Villa Bertramka** (✉ Mozartova 169, Smíchov, ☎ 257–318–461, WEB www.bertramka.cz) emphasize the music of Mozart and his contemporaries.

If a film was made in the United States or Britain, the chances are good that it will be shown with Czech subtitles rather than dubbed. (Film titles, however, are usually translated into Czech, so your only clue to the movie's country of origin may be the poster used in advertisements.) Movies in the original language are normally indicated with the note *českými titulky* (with Czech subtitles). Prague's English-language publications carry film reviews and full timetables. Many downtown cinemas cluster near Wenceslas Square. A wave of new construction has left the city with several modern multiplexes that have giant screens and digital sound. **Slovanský dům** (✉ Na Příkop22, Nové Město, ☎ 257–181–212, WEB www.stercentury.cz) is the most central, but also the most expensive. Among the largest cinemas in Prague is **Blaník** (✉ Václavské nám. 56, ☎ 224–033–172). At this writing, an IMAX theater was scheduled to open by early 2003 at **Flora Plaza** (✉ Vinohradská and Jičínská, Žižkov) right above the metro Flora stop on the A line. **Lucerna** (✉ Vodičkova 36, Nové Město, ☎ 224–216–972) is a classic picture palace in the shopping arcade of the same name.

The Czech Republic has a strong operatic tradition. Unlike during the Communist period, operas are almost always sung in their original tongue, and the repertoire offers plenty of Italian favorites as well as the Czech national composers Janaček, Dvořák, and Smetana. (Czech operas are supertitled in English.) The major opera houses also often stage ballets. Appropriate attire is recommended for all venues; the National and Estates theaters instituted a "no jeans" rule in 1998. Ticket prices are still quite reasonable, at 40 Kč–900 Kč.

A great venue for a night at the opera is the plush **Národní divadlo** (National Theater; ⌧ Národní tř. 2, Nové Měesto, ☎ 224–901–448, WEB www.narodni-divadlo.cz). Performances at the **Statní Opera Praha** (State Opera House; ⌧ Wilsonova 4, Nové Město, ☎ 224–227–266, WEB www.opera.cz), near the top of Wenceslas Square, can also be excellent. The historic **Stavovské divadlo** (Estates Theater; ⌧ Ovocný tř. 1, Staré Měesto, ☎ 224–215–001, WEB www.narodni-divadlo.cz), where Mozart's *Don Giovanni* premiered in the 18th century, plays host to a mix of operas and dramatic works.

PUPPET SHOWS

This traditional form of Czech popular entertainment has been given new life thanks to the productions mounted at the **Národní divadlo marionet** (National Marionette Theater; ⌧ Žatecká 1, ☎ 224–819–322; in season, shows are also performed at Celetná 13). Children and adults alike can enjoy the hilarity and pathos of famous operas adapted for nonhuman "singers." The company's bread and butter is a production of Mozart's *Don Giovanni*.

THEATER

A dozen or so professional theater companies play in Prague to ever-packed houses. Visiting the theater is a vital activity in Czech society, and the language barrier can't obscure the players' artistry. Nonverbal theater also abounds: not only tourist-friendly mime and "Black Light Theater"—a melding of live acting, mime, video, and stage trickery—but also serious (or incomprehensible) productions by top local and foreign troupes. Several English-language theater groups operate sporadically. For complete listings, pick up a copy of the *Prague Post*. The famous **Laterna Magika** (Magic Lantern) puts on a multimedia extravaganza in the National Theater's glass-encased modern hall (⌧ Národní tř. 4, Nové Město, ☎ 224–914–129). The popular **Archa Theater** (⌧ Na Poříčí 26, Nové Město, ☎ 221–716–333) offers avant-garde and experimental theater, music, and dance and has hosted world-class visiting ensembles such as the Royal Shakespeare Company.

Outdoor Activities and Sports

Boatings

Rowboats and paddle boats can be rented on Slovanský ostrov, the island in the Vltava just south of the National Theater.

Fitness Clubs

Some luxury hotels have well-equipped fitness centers with swimming pools. The centrally located **Hilton** (⌧ Pobřežní 1, Karlín, ☎ 224–841–111, WEB www.hilton.com; metro: Florenc [Line B or C]) has full fitness facilities and tennis courts. Excellent and inexpensive facilities can be found at the **Hotel Axa** (⌧ Na Poříčí 40, Nové Město, ☎ 224–812–580, WEB www.vol.cz/axa).

Jogging

The best place for jogging is **Stromovka,** a large, flat park adjacent to the Výstaviště fairgrounds in Prague 7 (take Tram 5, 12, or 17 to the Výstaviště stop). Closer to the center, another popular park is **Letenské sady** (Letna Park), the park east of the Royal Garden at Prague

Castle, across Chotkova Street. For safety's sake, unaccompanied women should avoid the more remote corners of this park.

Spectator Sports

The best place to find out what's going on (and where) is the weekly sports page of the *Prague Post,* or you can inquire at your hotel.

SOCCER

National and international matches are played regularly at the home of Prague's Sparta team, **Stadión Spartra Praha** (Sparta Stadium; ⊠ Milady Horákové, Letná, ☎ 220–571–167 box office, WEB www. sparta.cz), behind Letna Park. To reach the stadium, take Tram 1, 25, or 26 to the Sparta stop.

Swimming

The **Hilton** (⊠ Pobřežní 1, Karlín, ☎ 224–841–111, WEB www.hilton.com; metro: Florenc [Line B or C]) has a pool that is open to the public. **Hotel Axa** (⊠ Na Poříčí 40, Nové Město, ☎ 224–812–580, WEB www. vol.cz/axa) has a nice indoor pool. The best public swimming pool in Prague is at the **Plavecký Stadión Podolí** (Podolí Swimming Stadium; ⊠ Podolská 74, Podolí, ☎ 241–433–952), which you can get to from the city center in 15 minutes or less by taking Tram 3 or 17 to the Kublov stop. The indoor pool is 50 meters long, and the complex also includes two open-air pools, a sauna, a steam bath, and a wild-ride water slide. A word of warning: Podolí, for all its attractions, is notorious as a local hot spot of petty thievery. Don't entrust any valuables to the lockers— it's best either to check them in the safe with the *vrátnice* (superintendent), or better yet, don't bring them at all.

Shopping

While Prague has a long way to go before it can match such great European shopping cities as Paris and Rome, the Czech Republic capital is a great place to pick up gifts and souvenirs. Bohemian crystal and porcelain deservedly enjoy a worldwide reputation for quality, and plenty of shops offer excellent bargains. The local market for antiques and art is still relatively undeveloped, although dozens of antiquarian bookstores harbor some excellent finds, particularly German and Czech books and graphics.

Shopping Districts

The major shopping areas are **Na Příkopě,** which runs from the foot of Wenceslas Square to náměstí Republiky (Republic Square), and the area around **Old Town Square.** The Old Town **Pařížská ulice** and **Karlova ulice** are streets dotted with boutiques and antiques shops. In the Lesser Quarter, try **Nerudova ulice,** the street that runs up to Hradčany. An artistically designed modern glass shopping mall, **Anděl City** (⊠ Corner of Plzeňská and Nádražní, Smiov, WEB www. angelcity.com; metro: Anděl) covers an entire city block. It partly opened in 2001 and eventually will include a multiplex cinema, a four-star hotel, and bowling alley plus clothing, perfume, electronics, and book stores. A large Carrefour supermarket and another multiplex are right across the street.

Department Stores

Prague's department stores are catching up quickly to their Western counterparts. **Bílá Labuť'** (⊠ Na Poříčí 23, Nové Město, ☎ 224–811–364, WEB www.bilalabut.cz) has a decent selection, but the overall shabbiness harks back to socialist times. **Kotva** (⊠ Nám. Republiky 8, Nové Město, ☎ 224–801–111, WEB www.od-kotva.cz) is comparatively upscale, with a nice stationery section and a basement supermarket with wine and cheese aisles. The centrally located **Tesco** (⊠ Národní tř. 26, ☎ 222–003–111) is generally the best place for one-stop shopping and a supermarket with peanut butter and other hard-to-find items.

Street Markets

For fruits, vegetables, and souvenirs, the best street market in central Prague is on **Havelská ulice** in the Old Town. The biggest market is the one in **Holešovice,** north of the city center; it offers food, jewelry, electronic goods, clothes, and imported liquor. Take the metro (Line C) to the Vltavská station and then catch any tram heading east (running to the left as you exit the metro station). Exit at the first stop and follow the crowds. It's better to shop in the week, as both are closed Saturday afternoon and all day on Sunday.

Specialty Stores

ANTIQUES

For antiques connoisseurs, Prague can be a bit of a letdown. Even in comparison to other former Communist capitals such as Budapest, the choice of antiques in Prague can seem depressingly slim, as the city lacks large stores with a diverse selection of goods. The typical Prague *starožitnosti* (antiques shop) tends to be a small, one-room jumble of old glass and bric-a-brac. The good ones distinguish themselves by focusing on one particular specialty.

On the pricey end of the scale is the Prague affiliate of the Austrian auction house **Dorotheum** (✉ Ovocný tř. 2, Nové Město, ☎ 224–222–001, ⓦⓔⓑ www.dorotheum.cz), an elegant pawnshop that specializes in small things: jewelry, porcelain knickknacks, and standing clocks, as well as the odd military sword. The small **JHB Starožitnosti** (✉ Panská 1, Nové Město, ☎ 222–245–836) is the place for old clocks: everything from rococo to Empire standing clocks and Bavarian cuckoo clocks. The shop also sells antique pocket watches. **Nostalgie Antique** (✉ Jánský Vršek 8, Malá Strana, ☎ 257–530–049) specializes in old textiles and jewelry. Most of the textiles are pre–World War II and include clothing, table linens, curtains, hats, and laces. **Papillio** (✉ Týn 1, Staré Město, ☎ 224–895–454, ⓦⓔⓑ www.papilio.cz), in the elaborately refurbished medieval courtyard behind the Church of the Virgin Mary Before Týn, is probably one of the best antiques shops in Prague, offering furniture, paintings, and especially museum-quality antique glass. Here you can find colorful Biedermeier goblets by Moser and wonderful Loetz vases. **Zlatnictví František Vomáčka** (✉ Náprstkova 9, Staré Město, ☎ 222–222–017) is a cluttered shop that redeems itself with its selection of old jewelry in a broad price range, including rare Art Nouveau rings and antique garnet brooches. In the shop's affiliate next door, jewelry is repaired, cleaned, and made to order.

ART GALLERIES

The best galleries in Prague are quirky and eclectic affairs, places to sift through artworks rather than browse at arms' length. Many are also slightly off the beaten track and away from the main tourist thoroughfares. Prague's as-yet-untouristed Nový Svět neighborhood is something of a miniature artist's quarter. **Galerie Litera** (✉ Karlinske nám. 13, Karlín, ☎ 222–317–195) is in a neighborhood where tourists rarely set foot—it's not rough but pretty seedy. (Karlín is northeast of the city center; get off the metro at Florenc and walk five minutes up Sokolovská.) Most of the gallery space is given over to temporary shows of unique, high-quality graphics. There are also some lovely ceramics as well as a refined selection of antiquarian art books. **Galerie Nový Svět** (✉ Nový Svět 5, Hradčany, ☎ 220–514–611) displays interesting paintings and drawings by somewhat obscure Czech artists, as well as ceramics, glass, and art books. At the high end is **Galerie Peithner-Lichtenfels** (✉ Michalská 12, Staré Město, ☎ 224–227–680) in the Old

Town, which specializes in modern Czech art. Paintings, prints, and drawings crowd the walls and are propped against glass cases and window sills. Comb through works by Czech Cubists, currently fetching high prices at international auctions.

BOOKS AND PRINTS

Like its antiques shops, Prague's rare-book shops, or *antikvariáts,* were once part of a massive state-owned consortium that, since privatization, has split up and diversified. Now most shops tend to cultivate their own specialties. Some have a small English-language section with a motley blend of potboilers, academic texts, classics, and tattered paperbacks. Books in German, on the other hand, are abundant.

For new books in English, try **Anagram Books** (⊠ Týn 4, Staré Město, ☎ 224–895–737). **Antikvariát Karel Křenek** (⊠ Celetná 31, Staré Město, ☎ 222–322–919), near the Powder Tower, specializes in books with a humanist slant. It has a good selection of modern graphics and prides itself on its avant-garde periodicals and journals from the 1920s and 1930s. It also has a small collection of English books. There's a great selection of English-language books at **Big Ben Bookshop** (⊠ Malá Štupartská 5, Staré Město, ☎ 224–826–565). If you'd just like a good read, be sure to check out the **Globe Bookstore and Coffeehouse** (⊠ Pšstrossova 6, Nové Město, ☎ 224–916–264), a longtime magnet for the local English-speaking community, in its new, more central site. For hiking maps and auto atlases, try the downstairs level of the **Jan Kanzelsberger bookshop** (⊠ Václavské nám. 42, Nové Město, ☎ 224–217–335) on Wenceslas Square. **U Karlova Mostu** (⊠ Karlova 2, Staré Město, ☎ 222–220–286) is the preeminent Prague bookstore. In a suitably bookish location opposite the Klementinum, it's the place to go if you are looking for that elusive 15th-century manuscript. In addition to housing ancient books too precious to be leafed through, the store has a good selection of books on local subjects, a small foreign-language section, and a host of prints, maps, drawings, and paintings.

GLASS

Glass has traditionally been Bohemia's biggest export, and it was one of the few products manufactured during Communist times that managed to retain an artistically innovative spirit. Today Prague has plenty of shops selling Bohemian glass, though much of it is tourist kitsch. A good place to find modern works of art in glass is **Galerie Pyramida** (⊠ Národní 11, Nové Město, ☎ 224–213–117). **Galerie 'Z'** (⊠ U lužického semináře 7, ☎ 257–535–563) sells limited-edition mold-melted and blown glass. **Moser** (⊠ Na Příkopě 12, Nové Město, ☎ 224–211–293, WEB www.moser.cz), the opulent flagship store of the world-famous Karlovy Vary glassmaker, offers the widest selection of traditional glass. Even if you're not in the market to buy, stop by the store simply to look at the elegant wood-paneled salesrooms on the second floor. The staff will gladly pack goods for traveling.

HOME DESIGN

Czech design is wonderfully rich both in quality and imagination, emphasizing old-fashioned craftsmanship while often taking an offbeat, even humorous approach. Strained relations between Czech designers and producers have reined in the potential selection, but there are nevertheless a handful of places showcasing Czech work. **Arzenal** (⊠ Valentinská 11, Josefov, ☎ 224–814–099, WEB www.arzenal.cz) is a design shop that offers Japanese and Thai food in addition to vases and chairs; it exclusively sells work by Bořek Šípek, President Havel's official designer. **Fast** (⊠ Sázavská 32, Vinohrady, ☎ 224–250–538, WEB www.fast.cz) is a little bit off the beaten track but worth the trek. Besides ultramodern furniture, there are ingenious (and more portable) pens, binders, and other office and home accoutrements. **Galerie Bydlení** (✉ Truhlářská 20, Nové Město, ☎ 222–312–383) is a father-and-son operation focusing exclusively on Czech-made furniture.

JEWELRY

Alfons Mucha is perhaps most famous for his whiplash Art Nouveau posters, but he also designed furniture, lamps, clothing, and jewelry. **Art Décoratif** (✉ U Obecního domu, Staré Město, ☎ 222–002–350, WEB www.artdecoratif.cz), right next door to the Art Nouveau Obecní Dům, sells Mucha-inspired designs—the jewelry is especially remarkable. **Granát** (✉ Dlouhá 28, Staré Město, ☎ 222–315–612, WEB www.granat.cz) has a comprehensive selection of garnet jewelry, plus contemporary and traditional pieces set in gold and silver. **Halada** (✉ Karlova 25, Staré Město, ☎ 224–228–938, WEB www.halada.cz) sells sleek, Czech-designed silver jewelry; an affiliate shop at Na Příkopě 16 specializes in gold, diamonds, and pearls.

MARIONETTES

Marionettes have a long tradition in Bohemia, going back to the times when traveling troupes used to entertain children with morality plays on town squares. Now, although the art form survives, it has become yet another tourist lure, and you'll continually stumble across stalls selling almost identical marionettes. Secondhand and antique marionettes are surprisingly hard to find. One place to look is **Antikva Ing. Bürger** (✉ Betlémské nám. 8, in courtyard, Nové Město, ☎ 222–221–595; Karlova 12, Staré Město, ☎ 0/602–315–729). The marionettes at **Obchod Pod lampou** (✉ U Lužického semináře 5, Malá Strana, ☎ no phone) are the real thing. These puppets—hand-crafted knights, princesses, and pirates—are made by the same artists who supply professional puppeteers. Prices may be higher than for the usual stuff on the street, but the craftsmanship is well worth it.

TOYS AND GIFTS FOR CHILDREN

Nearly every stationery store has beautiful watercolor and colored-chalk sets available at rock-bottom prices. The Czechs are also master illustrators, and the books they've made for young "pre-readers" are some of the world's loveliest. For the child with a theatrical bent, a marionette—they range from finger-size to nearly child-size—can be a wonder. For delightful and reasonably priced Czech-made wooden toys and wind-up trains, cars, and animals, look in at **Hračky** (✉ Pohořelec 24, Hradčany, ☎ 0/603–515–745).

Prague Essentials

AIR TRAVEL

ČSA (Czech Airlines), the Czech national carrier, offers the only direct flights from New York (JFK) to Prague, with six flights a week most times (daily flights during the busiest season). It's also possible to connect through a major European airport and continue to Prague. The flight from New York to Prague takes about 8 hours; from the West Coast, including a stopover, 12 to 16 hours. Go Airways offers discount flights to Prague from Britain, but you must leave from Stansted or East Midlands airport. Another way to save money is either changing flights in Frankfurt or catching a bus from Frankfurt to Prague.
➤ CARRIERS: Air Canada (☎ 224–810–181). Air France (☎ 224–227–164). Alitalia (☎ 224–194–150). Austrian Airlines (☎ 224–826–199). American Airlines (☎ 224–234–985). British Airways (☎ 222–114–444). British Midland (☎ 224–810–180). ČSA (☎ 220–104–310, WEB www.csa.cz). Delta (☎ 224–946–733). Go (☎ 296–333–333, WEB

www.go-fly.com). **KLM** (☎ 233–090–933). **Lufthansa** (☎ 224–811–007). **SAS** (☎ 220–114–456). **Swiss** (☎ 224–812–211).

AIRPORTS AND TRANSFERS

Ruzyně Airport is 20 km (12 mi) northwest of the downtown area. It's small but easily negotiated. A still-expanding main terminal has eased traffic flow. The trip to downtown is a straight shot down Evropská Boulevard and takes approximately 20 minutes. The road is not usually busy, but anticipate an additional 20 minutes during rush hour (7 AM–9 AM and 3 PM–6 PM).

➤ AIRPORT INFORMATION: **Ruzyně Airport** (☎ 220–111–111, WEB www.csl.cz).

TRANSFERS

The Cedaz minibus shuttle links the airport with náměstí Republiky (Republic Square, just off the Old Town). It runs hourly, more often at peak periods, between 5:30 AM and 9:30 PM daily and makes an intermediate stop at the Dejvická metro station. The one-way fare is 90 Kč. The minibus also serves many hotels for 370 Kč—650 Kč, which is sometimes less than the taxi fare. Regular municipal bus service (Bus 119) connects the airport and the Dejvická station; the fare is 12 Kč (15 Kč if purchased from the driver), and the ticket is transferrable to trams or the metro. From Dejvická you can take the metro to the city center. To reach Wenceslas Square, get off at the Můstek station.

The transportation company FIX has cars waiting at the airport, and these are your only choice if you want a taxi. Technically, though, these aren't taxis and they charge a fixed rate based on zones. The fees range from 120 Kč to 870 Kč for travel into the city. Be sure to find out how much it will cost—preferably in writing from their airport representative—before entering the car, because overcharging is a problem. The ride should cost 500 Kč–700 Kč.

You can call a taxi on your own; the rates might be a little cheaper than if you use a FIX car, but beware of dishonest taxi drivers.
➤ CONTACTS: **Cedaz** (☎ 220–114–296), WEB www.aas.cz/cedaz).

BUS TRAVEL TO AND FROM PRAGUE

The Czech complex of regional bus lines known collectively as ČSAD operates its dense network from the sprawling Florenc station. For information about routes and schedules, call, consult the confusingly displayed timetables posted at the station, or visit the information window in the lower level lobby, which is open daily 6 AM–9 PM. The company's Web site will give you bus and train information in English (click on the British flag).
➤ BUS LINES: **ČSAD** (✉ Florenc station, Křižíkova, Karl'n, ☎ 12999; 224–214–990 route and schedule information; WEB www.jizdnirady.cz; metro: Florenc [Line B or C]).

BUS AND TRAM TRAVEL WITHIN PRAGUE

Prague's extensive bus and streetcar network allows for fast, efficient travel throughout the city. Tickets are the same as those used for the metro, although you validate them at machines inside the bus or tram. Tickets (*jízdenky*) can be bought at hotels, some newsstands, and from dispensing machines in the metro stations. The basic, transferrable ticket costs 12 Kč. It permits one hour's travel throughout the metro, tram, and bus network between 5 AM and 8 PM on weekdays, or 90 minutes' travel at other times. Single-ride tickets cost 8 Kč and allow one 15-minute ride on a tram or bus, without transfer, or a metro journey of up to four stations lasting less than 30 minutes (transfer between lines is allowed). You can also buy a one-day pass allowing unlimited use of the system for 70 Kč, a three-day pass for 200 Kč, a seven-day pass for 250 Kč, or a 15-day pass for 280 Kč. The passes can be purchased at the main metro stations, from ticket machines, and at some newsstands in the center. A pass is not valid until stamped in the orange machines in metro stations or aboard trams *and* the required information is entered on the back (there are instructions in English). A refurbished old tram, No. 91, travels through the Old Town and Lesser Quarter on summer weekends. The metro shuts down at midnight, but Trams 50–59 and Buses 500 and above run all night. Night trams run at 40-minute intervals, and all routes intersect at the corner of Lazarská and Spálená streets in the New Town near the Národní třída metro station. Schedules and regulations in English are on the transportation department's official Web site.

➤ INFORMATION: **Dopravní Podnik** (WEB www.dp-praha.cz).

CAR RENTALS

Several major agencies have offices at the airport and also in the city. It's usually cheaper if you make a reservation for your rental car before you leave home.

➤ MAJOR AGENCIES: **Alamo** (✉ Ruzyně Airport, Ruzyně, ☎ 220–114–340; ✉ Hilton, Pobřežní 1, Karlín, ☎ 224–842–407). **Avis** (✉ Ruzyně Airport, Ruzyně, ☎ 220–114–270; Klimentská 46, Nové Město, ☎ 221–851–225). **Budget** (✉ Ruzyně Airport, Ruzyně, ☎ 220–113–253; Hotel Inter-Continental, nám. Curieových 5, Staré Město, ☎ 224–889–995). **Europcar** (✉ Ruzyně Airport, Ruzyně, ☎ 235–364–531; Pařižská 28, Staré Město, ☎ 224–811–290). **Hertz** (✉ Ruzyně Airport, Ruzyně, ☎ 220–114–340; Karlovo nám. 28, Nové Město, ☎ 222–231–010; Diplomat hotel, Evropská 15, Dejvice, ☎ 224–394–175).

CAR TRAVEL

If your visit is restricted to the Czech capital, you'll do better not to rent a car. The capital is congested, and you'll save yourself a lot of hassle if you rely on public transportation. If you are planning to take excursions into the country, then a car will be useful, but don't pick it up until you are ready to depart. If you are arriving by car, you'll find that Prague is well served by major roads and highways from anywhere in the country. On arriving in the city, simply follow the signs to CENTRUM (city center).

PARKING

Parking is permitted in the center of town on a growing number of streets with parking meters or in the few small lots within walking distance of the historic center—but parking spaces are scarce. A meter with a green stripe lets you park up to six hours; an orange-stripe meter gives you two. (Use change in the meters.) A sign with a blue circle outlined in red with a diagonal red slash indicates a no-parking zone. Avoid the blue-marked spaces, which are reserved for local residents. Violaters may find a "boot" immobilizing their vehicle. If your hotel offers parking, you will have to pay a daily rate.

There's an underground lot at náměstí Jana Palacha, near Old Town Square. There are also park-and-ride (P+R) lots at some suburban metro stations, including Skalka (Line A), Zličín and Černý Most (Line B), and Nádraží Holešovice and Opatov (Line C).

TRAFFIC

During the day, traffic can be stop-and-go. Pay particular attention to the trams, which have the right-of-way in every situation. Avoid, when possible, driving in the congested and labyrinthine Old Town.

EMBASSIES AND CONSULATES

All embassies and consulates are in Prague. *See* the A to Z section at the end of this chapter for addresses.

➤ CONTACTS: **Canadian Embassy** (✉ Mickiewiczova 6, Hradčany, ☎ 272–101–890, WEB www.dfait-maeci.gc.ca/prague). **U.K. Embassy** (✉ Thunovská 14, Malá Strana, ☎ 257–530–278, WEB www.britain.cz). **U.S. Embassy** (✉ Tržiště 15, Malá Strana, ☎ 257–530–663, WEB www.usembassy.cz).

EMERGENCIES

➤ DOCTORS AND DENTISTS: **Dentist Referrals** (✉ Palackého 5, ☎ 224–946–981 24-hr emergency service). **Lékařská služba první pomoci** (district first-aid clinic; ✉ Palackého 5, Nové Město, ☎ 224–946–982).

➤ EMERGENCY SERVICES: **Ambulance** (☎ 155). **Federal Police** (☎ 158). **Prague city police** (☎ 156).

➤ HOSPITALS: **American Medical Center** (✉ Janovského 48, Holešovice, ☎ 220–807–756 24-hr service). **First Medical Clinic of Prague** (✉ Tylovo nám. 3/15, Nové Město, ☎ 224–251–319). **Na Homolce Hospital** (✉ Roentgenova 2, Prague 5, ☎ 257–272–146 weekdays [foreigners' department]; 257–211–111; 257–272–191).

➤ LATE-NIGHT PHARMACIES: **Lékárna U Anděla** (✉ Štefánikova 6, Smíchov, ☎ 257–320–918). **Lékárna** (✉ Belgická 37, Nové Město, ☎ 222–513–396).

ENGLISH-LANGUAGE MEDIA

In the city center nearly every bookstore carries a few guidebooks and paperbacks in English. Street vendors on Wenceslas Square and Na Příkopě carry leading foreign newspapers and periodicals. To find out what's on and to get the latest tips for shopping, dining, and entertainment, consult Prague's weekly English-language newspaper, the *Prague Post* (WEB www.praguepost.com). It prints comprehensive entertainment listings and can be bought at most downtown newsstands as well as in major North American and European cities.

SUBWAY TRAVEL

Prague's subway system, the metro, is clean and reliable; the stations are marked with an inconspicuous M sign. Trains run daily 5 AM–midnight. Validate your ticket at an orange machine before descending the escalator. Trains are patrolled often; the fine for riding without a valid ticket is 400 Kč. Beware of pickpockets, who often operate in large groups on crowded trams and metro cars.

TAXIS

Dishonest taxi drivers are the shame of the nation. Luckily you probably won't need to rely on taxis for trips within the city center (it's usually easier to walk or take the subway). Typical scams include drivers doctoring the meter or simply failing to turn the meter on and then demanding an exorbitant sum at the end of the ride. In an honest cab, the meter starts at 30 Kč and increases by 22 Kč per km (½ mi) or 4 Kč per minute at rest. Most rides within town should cost no more than 80 Kč–150 Kč. To minimize the chances of getting ripped off, avoid taxi stands in Wenceslas Square, Old Town Square, and other heavily touristed areas. The best alternative is to phone for a taxi in advance. Many radio-taxi firms have English-speaking operators.

➤ CONTACTS: **AAA Taxi** (☎ 233–113–311, WEB www.aaa.radiotaxi.cz). **Profitaxi** (☎ 261–314–151).

TOURS

Čedok offers a 3½-hour "Grand City Tour," a combination bus and walking venture that covers all the major sights with commentary in

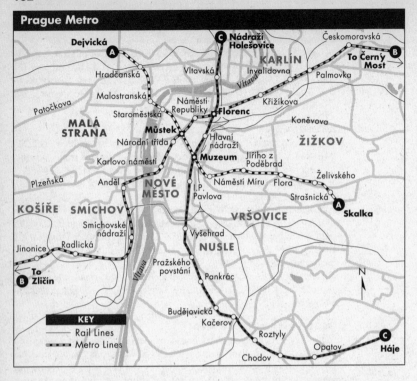

Prague Metro

KEY

Rail Lines
Metro Lines

English. It departs daily at 9:30 AM year-round, and also at 2 PM from April through October, from opposite the Prašná brána (Powder Tower) on Republic Square, near the main Čedok office. The price is about 750 Kč. "Historic Prague on Foot" is a slower-paced, three-hour walking tour for 400 Kč. From April through October, it departs Republic Square on Wednesday, Friday, and Sunday at 9:30 AM; in the off-season, it departs Friday at 9:30 AM. More tours are offered, especially in summer, and the schedules may well vary according to demand. You can also contact Čedok's main office to arrange a personalized walking tour. Times and itineraries are negotiable; prices start at around 500 Kč per hour.

Very similar tours by other operators also depart daily from Republic Square, Národní třída near Jungmannovo náměstí, and Wenceslas Square. Prices are generally a couple hundred crowns less than for Čedok's tours. Themed walking tours are very popular as well. You can choose medieval architecture, "Velvet Revolution walks," visits to Communist monuments, and any number of pub crawls. Each year, four or five small operators do these tours, which generally last a couple of hours and cost 200 Kč–300 Kč. Inquire at Prague Information Service or a major ticket agency for the current season's offerings.

TRAIN TRAVEL

International trains arrive at and depart from either of two stations: the main station, Hlavní nádraží, is about 500 yards east of Wenceslas Square on Opletalova or Washingtonova street. Then there's the suburban Nádraží Holešovice, about 2 km (1 mi) north of the city center. This is an unending source of confusion—always make certain you know which station your train is using. Note also that trains arriving from the west usually stop at Smíchov station, on the west bank of the Vltava, before continuing to the main station. Prague's other central train station, Masarykovo nádraží, serves mostly local trains but has an international ticket window that is often much less crowded than those at the main station.

For train times, consult timetables in a station or get in line at the information office upstairs at the main station (for domestic trains, open daily 3 AM–11:45 PM) or downstairs near the exits under the ČD Centrum sign (open daily 6 AM–7:30 PM). The main Čedok office also provides train information and issues tickets.

Wenceslas Square is a convenient five-minute walk from the main station (best not undertaken late at night), or you can take the subway (Line C) one stop in the Háje direction to Muzeum. A taxi ride from the main station to the center should cost about 100 Kč, but the station cabbies are known for overcharging. To reach the city center from Nádraží Holešovice, take the metro (Line C) four stops to Muzeum; a taxi ride should cost roughly 200 Kč–250 Kč.

➤ CONTACTS: **Čedok** (✉ Na Příkopě 18, Staré Město, ☎ 224–197–111, WEB www.cedok.cz).

➤ TRAIN STATIONS: **Hlavní nádraží** (✉ Wilsonova ul., Nové Město, ☎ 224–224–200 schedules and fares). **Masarykovo nádraží** (✉ Hybernská 13, Nové Město). **Nádraží Holešovice** (✉ Vrbenskehóo, Holešovice).

TRAVEL AGENCIES

American Express and Thomas Cook, two big international agencies, have convenient offices in Prague. For bus tickets to just about anywhere in Europe, Bohemia Tour is useful. Čedok, the ubiquitous Czech travel agency, provides general tourist information and city maps. Čedok will also exchange money, book accommodations, arrange guided tours, and book passage on airlines, buses, and trains. You can pay for Čedok services, including booking rail tickets, with any major credit card. Note limited weekend hours. The main office is open weekdays 8:30–6 and Saturday 9–1.

➤ CONTACTS: **American Express** (✉ Václavské nám. 56, Nové Město, ☎ 224–219–992; Mostecká 12, Malá Strana, ☎ 257–313–636). **Bohemia Tour** (✉ Jungmannova 4, Nové Město, ☎ 224–947–707, WEB www.bohemiatour.cz). **Čedok** (✉ Na Příkopě 18, Staré Město, ☎ 224–197–111, WEB www.cedok.cz). **Thomas Cook** (✉ Karlova 3, Staré Město, ☎ 222–221–055).

VISITOR INFORMATION

The Czech Tourist Authority office on Old Town Square can provide information on tourism outside Prague but does not sell tickets or book accommodations. The Prague Information Service has four central offices. The Town Hall branch is open weekdays 9–6, weekends 9–5. The Na Příkopě office, just a few doors down from Čedok's main office, is open weekdays 9–6 and Saturday 9–3. The Hlavní nádraží branch is open April–October, weekdays 9–7 and weekends 9–4, and November–March, weekdays 9–6 and Saturday 9–3. The Charles Bridge tower office on the Malá Strana end of Charles Bridge, is open April–October, daily 10–6.

➤ CONTACTS: **Czech Tourist Authority** (✉ Staroměstské nám. 6, Staré Město, ☎ 227–158–111). There are four central offices of the municipal **Prague Information Service**, or PIS (✉ Staroměstská radnice [Old Town Hall], Staré Město, ☎ 224–482–562, WEB www.pis.cz; Na Příkopě 20, Nové Město, ☎ no phone; Hlavní nádraží, lower hall, Staré Měst, ☎ no phone; Malostranská mostecká věž, Malá Strana, ☎ no phone).

SOUTHERN BOHEMIA

With Prague at its heart and Germany and the former Austro-Hungarian Empire on its mountainous borders, the kingdom of Bohemia was for centuries buffeted by religious and national conflicts, invasions, and wars. But its position also meant that Bohemia benefited from the cultural wealth and diversity of Central Europe. The result is a glorious array of history-laden castles, walled cities, and spa towns set in a gentle, rolling landscape.

Southern Bohemia (separate sections on the northern and western areas follow) is particularly famous for its involvement in the Hussite religious wars of the 15th century, which revolved around the town of Tábor. But the area also has more than its fair share of well-preserved and stunning walled towns, built up by generations of noble families, who left behind layers of Gothic, Renaissance, and baroque architecture (particularly notable in Český Krumlov). Farther north and an easy drive east of Prague is the old silver-mining town of Kutná Hora, once a rival to Prague for the royal residence.

Český Krumlov (along with the spas of western Bohemia) offers some of the best accommodations in the Czech Republic outside the capital.

Numbers in the margin correspond to numbers on the Bohemia map.

Kutná Hora

❶ *70 km (44 mi) east of Prague.*

The approach to Kutná Hora looks much as it has for centuries. The long economic decline of this town, once Prague's chief rival in Bohemia for wealth and beauty, spared it the postwar construction that has blighted the outskirts of so many other Czech cities. Though it is undeniably beautiful, with an intact Gothic and baroque townscape, Kutná Hora feels a bit melancholy. The town owes its illustrious past to silver, discovered here during the 12th century. For some 400 years the mines were worked with consummate efficiency, the wealth going to support grand projects to rival those of Prague and the nearby Cistercian monastery of Sedlec. As the silver began to run out during the 16th and 17th centuries, however, Kutná Hora's importance faded. Since the early 1990s, the town has beautified itself to a degree, but despite a significant tourist industry, modern Kutná Hora is dwarfed by the splendors of the Middle Ages. The city became a UNESCO World Heritage Site in 1995.

★ Forget the town center for a moment and walk to the **Chrám svaté Barbory** (St. Barbara's Cathedral), a 10-minute stroll from the main Palackého náměstí along Barborská ulice. The approach to the church, overlooking the river, is magnificent. Baroque statues line the road in front of a vast former Jesuit college as you near St. Barbara's, which is really just a parish church that is commonly granted the grander title. From a distance, the three-peaked roof of the church gives the impression of a large, magnificent tent more than a religious center. St. Barbara's is undoubtedly Kutná Hora's masterpiece and a high point of the Gothic style in Bohemia. Begun in the 1380s, it drew on the talents of the Peter Parler workshop as well as two luminaries of the late-Gothic flowering a century later, Matyáš Rejsek and Benedikt Ried. The soaring roof was added as late as 1558, replaced in the 18th century, and finally restored, by Josef Mocker, late in the 1800s; the western facade also dates from the end of the 19th century. Once you arrive, you can

Bohemia

Bautzen
Görlitz
Dresden
Löbau
Pirna
Zittau
Freiberg
E40
Nový Bor
Chemnitz
E55
Špindlerův
Mlýn
Děčín 13
Liberec
Vrchlabí
Ústí nad
Labem
30
Teplice
15
Mimoň
Jablonec 21
Litvínov
Střekov
38
Turnov
Most
Castle
Doksy
Nová Paka
Terezín 19
Chomutov
8
Ohře
Elbe
9
Jičín
Vejprty
Mělník
Nelahozeves
16
Mladá
Kraslice
Louny
Boleslav
E442
Žatec
Zlonice
Neratovice
32
Františkovy
Ostrov
Veltrusy Château
18 17
E65
Poděbrady
Lázně 11
Karlovy Vary
and Gardens
Roztoky
Čelákovice
13
Sokolov
Bochov
E48
16
Labe
Cheb 12
Bečov
Kralovice
12
Kolín
Toužim
E49
Lidice
Prague
Mariánské
27
Beroun
333
1
Lázně 14
Chodová
Beroun ka
Rudná
Říčany
Uhlířské
Kutná
Planá
Zdice
E50
Janovice
E50
Hora
Tachov
Stříbro
Plzeň
Zbraslavice
Bor
21
15
Konopiště
2
Horšovský
Dobřany
Rokycany
3
Český
Týn
E53
20
Šternberk
20
Domažlice
Nepomuk
Vltava
Příbram
Sedlčany
Klatovy
20
Horažd'ovice
Zvíkov
19
Milevsko
E55
Pelhřimov
Castle
4
Sušice
Písek
Tábor
19
Cham
Strakonice
Otava
10
Soběslav
Kamenice
Veselí
Vimperk
Vodňany
22
34
Regen
Lužnice
Třeboň
Jindřichův
Hluboká nad Vltavou
9
5
Hradec
Deggendorf
České Budějovice
8
E49
Borovany
Český
7
Trhové Sviny
Krumlov
Passau
vod. nádrž
Lipno
Kaplice
Gmünd
Rožmberk
6
nad Vltavou
GERMANY
Freistadt
AUSTRIA
N
Stadl-Paura
0   20 miles
0   30 km

see the romantic view over the town, marked by the visibly tilting 260-ft-tower of St. James's Church. Though the view is impressive, a few modern buildings intrude.

St. Barbara is the patron saint of miners, and silver-mining themes dominate the interior of the church. Gothic frescoes depict angels carrying shields with mining symbols. The town's other major occupation, minting, can be seen in frescoes in the **Mintner's Chapel.** A statue of a miner, donning the characteristic smock, stands proudly in the nave and dates from 1700. But the main attraction of the interior is the vaulting itself—attributed to Ried—which carries the eye effortlessly upward. ⊠ *Barborská ul.,* ☎ *no phone,* WEB *www.kutnohorsko.cz.* 🎫 *30 Kč.* ☉ *May–Sept., Tues.–Sun. 9–5:30; Oct. and Apr., Tues.–Sun. 9–11:30 and 1–4; Nov.–Mar., Tues.–Sun. 9–11:30 and 2–3:30.*

The **Hrádek** (Little Castle) was once part of the town's fortifications and now houses a museum of mining and coin production and a claustrophobic medieval mine tunnel. ⊠ *Barborská ul.,* ☎ *327–512–159,* WEB *muzeum.kutnohorsko.cz.* 🎫 *110 Kč.* ☉ *Apr. and Oct., Tues.–Sun. 9–5; May–June and Sept., Tues.–Sun. 9–6; July–Aug., Tues.–Sun. 10–6.*

You'll easily find the **Vlašský dvůr** (Italian Court), the old mint, by following the signs through town. Coins were first minted here in 1300, struck by Italian artisans brought in from Florence—hence the mint's odd name. It was here that the Prague groschen, one of the most widely circulated coins of the Middle Ages, was minted until 1726 and here, too, that the Bohemian kings stayed on their frequent visits. There's a **coin museum,** where you can see the small, silvery groschen being struck and buy replicas. ⊠ *Havlíčkovo nám.,* ☎ *327–512–873,* WEB *www.kutnohorsko.cz.* 🎫 *40 Kč.* ☉ *Apr.–Sept., daily 9–6; Oct. and Mar., daily 10–5; Nov.–Feb., daily 10–4.*

If the door to the **Chrám svatého Jakuba** (St. James's Church), which is next door to the old mint, is open, peek inside. Originally a Gothic church dating from the 1300s, the structure was almost entirely transformed into baroque during the 17th and 18th centuries. The characteristic onion dome on the tower was added in 1737. The paintings on the wall include works of the best baroque Czech masters; the pietà is by the 17th-century painter Karel Škréta. ⊠ *Havlíčkovo nám.,* ☎ *no phone,* WEB *www.kutnohorsko.cz.*

Before leaving the city, stop in the nearby suburb of Sedlec for a bone-chilling sight: a chapel decorated with the bones of some 40,000 people. The Kaple všech svatých (All Saints' Chapel), commonly known as the **kostnice** (ossuary) or "Bone Church," just up the road from the former Sedlec Monastery, came into being in the 16th century, when development forced the clearing of a nearby graveyard. Monks of the Cistercian order came up with the bright idea of using the bones for decoration; the most recent creations date from the end of the 19th century. The Sedlec Monastery is now a cigarette factory. Its run-down **Church of the Assumption of the Virgin** exemplifies the work of Giovanni Santini (1667–1723). A master of expressive line and delicate proportion, this one-of-a-kind architect fathered a bravura hybrid of Gothic and baroque. ⊠ *Zamecka 127, Sedlec,* ☎ *327–561–143,* WEB *www.kostnice.cz.* 🎫 *30 Kč.* ☉ *Apr.–Sept., daily 8–6; Oct., daily 9–noon and 1–5; Nov.–Mar., daily 9–noon and 1–4. Church closed Sun.–Mon.*

Lodging

$$ 🏨 **Medínek.** The location, on the main square, puts you an easy stroll from the sights, and the ground-floor restaurant offers decent Czech cooking in an atmosphere more pleasant than that found in the local

beer halls. Unfortunately, the 1960s architecture blights the surrounding square. ✉ *Palackého nám. 316, 284 01,* ☎ *327–512–741,* ⓕⓐⓧ *327–512–743,* ⓦⓔⓑ *www.medinek.cz. 90 rooms, 43 with bath. Restaurant, café, cable TV, meeting rooms, some pets allowed (fee); no a/c. AE, MC, V. BP.*

$$ ⊡ **U Hrnčíře.** This is a quaint little inn situated next to a potter's shop near the town center. The rooms are very plain and the stairs very steep, but the friendly staff gives the hotel a decidedly homey feel. The restaurant in the back garden has a beautiful view overlooking St. James' Church. ✉ *Barborská 24, 284 01,* ☎ *327–512–113. 5 rooms. Restaurant, cable TV, some pets allowed (fee); no a/c. MC, V. BP.*

Český Šternberk

❷ *35 km (21 mi) southwest of Kutná Hora, 24 km (15 mi) from Benešov.*

At night this 13th-century castle looks positively forbidding, occupying a forested knoll over the Sázava River. In daylight, the structure, last renovated in the 18th century, is less haunting but still impressive. You can tour some of the rooms fitted out with period furniture (mostly rococo); little of the early Gothic has survived the many renovations. The Šternberk (Sternberg) family has owned the place since the 13th century, except during the Communist era. ✉ *Český Šternberk 1,* ☎ *317–855–166.* ▣ *120 Kč.* ☉ *Apr. and Oct., weekends 9–6; May and Sept., Tues.–Sun. 9–5; June–Aug., Tues.–Sun. 9–6; Nov.–Mar. only group tours by appointment.*

Konopiště

❸ *25 km (15 mi) west of Český Šternberk, 45 km (27 mi) southeast of Prague.*

Given its remote location, Český Šternberk is ill-equipped for a meal or an overnight stay. Instead, continue on to the superior facilities of Konopiště (via the industrial town of Benešov). The town is best known for its 14th-century castle, which served six centuries later as the residence of the heir to the Austrian crown, Franz Ferdinand. Scorned by the Austrian nobility for marrying a commoner, Franz Ferdinand wanted an impressive summer residence to win back the envy of his peers, and he spared no expense in restoring the castle to its original Gothic form, filling its 82 rooms with outlandish paintings, statues, and curiosities. His dream came to a fateful end in 1914 when he was assassinated at Sarajevo, an event that helped precipitate World War I. The Austrian defeat in the war ultimately led to the fall of the Hapsburgs. Ironically, the destiny of the Austrian Empire had been sealed at the castle a month before the assassination, when Austrian emperor Franz Joseph I met with German kaiser Wilhelm II and agreed to join forces with him in the event of war.

To visit **Zámek Konopiště** (Konopiště Castle), start from the Konopiště Motel, about 1 km (½ mi) off Highway E55, and walk straight for about 2 km (1 mi) along the trail through the woods. Before long, the rounded, neo-Gothic towers appear through the trees, and you reach the formal garden with its almost mystical circle of classical statues. Built by the wealthy Beneschau family, the castle dates from around 1300 and for centuries served as a bastion of the nobility in their struggle for power with the king. At the end of the 14th century, Catholic nobles actually captured the weak King Wenceslas (Václav) IV in Prague and held him prisoner in the smaller of the two rounded towers. To this day the tower is known affectionately as the Václavka. Several of the rooms, reflecting Archduke Franz Ferdinand's extravagant taste and lifestyle, are open to the public during the high season. A valuable collection of weapons from the 16th through 18th centuries can be seen in the Weapons Hall on the third floor. Less easy to miss are the hundreds of stuffed animals, rather macabre monuments to the archduke's obsession with hunting. The interior is only open to tours; the guides may not speak English, but there are English texts available. The castle is about 3 km [2 mi] west of Benešov's train and bus stations on red- or yellow-marked paths. ⊠ *Zámek Konopiště, Benešov,* ☎ *317–721–366,* WEB *www.zamek-konopiste.cz.* 🎟 *Tours 130 Kč–260 Kč.* ☉ *Apr. and Oct., Tues.–Sun. 9–3; May–Aug., Tues.–Sun. 9–5; Sept., Tues.–Sun. 9–4.*

Dining and Lodging

$$ ✕🛏 **Amber Hotel Konopiště.** Long a favorite with Prague-based diplomats, who come for the fresh air and outdoor sports, the motel is about 2 km (1 mi) from Konopiště Castle, on a small road about 1 km (½ mi) from the main Prague–Tábor highway (E55). Rooms are small but well appointed (ask for one away from the main road). Its lodgelike restaurant, Stodola (open for dinner only), boasts a fine reputation for Bohemian-style grilled meats, chicken, and fish dishes. The live folk music in the evening is romantic rather than obtrusive; the wines and service are excellent. ⊠ *Benešov, 256 01,* ☎ *317–722–732,* FAX *317–722–053,* WEB *www.hotelkonopiste.cz. 40 rooms. 2 restaurants, cable TV, tennis court, pool, gym, outdoor hot tub, massage, sauna, miniature golf, meeting room, some pets allowed (fee); no a/c. DC, MC, V.*

Tábor

★ ❹ *45 km (27 mi) south of Konopiště on Hwy. E55.*

It's hard to believe this dusty Czech town was built to receive Christ on his return to Earth in the Second Coming. But that's what the Hussites intended when they flocked here by the thousands in 1420 to construct a society modeled on the communities of the early Christians. Tábor's fascinating history is unique among Czech towns—it started out as a combination utopia and fortress.

Following the execution of Jan Hus, a vociferous religious reformer who railed against the Catholic Church and the nobility, reform priests drawing on the support of poor workers and peasants took to the hills of southern Bohemia. These hilltop congregations soon grew into permanent settlements, wholly outside the feudal order. The most important settlement, on the Lužnice River, became known in 1420 as Tábor. Tábor quickly evolved into the symbolic and spiritual center of the Hussites (now called Taborites) and, together with Prague, served as the bulwark of the reform movement.

The early 1420s in Tábor were heady days for religious reformers. Private property was denounced, and the many poor who made the pilgrimage to Tábor were required to leave their possessions at the town gates. Some sects rejected the doctrine of transubstantiation (the belief that the Eucharistic elements become the body and blood of Christ), turning Holy Communion into a bawdy, secular feast of bread and wine. Other reformers considered themselves superior to Christ—who by dying had shown himself to be merely mortal. Few, however, felt obliged to work for a living, and the Taborites had to rely increasingly on raids of neighboring villages for survival.

War fever in Tábor at the time ran high, and the town became one of the focal points of the Hussite wars (1419–1434), which pitted reformers against an array of foreign crusaders, Catholics, and noblemen. Under the brilliant military leadership of Jan Žižka, the Taborites enjoyed early successes, but the forces of the established church and the moderate Hussite nobility proved too mighty in the end. Žižka died in 1424, and the Hussite uprising ended at the rout of Lipany 10 years later. Still, many of the town's citizens resisted recatholicization. Fittingly, following the Battle of White Mountain in 1620 (the final defeat for the Czech Protestants), Tábor was the last city to succumb to the conquering Hapsburgs.

Žižkovo náměstí (Žižka Square) is dominated by a large, 19th-century bronze statue of the gifted Hussite military leader. The stone tables in front of the Gothic town hall and the house at No. 6 date from the 15th century and were used by the Hussites to give daily communion to the faithful. Walk, if you dare, the tiny streets around the square, as they curve around, branch off, and then stop; few lead back to the main square. The confusing street plan was purposely laid during the 15th century to thwart incoming invasions.

The **Husitské muzeum** (Hussite Museum), just behind the town hall, documents the history of the reformers. You can visit an elaborate network of tunnels below the Old Town, carved by the Hussites for protection in case of attack. ⊠ *Žižkovo nám. 2*, ☎ *381–254–286*, WEB *www.tabor.cz/1ja/index.htm.* ☑ *Museum and tunnel tours 40 Kč each.* ☉ *Apr.–Oct., daily 8:30–5; Nov.–Mar., weekdays 8:30–5.*

Pražská ulice, a main route to the newer part of town, is lined with beautiful Renaissance facades. If you turn right at Divadelní and head to the Lužnice River, you'll see the remaining walls and fortifications of the 15th century, irrefutable evidence of the town's vital function as a stronghold.

Hrad Kotnov (Kotnov Castle), rising above the river in the distance, dates from the 13th century and was part of the earliest fortifications. The large pond to the northeast of the Old Town was created as a reservoir in 1492; since it was used for baptism, the fervent Taborites named the lake Jordán. ⊠ *Klokotská*, ☎ *381–252–788*, WEB *www.tabor.cz/1ja/index.htm.* ☑ *Castle 64 Kč, tower 32 Kč.* ☉ *May–Sept. 8:30–5; other times by appointment.*

Lodging

$$ 🖭 **Pension 189 Karel Bican.** At this lovely family-run pension, the service couldn't be nicer, nor could the soothing view of the river from some rooms. The premises date from the 14th century, and the Bicans will gladly show you the house's own catacombs, which once linked up to the medieval tunnel network. When it's hot outside, you can chill out in the cool basement lounge. Some rooms have cooking facilities. The level of comfort exceeds that found in many a Czech "luxury" hotel. ⊠ *Hradební 189, 390 01*, ☎ FAX *381–252–109*, WEB *www.globalnet.cz/bican. 6 rooms. Some kitchenettes, sauna, cable TV, minibars, bicycles, some pets allowed; no a/c. AE, MC, V. BP.*

$ 🖭 **Kapital.** A good bargain, this small hotel on the main street leading from the train and bus stations to the Old Town boasts of its "in door toilets," but in truth offers more than most in its price range, such as a TV (and a bathroom) in every room and covered parking. ⊠ *Tř. 9 května 617, 390 01*, ☎ *381–256–096*, FAX *381–252–411*, WEB *web.quick.cz/hotel-kapital. 24 rooms. Restaurant, cable TV, bicycles, bar, parking (fee). AE, DC, MC, V. BP.*

Třeboň

❺ *48 km (28 mi) south of Tábor.*

Amid a plethora of ponds rests a jewel of a town with a far different historical heritage than Tábor's. Třeboň was settled during the 12th century by the Wittkowitzes (later called the Rožmberks, or Rosenbergs), once Bohemia's noblest family. From the 14th to the end of the 16th century, the dynasty dominated southern Bohemia; they amassed their wealth through silver, real estate, and fish farming. You can see their emblem, a five-petal rose, on castles, doorways, and coats of arms all over the region. Their official residence was 40 km (25 mi) to the southwest, in Český Krumlov, but Třeboň was an important second residence and repository of the family archives, which still reside in the town château. Thanks to the Rosenberg family, this unlikely landlocked town has become the center of the Czech Republic's fishing industry. During the 15th and 16th centuries, the Rosenbergs peppered the countryside with 6,000 enormous ponds, partly to drain the land and partly to breed fish. Carp breeding is still big business, and if you are in the area in the late autumn, you may be lucky enough to witness the great carp harvests, when tens of thousands of the glittering fish are netted. The closest pond, **Rybník Svět** (Svět Pond), is on the southern edge of town; try to fit in a stroll along its banks. You can even swim here in the summer (the pond has pleasant, sandy beaches), but it can get crowded.

Třeboň is an access point in the Czech Greenways network. Greenways is a Czech-American organization that is gradually establishing a chain of hiking, biking, and riding routes from Prague to Vienna, working with local authorities and property owners to develop "ecotourism" along the way. Around Třeboň, hiking and horseback trails snake through the area's ponds and peat bogs. For specific information, contact the local tourist office.

The partially intact town defenses, made up of walls, 16th-century gates, and three bastions, are among the best in the Czech Republic. Near the **Svinenská Gate**, there's an 18th-century brewery, still producing outstanding beer. First brewed in 1379, as the redbrick tower proudly boasts, beer enjoys nearly as long a tradition here as in Plzeň or České Budějovice. The main square, Masarykovo náměstí (Masaryk Square), has a typical collection of arcaded Renaissance and baroque houses. Look for the **Bílý Koníček** (Little White Horse), the best-preserved Renaissance house on the square, dating from 1544. It's now a modest hotel and restaurant. Stop by for some of the excellent local beer. Look for the castle-topped, white facade. ⊠ *Masarykovo nám.,* ☎ *384–721–213.*

The entrance to **Zámek Třeboň** (Třeboň Château) lies at the southwest corner of the square. From the outside it looks plain and sober, with its stark white walls, but the walls of the inner courtyard are covered with sgraffito. Several different tours of the interior feature sumptuous recreations of the Renaissance lifestyle enjoyed by the Rosenbergs and apartments furnished in late-19th-century splendor. The last of the Rosenbergs died in 1611, and the castle eventually became the property of the Schwarzenberg family, who built their family tomb in a grand park on the other side of Svět Pond. It is now a monumental neo-Gothic destination for Sunday-afternoon picnickers. ⊠ *Masarykovo nám.,* ☎ *384–721–193,* WEB *www.trebon-mesto.cz.* ⊡ *Tours 20 Kč–130 Kč.* ☉ *Apr.–May and Sept.–Oct., Tues.–Sun. 9–4; June–Aug., Tues.–Sun. 9–5.*

Lodging

$$ ⊞ **Zlatá Hvězda.** Less striking than the budget Bílý Koníček Hotel at the other end of the square, the "Golden Star" is a more comfortable alternative. Renovation in the late 1990s left the rooms still exuding a pre-capitalist spareness, while adding such conveniences as relatively spacious bathrooms and satellite TVs. ⊠ *Masarykovo nám. 107, 379 01,* ☎ *384–757–111,* FAX *384–757–300,* WEB *www.zhvezda.cz.* 42

rooms. Restaurant, cable TV, gym, pub, meeting room, Internet, some pets allowed (fee); no a/c. AE, DC, MC, V. BP.

Rožmberk nad Vltavou

⑥ *70 km (42 mi) southwest of Třeboň.*

This little village, just a few miles from the former Iron Curtain, was forgotten in the postwar years. It seems like a ghost town, especially at night. The darkened **Hrad Rožmberk** (Rosenberg Castle) keeps a lonely vigil atop the hill overlooking the Vltava River. The slender upper tower, the Jakobínka, dates from the 13th century, when the Rosenberg family built the original structure. Most of the exterior, however, is 19th-century neo-Gothic. In summer you can tour some of the rooms and admire the weapons and Bohemian paintings. Don't miss the painting of the White Lady, her ghost supposedly haunts the castle. ⊠ *Rožmberk nad Vltavou,* ☎ *380–749–838,* WEB *www.hrad-rozmberk.cz.* ☞ *120 Kč.* ☉ *Apr. and Oct., weekends 9–4; May and Sept., Tues.–Sun. 9–4; June–Aug., Tues.–Sun. 9–5.*

Český Krumlov

★ **⑦** *22 km (13 mi) north of Rožmberk nad Vltavou.*

Český Krumlov, the official residence of the Rosenbergs for some 300 years, is an eye-opener. None of the surrounding towns or villages, with their open squares and mixtures of old and new buildings, will prepare you for the beauty of the Old Town. Here the Vltava works its wonders as nowhere else but in Prague itself, swirling in a nearly complete circle around the town. Across the river stands the proud castle, rivaling any in the country in size and splendor.

For the moment, Český Krumlov's beauty is still intact, even though the dilapidated buildings that lend the town its unique atmosphere are slowly metamorphosing into boutiques and pensions. Visitor facilities are improving but can become overburdened during peak months. Overlook any minor inconveniences, however, and enjoy a rare, unspoiled trip in time back to the Bohemian Renaissance. Greenways trails lead to and from the town; for details, contact the tourist office.

The town's main square, **náměstí Svornosti** (Unity Square), may not seem impressive at first sight, diminutive as it is. The **town hall,** at No. 1, built in 1580, is memorable for its Renaissance friezes and Gothic arcades. Tiny alleys fan out from the square in all directions.

Just opposite the empty Hotel Krumlov, a street called Horní ulice leads off toward the **Městské muzeum** (City Museum). A quick visit will get you acquainted with the rise and fall of the Rosenberg dynasty. ⊠ *Horní 152,* ☎ *380–711–674,* WEB *www.ckrumlov.cz/uk.* ☞ *40 Kč.* ☉ *May–June and Sept., daily 10–5; July–Aug., daily 10–6; Oct.–Apr., Tues.–Fri. 9–4, weekends 1–4.*

Just opposite the City Museum are the Renaissance facades, complete with lively sgraffiti, of the former **Jesuitská škola** (Jesuit school)—now the semiluxurious Růže hotel. Like many of Krumlov's most lordly edifices, it owes its abundance of Renaissance detailing to the town's location on the main trading routes to Italy and Bavaria—a perfect site for absorbing incoming fashions. The view over the Old Town and castle is most spectacular from the hotel parking lot. ⊠ *Horní 154.*

The tower of the Gothic **Kostel svatého Víta** (St. Vitus's Church), built in the early 1400s, rises to offset the larger, older tower of the castle across the river. Within the church, a marble-column baldachin shelters an elaborate baptismal font. At one time, it covered the tomb of Vilém of Rosenberg (1535–1592), who was one of his line's most august heads and a great patron of the town. ⊠ *Kostelní ul.*

To get to **Hrad Krumlov** (Krumlov Castle), cross the peaceful Vltava on the main street, Radniční, and enter via the staircase leading up from Latrán Street, or continue to the massive main gateway. The oldest and most striking part of the castle is the round 13th-century **tower**, renovated in the 16th century to look something like a minaret, with its delicately arcaded Renaissance balcony. The tower is part of the old border fortifications, guarding the Bohemian frontiers from Austrian incursion. Now repainted in something like its Renaissance finery, from various perspectives it appears pompous, absurd, astonishingly lovely—or all of these at once. From dungeon to bells, its inner secrets can be seen from the interior staircase.

Vilém of Rosenberg oversaw a major refurbishment of the castle, adding buildings, heightening the tower, and adding rich decorations—generally making the place suitable for one of the grandest Bohemians of the day. The castle passed out of the Rosenbergs' hands, however, when Vilém's brother and last of the line, the dissolute Petr Vok, sold both castle and town to Rudolf II in 1602 to pay off his debts. Under the succeeding Eggenberg and Schwarzenberg dynasties, the castle's transformation into an opulent palace continued. The Eggenbergs' prime addition was a **theater** built in the 1680s and completed in 1766 by Josef Adam of Schwarzenberg. Much of the theater and its accoutrements—sets, props, costumes, stage machinery—survive intact as an extremely rare working display of period stagecraft. After a 30-year closure, the theater reopened for tours in 1997.

As you enter the castle area, look into the old moats, where two playful brown bears now reside—unlikely to be of much help in protecting the castle from attack. In season, the castle rooms are open to the public. Be sure to ask at the ticket office about newly accessible areas of this enormous monument, as renovations and additional openings are ongoing. One sightseeing tour focuses on the Renaissance, baroque, and rococo rooms, taking in the delightful **Maškarní Sál** (Masquerade Hall), with its richly detailed 18th-century frescoes. A second tour highlights the seigneurial apartments of the Schwarzenbergs, who owned the castle until the Gestapo seized it in 1940. (The castle became state property in 1947.)

The courtyards and passageways of the castle are open to the public all year round. After proceeding through the Renaissance-era third and fourth courtyards, you'll come to a wonderfully romantic elevated passageway with spectacular views of the huddled houses of the Old Town. The Austrian Expressionist painter Egon Schiele often stayed in Český Krumlov in the early 1900s and liked to paint this particular view over the river; he titled his now-famous Krumlov series *Dead City*. From the river down below, the elevated passageway is revealed as the middle level of **most Na plášti** (Cloaked Bridge), a massive construction spanning a deep ravine. Below the passageway are three levels of high arches, looking like a particularly elaborate Roman viaduct. On top runs a narrow three-story block of enclosed passages dressed in light blue and white. At the end of the passageway you'll come to the theater, then to the luxuriously appointed **castle garden,** formal at the near end, leafy and contemplative on the other. In the middle is an 18th-century summer house with a modern, revolving open-air stage in front. Performances are held here in the summer. ⊠ *Český Krumlov,* ☎ *380–711–687,* WEB *www.ckrumlov.cz/uk.* ⊿ *Garden free, castle tours 140 Kč, tower 25 Kč, theater tours 170 Kč.* ☉ *Garden Apr.–Oct., daily.*

*Castle interior Apr. and Oct., Tues.–Sun. 9–4; May and Sept., Tues.–
Sun. 9–5; June–Aug., Tues.–Sun. 9–6. Tower May and Sept., daily 9–
5; June–Aug., Tues.–Sun. 9–4. Theater May–Sept., daily 10–4; Oct.,
daily 10–3.*

The **Egon Schiele Center** exhibits the work of Schiele and other 20th-
century and contemporary Austrian, German, and Czech artists in a
rambling Renaissance building near the river. The museum closes occasionally during the winter season. ⊠ *Široká 70–72,* ☎ *380–704–
011,* WEB *www.ckrumlov.cz/uk.* 🎟 *150 Kč.* ☉ *Daily 10–6.*

Dining and Lodging

Český Krumlov is crammed with pensions and private rooms for rent,
many priced around $20 per person per night. The best place to look
is along the tiny Parkán ulice, which parallels the river just off the main
street. A safe bet is the house at **Parkán No. 107** (☎ 380–716–396),
blessed with several nice rooms and friendly management.

$$ ✕🏠 **Na louži.** Lovingly preserved wood furniture and paneling lends
★ a traditional touch to this warm, inviting, family-run pub. The food
is unfussy and satisfying; look for the *pstruh* (Vltava trout) with pota-
toes. The country-style rooms upstairs are small but comfortable. ⊠
Kájovská 66, 381 01, ☎ FAX *380–711–280,* WEB *www.nalouzi.cz. 5 rooms.
Restaurant, cable TV, some pets allowed; no a/c. No credit cards.*

$$$$ 🏠 **Růže.** This Renaissance monastery has been transformed into an ex-
★ cellent hotel, only a two-minute walk from the main square. The decor
is Ye Olde Bohemian but tastefully done, even extending to the bath-
room "thrones." The rooms are spacious, and a few have drop-dead
views of the castle, so ask to see several before choosing. Note that
some double rooms have two narrow single beds, while some singles
have beds large enough for two. The restaurant, too, is top-rate, and
the elegant dining room is formal but not stuffy. ⊠ *Horní 154, 381
01,* ☎ *380–772–100,* FAX *380–713–146,* WEB *www.hotelruze.cz. 71
rooms. 2 restaurants, café, cable TV, indoor pool, gym, hair salon, mas-
sage, sauna, bicycles, dry-cleaning, laundry service, business services,
meeting room, some pets allowed; no a/c. AE, MC, V. BP.*

$$$ 🏠 **Dvořák.** Eminently comfortable, and completely modernized in
1999, this small hotel has three other things going for it: location, lo-
cation, location. It's situated smack in the center of the historic district, right by the old Barber's Bridge. ⊠ *Radniční 101, 381 01,* ☎ *380–
711–020,* FAX *380–711–024,* WEB *www.hoteldvorak.cz. 17 rooms, 3
suites. Restaurant, in-room safes, cable TV, sauna, bar, dry cleaning,
laundry service, business services; no a/c. AE, DC, MC, V. BP.*

Nightlife and the Arts

Český Krumlov hosts numerous summertime cultural events, including Renaissance fairs, a chamber-music festival (in June and July),
organ and piano festivals (July), and the top-notch International Music
Festival, held at the castle every August, with performances by leading Czech and foreign classical ensembles.

České Budějovice

❽ *22 km (13 mi) north of Český Krumlov.*

After the glories of Český Krumlov, any other town is a letdown—and
České Budějovice, famous primarily for its beer, is no exception. That
said, this industrial city of 100,000 has a much livelier scene than its
more picturesque neighbors and a large Old Town with several worthwhile sights, notably the well-preserved Gothic Dominican monastery
and Church of the Virgin on Piaristické náměstí. The major attraction
is the enormously proportioned main square—a rarity, it actually *is*

square—named after King Přemysl Otakar II, lined with arcaded houses and worth an hour or two of wandering. For a bite to eat and a sampling of locally brewed Budvar beer in an atmospheric setting, stop by Masné Krámy on Krajinská 13, two blocks north of the square. The delicious local beer is known to Germans as Budweiser (they call the town Budweis)—but this is not the stuff made in St. Louis.

To get a good view over the city, climb the 360 steps up to the Renaissance gallery of the **Černá věž** (Black Tower), at the northeast corner of the square next to St. Nicholas's Cathedral. ✉ *Nám. Přemysla Otakara II.* 🎟 *10 Kč.* ⊙ *Apr.–June and Sept.–Oct., Tues.–Sun. 10–6; July–Aug., daily 10–6.*

Lodging

$$$–$$$$ 🏨 **Zvon.** Old-fashioned, well kept, and comfortable, the historic hotel has an ideal location right on the main square. A room with a view, however, costs extra, but these rooms are considerably larger and brighter and come with large period bathtubs. ✉ *Nám. Přemysla Otakara II 28, 307 01,* ☎ *387–311–384,* ℻ *387–311–385,* 🌐 *www. hotel-zvon.cz. 75 rooms. 2 restaurants, café, cable TV, some minibars, pub, room, some pets allowed (fee); no a/c. AE, DC, MC, V. BP.*

Hluboká nad Vltavou

★ ❾   *9 km (5½ mi) north of České Budějovice.*

This is one of the Czech Republic's most curious châteaus. Although the structure dates from the 13th century, what you see is pure 19th-century excess, perpetrated by the wealthy Schwarzenberg family as proof of their "good taste." If you think you've seen it somewhere before, you're probably thinking of Windsor Castle, near London, on which it was carefully modeled. Take a tour; the rather pompous interior reflects the no-holds-barred tastes of the time, but many individual pieces are interesting. The wooden Renaissance ceiling in the large dining room was removed by the Schwarzenbergs from the castle at Český Krumlov and brought here. Also look for the beautiful late-baroque bookshelves in the library. If your interest in Czech painting wasn't satisfied in Prague, have a look at the **Galerie Mikoláše Aleše** (Aleš Art Gallery) in the Riding Hall, featuring a major collection of Gothic art and a new exhibition of modern Czech works. ✉ *Zamék 142, off Rte. 105 or 146, Hluboká nad Vltavou,* ☎ *387–967–045 château; 387–967–041 gallery;* 🌐 *www.hluboka.cz.* 🎟 *Château 150 Kč, gallery 30 Kč.* ⊙ *Château Apr.–June and Sept.–Oct., Tues.–Sun. 9–4:30; July–Aug., daily 9–5. Gallery May–Sept., daily 9–5; Oct.–Apr., daily 9–3:30.*

If you're in the mood for a brisk walk, follow the yellow trail signs 2 km (1 mi) to the **Lovecká chata Ohrada** (Ohrada Hunting Lodge), which houses a museum of hunting and fishing and also has a small zoo for children. ✉ *Zamék Ohrada 1, off Rte. 105, Hluboká nad Vltavou,* ☎ *387–965–340.* 🎟 *40 Kč.* ⊙ *June–Aug., daily 9–5:30; May and Sept., Tues.–Sun. 9–5:30; Apr.–Oct., Tues.–Fri. 9–3; Nov.–Mar. by appointment.*

Písek

❿   *60 km (37 mi) northwest of České Budějovice.*

If it weren't for Písek's 700-year-old **Gothic bridge,** peopled with baroque statues, you could easily bypass the town and continue on to Prague. After the splendors of Český Krumlov or even Třeboň, Písek's main square, Velké náměstí, is plain, despite its many handsome Renaissance and baroque houses. The bridge, a five-minute walk from the main square along Karlova ulice, was commissioned in the 1260s—making it the oldest bridge in the land, surpassing by 90 years Prague's Charles Bridge—by Přemysl Otakar II, who sought a secure crossing over the difficult Otava River for his salt shipments from nearby Prachatice. As early as the 9th century, Písek stood at the center of one of the most important trade routes to the west, linking Prague to Passau and the rest of Bavaria, and in the 15th century it became one of five major Hussite strongholds. The statues of saints weren't added to the bridge until the 18th century. One of the statues was damaged and all the paving stones washed away during the devastating floods of 2002. The oldest bridge managed to survive, however, and will be repaired.

Just off the main square, look for the 240-ft tower of the early-Gothic **Mariánský chrám** (Church of Mary). Construction was started at about the time the bridge was built. The lone surviving tower was completed in 1487. On the inside, look for the *Madonna of Písek*, a 14th-century Gothic altar painting. On a middle pillar is a rare series of early Gothic wall paintings dating from the end of the 13th century. ⊠ *Bakaláře at Leoše Janáčka.*

OFF THE BEATEN PATH	**ZVÍKOV** – If you've got room for still another castle, head for Zvíkov Castle, about 18 km (11 mi) north of town. The castle, at the confluence of the Otava and Vltava rivers, is impressive for its authenticity. Unlike many other castles in Bohemia, Zvíkov survived the 18th and 19th centuries unrenovated and still looks just as it did 500 years ago. ⊠ *Rte. 138, 18 km (11 mi) north of Písek,* ☎ *382–899–676.* ⊡ *80 Kč.* ☉ *Apr. and Oct., weekends 9:30–3:30; May and Sept., Tues.–Sun. 9:30–4; June–Aug., Tues.–Sun. 9–5.*

Southern Bohemia Essentials

BUS TRAVEL
All the major destinations in the region are reachable from Prague and České Budějovice on the ČSAD bus network (☞ Bus Travel to and from Prague *in* Prague Essentials, *above*).

CAR TRAVEL
Car travel affords the greatest ease and flexibility in this region. The main artery through the region, the two-lane E55 from Prague south to Tábor and České Budějovice, though often crowded, is in relatively good shape. If you are driving from Vienna, take the E49 toward Gmünd.

TOURS
Čedok offers several specialized tours from Prague that include visits to České Budějovice, Hluboká Castle, Český Krumlov, Kutná Hora, and Konopiště. The main Prague departure point is náměstí Republiky (Republic Square) in central Prague, opposite the Prašná brána (Powder Tower). Most tours need to be booked a day in advance.
➤ CONTACTS: Čedok (☎ 224–197–111, WEB www.cedok.cz).

TRAIN TRAVEL
Benešov (Konopiště), Tábor, and České Budějovice lie along the major southern line in the direction of Linz, and train service to these cities from Prague is frequent and comfortable. Most Vienna–Prague trains travel through Moravia, but a few stop at Třeboň and Tábor (with a change at Gmünd).

VISITOR INFORMATION
➤ CONTACTS: **České Budějovice Tourist Center** (✉ Nám. Přemysla Otakára II 1, ☎ 386–359–480, WEB www.c-budejovice.cz). **Český Krumlov Tourist Information** (✉ Nám. Svornosti 1, ☎ 380–711–183, WEB www.ckrumlov.cz). **Kutná Hora Tourist Information** (✉ Palackého nám. 377, ☎ 327–512–378, WEB www.kutnahora.cz). **Písek Tourist Information** (✉ Heydukova 97, ☎ 382–213–592, WEB www.icpisek.cz). **Tábor Tourist Information** (✉ Žižkovo nám. 2, ☎ 381–486–230, WEB www.tabor.cz). **Třeboň Tourist Information** (✉ Masarykovo nám. 103, ☎ 384–721–169, WEB www.trebon.cz).

WESTERN BOHEMIA

Until World War II, western Bohemia was the playground of Central Europe's rich and famous. Its three well-known spas, Karlovy Vary, Mariánské Lázně, and Františkovy Lázně (better known by their German names, Karlsbad, Marienbad, and Franzensbad, respectively), were the annual haunts of everybody who was anybody: Johann Wolfgang von Goethe, Ludwig van Beethoven, Karl Marx, and England's King Edward VII, to name but a few. Although strictly "proletarianized" in the Communist era, the spas still exude a nostalgic aura of a more elegant past and, unlike most of Bohemia, offer a basic tourist infrastructure that makes dining and lodging a pleasure.

Karlovy Vary

★ ⓫ *132 km (79 mi) due west of Prague on Rte. 6 (E48).*

Karlovy Vary, better known outside the Czech Republic by its German name, Karlsbad, is the most famous Bohemian spa. It is named for Emperor Charles IV, who allegedly happened upon the springs in 1358 while on a hunting expedition. As the story goes, the emperor's hound—chasing a harried stag—fell into a boiling spring and was scalded. Charles had the water tested and, familiar with spas in Italy, ordered baths to be established in the village of Vary. The spa reached its heyday in the 19th century, when royalty came here from all over Europe for treatment. The long list of those who "took the cure" includes Peter the Great, Goethe (no fewer than 13 times, according to a plaque on one house by the main spring), Schiller, Beethoven, and Chopin. Even Karl Marx, when he wasn't decrying wealth and privilege, spent time at the resort; he wrote some of *Das Kapital* here between 1874 and 1876.

After decades of neglect under the Communists that left many buildings crumbling behind their beautiful facades, the town leaders today face the daunting task of carving out a new role for Karlovy Vary, since few Czechs can afford to set aside weeks or months at a time for a leisurely cure. To raise some quick cash, many sanatoriums have turned to offering short-term accommodations to foreign visitors (at rather expensive rates). By the week or by the hour, "classical" spa procedures, laser treatments, plastic surgery, and even acupuncture are purveyed to German clients or to large numbers of Russians who bought property in town in the late 1990s. For most visitors, though, it's enough simply to stroll the streets and parks and allow the eyes to feast awhile on the splendors of the past.

Whether you're arriving by bus, train, or car, your first view of the town on the approach from Prague will be of the ugly new section on the banks of the Ohře River. Don't despair: continue along the main road—following the signs to the Grandhotel Pupp—until you reach the lovely main street of the older spa area, situated gently astride the banks of the little Teplá ("Warm") River. (Drivers, note that driving through or parking in the main spa area is allowed only with a permit obtainable from your hotel.) The walk from the new town to the spa area is about 20 minutes.

The **Historická čtvrt** (Historic District) is still largely intact. Tall 19th-century houses, boasting decorative and often eccentric facades, line the spa's proud riverside streets. Throughout you'll see colonnades full of people sipping the spa's hot sulfuric water from odd pipe-shape drinking cups. At night the streets fill with steam escaping from cracks in the earth, giving the town a slightly macabre feel.

Karlovy Vary's jarringly modern **Vřídelní kolonáda** (Vřídlo Colonnade; ⊠ Vřídelní ul. near Kosterní nám.) is built around the spring of the same name, the town's hottest and most dramatic gusher. The Vřídlo is indeed unique, shooting its scalding water to a height of some 40 ft. Walk inside the arcade to watch the hundreds of patients here take the famed Karlsbad drinking cure. They promenade somnambulistically up and down, eyes glazed, clutching drinking glasses filled periodically at one of the five "sources." The waters are said to be especially effective against diseases of the digestive and urinary tracts. They're also good for gout (which probably explains the spa's former popularity with royals). If you want to join the crowds and take a sip, you can buy your own spouted cup from vendors within the colonnade.

To the right of the Vřídlo Colonnade are steps up to the white **Kostel Mařì Magdaleny** (Church of Mary Magdalene). Designed by Kilian Ignaz Dientzenhofer (architect of the two Churches of St. Nicholas in Prague), this church is the best of the few baroque buildings still standing in Karlovy Vary. ⊠ *Moravská ul.,* ☎ *no phone.* ☉ *Daily 9–6.*

The neo-Renaissance pillared hall **Mlýnská kolonáda** (Mill Colonnade), along the river, is the spa town's centerpiece. Built from 1871 to 1881, it has four springs: Rusalka, Libussa, Prince Wenceslas, and Millpond. ⊠ *Mlýnské nábřeží.*

The very elegant **Sadová kolonáda** (Park Colonnade) is a white, wrought-iron construction. It was built in 1882 by the Viennese architectural duo Fellner and Helmer, who sprinkled the Austro-Hungarian Empire with many such edifices during the late 19th century and who also designed the town's theater, the quaint wooden Tržní kolonáda (Market Colonnade) next to the Vřídlo Colonnade, and one of the old bathhouses. ⊠ *Zahradní.*

The 20th century emerges at its most disturbing across the river from the historic district in the form of the huge, bunkerlike **Thermal Hotel,** built in the late 1960s. Although the building is a monstrosity, the view of Karlovy Vary from the rooftop pool is nothing short of spectacular. (The pool is open 8 AM –8 PM.) Even if you don't feel like a swim, it's worth taking the winding road up to the baths for the view. ⊠ *I. P. Pavlova 11.*

A five-minute walk up the steep Zámecký vrch from the Market Colonnade brings you to the redbrick Victorian **Kostel svatého Lukáše** (St. Luke's Church), once used by the local English community. ⊠ *Zámecký vrch at Petra Velikého.*

From Kostel svatého Lukáše, take a sharp right uphill on the redbrick road. Then turn left onto a footpath through the woods, following the signs to **Jelení skok** (Stag's Leap). After a while you'll see steps leading up to a bronze statue of a deer looking over the cliffs, the symbol of Karlovy Vary. From here a winding path leads up to a little red gazebo opening onto a fabulous panorama. ⊠ *Sovava trail in Petrova Výšina park.*

Reward yourself for making the climb to Stag's Leap with a light meal at the nearby restaurant **Jeleni skok.** You may have to pay an entrance fee if there is a live band (but you'll also get the opportunity to polka). If you don't want to walk up, you can drive up a signposted road from the Victorian church.

The splendid Russian Orthodox **Kostel svatých Petra a Pavla** (Church of Sts. Peter and Paul) has five domes. It dates from the end of the 19th century and was built with help from the Russian aristocracy. ⊠ *Tř. Krále Jiřího.*

It's not necessary to walk to one of the best views of the town. Higher even than Stag's Leap is an observation tower, **rozhledna Diana,** accessible by funicular from behind the Grandhotel Pupp. There's an elevator to the top of the tower. ⊠ *Výšina přátelství.* ☜ *Funicular 25 Kč one-way, 40 Kč round-trip; tower 10 Kč.* ☉ *June–Sept., Mon.–Thurs. and Sun. 11–9, Fri.–Sat. 11–11; May and Oct., Tues.–Wed. and Sun. 11–6, Fri.–Sat. 11–7; Mar.–Apr. and Nov.–Dec., Wed.–Sun. 11–5.*

On one of the town's best shopping streets you'll find **Elefant,** one of the last of a dying breed of sophisticated coffeehouses. Happily, the café as an institution is making a real comeback in the Czech Republic. ⊠ *Stará louka 30.*

Dining and Lodging

$$–$$$ ✕ **Embassy.** This cozy, sophisticated wine restaurant, conveniently near the Grandhotel Pupp, serves an innovative menu by local standards. Tagliatelle with smoked salmon in cream sauce makes an excellent main course, as does roast duck with cabbage and dumplings. The wine list features Czech varieties like the dry whites Rulandské bílé and Ryzlink Rýnský (the latter being the domestic version of the Riesling grape) and some pricey imports. ⊠ *Nová louka 21,* ☎ *353–221–161. AE, DC, MC, V.*

$$–$$$ ✕ **Karel IV.** This restaurant's location atop an old castle tower not far from the Market Colonnade gives diners the best view in town. Good renditions of traditional Czech standbys—*bramborák* (potato pancake) and chicken breast with peaches—are served in small, secluded dining areas that are particularly intimate after sunset. ⊠ *Zámeckývrch 2,* ☎ *353–227–255. AE, MC, V.*

$$$–$$$$ ☷ **Grandhotel Pupp.** This enormous hotel with a 215-year history is
★   one of Central Europe's most famous resorts. Standards and service slipped under the Communists, but the highly professional management has more than made up for the decades of neglect. Some rooms are furnished in 18th-century period style. The vast public rooms exude the very best taste, circa 1913, when the present building was completed. Every July, the Pupp houses international movie stars in town for the Karlovy Vary International Film Festival. (The adjacent Parkhotel Pupp, under the same management, is a more affordable alternative.) Breakfast is 400 Kč extra. ⊠ *Mírové nám. 2, 360 91,* ☎ *353–109–111,* ℻ *353–109–620 or 353–224–032,* ⓦⒺⒷ *www.pupp.com. 75 rooms, 34 suites. 4 restaurants, cable TV with movies, in-room safes, minibars, health club, sauna, spa, casino, lounge, 2 nightclubs, Internet, some pets allowed (fee); no a/c in some rooms. AE, DC, MC, V.*

$$$ ☷ **Dvořák.** Consider a splurge here if you're longing for Western standards of service and convenience. Opened in late 1990, this Austrian-owned hotel occupies three renovated town houses that are just a five-minute walk from the main spas. If possible, request a room with a bay-window view of the town. Spa treatments here run to about $750 per person per week in the high season. ⊠ *Nová louka 11, 360 21,* ☎ *353–224–145,* ℻ *353–222–814,* ⓦⒺⒷ *www.hotel-dvorak.cz. 76 rooms,*

3 suites. Restaurant, café, cable TV with movies, pool, gym, hair salon, massage, sauna, casino, Internet, some pets allowed (fee). AE, DC, MC, V. BP.

$$$ 🏨 **Elwa.** Renovations have successfully integrated modern comforts into this older, elegant spa resort midway between the old and new towns. Modern features include clean, comfortable rooms with contemporary furnishings, including overstuffed chairs. There's also an on-site fitness center. The spa specializes in digestive diseases. ⊠ *Zahradní 29, 360 01,* ☎ *353–228–472,* FAX *353–228–473,* WEB *www.hotelelwa.com. 10 rooms, 7 suites. Restaurant, cable TV, minibars, hair salon, health club, spa, bar, some pets allowed (fee); no a/c. AE, MC, V. BP.*

$$ 🏨 **Růže.** More than adequately comfortable and well priced given its location smack in the center of the spa district, this is a good choice for those who prefer a hotel to a pension or private room. ⊠ *I. P. Pavlova 1, 360 01,* ☎ FAX *353–221–846 or 353–221–853. 20 rooms. Restaurant, cable TV; no a/c. AE, V. BP.*

Nightlife and the Arts

Club Propaganda (⊠ Jaltská 7, ☎ 353–233–792) is Karlovy Vary's best venue for live rock and new music. The upscale action centers on the two nightclubs and the casino of the **Grandhotel Pupp** (⊠ Mírové nám. 2, ☎ 353–109–111). The Karlovy Vary Symphony Orchestra plays regularly at **Lázně III** (⊠ Mlýnské nábř. 5, ☎ 353–225–641).

Outdoor Activities and Sports

Karlovy Vary's warm, open-air public pool on top of the **Thermal Hotel** (⊠ I. P. Pavlova) offers the unique experience of swimming comfortably even in the coolest weather; the view over the town is outstanding. Marked **hiking trails** snake across the beech-and-pine-covered hills that surround the town on three sides. The **Karlovy Vary Golf Club** (⊠ Pražská 125, ☎ 353–331–101) is just out of town on the road to Prague.

Shopping

The town's most exclusive shopping clusters around the Grandhotel Pupp and back toward town along the river on Stará louka. A number of outlets for lesser-known, although high-quality, makers of glass and porcelain can be found along this street. If you are looking for an inexpensive but nonetheless unique gift from Karlovy Vary, consider a bottle of the ubiquitous bittersweet (and potent) Becherovka, a liqueur produced by the town's own Jan Becher distillery. Another neat gift would be one of the pipe-shaped ceramic drinking cups used to take the drinking cure at spas; you can find them at the colonnades. You can also buy boxes of tasty *oplatky* (wafers), sometimes covered with chocolate, at shops in all of the spa towns.

In western Bohemia, Karlovy Vary is best known to glass enthusiasts as the home of **Moser** (⊠ Tržiště 7, ☎ 353–235–303, WEB www.moser.cz), one of the world's leading producers of crystal and decorative glassware. For excellent buys in porcelain, try **Karlovarský porcelán** (⊠ Tržiště 27, ☎ 353–225–660, WEB www.dolphin.cz/thun).

Cheb

⓬ *42 km (26 mi) southwest of Karlovy Vary.*

Known for centuries by its German name of Eger, the old town of Cheb lies on the border with Germany in the far west of the Czech Republic. The town has been a fixture of Bohemia since 1322 (when it was handed over to King Jan, or Johann, as thanks for his support of a Bavarian prince), but as you walk around the beautiful medieval square, it's difficult not to think you're in Germany. The tall merchants' houses surrounding the main square, with their long, red-tile, sloping roofs dotted with windows like droopy eyelids, are more Germanic in style than anything else in Bohemia. You'll also hear a lot of German on the streets—more from the many German visitors than from the town's residents.

Germany took full possession of the town in 1938 under the terms of the notorious Munich Pact. But following World War II, virtually the entire German population was expelled, and the Czech name of Cheb was officially adopted. A more notorious German connection emerged in the years following the 1989 revolution: Cheb, like other border towns, became an unofficial center of prostitution. Don't be startled to see young women, provocatively dressed, lining the highways and roads into town.

The **statue** in the middle of the central square, náměstí Krále Jiřího z Poděbrad, similar to the Roland statues you see throughout Bohemia and attesting to the town's royal privileges, represents the town hero, Wastel of Eger. Look carefully at his right foot, and you'll see a small man holding a sword and a head—this shows the town had its own judge and executioner.

On the lower part of náměstí Krále Jiřího z Poděbrad are two rickety groups of timbered medieval buildings, 11 houses in all, divided by a narrow alley. The houses, forming the area known as **Špalíček,** date from the 13th century and were home to many Jewish merchants. **Židovská ulice** (Jews' Street), running uphill to the left of the Špalíček, served as the actual center of the ghetto. Note the small alley running off to the left of Židovská. This calm street, with the seemingly inappropriate name ulička Zavražděných (Lane of the Murdered), was the scene of an outrageous act of violence in 1350. Pressures had been building for some time between Jews and Christians. Incited by an anti-Semitic bishop, the townspeople finally chased the Jews into the street, closed off both ends, and massacred them. Now only the name attests to the slaughter. ⊠ *Nám. Krále Jiřího z Poděbrad.*

NEED A BREAK?   Cheb's main square abounds with cafés and little restaurants, all offering a fairly uniform menu of schnitzel and sauerbraten aimed at visiting Germans. The **Kavárna Špalíček,** nestled in the Špalíček buildings, is one of the better choices and has the added advantage of a unique architectural setting.

The **Chebské muzeum** (Cheb Museum) in the Pachelbel House on the main square documents the history of Cheb, with particular emphasis on the Hapsburg era. It was in this house that the great general of the Thirty Years' War, Albrecht von Wallenstein, was murdered in 1634 on the orders of his own emperor, the Hapsburg Ferdinand II, who was provoked by Wallenstein's increasing power and rumors of treason. According to legend, Wallenstein was on his way to the Saxon border to enlist support to fight the Swedes when his own officers barged into his room and stabbed him through the heart with a stave. In his memory, the stark bedroom with its four-poster bed and dark red velvet curtains has been left as it was. (The story also inspired playwright Friedrich Schiller to write the *Wallenstein* trilogy; he planned the work while living at the top of the square at No. 2.) The museum is interesting in its own right: it has a selection from the Wallenstein family picture gallery, a section on the history of Cheb, and a collection of minerals (including one discovered by Goethe). There's also the stuffed remains of Wallenstein's horse, who died in battle. ⊠ *Nám. Krále Jiřího z Poděbrad 3,* ☎ *354–422–246,* WEB *www.muzeumcheb.cz.* ⬛ *50 Kč.* ☉ *Mar.–Dec., Tues.–Sun. 9–noon and 1–5.*

The plain but imposing **Kostel svatého Mikuláše** (Church of St. Nicholas) was begun in 1230, when the church belonged to the Order of the Teutonic Knights. You can still see Romanesque windows on the towers; renovations throughout the centuries added an impressive Gothic portal and a baroque interior. Just inside the Gothic entrance is a wonderfully faded plaque commemorating the diamond jubilee of Hapsburg emperor Franz Joseph in 1908. ⊠ *Kostelní nám.,* ☎ *354–422–458.*

Follow Křižovnická, behind the Church of St. Nicholas, up to **Chebský hrad** (Cheb Castle), which stands on a cliff overlooking the Ohře River. The castle—now a ruin—was built in the late 12th century for Holy Roman Emperor Frederick Barbarossa. The square black tower was built with blocks of lava taken from the nearby Komorní Hůrka volcano; the red-brick walls are 17th-century additions. Inside the castle grounds is the carefully restored double-decker Romanesque chapel, which was restored in 2002, and notable for the many lovely columns with heads carved into their capitals. The rather dark ground floor was used by commoners. The bright, ornate top floor was reserved for the emperor and his family, who entered via a wooden bridge leading to the royal palace. ⊠ *Dobrovského 21,* ☎ *354–422–942,* WEB *www.muzeumcheb.cz/Hrad.htm.* 🎫 *30 Kč.* ☉ *Apr. and Oct., Tues.–Sun. 9–4; May and Sept., Tues.–Sun. 9–5; June–Aug., Tues.–Sun. 9–6.*

Dining and Lodging

$–$$ ✕ **Eva.** Of the many restaurants opened on and around the main square since the tourism boom began in the early 1990s, Eva is certainly one of the best. A decent array of mostly Czech and German dishes—with an emphasis on game—is served by a troop of attentive waiters. ⊠ *Jateční 4,* ☎ *354–422–498. No credit cards.*

$–$$$ 🏨 **Hvězda.** Three charming baroque buildings, with bright pastel facades, were joined in 2000 into one of the few hotels in downtown Cheb. The location on a main square gives easy access to the city's sites and eateries. Some rooms offer spectacular views, and the hotel's sidewalk café is a pleasant place to watch the endless parade of strollers. One room has six beds. ⊠ *Nám. Krále Jiřího z Poděbrad 5, 350 02,* ☎ *354–422–705,* FAX *354–422–546,* WEB *www.hotel-hvezda.cz. 41 rooms, some with shared bath. Restaurant, cable TV, some pets allowed (fee), parking (fee); no a/c. AE, MC, V. BP.*

Františkovy Lázně

13 *6 km (4 mi) from Cheb.*

Františkovy Lázně, or Franzensbad, the smallest of the three main Bohemian spas, isn't really in the same league as the other two (Karlovy Vary and Mariánské Lázně). Built on a more modest scale at the start of the 19th century, the town's ubiquitous kaiser-yellow buildings have been spruced up after their neglect under the previous regime and now present cheerful facades, almost too bright for the few strollers. The poorly kept parks and the formal yet human-scale neoclassical architecture retain much of their former charm. This little spa town couldn't be a more distinct contrast to nearby Cheb's slightly seedy, hustling air and medieval streetscapes. Overall, a pleasing torpor reigns in Františkovy Lázně. There is no town to speak of, just **Národní ulice,** the main street, which leads down into the spa park. The waters, whose healing properties were already known in the 16th century, are used primarily for treating heart problems—and infertility, hence the large number of young women wandering the grounds.

You might enjoy walking the path, indicated with red markers, from Cheb's main square westward along the river and then north past **Ko-**

morní Hůrka. The extinct volcano is now a tree-covered hill, but excavations on one side have laid bare the rock, and one tunnel is still open. Goethe instigated and took part in the excavations, and you can still—though barely—make out a relief of the poet carved into the rock face.

The most interesting sight in town may be the small **Lázeňský muzeum** (Spa Museum), just off Národní ulice. There is a wonderful collection of spa-related antiques, including copper bathtubs and a turn-of-the-20th-century exercise bike called a Velotrab. The guest books provide an insight into the cosmopolitan world of pre–World War I Central Europe. The book for 1812 contains the entry "Ludwig van Beethoven, composer from Vienna." ⊠ *Ul. Doktora Pohoreckého 8,* ☎ *354–542–344.* 🖾 *20 Kč.* ☉ *Tues.–Fri. 10–5, weekends 10–4 (usually closed mid-Dec.–mid-Jan.).*

The main spring, **Františkův pramen,** is under a little gazebo filled with brass pipes. The colonnade to the left was decorated with a bust of Lenin that was replaced in 1990 by a memorial to the American liberation of the town in April 1945. The oval neoclassical temple just beyond the spring (amazingly, *not* painted yellow and white) is the **Glauberova dvorana** (Glauber Pavilion), where several springs bubble up into glass cases. ⊠ *Národní ul.*

Dining and Lodging

Most of the establishments in town do a big trade in spa patients, who generally stay for several weeks. Spa treatments usually require a medical check and cost substantially more than the normal room charge. Walk-in treatment can be arranged at some hotels or at the information center. Signs around town advertise massage therapy and other treatments for casual visitors.

$$ ✕🖾 **Slovan.** This gracious place is the perfect complement to this re-
★ laxed little town. The eccentricity of the original turn-of-the-20th-century design survived a thorough renovation during the 1970s. The airy rooms are clean and comfortable, and some have a balcony overlooking the main street. The main-floor restaurant serves above-average Czech dishes such as tasty *svíčková* (beef sirloin in a citrusy cream sauce) and roast duck. ⊠ *Národní 5, 351 01,* ☎ *354–542–841,* 🖾 *354–542–843. 25 rooms, 19 with bath. Restaurant, café, refrigerators, cable TV, bar, meeting room, Internet, some pets allowed (fee). AE, MC, V.*

$$ 🖾 **Centrum.** Rooms in this barnlike building are well appointed, if a bit sterile. Still, it is among the best-run hotels in town and only a short walk from the main park and central spas. ⊠ *Anglická 392, 351 01,* ☎ *354–543–156,* 🖾 *354–543–157. 30 rooms. Restaurant, cable TV, bar, some pets allowed. AE, MC, V. BP.*

$$ 🖾 **Tři Lilie.** Reopened in 1995 after an expensive refitting, the "Three Lilies," which once accommodated the likes of Goethe and Metternich, immediately reestablished itself as the most comfortable spa hotel in town. It is thoroughly elegant, from guest rooms to brasserie. ⊠ *Národní 3,* ☎ 🖾 *354–542–415. 31 rooms. Restaurant, brasserie, café, cable TV, some pets allowed (fee). AE, MC, V. BP.*

Mariánské Lázně

★ ⑭ *30 km (18 mi) southeast of Cheb, 47 km (29 mi) south of Karlovy Vary.*

Your expectations of what a spa resort should be may come nearest to fulfillment here. It's far larger and more active than Františkovy Lázně and greener and quieter than Karlovy Vary. This was the spa favored by Britain's Edward VII. Goethe and Chopin also repaired here frequently. Mark Twain, on a visit to the spa in 1892, labeled the town a "health factory" and couldn't get over how new everything looked. Indeed, at that time everything was new. The sanatoriums, most built during the 19th century in a confident, outrageous mixture of "neo" styles, fan out impressively around a finely groomed oblong park. Cure takers and curiosity seekers alike parade through the Empire-style Cross Spring pavilion and the long colonnade near the top of the park. Buy a spouted drinking cup (available at the colonnades) and join the rest of the sippers taking the drinking cure. Be forewarned, though: the waters from the Rudolph, Ambrose, and Caroline springs, though harmless, all have a noticeable diuretic effect. For this reason they're used extensively in treating disorders of the kidney and bladder.

A stay in Mariánské Lázně can be healthful even without special treatment. Special walking trails of all difficulty levels surround the resort in all directions. The best advice is simply to put on comfortable shoes, buy a hiking map, and head out. One of the country's few golf courses lies about 3 km (2 mi) to the east of town. Hotels can also help to arrange special activities, such as tennis and horseback riding. For the less intrepid, a simple stroll around the gardens, with a few deep breaths of the town's famous air, is enough to restore a healthy sense of perspective.

For information on spa treatments, inquire at the main **spa offices** (⊠ Masarykova 22, ☎ 354–623–061, WEB www.marienbad.cz). Walk-in treatments can be arranged at the **Nové Lázně** (New Spa; ⊠ Reitenbergerova 53, ☎ 354–644–111).

OFF THE BEATEN PATH

CHODOVÁ PLANÁ – If you need a break from the rigorous healthiness of spa life, the Pivovarská restaurace a muzeum ve skále (Brewery Restaurant and Museum in the Rock) is just a few miles south of Mariánské Lázně in an underground complex of granite tunnels that have been used to age beer since the 1400s. Generous servings of Czech dishes including a whole roast suckling pig can be ordered to accompany the strong, fresh Chodovar beer tapped directly from granite storage vaults. Giant tanks of aging beer and brewing memorabilia can be seen through glass windows on the way in. You can tour the brewery, but at this writing, tours were conducted in German only. ⊠ *Pivovarská 107, Chodová Planá*, ☎ *374–798–122*, WEB *www.chodovar.cz.* ☜ *Museum free, tour 50 Kč.* ☉ *Daily 11–11; brewery tours daily at 2.*

Dining and Lodging

The best place to look for private lodgings is along Paleckého ulice and Hlavní třída, south of the main spa area. Private accommodations can also be found in the neighboring villages of Zádub and Závišín in the woods to the east of town.

$–$$$ ✗ **Koliba.** This combination hunting lodge and wine tavern, set in the ★ woods roughly 10 minutes on foot from the spas, is an excellent alternative to the hotel restaurants in town. Grilled meats and shish kebabs, plus tankards of Moravian wine (try the dry, cherry red Rulandské červené), are served with traditional gusto while fiddlers play rousing Moravian tunes. ⊠ *Dusíkova 592, in the direction of Karlovy Vary,* ☎ *354–625–169.* V.

$–$$ ✗ **Filip.** This bustling wine bar is where locals come to find relief from the sometimes large hordes of tourists. There's a tasty selection of traditional Czech dishes—mainly pork, grilled meats, and steaks. ⊠ *Poštovní 96,* ☎ *354–626–161. No credit cards.*

$$$$ ▣ **Excelsior.** This lovely older hotel is on the main street and is convenient to the spas and colonnade. Rooms have traditional cherry-wood furniture and marble bathrooms, and the views over the town are en-

chanting. The staff is friendly and multilingual. While the food in the restaurant is only average, the romantic setting provides adequate compensation. ✉ *Hlavní tř. 121, 353 01,* ☎ *354–622–705,* FAX *354–625–346,* WEB *www.orea.cz/excelsior. 64 rooms. Restaurant, café, cable TV with movies, minibars, massage, sauna, some pets allowed (fee); no a/c. AE, DC, MC, V. BP.*

$$$$ 🏨 **Parkhotel Golf.** Book in advance to secure a room at this stately villa situated 3½ km (2 mi) out of town on the road to Karlovy Vary. The large, open rooms are cheery and modern. The restaurant on the main floor is excellent, but the big draw is the 18-hole golf course on the premises, one of the few in the Czech Republic. The course was opened in 1905 by King Edward VII. ✉ *Zádub 55, 353 01,* ☎ *354–622–651 or 354–622–652,* FAX *354–622–655,* WEB *web.telecom.cz/parkhotel-golf. 25 rooms. Restaurant, minibars, cable TV, pool, 18-hole golf course, tennis court, nightclub, meeting room, Internet, some pets allowed (fee). AE, DC, MC, V. BP.*

$$$ 🏨 **Bohemia.** At this gracious, late-19th-century hotel, beautiful crys-
★   tal chandeliers in the main hall set the stage for a comfortable and el-egant stay. The crisp beige-and-white rooms let you spread out and *really* unpack; they're spacious and high ceilinged. (If you want to indulge, request one of the enormous suites overlooking the park.) The helpful staff can arrange spa treatments and horseback riding. A renovation in 2001 brightened up the facade and modernized the kitchen. ✉ *Hlavní tř. 100, 353 01,* ☎ *354–623–251,* FAX *354–622–943,* WEB *www.orea.cz/bohemia. 73 rooms, 4 suites. Restaurant, café, cable TV, lounge, some pets allowed (fee); no a/c. AE, MC, V. BP.*

Nightlife and the Arts

The West Bohemian Symphony Orchestra performs regularly in the New Spa (Nové Lázně). The town's annual Chopin festival each August brings in pianists from around Europe to perform the Polish composer's works.

Casino Lil (✉ Anglická 336, ☎ 354–623–293) is open daily 2 PM–7 AM. For late-night drinks, try the **Parkhotel Golf** (✉ Zádub 55, ☎ 354–622–651 or 354–622–652), which has a good nightclub with dancing in season.

Plzeň

🟤 *92 km (55 mi) west of Prague.*

The sprawling industrial city of Plzeň is hardly a tourist mecca, but it's worth stopping off for an hour or two on the way back to Prague. Two sights here are of particular interest to beer fanatics. The **Pilsner Urquell Brewery** is east of the city near the railway station. The beer was created in 1842 using the excellent Plzeň water, a special malt fermented on the premises, and hops grown in the region around Žatec. On a group tour of the 19th-century redbrick building you can taste the valuable brew, exported around the world. You can only visit the brewery on one of the daily guided tours, weekdays at 12:30 PM (sometimes also at 2 PM in the summer). You can only visit via the tour. ✉ *U Prazdroje 7,* ☎ *377–061–111,* WEB *www.pilsner-urquell.com.* 🎫 *120 Kč.* ☉ *Tours Apr.–May and Sept., daily at 12:30; July–Aug., daily at 12:30 and 2; Oct.–Mar., weekdays at 12:30.*

NEED A   You can continue drinking and find some cheap traditional grub at the
BREAK?   large **Na Spilce** beer hall just inside the brewery gates. The pub is open weekdays and Saturday 11 AM–10 PM, Friday 11 AM–11 PM, and Sunday 11 AM–7 PM.

The **Pivovarské muzeum** (Brewery Museum) is in a late-Gothic malt house one block northeast of náměstí Republiky. All kinds of paraphernalia trace the region's brewing history, including the horse-drawn carts used to haul the kegs. ⊠ *Veleslavinova 6,* ☎ *377–235–574,* WEB *www.pilsner-urquell.com.* ▨ *100 Kč.* ⊘ *Daily 10–6.*

The city's architectural attractions center on the main **náměstí Republiky** (Republic Square). The square is dominated by the enormous Gothic **Chrám svatého Bartoloměje** (Church of St. Bartholomew). Both the square and the church towers hold size records: the former is the largest in Bohemia and the latter, at 335 ft, the tallest in the Czech Republic. Around the square, mixed in with its good selection of stores, are a variety of other architectural jewels, including the town hall, adorned with sgraffiti and built in the Renaissance style by Italian architects during the town's heyday in the 16th century. The Moorish **synagogue,** one of the largest in Europe, is four blocks west of the square, just outside the green strip that circles the old town.

Dining and Lodging

$$ ✕▥ **Continental.** Just five minutes on foot from the main square, this late-19th-century restaurant remains a good choice, and the current owners are working to return the hotel to its former glory, when movie stars like Ingrid Bergman and Marlene Dietrich stayed there. The restaurant serves dependably satisfying traditional Czech dishes such as *cibulka* (onion soup) and *svíčková* (beef sirloin in a citrusy cream sauce). ⊠ *Zbojnická 8, 305 31,* ☎ *377–236–477,* FAX *377–722–1746,* WEB *www.hotelcontinental.cz. 46 rooms, 23 with bath. Restaurant, café, cable TV, some pets allowed, Internet, meeting room; no a/c. AE, DC, MC, V.*

$$ ▥ **Central.** This angular 1960s structure is recommendable for its sunny rooms, friendly staff, and great location, right on the main square. Indeed, even such worthies as Czar Alexander of Russia stayed here in the days when the hotel was a charming inn known as the Golden Eagle. Breakfast costs 120 Kč extra. ⊠ *Nám. Republiky 33, 305 31,* ☎ *377–226–757,* FAX *377–226–064,* WEB *web.telecom.cz/hotel-central. 77 rooms. Restaurant, café, cable TV, bar, Internet, some pets allowed (fee); no a/c. AE, DC, MC, V.*

Western Bohemia Essentials

BUS TRAVEL
Most major towns are easily reachable by bus service. Smaller towns, though, might only have one bus a day or even fewer. Be sure to know when the next bus comes so you won't be stranded. Frequent bus service between Prague and Karlovy Vary makes the journey only about two hours each way. Many places such as Plzeň are reachable by both bus and train. Both the price and time differences can be great (☞ Bus Travel to and from Prague *in* Prague Essentials).

CAR TRAVEL
If you're driving, you can take the E48 directly from Prague to Karlovy Vary. Roads in the area tend to be in good condition, though they can sometimes be quite narrow.

TOURS
Most of Prague's tour operators offer excursions to Karlovy Vary. Čedok offers one-day and longer tours covering western Bohemia's major sights, as well as curative vacations at many Czech spas.
➤ CONTACTS: Čedok (☎ 224–197–111, WEB www.cedok.cz).

TRAIN TRAVEL

Good, if slow, train service links all the major towns west of Prague. The best stretches are from Františkovy Lázně to Plzeň and from Plzeň to Prague. The Prague–Karlovy Vary run takes far longer than it should—more than three hours by the shortest route.

TRAVEL AGENCIES

The American Express representative in Karlovy Vary is Incentives CZ. ➤ CONTACTS: **Incentives CZ** (✉ Vřídelní 51, Karlovy Vary, ☎ 353–226–027, WEB www.incentives.cz).

VISITOR INFORMATION

➤ CONTACTS: **Cheb Tourist Information** (✉ Nám. Krále Jiřího z Poděbrad 33, Cheb, ☎ 354–434–385 or 354–422–705, WEB www.mestocheb.cz). **Františkovy Lázně Tourist Information** (✉ Tři Lilie Travel Agency, Národní 3, Františkovy Lázně, ☎ 354–542–430, WEB www.franzensbad.cz). **Karlovy Vary Tourist Information** (Kur-Info; ✉ Vřídelní kolonáda [Vřídlo Colonnade], Karlovy Vary, ☎ 353–322–4097, WEB www.karlovyvary.cz; Nám. Dr. M. Horákové 18, Karlovy Vary [near bus station], ☎ 353–222–833). **Mariánské Lázně Tourist Information** (Cultural and Information Center; ✉ Hlavní 47, Mariánské Lázně, ☎ 354–625–892 or 354–622–474, WEB www.marianskelazne.cz). **Plzeň Tourist Information** (✉ Nám. Republiky 41, Plzeň, ☎ 378–032–750, WEB info.plzen-city.cz). **Teplá Information** (✉ Masarykovo nám. c.p. 143, Teplá, ☎ 353–391–130, WEB www.tepla.cz).

NORTHERN BOHEMIA

Northern Bohemia is a paradox: much of it was despoiled by 40 years of rampant postwar industrialization, but here and there you can still find areas of great natural beauty. Along the Labe River, rolling hills, perfect for walking, guard the country's northern frontiers with Germany and Poland. Hikers and campers head for the Krkonoše range on the Polish border. As you move toward the west, the interest is more historical, in an area where the influence of Germany was felt in less pleasant ways than in the spas. You don't have to drive too far to reach the Sudetenland, the German-speaking border area that was handed over to Hitler by the British and French in 1938. The landscape here is riddled with the tragic remains of the Nazi occupation of Czech lands from 1939 to 1945. Most drastically affected was Terezín, better known as the infamous concentration camp Theresienstadt.

As tourist amenities keep improving, reasonably priced, adequately comfortable small-to-middling hotels are now not too difficult to find. Dining options still generally are standard Czech and German cooking, although Asian restaurants are now a less-than-amazing sight in the area's larger towns, thanks to the presence of sizable Chinese and Vietnamese communities in border areas. Pizzerias, which range from ghastly to quite congenial, are now ubiquitous.

Lidice

⑯ *18 km (11 mi) from Prague on Rte. 7 (the road to Ruzyně Airport). Head in the direction of Slaný. Turn off at Lidice exit and follow country road 3 km (2 mi).*

The Lidice story really begins with the notorious Munich Pact of 1938, under which the leaders of Great Britain and France permitted Hitler to occupy the largely German-speaking border regions of Czechoslovakia (the so-called Sudetenland). Less than a year later, in March 1939, Hitler used his forward position to occupy the whole of Bohemia and

Moravia, making the area into a protectorate of the German Reich. To guard his new possessions, Hitler appointed ruthless Nazi Reinhard Heydrich as Reichsprotektor. Heydrich immediately implemented a campaign of terror against Jews and intellectuals while currying favor with average Czechs by raising rations and wages. As a result, the Czech army-in-exile, based in Great Britain, soon began planning Heydrich's assassination. In the winter of 1941–42 a small band of parachutists was flown in to carry out the task.

The attack took place in the north part of Prague on May 27, 1942, and Heydrich died from his injuries on June 4. Hitler immediately ordered the little mining town of Lidice, west of Prague, "removed from the face of the earth," since it was alleged (although later found untrue) that some of the assassins had been sheltered by villagers there. On the night of June 9, a Gestapo unit entered Lidice, shot the entire adult male population (192 men), and sent the 196 women to the Ravensbrück concentration camp. A handful of the 103 children in the village were sent to Germany to be "Aryanized"; the others perished in death camps. On June 10, the entire village was razed. The assassins and their accomplices were found a week later in the Orthodox Church of Sts. Cyril and Methodius in Prague's New Town. There, the men committed suicide after a shoot-out with Nazi militia.

Lidice was rebuilt after the war on the initiative of a group of miners from Birmingham, England, who called their committee "Lidice Must Live." The wooden cross in the field, starkly decorated with barbed wire, marks the place in Old Lidice where the men were executed. Remains of brick walls are visible here, left over from the Gestapo's dynamite and bulldozer exercise. Still, Lidice is a sad town, not a place to linger.

The **Lidice museum and monument** are unforgettable sights. The empty field to the right, with a large cross at the bottom, is where the town of Lidice stood until 1942, when it was viciously razed by the Nazis in retribution for the assassination of the German overlord of the Czech lands, Reinhard Heydrich.

The monument to these events is a sober place. The arcades are graphic in their depiction of the deportation and slaughter of the inhabitants. The museum itself is dedicated to those killed, with photographs of each person and a short description of his or her fate. You'll also find reproductions of the German documents ordering the village's destruction, including the Gestapo's chillingly bureaucratic reports on how the massacre was carried out and the peculiar problems encountered in Aryanizing the deported children. The exhibits highlighting the international response (a suburb of Chicago was even renamed for the town) are heartwarming. An absorbing 18-minute film in Czech (worthwhile even for non-Czech speakers) tells the Lidice story. ✉ *Ul. 10. června 1942,* WEB *www.lidice-memorial.cz.* 🎫 *50 Kč.* ⏲ *Apr.–Oct., daily 8–6; Nov.–Mar., daily 9–3.*

Veltrusy Château and Gardens

⓱ *25 km (15 mi) north of Prague.*

The aristocratic retreat of Veltrusy contrasts vividly with the ordinariness of nearby Kralupy, an industrial town better left unexplored. The mansion's late-baroque splendor lies hidden in a carefully laid out English park full of old and rare trees and scattered with 18th-century architectural follies. Until the end of World War II the château belonged to the Chotek family, whose most famous scion was Sophie Chotek, wife of Archduke Franz Ferdinand. Today the palace is given over to a museum showcasing the cosmopolitan lifestyle of the imperial aristocracy, displaying Japanese and Chinese porcelain, English chandeliers, and 16th-century tapestries from Brussels. ⊠ *Off Rte. E55, Veltrusy,* ☎ *315–781–146.* ▦ *Tours 70 Kč–130 Kč, cycling tour 30 Kč.* ☉ *Park daily. Château Apr.–Aug., Tues.–Sun. 8–5; Sept., Tues.– Sun. 9–5; Mar. and Oct.–Nov., weekends 9–4.*

Nelahozeves

⑱ *25 km (15 mi) north of Prague, or 2½ km (1½ mi) on foot by marked paths from Veltrusy Château. By car: turn right out of Veltrusy onto Rte. 101 and over the Vltava River, then make a sharp left back along the river to Nelahozeves.*

Nelahozeves was the birthplace of Antonín Dvořák (1841–1904), the Czech Republic's greatest composer, who was known for weaving folk influences into Romantic music.

Squatting above the village, the brooding Renaissance **Nelahozeves Castle,** with its black-and-white sgraffito, is an increasingly popular attraction. The owners, a branch of the wealthy Lobkowicz family, lost the property to the Communist state in the 1950s, then regained it, along with their fabulous art collection, in the 1990s. The collection, one of the finest in private hands in Central Europe, includes such masterpieces as one of the paintings from Pieter Brueghel the Elder's six-canvas series depicting the seasons. This painting alone is worth the short, scenic train journey from Prague's Masarykovo station (change in Kralupy nad Vltavou and get off at the next stop, Nelahozeves-zastávka, or walk the 3 km [2 mi] from Kralupy along the peaceful Vltava bank). The one-hour main tour also includes paintings by Rubens and Velázquez, as well as a wonderful pair of London views by Canaletto. There is also valuable memorabilia of the family's musical patronage, including original manuscripts by Beethoven and a score of Handel's *Messiah* annotated by Mozart on the main tour. A second tour shows off the knights' hall with Renaissance decor, plus rooms with collections of period furniture, family portraits and imported porcelain. ⊠ *Nelahozeves,* ☎ *315–709–111,* WEB *www.lobkowicz.org.* ▦ *Main tour 330 Kč, second tour 100 Kč, both tours 380 Kč.* ☉ *Tues.–Sun. 9–5.*

Terezín

⑲ *36 km (22 mi) northwest of Nelahozeves on Rte. 8.*

During World War II, the town of Terezín—called Theresienstadt by the Germans—served as a detention center for thousands of Jews and was used by the Nazis as an elaborate prop in a nefarious propaganda ploy. The large barracks buildings around town, once used in the 18th and 19th centuries to house Austrian soldiers, became living quarters for thousands of interred Jews. But in 1942, to placate international public opinion, the Nazis cynically decided to transform the town into a showcase camp—to prove to the world their "benevolent" intentions toward the Jews. To give the place the image of a spa town, the streets were given new names such as Lake Street, Bath Street, and Park Street. Numerous elderly Jews from Germany were taken in by the deception and paid large sums of money to come to the new "retirement village." Just before the International Red Cross inspected the town in early 1944, Nazi authorities began a beautification campaign: they painted the buildings, set up stores, laid out a park with benches in front of the town hall, and arranged for concerts and sports. The map just off the main square shows the town's street plan as the locations of various buildings between 1941 and 1945. The Jews here were able, with great difficulty, to establish a cultural life of their own under the limited self-government that was set up in the camp. The inmates created a library and a theater, and lectures and musical performances were given on a regular basis.

Once it was clear that the war was lost, however, the Nazis dropped any pretense and quickly stepped up transport of Jews to the Auschwitz death camp in Poland. Transports were not new to the ghetto; to keep the population at around 30,000, a train was sent off every few months or so "to the east" to make room for incoming groups. In the fall of 1944, these transports were increased to one every few days. In all, some 87,000 Jews from Terezín were murdered in this way, and another 35,000 died from starvation or disease. The conductor Karel Ančerl, who died in 1973, and the novelist Ivan Klíma are among the few thousand who survived imprisonment at Terezín.

The enormity of Theresienstadt's role in history is difficult to grasp at first because the Czechs have put up few signs to tell you what to see, ★ but the **Památník Terezín** (Terezín Memorial) encompasses the existing buildings that are open to the public. Buildings include the **Magdeburg Barracks,** where the Jewish Council of Elders met, and the **Jewish cemetery's crematorium** just outside the town walls.

The town's horrific story is told in words and pictures at the **Museum of the Terezín Ghetto** (✉ Komenského ul., ☎ 416–782–577), just off the central park in town.

The **Malá Pevnost** (Small Fortress; ✉ Principova alej 304, ☎ 416–782–225), the actual prison and death camp, is 1 km (½ mi) east of Terezín. In the strange redbrick complex you'll see the prison more or less as it was when the Nazis left it in 1945. About 32,000 inmates came through the fortress, mostly POWs or political prisoners; those that did not die here were shipped off to other concentration camps. Above the entrance to the main courtyard stands the cynical motto ARBEIT MACHT FREI (Work Brings Freedom). Take a walk around the rooms, still housing a sad collection of rusty bed frames, sinks, and shower units. At the far end of the fortress, opposite the main entrance, is the special wing built by the Nazis when space became tight. The windowless cells are horrific; try going into one and closing the door—and then imagine being crammed in with 14 other people. In the center of the fortress is a museum and a small theater. WEB *www.pamatnik-terezin.cz.* 🎟 *One unit 140 Kč; all units 160 Kč.* ☯ *Museum and Magdeburg Barracks Apr.– Sept., daily 9–6; Oct.–Mar., daily 9–5:30. Small Fortress Apr.–Sept., daily 8–6; Oct.–Apr., daily 8–4:30. Crematorium Apr.–Nov., Sun.–Fri. 10–5.*

OFF THE
BEATEN PATH

STŘEKOV CASTLE – The Vltava River north of Litoměřice flows through a long, unspoiled, winding valley, packed in by surrounding hills. As you near heavily industrialized Ústí nad Labem, your eyes are suddenly assaulted by the towering mass of Střekov Castle, perched precariously on huge cliffs and rising abruptly above the right bank. The fortress was built in 1319 by King John of Luxembourg to control the rebellious nobles of northern Bohemia. During the 16th century it became the residence of Wenceslas of Lobkowicz, who rebuilt the castle in the Renaissance style. The lonely ruins have inspired many German artists and poets, including Richard Wagner, who came here on a moonlit night in the summer of 1842 and was inspired to write his romantic opera *Tannhäuser.* But if you arrive on a dark night, about the only classic that comes to mind is Mary Shelley's *Frankenstein.* Inside is a small historical exhibit about the Lobkowicz family and wine making. ✉ *Na*

Zachazce, Ústí nad Labem, ☎ *475–530–682.* 🎫 *60 Kč.* ☉ *May–*
Aug., Tues.–Sun. 9–5; Apr. and Sept.–Oct., Tues.–Sun. 9–4.

Mělník

⑳ *65 km (40 mi) southeast of Střekov Castle, about 40 km (23 mi) north*
of Prague.

Mělník is a lively town, known best perhaps for its autumn wine festival and the special Ludmila wine made from local grapes. If coming
by car, park on the small streets just off the pretty but hard-to-find main
square (head in the direction of the towers to find it). The town's **zámek,**
a smallish castle a few blocks from the main square, majestically guards
the confluence of the Labe (Elbe) River and two arms of the Vltava.
The view here is stunning, and the sunny hillsides are covered with vineyards. As the locals tell it, Emperor Charles IV was responsible for bringing wine production to the area. Having a good eye for favorable
growing conditions, he encouraged vintners from Burgundy to come
here and plant their vines.

The courtyard's three dominant architectural styles, reflecting alterations
to the castle over the years, fairly jump out at you. On the north side,
note the typical arcaded Renaissance balconies, decorated with sgraffiti. To the west, a Gothic tract is still easy to make out. The southern
wing is clearly baroque (although also decorated with arcades). Inside
the castle at the back, you'll find a *vinárna* with mediocre food but excellent views overlooking the rivers. On the other side is a **museum** of
paintings, furniture, and porcelain belonging to the Lobkowicz family—
an old aristocratic clan that has recovered quite a few castles and estates from the state. You can also tour the wine cellars under the castle.
✉ *Náměstí Míru 54,* ☎ *315–622–121,* WEB *www.lobkowicz-melnik.cz.*
🎫 *Museum 60 Kč; cellar tour 25 Kč, up to 220 Kč with wine tasting.*
☉ *Museum daily 10–5, wine cellar daily 10–6.*

Lodging

$$ 🏨 **Ludmila.** Though the hotel is an inconvenient 4 km (2½ mi) outside
the center of town, the pleasant English-speaking staff keeps the plain
rooms impeccably clean, and the restaurant is better than many you
will find in Mělník itself. ✉ *Pražská 2639, 276 01,* ☎ *315–622–423,*
FAX *315–623–390. 79 rooms. Restaurant, cable TV, Internet. AE, MC,*
V. BP.

Špindlerův Mlýn and the Krkonoše Range

㉑ *About 150 km (90 mi) northeast of Prague.*

If you're not planning to go to the Tatras in Slovakia but nevertheless
want a few days in the mountains, head for the **Krkonoše range**—the
so-called Giant Mountains—near the Polish frontier. Here you'll find
the most spectacular scenery in Bohemia, although it's something of
an exaggeration to call these rolling hills "giant" (the highest point is
5,256 ft). Not only is the scenery beautiful, but the local architecture
is refreshingly rural after all the towns and cities. The steep-roof tim-
ber houses, painted in warm colors, look just right pitched against sun-
lit pinewoods or snowy pastures. **Špindlerův Mlýn** is attractively placed
astride the rippling Labe (Elbe) River, here in its formative stages; it's
a good town to use as a hiking base. Hotel rooms are much more ex-
pensive in the ski season.

Lodging

$$ ☎ **Montana.** This "modern" 1970s hotel doesn't fit in with the rustic setting, and the rooms are quite spartan (though they have TVs). But the service is attentive, and the staff can offer good advice for planning walks around this popular resort town. ✉ *Bedřichov 70, 543 51,* ☎ *499–433–251,* FAX *499 433–156,* WEB *www.hotel.cz/montana. 70 rooms. Restaurant, café, cable TV, bar, some pets allowed; no a/c. MC, V. BP.*

$$ ☎ **Nechanický.** This 1920s lodge near the bridge in the center of town was restored to its original owners following the Velvet Revolution, and they have been working to brighten up its somewhat timeworn face. Rooms are cheery, clean, and well-proportioned. Front-facing rooms enjoy an excellent view of town. ✉ *Harrachova 43, 543 51,* ☎ *499–433–163,* FAX *499–433–134. 16 rooms. Restaurant, cable TV, some pets allowed; no a/c. MC, V. BP.*

$$ ☎ **Savoy.** This Tudor-style chalet, more than a century old, has a com-
★ fortable, fresh-air feeling—its cozy reception area is more typical of a family inn than a large hotel. The rooms, although on the smallish side and sparsely furnished, are immaculately clean. The restaurant serves fine traditional Czech dishes in a mellow setting. ✉ *Harrachova 22, 543 51,* ☎ *499–433–221,* FAX *499–433–241,* WEB *www.savoy.cz. 50 rooms. Restaurant, cable TV, gym, bar, meeting room, Internet, some pets allowed (fee); no a/c. AE, MC, V. BP.*

Outdoor Activities and Sports

Janské Lázně (another spa), Pec pod Sněžkou, and Špindlerův Mlýn are the principal resorts of the area, the last the most sophisticated in its accommodations and facilities. To get out and experience the mountains, take a bus from Špindlerův Mlýn via Janské Lázně to Pec pod Sněžkou—a deceptively long journey of around 50 km (31 mi). From there, embark on a two-stage chairlift to the top of **Sněžka** (the area's highest peak); then walk along the ridge overlooking the Polish countryside. You'll eventually drop into deep, silent pinewoods and return to Špindlerův Mlýn. This hike is just 11 km (7 mi)—three to four hours in good weather. The path actually takes you into Poland at one point; you won't need a visa, but take your passport along just in case. The weather can turn quickly in this high, treeless country, so carry rain gear and wear sturdy shoes.

The Labe's source is on the boggy heights near the Polish border. From the town of Harrachov, you can reach it on foot by a marked trail that heads eastward up the mountain. The distance is about 10 km (6 mi). From Špindlerův Mlýn, a beautiful but sometimes steep trail follows the Labe Valley northwest up 2,000 vertical ft to the source near Labská Bouda. Allow at least a half-day for this walk and take good shoes and a map.

Northern Bohemia Essentials

BUS TRAVEL

There are direct buses from Prague to Terezín, Litoměřice, Mělník, Špindlerův Mlýn, and Pec pod Sněžkou (☞ Bus Travel to and from Prague *in* Prague Essentials).

CAR TRAVEL

If you are driving, the E55 leads directly into the Czech Republic from Dresden and winds down to Prague via the old spa town of Teplice. The main road from Prague in the direction of the Krkonoše range is the E65, which is a four-lane highway for most of the distance. If you are driving through northern Bohemia, you'll be rewarded with a particularly picturesque drive on Route 261 along the Labe (Elbe) River on the way to Střekov Castle near Ústí nad Labem.

TOURS
Several private companies offer trips from Prague to Lidice, Mělník, Nelahozeves, Terezín, and Veltrusy Château. Wittmann Tours has a good tour to Terezín; buses leave Prague from the Inter-Continental Hotel, on Pařížská near the Staronová synagóga (Old-New Synagogue), daily from mid-March to December at 10 AM, returning around 5 PM, for a fare of 1,150 Kč.

➤ CONTACTS: **Wittmann Tours** (☎ 222–252–472, WEB www. wittman-tours.com).

TRAIN TRAVEL
Train connections in the north are spotty at best; bus is the preferred means of travel. Regular express trains connect Prague with Ústí nad Labem, but to reach other towns you'll have to take slower local trains or the bus (☞ Train Travel to and from Prague *in* Prague Essentials).

VISITOR INFORMATION
➤ CONTACTS: **Litoměřice Tourist Information** (✉ Mírové nám., Litoměřice, ☎ 416–732–440, WEB www.litomerice.cz). **Mělník Tourist Information** (✉ Nám. Míru 30, Mělník, ☎ 315–627–503, WEB www.melnik.cz). **Špindlerův Mlýn Tourist Information** (✉ Svatopetrská 173, Špindlerův Mlýn, ☎ 499–523–656, WEB www.mestospindleruvmlyn.cz). **Ústí nad Labem Tourist Information** (✉ Hrnčířská 1/10, Ústí nad Labem, ☎ 475–220–421, WEB www.usti-nl.cz).

SOUTHERN MORAVIA

Lacking the turbulent history of Bohemia to the west or the stark natural beauty of Slovakia farther east, Moravia, the easternmost province of the Czech Republic, is frequently overlooked as a travel destination. Still, although Moravia's cities do not match Prague for beauty and its gentle mountains hardly compare with Slovakia's strikingly rugged Tatras, Moravia's colorful villages and rolling hills certainly do merit a few days of exploration. Come here for the good wine, the folk music, the friendly faces, and the languid pace.

Moravia has a bit of both Bohemia and Slovakia. It is closer culturally to Bohemia: the two were bound together as one kingdom for some 1,000 years, following the fall of the Great Moravian Empire (Moravia's last stab at Slavonic statehood) at the end of the 10th century. All the historical and cultural movements that swept through Bohemia, including the religious turbulence and long period of Austrian Hapsburg rule, were felt strongly here as well. But, oddly, in many ways Moravia resembles Slovakia more than its cousin to the west. The colors come alive here in a way that is seldom seen in Bohemia. The subdued earthen pinks and yellows in towns such as Telč and Mikulov suddenly erupt into the fiery reds, greens, and purples of the traditional folk costumes farther to the east. Folk music, all but gone in Bohemia, is still very much alive in Moravia.

Southern Moravia's highlands define the "border" with Bohemia. Here, towns such as Jihlava and Telč are virtually indistinguishable from their Bohemian counterparts. The handsome squares, with their long arcades, bear witness to the prosperity enjoyed by this part of Europe during the 16th and early 17th century, until the Hapsburg crackdown on the Czech lands at the outset of the Thirty Years' War. In the south along the frontier with Austria—until the late 1980s a heavily fortified expanse of the Iron Curtain—the towns and people on both sides of the border seek to reestablish ties going back centuries. One of their common traditions is wine making. Znojmo, Mikulov, and Valtice are to the Czech Republic what the small towns of the *Weinviertel* on the other side of the border are to Austria.

Don't expect gastronomic delights in Moravia. The choices—especially outside Brno—are usually limited to roast pork with sauerkraut and dumplings, ho-hum chicken dishes, and the ever-reliable trout. Hotels are getting better, and the shabby, dim, bathroom-down-the-hall places are practically a thing of the past. In mountainous areas inquire locally about the possibility of staying in a *chata* (cabin). These are abundant, and they are often a pleasant alternative to the faceless modern hotels. Many lack modern amenities, though, so be prepared to rough it.

Numbers in the margin correspond to numbers on the Moravia map.

Jihlava

❶ *124 km (75 mi) southeast of Prague.*

On the Moravian side of the rolling highlands that mark the border between Bohemia and Moravia, just off the main highway from Prague to Brno, lies the old mining town of Jihlava, a good place to begin an exploration of Moravia. If the silver mines here had held out just a few more years, the townspeople claim, Jihlava could have become a great European city. There are several interesting churches clustered on or around the town's main square. During the 13th century, the town's enormous main square, **náměstí Míru** (Square of Peace), was one of the largest in Europe, rivaled in size only by those in Cologne and Kraków. But history can be cruel: the mines went bust during the 17th century, and the square today bears witness only to the town's once oversize ambitions.

The **Kostel svatého Ignáce** (St. Ignatius Church; ⊠ nám. Míru) in the northwest corner of the square is relatively young for Jihlava, built at the end of the 17th century, but look inside to see a rare Gothic crucifix, created during the 13th century for the early Bohemian king Přemysl Otakar II. The town's most striking structure is the Gothic **Kostel svatého Jakuba** (St. James Church; ⊠ Farní ul.) to the east of the main square. The church's exterior, with its uneven towers, is Gothic; the interior is baroque; and the font is a masterpiece of the Renaissance style, dating from 1599. Note also the baroque Chapel of the Holy Virgin, sandwiched between two late-Gothic chapels, with its oversized 14th-century pietà.

Dining and Lodging

\$–\$\$ ✕🏨 **Zlatá Hvězda.** Centrally located on the main square, this reconstructed old hotel in a beautiful Renaissance house is comfortable and surprisingly elegant. In keeping with the building, rooms are modestly harmonious, with wood ceilings and down comforters. You're a short walk from Jihlava's restaurants and shops, though the on-site café and wine bar are among the best in town. ⊠ *Nám. Míru 32, 586 01,* ☎ *567–309–421,* 📠 *567–309–496,* 🌐 *www.zlatahvezda.cz. 17 rooms, 1 apartment. Restaurant, café, cable TV, bar, meeting room, some pets allowed; no a/c. AE, MC, V.*

Telč

★ ❷ *30 km (19 mi) south of Jihlava, via Rte. 406.*

The little town of Telč has an even more impressive main square than that of Jihlava—it has been on the UNESCO World Heritage list since

Moravia

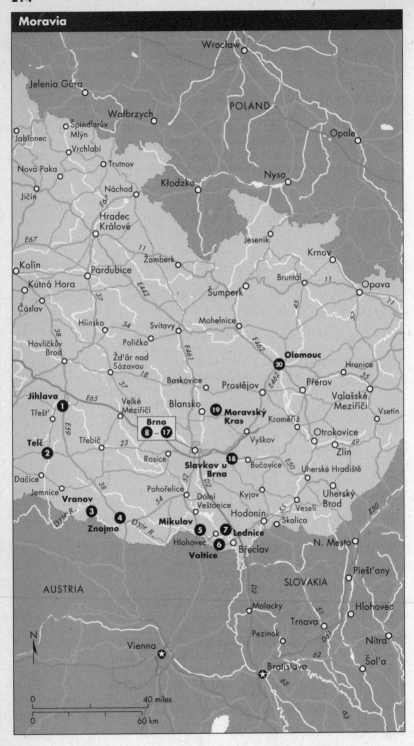

1992, but what strikes the eye most here is not its size but the unified style of the buildings. On the lowest levels are beautifully vaulted Gothic halls, just above are Renaissance floors and facades, and all the buildings are crowned with rich Renaissance and baroque gables. The square is so perfect you feel like you've entered a film set, not a living town. The town allegedly owes its architectural unity to Zacharias of Neuhaus, and the main square, **náměstí Zachariáše z Hradce,** is named after him. During the 16th century, so the story goes, the wealthy Zacharias had the castle—originally a small fort—rebuilt into a Renaissance château. But the contrast between the new castle and the town's rather ordinary buildings was so great that Zacharias had the square rebuilt to match the castle's splendor. Luckily for architecture fans, the Neuhaus dynasty died out shortly thereafter, and succeeding nobles had little interest in refashioning the town according to the vogue of the day.

It's best to approach Telč's main square on foot. If you've come by car, park outside the main walls on the side south of town and walk through the **Great Gate,** part of the original fortifications dating to the 13th century. As you approach on Palackého ulice, the square unfolds nobly in front of you, with the château at the northern end and beautiful houses, bathed in pastel reds and golds, gracing both sides. If you're a fan of Renaissance reliefs, note the black-and-white sgraffito corner house at No. 15, which dates from the middle of the 16th century. The house at No. 61, across from the Černý Orel Hotel, is also noteworthy for its fine detail.

The **château** forms a complex with the former **Jesuit college** and **Kostel svatého Jakuba** (Church of St. James). The château, originally Gothic, was built during the 14th century, perhaps by King John of Luxembourg, the father of Charles IV. It was given its current Renaissance appearance by Italian masters between 1553 and 1568. In season, you can tour the castle and admire the rich Renaissance interiors. Given the reputation of nobles for lively, lengthy banquets, the sgraffito relief in the dining room depicting gluttony (in addition to the six other deadly sins) seems odd indeed. Other interesting rooms with sgraffiti include the Treasury, the Armory, and the Blue and Gold chambers. A curious counterpoint to all this Renaissance splendor is the castle's permanent exhibit of paintings by leading Czech modernist Jan Zrzavý. There are two tours: the first goes through the Renaissance chambers; the second displays the rooms that were used as recently as 1945. ⊠ *Statní zámek Telč, nám. J. Kypty,* ☎ *567–243–943,* WEB *www.zamek-telc.cz.* ⊠ *Tours 120 Kč each, gallery 20 Kč.* ☉ *Apr. and Oct., Tues.–Sun. 9–4; May–Sept., Tues.–Sun. 9–5.*

NEED A BREAK? If you're looking for sweets, you can get good homemade cakes at a little private café, **Cukrárna u Matěje,** at Na baště 2, on the street leading past the château to a small lake.

A tiny street leading off the main square takes you to the 160-ft Romanesque tower of the **Kostel svatého Ducha** (Church of the Holy Spirit; ⊠ Palackého ul.). This is the oldest standing structure in Telč, dating from the first quarter of the 13th century. The interior, however, is a stylistic hodgepodge, as it was given a late-Gothic make-over and then, due to fire damage, refashioned through the 17th century.

Dining and Lodging

$$ ✕▦ **Černý Orel.** Here you'll get a very rare treat: an older, refined hotel ★ that puts modern amenities in a traditional setting. The public areas mix architectural details such as vaulted ceilings with plush, contem-

porary armchairs, and the basic but inviting rooms are well balanced and comfortably furnished. Ask for a room overlooking the square, as the baroque facade provides a perfect backdrop from which to view it. Even if you don't stay here, take a meal at the excellent hotel restaurant, a great spot for straightforward beef or pork dishes. ✉ *Nám. Zachariáše z Hradce 7, 588 56,* ☎ *567–243–222,* FAX *567–243–221,* WEB *www.cernyorel.cz. 30 rooms, 25 with bath. Restaurant, cable TV, bar, meeting room, some pets allowed (fee); no a/c. AE, MC, V.*

$$ 🖬 **Telč.** This is a slightly upscale alternative in town, even though the bright, polished appearance of the reception area doesn't quite carry over to the functional but pleasant rooms. (Some rooms open onto a courtyard.) The location, in a corner of the main square, is ideal. ✉ *Na Můstku 37, 588 56,* ☎ *567–243–109,* FAX *567–223–887. 10 rooms. Restaurant, cable TV, some pets allowed (fee). AE, DC, MC, V. BP.*

Vranov

❸ *55 km (34 mi) southeast of Telč.*

As a swimming and boating center for southern Moravia, Vranov would be a good place to stop in its own right. But what makes the
★ town truly noteworthy is the enormous and colorful **Vranovský hrad** (Vranov Castle), rising 200 ft from a rocky promontory. For nearly 1,000 years, this was the border between Bohemia and Austria, and thus it required a fortress of these dimensions. You'll either love or hate this proud mongrel of a building as its multicolored Gothic, Renaissance, and baroque elements vie for your attention. In the foreground, the solemn Renaissance tower rises over some Gothic fortifications. On its left is a golden baroque church, and there's a beautiful pink-and-white baroque dome to the back. Each unit is spectacular, but the overall effect of so many styles mixed together is jarring.

Take your eyes off the castle's motley exterior and tour its mostly baroque (and more harmonious) interior. The most impressive room is certainly the 43-ft-high elliptical Hall of Ancestors, the work of the Viennese master Johann Bernhard Fischer von Erlach (builder of the Clam-Gallas Palace in Prague and the Hofburg in Vienna). From June to August you can look inside the castle church as well. The rotunda, altar, and organ were designed by Fischer von Erlach at the end of the 17th century. ✉ *Zámecka ul. 93,* ☎ *515–296–215.* 💷 *Castle 60 Kč, English-language castle tour 120 Kč, church 15 Kč.* 🕙 *Castle Apr. and Oct., weekends 9–4; May–June and Sept., Tues.–Sun. 9–5; July–Aug., Tues.–Sun. 9–6. Church June, weekends 9–5; July–Aug., Sun.–Tues. 9–6; other times by arrangement.*

Znojmo

❹ *20 km (12 mi) east of Vranov.*

Znojmo enjoys a long history as an important frontier town between Austria and Bohemia and is the cultural center of southern Moravia. The Přemyslid prince Břetislav I had already built a fortress here in the 11th century, and in 1226 Znojmo became the first Moravian town (ahead of Brno) to receive town rights from the king. But modern Znojmo, with its many factories and high-rises, isn't really a place for lingering. Plan on spending no more than a few hours walking through the Old Town and visiting the remaining fortifications and churches that stand between the New Town and the river.

Znojmo's tumbledown **main square,** now usually filled with peddlers selling everything from butter to cheap souvenirs, isn't what it used to be when it was crowned by Moravia's most beautiful **town hall.** Unfortunately, the 14th-century building was destroyed in 1945, just before the end of the war, and all that remains of the original structure is the 250-ft Gothic tower you see at the top of the square—looking admittedly forlorn astride the modern department store that now occupies the space. From here, you can follow the run-down Zelinářská ulice, which trails from behind the town hall's tower to the southwest in the direction of the Old Town and the river.

The grand, Gothic **Kostel svatého Mikuláše** (Church of St. Nicholas; ✉ nám. Mikulášské) dates from 1338, but its neo-Gothic tower was not added until the 19th century. If you can get into the church (it's often locked), look for the impressive sacraments house, which was built around 1500 in late-Gothic style. Just behind the Kostel svatého Mikulášle is the curious, two-layer **Kostel svatého Václava** (Church of St. Wenceslas; ✉ nám. Mikulášské), built at the end of the 15th century. The upper level of this tiny white church is dedicated to St. Anne, the lower level to St. Martin. Along the medieval ramparts that separate the town from the river stands the original 11th-century **Rotunda svaté Kateřiny** (St. Catherine's Rotunda; ✉ Hradní), still in remarkably good condition. Step inside to see a rare cycle of restored frescoes from 1134 depicting various members of the early Přemyslid dynasty.

Dining and Lodging

Znojmo has two claims to fame that have endeared the town to the hearts (and palates) of Czechs everywhere. The first is the Znojmo gherkin, first cultivated in the 16th century. You'll find this tasty accompaniment to meals at restaurants all over the country. Just look for the *Znojmo* prefix—as in *Znojemský guláš*, a tasty stew spiced with pickles. Znojmo's other treat is wine. As the center of the Moravian wine industry, this is an excellent place to pick up a few bottles of your favorite grape. The best designations to look for, in addition to Znojmo, are Mikulov and Valtice. Some of the best varieties of grapes are Rulandské and Vavřinecké (for red) and Ryzlink and Müller Thurgau (for white).

✕🏨 **Hotel Morava.** A pretty, moderately ornate pink-and-yellow building on one of the town's squares in the historic district offers exceptionally large rooms with folksy furnishings. The rooms, which can comfortably hold up to four people, have pleasant views of the square's fountain. The hotel restaurant offers outdoor dining in the summer and a selection of local wines. ✉ *Horní nám. 16, 669 01,* ☎ *515–224–157,* WEB *www.znojman.cz/morava. 2 rooms. Restaurant, some pets allowed (fee); no a/c, no room phones. AE, MC, V. BP.*

$ 🏨 **Penzion Kim-Ex.** A family home with a terrace in a quiet residential neighborhood offers a relaxed atmosphere right on the Dyje River, facing a national park. Znojmo's historical center is about a mile away, but public transportation is close by. The wood-paneled rooms are bright and airy. ✉ *Vinohrady 26, 669 02,* ☎ *515–222–580,* WEB *penzionkimex.ic.cz/ 4. Cable TV, some pets allowed; no a/c. No credit cards. BP.*

Mikulov

❺ *54 km (34 mi) east of Znojmo.*

In many ways, Mikulov is the quintessential Moravian town. The soft pastel pinks and yellows of its buildings look almost mystical in the afternoon sunshine against the greens of the surrounding hills. But aside from the busy wine industry, not much goes on here, even though this is the main border crossing on the Vienna–Brno highway. It's as though the waning of the town's Jewish community left a breach that has never been filled.

If you happen to arrive at grape-harvesting time in October, head for one of the many private *sklípeks* (wine cellars) built into the hills surrounding the town. The tradition in these parts is simply to knock on the door; more often than not, you'll be invited in by the owner to taste a recent vintage. If you visit in early September, try to hit Mikulov's renowned wine-harvest festival, which is celebrated with traditional music, folk dancing, and much quaffing of local Riesling.

The striking **château** dominates the tiny main square and surrounding area. The château started out as the Gothic residence of the noble Liechtenstein family in the 13th century and was given its current baroque appearance some 400 years later. The most famous resident was Napoléon, who stayed here in 1805 while negotiating peace terms with the Austrians after winning the Battle of Austerlitz (Slavkov, near Brno). Sixty-one years later, Bismarck used the castle to sign a peace treaty with Austria. The castle's darkest days came at the end of World War II, when retreating Nazi SS units set fire to it. The château now houses the **Regionální Muzeum** (Regional Museum). Along with the expected rooms of period furniture, objects related to local wine-making are displayed. The most remarkable exhibit is a wine cask made in 1643, with a capacity of more than 22,000 gallons. This was used for collecting the vintner's obligatory tithe. ⊠ *Zámek 5,* ☎ *519–510–255,* WEB *www.rmm.cz.* ☜ *40 Kč.* ☉ *Apr., weekends 9–4; May–Sept., Tues.–Sun. 8–6.*

During the 19th century, Jews constituted nearly half the population of Mikulov. The town was the seat of the chief rabbi of Moravia from the 17th to the 19th century and a center of Jewish learning. Great Talmudic scholars, including Rabbis Jehuda Loew and David Oppenheimer, lived and taught here. Today, precious little is left of this heritage, but the **Jewish cemetery** remains as a potent evocation of the past. It is tended with care, and some of the most imposing tombstones on "Rabbis' Hill" are being restored. The cemetery sits above the castle. The gate is usually locked, but the key may be borrowed from the Částek family at Brněnská 28 (ring the buzzer). Out of respect for Jewish customs, the key is not lent out on Saturday. ⊠ *Off Brněnská ul.*

The Jewish quarter once spread along the western side of the castle hill. Of the many synagogues, baths, schools, and other structures that served the community, one of the few intact survivors is the 16th-century **Altschul** (Old Synagogue), which has been restored and now houses a small exposition and gallery. ⊠ *Husova 11.* ☜ *10 Kč.* ☉ *May–Sept., Tues.–Sun. 1–5.*

Dining and Lodging

$–$$ ✕🏠 **Rohatý Krokodýl.** This is a prim, nicely renovated hotel in the old
★   chief rabbi's house, under the castle. The doubles are on the small side, but the suites, which cost just a little more, are quite roomy. The facilities are the best in Mikulov, particularly the ground-floor restaurant, which serves a typical but delicately prepared selection of traditional Czech dishes. The front desk can arrange for hot-air balloon rides. ⊠ *Husova 8, 692 01,* ☎ *519–510–692,* FAX *519–511–695,* WEB *www.rohatykrokodyl.cz. 14 rooms. Restaurant, cable TV, pub, some pets allowed (fee); no a/c. AE, MC, V.*

Outdoor Activities and Sports

For walking enthusiasts, the white limestone **Pavlovské vrchy** (Pavlov Hills), where the Stone Age remains in Dolní Věstonice were found, are a challenging climb with views of a couple of castle ruins. From

Děvín Peak (1,800 ft), just south of Dolní Věstonice, a series of clearly marked paths follow the ridges the 10 km (6 mi) to Mikulov.

Shopping

The secret of Moravian wine is only now beginning to extend beyond the country's borders. A vintage bottle from one of the smaller but excellent vineyards in Bzenec, Velké Pavlovice, or Hodonín would be appreciated by any wine connoisseur.

Valtice

❻ *13 km (8 mi) east of Mikulov along Hwy. 414.*

This small town would be wholly nondescript except for the fascinating **château,** just off the main street, built for the Liechtenstein family by a group of leading baroque architects, among them Fischer von Erlach. Next to the town's dusty streets, with their dilapidated postwar storefronts, the castle looks positively grand, a glorious if slightly overexuberant holdover from a long-lost era. There are some 365 windows, painted ceilings, and much ornate woodwork. But best of all is the lure of spending the night—a rare practice in the Czech Republic. The left wing of the castle has been converted into the Hubertus hotel. You can also tour more than a dozen rooms, the chapel, and a picture gallery. The Valtice winery is behind and to the right of the castle, but it is not open to the public. ⊠ *Zámek 1,* ☎ *519–352–423,* WEB *www.valtice.cz.* 🖾 *40 Kč; guided tour in German (occasionally in English) 80 Kč.* ☉ *Apr. and Sept.–Oct., Tues.–Sun. 9–4; May–Aug., Tues.–Sun. 8–5.*

OFF THE
BEATEN PATH

HLOHOVEC – An abandoned summer palace lies just to the north of Valtice, not far from the tiny town of Hlohovec. In winter you can walk or skate across the adjoining Hlohovec Pond to the golden-yellow building; otherwise follow the tiny lane to Hlohovec, just off Route 422 outside Valtice. Emblazoned across the front of the palace is the German slogan ZWISCHEN ÖSTERREICH UND MÄHREN (Between Austria and Moravia), another reminder of the proximity of the border and the long history that these areas share. Consult Greenways maps for scenic horseback and bike tours of the area.

Dining and Lodging

$$ ✕🖾 **Hotel Hubertus.** This comfortable hotel is not hard to find. Just
★ look for the only palace in town; the hotel is on the left-hand side. Though the rooms are neither palatial nor furnished in period style, they are nevertheless inviting, with high ceilings and fresh flowers. The restaurant, with its garden terrace, has an ample selection of fish, including carp, trout, and pike. Book ahead in summer, as the hotel is popular with Austrians who like to slip across the border for an impromptu holiday. ⊠ *Zámek 1, 691 42,* ☎ *519–352–537,* FAX *519–352–538,* WEB *www.hotelhubertus.cz. 29 rooms, 22 with bath. Restaurant, bar, some pets allowed, meeting room; no TV in some rooms. AE, MC, V. BP.*

Lednice

❼ *7 km (4½ mi) from Valtice.*

As a display of their wealth and taste, the Liechtenstein family sprinkled neoclassical temples and eclectic follies across a huge swath of parkland around Valtice and Lednice throughout the 18th and 19th centuries. The extravagantly neo-Gothic **château** at Lednice, though obviously in disrepair, has a sumptuous interior; particularly resplendent are the blue-and-green silk wall coverings embossed with the Moravian eagle in the formal dining room and bay-window drawing room. The grounds, now a pleasant park open to the public, have a 200-ft-tall minaret and a massive greenhouse filled with exotic flora. The landscaped area has been on the UNESCO World Heritage list since 1996. ⊠ *Lednice,* ☎ *519–340–128,* WEB *www.lednice.cz.* ⊠ *Tours 110 Kč–150 Kč, minaret 10 Kč.* ☉ *Apr. and Oct., Tues.–Sun. 9–4; May–Sept., Tues.–Sun. 9–6.*

Southern Moravia Essentials

BUS TRAVEL

Brno, a regional transport hub, is the best base from which to head off into southern Moravia. There are also frequent direct bus connections from Prague to Jihlava (two hours); the bus journey to the other towns on the tour will take three to five hours from Prague.

Getting around the region is more difficult. In general, buses run sporadically, especially on weekends. If you're planning a day trip or two, Mikulov may be the best base, as there is regular bus service to Lednice, Valtice, and Brno.

CAR TRAVEL

Southern Moravia is within easy driving distance of Prague and Bratislava. Jihlava is 124 km (75 mi) southeast of Prague along the excellent D1/E65 freeway. From here, it's easy to continue to Brno, or to take the E59, which goes down to Vranov and Znojmo. Southern Moravia is also easily reached by car from Austria; there are major border crossings at Háté (below Znojmo) and Mikulov.

VISITOR INFORMATION

➤ CONTACTS: **Jihlava Tourist Information** (⊠ Masarykovo nám. 19, Jihlava, ☎ 567–731–1926, WEB www.jihlava.cz). **Mikulov Tourist Information** (⊠ Nám. 1, Mikulov, ☎ 625–510–855, WEB www.mikulov.cz). **Telč Tourist Information** (⊠ Nám. Zachariáše z Hradce 10, Telč, ☎ 567–724–3145, WEB www.telc-etc.cz). **Valtice Tourist Information** (⊠ Nám. Svobody 4, Valtice, ☎ 519–352–977, WEB www.valtice.cz).

BRNO

Moravia's cultural and geographic center, Brno (pronounced *burr*-no) grew rich in the 19th century and has a different feel from any other Czech or Slovak city. Beginning with a textile industry imported from Germany, Holland, and Belgium, Brno became the industrial heartland of the Austro-Hungarian Empire during the 18th and 19th centuries—hence its nickname Manchester of Moravia. You'll search in vain for an extensive old town; you'll also find few of the traditional arcaded storefronts that typify other historic Czech towns. Instead you'll see fine examples of the Empire and neo-Renaissance styles, their formal, geometric facades more in keeping with the conservative tastes of the 19th-century middle class.

In the early 20th century, the city became home to the best young architects working in the cubist and constructivist styles. Experimentation wasn't restricted to architecture. Leoš Janáček, an important composer of the early modern period, lived and worked in Brno, as did Austrian novelist Robert Musil. The modern tradition continues even today, and the city is considered to have the best theater and performing arts in Moravia, as well as a small but thriving café scene.

It's best to avoid Brno at trade-fair time (the biggest are in early spring and early autumn), when hotel and restaurant facilities are strained.

If the hotels are booked, the accommodation services at the town hall or main station will help you find a room.

Numbers in the text correspond to numbers in the margin and on the Brno map.

Exploring Brno

A Good Walk

Begin the walking tour at the triangular **náměstí Svobody** ⑧ in the heart of the commercial district. Then walk up Masarykova ulice toward the train station and make a right through the little arcade at No. 6 to see the animated Gothic portal of the **Stará radnice** ⑨. Leave through the portal and turn right into the old **Zelný trh** ⑩. On the far side of the market, dominating the square, stands the severe Renaissance Dietrichsteinský palác at No. 8. Go through an archway into the palace garden, from where stairs lead down to the baroque **Kostel Nalezení svatého Kříže** ⑪.

Towering above the church and market is the **Chrám svatých Petra a Pavla** ⑫, Brno's main church and a fixture of the skyline. The best way to get to it is to return to Zelný trh (via the little street off Kapucínské náměstí), make a left, and walk up narrow Petrská ulice, which begins just to the right of the Dietrichsteinský palác. Before leaving the church area, stroll around the pretty park and grounds. Return to the juncture of Petrská and Biskupská and follow Biskupská to Starobrněnská ulice. Turn left and cross the busy Husova třída onto Pekařská ulice. At the end of the street you'll come to a square named for Gregor Mendel (Mendlovo náměstí) and a medieval monastery with a large Gothic church, Starobrněnský klášter.

Continue the tour along the busy and somewhat downtrodden Úvoz ulice. Take the first right and climb the stairs to the calmer residential street of Pellicova. If there's a unique beauty to Brno, it's in neighborhoods such as this one, with its attractive houses, each in a different architectural style. Many houses incorporate cubist and geometric elements of the early modern period (1920s and 1930s). Begin the ascent to the **Špilberk hrad** ⑬. There is no direct path to the castle; just follow your instincts (or a detailed map) upward, and you'll get there. After taking in the view, stroll back down one of the windy paths to Husova třída and have a look in two of the Czech Republic's finest museums: the **Uměleckoprůmyslové muzeum** ⑭ and, just a block farther down Husova, Brno's modern art museum, the **Pražákův palác** ⑮. For old art culled from Moravian churches and estates, make sure to pay a visit to the **Místodržitelský palác** ⑯. It's also worth it to find a way to Ludwig Mies van der Rohe's **Villa Tugendhat** ⑰, the city's most famous work of architecture. The house is a bit off the beaten track, so you will need to travel there by car, taxi, or tram.

TIMING

The walking tour should take two to three hours at a leisurely pace. Allow a couple of hours to fully explore the Špilberk castle. Museum enthusiasts could easily spend a half-day or more browsing through the city's many collections. Brno is relatively busy on weekdays, surprisingly slow on weekends.

Sights to See

⑫ **Chrám svatých Petra a Pavla** (Cathedral of Sts. Peter and Paul). This is one church that probably looks better from a distance. The interior, a blend of baroque and Gothic, is light and tasteful but hardly mindblowing. Still, the slim neo-Gothic twin spires, added in this century to give the cathedral more of its original Gothic dignity, are a nice touch.

Brno

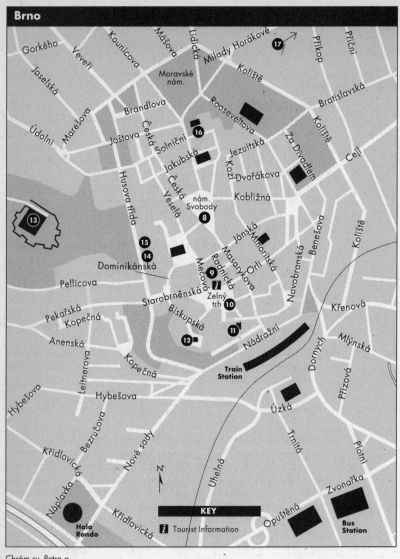

KEY

i Tourist Information

Don't be surprised if you hear the noon bells ringing from the cathedral at 11. The practice dates from the Thirty Years' War, when Swedish troops were massing for an attack outside the town walls. Brno's resistance had been fierce, and the Swedish commander decreed that he would give up the fight if the town could not be taken by noon the following day. The bell ringer caught wind of the decision and the next morning, just as the Swedes were preparing a final assault, rang the noon bells—an hour early. The ruse worked, and the Swedes decamped. Ever since, the midday bells have been rung an hour early as a show of gratitude. Although the city escaped, the cathedral caught a Swedish cannon shot and suffered severe damage in the resulting fire. ⊠ *Petrov at Petrská ul..* 🎟 *Free.* ⊙ *Daily dawn–dusk; closed during services.*

⓫ **Kostel Nalezení svatého Kříže** (Church of the Holy Cross). Formerly part of the Capuchin Monastery, this church combines a baroque silhouette with a rather stark facade. If you've ever wondered what a mummy looks like without its bandages, then enter the door to the monastery's *krypta* (crypt). In the basement are the mummified remains of some 200 nobles and monks from the late 17th and 18th centuries, ingeniously preserved by a natural system of air circulating through vents and chimneys. The best-known mummy is Colonel František Trenck, commander of the brutal Pandour regiment of the Austrian army, who, at least in legend, spent several years in the dungeons of Špilberk castle before finding his final rest here in 1749. Experts have concluded that his head is real, contrary to stories of its removal by a thief. A note of caution about the crypt: the graphic displays may frighten small children, so ask at the admission desk for the small brochure (20 Kč) with pictures that preview what's to follow. ⊠ *Kapucínské nám. 5,* ☎ *542–213–232,* WEB *www.volny.cz/kapucini.brno.* 🎟 *40 Kč.* ⊙ *May–Sept., Mon.–Sat. 9–11:45 and 2–4:30, Sun. 11–11:45 and 2–4:30; Oct.–mid-Dec. and mid-Jan.–Apr., Tues.–Sat. 9–11:45 and 2–4:30, Sun. 11–11:45 and 2–4:30.*

⓰ **Místodržitelský palác** (Governor's Palace). Moravia had much stronger artistic ties to Austria than Bohemia did, as can be seen in the impressive collection of Gothic, baroque, and 19th-century painting and sculpture found in this splendid baroque palace. Particularly fetching are Austrian painter Franz Anton Maulbertsch's ethereal rococo pageants. ⊠ *Moravské nám. 1A,* ☎ *542–321–100,* WEB *www.moravska-galerie.cz.* 🎟 *40 Kč.* ⊙ *Apr.–Sept., Wed. and Fri.–Sun. 10–6, Thurs. 10–7; Oct.–Mar., Wed. and Fri.–Sun. 10–5, Thurs. 10–6.*

❽ **Náměstí Svobody** (Freedom Square). The square itself is architecturally undistinguished, but here and along the adjoining streets you'll find the city's best stores and shopping opportunities. Anyone who has been to Vienna might experience a feeling of déjà vu here, as many of the buildings were built by 19th-century Austrian architects. Especially noteworthy is the stolid Klein Palace at No. 15, built by Theophil Hansen and Ludwig Foerster, both prominent for their work on Vienna's Ringstrasse.

⓯ **Pražákův palác** (Pražák Palace). This handsome, 19th-century neo-Renaissance building houses the largest collection of modern and contemporary Czech art outside Prague. While works by many of the same artists represented in Prague's major galleries can be seen here, the emphasis is on Moravian artists, who tended to prefer rural themes—their avant-garde concoctions have a certain folksy flavor. ⊠ *Husova 18,* ☎ *542–215–758,* WEB *www.moravska-galerie.cz.* 🎟 *40 Kč.* ⊙ *Apr.–Sept., Wed. and Fri.–Sun. 10–6, Thurs. 10–7; Oct.–Mar., Wed. and Fri.–Sun. 10–5, Thurs. 10–6.*

🔞 **Špilberk hrad** (Spielberg Castle). Once among the most feared places in the Hapsburg Empire, this fortress-cum-prison still broods over the town from behind its menacing walls. The castle's advantageous location was no secret to the early lords of the city, who moved here during the 13th century from neighboring Petrov Hill. Successive rulers gradually converted the old castle into a virtually impregnable fortress. Indeed, it successfully withstood the onslaughts of Hussites, Swedes, and Prussians over the centuries; only Napoléon, in 1809, succeeded in occupying the fortress. But the castle is best known for its gruesome history as a prison for enemies of the Austro-Hungarian monarchy and, later, of the Nazis in World War II. Although tales of torture during the Austrian period are probably untrue (judicial torture had been prohibited prior to the first prisoners' arrival in 1784), conditions for the hardest offenders were hellish: they were shackled day and night in dark, dank catacombs and fed only bread and water. The most brutal corrections ended with the death of the harsh, rationalist ruler Joseph II in 1790. The casemates (passages within the walls of the castle) have been turned into an exhibition of the late-18th-century prison and their Nazi-era use as an air-raid shelter. Parents should note that young children can easily become lost in the spooky, dim casemates. More dangerous, the low parapets atop the castle walls near the restaurant provide little security for over-curious climbers.

Aboveground, a recently opened museum in the fortress starts off with more displays on the prison era, installed in a row of cells on the ground floor, with detailed English texts. Above that is a new exhibition on the history of Brno, including several panoramic paintings showing the city in the 17th century, and photos showing then-and-now views of 19th- and 20th-century redevelopment in the Old Town. The third floor houses an attractive collection of paintings made by local artists or commissioned by local patrons over a four-century span; visitors who were intrigued by the modern art in the Pražákův palác will be interested to find more paintings by the prolific modernist Antonín Procházka here. There is also an exhibit on architecture and design in the 1920s and 1930s, with a turgid English explanation of this fertile period in the city's cultural development. ⊠ *Špilberk 1,* ☎ *542–214–145,* WEB *www.spilberk.cz.* 🎫 *Casemates 30 Kč, museum 30 Kč, tower 20 Kč, gate 10 Kč.* ☯ *Casemates and tower May–June and Sept., Tues.–Sun. 9–6; July–Aug., daily 9–6; Oct.–Apr., Tues.–Sun. 9–5. Museum Apr.–Sept., Tues.–Sun. 9–6; Oct.–Mar., Wed.–Sun. 10–5. Tower Tues.–Sun. 10–6.*

NEED A BREAK?	After a long walk and a good climb, what could be better than one of the best beers you'll ever have? The **Stopkova pivnice** (⊠ Česká 5) will set you up with one, or a soft drink. If you're hungry, try the house goulash, a tangy mixture of sausage, beef, rice, egg, and dumpling. For something more substantial, head for the restaurant on the second floor.

🔟 **Stará radnice** (Old Town Hall). The oldest secular building in Brno has an important Gothic portal. The door is the work of Anton Pilgram, architect of Vienna's St. Stephen's Cathedral. It was completed in 1510, but the building itself is about 200 years older. Look above the door to see a badly bent pinnacle that looks as if it wilted in the afternoon sun. This isn't the work of vandals but was apparently done by Pilgram himself out of revenge against the town. According to legend, Pilgram had been promised an excellent commission for his portal, but when he finished, the mayor and city councillors reneged on their offer. Pilgram was so angry at the duplicity that he purposely bent the pinnacle and left it poised, fittingly, over the statue of justice.

Just inside the door are the remains of two other famous Brno legends, the **Brno Dragon** and the **wagon wheel.** The dragon—a female alligator, to be anatomically correct—apparently turned up at the town walls one day in the 17th century and began eating children and livestock. A gatekeeper came up with the novel idea of filling a sack with limestone and placing it inside a freshly slaughtered goat. The dragon devoured the goat, swallowing the limestone as well, and went to quench its thirst at a nearby river. The water mixed with the limestone, bursting the dragon's stomach (the scars on the preserved dragon's stomach are still clearly visible). The story of the wagon wheel, on the other hand, concerns a bet placed some 400 years ago that a young wheelwright, Jiří Birk, couldn't chop down a tree, fashion the wood into a wheel, and roll it from his home at Lednice (33 mi [53 km] away) to the town walls of Brno—all between sunup and sundown. The wheel stands as a lasting tribute to his achievement. (The townspeople, however, became convinced that Jiří had enlisted the help of the devil to win the bet, so they stopped frequenting his workshop; poor Jiří died penniless.)

No longer the seat of the town government, the Old Town Hall holds exhibitions and performances. To find out what's on, ask in the information center just inside Pilgram's portal. The view from the top of the tower is one of the best in Brno, but the climb (five flights) is strenuous. What catches the eye is not so much any single building—although the cathedral does look spectacular—but the combination of old and new that defines modern Brno. In the distance, next to the crooked roofs and baroque onion domes, a power plant looks startlingly out of place. ✉ *Radnická 8.* 🎫 *Tower 20 Kč.* 🕐 *Apr.–Sept., daily 9–5.*

⑭ **Uměleckoprůmyslové muzeum** (Museum of Decorative Arts). Open again after a long renovation that ended in 2001, this is doubtless the best arts-and-crafts museum in the Czech Republic. It has an assemblage of artifacts far more extensive than the truncated collection in Prague's museum of the same name. The collection includes Gothic work, Art Nouveau and Secessionist pieces, and an excellent, comprehensive overview of Bohemian and Moravian glass. Keep an eye out for the elegant furniture from Josef Hoffmann's Wiener Werkstätte (Vienna Workshop). A jagged, candy-color table by Milan Knížák is a striking example of contemporary work. ✉ *Husova 14,* 📞 *532–169–111,* WEB *www.moravska-galerie.cz.* 🎫 *40 Kč.* 🕐 *Tues.–Sun. 9–5.*

⑰ **Villa Tugendhat.** Designed by Ludwig Mies van der Rohe and completed in 1930, this austere, white Bauhaus villa counts among the most important works of the modern period and is now a UNESCO World Heritage Site. The emphasis here is on function and the use of geometric forms, but you be the judge as to whether the house fits the neighborhood. The Tugendhat family fled before the Nazis, and their original furnishings vanished during the war or the house's subsequent heavy-handed remodeling. Replicas of Mies's cool, functional designs have been installed in the downstairs living area. Some of the original exotic wood paneling and an eye-stopping onyx screen remain in place. The best way to get there is to take a taxi or Tram 3, 5, or 11 to the Dětská nemocnice stop and then walk up unmarked Černopolní ulice for 10 minutes or so; you'll be able to see the modernist structure up on the hill. Advance reservations for tours are highly recommended. At this writing, a five-year renovation was planned to begin in 2003, so check to make sure it is open. ✉ *Černopolní 45,* 📞 *545–212–118,* WEB *www.spilberk.cz.* 🎫 *80 Kč.* 🕐 *Wed.–Sun. 10–6.*

⑩ **Zelný trh** (Cabbage Market). The only place where Brno begins to look like a typical Czech town, the Cabbage Market is immediately recognizable, not just for the many stands from which farmers still sell vegetables but also for the unique **Parnassus Fountain** that adorns its center. This baroque outburst (you either love it or hate it) couldn't be more out of place amid the formal elegance of most of the buildings on the square. But when Johann Bernhard Fischer von Erlach created the fountain in the late 17th century, it was important for a striving town like Brno to display its understanding of the classics and of ancient Greece. Thus, Hercules slays a three-headed dragon, while Amphitrite awaits the arrival of her lover—all incongruously surrounded by farmers hawking turnips and onions.

Dining and Lodging

$$–$$$ ✕ **Černý Medvěd.** Redecorated in cottage fashion with floral rather than red-plush upholstery, this is still one of Brno's most comfortable dining rooms. Wild game is the key ingredient in a traditionally Czech menu. ✉ *Jakubské nám. 1,* ☎ *542–214–548. AE, MC, V. Closed Sun.*

$–$$$ ✕ **La Braseria.** Delicious pastas and pizzas (a welcome alternative to the heavy local fare) are served here in an unhurried setting. Take a taxi, walk the 15 minutes from the center, or ride Tram 5 or 6 to the stop called Nemocnice u sv. Anny. ✉ *Pekařská 80,* ☎ *543–232–042. AE, DC, MC, V.*

$–$$ ✕ **Indická restaurace Taj.** One of the few places in the city to make a real try at any kind of ethnic food, this eatery hidden upstairs in a Victorian house creates a nice atmosphere as well. Once you cross the tiny bridge over a man-made indoor stream, you can sit in the Indian-theme main room and choose from the vegetarian or meat dishes. Some can be prepared at a lava grill at your table. Lunch specials are a real value. ✉ *Běhounská 12,* ☎ *542–214–372. AE, DC, MC, V.*

$–$$ ✕ **Zemanova kavárna.** This contemporary re-creation of a 1920s coffeehouse (the original was razed by the Communists to make way for a theater) is extremely stylish. Everything from the light fixtures to the furniture is faithfully copied from the original interior. The lofty ceilings provide pleasant, lilting acoustics, and the food isn't bad either: Czech with a dash of French, such as pepper steak with fries. ✉ *Jezuitská 6 (between Za Divadlem and Koliště),* ☎ *542–217–509,* WEB *www. zemanka.cz. DC, MC, V.*

$ ✕🏨 **U Královny Elišky.** Few restaurants can match this 14th-century wine cellar ($–$$$) for historical atmosphere. Local specialties including wild game and fish are served in rooms with names such as "The Musketeer" and "The Napoléon." In summer you can sit in the garden and order roast suckling pig or lamb while watching fencers in historical dress cross swords. The adjacent pension offers reasonable comfort at a good price (rates double during major trade fairs, however). Breakfast is extra, which is unusual here. ✉ *Mendlovo nám. 1A, 603 00,* ☎ *543–216–898 pension; 543–212–578 restaurant;* FAX *543–247–872;* WEB *www.itn.cz/penzion. 8 rooms. Some pets allowed; no a/c. No credit cards. No lunch; restaurant closed Sun.–Mon.*

$$$$ 🏨 **Holiday Inn.** Opened in 1993, this handsome representative of the American chain has become the hotel of choice for business travelers. It has all you'd expect for the price, including a well-trained, multilingual staff. There are two classes of rooms, standard and executive; the main difference is that standard rooms lack air-conditioning. Executive rooms also have some extra perks, such as a modem line and trouser press. The location, at the exhibition grounds about a mile from the city center, is inconvenient for those who don't have a car. Prices go up significantly during trade fairs and conventions. ✉ *Křížkovského 20, 603 00,* ☎ *543–122–111,* FAX *543–236–990,* WEB *www.hibrno.cz. 205 rooms. Restaurant, café, sauna, meeting rooms, Internet, some pets allowed (fee); no a/c in some rooms. AE, DC, MC, V. BP.*

$$$–$$$$ 🏨 **Grandhotel Brno.** Though not really grand, this hotel, built in 1870 and thoroughly remodeled in 1988, is certainly comfortable and convenient. High standards are maintained through the hotel's association with an Austrian chain. Service is attentive; the rooms, though small, are well appointed, with coffered ceilings and leather sofas. Ask for a room at the back, facing the town, as the hotel is on a busy street opposite the train station. ⊠ *Benešova 18/20, 657 83,* ☎ *542–518–111,* FAX *542–210–345,* WEB *ww.grandhotelbrno.cz. 116 rooms. 3 restaurants, minibars, cable TV with movies, sauna, gym, casino, nightclub, meeting rooms, Internet, some pets allowed (fee); no a/c. AE, DC, MC, V. BP.*

$$ 🏨 **Pegas.** This little inn makes an excellent choice given its reasonable
★ price and central location. The plain rooms are snug and clean, with wood paneling and down comforters, and the staff is helpful and friendly (and speaks English). Even if you don't stay here, be sure to have a meal and home-brewed beer at the house microbrewery. ⊠ *Jakubská 4, 602 00,* ☎ *542–210–104,* FAX *542–211–232. 15 rooms. Restaurant, TV, minibars, pub, some pets allowed. DC, MC, V. BP.*

$$ 🏨 **Slavia.** The century-old Slavia, just off the main Česká ulice, was thoroughly renovated in 1987. The grace of the fin-de-siècle facade and stucco-ceiling lobby is now oddly paired with utilitarian (though relatively spacious) rooms. The café, with adjacent terrace, is a good place to enjoy a cool drink on a warm afternoon. ⊠ *Solniční 15/17, 622 16,* ☎ *542–215–080,* FAX *542–211–769,* WEB *www.hotel.cz/slavia. 81 rooms. Restaurant, café, minibars, cable TV, some pets allowed; no a/c. AE, DC, MC, V. BP.*

Nightlife and the Arts

Brno is renowned throughout the Czech Republic for its theater and performing arts. There are a couple of main venues for jacket-and-tie cultural events, both slightly northwest of the center of town, just a five-minute walk from náměstí Svobody. Check the schedules at the theaters or pick up a copy of *Do města/Downtown,* Brno's free fortnightly bulletin of cultural events. For more sophisticated entertainment than a conversational evening at the local *pivnice* or *vinárna,* head for one of Brno's casinos. The tables usually stay open until 3 or 4 AM.

One of the country's best-known fringe theater companies, **Divadlo Husa na provázku** (Goose on a String Theater; ⊠ Zelný tř. 9, ☎ 542–211–630), has its home where Petrská ulice enters Zelný tř. The **Mahen Theater** (⊠ Rooseveltova 1, ☎ 542–321–285, WEB www.ndbrno.cz) is the principal venue for drama. Opera and ballet productions are held at the modern **Janáček Theater** (⊠ Rooseveltova 7, ☎ 542–321–285, WEB www.ndbrno.cz). Buy tickets directly at theater box offices or at the central **Předprodej vstupenek** (ticket office; ⊠ Běhounská 17).

The **Grandhotel Brno** (⊠ Benešova 18/20, ☎ 542–518–111) has the Grand Casino. The Star Club Casino at the **Hotel International** (⊠ Husova 16, ☎ 542–122–111) has roulette, blackjack, and poker tables, among others.

A few blocks north of the city center, **Klub Alterna** (⊠ Kounicova 48, ☎ 541–212–091, WEB www.alterna.cz) hosts good Czech jazz and folk performers.

Shopping

Moravia produces very attractive folk pottery, painted with bright red, orange, and yellow flower patterns. You can find these products in stores and hotel gift shops throughout the region. For sophisticated artwork, including paintings and photography, stop by **Ambrosiana** (✉ Jezuitská 11, ☎ 542–214–439). For rare books, art monographs, old prints, and a great selection of avant-garde 1920s periodicals, stop by **Antikvariát Alfa** (✉ Jánská 11, in the arcade, ☎ 542–211–947). **Český Design** (✉ Kapucínské nám. 5, ☎ 542–221–358) stocks handmade textiles, ceramics, and glass. You can buy English-language paperbacks and art books at **Knihkupectví Jiří Šedivý** (✉ Masarykova 6, ☎ 542–215–456).

Brno Essentials

AIR TRAVEL

It's possible to fly from Prague to Brno on Air Ostrava, but the distances between the cities are short, and it's ultimately cheaper and quicker to travel by road or rail. During the two large Brno trade fairs, in April and September, foreign carriers also connect the city with Frankfurt and Vienna. These flights are usually crowded with businesspeople, so you'll have to book well in advance.

➤ AIRLINES: **Air Ostrava** (✉ Prague, ☎ 220–113–406, WEB www.airport-brno.cz).

BED-AND-BREAKFAST RESERVATION AGENCIES

If you've arrived at Brno's main train station and are stuck for a room, try the accommodations service on the far left of the main hall, nominally open around the clock; you can place a sports bet there, too.

BUS TRAVEL

Bus connections from Prague's Florenc terminal to Brno are frequent, and the trip is a half-hour shorter than by train. Most buses arrive at the main bus station, a 10-minute walk from the train station. Some buses stop next to the train station. Buses also run between Brno and Vienna's Wien-Mitte station, stopping at Mikulov. Departures leave Brno for Vienna at 7:30 AM daily and at 5:30 PM every day except Tuesday.

➤ CONTACTS: **Main bus station** (UˇAN Zvonařka; ✉ Zvonařka 1, ☎ 543–217–733).

CAR TRAVEL

Brno, within easy driving distance of Prague, Bratislava, and Vienna, is 196 km (122 mi) from Prague and 121 km (75 mi) from Bratislava. The E65 highway links all three cities.

EMERGENCIES

➤ EMERGENCY SERVICES: **Ambulance** (☎ 155). **Police** (☎ 158).
➤ PHARMACIES: **Droxi Lékárna** (✉ Zelný tř. 16, ☎ 542–221–190).

PUBLIC TRANSPORTATION

Trams are the best way to get around the city. Tickets cost 7 Kč–19 Kč, depending on the time and zones traveled, and are available at newsstands, yellow ticket machines, or from the driver. Single-day, three-day and other long-term tickets are available. Most trams stop in front of the main station (Hlavní nádraží). Buses to the city periphery and nearby sights such as Moravský Kras in northern Moravia congregate at the main bus station, a 10-minute walk behind the train station. To find it, simply go to the train station and follow the signs to ČSAD.

TAXIS

The nominal taxi fare is about 18 Kč per km (½ mi). There are taxi stands at the main train station, Výstaviště exhibition grounds, and on Joštova Street at the north end of the Old Town. Dispatchers tend not to understand English.

TRAIN TRAVEL

Six comfortable EuroCity or InterCity trains daily make the three-hour run from Prague to Brno's station. They depart either from Prague's main station, Hlavní nádraží, or the suburban nádraží Holešovice. Trains leaving Prague for Bratislava, Budapest, and Vienna normally stop in Brno (check timetables to be sure).

➤ TRAIN STATIONS: **Hlavní nádraží** (✉ Nádražní 1, ☎ 542–214–803, WEB www.jizdnirady.cz).

TRAVEL AGENCIES

➤ CONTACTS: **Čedok** (✉ Nádražní 10/12, ☎ 542–321–267, WEB www.cedok.cz).

VISITOR INFORMATION

➤ CONTACTS: **Brno Tourist Information** (✉ Radnická 8 [Old Town Hall], ☎ 542–211–090, WEB www.kultura-brno.cz; Nádražní 6 [across from train station], ☎ 542–221–450).

NORTHERN MORAVIA

Just north of Brno is the Moravský Kras, a beautiful wilderness area with an extensive network of caves, caverns, and underground rivers. Many caves are open to the public, and one tour even incorporates an underground boat ride. Farther to the north lies Moravia's "second capital," Olomouc, an industrial but charming city with a long history as a center of learning. Paradoxically, despite its location far from the Austrian border, Olomouc remained a bastion of support for the Hapsburgs and the empire at a time when cries for independence could be heard throughout Bohemia and Moravia. In 1848, when revolts everywhere threatened to bring the monarchy down, the Hapsburg family fled here for safety. Franz Joseph, who went on to personify the stodgy permanence of the empire, was even crowned here as Austrian emperor that same year.

The green foothills of the Beskydy range begin east of Olomouc, perfect for a day or two of walking in the mountains. A half-day's journey farther to the east, in northern Slovakia, you'll find the spectacular peaks of the Tatras, a good jumping-off point for exploring eastern Slovakia or southern Poland.

Slavkov u Brna

18 *20 km (12 mi) east of Brno.*

Slavkov, better known as **Austerlitz,** was the scene of one of the great battlefields of European history, where the armies of Napoléon met and defeated the combined forces of Austrian emperor Franz II and Czar Alexander I in 1805. If you happen to have a copy of *War and Peace* handy, you will find no better account of it anywhere. Scattered about the rolling agricultural landscapes between Slavkov and Brno are a number of battle monuments linked by walking paths. Napoléon directed his army from Žuráň Hill, above a small town called Šlapanice (which can be reached from Brno by train or bus). Several miles southeast of Šlapanice an impressive memorial to the fallen of all three nations, the Mohyla míru (Cairn of Peace), crowns a hill above the village of Prace. Alongside the cairn is a small museum devoted to the battle. Several days of events commemorate the battle every year around December 2.

In Slavkov, the baroque château houses the **Historické muzeum** (History Museum), which displays memorabilia about the battle of Austerlitz; it's well worth visiting. ✉ *Palackého nám. 126, Slavkov u Brna,*

☏ 544–221–685, [WEB] *www.zamek-slavkov.cz.* ▨ 45 Kč. ☉ *Apr. and Oct.–Nov., Tues.–Sun. 9–4; May and Sept., Tues.–Sun. 9–5; June, daily 9–5; July–Aug., daily 9–6; by appointment Dec.–Feb.*

Moravský Kras

⑲ *30 km (19 mi) north of Brno.*

If it's scenic rather than military tourism you want, take a short trip north from Brno up the Svitava Valley and into the Moravský Kras (Moravian Karst), an area of limestone formations, underground stalactite caves, rivers, and tunnels. The most interesting part of the karst is in the vicinity of Blansko and includes several **caves.** You can arrange tours 8 km (5 mi) from the outskirts of Blansko at the Skalní Mlýn Hotel or the Moravian Karst information office. **Kateřinská jeskyně** (Catherine Cave; ✉ Skalní mlýn) is set amid thickly forested ravines, and visitors taking the half-hour tour are serenaded by recorded opera tunes. The 90-minute tour of **Punkevní jeskyně** (Punkva Cave) includes a boat trip along an underground river to the watery bottom of **Macocha Abyss,** the deepest drop of the karst (more than 400 ft). On this tour, a little motorized "train" links the Skalní Mlýn Hotel to the Punkva Cave, from where a **funicular** climbs to the lip of Macocha Abyss. Only the Punkva Cave is normally open year-round; check with the information service for up-to-date information. It's always advisable to arrive at least an hour before scheduled closing time in order to catch the day's last tour. ✉ *Informacní centrum, Skalní mlýn,* ☏ *516–413–161 Catherine Cave; 516–418–602 or 516–419–701 Punkva Cave; 516–413–575 or 516–410–024 advance tickets for both caves;* [WEB] *www.nature.cz/jeskyne/uvod en.htm.* ▨ *Catherine Cave 40 Kč, Punkva Cave (including underground boat ride) 80 Kč, funicular 50 Kč. ☉ Catherine Cave Apr.–Sept., daily 8–4; Mar. and Oct., daily 8–2. Punkva Cave Apr.–Sept., daily 8–3:30; Oct.–Mar., daily 8–2. Funicular Apr.–Sept., daily 8–5; Oct.–Mar., hrs vary depending on number of visitors.*

Outdoor Activities and Sports

Underground or on the surface, the walking is excellent in the karst, and if you miss one of the few buses running between the town of Blansko and the cave region, you may have to hoof it. Try to obtain a map in Brno or from the Moravian Karst information office in the settlement of Skalní Mlýn. Look for Čertův most (Devil's Bridge), a natural bridge high over the road just past the entrance to Catherine Cave. You can follow the path, indicated with yellow markers, from the cave for another couple of miles to the Macocha Abyss. Before setting out, check with the information office or at the bus station for current bus schedules; for much of the year the last bus from Skalní Mlýn back to Blansko leaves at around 3 PM.

Olomouc

★ **⑳** *77 km (48 mi) northeast of Brno.*

Olomouc is a paradox—so far from Austria yet so supportive of the empire. The Hapsburgs always felt at home here, even when they were being violently opposed by Czech nationalists and Protestants throughout Bohemia and much of Moravia. During the revolutions of 1848, when the middle class from all over the Austro-Hungarian Empire seemed ready to boot the Hapsburgs out of their palace, the royal family fled to Olomouc.

Despite being overshadowed by Brno, Olomouc, with its proud square and prim 19th-century buildings, still has the feel of a provincial imperial capital, not unlike similarly sized cities in Austria. The Old

Town, situated on a slight rise over a tributary of the River Morava, luckily managed to escape damage during the July 1997 floods that inundated a huge swath of Moravia, Poland, and eastern Germany. The focal point here is the triangular **Horní náměstí** (Upper Square). The eccentric **Morový sloup** (Trinity Column), in the northwest corner of the square, is the largest of its kind in the Czech Republic and houses a tiny chapel. Four of the city's half-dozen renowned **baroque fountains,** depicting Hercules (1687), Caesar (1724), Neptune (1695), and Jupiter (1707), dot the main square and the adjacent Dolní náměstí (Lower Square) to the south.

Olomouc's central square is marked by the bright, spire-bedecked Renaissance **radnice** (town hall) with its 220-ft tower. The tower was begun in the late 14th century and given its current appearance in 1443; the astronomical clock on the outside was built in 1422, but its inner mechanisms and modern mosaic decorations date from immediately after World War II. Be sure to look inside at the beautiful Renaissance stairway. You can also visit a large Gothic banquet room in the main building, with scenes from the city's history, and a late-Gothic chapel. Tours of the tower and chapel are given several times daily; contact the tourist office in the town hall. ⊠ *Horní nám.* ✉ *Tours 10 Kč.* ☉ *Mar.–Oct., daily 9–7; Nov.–Feb., daily 9–5.*

NEED A BREAK?	The wooden paneling and floral upholstery in the **Café Mahler** (⊠ Horní nám. 11) recall the taste of the 1880s, when Gustav Mahler briefly lived just around the corner while working as a conductor at the theater on the other side of the Upper Square. It's a good spot for ice cream, cake, or coffee.

On a small street just north of the Horní náměstí stands the Gothic **Chrám svatého Mořice** (Church of St. Maurice). Construction began in 1412, but a fire 40 years later badly damaged the structure; its current fierce, gray exterior dates from the middle of the 16th century. The baroque organ inside, the largest in the Czech Republic, originally contained 2,311 pipes until it was expanded in the 1960s to more than 10,000 pipes. ⊠ *Jana Opletalova ul.*

The interior of triple-domed **Kostel svatého Michala** (St. Michael's Church) casts a dramatic spell. The frescoes, the high and airy central dome, and the shades of rose, beige, and gray trompe-l'oeil marble on walls and arches blend to a harmonious, if dimly glimpsed, whole. The decoration followed a fire in 1709, only 30 years after the original construction. Architect and builder are not known, but it's surmised they are the same team that put up the Church of the Annunciation on Svatý Kopeček (Holy Hill), a popular Catholic pilgrimage site just outside Olomouc. ⊠ *Žerotínovo nám., 1 block uphill from Upper Square along Školní ul.*

Between the main square and the **Dóm svatého Václava** (Cathedral of St. Wenceslas) lies a peaceful neighborhood given over to huge buildings, mostly belonging either to the university or the archbishopric. As it stands today, the cathedral is just another example of the overbearing neo-Gothic enthusiasm of the late 19th century, having passed through just about every other architectural fad since its true Gothic days. ⊠ *Václavské nám.* ☉ *Daily 9–6.*

Next to the cathedral is the entrance to the **Palác Přemyslovců** (Přemyslid Palace), now a museum, where you can see early 16th-century wall paintings decorating the Gothic cloisters and, upstairs, a wonderful series of two- and three-arch Romanesque windows. This part of the building was used as a schoolroom some 700 years ago, and you can still make out drawings of animals engraved on the walls by early vandals. You can get an oddly phrased English-language pamphlet at the entrance to help you around the building. ⊠ *Václavské nám.* 🎫 *20 Kč.* ⊙ *Apr.–Oct., Tues.–Sun. 9–12:30 and 1–5.*

The **Děkanství** (Deacon's House), opposite the cathedral, now part of Palacký University, has two unusual claims to fame. Here, in 1767, the young musical prodigy Wolfgang Amadeus Mozart, age 11, spent six weeks recovering from a mild attack of chicken pox. The 16-year-old King Wenceslas III suffered a much worse fate here in 1306, when he was murdered, putting an end to the Přemyslid dynasty. The house is not open to the public. ⊠ *Václavské nám.*

Lodging

$$ 🏨 **Flora.** Don't expect luxury at this 1960s cookie-cutter high-rise, about a 15-minute walk from the town square. To its credit, the staff is attentive (English is spoken), and the pleasant, if anonymous, rooms are certainly adequate for a short stay. ⊠ *Krapkova 34, 779 00,* ☎ *585-422–200,* 📠 *585–421–211,* 🌐 *www.hotel-flora.cz. 140 rooms, 4 suites. Restaurant, cable TV, some pets allowed (fee); no a/c. AE, DC, MC, V. BP.*

$$ 🏨 **U Dómu svatého Václava.** This pleasant place represents a new class of Czech hotel and pension: you'll find modernized fittings installed in the old house. The six small suites all have kitchenettes. It's just down the street from the sleepy Václavské náměstí (where the Cathedral of St. Wenceslas is). ⊠ *Dómská 4, 772 00,* ☎ *585-220–502,* 📠 *585–220–501,* 🌐 *www.mcs.cz/udomu/brindex.htm. 6 rooms. Kitchenettes, cable TV; no a/c. AE, MC, V. BP.*

Outdoor Activities and Sports

The gentle, forested peaks of the **Beskydy Mountains** are popular destinations for hill walking, berry picking, and (in winter) cross-country skiing; several resorts have ski lifts as well. The year-round resort town of Rožnov pod Radhoštěm is connected by bus to all major cities in the country, and Velké Karlovice lies at the end of a rail line from Vsetín. Be sure to take along a good map; some roads may be closed during the winter. If you want to stay longer than a day, you can spend the night at one of the modest but comfortable mountain chalets in the area.

Northern Moravia Essentials

BUS TRAVEL

Brno is the gateway to northern Moravia. You'll sometimes have to resort to the bus to reach the smaller, out-of-the-way places throughout northern Moravia. To get to the Moravian Karst, you can take a bus from Brno to Vilémovice, a village not far from the Macocha Abyss.

CAR TRAVEL

Northern Moravia is a lost corner when it comes to car travel. None of the roads in northern Moravia really meet international highway standards, and the closer to Poland one gets, the worse the roads become before, in many cases, simply ending a few yards from the Polish border. Roads to Slovakia are in somewhat better shape. Highway 11 from Hradec Králové is a pleasant northern passage through mountains toward Opava. Highway 18 takes you south through farmland, near Olomouc, and then on to Slovakia.

TRAIN TRAVEL

Comparatively good trains, including several InterCity dailies, run frequently on the Prague–Olomouc–Ostrava line, one of the main rail cor-

ridors to Poland and Slovakia. Other long-distance trains branch off
south to Vsetín and on into Slovakia.

VISITOR INFORMATION
➤ CONTACTS: **Moravian Karst Central Information Service** (✉ Skalní
Mlýn 65, Blansko, ☎ 516–413–575 or 516–410–024, WEB www.
nature.cz/jeskyne/uvod_EN.htm). **Olomouc Tourist Information** (✉ Rad-
nice, Horní nám., Olomouc, ☎ 585–513–385, WEB www.olomoucko.cz).
Slavkov Historical Museum and Cultural Services Center Austerlitz (✉
Palackého nám. 126, Slavkov, ☎ 544–227–305 or 544–221–685, WEB
www.zamek-slavkov.cz).

THE CZECH REPUBLIC A TO Z

ADDRESSES
Navigation is relatively simple once you know the basic street-sign words:
ulice (street, abbreviated to ul., commonly dropped in printed addresses); *náměstí* (square, abbreviated to nám.); and *třída* (avenue). In
most towns, each building has two numbers, a confusing practice with
historic roots. In Prague, the blue tags mark the street address (usually); in Brno, ignore the blue tags and go by the white ones.

AIR TRAVEL
All international flights go into Prague. For detailed information, *see*
Prague Essentials. Air Ostrava flies from Prague to Ostrava and Brno,
both in Moravia, though it's usually more cost-effective to drive or take
a bus or train. Czech Airlines also flies to Ostrava.
➤ CARRIERS: **Air Ostrava** (☎ 220–113–406 in Prague). **ČSA** (☎ 220–
104–310, WEB www.csa.cz).

AIRPORTS
All international flights to the Czech Republic fly into Prague's Ruzyně
Airport, which is about 20 km (12 mi) northwest of downtown. Brno
and Ostrava airports handle domestic flights only.
➤ AIRPORTS: **Brno-Turany Airport** (☎ 545–521–310, WEB www.
airport-brno.cz). **Ruzyně Airport** (☎ 220–111–111, WEB www.csa.cz).

BUS TRAVEL
Several bus companies run direct services between major Western European cities and Prague. Kingscourt Express has several departures a
week between London and Prague and costs about $75 one-way and
$95 round-trip. The trip takes about 20 hours. Eurolines offers ser-
vice between Brno and many other cities in Europe.

The Czech Republic's extremely comprehensive state-run bus service,
ČSAD, is usually much quicker than the normal trains and more frequent than express trains, unless you're going to the major cities. Prices
are quite low—essentially the same as those for second-class rail tickets. Buy your tickets from the ticket window at the bus station or directly from the driver on the bus. Buses can be full to bursting. On
long-distance trips, it's a good idea to buy advance tickets when available (indicated by an "R" in a circle on timetables); get them at the local
station or at some travel agencies. The only drawback to traveling by
bus is figuring out the timetables. They are easy to read, but beware of
the small letters denoting exceptions to the times given. If in doubt, inquire at the information window or ask someone for assistance.
➤ BUS LINES: **ČSAD** (☎ 222–630–851 in Prague, WEB www.
jizdnirady.cz). **Eurolines** (☎ 542–215–448 in Brno, WEB www.
eurolines.cz/english/index.php). **Kingscourt Express** (☎ 020/8673–
7500 in London; 224–234–583 in Prague; WEB www.kce.cz).

BUSINESS HOURS

Though hours vary, most banks are open weekdays 8–5. Private currency exchange offices usually have longer hours, and some are open all night. It used to be that many sights outside the large towns, including most castles, were open daily except Monday only from May through September and in April and October were open only on weekends. Lately the trend is toward a longer season, although off-season hours may change capriciously, and many places still close from November to March. Stores are open weekdays 9–6. Some grocery stores open at 6 AM. Western-operated supermarkets are open much longer hours and on weekends; some larger supermarkets never close. Department stores often stay open until 7 PM. Outside Prague, most stores close for the weekend at noon on Saturday, although you can usually find a grocery open nights and weekends.

CAR RENTALS

There are no special requirements for renting a car in the Czech Republic, but be sure to shop around, as prices can differ greatly. Major firms like Avis and Hertz offer Western makes starting at around $45 per day or $300 per week, which includes insurance, damage waiver, and VAT (value-added tax); cars equipped with automatic transmission and air-conditioning are available, but it's best to reserve your rental car before you leave home, and it may be less expensive as well. Smaller local companies, on the other hand, can rent Czech cars for significantly less, but the service and insurance coverage may be inferior. A surcharge of 5%–12% applies to rental cars picked up at Prague's Ruzyně Airport. *See* Car Rentals *in* Prague Essentials for a list of agencies.

CAR TRAVEL

Traveling by car is the easiest and most flexible way of seeing the Czech Republic; however, if you intend to visit only the capital, you can do without a car. The city center is congested and difficult to navigate, and you'll save yourself a lot of hassle by sticking to public transportation.

A permit is required to drive on expressways and other four-lane highways. They cost 100 Kč for 10 days, 200 Kč for one month, and 800 Kč for one year and are sold at border crossings, some service stations, and all post offices.

In case of an accident or breakdown, *see* Emergencies, *below.*

PARKING

Parking is rarely a problem except in Prague (☞ Car Travel *in* Prague Essentials).

ROAD CONDITIONS

The Prague city center is mostly a snarl of traffic, one-way streets, and tram lines. If you plan to drive outside the capital, there are few four-lane highways, but most of the roads are in reasonably good shape, and traffic is usually light. Roads can be poorly marked, however, so before you start out, buy one of the inexpensive multilingual auto atlases available at any bookstore.

RULES OF THE ROAD

The Czech Republic follows the usual Continental rules of the road. A right turn on red is permitted only when indicated by a green arrow. Signposts with yellow diamonds indicate a main road where drivers have the right of way. The speed limit is 130 kph (78 mph) on four-lane highways, 90 kph (56 mph) on open roads, and 50 kph (30 mph) in built-up areas. Seat belts are compulsory, and drinking before driving is absolutely prohibited. Passengers under 12 years of age, or less than 150 cm (5 ft) in height, must ride in the back seat.

CUSTOMS AND DUTIES

The export of items considered to have historical value is not allowed. To be exported, an antique or work of art must have an export certificate. Reputable shops should be willing to advise customers on how to comply with the regulations. If a shop can't provide proof of the item's suitability for export, be wary. The authorities do not look kindly on unauthorized "export" of antiques, particularly of baroque religious pieces. Under certain circumstances, the value-added tax (VAT) on purchases over 1,000 Kč can be refunded if the goods are taken out of the country within 30 days.

EMBASSIES AND CONSULATES

➤ CONTACTS: **Canadian Embassy** (⊠ Mickiewiczova 6, Hradčany, Prague, ☎ 272–101–890, WEB www.dfait-maeci.gc.ca/prague). **U.K. Embassy** (⊠ Thunovská 14, Malá Strana, Prague, ☎ 257–530–278, WEB www.britain.cz). **U.S. Embassy** (⊠ Tržiště 15, Malá Strana, Prague, ☎ 257–530–663, WEB www.usembassy.cz).

EMERGENCIES

Emergency roadside assistance is offered by the Central Automobile Club and the Autoklub Bohemia Assistance unit, both of which operate 24 hours. There is also a general number to call if you have a breakdown on a highway and need assistance. The Autoklub Bohemia Assistance unit offers memberships but also has set rates for helping nonmembers in emergency situations. It is not affiliated with other international auto clubs. The ÚAMK, or Central Automobile Club, used to be known as the Yellow Angels because they roamed the highways in yellow cars looking for accidents. Now they wait by the phone. They have joined a number of international motoring organizations such as AIT and FAI and have emergency service agreements with many European insurance companies and car manufacturers.

➤ CONTACTS: **Police** (☎ 158). **Ambulance** (☎ 155). **Autoklub Bohemia Assistance** (☎ 1240, WEB www.aba.cz). **Fire** (☎ 150). **ÚAMK Emergency Roadside Assistance** (☎ 1230, WEB www.uamk.cz).

HOLIDAYS AND LANGUAGE

HOLIDAYS

January 1; Easter Monday; May 1 (Labor Day); May 8 (Liberation Day); July 5 (Sts. Cyril and Methodius Day); July 6 (Jan Hus Day); September 28 (Day of Czech Statehood); October 28 (Czech National Day); November 17 (Day of a Struggle for Liberty and Democracy); and December 24, 25, and 26.

LANGUAGE

Czech, a Slavic language closely related to Slovak and Polish, is the official language of the Czech Republic. Learning English is popular among young people, but German is still the most useful language for tourists, especially outside Prague.

LODGING

BED-AND-BREAKFAST RESERVATION AGENCIES

Most local information offices also book rooms in hotels, pensions, and private accommodations. Do-it-yourself travelers should keep a sharp eye out for room-for-rent signs reading ZIMMER FREI, PRIVAT, or UBYTOVÁNÍ. The Good Bed Agency specializes in Prague and Karlovy Vary. Many other B&Bs have home pages on the Web site of the IDS International Database System.

➤ CONTACTS: **The Good Bed Agency** (⊠ Kříženeckého nám. 322, Prague, ☎ 267–073–456, WEB www.goodbed.cz). **International Database System** (WEB www.hotel.cz).

MAIL AND SHIPPING

POSTAL RATES

At this writing, postcards to the United States and Canada cost 12 Kč; letters up to 20 grams in weight, 14 Kč. Postcards to Great Britain cost 9 Kč; letters, 9 Kč. You can buy stamps at post offices, hotels, and shops that sell postcards.

RECEIVING MAIL

If you don't know where you'll be staying, American Express mail service is a great convenience, available at no charge to anyone holding an American Express credit card or carrying American Express traveler's checks. There are several offices in Prague; the American Express representative in Karlovy Vary is Incentives CZ. You can also have mail held *poste restante* (general delivery) at post offices in major towns, but the letters should be marked *Pošta 1,* to designate the city's main post office; in Prague, the poste restante window is at the main post office. You will be asked for identification when you collect your mail.

➤ CONTACTS: **American Express** (⊠ Václavské nám. 56, Nové Město, ☎ 224–219–992, WEB www.americanexpress.com; Mostecká 12, Malá Strana, ☎ 257–313–636). **Incentives CZ** (⊠ Vřídelní 51, ☎ 353–226–027, WEB www.incentives.cz). **Prague Main Post Office** (⊠ Jindřišská ul. 14, WEB www.cpost.cz/postaAn).

MONEY MATTERS

The Czech Republic is still generally a bargain by Western standards. Prague remains the exception. Hotel prices in particular are often higher than the facilities would warrant, but prices at tourist resorts outside the capital are lower and, in the outlying areas and off the beaten track, very low. Unfortunately, many museums, castles, and certain clubs charge a higher entrance fee for foreigners than they charge for Czechs. A few hotels still follow this practice, too.

CREDIT CARDS

Visa, MasterCard, and American Express are widely accepted by major hotels and stores, Diners Club less so. Smaller establishments and those off the beaten track are less likely to accept a wide variety of credit cards.

➤ LOST CREDIT CARDS: **American Express** (☎ 336–393–111). **Diners Club** (☎ 267–314–485). **MasterCard** (☎ 261–354–650). **Visa** (☎ 224–125–353).

CURRENCY

The unit of currency in the Czech Republic is the koruna, or crown (Kč), which is divided into 100 haléřů, or hellers. There are (little-used) coins of 10, 20, and 50 hellers; coins of 1, 2, 5, 10, 20, and (rarely) 50 Kč; and notes of 50, 100, 200, 500, 1,000, 2,000, and 5,000 Kč. Notes of 1,000 Kč and up may not always be accepted for small purchases.

CURRENCY EXCHANGE

Try to avoid exchanging money at hotels or private exchange booths, including the ubiquitous Chequepoint and Exact Change booths. They routinely take commissions of 8%–10%. The best places to exchange are at bank counters, where the commissions average 1%–3%, or at ATMs. The koruna is fully convertible, which means it can be purchased outside the country and exchanged into other currencies. Of course, never change money with people on the street. Not only is it illegal, you will almost definitely be ripped off.

At this writing the exchange rate was around 33 Kč to the U.S. dollar, 21 Kč to the Canadian dollar, 48 Kč to the pound sterling, and 30 Kč to the euro.

PASSPORTS AND VISAS

United States and British citizens need only a valid passport to visit the Czech Republic as tourists. U.S. citizens may stay for 30 days without a visa; British citizens three or six months, depending on the type of passport. Canadian citizens require a visa, which is valid for up to 90 days and which must be obtained in advance. Long-term and work visas for all foreigners now must be obtained from outside the country. Those interested in working or living in the Czech Republic are advised to contact the Czech embassy or consulate in their home country well in advance of their trip.

TELEPHONES

The country code for the Czech Republic is 420. The country dropped regional codes and adopted a nationwide nine-digit standard in late 2002. Prefixes 0/601 to 0/777 denote mobile phones (omit the "0" when calling from outside the country).

Now that most people have mobile phones, working phone booths are harder to find. If you can't find a booth, the telephone office of the main post office is the best place to try. Once inside, follow signs for TELEGRAF/TELEFAX.

INTERNATIONAL CALLS

The international dialing code is 00. For calls to the United States, Canada, or the United Kingdom, dial the international operator. Otherwise, ask the receptionist at any hotel to put a call through for you, but the surcharges and rates will be tremendously high.

With the prepaid Karta X (300 Kč–1,000 Kč), rates to the U.S. are roughly 13 Kč per minute; a call to the U.K. costs about 12 Kč per minute. The cards are available at many money-changing stands and can work with any phone once you enter a 14-digit code. You do not need to find a booth with a card slot to use the cards.

You can reach an English-speaking operator from one of the major long-distance services on a toll-free number. The operator will connect your collect or credit-card call at the carrier's standard rates. In Prague, many phone booths allow direct international dialing.
➤ LONG-DISTANCE ACCESS NUMBERS: **AT&T** (☎ 0/042–000–101). **BT Direct** (☎ 0/042–004–401). **CanadaDirect** (☎ 0/042–000–151). **MCI** (☎ 0/042–000–112). **Sprint** (☎ 0/042–087–187).
➤ OTHER CONTACTS: **International Operator** (☎ 133004). **International Directory Assistance** (☎ 1181).

LOCAL CALLS

Coin-operated pay phones are hard to find. Most newer public phones operate only with a special telephone card, available from post offices and some newsstands in denominations of 150 Kč and up. Since the boom in mobile phone use, both the cards and working pay phones are harder to find. A short call within Prague costs a minimum of 4 Kč from a coin-operated phone or the equivalent of 3.5 Kč (1 unit) from a card-operated phone. The dial tone is a series of alternating short and long buzzes.

TIPPING

Service is usually not included in restaurant bills. Round the bill up to the next multiple of 10 (if the bill comes to 83 Kč, for example, give the waiter 90 Kč); 10% is considered appropriate in all but the most expensive places. Tip porters who bring bags to your rooms 40 Kč total. For room service, a 20 Kč tip is enough. In taxis, round the bill up by 10%. Give tour guides and helpful concierges between 50 Kč and 100 Kč for services rendered.

TOURS

Several Prague-based companies offer tours of the capital and other regions of the country. Čedok has a wide range of offerings, including driving and cycling tours. Precious Legacy Tours arranges tours to Jewish sites. Sportturist Special has regional and local tours and is the local office for Western Union. Wittmann Tours specializes in tours to sites of Jewish interest throughout the country and Central Europe. Contact Wolff Travel for regional and capital tours and international transportation tickets.

➤ TOUR COMPANIES: **Čedok** (⊠ Na Příkopě 18, Prague, ☎ 224–197–111, WEB www.cedok.cz). **Precious Legacy Tours** (⊠ Maiselova 16, Prague, ☎ 222–320–398, WEB www.legacytours.cz). **Sportturist Special** (⊠ Národní tř. 33, Prague, ☎ 224–228–518, WEB www.sportturistspecial.cz). **Wittmann Tours** (⊠ Manesova 8, Prague, ☎ 222–252–472, WEB www.wittmann-tours.com). **Wolff Travel** (⊠ Dykova 31, Prague, ☎ 222–511–333, WEB www.wolff-travel.com).

TRAIN TRAVEL

You can take a direct train from Paris via Frankfurt to Prague (daily) or from Berlin via Dresden to Prague (five times a day). Vienna is a good starting point for Prague, Brno, or Bratislava. There are three trains a day from Vienna's Südbahnhof (South Station) to Prague (five hours). Southern Moravia and southern Bohemia are served by trains from Vienna and Linz.

The state-run rail system is called České dráhy (ČD). On longer runs, it's not really worth taking anything less than an express (*rychlík*) train, marked in red on the timetable. Tickets are still very inexpensive: a second-class ticket from Prague to Brno cost 182 Kč at this writing. First-class is considerably more spacious and comfortable and well worth the cost (50% more than a standard ticket). A 40 Kč–60 Kč supplement is charged for the excellent international expresses, EuroCity (EC) and InterCity (IC), and for domestic SuperCity (SC) schedules. A 20 Kč supplement applies to reserved seats on domestic journeys. If you haven't bought a ticket in advance at the station (mandatory for seat reservations), you can buy one aboard the train from the conductor. On timetables, departures (*odjezd*) appear on a yellow background; arrivals (*příjezd*) are on white. It is possible to book sleepers (*lůžkový*) or the less-roomy couchettes (*lehátkový*) on most overnight trains.

➤ CONTACTS: **České dráhy** (ČD; ☎ 224–224–200 information, WEB www.cdrail.cz).

RAIL PASSES

The Eurail Pass and the Eurail Youthpass are not valid for travel within the Czech Republic, and most rail passes, such as the Czech Flexipass, will wind up costing more than what you'd spend buying tickets on the spot, particularly if you intend to travel mainly in the Czech Republic, since international tickets normally are more expensive. The European East Pass, for example, is good for first-class travel on the national railroads of the Czech Republic, Austria, Hungary, Poland, and Slovakia. The pass allows five days of unlimited travel within a one-month period for $220), and it must be purchased from Rail Europe before your departure.

➤ CONTACTS: **Rail Europe** (⊠ 226–230 Westchester Ave., White Plains, NY 10604, ☎ 877/257–2887, WEB www.raileurope.com; 2087 Dundas E, Suite 106, Mississauga, Ontario, Canada L4X 1M2, ☎ 800/361–7245).

TRAVEL AGENCIES

Prague's American Express (☞ Travel Agencies *in* Prague Essentials) provides full travel services in addition to changing money and selling traveler's checks. Local Czech travel agencies offer extensive information on regional activities and tours, and larger agencies can supply you with hotel and travel information and book air and rail tickets. Agencies with branches nationwide include Čedok (the former state-owned tourist bureau) and Sportturist Special (☞ Tours, *above*).

VISITOR INFORMATION

Most major towns have a local information office (Infocentrum or Informační středisko), usually in the central square and identified by a green-and-white sign with a lowercase "i" on the facade. These offices are often good sources for maps and guidebooks and can usually help you book hotel and private accommodations. In season (generally April through October), most are open during normal business hours and often on Saturday morning, sometimes even Sunday. In the winter, most are closed weekends. The Czech Tourist Authority, official provider of tourist information to the Czech Republic, has offices in the United States, Canada, Great Britain, European countries, and Japan, as well as in Prague. They stock maps and brochures on tourism outside Prague and dispense advice but do not book tickets or accommodations.

➤ CONTACTS: **Czech Tourist Authority** (✉ Staroměstské nám. 6, Prague, ☎ 224–810–411, WEB www.visitczech.cz).

5 HUNGARY

Budapest, an old-world city with a throbbing urban pulse, is a must-stop on any trip to Central Europe. Szentendre, Eger, Pécs, and Debrecen have their own charms, including majestic hilltop castles and cobblestone streets winding among lovely baroque buildings. Lake Balaton's popularity tells you much about this landlocked nation's fascination with water. On the Great Plain, traditional life continues much as it has for centuries, often on horseback. All this, and the generosity of the Magyar soul, sustains visitors to this land of vital spirit and beauty.

By Alan Levy
and Julie
Tomasz

Updated
by Scott
Alexander
Young

HUNGARY SITS AT THE CROSSROADS of Central Europe, having retained its own identity by absorbing countless invasions and foreign occupations. Its industrious, resilient people have a history of brave but unfortunate uprisings: against the Turks in the 17th century, the Hapsburgs in 1848, and the Soviet Union in 1956. With the withdrawal of the last Soviet soldiers from Hungarian soil in 1991, Hungary embarked on a decade of sweeping changes. The adjustment to a free-market economy has not all been easy sailing, but Hungary at long last has regained self-determination and a chance to rebuild an economy devastated by years of Communist misrule.

At the beginning of a new millennium much indeed seems possible. Hungary joined NATO in 1999, and European Union (EU) membership could come as soon as 2004. In 2002, then 39-year-old Prime Minister Viktor Orbán was the subject of gentle mockery when he suggested that the Hungarian economy was like a guided missile that had taken off and which could not be shot down. At the same time, people knew what he was talking about. For international investors, too, Hungary is seen as a good bet, one of the better in this fast-developing region.

An entire generation is coming of age in Hungary for whom foreign occupation, long lines to buy bananas, coupon books, and repression of the press are an increasingly distant memory. Their parents remember every precious, incremental gain in freedom during the years of so-called "goulash socialism" of the 1960s and '70s. Their grandparents may even look back to this time of protectionist economic policies and cradle-to-the-grave social welfare with a certain nostalgia.

The stage was set then for a tightly fought electoral contest in 2002 and a battle of ideologies, between Orbán's increasingly right-wing FIDESZ party and the Hungarian Socialist Party, which narrowly won the parliamentary elections.

Because Hungary is a small, agriculturally oriented country, visitors are often surprised by its grandeur and charm, especially in the capital, Budapest, which bustles with life as never before. These days most are spared bureaucratic hassles at border crossings, and most Westerners can stay in the country for three months (out of every six) without obtaining a visa.

Two rivers cross the country: the famous Duna (Danube) flows from the west through Budapest on its way to the southern frontier, and the smaller Tisza flows from the northeast across the Nagyalföld (Great Plain). What Hungary lacks in size it makes up for in beauty and charm. Western Hungary is dominated by the largest lake in Central Europe, Lake Balaton. Although some overdevelopment has blighted its splendor, its shores are still lined with baroque villages, relaxing spas, magnificent vineyards, and shaded garden restaurants serving the catch of the day. In eastern Hungary, the Nagyalföld offers opportunities to explore the folklore and customs of the Magyars (the Hungarians' name for themselves and their language). It is an area of spicy food, strong wine, and the proud *csikósok* (horsemen).

Hungarians are known for their hospitality. Although their unusual and difficult language is anything but a quick study, English is fast becoming the second language of Hungary, even superceding German. But what all Hungarians share is a deep love of music, and the calendar is studded with it, from Budapest's famous opera to its annual spring music festival. And at many restaurants Gypsy violinists serenade you during your evening meal.

Hungary (Magyarország)

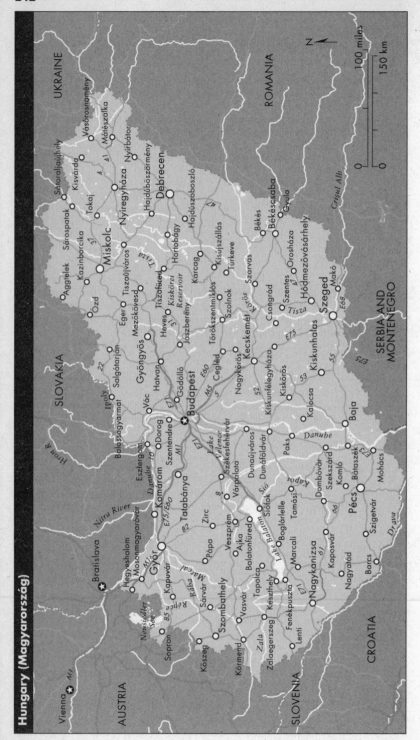

Pleasures and Pastimes

Beaches and Water Sports

Lake Balaton, the largest lake in Central Europe, is the most popular playground of this landlocked nation. If you're looking to relax in the sun and do a little windsurfing, swimming, or boating, settle in here for several days, basing yourself in either the northern shore's main town, Balatonfüred, or the more tranquil Tihany.

Dining

Through the lean postwar years the Hungarian kitchen lost none of its spice and sparkle. Meats, rich sauces, and creamy desserts predominate, but the more health-conscious will also find salads, even out of season. (Strict vegetarians should note, however, that even meatless dishes are often cooked with lard [*zsír*].) In addition to the ubiquitous dishes most foreigners are familiar with, such as chunky beef *gulyás* (goulash) and *paprikás csirke* (chicken paprika) served with *galuska* (little pinched dumplings), traditional Hungarian classics include fiery *halászlé* (fish soup), scarlet with hot paprika; *fogas* (pike perch) from Lake Balaton; and goose liver, duck, and veal specialties. Lake Balaton is the major source of fish in Hungary, particularly for *süllő,* a kind of perch. Hungarians are also very fond of carp (*ponty*), catfish (*harcsa*), and eel (*angolna*), which are often stewed in a garlic-and-tomato sauce. There's also *turós csusza,* which is a strange mixture of lukewarm pasta covered in curded cheese. It may not be to everyone's taste, but it is most definitely authentically Hungarian.

Portions are large, so don't plan to eat more than one main Hungarian meal a day. Desserts are lavish, and every inn seems to have its house *torta* (cake), though *rétes* (strüdels), *Somlói galuska* (a steamed sponge cake soaked in chocolate sauce and whipped cream), and *palacsinta* (stuffed crêpes) are ubiquitous. Traditional rétes fillings are *mák* (sugary poppy seeds), *meggy* (sour cherry), and *túró* (sweetened cottage cheese); palacsintas always come rolled with *dió* (sweet ground walnuts), *túró,* or *lekvár* (jam)—often *sárgabarack* (apricot). Finally, try the *Zserbó,* a delicious layered cake with apricot-jam and walnut filling.

In major cities, there is a good selection of restaurants, from the grander establishments that echo the imperial past of the Hapsburg era to trendy new international restaurants to cheap but cheerful spots favored by the working populus. In addition to trying out the standard *vendéglő* or *étterem* (restaurants), you can eat at a *bisztró étel bár* (sit-down snack bar), a *büfé* (snack counter), an *eszpresszó* (café), or a *söröző* (pub). And no matter how strict your diet, don't pass up a visit to at least one *cukrászda* (pastry shop). Finally, if you find yourself longing for something non-Hungarian—anything from pizza to Indian, Turkish to Korean, Greek to American-style fast food—you can find it aplenty in the larger cities.

Although prices are steadily increasing, there are plenty of good, affordable restaurants offering Hungarian and international dishes. Even in Budapest, eating out can provide you with some of the best value for the money of any European capital. In almost all restaurants, an inexpensive prix-fixe lunch called a *menü* is available, usually for as little as 1,000 Ft. It includes soup or salad, a main course, and a dessert. The days of charging customers for each slice of bread taken from the bread basket and of embellishing tourists' bills are, happily, fast receding. The glaring exception to this is along Váci utca, a downtown pedestrian thoroughfare in Budapest. If someone (usually a young lady) approaches you on this street and invites you to join her at a nearby café or restaurant, politely decline: unless you want to be presented later with a three-figure bill for a cup of coffee by a burly and intimidating "waiter."

Hungarians eat early—you still risk offhand service and cold food if you arrive at some traditional Hungarian restaurants after 9 PM. Lunch, the main meal for many, is served from noon to 2. At most moderately priced and inexpensive restaurants, casual but neat dress is acceptable.

CATEGORY	COST*
$$$$	over 3,500 Ft.
$$$	2,500 Ft.–3,500 Ft.
$$	1,500 Ft.–2,500 Ft.
$	under 1,500 Ft.

*per person for a main course at dinner

Folk Art

Hungary's centuries-old traditions of handmade, often regionally specific folk art are still beautifully alive. Intricately carved wooden boxes, vibrantly colorful embroidered tablecloths and shirts, matte-black pottery pitchers, delicately woven lace collars, ceramic plates splashed with painted flowers and birds, and decorative heavy leather whips are among the favorite handcrafted pieces you can purchase. You'll find them in folk-art stores around the country but can purchase them directly from the artisans at crafts fairs and from peddlers on the streets. Dolls dressed in national costume are also popular souvenirs.

Hiking

Northern Hungary offers places to get out and walk in nature. Base yourself in Eger—for lovely sightseeing, excellent wine, and good lodging—and make day trips north to Szilvásvárad for hiking or biking in the hills of the Bükk range and south for the same in the Mátra range, near Gyöngyös. Moving slightly farther north, you can spend a night or two in the magical palace hotel in Lillafüred, making excursions to the magnificent caves at Aggtelek, near the Slovak border, and to Tokaj, farther east, for some less athletic wine tasting.

Lodging

Outside Budapest there are not many expensive hotels, so you will improve your chances of having a memorable lodging experience by arranging a stay in one of the alternative options noted below. For specific recommendations or information about how to book lodging in these accommodations, see the lodging and information sections throughout the chapter.

Bought back from the government over the last several years, more and more of Hungary's magnificent, centuries-old castles and mansions are being restored and opened as country resorts; a night or two in one of these majestic old places makes for an unusual and romantic (but not always luxurious) lodging experience. Northern Hungary has some of the best.

Guest houses, also called *panziók* (pensions), provide simple accommodations—well suited to people on a budget. Like B&Bs, most are run by couples or families and offer simple breakfast facilities and usually have private bathrooms; they're generally outside the city or town center. Arrangements can be made directly with the panzió or through local tourist offices and travel agents abroad. Another good budget option is renting a room in a private home. In the provinces it is safe to accept rooms offered to you directly; they will almost always be clean and in a relatively good neighborhood, and the prospective landlord will probably not cheat you. Look for signs reading SZOBA KIADÓ (or the German ZIMMER FREI). Reservations and referrals can also be made by any tourist office, and if you go that route, you have someone to complain to if things don't work out.

Village tourism is a growing trend in Hungary, affording a chance to sink into life in tiny, typical villages around the country. The Hungarian Tourist Board produces a guide called *Village Tourism* with descriptions and color photos of many of the village homes now open to guests, either by the week or the night. Apartments in Budapest and cottages at Lake Balaton are available for short- and long-term rental and can make the most economic lodging for families—particularly for those who prefer to cook their own meals. Rates and reservations can be obtained from tourist offices in Hungary and abroad. Also consult the free annual accommodations directory published by **Tourinform**; published in five languages, it lists basic information about hotels, pensions, bungalows, and tourist hostels throughout the country. A separate brochure lists the country's campgrounds.

For single rooms with bath, count on paying about 80% of the double-room rate. During the off-season (in Budapest, September through March; at Lake Balaton, September through May), rates can drop considerably. Prices at Lake Balaton tend to be significantly higher than those in the rest of the countryside. Note that most large hotels set their rates and require payment in U.S. dollars or euros. Breakfast and VAT are usually—but not always—included in your quoted room rate. There is also a "tourist tax" of 3% in Budapest; outside the capital it varies region to region but is always less than a 1,000 Ft. This tax is usually not included in the quoted rates.

CATEGORY	BUDAPEST*	OTHER AREAS*
$$$$	over 50,000 Ft.	over 19,000 Ft.
$$$	35,000 Ft.–50,000 Ft.	14,000 Ft.–19,000 Ft.
$$	25,000 Ft.–35,000 Ft.	8,100 Ft.–14,000 Ft.
$	under 25,000 Ft.	under 8,100 Ft.

All prices are for a standard double room with bath and breakfast during peak season (June–August).

Porcelain

Among the most sought-after items in Hungary are the exquisite hand-painted Herend and Zsolnay porcelain. Unfortunately, the prices on all makes of porcelain have risen considerably in the last few years. For guaranteed authenticity, make your purchases at the specific Herend and Zsolnay stores in major cities, or at the factories themselves in Herend and Pécs, respectively.

Spas and Thermal Baths

Several thousand years ago, the first settlers of the area that is now Budapest chose their home because of its abundance of hot springs. Centuries later, the Romans and the Turks built baths and developed cultures based on medicinal bathing. Now there are more than 1,000 medicinal hot springs bubbling up around the country. Budapest alone has some 14 historic working baths, which attract ailing patients with medical prescriptions for specific water cures as well as "recreational" bathers—locals and tourists alike—wanting to soak in the relaxing waters, try some of the many massages and treatments, and experience the architectural beauty of the bathhouses themselves.

For most, a visit to a bath involves soaking in several thermal pools of varying temperatures and curative contents—perhaps throwing in a game of aquatic chess—relaxing in a steam room or sauna, and getting a brisk, if not brutal, massage (average cost: 800 Ft. for 15 minutes). Many bath facilities are single-sex or have certain days set aside for men or women only, and most people walk around nude or with miniature loincloths, provided at the door. Men should be aware that some men-only baths have a strong gay clientele.

In addition to the ancient beauties there are newer, modern baths open to the public at many spa hotels. They lack the charm and aesthetic appeal of their older peers but provide the latest treatments in sparkling facilities. Debrecen, Hévíz, and Eger are famous spa towns with popular bath facilities. For more information, look through the "Hungary: Land of Spas" brochure published by the Hungarian Tourist Board, available free from most tourist offices.

Wine, Beer, and Spirits

Hungary tempts wine connoisseurs with its important wine regions, especially Villány, near Pécs, in the south; Eger and Tokaj in the north; and the northern shore of Lake Balaton. Szürkebarát (a pinot gris varietal) and especially Olaszrizling (a milder Rhine Riesling) are common white table wines; Tokay, one of the great wines of the world, can be heavy, dark, and sweet, and its most famous variety is drunk as an aperitif or a dessert wine. Good Tokay is expensive, especially by Hungarian standards, so it's usually reserved for special occasions.

The red table wine of Hungary, Egri Bikavér (Bull's Blood of Eger, usually with *el toro* himself on the label), is the best buy and the safest bet with all foods. Villány produces superb reds and the best rosés; the most adventurous reds—with sometimes successful links to both Austrian and Californian wine making and viticulture—are from the Sopron area.

Before- and after-dinner drinks tend toward schnapps, most notably *Barack-pálinka*, an apricot brandy. A plum brandy called *Kosher szilva-pálinka*, bottled under rabbinical supervision, is the very best of the brandies available in stores. *Vilmos körte-pálinka*, a pear variety, is almost as good. Note than any bottle under 1,000 Ft. or so probably contains more ethyl alcohol than pure fruit brandy. Unicum, Hungary's national liqueur, is a dark, thick, and potent herbal bitter that could be likened to Germany's Jägermeister. Its chubby green bottle makes it a good souvenir to take home.

Major Hungarian beers are Dreher, Kőbányai, and Aranyászok, and several good foreign beers are produced in Hungary under license.

Exploring Hungary

Hungary's main geographical regions begin with the capital city and thriving urban heart of **Budapest.** Just north of Budapest, the Danube forms a gentle heart-shape curve along which lie the romantic and historic towns of the region called the **Danube Bend.** Southwest of Budapest are the vineyards, quaint villages, and popular, developed summer resorts around **Lake Balaton.** The verdant, rolling countryside of **Transdanubia** stretches west of the Danube to the borders of Austria, Slovenia, and Croatia; in the northern hills nestle the gemlike, beautifully restored towns of Sopron and Kőszeg and in the south, the culturally rich, dynamically beautiful city of Pécs. Given Hungary's relatively small size, most of these points are less than a few hours away from Budapest by car. The more rural and gently mountainous stretch of **northern Hungary** also includes the handsome, vibrant town of Eger and the famous wine village of Tokaj; the contrastingly flat and dry expanses of the **Great Plain,** in the east, are spiced with legendary traditions of horsemanship and agriculture and anchored by the interesting and lively cities of Kecskemét and Debrecen.

Great Itineraries

IF YOU HAVE 3 DAYS

⊞ **Budapest** alone offers a full vacation's worth of things to see and experience, but in one day an efficient and motivated visitor can pack in some of the don't-misses: exploration of **Várhegy**, a stroll on the **Danube korzó**, a glimpse of **Országház**, a look at **Hősök tere**, followed by a dip in the **Széchenyi Fürdő**, a hearty meal, and a night at the **Magyar Állami Operaház**. After a night's rest in Budapest, hop on an early boat to explore the time-honored artists' village of **Szentendre** and the majestic fortress of **Visegrád**, upriver in the Danube Bend. You can spend another night in Budapest; the next morning, drive down to **Badacsony** on Lake Balaton's northern shore. Follow a refreshing swim with a lunch of fresh Balaton fish and some wine tasting in the cool cellars on Mt. Badacsony's vineyard-covered slopes. On your way back to Budapest, stop for a stroll on **Tihany**'s cobblestone streets and drink in the views from its lovely hilltop abbey.

IF YOU HAVE 6 DAYS

Spend two full days exploring ⊞ **Budapest**; on your third day visit the Danube Bend's crown jewels, the villages of **Szentendre** and **Visegrád**, making the trip by scenic boat or by car. Return to Budapest for the night and head out the next morning for a day on the Great Plain, strolling among the sights of lovely ⊞ **Kecskemét** before venturing out to the *puszta* (prairie) in **Kiskunsági Nemzeti Park** (Kiskunsági National Park) or **Kerekegyháza** to experience the unique horsemanship stunts and demonstrations of Hungary's legendary cowboys, the csikós. Depending on how much you want to drive and how much of Budapest's nightlife you want to take in, you can either go back to Budapest (85 km [53 mi] from Kecskemét) for the night or spend it here in Kecskemét. On day five, drive down to ⊞ **Pécs** to see its beautiful town square, cathedral, and excellent museums. After a night's rest, make your way on scenic secondary roads through southern Transdanubia to **Keszthely** on the northwestern tip of Lake Balaton, visiting the spectacular Festetics mansion before moving east along the northern shore to ⊞ **Badacsony.** On the way, make a stop in **Szigliget** and scale its castle hill to gaze at the sweeping Lake Balaton view. In Badacsony, spend the rest of the afternoon hiking up the vineyard-carpeted slopes of Mount Badacsony, rewarded by generous wine tastings in the local cellars and a big fish dinner with live Gypsy music. Depending on your traveling speed (and the amount of wine you've tasted), instead of sleeping in Badacsony, you may prefer to move on along the northern shore and spend the fifth night in ⊞ **Tihany** or ⊞ **Balatonfüred,** both of which have good lodging possibilities with more facilities and amenities. Either way, you can spend your sixth day exploring Tihany and Balatonfüred, cooling off with a swim in the lake before heading back to Budapest.

When to Tour

The ideal times to visit Hungary are in the spring (May–June) and end of summer and early fall (late August–September). July and August, peak vacation season for Hungarians as well as foreign tourists, can be extremely hot and humid; Budapest is stuffy and crowded, and the entire Lake Balaton region is overrun with vacationers. Many of Hungary's major fairs and festivals take place during the spring and fall, including the Spring Festival (in many cities and towns) from late March to early April and the myriad wine-harvest festivals in late summer and early fall. Lake Balaton is the only area that gets boarded up during the low season, generally from mid- or late September until at least Easter, if not mid-May. Summer holds the unforgettable and quintessentially Hungarian sights of sweeping fields of swaying golden sunflowers and giant white storks summering in their bushy nests built on chimney tops.

BUDAPEST

Situated on both banks of the Danube, Budapest unites the colorful hills of Buda and the wide, businesslike boulevards of Pest. Though it was the site of a Roman outpost during the 1st century, the city was not officially created until 1873, when the towns of Óbuda, Pest, and Buda united. Since then, Budapest has been the cultural, political, intellectual, and commercial heart of Hungary; for the 20% of the nation's population who live in the capital, anywhere else is simply *vidék* ("the country").

Budapest has suffered many ravages in the course of its long history. It was totally destroyed by the Mongols in 1241, captured by the Turks in 1541, and nearly destroyed again by Soviet troops in 1945. But this bustling industrial and cultural center survived as the capital of the People's Republic of Hungary after the war—and then, as the 1980s drew to a close, it became renowned for "goulash socialism," a phrase used to describe the state's tolerance of an irrepressible entrepreneurial spirit. Budapest has undergone a radical makeover since the free elections of 1990. Change is still in the air. As more and more restaurants, bars, shops, and boutiques open their doors—and with fashion-conscious youths parading the streets—almost all traces of Communism may seem to have disappeared. But then look again: the elderly ladies selling flowers at the train station are a poignant reminder that some Hungarians have been left behind in this brave new world of competition.

Much of the charm of a visit to Budapest lies in unexpected glimpses into shadowy courtyards and in long vistas down sunlit cobbled streets. Although some 30,000 buildings were destroyed during World War II and in the 1956 Revolution, the past lingers on in the often crumbling architectural details of the antique structures that remain.

The principal sights of the city fall roughly into three areas, each of which can be comfortably covered on foot. The Budapest hills are best explored by public transportation. Note that, by tradition, the district number—a Roman numeral designating one of Budapest's 22 districts—precedes each address. For the sake of clarity, in this book, the word "District" precedes the number. Districts V, VI, and VII are in downtown Pest; District I includes Castle Hill, the main tourist district of Buda.

Exploring Budapest

Várhegy (Castle Hill)

Most of the major sights of Buda are on Várhegy (Castle Hill), a long, narrow plateau laced with cobblestone streets, clustered with beautifully preserved baroque, Gothic, and Renaissance houses and crowned by the magnificent Royal Palace. The area is theoretically banned to private cars (except for those of neighborhood residents and Hilton hotel guests), but the streets manage to be lined bumper to bumper with Trabants and Mercedes all the same—sometimes the only visual element to verify you're not in a fairy tale. As in all of Budapest, thriving urban new has taken up residence in historic old; international corporate offices, diplomatic residences, restaurants, and boutiques occupy many of its landmark buildings. The most striking example, perhaps, is the Hilton hotel on Hess András tér, which has ingeniously incorporated remains of Castle Hill's oldest church (a tower and one wall), built by Dominican friars in the 13th century.

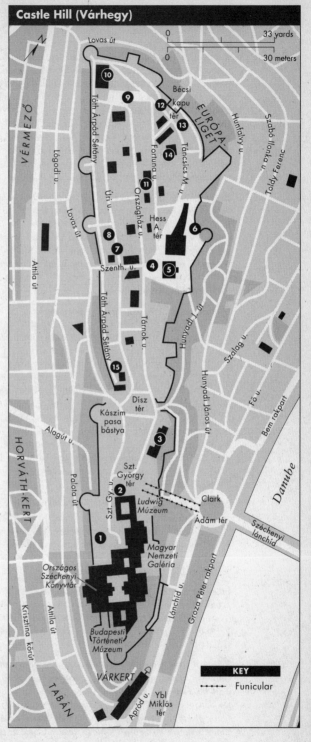

Castle Hill (Várhegy)

0   33 yards

0   30 meters

Lovas út

10

9

12 Bécsi kapu tér

13

EURÓPA LIGET

14 Fortuna u.

Tóth Árpád sétány

Úri u.

Lógodi u.

Lovas út

Országház u.

Táncsics M. u.

Hunfalvy u.

Szabó Ilonka u.

Toldy Ferenc

VÉRMEZŐ

11

8

7

Hess A. tér

6

4 **5**

Szenth. u.

Athila út

Tóth Árpád Sétány

Tárnok u.

Hunyadi J. út

Szalag u.

Fő u.

Bem rakpart

15

Dísz tér

Kászim pasa bástya

Alagút u.

HORVÁTH KERT

3

Hunyadi János út

Danube

Szt. György tér

Palota út

Szt. Gy.

2

Ludwig Múzeum

Clark

Ádám tér

Széchenyi lánchíd

1

Országos Széchenyi Könyvtár

Magyar Nemzeti Galéria

Lánchíd u.

Groza Péter rakpart

Kriszina körút

Athila út

Apród u.

Budapesti Történeti Múzeum

VÁRKERT

TABÁN

Ybl Miklós tér

KEY

┅┅┅ Funicular

Numbers in the text correspond to numbers in the margin and on the Castle Hill (Várhegy) map.

A GOOD WALK

Castle Hill's cobblestone streets and numerous museums are best explored on foot: plan to spend about a day here. Most of the transportation options for getting to Castle Hill deposit you on Szent György tér or Dísz tér. It's impossible not to find Castle Hill, but it is possible to be confused about how to get on top of it. If you're already on the Buda side of the river, you can take the Castle bus—*Várbusz*—from the Moszkva tér metro station, northwest of Castle Hill. If you're starting out from Pest, you can take a taxi or Bus 16 from Erzsébet tér or, the most scenic alternative, cross the Széchenyi Lánchíd (Chain Bridge) on foot to Clark Ádám tér and ride the *Sikló* (funicular) up Castle Hill.

Begin your exploration by walking slightly farther south to visit the **Királyi Palota** ① at the southern end of the hill. Of the palace's wealth of museums, the Ludwig Múzeum, the Magyar Nemzeti Galéria, the Budapesti Történeti Múzeum, and Országos Széchenyi Könyvtár are all interesting. Stop to take a look at the **Statue of Prince Eugene of Savoy** ② outside the entrance to Wing C before moving on. From here, you can cover the rest of the area by walking north along its handful of cobbled streets.

From Dísz tér, you can visit the **Várszínház** ③ theater on Szinház utca, then walk up Tárnok utca, whose houses and usually open courtyards offer glimpses of how Hungarians have integrated contemporary life into Gothic, Renaissance, and baroque settings. Of particular interest are the houses at No. 16, now the Aranyhordó restaurant, and at No. 18, the 15th-century Arany Sas Patika (Golden Eagle Pharmacy Museum), with a naïf Madonna and child in an overhead niche. This tiny museum displays instruments, prescriptions, books, and other artifacts from 16th- and 17th-century pharmacies. Modern commerce is also integrated into Tárnok utca's historic homes; you'll encounter numerous folk souvenir shops and tiny boutiques lining the street. Tárnok utca funnels into **Szentháromság tér** ④ and the Trinity Column; this is also where you'll find the **Mátyás templom** ⑤ and, just behind it, the **Halászbástya** ⑥.

After exploring them, double back to Dísz tér and set out northward again on **Úri utca** ⑦, which runs parallel to Tárnok utca; this long street is lined with beautiful, genteel homes. The **Budavári Labirintus** ⑧, at No. 9, is worth a stop, as is the amusing little Telefónia Museum, at No. 49. At the end of Úri utca you'll reach **Kapisztrán tér** ⑨, where you'll find the **Hadtörténeti Múzeum** ⑩.

From here, you can walk south again on Országház utca (Parliament Street), the main thoroughfare of 18th-century Buda; it takes its name from the building at No. 28, which was the seat of Parliament from 1790 to 1807. You'll end up back at Szentháromság tér, with just two streets remaining to explore.

You can stroll up little Fortuna utca, named for the 18th-century Fortuna Inn, which now houses the **Magyar Kereskedelmi és Vendéglátóipari Múzeum** ⑪. At the end of Fortuna utca you'll reach **Bécsi kapu tér** ⑫, opening to Moszkva tér just below. Head back on Táncsics Mihály, where you will find both the **Középkori Zsidó Imaház** ⑬ and the **Zenetörténeti Múzeum** ⑭. Next door, at No. 9, is the baroque house (formerly the Royal Mint) where rebel writer Táncsics Mihály was imprisoned in the dungeons and freed by the people on the Day of Revolution, March 15, 1848. Continue down this street, and you'll find yourself in front of the Hilton hotel, back at Hess András tér, bordering Szentháromság tér.

Those whose feet haven't protested yet can finish off their tour of Castle Hill by strolling south back to Dísz tér on **Tóth Árpád sétány** ⑮, the romantic, tree-lined promenade along the Buda side of the hill.

TIMING

Castle Hill is small enough to cover in one day, but perusing its major museums and several tiny exhibits will require more time.

SIGHTS TO SEE

⑫ **Bécsi kapu tér** (Vienna Gate Square). Marking the northern entrance to Castle Hill, the stone gateway (rebuilt in 1936) called Vienna Gate opens toward Vienna—or, closer at hand, Moszkva tér a few short blocks below. The square named after it has some fine baroque and rococo houses but is dominated by the enormous neo-Romanesque (1913–17) headquarters of the **Országos Levéltár** (Hungarian National Archives), which resembles a cathedral-like shrine to paperwork. ⊠ *District I.*

⑧ **Budavári Labirintus** (Labyrinth of Buda Castle). Used as a wine cellar during the 16th and 17th centuries and then as an air-raid shelter during World War II, the labyrinth—entered at Úri utca 9 below an early 18th-century house—can be explored with a tour or, if you dare, on your own. There are some English-language brochures available. ⊠ *District I, Úri u. 9,* ☎ *1/375–6858.* 🎟 *800 Ft.* ☉ *Daily 9:30–7:30.*

⑩ **Hadtörténeti Múzeum** (Museum of Military History). Fittingly, this museum is lodged in a former barracks, on the northwestern corner of Kapisztrán tér. The exhibits, which include collections of uniforms and military regalia, trace the military history of Hungary from the original Magyar conquest in the 9th century through the period of Ottoman rule to the mid-20th century. You can arrange an English-language tour in advance for around 1,000 Ft. ⊠ *District I, Tóth Árpád sétány 40,* ☎ *1/356–9522,* 🌐 *www.militaria.hu.* 🎟 *270 Ft.* ☉ *Apr.–Sept., Tues.– Sun. 10–6; Oct.–Mar., Tues.–Sun. 10–4.*

★ ⑥ **Halászbástya** (Fishermen's Bastion). The wondrous porch overlooking the Danube and Pest is the neo-Romanesque Fishermen's Bastion, a merry cluster of white stone towers, arches, and columns above a modern bronze statue of St. Stephen, Hungary's first king. Medieval fishwives once peddled their wares here, but now you see souvenirs and crafts merchants and musicians. ⊠ *District I, East of Szentháromság tér.*

⑨ **Kapisztrán tér** (Capistrano Square). Castle Hill's northernmost square was named after St. John of Capistrano, an Italian friar who in 1456 recruited a crusading army to fight the Turks who were threatening Hungary. There's a statue of this honored Franciscan on the northwest corner; also here are the **Museum of Military History** and the remains of the 12th-century Gothic Mária Magdolna templom (Church of St. Mary Magdalene). Its *torony* (tower), completed in 1496, is the only part left standing; the rest of the church was destroyed by air raids during World War II.

★ ❶ **Királyi Palota** (Royal Palace). A palace was built on this spot in the 13th century for the kings of Hungary and then reconstructed under the supervision of King Matthias during the 15th century. That in turn was demolished during the Turkish siege of Budapest in 1686. The Hapsburg empress Maria Theresa directed the building of a new palace in the 1700s. It was damaged during an unsuccessful attack by revolutionaries in 1849, but the Hapsburgs set about building again, completing work in 1905. Then, near the end of the Soviets' seven-week siege in February 1945, the entire Castle Hill district of palaces, mansions, and churches was reduced to rubble. Decades passed before reconstruction and whatever restoration was possible were completed. Archaeologists were able to recover both the original defensive walls and royal chambers, due in part to still surviving plans and texts from the reigns of Holy Roman Emperor Sisigimund and King Matthias.

Freed from mounds of rubble, the foundation walls and medieval castle walls were completed, and the ramparts surrounding the medieval royal residence were re-created as close to their original shape and size as possible. If you want an idea of the Hungarian home-life of Franz Josef and Sissi, however, you'll have to visit the baroque Gódólló Palace. The Royal Palace today is used as a cultural center and museum complex.

The Royal Palace's baroque southern wing (Wing E) contains the **Budapesti Történeti Múzeum** (Budapest History Museum), displaying a fascinating permanent exhibit of modern Budapest history from Buda's liberation from the Turks in 1686 through the 1970s. Viewing the vintage 19th- and 20th-century photos and videos of the castle, the Széchenyi Lánchíd, and other Budapest monuments—and seeing them as the backdrop to the horrors of World War II and the 1956 Revolution—helps to put your later sightseeing in context; while you're browsing, peek out one of the windows overlooking the Danube and Pest and let it start seeping in.

Through historical documents, objects, and art, other permanent exhibits depict the medieval history of the Buda fortress and the capital as a whole. This is the best place to view remains of the medieval Royal Palace and other archaeological excavations. Some of the artifacts unearthed during excavations are in the vestibule in the basement; others are still among the remains of medieval structures. Down in the cellars are the original medieval vaults of the palace; portraits of King Matthias and his second wife, Beatrice of Aragon; and many late-14th-century statues that probably adorned the Renaissance palace. ⊠ *Királyi Palota (Wing E), District I, Szt. György tér 2*, ☎ *1/375–7533*, WEB *www.btm.hu.* 🎫 *400 Ft.* ☉ *Mar.–mid-May and mid-Sept.–Oct., Wed.–Mon. 10–6; mid-May–mid-Sept., daily 10–6; Nov.–Feb., Wed.–Mon. 10–4.*

The collection at the **Ludwig Múzeum** includes more than 200 pieces of Hungarian and contemporary international art, including works by Picasso and Lichtenstein, and occupies the castle's northern wing. ⊠ *Királyi Palota (Wing A), District I, Dísz tér 17*, ☎ *1/375–7533*, WEB *www.ludwigmuseum.hu.* 🎫 *300 Ft.; free Tues.* ☉ *Tues.–Sun. 10–6.*

The **Magyar Nemzeti Galéria** (Hungarian National Gallery), which is made up of the immense center block of the Royal Palace (Wings B, C, and D), exhibits Hungarian fine art, from medieval ecclesiastical paintings and statues through the Gothic, Renaissance, and baroque art, to a rich collection of 19th- and 20th-century works. Especially notable are the works of the romantic painter Mihály Munkácsy, the impressionist Pál Szinyei Merse, and the surrealist Mihály Tivadar Kosztka Csontváry, whom Picasso much admired. There is also a large collection of modern Hungarian sculpture. Labels and commentary for both permanent and temporary exhibits are in English. If you contact the museum in advance, you can book a tour for up to five people with an English-speaking guide. ⊠ *Királyi Palota (entrance in Wing C), District I, Dísz tér 17*, ☎ *1/375–7533*, WEB *www.mng.hu.* 🎫 *Gallery 600 Ft., tour 1,300 Ft.* ☉ *Mid-Mar.–Oct., Tues.–Sun. 10–6; Nov.–mid-Jan., Tues.–Sun. 10–4; mid-Jan.–mid-Mar., Tues.–Fri. 10–4, weekends 10–6.*

The western wing (F) of the Royal Palace is the **Országos Széchenyi Könyvtár** (Széchenyi National Library), which houses more than 2 million volumes. Its archives include well-preserved medieval codices, manuscripts, and historic correspondence. This is not a lending library, but the reading rooms are open to the public (though you must show a passport), and even the most valuable materials can be viewed on microfilm. Small, temporary exhibits on rare books and documents are usually on display; the hours and admission fees for these are quite variable. Note that the entire library closes for one month every summer, usually in July or August. ⊠ *Királyi Palota (Wing F), District I, Dísz tér 17,* ☎ *1/224–3745 to arrange tour with English-speaking guide,* WEB *www.oszk.hu.* 🎫 *Tours 300 Ft.; exhibits vary.* ☉ *Reading rooms Mon. 1–9, Tues.–Sat. 9–9; exhibits Mon. 1–6, Tues.–Sat. 10–6.*

⓭ **Középkori Zsidó Imaház** (Medieval Synagogue). The excavated one-room Medieval Synagogue is now used as a museum. On display are objects relating to the Jewish community, including religious inscriptions, frescoes, and tombstones dating to the 15th century. ⊠ *District I, Táncsics Mihály u. 26,* ☎ *1/375–7533 Ext. 243.* 🎫 *120 Ft.* ☉ *May–Oct., Tues.–Sun. 10–6.*

⓫ **Magyar Kereskedelmi és Vendéglátóipari Múzeum** (Hungarian Museum of Commerce and Catering). The 18th-century Fortuna Inn now serves visitors in a different way—as the Catering Museum. Displays in a permanent exhibit show the city as a tourist destination from 1870 to the 1930s; you can see, for example, what a room at the Gellért Hotel, still operating today, would have looked like in 1918. The Commerce Museum, just across the courtyard, chronicles the history of Hungarian commerce from the late 19th century to 1947, when the new, Communist regime "liberated" the economy into socialism. The four-room exhibit includes everything from an antique chocolate-and-caramel vending machine to early shoe-polish advertisements. You can rent an English-language recorded tour for 300 Ft. ⊠ *District I, Fortuna u. 4,* ☎ *1/212–1245.* 🎫 *200 Ft.* ☉ *Wed.–Fri. 10–5, weekends 10–6.*

★ ❺ **Mátyás templom** (Matthias Church). The ornate white steeple of the Matthias Church is the highest point on Castle Hill. It was added in the 15th century, above a 13th-century Gothic chapel. Officially the Buda Church of Our Lady, it has been known as the Matthias Church since the 15th century, in remembrance of the so-called "just king," who greatly added to and embellished it during his reign. Many of these changes were lost when the Turks converted it into a Mosque. The intricate white stonework, mosaic roof decorations, and some of its geometric patterned columns seem to suggest Byzantine, yet it was substantially rebuilt again in the neo-baroque style, 87 years after the Turkish defeat in 1686. One fortunate survivor of all the changes was perhaps the finest example of Gothic stone carving in Hungary, the Assumption of the Blessed Virgin Mary, visible above the door on the side of the church that faces the Danube.

The **Szentháromság Kápolna** (Trinity Chapel) holds an *encolpion,* an enameled casket containing a miniature copy of the Gospel to be worn on the chest; it belonged to the 12th-century king Béla III and his wife, Anne of Chatillon. Their burial crowns and a cross, scepter, and rings found in their excavated graves are also displayed here. The church's **treasury** contains Renaissance and baroque chalices, monstrances, and vestments. High Mass is celebrated every Sunday at 10 AM, sometimes with full orchestra and choir—and often with major soloists; get here early if you want a seat. During the summer there are usually organ recitals on Friday at 8 PM. Tourists are asked to remain at the back of the church during weddings and services (it's least intrusive to come after 9 AM weekdays and between 1 and 5 PM Sunday and holidays). ⊠ *District I, Szentháromság tér 2,* ☏ *1/355–5657.* ☾ *Church daily 9–5; treasury Mon.–Sat. 9:30–5:30, Sun. 1–5:30.* ⊡ *300 Ft., treasury 300 Ft.*

②   Statue of Prince Eugene of Savoy. In front of the Royal Palace, facing the Danube by the entrance to Wing C, stands an equestrian statue of Prince Eugene of Savoy, a commander of the army that liberated Hungary from the Turks at the end of the 17th century. From here there is a superb view across the river to Pest. ⊠ *Királyi Palota (by Wing C entrance), District I, Dísz tér 17.*

④   Szentháromság tér (Holy Trinity Square). This square is named for its baroque Trinity Column, erected in 1712–13 as a gesture of thanksgiving by survivors of a plague. The column stands in front of the famous Gothic Matthias Church, its large pedestal a perfect seat from which to watch the wedding spectacles that take over the church on spring and summer weekends: from morning till night, frilly engaged pairs flow in one after the other and, after a brief transformation inside, back out onto the square. ⊠ *District I.*

★ **⑮   Tóth Árpád sétány** (Árpád Tóth Promenade). This romantic, tree-lined promenade along the Buda side of the hill is often mistakenly overlooked by sightseers. Beginning at the Museum of Military History, the promenade takes you "behind the scenes" along the back sides of the matte-pastel baroque houses that face Úri utca, with their regal arched windows and wrought-iron gates. On a late spring afternoon, the fragrance of the cherry trees and the sweeping view of the quiet Buda neighborhoods below may be enough to revive even the most weary. ⊠ *District I, from Kapisztrán tér to Szent György u.*

⑦   Úri utca (Úri Street). Running parallel to Tárnok utca, Úri utca has been less commercialized by boutiques and other shops. The longest and oldest street in the castle district, it is lined with many stately houses, all worth special attention for their delicately carved details. Both gateways of the baroque palace at Nos. 48–50 are articulated by Gothic niches. The **Telefónia Múzeum** (Telephone Museum) is an endearing little museum entered through a central courtyard shared with the local district police station. Although vintage telephone systems are still in use all over the country, both the oldest and most recent products of telecommunication—from the 1882 wooden box with hose attachment to the latest digital marvels—can be observed and tested here. ⊠ *District I, Úri u. 49,* ☏ *1/201–8188.* ⊡ *100 Ft.* ☾ *Tues.–Sun. 10–4.*

NEED A   For a light snack, pastry, and coffee, **Café Miro** (⊠ District I, Úri u. 30,
BREAK?   ☏ 1/375–5458) is a fresh, hip alternative to the old-world Budapest
           cafés.

---

③   Várszínház (Castle Theater). This former Franciscan church was transformed into a more secular royal venue in 1787 under the supervision of courtier Farkas Kempelen. The first theatrical performance in Hungarian was held here in 1790. Heavily damaged during World War II, the theater was rebuilt and reopened in 1978. While the building retains its original late-baroque-style facade, the interior was renovated with marble and concrete. It is now used as the studio theater of the National Theater and occasionally for classical recitals, and there is usually a historical exhibition in its foyer—usually theater-related, such as a display of costumes. ⊠ *District I, Színház u. 1–3,* ☏ *1/375–8649.*

⑭ Zenetörténeti Múzeum (Museum of Music History). This handsome gray-and-pearl-stone 18th-century palace is where Beethoven allegedly stayed in 1800 when he came to Buda to conduct his works. Now a museum, it displays rare manuscripts and old instruments downstairs in its permanent collection and temporary exhibits upstairs in a small, sunlit hall. The museum also often hosts intimate classical recitals. ⊠ *District I, Táncsics Mihály u. 7,* ☎ *1/214–6770 Ext. 250,* ⓦⓔⓑ *www.zti.hu/museum.htm.* 🎫 *400 Ft.; free Sun.* ⊘ *Feb.–Nov., Tues.–Sun. 10–6.*

Tabán and Gellért-hegy (Tabán and Gellért Hill)

Spreading below Castle Hill is the old quarter called Tabán (from the Turkish word for "armory"). A onetime suburb of Buda, it was known at the end of the 17th century as Little Serbia (*Rác*) because so many Serbian refugees settled here after fleeing from the Turks. It later became a district of vineyards and small taverns. Though most of the small houses characteristic of this district have been demolished—mainly in the interest of easing traffic—a few traditional buildings remain.

Gellért-hegy (Gellért Hill), 761 ft high, is the most beautiful natural formation on the Buda bank. It takes its name from St. Gellért (Gerard) of Csanad, a Venetian bishop who came to Hungary in the 11th century and, legend has it, was rolled off the top of the hill in a cart by pagans. The walk up can be tough, but take solace from the cluster of hot springs at its foot; these soothe and cure bathers at the Rác, Rudas, and Gellért baths.

Numbers in the text correspond to numbers in the margin and on the Exploring Budapest map.

A GOOD WALK

From the **Semmelweis Orvostörténeti Múzeum** ⑯, walk around the corner to Szarvas tér, where you will find the **Szarvas-ház** ⑰ at No. 1, and a few yards toward the river to the **Tabán plébánia-templom** ⑱. Walking south on Attila út and crossing to the other side of Hegyalja út will take you to the foot of Gellért Hill. You are now close to two Turkish baths, the **Rác Fürdő** (Rác Baths) ⑲ and, on the other side of the **Erzsébet híd** ⑳, the **Rudas Fürdő** (Rudas Baths) ㉑. You might need to take a soak in one or the other after climbing the stairs to the top of the hill, a 30 minute walk. Here, overlooking Budapest, is the **Citadella** ㉒, with its panoramic views of Budapest and the nearby Liberation Monument. After exploring the area, you can descend the hill and treat yourself to a soak or a swim at one of the baths. Either return the way you came, or go down the southeastern side of the hill to the **Gellért Szálloda és Thermál Fürdő** ㉓ at its southeastern foot. If you don't feel like walking to the Gellért baths, you can also take Bus 27 down the back of the hill to Móricz Zsigmond körtér and walk back toward the Gellért on busy Bartók Béla út, or take Tram 47, 49, 18, or 19 a couple of stops to Szent Gellért tér.

TIMING

The Citadella and Szabadság szobor are lit in golden lights every night, but the entire Gellért-hegy is at its scenic best every year on August 20, when it forms the backdrop to the spectacular St. Stephen's Day fireworks display.

SIGHTS TO SEE

★ ㉒ **Citadella.** The sweeping views of Budapest from this fortress atop the hill were once valued by the Austrian army, which used it as a lookout after the 1848–49 War of Independence. Some 60 cannons were housed in the citadel, though never used on the city's resentful populace. In the 1960s the Citadel was converted into a tourist site. It has cafés, a beer garden, wine cellars, and a hostel. In its inner wall is a

256

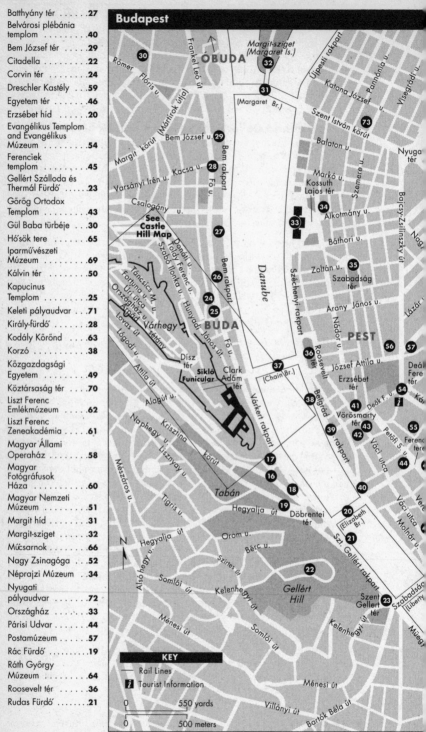

Budapest

KEY

— Rail Lines

ℹ️ Tourist Information

0   550 yards

0   500 meters

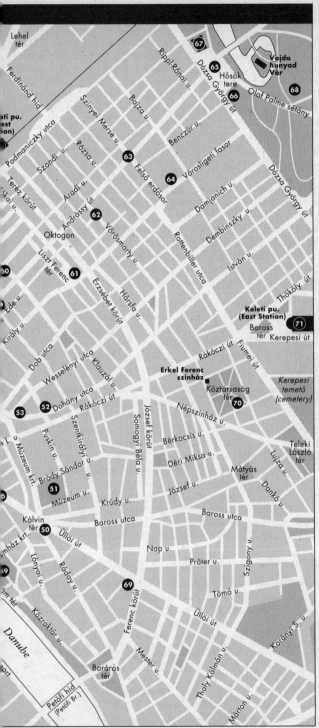

small graphic exhibition (with some relics) of Budapest's 2,000-year history.

Visible from many parts of the city, the 130-ft-high **Szabadság szobor** (Liberation Monument), which sits just below the southern edge of the Citadella, was originally planned as a memorial to a son of Hungary's then-ruler, Miklós Horthy, whose warplane had crashed in the Ukraine in 1942. However, by the time of its completion in 1947 (three years after Horthy was ousted), it had become a memorial to the Russian soldiers who fell in the 1944–45 siege of Budapest; and hence for decades it was associated chiefly with this. From afar it looks light, airy, and even liberating. A sturdy young girl, her hair and robe swirling in the wind, holds a palm branch high above her head. Until recently, she was further embellished with sculptures of giants slaying dragons, Red Army soldiers, and peasants rejoicing at the freedom that Soviet liberation promised (but failed) to bring to Hungary. Since 1992, her mood has lightened: in the Budapest city government's systematic purging of Communist symbols, the Red Combat infantrymen who had flanked the Liberation statue for decades were hacked off and carted away. A few are now on display among the other evicted statues in Szobor Park in the city's 22nd district. ⊠ *District XI, Citadella sétány,* ☎ *no phone.* ⌑ *Free.* ⊙ *Fortress daily.*

㉒ Erzsébet híd (Elizabeth Bridge). This bridge was named for Empress Elizabeth (1837–1898), called Sissi, of whom the Hungarians were particularly fond. The beautiful but unhappy wife of Franz Joseph, she was stabbed to death in 1898 by an anarchist while boarding a boat on Lake Geneva. The bridge was built between 1897 and 1903; at the time, it was the longest single-span suspension bridge in Europe.

★ **㉓ Gellért Szálloda és Thermál Fürdő** (Gellért Hotel and Thermal Baths). At the foot of Gellért Hill are these beautiful Art Nouveau establishments. The Danubius Hotel Gellért is the oldest spa hotel in Hungary, with hot springs that have supplied curative baths for nearly 2,000 years. It is the most popular among tourists, as you don't need reservations, and there's a wealth of treatments—including chamomile steam baths, salt-vapor inhalations, and hot mud packs. Many of these treatments require a doctor's prescription; they will accept prescriptions from foreign doctors. Because most staff speak English, it's quite easy to communicate. Men and women have separate steam and sauna rooms; both the indoor pool and the outdoor wave pool are coed. ⊠ *District XI, Gellért tér 1,* ☎ *1/466–5747 baths.* ⌑ *Indoor bath, steam rooms, and swimming pool 1,800 Ft. per day, 2,200 Ft. with cabin; treatments extra.* ⊙ *Baths weekdays 6 AM–6 PM, weekends 6 AM–4 PM.*

㉑ Rác Fürdő (Rác Baths). The Rá Baths take their name from the Serbians who settled in this area after fleeing the Turks, and it is said that King Matthias II used to visit these baths via secret tunnels from his palace on Castle Hill. Such antiquity will not be obvious from without: the canary-yellow building was rebuilt by Miklós Ybl in the mid-19th century. The Ottoman-era octagonal pool and cupola were retained during reconstruction. The waters are high in sodium and thought to be medicinal; you can also get a massage. Women can bathe on Monday, Wednesday, and Friday; men on Tuesday, Thursday, and Saturday. These baths are particularly popular with the gay community. ⊠ *District I, Hadnagy u. 8–10,* ☎ *1/356–1322.* ⌑ *700 Ft.* ⊙ *Mon.–Sat. 6:30–6.*

㉑ Rudas Fürdő (Rudas Baths). This bath is on the riverbank, the original Turkish pool making its interior possibly the most dramatically beautiful of Budapest's baths. A high, domed roof admits pinpricks of bluish-green light into the dark, circular stone hall with its austere columns and arches. Fed by eight springs with a year-round temperature of 44°C (111°F), the Rudas's highly fluoridated waters have been known for 1,000 years. The facility is open to men only and does not have a large gay following; a less interesting outer swimming pool is open to both sexes. Massages are available. ⊠ *District I, Döbrentei tér 9,* ☎ *1/201–1577.* ⌨ *900 Ft.* ☉ *Weekdays 6 AM–6 PM, weekends 6 AM–noon.*

🔟 **Semmelweis Orvostörténeti Múzeum** (Semmelweis Museum of Medical History). This splendid baroque house was the birthplace of Ignác Semmelweis (1818–65), the Hungarian physician who proved the contagiousness of puerperal (childbed) fever. It's now a museum that traces the history of healing. Semmelweis's grave is in the garden. ⊠ *District I, Apród u. 1–3,* ☎ *1/375–3533.* ⌨ *150 Ft.* ☉ *Tues.–Sun. 10:30–5:30.*

🔟 **Szarvas-ház** (Stag House). This Louis XVI–style building is named for the former Szarvas Café or, more accurately, for its extant trade sign, with an emblem of a stag not quite at bay, which can be seen above the arched entryway. The structure houses the Aranyszarvas restaurant, which preserves some of the mood of the old Tabán. ⊠ *District I, Szarvas tér 1.*

OFF THE
BEATEN PATH

SZOBOR PARK (STATUE PARK) – After the collapse of the Iron Curtain, Hungarians were understandably keen to rid Budapest of the symbols of Soviet domination. The Communist statues and memorials that once dotted Budapest's streets and squares have been moved to this open-air "Disneyland of Communism." As well as the huge figures of Lenin and Marx, there are statues of the Hungarian worker shaking hands with his Soviet army comrade, and Hungarian puppet prime minister János Kádár. Sometimes tacky but amusing souvenirs are for sale, and songs from the Hungarian and Russian workers' movements play on a tinny speaker system. To get there, take a red-numbered bus 7-173 to Etele tér, then the yellow Volán bus from platform 2. ⊠ *District XXII, Balatoni út, corner of Szabadkai út,* ☎ *1/427–7500,* WEB *www.szobopark.hu.* ⌨ *300 Ft.* ☉ *Daily 10–dusk.*

🔟 **Tabán plébánia-templom** (Tabán Parish Church). In 1736, this church was built on the site of a Turkish mosque and subsequently renovated and reconstructed several times. Its present form—mustard-colored stone with a rotund, green clock tower—could be described as restrained baroque. ⊠ *District I, Attila u. 1.*

North Buda and Margaret Island

Most of these sights are along Fő utca (Main Street), a long, straight thoroughfare that starts at the Chain Bridge and runs parallel to the Danube. It is lined on both sides with multistory late-18th-century houses—many darkened by soot and showing their age more than those you see in sparklingly restored Castle Hill. This northbound exploration can be done with the help of Bus 86, which covers the waterfront, or on foot, although this is a fairly large area.

Numbers in the text correspond to numbers in the margin and on the Exploring Budapest map.

A GOOD WALK

The walk begins along Fő utca. Stop first to take in the arresting beauty of the **Corvin tér** ㉔; just a block down Fő utca is the **Kapucinus Templom** ㉕, which was originally a Turkish mosque. Continue your walk up Fő utca, stopping at two other scenic squares, **Szilágyi Dezső**

tér ㉖ and **Batthyány tér** ㉗, with its head-on view of Parliament across the Danube. From there, continue north on Fő utca, passing (or stopping to bathe at) the famous Turkish **Király-fürdő** ㉘. From **Bem József tér** ㉙, go one block north, turn left (away from the river) and walk up Fekete Sas utca, crossing busy Margit körút and turning right, one block past, up Mecset utca. This will take you up the hill to **Gül Baba türbéje** ㉚. From here, walk back to the river and cross the **Margit híd** ㉛ to explore **Margit-sziget** ㉜ and island park in the middle of the Dunda.

TIMING

The tour can fit easily into a few hours, including a good 1½-hour soak at the baths, unless you want to do a thorough exploration of Margaret Island; expect the walk from Bem József tér up the hill to Gül Baba türbéje to take about 25 minutes. Fő utca and Bem József tér can get congested during rush hours (from around 7:30 AM to 8:30 AM and 4:30 PM to 6 PM). A leisurely stroll from one end of Margaret Island to the other takes about 40 minutes, but it's nice to spend some extra time wandering. Remember that museums are closed Monday and that the Király Baths are open to men and women on different days of the week.

SIGHTS TO SEE

㉗ **Batthyány tér.** There are tremendous views of Parliament from this square named after Count Lajos Batthyány, the prime minister shot dead in the 1848 revolution. The M2 subway, the HÉV electric railway from Szentendre, and various suburban and local buses converge on the square, and there's a covered market—as there has been since 1902. At No. 7 Batthyány tér is the beautiful, baroque twin-tower **Szent Anna-templom** (Church of St. Anne), dating from 1740–1762, its oval cupola adorned with frescoes and statuary. ⊠ *District I, Fő u. at Batthyány u.*

NEED A
BREAK?

The **Angelika** café (⊠ District I, Batthyány tér 7, ☎ 1/212–3784), in the rectory of the Church of St. Anne, serves swirled meringues, chestnut-filled layer cakes, and delicious pastries, as well as a selection of salads and grilled meat dishes. You can sit inside on small velvet chairs at marble-top tables or at one of the umbrella-shaded tables outdoors. It's open daily 9 AM–midnight.

㉙ **Bem József tér.** This square near the river is not particularly picturesque and can get heavy with traffic, but it houses the statue of its important namesake, Polish general József Bem, who offered his services to the 1848 revolutionaries in Vienna and then Hungary. Reorganizing the rebel forces in Transylvania, he was the war's most successful general. It was at this statue on October 23, 1956, that a great student demonstration in sympathy with the Poles' striving for liberal reforms exploded into the brave and tragic Hungarian uprising suppressed by the Red Army. ⊠ *District II, Fő u. at Bem József u.*

㉔ **Corvin tér.** This small, shady square on Fő utca is the site of the turn-of-the-20th-century Folk Art Association administration building and the Budai Vigadó concert hall, at No. 8. ⊠ *District I, Fő u. at Ponty u.*

㉚ **Gül Baba türbéje** (Tomb of Gül Baba). Gül Baba, a 16th-century dervish and poet whose name means "father of roses" in Turkish, was buried in a tomb built of carved stone blocks with four oval windows. He fought in several wars waged by the Turks and fell during the siege of Buda in 1541. The tomb remains a place of pilgrimage; it is considered Europe's northernmost Muslim shrine and marks the spot where he was slain. Set at an elevation on Rózsadomb (Rose Hill), the tomb is near a good lookout for city views. ⊠ *District II, Mecset u. 14.* ☜ *300 Ft.* ☽ *May–Sept., Tues.–Sun. 10–6; Oct., Tues.–Sun. 10–4.*

OFF THE
BEATEN PATH

GYERMEK VASÚT – The 12-km (7-mi) Children's Railway—so called because it's operated primarily by children—runs from Széchenyi-hegy to Hűvösvölgy. The sweeping views make the trip well worthwhile for children and adults alike. Departures are from Széchenyi-hegy. To get to Széchenyi-hegy, take Tram 56 from Moszkva tér, and change to the cog railway (public transport tickets valid) at the Fogaskereku Vasút stop. Take the cog railway uphill to the last stop and then walk a few hundred yards down a short, partly forested road to the left, in the direction most others will be going. The railway terminates at Hűvösvölgy, where you can catch Tram 56 back to Moszkva tér. ⊠ *District XII, Szillágyi Erzsébet fasor and Pasaréti út,* WEB *www.gyermekvasut.com.* ▭ *One-way 150 Ft.* ⊙ *Late Apr.–Oct., daily 8:45–5; Nov.–mid-Mar., Tues.–Fri. 10–4, weekends 10–5 (sometimes closed Tues.); mid-Mar.–late Apr., Tues.–Fri. 9:30–5, weekends 10–5.*

JÁNOSHEGY – A *libegő* (chairlift) will take you to János Hill—at 1,729 ft, the highest point in Budapest—where you can climb a lookout tower for the best view of the city. To get there, take Bus 158 from Moszkva tér to the last stop, Zugligeti út. ⊠ *Chairlift: District XII, Zugligeti út 97,* ☎ *1/394–3764.* ▭ *One-way 400 Ft., round-trip 500 Ft.* ⊙ *Mid-May–Aug., daily 9–6; Sept.–mid-May (depending on weather), daily 9:30–4; closed every other Mon.*

㉕ **Kapucinus templom** (Capuchin Church). This church was converted from a Turkish mosque at the end of the 17th century. Damaged during the revolution in 1849, it acquired its current romantic-style exterior when it was rebuilt a few years later. ⊠ *District II, Fő u. 32.*

㉘ **Király-fürdő** (King Baths). In 1565 Sokoli Mustapha, the Turkish pasha of Buda, ordered the construction of Turkish baths within the old city walls, to ensure that the Turks could still bathe in the event of siege. A stone cupola, crowned by a golden moon and crescent, arches over the steamy, dark pools indoors. It is open to men on Monday, Wednesday, and Friday; to women on Tuesday, Thursday, and Saturday. These baths are very popular with the gay community. ⊠ *District II, Fő u. 84,* ☎ *1/202–3688.* ▭ *500 Ft.* ⊙ *Weekdays 6:30–6, Sat. 6:30–noon.*

㉛ **Margit híd** (Margaret Bridge). At the southern end of the island, the Margaret Bridge is the closer of the two entrances for those coming from downtown Buda or Pest. Just north of the Chain Bridge, the bridge walkway provides gorgeous mid-river views of Castle Hill and Parliament. The original bridge was built during the 1840s by French engineer Ernest Gouin in collaboration with Gustave Eiffel. Toward the end of 1944, the bridge was blown up by the retreating Nazis while it was still crowded with rush-hour traffic. It was rebuilt in the same unusual shape—forming an obtuse angle in midstream, with a short leg leading down to the island.

㉜ **Margit-sziget** (Margaret Island). More than 2½ km (1½ mi) long and covering nearly 200 acres, this island park is ideal for strolling, jogging, sunbathing, or just loafing. In good weather, it draws a multitudinous cross-section of the city's population out to its gardens and sporting facilities. The outdoor pool complex of the Palatinus Baths (toward the Buda side), built in 1921, can attract tens of thousands of people on a summer day. Nearby are a tennis stadium, a youth athletic center, boathouses, sports grounds, and, most impressive of all, the Nemzeti Sportuszoda (National Sports Swimming Pool), designed by the architect Alfred Hajós (while still in his teens, Hajós won two gold medals in swimming at the first modern Olympic Games, held in Athens in 1896). In addition, walkers, joggers, bicyclists, and rollerbladers do laps around the island's perimeter and up and down the main road, closed to traffic except for Bus 26 (and a few official vehicles), which travels up and down the island and across the Margaret Bridge to and from Pest.

The island's natural curative hot springs have given rise to the Danubius Grand and Thermal hotels on the northern end of the island and are piped into two spa hotels on the mainland, the Aquincum on the Buda bank and the Hélia on the Pest side.

To experience Margaret Island's role in Budapest life fully, go on a Saturday or Sunday afternoon to join and/or watch people whiling away the day. Sunday is a particularly good choice for strategic sightseers, who can utilize the rest of the week to cover those city sights and areas that are closed on Sunday. On weekdays, you'll share the island only with joggers and children playing hooky from school.

The island was first mentioned almost 2,000 years ago as the summer residence of the commander of the Roman garrison at nearby Aquincum. Later known as Rabbit Island (Insula Leporum), it was a royal hunting ground during the Árpád dynasty. King Imre, who reigned from 1196 to 1204, held court here, and several convents and monasteries were built here during the Middle Ages. (During a walk round the island, you'll see the ruins of a few of these buildings.) It takes its current name from St. Margaret, the pious daughter of King Béla IV, who at the ripe old age of 10 retired to a Dominican nunnery here.

Through the center of the island runs the **Művész sétány** (Artists' Promenade), lined with busts of Hungarian visual artists, writers, and musicians. Shaded by giant plane trees, it's a perfect place to stroll. The promenade passes close to the **rose garden** (in the center of the island), a large grassy lawn surrounded by blooming flower beds planted with hundreds of kinds of flowers. It's a great spot to picnic or to watch a game of soccer or Ultimate Frisbee, both of which are regularly played here on weekend afternoons. Just east of the rose garden is a small, free would-be petting zoo, the **Margit-sziget Vadaspark,** if the animals were allowed to be petted. A fenced-in compound houses a menagerie of goats, rabbits, donkeys, assorted fowl and ducks, and gargantuan peacocks that sit heavily on straining tree branches.

At the northern end of the island is a copy of the water-powered **Marosvásárhelyi zenélő kút** (Marosvásárhely Musical Fountain), which plays songs and chimes. The original was designed more than 150 years ago by a Transylvanian named Péter Bodor. It stands near a serene, artificial rock garden with Japanese dwarf trees and lily ponds. The stream coursing through it never freezes, for it comes from a natural hot spring causing it instead to give off thick steam in winter that enshrouds the garden in a mystical cloud.

㉖ Szilágyi Dezső tér. This is another of the charming little squares punctuating Fő utca; here you'll find the house where composer Béla Bartók lived, at No. 4. ⊠ *District I, Fő u. at Székely u.*

Downtown Pest and the Kis Körút (Little Ring Road)

Budapest's urban heart is full of bona fide sights plus innumerable tiny streets and grand avenues where you can wander for hours admiring the city's stately old buildings—some freshly sparkling after their first painting in decades, others silently but still gracefully crumbling.

Dominated by the Parliament building, the district surrounding Kossuth tér is the legislative, diplomatic, and administrative nexus of Budapest; most of the ministries are here, as are the National Bank and Courts of Justice. Downriver, the romantic Danube promenade, the Duna korzó, extends along the stretch of riverfront across from Castle Hill. With Vörösmarty tér and pedestrian shopping street Váci utca just inland, this area forms Pest's tourist core. Going south, the korzó ends at Március 15 tér. One block in from the river, Ferenciek tere marks the beginning of the university area, spreading south of Kossuth Lajos utca. Here, the streets are narrower and the sounds of your footsteps echo off the elegantly aging stone buildings.

Pest is laid out in broad circular *körúts* ("ring roads" or boulevards). Vámház körút is the first sector of the 2½-km (1½-mi) Kis körút (Little Ring Road), which traces the route of the Old Town wall from Szabadság híd (Liberty Bridge) to Deák tér. Construction of the inner körút began in 1872 and was completed in 1880. Changing names as it curves, after Kálvin tér it becomes Múzeum körút (passing by the National Museum) and then Károly körút for its final stretch ending at Deák tér. Deák tér, the only place where all three subway lines converge, could be called the dead-center of downtown. East of Károly körút are the weathered streets of Budapest's former ghetto.

A GOOD WALK

After starting at Kossuth tér to see the **Országház** ㉝ and the **Néprajzi Múzeum** ㉞, it's worth walking a few blocks southeast to take in stately **Szabadság tér** ㉟ before heading back to the Danube and south to **Roosevelt tér** ㊱, which is at the foot of the **Széchenyi Lánchíd** ㊲. As this tour involves quite a bit of walking, you may want to take Tram 2 from Kossuth tér a few stops downriver to Roosevelt tér to save your energy. While time and/or energy may not allow it just now, at some point during your visit, a walk across the Chain Bridge is a must.

From Roosevelt tér go south, across the street, and join the **Korzó** ㊳ along the river, strolling past the **Vigadó** ㊴ at Vigadó tér, all the way to the **Belvárosi plébánia templom** ㊵ at Március 15 tér, just under the Elizabeth Bridge. Double back up the korzó to Vigadó tér and walk in from the river on Vigadó utca to **Vörösmarty tér** ㊶. Follow the crowds down pedestrian-only **Váci utca** ㊷, and when you reach Régiposta utca, take a detour to the right to see the **Görög Ortodox templom** ㊸. Return to Váci utca and continue south; at Ferenciek tere, look for the grand **Párisi Udvar** ㊹ arcade. Across busy Kossuth Lajos utca, you will find the **Ferenciek templom** ㊺. From here, stroll Petőfi Sándor utca, passing the Greek Orthodox temple, and **Egyetem tér** ㊻. Take a right on Szerb utca until you get to Veres Pálné utca, where you will find a 17th-century **Szerb Ortodox templom** ㊼. Continuing down Szerb utca, you'll find yourself at the southern end of Váci utca, facing **Vásárcsarnok** ㊽, the huge market hall. Across Vámház körút is the campus of the **Közgazdagsági Egytem** ㊾, the University of Economics, which was called Karl Marx University in the Communist days.

From here you can either walk or take Tram 47 or 49 to **Kálvin tér** ㊿. Just north of Kálvin tér on Múzeum körút is the **Magyar Nemzeti Múzeum** (51). The **Nagy Zsinagóga** (52) is about ¾ km (⅓ mi) farther north along the Kis körút (Small Ring Road)—a longish walk or one short stop by tram; around the corner from the synagogue is the **Zsidó Múzeum** (53). From here, more walking along the körút, or a tram ride to the last stop, brings you to Pest's main hub, Deák tér, where you'll find the **Evangelikus templom** (54). From here it's a short walk to the **Városház** (55), Budapest's old city hall building. The **Szent István Bazilika** (56) is an extra but rewarding 500-yard walk north on Bajcsy-Zsilinszky út.

TIMING

This is a particularly rich part of the city; the suggested walk will take the better part of a day, including time to visit the museums, stroll on the Korzó, and browse on Váci utca—not to mention time for lunch. Keep in mind that the museums are closed on Monday.

SIGHTS TO SEE

40 Belvárosi plébánia templom (Inner City Parish Church). Dating to the 12th century, this is the oldest ecclesiastical building in Pest. It's actually built on something even older—the remains of the Contra Aquincum, a 3rd-century Roman fortress and tower, parts of which are visible next to the church. There is hardly any architectural style that cannot be found in some part or another, starting with a single Romanesque arch in its south tower. The single nave still has its original Gothic chancel and some 15th-century Gothic frescoes. Two side chapels contain beautifully carved Renaissance altarpieces and tabernacles of red marble from the early 16th century. During Budapest's years of Turkish occupation, the church served as a mosque—a *mihrab*, a Muslim prayer niche, is a reminder of this. During the 18th century, the church was given two baroque towers and its present facade. In 1808 it was enriched with a rococo pulpit, and still later a superb winged triptych was added to the main altar. From 1867 to 1875, Franz Liszt lived only a few steps away from the church, in a town house where he held regular "musical Sundays" at which Richard and Cosima Wagner were frequent guests and participants. Liszt's own musical Sunday mornings often began in this church. An admirer of its acoustics and organ, he conducted many masses here, including the first Budapest performance of his *Missa Choralis*, in 1872. ⊠ *District V, Március 15 tér 2,* ☎ *1/318–3108.*

46 Egyetem tér (University Square). Budapest's University of Law sits here in the heart of the city's university neighborhood. On one corner is the cool gray-and-green marble **Egyetemi Templom** (University Church), one of Hungary's most beautiful baroque buildings. Built between 1725 and 1742, it has an especially splendid pulpit. ⊠ *District V.*

NEED A BREAK?	Though billed as a café, **Centrál** (⊠ District V, Károlyi Mihály u. 9, ☎ 1/266–4572) is actually more a living museum. It enjoyed fame as an illustrious literary café during Budapest's late-19th- and early 20th-century golden age and, after years of neglect, was finally restored to its former glory a few years ago. Centrál's menu includes, with each main dish, a recommended wine by the glass—as well as a good selection of vegetarian dishes and desserts. Quite apart from anything else, it has some of the most spotless toilets in all of Budapest.

54 Evangélikus Templom and Evangélikus Múzeum (Lutheran Church and Lutheran Museum). The neoclassical Lutheran Church sits in the center of it all on busy Deák tér. Classical concerts are regularly held here. The church's interior designer, János Krausz, flouted then-traditional church architecture by placing a single large interior beneath the huge vaulted roof structure. The adjoining school is now the Lutheran Museum, which traces the role of Protestantism in Hungarian history and contains Martin Luther's original will. ⊠ *District V, Deák Ferenc tér 4,* ☎ *1/317–4173.* 🎫 *Museum 300 Ft. (includes tour of church).* ☉ *Museum Mar.–Dec., Tues.–Sun. 10–6; Jan.–Feb., 10–5. Church only in conjunction with museum visit and during services (Sun. at 9, 11, and 6).*

45 Ferenciek templom (Franciscan Church). This pale yellow church was built in 1743. On the wall facing Kossuth Lajos utca is a bronze relief showing a scene from the devastating flood of 1838; the detail is so vivid that it almost makes you seasick. A faded arrow below the relief indicates the high-water mark of almost 4 ft. Next to it is the Nereids

Fountain, a popular meeting place for students from the nearby Eötvös Loránd University. ✉ *District V, Felszabadulás tér.*

㊸ **Görög Ortodox templom** (Greek Orthodox Church). Built at the end of the 18th century in late-baroque style, the Greek Orthodox Church was remodeled a century later by Miklós Ybl, who designed the Opera House and many other important Budapest landmarks. The church retains some fine wood carvings and a dazzling collection of icons by late-18th-century Serbian master Miklós Jankovich. ✉ *District V, Petőfi tér 2/b.*

㊿ **Kálvin tér** (Calvin Square). Calvin Square takes its name from the neoclassical Protestant church that tries to dominate this busy traffic hub; more glaringly noticeable, however, is a Pepsi billboard as tall and wide as the bottom half of the church. The Kecskeméti Kapu, a main gate of Pest, once stood here, as well as a cattle market that was a notorious den of thieves. At the beginning of the 19th century, this was where Pest ended and the prairie began. ✉ *District V.*

㊾ **Közgazdagsági Egyetem** (University of Economics). Just below the Liberty Bridge on the waterfront, the monumental neo-Renaissance building was once the Customs House. Built in 1871–1874 by Miklós Ybl, it is now also known as *közgáz* ("econ."), following a stint during the Communist era as Karl Marx University. ✉ *District V, Fővám tér.*

★ ㊳ **Korzó** (Promenade). The neighborhood to the south of Roosevelt tér has regained much of its past elegance—if not its architectural grandeur—with the erection of the Atrium Hyatt, Inter-Continental, and Budapest Marriott luxury hotels. Traversing all three and continuing well beyond them is the riverside *korzó,* a pedestrian promenade lined with park benches and appealing outdoor cafés from which one can enjoy postcard-perfect views of Gellért Hill and Castle Hill directly across the Danube. Try to take a stroll in the evening, when the views are lit up in shimmering gold. ✉ *District V, from Eötvös tér to Március 15 tér.*

(51) **Magyar Nemzeti Múzeum** (Hungarian National Museum). Built between 1837 and 1847, the museum is a fine example of 19th-century classicism—simple, well proportioned, and surrounded by a large garden. In front of this building on March 15, 1848, Sándor Petőfi recited his revolutionary poem, the "National Song" ("Nemzeti dal"), and the "12 Points," a list of political demands by young Hungarians calling on the people to rise up against the Hapsburgs. Celebrations of the national holiday commemorating the failed revolution are held on these steps every year on March 15.

What used to be the museum's biggest attraction, the **Szent Korona** (Holy Crown), was moved to the Parliament building in early 2000 to mark the millenary of the coronation of Hungary's first king, St. Stephen. The museum still has worthwhile rarities, however, including a completely furnished Turkish tent; masterworks of cabinetmaking and woodcarving, including pews from churches in Nyírbátor and Transylvania; a piano that belonged to both Beethoven and Liszt; and, in the treasury, masterpieces of goldsmithing, among them the 11th-century Constantions Monomachos crown from Byzantium and the richly pictorial 16th-century chalice of Miklós Pálffy. Looking at it is like reading the "Prince Valiant" comic strip in gold. The epic Hungarian history exhibit chronicles, among other things, the end of Communism and the much-celebrated exodus of the Russian troops. ✉ *District IX, Múzeum krt. 14–16,* ☎ *1/338–2122.* 🎫 *600 Ft., free for families (2 adults, 2 children) on weekends.* ⏲ *Mid-Mar.–mid-Oct., Tues.–Sun. 10–6; mid-Oct.–mid-Mar., Tues.–Sun. 10–5.*

★ ⑤ **Nagy Zsinagóga** (Great Synagogue). Seating 3,000, Europe's largest synagogue was designed by Ludwig Förs and built between 1844 and 1859 in a Byzantine-Moorish style described as "consciously archaic Romantic-Eastern." Desecrated by German and Hungarian Nazis, it was painstakingly reconstructed with donations from all over the world; its doors reopened in the fall of 1996. While used for regular services during much of the year, it is generally not used in midwinter, as the space is too large to heat; between December and February, visiting hours are erratic. In the courtyard behind the synagogue, a weeping willow made of metal honors the victims of the Holocaust. Liszt and Saint-Saëns are among the great musicians who have played the synagogue's grand organ. ✉ *District VII, Dohány u. 2–8,* ☎ *1/342–1335.* 🎫 *Free.* ☉ *Weekdays 10–3, Sun. 10–2.*

★ ㉞ **Néprajzi Múzeum** (Museum of Ethnography). The 1890s neoclassical temple formerly housed the Supreme Court. Now an impressive permanent exhibition, "The Folk Culture of the Hungarian People," explains all aspects of peasant life from the end of the 18th century until World War I; explanatory texts are provided in both English and Hungarian. Besides embroideries, pottery, and carvings—the authentic pieces you can't see at touristy folk shops—there are farming tools, furniture, and traditional costumes. The central room of the building alone is worth the entrance fee: a majestic hall with ornate marble staircases and pillars, and towering stained-glass windows. ✉ *District V, Kossuth tér 12,* ☎ *1/332–6340,* 🌐 *www.neprajz.hu.* 🎫 *500 Ft.* ☉ *Mar.–mid-Oct., Tues.–Sun. 10–5:30; mid-Oct.–Feb., Tues.–Sun. 10–4:30.*

★ ㉝ **Országház** (Parliament). The most visible symbol of Budapest's left bank is the huge neo-Gothic Parliament. Mirrored in the Danube much the way Britain's Parliament is reflected by the Thames, it lies midway between the Margaret and Chain bridges and can be reached by the M2 subway (Kossuth tér station) and waterfront Tram 2. A fine example of historicizing, eclectic fin-de-siècle architecture, it was designed by the Hungarian architect Ímre Steindl and built by a thousand workers between 1885 and 1902. The grace and dignity of its long facade and 24 slender towers, with spacious arcades and high windows balancing its vast central dome, lend this living landmark a refreshingly baroque spatial effect. The exterior is lined with 90 statues of great figures in Hungarian history; the corbels are ornamented by 242 allegorical statues. Inside are 691 rooms, 10 courtyards, and 29 staircases; some 88 pounds of gold were used for the staircases and halls. These halls are also a gallery of late-19th-century Hungarian art, with frescoes and canvases depicting Hungarian history, starting with Mihály Munkácsy's large painting of the Magyar Conquest of 896.

Since early 2000 Parliament's most sacred treasure has not been the Hungarian legislature but the newly exhibited **Szent Korona** (Holy Crown), which reposes with other royal relics under the cupola. The crown sits like a golden soufflé above a Byzantine band of holy scenes in enamel and pearls and other gems. It seems to date from the 12th century, so it could not be the crown that Pope Sylvester II presented to St. Stephen in the year 1000, when he was crowned the first king of Hungary. Nevertheless, it is known as the Crown of St. Stephen and has been regarded—even by Communist governments—as the legal symbol of Hungarian sovereignty and unbroken statehood. In 1945 the fleeing Hungarian army handed over the crown and its accompanying regalia to the Americans rather than have them fall into Soviet hands. They were restored to Hungary in 1978. The crown can be seen in the scope of daily tours of the Parliament building, which is the only way you can visit the Parliament, except during ceremonial events and when the legislature is in session (usually Monday and Tuesday from late summer to spring); its permanent home beyond that date has yet to be decided at this writing. Lines may be long, so it's best to call in advance for reservations. The building can also be visited on group tours organized by IBUSZ Travel. ⊠ *District V, Kossuth tér,* ☎ *1/441–4904; 1/441–4415 tour reservations;* ㏌ *www.mkogy.hu.* ☎ *1,700 Ft.* ☉ *Weekdays 8–6, Sat. 8–4, Sun. 8–2; daily tours in English at 10 and 2, starting from Gate No. 10, just right of main stairs.*

㊹ Párisi Udvar (Paris Court). This glass-roof arcade was built in 1914 in richly ornamental neo-Gothic and eclectic styles. Nowadays it's filled with touristy boutiques. ⊠ *District VI, corner of Petőfi Sándor u. and Kossuth Lajos u.*

㊱ Roosevelt tér (Roosevelt Square). This square opening onto the Danube is less closely connected with the U.S. president than with the progressive Hungarian statesman Count István Széchenyi, dubbed "the greatest Hungarian" even by his adversary, Kossuth. The neo-Renaissance palace of the **Magyar Tudományos Akadémia** (Academy of Sciences) on the north side was built between 1862 and 1864, after Széchenyi's suicide. It is a fitting memorial, for in 1825, the statesman donated a year's income from all his estates to establish the academy. Another Széchenyi project, the Széchenyi Lánchíd, leads into the square; there stands a statue of Széchenyi near one of another statesman, Ferenc Deák, whose negotiations led to the establishment of the dual monarchy after Kossuth's 1848–1849 revolution failed. Both men lived on this square. ⊠ *District V.*

★ ㉟ Szabadság tér (Liberty Square). This sprawling square is dominated by the longtime headquarters of **Magyar Televízió** (Hungarian Television), a former stock exchange with what look like four temples and two castles on its roof. Across from it is a solemn-looking neoclassical shrine, the **Nemzeti Bank** (National Bank). The bank's Postal Savings Bank branch, adjacent to the main building but visible from behind Szabadság tér on Hold utca, is another exuberant Art Nouveau masterpiece of architect Ödön Lechner, built in 1901 with colorful majolica mosaics, characteristically curvaceous windows, and pointed towers ending in swirling gold flourishes. In the square's center remains a gold hammer and sickle atop a white stone obelisk, one of the few monuments to the Russian "liberation" of Budapest in 1945. There were mutterings that it, too, would be pulled down, which prompted a Russian diplomatic outcry; the monument, after all, marks a gravesite of fallen Soviet troops. With the Stars and Stripes flying out in front, and a high security presence, the **American Embassy** is at Szabadság tér 12. ⊠ *District V.*

㊳ Széchenyi Lánchíd (Chain Bridge). This is the oldest and most beautiful of the seven road bridges that span the Danube in Budapest. Before it was built, the river could be crossed only by ferry or by a pontoon bridge that had to be removed when ice blocks began floating downstream in winter. It was constructed at the initiative of the great Hungarian reformer and philanthropist Count István Széchenyi, using an 1839 design by the French civil engineer William Tierney Clark. This classical, almost poetically graceful and symmetrical suspension bridge was finished by his Scottish namesake, Adam Clark, who also built the 383-yard tunnel under Castle Hill, thus connecting the Danube quay with the rest of Buda. After it was destroyed by the Nazis, the bridge was rebuilt in its original form (though slightly widened for traffic) and was reopened in 1949, on the centenary of its inauguration. At the Buda end of the bridge is Clark Ádám tér (Adam Clark Square), where you can zip up to Castle Hill on the sometimes crowded **Sikló**

funicular. ⊠ *District I, linking Clark Ádám tér with Roosevelt tér.* 🚠 *Funicular 400 Ft. uphill, 300 Ft. downhill.* ⊙ *Funicular daily 7:30 AM– 10 PM (closed every other Mon.).*

★ ❺❻ **Szent István Bazilika** (St. Stephen's Basilica). Handsome and massive, this is one of the chief landmarks of Pest and the city's largest church— it can hold 8,500 people. Its very Holy Roman front porch greets you with a tympanum bustling with statuary. The basilica's dome and the dome of Parliament are by far the most visible in the Pest skyline, and this is no accident: with the Magyar Millennium of 1896 in mind (the lavishly celebrated thousandth anniversary of the settling of the Carpathian Basin in 896), both domes were planned to be 315 ft high.

The millennium was not yet in sight when architect József Hild began building the basilica in neoclassical style in 1851, two years after the revolution was suppressed. After Hild's death, the project was taken over in 1867 by Miklós Ybl, the architect who did the most to trans- form modern Pest into a monumental metropolis. Wherever he could, Ybl shifted Hild's motifs toward the neo-Renaissance mode that Ybl favored. When the dome collapsed, partly damaging the walls, he made even more drastic changes. Ybl died in 1891, five years before the 1,000-year celebration, and the basilica was completed in neo-Re- naissance style by József Kauser—but not until 1905.

Below the cupola is a rich collection of late-19th-century Hungarian art: mosaics, altarpieces, and statuary (what heady days the Magyar Millennium must have meant for local talents). There are 150 kinds of marble, all from Hungary except for the Carrara in the sanctuary's centerpiece: a white statue of King (St.) Stephen I, Hungary's first king and patron saint. Stephen's mummified right hand is preserved as a relic in the **Szent Jobb Kápolna** (Holy Right Chapel); press a button and it will be illuminated for two minutes. You can also climb the 364 stairs (or take the elevator) to the top of the cupola for a spectacular view of the city. Extensive restorations have been under way at the aging basilica for years and should wrap up by 2010. ⊠ *District V, Szt. István tér,* 🕿 *1/311–0839.* 🎫 *Church free, Szt. Jobb chapel 150 Ft., cupola 500 Ft.* ⊙ *Church Mon.–Sat. 9–7, Sun. 1–5. Szt. Jobb Chapel Apr.– Oct., Mon.–Sat. 9–5, Sun. 1–5; Nov.–Mar., Mon.–Sat. 10–4, Sun. 1– 4. Cupola Apr. and Sept.–Oct., daily 10–5; May–Aug., daily 9–6.*

❹❼ **Szerb Ortodox templom** (Serbian Orthodox Church). Built in 1688, this lovely burnt-orange church, one of Budapest's oldest buildings, sits in a shaded garden surrounded by thick stone walls decorated with a large tile mosaic of St. George defeating the dragon. Its opening hours are somewhat erratic, but if the wrought-iron gates are open, wander in for a look at the beautiful hand-carved wooden pews. ⊠ *District V, Szerb u.*

❹❷ **Váci utca.** Immediately north of Elizabeth Bridge is Budapest's best- known shopping street and most unabashed tourist zone, Váci utca, a pedestrian precinct with electrified 19th-century lampposts and smart shops with credit-card emblems on ornate doorways. No bargain base- ment, Váci utca gets its special flavor from the mix of native furriers, tailors, designers, shoemakers, and folk artists, as well as an increas- ing number of internationally known boutiques. There are also book- stores and china and crystal shops, as well as food stores redolent of paprika. Váci utca's second half, south of Kossuth Lajos utca, was trans- formed into another pedestrian-only zone in the 1990s. This somewhat broader stretch of road, while coming to resemble the northern side, still retains a flavorful, more soothing ambience of its own. On both halves of Váci utca, watch your purses and wallets—against inflated prices *and* active pickpockets. ⊠ *District V, from Vörösmarty tér to Fővám tér.*

⑤ Városház (City Hall). The monumental former city council building, which used to be a hospital for wounded soldiers and then a resort for the elderly ("home" would be too cozy for so vast a hulk), is now Budapest's city hall. It's enormous enough to loom over the row of shops and businesses lining Károly körút in front of it but can only be entered through courtyards or side streets (it is most accessible from Gerlóczy utca). The Tuscan columns at the main entrance and the allegorical statuary of *Atlas, War,* and *Peace* are especially splendid. There was once a chapel in the center of the main facade, but now only its spire remains. ⊠ *District V, Városház u. 9–11,* ☎ *1/327–1000.* ⊡ *Free.* ☉ *Weekdays 9–5.*

⑱ Vásárcsarnok (Central Market Hall). The magnificent hall, a 19th-century iron-frame construction, was reopened in late 1994 after years of renovation (and disputes over who would foot the bill). Even during the leanest years of Communist shortages, the abundance of food came as a revelation to shoppers from East and West. Today, the cavernous, three-story market once again teems with people browsing among stalls packed with salamis and red-paprika chains. Upstairs you can buy folk embroideries and souvenirs. ⊠ *District IX, Vámház krt. 1–3,* ☎ *1/217–6067.* ☉ *Mon. 6 AM–5 PM, Tues.–Fri. 6 AM–6 PM, Sat. 6 AM–2 PM.*

㉟ Vigadó (Concert Hall). Designed in a striking romantic style by Frigyes Feszl and inaugurated in 1865 with Franz Liszt conducting his own *St. Elizabeth Oratorio,* the concert hall is a curious mixture of Byzantine, Moorish, Romanesque, and Hungarian motifs, punctuated by dancing statues and sturdy pillars. Brahms, Debussy, and Casals are among the other phenomenal musicians who have graced its stage. Mahler's *Symphony No. 1* and many works by Bartók were first performed here. While you can go into the lobby on your own, the hall is open only for concerts. ⊠ *District V, Vigadó tér 2,* ☎ *1/318–9167 box office.*

NEED A BREAK? If you only visit one café in Budapest, stop on Vörösmarty Square at the **Gerbeaud** café and pastry shop (⊠ District V, Vörösmarty tér 7, ☎ 1/429–9000), founded in 1858 by Hungarian Henrik Kugler and a Swiss, Emil Gerbeaud. The decor (green-marble tables, Regency-style marble fireplaces) is as sumptuous as the tempting selection of cake and sweets. The Gerbeaud's piano was originally intentioned for the *Titanic* but was saved because it wasn't ready in time for the voyage.

★ ㊶ Vörösmarty tér (Vörösmarty Square). This large, handsome square at the northern end of Váci utca is the heart of Pest's tourist life. Street musicians and sidewalk cafés make it one of the liveliest places in Budapest and a good spot to sit and relax—if you can ward off the aggressive caricature sketchers. Grouped around a white-marble statue of the 19th-century poet and dramatist Mihály Vörösmarty are luxury shops, an airline office, and an elegant former pissoir. Now a lovely kiosk, it displays gold-painted historic scenes of the square's golden days. ⊠ *District V, at northern end of Váci u.*

㊽ Zsidó Múzeum (Jewish Museum). The four-room museum, around the corner from the Great Synagogue, has displays explaining the effect of the Holocaust on Hungarian and Transylvanian Jews. (There are labels in English.) In late 1993, burglars ransacked the museum and got away with approximately 80% of its priceless collection; several months later, the stolen objects were found in Romania and returned to their home. ⊠ *District VII, Dohány u. 2,* ☎ *1/342–8949.* ⊡ *600*

Ft. ☉ *Mid-Mar.–mid-Oct., Mon.–Thurs. 10–5, Fri. and Sun. 10–2; mid-Oct.–mid-Mar., weekdays 10–3, Sun. 10–1.*

Andrássy Út

Behind St. Stephen's Basilica, at the crossroad along Bajcsy-Zsilinszky út, begins Budapest's grandest avenue, Andrássy út. For too many years, this broad boulevard bore the tongue-twisting name Népköztársaság útja (Avenue of the People's Republic) and, for a while before that, Stalin Avenue. In 1990, however, it reverted to its old name honoring Count Gyula Andrássy, a statesman who in 1867 became the first constitutional premier of Hungary. The boulevard that would eventually bear his name was begun in 1872, as Buda and Pest (and Óbuda) were about to be unified. Most of the mansions that line it were completed by 1884. It took another dozen years before the first underground railway on the Continent was completed for—you guessed it—the Magyar Millennium in 1896. Though preceded by London's Underground (1863), Budapest's was the world's first electrified subway. Only slightly modernized but refurbished for the 1996 millecentenary, this "Little Metro" is still running a 4-km (2½-mi) stretch from Vörösmarty tér to the far end of City Park. Using tiny yellow trains with tanklike treads, and stopping at antique stations marked FÖLDALATTI (Underground) on their wrought-iron entranceways, Line 1 is a tourist attraction in itself. Six of its 10 stations are along Andrássy út.

A GOOD WALK

A walking tour of Andrássy út's sights is straightforward: begin at its downtown end, near Deák tér, and stroll its length (about 2 km [1 mi]) all the way to Hősök tere, at the entrance to Budapest's popular City Park. The first third of the avenue, from Bajcsy-Zsilinszky út to the eight-sided intersection called Oktogon, is framed by rows of eclectic city palaces with balconies held up by stone giants. First stop is the mansion of the **Postamúzeum** ⑤⑦. Continue until you reach the imposing **Magyar Állami Operaház** ⑤⑧ and across the street the **Drechsler Kastély** ⑤⑨. A block or two farther, on "Budapest's Broadway," Nagymező utca, where you'll find theaters, nightclubs, and cabarets, is the **Magyar Fotógráfusok Háza (Mai Manó Ház)** ⑥⓪ photographic museum. Continuing down Andrássy, turn right onto Liszt Ferenc tér, a pedestrian street dominated by the **Liszt Ferenc Zeneakade**mia ⑥①. Return to Andrássy, and continue until you come to Vörösmarty, where a short detour right will take you to **Liszt Ferenc Emlékmúzeum** ⑥②.

The Parisian-style boulevard of Andrássy alters when it crosses the Nagy körút (Outer Ring Road), at the Oktogon crossing. Four rows of trees and scores of flower beds make the thoroughfare look more like a garden promenade, but its cultural character lingers. Farther up, past **Kodály körönd** ⑥③, the rest of Andrássy út is dominated by widely spaced mansions surrounded by private gardens. At Kodály körönd take another detour, turning right onto Felsőerdősor, then left onto Varosligeti fasor, where you will find the **Ráth György Múzeum** ⑥④ of Indian and Chinese art. Andrássy út ends at **Hősök tere** ⑥⑤. Finish your tour by browsing through the **Műcsarnok** ⑥⑥ and/or the **Szépművészeti Múzeum** ⑥⑦, and then perhaps take a stroll into the **Városliget** ⑥⑧. You can return to Deák tér on the Millenniumi Földalatti (Millennial Underground).

TIMING

As most museums are closed Monday, it's best to explore Andrássy út on other days, preferably weekdays or early Saturday, when stores are also open for browsing. During opera season, you can time your exploration to land you at the Operaház stairs just before 7 PM to watch the spectacle of opera goers flowing in for the evening's performance. City Park is best explored on a clear day.

SIGHTS TO SEE

59 **Drechsler Kastély** (Drechsler Palace). Across the street from the Operaház is the French Renaissance–style Drechsler Palace. An early work by Ödön Lechner, Hungary's master of Art Nouveau, it is now the home of the National Ballet School and is generally not open to tourists. ⊠ *District VI, Andrássy út 25.*

★ **65** **Hősök tere** (Heroes' Square). Andrássy út ends in grandeur at Heroes' Square, with Budapest's answer to Berlin's Brandenburg Gate. Cleaned and refurbished in 1996 for the millecentenary (1100th anniversary), the **Millenniumi Emlékmű**(Millennial Monument) is a semicircular twin colonnade with statues of Hungary's kings and leaders between its pillars. Set back in its open center, a 118-ft stone column is crowned by a dynamic statue of the archangel Gabriel, his outstretched arms bearing the ancient emblems of Hungary. At its base ride seven bronze horsemen: the Magyar chieftains, led by Árpád, whose tribes conquered the land in 896. Before the column lies a simple marble slab, the **Nemzeti Háborús Emlék Tábla** (National War Memorial), the nation's altar, at which every visiting foreign dignitary lays a ceremonial wreath. England's Queen Elizabeth upheld the tradition during her royal visit in May of 1992. In 1991 Pope John Paul II conducted a mass here. Just a few months earlier, half a million Hungarians had convened to recall the memory of Imre Nagy, the reform-minded Communist prime minister who partially inspired the 1956 revolution. Little would anyone have guessed then that in 1995, palm trees—and Madonna—would spring up on this very square in a scene from the film *Evita* (set in Argentina, not Hungary), nor that Michael Jackson would do his part to consecrate the square with a music video. ⊠ *District VI.*

63 **Kodály körönd.** A handsome traffic circle with imposing statues of three Hungarian warriors—leavened by a fourth one of a poet—Kodály körönd is surrounded by plane and chestnut trees. Look carefully at the towered mansions on the north side of the circle—behind the soot you'll see the fading colors of ornate frescoes peeking through. The circle takes its name from the composer Zoltán Kodály, who lived just beyond it at Andrássy út 89. ⊠ *District VI, Andrássy út at Szinyei Merse u.*

62 **Liszt Ferenc Emlékmúzeum** (Franz Liszt Memorial Museum). Andrássy út No. 67 was the original location of the old Academy of Music and Franz Liszt's last home; entered around the corner, it now houses a museum. Several rooms display the original furniture and instruments from Liszt's time there; another room shows temporary exhibits. The museum hosts excellent, free classical concerts year-round, except in August 1–20, when it is closed. ⊠ *District VI, Vörösmarty u. 35,* ☎ *1/300–9804,* 𝖶𝖤𝖡 *www.lisztmuseum.hu.* 💰 *300 Ft.* ☉ *Weekdays 10–6, Sat. 9–5. Classical concerts (free with admission) Sept.–July, Sat. at 11 AM.*

61 **Liszt Ferenc Zeneakadémia** (Franz Liszt Academy of Music). This magnificent Art Nouveau building presides over the cafés and gardens of Liszt Ferenc tér. Along with **Vigadó**, this is one of the city's main concert halls. On summer days, the sound of daytime rehearsals adds to the sweetness in the air along this pedestrian oasis of café society, just off buzzing Andrássy út. The academy itself has two auditoriums: a green-and-gold 1,200-seat main hall and a smaller hall for chamber music and solo recitals. Further along the square is a dramatic statue of Liszt Ferenc (Franz Liszt) himself, hair blown back from his brow, seemingly in a flight of inspiration. Pianist Ernő(Ernst) Dohnányi and composers Béla Bartók and Zoltán Kodály were teachers here. ⊠ *District VI, Liszt Ferenc tér 8,* ☎ *1/342–0179.*

★ **58** **Magyar Állami Operaház** (Hungarian State Opera House). Miklós Ybl's crowning achievement is the neo-Renaissance Opera House, built between 1875 and 1884. Badly damaged during the siege of 1944–1945, it was restored for its 1984 centenary. Two buxom marble sphinxes guard the driveway; the main entrance is flanked by Alajos Strobl's "romantic-realist" limestone statues of Liszt and of another 19th-century Hungarian composer, Ferenc Erkel, the father of Hungarian opera (his patriotic opera *Bánk bán* is still performed for national celebrations).

Inside, the spectacle begins even before the performance does. You glide up grand staircases and through wood-paneled corridors and gilt lime-green salons into a glittering jewel box of an auditorium. Its four tiers of boxes are held up by helmeted sphinxes beneath a frescoed ceiling by Károly Lotz. Lower down there are frescoes everywhere, with intertwined motifs of Apollo and Dionysus. In its early years, the Budapest Opera was conducted by Gustav Mahler (from 1888 to 1891) and, after World War II, by Otto Klemperer.

The best way to experience the Opera House's interior is to see a ballet or opera; and while performance quality varies, tickets are relatively cheap and easy to come by, at least by tourist standards. And descending from *La Bohème* into the Földalatti station beneath the Opera House was described by travel writer Stephen Brook in *The Double Eagle* as stepping "out of one period piece and into another." There are no performances in summer, except for the weeklong BudaFest international opera and ballet festival in mid-August. You cannot view the interior on your own, but 45-minute tours in English are usually conducted daily; buy tickets in the Opera Shop, by the sphinx at the Hajós utca entrance. (Large groups should call in advance.) ✉ *District VI, Andrássy út 22,* ☎ *1/331–2550 (Ext. 156 for tours).* 🎫 *Tours 1,200 Ft.* 🕐 *Tours daily at 3 and 4.*

60 **Magyar Fotográfusok Háza (Mai Manó Ház)** (Hungarian Photographers' House [Manó Mai House]). This ornate turn-of-the-20th-century building was built as a photography studio, where the wealthy bourgeoisie would come to be photographed by imperial and royal court photographer Manó Mai. Inside, ironwork and frescoes ornament the curving staircase leading up to the exhibition space, the largest of Budapest's three photo galleries. ✉ *District VI, Nagymező u. 20,* ☎ *1/302–4398.* 🎫 *200 Ft.* 🕐 *Weekdays 2–6.*

66 **Műcsarnok** (Palace of Exhibitions). The city's largest hall for special exhibitions is a striking 1895 temple of culture with a colorful tympanum. Its program of events includes exhibitions of contemporary Hungarian and international art and a rich series of films, plays, and concerts. ✉ *District XIV, Hősök tere,* ☎ *1/460–7000.* 🎫 *600 Ft.; free Tues.* 🕐 *Tues.–Sun. 10–6.*

57 **Postamúzeum** (Postal Museum). The best of Andrássy út's many marvelous stone mansions can be visited now, for the Postal Museum occupies an apartment with frescoes by Károly Lotz (whose work adorns St. Stephen's Basilica and the Opera House). Among the displays is an exhibition on the history of Hungarian mail, radio, and telecommunications. English-language pamphlets are available. Even if the exhibits don't thrill you, the venue, which was restored in 2001, is worth the visit. ✉ *District VI, Andrássy út 3,* ☎ *1/269–6838.* 🎫 *70 Ft.* 🕐 *Apr.–Oct., Tues.–Sun. 10–6; Nov.–Mar., Tues.–Sun. 10–4.*

64 **Ráth György Múzeum** (György Ráth Museum). Just off Andrássy út, the museum houses a rich collection of exotica from the Indian subcontinent and Chinese ceramics. The **Hopp Ferenc Kelet-Ázsiai Művészeti Múzeum** (Ferenc Hopp Museum of Eastern Asiatic Arts; ✉ District VI,

Andrássy út 103, ☎ 1/322–8476), which is affiliated with the György Ráth, hosts changing exhibits. ⊠ *District VI, Városligeti fasor 12,* ☎ *1/342–3916.* 🖼 *160 Ft. (combined ticket for both museums).* ⊙ *Oct.– mid-Apr., Tues.–Sun. 10–4; mid-Apr.–Sept., Tues.–Sun. 10–6.*

NEED A
BREAK?

The **Müvész** café (⊠ District VI, Andrássy út 29, ☎ 1/352–1337) is perhaps the only surviving "writer's café" where you will occasionally see a writer at work. The tarnished windows and wallpaper curling up at the edges give it a shabby chic appeal. Sit at a table outside during summer to watch the world passing by on Andrássy út.

★ ⑥⑦ **Szépmüvészeti Múzeum** (Museum of Fine Arts). Across Heroes' Square from the Palace of Exhibitions and built by the same team of Albert Schickedanz and Fülöp Herzog, the Museum of Fine Arts houses Hungary's best art collection, rich in Flemish and Dutch old masters. With seven fine El Grecos and five beautiful Goyas as well as paintings by Velázquez and Murillo, the collection of Spanish old masters is one of the best outside Spain. The Italian school is represented by Giorgione, Bellini, Correggio, Tintoretto, and Titian masterpieces and, above all, two superb Raphael paintings: *Eszterházy Madonna* and his immortal *Portrait of a Youth,* rescued after a world-famous art heist. Nineteenth-century French art includes works by Delacroix, Pissarro, Cézanne, Toulouse-Lautrec, Gauguin, Renoir, and Monet. There are also more than 100,000 drawings (including five by Rembrandt and three studies by Leonardo), Egyptian and Greco-Roman exhibitions, late-Gothic winged altars from northern Hungary and Transylvania, and works by all the leading figures of Hungarian art up to the present. A 20th-century collection was added to the museum's permanent exhibits in 1994, comprising an interesting series of statues, paintings, and drawings by Chagall, Le Corbusier, and others. Labels are in both Hungarian and English; there's also an English-language booklet for sale about the permanent collection. ⊠ *District XIV, Hősök tere,* ☎ *1/343–9759.* 🖼 *500 Ft.* ⊙ *Tues.–Sun. 10–5:30.*

Ⓒ ⑥⑧ **Városliget (City Park).** Heroes' Square is the gateway to a square kilometer (almost ½ square mi) of recreation, entertainment, beauty, and culture. A bridge behind the Millennial Monument leads across a boating basin that becomes an artificial ice-skating rink in winter; to the south of this lake stands a statue of George Washington, erected in 1906 with donations by Hungarian emigrants to the United States. You can soak or swim at the turn-of-the-20th-century Széchenyi Fürdő, jog along the park paths, or careen on Vidám Park's roller coaster. There's also the Petőfi Csarnok, a leisure-time youth center and major concert hall on the site of an old industrial exhibition. The restaurant Gundel is once again charming diners with its turn-of-the-20th-century ambience. Fair-weather weekends, when the children's attractions are teeming with youngsters and parents and the Széchenyi Fürdő brimming with bathers, are the best times for people-watchers to visit the park; if you go on a weekday, the main sights are rarely crowded.

The renovation that began in the once-depressing **Budapesti Állatkert** (Budapest Zoo) in the late 1990s is not expected to be finished until 2004, but the place is already cheerier, at least for humans—with petting opportunities aplenty and a new monkey house where endearing, seemingly clawless little simians climb all over you (beware of pickpockets). Don't miss the elephant pavilion, decorated with Zsolnay majolica and glazed ceramic animals. ⊠ *Városliget, District XIV, Állatkerti krt. 6–12,* ☎ *1/343–6075.* 🖼 *650 Ft.* ⊙ *Mar. and Oct., daily 9–5; Apr. and Sept., daily 9–6; May, daily 9–6:30; June–Aug., daily 9–7; Nov.– Feb., daily 9–4 (last tickets sold 1 hr before closing).*

At the **Fővárosi Nagycirkusz** (Municipal Grand Circus), colorful performances by local acrobats, clowns, and animal trainers, as well as by international artists, are staged here in a small ring. ⊠ *Városliget, District XIV, Állatkerti krt. 7,* ☎ *1/343–9630.* 🖼 *Weekdays 500 Ft.– 900 Ft., weekends 550 Ft.–950 Ft.* ☉ *July–Aug., Wed.–Fri. at 3 and 7; Thurs. at 3, Sat. at 10, 3, and 7; Sun. at 10 and 3; Sept.–June, schedule varies.*

Széchenyi Fürdő (Széchenyi Baths), the largest medicinal bathing complex in Europe, is housed in a beautiful neo-baroque building in the middle of City Park. There are several thermal pools indoors as well as two outdoors, which remain open even in winter, when dense steam hangs thick over the hot water's surface—you can just barely make out the figures of elderly men, submerged shoulder deep, crowded around waterproof chessboards. Note that to use the baths, you pay a 1,500 Ft. deposit: the balance (minus the changing room or cabin fee) is returned when you leave. Facilities include medical and underwater massage treatments, carbonated bath treatments and mud wraps. ⊠ *Városliget, District XIV, Állatkerti krt. 11,* ☎ *1/321–0310.* 🖼 *Changing room 400 Ft., cabin 700 Ft.* ☉ *Weekdays 6 AM–6 PM, weekends 6 AM–5 PM.*

Beside the City Park's lake stands **Vajdahunyad Vár** (Vajdahunyad Castle), a fantastic medley of Hungary's historic and architectural past, starting with the Romanesque gateway of the cloister of Jak in western Hungary. A Gothic castle, Transylvanian turrets, Renaissance loggia, baroque portico, and Byzantine decoration are all guarded by a spooky modern (1903) bronze statue of the anonymous medieval chronicler, who was the first recorder of Hungarian history. Designed for the millennial celebration in 1896, it was not completed until 1908. This hodgepodge houses the the surprisingly interesting **Mezőgazdasági Múzeum** (Agricultural Museum), with intriguingly arranged sections on animal husbandry, forestry, horticulture, hunting, and fishing. ⊠ *Városliget, District XIV, Széchenyi Island,* ☎ *1/343–3198.* 🖼 *200 Ft.* ☉ *Mid-Feb.–mid-Nov., Tues.–Fri. and Sun. 10–5, Sat. 10–6; mid-Nov.–mid-Feb., Tues.–Fri. 10–4, weekends 10–5.*

� Budapest's somewhat weary amusement park, **Vidám Park,** is next to the zoo and is crawling with happy children with their parents or grandparents in tow. Rides are inexpensive (some are for preschoolers). There are also game rooms and a scenic railway. Next to the main park is a separate, smaller section for toddlers. In winter, only a few rides operate. ⊠ *Városliget, XIV, Állatkerti krt. 14–16,* ☎ *1/343–0996.* 🖼 *400 Ft.* ☉ *Apr.–Oct., weekdays noon–7, weekends 10–7; Nov.–Mar., weekdays noon–6, weekends 10–7.*

Eastern Pest and the Nagy körút (Great Ring Road)

This section covers primarily Kossuth Lajos–Rákóczi út and the Nagykörút (Great Ring Road)—busy, less-touristy urban thoroughfares full of people, cars, shops, and Budapest's unique urban flavor.

Beginning a few blocks from the Elizabeth Bridge, Kossuth Lajos utca is Budapest's busiest shopping street. Try to look above and beyond the store windows to the architecture and activity along Kossuth Lajos utca and its continuation, Rákóczi út, which begins when it crosses the Kis körút (Little Ring Road) at the busy intersection called Astoria. Most of Rákóczi út is lined with hotels, shops, and department stores, and it ends at the grandiose Keleti (East) Railway Station, on Baross tér.

Pest's Great Ring Road, the Nagy körút, was laid out at the end of the 19th century in a wide semicircle anchored to the Danube at both ends; an arm of the river was covered over to create this 114-ft-wide thoroughfare. The large apartment buildings on both sides also date from this era. Along with theaters, stores, and cafés, they form a boulevard unique in Europe for its "unified eclecticism," which blends several different historic styles into a harmonious whole. Its entire length of almost 4½ km (2¾ mi) from Margaret Bridge to Petőfi Bridge is traversed by Trams 4 and 6, but strolling it in stretches is also a good way to experience the hustle and bustle of downtown Budapest.

Like its smaller counterpart, the Kis Körút (Small Ring Road), the Great Ring Road comprises sectors of various names. Beginning with Ferenc körút at the Petőfi Bridge, it changes to József körút at the intersection marked by the Museum of Applied Arts, then to Erzsébet körút at Blaha Lujza tér. Teréz körút begins at the busy Oktogon crossing with Andrássy út and ends at the Nyugati (West) Railway Station, where Szent István takes over for the final stretch to the Margaret Bridge.

A GOOD WALK

Beginning with a visit to the **Iparművészeti Múzeum** ⑥⑨, near the southern end of the boulevard, walk or take Tram 4 or 6 north (away from the Petőfi Bridge) to **Köztársaság tér** ⑦⑩. The neo-Renaissance **Keleti pályaudvar** ⑦⑴ is a one-metro-stop detour away from Blaha Lujza tér. Continuing in the same direction on the körút, go several stops on the tram to **Nyugati pályaudvar** ⑦⑵ and walk the remaining sector, Szent István körút, past the **Vígszínház** ⑦⑶ to Margaret Bridge. From the bridge, views of Margaret Island, to the north, and Parliament, Castle Hill, the Chain Bridge, and Gellért Hill, to the south, are gorgeous.

TIMING

As this area is packed with stores, it's best to explore during business hours—weekdays until around 5 PM and Saturday until 1 PM; Saturday will be most crowded. Keep in mind that the Iparművészeti Múzeum is closed Monday.

SIGHTS TO SEE

★ ⑥⑨ **Iparművészeti Múzeum** (Museum of Applied and Decorative Arts). The templelike structure housing this museum is indeed a shrine to Hungarian Art Nouveau, and in front of it, drawing pen in hand, sits a statue of its creator, Hungarian architect Ödön Lechner. Opened in the Magyar Millennial year of 1896, it was only the third museum of its kind in Europe. Its dome of tiles is crowned by a majolica lantern from the same source: the Zsolnay ceramic works in Pécs. Inside its central hall are playfully swirling whitewashed, double-decker, Moorish-style galleries and arcades. The museum, which collects and studies objects of interior decoration and use, has five departments: furniture, textiles, goldsmithing, ceramics, and everyday objects. ⊠ *District VIII, Üllői út 33–37,* ☎ *1/217–5222,* WEB *www.imm.hu.* ⊡ *300 Ft.* ☉ *Mid-Mar.– Oct., Tues.–Sun. 10–6; Nov.–mid-Mar., Tues.–Sun. 10–4.*

OFF THE BEATEN PATH
GÖDÖLLŐI KIRÁLYI KASTÉLY – The Royal Palace of Gödöllői has been referred to as the Hungarian Versailles, though this baroque mansion and former royal residence does suffer by comparison. This is because the palace was used as a barracks by Soviet troops after 1945, and much of the palace was still under restoration at this writing. Still, those interested in Emperor Franz Josef I and his legendarily beautiful and charismatic wife, Elizabeth (known as Sissi), will find this a rewarding half-day excursion. Sissi's violet-colored rooms contain secret doors, which allowed her to avoid tiresome guests. To get there, go to the Örs Vezér tere—last stop on the red metro line, and take the HÉV suburban train to the Szabadság tere stop. The palace sits across the street. ⊠ *Grassalkovich Kastély, Gödöllő,* ☎ *1/329–2340.* ⊡ *600 Ft.* ☉ *Tues.–Sun. 10–6.*

⓲ Keleti pályaudvar (East Railway Station). The grandiose, imperial-looking station was built in 1884 and considered Europe's most modern until well into the 20th century. Its neo-Renaissance facade, which resembles a gateway, is flanked by statues of two British inventors and railway pioneers, James Watt and George Stephenson. ⊠ *District VIII, Baross tér.*

⓱ Köztársaság tér (Square of the Republic). Surrounded by faceless concrete buildings, this square is not particularly alluring aesthetically but is significant because it was where the Communist Party of Budapest had its headquarters, and it was also the scene of heavy fighting in 1956. Here also is the city's second opera house, and Budapest's largest, the **Erkel Ferenc színház** (Ferenc Erkel Theater). ⊠ *District VIII, between Luther u. and Berzeriyi u.*

⓳ Nyugati pályaudvar (West Railway Station). The iron-laced glass hall of the West Railway Station is in complete contrast to—and much more modern than—the newer East Railway Station. Built in the 1870s, it was designed by a team of architects from Gustav Eiffel's office in Paris. ⊠ *District XIII, Teréz krt.*

★ **⓴ Vígszínház** (Comedy Theater). This neo-baroque, late-19th-century, gem-like theater twinkles with just a tiny, playful anticipation of Art Nouveau and sparkles inside and out since its 1994 refurbishment. The theater hosts primarily musicals, such as Hungarian adaptations of *Cats*, as well as dance performances and classical concerts. ⊠ *District XIII, Pannónia u. 1,* ☎ *1/329–2340 box office,* WEB *www.vigszinhaz.hu.*

NEED A BREAK? | Hands down the best café in this part of town, the **Európa kávéház** (⊠ District XIII, Szent István krt. 7–9, ☎ 1/312–2362) has marble-top tables; top-notch elegance; and, yes, delectable sweets. While it seems (in the best sense) a century old, it's in fact only been around since the late 1990s. Here you can sample some Eszterházy torta (a rich, buttery cake with walnut batter and, here at least, a walnut on top) or a Tyrolean strudel with poppy-seed filling.

Óbuda

Until its unification with Buda and Pest in 1872 to form the city of Budapest, Óbuda (meaning Old Buda) was a separate town that used to be the main settlement; now it is usually thought of as a suburb. Although the vast new apartment blocks of Budapest's biggest housing project and busy roadways are what first strike the eye, the historic core of Óbuda has been preserved in its entirety.

A GOOD WALK

Óbuda is easily reached by car, bus, or streetcar via the Árpád Bridge from Pest or by the HÉV suburban railway from Batthyány tér to the Árpád Bridge. Once you're there, covering all the sights on foot involves large but manageable distances along major exhaust-permeated roadways. One way to tackle it is to take Tram 17 from its southern terminus at the Buda side of the Margaret Bridge to Kiscelli utca and walk uphill to the **Kiscelli Múzeum.** Then walk back down the same street all the way past **Flórián tér,** continuing toward the Danube and making a left onto Hídfőutca or Szentlélek tér to enter **Fő tér.** After exploring the square, walk a block or two southeast to the HÉV suburban railway stop and take the train just north to the museum complex at **Aquincum.**

TIMING

It's best to begin touring Óbuda during the cooler, early hours of the day, as the heat on the area's busy roads can get overbearing. Avoid Monday, when museums are closed.

Aquincum. This complex comprises the reconstructed remains of a Roman settlement dating from the 1st century AD and the capital of the Roman province of Pannonia. Careful excavations have unearthed a varied selection of artifacts and mosaics, giving a tantalizing inkling of what life was like in the provinces of the Roman Empire. A gymnasium and a central heating system have been unearthed, along with the ruins of two baths and a shrine to Mithras, the Persian god of light, truth, and the sun. The **Aquincum múzeum** (Aquincum Museum) displays the dig's most notable finds: ceramics; a red-marble sarcophagus showing a triton and flying Eros on one side and on the other, Telesphorus, the angel of death, depicted as a hooded dwarf; and jewelry from a Roman lady's tomb. ⊠ *District III, Szentendrei út 139,* ☎ *1/250–1650.* 🖭 *700 Ft.* ☉ *Apr. and Oct., Tues.–Sun. 10–5; May–Sept., Tues.–Sun. 10–6. Grounds open an hr earlier than museum.*

Flórián tér (Flórián Square). The center of today's Óbuda is Flórián tér, where Roman ruins were first discovered when the foundations of a house were dug in 1778. Two centuries later, careful excavations were carried out during the reconstruction of the square, and today the restored ancient ruins lie in the center of the square in mind-boggling contrast to the racing traffic and cement-block housing projects. ⊠ *District III, Vörösvári út at Pacsirtamező u.*

Fő tér (Main Square). Óbuda's old main square is its most picturesque part. The square has been spruced up in recent years, and there are now several good restaurants and interesting museums in and around the baroque **Zichy Kúria** (Zichy Mansion), which has become a neighborhood cultural center. Among the most popular offerings are the summer concerts in the courtyard and the evening jazz concerts. ⊠ *District III, Kórház u. at Hídfő u.*

Hercules Villa. A fine 3rd-century Roman dwelling, it takes its name from the myth depicted on its beautiful mosaic floor. The ruin was unearthed between 1958 and 1967 and is now only open by request (inquire at the Aquincum Museum). ⊠ *District III, Meggyfa u. 19–21.*

Kiscelli Múzeum (Kiscelli Museum). A strenuous climb up the steep, dilapidated sidewalks of Remetehegy (Hermit's Hill) will deposit you at this elegant, mustard-yellow baroque mansion. Built between 1744 and 1760 as a Trinitarian monastery, today it holds an eclectic mix of paintings, sculptures, engravings, and sundry items related to the history of Budapest. Included here is the printing press on which poet and revolutionary Sándor Petőfi printed his famous "Nemzeti Dal" ("National Song"), in 1848, inciting the Hungarian people to rise up against the Hapsburgs. ⊠ *District III, Kiscelli u. 108,* ☎ *1/388–7817.* 🖭 *300 Ft.* ☉ *Nov.–Mar., Tues.–Sun. 10–4; Apr.–Oct., Tues.–Sun. 10–6.*

Római amfiteátrum (Roman Amphitheater). Probably dating back to the 2nd century AD, Óbuda's Roman military amphitheater once held some 16,000 people and, at 144 yards in diameter, was one of Europe's largest. A block of dwellings called the Round House was later built by the Romans above the amphitheater; massive stone walls found in the Round House's cellar were actually parts of the amphitheater. Below the amphitheater are the cells where prisoners and lions were held while awaiting confrontation. ⊠ *District III, Pacsirtamező u. at Nagyszombat u.*

Zichy Kúria (Zichy Mansion). One wing of the Zichy Mansion is taken up by the **Óbudai Helytörténeti Gyüjtemény** (Óbuda Local History Collection). Permanent exhibitions here include traditional rooms from typical homes in the district of Békásmegyer and a popular exhibit covering the history of toys from 1860 to 1960. Another wing houses the **Kassák Múzeum,** which honors the literary and artistic works of a pioneer of the Hungarian avant-garde, Lajos Kassák. ✉ *District III, Fő tér 1,* ☎ *1/250–1020 History Collection; 1/368–7021 Kassák Museum.* 🎫 *History Collection 120 Ft., Kassák Museum 100 Ft.* ☽ *History Collection mid-Mar.–mid-Oct., Tues.–Fri. 2–6, weekends 10–6; mid-Oct.– mid-Mar., Tues.–Fri. 2–5, weekends 10–5. Kassák Museum Mar.– Sept., Tues.–Sun. 10–6; Oct.–Feb., Tues.–Sun. 10–4.*

Dining

A far cry from the smattering of options available in the socialist era, Budapest's culinary scene now offers variety and quality both in satisfyingly large portions. It's possible, for instance, to eat very good sushi in Budapest, and the range of styles encompassed by the culinary classification "Hungarian" runs to more than just paprika and goulash served up in faux Gypsy surroundings.

A few of the city's grander dining establishments overlook the Danube and downtown from the imperious Buda Hill, while Pest has a busy restaurant scene, including bustling lunchtime bistros and late night cafés. To be right up to the latest minute on the restaurant scene, you can always rifle through local English-language press for fresh ideas on where to dine. The *Budapest Sun* has fairly impartial restaurant reviews (in English) and is available in most centrally located newsstands.

For price range information, *see* Dining *in* Pleasures and Pastimes.

Downtown Pest and the Small Ring Road

$$–$$$$ ✕ **Múzeum.** The gustatory anticipation sparked by this elegant, candlelit salon with mirrors, mosaics, and swift-moving waiters is matched by wholly satisfying, wonderful food. The salads are generous, the Hungarian wines excellent, and the chef dares to be creative. Unusual for a restaurant of this standing, Múzeum does not take all major credit cards—there's an ATM on the premises, however. ✉ *District VIII, Múzeum krt. 11,* ☎ *1/338–4221. Jacket and tie. AE. Closed Sun.*

$$–$$$$ ✕ **Café Kör.** The wrought-iron tables, vaulted ceilings, and crisp white
★ tablecloths give this chic bistro a decidedly downtown feel. In the heart of the busy fifth district, Café Kör is ideal for lunch or dinner when touring nearby Andrássy út or St. Stephen's Basilica. The specialty plate is a feast of rich goose liver paté, grilled meats, and cheeses, to be savored with a glass of Hungarian pezsgő (sparkling wine). True to its bistro aspirations, the daily specials are scribbled on the wall, in both Hungarian and English. ✉ *District V, Sas u. 17,* ☎ *1/311–0053. Reservations essential. MC, V. Closed Sun.*

✕ **Tom-George Restaurant & Bar.** Well-situated in the heart of downtown, Tom-George is Budapest's answer to urban chic. The spacious bar blends blondwood and wicker, giving the interior a relaxed yet sophisticated feel. Weekends find a young and stylish crowd choosing from the expansive cocktail menu. Minimalism at the table, though, belies exotic creativity in the kitchen. House specialties include nasi goreng with chicken breast and lamb with satay sauce. Sushi—perhaps Budapest's best—is glamorously prepared in a corner of the dining room. ✉ *District V, Oktober 6th utca 8,* ☎ *1/266–3525. Reservations essential. AE, V.*

$$–$$$ ✕ **Empire.** This is one eating and drinking establishment that anyone
★ nostalgic for Hapsburg-era magnificence shouldn't miss out on. After sinking into one of the very comfortable leather chairs, you'll enjoy the insulation from the traffic outside on Kossuth Lajos street—and indeed the whole 21st century. Game dishes are the noted specialty. ✉ *District V, Kossuth Lajos u. 19,* ☎ *1/317–3411. Reservations essential. AE, DC, MC, V.*

$-$$$ ✕ **Cyrano.** This smooth young bistro just off Vörösmarty tér has an
★ arty, contemporary bent, with wrought-iron chairs, green-marble
floors, and long-stem azure glasses. The creative kitchen sends out el-
egantly presented Hungarian and Continental dishes, from standards
such as goulash and chicken paprikás to more eclectic tastes such as
tender fried Camembert with blueberry jam. ⊠ *District V, Kristóf tér
7–8,* ☎ *1/266–3096. Reservations essential. AE, DC, MC, V.*

$$-$$$$ ✕ **Kárpátia.** As many a Hungarian will remind you, much of what is
now Romanian Transylvania, including the Carpathian mountains, was
once considered part of Hungary. The neo-Gothic interior and Gypsy
musicians here conjure up that lost world, along with a menu that includes "forgotten delicacies." There are in fact some 170 dishes, including the best *Hortobágyi* pancakes this side of the Puszta, and
stuffed Transylvanian cabbage. You can dine outdoors, under a mar-
quee, on summer nights. ⊠ *District V, Ferenciek tere 7–8,* ☎ *1/317–
3596. Reservations essential. AE, DC, MC, V.*

$-$$ ✕ **Baraka.** The deep velvet-red walls and airy balcony are offset by
★ the glean of varnished floorboards in this elegant and refreshingly
modern and hospitable restaurant tucked discreetly around the corner
from so much downtown action on quiet Magyar utca. The chicken
in sweet chili sauce is recommended, as is the New York cheesecake—
so called simply because the chef is from New York, but it's delicious
all the same. It's a welcome addition to the serious restaurant scene.
⊠ *District V, Magyar u. 12–14,* ☎ *1/483–1355. Reservations essential. AE, DC, MC, V. Closed Sun.*

$-$$ ✕ **Stex Ház.** In its own way, this three-level restaurant is every bit as
much of a classic as Gundel. Alfred Stex, a Hungarian, became a successful bootlegger in Prohibition America and then returned home to
open this restaurant. Faultlessly high-cholesterol working-class fodder
is paired with slightly sullen service. The food, when it arrives, makes
up for the waiters' sometimes frosty demeanor. If you like people-watching, there's a constant stream of customers in this gymnasium-size pro-
letarian palace. ⊠ *District XIII, Jószef krt. 55–57,* ☎ *1/318–5716. AE,
DC, MC, V.*

$-$$ ✕ **Vista Travel Café.** A favorite of lunching Hungarian businesspeo-
★ ple, backpackers, second-tier expatriates, and other assorted oddities,
Vista is a curious but successful hybrid of brassiere, café, cybercafé,
meeting place, and information center. The action in the kitchen can
creak at times, though it must be owed that dual-language menus
cheerfully warn you of that fact. You can fill in the paper place-mat
feedback forms while you wait for healthy, nutritious food to arrive.
Highlights include the Rarotonga sandwich, quiche Lorraine, pastas,
and all-day breakfast menu. ⊠ *District VII, Paulay Ede u. 7,* ☎ *1/268–
0888. AE, DC, MC, V.*

North Buda

$$-$$$$ ✕ **Fuji Japan.** If you need further convincing that Budapest now has
a truly international restaurant scene—or even if you just like excel-
lent Japanese food—then you'll make the trek to the Buda Hills and
this powerhouse of cuisine from the land of the rising sun. It's a spa-
cious place, with tables set a comfortable distance apart so that you
can watch the Japanese and Hungarian chefs at work and choose from
a menu of considerable depth, considering how far you are from the
sea. There's even a separate dining room where you can eat at low ta-
bles, in traditional Japanese style. ⊠ *District III, Csatárka u. 54/b,* ☎
1/325–7111. AE, DC, MC, V.

Dining

Lodging

Budapest Dining and Lodging

Lehel tér

Visegrádi u.

Váci út

Ferdinánd híd

Rippl-Rónai u.

Dózsa György út

Hősök tere

Városliget

Olof Palme sétány

Szinyei Merse u.

Bajza u.

Benczúr u.

Andrássy Dürer sor

Nyugati (West) Station

Podmaniczky utca

Nyugati tér

Teréz körút

Szondi u.

Rózsa u.

Aradi u.

Felső erdősor

Városligeti fasor

38

Dózsa György út

Bajcsy-Zsilinszky út

Jókai u.

37

Eötvös u.

Damjanich u.

Dembinszky u.

István u.

Nagymező u.

Mozsár u.

Andrássy út

Oktogon (Square)

Vörösmarty u.

Dob u.

Rottenbiller utca

Liszt Ferenc tér

Hajós u.

Lázár u.

Paulay Ede u.

Király u.

Erzsébet körút

Hárfa u.

Thököly út

Verseny u.

Keleti (East) Station

Baross tér

Kerepesi út

34

33

Dob utca

Nagy Diófa u.

Wesselényi utca

Klauzál u.

Kertész u.

Akácfa u.

Rákóczi út

Köztársaság tér

Fiumei út

Kerepesi temető (Cemetery)

Deák Ferenc tér

Károly krt.

Dohány utca

Rákóczi út

Szentkirályi u.

35

József körút

Népszínház u.

dor u.

Kossuth L. u.

21

Magyar u.

Múzeum krt.

Puskin u.

Brády Sándor u.

Somogyi Béla u.

Bérkocsis u.

Déri Miksa u.

Mátyás tér

Luzja u.

Danko u.

Teleki László tér

erenciek re

20

22

Kecskeméti u.

Múzeum u.

Krúdy u.

József u.

Baross utca

Szigony u.

N

Veres Pálné u.

Kálvin tér

Baross utca

Váci utca

Molnár u.

Lónyay u.

Üllői út

Nap u.

Práter u.

Tömő u.

Diószeghy Sámuel u.

Fővám tér

Vámház krt.

Ráday u.

Ferenc körút

36

Üllői út

Korányi S. u.

Liberty híd (Liberty Br.)

Kinizsi u.

Knézis u.

KEY

Köztaktár u.

Danube

Rail Lines

Tourist Information

Műegyetem rakpart

Petőfi híd (Petőfi Br.)

Boráros tér

Mester u.

Thaly Kálmán u.

Márton u.

0   550 yards

0   500 meters

$–$$$ ✗ **Udvarház.** The views from this Buda hilltop restaurant are unsurpassed. As you dine indoors at tables set with white linens or outdoors on the open terrace, your meals are accompanied by vistas of the Danube bridges and Parliament far below. Excellent fresh fish is prepared tableside; you could also try veal and goose liver in paprika sauce, served with salty cottage cheese dumplings. Catering to the predominantly tourist crowd, folklore shows and live Gypsy music frequently enliven the scene. The buses up here are infrequent, so it's easier to take a car or taxi. ✉ *District III, Hármashatárhegyi út 2,* ☏ *1/388–6921. AE, DC, MC, V. Closed Mon. Nov.–Mar. No lunch weekdays Nov.–Mar.*

$–$$ ✗ **Náncsi Néni.** "Auntie Nancsi" has built a loyal following by serv-
★   ing up straightforward, home-style Hungarian cuisine in rustic surroundings. Chains of paprika and garlic dangle from the low wooden ceiling above tables set with red-and-white gingham tablecloths and fresh bread tucked into tiny baskets. Shelves along the walls are crammed with jars of home-pickled vegetables, which you can purchase to take home. The menu includes turkey breast fillets stuffed with apples, peaches, mushrooms, cheese, and sour cream. There is a garden dining area open during warmer months, when reservations are essential. ✉ *District III, Ördögárok út 80,* ☏ *1/397–2742. AE, DC, MC, V.*

$ ✗ **Marxim.** Relive the good old bad days of "goulash socialism" in this tongue-in-cheek tribute to Hungary's socialist past, a pizza joint across the street from a factory. Vintage propaganda covers the walls, and dining booths are even separated by barbed wire. The pizza here is perfectly serviceable, although the blaring techno and house music that sometimes play in the background might be too revolutionary for some. As well as many standard pizzas, the menu includes made-up theme pizzas such as the Gulag Pizza, which is more nourishing than it sounds. ✉ *District II, Kisrókus u. 23,* ☏ *1/316–0231. AE, DC, MC, V. Closed Sun.*

Óbuda

$$–$$$ ✗ **Kéhli.** This pricey but laid-back, sepia-toned neighborhood tavern is on a hard-to-find street near the Óbuda end of the Árpád Bridge. Practically all the food here arrives in huge servings, which was just the way that Hungarian writer Gyula Krúdy (to whom the restaurant is dedicated) liked it, when he was a regular customer. Dishes like their hot pot with marrow bone and toast, or *lecsö* (a stew with a base of onions, peppers, tomatoes, and paprika) make for great comfort food on a cool day. ✉ *District III, Mókus u. 22,* ☏ *1/250–4241 or 1/368–0613. AE, DC, MC, V. No lunch weekdays.*

$–$$$ ✗ **Kisbuda Gyöngye.** Considered by many the finest restaurant in
★   Óbuda, this intimate place is filled with antique furniture, and its walls are creatively decorated with an eclectic but elegant patchwork of carved, wooden cupboard doors and panels. A violin-piano duo sets a romantic mood, and in warm weather you can dine outdoors in the cozy back garden. Try the tarragon ragoût of game, or their Flavors of the Forest platter (with pheasant breast, wild duck and wild mushrooms, or stuffed plum wrapped in venison sirloin). ✉ *District III, Kenyeres u. 34,* ☏ *1/368–6402 or 1/368–9246. Reservations essential. AE, DC, MC, V. Closed Sun.*

Tabán and Gellért Hill

$$$–$$$$ ✗ **Kacsa.** As its name ("The Duck") implies, the specialty in this up-
★   market Hungarian restaurant is duck. A special selection of duck dishes includes duck stuffed with ox tongue and plums. Though the street-corner frontage is rather unprepossessing, inside you'll experience true silver-service dining in what could pass for the dining room of a Hapsburg-era noble house. Yet the waiters and management are all rel-

atively young and energetic. You can ask to sit in the anteroom if the rather spirited piano and violin duet is too much for you. ⊠ *District I, Fő u. 75,* ☎ *1/209–9992. Reservations essential. AE, DC, MC, V.*

$$–$$$$ ✕ **Hemingway.** It takes some brio to pull off a restaurant with the style of Ernest Hemingway, but when that restaurant is housed in what looks like a 19th-century hunting lodge—complete with wooden balcony and lake views—the odds for success start to look better. The menu includes several kinds of seafood cooked on Mediterranean lava stone. Fans of heroic consumption will also appreciate a cocktail menu, with some 100 drinks, and a selection of after-dinner cigars. ⊠ *District XI, Kosztolányi Dezso tér 2 (on Feneketlen Lake),* ☎ *1/489–0236. Reservations essential. AE, DC, MC, V.*

$$–$$$$ ✕ **Rivalda.** On summer nights, you can choose to dine outside in an 18th-century courtyard or in the restaurant's rather rococo interior—with poplin stage curtains, theatrical masks, and peach-colored walls. The food is a lighter take on Hungarian cuisine, with some excellent seafood dishes including cream of pumpkin bisque with smoked salmon, and fillet of pike perch. A terrific place for a celebration, whether intimate or with a group, Rivalda has a substantial vegetarian menu, still something of a rarity in Budapest. ⊠ *District I, Színház u. 5–9,* ☎ *1/ 489–0236. Reservations essential. AE, DC, MC, V.*

$–$$$ ✕ **Villa Doria.** A baroque villa near Castle Hill is the venue for this el-
★ egant yet friendly Italian restaurant. The interior is all high ceilings, chandeliers, and polished parquet floors, while a terrace looking onto a garden is perfect for summer dining. The menu runs the gamut from good old spaghetti Bolognese to a large selection of traditional Italian antipasta, pasta, fish, and meat dishes, as well as southern Italian specialties. ⊠ *District I, Döbrentei u. 9,* ☎ *1/225–3233. Reservations essential. AE, DC, MC, V. Closed Mon.*

City Park

$$$–$$$$ ✕ **Gundel.** This is the restaurant to boast about when you return
★ home. In a late-19th-century palazzo, Gundel has been open since 1894 and under the direction of Hungary's best-known restaurateur, George Lang, since 1992. Try some of his signature dishes, such as pan-roasted fillet of Balaton fogas Gundel-style, or the goose liver pâtés. The budget-conscious can still enjoy this famous restaurant by ordering one of the weekday business menus, a three-course meal for 3,000 Ft.–4000 Ft. A cheaper cellar restaurant, 1894, with a separate entrance opened in mid-2002. ⊠ *District XIV, Várisoliget, Állatkerti út 2,* ☎ *1/321–3550. Reservations essential. Jacket and tie. AE, DC, MC, V.*

$$–$$$$ ✕ **Robinson Restaurant.** Robinson can certainly lay claim to one of the more exotic locations in Budapest dining—on wooden platforms atop an artificial lake. Diners look out across the lake to the delightful architectural folly of Vajdahunyad Castle. You can sit outside on the terrace during summer, or enjoy the warm pastel interior in colder months. Service is doting and the menu creative, with dishes such as crisp roast suckling pig with champagne-drenched cabbage or fresh fogas stuffed with spinach. ⊠ *District XIV, Várisoliget, Városligeti-tó (City Park Lake),* ☎ *1/422–0222. Reservations essential. AE, DC, MC, V.*

$–$$$ ✕ **Bagolyvár.** George Lang opened this restaurant next door to his gastronomic palace, Gundel, in 1993. The informal yet polished dining room has a soaring wood-beam ceiling, and the kitchen produces first-rate daily menus of home-style Hungarian specialties. Soups, served in shiny silver tureens, are particularly good. Musicians entertain with *cimbalom* (hammered dulcimer) music nightly from 7 PM. In warm weather there is outdoor dining in a lovely back garden. ⊠ *District XIV, Várisoliget, Állatkerti út 2,* ☎ *1/468–3110. AE, DC, MC, V.*

Lodging

Budapest has seen a steady increase in the variety and overall quality of its tourist accommodations since 1989, including a number of upscale, international-standard hotels that were due to open soon at this writing. Perhaps the most highly anticipated is the new Four Seasons Budapest in the palatial Gresham insurance building facing Erzebet Hid (Elizabeth Bridge).

All room rates given are based on double occupancy in high season. For luxury hotels, VAT of 12% and sometimes breakfast and a tourist tax of 3% will not be included in the room rate. Assume they are included unless there is a note to the contrary.

Advance reservations are strongly advised in the summer. In winter it's not anywhere near as difficult to find a hotel room, even at the last minute, and prices are usually reduced by 20%–30%. The best budget option is to book a private room or an entire apartment. Expect to pay between $20–$30 for a double room. The number of rooms available can be limited in high season, so if you're booking your accommodation on the spot, it may be best arrive in Budapest early in the morning.

Addresses below are preceded by the district number (in Roman numerals) and include the Hungarian postal code. Districts V, VI, and VII are in downtown Pest; District I includes Castle Hill, the main tourist district of Buda. For price ranges *see* Lodging *in* Pleasures and Pastimes.

APARTMENT RENTALS

Apartments, available for short- and long-term rental, are often an economical alternative to staying in a hotel, with an increasing number of options available, as Hungarian entrepreneurs find new uses for old family homes and inherited apartments. A short-term rental in Budapest will probably cost anywhere from $30 to $60 a day.

IBUSZ (✉ District V, Petöfi tér, H-1051, ☎ 01/318-5707, FAX 1/485-2769) is open 24 hours, renting out apartments in downtown Budapest, each consisting of two rooms plus a fully equipped kitchen and bathroom. Accommodation can also be arranged in private rooms—your host is usually a kindly elderly Hungarian lady. The two-person, high-season rate is approximately $40 a night. **To-Ma Tours** (✉ District XI, Bartók Béla út 4, ☎ 1/353-0819, FAX 1/269-5715) arranges private apartments and rooms. The apartments are remarkably spacious and resemble 1950s executive suites, without the telephone but with satellite TV and fully equipped kitchens. They're available for around $40 a night. **TRIBUS Hotel Service** (✉ District V, Apáczai Csere János u. 1, ☎ 1/318-5776, FAX 1/317-9099) has the advantage of being open 24 hours a day, booking private apartments and rooms in private homes; the company can also make hotel reservations.

Budapest Hotels

$$$$ 🏨 **art'otel.** Boutique hotels may not be anything new in the West, but art'otel has the distinction of being Budapest's only boutique hotel, and it is a tribute to its class. From the multi-million-dollar art collection on the walls to the carpet and water fountains, the interior is all the work of one man, American artist Donald Sultan. Encompassing one new building and four 18th-century baroque houses on the Buda riverfront, the art'otel adroitly blends old and new. Some rooms also have splendid views of Fisherman's Bastion and the Matthias Church. ✉ *District I, Bem rakpart 16–19, H-1011,* ☎ *1/487-9487,* FAX *1/487-9488,* WEB *www.parkplazaww.com. 156 rooms, 9 suites. Restaurant, café, cable TV with movies, in-room data ports, in-room safes, minibars, hair salon,* *sauna, meeting rooms, parking (fee); no-smoking rooms. AE, DC, MC, V.*

$$$$ 🏨 **Budapest Hilton.** You'll have to decide for yourself if this hotel, built in 1977 around the remains of a 17th-century Gothic chapel and adjacent to the Matthias Church, is a successful integration or not. The exterior certainly betrays the hotel's 1970s origins, but the modern and tasteful rooms and great views from Castle Hill will soothe the most delicate of aesthetic sensibilities. Rooms with the best Danube vistas cost more. Children, regardless of age, get free accommodation when sharing a room with their parents. VAT, tourist tax, and breakfast are not included in the rates. ✉ *District I, Hess András tér 1–3, H-1014,* ☎ *1/488–6600; 800/445–8667 in the U.S. and Canada;* FAX *1/488–6644;* WEB *www.hilton.com. 295 rooms, 26 suites. 3 restaurants, café, in-room data ports, gym, hair salon, sauna, 2 bars, dry cleaning, laundry service, business services, meeting rooms, travel services, parking (free and fee). AE, DC, MC, V.*

$$$$ 🏨 **Budapest Marriott.** North American–style hospitality on the Pest side of the Danube begins with the buffet of glazed pastries served daily in the lobby and even the feather-light ring of the front-desk bell. Guest rooms have lushly patterned carpets, floral bedspreads, and etched glass. The hotel's prime Danube location makes for some breathtaking views. Gellért Hill, the Chain and Elizabeth bridges, and Castle Hill are visible from all guest rooms, as well as the lobby, ballroom, every guest room, and even the impressive hotel fitness center. ✉ *District V, Apáczai Csere János u. 4, H-1052,* ☎ *1/266–7000; 800/831–4004 in the U.S. and Canada;* FAX *1/266–5000;* WEB *www.marriott.com. 362 rooms, 11 suites. 3 restaurants, in-room data ports, health club, sauna, squash, bar, shops, baby-sitting, dry cleaning, laundry service, business services, meeting rooms, travel services, parking (fee); no-smoking rooms. AE, DC, MC, V.*

$$$$ 🏨 **Hotel Inter-Continental Budapest.** Its days as the socialist-era Fórum Hotel now firmly consigned to the past, the Inter-Continental appeals to the modern business traveler. Every room has an executive-style work desk, and business rooms even contain a printer. The hotel is located right next to the Chain Bridge in Pest, and 60% of the rooms have views across the Danube to Castle Hill (these are more expensive). Rooms on higher floors ensure the least noise. All are decorated in pleasant pastels and furnished in the Biedermeier style typical of Central Europe. Rates do not include VAT, tourist tax, or breakfast. ✉ *District V, Apáczai Csere János u. 12–14 (Box 231, H-1368),* ☎ *1/327–6333,* FAX *1/327–6357,* WEB *www.budapest.intercontinental.com. 398 rooms, 16 suites. 2 restaurants, café, in-room data ports, pool, health club, bar, business services, meeting rooms, car rental, parking (fee); no-smoking floors. AE, DC, MC, V.*

$$$$ 🏨 **Hyatt Regency Budapest.** The spectacular 10-story atrium—a mix
★ of glass-capsule elevators, cascading tropical greenery, an actual prop plane suspended over an open bar, and café—is surpassed only by the Hyatt's views across the Danube to Castle Hill. All rooms are decorated and furnished in muted blues and light woods, and many overlook the Danube or Roosevelt tér. These, of course, are more expensive than those with less commanding views. ✉ *District V, Roosevelt tér 2, H-1051,* ☎ *1/266–1234,* FAX *1/266–9101,* WEB *www.budapest.hyatt.com. 330 rooms, 23 suites. 3 restaurants, in-room data ports, indoor pool, gym, hair salon, sauna, 2 bars, casino, business services, meeting rooms, travel services, parking (fee); no-smoking rooms. AE, DC, MC, V.*

$$$$ 🏨 **Kempinski Hotel Corvinus Budapest.** Madonna stayed here while
★ filming *Evita*, and so did Michael Jackson while shooting his "History" video on Heroes' Square. Rather cold and futuristic-looking on the outside, the hotel has rooms and suites that are spacious, with custom-

made art deco fittings and furniture, as well as an emphasis on functional touches like three phones in every room. Large, sparkling bathrooms—most with tubs and separate shower stalls and stocked with every toiletry—are the best in Budapest. Rates do not include VAT, tourist tax, or breakfast. ⊠ *District V, Erzsébet tér 7–8, H-1051,* ☎ *1/429–3777; 800/426–3135 in the U.S. and Canada;* FAX *1/429–4777;* WEB *www.kempinski-budapest.com. 342 rooms, 27 suites. 2 restaurants, in-room data ports, indoor pool, hair salon, health club, massage, bar, lobby lounge, pub, shops, dry cleaning, laundry service, business services, meeting rooms, travel services, parking (fee); no-smoking rooms. AE, DC, MC, V.*

$$$$ ⊞ **Le Méridien Budapest.** There could scarcely be more contrast be-
★ tween the Le Méridien and its pointedly modern neighbor, the Kempinski. The rooms of this entirely renovated early 20th-century building are decorated in the French Empire style and are both comfortable and plush. Those on the higher floors are slightly smaller but come with an individual balcony. The elegant hotel restaurant is home to splendid afternoon teas prepared by pastry chef Alain Lagrange. Rates do not include VAT, tourist tax, or breakfast. ⊠ *District V, Erzsébet tér 9–10, H-1051,* ☎ *1/429–5500,* FAX *1/429–5555,* WEB *www.lemeridien-budapest.com. 218 rooms, 27 suites. Restaurant, café, cable TV, indoor pool, health club, bar, business services, meeting rooms. AE, DC, MC, V.*

$$$–$$$$ ⊞ **Danubius Hotel Gellért.** Budapest's most renowned hotel has a col-
★ orful past. Built between 1912 and 1918, the German Art Nouveau Jugendstil-style Gellért was favored by Otto von Hapsburg, son of the last emperor. The Gellért is undergoing an incremental overhaul, as bit by bit rooms are refurnished in the original Jugendstil style, with no end in sight. It is therefore a very good idea to inquire about completed rooms when you reserve. Weekend rates can be more friendly. All guests have free access to the monumental and ornate thermal baths. ⊠ *District XI, Gellért tér 1, H-1111,* ☎ *1/385–2200,* FAX *1/466–6631,* WEB *www.danubiusgroup.com/gellert. 220 rooms, 14 suites. 2 restaurants, café, room service, indoor pool, hair salon, spa, Turkish bath, bar, baby-sitting, dry-cleaning, laundry service, business services, meeting rooms, parking (fee); no-smoking rooms. AE, DC, MC, V. BP.*

$$$ ⊞ **Danubius Hotel Astoria.** Constructed as a hotel between 1912 and 1914, the Astoria has a fascinating and turbulent history. The first independent Hungarian government was formed here in 1918. On a darker note, Nazi high command used the Astoria more or less as its headquarters, as did the Soviet forces during the ill-fated revolution of 1956. For the present, rooms today at the Astoria are genteel, spacious, and comfortable, with renovations faithful to the original Empire-style decor. The Café Mirror, with its dripping chandeliers, is a wonderful place to relive the Mittel-European coffeehouse tradition. Rates do not include breakfast. ⊠ *District V, Kossuth Lajos u. 19–21, H-1053,* ☎ *1/317–3411,* FAX *1/318–6798,* WEB *www.danubiusgroup.com/astoria. 125 rooms, 5 suites. Restaurant, café, room service, in-room safes, minibars, cable TV, bar, nightclub, dry-cleaning, laundry service, baby-sitting, business services, meeting rooms, Internet, free parking; no-smoking rooms. AE, DC, MC, V.*

$$$ ⊞ **Danubius Thermal Hotel Helia.** A sleek Scandinavian design and less hectic location upriver from downtown make this spa hotel on the Danube a change of pace from its Pest peers. Rooms are reasonably spacious and also kitted out in the ubiquitous "Scandinavian" style popularized by IKEA. The spa facilities are the most spotlessly clean in Budapest, and an on-site medical clinic caters to English-speaking clients—including everything from electrotherapy to fitness tests. The staff is friendly and helpful, and most of the comfortable rooms have

Danube views. All the room rates include use of the thermal bath and free parking. ✉ *District XIII, Kárpát u. 62–64, H-1133,* ☎ *1/452–5800;* FAX *1/452–5801;* WEB *www.danubiusgroup.com/helia. 254 rooms, 8 suites. Restaurant, café, indoor pool, tennis court, hair salon, health club, hot tub, massage, sauna, spa, steam room, Turkish bath, bar, business services, meeting rooms, free parking. AE, DC, MC, V. BP.*

$$$ 🏨 **K+K Hotel Opera.** Location, location, location: the K+K Hotel Opera has it all, around the corner from Budapest's beautiful opera house and just far enough away from busy Andrássy utca to block out the noise of traffic. Sunflower-yellow walls and bamboo and wicker furniture give the rooms a cheerful aspect. A hearty breakfast buffet will set you up well for a day's sightseeing.✉ *District VI, Révay u. 24, H-1065,* ☎ *1/269—0222,* FAX *1/269—0230,* WEB *www.kkhotels.com. 90 rooms. Restaurant, cable TV, in-room data ports, in-room safes, minibars, gym, bar, laundry service, business services, concierge, meeting rooms, free parking. AE, DC, MC, V. BP.*

$$$ 🏨 **Park Hotel Flamenco.** This glass-and-concrete socialist-era leviathan looks out onto the supposedly bottomless Feneketlen Lake. Happily, once inside, you can almost forget the Stalinist architecture, due to the pleasant, contemporary furnishings. Service is thoroughly professional, and the terrace restaurant has nice views of the lake and park surrounding it. ✉ *District XI, Tas Vezér u. 7, H-1113,* ☎ *1/372–2000,* FAX *1/365–8007,* WEB *www.danubiusgroup.com/flamenco. 350 rooms, 8 suites. 2 restaurants, indoor pool, hair salon, sauna, business services, laundry services, meeting rooms, travel services, parking (fee). AE, DC, MC, V.*

$$$ 🏨 **Radisson SAS Béke Hotel Budapest.** If you are arriving in Budapest's Nyugati Pal train station from Prague or Berlin, the Radisson could scarcely be better located, situated as it is on a bustling stretch of the Körút. Upon arrival at the Radisson, top-hat wearing bellmen will usher you through revolving doors into an impressive reception area, replete with sweeping marble staircase. The bland though comfortable and modern rooms are a faint disappointment after such grandeur, but snappy service and a great location compensate. Rates do not include VAT, tourist tax, or breakfast. ✉ *District VI, Teréz krt. 43, H-1067,* ☎ *1/301–1600,* FAX *1/301–1615,* WEB *www.radisson.com. 238 rooms, 8 suites. 2 restaurants, café, in-room data ports, in-room safes, minibars, cable TV with movies, pool, hair salon, massage, sauna, 2 bars, baby-sitting, business services, meeting rooms, travel services, parking (fee); no-smoking rooms. AE, DC, MC, V.*

$$$ 🏨 **Sydney Apartment Hotel.** Most of the clientele here are business executives on longer-term stays in Budapest, but that shouldn't deter you from the home-away-from-home apartments and such amenities as self-catering kitchens and one of the nicest indoor pools in town. If it's room service you need, you might choose to give these 45- to 110-square-meter (484- to 1180-square ft) apartments a miss, though it should be noted that there is a very helpful 24-hour front-office service. Breakfast is an extra 2,700 Ft. ✉ *District XIII, Hegedus Gyűla u. 52—54, H-1133,* ☎ *1/236–8888;* FAX *1/236–8899;* WEB *www.sydneyaparthotel.hu. 164 rooms, 10 suites. Kitchens, in-room data ports, indoor pool, gym, sauna, spa, meeting rooms, travel services, laundry facilities, free parking; no-smoking rooms. AE, DC, MC, V.*

$$ 🏨 **Carlton Hotel.** The Carlton is proof that you can stay in the Castle Hill district—even nestled at the foot of the hill itself—without paying a fortune. Rooms on the upper floors offer great Danube views. Both the reception area and the rooms are simply furnished and may even prove a little too stark for some tastes, but it's hard to do better for location and price. A large buffet breakfast is served every morning. ✉ *District I, Apor Péter u. 3, H-1011,* ☎ *1/224–0999,* FAX *1/224–0990,* WEB *www.carltonhotel.hu. 95 rooms. Cable TV with movies, in-*

room data ports, in-room safes, minibars, bar, business services, meeting room, parking (fee); no-smoking rooms. AE, DC, MC, V. BP.

$$ 🔲 **Mercure Hotel Budapest Nemzeti.** The egg-shell blue baroque facade of this turn-of-the-20th-century building is difficult to miss, even in this busy part of Pest. The high-ceiling lobby and public areas are festooned with pillars, arches, and wrought-iron railings. Rooms are comparatively plain but not unpleasant. Quadruple-glazed windows shield the front rooms from the noise of the busy intersection below. One should also be made aware that this area can be a hangout for streetwalkers. ⊠ *District XIII, József krt. 4, H-1088,* ☎ *1/303–9310,* 𝐅𝐀𝐗 *1/314–0019,* ☎ 𝐅𝐀𝐗 *1/303–9162,* 𝐖𝐄𝐁 *www.mercure.com. 75 rooms, 1 suite. Restaurant, minibars, bar, meeting room, travel services. AE, DC, MC, V.*

$ 🔲 **Hotel Benczúr.** The leafy lanes of Budapest's embassy district are where you will find this quiet, simply furnished hotel. Majestic Heroes' Square is but a short walk away, and you can even travel back and forth to the center via the antique underground railway line, the Földalatti, by descending downstairs on Andrássy út to the well-signposted Hösök tere metro stop. Rooms come with modern phones and larger-than-usual bathrooms. The Benczúr shares the building with Hotel Pedagógus. ⊠ *District VI, Benczúr u. 35, H-1068,* ☎ *1/342–7970,* 𝐅𝐀𝐗 *1/342–1558,* 𝐖𝐄𝐁 *www.hotelbenczur.hu. 93 rooms. Restaurant, minibars, massage, laundry service, meeting rooms, free parking; no-smoking rooms. MC, V. BP.*

$ 🔲 **Hotel Citadella.** The Citadella will appeal to the energetic, though its hilltop location can entail something of an upward hike after a day's sightseeing. This hotel and hostel combination is housed within a historical fort and does offer marvelous views from many of the room's small windows. None of the rooms has a bathtub, but half have showers. Continental breakfast is included in the rates. ⊠ *District XI, Citadella sétány, Gellérthegy, H-1118,* ☎ *1/466–5794,* 𝐅𝐀𝐗 *1/386–0505,* 𝐖𝐄𝐁 *www.hotels.hu/hotelcitadella. 20 rooms, 10 with shared bath. Restaurant, shop, dance club, parking (fee). No credit cards. CP.*

$ 🔲 **Kulturinov.** This budget hotel can be found in rather noble quar-
★ ters, in this instance one wing of a magnificent 1902 neo-baroque castle. Rooms come with two or three beds and are clean and peaceful; they have showers but no tubs. The neighborhood—one of Budapest's most famous squares in the luxurious castle district—is magical. ⊠ *District I, Szentháromság tér 6, H-1014,* ☎ *1/355–0122 or 1/375–1651,* 𝐅𝐀𝐗 *1/375–1886. 16 rooms. Snack bar, refrigerators, library, meeting rooms. AE, DC, MC, V. BP.*

Nightlife and the Arts

Nightlife

There is a mysterious quiet around the inner-city streets of Pest, even on some summer nights: mysterious because behind closed doors, on almost any night, you can indeed find hopping nightlife. For basic beer and wine drinking, *sörözős* and *borozós* (wine bars) abound, though it may help to master some basic Hungarian, as these places are unused to catering to tourists. The worst of them are little more than drunk tanks. For quiet conversation there are the so-called *drink-bárs* in most hotels and all over town, but some of these places tend to be a little seedy and will sometimes tack on a special foreigner surcharge.

Most nightspots and clubs have bars and dance floors, and some also have pool tables. Although some places do accept credit cards, it is still much more usual to pay in cash for your night on the town. As is the case in most other cities, the life of a club or disco in Budapest can be somewhat ephemeral. Those listed below are quite popular and seem to be here to stay. But for the very latest on the more transient "in" spots, consult the "Nightlife" section of the weekly *Budapest Sun* or *Budapest in Your Pocket,* published six times a year.

Budapest also has its share of seedy go-go clubs and "cabarets," some of which are known for scandalous billing and physical intimidation. Many a hapless single man has found himself having to pay an exorbitant drinks bill after accepting an invitation from a woman asking to join her for a drink. This scam is particularly prevalent on Váci utca. To avoid such rip-offs, at least make sure you don't order anything without first seeing the price.

Some of the most lively nightlife in Budapest hinges around the electronica scene; trance, techno, drum and bass, etc. Recreational drug use is fairly common, but travelers should be aware that penalties for possessing even small amounts of so-called soft drugs can be quite stiff.

A word of warning to the smoke-sensitive: although a 1999 law requiring smoke-free areas in many public establishments has already had a discernible impact in restaurants, the bar scene is a firm reminder that Budapest remains a city of smokers. No matter where you spend your night out, chances are you'll come home smelling of cigarette smoke.

BARS AND CLUBS

Angel Bar and Disco (⊠ District VII, Szövetség u. 33, ☎ 1/351–6490) is Budapest's busiest gay dance club, which attracts a mixed gay-straight crowd, who pack the floor to groove along to souped-up disco and happy house. It's closed Monday–Wednesday, and Saturday night is for men only. The biggest Irish pub in Central Europe, **Becketts** (⊠ District V, Bajcsy-Zsilinszky út 72, ☎ 1/311–1035) is a great place for a pub lunch, a quiet afternoon pint, or a rollicking good time in the evening as a band comes on and the place fills up. A gay-friendly crowd flocks to **Café Capella** (⊠ District V, Belgrád rakpart 23, ☎ 1/318–6231) for the frequent, glittery drag shows and club music until dawn. Of all the see-and-be-seen cafés in Budapest, **Cafe Vian** (⊠ District VI, Liszt Ferenc tér 9, ☎ 1/342–8991) is perhaps the most renowned, partly because of its unbeatable spot in "the tér"—Liszt Ferenc tér; it's a great place to while away the hours chatting and people-watching, either inside and surrounded by an ever-changing exhibit of modern art or outside in the summer under a canopy. Don't be put off by the surly bouncers; **Club Seven** (⊠ District VII, Akácfa 7, ☎ 1/478–9030) has more than one place to play, including an elegant cocktail bar separate from the main room, where an outgoing Hungarian crowd grooves to a mixture of live jazz, rock cover bands, and recorded dance music. Budapest has a truly glitzy international disco, **Dokk Backstage**)

CASINOS

Casinos all open daily 2 PM –4 or 5 AM. The centrally located and popular **Las Vegas Casino** (⊠ District V, Roosevelt tér 2, ☎ 1/317–6022) is in the Hyatt Regency hotel. In an 1879 building designed by prolific architect Miklós Ybl, who also designed the State Opera House, the **Várkert Casino** (⊠ District I, Miklós Ybl tér 9, ☎ 1/202–4244) is the most visually striking of the city's casinos.

The Arts

For the latest on arts events, consult the entertainment listings of the English-language press. Their entertainment calendars map out all that's happening in Budapest's arts and culture world—from thrash bands in wild clubs to performances at the Opera House. Hotels and tourist offices will provide you with a copy of the monthly publication *Programme,* which contains details of all cultural events.

Tickets can be bought at the venues themselves, but many ticket offices sell them without an extra charge. Prices are still very low, so markups of even 30% shouldn't dent your wallet if you book through your hotel. Inquire at Tourinform if you're not sure where to go. Ticket availability depends on the performance and season—it's usually possible to get tickets a few days before a show, but performances by major international artists sell out early. Tickets to Budapest Festival Orchestra concerts and festival events also go particularly quickly.

Theater and opera tickets are sold at the **Central Theater Booking Office** (⊠ District VI, Andrássy út 18, ☎ 1/267–9737). For classical music concert, ballet, and opera tickets, as well as tickets for major pop and rock shows, go to the **National Philharmonic Ticket Office** (⊠ District V, Mérleg u. 10, ☎ 1/318–0281). You can also stop in at the office and browse through the scores of free programs and fliers and scan the walls coated with upcoming concert posters. **Music Mix Ticket Service** (⊠ District V, Váci utca 33, ☎ 1/317–7736) specializes in popular music but handles other genres as well.

CLASSICAL MUSIC AND OPERA

The tiny recital room of the **Bartók Béla Emlékház** (Bartók Béla Memorial House; ⊠ District II, Csalán út 29, ☎ 1/394–4472) hosts intimate Friday-evening chamber music recitals by well-known ensembles from mid-March to June and September to mid-December. The **Budapest Kongresszusi Központ** (Budapest Convention Center; ⊠ District XII, Jagelló út 1–3, ☎ 1/209–1990) is the city's largest-capacity (but least atmospheric) classical concert venue and usually hosts the largest-selling events of the Spring Festival. The homely little sister of the Opera House, the **Erkel Színház** (Erkel Theater; ⊠ District VII, Köztársaság tér 30, ☎ 1/333–0540) is Budapest's other main opera and ballet venue. There are no regular performances in the summer, however. The **Liszt Ferenc Zeneakadémia** (Franz Liszt Academy of Music; ⊠ District VI, Liszt Ferenc tér 8, ☎ 1/342–0179), usually referred to as the Music Academy, is Budapest's premier classical concert venue, hosting orchestra and chamber music concerts in its splendid main hall. It's sometimes possible to grab a standing-room ticket just before a performance here. The glittering **Magyar Állami Operaház** (Hungarian State Opera House; ⊠ District VI, Andrássy út 22, ☎ 1/331–2550), Budapest's main venue for opera and classical ballet, presents an international repertoire of classical and modern works as well as such Hungarian favorites as Kodály's *Háry János*. Except during the one-week BudaFest international opera and ballet festival in mid-August, the Opera House is closed during the summer. Colorful operettas, such as those by Lehár and Kálmán, are staged at their main Budapest venue, the **Operetta Theater** (⊠ District VI, Nagymező u. 19, ☎ 1/353–2172). Classical concerts are held regularly at the **Pesti Vigadó** (Pest Concert Hall; ⊠ District V, Vigadó tér 2, ☎ 1/318–9167).

ENGLISH-LANGUAGE MOVIES

Many of the English-language movies that come to Budapest are subtitled in Hungarian rather than dubbed; this applies less so, however, to independent and art films, as well as—paradoxically—some of the major blockbusters and children's movies. Tickets are very inexpensive by Western standards (400 Ft.–700 Ft.). Consult the movie matrix in the *Budapest Sun* (WEB www.budapestsun.com) for a weekly list of what's showing. The centrally located multiplex **WestEnd Ster Century** (⊠ District VI, Váci út 1–3, ☎ 1/238–7222) usually has several mainstream movies playing.

FOLK DANCING

Many of Budapest's district cultural centers regularly hold traditional regional folk-dancing evenings, or dance houses (*táncház*), often with general instruction at the beginning. These sessions provide a less touristy way to taste Hungarian culture.

Almássy téri Szabadidő központ (Almássy Square Recreation Center; ⊠ District VII, Almássy tér 6, ☎ 1/352–1572) holds numerous folk-dancing evenings, representing Hungarian as well as Greek and other ethnic cultures. Traditionally the wildest táncház is held Saturday night at the **Belvárosi Ifjúsági ház** (City Youth Center; ⊠ District V, Molnár u. 9, ☎ 1/317–5928), where the stomping and whirling go on way into the night; the center, like many such venues, closes from mid-July to mid-August. A well-known Transylvanian folk ensemble, Tatros, hosts a weekly dance house at the **Marczibányi téri Művelődési ház** (Marczibányi Square Cultural Center; ⊠ District II, Marczibányi tér 5/a, ☎ 1/212–5789), from 8 until midnight on Wednesday night.

FOLKLORE PERFORMANCES

The **Hungarian State Folk Ensemble** performs regularly at the **Budai Vigadó** (⊠ District I, Corvin tér 8, ☎ 1/201–3766); shows incorporate instrumental music, dancing, and singing. The **Folklór Centrum** (⊠ District XI, Fehérvári út 47, ☎ 1/203–3868) has been a major venue for folklore performances for more than 30 years. It hosts regular traditional folk concerts and dance performances from spring through fall. The **Várszínház** (National Dance Theater; ⊠ District I, Színház u. 19, ☎ 1/201–4407 or 1/356–4085) stages modern dance productions and is also a venue for performances by popular, local folk bands.

THEATER

The **Budapest Bábszínház** (Budapest Puppet Theater; ⊠ District VI, Andrássy út 69, ☎ 1/321–5200) produces colorful shows that both children and adults enjoy even if they don't understand Hungarian. Watch for showings of *Cinderella* (*Hamupipőke*) and *Snow White and the Seven Dwarfs* (*Hófehérke*), part of the theater's regular repertoire. The **Madách Theater** (⊠ District VII, Erzsébet krt. 31–33, ☎ 1/478–2041) produces colorful musicals in Hungarian, including a popular adaptation of *Cats*. For English-language dramas check out the **Merlin Theater** (⊠ District V, Gerlóczy u. 4, ☎ 1/317–9338). The **Thália Theater** (⊠ District VI, Nagymező u. 22–24, ☎ 1/331–0500) specializes in musicals. The sparkling **Vígszínház** (Comedy Theater; ⊠ District XIII, Pannónia u. 1, ☎ 1/329–2340) hosts classical concerts and dance performances but is primarily a venue for musicals, such as the Hungarian adaptation of *West Side Story*.

Outdoor Activities and Sports

Bicycling

Because of constant thefts, bicycle rentals are difficult to find in Hungary. For more information on bicycle rental, try Tourinform. **Bringóhintó** (⊠ District VIII, Hajós Alfréd sétány 1, across from Thermal Hotel, ☎ 1/329–2072), a rental outfit on Margaret Island, offers popular four-wheel pedaled contraptions called *Bringóhintók,* as well as traditional two-wheelers; standard bikes cost about 800 Ft. per hour or 1,500 Ft. until 8 AM the next day, with a 10,000 Ft. deposit. For brochures and general information on bicycling conditions and suggested routes, contact the **Magyar Kerékpáros Túrázók Szövetsége** (Bicycle Touring Association of Hungary; ⊠ District V, Bajcsy-Zsilinszky út 31, 2nd floor, Apt. 3, ☎ 1/332–7177).

Health and Fitness Clubs

Gold's Gym (⊠ District VIII, Szentkirályi u. 26, ☎ 1/267–4334) has good weight-training and cardiovascular equipment and hourly aerobics classes in larger-than-usual spaces. **Michelle's Health & Fitness** (⊠ District II, Rózsakert Shopping Center, Gábor Áron u. 74, ☎ 1/391–5808) is a popular and well-equipped fitness center in the Buda hills. The **World Class Fitness Centre** (⊠ District V, Marriott hotel, Apáczai Csere János u. 4, ☎ 1/266–4290) really does live up to its name, with a well-equipped gymnasium, regular aerobics classes, plus sauna and squash court.

Horseback Riding

Note that English saddle, not Western, is the standard in Hungary. Experienced riders can ride at the **Budapesti Lovas Klub** (Budapest Equestrian Club; ⊠ District VIII, Kerepesi út 7, ☎ FAX 1/313–5210) for about 1,500 Ft. per hour. Call about two weeks ahead to assure yourself a horse. In the verdant outskirts of Buda, the **Petneházy Lovas Centrum** (Petneházy Equestrian Center; ⊠ District II, Feketefej út 2, Adyliget, ☎ 1/397–5048) offers horseback-riding lessons and trail rides for 1,800 Ft.–2,500 Ft. per hour.

Jogging

The path around the perimeter of **Margaret Island,** as well as the numerous pathways in the center, is level and inviting for a good run. **Városliget** (City Park) in flat Pest has paths good for jogging.

Spas and Thermal Baths

Newer, modern baths are open to the public at hotels, such as the **Danubius Grand Hotel Margitsziget** and the **Danubius Thermal Hotel Helia.** They lack the charm of their older peers but provide the latest treatments.

Gellért Thermal Baths (⊠ District XI, Gellért tér 1, ☎ 1/466–5747) are the most famous in Budapest. The baths are open weekdays 6 AM–6 PM, weekends 6 AM–4 PM. Admission is 1,800 Ft. per day, 2,200 Ft. with a cabin. **Király Baths** (⊠ District II, Fő u. 84, ☎ 1/202–3688) are open weekdays 6:30 AM–6 PM, Saturday 6:30–noon. The baths are open to men on Monday, Wednesday, and Friday; to women on Tuesday, Thursday, and Saturday. These baths are very popular with the gay community. Admission is 500 Ft. The **Lukács Baths** (⊠ District II, Frankel Leó u. 25–29, ☎ 1/326–1695) were built in the 19th century but modeled on the Turkish originals and fed with waters from a source dating from the Bronze Age and Roman times. The complex is open Monday–Saturday 6 AM–7 PM, Sunday 6 AM–5 PM; the facilities are coed. Admission to the baths is 450 Ft. The **Rác Baths** (⊠ District I, Hadnagy u. 8–10, ☎ 1/356–1322) are among the oldest in Budapest. Admission is 700 Ft. They are open Monday–Saturday 6:30 AM–6 PM. Women can bathe on Monday, Wednesday, and Friday; men on Tuesday, Thursday, and Saturday. These baths are particularly popular with the gay community. The **Rudas Baths** (⊠ District I, Döbrentei tér 9, ☎ 1/201–1577) are open to men only and do not have a large gay following; a less interesting outer swimming pool is open to both sexes. Massages are available. Admission is 900 Ft. The baths are open weekdays 6 AM–6 PM, weekends 6–noon. **Széchenyi Baths** (⊠ Városliget, District XIV, Állatkerti krt. 11, ☎ 1/321–0310) are the largest medicinal bathing facility in Europe. Admission is 400 Ft., 700 Ft. for a cabin. The baths are open weekdays 6 AM–6 PM, weekends 6 AM–5 PM.

Shopping

Shopping Districts

You'll find plenty of expensive boutiques, folk-art and souvenir shops, foreign-language bookstores, and classical-record shops on or around touristy **Váci utca,** Budapest's famous, upscale pedestrian-only promenade in District V. While a stroll along Váci utca is integral to a Budapest visit, browsing among some of the smaller, less touristy, more typically Hungarian shops in Pest—on the **Kis körút** (Small Ring Road) and **Nagy körút** (Great Ring Road)—may prove more interesting and less pricey. Lots of arty boutiques are springing up in the section of District V **south of Ferenciek tere** and **toward the Danube,** and around **Kálvin tér. Falk Miksa utca,** also in District V, running south from Szent István körút, is one of the city's best antiques districts, lined on both sides with atmospheric little shops and galleries.

Department Stores and Malls

Proof perhaps of this region's emerging consumer class, Budapest in the last few years has seen a swag of new department stores opening and a shopping-mall building boom. **Duna Plaza** (⊠ District XIII, Váci út 178, ☎ 1/465–1666) has 170 shops, a bowling alley, a Greek taverna, and an ice-skating rink. A special shoppers' bus leaves every half hour from Keleti train station to the **Polus Centre** (⊠ District XV, Szentmihályi út 131, ☎ 1/415–2114). There's a huge Tesco, some Hungarian department stores, fast food restaurants, and a bowling alley. **Skála Metro** (⊠ District VI, Nyugati tér 1–2, ☎ 1/353–2222) is definitely not the newest, but it is centrally located above the Nyugati underground rail station. Central Europe's biggest mall, the **Westend City Center** (⊠ District VI, Váci út 1–3, ☎ 1/238–7777), sits behind the Nyugati (West) Railway Station and teems with activity day and night, staying open weekdays until 9.

Markets

For true bargains and possibly an adventure, make an early morning trip to the vast **Ecseri Piac** (⊠ District IX, Nagykőrösi út 156 [Bus 54 from Boráros tér], ☎ 1/282–9563), on the outskirts of the city. A colorful, chaotic market that shoppers have flocked to for decades, it is an arsenal of secondhand goods, where you can find everything from frayed Russian army fatigues to Herend and Zsolnay porcelain vases to antique silver chalices. Goods are sold at permanent tables set up in rows, from trunks of cars parked on the perimeter, and by lone, shady characters clutching just one or two items. As a foreigner, you may be overcharged, so prepare to haggle—it's part of the flea-market experience. Also, watch out for pickpockets. Ecseri is open weekdays 6 AM– 1 PM, Saturday 8–3, but the best selection is on Saturday morning. A colorful outdoor flea market is held weekend mornings from 7 to 2 at **Petőfi Csarnok** (⊠ District XIV, Városliget, Zichy Mihály út 14, ☎ 1/ 251–7266). The quantity and selection are smaller than at Ecseri Piac, but it's a fun flea-market experience closer to the city center. Red-star medals, Russian military watches, and other memorabilia from Communist days are popular buys here. Although it's mostly a food market, you can get souvenirs and other trinkets upstairs at the **Vásárcsarnok** (⊠ District IX, Vámház krt. 1–3, ☎ 1/217–6067), which is open Monday 6 AM–5 PM, Tuesday–Friday 6 AM–6 PM, and Saturday 6 AM– 2 PM.

Specialty Stores

ANTIQUES

Falk Miksa utca, lined with antiques stores, is a delightful street for multiple-shop browsing. The shelves and tables at tiny **Anna Antikvitás**

(⊠ District V, Falk Miksa u. 18–20, ☎ 1/302–5461) are stacked with exquisite antique textiles—from heavily embroidered wall hangings to dainty lace gloves. The store also carries assorted antique objets d'art. **BÁV Műtárgy** (⊠ District V, Ferenciek tere 12, ☎ 1/318–3381; District V, Kossuth Lajos u. 1–3, ☎ 1/318–6934; District V, Szent István krt. 3, ☎ 1/331–4534), the State Commission Trading House, has antiques of all shapes, sizes, kinds, and prices at its several branches around the city. Porcelain is the specialty at the branch on Kossuth Lajos utca, and paintings at the Szent István körút store.**Darius Antiques** (⊠ District V, Falk Miksa u. 24–26, ☎ 1/311–2603) specializes in Biedermeier furniture and the Viennese baroque style. If antique weapons are your interest, then **Móró Régiség** (⊠ District V, Szent István krt. 1, ☎ 1/312–7877), with its range of militaria and firearms, is definitely worth a stop. **Polgár Galéria és Aukciósház** (⊠ District V, Kossuth Lajos u. 3, ☎ 1/318–6954) sells everything from jewelry to furniture and also holds several auctions a year. **Style Antique** (⊠ District V, Király u. 25, ☎ 1/321–3473) deals in expertly restored antique pinewood furniture.

ART GALLERIES

Budapest has dozens of art galleries showing and selling old works as well as the very latest. **Budapest Galéria Kiállítóterme** (Budapest Exhibition Hall; ⊠ District III, Lajos u. 158, ☎ 1/388–6771) specializes in Hungarian contemporary paintings. In a Bauhaus-era building is the **Fészek Galéria** (⊠ District VII, Kertész u. 36, ☎ 1/342–6548), which displays works by up-and-coming Hungarian artists and hosts concerts and theater performances in its often smoke-filled club room. New York celebrity Yoko Ono opened **Gallery 56** (⊠ District V, Falk Miksa u. 7, ☎ 1/269–2529) to show art by internationally known artists, such as Keith Haring, as well as works by up-and-coming Hungarian artists.

BOOKS

You'll encounter book-selling stands throughout the streets and metro stations of the city, many of which sell English-language souvenir picture books at discount prices. **Váci utca** is lined with bookstores that sell glossy coffee-table books about Budapest and Hungary. Whet your appetite for further travels at **Bamako** (⊠ District VI, Andrássy út 1), Budapest's best source for English-language travel guides. **Bestsellers** (⊠ District V, Október 6 u. 11, ☎ 1/312–1295) sells almost entirely English-language books and publications, including Hungarian classics translated into English, popular British and American best-sellers, and newspapers and magazines. The **Central European University Bookshop** (⊠ District V, Nádor u. 9, ☎ 1/327–3096), in the Central European University, should be your first stop for books concerned with Central European politics and history. **Kiŕly Books** ⊠ District I, Fö u. 79, ☎ 1/214–0972) has two floors of books in English and French. **Párisi Udvar Könyvesbolt** (⊠ District V, Petőfi Sándor u. 2, ☎ 1/235–0380) specializes in foreign-language books, especially travel-related. You will find the store inside the arcade.

CHINA, CRYSTAL, AND PORCELAIN

Hungary is famous for its age-old Herend porcelain, which is hand-painted in the village of Herend near Lake Balaton. High-quality Hungarian and Czech crystal is considerably less expensive here than in the United States. Crystal and porcelain dealers also sell their wares at the Ecseri Piac flea market, often at discount prices, but those looking for authentic Herend and Zsolnay should beware of imitations.

Goda Kristály (⊠ District V, Váci u. 9, ☎ 1/318–4630) has beautiful colored and clear pieces. **Haas & Czjzek** (⊠ District VI, Bajcsy-Zsilinszky út 23, ☎ 1/311–4094) has been in the business for more than 100 years, selling porcelain, glass, and ceramic pieces in traditional and contemporary styles. The brand's largest Budapest store, **Herendi Porcelain Shop** (⌧ District V, József Nádor tér 11, ☎ 1/317–2622), sells the delicate (and pricey) pieces, from figurines to dinner sets. For the Herend name and quality without the steep price tag, visit **Herend Village Pottery** (⌧ District II, Bem rakpart 37, ☎ 1/356–7899), where you can choose from Herend's practical line of durable ceramic cups, dishes, and table settings. Crystal, porcelain, and jewelry are all available at **Monarch Porcelain** (⌧ District V, Váci u. 42, ☎ 1/318–1117), in a large exhibition area. Shipping or free hotel delivery can be arranged. Hungary's exquisite Zsolnay porcelain, created and hand-painted in Pécs, is sold at the **Zsolnay Porcelain Shop** (⌧ District V, Kígyó u. 4, ☎ 1/318–3712) and a few other locations.

CLOTHING

Budapest is not Milan, though many of the big European and American brand names are represented in shopping centers like the Westend City Center. **Manier** (⌧ District V, Váci u. 48 [entrance at Nyári Pál u. 4], ☎ 1/318–1812) is a popular haute couture salon run by talented Hungarian designer Anikó Németh offering women's pieces ranging from quirky to totally outrageous. The store's second branch is across the street at Váci utca 53. Hungarian haute couture is represented by **Monarchia** (⌧ District V, Szabad sajtó út 6, ☎ 1/318–3146), even on Saturday mornings. **Orlando** (⌧ District VI, Rózsa u. 55, ☎ 341–4795), showcases fashions by four young Hungarian designers, both off-the-rack and tailor-made. A reputable men's bespoke suit service resides at **Taylor & Schneider** (⌧ District VI, Nagymezö u. 31, ☎ 312–0842), but you had best bring a translator to specify what you want.

FOLK ART

Handmade articles, such as embroidered tablecloths and painted plates, are sold all over the city by Transylvanian women wearing traditional scarves and colorful skirts. You can usually find them standing at **Moszkva tér, Jászai Mari tér,** outside the **Kossuth tér** metro, around **Váci utca,** and in the larger metro stations. **Holló Műhely** (⌧ District V, Vitkovics Mihály u. 12, ☎ 1/317–8103) sells the work of László Holló, a master wood craftsman who has resurrected traditional motifs and styles of earlier centuries. There are lovely hope chests, chairs, jewelry boxes, candlesticks, and more, all hand-carved and hand-painted with cheery folk motifs—a predominance of birds and flowers in reds, blues, and greens.

HOME DECOR AND GIFTS

Impresszió (⌧ District V, Károly krt. 10, ☎ 1/337–2772) is a little boutique packed with home furnishings, baskets, picture frames, and decorative packaging, all made of natural materials and reasonably priced. The courtyard it calls home includes similar shops and a pleasant café. A few blocks away, just down the street from the Holló Műhely, lies the **Interieur Stúdió** (⌧ District V, Vitkovics Mihály u. 6, ☎ 1/266–1666), offering wooden brushes, bookmarks, and even a birdcage; candles of all shapes and sizes; and sundry other objects for the home.

MUSIC

Recordings of Hungarian folk music or of pieces played by Hungarian artists are widely available on compact discs, though cassettes and records are much cheaper and are sold throughout the city. CDs are normally quite expensive—about 4,000 Ft.

FOTEX Records (⌧ District V, Szervita tér 2, ☎ 1/318–3395; District V, Váci u. 13, ☎ 1/318–3128; District VI, Teréz krt. 27, ☎ 1/332–7175; District XII, Alkotás út 11, ☎ 1/355–6886) is a flashy, western-style music store with a cross section of musical types but focused on contemporary pop. **MCD Amadeus** (⊠ District V, Szende Pál u. 1, ☎ 1/318–6691), just off the Duna korzó, has an extensive selection of classical CDs. **MCD Zeneszalon** (⊠ District V, Vörösmarty tér 1, ☎ no phone) has a large selection of all types of music and is centrally located. Its separate, extensive section on Hungarian artists is great for gift- or souvenir-browsing. The **Rózsavölgyi Zenebolt** (⊠ District V, Szervita tér 5, ☎ 1/318–3500) is an old, established music store crowded with sheet music and largely classical recordings but with other selections as well.

TOYS

For a step back into the world before Pokémon cards and action figures, stop in at the tiny **Játékszerek Anno** (Toys Anno; ⊠ District VI, Teréz krt. 54, ☎ 1/302–6234) store, where fabulous repros of antique European toys are sold. From simple paper puzzles to lovely stone building blocks to the 1940s wind-up metal monkeys on bicycles, these "nostalgia toys" are beautifully simple and exceptionally clever. Even if you're not a collector, it's worth a stop just to browse.

WINE

The burgeoning awareness of Hungary's wine culture has seen a number of upmarket wine stores specializing in Hungarian wines. A good place to start looking for Hungarian wines is **Budapest Bortársaság** (Budapest Wine Society; ⊠ District I, Batthyány u. 59, ☎ 1/212–2569 or 1/212–0262, FAX 1/212–5285); the cellar shop at the base of Castle Hill always has an excellent selection of Hungarian wines. In Pest, **In Vino Veritas** (⊠ District VII, Dohány u. 58–62, ☎ 1/341–3174 or 1/341–0646, FAX 1/321–1953) is a well-stocked store. **Monarchia Wine Shop** (⊠ District IX, Kinizsi u. 30–36, ☎ 1/456–9898) stocks well-presented selections of Hungarian and international wines and is open until 6 PM on Saturday.

Budapest Essentials

AIR TRAVEL

The most convenient way to fly between Hungary and the United States is with Malév Hungarian Airlines' nonstop direct service between JFK International Airport in New York and Budapest's Ferihegy Airport—still the only such flight that exists. Several other airlines offer connecting service from North America, including Austrian Airlines (through Vienna), British Airways (through London), Czech Airlines (through Prague), and Lufthansa (through Frankfurt or Munich). Carriers**Austrian Airlines** (☎ 1/296–0660). **British Airways** (☎ 1/411–5555). **ČSA** (Czech Airlines; ☎ 1/318–3175). **Lufthansa** (☎ 1/429–8011). **Malév** (☎ 1/235–3535 ticketing; 1/235–3888 flight information). **Swiss** (☎ 1/328–5000).

AIRPORTS AND TRANSFERS

Ferihegy Repülőtér, Hungary's only commercial airport with regularly scheduled service, is 24 km (15 mi) southeast of downtown Budapest. All non-Hungarian airlines operate from Terminal 2B; those of Malév, from Terminal 2A. (The older part of the airport, Terminal 1, no longer serves commercial flights, so the main airport is now often referred to as Ferihegy 2 and the terminals simply as A and B.)
➤ AIRPORT INFORMATION: **Ferihegy Repülőtér** (☎ 1/296–9696; 1/296–8000 same-day arrival information; 1/296–7000 same-day departure information).

TRANSFERS

Many hotels offer their guests car or minibus transportation to and from Ferihegy, but all of them charge for the service. You should arrange for a pickup in advance. If you're taking a taxi, allow anywhere between just 25 minutes during nonpeak hours and at least an hour during rush hours (7 AM–9 AM from the airport, 4 PM–6 PM from the city).

Official airport taxis are queued at the exit and overseen by a taxi monitor; their rates are fixed according to the zone of your final destination. A taxi ride to the center of Budapest will cost around 4,500 Ft. Trips to the airport are about 3,500 Ft. from Pest, 4,000 Ft. from Buda. Avoid taxi drivers who approach you before you are out of the arrivals lounge.

Minibuses run every half hour from 5:30 AM to 9:30 PM from the Hotel Kempinski on Erzsébet tér (near the main bus station and the Deák tér metro hub) in downtown Budapest. It takes almost the same time as taxis but costs only 800 Ft.

The LRI Airport Shuttle provides convenient door-to-door service between the airport and any address in the city. To get to the airport, call to arrange a pickup; to get to the city, make arrangements at LRI's airport desk. Service to or from either terminal costs 1,800 Ft. per person; since it normally shuttles several people at once, remember to allow time for a few other pickups or drop-offs.

➤ CONTACTS: **Airport Minibus** (☎ 1/296–8555). **Airport Taxis** (☎ 1/ 341–0000). **LRI Airport Shuttle** (☎ 1/296–8555).

BOAT TRAVEL

From late July through early September, two swift hydrofoils leave Vienna daily at 8 AM and 1 PM (once-a-day trips are scheduled mid-April– late July and September–late October). After a 5½-hour journey downriver, with a stop in the Slovak capital, Bratislava, and views of Hungary's largest church, the cathedral in Esztergom, the boats head into Budapest via its main artery, the Danube. The upriver journey takes about an hour longer.

➤ BOAT AND FERRY LINES: **MAHART Tours** (in Budapest: ✉ International Mooring Point, V, Belgrád rakpart, ☎ 1/318–1743; in Vienna: Handelskai 265, Vienna, ☎ 1/729–2161 or 1/729–2162, WEB www. maharttours.com).

BUS AND TRAM TRAVEL WITHIN BUDAPEST

Trams (*villamos*) and buses (*autóbusz*) are abundant and convenient. A one-fare ticket (106 Ft.; valid on all forms of public transportation) is valid for only one ride in one direction. Tickets are widely available in metro stations and newsstands and must be validated on board by inserting them downward facing you into the little devices provided for that purpose, then pulling the knob. Alternatively, you can purchase a *napijegy* (day ticket, 850 Ft.; a three-day "tourist ticket" costs 1,500 Ft.), which allows unlimited travel on all services within the city limits. Hold on to whatever ticket you have; spot checks by aggressive undercover checkers (look for the red armbands) are numerous and often targeted at tourists. Trolley-bus stops are marked with red, rectangular signs that list the route stops; regular bus stops are marked with similar light blue signs. (The trolley buses and regular buses themselves are red and blue, respectively.) Tram stops are marked by light blue or yellow signs. Most lines run from 5 AM and stop operating at 11 PM, but there is all-night service on certain key routes. Consult the separate night-bus map posted in most metro stations for all-night service.

CAR RENTALS

Rates are high. Daily rates for automatics begin around $55–$60 plus 60¢ per kilometer (½ mi); personal, theft, and accident insurance (not required but recommended) runs an additional $25–$30 per day. Rates tend to be significantly lower if you arrange your rental *from home* through the American offices. Locally based companies usually offer lower rates. Americana Rent-a-Car, for example, has unlimited-mileage weekend specials, and rates include free delivery and pickup of the car anywhere in Budapest. SPQR rents limousines.

➤ Major Agencies: **Avis** (✉ District V, Szervita tér 8, ☎ 1/318–4240; Ferihegy Repülőtér, Terminal 2A, ☎ 1/296–7265; Ferihegy Repülőtér, Terminal 2B, ☎ 1/296–6421). **Budget** (✉ Hotel Mercure Buda, District I, Krisztina krt. 41–43, ☎ 1/214–0420; Ferihegy Repülőtér, Terminal 2A, ☎ 1/296–8481; Ferihegy Repülőtér, Terminal 2B, ☎ 1/296–8197). **Europcar** (✉ District VIII, Ulloi út 60–62, ☎ 1/477–1080; Ferihegy Repülőtér, Terminal 2A, ☎ 1/296–6688; Ferihegy Repülőtér, Terminal 2B, ☎ 1/296–6610). **Hertz** (also known in Hungary as Mercure Rent-a-Car; ✉ Marriott hotel, District V, Apáczai Csere János u. 4, ☎ 1/266–4361; Ferihegy Repülőtér, Terminal 2A, ☎ 1/296–6988; Ferihegy Repülőtér, Terminal 2B, ☎ 1/296–7171).

➤ Local Agencies: **Americana Rent-a-Car** (✉ Ibis Hotel Volga, District XIII, Dózsa György út 65, ☎ 1/350–2542 or 1/320–8287). **EUrent** ✉ District XXIII, Szentlörinc út, ☎ 1/421–8333 or 1/421–8300). **Fox Autorent** ✉ District XI, Vegész u. 17–25, ☎ 1/382–9000). **SPQR** (✉ District XIII, Váci út 175, ☎ 1/237–7334 or 1/237–7300).

CAR TRAVEL

The main routes into Budapest are the M1 from Vienna (via Győr), the M3 from near Gyöngyös, the M5 from Kecskemét, and the M7 from the Balaton; the M3 and M5 are being upgraded and extended to Hungary's borders with Slovakia and Yugoslavia, respectively. Budapest, like any Western city, is plagued by traffic jams during the day, but motorists should have no problem later in the evening. Motorists not accustomed to sharing the city streets with trams should pay extra attention. You should be prepared to be flagged down numerous times by police conducting routine checks for drunk driving and stolen cars. Be sure all of your papers are in order and readily accessible; unfortunately, the police have been known to give foreigners a hard time.

PARKING

Gone are the "anything goes" days of parking in Budapest, when cars parked for free practically anywhere in the city, straddling curbs or angled in the middle of sidewalks. Now most streets in Budapest's main districts have restricted, fee-based parking; there are either parking meters that accept coins (usually for a maximum of two hours) or attendants who approach your car as you park and charge you according to how many hours you intend to stay. Hourly rates average 200 Ft. In most cases; overnight parking (generally after 6 PM and before 8 AM) in these areas is free. Budapest also has a number of parking lots and a few garages; two central-Pest garages in District V are at Szervita tér and Aranykéz utca 4–6.

EMBASSIES AND CONSULATES

All embassies and consulates are in Budapest. *See* the A to Z section at the end of this chapter for addresses.

EMERGENCIES

You call for a general ambulance or call Falck-SOS, a 24-hour private ambulance service with English-speaking personnel. If you need a doctor, ask your hotel or embassy for a recommendation, or visit R-Clinic, a private clinic staffed by English-speaking doctors offering 24-hour medical and ambulance service. The clinic accepts major credit cards and prepares full reports for your insurance company. Profident Dental Services is a private, English-speaking dental practice consisting of

Western-trained dentists and hygienists, with service available 24 hours a day. Most pharmacies close between 6 PM and 8 PM, but several stay open at night and on the weekend, offering 24-hour service, with a small surcharge for items that aren't officially stamped as urgent by a physician. You must ring the buzzer next to the night window and someone will respond over the intercom. Staff is unlikely to speak English. Late-night pharmacies are usually located across from the train stations.

➤ EMERGENCY SERVICES: **Ambulance** (☎ 104). **Falck–SOS** (☎ 1/200–0100). **Police** (☎ 107).

➤ DOCTORS AND DENTISTS: **R-Clinic** (⊠ District II, Felsőzöldmáli út 13, ☎ 1/325–9999). **Profident Dental Services** (⊠ District VII, Karoly Körót u. 1, ☎ 1/342–6972).

➤ LATE-NIGHT PHARMACIES: **Eighth District** (⊠ District VIII, Rákóczi út 39, near the Keleti train station, ☎ 1/314–3695). **Sixth District** (⊠ District VI, Teréz körút 41, near the Nyugati train station, ☎ 1/311–4439). **Twelfth District** (⊠ District XII, Alkotás utca 1/b, across from the Déli train station, ☎ 1/355–4691).

ENGLISH-LANGUAGE MEDIA

Several English-language weeklies have sprouted up to placate Budapest's large expatriate community. The *Budapest Sun* and the *Budapest Business Journal* are sold at major newsstands, hotels, and tourist points. The mini-guidebook *Budapest in Your Pocket* appears six times a year and is also widely available. *Where Budapest,* a free monthly magazine, is available only at major hotels.

SUBWAY TRAVEL

Service on Budapest's subways is cheap, fast, and frequent; stations are easily located on maps and streets by the big letter "M" (for metro). Tickets—106 Ft.; valid on all forms of mass transportation—can be bought at hotels, metro stations, newsstands, and kiosks. They are valid for one ride only; you can't change lines or direction. Tickets must be validated in the time-clock machines in station entrances and should be kept until the end of the journey, as there are frequent checks by undercover inspectors; a fine for traveling without a ticket is 2,500 Ft. Other options include a one-day ticket (850 Ft.), a three-day "tourist ticket" (1,700 Ft.), and a seven-day ticket (2,100 Ft., passport photo required); all allow unlimited subway travel within city limits.

Line 1 (marked FÖLDALATTI), which starts downtown at Vörösmarty tér and follows Andrássy út out past Gundel restaurant and City Park, is an antique tourist attraction in itself, built in the 1890s for the Magyar Millennium; its yellow trains with tank treads still work. Lines 2 and 3 were built 90 years later. Line 2 (red) runs from the eastern suburbs, past the Keleti (East) Railway Station, through the city center, and under the Danube to the Déli (South) station. One of the stations, Moszkva tér, is where the Várbusz (Castle Bus) can be boarded. Line 3 (blue) runs from the southeastern suburbs to Deák tér, through the city center, and northward to the Nyugati (West) station and the northern suburbs. On all three lines, fare tickets are canceled in machines at the station entrance. All three metro lines meet at the Deák tér station and run from 4:30 AM to shortly after 11 PM.

TAXIS

There are plenty of honest taxi drivers in Budapest and a few too many dishonest ones. Fortunately, the reliable ones are easy to spot: they will have a company logo and phone number, and a working meter. If one is hailed on the street, the base fare is generally 200 Ft. and then 200 Ft. each kilometer thereafter. When ordering a taxi by phone (and all the companies here have English-speaking operators), the rate falls to around 200 Ft. base fare, then 150 Ft.–180 Ft. per kilometer.

➤ CONTACTS: **BudaTaxi** (☎ 1/233–3333). **Citytaxi** (☎ 1/211–1111). **Est Taxi** (☎ 1/244–4444). **Fő taxi** (☎ 1/222–2222). **Radio Taxi** (☎ 1/377–7777). **6x6 Taxi** (☎ 1/266–6666).

TOURS

ORIENTATION TOURS

IBUSZ Travel conducts three-hour bus tours of the city that operate all year and cost about 5,500 Ft. Starting from Erzsébet tér, they take in parts of both Buda and Pest. They can also provide English-speaking personal guides on request. Cityrama also offers a three-hour city bus tour (about 5,500 Ft. per person). Both have commentary in English.

➤ CONTACTS: **Cityrama** (✉ District V, Báthori u. 22, ☎ 1/302–4382, WEB www.cityrama.hu). **IBUSZ Travel** (✉ District V, Petőfi tér 3, ☎ 1/318–5707, WEB www.ibusz.hu).

BOAT TOURS:

Hour-long evening sightseeing cruises on the *Danube Legend* depart nightly at 8:15 in April and October and three times nightly (at 8:15, 9, and 10) from May through September. Guests receive headphones with recorded explanations of the sights (available in some 24 languages). Boats depart from Pier 6–7 at Vigadó tér.

The *Duna-Bella* takes six two-hour Danube cruises a day—daylight hours only, but tours do include a one-hour walk on Margaret Island. Recorded commentary is provided through earphones. The tour is offered July through August six times a day; May through June and in September three times a day; and April and October once a day. Boats depart from Pier 6–7 at Vigadó tér.

From March until October at noon every day boats leave from the dock at Vigadó tér on 1½-hour cruises between the railroad bridges north and south of the Árpád and Petőfi bridges, respectively. The trip, organized by MAHART Tours, runs only on weekends and holidays (once a day, at noon) in March and April; then there are regular daytime services until October 31. Evening cruises are at 7:30, except between mid-June and the end of August, when boats leave at 8:15 PM. The cost is 1,200 Ft., 1,500 Ft. on summer evening cruises, with a band and disco on board.

➤ CONTACTS: *Danube Legend* (District V, Vigadó tér, Pier 6–7, ☎ 1/317–2203 reservations and information). *Duna-Bella* (District V, Vigadó tér, Pier 6–7, ☎ 1/317–2203 reservations and information). **MAHART Tours** (District V, Vigadó tér, ☎ 1/484–4000, 1/484–4013, WEB www.maharttours.com).

SPECIAL-INTEREST TOURS

Absolute Walking Tours has broken the mold for guided walking tours in Central Europe. The company offers historical and general interest tours but also creatively executed theme tours, such as the "Hammer & Sickle Tour" and a "Budapest Dark Side" night tour. The 3½-hour Budapest walk costs 3,500 Ft., 3,000 Ft. for students, with no reservations necessary; just show up at 10:30 AM on Deák tér in front of the Evangélikus Templon, a pale yellow Lutheran church.

Chosen Tours offers a three-hour combination bus and walking tour (2,600 Ft.) called "Budapest Through Jewish Eyes," highlighting the sights and cultural life of the city's Jewish history. Tours run daily except Saturday and include free pickup and drop-off at central locations. Arrangements can also be made for off-season tours, as well as custom-designed tours.

➤ CONTACTS: **Absolute Walking Tours** (✉ District XV, Bocskai u. 143a, ☎ 1/266–1729, 🆆🅴🅱 www.budapestours.com). **Chosen Tours** (✉ District XII, Pagony u. 40, ☎ 🄵🄰🅇 1/355–2202).

TRAIN TRAVEL

There are three main *pályaudvar* (train stations) in Budapest: trains to and from Vienna usually operate from the Keleti station, while those to the Lake Balaton region depart from the Déli. You can get information, regardless of the station, 24 hours a day through a central train information number.

➤ TRAIN STATIONS: **Keleti** *Pályaudvar* (East Railway Station; ✉ District VIII, Baross tér). **Nyugati** *Pályaudvar* (West Railway Station; ✉ District V, Nyugati tér). **Déli** *Pályaudvar* (South Railway Station; ✉ District XII, Alkotás u.). **Train Information** (☎ 1/461–5500 international train information; 1/461–5400 domestic train information).

TRAVEL AGENCIES

➤ CONTACTS: **American Express** (✉ District V, Deák Ferenc u. 10, ☎ 1/235–4330, 🄵🄰🅇 1/267–2028). **Getz International** (✉ V, Falk Miksa u. 5, ☎ 1/312–0645 or 1/312–0649, 🄵🄰🅇 1/312–1014). **Vista Travel Center** (✉ VI, Andrássy út 1, ☎ 1/269–6032 or 1/269–6033, 🄵🄰🅇 1/269–6031).

VISITOR INFORMATION

Tourinform has continued to expand and smarten up its act. It's main office is now open 24 hours, and it has several other help desks around town. The Tourism Office of Budapest has developed the Budapest Card, which entitles holders to unlimited travel on public transportation; free admission to many museums and sights; and discounts on various services from participating businesses. The cost at this writing was 3,700 Ft. for two days, 4,500 Ft. for three days; one card is valid for an adult plus one child under 14.

➤ CONTACTS: **Tourinform** (✉ District V, Vörösmarty tér, ☎ 1/438–8080, 🄵🄰🅇 1/356–1964; ✉ District V, Sütő u. 2, ☎ 1/317–9800; ✉ District VI, Liszt Ferenc tér 11, ☎ 1/342–9390). **Tourism Office of Budapest** (✉ District V, Március 15 tér 7, ☎ 1/266–0479; ✉ District VI, Nyugati pályaudvar, ☎ 1/302–8580).

THE DANUBE BEND

About 40 km (25 mi) north of Budapest, the Danube abandons its eastward course and turns abruptly south toward the capital, cutting through the Börzsöny and Visegrád hills. This area is called the Danube Bend and includes the baroque town of Szentendre, the hilltop castle ruins and town of Visegrád, and the cathedral town of Esztergom, all on the Danube's west bank. The most scenically varied part of Hungary, the region is best known for a chain of riverside spas and beaches, bare volcanic mountains, and limestone hills. Here, in the heartland, are the traces of the country's history—the remains of the Roman Empire's frontier, the battlefields of the Middle Ages, and the relics of the Hungarian Renaissance.

The district can be covered by car in one day, the total round-trip no more than 112 km (70 mi), although this affords only a cursory look around. A day trip to Szentendre from Budapest plus two days for Visegrád and Esztergom, with a night in either (both have lovely small hotels), would be best.

On the Danube's eastern bank, Vác is the only larger town of any real interest. No bridges span the Danube in this region, but there are numerous ferries (between Visegrád and Nagymaros, Basaharc and Szob,

Szentendre Island and Vác), making it possible to combine a visit to both sides of the Danube on the same excursion.

Though the Danube Bend's west bank contains the bulk of historical sights, the less-traveled east bank has the excellent hiking trails of the Börzsöny mountain range, which extends along the Danube from Vác to Zebegény before curving toward the Slovak border. The Pilis and Visegrád hills on the Danube's western side and the Börzsöny Hills on the east are popular nature escapes.

Numbers in the margin correspond to numbers on the Danube Bend map.

Szentendre

★ ❶ *21 km (13 mi) north of Budapest.*

A romantic, lively little town with a flourishing artists' colony, this is the highlight of the Danube Bend. With its profusion of enchanting church steeples, colorful baroque houses, and winding, narrow cobblestone streets, it's no wonder Szentendre attracts swarms of visitors, tripling its population in peak season.

Szentendre was first settled by Serbs and Greeks fleeing the advancing Turks in the 16th and 17th centuries. They built houses and churches in their own style—rich in reds and blues seldom seen elsewhere in Hungary. To truly savor Szentendre, duck into any and every cobblestone side street that appeals to you. Baroque houses with shingle roofs (often with an arched eye-of-God upstairs window) and colorful stone walls will enchant your eye and pique your curiosity.

Fő tér is Szentendre's main square, the centerpiece of which is an ornate **Memorial Cross** erected by Serbs in gratitude because the town was spared from a plague. The cross has a crucifixion painted on it and stands atop a triangular pillar adorned with a dozen icon paintings.

Every house on Fő tér is a designated landmark, and three of them are open to the public: the **Ferenczy Múzeum** (Ferenczy Museum) at No. 6, with paintings of Szentendre landscapes; the **Kmetty Múzeum** (Kmetty Museum) at No. 21, with works by János Kmetty, a pioneer of Hungarian avant-garde painting; and the **Szentendrei Képtár** (Municipal Gallery) at Nos. 2–5, with an excellent collection of local contemporary art and international changing exhibits. ▣ *Szentednrei Képtár and Kmetty Múzeum 150 Ft., Ferenczy Múzeum 300 Ft. ☉ Szentednrei Képtár and Kmetty Múzeum Wed.–Sun. 10–4, Ferenczy Múzeum Mon.–Thurs. 10–4.*

Gracing the corner of Görög utca (Greek Street) and Szentendre's main square, Fő tér, the so-called **Görög templom** (Greek Church, also known as Blagovestenska Church) is actually a Serbian Orthodox church that takes its name from the Greek inscription on a red-marble gravestone set in its wall. This elegant edifice was built between 1752 and 1754 by a rococo master, Andreas Mayerhoffer, on the site of a wooden church dating to the Great Serbian Migration (around 690). Its greatest glory—a symmetrical floor-to-ceiling panoply of stunning icons—was painted between 1802 and 1804 by Mihailo Zivkovic, a Serbian painter from Buda. ⊠ *Görög u. at Fő tér.* ▣ *100 Ft. ☉ Mar.–Oct., Tues.–Sun. 10–5.*

If you have time for only one of Szentendre's myriad museums, don't
★ miss the **Kovács Margit Múzeum,** which displays the collected works of Budapest ceramics artist Margit Kovács, who died in 1977. She left

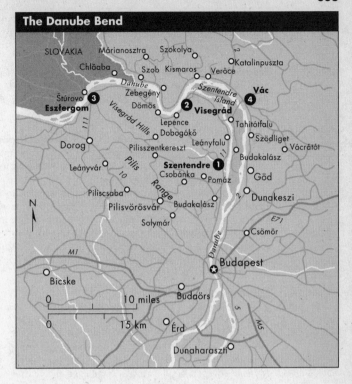

The Danube Bend

SLOVAKIA
Chlǎaba
Štúrovo ③
Eszfergom
Márianosztra Szokolya
Szob Kismaros
Danube Veröce Katalinpuszta
Zebegény
Szentendre Island
Dömös Vác ④
Visegrád ② Visegrád
Lepence
Dobogókő Tahitótfalu
Dorog Pilisszentkereszt Leányfalu Szödliget Vácrátót
Leányvár Budakalász
Pilis Szentendre ①
Csóbánka Csobánka Pomáz Göd
Piliscsaba Range
Pilisvörösvár Budakalász Dunakeszi
Solymár
Csömör
M1
Budapest
Bicske
Budaörs
0   10 miles
0   15 km Érd
Dunaharaszti

N

behind a wealth of richly textured work that ranges from ceramics to life-size sculptures. Admission to the museum is limited to 15 persons at a time, so it is wise to line up early or at lunchtime, when the herds of tour groups are occupied elsewhere. ⊠ *Vastagh György u. 1, off Görög u.*, ☎ *26/310–244 Ext. 114,* WEB *www.pmmi.hu.* ⊡ *400 Ft.* ☉ *Mid-Mar.–early Oct., daily 10–6; early Oct.–mid-Mar., Tues.–Sun. 10–5.*

Perched atop Vár-domb (Castle Hill) is Szentendre's oldest surviving monument, the **Katolikus plébánia templom** (Catholic Parish Church), dating to the 13th century. After many reconstructions, its oldest visible part is a 15th-century sundial in the doorway. The church's small cobblestone yard hosts an arts-and-crafts market and, often on weekends in summer, street entertainment. From here, views over Szentendre's angular tile rooftops and steeples and of the Danube beyond are superb. ⊠ *Vár-domb.* ⊡ *Free.* ☉ *Daily but hrs are sporadic.*

★ The **Szerb Ortodox Egyházi Gyüjtemény** (Serbian Orthodox Collection of Religious Art) displays exquisite artifacts relating to the history of the Serbian Orthodox Church in Hungary. Icons, altars, robes, 16th-century prayer books, and a 17th-century cross with (legend has it) a bullet hole through it were collected from all over the country, after being sold or stolen from Serbian churches that were abandoned when most Serbs returned to their homeland at the turn of the 20th century and following World War I. The museum shares a tranquil yard with the imposing Serbian Orthodox Cathedral. ⊠ *Pátriárka u. 5,* ☎ *26/312–399.* ⊡ *200 Ft.* ☉ *May–Sept., Tues.–Sun. 10–6; Oct.–Dec. and Mar.–Apr., Tues.–Sun. 10–4; Jan.–Feb., Fri.–Sun. 10–4.*

The crimson steeple of the handsome **Szerb Ortodox Bazilika** (Serbian Orthodox Cathedral) presides over a restful tree-shaded yard crowning the hill just north of Vár-domb (Castle Hill). It was built in the 1740s with a much more lavish but arguably less beautiful iconostasis than is found in the Greek Church below it. ⊠ *Pátriárka u. 5*, ☎ *26/314–456.* ⌨ *Free.* ☉ *Tues.–Sun. 10–4.*

NEED A
BREAK? For a quick cholesterol boost, grab a floppy, freshly fried *lángos* (flat, salty fried dough) drizzled with sour cream or brushed with garlic at **Piknik Büfé** (⊠ Dumtsa Jenő u. 22), just next door to the Tourinform office.

Szentendre's farthest-flung museum is the **Szabadtéri Néprajzi Múzeum** (Open-Air Ethnographic Museum), the largest open-air museum in the country. It is a living re-creation of 18th- and 19th-century village life from different regions of Hungary—the sort of place where blacksmith shops and a horse-powered mill compete with wooden houses and folk handicrafts for your attention. During regular crafts demonstrations, you can sit back and watch or give it a try yourself. Five kilometers (3 mi) to the northwest, the museum is reachable by bus from the Szentendre terminus of the HÉV suburban railway. ⊠ *Szabadságforrás út*, ☎ *26/314–456*, ⱳ *www.sznm.hu.* ⌨ *500 Ft.* ☉ *Apr.–Oct., Tues.–Sun. 9–5.*

Dining and Lodging

$–$$$ ✕ **Aranysárkány.** Though this spot was once a favorite of Hungarian
★ writer Frigyes Karinthy, more recent high-profile guests have included François Mitterrand. The food is all prepared in an open kitchen, and as there are only seven large tables, on a busy night you may share with strangers. Begin with a cold Tokaji wine soup or the hot *sárkány erőleves* (dragon bouillon) with quail eggs and sesame seeds. Main-course specialties include steak tartare and trout steamed in sherry. If you can still face dessert, try the plum pudding or cottage cheese dumplings. A wine list with 75 varieties of Hungarian will tempt the inquisitive palate. Reservations are a must during the busy summer months. ⊠ *Alkotmány u. 1/a*, ☎ *26/301–479. AE, DC, MC, V.*

$–$$$ ✕ **Régimódi.** This upstairs restaurant with fine wines and game specialties is practically on Fő tér. Lace curtains and antique knickknacks give the small dining room a homey intimacy. The summer terrace is a delightful place to dine alfresco and look out over the red-tile rooftops. ⊠ *Dumtsa Jenő u. 2*, ☎ *26/311–105. AE, DC, MC, V.*

$–$$ ✕ **Rab Ráby.** Hungarian home-style cooking with an emphasis on
★ fresh-water fish is the mark of this hospitable and often busy restaurant. Old lanterns, cowbells, and musical instruments decorate the walls of this converted 18th-century blacksmith's workshop. Reservations are a must during the busy summer months. ⊠ *Péter Pál u. 1*, ☎ *26/310–819. AE, MC, V.*

$–$$ ✕ **Vidám Szerzetesek.** The Happy Monks is well-touristed, but it's also popular with locals. The reasonably priced menu (in 19 languages) includes hearty, heavy Hungarian favorites such as lamb stew with ewe cheese. Try the *suhajda* (literally, "monk's pleasure"), a savory brew of smoked meat with a tasty dough cap baked over an earthenware pot. ⊠ *Bogdányi út 3–5*, ☎ *26/310–544. AE, DC, MC, V. Closed Mon.*

$$$$ 🏨 **Kentaur Ház.** This handsome, modern, chalet-style hotel is a two-minute walk from Fő tér, on what may be Hungary's last surviving square still to bear Karl Marx's name. Rooms are clean and simple, with pale gray carpeting, blond unfinished-wood paneling, and pastel-pink walls hung with original paintings by local artists. Children under 10 may stay for free. ⊠ *Marx tér 3–5, H-2000*, ☎ *26/318–184*, 🅕🅐🅧 *26/312–125*, ⱳ *www.hotels.hu/kentaur. 16 rooms. Restaurant, café, room service, cable TV, minibars, bar, meeting room, pets allowed, parking (fee). No credit cards. BP.*

$$ ⊡ **Centrum Panzió.** Szentendre's newest and most pristine inn has only six rooms, but two are family-size, and all are pleasantly furnished in shades of blue and gray. Just a short step from Szerb utca, the Centrum has pleasant Danube views and an attentive and genuinely friendly English-speaking management. The rooms are spotless and bright and even come with cable TV.⊠ *Bogdányi u. 15, H-2000,* ☎ ᶠᴬˣ *26/302–500,* ᵂᴱᴮ *www.hotels.hu/centrum_panzio. 6 rooms. Cable TV, laundry service, pets allowed, parking. No credit cards.*

$ ⊡ **St. Andrea Panzió.** This remodeled *panzió* (pension) atop a grassy incline has all the makings of a Swiss chalet. Attic space has been converted into modernized rooms with clean tiled showers. On a warm day you can eat breakfast on the outside patio. The owners are very friendly; they've even been known to specially cook meals for guests arriving late at night. ⊠ *Egres u. 22, H-2000,* ☎ *26/301–800,* ᶠᴬˣ *26/500–804,* ᵂᴱᴮ *www.hotels.hu/st_andrea. 16 rooms, 2 suites. Restaurant, room service, cable TV, bar, meeting room, parking. No credit cards.*

Outdoor Activities and Sports

BICYCLING

The waterfront and streets beyond Szentendre's main square are perfect for a bike ride—free of jostling cobblestones and relatively calm and quiet. Check with Tourinform for local rental outfits. Rentals are possible in Budapest; bicycles are permitted in a designated car of each HÉV suburban railway train. Many people make the trip between Budapest and Szentendre on bicycle along the designated bike path, which runs on busy roads in some places, but is pleasant and separate from the road for the stretch between Békásmegyer and Szentendre.

Nightlife and the Arts

Most of Szentendre's concerts and entertainment events occur during the spring and summer. The annual **Spring Festival,** usually held from mid-March through early April, offers classical concerts in some of Szentendre's churches, as well as jazz, folk, and rock performances in the cultural center and other venues about town. In July, the **Szentendre Summer Days** festival brings open-air theater performances and jazz and classical concerts to Fő tér and the cobblestone courtyard fronting the town hall. Although the plays are usually in Hungarian, the setting alone can make it an enjoyable experience. If you would just like a drink in amiable surroundings, the **Red Lion Pub** (⊠ Szerb u. 2a, ☎ 26/318–607) has a quiet courtyard and Victorian "gas-lit" interior, authentically stodgy pub food, and 36 kinds of whiskey to please the most picky pub goer.

Shopping

Flooded with tourists in summer, Szentendre is saturated with the requisite souvenir shops. Among the attractive but overpriced goods sold in every store are dolls dressed in traditional folk costumes, wooden trinkets, pottery, and colorful hand-embroidered tablecloths, doilies, and blouses. The best bargains are the hand-embroidered blankets and bags sold by dozens of elderly women in traditional folk attire, who stand for hours on the town's crowded streets. (Because of high weekend traffic, most Szentendre stores stay open all day on weekends, unlike those in Budapest. Galleries are closed Monday and accept major credit cards, although other stores may not.)

The one tiny room of **art-éria galéria** (⊠ Városház tér 1, ☎ 26/310–111) is crammed with paintings, graphics, and sculptures by 21 of Szentendre's best contemporary artists. The sophisticated **Erdész Galéria** (⊠ Fő tér 20, ☎ 26/310–139), on Szentendre's main square (not to be confused with the similarly named Gallery Erdész), displays paintings, statues, and other works by some 30 local artists. Topped with an abstract-statue trio of topless, pale-pink and baby-blue women in polka-dot bikini panties, the **Christoff Galéria** (✉ Bartók Béla u. 8, ☎ 26/317–031) is hard to miss as you climb the steep hill to its door. The gallery sells works by local and Hungarian contemporary artists, including those of popular visual artist and musician ef Zambo, creator of its crowning females. It's best to call ahead to check opening times. The **Gallery Erdész** (✉ Bercsényi u. 4, ☎ 26/317–925) displays an impressive selection of contemporary Hungarian art, as well as gifts such as leather bags, colored-glass vases, and handmade paper—not to mention some unique, curvaceous silver pieces made by a famous local jeweler. Beautiful stationery, booklets, and other handmade paper products are displayed and sold at the **László Vincze Paper Mill** (✉ Angyal u. 5, ☎ 26/314–328). In this small workshop at the top of a broken cobblestone street, Mr. Vincze lovingly creates his thick, watermarked paper, using traditional, 2,000-year old bleaching methods. Traditional crafts take a back seat in the refreshingly contemporary **Palmetta Design Galéria** (✉ Bogdányi u. 14, ☎ FAX 26/313–649), where you'll find textiles, ceramics, lamps, jewelry, and artwork by Hungarian and international artists and designers.

Visegrád

❷ *23 km (14 mi) north of Szentendre.*

Visegrád was the seat of the Hungarian kings during the 14th century, when a fortress built here by the Angevin kings became the royal residence. Today, the imposing fortress at the top of the hill towers over the peaceful little town of quiet, tree-lined streets and solid old houses. The forested hills rising just behind the town offer popular hiking possibilities. For a taste of Visegrád's best, climb to the Fellegvár, and then wander and take in the views of the Danube curving through the countryside; but make time to stroll around the village center a bit—on Fő utca and other streets that pique your interest.

★ Crowning the top of a 1,148-ft hill, the dramatic **Fellegvár** (Citadel) was built in the 13th century and served as the seat of Hungarian kings in the early 14th century. In the Middle Ages, the citadel was where the Holy Crown and other royal regalia were kept, until they were stolen by a dishonorable maid of honor in 1440; 23 years later, King Matthias had to pay 80,000 Ft. to retrieve them from Austria. (For the time being, the crown is safe in the Parliament building in Budapest.) A *panoptikum* (akin to slide projection) show portraying the era of the kings is included with admission. The breathtaking views of the Danube Bend below are ample reward for the strenuous 40-minute hike up. ☎ 26/398–101. 🎫 250 Ft. ☉ Mid-Mar.–mid-Nov., daily 9–5; mid-Nov.–mid-Mar., weekends 10–dusk; closed in snowy conditions.

In the 13th through 14th centuries, King Matthias Corvinus had a separate palace built on the banks of the Danube below the citadel. It was eventually razed by the Turks, and not until 1934 were the ruins finally excavated. Nowadays you can see the disheveled remnants of the **Királyi palota** (Royal Palace) and its **Salamon torony** (Salomon Tower), referred to together as the **Mátyás Király Múzeum** (King Matthias Museum). The Salomon Tower houses two small exhibits displaying ancient statues and well structures from the age of King Matthias. Especially worth seeing is the red-marble well, built by a 15th-century Italian architect. Above a ceremonial courtyard rise the palace's various halls; on the left you can still see a few fine original carvings, which give an idea of how magnificent the palace must once have been. Inside the palace is a small exhibit on its history, as well as a collection of gravestones dating from Roman times to the 19th century. Fridays in May, the museum hosts medieval-crafts demonstrations. ☒ *Fő u. 23,* ☎ *26/398–026,* WEB *www.visegrad.hu/muzeum.* ☒ *Royal Palace 300 Ft., Salomon Tower 300 Ft.* ☉ *Royal Palace Tues.–Sun. 9–4:30. Salomon Tower May–Sept., Tues.–Sun. 9–4:30.*

Like a tiny, precious gem, the miniature **Millennial Chapel** sits in a small clearing, tucked away on a corner down Fő utca, Visegrád's main street. The bite-size, powder-yellow church was built in 1896 to celebrate the Magyar Millennium and is open only on Pentecost and a few other holidays. ☒ *Fő u. 113.*

Dining and Lodging

$–$$ ✕ **Gulyás Csárda.** This cozy little restaurant, decorated with antique
★ folk art and memorabilia, complements its eight indoor tables with additional seating outside during the summer. The cuisine is typical homestyle Hungarian, with a limited selection of tasty traditional dishes. Try the halászlé, served in a pot and kept warm on a small spirit burner. ☒ *Nagy Lajos király u. 4,* ☎ *26/398–329. MC, V.*

$–$$ ✕ **Sirály Restaurant.** Now under the management of the Visegrád Hotel, this restaurant sits opposite the ferry station and is well known for its rolled fillet of venison and its many vegetarian dishes, including fried soy steak with vegetables. In summer, when cooking is often done on the terrace overlooking the Danube, expect barbecued meats and stews, soups, and gulyás served in old-fashioned pots. ☒ *Rév u. 15,* ☎ *26/398–376. AE, MC, V. Closed Nov.–Feb.*

$$ ✕ **Fekete Holló.** The popular "Black Raven" restaurant has an elegant yet comfortable atmosphere—a great place for a full meal or just a beer. Try the chef's creative specialties, such as coconut chicken leg with pineapples, or stick to such regional staples as fresh, grilled fish; either way save room for the palacsinta with nuts and chocolate. ☒ *Rév út 12,* ☎ *26/397–289. No credit cards. Closed Nov.–Mar.*

$$$$ ▥ **Beta Hotel Silvanus.** With 24 new rooms and an executive floor, this hotel seems to be remodeling itself as an executive retreat. As such, it is ideally situated high up on Fekete Hill, with commanding forest and Danube views. The expanded amenities also include a wellness center with tepidarium (salt therapy). Because of the location, it's best to have a car if you stay here (although a bus does stop nearby); hikers and bikers will find linking trails in the forest behind. ☒ *Fekete-hegy, H-2025,* ☎FAX *26/398–311,* WEB *www.betahotels.hu. 102 rooms, 5 suites. Restaurant, café, room service, minibars, cable TV with movies, indoor pool, hair salon, massage, sauna, steam room, bowling, mountain bikes, bar, dry-cleaning, laundry service, playground, meeting rooms, pets allowed. AE, DC, MC, V.*

$$ ▥ **Hotel & Haus Honti.** This 21-room hotel and its older, alpine-style sibling pension share the same yard in a quiet residential area, a three-minute walk from the town center. Apple trees and a gurgling brook create a peaceful, rustic ambience. The pension has seven tiny, clean rooms tucked under sloping ceilings with balconies, some with lovely Danube views; the rooms in the hotel are more spacious and more expensive, some with balconies affording a splendid view of the Citadel in the distance. ☒ *Fő u. 66, H-2025,* ☎ *26/398–120. 28 rooms. Restaurant, minibars, meeting room, some pets allowed, no-smoking rooms, free parking. No credit cards.*

$$ ▥ **Hotel Visegrád.** This is possibly the best place to stay in Visegrád, because this newly built, centrally located hotel also has an in-house travel agency, organizing local excursions in the area for both groups and individuals. Every room has a balcony with views of the Danube or the castle, and all are pristine yet comfortable, many in warm lemony and ochre hues. The suites are suitable for a family with three children. The hotel's Renaissance Restaurant is a slightly tacky but lik-

able medieval-theme restaurant. ⊠ *Rév út 15, H-2025,* ☎ *26/397–034,* FAX *26/597–088,* WEB *www.visegradtours.hu. 30 rooms, 7 suites. 2 restaurants, in-room safes, minibars, meeting room, travel services. AE, DC, MC, V.*

Nightlife and the Arts

The **Visegrád International Palace Games,** held annually on the second weekend in July, take the castle complex back to its medieval heyday, with horseback jousting tournaments, archery games, a medieval music and crafts fair, and other festivities.

Outdoor Activities and Sports

HIKING

Visegrád makes a great base for exploring the trails of the Visegrád and Pilis hills. A hiking map is posted on the corner of Fő utca and Rév utca, just above the pale-green Roman Catholic Parish Church. A well-trodden, well-marked hiking trail (posted with red signs) leads from the edge of Visegrád to the town of Pilisszentlászló, a wonderful 8½-km (5⅓ mi) journey that takes about three hours, through the oak and beech forests of the Visegrád Hills into the Pilis conservation region. Deer, wild boars, and mouflons roam freely here, and there are fields of yellow-blooming spring pheasant's eye and black pulsatilla.

SWIMMING

The outdoor thermal pools at **Lepence,** 3 km (2 mi) southwest of Visegrád on Route 11, combine good soaking with excellent Danube Bend views. ⊠ *Lepence-völgyi Termál és Strandfürdő, Lepence,* ☎ *26/ 398–208.* ⊠ *400 Ft.* ☉ *May–Sept., daily 9–6:30.*

TOBOGGAN SLIDE

ⓒ Winding through the trees on Nagy-Villám Hill is the **Wiegand Toboggan Run,** one of the longest slides you've ever seen. You ride on a small cart that is pulled uphill by trolley, then careen down the slope in a small, steel trough that resembles a bobsled run. ⊠ *Panoráma út, ½ km (¼ mi) from Fellegvár,* ☎ *26/397–397.* ⊠ *180 Ft. weekdays, 220 Ft. weekends; 1,000 Ft. for six runs weekdays, 1,200 Ft. weekends.* ☉ *May– Sept., daily 10–7; Apr. and Oct., daily 11–4; Nov.–Mar. (weather permitting), weekends 11–4.*

Esztergom

❸ *21 km (13 mi) north of Visegrád.*

Esztergom stands on the site of a Roman fortress, at the westernmost curve of the heart-shape Danube Bend, where the Danube marks the border between Hungary and Slovakia. (The bridge that once joined these two countries was destroyed by the Nazis near the end of World War II, though parts of the span can still be seen.) St. Stephen, the first Christian king of Hungary and founder of the nation, was crowned here in AD 1000, establishing Esztergom as Hungary's first capital, which it remained for the next 250 years. The majestic Bazilika, Hungary's largest, is Esztergom's main draw, followed by the fine art collection of the Primate's Palace. If you like strolling, leave yourself a little time to explore the narrow streets of Viziváros (Watertown) below the Bazilika, lined with brightly painted baroque buildings.

To the south of the cathedral, on **Szent Tamás Hill,** is a small church dedicated to St. Thomas à Becket of Canterbury. From here you can look down on the town and see how the Danube temporarily splits, forming an island, **Prímás-sziget,** that locals use as a base for waterskiing and swimming, in spite of the pollution. To reach it, cross the Kossuth Bridge.

★ Esztergom's **Bazilika** (cathedral), the largest in Hungary, stands on a hill overlooking the town; it is now the seat of the cardinal primate of Hungary. It was here, in the center of Hungarian Catholicism, that the famous anti-Communist cleric, Cardinal József Mindszenty, was finally reburied in 1991 (he was originally buried in Austria when he died in 1975), ending an era of religious intolerance and prosecution and a sorrowful chapter in Hungarian history. Its most interesting features are the Bakócz Chapel (1506), named for a primate of Hungary who only narrowly missed becoming pope; and the sacristy, which contains a valuable collection of medieval ecclesiastical art. If your timing is lucky, you could attend a concert during one of the various classical music festivals held here in summer. ⊠ *Szent István tér,* ☎ *33/311–895.* ⊡ *Free.* ⊙ *Apr.–late Oct., daily 7–4; late Oct.–Mar., weekdays 7–4, weekends 7–5.*

Considered by many to be Hungary's finest art gallery, the **Keresztény Múzeum** (Museum of Christian Art), in the Primate's Palace, has a thorough collection of early Hungarian and Italian paintings (the 14th- and 15th-century Italian collection is unusually large for a museum outside Italy). Unique holdings include the *Coffin of Our Lord* from Garamszentbenedek (today Hronský Beňadik, Slovakia); the wooden statues of the Apostles and of the Roman soldiers guarding the coffin are masterpieces of Hungarian baroque sculpture. The building also holds the Primate's Archives, which contain 20,000 volumes, including several medieval codices. Permission to visit the archives must be obtained in advance. ⊠ *Primate's Palace, Mindszenty tér 2,* ☎ *33/413–880.* ⊡ *200 Ft.* ⊙ *Mid-Mar.–Sept., Tues.–Sun. 10–6; Jan.–mid-Mar., Tues.–Sun. 10–5.*

Dining and Lodging

$–$$ ✕ **Prímás Pince.** Arched ceilings and exposed brick walls make a charming setting for refined Hungarian fare at this touristy but good restaurant just below the cathedral. Try the tournedos Budapest style (tender beef with sautéed vegetables and paprika) or the thick turkey breast Fiaker style (stuffed with ham and melted cheese). ⊠ *Szent István tér 4,* ☎ *33/313–495. AE, DC, MC, V. No dinner Jan.–Feb.*

$ ✕🏠 **Szalma Csárda & Panzió.** This inn (i.e., restaurant) and pension is on a tranquil, fairly undeveloped stretch of the Danube. The restaurant is splendidly rustic, complete with a large earthenware stove in the main room. Listen to live Gypsy music while enjoying "long-forgotten peasant dishes"—such as chicken paprika with wax beans and dill-spiced dumplings on the side. The 20-room pension, which from the outside resembles a ranch house, is run by the same family as the restaurant. The small rooms are clean and bright and furnished simply with low, summer-camp-like pinewood beds. ⊠ *Nagy-Duna sétány 2, on Prímás-sziget, H-2500,* ☎ FAX *33/315–336 or 33/403–838. MC.*

$$ 🏠 **Alabárdos Panzió.** Conveniently downhill from the cathedral, this cozy, remodeled home provides excellent views from upstairs. Rooms (doubles and quads) are small but less cramped than at other small pensions. Breakfast is included. ⊠ *Bajcsy-Zsilinszky u. 49, H-2500,* ☎ FAX *33/312–640. 22 rooms. Laundry facilities, meeting room. No credit cards.*

$$ 🏠 **Hotel Esztergom.** Simply furnished and sports-oriented, this hotel has a good location on Prímás-szíget. Tennis, swimming, bowling, horseback riding, and water-sports facilities are nearby. All rooms have balconies, though the largest—and nicest—rooms face away from the river. ⊠ *Prímás-szíget, Nagy Duna Sétány, H-2500,* ☎ *33/412–883,* FAX *33/412–853,* WEB *www.betahotels.hu. 34 rooms, 2 suites. Restaurant, meeting room. AE, DC, MC, V.*

Nightlife and the Arts

Every two years Esztergom hosts the **Nemzetközi Gitár Fesztivál** (International Guitar Festival), during which renowned classical guitarists from around the world hold master classes and workshops for participants. Recitals are held nearly every night in Esztergom's **Zöldház Művelődési Központ** (Green House Cultural Center) or the **Tanítóképző Főiskola** (Teachers College), where the festival is based, or elsewhere in Budapest and neighboring towns. The climax of it all is the glorious closing concert, held in the basilica, in which the hundreds of participants join together and perform as a guitar orchestra. The festival runs for two weeks, usually beginning in early August in odd-numbered years. Tickets and information are available at the tourist offices.

Vác

❹ *34 km (21 mi) north of Budapest; 20 km (12 mi) south of Nagymaros, which is accessed by ferry from Visegrád.*

With its lovely riverfront promenade, its cathedral, and less delightful Triumphal Arch, the small city of Vác, on the Danube's east bank, is well worth a short visit if only to watch the sun slowly set from the promenade. Vác's historic town center is full of pretty baroque buildings in matte yellows and reds and offers many visual rewards and photo opportunities for those who wander onto a few of its narrow cobblestone side streets heading in toward the river.

Vác's 18th-century **Székesegyház** (cathedral) on Konstantin tér is an outstanding example of Hungarian neoclassicism. It was built between 1763 and 1777 by Archbishop Kristóf Migazzi to the designs of the Italian architect Isidor Carnevale; the most interesting features are the murals by the Austrian Franz Anton Maulbertsch, both on the dome and behind the altar. Exquisite frescoes decorate the walls inside. Due to recent break-ins, you can view the interior only through a locked gate, except during Mass (daily 8–9 AM and 6–7 PM). ⊠ *Konstantin tér 11,* ☎ *27/317–010.* ☎ *Free.* ☙ *Daily 8–7.*

In 1764, when Archbishop Migazzi heard that Queen Maria Theresa planned to visit his humble town, he hurriedly arranged the construction of a **triumphal arch.** The queen came and left, but the awkward arch remains, at the edge of the city's historic core next to a cement-and-barbed-wire prison complex. ⊠ *Köztársaság út just past Barabás u.*

The **promenade** along the Danube is a wonderful place to stroll or picnic, looking out at the glistening river or back toward the pretty historic town. The main entrance to the riverfront area is from Petróczy utca, which begins at the cathedral on Konstantin tér and feeds straight into the promenade.

Vácrátóti Arborétum, 4 km (2½ mi) from Vác, is Hungary's biggest and best botanical garden, with more than 12,000 plant species. The arboretum's top priority is botanical research and collection under the auspices of the Hungarian Academy of Sciences, but you're welcome to stroll along the paths and sit on benches in the leafy shade. If you're driving from Vác, follow signs toward Gödöllő, then toward Vácrátót. ⊠ *Alkotmány u. 2–4,* ☎ *28/360–122 or 28/360–147.* ☎ *160 Ft.* ☙ *Apr.–Oct., daily 8–6; Nov.–Mar., daily 8–4.*

Dining

$–$$ ✕ **Halászkert Étterem.** The large terrace of this contemporary riverfront restaurant next to the ferry landing is a popular place for a hearty lunch or dinner in warmer months. The menu includes some

250 dishes, including Hungarian fish specialties. ⊠ *Liszt Ferenc rak-part 9,* ☎ *27/315–985. AE, DC, MC, V.*

Nightlife and the Arts

In July and August, a series of outdoor classical concerts are held in the verdant **Vácrátóti Arborétum.** The last weekend in July brings the **Váci Világi Vigalom** (Vác World Jamboree) festival, with folk dancing, music, crafts fairs, and other festivities throughout town.

Outdoor Activities and Sports

Vác is the gateway to hiking in the forests of the **Börzsöny Hills,** rich in natural springs, castle ruins, and splendid Danube Bend vistas. Consult the Börzsöny hiking map, available at Tourinform, for planning a walk on the well-marked trails. The **Börzsöny Természetjáró Kör** (Börzsöny Hiking Club) organizes free guided nature walks every other Sunday all year round. Naturally, Hungarian is the official language, but chances are good that younger group members will speak English—however, even without understanding what is spoken, the trips afford a nice opportunity to be guided through the area. Contact Tourinform for details.

Danube Bend Essentials

BICYCLE TRAVEL

The Danube Bend is a great place to explore by bike; most towns are relatively close together. Some routes have separate bike paths, while others run along the roads. Consult the "Danube Bend Cyclists' Map" (available at tourist offices) and Tourinform for exact information.

BOAT AND FERRY TRAVEL

If you have enough time, you can travel to the west-bank towns by cruise boat or jet foil from Budapest, a leisurely and pleasant journey, especially in summer and spring. Boating from Budapest to Esztergom takes about five hours, to Visegrád about three hours. Boats leave from the main Pest dock at Vigadó tér. The disadvantage of boat travel is that a round-trip by slow boat doesn't allow much time for sightseeing; the Esztergom route, for example, allows only under two hours before it's time to head back. Many people head upriver by boat in the morning and back down by bus or train as it's getting dark. There is daily service from Budapest to Visegrád, stopping in Szentendre. Less frequent boats go to Vác, on the east bank, as well.

As there are no bridges across the Danube in this region, there is regular daily passenger and car ferry service between several points on opposite sides of the Danube (except in winter when the river is too icy). The crossing generally takes about 10 minutes and costs roughly 600 Ft. per car and driver, 120 Ft. per passenger. The crossing between Nagymaros and Visegrád is recommended, as it affords gorgeous views of Visegrád's citadel and includes a beautiful drive through rolling hills on Route 12 south and then west of Nagymaros.

➤ CONTACTS: **MAHART Tours** (District V, Vigadó tér, Budapest, ☎ 1/484–4000 or 1/484–4013, WEB www.maharttours.com).

BUS TRAVEL

Buses, which are cheap and relatively comfortable—if you get a seat and don't have to stand—run regularly between Budapest's Árpád híd bus station and most towns along both sides of the Danube. The ride to Szentendre takes about half an hour. If you don't have a car, this is the best way to get around, since train service is spotty.

CAR TRAVEL

Route 11 runs along the western shore of the Danube, connecting Budapest to Szentendre, Visegrád, and Esztergom. Route 2 runs along the eastern shore for driving between Budapest and Vác.

TOURS

Cityrama runs its popular "Danube Tour" (approximately 16,000 Ft.) daily during the high season (May until September) from Wednesday to Sunday; from October to May the tour is offered only once a week, so call ahead for exact dates and times. Departing from Budapest, the full-day tour begins with sightseeing in Visegrád, then Esztergom. After lunch, the tour moves on to Szentendre for a guided walk and makes a scenic return to Budapest down the Danube. (The tour returns by bus when the water level is low.) IBUSZ Travel organizes day-long bus trips from Budapest along the Danube (May to October on Tuesday, Friday, and Sunday; November to April on Saturday only), stopping in Esztergom, Visegrád, and Szentendre. There's commentary in English; the cost, including lunch and admission fees, is about 16,000 Ft.

➤ CONTACTS: **Cityrama** (☎ 1/302–4382 in Budapest). **IBUSZ Travel** (☎ 1/485–2762 or 1/317–7767 in Budapest).

TRAIN TRAVEL

Vác and Esztergom have frequent daily express and local train service to and from Budapest's Nyugati (West) Station, but there are no direct connections between Szentendre and Esztergom. Trains do not run to Visegrád, either. The HÉV suburban railway runs between Batthyány tér (or Margaret Island, one stop north) in Budapest and Szentendre about every 10–20 minutes daily; the trip takes 40 minutes, and a *kiegészítő* (supplementary) ticket—which you need in addition to a Budapest public transport pass or ticket—costs 268 Ft. one-way.

VISITOR INFORMATION

➤ CONTACTS: **Esztergom Grantours** (✉ Széchenyi tér 25, Esztergom, ☎ FAX 33/413–756). **Esztergom IBUSZ** (✉ Kossuth L. u. 5, Esztergom, ☎ 33/412–552). **Esztergom Komtourist** (✉ Lőrinc u. 6, Esztergom, ☎ 33/312–082). **Szentendre Tourinform** (✉ Dumtsa Jenő u. 22, Szentendre, ☎ 26/317–965 or 26/317–966). **Vác Tourinform** (✉ Március 15 tér 16–18, Vác, ☎ 27/316–160). **Visegrád Tours** (✉ Sirály Restaurant, Rév u. 15, Visegrád, ☎ 26/398–160).

LAKE BALATON

Lake Balaton, the largest lake in Central Europe, stretches 80 km (50 mi) across Hungary. Its vast surface area contrasts dramatically with its modest depths: only 9¾ ft at the center and just 52½ ft at its deepest point, at the Tihany Félsziget (Tihany Peninsula). The Balaton—the most popular playground of this landlocked nation—lies just 90 km (56 mi) to the southwest of Budapest, so it's within easy reach of the capital by car, train, bus, and even bicycle. On a hot day in July or August, it seems the entire country and half of Germany are packed towel to towel on the lake's grassy public beaches, paddling about in the warm water and consuming fried meats and beer at the omnipresent snack bars.

On the lake's hilly northern shore, ideal for growing grapes, is Balatonfüred, Hungary's oldest spa town, famed for natural springs that bubble out curative waters. The national park on the Tihany Peninsula lies just to the south, and regular boat service links Tihany and Balatonfüred with Siófok on the southern shore. Flatter and more crowded with resorts, cottages, and trade-union rest houses, the southern shore (beginning with Balatonszentgyörgy) has fewer sights and is not as attractive as the northern one: north-shore locals say the only redeeming quality of the southern shore is its views back across the lake to the north. Families with small children prefer the southern shore for its shallower, warmer waters—you can walk for almost 2 km (1 mi) before it deepens. The water warms up to 25°C (77°F) in summer.

Every town along both shores has at least one *strand* (beach). The typical Balaton strand is a complex of blocky wooden changing cabanas and snack bars, fronted by a grassy flat stretch along the water for sitting and sunbathing. Most have paddleboat and other simple boat rentals. A small entrance fee is usually charged.

If you're interested in exploring beyond the beach you can set out by car, bicycle, or foot, on beautiful village-to-village tours—stopping to view lovely old baroque churches, photograph a stork family perched high in its chimney-top nest, or climb a vineyard-covered hill for sweeping vistas. Since most vacationers keep close to the shore, a small amount of exploring into the roads and countryside heading away from the lake will reward you with a break from the summer crowds.

Numbers in the margin correspond to numbers on the Lake Balaton and Transdanubia map.

Veszprém

❶ *116 km (72 mi) southwest of Budapest.*

Hilly Veszprém is the center of cultural life in the Balaton region. ★ **Várhegy** (Castle Hill) is the most picturesque part of town, north of Szabadság tér. **Hősök kapuja** (Heroes' Gate), at the entrance to the castle, houses a small exhibit on Hungary's history. Just past the gate and down a little alley to the left is the **Tűztorony** (Fire Tower); note that the lower level is medieval, while the upper stories are baroque. There is a good view of the town and surrounding area from the balcony. *Tower:* ☎ *88/425–204.* 🏛 *150 Ft.* ☉ *Apr.–mid-Oct., daily 10–6.*

Vár utca, the only street in the castle area, leads to a small square in front of the **Bishop's Palace** and the **cathedral**; outdoor concerts are held here in the summer. Vár utca continues past the square up to a terrace erected on the north staircase of the castle. Stand beside the modern statues of St. Stephen and his queen, Gizella, for a far-reaching view of the old quarter of town.

OFF THE BEATEN PATH

HEREND – This is the home of Hungary's renowned hand-painted porcelain. The factory here, founded in 1839, displays many valuable pieces in its **Herend Porcelán Művészeti Múzeum** (Herend Museum of Porcelain Arts). You can also tour the factory itself. In the adjoining Apicius Restaurant, you can even dine off their collection of porcelain, worth several million forint. Herend lies 16 km (10 mi) northwest of Veszprém on Road 8. ✉ *Kossuth Lajos u. 144,* ☎ *88/261–518,* WEB *www.herend.com.* 🏛 *Factory and museum 1,000 Ft., museum only, 300 Ft.* ☉ *Apr.–Oct., daily 9–5:30; Nov.–Mar., Mon.–Sat. 9–4:30.*

Dining

$ ✕ **Szürkebarát Borozó.** The plain off-white walls of the Gray Monk Tavern may be less than inspiring, but the hearty Hungarian fare at this cellar restaurant in the city center more than compensates. For an unusual (but very Hungarian) appetizer, try the paprika-spiced *velős piritós* (marrow on toast; missing from the English menu and some-

Lake Balaton and Transdanubia

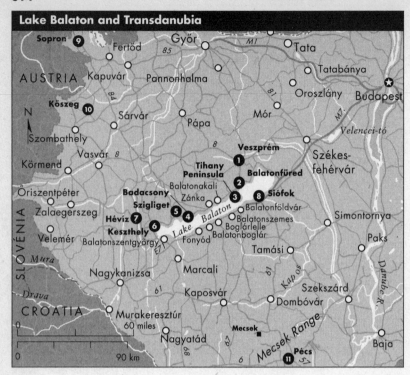

times unavailable); or for a main course, gnaw away at "Ms. Baker's pork hoofs." ⊠ *Szabadság tér 12,* ☎ *88/327–684. No credit cards.*

$$ ⊞ **Élló Panzió.** In this 18-room pension just southwest of the town center, you'll find ubiquitous golden lamp shades coupled with no lack of red—on the carpeting, the velvety chairs, and the curtains. Rooms in the newer annex building are more spacious than those in the chalet-like main house. Service is friendly. ⊠ *József Attila u. 25, H-8200,* ☎ *88/420–097 or 88/424–118,* ℻ *88/329–711,* ⓌⒺⒷ *www.hotels.hu/ello. 18 rooms. Breakfast room. DC, MC, V.*

Balatonfüred

❷ *18 km (11 mi) south of Veszprém, 115 km (71 mi) southwest of Budapest.*

Fed by 11 medicinal springs, Balatonfüred first gained popularity as a health resort (the lake's oldest) where ailing people with heart conditions and fatigue would come to take or, more accurately, to drink a cure. The waters, said to have stimulating and beneficial effects on the heart and nerves, are still an integral part of the town's identity and consumed voraciously, but only the internationally renowned cardiac hospital has actual bathing facilities. Today Balatonfüred, also known simply as Füred, is probably the Balaton's most popular destination, with every amenity to match. Above its busy boat landing, beaches, and promenade lined with great plane and poplar trees, the twisting streets of the Old Town climb hillsides thickly planted with vines. The climate and landscape also make this one of the best wine-growing districts in Hungary. Every year in July, the most elaborate of Lake Balaton's debutante cotillions, the Anna Ball, is held here.

The center of town is **Gyógy tér** (Spa Square), where the bubbling waters from five volcanic springs rise beneath a slim, colonnaded pavilion. In the square's centerpiece, the neoclassical **Well House** of the Kossuth Spring, you can sample the water, which has a pleasant, surprisingly refreshing taste despite the sulfurous aroma; for those who can't get enough, a 30-liter-per-person limit is posted. All the buildings on the square are pillared like Greek temples. At No. 3 is the **Horváth Ház** (Horváth House), where the Szentgyörgyi-Horváth family arranged the first of what was to become the Anna Ball in 1825 in honor of their daughter Anna.

The Anna Ball now takes place every July in another colonnaded building on the square, the **former Trade Unions' Sanatorium** (1802). Under its arcades is the **Balatoni Pantheon** (Balaton Pantheon): aesthetically interesting tablets and reliefs honoring Hungarian and foreign notables who either worked for Lake Balaton or spread the word about it. Among them is Jaroslav Hašek, the Czech author of the *Good Soldier Schweik,* who also wrote tales about Balaton.

On the eastern side of the square is the **Állami Kórház** (State Hospital), where hundreds of patients from all over the world are treated. Here, too, Rabindranath Tagore, the Indian author and Nobel Prize winner, recovered from a heart attack in 1926. The tree that he planted to commemorate his stay stands in a little grove at the western end of the paths leading from the square down to the lakeside. Tagore also wrote a poem for the planting, which is memorialized beneath the tree on a strikingly animated bust of Tagore: WHEN I AM NO LONGER ON EARTH, MY TREE,/LET THE EVER-RENEWED LEAVES OF THY SPRING/MURMUR TO THE WAYFARER:/THE POET DID LOVE WHILE HE LIVED. In the same grove are trees honoring visits by another Nobel laureate, the Italian poet Salvatore Quasimodo, in 1961, and Indian prime minister Indira Gandhi, in 1972. An adjoining grove honors Soviet cosmonauts and their Hungarian partner-in-space, Bertalan Farkas.

Trees, restaurants, and shops line the **Tagore sétány** (Tagore Promenade), which begins near the boat landing and runs for nearly a kilometer (almost ½ mi).

A stroll up **Blaha Lujza utca** from Gyógy tér will take you past several landmarks, such as the **Blaha Lujza Ház** (Lujza Blaha House), a neoclassical villa built in 1867 and, later, the summer home of this famous turn-of-the-20th-century actress, humanist, and singer (today it's a hotel). The sweet little **Kerek templom** (Round Church), consecrated in 1846, was built in a classical style and has a truly rounded interior.

NEED A BREAK? The plush **Kedves Café** (✉ Blaha Lujza u. 7, ☎ 87/343–229), built in 1795, was once the favorite summer haunt of well-known Hungarian writers and artists. Now more touristy than literary, it is still one of Lake Balaton's most popular and famous pastry shops.

Dining and Lodging

$$–$$$ ✕ **Baricska Csárda.** This rambling reed-thatched inn has wood-beamed
★ rooms, vaulted cellars, terraces, and views of both vineyards and the lake. The food is hearty yet ambitious: roasted trout, fish paprikás with gnocchi to soak up the creamy sauce, and delicious desserts mixing pumpkin and poppy seeds. In summer, Gypsy wedding shows are held nightly under the grape arbors. ✉ *Baricska dülő off Rte. 71 (Széchenyi út) behind Shell station,* ☎ *87/343–105. Reservations essential. AE, DC, MC, V. Closed Nov.–mid-Mar.*

$$–$$$ ✕ **Tölgyfa Csárda.** Perched high on a hilltop, the Oak Tree Tavern has breathtaking views over the steeples and rooftops of Balatonfüred and the Tihany Peninsula. The dining room and menu are worthy of a first-class Budapest restaurant, and nightly live Gypsy music keeps things

festive. ⊠ *Meleghegy (up the hill at the end of Csárda u.)*, ☎ *87/343–036. No credit cards. Closed late Nov.–Apr.*

$$$$ ★ 🏨 **Annabella.** The cool, spacious guest quarters in this large, Miami-style high-rise are especially pleasant in summer heat. The resort overlooks the lake and Tagore Promenade and has access to excellent swimming and water-sports facilities. All rooms have balconies; for the best views, request a room on a high floor with a view of the Tihany Peninsula. ⊠ *Deák Ferenc u. 25, H-8231*, ☎ *87/342–222*, FAX *87/483–029*, WEB *www.danubiusgroup.com. 383 rooms, 5 suites. Restaurant, café, indoor pool, pool, hair salon, massage, sauna, bicycles, bar, nightclub, baby-sitting, laundry service, travel services. AE, DC, MC, V. Closed late Oct.–mid-Apr.*

$$$$ 🏨 **Marina.** A central beachfront location is the Marina's main draw. Rooms in the homey 12-story building range from snug to small; suites have balconies but suffer from tiny bathrooms and dark bedrooms. Your safest bet is to get a high-floor "Superior" room with a lake view. Or better yet, stay in the "Lido" wing, which opens directly onto the water and where rooms (suites only) get plenty of sun. ⊠ *Széchenyi út 26, H-8230*, ☎ *87/343–460*, FAX *87/343–052*, WEB *www.danubiusgroup.com. 349 rooms, 34 suites, 34 apartments. Restaurant, indoor pool, hair salon, massage, sauna, beach, boating, bowling, bar, pub, nightclub, laundry service, travel services. AE, DC, MC, V. Closed Oct.–late Apr.*

$$ 🏨 **Park.** Hidden on a side street in town but close to the lakeshore, the Park is noticeably calmer than Füred's bustling main hotels. Rooms are large and bright, with high ceilings and tall windows. Suites have large, breezy balconies but small bathrooms. ⊠ *Jókai u. 24, H-8230*, ☎ FAX *87/343–203 or 87/342–005. 27 rooms, 5 suites. Restaurant, gym, sauna, bar, meeting room, free parking. No credit cards.*

$ 🏨 **Blaha Lujza Ház.** Hungary's fin-de-siècle songbird and actress Lujza Blaha spent her summers at this neoclassical villa, which has been converted into a hotel. The rooms are a bit cramped—there's not much room to negotiate your way around the bed sometimes. But the front-desk staff is helpful, and the breakfast room, which functions as a restaurant on summer evenings, is a pleasant place to begin the day with a buffet or cooked breakfast. ⊠ *Blaha u. 4, H-8230*, ☎ *87/581–210*, FAX *87/581–219. 22 rooms. Restaurant, gym, bar, free parking; no-smoking rooms. No credit cards.*

Outdoor Activities and Sports

BEACHES

Most hotels have their own private beaches, with water-sports facilities and equipment or special access to these nearby. Besides these, Balatonfüred has three public beaches, where you can rent sailboards, paddleboats, and other water toys; these are also available at Hungary's largest campground, **Füred Camping** (⊠ Széchenyi u. 24, next to the Marina hotel, ☎ 87/343–823). Although motorboats are banned from the lake, if you're desperate to water-ski you can try the campground's electric water-ski machine, which tows enthusiasts around a 1-km (½-mi) circle. A two-tow ticket runs around 900 Ft.

BICYCLING

In season you can rent bicycles from temporary, private outfits set up in central locations around town and near the beaches; one is usually working at the entrance to Füred Camping (⊠ Széchenyi u. 24, next to the Marina hotel). Inquire at the tourist office for other current locations. Average prices for mountain-bike rentals are 1,000 Ft. per hour or 3,500 Ft. per day. You can also usually rent mopeds in front of the Halászkert restaurant (⊠ Széchenyi út 2) for around 1,300 Ft. per hour and 5,000 Ft. per day.

HORSEBACK RIDING

Trail rides and horseback-riding lessons are available from mid-May to the end of September for about 2,500 Ft. an hour at the **Diana Lovasudvar** (Diana Riding Center; ⊠ Rte. 71 just southwest of the town center; turn right at the sign about 100 yards beyond the giant campground on the lake, ☎ 87/481–894).

Tihany and the Tihany Félsziget (Tihany Peninsula)

❸ *11 km (7 mi) southwest of Balatonfüred.*

The famed town of Tihany, with its twisting, narrow cobblestone streets and hilltop abbey, is on the Tihany Félsziget (Tihany Peninsula), joined to the mainland by a narrow neck and jutting 5 km (3 mi) into the lake. Only 12 square km (less than 5 square mi), the peninsula is not only a major tourist resort but perhaps the most historic part of the Balaton area. In 1952 the entire peninsula was declared a national park, and because of its geological rarities, it became Hungary's first nature-conservation zone. On it are more than 110 geyser craters, remains of former hot springs, reminiscent of those found in Iceland, Siberia, and Wyoming's Yellowstone Park.

The smooth Belső Tó (Inner Lake), 82 ft higher than Lake Balaton, is one of the peninsula's own two lakes; around it are barren yellowish-white rocks and volcanic cones rising against the sky. Though the hills surrounding the lake are known for their white wines, this area produces a notable Hungarian red, Tihany cabernet.

★ On a hilltop overlooking the old town is the **Bencés Apátság** (Benedictine Abbey), with foundations laid by King András I in 1055. Parts of the abbey were rebuilt in baroque style between 1719 and 1784. The abbey's charter—containing some 100 Hungarian words in its Latin text, making it the oldest written source of the Hungarian language—is kept in Pannonhalma, but a replica is on display in the abbey's 11th-century crypt. The contrast between the simple crypt, where a small black crucifix hangs over the tomb of King András, and the abbey's lavish baroque interior—all gold, gilted silver, and salmon—could scarcely be more marked. The altar, abbot's throne, choir parapet, organ case, and pulpit were all the work of Sebestyén Stuhloff. Local tradition says he immortalized the features of his doomed sweetheart in the face of the angel kneeling on the right-hand side of the altar to the Virgin Mary. A magnificent baroque organ, adorned by stucco cherubs, can be heard during evening concerts in summer.

In a baroque house adjoining and entered through the abbey is the **Bencés Apátsági Múzeum** (Benedictine Abbey Museum). The best exhibits are in the basement lapidarium: relics from Roman colonization, including mosaic floors; a relief of David from the 2nd or 3rd century; and 1,200-year-old carved stones—all labeled in English as well as Hungarian. Three of the upstairs rooms were lived in for five days in 1921 by the last emperor of the dissolved Austro-Hungarian monarchy, Karl IV, in a futile foray to regain the throne of Hungary. Banished to Madeira, he died of pneumonia there a year later. The rooms are preserved with nostalgic relish for Emperor Franz Joseph's doomed successor. ⊠ *Első András tér 1,* ☎ *87/448–405 abbey; 87/448–650 museum.* ▣ *250 Ft.* ☉ *May–Sept., Mon.–Sat. 9–5:30, Sun. 11–5:30; Apr. and Oct., Mon.–Sat. 10–4:30, Sun. 11–4:30; Nov.–Mar. (church and lapidarium only), Mon.–Sat. 11–4.*

The **Szabadtéri Múzeum** (Open-air Museum), Tihany's outdoor museum of ethnography, assembles a group of old structures, including a potter's shed, complete with a local artist-in-residence. Also here is the former house of the Fishermen's Guild, with an ancient boat—used until 1934—parked inside. ⊠ *Along Batthyány u. and neighboring streets,* ☎ *no phone.* ☉ *May–Sept., Tues.–Sun. 10–6.*

It's said that from **Visszhang domb** (Echo Hill), just a brief stroll from the Benedictine Abbey, as many as 16 syllables can be bounced off the abbey wall. With noise from builders and traffic, these days you may have to settle for a two-second echo. The hill is at the end of Piski István sétány.

<table>
<tr><td>NEED A
BREAK?</td><td>You can practice projecting from the terraces of the **Echo Restaurant** (⊠ Visszhang út 23, ☎ 87/448–460), an inn atop Echo Hill. While you're at it, try some fogas, carp, and catfish specialties.</td></tr>
</table>

Dining and Lodging

$–$$ ✕ **Halásztanya.** Views of the inner lake and local fish specialties—such as fogas fillets with garlic—contribute to this restaurant's popularity. ⊠ *Visszhang u. 11,* ☎ *87/448–771. Reservations not accepted. AE, MC, V. Closed Nov.–Easter.*

$–$$ ✕ **Pál Csárda.** Two thatch cottages house this simple restaurant, where cold fruit soup and fish stew are the specialties. You can eat in the garden, which is decorated with gourds and strands of dried peppers. ⊠ *Visszhang u. 19,* ☎ *87/448–605. Reservations not accepted. AE, MC, V. Closed Oct.–Apr.*

$$$$ ▦ **Club Tihany.** Picture Club Med transposed to late-1980s Central Europe, and you'll have some idea of what to expect at Club Tihany. This 32-acre lakeside holiday village stays busy year-round. Accommodations include standard hotel rooms and 160 bungalows, all with kitchen facilities. The list of activities is impressive—from fishing to thermal bathing at the spa. In summer, when the hotel is filled to capacity, the scramble for the breakfast buffet can be a little unnerving. ⊠ *Rév u. 3, H-8237,* ☎ *87/448–088 or 87/538–500,* ℻ *87/448–083,* ᴡᴇʙ *www. clubtihany.hu. 330 rooms, 161 bungalows. 3 restaurants, kitchens, tennis court, pool, gym, hair salon, spa, tennis, beach, fishing, 2 bars, wine bar, meeting rooms. AE, DC, MC, V.*

$$$–$$$$ ▦ **Kastély Hotel.** Lush landscaped lawns surround this stately neo-
   ★   baroque mansion on the water's edge, built in the 1920s for Archduke József Hapsburg and taken over by the Communist state in the '40s (it is still owned by the government). Inside, it's all understated elegance; rooms have soaring ceilings and crisp sheets. Rooms with lake-facing windows and/or balconies (slightly more expensive) are the best. Next door, a newer, uninviting concrete building houses the Kastély's sister, the Park Hotel, with 44 less expensive, though dated, rooms. ⊠ *Fürdő telepi út 1, H-8237,* ☎ *87/448–611,* ℻ *87/448–409,* ᴡᴇʙ *www.hotelfured.hu. 25 rooms, 1 suite. Restaurant, café, miniature golf, 2 tennis courts, sauna, beach, bar. AE, DC, MC, V. Closed mid-Oct.–mid-Apr.*

Nightlife and the Arts

Well-known musicians perform on the Benedictine Abbey's magnificent organ during the popular summer **organ-concert series,** which runs from July to August 20. Concerts are generally held weekends at 8:30 PM. Contact the abbey (☎ 87/448–405) for information and tickets.

Outdoor Activities and Sports

FISHING

Belső-tó (Inner Lake) is a popular angling spot in which you can try your luck at hooking ponty, catfish, and other local fish. Fishing permits can be bought on site at the fishing warden's office (☎ 87/448–082), on the premises of the Horgásztanya restaurant, on the southwest side of the lake.

Footpaths crisscross the entire peninsula, allowing you to climb the small hills on its west side for splendid views of the area or hike down Belső-tó (Inner Lake). If in midsummer you climb the area's highest hill, the **Csúcshegy** (761 ft—approximately a two-hour hike), you'll find the land below carpeted with purple lavender. Introduced from France into Hungary, lavender thrives on the lime-rich soil and strong sunshine of Tihany. The State Lavender and Medicinal Herb Farm here supplies the Hungarian pharmaceutical and cosmetics industries.

En Route The miniature town of Örvényes, about 7 km (4½ mi) west of Tihany, has the only working *vízi malom* (water mill) in the Balaton region. Built in the 18th century, it still grinds grain into flour while also serving as a tiny museum. In the miller's room is a collection of folk art, wood carvings, pottery, furniture, and pipes. On a nearby hill stand the ruins of a **Romanesque church**; only its chancel has survived. On Templom utca, a few steps from the bridge, is the baroque **St. Imre templom** (St. Imre Church), built in the late 18th century. *Water mill:* ⊠ *Szent Imre u. 1,* ☎ *87/449–360.* ⬚ *100 Ft.* ☉ *May–Sept., Tues.–Sun. 9–4.*

Balatonudvari, another kilometer (½ mi) west of Örvényes, is a pleasant beach resort famous for its cemetery, which was declared a national shrine because of its beautiful, unique heart-shape tombstones carved from white limestone at the turn of the 18th century. The cemetery is essentially on the highway, at the eastern end of town; it is easily visible from the road. Balatonudvari's beach itself is at **Kiliántelep,** 2 km (1 mi) to the west.

Badacsony

★ ❹ *41 km (25 mi) southwest of Tihany.*

One of the northern shore's most treasured images is the slopes of Mt. Badacsony (1,437 ft high), simply called the Badacsony, rising from the lake. The mysterious, coffinlike basalt peak of the Balaton Highlands is actually an extinct volcano flanked by smaller cone-shape hills. The masses of lava that coagulated here created bizarre and beautiful rock formations. At the upper edge, salt columns tower 180 to 200 ft like organ pipes in a huge semicircle. In 1965 Hungarian conservationists won a major victory that ended the quarrying of basalt from Mt. Badacsony, which is now a protected nature-preservation area.

The land below has been tilled painfully and lovingly for centuries. There are vineyards everywhere and splendid wine in every inn and tavern. In descending order of dryness, the best-loved Badacsony white wines are Rizlingszilváni, Kéknyelű, and Szürkebarát. Their proud producers claim that "no vine will produce good wine unless it can see its own reflection in the Balaton." They believe it is not enough for the sun simply to shine on a vine; the undersides of the leaves also need light, which is reflected from the lake's mirrorlike surface. Others claim the wine draws its strength from the fire of old volcanoes.

Many restaurants and inns have their own wine tastings, as do the numerous smaller, private cellars dotting the hill. Look for signs saying *bor* or *Wein* (wine, in Hungarian and German, respectively) to point the way. Most places are open mid-May to mid-September daily from around noon until 9 or 10.

Badacsony is really an administrative name for the entire area and includes not just the mountain but also five settlements at its foot. A good starting point for Badacsony sightseeing is the **Egry József Múzeum** (József Egry Museum), formerly the home and studio of a famous painter of

Balaton landscapes. His evocative paintings depict the lake's constantly changing hues, from its angry bright green during storms to its tranquil deep blues. ✉ *Egry sétány 12,* ☎ *87/431–044.* 🎫 *200 Ft.* ⊙ *May–Sept., Tues.–Sun. 10–6.*

Szegedy Róza út, the steep main street climbing the mountain, is flanked by vineyards and villas. This is the place to get acquainted with the writer Sándor Kisfaludy and his beloved bride from Badacsony, Róza Szegedy, to whom he dedicated his love poems. At the summit of her street is **Szegedy Róza Ház** (Róza Szegedy House), a baroque winepress house built in 1790 on a grand scale—with thatched roof, gabled wall, six semicircular arcades, and an arched and pillared balcony running the length of the four raftered upstairs rooms. It was here that the hometown girl met the visiting bard from Budapest. The house now serves as a memorial museum to both of them, furnished much the way it was when Kisfaludy was doing his best work immortalizing his two true loves, the Badacsony and his wife. ✉ *Szegedy Róza út 87,* ☎ *87/ 430–906.* 🎫 *200 Ft.* ⊙ *May–Sept., Tues.–Sun. 10–6.*

The steep climb to the **Kisfaludy kilátó** (Kisfaludy Lookout Tower) on Mt. Badacsony's summit is an integral part of the Badacsony experience and a rewarding bit of exercise. Serious summitry begins behind the Kisfaludy House at the **Rózsakő** (Rose Stone), a flat, smooth basalt slab with many carved inscriptions. Local legend has it that if a boy and a girl sit on it with their backs to Lake Balaton, they will marry within a year. From here, a trail marked in yellow leads up to the foot of the columns that stretch to the top. Steep flights of stone steps take you through a narrow gap between rocks and basalt walls until you reach a tree-lined plateau. You are now at the 1,391-ft level. Follow the blue triangular markings along a path to the lookout tower. Even with time out for rests and views, the ascent from Rózsakő should take less than an hour.

Just outside of town, **Rizapuszta** (✉ Káptalantóti út, Badacsonytomaj, Rizapuszta, ☎ 87/471–243) is a cellar and restaurant with regular tastings.

Dining and Lodging

$$–$$$$ ✕ **Halászkert.** The festive Fish Garden has won numerous international awards for its fine Hungarian cuisine. Inside are wooden rafters and tables draped with cheerful traditional blue-and-white *kékfestő* tablecloths; outside is a large terrace with umbrella-shaded tables. The extensive menu has such fresh-from-the-lake dishes as the house halászlé, and *párolt* (steamed) harcsa drenched with a paprika-caper sauce. ✉ *Park u. 5,* ☎ *87/431–054 or 87/431–113. AE, DC, MC, V. Closed Nov.– Apr.*

$–$$$ ✕ **Kisfaludy-ház.** Perched above the Szegedy Róza House is this Badacsony institution, once a winepress house owned by the poet Sándor Kisfaludy's family. Its wine cellar lies directly over a spring, but the main draw is a vast two-tier terrace that affords a breathtaking view of virtually the entire lake. Naturally, the wines are excellent and are incorporated into some of the cooking, such as creamy wine soup. ✉ *Szegedy Róza u. 87,* ☎ *87/431–016. AE, DC, MC, V. Closed Nov.– Apr.*

$–$$ ✕ **Szent Orbán Borház.** Part of the illustrious Szent Orbán winery, this restaurant overlooks some of the vineyard's 30 acres. On summer days golden light bathes the 19th-century former farmhouse, which has heavy wooden heirloom furniture and an antique porcelain stove. There are written menus, but charming servers also recite the dishes (in English and other languages), and they'll steer you toward sampling two unique house wines, Budai zöld and Kéknyelű—both based on legendary varietals from Roman times. Smoked goose liver paté is frequently available as an appetizer; changing seasonal specialties often feature fresh fish from Lake Balaton, including fogas. ⊠ *Szegedy Róza u. 22,* ☎ *87/431–382. AE, DC, MC, V.*

$$$–$$$$ 🏨 **Club Hotel Badacsony.** A private beach is just a step away from this hotel right on the shore of Lake Balaton. The Club Hotel, in the Badacsonytomaj neighborhood, is the largest in the area. Rooms are bright and clean. ⊠ *Balatoni út 14, H-8258 Badacsonytomaj,* ☎ *87/471–040,* FAX *87/471–059,* WEB *www.hotels.hu/club_hotel_badacsony. 52 rooms, 4 suites. Restaurant, café, tennis court, hair salon, massage, sauna, beach, bowling, meeting rooms. AE, DC, MC, V. Closed Nov.–Apr.*

$$ 🏨 **Hotel Volán.** This bright yellow, restored 19th-century mansion is a cheerful, family-oriented inn with a manicured yard for sunning and relaxing. Well-kept rooms are in the main house and in four modern additions behind it. ⊠ *Római út 168, H-8261 Badacsony,* ☎ FAX *87/ 431–013,* WEB *www.hotels.hu/volan_badacsony. 23 rooms. Restaurant, bar, pool. No credit cards. Closed Nov.–mid-Feb.*

Outdoor Activities and Sports

The upper paths and roads along the slopes of Mt. Badacsony are excellent for scenic walking. Well-marked trails lead to the summit of Mt. Badacsony.

For beach activities, you can go to one of Badacsony's several beaches or head 6 km (4 mi) northeast, to those at Balatonrendes and Ábrahámegy, combined communities forming quiet resorts.

Szigliget

★ ❺   *11 km (7 mi) west of Badacsony.*

The village of Szigliget is a tranquil, picturesque town with fine thatchroof winepress houses and a small beach. Towering over the town is the ruin of the 13th-century **Óvár** (Old Castle), a fortress so well protected that it was never taken by the Turks; it was demolished in the early 18th century by Hapsburgs fearful of rebellions. A steep path starting from Kisfaludy utca brings you to the top of the hill, where you can explore the ruins, under ongoing archaeological restoration (a sign maps out the restoration plan), and take in the breathtaking views.

Down in the village on Iharos út, at the intersection with the road to Badacsony, the Romanesque remains of the **Avas templom** (Avas Church), from the Arpad dynasty, still contain a 12th-century basalt tower with a stone spire. The **Eszterházy summer mansion** in the main square, Fő tér, was built in the 18th century and rebuilt in neoclassical style in the 19th. In recent decades a retreat for writers, it is closed to the public—but just as well, for the bland inside has little to do with its former self. The mansion has a 25-acre park with yews, willows, walnuts, pines, and more than 500 kinds of ornamental trees and shrubs.

Keszthely

❻   *18 km (10 mi) west of Szigliget.*

With a beautifully preserved pedestrian avenue (Kossuth Lajos utca) in the historic center of town, the spectacular baroque Festetics Kastély, and a relative absence of honky-tonk, Keszthely is far more classically attractive and sophisticated than other large Balaton towns. Continuing the cultural and arts tradition begun by Count György Festetics two centuries ago, Keszthely hosts numerous cultural events, including an annual summer arts festival. Just south of town is the vast swamp called Kis-Balaton (Little Balaton), formerly part of Lake Balaton and now a nature preserve filled with birds. Water flowing into Lake Balaton from its little sibling frequently churns up sediment, making the water around Keszthely's beaches disconcertingly cloudy.

The **Pethő Ház** (Pethő House), a striking town house of medieval origin, was rebuilt in baroque style with a handsome arcaded gallery above its courtyard. Hidden deep inside its courtyard is the restored 18th-century **synagogue,** in front of which stands a small memorial honoring the 829 Jewish people from the neighborhood, turned into a ghetto in 1944, who were killed during the Holocaust. ⊠ *Kossuth Lajos u. 22.*

★ Keszthely's magnificent **Festetics Kastély** (Festetics Palace) is one of the finest baroque complexes in Hungary. Begun around 1745, it was the seat of the enlightened and philanthropic Festetics dynasty, which had acquired Keszthely six years earlier. The palace's distinctive church-like tower and more than 100 rooms were added between 1883 and 1887; the interior is lush. The **Helikon Könyvtár** (Helikon Library) in the south wing contains some 52,000 volumes, with precious codices and documents of Festetics family history. Chamber and orchestral concerts are held in the **Mirror Gallery** ballroom or, in summer, in the courtyard. The palace opens onto a splendid park lined with rare plants and fine sculptures. ⊠ *Kastély u. 1,* ☎ *83/312–191.* ⊡ *1,500 Ft. (1,200 Ft. extra for videotaping, 500 Ft. for no-flash photos).* ۞ *June, Tues.–Sun. 9–5; July–Aug., daily 9–6; Sept.–May, Tues.–Sun. 10–5.*

Supposedly the largest of its kind in Central Europe, Keszthely's **Babamúzeum** (Doll Museum) exhibits some 450 porcelain figurines dressed in 240 types of colorful folk dress. The building has a pastoral look, created not only by the figurines—which convey the multifarious beauty of village garb—but also by the ceiling's huge, handcrafted wooden beams. On the two upper floors are wooden models of typical homes, churches, and ornate wooden gates representative of all regions in and near present-day Hungary that Magyars have inhabited since conquering the Carpathian basin in 896. The museum's pièce de résistance is the lifework of an elderly peasant woman from northern Hungary: a 9-yard-long model of Budapest's Parliament building, patched together over 14 years from almost 4 million snail shells (which are 28 million years old, no less) originating from the Pannon Sea, which once covered much of Hungary. ⊠ *Kossuth u. 11,* ☎ *83/318–855.* ⊡ *Doll Museum 250 Ft., model of Parliament 200 Ft.* ۞ *May–Sept., daily 10–5; Oct.–Apr., daily 9–5.*

Dining and Lodging

$–$$ ✕ **Hungária Gösser Söröző.** This beer garden keeps long hours and plenty of beer on tap. The food is better than you might guess judging just from the touristy atmosphere. Aside from barroom snacks, the huge menu includes *ropogós libacomb hagymás törtburgonyával* (crunchy goose drumstick with mashed potatoes and onions) and *töltött paprika* (stuffed peppers). ⊠ *Kossuth Lajos u. 35, north of Fő tér,* ☎ *83/312–265. AE, DC, MC, V.*

$$$$ ▥ **Danubius Hotel Helikon.** There are plenty of sports facilities at this large lakeside hotel: an indoor swimming pool, indoor tennis courts, sailing, surfing, rowing, fishing, and, in winter, skating. The comfortable modern rooms are on the small side, but they have soothing cream-and-blue bedspreads and curtains. ⊠ *Balaton part 5, H-8360,* ☎ *83/311–330,* FAX *83/315–403,* WEB *www.danubiusgroup.com. 224 rooms, 8 suites. Restaurant, 2 tennis courts, indoor pool, hair salon, health club, sauna, beach, boating, fishing, bowling, ice-skating, bar. AE, DC, MC, V.*

$$$ 🏨 **Béta Hotel Hullám.** This turn-of-the-20th-century mansion with an elegant twin tower sits right on the Balaton shore. Rooms are clean and simply furnished with functional brown furniture. You can use the pool and the numerous recreational facilities at the nearby Danubius Hotel Helikon. ⊠ *Balatonpart 1, H-8360,* ☎ *83/312–644,* ⨯⨯ *83/315– 338,* WEB *www.betahotels.hu. 28 rooms, 6 suites. Restaurant, minibars, beach, bar; no room phones. AE, DC, MC, V. Closed Nov.–Apr.*

Nightlife and the Arts

The **Balaton Festival,** held annually in May, includes high-caliber classical concerts and other festivities in venues around town and outdoors on Kossuth Lajos utca. In summer, classical concerts and master classes take place almost daily in the Festetics Palace's Mirror Hall.

Outdoor Activities and Sports

BALLOONING

Hot-air balloon rides in the Keszthely region have become popular, despite the high price (28,000 Ft. per person). Dr. Bóka György (a practicing M.D. and balloon pilot) and his friendly team will take you up in his blue-and-yellow balloon for an hour-long tour—the trip includes a post-landing champagne ritual. Flights depend strongly on wind and air-pressure conditions; in summer, they can usually fly only in early morning and early evening. Transportation to and from the site is included. Contact **Med-Aer** (⊠ Móricz Zsigmond u. 7, ☎ 83/312–421 or 06/309–576–321) at least one week in advance to reserve your spot.

HORSEBACK RIDING

János Lovarda (János Stable; ⊠ Sömögyedüllő, ☎ 83/314–855) offers lessons, rides in the ring, and carriage rides.

WATER SPORTS

You can rent paddleboats and other water toys at the public beach next to the Béta Hotel Hullám or from the Danubius Hotel Helikon.

Hévíz

❼ *6 km (4 mi) northwest of Keszthely.*

Hévíz is one of Hungary's biggest and most famous spa resorts, with the largest natural curative thermal lake in Europe. Lake Hévíz covers nearly 60,000 square yards, with warm water that never grows cooler than 33°C– 35°C (91.4°F–95°F) in summer and 30°C–32°C (86°F–89.6°F) in winter, thus allowing year-round bathing, particularly where the lake is covered by a roof and looks like a racetrack grandstand. Richly endowed with sulfur, alkali, calcium salts, and other curative components, the Hévíz water is recommended for spinal, rheumatic, gynecological, and articular disorders and is drunk to help digestive problems and receding gums. Fed by a spring producing 86 million liters (22.7 million gallons) of water a day, the lake cycles through a complete water change every 28 hours. Squeamish bathers, however, should be forewarned that along with its photogenic lily pads, the lake naturally contains assorted sludgy mud and plant material. It's all supposed to be good for you, though—even the mud, which is full of iodine and estrogen.

The vast spa park has hospitals, sanatoriums, expensive hotels, and a casino. The public bath facilities are in the **Szent András Kórház** (St. Andrew Hospital), a large, turreted medicinal bathing complex on the lakeshore with a large staff on hand to treat rheumatological complaints. Bathing for more than three hours at a time is not recommended. ⊠ *Dr. Schulhof Vilmos sétány 1,* ☎ *83/340–587.* 💶 *500 Ft. (valid for 3 hrs).* ⊙ *May–Sept., daily 8:30–5:30; Oct.–Apr., daily 9–4:30.*

The beautifully furnished **Talpasház** (House on Soles) takes its name from an interesting architectural detail: its upright beams are encased in thick foundation boards. Exquisite antique peasant furniture, textiles, and pottery fill the house along with the work of contemporary local folk artists. Some of their work is for sale on the premises, and you can also create your own works on a pottery wheel. Contact the caretaker, Csaba Rezes, who lives next door at No. 15, if the door happens to be closed. ⊠ *Dózsa György u. 17,* ☎ *85/377–364 caretaker.* ⊠ *100 Ft.* ⊙ *Late May–Sept., Tues.–Sun. variable hrs (call the caretaker to let you in).*

OFF THE BEATEN PATH
CSILLAGVÁR (STAR CASTLE) – It's worth stopping in Balatonszentgyörgy to see this castle, hidden away at the end of a dirt road past a gaping quarry. The house was built in the 1820s as a hunting lodge for László, the Festetics family's eccentric. Though it's not star-shape inside, wedge-shape projections on the ground floor give the outside this effect. Today the castle houses a museum of 16th- and 17th-century life in the border fortresses of the Balaton. ⊠ *Irtási dűlő,* ☎ *85/377–532.* ⊠ *100 Ft.* ⊙ *May–Aug., daily 9–6.*

Lodging

$$$$ ⊞ **Danubius Thermal Hotel Aqua.** This large, luxurious spa-hotel in the city center has its own thermal baths and physiotherapy unit (plus a full dental service!). The rooms are smaller than average and therefore not suited to families who intend to share a single room. Numerous cure packages are available. ⊠ *Kossuth Lajos u. 13–15, H-8380,* ☎ *83/341–090,* FAX *83/340–970,* WEB *www.danubiusgroup.com.* 227 *rooms. Restaurant, pool, hair salon, massage, sauna, spa, bar. AE, DC, MC, V.*

$$$$ ⊞ **Hotel Palace Hévíz.** There's a suggestion of Hercule Poirot about the art-deco exterior and atrium of the Hevis, as though the Belgium detective might wander in wagging his finger at you at any moment. All those gleaming white surfaces turn out to be new, however, as the hotel is a recent construction. The hotel has thermal baths, various treatments, and its own dental center. ⊠ *Rákóczi u. 1–3, H-8380,* ☎ *83/ 545–900,* FAX *83/545–901,* WEB *www.palace-heviz.hu.* 160 *rooms. Restaurant, café, indoor pool, hair salon, massage, sauna, bar, some pets allowed. AE, DC, MC, V.*

$$$$ ⊞ **Rogner Hévíz Hotel Lotus Therme.** No expense has been spared at this spa and "wellness" hotel promoting relaxation and invigoration. In addition to enjoying thermal baths, a fitness center, and various purification and detoxification therapies, you can join in golf and tennis excursions. There are even in-house dieticians. The hotel itself is a large, crescent-shape building just off the E71. ⊠ *Lótuszvirág u. 80, H-8380,* ☎ *83/500–501,* FAX *83/500–513,* WEB *www.lotustherme.com.* 231 *rooms. Restaurant, café, cable TV, indoor pool, hair salon, health club, massage, sauna, bar, shops; no-smoking rooms. AE, DC, MC, V.*

Siófok

❽ *110 km (68 mi) east of Hévíz, 105 km (65 mi) southwest of Budapest.*

Siófok is the largest city on the southern shore and one of Hungary's major tourist and holiday centers. It is also arguably the least beautiful. In 1863 a railway station was built for the city, paving the way for its "golden age" at the turn of the 20th century. In the closing stages of World War II the city sustained heavy damage; to boost tourism during the 1960s, the Pannonia Hotel Company built four of what many consider to be the ugliest hotels in the area. If, however, these were Sió-fok's *only* ugly buildings, there would still be hope for a ray of aesthetic redemption. With the exception of the twin-tower train station and the adjacent business district stretching a few blocks to the *Víztorony* (water tower), dating from 1912, the city is overrun by drab modern structures. Its shoreline is now a long, honky-tonk strip crammed with concrete-bunker hotels, discos, go-go bars, and tacky restaurants. So while Siófok is not for those seeking a peaceful lakeside getaway, it is exactly what hordes of action-seeking young people want—an all-in-one playground.

One worthwhile attraction is the **Kálmán Imre Múzeum** (Imre Kálmán Museum), housed in the birthplace of composer Kálmán (1882–1953), known internationally as the Prince of Operetta. Inside this small house-cum-museum are his first piano, original scores, his smoking jacket, and lots of old pictures. ⊠ *Kálmán Imre sétány 5,* ☎ *84/311–287.* 🖾 *200 Ft.* ☉ *Tues.–Sun. 9–5.*

Dining and Lodging

$$–$$$ ✗ **Millennium Étterem.** Imre Makovecz, one of Hungary's preeminent architects, oversaw renovation of this elegant restaurant, once an old villa, in the early '90s. The menu lists several Hungarian specialties as well as fresh, local fish, including whole trout and pike perch. ⊠ *Fő u. 93–95,* ☎ *84/312–546. AE, DC, MC, V.*

$–$$ ✗ **Csárdás Étterem.** The oldest and one of the best restaurants in Sió-
★ fok, the Csárdás Étterem consistently wins awards for its hearty, never-bland Hungarian cuisine. House specialties include a breaded and fried pork fillet stuffed with cheese, ham, and smoked bacon. ⊠ *Fő u. 105,* ☎ *84/310–642. AE, MC, V.*

$$$$ 🏨 **Hotel Atrium Janus Siófok.** Every room in this bright luxury hotel is clean and comfortably contemporary. The "relaxation center" downstairs has a swimming pool, sauna, and whirlpool. ⊠ *Fő u. 93–95, H-8600,* ☎ *84/312–546,* 𝔽𝔸𝕏 *84/312–432,* 𝕎𝔼𝔹 *www.janushotel.hu. 22 rooms, 7 suites. Restaurant, café, in-room safes, minibars, indoor pool, gym, sauna, bar, meeting rooms. AE, DC, MC, V.*

$$$ 🏨 **Hotel Fortuna.** This three-story, bright-yellow rectangular block has the advantage of being somewhat removed from the multilane traffic of the city's main street and about 100 yards from the lakeshore. The rooms are modern and, like the building's facade, awash in a soothing yellow; all have balconies. ⊠ *Erkel Ferenc u. 51, H-8600,* ☎ 𝔽𝔸𝕏 *84/311–087 or 84/313–476. 41 rooms, 5 suites. Restaurant, bar, playground, meeting rooms. AE, DC, MC, V.*

Nightlife and the Arts

The town remains loyal to Siófok-born operetta composer Imre Kálmán and hosts popular operetta concerts regularly in the summer at the **Kulturális Központ** (Cultural Center; ⊠ Fő tér 2, ☎ 84/311–855).

Outdoor Activities and Sports

GO-CARTS

Speed demons can whiz around the **Go-Cart Track** (⊠ Rte. 70, by railroad crossing, ☎ 84/311–917 or 06/209–512–510), which is open from mid-May through September; a 10-minute drive costs about 1,800 Ft.

TENNIS

The **Sport Centrum** (⊠ Küszhegyi út, ☎ 84/314–523) has eight tennis courts as well as a handball court, sauna, and, lest things get too athletic, a bar.

WATER SPORTS

Boating and other water-sports equipment is available for hire at the **MOL Water Sports Center** (☎ 84/311–161), on the waterfront on Vitorlás utca 10. Kayaks and canoes cost 500 Ft.–600 Ft. per hour, sailboats around 6,000 Ft. per hour.

Lake Balaton Essentials

BUS TRAVEL

Buses headed for the Lake Balaton region depart from Budapest's Erzsébét tér station daily; contact Volánbusz for current schedules.

Buses frequently link Lake Balaton's major resorts. Arrive at the bus station early. Tickets with seat reservations can be bought in the stations up to 20 minutes prior to departure, otherwise from the driver; reservations cannot be made by phone. Contact the tourist offices or Volánbusz for schedule and fare information.

➤ Bus Schedules: **Volánbusz** (☎ 1/485–2162 in Budapest).

CAR TRAVEL

Driving is the most convenient way to explore the area, but keep in mind that traffic can be heavy during summer weekends.

Expressway E71/M7 is the main artery between Budapest and Lake Balaton. At press time still under construction, it had gotten as far as the lake's northeastern point and will eventually reach southwestern Hungary. From here Route 7 from Budapest joins the E71 and continues along the lake's southern shore to Siófok and towns farther west. Route 71 goes along the northern shore to Balatonfüred and lakeside towns southwest. The drive from Budapest to Siófok takes about 1½ hours, except on weekends, when traffic can be severe. From Budapest to Balatonfüred is about the same.

FERRY TRAVEL

The slowest but most scenic way to travel among Lake Balaton's major resorts is by ferry. Schedules for MAHART Tours, the national ferry company, are available from most of the tourist offices in the region.

➤ Ferry Information: **MAHART Tours** (☎ 1/318–1704 in Budapest).

TOURS

You can arrange tours directly with the hotels in the Balaton area and with the help of Tourinform offices; these can include boat trips to vineyards, folk-music evenings, and overnight trips to local inns.

FROM BUDAPEST

Cityrama takes groups twice a week from April to October from Budapest to Balatonfüred for a walk along the promenade and then over to Tihany for a tour of the abbey. After lunch, you'll take a ferry across the Balaton and then head back to Budapest, with a wine-tasting stop on the way.

IBUSZ Travel has several tours to Balaton from Budapest; inquire at the office in Budapest.

➤ Contact: **Cityrama** (☎ 1/302–4382 in Budapest). **IBUSZ Travel** (✉ District V, Ferenciek tere 10, ☎ 1/485–2762 or 1/317–7767, WEB www.ibusz.hu).

BOAT TOURS

MAHART arranges several sailing excursions on Lake Balaton. From Balatonfüred, the *Csongor* sets out several times daily in July and August for an hour-long jaunt around the Tihany Peninsula. Most other tours depart from Siófok also in the same period, including the "Tihany Tour," on Saturday at 10 AM, with stops for guided sightseeing in Balatonfüred and Tihany; and the "Sunset Tour," a 1½-hour cruise at 7:30 PM daily during which you can sip a glass of champagne while watching the sun sink. The "Badacsony Tour" departs from Keszthely and goes to Badacsony at 10:30 AM Thursday.

➤ CONTACT: **MAHART** (☎ 84/312–308).

TRAIN TRAVEL

Daily express trains run from Budapest's Déli (South) Station to Siófok and Balatonfüred. The roughly two-hour trip costs about 900 Ft. each way.

Trains from Budapest serve the resorts on the northern shore; a separate line links resorts on the southern shore. There is no train service to Tihany. While most towns are on a rail line, it's inconvenient to decipher the train schedules; trains don't run very frequently, so planning connections can be tricky. Since many towns are just a few miles apart, getting stuck on a local train can feel like an endless stop-start cycle. Also bear in mind that, apart from some trains between Budapest and Veszprém, you cannot reserve seats on the Balaton trains—it's first come, first seated.

➤ TRAIN STATIONS: **Balatonfüred train station** (✉ Castricum tér, ☎ 87/343–652). **Siófok train station** (✉ Millenium tér, ☎ 84/310–061). **Veszprém train station** (✉ Jutasi út 34, 2 km [1 mi] outside of town, ☎ 88/329–999).

VISITOR INFORMATION

The Balaton Communication and Information Hotline is an excellent source of travel information for the region (in Hungarian only), with a comprehensive Web site (with some English information).

➤ TOURIST INFORMATION: **Badacsony Tourinform** (✉ Park u. 6, ☎ FAX 87/431–046). **Balaton Communication and Information Hotline** (☎ 88/406–963, WEB www.balaton.hu). **Balatonfüred Tourinform** (✉ Széchenyi u. 47, ☎ 87/580–480). **Balatontourist** (✉ Tagore sétány 1, ☎ 87/342–822 or 87/343–471). **Hévíz Tourist** (✉ Rákóczi u. 4, ☎ 83/341–348). **Keszthely Tourinform** (✉ Kossuth u. 28, ☎ FAX 83/314–144). **Siófok IBUSZ** (✉ Fő u. 174, ☎ 84/315–213). **Siófok Tourinform** (✉ Víztorony, ☎ 84/315–355). **Tihany Tourinform** (✉ Kossuth u. 20, ☎ FAX 87/448–804). **Veszprém Tourinform** (✉ Vár u. 4, ☎ FAX 88/404–548).

TRANSDANUBIA

Western Hungary, often referred to as Transdanubia (Dunántúl in Hungarian), is the area south and west of the Danube, stretching to the Slovak and Austrian borders in the west and north and to Slovenia and Croatia in the south. It presents a highly picturesque landscape, including several ranges of hills and small mountains. Most of its surface is covered with farmland, vineyards, and orchards—all nurtured and made verdant by a climate that is noticeably more humid than in the rest of the country.

The Romans called the region Pannonia. For centuries it was a frontier province; today it is far richer in Roman ruins than the rest of Hungary. Centuries later, the 150-year Turkish occupation left its mark on the region, particularly in the south, where it's not uncommon to see a former mosque serving as a Christian church. Austrian influence is clearly visible in the region's baroque buildings, particularly in the magnificent Eszterházy Palace in Fertőd, outside of Sopron. Vienna, after all, is just a few hours' drive away.

Numbers in the margin correspond to numbers on the Lake Balaton and Transdanubia map.

En Route   Perched proudly above the countryside on top of a high hill on the way to Sopron—135 km (84 mi) west of Budapest, 100 km (62 mi) ★ east of Sopron—the vast, 1,000-year old Benedictine **Pannonhalma Apátság** (Pannonhalma Abbey) gleams like a gift from heaven. During the Middle Ages, it was an important ecclesiastical center and wielded considerable political influence. The abbey housed Hungary's first school and is said to be the first place the Holy Scriptures were read on Hungarian soil. It's still a working monastery and school; 60 monks and 320 students live here. A late-Gothic cloister and a 180-ft neoclassical tower are the two stylistic exceptions to the predominantly baroque architecture. The library of more than 300,000 volumes houses some priceless medieval documents, including the first to contain a large number of Hungarian words: the 11th-century deed to the abbey of Tihany. Visits are permitted only with a guide, which is included in the admission price. Tours begin every hour on the hour; the last one of the day begins at the closing hour listed below. There are regularly scheduled English- and other foreign-language tours at 11 and 1 from late March to mid-November. Occasional organ recitals are held in the basilica in summer. ✉ *Pannonhalma, off Rte. 82 south of Győr,* ☎ *96/570–191,* 𝖥𝖠𝖷 *96/570–192,* 𝖶𝖤𝖡 *www.osb.hu.* 💷 *500 Ft. (foreign-language guide 800 Ft.).* ◷ *Late Mar.–May and Oct.–mid-Nov., Tues.–Sun. 9–4; June–Sept., daily 9–5; mid-Nov.–late Mar., Tues.–Sun. 10–3. Monastery closed Sun. mornings except for those wishing to attend mass; library and yard remain open to tours.*

Sopron

★ ❾   *211 km (131 mi) northwest of Budapest, 100 km (62 mi) west of Pannonhalma.*

Sopron, which lies on the Austrian frontier, between Lake Fertő (in German, Neusiedlersee) and the Sopron Hills, is one of Hungary's most picturesque towns. Barely an hour away from Vienna by car, it is a bargain shopping center for many Austrians, who flock here for the day. The joke in Sopron is that every day at noon, "We play the Austrian national hymn so that the Austrians have to stand still for two minutes while we Hungarians shop."

There is much more to Sopron, however, than conspicuous consumption by foreigners. Behind the narrow storefronts along the City Ring Várkerület (called Lenin Boulevard until 1989) and within the city walls (one set built by Romans, the other by medieval Magyars) lies a horseshoe-shape inner city that is a wondrous mix of Gothic, baroque, and Renaissance. In the center of this inner city is Fő tér, the main square of perfectly proportioned Italianate architecture. Sopron's faithful and inspired restoration won a 1975 Europe Prize Gold Medal for Protection of Monuments, and the work continues slowly and carefully.

Today's city of 60,000 was a small Celtic settlement more than 2,300 years ago. During Roman times, under the name of Scarabantia, it stood on the main European north–south trade route, the Amber Road; it also happened to be near the junction with the east–west route used by Byzantine merchants. In 896 the Magyars conquered the Carpathian basin and later named the city Suprun for a medieval Hungarian warrior. After the Hapsburgs took over the territory during the Turkish wars of the 16th and 17th centuries, they renamed the city Ödenburg (Castle on the Ruins) and made it the capital of the rich and fertile Austrian Burgenland. Ferdinand III, later Holy Roman Emperor, was crowned king of Hungary here in 1625, and at a special session of the Hungarian parliament in 1681, Prince Paul Esterházy was elected palatine (ruling deputy) of Hungary. And always, under any name or regime, Sopron was a fine and prosperous place in which to live.

A sightseeing note: for those who plan to visit as many museums as they can, one collective ticket covering most of Sopron's museums is available from the Storno Ház for about 900 Ft.

The symbol of the town's endurance—and entranceway to the Old City— is the 200-ft-high **Tűztorony** (Fire Tower), with foundations dating to the days of the Árpád dynasty (9th–13th centuries) and perhaps back to the Romans. The tower is remarkable for its uniquely harmonious blend of architectural styles: it has a Romanesque base rising to a circular balcony of Renaissance loggias topped by an octagonal clock tower that is itself capped by a brass baroque onion dome and belfry. The upper portions were rebuilt after most of the earlier Fire Tower was, appropriately, destroyed by the Great Fire of 1676, started by students roasting chestnuts in a high wind. Throughout the centuries the tower bell tolled the alarm for fire or the death of a prominent citizen, and from the loggias musicians trumpeted the approach of an enemy or serenaded the citizenry. Both warning concerts were accompanied by flags (red for fire, blue for enemy) pointing in the direction of danger. Today you can take in good views of the town and surrounding countryside from the top of the tower. ⊠ *Fő tér,* ☎ *99/311–327.* ▣ *200 Ft.* ⊙ *Apr.–Oct., Tues.–Sun. 10–5.*

★ At No. 8 on Fő tér, the exquisite main square, is the city's finest Renaissance building: the turreted **Storno Ház** (Storno House). Inside its two-story loggia, a museum houses a remarkable family collection of furniture, porcelain, sculptures, and paintings. Tape-recorded tours are available in English. The Stornos were a rags-to-riches dynasty of chimney sweeps who over several generations bought or just relieved grateful owners of unwanted treasures and evolved into a family of painters and sculptors themselves. The dynasty died out in Hungary a few years ago, but its heirs and the Hungarian state have agreed nothing will be removed from the Storno House. On an exterior wall hangs a plaque commemorating visits by King Matthias Corvinus (winter 1482–1483) and Franz Liszt (1840 and 1881). ⊠ *Fő tér 8,* ☎ *99/311–327.* ▣ *200 Ft.* ⊙ *Apr.–Oct., Tues.–Sun. 10–6; Nov.–Mar., Tues.–Sun. 10–2. Upstairs museum can be visited by guided tour only, given every ½ hr (last one begins ½ hr before closing).*

A fine Renaissance courtyard leads to the **Rómaikori Kőtár** (Roman Archaeology Museum) in a churchlike vaulted medieval cellar—a perfect setting for the gigantic statues of Jupiter, Juno, and Minerva unearthed beneath the main square during the digging of foundations for the city hall in the late 19th century. On the second floor a separate museum (with identical hours and admission prices) re-creates the living environment of 17th- and 18th-century Sopron apartments. ⊠ *Fő tér 6,* ☎ *99/311–327.* ▣ *150 Ft.* ⊙ *Apr.–Oct., Tues.–Sun. 10–6; Nov.–Mar., Tues.–Sun. 10–2.*

The 19th-century Angels' Drugstore is now the **Angyal Patika Múzeum** (Angel Pharmacy Museum), with old Viennese porcelain vessels and papers pertaining to Ignaz Philipp Semmelweis (1815–1865), the Hungarian physician whose pioneering work in antiseptics, while he was in Vienna, made childbirth safer. ⊠ *Fő tér 2,* ☎ *99/311–327.* ▣ *100 Ft.* ⊙ *Apr.–Oct., usually Tues.–Sun. 9:30–2. If closed, request entry at Soproni Múzeum office in Storno Ház, Fő tér 8.*

The centerpiece of Fő tér is a sparkling, spiraling three-tier **Szentháromság szobor** (Holy Trinity Column), aswirl with gilded angels—

the earliest (1701) and loveliest baroque monument to a plague in all of Hungary.

Legend has it that the early Gothic (1280–1300) **Kecske templom** (Goat Church) takes its name from a medieval billy goat that scratched up a treasure, enabling early day Franciscans to build a church on the site (the Benedictines took over in 1802). More likely, however, the name comes from the figures of goats carved into its crests: the coat of arms of the Gutsch family, who financed the church. The Goat Church has a soaring, pointed, 14th-century steeple; three naves; its original Gothic choir (betraying French influence); and, after several rebuildings, a Hungarian Gothic-baroque red-marble pulpit, a rococo main altar, baroque altars, and a painting of St. Stephen by one of the Stornos. The church stands before the Holy Trinity Column in Fő tér. ⊠ *Fő tér at Templom u.* 🖭 *Free.* ☉ *Daily 10–noon and 2–5.*

In the Gothic **Középkori Káptalan** (Medieval Chapter Room) of the ☞ **Goat Church,** monks meditated, contemplating on the curved pillars the sins in sculptures similar to those atop Notre-Dame Cathedral in Paris. Avarice is a monkey; Lewdness, a bear; Incredulity, a griffin; Inconstancy, a crab crawling backward; and Vanity, a woman with a mirror in hand. ⊠ *Templom u. 1.* 🖭 *Free (donations accepted).* ☉ *Apr.– mid-Oct., daily 10–noon and 2–5.*

The medieval **Ó-zsinagóga** (Old Synagogue), complete with a stone *mikva,* a ritual bath for women, is now a religious museum with old Torahs on display and an exhibit about the World War II deportation of the Jews. Built around 1300, it endured several incarnations over the centuries, including that as a hospital (in the 1400s) and later as a residential building, before being restored in 1973; the facade dates from 1734. A plaque honors the 1,640 Jews of Sopron who were murdered by the Nazis—the quiet street that is home to this and another old synagogue a few doors away, at No. 11, became the city's Jewish ghetto in May 1944. Only 274 of Sopron's Jews survived, and today there are scarcely enough to muster a *minyan* (quorum of 10), let alone a congregation. ⊠ *Új u. 22,* ☎ *99/311–327.* 🖭 *150 Ft.* ☉ *May–Sept., Wed.–Mon. 9–5; Oct., Wed.–Mon. 10–2.*

The **Cézár Ház** (Cézár House) has a wine cellar downstairs, but upstairs, in rooms where the Hungarian Parliament met in 1681, is a private museum created by the widow of József Soproni-Horváth (1891– 1961), a remarkable artist who prefixed his hometown's name to his own so he wouldn't be just another Joe Croat (*Horváth* means "Croat," in Hungarian). This Horváth nevertheless stands out for the wonders he worked with watercolors. He used that fragile medium to bring large surfaces to life in a density usually associated with oil paintings, while depicting realistic scenes, such as a girl grieving over her drowned sister's body. ⊠ *Hátsókapu u. 2,* ☎ *99/312–326.* 🖭 *120 Ft.* ☉ *Thurs.– Fri. and Sun. 10–1, Sat. 10–1 and 3–6.*

Along **Szent György utca** (St. George Street), numerous dragons of religion and architecture coexist in sightly harmony. The **Erdődy Vár** (Erdődy Palace) at No. 16 is Sopron's richest rococo building. Two doors down, at No. 12, stands the **Eggenberg Ház** (Eggenberg House), where the widow of Prince Johann Eggenberg held Protestant services during the harshest days of the Counter-Reformation and beyond. But the street takes its name from **Szent György templom** (St. George's Church), a 14th-century Catholic church so sensitively "baroqued" some 300 years later that its interior is still as soft as whipped cream. The church is generally open daily 9–5; the other buildings are not open to the public.

Mária szobor (St. Mary's Column), with its finely sculpted biblical reliefs, is a superb baroque specimen. It was built in 1745 to mark the former site of the medieval Church of Our Lady, destroyed by Sopron citizens in 1632 because they feared the Turks would use it as a strategic firing tower. ⊠ *At the Előkapu (Outer Gate).*

NEED A
BREAK?

Red-velvety chairs, an ornate chandelier, a semi-spiraling wooden staircase, and scrumptious pastry are the hallmarks of the **Dömötöri cukrászda** (⊠ Széchenyi tér at the corner of Erszébet u., ☎ 99/312-781), a cozy little café on Sopron's second most famous, but largest, square.

Strolling along **Várkerület,** the circular boulevard embracing Sopron's inner core, allows you to take in the vibrant harmony of beautifully preserved baroque and rococo architecture and the fashionable shops and cafés of Sopron's thriving downtown business district.

OFF THE
BEATEN PATH

ESZTERHÁZY PALACE – The magnificent yellow baroque palace built in 1720–1760 as a residence for the Hungarian noble family, is prized as one of the country's most exquisite palaces. Though badly damaged in World War II, it has been painstakingly restored, making it clear why in its day the palace was referred to as the Hungarian Versailles. Its 126 rooms include a lavish Hall of Mirrors and a three-story-high concert hall, where classical concerts are held in summer (usually Saturday at 6 PM). Joseph Haydn, court conductor to the Eszterházy family here for 30 years, is the subject of a small museum inside. Slippers—mandatory, to preserve the palace floors—are provided at the entrance. The palace lies 27 km (17 mi) southeast of Sopron, in Fertőd. ⊠ *Bartók Béla u. 2, Fertőd (just off Rte. 85),* ☎ *99/370-971.* ☑ *700 Ft.* ☉ *Mid-Mar.–mid-Oct., Tues.–Sun. 9–5; mid-Oct.–mid-Mar., Tues.–Sun. 9–4.*

Dining and Lodging

$–$$ ✕ **Barokk Étterem.** Specialties at the BaroqueRestaurant include meat fondue for two, trout, and veal with chicken-liver stuffing. Entrance to the restaurant is through a lovely courtyard, which is crammed by day with racks of merchandise from the neighboring boutiques. Pastels and modern fixtures fill the dining room, which has an arched ceiling. ⊠ *Várkerület 25,* ☎ *99/312-227. AE, MC, V. Closed Sun.*

$–$$ ✕ **Corvinus.** The location, in the 700-year-old Storno House off Sopron's delightful cobblestone main square—the city's historic heart—couldn't be better. The Corvinus itself combines a café, pub, pizzeria, and restaurant all in one. Among the Hungarian specialties are a meaty soup with a baked-on pastry cap, and roasted goose liver. Service is formal yet friendly, whether you dine inside under vaulted ceilings or at an outdoor table. ⊠ *Fő tér 7–8,* ☎ *99/314-841. AE, DC, MC, V.*

$–$$ ✕ **Gambrinus.** This comfortable, simply furnished restaurant serves up Hungarian fare and grilled meats with few frills and is especially popular at lunchtime, when a crowd of Austrian shoppers from across the border fills its tables. Gambrinus, and its attached hotel, sits in a 700-year-old building on Sopron's main square. ⊠ *Fő tér 3,* ☎ *99/339-966. No credit cards.*

$$$–$$$$ ▥ **Best Western Pannonia Med Hotel.** There has been a hotel here since the 17th century, when the Golden Hind welcomed stagecoaches traveling between Budapest and Vienna. It was destroyed in a fire but rebuilt in neoclassical style in 1893. With soaring ceilings, dripping chandeliers, and a breakfast room with gilt-edge mirrors and little golden chairs, the hotel is elegant. Standard rooms are comfortable and smart but pale in comparison to the handsome suites, with huge wooden beds and antiques. Facilities are good, as well: it's not every hotel that has its own cosmetic-

surgery consultant. ✉ *Várkerület 75, H-9400,* ☎ *99/312–180,* ℻ *99/340–766,* 🌐 *www.pannoniahotel.com or www.bestwestern.com. 48 rooms, 14 suites. Restaurant, in-room data ports, pool, gym, hair salon, sauna, spa, bar, meeting rooms, free parking. AE, DC, MC, V.*

$$$ 🔲 **Hotel Sopron.** There's no getting around the Hotel Sopron's out-
★ dated early '80s appearance, so the management wisely emphasizes the panoramic city views and services and amenities. Many, but not all, of the brown and beige rooms do have great views of Sopron's old town. As for services, the hotel can organize everything from wine-tasting tours to scenic train trips, as well as the ubiquitous (in this part of the world) dental services. ✉ *Fövényverem u. 7, H-9400,* ☎ *99/512–261,* ℻ *99/311–090,* 🌐 *www.hotelsopron.hu. 106 rooms, 6 suites. Restaurant, 2 tennis courts, pool, gym, sauna, bicycles, bar, playground, meeting room; no a/c in some rooms. AE, DC, MC, V.*

Nightlife and the Arts

From mid- to late March, Sopron's cultural life warms up during the annual **Tavaszi Fesztivál** (Spring Festival), with classical concerts, folk-dance performances, and other events. Peak season for cultural events is from mid-June through mid-July, when the **Sopron Ünnepi Hetek** (So-pron Festival Weeks) brings music, dance, and theater performances and art exhibits to churches and venues around town. Contact Tour-inform (☎ 99/338–592) or the Theater and Festival Office (✉ Széchenyi tér 17–18, ☎ 99/511–730) for details.

Outdoor Activities and Sports

The forested hills of the Fertő-Hanság National Park around Sopron have many well-marked hiking trails. Ask for a map and advice at the **Tourinform** information center (✉ Előkapu u. 11, ☎ 99/338–592, ℻ 99/338–892).

Shopping

Várkerület is Sopron's main shopping street. **Herend Village Pottery** (✉ Új u. 5, ☎ 99/338–546) sells high-quality Herend ceramics hand-painted with tiny blue flowers and other cheerful, colorful patterns. If you can't make it to the less expensive factory outlet in Pécs, you can purchase exquisite Zsolnay porcelain at the **Zsolnay Márkabolt** (✉ Előkapu u. 11, ☎ 99/311–367), a tiny room lined with glass cabinets displaying the delicate wares.

Kőszeg

 45 km (28 mi) south of Sopron.

At an altitude of 886 ft in the forested hills near the Austrian border, Kőszeg is Hungary's highest and also one of its most enchanting little cities. Justly called the "jewel box of Hungary," Kőszeg resembles a living postcard of quiet cobblestone streets winding among Gothic and baroque houses, with picturesque church steeples and a castle tower rising in the background.

Continually quarreled over by the Austrians and Hungarians, Kőszeg, established in 1263, was designed with an eye to defense—a moat, a draw-bridge, thick ramparts, and a 14th-century fortified castle were essen-tial to its survival. It was from this castle in 1532 that a few hundred Hungarian peasant soldiers beat back a Turkish army of nearly 200,000 and forced Sultan Suleiman I to abandon his attempt to conquer Vienna. To celebrate Christianity's narrow escape, the bells of Kőszeg's churches and castle toll every day at 11 AM, the hour the Turks turned tail.

Music, too, reigned in Kőszeg: Haydn spent many of his creative years here as court composer to the Eszterházys, and Franz Liszt gave a concert in 1846 in what is now just the shabby shell of Kőszeg's grandiose but beloved Ballhouse.

Jézus Szíve Plébánia templom (Sacred Heart Church), erected between 1892 and 1894, is a creamy neo-Gothic concoction by Viennese architect Ludwig Schöne. It is reminiscent both of Vienna's St. Stephen's Cathedral (for its mosaic roof and spires) and, inside, of Venice's San Marco (for the candy-stripe pillars supporting its three naves). While the church is generally open daily 8 AM–8 PM (until 6 in the off-season, roughly October–May), it is only accessible during mass. If you come to see the interior during a service, you must remain in the back of the church; there's usually a small window of opportunity just after morning mass (which ends at 8:30) to explore the whole interior. A small admission may be charged. ⊠ *Fő tér at Várkör,* ☎ *94/360–121.*

Szent Jakab templom (St. James Church) is the treasure of the city. The church dates much further back than its 18th-century baroque facade and even beyond its Gothic interior; in fact, it is the oldest church in Kőszeg. Inside are astonishingly well preserved 15th-century wall paintings, one of the Virgin Mary with mantle (painted, in fresco technique, on wet plaster) and one of a giant St. Christopher (painted *al secco*, on dry wall). If a mass is taking place when you arrive, it's best to wait outside until it's over. ⊠ *Jurisics tér at Rajnis u.* ☜ *Free.* ☯ *Daily 9–6.*

Not long after the Counter-Reformation, **Szent Imre templom** (St. Emerich's Church), the smaller church right next to St. James's Church, converted to Catholicism and replaced many of its Protestant trappings with baroque furnishings, most notably a high altar flanked by vivid statues of St. Stephen inviting and St. Ladislas defending the Virgin Mary. This church and St. James's next door, two landmarks planted side by side, symbolize Kőszeg's ethnic mix, formed over the centuries by Hungarian tribes moving west and by Germans expanding to the east. ⊠ *Jurisics tér at Chernel u.* ☜ *Free.* ☯ *Daily 8:30–6.*

Jurisics tér (Jurisics Square) was named after the Croatian captain Miklós Jurisics, who commanded Kőszeg's dramatic defense against the Turks in 1532. Like other fine "squares" in this part of Hungary, this one is not square but triangular.

The sprightly Gothic dowager of a building, **Városház** (City Hall), on one side of Jurisics Square, is dressed for a midsummer ball with cream- and cinnamon-color stripes skirting the ground floor. Fresco medallions of the Kőszeg, Hungarian, and Jurisics crests, painted in 1712, decorate the upper level. Inside the front door is a surprising courtyard whose brown window frames contrast with walls painted cool white, reminiscent of a Hungarian *csárda* (inn). The interior is not open to the public. ⊠ *Jurisics tér 8.*

Jurisics Square converges on the handsome **Hősi kapu** (Heroes' Gate), whose imposing tower's Renaissance-Gothic facade belies its fairly recent construction, in 1932, to celebrate the 400th anniversary of the Turkish siege. This historic victory is commemorated in relief inside the portal, where another relief mourns Kőszeg's loss of life in World War I, a defeat that also cost the city two-thirds of its market for textiles and agriculture after the breakup of the Austro-Hungarian Empire. The observation tower affords fine views. ⊠ *Jurisics tér 6,* ☎ *94/360–240.* ☜ *120 Ft.* ☯ *Apr.–Oct., Tues.–Sun. 10–5.*

The **Sgraffító ház** dates to the Renaissance, when sgraffito (design in which part of a surface layer is scratched away to reveal a different colored layer) was still a respectable art form. It now houses a funky pizzeria with live music every other Thursday night. ⊠ *Jurisics tér 7.*

Beneath a loft for drying medicinal herbs, the **Apotéka az Arany Egyszarvúhoz** (Golden Unicorn Pharmacy) is now a pharmacy museum (Patika Múzeum) with antique furniture, equipment, and paintings related to the pharmacy's history. ⊠ *Jurisics tér 11,* ☎ *94/360–337.* ⊠ *120 Ft.* ☉ *Apr.–Oct., Tues.–Sun. 10–5.*

On the corner of Rájnis József utca and Várkör (City Ring), the street that girdles the inner town, **statues of Sts. Leonard and Donatus** welcome you into the old quarter. The former carries a chain, for he is patron saint of prisoners and blacksmiths, as well as shepherds, animals, and sick people. The latter, the patron saint of wine, should hang his holy head a little. Kőszeg wine growers thrived until the turn of the 20th century, when phylloxera wiped out their industry. Now Kőszeg "imports" its wine from nearby Sopron. Rájnis utca nevertheless still has a few wine cellars, where the stuff is happily drunk with gusto.

NEED A BREAK?

In the town's historic wine district, it's only fitting to raise a glass or two at the **Kőszeg Szöllő Termelői Szövetkezete Borozója** (Kőszeg Vintners Association Winery; ⊠ Rajnis u. 10), in the cellar of a 15th-century Gothic house. It's usually closed on Monday.

The **Jurisics Vár** (Jurisics Castle), which you enter by crossing two former moats, is named not for the nobility who have inhabited it over the years but for the Croatian captain Miklós Jurisics, who commanded its victorious defense against the Turks in 1532. In the first enclosure are a youth hostel, a bathhouse where the local brass band rehearses, and a modern (1963) statue of the heroic Jurisics. One of the most interesting exhibits in the **Jurisics Miklós Vármúzeum** (Jurisics Castle Museum), which has exhibits on the city's and the castle's histories, is the "Book of the Vine's Growth": a chronicle kept for more than a century and a half, starting in 1740, by a succession of town clerks whose duty was to trace the sizes and shapes of vine buds on April 24 of each year. The tradition is still carried out at the same time every year. ⊠ *Rájnis József u. 9,* ☎ *94/360–240.* ⊠ *120 Ft. (castle grounds 40 Ft. additional).* ☉ *Tues.–Sun. 10–5.*

Dining and Lodging

$–$$ ✕ **Ibrahim Kávézó.** Named after a Turkish pasha, this small café has a strong Turkish theme, with a red canopy hanging above the tiny bar and bright-blue painted ceilings peppered with bronze studs. The larger back room has a kitschy fountain with a bronze cobra spitting water. The food, however, is Continental. Try the venison bourguignonne with potato dumplings, and don't overlook the delicious strudels (they even have blueberry, a rarity in Hungary). ⊠ *Fő tér 17,* ☎ *94/360–854. No credit cards.*

$–$$ ✕ **Kulacs Vendéglő.** A central location near Fő tér, home-style fare, and low prices make this informal eatery popular. Try the *Kulacs pecsenye* (roast meat "Canteen-style")—spareribs covered with fried onions and a gravy with steamed broccoli and chopped carrots. Typical Hungarian red-and-white embroidered tablecloths and curtains add a cheerful touch to the small dining room. ⊠ *Várkör 12,* ☎ *94/362–318. DC, MC, V.*

$$ ▣ **Alpokalja Panzió.** On the western edge of town along the highway to Austria, this cheerful chalet-style pension is convenient if you're traveling by car. Clean rooms, with either white or wooden walls, are small and sunny. Avoid rooms that face the auto yard and train tracks out back. Bathroms have showers only and no tubs. Breakfast costs a few dollars extra. ⊠ *Szombathelyi u. 8, H-9730,* ☎ ℻ *94/360–056,* WEB *www.hotels.hu/alpokalja. 27 rooms. Restaurant, billiards. DC, MC, V.*

$$ ⊞ **Írottkő.** This modern hotel on the town's main square manages to blend in with the neighboring old houses. Its four-story atrium is sleek, and the guest rooms are functional but not so luxurious that you'd want to stay indoors when there's so much to see outside. The staff is friendly and multilingual. ⊠ *Fő tér 4, H-9730,* ☎ FAX *94/360–373,* WEB *www.hotelirottko.hu. 52 rooms. Pub. AE, DC, MC, V.*

$ ⊞ **Szálloda az Arany Strucchoz.** Built in 1718, this inn is one of the oldest hotels in Hungary. Although it is definitely showing its age, it has an excellent location: on the main square next to the Sacred Heart church. But for color TVs and renovated bathrooms, most of the spacious rooms have wilting, bare-bones furnishings adequate for a decent night's sleep. The corner room with 19th-century Biedermeier furnishings and a balcony overlooking the main square is the prize of the hotel—it and three other rooms with a similar look are just a few dollars more than the standard rooms. ⊠ *Várkör 124, H-9730,* ☎ FAX *94/360–323. 18 rooms. Restaurant. No credit cards.*

Nightlife and the Arts

Kőszeg is anything but a nightlife hot spot. A big night out might center on dinner and a pre-bedtime stroll.

Each year in late April, music and dance festivities are organized to celebrate the *szöllő rajzolás* (grape drawing), a tradition since 1740 in which the town clerks record the sizes and shapes of the year's vine buds in a special book on April 24. The town's biggest cultural event is the annual **Ost-West Fesztival** (East-West Festival) in early June—a weekend of open-air international folk music and dance performances on Fő tér, in the castle courtyard, and throughout the inner town. The **grape harvest** is usually celebrated in late September with a series of woodwind ensemble concerts and a harvest parade.

For exact schedule and ticket information on cultural events, contact **Savaria Tourist** (⊠ Várkör 69, ☎ FAX 94/360–238).

Pécs

❶ *365 km (226 mi) southeast of Kőszeg, 197 km (122 mi) southwest of Budapest.*

The southwest's premier city and the fifth largest in Hungary, Pécs (pronounced *paytch*) is a vibrant, cultured, beautiful city that leaves most visitors aesthetically and intellectually satiated. Pécs went through various incarnations in the course of its long history. The Franks called it Quinque Ecclesiae; the Slavs, Pet Cerkve; and the Hapsburgs, Fünfkirchen; all three names mean "five churches." Today there are many more churches, plus two mosques and a handsome synagogue. In any language, however, Pécs could just as well be renamed City of Many Museums, for on one square block alone there are seven. (A one-day pass covering most of them can be purchased at any participating museum for about 800 Ft.) Three of them—the Zsolnay, Vasarely, and Csontváry—justify a two- or three-day stay in this sparkling, eclectic city in the Mecsek Hills, just 30 km (19 mi) north of the Croatian border.

At the foot of Széchenyi tér, the grand sloping monumental thoroughfare that is the pride of the city, stands the dainty **Zsolnay Fountain,** a petite Art Nouveau majolica temple guarded by shiny ox-head gargoyles made of green eosin porcelain that gush pure drinking water piped into Pécs via Roman aqueducts. The fountain was built in the early 19th century by the famous Zsolnay family, who pioneered and developed their unique porcelain art here in Pécs.

NEED A
BREAK?   A short walk down pedestrians-only Király utca, opening from Széchenyi
tér, is the **Caflisch Cukrászda** (⊠ Király u. 32, ☎ 72/310–391), a cozy,
informal café established in 1869—in a building dating to 1789—with
tiny round, marble-top tables and small chandeliers. It's open until 10 PM.

Széchenyi tér is crowned by a delightful Turkish construction: a 16th-
century mosque. Dating from the years of Turkish occupation (1543–
★ 1686), the mosque is now the Catholic **Belvárosi plébánia templom**
(Inner City Parish Church), which you might infer from the cross sur-
mounting a gilded crescent atop the dome. Despite the fierce religious
war raging on its walls—Christian statuary and frescoes beneath Turkish arcades and mihrabs (prayer niches)—this church, also referred to
as the Gazi Khassim Pasha Jammi, remains the largest and finest relic
of Turkish architecture in Hungary. ⊠ *Széchenyi tér.* ☜ *Free.* ☉ *Mid-
Apr.–mid-Oct., Mon.–Sat. 10–4, Sun. 11:30–4; mid-Oct.–mid-Apr.,
Mon.–Sat. 11–noon, Sun. 11:30–2.*

Occupying the upper floor of the oldest surviving building in Pécs, the
★ **Zsolnay Múzeum** (Zsolnay Museum) dates from 1324 and was built
and rebuilt in Romanesque, Renaissance, and baroque styles during
its checkered history. A stroll through its rooms is a merry show-and-
tell waltz through a revolution in pottery that started in 1851, when
Miklós Zsolnay, a local merchant, bought the site of an old kiln and
set up a stoneware factory for his son Ignác to run. Ignác's brother,
Vilmos, a shopkeeper with an artistic bent, bought the factory from
him in 1863, imported experts from Germany, and, with the help of
a Pécs pharmacist for chemical glaze experiments and his daughters
for hand painting, created the distinctive namesake porcelain.

Among the museum's exhibits are Vilmos's early efforts at Delft-blue
handmade vases, cups, and saucers; his two-layer ceramics; examples
of the gold-brocade rims that became a Zsolnay trademark; and table
settings for royal families. Be sure to look up and notice the unusual
Zsolnay chandeliers lighting your way. The Zsolnay store in the center of Pécs, at Jokai tér 2, sells a wide selection of ceramics. ⊠ *Káptalan u. 2,* ☎ *72/310–172,* WEB *www.zsolnay.hu.* ☜ *250 Ft.* ☉ *Tues.–
Sun. 10–6.*

If you haven't had enough Zsolnay after visiting the Zsolnay Museum,
join the groups of tourists (usually German or Hungarian) braving heavily trafficked Zsolnay Vilmos utca to visit the **Zsolnay porcelán gyár**
(Zsolnay Porcelain Factory), where gleaming monumental towers and
statuary of seemingly pollution-proof porcelain hold their own among
giant smokestacks. The factory can be visited by guided tour only, in
groups of 10–30. Call the factory or ask **Tourinform** (⊠ Széchenyi tér
9, ☎ 72/213–315) to help find out when the next group is visiting so
that you can tag along.

On a hill behind the factory stands the ultimate monument to the dynasty's founder, who died in 1900: the **Zsolnay Mausoleum**, with the
bones of Vilmos and his wife in a blue ceramic well and, over the doorway, a relief of Vilmos, with disciples resembling his wife, daughters,
and son kneeling before him. The mausoleum is open Tuesday–Sunday 11–3. Admission is 500 Ft. Call ahead (☎ 06/309–297–803) for
a one-hour tour in English, which runs about 100 Ft. extra per person, proportionally more if there are fewer than 10 people on hand.
⊠ *Zsolnay Vilmos u. 69,* ☎ *72/325–266 factory tour information.* ☜
Factory 200 Ft. English-language tour 300 Ft.

The pioneer of Op Art (who later settled in France) was born Győző
Vásárhelyi in 1908 in the funhouse that is the **Vasarely Múzeum**

(Vasarely Museum). The first hall is a corridor of visual tricks devised by his disciples, at the end of which hangs a hypnotic canvas of shifting cubes by Jean-Pierre Yvaral. Upstairs, the illusions grow profound: a zebra gallops by while chess pieces and blood cells seem to come at you. ✉ *Káptalan u. 3,* ☎ *72/324–822.* 💰 *250 Ft.* ☉ *Tues.–Sun. 10–6.*

The **Endre Nemes Múzeum** (Endre Nemes Museum) displays the ceramics of Vilmos Zsolnay and his followers (accompanied by English texts). Another section of the museum contains a street scene titled *Utca* ("street"), constructed entirely of white foam plastic by the sculptor Erzsébet Schaár. The people on the street are made of gypsum, simple in body structure but with finely drawn heads and faces of historical figures such as Karl Marx and Sándor Petőfi, the famous Hungarian poet. ✉ *Káptalan u. 5,* ☎ *72/324–822.* 💰 *250 Ft.* ☉ *Apr.–Oct., Tues.–Sun. 10–6; Nov.–Mar., Tues.–Sun. 2–6.*

Mihály Tivadar Csontváry Kosztka (1853–1919) was a pharmacist who worked, as he put it, to "catch up with, let alone surpass, the great masters." An early expressionist and forerunner of surrealism, Csontváry influenced Picasso; his work is to be found almost exclusively here, at

★ the **Csontváry Múzeum** (Csontváry Museum), and in a room of the Hungarian National Gallery in Budapest.

The paintings in the five rooms of this museum are arranged to show Csontváry's progression from soulful portraits to seemingly conventional landscapes executed with decidedly unconventional colors to his 1904 *Temple of Zeus in Athens*—about which Csontváry said, "This is the first painting in which the canvas can no longer be seen." After a 1905 tryout in Budapest, Csontváry was ready for a 1907 exhibition in Paris, which turned out to be a huge critical success. Not long after finishing his last great epic painting, *Mary at the Well in Nazareth* (1908), megalomania gripped him. Though his canvases grew ever larger, Csontváry finished nothing that he started after 1909 except a patriotic drawing of Emperor Franz Joseph, completed at the start of World War I in 1914. The last room of the exhibit is filled only with sketches. After he died in Budapest in 1919, Csontváry's canvases were about to be reused as furniture covers when a collector from Pécs named Gedeon Gerlóczy rescued them with a ransom of 10,000 Ft. The collection in Pécs is now valued at more than 2.85 billion Ft. ($10 million).

The museum, which is considered to be one of the three major galleries in Pécs, sits just around the corner from its peers. If you've just left the Vasarely and you have the time, it's probably best to wait a day and bring a fresh eye here. ✉ *Janus Pannonius u. 11,* ☎ *72/310–544.* 💰 *250 Ft.* ☉ *Tues.–Sun. 10–6.*

★ One of Europe's most magnificent cathedrals is the **Pécs Bazilika** (Pécs Basilica), promoted from cathedral to basilica rank after Pope John Paul II's visit in 1991. At the beginning of the 19th century, Mihály Pollack directed the transformation of the exterior, changing it from baroque to neoclassical; its interior remained Gothic. Near the end of the 19th century, Bishop Nándor Dulánszky decided to restore the cathedral to its original, Árpád-period style—the result is a four-spired monument that has an utterly breathtaking interior frescoed in shimmering golds, silvers, and blues. ✉ *Szent István tér.* 💰 *250 Ft. (including treasury and crypt), full lighting 500 Ft., English-language tour 1,000 Ft.* ☉ *Apr.–Oct., weekdays 9–5, Sat. 9–2, Sun. 1–5; Nov.–Mar., Mon.–Sat. 10–4, Sat. 10–1, Sun. 1–4.*

In front of Pécs Basilica is a serene little park, just beyond which is the 4th-century **Ókeresztény mauzóleum** (Early Christian Mausoleum),

Hungary's largest and most important early Christian mausoleum and a World Heritage Site. Some of the subterranean crypts and chapels date to its earliest days; the murals on the walls (Adam and Eve, Daniel in the lion's den, the Resurrection) are in remarkably good condition. ⊠ *Szent István tér,* ☎ *no phone.* ▣ *200 Ft.* ☉ *Tues.–Sun. 10–6.*

<table>
<tr><td>OFF THE
BEATEN PATH</td><td>VILLÁNY – The town of Villány, 30 km (19 mi) south of Pécs and nestled in the low, verdant Villányi Hills, is the center of one of Hungary's most famous wine regions. Villány's exceptional and unique red wines are heralded here and abroad; its burgundies, cabernets, and ports are said to give the best of their French and Italian peers a run for the money. Many wine cellars offer regular wine tastings and sales. Tourinform (⊠ Széchenyi tér 9, ☎ 72/213–315) in Pécs has an informative brochure and listing of cellars. If you wish to learn about the wine before imbibing, stop in at the Bor Múzeum (Wine Museum; ⊠ Bem u. 8, ☎ 72/492–130) for a look at the history of the region's viticulture, which dates back some 2,000 years. The museum is open Tuesday–Sunday 9–5; admission is free.</td></tr>
</table>

Dining and Lodging

$–$$ ✕ **Pannonia.** The menu at this classy cellar restaurant has been designed to complement the sparkling wines from the on-site winery—with five floors of underground wine cellars—of the same name. Among the dishes are poached salmon in green champagne sauce and panfried butter fish with wok-fried vegetables. The seafood is flown in weekly from Sweden, the country that happens to be the biggest importer of Pannonia wines. The restaurant's location near Pécs Basilica makes it a perfect spot for lunch while sightseeing. ⊠ *Szent István tér 12,* ☎ *72/210–084. MC, V.*

$–$$ ✕ **Vasváry Ház.** A life-size Elvis Presley gyrates on one end of the long bar at this Hungarian version of a T. G. I. Friday's restaurant, while at the other end, a model Marilyn Monroe fights a breeze, à la *The Seven Year Itch.* Food ranges from contemporary Hungarian dishes—such as *pulykajavka Rézi nén módra* ("Aunt Rezi's prime turkey")—to Mediterranean-influenced fare, including seafood paella. ⊠ *Király u. 19,* ☎ *72/212–224. AE, DC, MC, V.*

$$$ ⌑ **Hotel Millennium Szálló.** Renowned Hungarian architect Sándor Dévényi designed this chintzy suburban castle on Kálvária hill, amidst a nature reserve and just outside the old city wall. The rooms are pleasantly low-key, and four of them look out onto the four spires of the Pécs Basilica. ⊠ *Kálvária u. 58, H-7625,* ☎ 匧 *72/512–222 or 72/512–223,* ⟨WEB⟩ *www.hotels.hu/hotelmillennium. 25 rooms. Restaurant, free parking, some pets allowed. AE, DC, MC, V.*

$$$ ⌑ **Hotel Palatinus.** Art Nouveau prevails on the streets of many of Hun-
★   gary's cities and towns, but for some pure art deco, spend a night at this central Pés hotel. (Or at the very least, wander in from the pedestrian arcade for a drink in the Gösser Brasserie and have a look around.) The hotel's public grand areas—lobby, sweeping staircases, restaurant, and ballroom—are all stunning. The modern rooms are somewhat disappointing after the public areas, but are well equipped. ⊠ *Király u. 5, H-7621,* ☎ *72/514–260,* 匧 *72/514–738,* ⟨WEB⟩ *www.danubiusgroup.com. 88 rooms, 6 suites. 2 restaurants, minibars, room TVs with movies, massage, sauna. AE, DC, MC, V.*

$$ ⌑ **Szinbád Panzio.** This establishment stands out among Pécs's several smaller inns because of its on-site Turkish restaurant. The good-value accommodations have spacious bathrooms, balconies, and outdoor areas with tables and chairs. ⊠ *Klimó Gy. u. 9, H-7625,* ☎ 匧 *72/512–222 or 72/512–223,* ⟨WEB⟩ *www.hotels.hu/szinbad_restaurant_panzio. 25 rooms. Restaurant, free parking; no a/c. AE, DC, MC, V.*

Nightlife and the Arts

THE ARTS

September brings harvest-related festivities such as classical concerts, folk-music and -dance performances, and a parade or two to venues in and around Pécs. Inquire at **Tourinform** (⊠ Széchenyi tér 9, ☎ 72/213–315) for specifics. Tourinform publishes a monthly arts and events calendar in English and can help with further schedule and ticket information.

The **Pécsi Nemzeti Színház** (Pécs National Theater; ⊠ Színház tér 1, ☎ 72/211–965) is the main venue for regular performances by the Pécs Symphony Orchestra and the theater's opera and modern ballet companies. The theater is closed from late May until September.

NIGHTLIFE

Murphy's Pub (⊠ Király u. 2, ☎ 72/325–439), with dark woods and polished brass, keeps an ample supply of Guinness on tap. The **Fregatt Arizona Pub** (⊠ Király u. 21, ☎ 72/210–486) has low-vaulted ceilings and Guinness on tap.

Outdoor Activities and Sports

The **Mecsek Hills** rise up just behind Pécs, with abundant well-marked hiking trails through its forests and fresh air. Guided walks are often organized on weekends by local nature clubs; contact **Tourinform** (⊠ Széchenyi tér 9, ☎ 72/213–315) for dates and times.

Shopping

Király utca, a vibrant, pedestrians-only street lined with beautifully preserved romantic and baroque facades, is Pécs's main shopping zone, full of colorful boutiques and outdoor cafés.

The best place in the whole country to buy exquisite Zsolnay porcelain is at the **Zsolnay Márkabolt** (⊠ Jókai tér 2, ☎ 72/310–220). As the Zsolnay factory's own outlet, the store offers guaranteed authenticity and the best prices on the full spectrum of pieces—from tea sets profusely painted with colorful, gold-winged butterflies to white-and-night-blue dinner services.

Pécs's **kirakodóvásár** (flea market; ⊠ Vásár tér, ☎ 72/224–313) provides great browsing and bargain hunting among its eclectic mix of goods—from used clothing and handcrafted folk art to antiques and fresh vegetables. It's held every day (from 6 until 1), but weekends draw many more sellers, and the first Sunday of every month is the best for quantity and variety, especially in terms of antiques.

Transdanubia Essentials

BUS TRAVEL

If you visit without a car, you'll need to rely on buses to get you to smaller towns such as Pannonhalma, which are not on the rail lines. Regular buses link the towns in the area. Inquire at tourist offices for more information.

CAR TRAVEL

Traveling around Transdanubia is done best by car. From Budapest, you can get to Pannonhalma, Fertőd, and Sopron via the M1 through Győr, switching onto the appropriate secondary route there. Pécs and Budapest are directly connected by Route 6. The M1 runs into Austria, Route 6 to the border of Croatia.

Kőszeg and Sopron are a fairly short driving distance from one another. Significantly farther south and east, Pécs can be reached from Kőszeg along connecting major secondary roads past the southern tip of the Balaton and through Kaposvár. It's a beautiful drive.

TRAIN TRAVEL

There are good rail connections from Budapest to Sopron and Pécs; the trip—by InterCity (IC) trains, which run several times daily—takes 2½ hours to Sopron, 3 to Pécs. Trains to Sopron and Fertőd go north through Győr. There are direct connections between Vienna and Sopron and Bratislava and Győr.

The trip from Sopron to Kőszeg is not direct; you'd have to change in Szombathely, south of Kőszeg, which sends you a good 30 minutes out of your way. The trip from Sopron to Pécs is quite long—about 1½ hours from Sopron to Szombathely, where you transfer to the train to Pécs, which takes nearly 4½ hours.

➤ TRAIN STATIONS: Kőszeg **train station** (✉ Alsó krt. 2, ☎ 94/360–053). **Pécs train station** (✉ Indóhász tér, ☎ 72/312–443). **Sopron train station** (✉ Vasútállomás, ☎ 99/517–212).

VISITOR INFORMATION

➤ TOURIST INFORMATION: **Pécs: Tourinform** (✉ Széchenyi tér 9, ☎ 72/213–315, ℻ 72/212–632). **Savaria Tourist**, Kőszeg (✉ Várkör 69, ☎ ℻ 94/360–238). **Sopron: Tourinform** (✉ Előkapu u. 11, ☎ 99/338–592, ☎ ℻ 338–892, WEB www.sopron.hu).

NORTHERN HUNGARY

Northern Hungary stretches from the Danube Bend, north of Budapest, along the northeastern frontier with Slovakia as far west as Sátoraljaújhely. It is a clearly defined area, marked by several mountain ranges of no great height but of considerable scenic beauty. Most of the peaks reach 3,000 ft and are thickly wooded almost to their summit. Grottoes and caves abound, as well as thermal baths. In the state game reserves, it's not uncommon to spot herds of deer, wild boars, and eagles.

Historically, the valleys of northern Hungary have always been of considerable strategic importance, as they provided the only access to the Carpathian Mountains. The city of Eger, renowned throughout Hungarian history as one of the guardians of these strategic routes, retains its splendor, with many ruins picturesquely dotting the surrounding hilltops. The Mátra Mountains, less than 90 km (56 mi) from Budapest, are a center for winter sports—they also allow for year-round recreation. Last but not least, this is one of the great wine-growing districts of Hungary, with Gyöngyös and Eger contributing the "Magyar nectar" and Tokaj producing the "wine of kings."

Numbers in the margin correspond to numbers on the Northern Hungary and the Great Plain map.

Hollókő

★ ❶   *100 km (62 mi) northeast of Budapest.*

UNESCO lists this tiny mountain village close to the Slovakian border as one of its World Heritage Sites because of Hollókő's unique medieval structure and age-old Palóc (ethnographic group indigenous to northern Hungary) cultural and handcrafting traditions still practiced today by the village's 400 inhabitants. The most famous of these traditions are apparent during Easter, when the villagers dress in colorful embroidered costumes. During this time, thousands of visitors descend upon the village.

Hollókő is authentically enchanting: old whitewashed houses, some of them built in the 17th century, cluster together on narrow cobblestone pathways; directly above them loom the hilltop ruins (now being restored) of a 13th-century castle. For information on Hollókő's Easter festivities and other events, contact the village's cultural foundation, **Hollókőért közalapítvány** (✉ Kossuth u. 68, H-3176, ☎ 🗺 32/579–010).

Dining and Lodging

$–$$ ✕ **Muskátli Vendéglő.** Named for the bright red and pink flowers lining its windowsills, the Geranium Restaurant is a cozy little eatery on Hollókő's main street. Specialties include *Palócgulyás,* a rich local goulash thick with chunks of pork and beans, and *Nógrádi palócpecsenye,* pork cutlets smothered in mustard-garlic sauce. ✉ *Kossuth út 61,* ☎ *32/379–262. AE, DC, MC, V. Closed Mon. Mar.–Dec. and Mon.–Wed. Jan.–Feb.*

$$$ 🏨 **Kastély Szirák.** One of Hungary's best castle hotels was built in 1748, on the foundations of a 13th-century knights' hostel, for Count József Teleki: an arts patron who created a vast library and covered the main hall with frescoes depicting Ovid's *Metamorphoses.* Double rooms cost about 15,000 Ft. per night, including breakfast. A newer wing houses the "tourist hotel," comprising bland, dated units that share nothing of the castle's aura. You can also go horseback riding, even if you're not a guest. The hotel lies about 35 km (22 mi) along Route 21 and then some lovely side roads from Hollókő. ✉ *Petőfi út 26, H–3044 Szirák,* ☎ 🗺 *60/353–053. 21 rooms, 4 suites. Restaurant, tennis court, sauna, horseback riding, meeting rooms. AE, DC, MC, V.*

Gyöngyös

❷ *40 km (25 mi) southeast of Hollókő, 75 km (47 mi) northeast of Budapest.*

The city of Gyöngyös, famous for its excellent wines, lies at the base of the volcanic Mátra mountain range, Hungary's best-developed mountain vacation area. (While you're here, don't pass up the chance to sample the Debrői hárslevelű, a magnificent white wine produced in a nearby village.) Early in the 1960s huge lignite deposits were discovered, and the large-scale mines and power stations established since then have changed the character of the entire region.

Although it offers few reasons to linger in its own right, Gyöngyös serves as the gateway to the Mátras and is a good starting point for visiting the many beautiful resorts that lie just north of it. The best known is Mátrafüred, at 1,300 ft, which can be reached by narrow-gauge railway from Gyöngyös. Just a few miles from Mátrafüred is Kékestető, the highest point in Hungary (3,327 ft).

The 15th-century beautifully restored **Szent Bertalan templom** (Church of St. Bartholomew), on Fő tér, is one of Hungary's largest Gothic churches. Next to the altar is a 16th-century bronze baptismal font; there's also a fresco of King Károly IV's visit to Gyöngyös after a serious fire. ✉ *Fő tér; treasury: Szent Bertalan út 3,* ☎ *37/311–143.* 🏛 *Church free, treasury 50 Ft.* ☉ *Church daily 7–4; treasury Tues.–Sun. 10–noon and 2–4.*

The **Mátra Múzeum** (Mátra Museum), in a handsome neoclassical mansion, provides a helpful preparation for excursions into the Mátras with its extensive exhibits on the flora and fauna of the region, as well as geological and historical displays. In addition to hearing recorded sounds of indigenous bird songs, you can examine deer, eagles, and other fauna you may encounter, as well as those you'll be luckier to avoid, such as the sharp-tusked wild boar. Also on display is "Bruno," the hulking

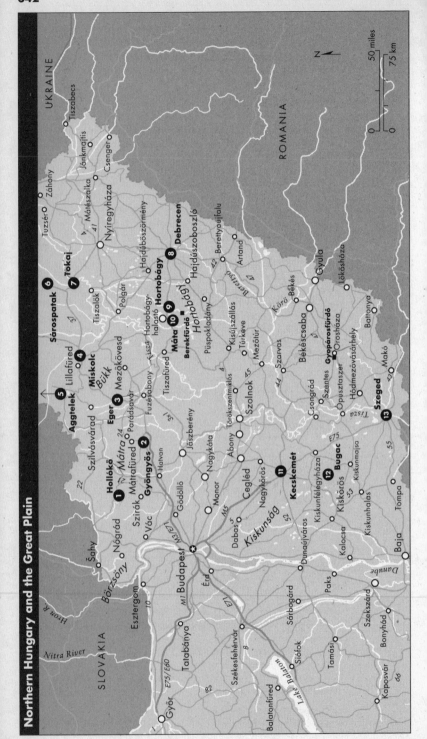

Northern Hungary and the Great Plain

1- to 2-million-year-old skeleton of a young mammoth found in the northern Mátra. Unless you're a fan of dank cellars filled with snakes and bugs (and their smell), avoid the "Mikro-varium" exhibit downstairs. ⊠ *Kossuth Lajos u. 40,* ☎ *37/311–447.* ☒ *200 Ft.* ☉ *Mar.–Oct., Tues.–Sun. 9–5; Nov.–Feb., Tues.–Sun. 10–2.*

Dining and Lodging

$$$$ ✕▥ **Kastély Hotel Sasvár.** The Sasvár Castle Hotel is in an early 19th-century mansion, expanded in 1882 in German Renaissance style by virtuoso architect Miklós Ybl. Majestic details include a minaretlike tower, a soaring steeple sublimely topped off by a spire, and a spacious, colonnaded courtyard flanked on three sides by the hotel's low wings. The rooms, which look out either onto sloping forests, the courtyard, or the quiet road leading past the village, have neo-Renaissance or neo-baroque furnishings; suites also include hot tubs and saunas. The hotel nestles deep in the Mátra Hills, about 25 km (15 mi) north of Gyöngyös. ⊠ *Kossuth u. 1, H–3242 Parádsasvár,* ☎ *36/444–444,* ⅎ⅍ *36/544–010,* ᴡᴇʙ *www.sasvar.hu. 54 rooms, 5 suites. Restaurant, tennis court, 2 pools (1 indoor), hot tub, sauna, steam room, bowling, squash, baby-sitting, meeting rooms. MC, V.*

Outdoor Activities and Sports

Stop at the Eger **Tourinform** office (⊠ Dobó tér 2, ☎ 36/517–715) for maps, books, and advice about the area's rich outdoor offerings.

BICYCLING

Avar Túrakerékpár Klub (⊠ Bene út 33, ☎ ⅎ⅍ 37/309–116), a good source for bicycle rental and touring information, organizes custom-designed bicycle tours for all abilities. From mid-May through late August it holds regular Saturday-afternoon trips open to all; call ahead for details.

HIKING

Mátrafüred and Mátraháza are popular starting points for hikes up Kékestető, Hungary's highest peak at 3,327 ft. Views from the TV and lookout tower are phenomenal. Don't expect to find yourself alone with only the rushing wind at the top of the peak; it's actually somewhat developed, with a couple of hotels where you can spend a night dozing in one of the highest beds in Hungary.

En Route Route 24 is the scenic route between Gyöngyös and Eger, climbing and twisting through the Mátras. You can pause in **Sirok** to snap a photo of its castle ruins, piled high on a hill looming over the village.

Eger

★ ❸ *40 km (25 mi) east of Gyöngyös.*

With vineyard surroundings and more than 175 of Hungary's historic monuments—a figure surpassed only by Budapest and Sopron—the picture-book baroque city of Eger is ripe for exploration. The city, which lies in a fertile valley between the Mátra Mountains and their eastern neighbor, the Bükk range, has borne witness to much history, heartbreak, and glory. It was settled quite early in the Hungarian conquest of the land, and it was one of five bishoprics created by King Stephen I when he Christianized the country almost a millennium ago.

In 1552 the city was attacked by the Turks, but the commander, István Dobó, and fewer than 2,000 men and women held out for 38 days against 80,000 Turkish soldiers and drove them away. One of Hungary's great legends tells of the women of Eger pouring hot pitch onto the heads of the Turks as they attempted to scale the castle walls (the event is depicted in a famous painting now in the National Gallery in Budapest). Despite such heroism, however, Eger fell to the Turks in 1596 and became one of the most important northern outposts of Muslim power until its reconquest in 1687.

Today, restored baroque and rococo buildings line Eger's cobblestone streets, making for excellent strolling and sightseeing. Wherever you wander, make a point of peeking into open courtyards, where you may happen upon otherwise hidden architectural gems.

The grand, neoclassical **Bazilika** (Basilica), the second-largest cathedral in Hungary, was built in the center of town early in the 19th century. It is approached by a stunning stairway flanked by statues of Sts. Stephen, László, Peter, and Paul—the work of Italian sculptor Marco Casagrande, who also carved 22 biblical reliefs inside and outside the building. From May 15 through October 15, organ recitals are held Monday through Saturday at 11:30 AM and Sunday at 12:45 PM. It's best to visit when no masses are taking place—from 9 until 6. ⊠ *Eszterházy tér*, ☎ *36/316–592.* ▧ *Free.* ☉ *Daily 5:45 AM–7:30 PM.*

The square block of a baroque building opposite the basilica is a former lyceum, now the **Eszterházy Károly főiskola** (Károly Eszterházy Teachers College). The handsome library has a fine trompe-l'oeil ceiling fresco that gives an intoxicating illusion of depth. High up in the structure's six-story observatory, now a museum, is a horizontal sundial with a tiny gold cannon, which, when filled with gunpowder, used to let out a burst at exactly high noon. Also here, the noonday sun, shining through a tiny aperture, makes a palm-size silvery spot on the meridian line on the marble floor. Climb higher to the "Specula Periscope" grand finale: in a darkened room a man manipulates three rods of a periscope—in operation since 1776—to project panoramic views of Eger onto a round table. Children squeal with delight as real people and cars hurry and scurry across the table like hyperactive Legos. ⊠ *Eszterházy tér 1*, ☎ *36/410–466.* ▧ *Library and museum 330 Ft.; on request, half-price for museum only.* ☉ *Mid-Apr.–Sept., Tues.– Sun. 9:30–3; mid-Mar.–mid-Apr. and Oct.–mid-Dec., Tues.–Fri. 9:30– 1, weekends 9:30–noon; Jan.–mid-Mar., weekends 9:30–noon.*

Eger's rococo **Cistercia templom** (Cistercian Church) was built during the first half of the 18th century. A splendid statue of St. Francis Borgia kneeling beneath Christ on the cross dominates the main altar, which dates to 1770. The church can be visited during mass on weekdays (held at 7:15 AM and 8 AM) and on Sunday (held at 7 AM, 8 AM, 10 AM and 7 PM); other times it can be viewed through a locked gate. ⊠ *Széchenyi u. 15*, ☎ *36/313–496.* ▧ *Free.*

NEED A BREAK?	**Dobos Cukrászda** (⊠ Széchenyi u. 6, ☎ 36/413–335), on Eger's central pedestrian street, is a great spot to revive after sightseeing; try the house specialty, *dobos bomba* (chocolate-covered cake).

The light, lovely, dove-gray **Rác templom** (Serbian Orthodox Church) contains more than 100 icon paintings on wood that look as though they were fashioned from gold and marble. The church sits on a hilltop almost 1 km (½ mi) away from the end of Széchenyi utca. ⊠ *Vitkovits u. 30*, ☎ *36/320–129.* ▧ *100 Ft.* ☉ *Tues.–Sun. 10–4.*

The **Nagypréposti palota** (Provost's House), on Kossuth Lajos utca, is a small rococo palace still considered one of Hungary's finest mansions despite abuse by the Red Army (soldiers ruined several frescoes by heating the building with oil). The building now serves as European headquarters of the International Committee of Historic Towns (ICO-

MOS) but is also regularly open for public viewing and has a museum and library. ⊠ *Kossuth Lajos u. 4.* 🖂 *Library and museum 330 Ft.; on request, half-price for museum only.* ⊙ *Jan.–June, Tues.–Fri. 10–7, Sat. 10–4; July–Aug., Mon. 1–7, Tues.–Fri. 10–7; Sept.–Dec., Mon. 1–7, Tues.–Fri. 10–7, Sat. 10–4.*

During a brief stay in Eger (1758–1761), German artist Henrik Fazola graced many buildings with his work but none so exquisitely as the wrought-iron twin gates that, facing each other just inside the entryway of the **Megye Ház** (County Council Hall), frame the inner entrances to the building's two wings. Sent to Paris in 1889 for the international exposition, the richly ornamented, mirror-image gates—which have not only numerous flowers and leaves but clusters of grapes and a stork with a snake in its beak—won a gold medal 130 years after their creation. On the wall to the right of the building's street entrance, a sign indicates the level of floodwaters during the flooding of the Eger stream on August 31, 1878. Similar signs can be seen throughout this area of the city. ⊠ *Kossuth Lajos u. 9,* ☎ *36/312–744.* 🖂 *Free.* ⊙ *Apr.–Oct., Tues.–Sun. 9–5.*

Eger Vár (Eger Castle) was built after the devastating Tartar invasion of 1241–1242. When Béla IV returned from exile in Italy, he ordered the erection of mighty fortresses like those he had seen in the West. Within the castle walls an imposing Romanesque cathedral was built and then, during the 15th century, rebuilt in Gothic style; today only its foundations remain. Inside the foundation area, a statue of Szent István (St. Stephen), erected in 1900, looks out benignly over the city. Nearby are catacombs that were built in the second half of the 16th century by Italian engineers. By racing back and forth through this labyrinth of underground tunnels and appearing at various ends of the castle, the hundreds of defenders tricked the attacking Turks into thinking there were thousands of them. The Gothic-style **Püspök Ház** (Bishop's House) contains the castle history museum and, in the basement, a numismatic museum where coins can be minted and certified (in English). Also here are an art gallery, displaying Italian and Dutch Renaissance works; a prison exhibit, near the main entrance; and a wax museum, depicting characters from the Hungarian historical novel *Eclipse of the Crescent Moon,* about Hungary's final expulsion of the Turks. Videotaping is not allowed, but photography (no flash) is allowed for a fee. ⊠ *Dózsa György tér,* ☎ *36/312–744.* 🖂 *Museums (including general castle admission) 300 Ft.; castle grounds 120 Ft.; photography fee (no flash) 300 Ft. per camera.* ⊙ *Castle grounds Apr.–Oct., daily 6 AM–8 PM; Nov.–Mar., daily 6–5. Museums Apr.–Aug. and Nov.–Feb., Tues.–Sun. 8–5; Sept., Tues.–Sun. 8–7; Mar. and Oct., Tues.–Sun. 8–6. Prison exhibit and catacombs Apr.–Sept., Tues.–Sun. 9–5 (catacombs remain open on Mon.). Wax museum daily 9–6.*

Downtown, picturesque **Dobó tér** is marked by two intensely animated statues produced in the early 20th century by a father and son: *Dobó the Defender* is by Alajos Stróbl, and the sculpture of a Magyar battling two Turks is by Stróbl's son, Zsigmond Kisfaludi-Stróbl. Their works flank the **Minorita templom** (Minorite Church), which with its twin spires and finely carved pulpit, pews, and organ loft is considered one of the best baroque churches in Central Europe. *Church:* ☎ *36/313–304.* 🖂 *Free.* ⊙ *Daily 10–5.*

A bridge over the Eger stream—it's too small to be classified as a river—leads to an early 17th-century Turkish **minaret,** from the top of which Muslims were called to prayer. This is the northernmost surviving Turkish building in Europe. ⊠ *Knézich K. u.* 🖂 *80 Ft.* ⊙ *Apr.–Oct., daily 10–6.*

Eger wine is renowned beyond Hungary. The best-known variety is *Egri Bikavér* (Bull's Blood of Eger), a full-bodied red wine. Other outstanding vintages are the Medoc Noir, a dark red dessert wine; Leányka, a delightful dry white; and the sweeter white Muskotály. The place to sample them is the **Szépasszony-völgy,** a vineyard area within Eger's city limits. Some 250 small wine cellars (some of them literally holes-in-the-wall and most of them now private) stand open and inviting in the warm weather, and a few are open in winter, too. You may be given a tour of the cellar, and wines will be tapped from the barrel into your glass by the vintners themselves at the tiniest cost (but it's prudent to inquire politely how much it will cost before imbibing).

OFF THE
BEATEN PATH

SZILVÁSVÁRAD – About 25 km (16 mi) from Eger up into the Bükk Mountains brings you to this village, one of Hungary's most important equestrian centers. For more than 500 years, the white Lipizzaner horses have been bred here, and every year on a weekend in early September they prance and pose in the Lipicai Lovasfesztivál, an international carriage-driving competition held in the equestrian stadium. At other times, you can see them grazing in the village fields. You can familiarize yourself with their proud history at the Lipicai Múzeum (Lipizzaner Museum; ✉ Park u. 8, ☎ 36/355–155). Admission is 80 Ft., and the museum is open April–October, Tuesday–Sunday 9–noon and 2–5. Szilvásvárad is also a popular base for hiking and bicycling through the surrounding gentle green hills of Bükk National Park.

Dining and Lodging

$–$$$ ✕ **Fehér Szarvas.** The name of this rustic cellar means "white stag," and game is the uncontested specialty. Favorites include venison fillet served in a pan sizzling with chicken liver, sausage, and herb butter; and wild boar cutlet with mushrooms, basil-spiced cabbage, and potato croquettes mixed with almonds. The skulls and skins hanging from rafters and walls make the inn look like Archduke Franz Ferdinand's trophy room. ✉ *Klapka György u. 8,* ☎ *36/411–129. AE, MC, V. No lunch.*

$–$$ ✕ **Efendi Vendéglő.** Excellent food makes this restaurant, in an arched
★   basement room a few doors away from Eger's castle gate, a regional favorite. The interior is "modern-medieval-romantic"—candlelighted tables among floral landscape paintings interspersed with a bit of medieval weaponry. A favorite on the menu, available in English, is *legényfogó leves* (wedding soup or, literally, "catcher of young men"). Made with meat, vegetables, cream, and liver, this stew is one of the lures that Hungarian women have used for centuries to attract potential husbands. It's a good idea to reserve ahead for a table. ✉ *Kossuth Lajos u. 19,* ☎ *36/410–323. AE, DC, MC, V.*

$ ✕ **HBH Bajor Sörház.** For substantial Hungarian fare at a good price, it's impossible to beat this spot, which has a great location on Dobó tér. The menu makes for an entertaining read, with main courses such as the Valiant Border Guard's Meal (chicken, ham, apple, and a cheese sauce) and the Favorite of the Hunter (a stag and wild boar dish). The latter will go down more than adequately with a glass of Bull's Blood—or perhaps even a Munich Hofbräuhaus, the beer that gives the restaurant its initials. ✉ *Bajcsy Zsilinszky u. 19, on Dobó tér,* ☎ *36/316–312. AE, DC, MC, V.*

$$$$ ⌂ **Imola Udvarház.** Apartments at the most upmarket small hotel in
★   Eger are pricey, but the location, facilities, and pleasant, spacious self-catering quarters justify the tariff. Imola Udvarház practically sits on the steps up to the castle, and the oak and wicker furnished apartments are spotless yet homey. The wine list at the hotel restaurant includes a hundred different wines. Breakfast costs an additional 1,500 Ft. ✉ *Dózsa György tér 4, H-3300,* ☎ FAX *36/516–180,* WEB *www.imolanet.hu.*

6 apartments. Restaurant, café, in-room data ports, kitchens, cable TV, bar, meeting room. AE, DC, MC, V.

$$$ ⊡ **Offi Ház.** Picturesque Dobó tér has an equally picturesque inn, with
★ a yellow-brick exterior and five suites tastefully furnished with repro-
duction period furniture. Upstairs there's a silver-service restaurant, dec-
orated with a series of sugar sculptures, including a full-size grandfather
clock that actually keeps the correct time. Downstairs you can eat a
pub lunch in a somewhat smoky, far more basic dining room. ⊠ *Dobó
tér 4, H-3300,* ☎ FAX *36/311–005 or 36/311–330,* WEB *www.offihaz.hu.
5 suites. 2 restaurants, in-room data ports, cable TV. AE, DC, MC, V.*

$$ ⊡ **Hotel Senator Ház.** This little inn sits on Eger's main square in a
★ lovely 18th-century town house. Whimsical paintings by local artist
András Győrffy hang in all the guest rooms, which are decidedly more
modern than the small, elegant lobby might have you believe but are
tastefully decorated in pale tans and whites. ⊠ *Dobó tér 11, H-3300,*
☎ FAX *36/320–466,* WEB *www.hotels.hu/senatorhaz. 11 rooms. Restaurant, minibars, free parking. AE, MC, V.*

$ ⊡ **Garten Vendégház.** This informal, family-run pension, named the
Garden Lodging House after its profusion of lilacs, geraniums, and aca-
cias, sits atop a quiet, rural hill, a 10-minute walk from Eger's main
square. Rooms here are clean, bright, and rich with pine furnishings.
The suites, with eat-in kitchens, are great for families. The cheerful owners, Olga and Sanyi, can arrange tennis at the neighboring courts. You
can request rates with or without breakfast. ⊠ *Legányi u. 6, H-3300,*
☎ *36/320–371,* WEB *www.hotels.hu/garten. 7 rooms, 2 suites. Breakfast room, some kitchens; no room phones. No credit cards.*

Nightlife and the Arts

THE ARTS

From June to mid-September live bands sometimes play folk music for
free out on Kis Dobó tér, part of Eger's main square.

The **Agria Nyári Játékok** (Agria Summer Festival) and associated
events run from July to early September, with folk-dance and theater
performances as well as concerts of musical genres from Renaissance
to jazz to laser karaoke. Performances are held in various locations.
For information, contact Tourinform (⊠ Dobó tér 2, ☎ 36/517–715).

For two weeks every summer, beginning around late July, **Ünnepi
Hetek a Barokk Egerben** (Festival Weeks in Baroque Eger) takes place,
a cultural festival of classical concerts, dance programs, and more in
Eger's venues and streets and squares. In early September, the three-
to four-day **Szüreti Kulturális Napok Egerben** (Eger Harvest Cultural
Festival) celebrates the grape harvest with a traditional harvest parade
through the town center, ample wine tastings in the main squares, appearances by the crowned Wine Queen, and an outdoor Harvest Ball
on Dobó tér.

NIGHTLIFE

Old Jack's Pub (⊠ Rákóczi út 28, ☎ 36/425–050) is a popular English-style pub just outside the center of town.

Outdoor Activities and Sports

BICYCLING

The forested hills of the Bükk National Park around the village of Szilvásvárad, north of Eger, comprise some of the country's most popular mountain-biking terrain. Rentals, maps, route advice, and tour guides
are available at Csaba Tarnai's **Mountain Bike Kölcsönző** (⊠ Szalajka-
völgy út, at entrance to Bükk National Park in Szilvásvárad, Szalajka
Valley, ☎ 60/352–695).

HIKING

Bükk National Park, just north of Eger, has plenty of well-marked, well-used trails. The most popular excursions begin in the village of Szil-vásvárad. Tourinform (⊠ Dobó tér 2, ☎ 36/517–715) can provide a hiking map and suggest routes according to the level of difficulty and duration.

HORSEBACK RIDING

A famous breeding center of the prized white Lipizzaner horses, the village of Szilvásvárad is the heart of the region's horse culture. The stables at **Mátyus Udvarház** (⊠ off Noszvaji út, ☎ 36/312–804) can accommodate your every equestrian need. Hourly rates in the area run around 2,000 Ft. for taking the reins into your own hands outdoors. A one-hour carriage ride for up to three people costs about 4,000 Ft.

SWIMMING

Eger's **Strandfürdő** (open-air baths; ⊠ Petőfi Sándor tér 2, ☎ 36/412–202) are set in a vast, lovely park in the center of town. You can pick where to plunge from among six pools of varying sizes, temperatures, and curative powers.

Miskolc

❹ *63 km (39 mi) northeast of Eger.*

East of the Bükk Mountains lies industrial Miskolc, the third-largest city (population 200,000) in Hungary. A sprawling city cluttered with factories and industrial plants (many of them now idle), Miskolc is often maligned as one of the country's least desirable places to visit. Yet it contains some interesting baroque buildings, as well as the medieval castle of Diósgyőr, clashing yet coexisting with the housing projects and traffic that surround it. And one of Miskolc's prime, unexpected assets is the nearby beautiful countryside. As you travel west toward Lillafüred, past behemoth factories and plants, it's hard not to be wary of just what sort of countryside lies ahead; but almost immediately after passing the LEAVING MISKOLC sign and just before despair settles in, the scenery changes dramatically: the tree-covered hills of the Bükk range rise and crowd together as the road curves up and around them.

The regal, ruined stone body of **Diósgyőri Vár** (Diósgyőr Castle) stands exposed in the midst of Miskolc's urban clamor, as if trapped in a land that was long taken over by an entirely new reality. With four mighty towers, the structure is considered to be one of Hungary's most beautiful medieval castles. Built between the mid-13th and late 14th centuries, it was originally a retreat for King Louis I, of the Angevin dynasty, but was later adopted by the queens (the castle is also known as Queen's Castle). The opening hours can be erratic in winter; it's best to call ahead. ⊠ *Vár u. 24,* ☎ *46/370–735.* ☒ *300 Ft.* ☉ *Daily 9–6.*

Dining and Lodging

$$$$ ✕▥ **Hotel Palota.** As you round the bend on the road from Miskolc, ★   the fairy-tale spire of this 1930 luxury hotel's tower rises majestically from a fold in the hills. The lobby and other public rooms have soaring, ornately sculpted ceilings; rich woodwork; and epic frescoes. Guest rooms are fairly simple, with low-key wood furnishings and large windows, most of which look out onto the surrounding greenery. The Mátyás Restaurant, in a round room with vaulted ceilings and stained-glass windows, specializes in game from the Bükk Mountains and trout from the nearby stocked lake. ⊠ *Erzsébet sétány 1, H-3517 Miskolc Lillafüred,* ☎ *46/331–179,* ℻ *46/379–273,* ⎍ℰℬ *www.hunguest.hu.* 115 *rooms, 18 suites. Restaurant, minibars, bar, indoor pool, gym, sauna, bowling, bar, meeting rooms, parking (fee). AE, DC, MC, V.*

Aggtelek

⑤ *55 km (34 mi) north of Miskolc.*

One of the most extensive cave systems in Europe lies at Aggtelek, right on the Slovak border. Containing the largest stalactite system in Europe, the largest of the caves, the Baradla, is 24 km (15 mi) long, extending under Slovakia; its stalactite and stalagmite formations are of extraordinary size—some more than 49 ft high. In one of the chambers of the cave is a 600-seat concert hall, where classical concerts are held every summer. When the lights are left off for a brief period, you experience the purest darkness there is; try holding your hand up to your face—no matter how hard you strain, you won't see it.

Additional caves are open to the public. There are three entrances: in Aggtelek, at Vörös-tó (Red Lake), and in the village of Jósvafő. Guided tours vary in length and difficulty, from the short, one-hour walks beginning at Aggtelek or Jósvafő to the five- to eight-hour, 7-km (4½-mi) exploration. Of the shorter tours, the medium-length (two-hour) tour beginning at Vörös-tó is considered the best; the group congregates at Jósvafő, takes a public bus (fare covered by tour admission) to the Vörös-tó entrance, then makes its way back to Jósvafő underground. Although tours are conducted in Hungarian, written English translations are available at the ticket offices. Requests for the long tour must be sent in writing to the National Park headquarters at least two weeks ahead of time so the unmaintained sections can be rigged with proper lighting.

The caves are open year-round—they maintain a constant temperature, regardless of the weather. Keep in mind that it's chilly and damp underground—bring a sweater or light jacket and wear shoes with good traction. ✉ *Directorate of Aggtelek National Park, Tengerszem oldal 1, H-3758 Jósvafő,* ☎ 🖷 *48/350–006 or 48/343–073. 1-hr tours beginning at Aggtelek* 🎫 *1,200 Ft.* ☉ *Mid-Apr.–Sept., daily at 10, 1, 3, and 5 (sometimes more often); Oct.–mid-Apr., daily at 10, 1, and 3. 1-hr tours from Jósvafő* 🎫 *900 Ft.* ☉ *Mid-Apr.–Sept., daily at noon and 5 (sometimes more often); Oct.–mid-Apr., daily at 10 and 3. 2-hr tours from Jósvafő* 🎫 *1,400 Ft.* ☉ *Apr.–Sept., daily at 10, noon, 1:30, and 3; Oct.–Mar., daily at 10 and 3. Long tour (with 2-wk prior written request) from Aggtelek:* 🎫 *7-km (4½-mi) 4,500 Ft., 9-km (5½-mi) 5,500 Ft. (minimum 5 adults or equivalent admission cost).*

Sárospatak

⑥ *80 km (50 mi) northeast of Miskolc.*

For hundreds of years, this northern town at the foot of the Zemplén Mountains thrived as the region's elite cultural and intellectual center, its progressive Calvinist College (now a state-run school) educating such famous national thinkers as statesman Lajos Kossuth and writer Zsigmond Móricz. In 1616, Sárospatak's golden age began when its gorgeous castle became home to the famous Hungarian noble family, the Rákóczi, and was the scene of their unsuccessful plot to free Hungary from the Hapsburgs. Today, however, Sárospatak's reality is more that of an economically struggling eastern town. Its rich, historic aura, however, remains in its majestic castle and many fine medieval houses.

The **library** of today's **Református kollégium** (Reformed College, formerly the Calvinist College) is treasured as one of the country's most beautiful. The main hall, designed by Mihály Pollack in 1817, is a grand yet refined open room with pillars stretching up to an ornately frescoed ceiling. Tours are given hourly; English-speaking guides are available. ✉ *Rákóczi út 1,* ☎ *47/311–057.* 🎫 *200 Ft.* ☉ *Apr.–Oct., Mon.–Sat. 9–5, Sun. 9–1; Nov.–Dec., weekdays 9–5.*

★ Poised on the bank of the Bodrog River, the part-Gothic, part-Renaissance, part-Baroque **Sárospatak vár** (Sárospatak Castle) is one of Hungary's most beautiful castles—now excellently restored. The castle was first constructed in the 11th century, but several additions were made over the centuries. A six-lanced rose emblem, which signifies silence, marks the spot in the castle's northeast corner where the Rákóczi family conspired to incite a revolution against the Hapsburgs. The first, though unsuccessful, uprising was led by Ferenc Rákóczi I on April 9, 1670; in 1703, after his father's death, Ferenc Rákóczi II led a nine-year rebellion that was ultimately fruitless. The museum houses an excellent collection of antique furniture from the 16th to 19th century, portraits of the Rákóczi family, various weapons, and antique clothing. ✉ *Szt. Erzsébet út 19,* ☎ *47/311–083.* 🎫 *300 Ft.* ☉ *Mar.–Oct., Tues.–Sun. 10–6; Nov.–Feb., Tues.–Sun. 10–5.*

Dining and Lodging

$$ ✕🏨 **Hotel Bodrog.** Sárospatak's main hotel and restaurant may be cloaked in charmless 1980s Communist institutionality, but it is central, clean, and adequately comfortable. Inside the drab cement-block exterior are accommodations with basic furnishings, though they do have televisions and minibars. The restaurant has an extensive selection of wines from nearby Tokaj and serves standard Hungarian fare. Gypsy Roast Sárospatak-style, a pork cutlet with an extra cholesterol booster on top in the form of an egg sunny-side up, is a popular choice. Venison and trout are also available. ✉ *Rákóczi u. 58, H-3950,* ☎ *47/311–744,* FAX *47/311–527,* WEB *www.hotels.hu/bodrog_hotel. 50 rooms. Restaurant, minibars, cable TV, gym, sauna, meeting rooms; no a/c in some rooms. DC, MC, V.*

Nightlife and the Arts

During the annual **Zempléni Művészeti Napok** (Zemplén County Arts Days) in mid- to late August, well-known musicians perform classical concerts in the Sárospatak Castle's courtyard. For information, contact the Sárospatak Cultural Center (✉ Eötvös u. 6, ☎ 47/311–811) or the IBUSZ office (☎ 1/485–2700 in Budapest).

Tokaj

❼ *54 km (33 mi) east of Miskolc.*

This enchanting little village is the center of one of Hungary's most famous wine regions. It's home to the legendary Aszú wine, a dessert wine made from grapes allowed to shrivel on the vine. Aszú is produced to varying degrees of sweetness, based on how many bushels of sweet grape paste are added to the wine essence, the already highly sweet juice first pressed from them; the scale goes from two *puttonyos* (bushels) to nectar-rich six puttonyos.

The region's famed wines, dubbed (allegedly by Louis XV) the "wine of kings and king of wines," are typically golden yellow with slightly brownish tints and an almost oily texture. They've been admired outside of Hungary since Polish merchants first became hooked in the Middle Ages. In 1562, after a few sips of wine from the nearby village of Tállya, Pope Pius IV is said to have declared, "*Summum pontificem talia vina decent*" ("These wines are fit for a pope"). Other countries—France, Germany, and Russia included—have tried without success to produce the wine from Tokaj grapes; the secret apparently lies in the combination of volcanic soil and climate.

The surrounding countryside is beautiful, especially in October, when the grapes hang from the vines in thick clusters. Before or after descending into the wine cellars for some epic tasting, be sure to pause while the bells toll at the lovely baroque Roman Catholic church (1770) on the main square and wend your way along some of the narrow side streets winding up into the vineyard-covered hills: views of the red-tile roofs and sloping vineyards are like sweet Aszú for the eyes. If you can still focus after a round of wine tasting, be sure to look up at the top of lampposts and chimneys, where giant white storks preside over the village from their big bushy nests. They usually return here to their nests in late April or May after wintering in warmer climes.

The third floor of the **Tokaj Múzeum** (Tokaj Museum), housed in a late-18th-century building, displays objects connected with the history of the wine's production. The first and second floors contain exhibits of ecclesiastical art and the history of the county, respectively. ⊠ *Bethlen Gábor u. 7,* ☎ *47/352–636.* ☜ *250 Ft.* ☼ *Tues.–Sun. 11–4.*

Tokaj's most famous wine cellar, the nearly 700-year-old **Rákóczi-pince** (Rákóczi Cellar), is also Europe's largest, comprising some 1½ km (1 mi) of branching tunnels extending into the hills (today, about 1,312 ft are in use). Here you can sample Tokaj's famed wines and purchase bottles of your favorites for the road (all major credit cards are accepted). A standard cellar tour with a tasting of six different wines and some *pogácsa* (salty biscuits) costs around 1,500 Ft. These tours are not given in English, but English-language pamphlets are available. ⊠ *Kossuth tér 13,* ☎ *47/352–408.* ☼ *Apr.–Oct., daily 10–7.*

The Várhelyi family offers wine tastings in the cool, damp cellar of their 16th-century house, called **Himesudvar.** After the initial tasting, you can purchase bottles of your favorite wines and continue imbibing in their pleasant garden. A standard sampling of five different wines starts at around 1,000 Ft. If you don't see anyone on arriving, don't hesitate to ring the bell. ⊠ *Bem út 2,* ☎ *47/352–416.* ☼ *Daily 9–9.*

Dining and Lodging
Tourinform (⊠ Serhaz u. 1, ☎ FAX 47/352–259) can book you a room in a private home as well as in other hotels and pensions in the area.

$–$$ ✕ **Róna Restaurant.** In this simple dining room you can order excellent Hungarian dishes from goose liver to fresh carp or pike perch. Original paintings by local artists decorate the pleasant dining room. ⊠ *Bethlen Gábor u. 19,* ☎ *47/352–116. No credit cards. Closed Jan.–Feb.*

$ ✕🏨 **Hotel Tokaj.** What could well be the weirdest-looking building in the country houses Tokaj's main hotel. Giant red balls that resemble clown's noses protrude from each boxy cement balcony under a rainbow-striped facade. If the exterior doesn't put you off, you'll find adequately comfortable rooms inside, most of which have balconies. The large, popular restaurant serves excellent fish specialties, including spicy halászlé with a swirl of sour cream. ⊠ *Rákóczi u. 5, H-3910,* ☎ *47/352–344,* FAX *47/352–759. 42 rooms. Restaurant. AE, DC, MC, V.*

$$ 🏨 **Toldi Fogadó.** A historic building with a pleasantly rustic interior houses this pension, right in the town center. Rooms are clean and spacious, with pinewood floors dappled by comely knots. ⊠ *Hajdú köz 2, H-3910,* ☎ FAX *47/353–403. 6 rooms. Restaurant, minibars, cable TV. AE, MC, V.*

Nightlife and the Arts
Classical concerts by well-known artists are performed here during the **Zemplén Művészeti Napok** (Zemplén Art Days), a countywide classical music festival held annually in mid-August.

Naturally, Tokaj's best festival is the annual **Szüreti Hét** (Harvest Week) in early October, celebrating the autumn grape harvest with a parade, a street ball, folk-art markets, and a plethora of wine tastings from the local vintners' stands erected on and around the main square.

Tourinform (✉ Serhaz u. 1, ☎ FAX 47/352–259) can provide information on both festivals.

Northern Hungary Essentials

BUS TRAVEL

Most buses to northern Hungary depart from Budapest's Népstadion station.

CAR TRAVEL

The M3 expressway is the main link between Budapest and northern Hungary, cutting toward the northeast and Slovakia, though it may take years of construction before it actually reaches the border. In the meantime, the smaller Route 3 goes the rest of the way from near Eger, and Route 37 branches eastward from Route 3 toward Tokaj and Sárospatak. Secondary roads through the Mátra and Bükk mountains are windy but in good shape and wonderfully scenic—this is the best way to see the region.

TRAIN TRAVEL

Trains between Eger and Budapest run several times daily from Keleti station. Trains run frequently all day between Budapest and Miskolc.

Several daily trains connect Miskolc with Sárospatak and Miskolc with Tokaj. Szilvásvárad and Eger are easily accessible from each other by frequent trains.

The Eger train station lies about 1 km (½ mi) from the center of town (a 20-minute walk). Miskolc's station is about 15 minutes by bus or tram from the center of town.

➤ TRAIN STATIONS: **Eger train station** (✉ Állomás tér 1, ☎ 36/314–264). **Miskolc train station** (✉ Tiszai pályaudvar, ☎ 46/412–665).

VISITOR INFORMATION

➤ TOURIST INFORMATION: **Eger Tourinform** (✉ Dobó tér 2, ☎ 36/517–715, FAX 36/518–815). **Gyöngyös Tourinform** (✉ Fő tér 10, ☎ FAX 37/311–155). **Miskolc Tourinform** (✉ Mindszent tér 1, ☎ FAX 46/348–921). **Sárospatak Tourinform** (✉ Eötvös u. 6, ☎ FAX 47/315–317). **Tokaj Tourinform** (✉ Serhaz u. 1, ☎ FAX 47/352–259).

THE GREAT PLAIN

Hungary's Great Plain—the Nagyalföld—stretches south from Budapest to the borders of Croatia and Yugoslavia and as far east as Ukraine and Romania. It covers an area of 51,800 square km (20,000 square mi) and is what most people think of as the typical Hungarian landscape. Almost completely flat, it is the home of shepherds and their flocks and, above all, of splendid horses and the csikósok, their riders. The plain has a wild, almost alien air; its sprawling villages consist mostly of one-story houses, though there are many large farms. The plain, which is divided into two almost equal parts by the Tisza River, also contains several of Hungary's most historic cities—it has much from medieval times (largely because it was never occupied by the Turks), and today it remains the least developed area of Hungary.

As you near the region, you will soon find yourself driving in a hypnotically straight line coming from Budapest through the dream landscape of the Hortobágy, a grassy *puszta,* or prairie. Here, the land flattens out like a palacsinta, opening into vast stretches of dusty grassland interrupted only by stands of trees and distant thatch-roof *tanyák* (ranches). The only detectable movement here comes from the herds of *racka* sheep or cattle drifting lazily across the horizon, guided by shepherds and their trusty *puli* herd dogs. Covering more than 250,000 acres, the Hortobágy became the first of Hungary's four national parks, in 1973. Its flora and fauna—including primeval breeds of longhorn cattle and racka sheep, prairie dogs, and *nóniusz* horses— are all under strict protection.

No matter how little time you have, you should make a point of taking in a traditional horse show, like the one arranged by the Epona Riding Center in Máta. As touristy as the shows are, they are an integral part of the Great Plain experience, not to mention a lot of fun.

Numbers in the margin correspond to numbers on the Northern Hungary and the Great Plain map.

Debrecen

❽ *226 km (140 mi) east of Budapest.*

With a population approaching a quarter of a million, Debrecen is Hungary's second-largest city. Though it has considerably less clout than Budapest, Debrecen was Hungary's capital twice, albeit only briefly. In 1849 it was here that Lajos Kossuth declared Hungarian independence from the Hapsburgs; in 1944, the Red Army liberated Debrecen from the Nazis and made the city the provisional capital until Budapest was taken.

Debrecen has been inhabited since the Stone Age. It was already a sizable village by the end of the 12th century and, by the 14th, an important market town. It takes its name from a Slavonic term for "good earth," and, indeed, much of the country's wheat, produce, meat, and poultry has been produced in this area for centuries.

Today, Debrecen is a vibrant, friendly city, with a sizable population of young people attending its several esteemed universities. There's only one tram line (appropriately numbered 1), but it runs fast and frequently in a nearly straight line from the railroad station along Piac utca and out to the Nagyerdő (Great Forest), a giant city park. All in all, it's a good place to spend a day exploring the sights before heading out for a puszta experience.

For almost 500 years, Debrecen has been the stronghold of Hungarian Protestantism—its inhabitants have called it "the Calvinist Rome." In 1536 Calvinism began to replace Roman Catholicism in Debrecen, and two years later the **Református Kollégium** (Reformed College) was founded on what is now Kálvin tér (Calvin Square). Early in the 19th century the college's medieval building was replaced by a pillared structure that provides a vivid lesson in Hungarian religious and political history: the facade's busts honor prominent students and educators as well as religious reformers John Calvin and Huldrych Zwingli. Inside, the main staircase is lined with frescoes of student life and significant moments in the college's history (all painted during the 1930s in honor of the school's 400th anniversary). At the top of the stairs is the **Oratory,** which has twice been the setting for provisional parliaments. In 1849 Lajos Kossuth first proclaimed Hungarian sovereignty here, and the new National Assembly's Chamber of Deputies met here during the last stages of the doomed revolution. Kossuth's pulpit and pew are marked, and two rare surviving flags of his revolution hang on the front wall. Some relics from 1944 line the back wall. Also worth seeing are the college's **library,** which rotates exhibitions of illuminated manuscripts and rare Bibles, and two **museums**—one on the school's history, the other on religious art. ✉ *Kálvin tér 16,* ☎ *52/414–744.* ⊡ *150 Ft.* ☉ *Tues.–Sat. 9–5, Sun. 9–1.*

Because the Oratory in the Reformed College was too small for a large crowd, Lajos Kossuth reread his declaration of independence by popular demand to a cheering public in 1849 in the twin-turreted, strikingly yellow **Nagytemplom** (Great Church). The Great Church opened its doors in 1817 after more than a decade of construction on the design of Mihály Pécsi; it was built on the site of a 14th-century church that had burned down in 1802. As befits the austerity of Calvinism, the church is devoid of decoration—but with all the baroque architecture throughout Hungary, you may welcome the contrast. ✉ *Kálvin tér,* ☎ *52/412–459.* ⊡ *Church 70 Ft., tower 100 Ft.* ☉ *Jan.–Mar., Mon.–Sat. 10–noon, Sun. 11–1; Apr.–Oct., weekdays 9–4, Sat. 9–noon, Sun. 10–4; Nov.–Dec., Mon.–Sat. 10–noon, Sun. 11–1.*

NEED A BREAK? Bright and modern it may be, but the **Kismandula Cukrászda** (Little Almond Pastry Shop; ✉ Liszt Ferenc u. 10, ☎ 52/310–873) has age-old favorites aplenty—not least, fresh, well-packed rétes and *madártej* (literally, bird's milk), a vanilla-flavored liquid custard with a meringue of sorts floating inside. On summer evenings, a large terrace—shared by the pastry shop with a restaurant under the same ownership—is sometimes the scene of mime dances and other performances.

The **Déri Múzeum** (Déri Museum) was founded in the 1920s to house the art and antiquities of a wealthy Hungarian silk manufacturer living in Vienna. Its two floors are devoted to local history, archaeology, and weapons as well as to Egyptian, Greek, Roman, Etruscan, and Far Eastern art. On the top floor are Hungarian and foreign fine art from the 15th to the 20th century, including the striking (and huge) *Ecce Homo* by Mihály Munkácsy and, on loan since 2000, two similar scenes from the life of Christ by the same famous 19th-century artist. ✉ *Déri tér 1,* ☎ *52/322–207.* ⊡ *300 Ft. (400 Ft. includes Munkácsy exhibit).* ☉ *Apr.–Oct., Tues.–Sun. 10–6; Nov.–Mar., Tues.–Sun. 10–4.*

Debrecen's main artery, **Piac utca** (Market Street), runs from the Great Church to the railroad station. At the corner of Széchenyi utca, the **Kistemplom** (Small Church; ✉ Révész tér 2, ☎ 52/343–872)—Debrecen's oldest surviving church, built in 1720—looks like a rococo chess-piece castle. This Calvinist venue is known to the locals as the "truncated church" because early in the 20th century, its onion dome was blown down in a gale. The church is kept closed, except during services, but the ministers and caretakers next door at the church office are happy to open it for you weekdays 9 AM–noon and Sunday 8:30 AM–11 AM.

Across the street from the Kistemplom is the **Megyeház** (county hall; ✉ Piac u. 54, ☎ 52/507–550), built in 1911–1912 in Transylvanian Art Nouveau, a darker and heavier version of the Paris, Munich, and Vienna versions. The ceramic ornaments on the facade are of Zsolnay majolica. Inside, brass chandeliers illuminate the stairs and halls, spotlighting the symmetry and delicate restraint of the interior. In the Council Hall upstairs, stained-glass windows by Károly Kernstock depict seven leaders of the tribes that conquered Hungary in 896. The building is open Monday–Thursday 8–4, Friday 8–1.

★ The **Timárház** (Tanner House), in a restored 19th-century building, is the center for preserving and maintaining the ancient folk-arts-and-crafts traditions of Hajdú-Bihar county. In its delightful, small complex you can wander into the artisans' workshops and watch them creating exquisite pieces—from impossibly fine, intricately handmade lacework to colorful hand-loomed wool rugs. The artisans—among the best in the country—encourage visitors of all ages to try their hand at the crafts. The complex's showroom displays magnificent leather whips, heavy wool shepherd robes, and other examples of the county's traditional folk art; the embroidered textiles are some of the best you'll see anywhere. Although the displayed pieces are not for sale, the staff can help you contact the artists to custom-order something. A tiny gift shop, however, does sell a small selection of representative goods at great prices. ⊠ *Nagy Gál István u. 6,* ☎ *52/368–857.* ☞ *100 Ft.* ☼ *Late Mar.–late Oct., Tues.–Fri. 10–6, Sat. 10–2; late Oct.–late Mar., Tues.–Fri. 10–5, Sat. 10–2.*

The 19th-century **Vörös templom** (Red Church) is as remarkable a Calvinist church as you'll find anywhere in Europe. On the outside this seems an undistinguished redbrick house of worship, built with the usual unadorned interior, but the church celebrated its 50th anniversary at the zenith of the applied-arts movement in Hungary. Its worshipers commissioned artist Jenő Haranghy to paint the walls with biblical allegories using no human bodies or faces (just an occasional limb) but rather plenty of grapes, trees, and symbols. Giant frescoes covering the walls, ceilings, niches, and crannies represent, among other subjects, a stag in fresh water, the Martin Luther anthem "A Mighty Fortress Is Our God," and the 23rd Psalm (with a dozen sheep representing the 12 Tribes of Israel and the 12 Apostles). The Red Church is open only during religious services (10 AM on Sunday and religious holidays), but you might try for a private church visit from the deaconage (☎ 52/ 325–736) on Kossuth Lajos utca. The church is just a 10-minute walk from the county hall along Kossuth Lajos utca. ⊠ *Méliusz tér.*

Debrecen's one tram line runs out to the **Nagyerdő** (Great Forest), a huge city park with a zoo, a sports stadium, swimming pools, an artificial rowing lake, a thermal-spa-cum-luxury-hotel (the Termál Hotel Debrecen), an amusement park, restaurants, and an open-air theater. Also here is the photogenic Kossuth Lajos University, its handsome neobaroque facade fronted by a large pool and fountain around which six bronze nudes pose in the sun. The university is one of the few in Central Europe with a real campus, and every summer, from mid-July to mid-August, it hosts a world-renowned Hungarian-language program.

Dining and Lodging

$–$$ ★ ✕ **Városháza.** A visit to the Városháza begins with your descent down a grand staircase into a small foyer flanked by glass cases packed with liquor bottles from around the world. As you enter the fairly small dining room, your eye will probably next fall on two wax-doll 19th-century ladies taking tea. This place has been consistently named one of the 10 best restaurants in Hungary, but the longtime chef has now departed. An illustrated wine list with explanations helps you match a Hungarian wine to your food. ⊠ *Piac u. 20,* ☎ *52/444–767. AE, DC, MC, V.*

$ ✕ **Serpince a Flaskához.** When you walk into this completely unpretentious and very popular neighborhood pub, you may be surprised to be presented with a nicely bound menu in four languages. For a light meal, try a *palócleves,* a thick, piquantly sourish meat-and-potatoes soup with tarragon and caraway. For something heavier, try the "boiled hock strips covered with ewe cheese, Túróczi style." ⊠ *Miklós u. 4,* ☎ *52/414–582. AE, DC, MC, V.*

$$$$ 🏨 **Termál Hotel Debrecen.** Other hotels may be attached to spas, but this hotel is actually located within a medical spa. You can detect the (not unpleasant) smell of alkaline chloride as soon as you check in at the front desk. The hotel's amenities span the seasons: in summer you can swim in a large outdoor pool; in winter you can warm yourself by the library fire. The decorators went a bit wild with pinkish beige and paisley in the guest quarters, but with a balcony in each room overlooking the Great Forest, that's a minor quibble. ✉ *Nagyerdei park 1, H-4032,* ☎ *52/514–111,* FAX *52/311–730,* WEB *www.termalhotel.hu. 56 rooms, 40 suites. Restaurant, bar, snack bar, indoor pool, sauna, spa, meeting rooms. AE, DC, MC, V.*

$$–$$$ 🏨 **Cívis Grand Hotel Aranybika.** From the outside the Golden Bull is
★   an Art Nouveau classic, but inside it's a bit of a patchwork quilt. Parts of the lobby, like the neo-baroque doorway to the cocktail bar, are gorgeous, as is the airy and elegant restaurant. Brown and beige leftover renovations from the 1970s spoil the effect a bit, but the staff is extremely attentive and friendly, and the hotel's location in the center of Debrecen is excellent. The guest rooms in the old Grand section of the hotel are being spruced up, while those in the newer "tourist" wing are a bit on the institutional side. ✉ *Piac u. 11–15, H-4025,* ☎ *52/ 508–600,* FAX *52/421–834. 230 rooms, 4 suites. Restaurant, café, indoor pool, gym, sauna, spa, casino, business services, meeting rooms; no a/c in some rooms. AE, DC, MC, V.*

$ 🏨 **Korona Panzió.** This cheery little inn is just down the street from
★   the Great Church. The immaculate rooms are a great value and have contemporary furnishings and terraces. Breakfast costs an extra 700 Ft. ✉ *Péterfia u. 54, H-4026,* ☎ *52/535–260,* FAX *52/535–261,* WEB *www.hotels.hu/koronapanzio1. 9 rooms. Cable TV, in-room VCRs; no smoking. No credit cards.*

Nightlife and the Arts

Debrecen summers are filled with annual cultural festivals. **Debrecen Tavaszi Fesztivál** (Debrecen Spring Festival) precedes the season, in mid- to late March, packing in two weeks full of concerts, dance and theater performances, and special art exhibits. Main events are held at the Csokonai Theater and Bartók Hall. The biannual **Bartók Béla Nemzetközi Kórusverseny** (Béla Bartók International Choral Festival), scheduled next for July 2004, is a competition for choirs from around the world and provides choral-music aficionados with numerous full-scale concerts in Bartók Hall. Jazz fans can hear local ensembles as well as groups from around Hungary and abroad during the **Debreceni Jazz Napok** (Debrecen Jazz Festival) in mid-March, in conjunction with the Spring Festival. One of the city's favorite occasions is the **Debreceni Virágkarnevál** (Flower Carnival) on St. Stephen's Day (August 20), when a festive parade of flower-encrusted floats and carriages makes its way down Debrecen's main street along the tram line all the way to the Nagyerdő Stadium.

For information on Debrecen's festivals, contact **Tourinform** (✉ Piac u. 20, ☎ 52/412–250, FAX 52/535–323).

One of Debrecen's main cultural venues is the **Csokonai Theater** (✉ Kossuth u. 10, ☎ 52/417–811), which is devoted to theater productions (though none in English).

Outdoor Activities and Sports

A visit to the Great Plain is hardly complete without at least some contact with horses. There are several horseback-riding outfits outside Debrecen on the puszta; **Tourinform** (✉ Piac u. 20, ☎ 52/412–250, FAX 52/535–323) can help arrange excursions.

The Great Forest bubbles with thermal baths and pools. The park's main complex, the **Nagyerdei Lido** (⊠ Nagyerdei Strand, ☎ 52/346–000), has eight pools, including a large pool for active swimming (most people soak idly in Hungary's public pools) and a wave pool.

Hortobágy

❾ *39 km (24 mi) west of Debrecen.*

The main visitor center for and gateway to the prairie is the little village of Hortobágy. Traveling from Debrecen, you'll reach this town just before you would cross the Hortobágy River. Before heading out to the prairie itself, you can take in Hortobágy's own sights: a prairie museum, its famous stone bridge, and the historic Hortobágyi Csárda inn.

Crossing the Hortobágy River is one of the puszta's famous symbols: the curving, white-stone **Kilenc-lyukú híd** (Nine-Arch Bridge). It was built in the early 19th century and is the longest stone bridge in Hungary (548 ft). ⊠ *Rte. 33 at Petőfi tér.*

Built in 1699, the **Hortobágyi Csárda** (Hortobágy Inn) has been a regional institution for most of the last three centuries. Its construction is typical of the Great Plain: a long, white stone structure with arching windows, brown-wood details, and a stork nest—and occasionally storks—on its chimney. Its restaurant is quite popular. ⊠ *Petőfi tér 2,* ☎ *52/369–139.* ☉ *Mid-Feb.–Sept., daily.*

For a glimpse into traditional Hortobágy pastoral life, visit the **Pásztormúzeum** (Shepherd Museum), across the street from the Hortobágy Inn. Exhibits focus on traditional costumes and tools, such as the shepherds' heavy embroidered cloaks and carved sticks. The lot in front of the museum is the tourism center for the area, bustling with visitors and local touristic enterprises, including the helpful local Tourinform office. ⊠ *Petőfi tér 1,* ☎ *52/369–119.* ☜ *300 Ft.* ☉ *Mid-May–Sept., daily 9–6; Oct. and Mar.–mid-May, daily 10–2; Nov.–Feb., with prior notice only.*

OFF THE BEATEN PATH

HORTOBÁGYHALASTÓ – About 5 km (3 mi) west of Hortobágy, Hortobágyhalastó (Great Plain Fish Pond) is a tiny, sleepy hamlet at the end of a dirt road, where chickens strut about and the center of town is essentially an old phone booth. However, it's not the village but the 5,000-acre-pond nature reserve of the same name at its edge that draws dedicated bird-watchers to look for some of the 150 species in residence. A nature walk around the entire reserve will take most of a day and requires advance permission from the **Hortobágyi Nemzeti Park Igazgatóság** (National Park's Headquarters; ⊠ Sumen u. 2, H-4024 Debrecen, ☎ 52/349–922, ⅀ 52/410–645); contact Tourinform in Debrecen for assistance.

Dining

$$
★
✕ Hortobágyi Csárda. Old flasks and saddles, antlers, and dried corn-and-paprika wreaths hang from the walls and rafters of this traditional Hungarian roadside inn. This is the place to order the regional specialty, *Hortobágyi húsospalacsinta* (Hortobágy pancakes), which are filled with beef and braised with a tomato-and-sour-cream sauce. Follow the pancakes with *bográcsgulyás*—spicy goulash soup puszta-style, with meat and dumplings. Veal paprikás and solid beef and lamb *pörkölt* (thick stews with paprika and sour cream) are also recommended, as are the cheese-curd and apricot-jam dessert pancakes. ⊠ *Petőfi tér 2,* ☎ *52/369–139. AE, DC, MC, V. Closed Oct.–mid-Feb.*

Nightlife and the Arts

The three-day **Hortobágyi hid vásár** (Hortobágy Bridge Fair), held annually around August 20, brings horse shows, a folk-art fair, ox roasts, and festive crowds to the plot beneath the famous Nine-Arch Bridge.

Máta

⑩ *About 2 km (1 mi) southwest of Hortobágy.*

The hamlet of Máta is home to the **Hortobágy Club Hotel,** a "rider's village" with some 500 champion horses and first-rate riders. This is the most important equestrian center in the region. From around May through September there is a daily half-hour-long "Rangeman's Show." Groups of 16 can ride the prairie in covered wagons pulled by horses of the prizewinning nóniusz breed and driven by herders. You'll see herds of racka sheep with twisted horns, gray cattle, and wild boars, all tended by shepherds, cowherds, and swineherds dressed in distinctive costumes and aided by shaggy puli herd dogs and Komondor sheepdogs. At various stops along the route of this minirodeo, csikós perform stunts with the animals; the best involves five horses piloted by one man who stands straddling the last two. You can even try a little (less risky) riding yourself with help from the csikós. In winter and in bad weather, indoor shows are organized. Call ahead to inquire about arranging for accommodations or an English-speaking guide. ✉ *Hortobágy-Máta,* ☎ *52/369–020.* 🎫 *Riding shows and wagon tours 1,800 Ft.* ☉ *Departures daily at 10, noon, 2, and 4 (more frequently if demand warrants).*

Lodging

$$$$ 🏨 **Hortobágy Club Hotel.** This vast, luxury equestrian complex is one
★ of Hungary's best and most imaginative resorts. The contemporary, puszta-style buildings house stables, two-story family cottages (for rent by the floor), and special "rider houses," complete with private three-horse stables. The main building contains standard rooms, all with balconies and contemporary furnishings. Tennis courts, a swimming pool, and myriad horse-related activities provide ample entertainment in an area otherwise considered to be the middle of nowhere. ✉ *H-4071 Hortobágy-Máta,* ☎ *52/369–092,* ℻ *52/369–027. 52 rooms, 4 suites, 20 cottages. 2 restaurants, 2 tennis courts, pool, gym, massage, sauna, horseback riding, 2 bars, business services, meeting rooms. AE, DC, MC, V.*

Nightlife and the Arts

Equestrian fans gather annually for the **Hortobágy International Horse Festival,** held for about four days in July or August. Exciting show-jumping and carriage-driving competitions are held, as well as traditional horseback stunts by the csikós, folk-music and dance performances, and a folk-art fair.

Outdoor Activities and Sports

The **Hortobágy Club Hotel** (✉ H-4071, Hortobágy-Máta, ☎ 52/369–092) arranges horseback riding lessons (1,800 Ft. per half hour, beginner; 2,800 Ft. per hour, intermediate and advanced dressage) and guided rides out on the puszta (about 2,300 Ft. per hour) on its excellent horses.

Kecskemét

⑪ *191 km (118 mi) southwest of Debrecen.*

With a name roughly translating as "Goat Walk," this sprawling town smack in the middle of the country never fails to surprise unsuspecting first-time visitors with its elegant landmark buildings, interesting museums, and friendly, welcoming people. Its splendid main square, Szabadság tér (Liberty Square), is marred only by two faceless cement-block buildings, one of which houses the city's McDonald's (a true sign the city is not just a dusty prairie town anymore). Home of the elite Kodály Institute, where famous composer and pedagogue Zoltán Kodály's methods are taught, the city also maintains a fairly active cultural life.

The Kecskemét area, fruit center of the Great Plain, produces *barack pálinka,* a smooth yet tangy apricot brandy that can warm the heart and blur the mind in just one shot. Ask for home-brewed *házi pálinka,* which is much better (and often stronger) than the commercial brews.

A short drive from town takes you into the expansive sandy grasslands of Kiskunság National Park, the smaller of the two protected areas (the other is Hortobágy National Park) of the Great Plain. You can watch a traditional horse show, do some riding, or immerse yourself in the experience by spending a night or two at one of the inns out on the prairie.

The **Magyar Fotográfia Múzeum** (Hungarian Photography Museum) is one of only a few museums in Hungary dedicated solely to photography. With a growing collection of more than 275,000 photos, documents, and equipment pieces, it continues to be the most important photography center in the country. The main exhibits are fine works by such pioneers of Hungarian photography as André Kertész, Brassaï, and Martin Munkácsi, all of whom moved and gained fame abroad. ⊠ *Katona József tér 12,* ☎ *76/483–221.* ⌸ *150 Ft.* ☉ *Wed.– Sun. 10–5.*

The handsome Moorish-style **zsinagóga** (synagogue) anchoring one end of Liberty Square is beautifully restored but has been stripped of its original purpose. Today it is the headquarters of the House of Science and Technology, with offices and a convention center, but it also houses a small collection of Michelangelo sculpture reproductions from Budapest's Museum of Fine Arts. ⊠ *Rákóczi út 2,* ☎ *76/487– 611.* ⌸ *Free.* ☉ *Weekdays 10–4; closed during special events.*

Kecskemét's most famous building is the **Cifrapalota** (Ornamental Palace), a unique and remarkable Hungarian-style Art Nouveau building built in 1902. A three-story cream-color structure studded with folksy lilac, blue, red, and yellow Zsolnay majolica flowers and hearts, it stands on Liberty Square's corner like a cheerful cream pastry. Once a residential building, it now houses the **Kecskeméti képtár** (Kecskemét Gallery), displaying artwork by Hungarian fine artists as well as occasional international exhibits. ⊠ *Rákóczi u. 1,* ☎ *76/480–776.* ⌸ *260 Ft.* ☉ *Tues.–Sat. 10–5, Sun. 2–5.*

NEED A BREAK?
: You can treat yourself to fresh pastries or ice cream at the café that shares this book's name, the **Fodor Cukrászda** (Fodor Confectionery; ⊠ Szabadság tér 2, ☎ 76/497–545). It's right on the main square and is open March–late December.

★ Built in 1893–1897 by Ödön Lechner in the Hungarian Art Nouveau style that he created, the **Városház** (town hall) is one of the style's finest examples. Window frames are arched here, pointed there, and the roof, covered with tiny copper- and gold-color tiles, looks as if it has been rained on by pennies from heaven. In typical Lechner style, the outlines of the central facade make a curving line to a pointed top, under which 37 little bells add the finishing visual and auditory touch: every hour from 7 AM to 8 PM, they flood the main square with ringing melodies from Kodaly, Beethoven, Mozart, and other major composers as well as traditional Hungarian folk songs. The building's **Dísz Terem** (Ceremonial Hall) is a spectacular palace of glimmering gold-painted vaulted ceilings, exquisitely carved wooden pews, colorful frescoes by Bertalan Székely (who also painted the frescoes for Budapest's Matthiás Church), and a gorgeously ornate chandelier that floats above the room like an ethereal bouquet of lights and shining brass. The hall is open only to tour groups that have made prior arrangements; call in advance and ask for the reception desk. ✉ *Kossuth tér 1,* ☎ *76/483–683 Ext. 2153.* 🎟 *Ceremonial hall 200 Ft.*

The oldest building on Kossuth tér is the **Szent Miklós templom** (Church of St. Nicholas), also known as the Barátság templom (Friendship Church) because of St. Nick's role as the saint of friendship. It was built in Gothic style in either the 13th or the 15th century (a subject of debate) but rebuilt in baroque style during the 18th century. ✉ *Kossuth tér 5.* 🎟 *Free.*

The unusual, one-of-a-kind **Szórakoténusz Játékmúzeum és Műhely** (Szórakoténusz Toy Museum and Workshop) chronicles the history of Hungarian toys, beginning with archaeological pieces such as stone figures and clay toys from medieval guilds. The museum also hosts changing international exhibits. In the workshop, artisans prepare traditional toys and invite you to try it yourself. Next door to the toy museum is the small **Magyar Naív Művészek Múzeuma** (Hungarian Naive Art Museum), where you can see a collection of this simple style of painting and sculpting created by Hungarian artists. ✉ *Gáspár András u. 11,* ☎ *76/481–469 Toy Museum; 76/324–767 Naive Art Museum.* 🎟 *200 Ft. each.* ☉ *Toy Museum Tues.–Sun. 10–12:30 and 1–5; Naive Art Museum Tues.–Sun. 10–5; Toy Workshop alternate Sat. 10–noon and 2:30–5, Sun. 10–noon.*

OFF THE BEATEN PATH **PIAC** – Kecskemét is Hungary's fruit capital, and it's worth experiencing the region's riches firsthand by visiting the bustling *piac* (market), where—depending on the season—you can indulge in freshly plucked apples, cherries, and the famous Kecskemét apricots. Provided there is no sudden spring freeze, apricot season is around June through August. ✉ *Budai u. near corner of Nagykörösi út.* ☉ *Tues.–Sat. 6–noon, Sun. 6 AM–11 AM.*

Dining and Lodging

$–$$$ ✕ **Kisbugaci Csárda.** This cozy eatery tucked away on a side street is warm and bright. The inner area has wood paneling and upholstered booths; the outer section has simple wooden tables covered with locally embroidered tablecloths and matching curtains. Food is heavy, ample, and tasty. Try the kitchen's goose specialties, such as the *Bugaci libatoros*—a sampling of goose liver, thigh, and breast with steamed cabbage and boiled potatoes. Request a plate of dried paprikas—usually crumbled into soup—if you really want to spice things up. ✉ *Munkácsy u. 10,* ☎ *76/486–782. MC, V. No dinner Sun.*

$–$$ ✕ **Liberté Kávéház.** The closest thing to a Viennese coffee house on the Great Plain—and pretty close at that—is this long Art Nouveau room with a restaurant-size menu. The menu runs the gamut from regional favorites such as Hortobágy pancakes to more adventurous dishes such as Hawaiian turkey-breast fillet with pineapple. In front of you is Liberty Square, the center of Kescemét; the windows at the back have a view through to the Reformed Church. ✉ *Szabadság tér 2,* ☎ *76/328–636. AE, DC, MC, V.*

$$ 🖼 **Arany Homok Hotel.** The staff is cheerful and friendly, and Kecskemét is right on your doorstep at this hotel on a small square close to the city center. The design leaves much to be desired, however: it doesn't require an overheated imagination to envisage this concrete-bunker-style hotel as a resting place for socialist-era bureaucrats. And as the hotel brochure puts it, "the architecture suits the fashion of the '60s." Most rooms have pared-down blond-wood furnishings, generic gray wall-to-wall carpeting, and small bathrooms. All doubles have balconies. ⊠ *Kossuth tér 3, H-6000,* ☎ *76/486–286,* 𝖥𝖠𝖷 *76/481–195,* 𝖶𝖤𝖡 *www.hotels.hu/aranyhomok. 111 rooms, 4 suites. Restaurant, gym, casino, laundry service, meeting rooms, travel services; some pets allowed. AE, DC, MC, V.*

$$ 🖼 **Hotel Centrál.** Facing a small park a few minutes walk away from Liberty Square, this hotel almost lives up to its name. The Central's contemporary furnishings and fittings adhere to an almost minimalistic aesthetic, with plain wooden chairs and simple white bed linens. The overall effect is pleasant. ⊠ *Kisfaludy u. 10, H-6000,* ☎ *76/502– 710,* 𝖥𝖠𝖷 *76/502–713. 17 rooms. Cable TV, laundry facilities, meeting room, free parking; no a/c in some rooms. AE, DC, MC, V.*

$$ 🖼 **Pongrácz Manor.** For total puszta immersion, spend a night or two
★ at this Great Plain ranch, about 25 km (16 mi) outside of Kecskemét. The manor, which sits adjacent to a complex of whitewashed buildings with reed roofs, has small, simple, comfortable rooms. The stables house some 70 horses; in addition to riding yourself you can watch resident champion csikósok perform daredevil stunts and stage mock 1848-revolution battles in full hussar dress. Anglers can try their luck in the nearby lake; the restaurant's kitchen will cook your catch (one fish per day). The ranch is popular, so reserve ahead. ⊠ *Kunpuszta 76, H-6041 Kerekegyháza,* ☎ *76/710–093,* 𝖥𝖠𝖷 *76/371–240,* 𝖶𝖤𝖡 *www. hotels.hu/pongracz. 26 rooms with bath, 5 rooms with shared bath, 4 suites. Restaurant, 2 tennis courts, pool, sauna, fishing, bowling, horseback riding, squash. No credit cards. Closed Jan.–Mar.*

$ 🖼 **Fábián Panzió.** It's hard to miss this very pink villa just off the main square. Inside, the pink (though muted) continues, mixing with white, turquoise, and lavender. The friendly owners keep their pension immaculate: floors in the tiny entranceway are polished until they look wet, and even the paths through the blooming back garden are spotless. Rooms are in the main house and in a comely, one-story motel-like building in the garden. The largest and quietest rooms are in the back. ⊠ *Kápolna u. 14, H-6000,* ☎ *76/477–677,* 𝖥𝖠𝖷 *76/477–175. 10 rooms. Laundry service. No credit cards.*

Nightlife and the Arts

Kecskemét's annual **Tavaszi Fesztivál** (Spring Festival) is held from mid-March to early April and includes concerts, dance performances, theater productions, and art exhibits by local and special guest artists from around the country and abroad. Every two years in July, the city hosts a giant children's festival, **Európa Jövője Gyermektalálkozó** (Future of Europe Children's Convention), during which children's groups from some 25 countries put on colorful folk-dance and singing performances outside on the main square; the next one will take place in 2004.

For schedule and ticket information on all cultural events, contact **Tourinform** (⊠ Kossuth tér 1, ☎ 𝖥𝖠𝖷 76/481–065).

The beautiful **Katona József Theater** (⊠ Katona József tér 5, ☎ 76/ 483–283) is known for its excellent dramatic productions (in Hungarian) and also hosts classical concerts, operas, and dance performances during the Spring Festival and other celebrations. The **Kodály Zoltán Zenepedagógiai Intézet** (Zoltán Kodály Music Pedagogy Institute; ⊠

Kéttemplom köz 1, ☎ 76/481–518) often holds student and faculty recitals, particularly during its biannual international music seminar in mid- to late July; the next one is scheduled for 2003.

Outdoor Activities and Sports

The nearby puszta is the setting for traditional horse-stunt shows, carriage rides, guided horseback rides, and other horsey activities. Full-length shows and daylong excursions are bus tour–centric (because of the costs involved), although essentially anything can be arranged if a smaller group or individuals are willing to pay for it. Contact Tourinform or Bugac Tours (☞ Visitor Information, *below, for both*) for other possibilities and for help making arrangements.

Nyakvágó Kft. (✉ Kunszentmiklós, Bösztörpuszta-Nagyállás, ☎ FAX 76/351–198 or ☎ 76/351–201) sometimes offers full- and half-day "Puszta Programs" for smaller groups of individuals who want to take part in the program on the same day. The program includes carriage rides, horse shows, a visit to a working farm, and folk dancing, all lubricated with wine and pálinka (brandy) and including typical puszta meals. A full-day program costs roughly 5,000 Ft., and a half day costs about 4,000 Ft. It's best to call a day or so in advance.

Bugac

⑫ *46 km (29 mi) south of Kecskemét.*

The Bugac puszta is the central and most-visited section of the 86,450-acre **Kiskunsági National Park**—the smaller sister of Hortobágy National Park (farther northeast); together they compose the entire Great Plain. Bugac puszta's expansive, sandy, impossibly flat grassland scenery has provided Hungarian poets and artists with inexhaustible material over the centuries. Although the dry, open stretches may seem numbingly uniform to the casual eye, the Bugac's fragile ecosystem is the most varied of the entire park; its primeval juniper trees, extremely rare in the region, are the area's most protected and treasured flora. Today, Bugac continues to inspire visitors with its strong equestrian traditions and the fun but touristy horse shows and tours offered in its boundaries. The park's half-hour traditional horse show, included in the entrance fee, takes place daily at 1:15 PM. You can also wander around the area and peek into the Kiskunság National Park Museum, which has exhibits about pastoral life on the prairie. ✉ *Park: Bugac puszta.* 🎫 *1,000 Ft. plus 1,000 Ft. per car.* ☉ *Apr.–Oct., daily 9–5 or 6. Information:* ✉ *Karikás Csárda,* ☎ *76/372–688; in Kecskemét,* ✉ *Bugac Tours, Szabadság tér 5/a,* ☎ *76/482–500.*

Dining

$–$$ ✗ **Bugaci Csárda.** Bugac's most famous and popular restaurant is a tour-bus magnet but is still considered a mandatory part of a puszta visit. It's at the end of a dirt road just past the park's main entrance, in a traditional whitewashed, thatch-roof house decorated inside with cheerful red-and-white folk embroideries. Here you can feast on all the Hungarian standards. ✉ *Rte. 54, next to park entrance,* ☎ *76/372–522. No credit cards. Closed Nov.–Mar.*

Outdoor Activities and Sports

The region specializes in equestrian sports. Contact either of the following two companies for horseback-riding lessons, trail rides, and horse carriage rides. **Bugaci Ménes** (✉ Bugac, ☎ FAX 76/372–617). **Bugac Tours** (✉ Szabadság tér 5/a, Kecskemét, ☎ 76/482–500, ☎ FAX 76/481–643; Karikás Csárda, Bugac, ☎ 76/372–688).

Szeged

🔟 *87 km (54 mi) south of Kecskemét.*

The largest city in southern Hungary was almost completely rebuilt after a disastrous flood in 1879, using a concentric plan not unlike that of the Pest side of Budapest, with avenues connecting two boulevards like the spokes of a wheel.

Szeged is famous mainly for two things: its open-air festival, held each year in July and August, and its paprika. But Szeged's paprikas are useful not only in goulash kettles but in test tubes as well: local biochemist Albert Szentgyörgyi won the Nobel Prize in 1937 for his discoveries about vitamin C, extracted from his hometown vegetable. In late summer and early autumn in Szeged, you can see rack after rack of red peppers drying in the open air.

While Szeged does hold architectural delights, they are few compared to cities of similar size; it makes up for this, however, with a dynamic atmosphere that peaks during the school year, when students from the city's schools and universities liven up the streets, cafés, and bars.

The heart of the city center is the large **Széchenyi tér,** lined with trees and surrounded by imposing buildings. Most notable is the bright yellow, eclectic neo-baroque **Városház** (town hall; ⊠ Széchenyi tér 10), built at the turn of the 19th century and, after suffering major damage during the flood of 1879, reconstructed by well-known eclectic Art Nouveau architect Ödön Lechner. At the square's opposite end stands the pale-green **Hotel Tisza** (⊠ Wesselényi u. 4); the guest rooms and lobby look tired and worn, but the lovely, still-active concert hall was the site of many piano recitals by legendary composer Béla Bartók. Its restaurant was a favorite haunt of famous poet Mihály Babits.

NEED A BREAK?
Grab a hot strudel stuffed with apple, poppy seed, or peppery cabbage at the counter of **Hatos Rétes** bakery-cum-café (⊠ Klauzal tér 6), a popular spot not only for a quick strudel but also *óriás palacsinta* (giant stuffed crepes)—salty (ham, cheese) or sweet (plum, raspberry, chestnut). This is also among the few places in Hungary that serve decaffeinated coffee.

★ Szeged's most striking building is the **Fogadalmi templom** (Votive Church), an imposing neo-Romanesque brick edifice built between 1912 and 1929 in fulfillment of a municipal promise made after the 1879 flood. One of Hungary's largest churches, it seats 6,000 and has a splendid organ with 12,000 pipes. The church forms the backdrop to the annual Szegedi Szabadtéri Játékok (Szeged Open-Air Festival), held in vast Dóm tér (Cathedral Square). Outstanding performances of Hungary's great national drama, Imre Madách's *Tragedy of Man,* are given each summer at the festival, as well as other theatrical pieces, operas, and concerts. A performance of a different sort takes place here daily at 12:15 PM, when the mechanical figures on the church's clock put on their five-minute show to music. ⊠ *Dóm tér,* ☎ *62/420–157 church; 62/420–953 crypt.* 🎫 *Church free, crypt 100 Ft.* ☉ *Church weekends 9–6, Sun. 12:30–6. Crypt Apr.–Oct., Tues.–Sun. 10–6; Nov.–Mar., Tues.–Sun. 10–4.*

Szeged's **Régi Zsinagóga** (Old Synagogue) was built in 1839 in neoclassical style. On its outside wall a marker written in Hungarian and Hebrew shows the height of the floodwaters in 1879. It is open only rarely for special events. ⊠ *Hajnóczi u. 12.* ☉ *Apr.–Sept., Sun.–Fri. 9–noon and 1–6.*

★ The **Új Zsinagóga** (New Synagogue), finished in 1905, is Szeged's purest and finest representation of Art Nouveau. Its wood and stone carvings, wrought iron, and furnishings are all the work of local craftspeople. A memorial in the entrance hall honors Szeged's victims of the Holocaust. The New Synagogue, at the corner of Gutenberg utca and Jósika utca, is not far from the smaller Old Synagogue. ⊠ *Gutenberg u. 20,* ☎ *62/423–849.* 🖼 *200 Ft.* ☉ *Apr.–Oct., Sun.–Mon. 9–noon and 1–5; Nov.–Mar., Sun.–Mon. 9–2. Closed Jewish holidays.*

OFF THE
BEATEN PATH

NEMZETI TÖRTÉNETI EMLÉKPARK – The ultimate in monuments to Hungarian history and pride is the enormous National Historic Memorial Park in Ópusztaszer, 29 km (18 mi) north of Szeged. It was built on the site of the first parliamentary congregation of the nomadic Magyar tribes, held in AD 895, in which they agreed to be ruled by mighty Árpád. Paths meander among an open-air museum of traditional village buildings. The main reason to come is the Feszty Körkép (Feszty Cyclorama), an astounding 5,249-ft, 360-degree panoramic oil painting depicting the arrival of the Magyar tribes to the Carpathian basin 1,105 years ago—effectively, the birth of Hungary. It was painted in 1892–1894 by Árpád Feszti and exhibited in Budapest to celebrate the Magyar millennium. Sixty percent of it was destroyed during a World War II bombing, and it wasn't until 1991 that a group of art restorers brought it here and started a painstaking project to resurrect it in time for Hungary's millecentennial celebrations in 1996. Today, housed in its own giant rotunda, the painting is viewable as part of a multimedia experience: groups of up to 100 at a time are let in every half hour for a 25-minute viewing of the painting, accompanied by a recorded explanation and, at the end, a special sound show in which different recordings are played near different parts of the painting—galloping horses, trumpeting horns, screaming virgins, rushing water—to the scene depicted. The attraction is so popular that on summer weekends it's a good idea to call ahead and reserve a spot in the slot of your choice (tickets are for a set showing). The explanation is in Hungarian, but English-language versions on CD, available at the entrance, can be listened to on headphones before or after the viewing. The cyclorama is the only park attraction open in winter. ⊠ *Szoborkert 68, Ópusztaszer,* ☎ *62/275–257 or 62/275–133.* 🖼 *Feszty körkép and park 1,600 Ft.* ☉ *Apr.–Oct., daily 9–6; Nov.–Mar., daily 9–4.*

Dining and Lodging

$$–$$$ ✕ **Alabárdos Étterem.** An 1810 landmark houses this elegant eatery, and its specialty is not just a meal but an experience: the lights are dimmed as waiters rush to your table with a flaming spear of skewered meats, which they then prepare in a spicy ragoût at your table. ⊠ *Oskola u. 13,* ☎ *62/420–914. MC, V. Closed Sun.*

$–$$ ✕ **Botond Restaurant.** Originally Szeged's first printing press, this 1810 neoclassical building now houses a popular restaurant. Specialties include *Tenkes-hegyi szűzérmek* (Tenkes Hill pork tenderloin), served with bacon, mushrooms, and paprika. The outdoor terrace is a prime dining spot in good weather. There's Gypsy music nightly from 7. ⊠ *Széchenyi tér 13,* ☎ *62/420–435. AE, DC, MC, V.*

$–$$ ✕ **Öreg Kőrössy Halászkert Vendéglő.** This thatch-roof fisherman's inn on the Tisza River first opened in 1930; decades later, this place mixes rustic charm and modern glitter. The menu still includes original house staples such as rich-red *Öreg Kőrössy halászlé* (Old Kőrös fish soup) and *Kőrössy* fish paprikás. It's not easy to find; take a car or bus, as it's a long walk from the city center. ⊠ *Sárga üdülőtelep 262 (head north from city center along river on Felső-Tiszapart and turn off after about 2 km [1 mi] where main road makes its first curve, to the left,* *at a sign pointing to restaurant; follow smaller road around several curves and past a restaurant with a similar name),* ☎ 62/495–481. MC, V.

\$\$ 🏨 **Marika Panzió.** This friendly inn sits on a historic street in the Alsóváros (Lower Town), a five-minute drive from the city center. Cozy rooms have light-wood paneling and larger-hotel amenities such as color TVs, minibars, and air-conditioning. The back garden has a small swimming pool. ⊠ *Nyíl u. 45, H-6725,* ☎ FAX *62/443–861,* WEB *www. hotels.hu/marika_szeged. 9 rooms. Minibars, pool, free parking. AE, DC, MC, V.*

Nightlife and the Arts

Szeged's own symphony orchestra, theater company, and famous contemporary dance troupe form the solid foundation for a rich cultural life. The **Szeged Nemzeti Színház** (Szeged National Theater; ⊠ Deák Ferenc u. 12, ☎ 62/479–279) stages Hungarian dramas, as well as classical concerts, operas, and ballets. Chamber-music concerts are often held in the conservatory and in the historic recital hall of the **Hotel Tisza** (⊠ Wesselényi u. 1). Szeged's most important event, drawing crowds from around the country, is the annual **Szegedi Szabadtéri Játékok** (Szeged Open-Air Festival), a tradition established in the 1930s, held mid-July through mid-September. The gala series of dramas, operas, operettas, classical concerts, and folk-dance performances by Hungarian and international artists is held outdoors on the vast cobblestone Cathedral Square. Tickets are always hot commodities; plan far ahead. For tickets and information, contact the ticket office (⊠ Kárász u. 15, ☎ 62/476–555).

Shopping

You'll have no trouble finding packages of authentic **Szegedi paprika** in all sizes and degrees of spiciness in most of the city's shops. Szeged's other famous product is its excellent **salami** made by the local Pick Salami factory, which has been producing Hungary's most-famous, most-exported salamis since 1869. You'll find an extensive salami selection at the **Pick** factory outlet stores (⊠ Jókai u. 7, in Nagyárúház Passage, ☎ 62/425–021; ⊠ Maros u. 21, next to factory, ☎ 62/421–879).

The Great Plain Essentials

BUS TRAVEL

Volánbusz operates service from Budapest's Népstadion terminal to towns throughout the Great Plain. Local buses connect most towns within the region.

➤ Bus Schedules: **Volánbusz** (☎ 1/485–2162 in Budapest).

CAR TRAVEL

From Budapest, Route 4 goes straight to Debrecen, but it's faster to take the M3 expressway and switch to Route 33 midway there; the M5 goes to Kecskemét and Szeged.

The flat expanses of this region make for easy, if eventually numbing, driving. Secondary-route 47 runs along the eastern edge of the country, connecting Debrecen and Szeged. Debrecen and Kecskemét are easily driven between as well via Route 4 through Szolnok, then dropping south in Cegléd. The puszta regions of Bugac and Hortobágy are accessible from Kecskemét and Debrecen by well-marked roads.

TRAIN TRAVEL

Service to the Great Plain from Budapest is quite good; daily service is available from the capital's Nyugati (West) and Keleti (East) stations. Intercity (IC) trains, the fastest, run between Budapest and Debrecen, Kecskemét, and Szeged; they require seat reservations. Trains also run from Romania into Debrecen.

Connections within the region are via the rail junctions in Szolnok and Cegléd, in the geometric center of the Great Plain. The Szeged train station is a 30-minute walk from the town center; you can also take a tram. The trains for Kecskemét are on the Szeged line; the trip between the towns takes roughly an hour. The ride from Szolnok to Debrecen takes about an hour and a half.

➤ TRAIN STATIONS: **Debrecen train station** (⊠ Petőfi tér 12, ☎ 52/346–777). **Kecskemét train station** (⊠ Kodály Zoltán tér 7, ☎ 76/322–460). **Szeged train station** (⊠ Tisza pályaudvar, ☎ 62/421–821).

TOURS

Cityrama runs day trips several times a week to the Great Plain from Budapest. They begin with a sightseeing walk through Kecskemét, then head out to the prairie town of Lajosmizse for drinking, dining, Gypsy music, carriage rides, and a traditional csikós horse show. The cost is approximately 16,000 Ft.

IBUSZ Travel also operates full-day tours out to the Great Plain, to Lajosmizse as well as to Bugac, both first taking in Keckemét's sights. Costs run 16,000 Ft.–17,000 Ft.

➤ CONTACTS: **Cityrama** (☎ 1/302–4382 in Budapest). **IBUSZ Travel** (☎ 1/485–2700 in Budapest, WEB www.ibusz.hu).

VISITOR INFORMATION

➤ TOURIST INFORMATION: **Bugac Tours** (⊠ Karikás Csárda, Bugac, ☎ 76/372–688; ⊠ Szabadság tér 5/a, Kecskemét, ☎ 76/482–500, FAX 76/481–643). **Debrecen Tourinform** (⊠ Piac u. 20, ☎ 52/412–250, FAX 52/535–323). **Hortobágy Pusztainform** (⊠ Pásztormúzeum, FAX 52/589–321). **Kecskemé Tourinform** (⊠ Kossuth tér 1, ☎ FAX 76/481–065). **Szeged Tourinform** (⊠ Victor Hugo u. 1, ☎ FAX 62/425–711).

HUNGARY A TO Z

To research prices, get advice from other travelers, and book travel arrangements, visit www.fodors.com.

AIR TRAVEL

See Air Travel *in* Budapest Essentials, *above.*

BIKE TRAVEL

For specifics on bicycling conditions and suggested routes, contact the Bicycle Touring Association of Hungary, which has English-language information available Monday only, 1–6. Tourinform in Budapest can provide you with the "Hungary by Bike" brochure and general information on current rental outfits.

➤ BIKE INFORMATION: **Bicycle Touring Association of Hungary** (⊠ District V, Bajcsy-Zsilinszky út 31, 2nd floor, Apt. 3, Budapest, ☎ 1/332–7177). **Tourinform** (☞ Visitor Information, *below*).

BOAT TRAVEL

Hungary is well equipped with nautical transport, and Budapest is situated on a major international waterway, the Danube. Vienna is five hours away by hydrofoil or boat. For more information, *see* Boat Travel *in* Budapest Essentials, *above.*

BUS TRAVEL

Long-distance buses link Budapest with most cities in Hungary as well as major cities in neighboring countries. From Budapest, buses to Bratislava and Prague, as well as Austria and points farther west, depart from the Erzsébet tér bus station. Buses to Kraków, Sofia, and parts of Romania and Serbia and Montenegro operate from the Népstadion station. Though inexpensive, these buses tend to be crowded, so buy your tickets days in advance at the stations. (Reservations cannot be made by phone, and a few routes allow purchases only from the driver.)

Buses to the eastern part of Hungary depart from the Népstadion station. For the Danube Bend, buses leave from the bus terminal at Árpád Bridge. For bus travel within the country arrive at least 20 minutes before departure to buy a ticket (this is not possible for all routes, as tickets for some routes can only be purchased directly from the driver). If there's a crowd pressing to get on, feel free to wave your pre-purchased ticket about as you jostle your way aboard. Technically speaking, reserved seats must be occupied by no later than 10 minutes before departure time.

➤ Bus Stations: **Árpád Bridge bus station** (⊠ District III, Budapest, ☎ 1/329–1450). **Erzsébet tér bus station** (⊠ District V, Budapest, ☎ 1/485–2100). **Népstadion bus station** (⊠ District XIV, Budapest, ☎ 1/252–4498).

BUSINESS HOURS
Banks are generally open weekdays until 3 or 4; most close by 2 on Friday.

Museums are usually open Tuesday–Sunday 10–6 and are closed on Monday; most stop admitting people 30 minutes before closing time. Some have a free-admission day; see individual listings in the chapter, but double-check, as the days tend to change.

Department stores are open weekdays 10–5 or 6, Saturday until 1. Grocery stores are generally open weekdays 7 AM to 6 or 7 PM, Saturday until 1 PM; "nonstops," or *éjjel-nappali,* are (theoretically) open 24 hours.

CAR RENTAL
Car-rental prices can vary greatly. Avis and Hertz rent Western models for as much as $550 or more per week. Smaller local companies, on the other hand, can rent Hungarian cars for as low as $150 per week. Try to make rental arrangements before you get to Hungary; renting a car when you get there costs quite a bit more than an advance reservation. *See* Car Rental *in* Budapest Essentials, *above,* for a list of agencies.

Foreign driver's licenses are generally accepted by car rental agencies but are technically not legally valid (☞ Car Travel, *below,* for more information).

CAR TRAVEL
To drive in Hungary, Americans and Canadians need an International Driver's License—although domestic licenses are usually accepted anyway. It can, however, get messy and expensive if you are stopped by a police officer who insists you need an International Driver's License (which, legally, you do), so it's best to obtain the international license. If you're from the United Kingdom you may use your domestic license.

Getting around by car is the best way to see Hungary. It's a small country, so even driving across the whole territory is manageable. Speed traps are numerous, so it's best to observe the speed limit; fines start from the equivalent of roughly $40, but they can easily reach $230. Using—even holding—a cell phone while driving is an offense. In an effort to forestall bribe-taking, the time-honored practice of on-the-spot payment for violations was abolished in 2000, so police must now give accused speeders an invoice payable at post offices. (Remember this should you feel innocent and an officer suggests an on-the-spot "discount.") Spot checks are frequent as well, and police occasionally try to take advantage of foreigners, so always have your papers on hand.

GASOLINE

Gas stations are plentiful in Hungary, and many on the main highways stay open all night, even on holidays. Major chains, such as MOL, Shell, and OMV, have Western-style full-facility stations with rest rooms, brightly lit convenience stores, and 24-hour service. Lines are rarely long, and supplies are essentially stable. Unleaded gasoline (*bleifrei* or *ólommentes*) is generally available at most stations and is usually the 95-octane-level choice. If your car requires unleaded gasoline, be sure to double-check that you're not reaching for the leaded before you pump.

EMERGENCY SERVICES

➤ CONTACT: **Hungarian Automobile Club's breakdown service** (☎ 1/ 345–1744 or 188).

PARKING

Smaller towns usually have free parking on the street and some hourly fee lots near main tourist zones. Throughout the country, no-parking zones are marked with the international "No Parking" sign: a white circle with a diagonal line through it. For information on parking in Budapest, *see* Car Travel *in* Budapest Essentials.

ROAD CONDITIONS

There are four classes of roads: expressways (designated by the letter "M" and a single digit), main highways (a single digit), secondary roads (a two-digit number), and minor roads (a three-digit number). Highways, expressways, and secondary roads are generally in good condition. The conditions of minor roads vary considerably; keep in mind that tractors and horse-drawn carts may slow your route down in rural areas. In planning your driving route with a map, opt for the larger roadways whenever possible; you'll generally end up saving time even if there is a shorter but smaller road. It's not so much the condition of the smaller roads but the kind of traffic on them and the number of towns (where the speed limit is 50 kph [30 mph]) they pass through that will slow you down. If you're in no hurry, however, explore the smaller roads!

At this writing, Hungary was continuing a massive upgrading and reconstruction of many of its expressways, gearing up for its role as the main bridge for future trade between the Balkan countries and the former Soviet Union and Western Europe. To help fund the project, tolls are required on several routes. Toll roads include the M1, which runs west from Budapest toward Vienna; the M3, which runs northeast toward Slovakia; and the M5, from Budapest to just south of Kecskemét (and eventually through Szeged to Serbia and Montenegro).

RULES OF THE ROAD

Hungarians drive on the right and observe the usual Continental rules of the road (but they revel in passing). Unless otherwise noted, the speed limit in developed areas is 50 kph (30 mph), on main roads 80–100 kph (50–62 mph), and on highways 120 kph (75 mph). Stay alert: speed-limit signs are few and far between. Seat belts are compulsory (front-seat belts in lower speed zones, both front and back in higher speed zones), and drinking alcohol is prohibited—there is a zero-tolerance policy, and the penalties are very severe.

CUSTOMS AND DUTIES

ON ARRIVAL

Objects for personal use may be imported freely. If you are over 16, you may bring in 250 cigarettes or 50 cigars or 250 grams of tobacco, plus 2 liters of wine, 1 liter of spirits, and 100 milliliters of perfume. (You also may leave Hungary with this much, plus 5 liters of beer). If you bring in more than $400 in cash and think you may be taking that much out, technically speaking you should declare it on arrival. A customs charge is made on gifts valued in Hungary at more than 30,500 Ft.

ON DEPARTURE

Take care when you leave Hungary that you have the right documentation for exporting goods. Keep receipts of any major purchases. A special permit is needed for works of art, antiques, or objects of museum value. Upon leaving, you are entitled to a value-added tax (VAT) refund on new goods (i.e., not works of art, antiques, or objects of museum value) valued at 50,000 Ft. or more (VAT inclusive). But applying for the refund may rack up more frustration than money: cash refunds are given only in forints, and you may find yourself in the airport minutes before boarding with a handful of soft currency; while you can take out up to 350,000 Ft., converting it back home will difficult. If you otherwise don't have much hard currency on you, you can convert up to about 100,000 of the forints into dollars to come up with the $400-in-cash export limit. If you made your purchases by credit card you can file for a credit to your card or to your bank account (again in forints), but don't expect it to come through in a hurry. If you intend to apply for the credit, make sure you get customs to stamp the original purchase invoice before you leave the country. For more information, pick up a tax refund brochure from any tourist office or hotel, or contact Intel Trade Rt. in Budapest. For further Hungarian customs information, inquire at the National Customs and Revenue Office. If you have trouble communicating, ask Tourinform (1/438–8080) for help.

➤ INFORMATION: **Intel Trade Rt.** (✉ District I, Csalogány u. 6-10, Budapest, ☎ 1/201–8120 or 1/356–9800). **National Customs and Revenue Office** (✉ Regional Directorate for Central Hungary, District XIV, Hungária krt. 112–114, Budapest, ☎ 1/470–4121 or 470–4122). **Tourinform** (☎ 1/438–8080).

EMBASSIES AND CONSULATES

Australian Consulate (✉ District VII, Királyhágó tér 8–9, Budapest, ☎ 1/457–9777). **British Embassy** (✉ District V, Harmincad u. 6, Budapest, ☎ 1/266–2888, FAX 1/266–0907). **Canadian Consulate** (✉ District XII, Budakeszi út 32, Budapest, ☎ 1/392–3360). **New Zealand Consulate** (✉ District VI, Teréz krt. 38, Budapest, ☎ 1/331–4908). **U.S. Embassy** (✉ District V, Szabadság tér 12, Budapest, ☎ 1/475–4400).

EMERGENCIES

➤ CONTACTS: **Ambulance** (☎ 104). **Fire** (☎ 105). **Police** (☎ 107).

HOLIDAYS

January 1, March 15 (Anniversary of 1848 Revolution); Easter Sunday and Easter Monday (in March, April, or May); May 1 (Labor Day); August 20 (St. Stephen's and Constitution Day); October 23 (1956 Revolution Day); December 24–26.

LANGUAGE

Hungarian (*Magyar*) tends to look and sound intimidating at first because it is not an Indo-European language. Generally, older people speak some German, and many younger people speak at least rudimentary English, which has become the most popular language to learn. It's a safe bet that anyone in the tourist trade will speak at least one of the two languages. Also note that when giving names, Hungarians put the family name before the given name, thus Janos Szabo (John Taylor) becomes Szabo Janos.

MAIL

Airmail letters and postcards generally take seven days to travel between Hungary and the United States, sometimes more than twice as long, however, during the Christmas season. Postage for an airmail letter to the United States costs about 160 Ft.; an airmail letter to the United Kingdom and elsewhere in Western Europe costs about 150 Ft. Airmail postcards to the United States cost about 110 Ft. and to the United Kingdom and the rest of Western Europe about 100 Ft.

Budapest's main post office branch is downtown. The post offices near Budapest's Keleti (East) and Nyugati (West) train stations stay open until 9 PM on weekdays, the former just as long on weekends while the latter shuts its doors at 8 PM. The American Express office in Budapest has poste restante services.

➤ POST OFFICE: **American Express** (✉ District V, Deák Ferenc u. 10 H-1052 Budapest, ☎ 1/235–4330). **Downtown Budapest post office branch** (✉ District V, Magyar Posta 4. sz., Viroshiz u. 18, H-1052 Budapest). **Keleti post office** (✉ District VIII, Baross tér 11/C, Budapest). **Nyugati post office** (✉ District VI, Teréz krt. 51, Budapest).

MONEY MATTERS

Even with inflation and the 25% value-added tax (VAT) in the service industry, enjoyable vacations with all the trimmings still remain less expensive in Hungary than in nearby Western European cities such as Vienna.

Eurocheque holders can cash personal checks in all banks and in most hotels. Many banks also cash American Express and Visa traveler's checks. American Express has a full-service office in Budapest, which also dispenses cash to its cardholders; a smaller branch on Castle Hill, at the Sisi Restaurant, has a currency exchange that operates daily from March to mid-January. Budapest also has a Citibank offering full services to account holders, including a 24-hour cash machine.

➤ CONTACTS: **American Express** (✉ District V, Deák Ferenc u. 10, Budapest, ☎ 1/235–4330, ℻ 1/267–2028; ✉ Sisi Restaurant, District 1, Castle Hill, ☎ 1/264–0118). **Citibank** (✉ District V, Vörösmarty tér 4).

CURRENCY

Hungary's unit of currency is the forint (Ft.). There are bills of 200, 500, 1,000, 2,000, 5,000, 10,000 and 20,000 forints and coins of 1, 2, 5, 10, 20, 50, and 100 forints.

CURRENCY EXCHANGE

At this writing, the exchange rate was approximately 249 Ft. to the U.S. dollar, 158 Ft. to the Canadian dollar, 386 Ft. to the pound sterling, and 243 Ft. to the euro. It is probably still wise to bring traveler's checks, which can be cashed all over the country in banks and hotels. There is still a black market in hard currency, but changing money on the street is risky and illegal, and the bank rate almost always comes close. Stick with banks and official exchange offices. There are also many cash-exchange machines in Budapest, into which you feed paper currency for forints. Most bank automats and cash-exchange machines are clustered around their respective bank branches throughout downtown Pest.

CREDIT CARDS

All major credit cards are accepted in Hungary, but don't rely on them in smaller towns or less expensive accommodations and restaurants. Twenty-four-hour cash machines have sprung up throughout Budapest and in major towns around the country. Some accept Plus-network bank cards and Visa credit cards, others Cirrus and MasterCard. You can withdraw forints only (automatically converted at the bank's official exchange rate) directly from your account. Some levy a 1% or $3 service charge. Instructions are in English.

➤ LOST CREDIT CARDS: **American Express** (☎ 336/393–111 collect to the U.S.). **Diners Club** (☎ 640–248–424). **Mastercard** (☎ 680–012–517). **Visa** (☎ 680–011–272).

PASSPORTS AND VISAS

Only a valid passport is required of U.S., British, Canadian, and New Zealand citizens; Australian citizens must obtain a visa.

➤ HUNGARIAN EMBASSIES: **Australia** (✉ 17 Beale Crescent Deakin Act., Canberra 2600, ☎ 6126/282–3226). **Canada** (✉ 299 Waverley St., Ottawa, Ontario K2P 0V9, ☎ 613/230–9614). **New Zealand** (Consulate General: ✉ 151 Orangi Kaupapa Rd., Wellington 6005, ☎ 4/938–0427). **United States** (✉ 3910 Shoemaker St. NW, Washington, DC 20008, ☎ 202/362–6730). **United Kingdom** (✉ 35b Eaton Pl., London SW1X 8BY, ☎ 0171/235–5218).

TELEPHONES

Within Hungary, most towns can be dialed directly: dial "06" and wait for the buzzing tone; then dial the local number. Cellular phone numbers are treated like long-distance domestic calls: dial "06" before the number (when giving their cellular phone numbers, most people include the 06 anyway). It is unnecessary to use the city code, 1, when dialing within Budapest

DIRECTORY AND OPERATOR ASSISTANCE

Dial "198" for directory assistance for all of Hungary. There is usually someone on-hand who can speak English. You can also consult *The Phone Book,* an English-language telephone directory full of important Budapest numbers as well as cultural and tourist information; it's provided in guest rooms of most major hotels, as well as at many restaurants and English-language bookstores. The slim but information-packed city guide *Budapest in Your Pocket* lists important phone numbers; it appears six times a year and can be found at newsstands and hotels.

INTERNATIONAL CALLS

Direct calls to foreign countries can be made from Budapest and all major provincial towns by dialing "00" and waiting for the international dialing tone; on pay phones the initial charge is 60 Ft.

The country code for Hungary is 36. When dialing from outside the country, drop the initial 06 prefix for area codes outside of Budapest. ➤ ACCESS CODES: **AT&T** (☎ 06/800–01111). **MCI** (☎ 06/800–01411). **Sprint** (☎ 06/800–01877).

PUBLIC PHONES

Coin-operated pay phones accept 10-Ft., 20-Ft., 50-Ft., and 100-Ft. coins; the minimum initial amount is 20 Ft. Given that these phones often swallow up change without allowing a call in exchange, however, it's best when possible to use gray card–operated telephones, which outnumber coin-operated phones in Budapest and the Balaton region. The cards—available at post offices and most newsstands and kiosks—come in units of 60 (800 Ft.) and 90 (1,800 Ft.) calls.

TIPPING

Taxi drivers and hairdressers expect 10%–15% tips, while porters should get 200 Ft.–400 Ft. Coatroom attendants receive 100 Ft.–200 Ft., as do gas-pump attendants if they wash your windows or check your tires; dressing-room attendants at thermal baths receive 50 Ft.–100 Ft. for opening and closing your locker. Gratuities are not included automatically on bills at most restaurants; when the waiter arrives with the bill, you should immediately add a 10%–15% tip to the amount, as it is not customary to leave the tip on the table. If a Gypsy band plays exclusively for your table, you should leave at least 200 Ft. in a plate discreetly provided for that purpose.

TOURS

BOAT TOURS

MAHART Tours runs boat excursions on Lake Balaton and on the Danube in and beyond Budapest.

➤ CONTACT: **MAHART Tours** (✉ District V, Belgrád rakpart, Budapest, ☎ 1/318–1743, WEB www.maharttours.com).

EXCURSIONS

IBUSZ Travel arranges bus tours to places around the country, from cave visits in the Mátra Mountains to wine tasting in the Tokaj region to traditional pig roasts on the Great Plain.

➤ CONTACT: **IBUSZ Travel** (central branch: ✉ District V, Ferenciek tere 10, Budapest, ☎ 1/485–2700, WEB www.ibusz.hu).

TRAIN TRAVEL

International trains are routed to two stations in Budapest (☞ Budapest Essentials, *above*). Keleti pályaudvar (East Station) receives most international rail traffic coming in from the west. Nyugati pályaudvar (West Station) handles a combination of international and domestic trains.

Travel by train from Budapest to other large cities or to Lake Balaton is cheap and efficient. Avoid *személyvonat* (local trains), which are extremely slow; instead, take Intercity (IC) trains—which are especially clean and fast but require a *helyjegy* (seat reservation) for about 350 Ft.—or gyorsvonat (express trains). On timetables, tracks (*vágány*) are abbreviated with a "v"; *indul* means departing, while *érkezik* means arriving. Trains get crowded during weekend travel in summer; you're more likely to have elbow room if you pay a little extra for first-class tickets.

Snacks and drinks are often not available on trains, so pack a lunch for the road; train picnics are a way of life. For more information about rail travel, contact or visit MAV Passenger Service.

➤ TRAIN INFORMATION: **MAV Passenger Service** (✉ District VI, Andrássy út 35, Budapest, ☎ 1/461–5500 international information; 1/461–5400 domestic information; WEB www.mav.hu/eng).

CUTTING COSTS

Only Hungarian citizens are entitled to student discounts on domestic train fares; all senior citizens (men over 60, women over 55), however, are eligible for a 20% discount.

For travel only within Hungary, there's a Hungarian Flexipass, which costs $67 for any 5 days of travel within a 15-day period, or $84 for for 10 days of within a one-month period.

The European East Pass, available in the United States, New Zealand, South Africa, and Australia, may be used on the national rail networks of Hungary, Austria, the Czech Republic, Poland, and Slovakia. The pass covers five days of unlimited first-class travel within a one-month period for US$220. Additional travel days may be purchased.

Hungary is also covered by the Eurailpass, which provides unlimited first-class rail travel, in all of the participating countries of Europe, for the duration of the pass. For further information on the Hungarian Flexipass, European East Pass, and Eurailpass, contact Rail Europe and *see* Train Travel *in* Smart Travel Tips A to Z.

➤ INFORMATION AND PASSES: **Rail Europe** (✉ 500 Mamaroneck Ave., Harrison, NY 10528, ☎ 914/682–5172 or 800/438–7245, FAX 800/432–1329; ✉ 2087 Dundas E, Suite 106, Mississauga, Ontario L4X 1M2, ☎ 800/361–7245, FAX 905/602–4198; WEB www.raileurope.com).

TRAVEL AGENCIES

➤ CONTACTS: **American Express** (✉ District V, Deák Ferenc u. 10, Budapest, ☎ 1/235–4330, FAX 1/267–2028). **Carlson Wagonlit Travel** (✉ District V, Dorottya u. 3, Budapest, ☎ 1/429–2111, FAX 1/429–2129). **Vista Travel Center** (✉ District VI, Andrássy út 1, Budapest, ☎ 1/269–6032 or 1/269–6033, FAX 1/269–6031, WEB www.vista.hu).

VISITOR INFORMATION

➤ TOURIST INFORMATION: **IBUSZ Travel** (central branch: ✉ District V, Ferenciek tere 10, Budapest, ☎ 1/485–2700). **Tourinform** (✉ District V, Sütő u. 2, Budapest, ☎ 1/438–8080). **TRIBUS Hotel Service** (✉ District V, Apáczai Csere János u. 1, Budapest, ☎ 1/318–5776), open 24 hours.

6 POLAND

From the Baltic coast, with its white sands
and pine forests, to the pristine lakes of
Mazuria, to the virgin forest of Bialowieża,
to the sharp granite peaks of the Tatra
mountains, Poland's infinite variety of
landscapes is arranged in latitudinal strips.
You will find beautiful cities with history
and culture, including dreamlike, medieval
Kraków, preserved like an insect in amber.
In Poland, you can rediscover the joy
of four clearly marked seasons: green,
moist, gentle spring; clear blue summer;
Technicolor autumn; and black-and-white
winter—nature and culture conspiring to
spin a wheel of seasonal delights.

Updated by
Dorota Wąsik
and Slawomir
Zurek

POLES ARE FOND OF QUOTING, with a wry grimace, an old Chinese valediction: "May you live in interesting times." The times are certainly interesting in Poland—home of the Solidarity political-labor-social movement that sent shock waves through the Soviet bloc beginning in 1980, and the first Eastern European state to shake off Communist rule. But as the grimace implies, being on the firing line of history is a challenge. There are constant reminders that the return to capitalism, after 45 years of Sovietism, is an experiment on a vast and unprecedented scale, bringing benefits for a growing percentage of the population but also hardships for many.

The reforms of more than a decade have brought little tangible benefits to the average Pole, and the people's resolve is faltering. The stress was seen in the mid-2000 breakup of the unpopular ruling coalition of the two reform-minded political parties. To ensure that reforms don't proceed too quickly, Poles have overwhelmingly thrown their support behind President Aleksander Kwaśniewski—himself a former Communist.

On the other hand, NATO membership, healthy IMF ratings, and the ever-increasing privatization of state companies all paint a hopeful economic picture. The new economy is part of the reason Warsaw and Kraków are enjoying a cultural renaissance. Travelers are now flocking to Central Europe's largest country in ever greater numbers. They're coming to visit the beautifully preserved medieval city of Kraków, breathtaking mountains, the Hanseatic town of Gdańsk, and the haunting Baltic seascapes. Most of all, they're coming to witness a nation in the process of rebirth.

The Communist era represented the most recent stage in the Poles' age-old struggle to retain their national identity in the face of pressure from more powerful neighbors to the west and east. Founded as a unified state during the 10th century on the great north-European plain, Poland lay for a thousand years at the heart of Europe, precisely at the halfway point between the Atlantic coast of Spain and the Ural Mountains. With no easily demarcated or defensible frontiers, this gave it an enviable geostrategic position. During the Middle Ages, Poland fought against German advances, uniting with its eastern neighbors in 1410 to roundly defeat the Teutonic Knights in the Battle of Grunwald. In the golden age of Polish history, the 16th and 17th centuries, Poland pushed eastward against its Slavic neighbors, taking Kiev and envisioning a kingdom that stretched from the Baltic to the Black Sea. It saw itself then as a bastion of Christendom holding back the hordes from the east, a role best symbolized when Polish king Jan III Sobieski led the allied Christian forces to defeat the Turks at Vienna in 1683.

By the end of the 18th century, powerful neighbors had united to obliterate Poland—with its outmoded tendency to practice democracy at the highest levels of state and elect foreigners to the throne—from the map of Europe. Its territories were to remain divided among the Austrian, Prussian, and Russian empires until the end of World War I. This period of partition is often used to explain patterns of character or public behavior—the Polish tendency to subvert organized authority, for example, or Polish allegiance to the role of the Roman Catholic Church as guardian of the national identity, a devotion that would survive intense and, on occasion, brutal pressure by the Communist secret police and other authorities.

Evidence of the period of partition remains throughout Poland, despite a tendency in the postwar years to impose uniformity. The formerly

Prussian-ruled regions of western Poland, centered in Poznań, are still regarded as cleaner and better organized than the formerly Russian-ruled central areas around the capital, Warsaw. The former Austrian zone in the south, particularly the city of Kraków, retains a reputation for formality and propriety reminiscent of the Hapsburg period. The architecture of the three regions also bears traces of distinct 19th-century imperial styles.

During the 20th century, after a brief period of revived independence in the interwar years, Poland once again fell victim to the old struggle between east and west. It was first crushed by Hitler's *Drang nach Osten* (drive toward the east), which killed 6 million Polish citizens, including 3 million of the Jews who had played such a major role in the nation's history. Then, in 1945, the Soviet Union imposed a Communist system in Poland. Poland's borders were shifted 240 km (150 mi) westward, and in the process lands formerly held by Germany were annexed and the *kresy*, or eastern territories, were lost. These mid-century experiences are embedded deeply in the Polish psyche. Poles show an almost mystical reverence for these struggles by remembering dozens of wartime anniversaries each year, which they celebrate with speeches, color guards, and candles placed at countless memorials and cemeteries. Since 1989, it has been possible to openly mourn those who died fighting Soviet power and the Polish Communist authorities during the 1940s and 1950s.

Poland's historic cities—Kraków, Warsaw, Gdańsk—tell much of the tale of European history and culture. Its countryside offers unrivaled possibilities of escape from the 21st century to a simpler time, to unspoiled nature, and to the remnants of the grand Polish past scattered throughout the country. Paradoxically, the Communists—who after 1956 dropped attempts to collectivize agriculture and kept the Polish peasant on his small plot of land—left much of rural Poland in a romantic, almost pre-industrial state. Cornflowers still bloom, storks perch atop untidy nests by cottage chimneys, and horse carts lazily make their way along worn field tracks. Travelers should try to ignore the legacy of Communism, which—though slowly disappearing—can be still encountered here and there (ugly Soviet-style buildings, pockets of terrible pollution), and concentrate on Poland's many attractions.

Despite a certain wary reserve in public behavior, the Poles will win you over with their strong individualism, their sense of humor, and their capacity for fun. Given a chance, perhaps, they will display their proverbial hospitality. Today, more than ever, they are very politically aware of both local and international issues. Whether or not they are for or against free-fall capitalism, one thing remains certain: *Puppies* (Polish yuppies) want to get their MTV.

Pleasures and Pastimes

Dining

Although, at a first glance, Polish food may seem somewhat monotonous and heavy, there is much more to it than the stereotypical collation of pork, potatoes, and cabbage. The cuisine reflects Poland's multicultural history. Dishes now considered "typically Polish" are often a mixture of Russian, German, Ukrainian, Italian, Jewish, Lithuanian, Turkish, French, and other cuisines, hence the variety and the unexpected juxtapositions of ingredients. Although the Communist reality tended to "equalize" everything, including the food, the post-Communist era has brought the revival of many of the old traditions of Polish cooking, and finer city restaurants are bringing a nouvelle flair to the tried-

and-true favorites. All in all, Polish food can be filling, tasty, and relatively cheap.

One of the joys of Polish cuisine is the soup, a fundamental part of the daily meal and potentially a meal in itself. Soups are invariably excellent, often thick and nourishing, with lots of peas and beans. Clear beet soup, *barszcz,* is the most traditional, but soured barley soup, *żurek,* should be sampled at least once. Pickled or soused herring is also a favorite Polish appetizer. The Polish chef's greatest love is pork in all its varieties, including suckling pig and wild boar. Traditional sausages, *kabanos,* usually dried and smoked, are delicious, as are the different kinds of *kiełbasa.*

A popular hunter's dish, *bigos,* is made from soured and fresh cabbage, stewed (for several days or weeks) together with many different kinds of meat and sausage. Delicious *gołąbki,* (literally "little pigeons" but having nothing to do with their flying namesakes) are cabbage leaves stuffed with rice and meat filling, served with tomato or mushroom cream sauce. *Pierogi* are boiled dumplings with different kinds of fillings. The two most popular kinds are *pierogi ruskie* (the Russian *pierogi*), with potatoes, cottage cheese, onion, salt and pepper, and the *pierogi z kapustą i grzybami,* with cabbage and mushrooms. Dessert remains a major institution in Polish life, and traditional sweets include *pączki* (full and round doughnuts, often filled with wild rose confiture); *nugat* (two wafers with very sweet filling made from honey, nuts, and egg yolks); *piszinger* (many layers of wafer with chocolate filling); *szarlotka* (apple pie); and *sernik* (cheesecake).

The traditional sit-down restaurant is still the main feature of the dining scene in Poland, across all price ranges. But if you are in a hurry there is more variety than ever. Next to the old low-cost, self-service *bar mleczny* (milk bars) and cheap cafeterias, you will find pizza parlors, burger joints, and other fast-food outlets. If you are really pressed for time, you will nearly always be able to find a street stall (usually housed in a small white caravan) that serves *zapiekanki,* French bread toasted with cheese and mushrooms.

Most restaurants these days have an adequate wine list, although wine tends to be rather expensive. Beer and vodka remain traditional Polish drinks. In addition to white vodkas, best consumed ice cold, there is a selection of flavored vodkas. *Żubrówka,* or bison vodka, is flavored with grass from Białowieża virgin forest and has a yellowish-green tint and a matching, subtly herbal flavor. *Szarlotka* and *tatanka* are very good apple-flavored vodkas. *Pieprzówka* has the sharp tang of pepper; *dzięgielówka* and *piołunówka* taste and smell of wild herbs. *Wiśniówka* is a sweet cherry vodka, and *krupnik* is a sweetish spirit made from mead. In the winter, nothing will keep you warm better than *gorący miód* (hot mead), and in the summer there is nothing more refreshing than cold beer—*piwo* (pronounced *pi*-vo). Polish beer is almost exclusively lager; popular brands include Żywiec, Okocim, and Leżajsk.

Although upscale city restaurants have adapted to Western mealtimes, Poles traditionally eat their main meal of the day, *obiad* (dinner), between 3 and 5. Many restaurants therefore open at 1 and do not get into full swing until mid-afternoon. Although in cities there is a growing trend to stay open later ("to the last customer" is a popular new slogan), many restaurants still close relatively early, and it may be difficult to order a meal after 9 PM. A few restaurants offer fixed-price meals between about 1 and 5, though these do not always represent a savings over à la carte prices.

Poland (Polska)

Baltic
Sea

Wejherowo
Gdynia · Zato
GdaŚ
Słupsk
Gdańsk
Sławno
Kołobrzeg · Koszalin
Kościerzyna
Tczew
21
Miastko
Malt
Świnoujście
Karlin
Starogard
Gdański
Sztur
Zalew
SzczeciŚski
Nowogard
Szczecinek
Chojnice
Kwidzy
23
Szczecin
Goleniów
Stargard
Szczeciński
Jastrowie
Grudziq
10
52
Kalisz
Pom.
Piła
Bydgoszcz
Wisła R.
Toruń
Pyrzyce
Chodzież
22
Notec R.
25
Odra R.
Gorzów
Wielkopolski
Rogoźno
Inowrocław
Wł
E65
E281
24
Pniewy
Gniezno
Skwierzyna
2
E30
Poznań
Września
Krośniewice
Świebodzin
Środa
Wielkopolska
32
Jarocin
25
Zgi
Zielona
Góra
Leszno
Kalisz
Warta R.
Krotoszyn
Kożuchów
Sieradz
Zduńs
Wola
Szprotawa
Rawicz
Ostrów
Wielkopolski
Lubin
14
Bolesławiec
Odra R.
Kępno
Wieluń
Nysse R.
Zgorzelec
Legnica
Oleśnica
Wrocław
Jelenia
Góra
Kluczbork
45
Brzeg
43
Wałbrzych
Opole
Lubliniec
Nysa
Bytom
Kudowa Zdroj
Kłodzko
Gliwice
Chorzów
Katowice
Wodzisław
91
Bi
Bi
CZECH
REPUBLIC

GERMANY

E65

E75

LITHUANIA

Kaliningrad

RUSSIA

Górowo
Iławeckie
olag
Bartoszyce
Węgorzewo
Suwałki
Pasłęk
Lidzbark
Warm.
Giżycko
Ełk
Augustów
Mrągowo
16
Olsztyn
16
Ostróda
Szczytno
Grajewo
Szczuczyn
52
53
Czarna
Białostocka
Nowe Miasto
Lubawskie
Nidzica
Łomża
Białystok
61
Mława
Ostrołęka
Ciechanów
Zambrów
Bielsk
Podlaski
18
60
Ostrów
Mazowiecki
19
wek
Płock
Wyszków
Siemiatycze
62
Sokołów
Podlaski
Kutno
Warsaw
Siedlce
E30
Brest
łowicz
Mińsk Mazowiecki
2
Otwock
Biała
Podlaska
Żyrardów
Garwolin
Grójec
Radzyń
Podl
Łódź
E67
Pilica R.
Kock
19
Włodawa
Tomaszów Mazowiecki
Puławy
Piotrków Trybunalski
Radom
44
Kazimierz
Dolny
Lublin
Radomsko
Skarżysko
Kamienna
74
Chełm
Ostrowiec
Świętokrzyski
Krasnystaw
Kraśnik
Kielce
17
Zamość
stochowa
Janów
78
Jędrzejów
Sandomierz
Tomaszów
Lubelski
Stalowa
Wola
osnowiec
Miechów
Leżajsk
aworzno
Mielec
19
E40
Jarosław
więcim
Kraków
Tarnów
E40
Dębica
Rzeszów
UKRAINE
52
Myślenice
Przemyśl
98
Nowy
Sącz
Krosno
Rabka
Gorlice
Sanok
Krynica

BELARUS

Wkra R.
Biebrza R.
Bug R.
Wisła R.
Wieprz R.
Bug R.
San R.
Wisła R.

N

0   60 miles

0   90 km

Zakopane
SLOVAKIA

CATEGORY	COST*
$$$$	over zł 50
$$$	zł 35–zł 50
$$	zł 20–zł 35
$	under zł 20

*per person for a main course at dinner

Hiking, Walking, and Cycling

There are nearly endless possibilities for hiking in Poland. The most spectacular terrain is in the south in the Tatra Mountains and the Podhale region, and in the wild and deserted Bieszczady region in the southeast (along the borders of Slovakia and Ukraine). All national parks have well-marked trails that traverse beautiful countryside. The parks also provide overnight accommodations at regular intervals in the form of walkers' huts and hostels, which can be fairly basic. Elsewhere in the country it is more difficult to guarantee you'll find a bed at the right point on your route. For biking, the flat areas of the north are perhaps best, and many parts of the country have touring tracks and byroads.

Lodging

Lodging options are getting better and better, although travelers seeking elegant accommodations have fewer options to choose from than in more popular cities in Central Europe like Prague. Cheap and comfortable bed-and-breakfast accommodations in private homes or pensions are widely available only in the mountains or on the coast; look for signs in windows that say POKOJE GOŚCINNE (guest rooms) or inquire at tourist information offices in resort towns.

The number of privately owned hotels and wayside motels has increased rapidly since 1989. Many of the more recent additions are smaller boutique hotels, but the number of hotels owned and managed by international chains is also growing. Orbis hotels—the former State-owned monopoly, now privatized—offers a standard of accommodations on a par with the international chains, usually at international prices. Standards at municipally owned hotels vary enormously; ask to see your room before checking in. Gromada cooperative runs excellent, inexpensive hotels. The Polish Tourist Association, PTTK, also has a network of very inexpensive hotels throughout Poland, but single and double rooms are limited in number, and most of the accommodations are in dormitories.

Room prices and standards can differ vastly. If you do your homework, you can find real bargains outside the major cities. Government star ratings (from five down to one) are outdated and refer to ownership category and size as much as to standards. They do, however, give an indication of price.

Service charges are included in the room price, as is a value-added tax (VAT) of 22%. Breakfast is included in most cases. The price does not necessarily reflect whether the bathroom has a tub or shower. Rates during the peak season on the coast (May–September) and in the southern mountain region (December–March and July–August) are up to 50% higher than off-season prices. Seasonal variations elsewhere in the country are less marked, apart from short-term increased rates for special occasions, such as in Poznań during the trade fair.

CATEGORY	COST*
$$$$	over zł 800
$$$	zł 400–zł 800
$$	zł 200–zł 400
$	under zł 200

*All prices are for two people in a double room, with a private bath and breakfast.

Music

Poland has a strong musical tradition, and in the big cities during the performance season (from October to May), you will have opportunities to hear outstanding musicians and orchestras—at very moderate prices. There are also a growing number of summer festivals to choose from. Cafés frequently host musical performances in the evenings, and many upmarket cafés have daytime pianists. Jazz is also popular, and jazz clubs can be found for all tastes in most larger towns.

Shopping

Poland is not yet a major shopping destination, though the country is well known for particular items. Leather products are well designed and cheaper than their Western counterparts. The best region for leather is the south: Kraków for more sophisticated products and the mountains for folk goods. Amber and silver jewelry are on sale all over Poland, but the best places to search for unusual pieces are on the Baltic coast. Wooden, woven, and embroidered folk arts and crafts are found in Cepelia stores all over Poland. Glassware, including cut glass, is beautifully designed and relatively cheap. And of course you can find Polish vodka (*wódka*) anywhere in the country. Polonez and Żytnia are clear rye vodkas; Żubrówka is pale green and flavored with bison grass from the Białowieska forest; Jarzębiak is flavored with rowan berries.

Exploring Poland

The savvy traveler will be enticed by Poland's delightful and wide variety of scenery and architecture. The silvery Baltic Sea coast and the Mazurian Lakes of the north lie 650 km (400 mi) from the towering Tatra Mountains of the south; in between are historic cities and castles. If you are using public transportation, Warsaw is the hub from which all fast trains radiate, and it is usually wise to begin and end your travels through Poland there.

Great Itineraries

IF YOU HAVE 3 DAYS

Begin in 🖼 **Warsaw,** taking in the city's Old Town—destroyed during the Second World War and reconstructed during the 1950s—as well as the baroque palace in Wilanów and the neoclassical palace in the Łazienki Park. On your second day, rent a car so that en route to Kraków you can visit 🖼 **Kazimierz Dolny,** a Renaissance village on the Vistula River, and catch at least a glimpse of Poland's lush countryside. Alternatively, you can go to Kraków by public transportation via 🖼 **Częstochowa,** where the 14th-century Pauline Monastery contains Poland's holiest relic: the icon of the Black Madonna. No matter how you get there, leave at least a whole day for 🖼 **Kraków,** the nation's capital before 1609. Its uniquely intact, medieval Old Town contains a wealth of works of art and is home to the university where Nicolaus Copernicus studied.

IF YOU HAVE 5 DAYS

Begin your stay in 🖼 **Gdańsk** and explore the historic Old Town, which was originally one of the main Hanseatic ports on the Baltic. By car, take the 1 (E75) and Route 50 to **Malbork** and see the vast castle that was the headquarters of the Teutonic Knights (to do this properly, you need at least half a day). From Malbork, rejoin the 1 (E75), and drop by another castle in Gniew before heading to 🖼 **Toruń,** a small walled town on the Vistula River and Copernicus's birthplace. From Toruń, take Route 10 and the 7 (E77) to Warsaw. This route can also be done easily by train. But if you instead wish to explore the Mazurian Lakes on your way to Warsaw, a car is essential: from Malbork, take the cross-country route via Dzierzgoń to Ostróda and then Route 16 to **Olsztyn,** before taking the 7 (E77) to Warsaw. After a day exploring Warsaw, make your way to Kraków. From here take a day-trip to **Zakopane,** two hours away by bus, on the way admiring the foothills of the Podhale region and the High Tatra range in the distance. A day in Zakopane will allow you to try regional cooking and get a feel for life in the mountains.

When to Tour

With its characteristically gray, cold weather and short daylight hours, the Polish winter may persuade you to spend your vacation in the Caribbean. Unless you are a skier, spring is a good time for intense, energetic sightseeing. Summers can be hot and humid, especially in southern Poland, but this is still the busiest tourist season. If you are interested in the arts, remember that theaters and concert halls close completely for the months of July and August and often do not get going with the new season's programs until October. The fabled Polish Golden Autumn, when the leaves do their thing, lasts until November and can be a good time for touring. The winter sports season is from December to March, when high-season rates are once again in effect in the mountains. In general, central heating is universal and efficient in Poland, but air-conditioning is a rarity.

WARSAW

Your first view of Warsaw (Warszawa) is likely to produce an impression of monotonous gray concrete, broken suddenly by a curious, wedding-cake edifice towering over the city: the Palace of Culture and Science, Stalin's early 1950s gift to the city. In the early 1990s, an American businessman wanted to purchase it to cut off the elaborate pinnacle and crenellated outbuildings and develop the remaining skyscraper into a business center. Suddenly, Warsovians, after decades of mocking this symbol of Russian imperialism, grudgingly admitted to a sentimental attachment. The entrepreneur's scheme fell through, and the Palace of Culture still stands to give visitors a useful orientation point.

Central Warsaw's predominating bleakness is a legacy of the tragedy that befell what had been, prior to World War II, a marvelous Central European city. Seventy-five percent of Warsaw was destroyed during a heroic uprising against the Nazis in 1944. Although rebuilt in the 1950s and 1960s in postwar "functional" styles, as economic times grew harder, it was largely left to decay. But as you start to explore, your initial reservations will fade away. Fragments of the Warsaw that survived the war acquire a special poignancy in their isolation: odd rows of Art Nouveau tenements, such as those on the south side of the great square around the Palace of Culture and on ulica Wilcza; the elegant aleje Ujazdowskie, now the diplomatic quarter, leading to the Belvedere Palace and the Łazienki Palace and Park. The reconstructed areas of the city—the historic Old Town area, rebuilt brick by brick in the 1950s; the Royal Castle; the Ujazdowski Castle—are moving tributes to the Poles' ability to survive and preserve their history.

Moreover, Warsaw is at last getting a face-lift, and the pace of change is so fast that even the locals can't keep up. The butcher shop where customers have faithfully lined up over the past 25 years closes down one evening only to be replaced the next day by a sleek, white-tiled computer outlet. The local grocery turns overnight into a well-lit boutique selling imported fashions at prices that former clients cannot afford. While some may live to regret the disappearance of the local shoemaker or tailor—those striking survivors whom Communism froze in a time warp—the new arrivals create a vibrant image. Visitors in search of old-world charm may be disappointed, but they can console themselves with the thought that the range of facilities available in many areas, especially for dining out, has improved tremendously. Future forward, the city is intent on resurrecting long-suppressed cultural activities, which can now be appreciated in an atmosphere of experimentation and possibility.

Exploring Warsaw

The geographical core and political center of Poland since 1611, when King Zygmunt III Waza moved the capital here from Kraków, Warsaw will doubtless shock the first-time visitor with its bleak postwar architecture. But the history of this city can turn dismay first to amazement and then to deep admiration for the surviving one-third of its inhabitants who so energetically rebuilt their city—literally from the ashes—starting in 1945. Warsaw was in the worst possible location during World War II, and perhaps nowhere else in Europe are there so many reminders of that time: plaques describing massacres of Poles by the Nazis are numerous. (The city's darkest hours came in April 1943, when the inhabitants of the Jewish ghetto rose up in arms against the Nazis and were brutally put down, and in the summer of 1944, when the Warsaw Uprising was ultimately defeated.)

Amid the drabness you will find a few architectural attractions. Although many of the buildings in central Warsaw were built in an austere, quasi-Gothic, Stalinist style, a large number of prewar buildings were carefully restored or, in many cases, completely reconstructed following clues in old prints and paintings. A case in point is the beautiful Rynek Starego Miasta (Old Town Square). The Zamek Królewski (Royal Castle), which houses a museum, is the greatest of the rebuilt monuments.

Apart from the embankment carved out by the Wisła (Vistula) River, which runs through the city south to north, Warsaw is entirely flat. Most sights, attractions, and hotels lie west of the river. Major thoroughfares include aleje Jerozolimskie, which runs east–west, and ulica Nowy Świat, which runs south–north through a main shopping district, passes the university, and ends at the entrance to the Stare Miasto (Old Town). Be careful about Nowy Świat: its name changes six times between its starting point in Wilanów (where it's called aleja Wilanowska) and its terminus (where it's named Krakowskie Przedmieście). To orient yourself, start at Central Station, the Marriott hotel (a glass skyscraper), or the Palace of Culture, all of which sit within a block of one another on aleje Jerozolimskie. Walk east toward the river on aleje Jerozolimskie two blocks to Nowy Świat. Heading north, this street is a main shopping district, closed to all traffic except buses, taxis, and government vehicles. In about 20 minutes the street (now called Krakowskie Przedmieście) will terminate at plac Zamkowy (Castle Square), the plaza that marks the entrance to the Old Town. North of this point is Nowe Miasto (New Town), primarily a residential area, and to the west lie Muranów and Mirów, former Jewish districts. Praga, a poorer quarter of workers and artisans that emerged from the war fairly intact, and the enormous Zoological Park are situated east of the Vistula River.

Numbers in the text correspond to numbers in the margin and on the Warsaw map.

Stare Miasto (Old Town) and Nowe Miasto (New Town)

The rebuilding of the historic Old Town, situated on an escarpment on the left bank of the Vistula, is a real phoenix-risen-from-the-ashes story. Postwar architects, determined to get it absolutely as it was before, turned to old prints, photographs in family albums, and paintings, in particular the detailed 18th-century views of Bernardo Bellotto (the nephew of Canaletto). Curiously, some of Bellotto's views were painted not from real life but from sketches of projects that were never realized. Whatever your feelings about reproduction architecture—and there's a lot of it in Warsaw—it seems to have worked. The Old Town is closed to traffic, and in its narrow streets you can leave the 21st century behind and relax for a while. Everything here is within easy walking distance. Just a short stroll beyond the Barbakan gate is the New Town, which also has sights well worth seeing.

A GOOD WALK

Begin at **plac Zamkowy** ①, first visiting the **Zamek Królewski** ②. Next make your way along narrow ulica Kanonia, and you'll find the great cracked Zygmunt bell in the middle of a quiet, cobbled square—exactly where it fell from the cathedral tower during the bombardment of 1939. Continue along ulica Jezuicka, turning through one of the archways to admire the view over the Vistula from the terrace that runs along the back of the houses. The **Rynek Starego Miasta** ③ is a place to relax and to take in buildings like the Klucznikowska Mansion at No. 21. (The Gothic brick portal and cellars of this structure, which now houses an elegant restaurant, are the originals from the 15th century.) Be sure to visit the **Muzeum Historyczna Warszawy** ④—don't miss its 20-minute film in English on the history of the city—and the **Muzeum Literatury im. Adama Mickiewicza** ⑤. Before leaving the square, take a look at the stone **Warszawska Syrenka** ⑥ in the fountain at its center; then head north along Krzywe Koło and the ramparts of the Old Town's walls to reach the **Barbakan** ⑦, marking the boundary between the Old and New Towns.

On ulica Freta you'll come upon the **Kościół Dominikanów** ⑧ and the house where Marie Curie Sklodowska was born, now the **Muzeum Marii Skłodowskiej-Curie** ⑨. Ulica Freta takes you to the **Rynek Nowego Miasta** ⑩, near which there are fine churches built from the 15th to 17th century, including **Kościół Najświętszej Marii Panny** ⑪ and the **Kościół Sakramentek** ⑫. Returning from the New Town, take ulica Świętojerska to plac Krasińskich, where you'll find the Baroque **Pałac Krasiński** ⑬ and the **Pomnik Bohaterów Warszawy 1939–1945** ⑭; then go back along ulica Długa to the Barbakan. Ulica Nowomiejska takes you back to the Rynek Starego Miasta, and then you can take ulica Świętojańska, with the **Kościół Jezuitów** ⑮ and the **Archikatedralna Bazylika świętego Jana** ⑯ on your left, to return to plac Zamkowy.

TIMING

The Old Town is not large in area. If you are content to admire the exteriors of buildings, you can easily see it in half a day. But to take it in fully you will need a whole day. At the Zamek Królewski, give yourself about three hours if you want to explore all of its exhibits. The Rynek Starego Miasta, with its cafés and restaurants, is a good place to relax in the evening.

SIGHTS TO SEE

⑯ **Archikatedralna Bazylika świętego Jana** (Cathedral of St. John). Ulica Świętojańska, leading from the Rynek Starego Miasta to the Zamek Królewski, takes its name from this cathedral, which was built at the turn of the 14th century; coronations of the Polish kings took place here from the 16th to 18th centuries. The crypts contain the tombs of the last two princes of Mazovia, the archbishops of Warsaw, and such famous Poles as the 19th-century novelist Henryk Sienkiewicz, the Nobel Prize–winning author of *Quo Vadis?* ✉ *Ul. Świętojańska 8, Stare Miasto.*

⑦ Barbakan. The pinnacled Barbakan, the mid-16th-century stronghold in the old city wall on ulica Freta, now marks the boundary between the Old Town and the New Town. From here you can see the partially restored wall that was built to enclose the Old Town. ✉ *Ul. Freta, Stare Miasto.*

⑧ Kościół Dominikanów (Dominican Church). This baroque church in the New Town was badly damaged in the aftermath of the 1943 uprising, when the adjoining monastery served as a field hospital for wounded insurrectionists. It was reconstructed in the 1950s. ✉ *Ul. Freta 8–10, Nowe Miasto.*

⑮ Kościół Jezuitów (Jesuit Church). On the left-hand side of the entrance to the Cathedral of St. John you'll find the early 17th-century Jesuit Church, founded by King Jan III Sobieski. Throughout the postwar years, a visit to this church at Eastertime was considered a must by Warsovians, and its Gethsemane decorations always contained a hidden political message. (In 1985 the risen Christ had the face of Father Jerzy Popiełuszko, the Warsaw priest murdered the previous year by the Polish secret police.) ✉ *On the east side of ul. Świętojańska, 1 block up from pl. Zamkowy, Stare Miasto.*

⑪ Kościół Najświętszej Marii Panny (St. Mary's Church). The oldest church in the New Town, St. Mary's was built as a parish church by the princes of Mazovia in the early 15th century. It has been destroyed and rebuilt many times throughout its history. ✉ *Przyrynek 2, Nowe Miasto.*

⑫ Kościół Sakramentek (Church of the Sisters of the Blessed Sacrament). Built as a thanksgiving offering by King Jan III Sobieski's queen, Marysieńka, after his victory against the Turks at Vienna in 1683, this cool, white church stands on the east side of Rynek Nowego Miasta (New Town Square). ✉ *Rynek Nowego Miasta 2, Nowe Miasto.*

④ Muzeum Historyczne Warszawy (Warsaw Historical Museum). Four fine examples of Renaissance mansions can be found on the northern side of the Old Town Square (note the sculpture of a black slave on the facade of No. 34, the **Negro House**). These historical homes, some of which contain Renaissance ceiling paintings, now house the Warsaw Historical Museum. The museum screens a short documentary film on the history of Warsaw daily at noon in English. ✉ *Rynek Starego Miasta 28–42, Stare Miasto,* ☎ *022/635–16–25,* WEB *www.gminacentrum.waw.pl/muzeum_historyczne.* 💳 *zł 8.* ⊘ *Tues. and Thurs. 11–5:30, Wed. and Fri. 11–3:30, weekends 10:30–4.*

⑤ Muzeum Literatury im. Adama Mickiewicza (Adam Mickiewicz Museum of Literature). Mickiewicz was Poland's greatest Romantic poet. He and other Polish writers are the focus of this museum of manuscripts, mementos, and portraits. The museum is closed on the first Sunday of each month. ✉ *Rynek Starego Miasta 20, Stare Miasto,* ☎ *022/831–40–61.* 💳 *zł 5.* ⊘ *Mon.–Tues. and Fri. 10–3, Wed.–Thurs. and Sat. 11–6, Sun. 11–5.*

⑨ Muzeum Marii Skłodowskiej-Curie (Marie Curie Museum). The house in which Marie Curie Sklodowska was born has a small museum inside dedicated to the great physicist, chemist, winner of two Nobel Prizes, and discoverer of radium. ✉ *Ul. Freta 16, Nowe Miasto,* ☎ *022/831–80–92.* 💳 *zł 6.* ⊘ *Tues.–Sat. 10–4, Sun. 10–2.*

⑬ Pałac Krasińskich (Krasiński Palace). This late-17th-century palace currently houses the historic-prints collection of Poland's National Library. It can be visited only by appointment. ✉ *Pl. Krasińskich 5, Nowe Miasto,* ☎ *022/831–32–41 tours.* 💳 *zł 12.*

386

Warsaw

NOWE MIASTO
(NEW TOWN)

Stawki

ul. Dzika

ul. Lewartowskiego

Generała Władysława Andersa

Bonifraterska

Franciszkańska

Świętojerska

ul. Świętojańska

Miodowa

MURANÓW

M. Anielewicza

ul. Zamenhofa

Nowolipki

Karmelicka

pl. Bankowy

Długa

STARE MIASTO
(OLD TOWN)

pl.
Teatralny

Senatorska

Wierzbowe

al. Solidarności

Elektoralna

Ogród
Saski

Królewska

Al. Jana Pawła II

Marszałkowska

Żelazna

Zielna

pl.
Grzybowski

Twarda

Świętokrzyska

Pereca

Pańska

Emilii Plater

pl.
Defilad

Prosta
Pańska

Sienna

Central
Station

Złota

al. Jerozolimskie

Chmielna

Poznańska

Towarowa

Emilii Plater

Wspólna

Hoża

KEY

ℹ️ Tourist Information

— Rail Lines

Koszykowa

0   750 yards

0   750 meters

al. Niepodległości

Nowowiejsk

Raszyńska

Filtrowa

Wawelska

Bonifraterska

a Dubois

Wałowa

Nowolipki

Miodowa

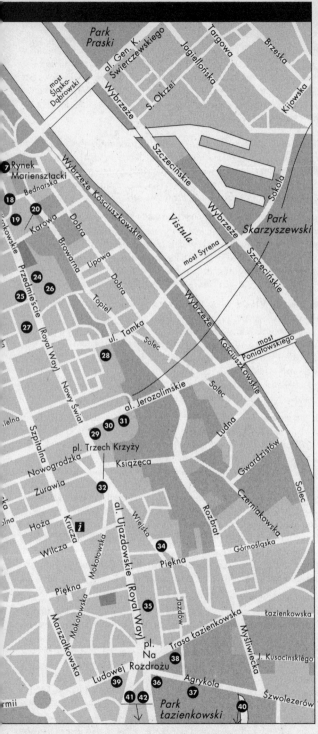

KOŚCIÓŁ ŚWIĘTEGO STANISŁAWA KOSTKI – In October 1984 Polish secret police officers murdered the popular parish priest Jerzy Popiełuszko
because of his sermons, which the Communist regime considered
gravely threatening. Thereafter the martyred Popiełuszko's church became the site of huge and very moving Solidarity meetings. You can visit
his grave on the grounds of this church north of the New Town. Take a
taxi or Bus 116 or 122 from ulica Bonifraterska to plac Wilsona; then
walk two blocks west along ulica Zygmunta Krasinskiego. ⊠ *Ul. Stanisława Hozjusza 2, Żoliborz.*

❶ Plac Zamkowy (Castle Square). Many visitors enter the Old Town
through this plaza area on the southern border of the district. You can't
miss the **Zygmunt Column,** which honors King Zygmunt III Waza, king
of Poland and Sweden, who in the early 17th century moved the capital to Warsaw from Kraków. ⊠ *Stare Miasto.*

⓮ Pomnik Bohaterów Warszawy 1939–1945 (Monument to the Heroes
of Warsaw). Unveiled in 1989, this monument constitutes a poignant
reminder of what World War II meant for the citizens of Warsaw. Massive bronze figures raise defiant fists above the sewer openings used
by Polish resistance fighters in Warsaw's Old Town to escape the Nazis
in 1944. ⊠ *Pl. Krasińkich and ul. Długa, Stare Miasto.*

⓾ Rynek Nowego Miasta (New Town Square). Warsaw's New Town was
actually founded at the turn of the 15th century. This part of the city,
however, was rebuilt after the war in 18th- and 19th-century styles and
has a more elegant and spacious feel about it than the Old Town. The
centerpiece of the district is the leafy New Town Square, slightly more
irregular and relaxed than its Old Town counterpart. The houses on
the square—and in such nearby streets as ulica Kościelna—have curiously stark and formalized wall paintings. ⊠ *Nowe Miasto.*

★ **❸ Rynek Starego Miasta** (Old Town Square). This is the hub of life in
Warsaw's Old Town. The earliest settlers arrived at this spot during
the 10th and 11th centuries. Legend has it that a peasant named Wars
was directed to the site by a mermaid named Sawa—hence the name
of the city in Polish, Warszawa. (Sawa has been immortalized in Warsaw's official emblem.) In the 14th century Warsaw was already a walled
city, and in 1413 its citizens obtained a borough charter from the
princes of Mazovia. The present layout of the Old Town dates from
that time, and traces of the original Gothic buildings still surround the
Old Town Square. The appearance of today's square, however, largely
dates from the 16th and early 17th centuries, when Warsaw's wealth
and importance grew rapidly as a result of the 1569 Polish-Lithuanian
union and Warsaw's new status as Poland's city.

The Old Town Square is usually very active, even though no traffic is
allowed and there is no longer a formal market. Artists and craftspeople
of all kinds still sell their wares here in the summer, but don't expect
many bargains—tourists are their prime targets. Musical performances
are often held here on weekends on a stage erected at the north end.
Horse-drawn cabs await visitors. To explore some of the square's
beautiful and historic houses, visit the Adam Mickiewicz Museum of
Literature on the east side of the square and the Warsaw Historical Museum on the north side. After being almost completely annihilated during World War II, these mansions were meticulously reconstructed using
old prints, plans, and paintings. For some of the best Gothic details,
look for No. 31, traditionally known as the House of the Mazovian
Dukes. At night the square is lit up romantically. If you're after good
food and atmosphere, this is one of Warsaw's best bets.

Krzywe Koło (Crooked Wheel Street) runs from the Old Town Square to the reconstructed ramparts of the city wall. From this corner you can see out over the Vistula and also over the New Town stretching to the north beyond the city walls. As you look out over the town walls and down the Vistula embankment, you will see the **Stara Prochownia** (Old Powder Tower), now a popular venue for poetry readings, music, and drama. ⊠ *Stare Miasto.*

❻ **Warszawska Syrenka** (Warsaw Mermaid). The mermaid is the symbol on the crest of the city of Warsaw. This particular stone statue had been traveling around the city for more than 70 years before in 2000 finding itself back where it was originally placed in 1855, in the center of a fountain in the Old Town Square. ⊠ *Stare Miasto.*

★ ❷ **Zamek Królewski** (Royal Castle). Warsaw's Royal Castle stands on the east side of Castle Square. The princes of Mazovia first built a residence on this spot overlooking the Vistula in the 14th century. Its present Renaissance form dates from the reign of King Zygmunt III Waza, who needed a magnificent palace for his new capital. Reconstructed in the 1970s, it now gleams as it did in its earliest years, with gilt, marble, and wall paintings. It also houses impressive collections of art—including the famous views of Warsaw by Canaletto's nephew Bernardo Bellotto (also known as Canaletto), which were used to rebuild the city after the war. Tours in English are available. ⊠ *Pl. Zamkowy 4, Stare Miasto,* ☎ *022/657–21–70.* 🎫 *zł 14.* ⊙ *Daily 10–4.*

NEED A
BREAK?

Kawiarnia Literacka (⊠ Krakowskie Przedmieście 87/89, Stare Miasto, ☎ 022/826–57–84), on the ground floor of the PEN club premises, is an airy café where you can listen to classic jazz on weekend evenings.

The Royal Route

All towns with kings had their "royal routes," and the one in Warsaw stretches south from Castle Square for 4 km (2½ mi), running through busy Krakowskie Przedmieście, along Nowy Świat, and on to the Park Łazienkowski (Łazienki Park). The route is lined with some of Warsaw's finest churches and palaces, but there are also landmarks of some of the city's most famous folk, including Frédéric Chopin. As a child Chopin played in the Kasimir Palace gardens, gave his first concert in the Radziwiłł Palace (now the Pałac Namiestnikowski [Presidential Palace]), then moved with his family to the building that now houses the city's Academy of Fine Arts. Today, the Chopin Society is headquartered in the Pałac Ostrogskich (Ostrogski Palace).

A GOOD WALK

The first stage of the route, from Castle Square to aleje Jerozolimskie, is about 3 km (2 mi). Krakowskie Przedmieście is a wide thoroughfare lined with fine churches and elegant mansions and palaces. First on the route is **Kościół świętej Anny** ⑰, on the south side of Castle Square, followed a block later by the **Pałac Kazanowskich** ⑱. From here you can make a detour down the hill via ulica Bednarska to the leafy 18th-century Rynek Mariensztacki (Mariensztat Square), a 10-minute walk. Back on Krakowskie Przedmieście, heading south, you come to the **Kościół Karmelitów** ⑲ and the **Pałac Namiestnikowski** ⑳.

Another detour—this one to the west along Królewska—brings you in two minutes to the wide-open spaces of the plac Piłsudskiego, site of the **Grób Nieznanego Żołnierza** ㉑ and the Teatr Wielki (Opera House). From the southwest corner of the square take ulica Mazowiecka south, passing the **Galeria Zachęta** ㉒ on your right; then turn right onto ulica Kredytowa. On your right is the 18th-century neoclassical Kościół Ewangelicko-Augsburski (J. B. Augsburg Protestant Community Church), which like Kościół świętego Aleksandra in plac Trzech Krzyży was modeled on Rome's pantheon. Across the street is the **Muzeum Etnograficzne** ㉓.

Retrace your steps to Krakowskie Przedmieście. Continuing south you pass the **Kościół Wizytek** ㉔, the **Pałac Czapskich** ㉕, and **Warsaw University** ㉖. Beyond the **Kościół świętego Krzyża** ㉗ the road narrows and becomes ulica Nowy Świat, a pedestrian precinct with elegant shops and cafés in 18th-century houses. You can detour down the hill to the east to the **Pałac Ostrogskich** ㉘, a 10-minute walk.

At the south end of ulica Nowy Świat you'll come to the massive **former headquarters of the Polish Communist Party** ㉙. East of this building you'll find the **Muzeum Narodowe** ㉚, in which you can easily spend half a day, and the **Muzeum Wojska Polskiego** ㉛. At the south end of plac Trzech Krzyży lies **Kościół świętego Aleksandra** ㉜, modeled on the Roman pantheon. If you have time, from the tram stop at the corner of Nowy Świat make the two-stop trip west along aleje Jerozolimskie to the **Pałac Kultury i Nauki** ㉝.

TIMING

Walking at a brisk pace, you can cover this route in an hour, but to soak in the sights along the way, allow a whole morning or afternoon.

SIGHTS TO SEE

㉙ **Former headquarters of the Polish Communist Party.** Anti-Communists love the irony of this once-despised symbol of oppression; for a decade after the Communist fall, until 2001, it was the seat of the Warsaw Stock Exchange. ⊠ *Al. Jerozolimskie and Nowy Świat, Royal Route.*

㉒ **Galeria Zachęta** (Zachęta Gallery). Built at the end of the 19th century by the Society for the Encouragement of the Fine Arts, this gallery has no permanent collection but organizes thought-provoking special exhibitions (primarily modern art) in high-ceilinged, well-lit halls. It was in this building in 1922 that the first president of the post–World War I Polish Republic, Gabriel Narutowicz, was assassinated by a right-wing fanatic. Admission costs to the exhibits vary. ⊠ *Pl. Małachowskiego 3, Royal Route,* ☎ *022/827–69–09,* WEB *www.ddg.com.pl/zacheta.* ☒ *Most exhibitions zł 20–zł 40.* ☉ *Tues.–Sun. 10–6.*

㉑ **Grób Nieznanego Żołnierza** (Tomb of the Unknown Soldier). Built as a memorial after World War I, the Tomb of the Unknown Soldier contains the body of a Polish soldier brought from the eastern battlefields of the Polish-Soviet war of 1919–1920—a war not much mentioned in the 45 years of Communist rule after World War II. Ceremonial changes of the guard take place at noon each Sunday; visitors may be surprised to see the Polish Army still using the goose step on such occasions. The memorial is a surviving fragment of the early 18th-century Saxon Palace, which used to stand here on the west side of plac Piłsudskiego. Behind the tomb are the delightful **Ogród Saski** (Saxon Gardens), which were once the palace's park and were designed by French and Saxon landscape gardeners. ⊠ *Pl. Piłsudskiego, Royal Route.*

㉙ **Kościół Karmelitów** (Church of the Discalced Carmelites). This late-17th-century baroque church sits at the back of a square off the main line of the street. ⊠ *Krakowskie Przedmieście 52, Royal Route.*

㉜ **Kościół świętego Aleksandra** (St. Alexander's Church). Built in the early 19th century as a replica of the Roman pantheon, St. Alexander's stands on an island in the middle of plac Trzech Krzyży, a name that is notoriously difficult for foreigners to pronounce and means "Three Crosses Square." One of the crosses is on the church itself. ⊠ *Pl. Trzech Krzyży, Royal Route.*

27 **Kościół świętego Krzyża** (Holy Cross Church). The heart of Poland's most famous composer, Frédéric Chopin, is immured in a pillar inside this baroque church. Atop the church steps is a massive, sculpted crucifix. Across from the church is the **statue of Nicolaus Copernicus,** standing in front of the neoclassical Staszic Palace, the headquarters of the Polish Academy of Sciences. Like many other notable Warsaw monuments, this statue is the work of the 19th-century Danish sculptor Bertel Thorvaldsen. ✉ *Krakowskie Przedmieście 3, Royal Route.*

17 **Kościół świętej Anny** (St. Anne's Church). Built in 1454 by Anne, princess of Mazovia, the church stands on the south corner of Castle Square. It was rebuilt in high-baroque style after being destroyed during the Swedish invasions of the 17th century, and thanks to 1990s redecoration and regilding it glows once again. A plaque on the wall outside marks the spot where Pope John Paul II celebrated mass in 1980, during his first visit to Poland after his election to the papacy. ✉ *Krakowskie Przedmieście 68, Royal Route.*

24 **Kościół Wizytek** (Church of the Visitation Sisters). In front of this late-baroque church stands a statue of Cardinal Stefan Wyszyński, primate of Poland from 1948 to 1981. Wyszyński was imprisoned during the 1950s but lived to see a Polish pope and the birth of Solidarity. The fresh flowers always lying at the foot of the statue are evidence of the warmth with which he is remembered. ✉ *Krakowskie Przedmieście 30, Royal Route.*

23 **Muzeum Etnograficzne** (Ethnographic Museum). On display here you'll find an interesting collection of Polish folk art, crafts, and costumes from all parts of the country. ✉ *Ul. Kredytowa 1, Royal Route,* ☎ *022/827–76–41.* 🖾 *zł 4, free Wed.* ☉ *Tues. and Thurs.–Fri. 9–4, Wed. 11–6, weekends 10–5.*

★ **30** **Muzeum Narodowe** (National Museum of Warsaw). In a functional 1930s building, the National Museum has an impressive collection of contemporary Polish and European paintings, Gothic icons, and works from antiquity. It's usually closed on the day after a major holiday. ✉ *Al. Jerozolimskie 3, Royal Route,* ☎ *022/621–10–31,* 🆆🅴🅱 *www.ddg.com.pl/nm.* 🖾 *zł 13, free Wed.* ☉ *Tues.–Wed. and Fri. 10–4, Thurs. noon–5, weekends 10–5.*

31 **Muzeum Wojska Polskiego** (Polish Army Museum). If you're interested in all things military, you might want to visit this museum's exhibits of weaponry, armor, and uniforms, which trace Polish military history for the past 10 centuries. Heavy armaments are displayed outside. ✉ *Al. Jerozolimskie 3, Royal Route,* ☎ *022/629–52–71.* 🖾 *zł 10; free Wed.* ☉ *May–Sept., Wed.–Sun. 11–5; Oct.–Apr., Wed.–Sun. 10–4.*

NEED A BREAK? **Blikle** (✉ Nowy Świat 35, Royal Route), Warsaw's oldest cake shop, has a black-and-white-tile café that serves savory snacks as well as Blikle's famous doughnuts.

25 **Pałac Czapskich** (Czapski Palace). Now the home of the Academy of Fine Arts, the Czapski Palace dates from the late 17th century but was rebuilt in 1740 in the rococo style. Zygmunt Krasiński, the Polish romantic poet, was born here in 1812, and Chopin once lived in the palace mews. ✉ *Krakowskie Przedmieście 5, Royal Route.*

18 **Pałac Kazanowskich** (Kazanowski Palace). This 17th-century palace was given a neoclassical front elevation in the 19th century. The courtyard at the rear still contains massive late-Renaissance buttresses and is worth a visit because of its plaque commemorating Zagloba's fight with the monkeys, from Sienkiewicz's historical novel *The Deluge*. In a small garden in front of the palace stands a **monument to Adam Mickiewicz,** the great Polish romantic poet. It was here that Warsaw University students gathered in March 1968, after a performance of Mickiewicz's hitherto banned play *Forefathers' Eve,* which set in motion the events that led to the fall of Poland's Communist leader Władysław Gomułka, a wave of student protests, and a regime-sponsored anti-Semitic campaign. Unfortunately, you cannot visit the interior. ⊠ *Krakowskie Przedmieście 62, Royal Route.*

🖐 ㉝ **Pałac Kultury i Nauki** (Palace of Culture and Science). This massive Stalinist-Gothic structure looks like a wedding cake and is the main landmark in the city. From the 30th floor you can get a panoramic view. The old joke runs that this is Warsaw's best view because it is the only place where you can't see the palace. To view all of urban Warsaw from 700 ft up, buy tickets at the booth near the east entrance. The building houses a number of facilities, including a swimming pool and the **Museum of Science and Technology.** Also in the palace is the **Teatr Lalek,** a good puppet theater (the entrance is on the north side). ⊠ *Pl. Defilad 1, Royal Route,* ☎ *022/620–02–11; 022/620–49–50 (theater).* 🎫 *zł 7.5.* ☉ *Daily 9–6.*

㉟ **Pałac Namiestnikowski** (Presidential Palace). This palace was built in the 17th century by the Radziwiłł family (into which Jackie Kennedy's sister Lee later married). In the 19th century it functioned as the administrative office of the czarist occupiers—hence its present name. In 1955 the Warsaw Pact was signed here; later the palace served as the headquarters for the Presidium of the Council of Ministers, and since 1995 it has been the official residence of Poland's president. In the forecourt is an **equestrian statue of Prince Józef Poniatowski,** a nephew of the last king of Poland and one of Napoléon's marshals. He was wounded and drowned in the Elster River during the Battle of Leipzig in 1813, following the disastrous retreat of Napoléon's Grande Armée from Russia. ⊠ *Krakowskie Przedmieście 46–48, Royal Route.*

㉘ **Pałac Ostrogskich** (Ostrogski Palace). The headquarters of the Towarzystwo im. Fryderyka Chopina (Chopin Society) is in this 17th-century palace, which towers above ulica Tamka. The best approach is via the steps from ulica Tamka. In the 19th century the Warsaw Conservatory was housed here (Ignacy Paderewski was one of its students). Now a venue for Chopin concerts, it is also home to the **Muzeum Fryderyka Chopina** (Frédéric Chopin Museum), a small collection of mementos, including the last piano played by the composer. The works of Chopin (1810–1849) took their roots from folk rhythms and melodies of exclusively Polish invention. Thanks to Chopin, Poland could fairly claim to have been the fountainhead of popular music in Europe, and the composer's polonaises and mazurkas whirled their way around the continent in the mid-19th century. ⊠ *Ul. Okólnik 1, Royal Route,* ☎ *022/827–54–71.* 🎫 *Free.* ☉ *Mon.–Sat. 10–2, Thurs. noon–6.*

NEED A BREAK?   **Nowy Świat** (⊠ Nowy Świat 63, Royal Route), on the corner of Nowy Świat and ulica Świętokrzyska, is a spacious, traditional café, with plenty of foreign-language newspapers for those who want to linger over coffee.

㉖ **Warsaw University.** The high wrought-iron gates of Warsaw University lead into a leafy campus. The **Pałac Kazimierzowski** (Kazimierzowski Palace) currently houses the university administration; in the 18th century it was the Military Cadet School where Tadeusz Kościuszko studied. ⊠ *Krakowskie Przedmieście 26–28, Royal Route.*

The Diplomatic Quarter
and Park Łazienkowski (Łazienki Park)

In the 19th century smart carriages and riders eager to be seen thronged aleje Ujazdowskie. Today the avenue is a favorite with Sunday strollers. It leads to the beautiful Łazienki Park and the white Pałac Łazienkowski (Łazienki Palace), the private residence of the last king of Poland.

A GOOD WALK

The diplomatic quarter and Łazienki Park lie along the Royal Route leading from the Old Town to Wilanów. From plac Trzech Krzyży it is about 3 km (2 mi) to the southern edge of the park. Start your walk at the north end of aleje Ujazdowskie, where during the 19th century the rich built residences, many of which now house foreign embassies. A five-minute walk down ulica Wiejska, on your left, brings you to the **Sejm** ㉞. As you continue south you may choose to stroll under the trees of the **Park Ujazdowski** ㉟, parallel to aleje Ujazdowskie below ulica Piękna and farther from the traffic. At plac Na Rozdrożu you leave the diplomatic quarter and enter Warsaw's Whitehall. On your left are the **Botanical Gardens** ㊱ and **Park Łazienkowski** ㊲. If you are interested in modern art, **Zamek Ujazdowski** ㊳, home of the Center for Contemporary Art, is 600 ft east of the intersection, down a path through the park parallel to the Trasa Łazienkowska. The wartime **Gestapo headquarters** ㊴ is 600 ft southwest of plac Na Rozdrożu on aleje Szucha. To reach the **Pałac Łazienkowski** ㊵, go south on aleje Ujazdowskie from plac Na Rozdrożu about 1 km (½ mi). Enter by the gates opposite ulica Bagatela, beside the **Pałac Belweder** ㊶.

At the top of the hill of the Vistula embankment, across from Pałac Belweder at ulica Bagatela, you can board Bus 116, 180, or E-2 for **Pałac Wilanów** ㊷. (The rest of the Royal Route, which until the 1980s ran through open countryside, is now lined with housing developments.)

TIMING

Take a morning or afternoon to explore this route. If you wish to linger at some of the sights, make it a whole day: Łazienki Park and the Łazienki Palace deserve three or four hours at the least. This tree-lined walk is good for a hot summer day.

SIGHTS TO SEE

㊱ **Botanical Gardens.** These gardens, covering an area of roughly 3 acres, were laid out in 1818. At the entrance stands the neoclassical **observatory**, now part of Warsaw University. ⊠ *Al. Ujazdowskie 4, Łazienkowski.* 🎟 *Free.* ☉ *Daily dawn–dusk.*

㊴ **Gestapo headquarters.** The building that currently houses the Ministry of Education was the Gestapo headquarters during World War II. A small museum details the horrors that took place behind its peaceful facade. ⊠ *Al. Szucha 25, Łazienkowski,* ☎ *022/629–49–19.* 🎟 *Free.* ☉ *Wed. 9–5, Thurs. and Sat. 9–4, Fri. 10–5, Sun. 10–4.*

㊶ **Pałac Belweder** (Belvedere Palace). Built in the early 18th century, the palace was reconstructed in 1818 in neoclassical style by the Russian governor of Poland, the grand duke Constantine. Until 1994 it was the official residence of Poland's president. Belvedere Palace stands just south of the main gates to Łazienki Park. ⊠ *Ul. Belwederska 2, Łazienkowski.*

★ ㊵ **Pałac Łazienkowski** (Łazienki Palace). This magnificent palace is the focal point of the Park Łazienkowski. This neoclassical summer residence was so faithfully reconstructed after the war that there is still no electricity—be sure to visit when it's sunny, or you won't see anything of the interior. The palace has some splendid 18th-century furniture as well as part of the art collection of King Słanisław August

Poniatowski. ✉ *Ul. Agrykola 1, Łazienkowski,* ☎ *022/621–62–41.* 🎫 *zł 10.* ⏲ *Tues.–Sun. 10–3:15.*

★ 42 **Pałac Wilanów** (Wilanów Palace). A baroque gateway and false moat lead to the wide courtyard that stretches along the front of Wilanów Palace, built between 1681 and 1696 by King Jan III Sobieski. After his death, the palace passed through various hands before it was bought at the end of the 18th century by Stanisław Kostka Potocki, who amassed a major art collection, laid out the gardens, and opened the first public museum here in 1805. Potocki's neo-Gothic tomb can be seen to the left of the driveway as you approach the palace. The palace interiors still hold much of the original furniture; there's also a striking display of 16th- to 18th-century Polish portraits on the first floor. English-speaking guides are available.

Outside of the Pałac Wilanów, to the left of the main entrance, is a romantic **park** with pagodas, summerhouses, and bridges overlooking a lake. Behind the palace is a formal Italian garden from which you can admire the magnificent gilt decoration on the palace walls. There's also a gallery of contemporary Polish art on the grounds. Stables to the right of the entrance now house a poster gallery, the Muzeum Plakatu. The latter is well worth visiting, for this is a branch of art in which Poles have historically excelled. ✉ *Ul. Wiertnicza 1, Wilanów,* ☎ *022/842–81–01,* WEB *www.wilanow-palac.art.pl.* 🎫 *Palace zł 15; park zł 3, free Thurs.* ⏲ *Palace Tues.–Sun. 9:30–2:30, Sun. until 6* PM *mid-June–mid-Sept.; park daily 9–dusk.*

37 **Park Łazienkowski** (Łazienki Park). The 180 acres of this park, commissioned during the late 18th century by King Słanisław August Poniatowski, run along the Vistula escarpment, parallel to the Royal Route. Look for the peacocks that wander through the park and the delicate red squirrels that in Poland answer to the name Basia, a diminutive of Barbara. In the old coach houses on the east side of the park you'll find the **Muzeum Łowiectwa i Jezdziectwa** (Museum of Hunting; ☎ 022/621–62–41), which contains a collection of stuffed birds and animals native to Poland. It is open Tuesday–Sunday 10–3; admission is zł5. One of the most beloved sights in Łazienki Park is the **Pomnik Frydericka Chopina** (Chopin Memorial), a sculpture under a streaming willow tree that shows the composer in a typical romantic pose. In summer, outdoor concerts of Chopin's piano music are held here every Sunday afternoon. ✉ *Al. Ujazdowskie, Łazienkowski.*

35 **Park Ujazdowski** (Ujazdów Park). At the entrance to the formal gardens, there is a **19th-century weighing booth,** just inside the gate, still in operation. There is also a well-equipped **playground** for small children, with sand, swings, and slides. ✉ *Corner of aleje Ujazdowskie and ulica Piękna, Diplomatic Quarter.*

34 **Sejm.** The Polish Houses of the Sejm (parliament) are housed in a round, white debating chamber that was built during the 1920s, after the rebirth of an independent Polish state. ✉ *Ul. Wiejska 6, Diplomatic Quarter.*

NEED A BREAK? **Modulor Cafe** (✉ pl. Trzech Krzyży 2, Diplomatic Quarter), up the street from the Sheraton, has great coffee and a variety of fresh-squeezed juices.

38 **Zamek Ujazdowski** (Ujazdowski Castle). If you are interested in modern art, you will find it in the somewhat unlikely setting of this 18th-century castle, reconstructed in the 1980s. Now the home of the **Center for Contemporary Art,** the castle hosts a variety of exhibitions by Pol-

ish, European, and North American artists. ✉ *Al. Ujazdowskie 6, Łazienkowski,* ☎ *022/628–12–71.* 🎫 *zł 4, free Thurs.* ⊙ *Tues.–Thurs. and weekends 11–5, Fri. 11–9.*

Jewish Warsaw

The quiet streets of Mirów and Muranów, which now contain mostly apartment buildings, once housed the largest Jewish population in Europe: about 380,000 people in 1939. The Nazis sealed off this area from the rest of the city on November 15, 1940, and the congested area became rapidly less populated as people died from starvation and disease. Between July and September 1942, the Nazis deported about 300,000 ghetto residents to the death camp at Treblinka. On April 19, 1943, the remaining inhabitants instigated the Warsaw Ghetto Uprising. Children threw homemade bombs at tanks, and men and women fought soldiers hand to hand. In the end, almost all of those remaining died in the uprising or fled through the sewers to the "Aryan side."

A GOOD WALK

The wartime ghetto area is northwest of Warsaw's Old Town. Begin on ulica Sienna to see the **fragment of ghetto wall** ㊸. Walk north along aleje Jana Pawła II until you reach ulica Twarda; then turn right. Go past a synagogue and across plac Grzybowski to **ulica Próżna** ㊹. Head east through a small market area to ulica Marszałkowska and take a left to reach plac Bankowy and the **Jewish Historical Institute and Museum** ㊺. From here, walk west along aleje Solidarności toward aleje Jana Pawła II, passing the **Femina cinema** ㊻ on your left. Turn north on aleje Jana Pawła II and walk to ulica Mordechaja Anielewicza; turn right here to reach the monument **Pomnik Bohaterów Getta** ㊼. From here take ulica Karmelicka north to ulica Stawki, where you'll find the **Umschlagplatz** ㊽. (Trams run along aleje Jana Pawła II to help you on your route.) From Umschlagplatz follow ulica Dzika north around the bend. After the intersection with aleje Jana Pawła II, continue west on ulica Dzika to ulica Okopowa. From this corner you can take any tram south along ulica Okopowa to reach the **Jewish Cemetery** ㊾.

TIMING

It is possible to see all of the sights in a few hours, although this would involve some energetic walking. If you allow a whole day, you'll have time for reflection and a full exploration of the cemetery.

SIGHTS TO SEE

㊻ **Femina cinema.** Before the war this area was the heart of Warsaw's Jewish quarter, which was walled off by the Nazis in November 1940 to isolate the Jewish community from "Aryan" Warsaw. The cinema is one of the few buildings in this district that survived the war. It was here that the ghetto orchestra organized concerts in 1941 and 1942. Many outstanding musicians found themselves behind the ghetto walls and continued to make music despite the dangers. ✉ *Al. Solidarności 115, Muranów.*

㊸ **Fragment of ghetto wall.** In the courtyard of this building, through the archway on the left, stands a 10-ft-tall fragment of the infamous ghetto wall that existed for one year from November 1940. ✉ *Ul. Sienna 55, Muranów*

㊾ **Jewish Cemetery.** Behind a high brick wall on ulica Okopowa you will find Warsaw's Jewish Cemetery, an island of continuity amid so much destruction of the city's Jewish heritage. The cemetery, which is still in use, survived the war, and although it was neglected and became badly overgrown during the postwar period, it is gradually being restored. Here you will find 19th-century headstones and much that testifies to the Jewish community's role in Polish history and culture. Ludwik

Zamenhof, the creator of the artificial language Esperanto, is buried here, as are Henryk Wohl, minister of the treasury in the national government during the 1864 uprising against Russian rule; Szymon Askenazy, the historian and diplomat; Hipolit Wawelberg, the cofounder of Warsaw Polytechnic; and poet Bolesław Leśmian. To reach the cemetery, take Bus 107, 111, or 516 from plac Bankowy. ☒ *Ul. Okopowa 49–51, Muranów.*

㊺ Jewish Historical Institute and Museum. You'll find the institute behind a glittering new office block on the southeast corner of plac Bankowy—the site of what had been the largest temple in Warsaw, the Tłomackie Synagogue. For those seeking to investigate their family history, the institute houses the **Ronald S. Lauder Foundation Genealogy Project,** which acts as a clearinghouse of information on available archival resources and on the history of towns and villages in which Polish Jews resided. English-speaking staff members are available. The institute also houses a museum that displays a permanent collection of mementos and artifacts and periodically organizes special exhibitions. ☒ *Ul. Tłomackie 3, Muranów,* ☎ *022/827–92–21,* WEB *www.jewishinstitute.org.pl.* ✉ *Free.* ☉ *Tues.–Fri. 10–6.*

㊼ Pomnik Bohaterów Getta (Monument to the Heroes of the Warsaw Ghetto). On April 19, 1943, the Jewish Fighting Organization began an uprising in a desperate attempt to resist the mass transports to Treblinka that had been taking place since the beginning of that year. Though doomed from the start, the brave ghetto fighters managed to keep up their struggle for a whole month. But by May 16, General Jürgen Stroop could report to his superior officer that "the former Jewish district in Warsaw had ceased to exist." The ghetto had become a smoldering ruin, razed by Nazi flamethrowers. A monument marks the location of the house at nearby **ulica Miła 18,** the site of the uprising's command bunker and where its leader, Mordechai Anielewicz, was killed. ☒ *Ul. Zamenhofa between ul. M. Anielewicza and ul. Lewartowskiego, Muranów.*

OFF THE
BEATEN PATH

POWĄZKI CEMETERY – Dating from 1790, Warsaw's oldest cemetery is worth a visit if you are in a reflective mood. Many well-known Polish names appear on the often elaborate headstones and tombs. There is also a recent memorial to the victims of the Katyn Massacre, when 4,000 Polish servicemen, who had been taken prisoner when the Soviets were still aligned with the Nazis, were murdered by the Soviet army on orders from Stalin in 1940 in the Katyn Forest. Enter from ulica Powązkowska. ☒ *Ul. Powązkowska 43–45, Muranów, next to the Jewish Cemetery.* ☉ *Sun.–Thurs. 9–3, Fri. 9–1.*

㊹ Ulica Próżna. This is the only street in Jewish Warsaw where tenement buildings have been preserved on both sides of the street. The Lauder Foundation has instigated a plan to restore the street to its original state. No. 9 belonged to Zelman Nożyk, founder of the ghetto synagogue. ☒ *Muranów.*

㊽ Umschlagplatz. This plaza was the rail terminus from which tens of thousands of the ghetto's inhabitants were shipped in cattle cars to the extermination camp of Treblinka, about 100 km (60 mi) northeast of Warsaw. The school building to the right of the square was used to detain those who had to wait overnight for transport; the beginning of the rail tracks survives on the right. At the entrance to the square is a memorial gateway, erected in 1988 on the 45th anniversary of the uprising. ☒ *Ul. Stawki and ul. Dzika, Muranów.*

OFF THE
BEATEN PATH

CHOPIN AND RADZIWIŁŁ ESTATES – If you have an extra day in Warsaw, a trip to the Puszcza Kampinoska (Kampinoski National Park), located about an hour west of the city, is highly recommended, for two of Warsaw's loveliest abodes are situated here: the birthplace of Chopin and the Radziwiłł country estate. The best way to view these two sights quickly is to take one of the many available tours. Both places can also be reached by bus from Warsaw's main bus station.

Żelazowa Wola (☎ 046/863–33–00 or 046/838–56–20) is a mecca for all Chopin lovers. The composer's birthplace, a small 19th-century manor house, is filled with original furnishings and is devoted to Chopin's life. Admission is zł 6, and it's open Tuesday–Sunday 9–4; on summer Sundays, concerts are held on the terrace at 11 AM and 3 PM. If driving, go 30 km (18½ mi) west of Warsaw on the 2 (E30), and at Sochaczew turn north on Route 580.

Nieborów (☎ 046/863–33–00 or 046/838–56–20), the stunning country estate of the Radziwiłł family, is centered on a baroque palace designed by Tilman van Gameren in the late 17th century. In 1945, the estate was taken over by the National Museum of Warsaw, and it still contains its historic furnishings. Admission is zł 6, and it's open Tuesday–Friday 10–4. The palace contains a small hotel (book ahead; no children allowed). To get here from Żelazowa Wola, return to the 2 (E30) and drive west to Łowicz; then take Route 70 southeast about 10 km (6 mi).

Dining

Like everything else in Warsaw, the dining scene is changing rapidly. New restaurants serve ethnic cuisine (Korean, Japanese, Chinese, and Italian are particularly popular), while others spin such hip variations as "Peasant Chic" and "Light Old Polish." Gone are the old, seedy bars, and in are clean and brightly tiled pizza parlors. Prices have risen spectacularly, and eating out in Warsaw is much more expensive than in other Polish cities. Check the price of the wine before ordering, as restaurants sometimes charge astronomical prices for an ordinary bottle. For the higher-priced dining spots, it is essential to make reservations. Almost all restaurants are closed on public holidays.

$$$–$$$$ ✕ **Belvedere.** You could not find a more romantic setting for lunch or
★ dinner than this elegant restaurant in the New Orangery at Łazienki Park. The lamp-lit park spreads out beyond the windows, and candles glitter below the high ceilings. Polish cuisine is a specialty, and many dishes are prepared with a variety of fresh mushrooms; try the mushroom soup. Also recommended is the roast boar, served with an assortment of vegetables. ⊠ *Łazienki Park, ul. Agrykola 1, Łazienki, enter from ul. Parkowa or ul. Gargarina,* ☎ *022/841–48–06. Jacket and tie. Reservations essential. AE, DC, MC, V.*

$$$–$$$$ ✕ **Dom Restauracyjny Gessler.** Come here partly for the atmospheric setting: a warren of candlelit bare-brick cellars and ground-floor rooms in one of the historic houses on the Rynek Starego Miasta (Old Town Square). Start with *łosoś książąt polskich* (salmon, Polish-prince-style, cooked in cream) or *bulion z kołdunami* (broth with dumplings). Then try duck in a marjoram-based sauce, served with noodles. ⊠ *Rynek Starego Miasta 19–21, Stare Miasto,* ☎ *022/831–44–27. Reservations essential. AE, DC, MC, V.*

$$$–$$$$ ✕ **Fukier.** This long-established wine bar on the Old Town Square has become a fascinating network of elaborately decorated dining rooms. There is a talking parrot in a cage, and candles adorn all available shelf space (sometimes set dangerously close to diners' elbows). The food is "Light Old Polish." Steak, served on a grill, is a specialty; follow it

398

Warsaw Dining and Lodging

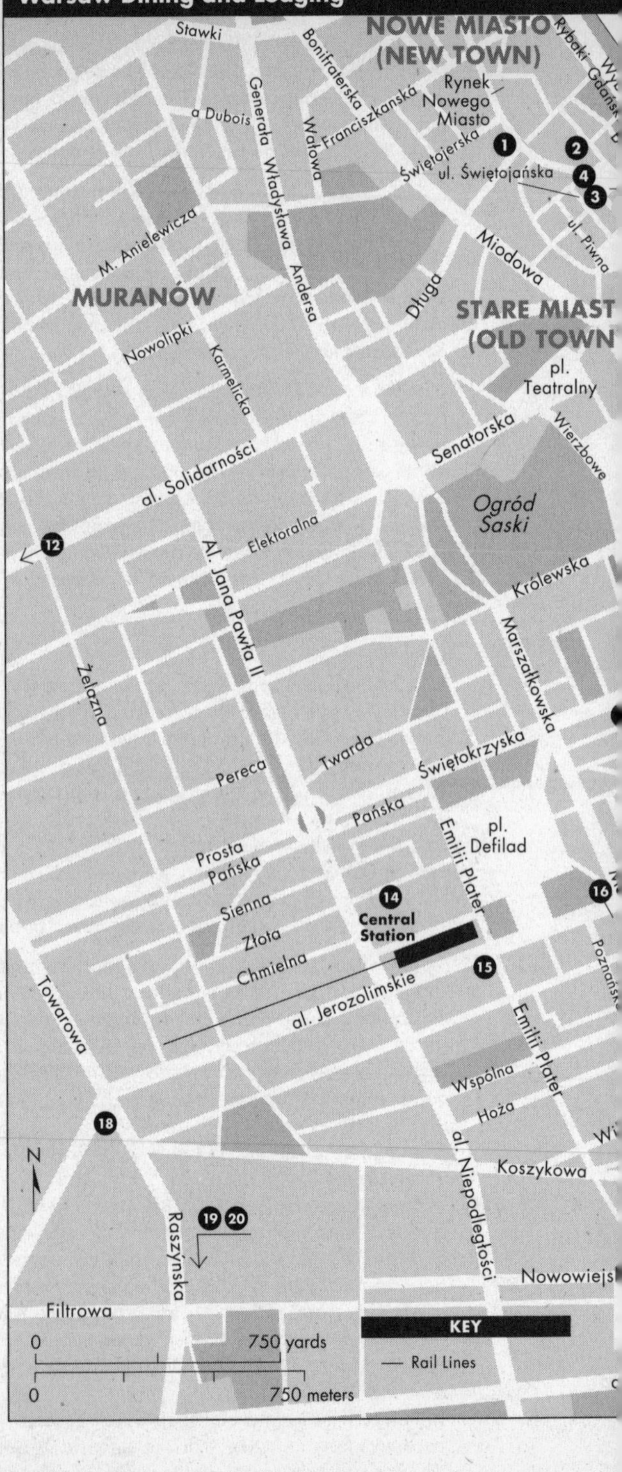

NOWE MIASTO (NEW TOWN)

MURANÓW

STARE MIAST (OLD TOWN)

Ogród Saski

Central Station

KEY

— Rail Lines

0   750 yards
0   750 meters

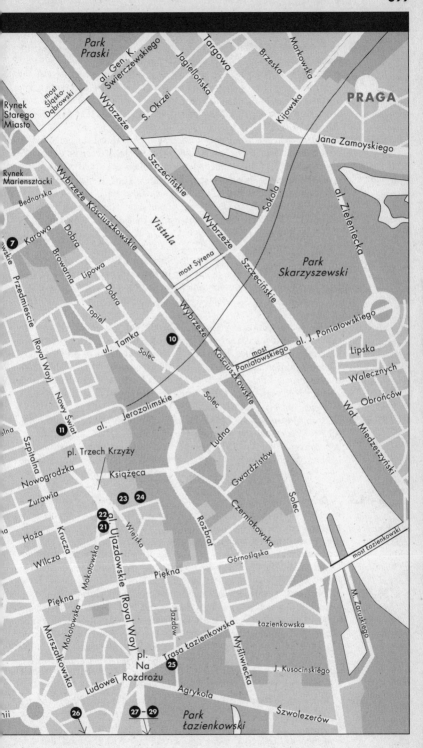

Park Praski

al. Gen. K. Świerczewskiego

Jagiellońska

Targowa

Brzeska

Markowska

PRAGA

Rynek Starego Miasto

Wybrzeże

S. Okrzei

Kijowska

Jana Zamoyskiego

Rynek Mariensztacki

Wybrzeże Kościuszkowskie

Szczecińskie

Sokola

al. Zieleniecka

Bednarska

Vistula

Wybrzeże

Szczecińskie

Park Skarzyszewski

7

Karowa

Dobra

Lipowa

most Syrena

Browarna

Przedmieście (Royal Way)

Dobra

Topiel

Wybrzeże

al. J. Poniatowskiego

Lipska

Waleczných

ul. Tamka

Solec

10

Kościuszkowskie

most Poniatowskiego

Obrońców

Nowy Świat

Jerozolimskie

Solec

Wał Miedzeszyński

Ilna

Szpitalna

al.

11

Solec

pl. Trzech Krzyży

Ludna

Nowogrodzka

Książęca

Gwardzistów

Żurawia

23

24

Czerniakowska

Solec

Hoża

22

21

al. Ujazdowskie (Royal Way)

Wiejska

Rozbrat

Krucza

Mokotowska

Wilcza

Piękna

Górnośląska

most Łazienkowski

Piękna

Mokotowska

Jazdów

Łazienkowska

M. Zaruskiego

Marszałkowska

Trasa Łazienkowska

Myśliwiecka

Ludowej

pl. Na

25

J. Kusocińskiego

Rozdrożu

Agrykola

26

27–29

Park Łazienkowski

Szwolezerów

nii

with one of the rich cream gâteaux. ☒ *Rynek Starego Miasta 27, Stare Miasto,* ☎ *022/831–10–13. Reservations essential. AE, DC, MC, V.*

$$$–$$$$ ✗ **Kamienne Schodki.** This restaurant with a vaulted ceiling in a 16th-century house on the corner of the Old Town Square is famous for its roast duck served with apples (actually, for a long time this was the only dish offered). The chicken or pork *à la polonaise* with garlic stuffing is also quite good. Save room for the light and creamy pastries. ☒ *Rynek Starego Miasta 26, Stare Miasto,* ☎ *022/831–08–22. AE, DC, MC, V.*

$$–$$$$ ✗ **Bazyliszek.** A second-floor restaurant in a 17th-century merchant's house on the Old Town Square, this place has long received top marks for atmosphere. You'll dine under high ceilings of carved wood. In the Knight's Room suits of armor and crossed swords decorate the walls. The restaurant serves traditional Polish fare, with an emphasis on game dishes. Try the stewed hare in cream sauce, served with beets and noodles. There is a good café downstairs that offers cheaper food. ☒ *Rynek Starego Miasta 3/9, Stare Miasto,* ☎ *022/831–18–41. Reservations essential. AE, DC, MC, V.*

$$–$$$$ ✗ **Café Ejlat.** This Warsaw institution, owned by the Polish-Israeli Friendship Society, has a menu rich in Jewish specialties (including a halvah dessert) and contemporary Polish dishes. ☒ *Al. Ujazdowskie 47, Srodmiescie,* ☎ *022/628–54–72. Reservations essential. AE, DC, MC, V.*

$$–$$$$ ✗ **Flik.** Set on a corner overlooking the Morskie Oko Park, this restaurant in Mokotów has a lovely geranium-frilled terrace. The dining room has well-spaced tables, light cane furniture, and lots of greenery. Try the fresh salmon starter followed by *zrazy* (rolled beef fillet stuffed with mushrooms). There is a self-service salad bar, and downstairs is a small, casual café. ☒ *Ul. Puławska 43, Morskie Oko Park,* ☎ *022/ 849–44–34. AE, DC, MC, V.*

$$–$$$$ ✗ **Klub Aktora.** An "in" place for expats and hip Warsovians, the Aktora thrives under the watchful eye of Stanisław Pruszyński, who escaped from Poland in 1955 to become a restaurateur in Canada, only to return to Poland after Communism fell. The most chic time to come may be afternoon tea. ☒ *Al. Ujazdowskie 45, Łazienki,* ☎ *022/628– 93–66. AE, DC, MC, V.*

$$–$$$$ ✗ **Qchnia Artystyczna.** This artsy place at the back of the Zamek Ujazdowski (Ujazdowski Castle) is not for the stodgy. The service is terrible, but the mainly vegetarian menu is creative and filling. Sample the *naleśniki* (crepes stuffed with sweet cheese or fruit). In summer, outdoor tables overlook a magnificent view of the park. ☒ *Zamek Ujazdowski, al. Ujazdowskie 6, Łazienki,* ☎ *022/625–76–27. AE, DC, MC, V.*

$$–$$$$ ✗ **Organza.** This trendy bar, restaurant, and night club—all in one—is quite a nice place to go for a dinner and stay for dancing later on. Regardless of what you want to do there, it is guaranteed you will be entertained; you might even take part in a fashion show, if you are lucky. The staff is friendly and helpful and will tell you all you want to know about the menu. The specialty is fish; the calamari with garlic-onion sauce is highly recommended. ☒ *Ul. Sienkiewicza 4, Srodmiescie,* ☎ *022/828–25–25. AE, MC, V.*

$$–$$$ ✗ **Restauracja Polska.** With a stylish room and some of the best food
★ in the city, this basement restaurant is the place to be seen in Warsaw these days. The tasteful main salon has antique furnishings and large bouquets of flowers. You can't go wrong here with the food, but definitely try the homemade pierogi or the bigos. For dessert, the chocolate-nut torte is outstanding. ☒ *Nowy Świat 21, Srodmiescie,* ☎ *022/ 826–38–77. AE, DC, MC, V.*

\$\$–\$\$\$ ✕ **Studio Buffo.** Just steps from the Sheraton, this restaurant offers patio dining in summer. The constantly changing menu is mainly a twist on Polish dishes. You can't go wrong with the chef's recommendations. ⊠ *Ul. Marii Konopnickiej 6, Srodmiescie,* ☎ *022/626–89–07. AE, DC, MC, V.*

\$\$ ✕ **Pod Barbakanem.** This milk bar situated under the Barbakan gate is the best deal in town if you can tolerate the grouchy cashier. Enjoy the enormous bowls of homemade soups, the chicken cutlets with mashed potatoes and fresh seasonal vegetables, and the naleśniki. ⊠ *Ul. Mostowka 28, Stare Miasto,* ☎ *022/831–47–37. No credit cards.*

Lodging

Warsaw is beginning to deal with its shortage of luxury hotel rooms for business travelers, but lower down the price scale, options still remain restricted. Bed-and-breakfast accommodations are difficult to find. In summer there are generally more options because student hostels rent out their spaces. Demand is high, so book well in advance.

Warsaw is a small city, and the location of your hotel is not of crucial importance in terms of travel time to major sights or night spots. Many hotels are clustered in the downtown area near the intersection of ulica Marszałkowska and aleje Jerozolimskie. This is not an especially scenic area; nevertheless, the neighborhood doesn't exactly become a "concrete desert" after business hours, since there are many residences, restaurants, and nightspots. Note that with a rising crime rate in the city, it is best to be cautious when strolling downtown at night—although the greatest hazards usually turn out to be uneven pavement and inadequate lighting.

The hotels on plac Piłsudskiego, which is close to parks and within easy walking distance of the Old Town, offer more pleasant surroundings. Most of the suburban hotels have no particular scenic advantage, though they do provide immediate access to larger tracts of open space and fresh air.

\$\$\$\$ 🏨 **Hotel Jan III Sobieski.** Since it opened in 1991, this hotel's bright pink, blue, and yellow illusionist facade has startled more than a few Warsovians. Inside, however, the decor is more conventional, and the service is impeccable. The rooms are reasonably sized and warmly furnished in soft rosewood and flowered prints. ⊠ *Pl. Zawiszy 1, 02-025, Srodmiescie,* ☎ *022/658–44–44,* FAX *022/659–88–28,* WEB *www.sobieski.com.pl. 377 rooms, 27 suites. 2 restaurants, café, room service, cable TV, some in-room safes, minibars, gym, hair salon, 2 hot tubs, massage, sauna, bar, shops, laundry service, business services, meeting rooms, parking (fee). AE, DC, MC, V. BP.*

\$\$\$\$ 🏨 **Le Royal Méridien Bristol.** Built in 1901 by a consortium headed by
★ Ignacy Paderewski—the concert pianist who served as Poland's prime minister from 1919 to 1920—the Bristol was long at the center of Warsaw's social life. Impressively situated on the Royal Route, next to the Pałac Namiestnikowski (Presidential Palace), the hotel survived World War II more or less intact. It continues to maintain a long tradition of luxury and elegance under the new ownership of Le Méridien. Additionally, the hotel has one of the best cafés in town—no one can resist its pastries. ⊠ *Krakowskie Przedmieście 42/44, 00–325, Royal Route,* ☎ *022/625–25–25,* FAX *022/625–25–77.* WEB *www.bristol.polhotels.com. 163 rooms, 43 suites. 2 restaurants, café, cable TV, in-room fax, in-room safes, minibars, indoor pool, gym, massage, sauna, steam room, bar, business services, meeting rooms, Internet; no-smoking floors. AE, DC, MC, V. BP.*

$$$$ ⊞ **Sheraton Warsaw Hotel and Towers.** Halfway down the Royal
★   Route from the Old Town, this curved six-story building overlooks plac
      Trzech Krzyży, while behind it lie the parks that run along the Vistula
      embankment. The interiors are bright, the rooms generously sized, and
      the well-trained staff succeeds in making the Sheraton the friendliest
      hotel in Warsaw. ⊠ *Ul. Bolesława Prusa 2, 00–504, Royal Route,* ☎
      022/657–61–00, FAX *022/657–62–00,* WEB *www.sheraton.pl. 350 rooms,
      20 suites. 3 restaurants, café, some in-room data ports, some in-room
      faxes, in-room safe, cable TV, aerobics, hair salon, health club, mas-
      sage, sauna, steam room, dry cleaning, laundry service, concierge floor,
      business services, parking (fee). AE, DC, MC, V. BP.*

$$$$ ⊞ **Sofitel Victoria Warsaw.** Opened in the late 1970s, the Victoria was
      until 1989 Warsaw's only luxury hotel, hosting a stream of official vis-
      itors and state delegations. The large and comfortably furnished guest
      rooms are decorated in tones of brown and gold. Health facilities in-
      clude a basement swimming pool and three exercise rooms, and the
      hotel is just across the street from the jogging (or walking) paths of
      the Ogród Saski (Saxon Gardens). ⊠ *Ul. Królewska 11, 00–065,
      Royal Route,* ☎ *022/657–80–11,* FAX *022/657–80–57,* WEB *www.sofi-
      tel.com. 347 rooms, 13 suites. 3 restaurants, room service, cable TV
      with movies and video games, in-room data ports, minibars, in-room
      safes, pool, health clubs, bar, casino, nightclub, shops, dry cleaning,
      laundry, business services, car rental, travel services, parking (fee),
      some pets allowed; no-smoking rooms. AE, DC, MC, V.*

$$$$ ⊞ **Warsaw Marriott.** Located in the high-rise Lim Center opposite Cen-
      tral Station, the Marriott currently has some of the city's best accom-
      modations. The staff is well trained and helpful; everyone speaks some
      English. The views from every room—of central Warsaw and far be-
      yond—are spectacular on a clear day. The Lila Veneda restaurant on
      the second floor hosts a special Sunday brunch, complete with Dix-
      ieland band. ⊠ *Al. Jerozolimskie 65/79, 00–697, Srodmiescie,* ☎ *022/
      630–63–06,* FAX *022/620–52–39,* WEB *www.marriott.com/waw.pl. 489
      rooms, 34 suites. 3 restaurants, café, room service, cable TV, in-room
      data ports, some kitchens, minibars, in-room safes, indoor pool, gym,
      hair salon, hot tub, sauna, 3 bars, casino, nightclub, shop, laundry ser-
      vice, business services, concierge, car rental, parking (fee). AE, DC, MC,
      V. BP.*

$$$–$$$$ ⊞ **Holiday Inn.** Designed, and later franchised, by Holiday Inn, this
      gleaming six-story complex opposite Warsaw's Central Station avoids
      some of the standard chain-hotel impersonality. It's softly carpeted and
      furnished throughout in shades of gray and blue. A tree-filled, steel-
      and-glass conservatory fronts the building up to the third floor. The
      generously proportioned guest rooms have projecting bay windows that
      overlook the very center of the city. ⊠ *Ul. złota 48, 00–120, Srodmi-
      escie,* ☎ *022/697–39–99,* FAX *022/697–38–99,* WEB *www.sixconti-
      nentshotels.com. 365 rooms, 8 suites. 3 restaurants, café, room service,
      cable TV, in-room data ports, minibars, gym, hot tub, sauna, shop, 2
      bars, concierge, dry cleaning, laundry service, business services, park-
      ing (fee), some pets allowed. AE, DC, MC, V. BP.*

$$$ ⊞ **Hotel Orbis Europejski.** Although it retains traces of its earlier
      grandeur, this hotel is now clearly struggling to maintain standards.
      The 19th-century building was reopened in 1962 after postwar re-
      construction; the renovators managed to retain some original features,
      including two grand marble staircases. The rooms, with somewhat
      shabby furnishings, are very diverse in size and shape. Almost all have
      views overlooking historic Warsaw—on one side, the Royal Route, on
      the other, plac Piłsudskiego. The hotel is not air-conditioned. Guests
      are allowed, for an extra fee, to use the pool and health club facilities

of the Sofitel Victoria Warsaw, which is under the same management. ⊠ *Krakowskie Przedmieście 13, 00–065, Royal Route,* ☎ *022/826–50–51,* FAX *022/826–11–11.* WEB *www.orbis.pl. 233 rooms, 13 suites. Restaurant, room service, minibars, hair salon, bar, shop, dry cleaning, laundry service, business services, meeting rooms, some pets allowed (fee); no a/c. AE, DC, MC, V.*

$$$ ⊞ **Metropol Hotel.** This 1960s hotel is right on Warsaw's main downtown intersection. Most of the rooms are singles and are large enough to contain a bed, armchairs, and desk without feeling crowded. Bathrooms, though small, are attractively tiled and fitted. Each room has a balcony overlooking busy ulica Marszałkowska, and traffic noise can be very intrusive when the windows are open. There is no air-conditioning. ⊠ *Ul. Marszałkowska 99A, 00–693, Srodmiescie,* ☎ *022/629–40–01,* FAX *022/625–30–14,* WEB *www.syrena.com.pl. 175 rooms, 16 suites. Restaurant, cable TV, business services, meeting room, parking (fee); no a/c. AE, DC, MC, V. BP.*

$$$ ⊞ **Novotel Warsaw Airport.** The Novotel can be recommended for a good night's sleep, as it is some distance away from the hustle and bustle of the city center. It's only five minutes from the airport (fortunately, *not* under any flight paths) and it's right across the road from a major area of gardens and parks. Though removed from the heart of the city, the hotel is on the main bus routes; Bus 175 will take you downtown in 15 minutes. The atmosphere is friendly, and the rooms are light, clean, and comfortable. ⊠ *Ul. 1 Sierpnia 1, 02–134, Mokotow,* ☎ *022/846–40–51,* FAX *022/846–36–86. 150 rooms. Restaurant, minibars, pool, gym, bar, meeting rooms, airport shuttle. AE, DC, MC, V. BP.*

$$$ ⊞ **Novotel Warsaw Centrum.** This dun-color, 30-story, Swedish-designed metal cube (formerly the Forum) has been a fixture on the Warsaw skyline since 1974. Guest rooms are of average size, and those on the east side of the building have good views—but don't choose this hotel if you're counting on cheerful surroundings. Depressing tones of brown and green predominate, and the furnishings seem to have been chosen for function rather than comfort. The staff, used to dealing with rapid-turnover group tours, can be offhand. The hotel is in the middle of a heavily built-up area. On the plus side, it is within easy reach of the entertainment districts. ⊠ *Ul. Nowogrodzka 24/26, 00–511, Srodmiescie,* ☎ *022/621–02–71,* FAX *022/625–04–76,* WEB *www.novotel.com. 750 rooms, 13 suites. 2 restaurants, cable TV, some minibars, some refrigerators, some in-room safes, hair salon, bar, shops, dry cleaning, laundry, some pets allowed. AE, DC, MC, V. BP.*

$$$ ⊞ **Parkowa Hotel.** This 1970s hotel, reserved for official government
★ delegations, frequently has rooms available to the general public. It is just south of the Pałac Belweder (Belvedere Palace) in a landscaped area adjacent to Łazienki Park. The hotel has been renovated since it has been privatized and offers Western-style accommodations (including air-conditioning). ⊠ *Ul. Belwederska 46/50, 00–594, Łazienki,* ☎ *022/694–80–00,* FAX *022/41–60–29,* WEB *www.hotelparkowa.pl. 44 rooms. Restaurant, cable TV, minibars, sauna, bar, business services, meeting rooms, free parking. AE, DC, MC, V. BP.*

$$–$$$ ⊞ **Hotel Gromada Warsaw.** Opened in 1995 and just under 1 km (½ mi) from Warsaw's airport and about 7 km (4½ mi) from the city center, the Gromada is run by a peasants' cooperative. The dining room is one of its attractions, and breakfast is particularly recommended. The rooms are comfortable, if standardized. The hotel stands well back from the busy main road and has wooded grounds. There is good bus service into town. ⊠ *Ul. 17 Stycznia 32, 02–148, Mokotow,* ☎ *022/576–46–00,* FAX *022/846–15–80. 140 rooms. Restaurant, bar, gym, sauna, nightclub. AE, DC, MC, V. BP.*

$$ ⊞ **Gromada Dom Chłopa.** With an excellent location in the center of Warsaw, this white five-story hotel was built during the late 1950s by the Gromada peasants' cooperative and originally had a plant-and-seed store on the ground floor. The hotel, which was renovated in 2000, offers clean and reasonably priced accommodations; rooms are rather small, but the colors are lively, and the bathrooms have been updated. There is no air-conditioning. ⊠ *Pl. Powstańców Warszawy 2, 00–030, Srodmiescie,* ☎ *022/625–15–45,* FAX *022/625–21–40. 282 rooms. Restaurant, bar, parking (fee); no a/c. AE, DC, MC, V. BP.*

$$ ⊞ **Ibis Warszawa Centrum.** This hotel in central Warsaw was built in 2000, providing convenient access to all places you need to visit. It's 2.5 km (1.5 mi) from Old Town. The rooms are light, clean, reasonably spacious, and comfortable. And the hotel staff are friendly and helpful. ⊠ *Aleja Solidarnosci 165, Wola, 00–876,,* ☎ *022/520–30–00,* FAX *022/520–30–30,* WEB *www.ibishotel.com. 189 rooms. Restaurant, cable TV, phone, in-room data ports, bar, business services, parking (fee), some pets allowed (fee). AE, MC, V.*

$–$$ ⊞ **Logos.** This hotel is situated in Powiśle, across the road from the Vistula River and 10 minutes by foot (admittedly all uphill) from the Royal Route. Traffic noise can be a big problem in front-facing rooms, but courtyard-facing rooms are peaceful. The decor throughout is dull, with plenty of dark-wood paneling and chocolate-brown paint, and there is no air-conditioning. Only the 10 doubles have private bathrooms. The rooms, though, are spacious and comfortable, and everything is clean. ⊠ *Wybrzeże Kościuszkowskie 31/33, 00–379, Powisle,* ☎ *022/622–55–61,* FAX *022/625–51–85. 360 rooms, 10 with bath. Restaurant, café; no a/c. AE, DC, MC, V.*

$ ⊞ **Hera.** This three-story socialist-realist building on the edge of Łazienki Park was taken over from the Communist Central Committee in 1990 by Warsaw University. It is used mainly for university guests, but overflow rooms are rented throughout the year. The spartanly decorated rooms are of good size, and many overlook the beautiful park. It is probably the best-located hotel in the price range. ⊠ *Ul. Belwederska 26/30, 00–594, Łazienki,* ☎ *022/553–10–00. 40 rooms. Restaurant. AE, DC, MC, V.*

Nightlife and the Arts

As throughout Central Europe, people tend to meet for drinks in the evenings in *kawiarnie* (cafés)—where you can linger for as long as you like over a serving of coffee or brandy—rather than in bars. (Most cafés are open until 10.) But Western-style bars have become more popular, and there is also a growing fashion for pubs. Discos and rock clubs are mushrooming; jazz clubs have a wide audience. Casinos are mainly the haunt of foreign visitors and the new, rich business class of Poles.

Nightlife

BARS AND LOUNGES

If you've got to know the score, **Champions** (⊠ Lim Center, al. Jerozolimskie 65/79, Srodmiescie, ☎ 022/630–40–33) sports bar and restaurant is a great place to watch American basketball, football games, and motor sports. **Harenda** (⊠ Krakowskie Przedmieście 4/6, Royal Route, enter from ulica Obożna, ☎ 022/826–29–00) occasionally hosts some good jazz and has an outdoor terrace that gets crowded in summer. The **John Bull Pub** (⊠ ul. Zielna 37, Srodmiescie, ☎ 022/620–06–56; ⊠ ul. Jezuicka 4, Stare Miasto, ☎ 022/831–37–62) is open until midnight and serves English draft beers in two locations. **Morgan's** (⊠ ul. Okólnik 1, Srodmiescie, enter from ul. Tamka, ☎ 022/826–81–38) is the Irish pub that is always open late.

CASINOS

The **Casino Warsaw** (⊠ al. Jerozolimskie 65/79, Srodmiescie, ☎ 022/ 830–01–78), on the second floor of the Marriott, is Warsaw's plushest and most sedate casino. The gamblers are often international businessmen or Polish jet-setters. It's open daily 11 AM–7 AM. The **Victoria Casino** (⊠ ul. Królewska 11, Royal Route, ☎ 022/827–66–33) is quite popular and open daily 2

DISCOS

Ground Zero (⊠ ul. Wspólna 62, Srodmiescie, ☎ 022/625–43–80), a former bomb shelter, is a large, crowded bi-level disco. **Hades** (⊠ al. Niepodległości 162, Ochota, ☎ 022/49–12–51) is a popular disco in the cellars of the Central School of Economics, with plenty of seating space. **Labirynt** (⊠ ul. Smolna 12, Srodmiescie, ☎ 022/826–22–20) attracts the young-professional crowd. In the Marriott, **Orpheus** (⊠ al. Jerozolimskie 65/79, Srodmiescie, ☎ 022/630–54–16) has an elegant air and is very expensive. There is a well-established disco at the student club **Stodoła** (⊠ Batorego 10, Ochota, ☎ 022/25–86–25). **Tango** (⊠ al. Jerozolimskie 4, Srodmiescie, ☎ 022/622–19–19) is a pricey disco.

JAZZ CLUBS

Blue Velvet (⊠ Krakowskie Przedmieście 5, Royal Route, ☎ 022/ 828–11–03) hosts regular modern jazz evenings. **Kawiarnia Literacka** (⊠ Krakowskie Przedmieście 87/89, Royal Route, ☎ 022/826–57–84) has classic jazz on weekends.

The Arts

You can find out about Warsaw's thriving arts scene in the English-language *Warsaw Insider,* available at most major hotels. If you read Polish, the monthlies *IKS* (*Informator Kulturalny Stolicy*) and *City Magazine* and the daily *Gazeta Wyborcza* have the best listings. Tickets for most performances are inexpensive, but if you want to spend even less, most theaters sell general-admission tickets—*wejściówki*—for a few złoty immediately before the performance. Wejściówki are often available for performances for which all standard tickets have been sold. Warsaw's only major ticket agency, **ZASP** (⊠ al. Jerozolimskie 25, Srodmiescie, ☎ 022/621–94–54), is a good source for information on arts happenings. If you speak Polish, call **Telefoniczny Informator Kulturalny** (☎ 022/629–84–89), which is open daily 10–6, for information on upcoming performances.

FILM

Since 1989, it seems every cinema in Warsaw has been showing foreign films—mainly U.S. box-office hits—nonstop. These are generally shown in the original language with added subtitles. In the year 2000, cineplexes burst onto the Warsaw scene, providing state-of-the-art cinematic environments. Don't count on seeing many Polish films while visiting Warsaw; only one cinema specializes in Polish features: **Iluzjon Filmoteki Narodowej** (⊠ ul. Narbutta 55A, Ochota, ☎ 022/ 48–33–33). **Relax** (⊠ ul. złota 8, Srodmiescie, ☎ 022/827–77–62) is a large, popular cinema in the center of town showing mostly American films. **Silver Screen** (⊠ ul. Puławska 21/29, Centrum, ☎ 022/852– 88–88), close to the city center, is one of the newest cinemas in town specializing in U.S. films. **Skarpa** (⊠ ul. Kopernika 7–9, Srodmiescie, ☎ 022/826–48–96), off ulica Nowy Świat, is large and modern, showing mostly American movies. **Wars** (⊠ Rynek Nowe Miasta 5–7, Nowe Miasto, ☎ 022/831–44–88), a cinema on the New Town Square, occasionally forgets about box-office success and shows an old Polish classic. This cinema also has a good program of foreign films.

MUSIC

In summer, free Chopin concerts are held at the Chopin Memorial in Łazienki Park on Sunday and at Chopin's birthplace, Żelazowa Wola, outside Warsaw. The **Filharmonia Narodowa** (National Philharmonic; ✉ ul. Sienkiewicza 10, Srodmiescie, ☎ 022/826–72–81) hosts an excellent season of concerts, with visits from world-renowned performers and orchestras as well as Polish musicians. Very popular concerts of classical music for children—run for years by Jadwiga Mackiewicz, who is herself almost a national institution—are held here on Sunday at 2; admission is from zł 5. The **Studio Koncertowe Polskiego Radia** (Polish Radio Concert Studio; ✉ ul. Woronicza 17, Mokotow, ☎ 022/645–52–52), open since 1992, has excellent acoustics and popular programs. The **Royal Castle** (✉ pl. Zamkowy 4, Stare Miasto, ☎ 022/657–21–70) has regular concerts in its stunning Great Assembly Hall. The Chopin Society, **Towarzystwo im. Fryderyka Chopina** (✉ ul. Okólnik 1, Srodmiescie, ☎ 022/827–54–71), organizes recitals and chamber concerts in the Pałac Ostrogskich (Ostrogski Palace).

OPERA AND DANCE

Housed in a beautifully restored 19th-century theater, **Opera Kameralna** (✉ al. Solidarności 76B, Muranów, ☎ 022/625–75–10), the Warsaw chamber opera, has an ambitious program and a growing reputation for quality performances. **Teatr Wielki** (Opera House; ✉ pl. Teatralny 1, Srodmiescie, ☎ 022/826–32–88), Warsaw's grand opera, stages spectacular productions of the classic international opera and ballet repertoire, as well as Polish operas and ballets. The massive neoclassical house, built in the 1820s and reconstructed after the war, has an auditorium with more than 2,000 seats. Stanisław Moniuszko's 1865 opera *Straszny Dwór* (Haunted Manor), a lively piece with folk costumes and dancing, is a good starting point if you want to explore Polish music: the visual aspects will entertain you, even if the music is unfamiliar. Plot summaries in English are available at most performances.

THEATER

The **Globe Theater Group** (☎ 022/620–44–29) performs American and British plays at various theater venues. **"Gulliver" Teatr Lalek** (✉ ul. Różana 16, Srodmiescie, ☎ 022/45–16–76) is one of Warsaw's excellent puppet theaters. **Teatr Narodowy** (✉ pl. Teatralny, Srodmiescie, ☎ 022/826–32–88), adjoining the opera house and under the same management, stages Polish classics. Warsaw's Jewish Theater, **Teatr Żydowski** (✉ Plac Grzybowski 12/16, Srodmiescie, ☎ 022/620–70–25), performs in Yiddish, but most of its productions are colorful costume dramas in which the action speaks as loudly as the words. Translation into English is provided through headphones.

Outdoor Activities and Sports

Health Clubs

The best health club in Warsaw is the **Fitness Center** at the Sheraton (✉ ul. Bolesława Prusa 2, Royal Route, ☎ 022/657–61–00). Open to nonmembers, the center has the latest equipment, aerobics and other classes, and child care.

Hiking

In Warsaw the local branch of PTTK (Polish Tourist Association) organizes daylong hikes in the nearby countryside on weekends. Watch the local papers for advertisements of meeting points and routes.

Horse Racing

You can reach Warsaw's beautiful but seedy **racecourse** (✉ ul. Puławska 266, Slozew, ☎ 022/843–14–41) by taking Tram 4 or 36 or one of the special buses marked WYŚCIGI, which run from the east side of the Pałac Kultury i Nauki (Palace of Culture and Science) on Saturday in season (May–October). Betting is on a tote system. Admission to the stands is zł 20.

Jogging

Along with dogs and bicycles, joggers are banned from Warsaw's largest and most beautiful park, Łazienki Park. The 9½ km (6 mi) trail through parkland and over footbridges from the Ujazdów Park to Mariensztat (parallel to the Royal Route) is a good route. The Vistula embankment makes for a good straight run (the paved surface runs for about 12 km [8 mi]). Piłsudski Park has a circular route of about 4½ km (3 mi). You can jog in the center of town on the somewhat restricted pathways of the Ogród Saski (Saxon Gardens).

Soccer

Warsaw's soccer team, **Legia** (☎ 022/621–08–96), plays at the field at ulica Łazienkowska 3. Admission is from zł 20.

Swimming

Warsaw's indoor pools tend to be overcrowded, and some restrict admission to those with season tickets; it's best to check first. For a swim your best bet is the indoor pool at the **Le Royal Méridien Bristol** (✉ Krakowskie Przedmieście 42/44, Royal Route, ☎ 022/625–25–25). **Klub Sportowy Warszawianka** (✉ ul. Dominika Merliniego 9, Mokotow, ☎ 022/844–62–07) is an option if you are not afraid of crowded places. This pool is usually used by the Polish professional swimmers before all major international tournaments. At the **Spartańska** (✉ ul. Spartańska 1, ☎ 022/48–67–46) you can usually persuade them to let you swim on a special one-day pass.

Shopping

Warsaw's shopping scene is booming, with more and more international chains—such as Marks & Spencer, London's noted department store—boutiques, and suburban shopping malls setting up shop. As a result, locally produced items are sometimes harder to find than ridiculously expensive imported ones. Shopping hours are usually from 11 AM to 7 PM on weekdays and from 10 AM to 1 PM on Saturday. RUCH kiosks, which sell bus and train tickets, newspapers, and cosmetics, are usually open from 7 to 7.

Shopping Districts

Warsaw has four main shopping streets, all in Srodmiescie. The larger stores lie on **ulica Marszałkowska** (from ulica Królewska to plac Zbawiciela) and **aleje Jerozolimskie** (from Central Station to plac Generala de Gaulle, in Srodmiescie). Smaller stores and more specialized boutiques can be found on **ulica Nowy Świat** and **ulica Chmielna.**

Department Stores

Warsaw's oldest department store, **Arka** (✉ ul. Bracka 25, Srodmiescie, ☎ 022/692–14–00), has a monumental staircase, Art Nouveau stained-glass windows, and stores selling clothing, jewelry, and household items. At the **Galeria Centrum** (✉ ul. Marszałkowska 104–122, Srodmiescie, ☎ 022/551–41–41)—divided into Wars, Sawa, and Junior sections—private boutiques sell mainly imported fashion items.

Specialty Stores

ANTIQUES

For fine antique furniture, art, and china try one of the branches of **Desa** (✉ ul. Marszałkowska 34, Srodmiescie, ☎ 022/621–66–15; ✉ ul. Nowy Świat 51, Srodmiescie, ☎ 022/827–47–60; ✉ Rynek Starego

Miasta 4/6, Stare Miasto, ☎ 022/831–16–81). Remember, however, that most antiques cannot be exported.

ART GALLERIES

Galeria Nowy Świat (✉ Nowy Świat 23, Srodmiescie, ☎ 022/826–35–01) has paintings, ceramics, and designer furniture. **Galeria Sztuki** (✉ ul. Świętokrzyska 32, Srodmiescie, ☎ 022/652–11–77) holds one of the finest collections of contemporary Polish art.

FOLK ART AND CRAFTS

Arex (✉ ul. Chopina 5B, Mokotow, ☎ 022/629–66–24) is the best place to go for traditional Polish wood carvings. The branches of **Cepelia** (✉ pl. Konstytucji 5, Srodmiescie, ☎ 022/621–26–18;✉ Rynek Starego Miasta 10, Stare Miasto, ☎ 022/831–18–05) sell folk art, including wood carvings and silver and amber jewelry.

GLASS AND CRYSTAL

A. Jabłonski (✉ ul. Nowy Świat 52, Royal Route) sells unique pieces of handblown glass and crystal. **Szlifierna skła** (✉ ul. Nowomeijska 1/3, Stare Miasto, ☎ 022/831–46–43), next to the Old Town Square, custom engraves all kinds of crystal goods.

JEWELRY

There are many jewelry (*jubiler*) stores clustered around the Old Town and ulica Nowy Świat. The **Art Gallery** (✉ Rynek Starego Miasto 13, Stare Miasto) has a great selection of silver and amber, although much of it is somewhat overpriced. One of the oldest and best-established jewelry stores in Poland is **W. Kruk** (✉ pl. Konstytucji 6, Srodmiescie, ☎ 022/628–75–34).

LEATHER

JKM (✉ Krakowskie Przedmieście 65, Royal Route, ☎ 022/827–22–62) is a small shop crammed with bags, suitcases, and gloves from the best Polish producers. **Pekar** (✉ al. Jerozolimskie 29, Srodmiescie, ☎ 022/621–90–82) carries a wide range of bags, gloves, and jackets.

Street Markets

The largest Warsaw market—known as the Russian market and composed largely of private sellers hawking everything from antiques to blue jeans—is at the **Tysiąclecie Sports Stadium,** east of the river at Rondo Waszyngtona in Grochow. If you go, watch out for pickpockets.

Warsaw Essentials

AIR TRAVEL

The Polish airline LOT makes the lion's share of the flights to and from Warsaw (from Chicago, Newark, and New York-JFK), but many international carriers offer direct and connecting service from North America and Europe. The flying time from New York to Warsaw is approximately 9 hours, from London approximately 2½ hours.

➤ AIRLINES: **Air France** (✉ ul. Krucza 21, Srodmiescie, ☎ 022/628–12–81; ✉ Okęcie Airport, ☎ 022/650–45–08). **Alitalia** (✉ J.B. Moliera 8, Srodmiescie, ☎ 022/826–28–01; ✉ Okęcie Airport, ☎ 022/846–78–46). **Austrian Airlines** (✉ Sienna 39, Srodmiescie, ☎ 22/627–52–90; ✉ Okęcie Airport, ☎ 022/650–35–16). **British Airways** (✉ ul. Krucza 49, Srodmiescie, ☎ 022/628–94–31; ✉ Okęcie Airport, ☎ 022/650–45–03). **Finnair** (✉ FIM Tower, al. Jerozolimskie 81, Srodmiescie, ☎ 022/695–08–11; ✉ Okęcie Airport, ☎ 022/650–35–70). **LOT** (✉ al. Jerozolimskie 65/79, Srodmiescie, ☎ 022/630–50–07; 0801/300–952 reservations; ✉ Okęcie Airport, ☎ 22/650–39–43 departures; 022/650–17–50 domestic information). **Lufthansa** (✉ Sienna 39, Srodmiescie, ☎ 22/338–13–00 or 0801/312–312; ✉ Okęcie Airport, ☎ 022/

650–45–10). **SAS** (✉ Sienna 39, Srodmiescie, ☎ 022/850–05–00; ✉ Okęcie Airport, ☎ 22/650–34–64). **Swiss** (✉ ul. Jana Pawla II 15, Srodmiescie, ☎ 22/697–66–00).

AIRPORTS AND TRANSFERS

Warsaw's Okęcie Airport, also known as Fredyryka Chopina International Airport, is 7 km (4½ mi) south of the city center and has the most international flights into and out of Poland.

➤ AIRPORT INFORMATION: **Okęcie Airport** (☎ 022/650–42–20 or 0801–300–952, WEB www.polish-airports.com).

TRANSFERS

The direct route to downtown, where almost all the hotels are, is along aleje Żwirki i Wigury and ulica Raszyńska. The AIRPORT–CITY bus leaves from Platform 4 outside Terminal 1 every 20 minutes and stops at all the major hotels and Central Station. Tickets cost zł 6, and the trip takes about 25 minutes. Alternatively, Bus 175 leaves Okęcie about every 10 minutes. It also runs past most major downtown hotels and is reliable and cheap, but beware of pickpockets. Purchase tickets for zł 2.40 at an airport RUCH kiosk. If your immediate destination is not Warsaw, Polski Express has direct service from Okęcie to major Polish cities. Avoid at all costs the taxi hawkers and unmarked vehicles (no number at the top) outside the arrivals hall: not only are these cabs expensive but they can also be dangerous. Your best bet is to call radio taxi from one of the radio taxi kiosks in the arrivals area, or call your hotel in advance and have them pick you up. A cab ride into the city should cost about zł 25.

➤ CONTACTS: **Radio Taxi** (☎ 22/919, 22/644–44–44, or 22/655–55–55).

BED-AND-BREAKFAST RESERVATION AGENCIES

The Bureau of Private Accommodations has many accommodations in the city center, although none include breakfast. The staff is helpful and speaks English.

➤ CONTACTS: **Bureau of Private Accommodations** (✉ ul. Krucza 17, Srodmiescie, ☎ 022/628–75–40).

BUS TRAVEL

Warsaw's main bus station, Dworzec PKS Zachodni, 10 minutes from Central Station on Bus 127 or 130, serves most long-distance routes. Tickets for all destinations can be purchased here regardless of which bus station you are leaving from.

Local services for points north of the city run from Dworzec PKS Marymont in the northern district of Żoliborz. Buses headed east leave from Dworzec PKS Stadion on the east bank of the Vistula.

The private long-distance bus service Polski Express, which goes to most major destinations in Poland, arrives and departs from Jana Pawła II between Central Station and the Holiday Inn. Polski Express also has a stop at the airport.

➤ CONTACTS: **Dworzec PKS Marymont** (✉ ul. Marymoncka and ul. Żeromskiego, Żoliborz, ☎ 022/823–63–94). **Dworzec PKS Stadion** (✉ intersection of ul. Targowa, ul. Zamoyskiego, and al. Zieleniecka, Praga, ☎ 022/823–63–94). **Dworzec PKS Zachodni** (✉ al. Jerozolimskie 144, Srodmiescie, 022/823–63–94). **Polski Express** (✉ Jana Pawła II, between Central Station and the Holiday Inn, Srodmiescie, ☎ 022/620–03–30, WEB wipos.p.lodz.pl/pex).

BUS, TRAM, AND SUBWAY TRAVEL WITHIN WARSAW

A trip on a city bus costs zł 2.40. Purchase tickets from RUCH kiosks or bus drivers, and cancel one in the machine on the bus for each ride.

Buses that halt at all stops along their route are numbered 100 and up. Express buses are numbered from E-1 upward. Buses numbered 500–599 stop at selected stops. Check details on the information board at the bus stop. Night buses (numbered 600 and up) operate between 11 PM and 5:30 AM; the fare is three tickets. Buses can be very crowded, and you should beware of pickpockets.

Trams are the fastest means of public transport, since they are not affected by traffic holdups but are also often crowded. Purchase tickets from RUCH kiosks or tram operators, and cancel one ticket in the machine on the tram for each ride. Trams run on a north–south and east–west grid system along most of the main city routes, pulling up automatically at all stops. Each tram has a diagram of the system.

Warsaw's underground opened in spring 1995. Although as yet it has only one line, running from the southern suburbs to the city center (Kabaty to Ratusz, at Plac Bankowy), it is clean and fast and costs the same as the tram or bus. Use the same tickets, canceling them at the entrance to the station.

CAR RENTALS
Major international car-rental agencies have offices in Warsaw's city center and at the airport as well.
➤ MAJOR AGENCIES: **Avis Poland** (✉ Marriott hotel, al. Jerozolimskie 65/79, Srodmiescie, ☎ 022/630–73–16; ✉ Okęcie Airport, ☎ 022/650–48–72). **Budget** (✉ Marriott hotel, al. Jerozolimskie 65/79, Srodmiescie, ☎ 022/630–72–80; ✉ Okęcie Airport, ☎ 22/9572 or 22/650–17–50). **Hertz** (✉ Nowogrodzka 27, Srodmiescie, ☎ 022/621–13–60; ✉ Okęcie Airport, ☎ 022/650–28–96).

CAR TRAVEL
Within the city, a car can be more a problem than a convenience. Warsaw currently has too many cars for its road network, and there are sometimes major snarls. Parking also can be very difficult. And there is a real threat of theft—of contents, parts, or the entire car—if you leave a Western model unattended, and it is not easy to get quick service or repairs. If you do bring your car, park it overnight in a guarded parking garage.

EMBASSIES AND CONSULATES
All embassies are in Warsaw. *See* the A to Z section at the end of this chapter for addresses.

EMERGENCIES
➤ CONTACTS: **Ambulance** (☎ 999). **Police** (☎ 997).
➤ DOCTORS AND DENTISTS: **American Medical Center** (✉ ul. Wilcza 23, Suite 29, Srodmiescie, ☎ 0602–243–024 24-hr service). **Austria-Dent Center** (✉ ul. Zelazna 54, Srodmiescie, ☎ 022/821–31–84).
➤ LATE-NIGHT PHARMACIES: **Apteka Grabowskiego** (✉ Central Station, 1st floor, al. Jerozolimskie 54, Srodmiescie, ☎ 022/25–69–86; ✉ ul. Freta 13, Srodmiescie, ☎ 022/831–50–91; ✉ ul. Widok 19, Srodmiescie, ☎ 022/827–35–93).

ENGLISH-LANGUAGE BOOKSTORES
Most major bookstores now have well-stocked sections of English-language books.
➤ CONTACTS: **Empik** (✉ ul. Nowy Świat 15/17, Srodmiescie, ☎ 022/627–06–50; ✉ ul. Marszałkowska 116–122, Srodmiescie, ☎ 022/827–82–96). **Bookland** (✉ al. Jerozolimskie 61, Srodmiescie, ☎ 022/646–57–27).

MONEY MATTERS

To change money, head to the Kantor Wymiany Walut, which has swift, friendly service and usually offers slightly better rates than hotels and banks. It is open weekdays 11–7 and Saturday 9–2. Another Kantor office is in the main post office, open 24 hours a day. TEBOS, in Central Station at the foot of the staircase leading from the main hall to the access passage for platforms, is also open 24 hours a day. (Remember to watch out for pickpockets.)

➤ CURRENCY EXCHANGE: **Kantor Wymiany Walut** (✉ ul. Marszałkowska 66, at ulica Wilcza, Srodmiescie;✉ Main Post Office, ul. Świętokrzyska 31, Srodmiescie). **TEBOS** (✉ Central Station, al. Jerozolimskie 54, Srodmiescie).

TAXIS

In Warsaw, it is always best to use the services of Radio Taxi because they are the most reliable and the operators usually speak English. The standard charge is zł 3.6 for the first kilometer (½ mi) and zł 1.4 for each kilometer thereafter. It is not customary to tip taxi drivers, although you can round up the fare to the nearest złoty. Avoid unmarked Mercedes cabs as well as taxis that do not have a number on the top (9622, 9623, etc.), as they are likely to charge far more than the going rate.

➤ CONTACTS: **Radio Taxi** (☎ 22/919, 22/644–44–44, or 22/655–55–55).

TOURS

Tours of the city or the country can be booked at major hotels or through the agencies directly. Mazurkas Travel leads daily tours of Warsaw as well as longer tours of Poland, as does Local Rent a Car Poland LTD. For tours that focus on Jewish Warsaw or Poland call Our Roots—Jewish Information and Tourist Bureau.

➤ CONTACTS: **Local Rent a Car Poland LTD** (✉ Europejski Hotel, ul. Krakowskie Przedmieście 13, Royal Route, ☎ 022/657–81–81). **Mazurkas Travel** (✉ ul. Długa 8/14, Srodmiescie, ☎ 022/635–66–33). **Our Roots—Jewish Information and Tourist Bureau** (✉ ul. Twarda 6, Srodmiescie, ☎ 022/620–05–56).

TRAIN TRAVEL

As the name implies, Warsaw's Warszawa Centralna (Central Station) is right in the heart of the city, between the Marriott and Holiday Inn. Beware of pickpockets and muggers who prey on passengers as they board or leave trains. Domestic trains run from Warszawa Śródmieście, next to Central Station on aleje Jerozolimskie. East of the river, domestic trains run from Dworzec Wileński. You can purchase train tickets at the train station or at travel agencies, including Orbis.

➤ CONTACTS: **Dworzec Wileński** (✉ ul. Targowa, Praga, ☎ 022/18–35–21). **Warszawa Centralna** (Central Station; ✉ al. Jerozolimskie 54, Srodmiescie, ☎ 022/25–50–00; 022/620–45–12 international rail information; 022/620–03–61 domestic rail information). Domestic trains run from **Warszawa Śródmieście** (✉ al. Jerozolimskie, Srodmiescie, next to Warszawa Centralna, ☎ 022/628–47–41).

TRAVEL AGENCIES

American Express sells traveler's checks, exchanges currency, rents cars, and provides other travel agency services. Carlson Wagonlit Travel is centrally located. Getz International Travel Ltd. is an efficient agency with friendly service. Orbis is the best place to buy train tickets.

➤ CONTACTS: **American Express** (✉ Krakowskie Przedmieście 11, Royal Route, ☎ 022/635–20–02; 022/630–69–52 24-hr service). **Carlson Wagonlit Travel** (✉ ul. Nowy Świat 64, Srodmiescie, ☎ 022/826–04–31). **Getz International Travel Ltd.** (✉ al. Jerozolimskie 56C, Srodmiescie, ☎ 022/630–27–60). **Orbis** (✉ ul. Bracka 16, Srodmiescie, ☎ 022/826–02–71).

VISITOR INFORMATION

The Center for Tourist Information, on Castle Square, is open week-days 9–6 and weekends 11–6. Branches of the Warsaw Tourist Infor-mation Office are open weekdays 8–7 and weekends 9–3. There is a branch at the arrivals hall of Warsaw's airport.

➤ CONTACTS: **Center for Tourist Information** (✉ pl. Zamkowy 1, Stare Miasto, ☎ 022/635–18–81). **Warsaw Tourist Information Of-fice** (✉ Gromada Dom Chłopa, pl. Powstańców Warszawy 2, Srod-miescie, ☎ 022/625–15–45).

KRAKÓW

Renaissance arcades, enchanting onion domes, baroque spires, story-book streets, and Leonardo da Vinci's sublime painting *Cecilia Gallerani*—little wonder the stunning beauty of this 1,000-year-old city and its sights attract hundreds of thousands of visitors annually. Kraków, seat of Poland's oldest university and once the nation's cap-ital (before finally relinquishing the honor to Warsaw in 1609), is one of the few Polish cities that escaped devastation by Hitler's armies dur-ing World War II. Today Kraków's fine towers, facades, and churches, reflecting seven centuries of Polish architecture, continue to make it the shop window of Poland. Its location, about 270 km (170 mi) south of Warsaw, also makes it a good starting point for hiking and skiing trips in the mountains of southern Poland.

Exploring Kraków

It would be almost unthinkable to visit the Małopolska region with-out visiting Kraków. Ten years ago, the Old Town's face was still stained by pollution from the steelworks in the outlying suburb of Nowa Huta and the nearby industrial area of Śląsk (Silesia). The countenance of the city today is much brighter, restored to its former glory. Start-ing as a market town in the 10th century, Kraków became Poland's capital in 1037. Until as recently as the 19th century there were walls encircling the Old Town; now there is the Planty, a ring of parkland.

To the immediate southeast of the Old Town is the old Jewish quar-ter of Kazimierz. This was once a separate town, chartered in 1335 by its founder, Kazimierz the Great. In 1495 Kraków's Jews were expelled from the city by King John Albert, and they resettled in Kazimierz. The Jewish community of Kazimierz came to an abrupt and tragic end dur-ing World War II. In 1941 the Jews of Kazimierz were moved first to a Jewish ghetto across the Vistula River in Podgórze, then to Płaszów concentration camp. Most who survived Płaszów were transported to their deaths in the much larger concentration camp at Auschwitz-Birkenau. Those who escaped Płaszów formed the basis of Thomas Ken-neally's book, and Steven Spielberg's film, *Schindler's List*.

Numbers in the text correspond to numbers in the margin and on the Kraków map.

Stare Miasto (Old Town)

Kraków's streets are a vast and lovely living museum, and the Stare Miasto (Old Town) in particular is a historical gold mine. Its ancient houses, churches, and palaces can overwhelm visitors with only a few days to see the sights. The heart of it all is Kraków's "drawing room"— the Rynek Główny, or Main Market Square.

A GOOD WALK

The Old Town is best explored on foot, beginning at the **Barbakan** ①
and city gate on **ulica Floriańska** ②. Here you should visit the Czartoryski Collection in the **Arsenał Miejski** ③, which contains Leonardo da
Vinci's legendary *Lady with an Ermine*; enter from św. Jana. But drop'
by the **Dom Jana Matejki** ④ and admire the medieval mansions as well.
Ulica Floriańska will take you to the **Rynek Główny** ⑤ at the center of
the town, where you will find the **Kościół Mariacki** ⑥, the Renaissance
Sukiennice ⑦, and a collection of magnificent Renaissance town houses.

The historic early buildings of the Jagiellonian University lie in streets
leading off to the southwest and south of the square. Take ulica świętej
Anny to reach ulica Jagiellońska, where you'll find the **Collegium
Maius** ⑧, where Copernicus once studied. Then go via the streets of
Gołębia and Bracka to plac Wszystkich Świętych and the 13th-century
Kościół Franciszkanów ⑨, hiding magnificent wall paintings and
stained-glass windows by the local Art Nouveau master Stanisław
Wyspiański. From here take ulica Grodzka south to another collegiate
building, the **Collegium Juridicum** ⑩, to the 11th-century **Kościół
świętego Andrzeja** ⑪, and to the wonderful baroque **Kościół świętego
Piotra i Pawła** ⑫. Cut through to Kraków's oldest street, **ulica Kanonicza** ⑬, where the canons of the cathedral once lived. Ulica Kanonicza
leads to the Wawel Hill, where you'll find the **Katedra Wawelska** ⑭
and the Renaissance **Zamek Królewski** ⑮. From the Wawel Hill, you
can stroll south down the Vistula embankment to visit the **Kościół na
Skałce** ⑯ and the fine 14th-century redbrick Gothic Kościół świętej
Katarzyny at the corners of Skałeczna and Augustiańska streets.

TIMING

The Wawel Hill sights alone require a whole morning or afternoon;
the rest of the Old Town, at least a day.

SIGHTS TO SEE

★ ❸ **Arsenał Miejski** (Municipal Arsenal). The surviving fragment of
Kraków's city wall opposite the Barbakan, where students and amateur artists hang their paintings for sale in the summer, contains the
Renaissance Municipal Arsenal, which now houses part of the National
Museum's **Czartoryski Collection,** including such celebrated paintings as Rembrandt's *Landscape with the Good Samaritan.* The prize
of the collection and to many observers the most beautiful portrait ever
painted is Leonardo da Vinci's *Cecilia Gallerani,* also known as the
Lady with an Ermine. ⊠ *Św. Jana 19 and Pijarska 8,* ☎ 012/422–55–
66. 🎟 *zł 7.* ☉ *Tues. and Thurs. 9–3:30, Wed. 11–6, Sat. 10–3:30.*

❶ **Barbakan.** Only one small section of Kraków's city wall still stands,
centered on the 15th-century Barbakan, one of the largest strongholds
of its kind in Europe. ⊠ *Basztowa, opposite Floriańska.*

⑩ **Collegium Juridicum.** This magnificent Gothic building, built in the early
15th century to house the Jagiellonian University's law students, lies
on one of Kraków's oldest streets. ⊠ *Grodzka 53.*

★ ❽ **Collegium Maius.** The Jagiellonian University was another innovation
of Kazimierz the Great. Established in 1364, it was the first university
in Poland and one of the earliest ones in Europe. The Collegium Maius
is the oldest surviving building of the university, though historians are
undecided where the very first one stood. The Jagiellonian's most famous student, Nicolaus Copernicus, studied here from 1491 to 1495.
The first visual delight is the arcaded Gothic courtyard. On the second floor, the museum and rooms are a must for all visitors to Kraków.
They can only be visited on a guided tour (call in advance for an English guide). On the tour you see the treasury, assembly hall, library,

414

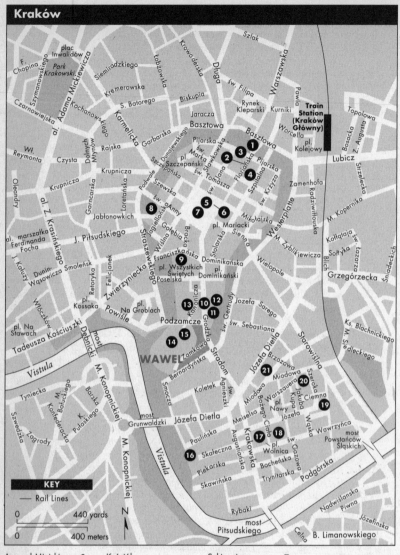

Kraków

Train Station (Kraków Główny)

WAWEL

KEY

— Rail Lines

0   440 yards

0   400 meters

N

and common room. The museum includes the so-called Jagiellonian globe, the first globe to depict the American continents. ⊠ *Jagiellońska 15,* ☎ *012/422–05–49.* 🎦 *Courtyard free, museum zł 8.* ⊙ *Museum Mon.–Thurs. 11–3, Sat. 11–1:30.*

❹ **Dom Jana Matejki** (House of Jan Matejko). The 19th-century painter Jan Matejko was born and died in this house, which now serves as a museum for his work. Even if you don't warm to his painting, Matejko was a prodigious collector of everything from Renaissance art to medieval weaponry, and this 16th-century building is in wonderful condition. ⊠ *Floriańska 41,* ☎ *012/22–59–26.* 🎦 *zł 5.* ⊙ *Tues. and Thurs. 9–3:30, Wed. 11–6, Sat. 10–3:30.*

★ ⓮ **Katedra Wawelska** (Wawel Cathedral). Wawel Hill, a 15-acre rocky limestone outcropping on the banks of the Vistula, dominates the old part of the city. The hill was a natural point for fortification on the flat Vistula Plain. During the 8th century it was topped with a tribal stronghold and since the 10th century has held a royal residence and served as the seat of the bishops of Kraków. Construction on the present Wawel Cathedral—the third cathedral in this very place—was begun in 1320, and the structure was consecrated in 1364. Little room for expansion on the hill has meant the preservation of the original austere structure, although a few Renaissance and baroque chapels have been crowded around it. The most notable of these is the **Kaplica Zygmuntowska** (Sigismund Chapel), built in the 1520s by the Florentine architect Bartolomeo Berrecci and widely considered to be the finest Renaissance chapel north of the Alps.

From 1037, when Kraków became the capital of Poland, Polish kings were crowned and buried in the Wawel Cathedral. This tradition continued up to the time of the partitions, even after the capital had been moved to Warsaw. During the 19th century, only great national heroes were honored by a Wawel entombment: Tadeusz Kościuszko was buried here in 1817; Adam Mickiewicz and Juliusz Słowacki, both great romantic poets, were also brought back from exile to the Wawel after their deaths; and Marshal Józef Piłsudski, the hero of independent Poland between the two world wars, was interred in the cathedral crypt in 1935.

The cathedral also has a treasury, archives, library, and museum. Among the showpieces in the library, one of the earliest in Poland, is the 12th-century *Emmeram Gospel* from Regensburg. After touring at ground level, you can climb the wooden staircase of the **Sigismund Tower,** entering through the sacristy. The tower holds the famous Sigismund Bell, which was commissioned in 1520 by King Sigismund the Old and is still tolled on all solemn state and church occasions. ⊠ *Wawel.* 🎦 *Museum zł 5.* ⊙ *Tues.–Sun. 10–5:30.*

❾ **Kościół Franciszkanów** (Franciscan Church and Monastery). The mid–13th-century church and monastery are among the earliest brick buildings in Kraków. The Art Nouveau stained-glass windows and wall decorations by Stanisław Wyspiański are true masterpieces. ⊠ *Plac Wszystkich Świętych 1.*

OFF THE BEATEN PATH **KOPIEC KOŚCIUSZKI (KOŚCIUSZKO'S MOUND) –** This mound on the outskirts of Kraków was built in tribute to the memory of Tadeusz Kościuszko in 1820, three years after his death. The earth came from battlefields on which he had fought; soil from the United States was added in 1926. The best place from which to get a panoramic view of the city, the mound presides above a 19th-century Austrian fort. Take Tram 1 or 6 from plac Dominikański to the terminus at Salwator and then walk up aleja Waszyngtona to the mound. ⊙ *Daily 10–dusk.*

★ **❻ Kościół Mariacki** (Church of Our Lady). Dominating the northeast corner of Rynek Główny is the twin-towered Church of Our Lady. The
first church was built on this site before the town plan of 1257, which
is why it stands slightly askew from the main square; the present
church, completed in 1397, was built on the foundations of its prede-
cessor. You'll note that the two towers, added in the early 15th century, are of different heights. Legend has it that they were built by two
brothers, one of whom grew jealous of the other's work and slew him
with a sword. You can still see the supposed murder weapon, hanging
in the gate of the Sukiennice. From the higher tower, a strange bugle
call—known as the "Hejnał Mariacki"—rings out to mark each hour.
It breaks off on an abrupt sobbing note to commemorate an unknown
bugler struck in the throat by a Tartar arrow as he was playing his call
to warn the city of imminent attack. The church's main showpiece is
the magnificent wooden altarpiece with more than 200 carved figures,
the work of the 15th-century artist Wit Stwosz (Veit Stoss). The pan-
els depict medieval life in detail; the figure in the bottom right-hand
corner of the Crucifixion panel is believed to represent Stwosz himself. ⊠ *Rynek Główny, entrance from the side of Pl. Mariacki.* 🕿 *Church
free, altar zł3.* ☉ *Altar Mon.–Sat. 11:30–6, Sun. 2–6.*

⓰ Kościół na Skałce (Church on the Rock). Standing on the Vistula embankment to the south of Wawel Hill, this church is the center of the
cult of St. Stanisław. The bishop and martyr was beheaded and dis-
membered by order of the king in the church that stood on this spot
in 1079—a tale of rivalry similar to that of Henry II and Thomas à
Becket. The story goes that the saint's body was miraculously re-
assembled, as a symbol of the restoration of Poland's unity after its
years of fragmentation. Beginning in the 19th century, the church also
became the last resting place for well-known Polish writers and artists;
among those buried here are the composer Karol Szymanowski and
the painter and playwright Stanisław Wyspiański. ⊠ *Between Paulińska
and Skałeczna on the Vistula embankment.*

⓫ Kościół świętego Andrzeja (Church of St. Andrew). The finest surviving example of Romanesque architecture in Kraków is this 11th-cen-
tury fortified church. Local residents took refuge in St. Andrew during
Tartar raids. The interior, remodeled during the 18th century, includes
a fanciful pulpit resembling a boat. ⊠ *At the midpoint of Grodzka,
on the east side.*

⓬ Kościół świętego Piotra i Pawła (Church of Sts. Peter and Paul). The
first baroque church in Kraków was commissioned for the Jesuit order.
It is one of the most faithful and successful examples of transplanting
the model of the famous del Gesu Church (the "prototype" Jesuit
church in Rome) to foreign soil. At the fence are the figures of the 12
apostles. ⊠ *At the midpoint of Grodzka, on the east side, next to St.
Andrew's Church.*

★ **❺ Rynek Główny** (Main Market Square). Europe's largest medieval marketplace is on a par in size and grandeur with St. Mark's Square in Venice.
It even has the same plague of pigeons, although legend tells us the ones
here are no ordinary birds: they are allegedly the spirits of the knights
of Duke Henry IV Probus, who in the 13th century were cursed and
turned into birds. This great square was not always so spacious. In an
earlier period it contained—in addition to the present buildings—a Gothic
town hall, a Renaissance granary, a large weighing house, a foundry,
a pillory, and hundreds of traders' stalls. A few flower sellers under
colorful umbrellas and some portable souvenir stalls are all that remain
of this bustling commercial activity. Above all, Rynek is Kraków's largest

outdoor café, from spring through autumn, with more than 20 cafés scattered around the perimeter of the square.

A pageant of history has passed through this square. From 1320 on, Polish kings came here on the day after their coronation to meet the city's burghers and receive homage and tribute in the name of all the towns of Poland. Albert Hohenzollern, the grand master of the Teutonic Knights, came here in 1525 to pay homage to Sigismund the Old, King of Poland. And in 1794 Tadeusz Kościuszko took a solemn vow to overthrow czarist Russia here.

The **Dom pod Jeleniami** (House at the Sign of the Stag), at No. 36, was once an inn where both Goethe and Czar Nicholas I found shelter. At No. 45 is the **Dom pod Orłem** (House at the Sign of the Eagle), where Tadeusz Kościuszko lived as a young officer in 1777; a little farther down the square, at No. 6, is the **Szara Kamienica** (Gray House), which he made his staff headquarters in 1794. In the house at No. 9, the young Polish noblewoman Maryna Mniszchówna married the False Dymitri, the pretender to the Russian throne, in 1605. (These events are portrayed in Pushkin's play *Boris Godunov* and in Mussorgsky's operatic adaptation of it.) At No. 16 is the **14th-century house** of the Wierzynek merchant family. In 1364, during a "summit" meeting attended by the Holy Roman Emperor, one of the Wierzyneks gave an elaborate feast for the visiting royal dignitaries; today the house is a restaurant.

At the southwest corner of Rynek square, the **Wieża Ratuszowa** (Town Hall Tower) is all that remains of the 16th-century town hall, which was demolished in the early 19th century. The tower houses a branch of the Muzeum Historyczne Miasta Krakowa (Kraków History Museum) and affords a panoramic view of the old city. Although the museum and tower are closed during the winter, it's possible to organize a group visit. ⊠ *Rynek Główny,* ☎ *012/422-15-04.* 🎟 *zł 4.* ☉ *Apr.– Oct., daily 10–5.*

★ ❼ **Sukiennice** (Cloth Hall). A statue of Adam Mickiewicz sits in front of the eastern entrance to the Renaissance Cloth Hall, which stands in the middle of the Main Market Square. The Gothic arches date from the 14th century, but after a fire in 1555 the upper part was rebuilt in Renaissance style. The inner arcades on the ground floor still hold traders' booths, now mainly selling local crafts. On the first floor, in a branch of the National Museum, you can view a collection of 19th-century Polish paintings. ⊠ *Rynek Główny 1–3,* ☎ *012/422-11-66.* 🎟 *zł 7.* ☉ *Tues. and Thurs. 11–6, Wed. 9–3:30, weekends 10–3:30.*

NEED A BREAK? The **Kawiarnia Noworolski** (⊠ Rynek Główny 1), next to the entrance to the National Museum in the Cloth Hall, is a wonderful place to sit and watch the goings-on in the square, as well as to observe the hourly trumpet call from the tower of the Church of Our Lady.

❷ **Ulica Floriańska.** The beautiful **Brama Floriańska** (Florian Gate) was built around 1300 and leads through Kraków's old city walls into this street, which was laid out according to the town plan of 1257. The Gothic houses of the 13th-century burghers still remain, although they were rebuilt and given Renaissance or neoclassical facades. The house at No. 24, decorated with an emblem of three bells, was once the workshop of a bell founder. The chains hanging on the walls of the house at No. 17 barred the streets to invaders when the city was under siege. The **Dom pod Murzynami** (Negroes' House), standing where ulica Floriańska enters the market square, is a 16th-century tenement decorated with two rather fancifully imagined African tribesmen—testimony to the fascination with Africa entertained by Europeans in the Age of Discovery. The house was also once known as Dom pod Etiopy (House under the Ethiopians).

NEED A BREAK?   In the Art Nouveau café **Jama Michalikowa** (⊠ Floriańska 45, ☏ 012/ 422–15–61), the walls are hung with caricatures by late-19th-century customers, who sometimes paid their bills in kind.

★ ⑬ **Ulica Kanonicza.** This street, which leads from almost the center of town to the foot of Wawel Hill, is considered by some the most beautiful street in Europe. Most of the houses here date from the 14th and 15th centuries, although they were "modernized" in Renaissance or later styles. The street was named for the many canons of Wawel Cathedral who have lived here, including Pope John Paul II, who lived in the Chapter House at No. 19 and later in the late-16th-century Dean's House at No. 21. The Chapter House is now the **Muzeum Archidiecezjalne** (Archdiocesan Museum), displaying 13th-century paintings and other art belonging to the archdiocese, not to mention Pope John Paul II's former room. ⊠ Ul. Kanonicza 19, ☏ 012/421–89–63. ☑ zł 5. ☉ Tues.– Thurs. 10–4, weekends 10–3.

★ ⑮ **Zamek Królewski** (Royal Castle). The castle that now stands here dates from the early 16th century, when the Romanesque residence that stood on this site was destroyed by fire. King Sigismund the Old brought artists and craftsmen from Italy to create his castle, and despite baroque reconstruction after another fire in the late 16th century, several parts of the Renaissance castle remain, including the beautiful arcaded courtyard. After the transfer of the capital to Warsaw at the beginning of the 17th century, the castle was stripped of its fine furnishings, and later in the century it was devastated by the Swedish wars. In 1905, a voluntary Polish society purchased the castle from the Austrian authorities and began restoration. It narrowly escaped destruction in 1945, when the Nazis almost demolished it as a parting shot. Today you can visit the royal chambers, furnished in the style of the 16th and 17th centuries and hung with the 16th-century Belgian arras tapestries that during World War II were kept in Canada. The Royal Treasury on the ground floor contains a somewhat depleted collection of Polish crown jewels; the most fascinating item displayed here is the *Szczerbiec,* the jagged sword used from the early 14th century onward at the coronation of Polish kings. The Royal Armory houses a collection of Polish and Eastern arms and armor. The west wing holds an imposing collection of Turkish embroidered tents.

For many Poles, the castle's importance extends beyond its history. Hindu esoteric thinkers claim it is one of the world's mystic energy centers, a chakhra. Polish believers—and there have been hundreds of thousands over the last few decades—think that by rubbing up against the castle wall in the courtyard they will absorb vital energy.

☕ Every Polish child knows the legend of the fire-breathing dragon that once terrorized local residents from his **Smocza Jama** (Dragon's Den), a cave at the foot of Wawel Hill. Follow the signs to the ticket office opposite the castle, in the direction of the river. The dragon threatened to destroy the town unless he was fed a damsel a week. The king promised half his kingdom and his daughter's hand in marriage to any man who could slay the dragon. The usual quota of knights tried and failed. But finally a crafty cobbler named Skuba tricked the dragon into eating a lambskin filled with salt and sulfur. The dragon went wild with thirst, rushed into the Vistula River, and drank until it exploded. The Dragon's Den is still there, however, and in warmer months smoke and flame belch out of it every 15 minutes to thrill young visitors. A bronze statue of the dragon itself stands guard at the entrance. The den is open May–September, Monday–Thursday and weekends 10–3; admission is zł 3. To reach the castle, go to the end of Grodzka or Kanonicza streets, and then walk up Wawel Hill. ⊠ *Wawel*, ☎ *012/422–16–17.* 🎫 *Royal chambers zł 12, treasury and armory zł 10.* ☉ *Royal chambers, treasury, and armory Tues.–Thurs. and Sat. 9:30–3, Fri. 9:30–4, Sun. 10–3; hrs may be reduced off-season.*

Kazimierz

Kazimierz was founded by King Kazimierz the Great as a separate city in 1335. By the end of 15th century, it had come to house a growing Jewish district at a time when industrious and enterprising Jews were welcomed by the Polish kings to escape persecution in Europe. Thus, Kazimierz became one of the most important centers of the Jewish diaspora in Europe. Here they thrived until World War II.

A GOOD WALK

Southeast of Wawel Hill, you can take a tram from the corner of Bernadyńska and Starowiślna to the Kazimierz district (or on a pleasant day you can walk). Get off at the second tram stop on ulica Krakowska for plac Wolnica, site of the **Muzeum Etnograficzne** ⑰, which is in the former Kazimierz town hall. From the plaza, head north on ulica Bożego Ciała, past the **Kościół Bożego Ciała** ⑱, from which the street takes its name. Turn right onto ulica Józefa, go past the Synagoga Wysoka (High Synagogue), and then turn left onto ulica Jakuba to see the Synagoga Izaaka (Isaac's Synagogue), which dates from 1638 and is now the Lauder Foundation Education Center. Then continue down ulica Józefa to ulica Szeroka, where you'll find the **Stara Synagoga** ⑲, now the Jewish Historical Museum. Farther north along ulica Szeroka are the **Synagoga Remuh** ⑳ and the Jewish cemetery. Across the street, at ulica Dajwór 26, is the Synagoga Poppera, dating from 1620.

Take ulica Warszauera—noting the Synagoga Kupa, built by subscription in 1590—to ulica Estery and turn north to reach ulica Miodowa. Walk west to see the **Synagoga Tempel** ㉑. From here you can continue west along ulica Miodowa until you rejoin the tram route.

TIMING

The main sights of Kazimierz can be visited in a morning or afternoon; however, this city-within-a-city can easily keep you busy for a whole day.

SIGHTS TO SEE

⑱ **Kościół Bożego Ciała** (Corpus Christi Church). This 15th-century church was used by King Charles Gustavus of Sweden as his headquarters during the Siege of Kraków in 1655. ⊠ *Northeast corner of Plac Wolnica.*

⑰ **Muzeum Etnograficzne im. Seweryna Udzieli w Krakowie** (Ethnographic Museum). Kazimierz's 15th-century Ratusz (town hall) stands in the middle of plac Wolnica. It is now the Ethnographic Museum, displaying a well-mounted collection of regional folk art. ⊠ *Plac Wolnica 1*, ☎ *012/656–28–63.* 🎫 *zł 5.* ☉ *Mon. 10–6, Wed.–Fri. 10–3, weekends 10–2.*

⑲ **Stara Synagoga** (Old Synagogue). The oldest surviving example of Jewish religious architecture in Poland, this synagogue was built in the 15th century and reconstructed in Renaissance style following a fire in 1557. It was here in 1775 that Tadeusz Kościuszko successfully appealed to the Jewish community to join in the national insurrection. Looted and partly destroyed during the Nazi occupation, it has been rebuilt and now houses the **Museum of the History and Culture of Kraków Jews.** It's always closed on the first weekend of the month. ⊠ *Szeroka 24,* ☏ *012/422–09–62.* 🎫 *zł 5.* ☉ *Wed.–Thurs. and weekends 9–3, Fri. 11–6.*

NEED A BREAK?

Alef Café (⊠ Szeroka 17, ☏ 012/421–38–70) is as close as you can get to a glimpse of the lost world of Kazimierz. Musical performances are often given here.

⓴ Synagoga Remuh. This 16th-century synagogue is still used for worship and is named after the son of its founder, Rabbi Moses Isserles, who is buried in the **cemetery** attached to the synagogue. Used by the Jewish community from 1533 to 1799, this is the only well-preserved Renaissance Jewish cemetery in Europe. (The so-called new cemetery on ulica Miodowa, which contains many old headstones, was established in 1800.) ⊠ *Szeroka 40.* 🎫 *zł 2.* ☉ *Weekdays 9–6.*

㉑ Synagoga Tempel. The 19th-century Reformed Tempel Synagogue is one of only two synagogues in Kraków still used for worship. At this writing, the synagogue was open only for prayers and an occasional concert. ⊠ *Corner of Miodowa and Podbrzezie.*

Dining

$$$–$$$$ ✕ **Copernicus.** This top-class restaurant situated in a hotel by the same name in one of Kraków's loveliest corners, at the foot of Wawel Hill, will delight you with its elegant and imaginative menu, cosmopolitan but also traditionally Polish at the same time. The venison rolled in bacon, served with cabbage-filled pierogi, is widely considered the best offering on the menu. The restaurant is expensive, but worth every złoty, considered by many gourmets Kraków's best restaurant. ⊠ *Hotel Copernicus, Kanonicza 16,* ☏ *012/431–10–44. Reservations essential. AE, DC, MC, V.*

$$$–$$$$ ✕ **Pod Róża.** Built in a converted courtyard of a tenement house,
★ Under the Rose is airy, spacious, and elegant, all under a glass roof. A seasonally changing, contemporary menu is matched by impeccable service; there is nightly live piano music. The chefs make their own pastas, ice cream, and bread. Adjoining is a sister restaurant, Amarone, with slightly cheaper Italian cuisine. ⊠ *Floriańska 14,* ☏ *0–12/424–33–81. Reservations essential. AE, DC, MC, V.*

$$$–$$$$ ✕ **Tetmajerowska.** Established in 1876, this second-floor restaurant sparkles with crystal and gleaming cutlery. It takes its name from the painter Włodzimierz Tetmajer, whose frieze decorates the room. Try the fried eel in cream and dill sauce or one of the excellent veal dishes. Also part of Tetmajerowska is Hawełka, a less pricey restaurant on the ground floor. ⊠ *Rynek Główny 34,* ☏ *012/422–06–31. Reservations essential. AE, DC, MC, V.*

$$–$$$$ ✕ **Padva.** Kraków's premier Italian restaurant is propitiously located just opposite the Renaissance courtyard of Collegium Maius. It is certainly hard to argue with Padva's comprehensive Italian menu featuring excellent antipasti and pastas and extra efforts, including seafood that is flown in directly from Italy twice a week. ⊠ *Jagiellońska 2,* ☏ *012/292–02–72. AE, DC, MC, V.*

$$–$$$ ✕ **Chłopskie Jadło.** This restaurant's name means "Peasant Kitchen,"
★ but this is the most upscale interpretation of that theme imaginable. For a starter try the żurek (stone soup) made from soured barley; then indulge in the very traditional main course of cabbage rolls stuffed with sauerkraut and grits in a mushroom sauce. All meals come with com-

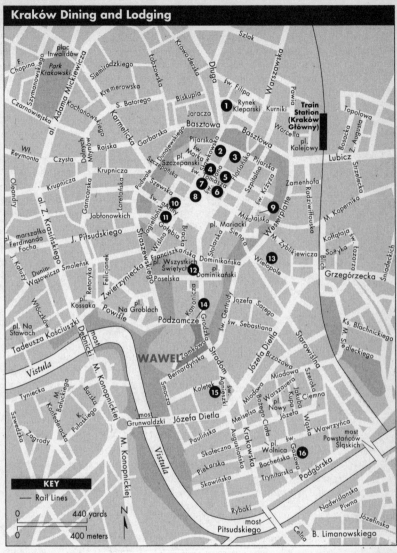

Kraków Dining and Lodging

Dining

Brasserie **16**
Cherubino **6**
Chimera Salad Bar . **10**
Chłopskie
Jadło **15**
Copernicus **14**
La Fontaine **7**
Padva **11**
Pod Aniołami **12**
Pod Różą **5**
Tetmajerowska **8**

Lodging

Amadeus Hotel **9**
Atrium **1**
Francuski
Orbis Hotel **2**
Grand Hotel **4**
Holiday Inn **13**
Hotel Copernicus . . **14**
Hotel Polski
(Pod Białym Orłem) . **3**
Pod Różą **5**

plimentary bread and lard, and the menu is an artery-clogging cross-section of traditional Polish peasant cuisine. ⊠ *Św. Agnieszki 1,* ☎ *012/421-85-20. Reservations essential. AE, DC, MC, V.*

$$-$$$ ✕ **La Fontaine.** Possibly the best French restaurant in town is just off the main square. Although the restaurant is snugly situated in a medieval cellar, in the summer a little garden opens in the courtyard. The owner and chef, Pierre Gaillard, a disciple of Paul Bocusse, is a true artist and his dishes little works of art. Try the snails, beautifully prepared and served in four different styles, or the very tempting desserts, particularly the crème brûlée. ⊠ *Sławkowska 1,* ☎ *012/431-09-30. Reservations essential. AE, DC, MC, V.*

$$-$$$ ✕ **Pod Aniołami.** Legend has it that this downstairs cellar was once ★ an alchemist's lab. These days, Under the Angels is one of the more tastefully furnished restaurants in Kraków, with excellent interpretations of Polish cuisine. Try smoked sheep's-milk cheese warmed under the grill, then the delectable Mr. John's Ribs. Patrons crowd onto the upstairs courtyard when the weather is warm. ⊠ *Grodzka 35,* ☎ *012/421-39-99. Reservations essential. AE, DC, MC, V.*

$-$$ ✕ **Brasserie.** Located slightly off the beaten track, Brasserie is a good ★ choice when you are touring the Kazimierz district. In the converted 19th-century tram terminal you'll find a truly Parisian ambiance, which manifests itself in the music, decor, and, above all, the menu. Try the spicy gratin of soft cheeses or a generous portion of *moules* (mussels). ⊠ *Gazowa 4,* ☎ *012/292-19-98. AE, DC, MC, V.*

$-$$ ✕ **Cherubino.** Cherubino must have one of the most intriguing menus ★ in Kraków, with a combination of Tuscan cuisine and lighter, more contemporary interpretations of Polish cuisine. Next to traditional gnocchi, carpaccio, and cannelloni, the menu features pierogi, roast duck, and buckwheat soup. The decor is also memorable: you can choose to dine under a winged boat or in one of four beautifully restored 19th-century carriages. ⊠ *Św. Tomasza 15,* ☎ *012/429-40-07. Reservations essential. AE, DC, MC, V.*

$ ✕ **Chimera Salad Bar.** In a downstairs cellar with arras and Victorian etchings on its walls, you'll find Kraków's most upmarket salad bar. The nourishing salads are a tremendous value, but some cooked meals are also available. Some savory staples include stuffed eggplant and a spinach soufflé. ⊠ *Św. Anny 3,* ☎ *012/429-11-68. No credit cards.*

Lodging

Kraków remains lamentably short on first-class accommodations close to the city center. Some satisfactory mid-range hotels have sprung up in the last year or so, but visitors should still book well in advance—even in winter, when the city plays host to many business conferences and hotels fill up. If you're staying in the Old Town, rooms facing the street can be noisy at night, so request a quiet room.

$$$$ 🛏 **Holiday Inn.** The four-star Holiday Inn Kraków opened in September 2001, in a newly refurbished and extended block of historic tenement houses. Although the rooms are very nice, they are also business-hotel standard and not terribly unique or nearly as atmospheric as the building itself. The hotel is next to the Main Post Office, just outside the Planty ring, within walking distance to both the Market Square and Main Railway Station. ⊠ *Wielopole 4, 31-072,* ☎ *012/619-00-00,* FAX *012/619-00-05,* WEB *www.krakow.globalhotels.pl. 154 rooms, 10 suites. Restaurant, café, room service, minibars, gym, sauna, laundry service, Internet, meeting rooms. AE, DC, MC, V. BP.*

$$$-$$$$ 🛏 **Hotel Copernicus.** Hotel Copernicus is a tastefully adapted medieval ★ tenement house in the oldest and, arguably, the most charming street in Kraków. A story goes that Copernicus himself (a graduate of the

Kraków University) stayed here once. Whether that's true or not, traces of history definitely remain in Renaissance portals, wall paintings, and floor mosaics, while all rooms are happily modern: air-conditioned and equipped with minibars, TV, and jetted bathtubs. ✉ *Kanonicza 16, 31-002,* ☎ *012/424–34–00,* FAX *012/424–34–05,* WEB *www.hotel.com.pl. 29 rooms, 8 suites. Restaurant, café, room service, in-room hot tubs, minibars, indoor pool, sauna, laundry service, meeting room, Internet. AE, DC, MC, V. BP.*

$$$ 🏨 **Amadeus Hotel.** A stone's throw from the Rynek, this small hotel
★ is among Kraków's newest. In style and ambience, it claims inspiration with Wolfgang Amadeus. This cozy and elegant establishment has hosted such celebrities as Mikhail Baryshnikov and Mrs. Vladimir Putin. The hotel's restaurant, in addition to the standard menu, features a selection of dishes from a different country each month. ✉ *Mikołajska 20, 30-027,* ☎ *012/429–60–70,* FAX *012/429–60–62,* WEB *www.hotel-amadeus.pl. 20 rooms, 2 suites. Restaurant, café, room service, cable TV, minibars, gym, sauna, bar, laundry service, Internet, meeting rooms. AE, DC, MC, V. BP.*

$$$ 🏨 **Francuski Orbis Hotel.** The "French" hotel is just across the street from Czartoryski Museum, where Leonardo Da Vinci's *Cecilia Gallerani* resides. A sweeping spiral staircase leads up from the large, high-ceilinged lobby to rooms decorated in faux fin-de-siècle grandeur. ✉ *Pijarska 13, 31–015,* ☎ *012/422–51–22,* FAX *012/422–52–70,* WEB *www.orbis.pl. 27 rooms, 15 suites. Restaurant, room service, cable TV, minibars, bar, dry-cleaning, laundry service, business services, meeting room, some pets allowed; no a/c in some rooms, no-smoking rooms. AE, DC, MC, V. BP.*

$$$ 🏨 **Grand Hotel.** Without question this hotel around the corner from Kraków's main square is the most elegant address for visitors to the city and the one most accessible to the major sights. The decor is Regency-inspired, though most of the furnishings are reproductions. Suite 11 has two large bathrooms, a gilded ceiling, and a bedroom fit for a potentate. The banquet room has its own miniature hall of mirrors. ✉ *Sławkowska 5–7, 31–016,* ☎ *012/421–72–55,* FAX *012/421–83–60,* WEB *www.grand.pl. 50 rooms, 6 suites. Restaurant, café, cable TV, minibars, bar. AE, DC, MC, V. BP.*

$$$ 🏨 **Pod Różą.** The management is still proud that both Chopin and Czar
★ Alexander I slept here. More recently, it has welcomed presidents and royals. Housed in a 14th-century building, the hotel offers guests spacious, high-ceilinged rooms on the fashionable shopping street Floriańska. The first-class Italian restaurant and 15th-century wine cellar add to the Pod Róża's attractions. ✉ *Floriańska 14, 31–021,* ☎ *012/424–33–00,* FAX *012/424–33–51.* WEB *www.hotel.com.pl. 51 rooms, 3 suites. 2 restaurants, café, cable TV, minibars, meeting rooms, wine bar. AE, DC, MC, V. BP.*

$$$ 🏨 **Hotel Polski (Pod Białym Orłem).** Located within the medieval city walls, opposite the open-air art gallery by the Florianska gate, the simple, unpretentious hotel Under the White Eagle upgraded its facilities in 2001. ✉ *Pijarska 17, 31–015,* ☎ *012/422–11–44,* FAX *012/422–15–29,* WEB *www.podorlem.com.pl. 50 rooms, 3 suites. AE, DC, MC, V. BP.*

$$ 🏨 **Atrium.** This neat hotel, which opened in 2000, is less fashionably located just outside the green girdle of Planty. It is still very near the Main Square—a mere five-minute walk. And it's a good value for money. ✉ *Krzywa 7, 31-149,* ☎ *012/430–02–03,* FAX *012/430–01–96,* WEB *www.hotelatrium.com.pl. 47 rooms, 4 suites, 3 apartments. Restaurant, cable TV, meeting rooms, parking (fee), some pets allowed. AE, DC, MC, V.*

Nightlife and the Arts

Kraków has a lively tradition in theater and music. Pick up a copy of *Karnet,* which gives detailed cultural information in Polish and English, or *Kraków in Your Pocket,* which has a reasonably comprehensive entertainment calendar and is available in kiosks all over town.

Nightlife

BARS

The mysterious **Alchemia** (✉ Estery 5) is a great bar in Kazimierz, near plac Nowy. **O'Morgan's Irish Pub** (✉ Garncarska 5) is headquarters for Kraków's English-speaking community. **Les Couleurs** (✉ Estery 10) is the Kazimierz address to seek out if you want a Parisian atmosphere along with your drinks. At trendy **Paparazzi** (✉ Mikołajska 9) you can observe Kraków's beautiful people in action and sip the best cocktails in town. **Singer** (✉ Estery 20) is a good, though smoky, bar in Kazimierz. **Stalowe Magnolie** (Steel Magnolias; ✉ św. Jana 15) is an elegant faux-fin-de-siècle music club (smart attire required). **Tam i z powrotem** (✉ pl. Nowy 9) is a Kazimierz bar with a decidedly British feel.

CABARET AND LIVE MUSIC

Like many restaurants in Kazimierz, **Alef** (✉ Szeroka 17) is a place where Klezmer music is on hand every night. **Harris Piano Jazz Bar** (✉ Rynek Główny 28), in Old Town, is a good spot for jazz. At **Jama Michalika** (✉ Floriańska 45), popular musical and comedic cabarets take place in a café that has remained essentially the same for a century. The underground venue **Klub Indigo** (✉ Floriańska 26) simulcasts concerts by Polish and international musicians on Poland's Jazz Radio. **Loch Camelot** (✉ św. Tomasza 17) is a traditional Polish café with regular cabaret performances held in its basement. The cabaret at **Pod Baranami** (✉ Rynek Główny 27) was founded in 1956 by Kraków theater legend Piotr Skrzynecki. Jazz sessions are regularly held at **U Muniaka** (✉ Floriańska 3).

The Arts

FILM

Kraków Cinema Centre ARS (✉ św. Jana 6, ☎ 012/421–41–99) shows movies from Hollywood and Europe, almost always in the original language with Polish subtitles. The center also screens contemporary Polish films.

MUSIC

If you're a fan of chamber music, there are occasional performances in the great hall of the Zamek Królewski (Royal Castle) on Wawel Hill, at the Municipal Arsenal, or at the Sukiennice Art Gallery. Kraków's symphony, **Filharmonia im. Karola Szymanowskiego** (✉ Philharmonic Hall, Zwierzyniecka 1, ☎ 012/422–94–77 tickets), gives frequent concerts. Look out for the performances of **Sinfonietta Cracovia** (☎ 012/415–00–97 schedule and ticket information); Kraków's young and brilliant city orchestra performs in different venues all over town.

OPERA AND DANCE

The stunning **Teatr im. Juliusza Słowackiego** (Słowacki Theater; ✉ pl. św. Ducha 1, ☎ 012/422–43–22) hosts traditional opera and ballet favorites as well as dramatic performances.

THEATER

The popular **Bagatela** (✉ Karmelicka 6, ☎ 012/422–45–44) is a venue for children's theater as well as adult drama and farce. **Scena pod Ratuszem** (✉ Wież Ratuszowa, ☎ 012/421–16–57), a tiny theater in the cellar of the Town Hall Tower, stages small-scale dramas in front of a bare-brick backdrop. The **Stary Teatr** (✉ Jagiellońska 5, ☎ 012/422–

85–66) is Kraków's oldest and most renowned theater. Every summer in July, Kraków hosts the **Street Theatre Festival** (☎ 012/633–89–47) with performances all around town, but mostly at Kraków's biggest outdoor stage, Rynek Główny.

Outdoor Activities and Sports

Hiking

In the immediate vicinity of Kraków, there are great hiking trails, notably in the Las Wolski (Wolski Forest), which hides nature reserves, a zoo, a horseback riding center, and a Camadolese Monastery. For details, pick up the brochure *Active Leisure* from the Tourist Information Point at Planty/Szpitalna. Farther afield, the Niepołomice Forest has extensive hiking trails over flat, sandy terrain. Ojców National Park has marked trails for hikers, some of which are steep and fairly rough.

Jogging

If you want to jog in Kraków, the Planty, a ring of gardens around the Old Town, makes an excellent 5-km (3-mi) route and is easily accessible from most hotels. The pathways along the Vistula also provide a good jogging route: west of the Dębnicki Bridge, take the path on the right bank; east of the bridge, the one on the left bank.

Shopping

In Kraków's Old Town, department stores and brand-name fashion and leisure-wear stores are on the increase, while the number of crafts and specialty shops is declining. Most shops are open weekdays 10–6, Saturday 9–2.

For regionally produced goods, head to the Rynek Główny (Main Market Square). At the booths in the Sukiennice you'll find tooled leather goods, local crystal and glass, wood carvings, and the embroidered felt slippers made in the Podhale region. Rabbit-skin slippers are also a local specialty.

Kraków Essentials

AIR TRAVEL

There are direct air connections on LOT, the Polish airline, between Kraków and Chicago, Newark, and New York (JFK), and the city can be reached by direct flight from most major European cities, including Frankfurt, London, Paris, Rome, Vienna, and Zurich. LOT flies several times daily between Kraków and Warsaw; the flight takes 40 minutes. LOT's Kraków office is open weekdays 9–6, Saturday 9–3. Most flights into Kraków–Balice are operated by LOT, though some flights are code shares with other airlines, and a number of seats are available to other airlines on LOT flights. Orbis is a good source for tickets.

➤ AIRLINES: **Alitalia** (✉ Intercrac Travel, ul. Krupnicza 3, ☎ 012/431–06–21). **Austrian Airlines** (✉ ul. Krakowska 41, ☎ 012/429–66–66). **LOT** (✉ Pope John Paul II Kraków–Balice Airport, Balice, ☎ 012/285–50–51; ✉ Basztowa 15, ☎ 012/422–42–15 or 012/422–66–83). **Orbis Travel** (✉ Rynek Główny 41, ☎ 012/428–19–91).

AIRPORTS AND TRANSFERS

The Pope John Paul II Kraków–Balice Airport, 11 km (7 mi) west of the city, is the region's only airport. In spring and fall fog can cause frustrating delays.

➤ CONTACTS: **Pope John Paul II Kraków–Balice Airport** (☎ 012/411–19–55, WEB www.lotnisko-balice.pl).

Bus 208 runs between the airport and the main train station, and Bus 192 between Rondo Mogilskie and the airport. The basic fare is zł 2.20 with an extra charge for luggage. Taxis are available from outside the terminal, and the fare into the city center is approximately zł 50.

BUS TRAVEL
Express bus service to Kraków runs regularly to and from most Polish cities. The journey to or from Warsaw's main PKS station takes three hours. All buses arrive at the main PKS station, just across from the train station on plac Kolejowy. From here you can transfer to buses headed for other destinations in the region.
➤ CONTACTS: **Kraków Main PKS Station** (✉ ul. Worcella, ☎ 012/9316, WEB www.eurolines.com.pl).

CAR TRAVEL
A car will not be of much use to you in Kraków, since most of the Old Town is closed to traffic and distances between major sights are short. A car will be invaluable, however, if you set out to explore the rest of the region. You can approach Kraków either on the E77 highway (from Warsaw and north) or via the E40 (from the area around Katowice). Use the parking facilities at your hotel or one of the attended municipal parking garages (try plac Szczepański or plac świętego Ducha). On the whole, parking space in Kraków is rather scarce and expensive—between zł 5 and zł 10 per hour.

EMBASSIES AND CONSULATES
There is a U.S. consulate in Kraków. See the A to Z section at the end of this chapter for the address.

EMERGENCIES
➤ LATE-NIGHT PHARMACIES: **Nonstop** (✉ Dunajewskiego 2, ☎ 012/422–65–04).

TRAIN TRAVEL
Nonstop express trains from Warsaw take just under three hours and run throughout the day. All trains arrive at Kraków Główny Station on the edge of the Old Town.
➤ CONTACTS: **Kraków Główny Station** (✉ pl. Dworcowy 1, ☎ 012/9436).

TOURS
All major hotels will arrange tours of the city as well as surrounding attractions. For tours of Jewish Kraków go to Jarden Tours or one of the smaller operators (such as Bell Travel and Individual Guided Tours), who provide well-informed, friendly guide services for both individuals and groups. Orbis, through its subsidiary Cracow Tours, organizes tours by bus, minibus, or limousine, at prices ranging from $30 for a half-day coach tour to $140 for a full-day tour in a chauffeur-driven car. Throughout the year they lead half-day visits to the Nazi concentration camp at Oświęcim (Auschwitz) or the Wieliczka salt mine, half-day tours of Kraków, and junkets to the Ojców National Park. In the summer they also offer a day-trip to the Dunajec River gorge (including a journey down the river by raft). Orbis will also arrange day trips to Pope John Paul II's birthplace at Wadowice, to the Bernadine Monastery at Kalwaria Zebrzydowska, and to the Pauline Monastery at Częstochowa.

On summer weekends (May–September), there Żegluga krakowska operates slow boat trips to Tyniec Abbey three times a day (10, 1, and

6), starting from a small wharf below the Wawel castle, by Grunwaldzki bridge. The trip lasts three hours, and a ticket costs zł 15.

➤ CONTACTS: **Bell Travel** (✉ ul. Pilotów 13, ☎ 012/411–48–16 or 48/601–520–885). **Individual Guided Tours** (✉ os. Przy Arce 13, ☎ 48/602–131–919). **Jarden Tours** (✉ Szeroka 2, ☎ 012/421–13–74, WEB www.jarden.pl). **Orbis/Cracow Tours** (✉ Rynek Główny 41, ☎ 012/422–11–57). **Żegluga krakowska** (✉ Wawel wharf, ☎ 012/422–08–55).

VISITOR INFORMATION

The Cultural Information Center is open weekdays 10–6, Saturday until 4. To change money and purchase air, train, and bus tickets, head to Orbis, which is open weekdays 9–5 and Saturday 9–2. The Tourist Information Point, in the Planty, between the Main Railway Station and Słowackiego Theatre, is open Monday–Friday 8–8, weekends 9–5. The privately run Tourist Information Office is open weekdays 9–6 and Saturday 9–2.

➤ CONTACTS: **Cultural Information Center** (✉ św. Jana 2, ☎ 012/421–77–87, WEB www.karnet.krakow2000.pl). **Orbis** (✉ Rynek Główny 41, ☎ 012/422–11–57). **Tourist Information Office** (✉ Rynek Główny, Sukiennice 1/3, ☎ 012/422–60–91). **Tourist Information Point** (✉ Szpitalna 25, ☎ 012/432–01–10 or 012/432–00–60).

MAŁOPOLSKA

Just to the south of Kraków, Poland's great plains give way to the gently folding foothills of the Carpathians, building to the High Tatras on the Slovak border. The fine medieval architecture of many towns in Małopolska (Little Poland) comes from a period when the area prospered as the intersection of thriving trade routes. In the countryside, wooden homesteads and strip-farmed tracts tell another story: of the hardships and poverty the peasantry endured before the 20th century brought tourists to the mountains. During the 19th century, when this part of Poland was under Austrian rule as the province of Western Galicia, hundreds of thousands of peasants fled from the grinding toil on poor soil to seek their fortune in the United States; it sometimes seems as if every family hereabouts has a cousin in America.

A visit to Kraków and Małopolska is incomplete without trips to at least two nearby destinations: the Wieliczka Salt Mine, where salt has been mined for a thousand years, and Auschwitz and Birkenau, sites of the Nazis' most gruesome and brutal concentration camps. Farther afield are Ojców National Park and Zakopane, both of which offer first-rate hiking in unadulterated natural surroundings. This is also Poland's main winter sports area. Zakopane is the self-styled winter capital of Poland, and the spa towns of Szczawnica, Krościenko, and Krynica are good bases for cross-country skiing. If you've been looking for insight into the devout Catholicism of the Poles, head to Częstochowa, where 5 million people a year come to pray before the famous ancient icon of the Virgin Mary and baby Jesus known as the Black Madonna.

Małopolska remains intensely Catholic and conservative, and the traditional way of life in the countryside is relatively intact. Folk crafts and customs are still very much alive in the mountains and foothills. *Podhale*, carved-wood beehives, stand in mountain gardens, and worshipers set out for Sunday church in embroidered white-felt trousers.

This is one of the only regions in Poland where you'll find a number of inexpensive bed-and-breakfast accommodations in private pensions. Pensions (generally small hotels) usually offer full board and hearty meals.

Numbers in the margin correspond to numbers on the Southeastern Poland map.

Częstochowa

❶ *120 km (74 mi) northwest of Kraków, 220 km (136 mi) southwest of Warsaw.*

★ An estimated 5 million pilgrims a year make their way, some on foot, to the town of Częstochowa. They come to see the 14th-century **Klasztor Paulinów** (Pauline Monastery) at the Jasna Góra (Hill of Light). The town itself grew with the monastery, and there is little else to draw visitors here. Although the Communist government planted industry here in the hope of overshadowing the cult, that didn't happen. Inside the monastery is Poland's holiest shrine, home to the *Black Madonna of Częstochowa,* a wood-pane painting of a dark-skinned Madonna and child, the origins of which are uncertain (legend attributes the work to Luke the Apostle himself, and it may have been executed anytime between the 6th and 14th centuries, anywhere between Byzantium and Hungary). It has a number of miracles attributed to it, including the repulsion of invading Swedish forces in the 16th century. The Black Madonna's designation as savior of Poland dates from those turbulent days. To see the Black Madonna, you have to join the faithful and walk on your knees behind a screen, where the eyes, according to believers, will fix directly on you. The monastery was rebuilt in baroque style during the 17th and 18th centuries, as was the interior of the Gothic church. The **Monastery Treasury** holds an important collection of manuscripts and works of art. ⊠ *al. Najświętszej Marii Panny 1.* ☎ *Free.* ☉ *Treasury daily 11–1 and 3–5.*

Dining and Lodging

$–$$ ✕ **Wiking.** You can take in the local color at this crowded restaurant. Try the herring in cream as a starter, followed by chicken with potatoes. ⊠ *Nowowiejska,* ☎ *034/324–57–68. No credit cards.*

$$ ☆ **Mercure Patria Częstochowa.** This six-story 1980s hotel, which is owned by Accor's Mercure group and managed by Orbis, offers predictable cuisine and accommodations close to the Jasna Góra Monastery. Rooms are brightly furnished and comfortable, the staff cheerful and friendly. ⊠ *Popiełuszki 2, 42–200,* ☎ *034/324–70–01,* FAX *034/324–63–32,* WEB *www.mercure.com. 96 rooms, 6 suites. 2 restaurants, tennis court, volleyball, bar. AE, DC, MC, V. BP.*

$$ ☆ **Hotel Inter.** This modern hotel is privately owned and reasonably priced. There is satellite TV in every room, and there's a small fitness center. ⊠ *Marszalka E. Rydza-Smiglego 26–34, 42–225,* ☎ *034/366–02–67,* FAX *034/366–04–57. 17 rooms, 40 beds. Cable TV, gym. AE, DC, MC, V.*

Ojców National Park

❷ *48 km (30 mi) northwest of Kraków.*

This national park covers the limestone gorge of the Prądnik River. The ridge above the gorge is topped by a series of ruined castles that once guarded the trade route from Kraków to Silesia. The Renaissance castle **Pieskowa Skała** (⊠ *Sułoszowa,* WEB www.wawel.krakow.pl), which now houses a branch of the Wawel Museum's art collection, is the best-preserved in Ojców National Park. Admission to the museum is zł 7, and it's open Tuesday–Friday 10–3:30 and weekends 10–5:30. The castle is on a side road that branches off from the main Olkusz–Kraków route; it's 22 km (13 mi) from Olkusz, 25 km (15 mi) from Kraków.

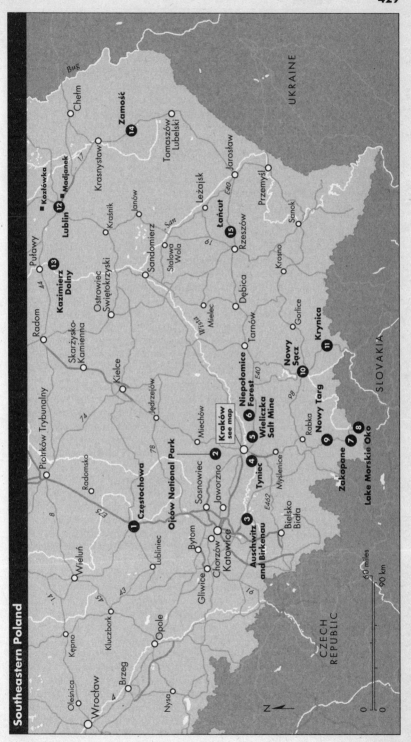

Southeastern Poland

Ojców's limestone caves are linked with many legends. In one, Władysław the Short, a medieval Polish king, is supposed to have escaped his German pursuers with the help of a spider that spun a web over the mouth of the cave in which he was hiding. You can visit **Władysław the Short's cave** (✉ Czajowice, ☎ 012/389–20–27; 012/389–20–10 guided tour reservations). Admission is zł 5 and 3, and it is open May–October, daily 9:30–6. The gorge is at its best in autumn, when shades of gold and red stand out against the white limestone. To reach the park from Kraków, take the E40 northwest and turn off at Jerzmanowice for Pieskowa Skała. For the cave, park at Czajowice and walk from there. PKS buses leave regularly from the bus station on plac Kolejowy in Kraków. ✉ *Ojców*.

Auschwitz and Birkenau

★ ❸ *50 km (31 mi) southwest of Ojców National Park, 60 km (38 mi) west of Kraków.*

Between 1940 and 1945 more than 1.5 million people, 90% of them Jews from Poland and throughout Europe, died here in the Nazis' largest death-camp complex. The camp in the small town of Oświęcim (better known by its German name, Auschwitz) has come to be seen as the epicenter of the moral collapse of the West, proof of the human capacity for tremendous evil. The gas chambers at nearby Brzezinka (Birkenau) could exterminate thousands in a single day. The first inmates were Polish political prisoners, and the first gas victims were Russian POWs; the dead eventually included Jews, Romanies (Gypsies), homosexuals, Jehovah's Witnesses, and so-called criminals.

The *Konzentrationslager* (concentration camp) had three parts: Auschwitz, Birkenau, and Monowitz (where a chemical plant was run by prison labor). The barracks at Auschwitz have been completely restored and made into the **Państwowe Muzeum Auschwitz-Birkenau w Oswiecimiu** (Auschwitz-Birkenau State Museum), which has been described by one survivor, the author Primo Levi, as "something static, rearranged, contrived." With that in mind, begin with the heart-rending movie filmed by Soviet troops on January 27, 1945, the day they liberated the few prisoners left behind by the retreating Germans. The English version runs a few times a day, although narration isn't really necessary. Purchase a guidebook in English (most exhibits are in Polish or German) and walk through the notorious gate marked ARBEIT MACHT FREI (Work Brings Freedom). The most provocative exhibits are the huge piles of belongings confiscated from victims, as well as the two tons of human hair intended for use in the German textile industry. The execution wall, the prison block, and the reconstructed crematorium at the end of the tour are harshly sobering.Far more affecting than the restored Auschwitz are the unaltered barracks, electric fences, and blown-up gas chambers at the enormous **Birkenau** camp 3 km (2 mi) away. More prisoners lived and died here than at Auschwitz, including hundreds of thousands who went directly to the gas chambers from boxcars in which they had been locked up for days. The camp has been preserved to look much the way it did after the Nazis abandoned it. A walk to the back area brings you to the Monument to the Glory of the Victims, designed by Polish and Italian artists and erected in 1967. Behind the trees to the right of the monument lies a farm pond, its banks still murky with human ashes and bone fragments. To hear the tape on the camp's history in English, ask the reception staff in the main guardhouse. There are regularly scheduled, guided tours in English for an additional fee (inquire at the museum). To reach the camps from Kraków, take the E22a or the train or bus from plac Kolejowy.

You can park at either camp, and from April 15 to October 31 a shuttle bus runs between them once an hour. ⊠ *Więźniów Oświęcimia 20, Oświęcim* ☎ *033/843–20–22,* WEB *www.auschwitz-muzeum.oswiecim.pl.* ▣ *Auschwitz and Birkenau free, film zł 2, guided tours in English zł 174.* ⊙ *Auschwitz museum daily 8–6, Birkenau daily 9–4.*

Tyniec Abbey

❹ *43 km (27 mi) east of Oświęcim, 12 km (7½ mi) southwest of Kraków.*

The **Benedictine Abbey** at Tyniec is perched high on a cliff above the Vistula River. Benedictine monks settled at Tyniec already in the 11th century. From this fortified cloister, the Confederates of Bar set off in 1772 to raid Kraków; as a result the abbey was destroyed later that year by the Russian army. In 1817 the Benedictine order was banned and the monks disbanded. It was not until 1939 that the order recovered the land and not until the late 1960s that it again became an abbey and the work of reconstruction began in earnest. From May to September recitals of organ music are held in the abbey church. From Kraków take Highway 7(E77) south to Highway A4, then take A4 about 4 km (2½ mi) to Tyniec; or take Bus 112 from most Grunwaldzki, near the Forum Hotel. On summer weekends, Żlegluga krakowska runs boat trips to the abbey from Kraków (*see* Tours *in* Kraków Essentials, above). ⊠ *Tyniec.* ▣ *Free.* ⊙ *Daily 9–4.*

Wieliczka Salt Mine

★ **❺** *12 km (7½ mi) southeast of Kraków on the E40.*

Although the beginnings of evaporated salt production in the Wieliczka area go back to prehistoric times, rock salt was discovered here in the second half of the 13th century. By the 14th century the salt was so prized that King Kazimierz the Great built city walls with 11 defense towers at Wieliczka to protect the mines from Tartar raids. Now the mine is a must-visit: the fascinating tour takes you through historic galleries and chambers 150 yards below ground level, including amazing underground lakes and underground chapels carved by medieval miners, the most magnificent of which is the **Chapel of the Blessed Kinga** (Kinga was a 14th-century Polish queen). Minibus tours to the salt mine leave from the Kraków train station. ⊠ *Daniłowicza 10, Wieliczka,* ☎ *012/278–73–02.* ▣ *zł 29.* ⊙ *Daily 7:30–7:30.*

Niepołomice Forest

❻ *12 km (7½ mi) east of Wieliczka, 25 km (15 mi) east of Kraków.*

The town of Niepołomice is on the western edge of the forest and has a 14th-century **hunting lodge** and **church** built by Kazimierz the Great. Animals, including bison, still live in the forest, and you may be lucky enough to see some of them as you stroll under the ancient oak trees. From Kraków, take the E40 east and turn north at Wieliczka, or take a PKS bus or train from plac Kolejowy. On summer weekends Kraków city transport also runs special buses to Niepołomice from plac Kolejowy. ⊠ *Niepołomice.* ▣ *Free.* ⊙ *Church daily dawn–dusk.*

Zakopane

★ **❼** *100 km (62 mi) south of Kraków on Hwy. E95.*

Nestled at the foot of the Tatra Mountains, at 3,281 ft above sea level, Zakopane is the highest town in Poland (it's the southernmost as well). Until the 19th-century romantic movement started a fashion for mountain scenery, Zakopane was a poor and remote village. During the 1870s, when the Tatra Association was founded, people began coming to the mountains for their health and recreation, and Zakopane developed into Poland's leading mountain resort. At the turn of the 20th century it was home to many writers, painters, and musicians. Of these, the most famous are the composer Karol Szymanowski and the artist and playwright Stanisław Witkiewicz (Witkacy). The father of the latter, also named Stanisław Witkiewicz, was responsible for creating the so-called Zakopane style inspired by traditional local wooden architecture.

The town is small, and its sights can easily be covered on foot. Ulica Krupówki, the main thoroughfare, runs downhill through the town from northwest to southeast. If you begin at the northwest end, you will pass many buildings in the Zakopane style. Ulica Kościuszki runs east to west across Krupówki and links the town with the railway and bus stations. At the bottom of the hill is ulica Kościeliska.

A cable railway can take you from the center of town up to the high ridge of **Gubałówka,** where on a clear day you will have a fine view of the Tatras and of the town. An alternative to riding the cable car back into town is to take the path along the ridge to Pałkówka and from there back down into town, about 9 km (5½ mi). Children can have their photograph taken on the Gubałówka terrace in a carriage drawn by four white mountain sheepdogs and driven by a man dressed in a white bearskin. *The cable railway station is down from the corner of ulica Krupówki and ulica Kościeliska, at the end of the path lined with souvenir stalls.*

At the foot of the hill in town is the mid-19th-century wooden **Kościół świętego Klemensa** (Church of St. Clement), the first church built in Zakopane. Witkiewicz is buried in the adjoining cemetery. ✉ *Ul. Kościeliska opposite Kasprusie.*

The **Muzeum Tatrzańskie** (Tatra Museum) on Zakopane's main street has two replicas of typical highland dwellings, mountain crafts, and a collection of Zakopane's flora and fauna. The first room is a portrait gallery of local heroes and famous visitors to Zakopane, who include writer Joseph Conrad and national hero Józef Piłsudski. Ask for an explanatory cassette in English. ✉ *Krupówki 10,* ☎ *018/201–52–05.* 💰 *zł 4.* 🕐 *Tues.–Thurs. and Sat. 9–5, Sun. 9–3.*

The **Willa Atma,** a wooden villa in the Zakopane style, was home to the Polish composer Karol Szymanowski in the 1920s. It is now a museum dedicated to his life and work. ✉ *Kasprusie 19,* ☎ *018/201–34–93.* 💰 *zł 5.* 🕐 *Tues.–Thurs. and weekends 10–3.*

Witkiewicz's very first project in the Zakopane style was the Willa Koliba, which is now the **Muzeum Stylu Zakopańskiego im. Stanisława Witkiewicza** (Stanisław Witkiewicz Museum of the Zakopane Style). ✉ *Kościeliska 18,* ☎ *018/201–36–02.* 💰 *zł 4.* 🕐 *Wed.–Thurs. and Sat. 9–5, Sun. 9–3.*

Willa pod Jedlami, an elaborate villa and another of Stanisław Witkiewicz's Zakopane buildings, is considered one of his most ambitious works. Unfortunately, the interior isn't open to the public, since it's a private home. ✉ *Koziniec 1.*

....

OFF THE
BEATEN PATH

DOLINA KOŚCIELISKA (KOŚCIELISKA VALLEY) – Nine kilometers (5 miles) southwest of Zakopane on the road to Kiry and Witów, this valley falls within the **Tatrzański Park Narodowy** (Tatra National Park), which covers the entire mountain range in both Poland and Slovakia. Remember that you are not allowed to pick flowers here—a strong temptation in spring, when the lower valley is covered with crocuses. The first part of the valley runs for roughly a mile through flat, open pasture, before the stream that gave the valley its name begins its descent through steep, rocky gorges. It ends at Ornak, 5½ km (3½ mi) from the road, where there are splendid views. Horse-drawn carriages (sleighs in winter) wait at the entrance to take visitors halfway up the valley (for about zł 30), but if you want to reach Ornak, you must cover the last stage on foot. Harnaś is a bar at the entrance to the valley, where locals come to drink beer and where dishes such as *fasolka po bretońsku* (baked beans) or *bigos* (a dish made with sauerkraut, cabbage, sausage, apples, and bacon) are available from 8 AM to 10 PM. *Take a bus or a minibus to Kiry from Zakopane's PKS bus station on Kościuszki.*

BUKOWINA TATRZAŃSKA – A village built largely out of wood and set high on a ridge 13 km (8 mi) northeast of Zakopane, Bukowina Tatrzańska was once famed for its number of beekeepers and its honey. The path at the top of the ridge, parallel to the main road to Łysa Polana, affords spectacular views of the Tatra range and is a favored spot for winter sunbathing. *Bukowina can easily be reached by PKS bus from the Zakopane station on Kościuszki. By car, take E95 (the main road to Kraków) north from Zakopane, and after 5 km (3 mi) turn east onto Hwy. 961, which leads to the border crossing point at Polana. The left turn into the village of Bukowina is clearly marked.*

Dining and Lodging

$$–$$$ ✕ **Murowana Piwnica.** The dining room in the Giewont Orbis Hotel is high-ceilinged and galleried, decorated with crystal chandeliers and crisp, white tablecloths on well-spaced tables. Service is elegant and discreet. The game dishes are the best items on the menu; try the roast pheasant when it's in season. ⊠ *Giewont Orbis Hotel, Kościuszki 1,* ☎ *018/201–20–11. AE, DC, MC, V.*

$–$$$ ✕ **Czarny Staw.** Hearty mountain fare in the traditional Zakopane "rustic" style is the trademark of the Black Pond. The restaurant's specialty is fish, especially the mountain trout that comes to you in a large, fish-shaped wooden bowl. Traditionally dressed staff prepare meat on an open grill in the middle of the room. ⊠ *Krupówki 2,* ☎ *018/201–38–56. AE, DC, MC, V.*

$–$$$ ✕ **Zbójecka.** Of all the restaurants in traditional Zakopane style, this
★ is the most inviting. A set of stairs leads down to a large basement, bathed in light and warmth from a fireplace and an open grill. Diners sink back into wool-covered chairs and enjoy a selection of carnivorous delights, snug and warm and a century away from the bustle of ulica Krupówki. ⊠ *Krupówki 28,* ☎ *018/201–38–54. AE, DC, MC, V.*

$$–$$$$ 🏨 **Litwor.** This is one of the best hotels in Małopolska. The rooms have
★ all the amenities you could crave, including towel warmers and heated floors in the plush bathrooms. Perhaps best of all, the friendly staff seem to enjoy perfecting their English. ⊠ *Krupówki 11, 34–500,* ☎ *018/201–71–89, FAX 018/201–71–90, WEB www.litwor.pl. 49 rooms, 6 suites. Restaurant, cable TV, tennis court, indoor pool, gym, hot tub, sauna, steam room, bar, business services, convention center, some pets allowed. AE, DC, MC, V. BP.*

$$$ 🏨 **Villa Marilor Hotel.** This comfortable upscale hotel, reminiscent of
★ a luxurious alpine lodge, opened in 2001 in a tastefully restored 19th-century palace. Located in the very center of Zakopane, it is pleasantly hidden away in a private park. ⊠ *Kościuszki 18, 34–500,* ☎ *018/206–44–12, FAX 018/206–44–10, WEB www.hotele-marilor.com.pl. 20 rooms. Restaurant, minibars, tennis court, hot tub, massage, sauna, bar, meeting room, free parking. AE, DC, MC, V. BP.*

$$-$$$ 🏠 **Sabała.** This large, historic hotel was built in 1897 in the then-emerging Zakopane style and named after a renowned 19th-century storyteller. The wood-paneled rooms are also furnished in beeswax-treated, solid wood furnishings; many of the rooms have original fixtures. ⊠ *Krupówki 11, 34–500,* ☎ *018/201–50–92,* FAX *018/201–50–93,* WEB *www.sabala.zakopane.pl. 20 rooms. Restaurant, some pets allowed. AE, DC, MC, V. BP.*

$-$$ 🏠 **Giewont Orbis Hotel.** This late-19th-century hotel is right in the center of town. The rooms are furnished in traditional style but vary greatly in size; it's a good idea to see the room before moving in. Try to get a room with a view of the peak after which the hotel is named. ⊠ *Kościuszki 1, 34–500,* ☎ *018/201–20–11,* FAX *018/201–20–15,* WEB *www.giewont.net.pl. 44 rooms. Restaurant, cable TV, meeting room. AE, DC, MC, V. BP.*

Nightlife and the Arts

Zakopane's theatrical and musical performances are often connected with the artists and writers who made the town their home, particularly Witkiewicz and Karol Szymanowski. Posters on kiosks announce performances. Traditional local folk orchestras also perform regularly. As for nightlife, Zakopane is not the all-night town that Kraków is, but there are some interesting options.

BARS

Caffe Sanacja (⊠ Krupówki 45) is a dark, wooden enclave for the small but vibrant artistic community. **Paparazzi** (⊠ Gen. Galicy 8), the sibling of Kraków's own Paparazzi, is Zakopane's après-ski alternative to folksy traditionalism. **Pstrąg Jazz Club** (⊠ Jagiellońska 18) is an eclectically furnished jazz venue hidden under the Warszawianka hotel.

MUSIC

A festival of Szymanowski's music, with concerts all over town, is held in July, and an autumn music festival is held in September and October. The **Kulczycki Gallery** (⊠ Koziniec 8, ☎ 018/201–29–36) occasionally hosts concerts and other events. Concerts are also sometimes given at the **Willa Atma** (⊠ Kasprusie 19, ☎ 018/206–31–50).

THEATER

The **Teatr im. Stanisława Ignacego Witkiewicza** (⊠ Chramcówki 15, ☎ 018/206–82–97) has two stages and often brings in well-known actors for the season.

Outdoor Activities and Sports

BIKING

Mountain biking has become increasingly popular in the area. **Rent a bike** (⊠ Sienkiewicza 37, ☎ 018/201–42–66) has a small selection of mountain bikes available. You can hire a bike at **Sport & Fun Company Ltd.** (⊠ Rondo 1, ☎ 018/201–56–03) for zł 50 per day.

HIKING

The Gorczański, Pieniński, and Tatrzański (Tatra) national parks all have hiking territory. The routes are well marked, and there are maps at entrance points that give the distances, times, and degrees of difficulty of the trails. On the lower reaches of trails out of major tourist points (such as Zakopane, Szczawnica, and Krynica), walkers crowd the paths, but they thin out as you go higher up.

JOGGING

In Zakopane the Droga pod Reglami, the road just below the line of the forest, which runs along the foot of the Tatra National Park, makes a relatively flat jogging route; it can be approached from various points in the town.

Zakopane acquired snow-making machinery in 1990 and is still the region's major center for downhill skiing, although Krynica and Krościenko also have facilities. Chairlifts bring skiers to the peaks of **Butorowy Wierch** (⊠ Powstańców Śląskich, ☎ 018/201–39–41). You'll find the most advanced runs at **Kasprowy Wierch** (⊠ Kuźnice, ☎ 018/201–45–10 lower station; 018/201–44–05 upper station); Kuźnice, where the cable lift is found, can be reached by a minibus from outside Zakopane's bus station). **Nosal** (⊠ Balcera, ☎ 018/201–31–81) has a small chairlift. Tickets can be hard to come by in season, so it may be easier to get them at **Orbis** (⊠ Krupówki 22), although you'll pay a surcharge of 30%.

Shopping

Leather and sheepskin products are local specialties, along with handknit socks, sweaters, and caps in white, gray, and black patterns made from rough, undyed wool. The best place to look for local hand-made goods is at the **Zakopane market** (⊠ ul. Krupówki), at the foot of the street on the way to the Gubałówka cable railway. Wednesday is the main market day, but some stalls are here all week. Street vendors are around daily and charge higher prices, as they do throughout the region. **Limba** (⊠ Kościeliska 1) has a fine assortment of handmade local costumes, as well as smaller items such as belts and walking sticks.

Lake Morskie Oko

8 *30 km (20 mi) southeast of Zakopane in the direction of Poronin or Cyrla.*

Morskie Oko is the largest and loveliest of the lakes in the High Tatras, 4,570 ft above sea level. The name means "Eye of the Sea," and an old legend claims it has a secret underground passage connecting it to the ocean. The **Mięguszowiecki** and **Mnich** peaks appear to rise straight up from the water, and the depth of the lake permanently colors it an intense blue. Orbis in Zakopane runs a regular bus service to within 10 minutes' walk of the lake, but you can get no closer by car. If you feel more energetic, you can take a PKS bus or a private minibus from the Zakopane bus station to Łysa Polana and follow the marked trail for 8 km (5 mi). ⊠ *Morskie Oko.*

Dining and Lodging

$ ✕🏨 **Schronisko Morskie Oko.** A climbers' and hikers' hostel, this establishment has a restaurant that serves large portions of such basic fare as *fasolka po bretońsku* (Breton-style baked beans, made with tomato sauce and bits of bacon) or pancakes with whipped cream. You can obtain a bed in a spartan, clean three-, four-, five-, or six-person room for very little. ⊠ *Morskie Oko (Box 201, Zakopane, 34–500),* ☎ *018/207–76–09. No credit cards.*

Nowy Targ

9 *24 km (15 mi) north of Zakopane, 90 km (56 mi) south of Kraków.*

The unofficial capital of the Podhale region, Nowy Targ has been a chartered borough since the 14th century, when it stood at an intersection of international trade routes, and it remains an important market center for the entire mountain region. It is worth visiting on Thursday, market day, when farmers bring their livestock in for sale and when several stalls offer local products, including rough wool sweaters and sheepskin coats. The White and Black Dunajec streams meet in Nowy Targ to form the Dunajec River, which then runs on through steep limestone gorges to Nowy Sącz. By car, take the main road from Zakopane to Kraków. Buses run from Zakopane every hour.

En Route   On the road to Szczawnica, 12 km (8 mi) east of Nowy Targ, is **Dębno.** This village in the valley of the Dunajec River has a tiny wooden church dating from the 15th century (it's believed to be the oldest wooden building in the Podhale region); inside are medieval wall paintings and wooden sculptures. *Buses run from the marketplace in Nowy Targ.*

Krościenko, 25 km (15 mi) east of Nowy Targ and 35 km (22 mi) south-west of Nowy Sącz, is one of the villages that became holiday resorts during the late 19th century, and it is still popular today as a center for walking vacations. It has many interesting Zakopane-style wooden structures. *The best access is by PKS bus from the train station in Nowy Sącz.*

The small spa of **Szczawnica,** 28 km (17½ mi) east of Nowy Targ and 35 km (22 mi) southwest of Nowy Sącz, dates from the late 19th century; you can stroll around in the high-vaulted pump rooms and sip the foul-tasting mineral waters. It is also a landing point of an unforgettable raft trip from Kąty through the Dunajec Gorge, a popular tourist attraction operated since the mid-19th century by the local mountaineer raftsmen (the price is only zł 31). The rafting season is April through October, and it's not necessary to purchase tickets in advance. *The best access to Szczawnica is by PKS bus from the marketplace in Nowy Targ or outside the train station in Nowy Sącz. From Szczawnica, there are frequent buses to the Kąty wharf, where you can hire a raftsman for the river trip.*

Nowy Sącz

⑩   *70 Km (44 mi) northeast of Nowy Targ.*

Nowy Sącz has existed as a market town since the 13th century. Remnants from this early period include a ruined 14th-century castle, about 10 minutes from the market square on ulica Piotra Skargi, as well as the church on the northeast side of the market square and the 15th-century church and chapter house on the square's east side.

Dining and Lodging

\$\$ ✕ **Zajazd Sądecki.** This restaurant emphasizes regional cuisine, such as pancakes highland-style, stuffed with pork and onions. The dining room is cozy, with pine furniture and crisp white tablecloths. ✉ *Królowej Jadwigi 67,* ☎ *018/443–67–17. No credit cards.*

\$\$ ⊞ **Orbis Hotel Beskid.** This standard high-rise is a typical product of the mid-1960s. It commands good views while being conveniently located near the rail and bus stations in the town center. The rooms are rather small and drab but comfortable, brightened with Podhale folk elements. Delicious breakfasts are served. ✉ *Limanowskiego 1, 33–330,* ☎ *018/443–57–70,* FAX *018/443–51–44,* WEB *www.orbis.pl. 63 rooms, 10 suites. Restaurant, minibars, bar. AE, DC, MC, V. BP.*

Krynica

⑪   *32 km (20 mi) southeast of Nowy Sącz on Hwy. 99.*

Krynica is a spa and winter-sports center in a high valley. In the late 19th century Krynica was developed in the classic spa style, gaining a tree-lined promenade, a pump room, and concert halls. The waters here are not appetizing to the unaccustomed palate. In fact, they are the most concentrated mineral waters in Europe. The salutary properties of Krynica's mineral waters were recognized during the 18th century, and the first **bathhouse** was built here in 1807. ✉ *Kraszewskiego 9.*

Lodging

In addition to more traditional hotels, also look for signs in windows advertising POKOJE (rooms).

$ ⊡ Hotel Meran. This is a friendly three-story hotel, with wooden balconies and good parking facilities. ⊠ *Kościelna 9, 33–380,* ☎ *018/471–21–09. 30 rooms. Free parking. www.hotele-marilor.com.pl*

$ ⊡ Pensjonat Wisła. This small, friendly pension is more than 100 years old. Famous for its old-fashioned hospitality and home cooking, Pensjonat Wisła is in the center of the Krynica spa area. If there are no available rooms here, the pension will provide information on vacancies elsewhere. Most rooms have a private bath. ⊠ *Bulwary Dietla 1, 33–380,* ☎ *018/471–55–12. 45 rooms. Restaurant, some microwaves; no TV in some rooms. No credit cards. BP, FAP.*

Małopolska Essentials

BUS TRAVEL
Zakopane is most easily accessible by bus from Kraków, a two-hour trip by express bus, and seats can be reserved in advance. There are also through services from Warsaw to Zakopane (five hours). Almost all villages in the region, however isolated, can be reached by PKS bus or a private minibus. The buses themselves can be ancient and slow, so take an express bus if one operates to your destination. The best deals are privately operated, frequent bus services, which stop just outside the "official" PKS bus stations.

➤ CONTACTS: **PKS Bus Station** (⊠ corner of Kościuski and Chramcówki, Zakopane, ☎ 018/201–44–53).

CAR TRAVEL
It is not necessary to have a car to explore the southern region. Public transport will take you to even the most remote and inaccessible places—but it will take time and can be uncomfortably crowded. On the other hand, the narrow mountain roads can be trying and dangerous for drivers.

The 7 (E77) highway, which takes you roughly halfway from Kraków to Zakopane, is four-lane all the way. The road that runs the rest of the way, E95, has recently been much improved, but some stretches are still single-lane, and horse-drawn carts can cause major delays. Side roads in the region can be very narrow and badly surfaced. In Zakopane and other towns in the region it would be wise to leave your car at a guarded parking lot.

To get to Częstochowa from Kraków, take the E40 to Katowice, where you get on the E75. There are usually plenty of places to park along the town's main boulevard.

EMERGENCIES
➤ EMERGENCY NUMBERS: **Emergency Ambulance** (☎ 999). **Nowy Sącz Hospital** (⊠ Młyńska 5, Nowy Sącz, ☎ 018/443–88–77). **Police Emergencies** (☎ 997).

➤ LATE-NIGHT PHARMACIES: **Apteka Pharbita Zakopane** (⊠ Chramcówki 34, Zakopane, ☎ 018/206–82–21). **Pharmacy Nowy Sącz** (⊠ Rynek 27, Nowy Sącz, ☎ 018/443–82–92). **Vita Pharmacy Krynica** (⊠ Kraszewskiego 61, Krynica, ☎ 018/471–39–47).

PRIVATE ACCOMMODATIONS
In Zakopane, there are two options for private accommodations. The tourist information center, BIT, can help you make arrangements for a private room. Tatra Tours and Travel, an Australian-operated agency, can arrange accommodations in pensions or hostels as well as tours of the region.

BIT (⊠ Kościuszki 17, Zakopane, ☎ 018/201–22–11). **Tatra Tours and Travel** (⊠ Kościeliska 1, Zakopane, ☎ 018/201–32–53).

TRAIN TRAVEL

From Kraków, the trip to Zakopane takes a full four to five hours because of the rugged nature of the terrain. Unless you take the overnight sleeper from Warsaw, which arrives in Zakopane at 6 AM, it's better to change to a bus in Kraków. A train runs daily to Częstochowa from Kraków (two hours).

Trains move slowly in the hilly region south of Kraków, but most towns are accessible by train from Zakopane, and the routes can be very picturesque. A ride on an old steam train from Chabówka to Zakopane is a tourist attraction in itself.

➤ CONTACTS: **Zakopane Train Station** (⊠ ul. Chramcówki, Zakopane, ☎ 018/201–50–31).

VISITOR INFORMATION

➤ CONTACTS: **Częstochowa Tourist Information** (IT; ⊠ al. Najświętszej Marii Panny 65, Częstochowa, ☎ 034/368–22–50). **Krynica Tourist Information** (⊠ Piłsudskiego 8, Krynica, ☎ 018/471–57–46). **Nowy Sącz Tourist Information** (⊠ Piotra Skargi 2, Nowy Sącz, ☎ 018/443–55–97). **Orbis Zakopane** (⊠ Krupówki 22, Zakopane, ☎ 018/201–22–38). **Zakopane Tourist Information** (BIT; ⊠ Kościuszki 17, Zakopane, ☎ 018/201–22–11).

LUBLIN AND EASTERN POLAND

Lublin's location in eastern Poland has "protected" it somewhat from the influences that have swept the country since it opened to the West in 1989. Visitors here can get a peek at the old Poland—less prosperous, more traditional. Historically, Lublin lay in the heart of Poland and served as a crossroads between east and west. It was in Lublin in 1569 that the eastern duchy of Lithuania joined the kingdom of Poland by signing the Union of Lublin, thus creating the largest empire in Europe at the time. Following World War II, when Poland's borders shifted westward, Lublin found itself near the Soviet border. This has led to considerable contact with the East, largely in the form of Russian and Ukrainian traders who flock to the city's marketplace to peddle their goods—everything from old auto parts to caviar and champagne—and, increasingly, to make purchases in Poland for resale in their own countries.

With its graying exterior and mild urban decay, Lublin may seem as if it has seen better days, but the city is taking steps to renew itself. One of the most important current projects is the restoration of Lublin's chief monument, its walled Old Town. In the district at the western end of Krakowskie Przedmieście, many of the buildings along the cobblestone streets have been beautifully restored, and the area is looking up. And Lublin is rich in parks, offering wild, lush greens in summer and golden yellows in autumn.

Lublin is also a good hub for exploring the villages and countryside of the eastern parts of the country. In less than an hour visitors can travel to Puławy to enjoy a picnic on the palace grounds or to the village of Kazimierz Dolny for a walk along the banks of the Vistula. It's also possible to make a day trip out of Zamość and Łańcut, though these places make nice stopovers if you have time.

Numbers in the margin correspond to numbers on the Southeastern Poland map.

Lublin

⑫ *160 km (100 mi) southeast of Warsaw, 270 km (170 mi) northeast of Kraków.*

The tourist attractions of Lublin are in three distinct regions of the city. The Stare Miasto (Old Town), a medieval walled city, is at the eastern end of Krakowskie Przedmieście, the main street. The castle and nearby Jewish cemetery are just outside the old city wall, to the northeast. The Catholic and Marie Skłodowska-Curie universities and the adjacent Saxon Gardens are on the western edge of the city, off aleja Racław-ickie (take a bus west from Krakowskie Przedmieście).

Situated at the eastern end of Lublin's main shopping street, Krakowskie Przedmieście, is the **Brama Krakowska** (Kraków Gate), a Gothic and baroque structure that served as the main entrance to the medieval city. Today it separates modern Lublin from the Old Town. The gate houses the **Muzeum Lubelskie** (Lublin History Museum), where you can learn about the area's history. ⊠ *Pl. Łokietka 3,* ☎ *081/532–60–01.* ☜ *zł 3.* ⊘ *Wed.–Sat. 9–4.*

Part of Lublin's tremendous success as a medieval trading center stemmed from a royal decree exempting the city from all customs duties. As a result, huge fortunes were made and kept, and the town's merchants were able to build the beautiful 14th- and 15th-century houses—complete with colorful frescoed facades—that surround the ★ **Rynek** (market square). The Rynek's unusual trapezoidal shape is the result of medieval builders adapting the construction of the town to the outline of the protective walls surrounding Lublin.

Filling the center of the Rynek is the reconstructed **Stary Ratusz** (Old Town Hall), built in the 16th century and rebuilt in neoclassical style in the 1780s by the Italian architect Domenico Merlini. Here a royal tribunal served as the seat of the Crown Court of Justice for Małopol-ska beginning in 1578; records of its activities can be seen in the town hall's history museum. On Saturday the hall fills with young couples waiting to be married. ⊠ *Rynek 1,* ☎ *081/532–68–66.* ☜ *Museum zł 3.* ⊘ *Wed.–Sun. 9–4.*

NEED A BREAK?
In one of the recently reconstructed medieval tenements you can visit the small ground-floor **Apteka–Muzeum** (Museum of Pharmacy; ⊠ Grodzka 5A), which is a reproduction of an early chemist's shop, and then drink a cup of coffee in the café behind it.

★ The **Kościół Dominikanów** (Dominican Church and Monastery) dating from 1342, is the jewel of Lublin's Old Town; the interior was reno-vated in rococo style in the 17th century. Two of its 11 chapels are par-ticularly noteworthy: the **Kaplica Firlejowska** (Firlej Family Chapel), with its late-Renaissance architecture, and the **Kaplica Tyszkiewskich** (Tyszkiewski Family Chapel), with its early baroque decoration. Cir-cling the walls above the chapels are paintings depicting the transport of a piece of the True Cross—the cross on which Jesus was crucified—to Lublin and the protection the relic has given the city through the ages. Unfortunately, this protection did not extend to the relic itself, which was stolen from the church in 1991. The church is often closed now, but try knocking on the monastery door to the right of the entrance. ⊠ *Ul. złota.* ☜ *Free.* ⊘ *Weekdays 9–noon and 3–6, weekends 3–6.*

Outside the old city wall, just around the corner from Kraków Gate, stands the **Katedra** (Lublin Cathedral), founded by the Jesuits in 1625 but now bearing later neoclassical features. Inside to the left of the baroque high altar, a reproduction of the *Black Madonna of Często-*

chowa is on display. You can reach the **Kaplica Akustyczna** (Whispering Chapel) by a passage to the right of the high altar. Watch what you say here—a whisper in one corner can be heard perfectly in another. Next to the chapel is the **treasury,** holding what remains of the original illusionistic frescoes that decorated the church interior: the images were painted so skillfully that they appear almost three dimensional. ⊠ *Królewska.* ☎ *Whispering Chapel and treasury zł 2.* ☉ *Tues.–Sun. 10–2 and 3–5.*

★ During the late 14th century, King Kazimierz the Great ordered the construction of the **Zamek** (Lublin Castle) as well as the defensive walls surrounding the city, to protect the wealthy trading center from invasion. Most of the castle was rebuilt in mock Gothic style during the 19th century, when it was converted to a prison. Run at various times by the Russian czar, the German Gestapo, and the Communist secret police, the castle prison witnessed its largest number of deaths during World War II, when the Nazis murdered more than 10,000 political prisoners here. The **Kaplica Trójcy świętego** (Chapel of the Holy Trinity), which has been restored in a decades-long project, is the most outstanding attraction in Lublin. The 14th-century chapel is covered with Byzantine-style murals. Note the ancient graffiti on the walls. The **Castle Museum** houses historical exhibits and an art gallery, which displays Jan Matejko's *Unia Lubelska* (1869), depicting the signing of the Lublin Union by the king of Poland and Grand Duke of Lithuania exactly three centuries earlier. ⊠ *Zamkowa 9,* ☎ *081/532–50–01.* ☐ *zł 7.* ☉ *Wed.–Sat. 9–4, Sun. 9–5.*

Lublin was a center of Jewish culture in the 16th century. The hill behind Lublin Castle is the site of the **Stary Cmentarz Żydowski** (Old Jewish Cemetery). The cemetery was destroyed during World War II by the German SS, which used the rubble from the headstones to pave the entranceway to Majdanek concentration camp. The park at the base of the castle hill was the site of the Jewish ghetto, in which Nazis imprisoned the Jewish population of Lublin until April 1943, when they sent them to Majdanek.

....

OFF THE BEATEN PATH   **MAJDANEK CONCENTRATION CAMP –** Reminders of the horrors of World War II are never far away in Poland, and 5 km (3 mi) southeast of Lublin's city center lie the remnants of the Majdanek concentration camp, second in scope only to Auschwitz. Established in July 1941, it grew to 1,235 acres, although the original plan was to make it five times as large. From 1941 to 1944 more than 360,000 people lost their lives here, either by direct extermination or through illness and disease. Standing at the camp entrance is one of two monuments designed for the 25th anniversary of the liberation of Majdanek. The **Monument of Struggle and Martyrdom** symbolizes the inmates' faith and hope; the mausoleum at the rear of the camp marks the death of that hope. Of the five fields constituting the original camp, only the gas chambers, watchtowers, and crematoriums, as well as some barracks on Field Three, remain. The **visitor center,** to the left of the monument at the entrance, shows a movie about the camp (in English) and has a bookstore as well as a restaurant. To reach the camp from Lublin, take Bus 153 or 156 from Krakowskie Przedmieście. ⊠ *Droga Męczenników Majdanka 67,* ☎ *081/744–26–47,* 🌐 *www.majdanek.pl.* ☐ *Free.* ☉ *Tues.–Sun. 8–6; last film at 2 PM.*

KOZŁÓWKA – In a beautiful and well-tended park, this 18th-century palace (41 km [25 mi] north of Lublin) was built for the Zamoyski family and is one of a handful of palaces in Poland whose interiors have remained intact. Housed in the palace annex is a fascinating relic of the

Stalinist era, the **Museum of the Art of Socialist Realism.** The palace is reachable by bus from Lublin. If you are driving, take Route 19 north of Lublin to Lubartów (29 km [18 mi]); then head west for 12 km (7 mi). ⊠ *Kozłówka* ☎ *081/852–70–91,* WEB *www.muzeumkozlowka.lublin.pl.* 🎟 *zł 7.* 🕐 *Mar.–Nov., Tues.–Sun. 10–4.*

Dining and Lodging

$$ ✕ **Club Hades.** Locals think this is the best place to dine in Lublin. Specialties include onion soup and all kinds of meat dishes. ⊠ *Al. Peowiaków 12,* ☎ *081/532–56–41. AE, DC, MC, V.*

$$ ✕ **Piwnica.** This popular restaurant serves traditional Polish fare. Try
★ the pickled herring for an appetizer, then roast pork, veal cutlet, or beef medallions with mashed potatoes for a main course. ⊠ *Skłodowskiej 12,* ☎ *081/534–39–19. AE, DC, MC, V.*

$$$ 🏨 **Mercure-Unia Hotel.** This six-story hotel is just off the main road
★ outside the Old Town. Most of the public spaces are fairly cramped, but the rooms are reasonably spacious and comfortably furnished. ⊠ *Al. Racławickie 12, 20–037,* ☎ *081/533–20–61,* FAX *081/533–30–21,* WEB *www.mercure.com. 2 restaurants, minibars, bar, casino. AE, DC, MC, V. BP.*

$$ 🏨 **Victoria Hotel.** This venerable hotel is large and situated within walking distance of all the Old Town's landmarks. The rooms are on the small side, but the service is efficient and friendly. Rooms over the street, which is on a hill, can be noisy. ⊠ *Narutowicza 58–60, 20–401,* ☎ *081/533–70–11,* FAX *081/532–90–261,* WEB *hotel.victoria.lublin.pl. 190 rooms, 63 with bath. Restaurant, room service, cable TV, hair salon, laundry service, some pets allowed, parking (fee). AE, DC, MC, V. BP.*

$ 🏨 **Dom Nauczyciela.** This hotel, which was formerly reserved for members of the Communist teachers union, is clean, comfortable, and efficiently run, if lacking in elegance. The rooms are small but adequate. ⊠ *Akademicka 4, 20–033,* ☎ *081/533–82–85,* FAX *081/533–37–45. 36 rooms. Restaurant, café. No credit cards. BP.*

Nightlife and the Arts

For up-to-date information about movies, theater, and concerts in Lublin, consult the local papers, *Kurier Lubelski* and *Dziennik Lubelski.* Theater tickets are available at **Centrum Kultury** (⊠ Peowiaków 12), the home of all theater groups in Lublin. Student nightlife centers on Marie Skłodowska-Curie University's **Chatka Żaka Club** (⊠ Radziszewskiego 16, ☎ 081/533–32–01). The club has a cafeteria, a bar, a popular disco, and a cinema that often shows American movies. Tickets for orchestral performances can be purchased at the **Philharmonic Hall** (⊠ Marii Skłodowskiej-Curie 5, ☎ 081/743–78–21) Tuesday –Sunday noon–7.

Outdoor Activities and Sports

On hot summer days Lublin residents head for Zalew Zembrzycki, a man-made lake about 4 km (2½ mi) south of central Lublin. The lake has sailing and canoe rentals. You can get there by taking Bus 25 or 42 from Lublin Cathedral.

Kazimierz Dolny

★ ⑬ *12 km (7 mi) south of Puławy, 40 km (25 mi) west of Lublin, 130 km (80 mi) southeast of Warsaw.*

This small town is so pleasing to the eyes that it has thrived for over a century as an artists' colony and vacation spot. It sits on a steep, hilly bank of the placid Vistula River, and whitewashed facades and steeply pitched red-tile roofs peek out over the treetops. Although the first settlement existed here in the 12th century, the town was formally founded by King Kazimierz the Great, after whom the town was named. This Kazimierz received the nickname Dolny (the Lower) to distinguish it from another newly founded Kazimierz upriver, now part of Kraków. Kazimierz Dolny prospered as a river port during the 16th and 17th centuries, but the partitioning of Poland left it cut off from the grain markets of Gdańsk. Thereafter, the town fell into decline until it was rediscovered by painters and writers during the 19th century. Today both artistic and nonartistic visitors can still enjoy the Renaissance architecture along the village's dusty cobblestone streets or hike through the nearby hills and gorges.

On the southeast corner of the town's market square lie the **Kamienice Przybyłów** (Przybyła Brothers' Houses), left behind by one of the most powerful families in Kazimierz Dolny, the Przybyłas. The ornate houses were built in 1615, and their facades are adorned with the two-story bas-relief figures of St. Nicholas (left) and St. Christopher (right), the brothers' patron saints. ⊠ *Rynek.*

The **Kamienica Celejowska** (Celej Family House), seat of a powerful Kazimierz clan, stands one block toward the river from the main square, and it is embellished with griffins, dragons, and salamanders. The former residence now houses the **Town Museum of Kazimierz Dolny** and many paintings depicting local life of past eras. ⊠ *Senatorska 11,* ☎ *081/881–01–04.* 🎫 *zł 5.* ☉ *Tues.–Sun. 10–3.*

A covered passageway off ulica Senatorska leads up to the walled courtyard of the **Kościół Reformatów** (Church and Monastery of the Reformati), which stands on the southern hill overlooking the town's market square. The Reformati were the reformed Franciscan Order. In the late 18th century an encircling wall was built to protect the monastery's buildings. A plaque inside the passageway memorializes the Nazis' use of the site as a house of torture during World War II. The climb up to the courtyard is worthwhile just for the spectacular view it affords of the town. ⊠ *Ul. Klasztorna, off ul. Senatorska.*

On the north side of the main square is the **Kościół Parafialny** (Parish Church), initially built in Gothic style but remodeled in the so-called Lublin-Renaissance style. Note the Renaissance stalls in the presbytery, the rococo confessionals, an ornate 17th-century organ and pulpit, and an unusual chandelier made from stags' antlers. ⊠ *Rynek, north side.*

The ruins of the 14th-century **Zamek** (Kazimierz Castle), which served as a watchtower to protect the Vistula trade route, stand on a steep hill to the northeast of the town's market square. From here there is a grand view over the town and the Vistula Valley.

The **Góra Trzech Krzyży** (Three Crosses Hill) lies to the east of the market square. The crosses were constructed in 1708 to commemorate the victims of a plague that ravaged the town. This vantage point affords perhaps the best view of the town.

Lodging

$–$$ 🏨 **SARP.** This ideally located hotel on the corner of the town square belongs and caters to the Architects' Association but will take other guests on a commercial basis. The rooms are large and irregular in shape, with simple but adequate furnishings. The restaurant is usually packed with intellectuals. ⊠ *Rynek 20, 24–120,* ☎ 𝐅𝐀𝐗 *081/881–05–44,* 𝐖𝐄𝐁 *www.kazimierz-dolny.pl/sarp.html. 35 rooms, 20 with shared bath. Dining room. No credit cards. BP.*

Outdoor Activities and Sports

BOATING

During the summer season (May–October), boat rides on the Vistula leave from the dock at ulica Puławska 6. The half-hour ride takes you south to Janowiec and its Firlej Castle ruins.

➤ CONTACTS: Żegluga Pasażerska po Wiśle (✉ ul. Puławska 6, ☎ 081/881–01–35).

HIKING

Take one of the numerous marked trails, ranging in length from 2 km to 6 km (1 mi to 4 mi), and explore the hilly landscape around Kazimierz. All trails converge on the market square. Tourist tracks lead north (marked red) and south (marked green) along the river from the square, along streets and cart paths, through orchards and quarries.

Zamość

⓮ *87 km (54 mi) southeast of Lublin, 318 km (198 mi) northeast of Kraków.*

The fortified town of Zamość has a wonderfully preserved, Renaissance-era central square, wide boulevards, and neat rows of colorful houses with brightly painted facades. The town was conceived in the late 16th century by Hetman Jan Zamoyski as an outpost along the thriving trade route between Lublin and Lwów. He commissioned Italian architect Bernardo Morando, who created a masterpiece of Renaissance urban planning. The town thrived, and its strong fortifications spared it from destruction during the Swedish onslaught of the 17th century. The Polish victory over Lenin's Red Army near Zamość in 1920 kept the way clear for the country's restored independence. World War II saw the town renamed Himmlerstadt, with thousands of its residents (45% of the town was Jewish) deported or exterminated to make way for German settlers.

★ Zamość's **Rynek** (market square) is a breathtaking arcaded plaza surrounded by the decorative facades of homes built by local merchants during the 16th and 17th centuries. Dominating the square is the impressive baroque **Ratusz** (town hall), topped by a 164-ft spire.

The **Muzeum Regionalne w Zamościu** (Zamość Regional Museum), housed in a charming town house next door to the town hall, has paintings of the Zamoyski clan and a scale model of Zamość. ✉ *Ormiańska 24,* ☎ *084/638–64–94.* 🎫 *zł 4.* ◷ *Tues.–Sun. 9–4.*

Kolegiata świętego Tomasza (St. Thomas Collegiate Church), one of Poland's most beautiful Renaissance churches, stands near the southwest corner of the market square. In the presbytery are four 17th-century paintings ascribed to Domenico Robusti, Tintoretto's son. The church is also the final resting place of Jan Zamoyski, buried in the **Zamoyski Chapel** to the right of the high altar. ✉ *Kolegiacka.*

The **Pałac Zamojskich** (Zamoyski Palace), home of the founding family of Zamość, lies near the market square beyond St. Thomas Collegiate Church. The palace was turned into a military hospital in the 1830s; now it serves as a courthouse. ✉ *Zamkowa.*

Behind the Zamoyski Palace is the **Arsenał** (Arsenal Museum), which houses a collection of Turkish armaments and rugs, as well as a model of the original town plan. ✉ *Zamkowa 2,* ☎ *084/638–40–76.* 🎫 *zł 4.50.* ◷ *Tues.–Sun. 10–4.*

Near the northwest corner of the main square, behind the town hall, is the **Akademia** (Old Academy), a distinguished center of learning during the 17th and 18th centuries and once the third-largest university after those in Kraków and Vilnius. It is now a high school. ✉ *Akademicka.*

The oldest entrance to Zamość, the **Brama Lubelska** (Lublin Gate) is to the northwest of the market square, across the road from the Old Academy. In 1588, Jan Zamoyski triumphantly led the Austrian archduke Maximilian into town through this gate after defeating him in his attempt to seize the Polish throne from Sigismund III. He then bricked up the gate to commemorate his victory. ✉ ukasińskiego.

What's left of Zamość's fortifications are at the bottom of ulica Staszica. This is the **Bastion i Brama Lwowska** (Lwów Gate and Bastion). With defenses like these—three stories high and 20 ft thick—it is easy to understand why Zamość was one of the few places to escape ruin in the Swedish attack. ✉ *Ul. Staszica.* 🖾 *zł 1.* ☉ *Tues.–Sun. 10–4.*

South of the town's marketplace is the **Rotunda,** a monument to a tragic era in Zamość's history. From 1939 to 1944 this fortified emplacement served as an extermination camp where tens of thousands of Poles, Jews, and Russians were brutally killed, some even burned alive. Now it serves as a memorial to the victims of Nazi brutality in the region. ✉ *Ul. Moranda.* 🖾 *zł 7.* ☉ *Daily 10–5.*

Lodging

$ 🏨 **Hotel Jubilat.** Built in the 1970s, this hotel offers comfortable rooms on the edge of the Old Town. The decor is dark, but everything is clean. ✉ *Wyszyńskiego 52, 22–400,* ☎ *084/638–64–01. 90 rooms. Restaurant, cable TV, refrigerators, gym, sauna, bar. AE, DC, MC, V. BP.*

$ 🏨 **Hotel Renesans.** This small hotel is located within a few blocks of the main square. It has cheerful rooms and modern bathrooms. ✉ *Grecka 6, 22–400,* ☎ 🖷 *084/629–20–01. 40 rooms. Restaurant, cable TV, refrigerators, hair salon, bar, meeting rooms. AE, DC, MC, V. BP.*

Łańcut

ⓕ   *130 km (81 mi) southwest of Zamość on Hwy. 4(E40).*

★   The neo-baroque **Łańcut Palace,** situated within a 76-acre park, is the main attraction in town. Built during the 16th century, the palace is one of the most grandiose aristocratic residences in Eastern Europe. In the 19th century it was willed to the Potocki family, who amassed an impressive art collection here. Count Alfred Potocki, the last owner, emigrated to Liechtenstein in 1944 as Russian troops approached, escaping with 11 train cars full of art objects and paintings. Much was left behind, however, and after the war a **museum** was established in the palace (which had survived intact). Today you can see the family collection of art and interior decorations, including Biedermeier, neoclassical, and rococo furnishings. Of particular interest are the intricate wood-inlay floors, the tiny theater off the dining hall, and the hall of sculpture painted to resemble a trellis of grapevines. More than 40 rooms are open to the public, including the Turkish and Chinese apartments, which reflect the 18th-century fascination with the Near and Far East. Outside, a moat and a system of bastions laid out like a five-point star separate the inner Italian and rose gardens from the rest of the park. The **Carriage Museum** in the old coach house outside the main gates contains more than 50 vehicles and is one of the largest museums of its kind in Europe. ✉ *Zamkowa 1,* ☎ *017/225–20–08.* 🖾 *zł 12.* ☉ *Museums Tues.–Sat. 8–2:30, Sun. 9–4; park daily dawn–dusk.*

OFF THE
BEATEN PATH

KLASZTOR OO.BERNARDYNÓW – This basilica and monastery of the Bernadine Fathers dates back to the 17th century and is a major pilgrimage site in the town of Leżajsk. Frequent musical performances are given on the 17th-century organ. There is also a museum attached to the monastery with exhibits of beautiful wood carvings. To reach the monastery, go 29 km (13 mi) north of Łańcut on Route 877. ⊠ *Pl. Mariacki 8, Leżajsk,* ☎ *017/242–00–06.*

Lodging

$
★

⊞ **Hotel Zamkowy.** Although the rooms in this 18th-century palace have 1970s furnishings, they are cozy and overlook the palace courtyard. There are only 42 beds, so reservations are imperative. ⊠ *Zamkowa 1, 37–100,* ☎ *017/225–26–71. 20 rooms, 13 with shared bath. Restaurant. AE, DC, MC, V. BP.*

Lublin and Eastern Poland Essentials

BUS TRAVEL

Lublin, which has two PKS bus stations, is the gateway to the region. Dworzec PKS Główny, just north of the Stare Miasto (Old Town) near the castle, connects Lublin with cities to the west and south. Buses run regularly between this station and Warsaw (3 hours). Another Lublin station, Dworzec PKS Północny, connects to points east. It lies about 4 km (2½ mi) southeast of Lublin's center; take Bus 155 or 159 between the city center and the station.

Buses run regularly from Lublin's Dworzec PKS Główny to Puławy (1 hour) and Kazimierz Dolny (1½ hours); buses for Zamość (1¾ hours) leave from Dworzec PKS Północny.
➤ CONTACTS: **Dworzec PKS Główny** (⊠ al. Tysiąclecia 4, Lublin, ☎ 081/747–89–22). **Dworzec PKS Północny** (⊠ Gospodarcza, Lublin).

CAR TRAVEL

From Warsaw, Route 17 (E372) takes you to Lublin and Zamość (with a convenient detour to Puławy and Kazimierz Dolny if you turn from the main road at Kurów, west into Route 44). From Kraków, the Tarnów-Rzeszów Route 4 (E40) will bring you farther south, close to ańcut and Leżajsk. A car can be useful if you wish to visit some of the smaller towns in this part of Poland and stay independent of bus and railway timetables.

EMERGENCIES

➤ LATE-NIGHT PHARMACIES: **Apteka** (⊠ Bramowa 8, Lublin, ☎ 081/532–05–21; ⊠ Krakowskie Przedmieście 49, Lublin, ☎ 081/532–24–25).

TRAIN TRAVEL

Lublin's main station, Lublin Główny, is about 4 km (2½ mi) south of the city center; take Bus 13 or 158 between the center and the station. Frequent train service connects Lublin with Warsaw (2½ hours) and Kraków (4½ hours). Trains run regularly between Lublin and Zamość (3 hours). A coach-class ticket costs about the same as the bus.
➤ CONTACTS: **Lublin Główny** (⊠ pl. Dworcowy, Lublin, ☎ 081/531–56–42).

TRAVEL AGENCIES

The local Orbis offices in Lublin and Zamość can book train tickets and exchange money.
➤ CONTACTS: **Orbis** (⊠ Narutowicza 31/33, Lublin, ☎ 081/532–22–56 or 081/532–22–59; ⊠ Grodzka 18, Zamość, ☎ 084/639–30–01).

VISITOR INFORMATION
➤ CONTACTS: **Lublin Centrum Informacji Turystycznej** (✉ Krakowskie Przedmieście 78, Lublin, ☎ 081/532–44–12). **Zamojski Ośrodek Informacji Turystycznej** (✉ Rynek Wielki 13, Zamość, ☎ 084/639–22–92).

GDAŃSK AND THE NORTHEAST

This region attracts visitors with Gdańsk (the bustling city that was the birthplace of Solidarity), Riviera-like resorts, and Poland's castle country. Until World War II, most of this area was included in Prussia and was referred to as "the sandbox of the Holy Roman Empire." It is indeed sandy, but it contains some startling landscapes and magnificent historic sites, such as the fortress of the Teutonic Knights at Malbork (close to and easily accessible by train from Gdańsk). In the northeast are 1,000 lakes and thousand-year-old forests (and the attendant mosquitoes during the summer). The Mazurian and Augustów-Suwałki lake area forms a labyrinth of interconnecting rivers and canals, against a backdrop of ancient forests. Olsztyn is the best starting point for exploring this area, and you need a car—or a canoe—to experience its delights fully.

Gdańsk, the third-largest city in Poland and the capital of this region, is linked with two smaller neighboring towns, Gdynia and Sopot, in an urban conglomeration called the Trójmiasto (Tri-City), on the western bank of the Bay of Gdańsk. These cities operate as a single organism and form one of Poland's most exciting and vibrant places.

Numbers in the margin correspond to numbers on the Gdańsk and the Northeast map.

Gdańsk

❶ *350 km (219 mi) north of Warsaw, 340 km (215 mi) east of Szczecin.*

Maybe it's the sea air, or maybe it's the city's history of political tumult. Whatever the reason, Gdańsk is special to Poles—and to Scandinavians and Germans, who visit the region in great numbers. Between 1308 and 1945, this Baltic port was an independent city-state called Danzig, a majority of whose residents were ethnic Germans. When the Nazis fired the first shots of World War II here on September 1, 1939, they began a process of systematic destruction of Poland that would last for six years and leave millions dead. Nevertheless, in 1997 Gdańsk celebrated its 1,000th year as a Baltic city.

The city remains famous for having been the cradle of the workers' movement that came to be known as Solidarity. Food-price increases in 1970 led to the first strikes at the (former) Lenin Shipyards in Gdańsk. The Communist authorities brutally put down the protest, killing 40 workers in December of that year. Throughout the 1970s, small groups of anti-Communist workers and intellectuals based in Gdańsk continued to organize. By August 1980, they had gained sufficient critical mass to form Solidarność (Solidarity), which the government was forced to recognize as the first independent trade union in the former Soviet bloc. Although the government attempted to destroy Solidarity after declaring martial law in December 1981, Solidarity activists continued to keep the objectives of democracy and independence from the Soviet Union alive. After the collapse of communism in 1989, Solidarity leader Lech Wałęsa became president of Poland in the nation's first free elections since World War II.

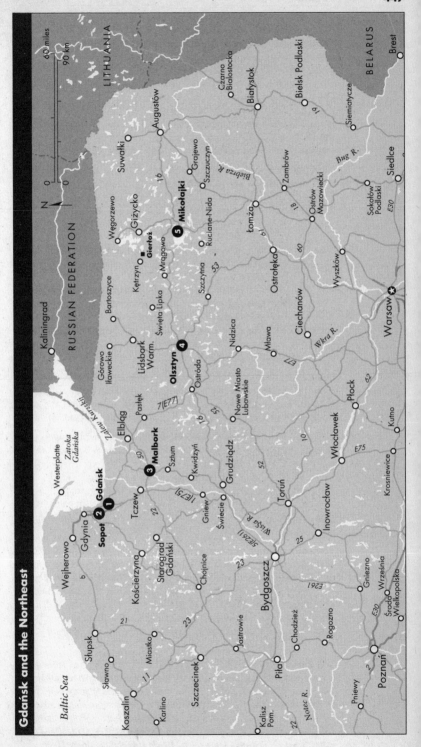

The historic core of this medieval city can easily be explored on foot. Although Gdańsk was almost entirely destroyed during World War II, the streets of its Główne Miasto (Main Town) have been lovingly restored and still retain their historical and cultural richness. North of Main Town, the Stare Miasto (Old Town) contains many newer hotels and shops, but several churches and the beautifully reconstructed Old Town Hall justify its name. At the north end of the Old Town sit the shipyards. This site, which captivated world attention during the many clashes between workers and militarized police units during the 1970s and 1980s, has now settled back into its daily grind, and the shipyards struggle to make the adjustment to the free market.

★ The largest brick church in the world and the largest church in Poland, the **Kościół Najświętszej Marii Panny** (St. Mary's Church), on the north side of ulica Piwna in Gdańsk's Main Town, can accommodate 25,000 people. Also referred to in abbreviated form as Kościół Mariacki, this enormous 14th-century church underwent major restoration after World War II, and 15 of its 22 altars have been relocated to museums in Gdańsk and Warsaw. The highlight of a visit is climbing the hundreds of steps up the church tower, where the view is sensational. It costs zł 3 to make the climb—which makes it cheaper than an aerobics class—and the view is spectacular. The church also contains a 500-year-old, 25-ft-high astronomical clock that has only recently been restored to working order after years of neglect. It keeps track of solar and lunar progressions, and it displays the signs of the zodiac, something of an anomaly in a Catholic church. ⊠ *Podkramarska 5, corner of Piwna and Podkramarska.* ☎ *Tower zł 3.* ☉ *Daily 9–5.*

Two blocks west of St. Mary's Church, the **Wielka Zbrojownia** (Great Armory) is a good example of 17th-century Dutch Renaissance architecture. The ground floor is now a trade center, and the upper floors house an art school. ⊠ *Ul. Piwna, near targ Węglowy.*

Three huge and somber crosses perpetually draped with flowers stand outside the gates of the **Stocznia Gdańska** (Gdańsk Shipyards). Formerly called the Lenin Shipyards, this place gave birth to the Solidarity movement. The crosses are only one **monument** to Solidarity in the shipyards. There are plaques that commemorate the struggle as well as a quotation by Pope John Paul II inspired by his visit to the monument in 1987: "The Grace of God could not have created anything better; in this place, silence is a scream." ⊠ *Jana z Kolna.*

The shipyard monument in the Gdańsk Shipyards clearly symbolizes the fundamental link in the Polish consciousness between Catholicism and political dissent; another example is the **Kościół świętej Brygidy** (St. Brigitte's Church), a few blocks north. After the government declared martial law in 1981 in an attempt to force Solidarity to disband, members began meeting here secretly during celebrations of mass. There is a statue of Pope John Paul II in the front. ⊠ *Profesorska 17, near Old Town Hall.*

The **Żuraw Gdański** (Harbor Crane), built in 1444, was medieval Europe's largest and oldest crane. Today it houses the **Muzeum Morskie** (Maritime Museum), with a collection of models of the ships constructed in the Gdańsk Shipyards since 1945. At the museum ticket office, inquire about tickets for tours of the *Sołdek,* a World War II battleship moored nearby on the canal. ⊠ *Ołowianka 9–13,* ☎ *058/301–86–11.* ☑ *zł 8.* ☉ *Oct.–June, Tues.–Sun. 10–4; July–Sept., daily 10–4.*

The **Muzeum Narodowe w Gdańsku** (National Museum in Gdańsk) is housed in a former Franciscan monastery just south of the old walls of the Main Town. Exhibits include 14th- to 20th-century art and ethnographic collections. Hans Memling's triptych *Last Judgment* is the jewel of the collection. ⊠ *Toruńska 1, off Okopowa*, ☏ *058/301–70–61.* ▣ *zł 5, Sun. free.* ☾ *Daily 10–3.*

The small **Museum Archeologiczne Gdańska** (Gdańsk Archaeological Museum) displays Slavic tribal artifacts, including jewelry, pottery, boats, and bones. ⊠ *Mariacka 25–26,* ☏ *058/301–50–31.* ▣ *zł 3.* ☾ *Tues.– Sun. 10–4.*

★ The historic entrance to the Old Town of Gdańsk is marked by the **Brama Wyżynna** (High Gate). This magnificent Renaissance gate, built in 1576, is adorned with the flags of Poland, Gdańsk, and the Prussian kingdom. As the king entered the city on his annual visit, he'd pass this gate first, then the **Brama złota** (Golden Gate), which is just behind it and dates from 1614, combining characteristics of the Italian and Dutch Renaissances. ⊠ *Off Wały Jagiellońskie, at Długa.*

One of the city's most distinctive landmarks is the elaborately gilded **Fontanna Neptuna** (Neptune Fountain), at the western end of Długi Targ. Every day after dusk, this 17th-century fountain is illuminated, adding a romantic glow to the entire area. Around the fountain, vendors selling amber jewelry and souvenirs maintain a centuries-old tradition of trade at this point. ⊠ *Długa, east of Wały Jagiellońskie.*

★ Behind the Fontanna Neptuna on Długi Targ is the **Dwór Artusa** (Artus Mansion). Constructed over a period from the 15th through the 17th centuries, the mansion was named for mythical King Arthur, who otherwise has no affiliation with the place (alas, there are no traces of Excalibur or Merlin). This and the other stately mansions on the Długi Targ are reminders of the traders and aristocrats who once resided in this posh district. The mansion's collection includes Renaissance furnishings, paintings, holy figures, and the world's largest Renaissance stove. ⊠ *Długi Targ 43,* ☏ *058/346–33–58.* ▣ *zł 5.* ☾ *Tues.–Sat. 10– 4, Sun. 11–4.*

At the water's edge is the eastern entrance to the medieval city of Gdańsk, the **Brama Zielona** (Green Gate). This 16th-century gate killed two birds with one stone, doubling as a royal residence. Unfortunately, the name no longer fits: the gate is now painted brown. ⊠ *At the eastern end of Długi Targ.*

The former parish church of Gdańsk's Old Town, **Kościół świętej Katarzyny** (St. Catherine's Church), near the corner of ulica Podmłyńska and ulica Katarzynki, is supposedly the oldest church in the city. The construction was begun in 1220s; the tower was constructed in the 1480s, the carillon of 37 bells added in 1634. The 17th-century astronomer Jan Hevelius was buried in the presbytery of the church, below which lies what's left of the town's oldest Christian cemetery (which dates from the 10th century). ⊠ *Ul. Wielki Młyn,* ☏ *058/301–15–95.*

On a small island in the canal, just north of St. Catherine's Church, stands the **Wielki Młyn** (Great Mill). The largest mill in medieval Europe, it operated from the time of its completion in 1350 until 1945. ⊠ *Intersection of Podmłyńska and Na Piaskach.*

★ Although Gdańsk's original **Ratusz Główny** (Old Town Hall) was completely destroyed during World War II, a careful reconstruction of the exterior and interior now re-creates the glory of Gdańsk's medieval past. Inside the town hall, the **Muzeum Historii Miasta Gdańska** (Gdańsk Historical Museum) covers more than five centuries of Gdańsk's history in exhibits that include paintings, sculptures, and weapons. ⊠ *Długa 47,* ☏ *058/301–48–72.* ▣ *Museum zł 4.* ☾ *Tues.– Sun. 11–4.*

The district of Oliwa, north of the city center, is worth visiting if only
★ for its magnificent **Katedra w Oliwie** (Oliwa Cathedral). Originally part
of a Cistercian monastery, the church was erected during the 13th century. Like most other structures in Poland, it has been rebuilt many
times, resulting in a hodgepodge of styles from Gothic to Renaissance
to rococo. The cathedral houses one of the most impressive rococo or-
gans you're ever likely to hear—and see. It has more than 6,000 pipes,
and when a special mechanism is activated, wooden angels ring bells
and a wooden star climbs up a wooden sky. Demonstrations of the
organ and a brief narrated church history are given almost hourly on
weekdays in summer, less frequently on weekends and the rest of the
year. ⊠ *Cystersów 10.*

In a beautiful park surrounding the cathedral in Oliwa is a museum
complex. The **Muzeum Sztuki Współczesnej** (Modern Art Museum) has
a large collection of works by Polish artists from the interwar period
onward. Connected to the Modern Art Museum administratively is the
Muzeum Etnograficzne (Ethnographic Museum; ul. Opacka 12, ☎ 058/
552–12–71), which has fine examples of local crafts from the 19th century and an interesting display of amber folk jewelry. The Oliwa district is best reached by train; get off at Gdańsk-Oliwa and walk west
up ulica Piastowska to ulica Opacka; or take Tram 2 or 6 toward Sopot.
⊠ *Pałac Opatów, Cystersw 15A,* ☎ *058/552–12–71.* 🎟 *zł 4, Wed.
free.* ☉ *Tues.-Sat. 9–4, Sun. 10–4.*

OFF THE   **WESTERPLATTE** – Ten kilometers (6½ miles) north of the Old Town, the
BEATEN PATH   peninsula of Westerplatte is home to a branch of the National Museum.
World War II broke out here, at the entrance to the northern port. On
September 1, 1939, a German warship, the *Schleswig Holstein,* began
a bombardment of the Polish army positions here. A monument to the
men who attempted to defend the Westerplatte for seven days against
impossible odds was erected in the 1960s. Westerplatte can be reached
by Bus 106 or 158 from ulica Okopowa, just outside the Main Town
wall, or by water bus. ⊠ *Majora Sucharskiego 1,* ☎ *058/343–69–72.*
🎟 *Museum zł 5.* ☉ *Museum May–Oct., daily 9–4.*

Dining and Lodging

$$–$$$$ ✕ **Euro.** The Euro serves up the closest thing to nouvelle cuisine in
Gdańsk, in a prime location. Specialties include the veal escallopes with
fettuccine in cream sauce and the substantial steak Madame Walewska
with croquettes, prunes, and sausage in red wine. ⊠ *Długi 79/80,* ☎
058/301–23–83. AE, DC, MC, V.

$$–$$$$ ✕ **Major.** On the main thoroughfare, the Major has large tables and se-
★ cluded booths; the dining room is painted in glowing colors, and its ap-
pearance is enhanced by fresh flowers and oversize dinner plates. Try
the game soup, followed by duck roasted with apples and buckwheat
grits (*kasza gryczana*). During warm weather you can people-watch from
the outside café. ⊠ *Długa 18,* ☎ *058/301–10–69. AE, DC, MC, V.*

$$–$$$$ ✕ **Pod Łososiem.** The Salmon is memorable for its elegant baroque-
★ era dining rooms, well-oiled maître d', attentive service, and excellent
seafood (the menu also extends to game and fowl dishes). Try the salmon
or smoked eel to start, followed by flounder or grilled trout. ⊠ *Sze-
roka 52/53,* ☎ *058/301–76–52. AE, DC, MC, V.*

$$–$$$$ ✕ **Tawerna.** The scale-model sailing ship outside leads you into a se-
★ ries of wood-paneled dining rooms overlooking the Motlawa Canal.
This is a pleasant place to linger over lunch or dinner. Tawerna's fresh
trout is always reliable, but ask the polite, multilingual waitstaff about
the fish of the day. ⊠ *Powroźnicza 19–20, off Długi Targ,* ☎ *058/301–
41–14. AE, DC, MC, V.*

$–$$$ ✕ **Retman.** This restaurant is just a stone's throw from the Green Gate, which you can make out through a stained-glass window. The candlelit interior tries to recapture the atmosphere of 18th-century Gdańsk. A long and varied menu in English includes schnitzel, chateaubriand, and a large selection of seafood. ✉ *Stągiewna 1,* ☎ *058/ 301–92–48. AE, DC, MC, V.*

$–$$ ✕ **Pod Jaszczurem.** A step up from the traditional milk bar, this restaurant serves perfectly acceptable, if not distinguished, Polish favorites, steaks, and rather Polish pastas and pizzas. ✉ *Długa 47/49,* ☎ *058/ 301–91–13. AE, DC, MC, V. BP.*

$$$ 🏨 **Hotel Hanza.** This hotel has the best location in town in a spank-
★ ing new building set right on the Motlawa Canal. Though modern, the Hanza blends in with its surroundings nicely. All rooms are air-conditioned for those few weeks in summer when cooling off really is necessary. Advance bookings, especially in peak season, are strongly recommended. ✉ *Tokarska 6, 80–888,* ☎ *058/305–34–27,* FAX *058/ 305–33–86.* WEB *www.hanza-hotel.com.pl. 53 rooms, 7 suites. Restaurant, cable TV, minibars, gym, hot tub, sauna, bar, Internet, meeting rooms, free parking. AE, DC, MC, V. BP.*

$$$ 🏨 **Hotel Podewils.** This luxurious hotel is located on the edge of the
★ Old Town, opposite the Gdańsk Główny train station. The rooms and staff are uniformly pleasant, and the facilities are up to date, with a trouser press, a hair dryer, and Internet access in every room. ✉ *Szafarnia 2/3, 80–755,* ☎ *058/301–26–34,* FAX *058/301–63–01,* WEB *www.podewils-hotel.pl. 20 rooms. Restaurant, gym, sauna, bar, Internet. AE, DC, MC, V. BP.*

Nightlife and the Arts

Although Sopot is where the Tri-City really goes to have fun, there's good nightlife in Gdańsk. On summer nights, the Old Town teems with street musicians, families, and high-spirited young people. For details about cultural events in Gdańsk, Sopot, and Gdynia, see the English-language periodical *Gdańsk in Your Pocket.* The **Cotton Club** (✉ al. złotników 25, ☎ 058/301–88–13) draws a mixed crowd to two levels of laid-back drinking and pool tables. The **Jazz Club** (✉ Długi Targ 39/40) has regular live jazz concerts and the best bar staff in town. **Kamienica** (✉ Mariacka 23) is a popular bar decorated in murals showing the street outside.

Local and international performers take to the stage at Gdańsk's **Opera i Filharmonia Bałtycka** (Baltic Opera and Philharmonic; ✉ al. Zwycięstwa 15, ☎ 058/341–05–63). Gdańsk has a well-known theater company, **Teatr Wybrzeże** (✉ św. Ducha 2, ☎ 058/301–70–21).

Sopot

❷ *12 km (7½ mi) north of Gdańsk.*

Sopot is one of Poland's leading seaside holiday resorts, with miles of sandy beaches—in theory now safe for bathing (efforts are being made to deal with the Baltic's chronic pollution problems). Sopot enjoyed its heyday in the 1920s and 1930s, when the wealthy flocked here to gamble and enjoy the town's demure, quiet atmosphere. Once the most elegant seaside resort in Poland, Sopot got a little too popular for its own good in the 1980s, when it began to look down-at-heel. Today it is restoring its Riviera-like atmosphere. Much of Sopot's life takes place close to the Grand Hotel, once *the* place to stay in the area. Sopot's marvelous 19th-century pier is the longest on the Baltic.

Lodging

$$$ 🏨 **Grand Orbis Hotel.** The Grand is not only Sopot's best-known
★   hotel, it's also one of its best-known landmarks. Though its beachfront
location and late-19th-century elegance are highly appealing, the rooms
themselves are overdue for a makeover. The Grand is also famous for
its men's urinals (impressive 6-ft porcelain vaults). ⊠ *Powstańców
Warszawy 8–12, 81–718,* ☎ *058/551–00–41,* FAX *058/551–61–24.* WEB
*www.orbis.pl. 112 rooms. Restaurant, coffee shop, room service, cable
TV, gym, hair salon, beach, billiards, 2 bars, casino, nightclub, dry clean-
ing, laundry service, business services, meeting rooms, some pets al-
lowed. AE, DC, MC, V. BP.*

$$–$$$ 🏨 **Villa Hestia.** This boutique hotel is an echo of gentler days when
Sopot was known as the Riviera of Poland. These fully equipped lux-
ury rooms and suites, popular with honeymooners, are surrounded by
a landscaped garden just a 10-minute walk to the beach. Each has a
fireplace. Downstairs is the renowned and beautifully decorated Fukier
restaurant. ⊠ *Władysława IV 3/5, 81–703,* ☎ *058/551–21–00,* FAX *058/
551–46–36,* WEB *www.villahestia.pl. 2 rooms, 3 suites. Restaurant,
pub. AE, DC, MC, V. BP.*

$$ 🏨 **Novotel Gdańsk Marina.** This large block on the beach is a little
out of the way, but it has great views and is a 15-minute stroll from
the pier in Sopot. The Marina is a good option when more central hotels are booked. There's a bowling alley downstairs and a miniature
golf course right outside. All business rooms have Internet connections,
and translators and interpreters are available. ⊠ *Jelitkowska 20, Sopot
80–341,* ☎ *058/553–20–79,* FAX *058/553–31–59,* WEB *www.novotel.com.
126 rooms, 23 suites, 2 apartments. Restaurant, cable TV, minibars,
miniature golf, 2 tennis courts, indoor pool, gym, hair salon, sauna,
bowling, nightclub, business services, Internet, some pets allowed.
AE, DC, MC, V. BP.*

Nightlife and the Arts

Stroll down ulica Bohaterów Monte Cassino to find the café, pub, or
nightclub of your choice. In August the Miedzynadodowy Festiwal
Piosenki (International Song Festival) is held in the open-air concert
hall (Muszla Koncertowa) in Skwer Kuracyjny in the center of town
near the pier.

Model types tend to congregate at **Number 5** (⊠ Bohaterów Monte
Cassino 5). The **Siouxie** (⊠ Bohaterów Monte Cassino 9) begins the
day as a quiet coffee place and as night falls turns into a popular bohemian hangout.

Opera Leśna (Forest Opera; ⊠ Moniuszki 12, ☎ 058/551–18–12) gives
performances during the summer at its open-air opera house in the forest to the west of town. Sopot is home to a branch of Gdańsk's Teatr
Wybrzeże, the **Scena Kameralna** (Chamber Theater; ⊠ Bohatcrów
Monte Cassino 55/57, ☎ 058/551–58–12).

Malbork Castle

❸   *45 km (28 mi) southeast of Gdańsk on Rte. 50.*

One of the most impressive strongholds of the Middle Ages, the huge
★ **Zamek w Malborku** (Malbork Castle) is the central feature of the
quiet town of Malbork (the former German city of Marienburg). In
1230 the Teutonic Knights arrived on the banks of the Vistula River
and settled here, aiming to establish their own state on these conquered
Prussian lands. The castle passed into Polish hands after the second
Toruń Treaty in 1466 concluded the 13-year war between the Poles
and the Order of Teutonic Knights. For the next three centuries, Mal-

bork served as the royal residence for Polish kings during their annual visit to Pomerania. The castle was half destroyed during World War II, after which the building underwent a major renovation. The two-hour tours are the best way to see the castle; tours are available in English, and there's an English-language guidebook in the gift shop. ⊠ *Malbork,* ☎ *055/272–33–64.* 🎫 *zł 13.* ⊘ *May–Sept., Tues.–Sun. 9–5; Oct.–Apr., Tues.–Sun. 9–3.*

OFF THE BEATEN PATH

GNIEW – Located 67 km (42 mi) south of Gdańsk on Route 1 (E75), the restored castle of Gniew specializes in medieval-style festivals. Staff stage realistic reenactments of jousting tournaments and sword fights, followed by wild boar roasts, in the town square and in the castle. The castle has a museum and a hotel. ⊠ *Pl. Zamkowy 2, 83–140,* ☎ *058/535–35–29.* 🎫 *Museum zł 8, English-language guide zł 25.* ⊘ *Museum May–Sept., Tues.–Sun. 9–4:30; Oct.–Apr. by appointment only.*

Olsztyn

❹ *130 km (81 mi) southeast of Malbork, 150 km (93 mi) southeast of Gdańsk, 215 km (133 mi) north of Warsaw.*

A city where Polish and Prussian influences overlap, Olsztyn has served as the region's primary industrial center since World War II. The city is large and has a good number of hotels and restaurants, making it a nice jumping-off point for the Mazurian Lakes.

The Gothic Brama Wysoka (High Gate) marks the entrance to Olsztyn's Old Town and the main square. Southeast of the square is the 15th-century Katedra świętego Jakuba (St. James Cathedral).

The **Zamek** (Castle), with its ethnographic and historical **museum,** stands just to the west of the town's square. Once again, Copernicus, that Renaissance man who really got around in northern Poland, is featured in an exhibit. He successfully directed the defense of the castle from 1516 to 1521 against the Teutonic Knights while serving as an administrator of Warmia province. ⊠ *Zamkowa 1,* ☎ *089/527–95–96.* 🎫 *Museum zł 6.* ⊘ *Museum Tues.–Sun. 9–3.*

OFF THE BEATEN PATH

LIDZBARK WARMIŃSKI – This town, 46 km (28½ mi) north of Olsztyn, is home to a well-preserved 14th-century **castle** of the Teutonic Knights, which survived World War II only because the local population refused to help the Germans demolish it. Buses run to Lidzbark from Olsztyn. ⊠ *Pl. Zamkowy,* ☎ *089/767–32–11.* 🎫 *zł 2.* ⊘ *Tues.–Sun. 9–2.*

Lodging

$–$$ 🏨 **HP Park.** This comfortable if blandly modern hotel sits in parkland and offers horseback riding and bicycles for rent. ⊠ *Warszawska 119, 10–701,* ☎ *089/524–06–04,* 🗎 *089/524–00–77.* 🖥 *www.beph.pl. 100 rooms. Restaurant, grill, room service, cable TV, horseback riding, bicycles, bar, shop, laundry service, business services, some pets allowed; no-smoking rooms. AE, DC, MC, V. BP.*

Mikołajki

❺ *85 km (53 mi) east of Olsztyn.*

One of the most popular resorts in the Mazurian Lakes region, Mikołajki is situated on the shores of Lake Tałty and Lake Mikołajskie. Boating is popular on nearby Lake Śniardwy. There is a nature preserve surrounding Lake Łukajno, 4 km (2½ mi) east of Mikołajki.

OFF THE
BEATEN PATH

WOLF'S LAIR – About 8 km (5 mi) east of Kętrzyn lies Hitler's onetime bunker, at Gierłoż, called Wilczy Szaniec (Wolf's Lair), built during World War II as his East Prussian military command post. Its massively fortified concrete bunkers were blown up, but you can still climb in and among the remains and get a feel for his megalomania. Wolf's Lair was also where a small group of German patriots tried—and failed—to assassinate Hitler on July 20, 1944. ⊠ Gierłoż, ☎ 089/752-44-29. ☞ zł 7, English-language tour zł 50. ☉ Daily 9–8.

Lodging

$$ 🏨 **Hotel Gołębiewski.** This enormous hotel has just about everything you might want, including an indoor pool with massive water slides. Set right on a lake, it is a popular resort spot. ⊠ Mrągowska 34, 11–730, ☎ 087/429-07-00, FAX 087/429-04-44. WEB www.golebiewski.pl. 576 rooms. 3 restaurants, cable TV, indoor pool, 4 tennis courts, horseback riding, bar, convention center. AE, DC, MC, V. BP.

Gdańsk and the Northeast Essentials

AIR TRAVEL

Gdańsk has the only airport in northeastern Poland with regular service. There are several daily flights to Gdańsk from Warsaw, Hamburg, and Copenhagen.

➤ AIRLINES: **LOT** (☎ 058/301-36-66). **SAS** (☎ 058/341-62-60).

AIRPORTS

Gdańsk's airport is 16 km (10 mi) out of town in Rębiechowo and can be reached by Bus 162, which picks you up and drops you off at the main train station, or by taxi.

➤ CONTACTS: **Gdańsk Airport** (☎ 058/341-52-51).

BOAT AND FERRY TRAVEL

Ferries travel daily from Gdańsk to Karlskrona and Oxelösund, Sweden. You can book tickets through Orbis in Gdańsk or Polferries or Lion Ferry, both in Gdynia. In summer, an hourly water-bus service links Gdańsk with Sopot and Gdynia, via Westerplatte and Hel.

➤ FERRY COMPANIES: **Lion Ferry** (⊠ Kwiatowskiego 60, Gdynia, ☎ 058/665-14-14). **Orbis** (⊠ Hotel Heweliusz, Heweliusza 22, Gdańsk, ☎ 058/301-34-56). **Polferries** (Polish Baltic Shipping Company; ⊠ Przemysłowa 1, Gdynia, ☎ 058/301-45-44).

➤ FERRY TERMINALS: In Gdańsk, the **Gdańsk Water-bus Station** (⊠ Długie Pobrzeże, near Brama Zielona, ☎ 058/301-49-26). The **Gdynia Water-bus Station** (⊠ al. Zjednoczenia 2, Gdynia, ☎ 058/620-21-54). **Sopot Water-bus Station** (⊠ Sopot Pier, ☎ 058/551-12-93).

BUS TRAVEL

Gdańsk is the major gateway for the Baltic coast and northeastern Poland. Gdańsk's PKS bus station is right next to the train station. Buses may be useful for those who want to venture to small towns off the beaten track; otherwise, trains are more frequent and more comfortable.

A regular service runs throughout the Tri-City area, taking you from Gdańsk through Oliwa and Sopot to Gdynia. The whole trip takes about 1¾ hours. The buses run from 5 AM to 11 PM; after 11 PM there is an hourly night-bus service. PKS buses link all the small towns and villages of the region.

➤ CONTACTS: **Gdańsk PKS Bus Station** (⊠ 3 Maja, ☎ 058/302-15-32).

CAR TRAVEL

From Warsaw, the 7 (E77), a two-lane road for part of its length, goes directly to Gdańsk. From the west, the quickest route to the coast from the border crossing at Frankfurt/Oder is to take the 2 (E30) to Poznań and then the 5 (E261) via Gniezno and Bydgoszcz to Świecie, where it becomes the 1 (E75) and continues via Tczew to the coast.

The road network in this part of Poland is relatively well developed and there are plenty of gas stations. Although Gdańsk's Stare Miasto (Old Town) and Główne Miasto (Main Town) areas are easily walkable, a car is useful if you wish to visit other parts of the Tri-City region, such as Sopot and the museums and cathedral at Oliwa, or sights farther afield.

EMERGENCIES

➤ CONTACTS: **Gdańsk Emergency Room** (⊠ al. Zwycięstwa 49, Gdańsk, ☎ 058/302–29–29). **Sopot Emergency Room** (⊠ Chrobrego 6/8, Sopot, ☎ 058/551–24–55).
➤ LATE-NIGHT PHARMACIES: **Apteka Dworcowa Gdańsk** (⊠ Gdańsk Główny [main train station], Podwale Grodzkie 1, Gdańsk, ☎ 058/346–25–40). **Apteka Kuracyjna Sopot** (⊠ al. Niepodległości 861, Sopot, ☎ 058/551–31–58). **Pod Gryfem Gdynia** (⊠ Starowiejska 34, Gdynia, ☎ 058/620–19–82).

TRAIN TRAVEL

The main station is Gdańsk Główny. Many daily trains leave here for Warsaw (four hours), Kraków (eight hours), Poznań (four hours), and Malbork (take the train to Warsaw, which stops in Malbork; local trains can take ages). All the towns of the region can be reached by train. Within the Tri-City area, a fast electric-train service runs every 15 minutes from Gdańsk Główny via Oliwa, Sopot, and Gdynia to Wejherowo. The service operates from 4 AM to 1 AM.
➤ CONTACTS: **Gdańsk Główny** (⊠ Podwale Grodzkie 1, Gdańsk, ☎ 058/94–36).

TRAVEL AGENCIES

➤ CONTACTS: **Orbis** (⊠ Heweliusza 22, Gdańsk, ☎ 058/301–34–56; ⊠ Podwale Staromiejskie 96, Sopot, ☎ 058/55–41–42).

VISITOR INFORMATION

➤ CONTACTS: **Agencja Infomacji Turystycznej Gdańsk** (⊠ Długa 45, Gdańsk, ☎ 058/301–93–27).

WESTERN POLAND

Comprising the provinces of Wielkopolska (Great Poland) and Dolny Śląsk (Lower Silesia), western Poland has always been the traditional heartland of the Polish state—despite spending much of the past 500 years under German, Prussian, and Austro-Hungarian control. Great Poland is part of the flat, vast plain that extends north through Europe and is characterized by smooth farmland, pockets of forest, and numerous lakes. There are many opportunities here for walking, swimming, fishing, and hunting. The hills of Lower Silesia rise gently to the Karkonosze Mountains, where trails draw energetic walkers and resorts lure skiers during winter. Wrocław and Poznań, two of western Poland's primary cities, attract crowds year-round for theater, music, and other cultural diversions.

Although the early Polish state had its origins in the west, the region has fallen (more than once) under German influence. The Poles of Great

Poland are affectionately mocked by their countrymen for having absorbed the archetypal German habits of cleanliness, order, and thrift. Lower Silesia and Pomerania were integrated with Poland only in 1945, so don't be surprised if the west feels sober, restrained, and altogether more Germanic than anything you'll find elsewhere in Poland.

Gniezno, the first capital of Poland, is worth visiting for its cathedral and, together with the nearby early settlement at Biskupin, could be a day trip from Poznań. Toruń, the birthplace of Nicolaus Copernicus, is also a good base from which to explore the northern part of this region.

Numbers in the margin correspond to numbers on the Western Poland map.

Wrocław

❶ *350 km (220 mi) southwest of Warsaw, 260 km (165 mi) northwest of Kraków.*

Midway between Kraków and Poznań on the Odra River, Wrocław, the capital of Dolny Śląsk (Lower Silesia), dates to the 10th century, when the Ostrów Tumski islet on the Odra became a fortified Slav settlement. There are now some 100 bridges spanning the city's 90-km (56-mi) network of slow-moving canals and tributaries, giving Wrocław its particular charm. Wrocław's population is also notable: almost half the residents of Poland's fourth-largest city are under the age of 30; most are students at one of the city's many institutions of higher learning.

Following the destruction that ravaged Wrocław during World War II, many of the city's historic buildings were restored. Wrocław's architectural attractions are its many brick Gothic churches, the majority of which lie in or around the Stare Miasto (Old Town) and Ostrów Tumski. This area is small enough to explore easily on foot.

The **Rynek** (market square) together with the adjoining **plac Solny** (Salt Square) form the heart of the Old Town, which stretches between the Fosa Miejska moat and the Odra River. Wrocław's market square is almost as grand as Kraków's and bustles with activity. Many of the houses were restored for the Pope's visit in 1997.

Just off the square to the northwest, the little **Jaś i Małgosia** (Hansel and Gretel) houses are linked by a baroque arcade—holding hands, so to speak. ✉ *Ul. Odrzańska and ul. Wita Stwosza.*

★ The magnificently ornate **Ratusz** (town hall) is the highlight of the market square. Mostly Gothic in style, with a dash of Renaissance and baroque thrown in, the town hall was under continuous construction from the 14th to the 16th century as Wrocław grew and prospered. In the center of the spired, pinnacled, and gabled **east facade** is a Renaissance **astronomical clock** from 1580. The **Gothic portal** was the main entrance of the Ratusz until 1616. The lavish **south facade,** dating from the 15th and 16th centuries, swarms with delicately wrought sculptures, friezes, reliefs, and oriels. Today the town hall houses the **Historical Museum of Wrocław.** ✉ *Sukiennice 9,* ☎ *071/344–36–38.* 🎫 *Museum zł 6.* ⊙ *Museum Wed.–Fri. 10–4, weekends 10–5.*

★ The massive 14th-century **Kościół świętej Marii Magdaleny** (St. Mary Magdalene's Church) has a 12th-century **Romanesque portal** on the south wall that is considered the finest example of Romanesque architecture in Poland. ✉ *Corner of ul. Szewska and ul. św. Marii Kaznodziejska, 1 block east of market square.*

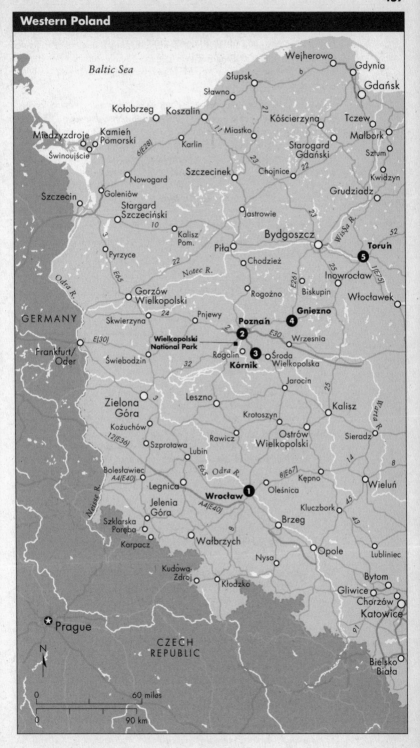

Western Poland

Baltic Sea

Wejherowo
Gdynia
Gdańsk
Słupsk
Sławno
Kościerzyna
Tczew
Kołobrzeg
Koszalin
Malbork
Miastko
Starogard
Gdański
Sztum
Miedzyzdroje
Kamień
Pomorski
Karlin
Kwidzyn
Świnoujście
Szczecinek
Chojnice
Grudziadz
Nowogard
Jastrowie
Szczecin
Goleniów
Stargard
Szczeciński
Kalisz
Pom.
Bydgoszcz
Toruń 5
Piła
Pyrzyce
Chodzież
Inowrocław
Włocławek
Notec R.
Rogożno
Biskupin
Gorzów
Wielkopolski
Gniezno 4
GERMANY
Skwierzyna
Pnjewy
Poznań 2
Wrzesnia
Wielkopolski
National Park
Rogalin
Środa
Wielkopolska
Frankfurt/
Oder
Świebodzin
Kórnik 3
Jarocin
Zielona
Góra
Leszno
Kalisz
Kożuchów
Krotoszyn
Sieradz
Szprotawa
Rawicz
Ostrów
Wielkopolski
Bolesławiec
Lubin
Odra R.
Kępno
Wieluń
Legnica
Wrocław 1
Oleśnica
Jelenia
Góra
Kluczbork
Szklarska
Poręba
Brzeg
Karpacz
Wałbrzych
Opole
Lubliniec
Nysa
Bytom
Kudowa-
Zdroj
Kłodzko
Gliwice
Chorzów
Katowice
Prague
CZECH
REPUBLIC
Bielsko
Biała

Odra R.
Nysa R.
Wisła R.
Warta R.

0   60 miles
0   90 km

The 14th-century brick **Kościół świętej Elżbiety** (Church of St. Elizabeth) was ravaged by fires in 1975 and 1976 and reopened only in the late 1990s. You can brave the 302-step climb to the top of the **tower** and look inside at the magnificent organ. The church can be reached through the arcade linking the Hansel and Gretel houses. ⊠ *Ul. Kiełbaśnicza.*

Wrocław's university district lies between ulica Uniwersytecka and the river. The vast 18th-century **Uniwersytet Wrocławski** (Wrocław University) was built between 1728 and 1741 by Emperor Leopold I on the site of the west wing of the former prince's castle. Behind the fountain and up the staircase is the magnificent assembly hall, **Aula Leopoldina.** The Aula is decorated with illusionist frescoes and life-size sculptures of great philosophers and patrons of learning. *Aula:* ⊠ *pl. Uniwersytecki 1.* 🕮 *zł 4.* ☉ *Thurs.–Tues. 10–3:30.*

NEED A
BREAK?

Café Uni (⊠ pl. Uniwersytecki 11), with its outdoor patio and frequent recitals, is a good place to sip coffee and admire the 565-ft facade of the university.

North of the university district, the Most Piaskowy (Sand Bridge) connects the left bank of the Odra with **Wyspa Piasek** (Sand Island). On the island directly across from the Sand Bridge is a former Augustinian monastery used as Nazi headquarters during the war; the building is now the **University Library.** The 14th-century **Kościół Najświętszej Marii Panny** (St. Mary's Church) is in the middle of the island. The church's Gothic interior was restored after World War II; it has a lofty vaulted ceiling and brilliant stained-glass windows.

★ Nine blocks northeast of the market square on the river's right bank, the district of **Ostrów Tumski** (Cathedral Island) is no longer an island. It is one of the city's oldest quarters, with winding streets, beautiful bridges—including two graceful, painted bridges, the Most Tumski (Cathedral Bridge) and Most Młyński (Mill Bridge)—and a cluster of churches. The **Kościół świętego Piotra i świętego Pawła** (Church of Sts. Peter and Paul) has no aisles. The early 14th-century **Kościół świętego Krzyża** (Holy Cross Church), just beyond the **statue of Pope John XXIII** (1968), is housed on the upper level of a rigid and forbidding building erected by Duke Henryk as his own mausoleum (the duke's Gothic sarcophagus has been moved to Wrocław's Historical Museum). On the lower level of Duke Henryk's mausoleum lies the 13th-century **Kościół świętego Bartłomieja** (St. Bartholomew's Church).

The 13th-century **Katedra świętego Jana Chrzciciela** (Cathedral of St. John the Baptist), with its two truncated towers, is the focal point of Cathedral Island. Its chancel is the earliest example of Gothic architecture in Poland. The cathedral houses the largest organ in the country, with 10,000 pipes. On the southern side of the cathedral is **St. Elizabeth's Chapel**; the bust of Cardinal Frederick above the entrance, along with numerous other sculptures and frescoes, came from the studio of Gian Lorenzo Bernini. The **Elector's Chapel,** in the northwestern corner of the cathedral, dates from the early 18th century and was designed by the baroque architect Johann Fischer von Erlach of Vienna. As these chapels are often closed, check at the sacristy for an update as well as for admission fees. ⊠ *Pl. Katedralny, Ostrów Tumski.*

The **Muzeum Archidiecezjalne** (Archdiocesan Museum), north of the Cathedral of St. John the Baptist, houses a collection of medieval Silesian art. ⊠ *Ul. Kanonia 12, Ostrów Tumski,* ☎ *071/322–17–55.* 🕮 *zł 4.* ☉ *Daily 10–3.*

Dining and Lodging

$$–$$$$ ✕ **Królewska and Karczma Piastow.** This beautifully decorated es-
★ tablishment in the heart of Wrocław is divided into two parts: a restau-
rant-nightclub and café–wine cellar. The restaurant, Królewska, serves
Polish and international fare. The *shashlik* (grilled beef and peppers)
served with brown rice is particularly tasty. The Renaissance-style
wine cellar, Karczma Piastow, is a good place to relax on a hot sum-
mer's day. ⊠ *Rynek 5,* ☎ *071/372–48–96. AE, DC, MC, V.*

$$–$$$$ ✕ **Spiż.** Located in the cellar of the town hall, this restaurant is the
place to go for a mix of Polish and European cuisine. Heading the menu
are *schabowy* (pork cutlet), with mashed potatoes and sauerkraut, and
golonka (pig's knuckle). ⊠ *Sukiennice 9,* ☎ *071/344–52–67. AE, DC,
MC, V.*

$$–$$$ 🏨 **Qubus Hotel Maria Magdalena.** Lying only a few hundred feet from
the market square, this hotel has immaculate rooms with all the modern conveniences, including air-conditioning. ⊠ *Ul. Marii Magdaleny
2, 50-103,* ☎ *071/341–08–98,* FAX *071/341–09–20,* WEB *www.hotel-
mm.com.pl. 50 rooms. Restaurant, cable TV, in-room data ports,
minibars, indoor pool, gym, hair salon, hot tub, sauna, bar, business
services, meeting room. AE, DC, MC, V.*

$–$$ 🏨 **Hotel Europejski.** Renovations in this hotel have been sporadic,
leaving it half old and half new. The small and simple older rooms are
cheaper than the refurbished ones. All guests can admire the exquisite
lobby. ⊠ *Ul. Józefa Piłsudskiego 88, 50–017,* ☎ *071/343–10–71,* FAX
071/344–34–33, WEB *www.odratourist.pl. 74 rooms. Restaurant, bar,
laundry facilities, meeting rooms. AE, DC, MC, V. BP.*

Nightlife and the Arts

Wrocław hosts two popular summer music festivals. One of the most
renowned of Wrocław's festivals is **Jazz on the Odra** (☎ 071/22–55–
42), a summertime event that has attracted an international group of
performers for the past 25 years. **Wratislavia Cantans** is a series of 24
summer concerts featuring Gregorian chants, German oratorios, operas, cantatas, and other choral performances. Concerts take place at
different points in the city.

If you get tired of the bars around the market square try the **Kalam-
bur** (⊠ ul. Kuźnicza 29A, ☎ 071/343–26–50). This Art Nouveau
café-bar is attached to a small, well-known theater, and there is sometimes live music.

The **Philharmonic** (⊠ ul. Piłsudskiego 19, ☎ 071/442–001) hosts classical performances several times each week.

Teatr Polski (⊠ ul. G. Zapolskiej 3, ☎ 071/343–86–53) is the occasional home of the Wrocław Pantomime Theater. **Wrocławski Teatr Lalek**
(⊠ pl. Teatralny 4, ☎ 071/344–12–17) is widely regarded as the best
puppet theater in Poland.

Poznań

2 *300 km (186 mi) west of Warsaw, 170 km (105 mi) north of Wrocław.*

Halfway between Warsaw and Berlin, in the middle of the monotonously
flat Polish lowlands, Poznań has been an east–west trading center for
more than 1,000 years. In the Middle Ages, merchants made a great
point of bringing their wares here on St. John's Day (June 23), and the
annual tradition has continued, though the markets have now been su-
perseded by the International Trade Fair, which has been held here since
1922. Until the 13th century, Poznań was, on and off, the capital of
Poland, and in 968 the first Polish bishopric was founded here by

Mieszko I. It still remains the capital of the Wielkopolska (Great Poland) region.

Despite its somewhat grim industrial outskirts, Poznań is one of the country's most charming old towns; consider making a trip through western Poland if only to visit Poznań's majestic market square. Poznań may be only the fifth-largest city in Poland, but to a tourist it will feel larger than that. While the majority of sights are near the Old Town's impressive Stary Rynek (Old Market Square), other attractions are off in the sprawling maze of ancillary streets. Walking is not recommended here. Invest in some tram tickets and a city map with the transit routes marked; your feet will thank you.

Poznań's **Stary Rynek** (Old Market Square) mainly dates from the 16th century. It has a somewhat cluttered feeling, since the center is occupied with both 20th-century additions and Renaissance structures.

★ Poznań residents will proudly tell you that the imposing Renaissance **Ratusz** (town hall) at the center of the Old Market Square is the most splendid building in Poland. Its clock tower is famous for the goats that appear every day at noon to butt heads before disappearing inside. Legend has it that the clock maker who installed the timepiece planned to give a party on the occasion. He ordered two goats for the feast, but the goats escaped and started fighting on the tower. The mayor was so amused by the event that he ordered the clock maker to construct a mechanism to reenact the goat fight. The town hall now houses a **Museum of City History,** which contains a room dedicated to Chopin. ⊠ *Stary Rynek 1,* ☎ *061/852–56–13.* 🎫 *zł 5.5.* ☉ *Mon.–Tues. and Fri. 10–4, Wed. noon–6, Thurs. and Sun. 10–3.*

The tiny arcaded shopkeepers' houses in the Old Market Square date to the mid-16th century. Some of them now house the **Muzeum Instrumentow Muzycznycy** (Museum of Musical Instruments), where you can see Chopin's piano and a plaster cast of the maestro's hands. ⊠ *Stary Rynek 45,* ☎ *061/852–08–57.* 🎫 *zł 6.* ☉ *Tues. and Thurs. 10–4, Wed. and Fri.–Sat. 9–5, Sun. 11–4.*

A few blocks west of the Old Market Square is the **Muzeum Narodowe** (National Museum), which has a good collection of Polish and Western European paintings. ⊠ *Al. Marcinkowskiego 9,* ☎ *061/852–80–11.* 🎫 *zł 4.* ☉ *Wed.–Sat. 10–4, Sun. 11–3.*

After a visit to the museum, walk across plac Wolności (Freedom Square) to the beautiful **Biblioteka Raczyńskich** (Raczyński Library), built in 1829 by the aristocratic Raczyński family. ⊠ *Pl. Wolności 19,* ☎ *061/852–94–42.* 🎫 *Free.* ☉ *Daily 9–5.*

Ostrów Tumski (Cathedral Island), an islet in the Warta River east of the Old Town, is the historic cradle of Poznań. This is where the Polanie tribe built their first fortified settlement and their first basilica in the 10th century.

Cathedral Island's **Poznań Cathedral** was rebuilt after World War II in pseudo-Gothic style, but 10th- and 11th-century remains can be seen in some interior details. Directly behind the main altar is the heptagonal **Golden Chapel,** worth seeing for the sheer opulence of its romantic Byzantine decor. Within the chapel is the **mausoleum** of the first rulers of Poland, Mieszko I and Bolesław the Great. ⊠ *Ul. Mieszka I.*

··

OFF THE BEATEN PATH   **WIELKOPOLSKI NATIONAL PARK –** This beautiful national park is 19 km (10 mi) southwest of Poznań on Route 430. The pine forests are punctuated with 16 lakes, 2 of which, Lake Rusałka and Lake Strzeszynek, have long beaches, tourist accommodations, and water-sports equipment for hire. There are several interesting legends associated with the park; for example, at the bottom of Lake Góreckie there is supposed to be a submerged town, and on still nights you can hear the faint ringing of the town bells. ✉ *Jeziory, 62-050 Mosina,* ☎ *061/813–22–06.*

Dining and Lodging

$$–$$$$ ✕ **Kresowa.** On the main town square, this popular restaurant specializes in cuisine from the *kresy,* or Poland's former eastern territories (Lithuania, Ukraine, and Belarus). ✉ *Stary Rynek 2,* ☎ *061/853–12–91. AE, DC, MC, V.*

$$$ 🏨 **Mercure Poznań.** This five-story, glass-front hotel is an Orbis product from the 1960s, now part of the French chain but still managed by Orbis. Identical brown doors lead from long corridors into nearly identical rooms. The rooms are furnished in dark shades but have the usual Orbis standard of comfort. Its strong suit is convenience: an excellent location and good parking facilities. ✉ *Ul. Roosevelta 20, 60–829,* ☎ *061/855–80–00,* FAX *061/847–31–41,* WEB *www.mercure.com. 203 rooms, 11 suites. Restaurant, café, cable TV, minibars, hair salon, bar, shops, laundry service, travel services, parking (fee). AE, DC, MC, V.*

$$$ 🏨 **Novotel Poznań Centrum.** This charmless high-rise in the city center next to the railway station has the familiar Orbis touch: rooms decorated in government-regulation brown with slightly outdated bathrooms. It's now part of Accor's Novotel chain, though still managed by Orbis. ✉ *Pl. Andersa 1, 61–898,* ☎ *061/858–70–00,* FAX *061/852–26–31.* WEB *www.novotel.com. 485 rooms, 10 suites. Restaurant, room service, minibars, massage, sauna, bar, nightclub, playground, car rental. AE, DC, MC, V.*

$–$$ 🏨 **Dom Turysty PTTK.** This hotel has only 18 rooms (of which 10 are singles), but if you can get in you'll like its location, right at the center of the Old Town. Rooms are comfortably furnished, with Polish folk elements, and the staff is friendly and well informed. ✉ *Stary Rynek 91, 61–001,* ☎ FAX *061/852–88–93. 18 rooms, 10 with shared bath. Restaurant, café. AE, DC, MC, V. BP.*

$–$$ 🏨 **Hotel Lech.** This older hotel near the university is a good base for exploring Poznań on foot. Rooms are on the small side but comfortably furnished. There is no restaurant service apart from breakfast, and the hotel bar sometimes attracts a rather rowdy crowd in the evening. ✉ *Ul. św. Marcin 74, 61–809,* ☎ *061/853–08–79,* FAX *061/853–08–80.* WEB *www.hotel-lech.poznan.pl. 79 rooms, 1 suite. Bar. AE, DC, MC, V. BP.*

Nightlife and the Arts

All the big hotels in Poznań have nightclubs with floor shows. The **Black Club** in the Mercure Poznań (✉ ul. Roosevelta 20, ☎ 061/847–08–01) is always crowded.

The **Filharmonia Poznańska** (Poznań Philharmonic; ✉ ul. św. Marcin 81, ☎ 061/852–47–08) holds concerts in Wrocław University's beautifully restored Aula, where the acoustics are excellent.

Stefan Stuligrosz's Boys Choir (✉ Teatr Wielki, ul. Fredry 9, ☎ 061/852–82–91)—the Poznań Nightingales—is one of Poznań's best-known musical attractions.

Kórnik

❸ *20 km (12 mi) southeast of Poznań on Rte. 42.*

Kórnik's biggest draw is an 18th-century **neo-Gothic castle,** which houses a museum full of antique furnishings and a library of more than 150,000 rare books (including manuscripts by Mickiewicz and Słowacki).

Note the magnificent wood-inlay floors. The castle is surrounded by Poland's largest **arboretum,** with more than 3,000 varieties of trees and shrubs. ⊠ *Kórnik,* ☎ *061/817–00–81.* 🎫 *zł 4.* ☽ *May–Sept., daily 9–5; Oct.–Apr., daily 9–3.*

OFF THE
BEATEN PATH
ROGALIN PALACE – Head 20 km (12 mi) south of Poznań to this baroque-era palace. It is now a branch of the National Museum in Poznań and includes a collection of 19th-century German and Polish art. The nearby English Garden contains some of the oldest oak trees in Europe. ⊠ *Rogalin,* ☎ *061/813–80–30.* 🎫 *zł 4.* ☽ *Tues.–Sun. 10–4.*

Gniezno

❹ *50 km (31 mi) northeast of Poznań on Hwy. 5 (E261).*

Lying along the Piast Route—Poland's historic memory lane running from Poznań to Kruszwica—Gniezno is the original capital of Poland and is surrounded by towns whose monuments date as far back as the origins of the Polish state. Legend has it that Lech, the founder of the country, spotted some white eagles nesting on the site; he then named the town Gniezno (nesting site) and proclaimed the white eagle the nation's emblem. On a more historical note, King Mieszko I made Gniezno the seat of the country's first bishop, St. Wojciech, after the king brought Catholicism to the Polish people during the 10th century.

★ The first **cathedral** in Gniezno was built by King Mieszko I before AD 977. The present 14th-century building is the most imposing Gothic cathedral in Poland. At the back of the church the 12th-century bronze-cast **Doors of Gniezno** have intricate bas-relief scenes depicting the life of St. Wojciech (Adalbert), a Czech missionary commissioned to bring Christianity to the Prussians in northern Poland. Not everyone appreciated his message: he was killed by pagans. It is said that his body was bought from his murderers for its weight in gold, which the Poles paid ungrudgingly. On the altar a silver sarcophagus, supported by four silver pallbearers, bears the remains of St. Wojciech. ⊠ *Ul. Laskiego 9.* 🎫 *Doors of Gniezno zł 3.* ☽ *Mon.–Sat. 10–5, Sun. 1:30–5:30.*

Housed in a characterless concrete school building in Gniezno, the **Muzeum Poczatkew Państwa Polskiego** (Museum of the Original Polish State) has multimedia exhibitions in five languages, including English, that describe medieval Poland. ⊠ *Ul. Kostrzewskiego 6,* ☎ *061/426–46–41.* 🎫 *zł 3.* ☽ *Tues.–Sun. 10–5.*

OFF THE
BEATEN PATH
BISKUPIN – Step back in time by wandering along the wood-paved streets and peering into the small wooden huts at the fortified settlement at Biskupin, 30 km (18 mi) north of Gniezno on route E261 toward Bydgoszcz. This 100-acre "Polish Pompeii" is one of the most fascinating archaeological sites in Europe. It was discovered in 1933, when a local school principal and his students noticed some wood stakes protruding from the water during an excursion to Lake Biskupieńskie. The lake was later drained, revealing a settlement largely preserved over the centuries by the lake waters. Dating to 550 BC, the settlement was surrounded by defensive ramparts of oak and clay and a breakwater formed from stakes driven into the ground at a 45-degree angle. A wooden plaque at the entrance shows a plan of the original settlement. The museum holds a yearly festival in the last week of September that includes historic reenactments. ⊠ *Biskupin,* ☎ *053/425–025,* 🌐 *www.biskupin.pl.* 🎫 *zł 4.* ☽ *May–Sept., daily 9–6; Oct.–Apr., daily 9–5.*

Toruń

★ ❺ *210 km (130 mi) northwest of Warsaw, 150 km (93 mi) east of Poznań.*

The birthplace of Nicolaus Copernicus, the medieval astronomer who first postulated that the earth travels around the sun, Toruń is a beautiful medieval city. It is also one of the few Polish cities to have survived World War II relatively unscathed. The Stare Miasto (Old Town) brims with ancient churches, civic buildings, and residences, its Gothic burgher houses and town hall blending harmoniously with the Renaissance and baroque of its later patrician mansions.

★ The **Muzeum Mikołaja Kopernika** (Nicolaus Copernicus Museum), one block south of the Rynek Staromiejski (Old Town Square), is dedicated to Toruń's most famous native son, who in 1617 wrote *De Revolutionibus Orbium Coelestium* (On the Revolutions of the Celestial Spheres), explaining his theory of a heliocentric universe. The museum consists of two houses: the house at ulica Kopernika 17, where Copernicus was born (in 1473) and lived until he was 17 years old, and the adjoining historic town house. The rooms have been restored with period furnishings, some of which belonged to the Copernicus family. There is also a scale model of Toruń, which is accompanied by a sound-and-light show (available in English) that tells the history of the city. ⊠ *Ul. Kopernika 15/17,* ☎ *056/622–67–48.* ▨ *zł 4.* ☼ *Tues.–Sun. 10–4.*

The Old Town Square is dominated by the 14th-century **Ratusz** (town hall), one of the largest buildings of its kind in northern Poland. It has 365 windows, and its four pinnacles are meant to represent the four seasons of the year. Built in 1274, the town hall's **tower** is the oldest in Poland, although it did receive some later Dutch Renaissance additions. You can go up into the tower to enjoy a spectacular view. Inside the town hall the **historical museum** houses a collection of painted glass, paintings, and sculptures from the region's craftsmen. Look for the gingerbread molds, which have been used since the 14th century to create the treats for which Toruń is famous. ⊠ *Rynek Staromiejski 1,* ☎ *056/622–70–38.* ▨ *Museum zł 4.* ☼ *Wed.–Sun. 10–5.*

NEED A BREAK?   Inside the town hall, around the corner from the historical museum, the atmospheric café **Piwnica Pod Aniołem** (Rynek Staromiejski 1) serves great coffee.

On the eastern side of the Old Town Square is **Pod Gwiazdą** (House under the Stars). Built in the 15th century, it was remodeled in the 17th century in the baroque style. It is now the **Far Eastern Art Museum**, which is worth visiting to see the interior of the house, especially the carved-wood staircase. ⊠ *Rynek Staromiejski 35,* ☎ *056/622–67–48.* ▨ *zł 6.* ☼ *Tues.–Sun. 10–4.*

Kościół świętego Jana (St. John's Church) was built in the 13th through 15th centuries. This is where Copernicus was baptized. The **tuba Dei**, a 15th-century bell in the church's tower, is one of the largest in Poland. ⊠ *Ul. Żeglarska, south of the Old Town Square.*

In a pleasant park northeast of Toruń's Old Town stands the **Muzeum Etnografiszne** (Ethnographic Museum). Outside the museum are brightly decorated farmhouses that have been restored and filled with antique furnishings. The grounds have been designed to replicate life in the Bydgoszcz region (west of Toruń) in the 19th and early 20th centuries. ⊠ *Wały Sikorskiego 19,* ☎ *056/622–80–91.* ▨ *zł 4.* ☼ *Mon., Wed., and Fri. 9–4; Tues., Thurs., and weekends 10–6.*

Dining and Lodging

$$–$$$$ ✕ **Restauracja Staromiejska.** Located in the old wine cellar of a 4th-
★   century building, this place has polished wood and stone floors, white-
washed walls, and red, brick-ribbed, vaulted ceilings. Enjoy the excellent
pizza as well as Polish fare. ⊠ *Ul. Szczytna 2–4,* ☎ *056/622–67–25.
AE, DC, MC, V.*

$$–$$$$ ✕ **Trzy Korony.** Inside an old house on the Old Town Square this
restaurant serves up regional dishes, including many varieties of meat-
filled dumplings (*pyzy*) and thick bean soup (*zupa fasolowa*). ⊠ *Rynek
Staromiejski 21,* ☎ *056/622–60–31. AE, DC, MC, V.*

$–$$ ✕ **Zajazd Staropolski.** This traditional Polish restaurant has a restored
★   17th-century interior and serves excellent meat dishes and soups. ⊠
Ul. Żeglarska 10–14, ☎ *056/622–60–60. AE, DC, MC, V.*

$$$ 🏨 **Kosmos.** A functional 1960s Orbis hotel, Kosmos is showing signs
of wear; however, one section of the hotel has recently been renovated.
It is near the river, in the city center. ⊠ *Ul. Popiełuszki 2, 87–100,* ☎
056/622–13–44, FAX *056/622–13–41,* WEB *www.orbis.pl. 57 rooms, 2
suites. Restaurant, room service, cable TV, bar, laundry service, Inter-
net, business services, meeting room. AE, DC, MC, V. BP.*

$$–$$$ 🏨 **Gromada Zajazd Staropolski.** Situated in three former tenement
★   houses off the Old Town Square, Zajazd Staropolski is without a doubt
the nicest hotel in town. ⊠ *Ul. Żeglarska 10–14, 87–100,* ☎ *056/622–
60–60,* FAX *056/622–60–62. 33 rooms. Restaurant. AE, MC, V.*

$$ 🏨 **Helios.** This friendly, medium-size Orbis hotel in the city center has
typical Orbis rooms (comfortable but plain) and a good restaurant. ⊠
Ul. Kraszewskiego 1/3, 87–100, ☎ *056/619–65–50,* FAX *80/655–54–
29,* WEB *www.orbis.pl. 108 rooms. Restaurant, room service, cable TV,
hair salon, sauna, nightclub. AE, DC, MC, V. BP.*

$ 🏨 **Hotel Polonia.** A favorite of Polish families, this antiquated hotel is
just across the street from the Municipal Theater near the Old Town
Square. The rooms are large, with high ceilings, and very simple. ⊠
Pl. Teatralny 5, 87–100, ☎ *056/622–30–29,* FAX *056/622–30–29. 46
rooms, 16 with shared bath. No credit cards. BP.*

Western Poland Essentials

AIR TRAVEL

LOT offers daily flights from Warsaw to Wrocław, where special LOT
buses shuttle passengers from Starachowice Airport to the LOT office
in town. Buses leave from the same point for the airport one hour before each flight. City Bus 106 will also take you the 10 km (6 mi) from
the city to the airport.

Poznań's Ławice Airport is to the west of the city in the Wola district.
Buses run regularly to and from the LOT office; allow about an hour
for the journey.
➤ CONTACTS: **LOT office Poznań** (⊠ ul. św. Marcin 69, Poznań, ☎
058/852–28–47). **LOT office Wrocław** (⊠ ul. Józefa Piłsudskiego 77,
Wrocław, ☎ 071/343–90–31).

BUS TRAVEL

Long-distance PKS buses from other Polish cities arrive in Wrocław at
Dworzec Centralny PKS, diagonally opposite the main train station.
The station also serves local routes, with frequent service to Jelenia Góra,
Częstochowa, Łódź, and the spa towns of Kudowa, Duszniki, and Polan-
ica. In Poznań the Dworzec PKS bus station is a short walk from the
train station. Frequent bus service is available to and from Kornik and
Gniezno. Toruń's PKS bus station is east of the Old Town. Take local
Bus 22 to and from the station.

➤ CONTACTS: **Dworzec Centralny PKS Wrocław** (✉ ul. Kościuszki 135, Wrocław, ☎ 071/344–44–61). **Dworzec PKS Bus Station Poznań** (✉ ul. Towarowa 17/19, Poznań, ☎ 061/833–12–12). **PKS Bus Station Toruń** (✉ ul. Dąbrowskiego, Toruń, ☎ 056/622–28–42).

CAR TRAVEL

Western Poland has good roads and plenty of gas and service stations. From the west, a four-lane divided highway extends most of the way between Wrocław and the German border town of Cottbus. From Warsaw, the best route is to take the 8 (E67) through Piotrków Tribunalski to Wrocław.

Poznań, on the main east–west route from Berlin to Moscow, is easily accessible by car. The 2 (E30), which leads from the border at Frankfurt/Oder through Poznań and Warsaw to the eastern border at Terespol/Brest in Belarus, is still mostly a two-lane road and is considered—because of its curves and lack of shoulders—one of the most dangerous roads in Europe.

TRAIN TRAVEL

Trains run frequently from the modern Poznań Główny to Szczecin (3 hours), Toruń (2½ hours), Wrocław (3 hours), Kraków (8 hours), and Warsaw (4 hours). International destinations include Berlin (4½ hours), Budapest (15 hours), and Paris (20 hours).

Toruń's PKP train station lies south of the city, across the Vistula River, and is connected to town by Bus 22. There is daily service to and from Poznań (three hours), Gdańsk (four hours), Warsaw (three hours), and Kraków (nine hours).

Wrocław Główny PKP connects Wrocław by rail to all major cities in Poland, with frequent service to and from Kraków (five hours), Warsaw (six hours), and Gdańsk (seven hours). Trains also leave here for many cities in Western and Eastern Europe: Dresden, Berlin, Prague, Budapest, and Frankfurt. The station is in the city center, a 30-minute walk south from the Rynek (market square). Wrocław Nadodrze is the hub for local routes to the east and southeast, including Gniezno. You might want to come to the Wrocław Świebodzki station just to admire the station building, which dates from 1848. You can also catch local trains from here. The station lies 1 km (½ mi) south of Wrocław's market square.

➤ CONTACTS: **PKP train station Toruń** (✉ Toruń ul. Kujawska 1, ☎ 056/621–30–44). **Poznań Główny** (✉ ul. Dworcowa 1, Poznań, ☎ 061/869–38–11). **Wrocław Główny PKP** (✉ ul. Józefa Piłsudskiego, Wrocław, ☎ 071/368–33–33). **Wrocław Nadodrze** (✉ ul. Staszica 50, Wrocław, ☎ 71/369–37–07).

VISITOR INFORMATION

IT in Poznań sells the cultural guide *IKS,* which has lots of useful information, much of it in English, and is open weekdays 9–5, Saturday 10–2. IT in Toruń is open Monday–Saturday 9–4. IT in Wrocław has good maps and English guidebooks and is open weekdays 9–5, Saturday 10–2. Orbis, which has offices in all of the three major towns in western Poland, is the best place to by train tickets.

➤ IT OFFICES: **IT Poznań** (✉ Stary Rynek 59, Poznań, ☎ 061/852–61–56). **IT Toruń** (✉ ul. Piekary 37/39, Toruń, ☎ 056/621–09–31). **IT Wrocław** (✉ Rynek 14, Wrocław, ☎ 071/344–31–11).

➤ ORBIS OFFICES: **Orbis Poznań** (✉ ul. Marcinkowskiego 21, Poznań, ☎ 061/853–20–52). **Orbis Toruń** (✉ ul. Mostwa 7, Toruń, ☎ 056/622–17–14). **Orbis Wrocław** (✉ Rynek 29, Wrocław, ☎ 071/344–76–79).

POLAND A TO Z

ADDRESSES
Finding your way around is pretty straightforward once you are familiar with the basic street-sign words. *Ulica,* usually abbreviated to ul., means street (the "ulica" prefix is often skipped, and streets are referred to by their names only); *aleje* (al.) is avenue; and *plac* (pl.) is square. In city centers most addresses are clearly marked by a big blue sign with a red stripe across the bottom.

AIR TRAVEL
Most direct flights from North America arrive in Warsaw, but there are nonstop flights from the U.S. to Kraków as well. LOT Polish Airlines has daily domestic services linking many major Polish cities: Warsaw, Gdańsk, Katowice, Kraków, Poznań, Rzeszów, Szczecin, and Wrocław. Flying time in each case is no longer than an hour. Compared with rail travel, flying is very expensive (although not by Western standards), and most airports are some distance from the city center. However, in a few instances, rail connections can be so limited that flying is a real time-saver (this is especially true between Wrocław and Warsaw, and Rzeszów and Warsaw).

AIRPORTS
For airport information, *see* Essentials in the individual regional sections.

BOAT AND FERRY TRAVEL
Lion Ferry offers service from Gdynia to Karlskrona, Sweden. Polferries operates regular ferry service from Denmark (Copenhagen, Ronne) and Sweden (Malmö, Nynashamn, Oxelösund) to Świnoujście, Kołobrzeg, or Gdańsk.

In the summer season, it is possible to take ferries or hydrofoils between various points on the Baltic coast. Two of the more popular routes are Szczecin to Świnoujście, near the German border on the coast, and Sopot to Hel, north of Gdańsk.
➤ Boat and Ferry Lines: **Lion Ferry** (✉ Kwiatowskiego 60, Gdynia, ☎ 058/665–14–14). **Polferries** (Polish Baltic Shipping Company; ✉ 8, Warsaw, ☎ 022/830–00–97).

BUS TRAVEL TO POLAND
A number of companies operate buses between major European cities and Polish cities. Many travel nonstop, and what you lose in comfort you make up for in savings: the bus fare is roughly half the train fare. You can purchase tickets from Anna Travel, an agency that specializes in international bus travel.
➤ Contacts: **Anna Travel** (✉ al. Jerozolimskie 54, Warsaw, ☎ 022/ 825–53–89).

BUS TRAVEL WITHIN POLAND
The national bus company, PKS, and the private and much more pleasant Polski Express both offer long-distance service to all cities. You can reserve seats on express buses, which often—except in the case of a few major intercity routes—get to their destinations more quickly than trains. For really out-of-the-way destinations, the bus is often the only means of transportation.
➤ Bus Lines: **PKS** (☎ 022/823–63–94 in Warsaw). **Polski Express** (☎ 022/620–03–30 in Warsaw).

BUSINESS HOURS

Food shops are open weekdays 7–7, Saturday 7–1. Other stores are open weekdays 11–7 and Saturday 9–1, although more and more stores are staying open later and on Sunday. Banks are generally open weekdays 8–3 or 8–6. Museum hours are unpredictable but are generally Tuesday–Sunday 10–5.

CAR RENTALS

A valid driver's license, issued in any country, will enable you to drive without a special permit in Poland. You do need green-card insurance, which can be purchased at the border, if you are driving your own car.

For agency numbers, *see* Essentials sections in individual regional sections.

CAR TRAVEL

In summer, the border-crossing points into Poland from Germany and out of Poland to the east are notoriously lengthy. Green-card insurance, which covers collision damage outside one's country of residence, can be bought at the border and is necessary if you are bringing in your own car. Rental companies outside Poland often do not permit their cars to cross the border due to the high incidence of theft (for example, Avis Germany will not allow you to take its rental cars to Poland).

The Polish Motoring Association (PZMot) provides tourist information about driving in Poland. It also provides emergency roadside assistance, as well as breakdown and repair services. If your car breaks down in a remote area, you can usually find a local farmer who will help with a tractor tow and some mechanical assistance.

➤ CONTACTS: **Polish Motoring Association** (PZMot; ☎ 022/629–83–36; 9637 countrywide for emergency roadside assistance).

ROAD CONDITIONS

Driving conditions in Poland continue to deteriorate as traffic density explodes. You will not yet find any Western-quality highways, although new east–west international highways are under construction and a few major roads (such as the one from Warsaw to Katowice) are now entirely four-lane divided highways. This is, however, still the exception rather than the rule. Horse-drawn traffic can cause congestion even on major roads, and carts, pedestrians, and cyclists make driving at night particularly hazardous. If you can avoid driving in Poland, do so.

RULES OF THE ROAD

Poles drive on the right, and there is an overall speed limit of 90 kph (54 mph), 110 kph (68 mph) on motorways. The speed limit in built-up areas is 60 kph (36 mph)—except in Warsaw, where it is 50 kph (30 mph); the beginning and end of the lower speed limits are marked by a sign bearing the name of the town in a white rectangle. At press time, the price of gas was about zł 36 for 10 liters (about 2½ gallons) of unleaded gas. Filling stations appear about every 40 km (25 mi) on major roads but can be difficult to find on side roads. They are usually open 6 AM–10 PM, although there are 24-hour stations, usually in cities.

CUSTOMS AND DUTIES

Persons over 18 may bring the following into Poland duty-free: personal belongings, including musical instruments; one computer; one radio; one camera with 24 rolls of film; up to 250 cigarettes or 50 cigars; 1 liter of spirits and 2 liters of wine; together with goods that are not for personal use up to the value of €70. Foreign currency over the value of €5,000 may be brought in but must be declared, as should antique jewelry or books published before 1945 (to avoid possible problems when taking them out of the country.

EMBASSIES AND CONSULATES
The U.S., Canadian, and British embassies are on or just off aleje Ujazdowskie; the British Consulate is closer to the center of town.
➤ CONTACTS: **British Embassy** (✉ al. Roż 1, Srodmiescie, Warsaw, ☎ 022/628–10–01). **British Consulate** (✉ ul. Emilii Plater 28, Srodmiescie, Warsaw, ☎ 022/625–30–99). **Canadian Embassy** (✉ ul. Matejki 1–5, Srodmiescie, Warsaw, ☎ 022/584–31–00). **U.S. Embassy** (✉ al. Ujazdowskie 29–31, Srodmiescie, Warsaw, ☎ 022/628–30–41). **U.S. Consulate** (✉ Stolarska 9, Kraków, ☎ 012/429–66–55).

EMERGENCIES
➤ CONTACTS: **Ambulance** (☎ 999). **Police** (☎ 997).

HOLIDAYS
January 1; Easter Sunday and Monday; May 1 (Labor Day); May 3 (Constitution Day); June 22 (Corpus Christi); August 15 (Assumption); November 1 (All Saints' Day); November 11 (rebirth of the Polish state, 1918); December 25, 26.

LANGUAGE
Polish is a Slavic language that uses the Roman alphabet but has several additional characters and diacritical marks. Because it has a higher incidence of consonant clusters than English, most English speakers find it a difficult language to decipher, much less pronounce. Take a phrase book and a pocket dictionary with you; the people you're trying to communicate with will at least appreciate the effort. The *Berlitz Polish Phrase Book and Dictionary* is a good starting point.

Younger Poles are likely to speak some English, while their elders are more likely to know French or German—and, of course, Russian, which they will not always admit to. In larger cities English is increasingly common, especially in hotels, restaurants, and tourism-related shops, but English speakers in the countryside are still a rarity.

MAIL AND SHIPPING
Airmail letters to the United States and Canada at press time cost zł 2.40; postcards, zł 2.20. Airmail letters to the United Kingdom or Europe cost zł 2.20; postcards, zł 2.10. (The price for a letter increases if it weights above 20 grams.) Airmail Express costs an extra zł 4 flat charge and cuts the travel time in half. Post offices are open weekdays 8 AM–8 PM. At least one post office is open 24 hours a day in every major city.

The main post office in every town has *poste restante* (general delivery) facilities. Friends and family who send you mail should write "No. 1" (signifying the main post office) after the name of the city.

MONEY MATTERS
At this writing, the złoty had strengthened and stabilized, and the annual rate of inflation had fallen to about 3.5%. The days when you could exchange $50 on the black market and feel like a millionaire are over. Although most goods and services are still cheaper than in the West, they are gradually rising to European levels. On the other hand, visitors have a greater range of options in selecting appropriate accommodations. Some top hotels still quote room prices in foreign currency (usually euros), but in the provinces simple rooms can be had for the equivalent of $10 per night. Overall, you can still get very good value for your money in Poland, and the farther you venture off the beaten track, the cheaper your vacation will be.

CURRENCY

The monetary unit in Poland is the złoty (zł), which is subdivided into 100 groszy (gr). Since the currency reform of 1995, there are notes of 10, 20, 50, 100, and 200 złotys, and coins in values of 1, 2, and 5 złoty and 1, 2, 5, 10, 20, and 50 groszys.

CURRENCY EXCHANGE

At press time, the bank exchange rate was about zł 4 to the U.S. dollar, zł 2.5 to the Canadian dollar, zł 3.5 to the euro, and zł 5.8 to the pound sterling. Foreign currency can be exchanged at banks or at private exchange bureaus (*Kantor Wymiany Walut*), where rates are usually slightly higher than at banks and service is swifter. With a major credit card and a PIN (personal identification number), you can also get money from cash machines, which you can find in most major cities.

PASSPORTS AND VISAS

U.S. and EU citizens do not need visas for entry to Poland (a valid passport will suffice).

Canadian citizens must pay C$89–C$207 for a single- or multi-entry visa. Apply at the nearest Polish consulate. Each visitor must complete one application form and provide two passport-size photographs. Allow about two weeks for processing. Visas are issued for 90 days but can be extended once in Poland, through the local police headquarters.

TAXES

A 22% value-added tax (VAT) is applied to most goods and services. A VAT refund is available for visitors; take your receipts to the refund service at any border or the Warsaw or Kraków airport. There are also taxes on airline tickets.

TELEPHONES

The country code for Poland is 48. The city code for Warsaw is 22. When calling from one Polish city to another, an additional prefix is required before the area code (you can choose between 1033, 1044, and 1055 corresponding to different phone companies); however, this does not apply when using public phones or when calling to from another country.

LOCAL CALLS

Phone booths that take calling cards have become widespread. There are two types of phones. Older, blue phones take magnetic cards. Newer, silver phones are gradually replacing the old ones and operate on electronic-chip chards. Either can be used for both local and long-distance calls. Cards, which cost zł 11.30, zł 20.40, or zł 37.20, are available at post offices, most newspaper kiosks, and hotels. When making a long-distance call, first dial "0," wait for the dial tone, and then dial the rest of your number.

INTERNATIONAL CALLS

International calls can be made from post offices or first-class hotels, where you can use your credit card or pay after making the call. You can also make calling card calls through a toll-free operator.

➤ ACCESS NUMBERS: **AT&T USA Direct** (☎ 0–0800–111–1111). **MCI** (☎ 0–0800–111–2122). **Sprint Global One** (☎ 0–0800–111–3115).

TIPPING

It is customary to round up on bills, for a total of not more than about 10% for waiters. For taxi drivers, round up to the nearest złoty or two. A tip of zł 2 per bag is in order for porters. Concierges and tour guides should get at least zł 5.

TRAIN TRAVEL

There are direct trains to Poland from major European cities. In Poland, Orbis and other international travel agencies such as Wagonlit sell international rail tickets, as do all main city stations.

Polish trains run at three speeds: *ekspresowy* (express), *pośpieszny* (fast), and the much cheaper *osobowy* (slow). Reservation is mandatory on many express lines, including Intercity trains. Intercity expresses between major cities are the most comfortable and include coffee and sandwiches in the price of the ticket. Only the first two categories have first-class accommodations, and you can reserve a seat only on express trains. *Couchettes* and sleeping cars (three berths to a car in second class, two berths in first class) are available on long-distance routes. Though restaurant cars are usually available on intercity trains and buffet cars on express trains, it is advisable when on a long trip to take along some food. Tickets can be bought at the station or through Orbis or any travel agency. Tickets are issued for a given date, after which you get only two days during which to travel; thereafter they become invalid.

RAIL PASSES

The European East Pass covers Poland, as well as Austria, the Czech Republic, Hungary, and Slovakia.

VISITOR INFORMATION

Orbis is partially privatized and is still the main Polish tourist information office, with branches throughout the country. It specializes in booking reservations in its own hotels and in selling tickets for both domestic and overseas travel. PTTK, a nationwide network of tourist clubs, can provide extensive information for the budget traveler or visitor with a particular interest in the history of individual regions or the outdoors. Look for signs marked IT on or near the main squares of cities and towns for complete tourist information services. For local offices of Orbis and PTTK, *see* Visitor Information *in* Essentials *sections*. Before you leave, contact the Polish National Tourist Office for information on the country.

➤ CONTACTS: **Polish National Tourist Office** (✉ 275 Madison Ave., Suite 1711, New York, NY 10016,☎ 212/338–9412, WEB www.poland-tour.org; ✉ Remo House, 310–312 Regent St., 1st floor, London W1R 5AJ, ☎ 44/171–580–88–11).

7 ROMANIA

Much of Romania seems lost in a time warp. Fir-covered mountains shelter picturesque villages. Women, often in traditional garb, coax wool onto spindles while red-tasseled horses pull wagons loaded with hay. Fortresses and palaces span the centuries, as do more than 2,000 monasteries, including the famed painted monasteries of Bucovina. In the east, the Black Sea coastline stretches north to the Danube Delta, home to 300-plus species of birds. Transylvanian cities such as Sibiu, Sighişoara, and Braşov have intriguing medieval districts, while Bucharest's wide avenues and mansions suggest why it was once hailed as the "Paris of the East."

Updated by
Joyce Dalton

CONSIDERED BY MANY THE MOST BEAUTIFUL COUNTRY in eastern Europe, Romania is full of wonders, both natural and human-made. The Carpathian Mountains cut north–south through the center of the country, affording marvelous drives through fir-covered forests. Several Transylvanian cities claim intact medieval districts (not to mention sights relating to the fictional Count Dracula and his real-life inspiration, Prince Vlad Țepeș), while fortified churches dominate villages. Maramureș, in the northwest, is the country's—and perhaps, all Europe's—most traditional zone, with towering hand-carved wooden gates, exquisite high-steepled wooden churches, and folk costume still the approved mode of dress, especially on Sunday. To the northeast, the five painted monasteries of Bucovina are UNESCO World Heritage monuments. The Black Sea and the watery wilderness of the Danube Delta mark Romania's eastern boundary, while Bucharest, the capital, retains the strong French cultural influence for which it has long been known.

In contrast to its idyllic geography, Romania's history has seldom been peaceful. Though the earliest inhabitants date to the Stone Age and the Greeks established trading settlements along the coast in the 7th century BC, it is to the Dacians, a Thracian tribe, and conquering Roman legions that Romanians trace their heritage. (In fact, Romanian is a Latin-based language, most similar to Italian.) Over the centuries, Tartar invasions, struggles against the Ottoman Turks, years of Austro-Hungarian domination in Transylvania, and five decades of Communist rule have led to what some term the "Mioritic complex." This refers to an old, beloved ballad in which two shepherds plot the death of a third for his wealth. Warned by Miorița, one of his lambs, the third shepherd calmly accepts his fate rather than fighting or fleeing. Of course, Romanians' resignation has limits. Many of the country's most magnificent monasteries were built by ruling princes to commemorate victories against invading Ottoman Turks, and in 1989, Communist dictator Nicolae Ceaușescu's rule (and life) ended with a brief, but violent, revolution. In many cities, citizens still place flowers by crosses commemorating those who died in the tumultuous events.

Following the revolution, Romania established a multiparty system with an elected president and a two-chamber parliament and approved a constitution guaranteeing individual rights. Most Romanians have embraced capitalism with enthusiasm, opening an ever-expanding network of shops, restaurants, hotels, travel agencies, and clubs. By publication time, Romanians' fervent desire for membership in NATO and the European Union may be a reality.

As elsewhere in the region, political and economic reforms here have not been unqualified successes. Corruption remains a serious problem (though visitors generally are blissfully unaware of its existence), and inflation and unemployment continue. Elderly beggars, whose pensions are no longer adequate, stand passively along city streets, and younger, more assertive beggars sometimes approach. In the latter cases, avoid opening your purse or showing money. Most visitors have no crime problems and return home rather overwhelmed by the friendliness of the average Romanian. Hospitality enjoys a long tradition here, and the popular expression "Come as a tourist; leave as a friend" rings true.

You can enjoy all that Romania has to offer at bargain prices. Food, entry fees, excursions, transportation, and hotels outside the capital remain very reasonable by Western standards. The exceptions are car rentals, gas, and upscale lodgings in Bucharest. Trains cover the country extensively; they're cheap, clean (though toilets are abominable), and reliable. Package tours, organized through operators in your home country or in Romania, can provide worry-free travel at good prices. If you prefer independent travel you can expect little difficulty exploring by train or rental car, though you should know that most roads are one lane in each direction and are not well maintained. Frequent passing of horse-drawn wagons and slow-moving trucks is a given. Road signs are abundant, so it's difficult to become lost except when negotiating city streets.

Romania is something of an unknown factor to many potential visitors. As one Romanian put it, "What do foreigners know about us? Dracula, Ceauşescu, and Nadia Comaneci!" Though more and more travelers are discovering Romania's charms, you still can enjoy a wealth of sights and experiences at great prices, free of busloads of tourists vying for photo ops. You'll find Romania a corner of Europe rich in tradition and natural beauty.

Pleasures and Pastimes

Churches, Monasteries, and Synagogues

Romania, a nation the size of Oregon, has some 2,000 monasteries, countless churches, and about 100 synagogues. Most are active, a fact all the more impressive considering that decades of Communist rule hardly encouraged religion.

From the multigabled roofs and towering spires of Maramureş's exquisite wooden gems to the fortified Saxon-influenced churches of Transylvania and the unique exterior frescoes of Bucovina's monasteries, these religious structures are also temples of history and culture. Many were built centuries ago by ruling princes to commemorate victories, usually against invading Ottoman Turks. Although Romania's extant Jewish population is small, most synagogues are well maintained.

Dining

New restaurants open at a rapid pace, especially in tourist- or business-oriented cities. Although international and ethnic restaurants abound in large cities, expect less variety elsewhere. Menus tend to be meat-oriented, emphasizing pork, though fish, chicken, and beef dishes are also available. Most entrées are fried or grilled. Vegetables appear on menus, but confirmed vegetarians may find choices slim. The exception is the tasty tomato, cucumber, and crumbled cheese salad served everywhere in season. Typically, each food item is ordered (and charged for) individually, right down to the butter. If you don't want bread, say so or it will be brought to your table and added to your bill.

Traditional dishes include *mămăligă* (polenta), *sarmale* (cabbage rolls stuffed with meat and rice), *caşcaval pane* (fried sheep's-milk cheese), *ghiveci* (casserole with vegetables), *mititei* (spicy sausages), *ciorbă* (slightly sour soup made with various ingredients), and *clătite* (pancakes filled with cheese, jam, or chocolate).

The familiar alcoholic and nonalcoholic drinks are readily available. In the former category, *ţuică*, a powerful plum brandy, is the national favorite. Romanian wines can be very good and are quite inexpensive. Strong Turkish-style coffee is favored, although instant coffee, commonly called *nes*, is also served. While tap water is considered safe except in the Danube Delta, it's a good idea to stick to bottled water, *apă minerală*, which is inexpensive and widely available in restaurants, groceries, and kiosks.

Most restaurants open before noon and continue serving until 11 or later. Small-town eateries close earlier. Fast-food chains have prolifer-

Romania (România)

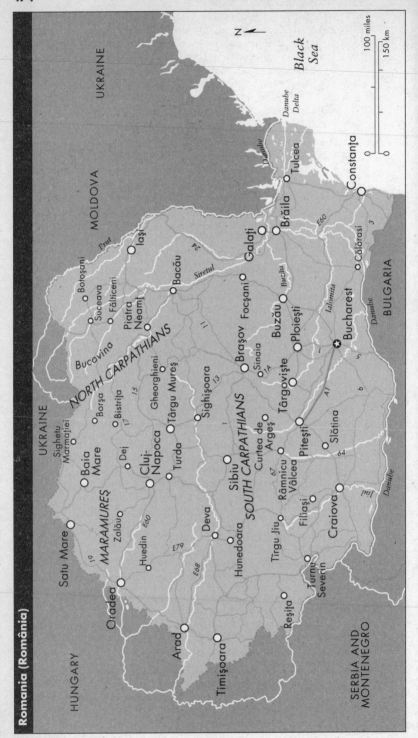

ated, as have kiosks şelling snacks. Along major roads are adequate to good eateries, some with menus in English, while larger gas stations have Western-style convenience stores selling food items.

CATEGORY	COST*
$$$$	over $15
$$$	$8–$15
$$	$4–$7
$	under $4

per person for a main course at dinner

Lodging

In Bucharest, the lodging picture is improving steadily as international chains increase their presence and smaller properties open, with comfortable rooms at reasonable prices. Throughout the country, people have turned their homes into bed-and-breakfast establishments, and home stays are also possible. Best Western, Hilton, Holiday Inn Crowne Plaza, Ibis, Inter-Continental, Marriott, and Sofitel are all represented. Continental Hotels, a Romanian chain with more than 10 properties around the country, provides reliable accommodations at reasonable prices. A rating system of one to five stars is in place, and rates are posted. Breakfast, often a nice buffet, is almost always included.

In cities and towns that see few tourists or business travelers, hotels often date to the socialist era and are sterile and not terribly attractive. Though frequently in need of refurbishment, rooms typically are clean and have private baths. The reception staff usually speaks at least some English. Away from major centers, hotels seldom accept credit cards or traveler's checks.

Some monasteries accept overnight guests. Facilities range from basic to attractive units constructed especially for tourists. Prices usually include two or three meals. Because English may not be spoken at the monasteries, it's best to book through a Romanian tour operator.

CATEGORY	BUCHAREST*	OTHER AREAS*
$$$$	over $200	over $95
$$$	$150–$200	$70–$95
$$	$80–$149	$35–$69
$	under $80	under $35

All prices are for a double room during peak season, including breakfast.

Shopping

If you love traditional crafts, pack a spare bag when visiting Romania, where you'll find variety, fine workmanship, and low prices. Items include hand-woven carpets; embroidered blouses, scarves, tablecloths, and bedspreads; painted and beaded eggs; wooden masks; ceramics; icons painted on glass or wood; and leather vests trimmed in fur, tassels, and embroidery. Monastery and museum shops are good places for making such purchases. Although customs officials seldom inspect foreigners' baggage, you should have receipts handy for antiques and art, just in case.

Walking and Hiking

Romania's Carpathian Mountains afford superb hiking for all levels. A well-organized trail system exists, although many markings are in need of maintenance. Hiking maps are not easy to find. Ask about routes and conditions at Salvamont stations in major hiking gateways such as Bran, Braşov, Buşteni, Poiana Braşov, Sinaia, Sibiu, and Zărneşti. Salvamont helps hikers in need; its members wear triangular badges bearing the organization's name.

Exploring Romania

Great Itineraries

Numbers in the text correspond to numbers in the margin and on the Bucharest map.

IF YOU HAVE 3 DAYS

Explore the sights of ⊞ **Bucharest** by strolling along Calea Victoriei to Piaţa Revoluţiei. View at least the exterior of Palatul Parlamentului and then visit Muzeul Ţăranului Român or Muzeul Satului, two museums well worth seeing. On the second day, head north to **Sinaia** to tour Castelul Peleş before continuing to ⊞ **Braşov** and its fine medieval section. Overnight in Braşov or nearby ⊞ **Poiana Braşov.** On the last day, visit the fortified churches at Prejmer and Hărman, just north of Braşov. Then head southwest on Route 73 to Castle Bran before returning to Bucharest via Piteşti.

IF YOU HAVE 5 DAYS

Follow the itinerary above for the first two days. On the third day, visit Castle Bran before heading northwest to **Sighişoara** and its intact medieval district; continue to ⊞ **Sibiu** to spend the night. On the fourth day, savor Sibiu's Old Town, the Astra outdoor museum, and the Muzeul de Icoane pe Sticlă (Icons on Glass Museum) in nearby Sibiel; overnight again in Sibiu. On the fifth day, return to Bucharest via Râmnicu Vâlcea and Curtea de Argeş, stopping in the latter to see the magnificent church and monastery.

When to Tour

Generally sunny but mild conditions make May through June and September through October ideal sightseeing months. Winters tend to be cold and snowy, while midsummer days are hot except in higher elevations and along the coast. Most Black Sea hotels are closed in the off-season. Folkloric festivals take place throughout the year, especially in summer and between Christmas and New Year's (☞ Festivals and Seasonal Events *in* Smart Travel Tips).

BUCHAREST

According to legend, a shepherd named Bucur settled on the site where the city of Bucharest now stands. However, it was Vlad Ţepeş, the 15th-century prince upon whom Bram Stoker based his fictional Dracula, who decreed the name Bucureşi. Two centuries later, this citadel on the Dâmboviţa River became the capital of the province of Wallachia and, later, the capital of Romania. Early 20th-century Bucharest was a lively center for trade and the arts. Its ornate mansions, spacious parks, wide boulevards, and sophisticated lifestyle earned the city the moniker "Paris of the East." Though the comparison is less obvious today, traces of the city's past glory remain.

Exploring Bucharest

Sightseeing can best be divided into two segments, to be covered in two days: first from Piaţa Revoluţiei north to Parcul Herăstrău, and second from Piaţa Universităţii south to the Dâmboviţa River, then west to Palatul Parlamentului and Palatul Cotroceni.

Bucharest is not laid out in a neat grid, and its many circular *pieţe* (plazas) add to the confusion. Street names are not always posted, nor are building numbers. Arm yourself with a good map, obtainable from the Romanian Tourist Office in your home country (☞ Visitor Information *in* Smart Travel Tips), bookstores, or hotels, and don't be shy about asking for assistance. Most Romanians are helpful, and many, especially young people, speak English.

Numbers in the text correspond to numbers in the margin and on the Bucharest map.

A Good Walk

Several imposing buildings surround Piaţa Revoluţiei, including **Muzeul Naţional de Artă** ①, **Ateneul Român** ②, and **Biserica Creţulescu** ③. Proceed north on Calea Victoriei past some of the city's fine old mansions, such as Casa Vernescu and the Muzeul Naţional George Enescu. Just across Piaţa Victoriei, take Şoseaua Kiseleff and you will come immediately to two museums: the **Muzeul de Istorie Naturală Grigore Antipa** ④ and the not-to-be-missed **Muzeul Ţăranului Român** ⑤. Continue up Kiseleff or take the Metro to the **Arcul de Triumf** ⑥. A short distance beyond this circle, in Parcul Herăstrău, is the entrance to **Muzeul Satului** ⑦, among the best of Romania's many outdoor village museums.

For a second tour, walk west from Piaţa Universităţii along B-dul Republicii, admiring the University of Bucharest's 19th-century buildings and the statues of scholars and statesmen. Turn south on Calea Victoriei, where you soon reach **Muzeul Naţional de Istorie** ⑧ with its marvelous gold exhibit. Farther along, the **Lipscani** district, or historic center, is a confusing maze of winding streets. Though less picturesque than it once was, the area houses antiques stores and galleries (especially surrounding the courtyard of Hanul cu Tei), **Biserica Curtea Veche** ⑨, **Curtea Veche** ⑩, and **Hanul lui Manuc** ⑪. Two churches, the **Biserica Stavropoleos** ⑫ and the onion-domed Russian Church, are nearby. Walk south down Calea Victoriei (or any of the many streets in this area heading south) until you reach the river; then turn left onto Splaiul Independenţei, which leads to Piaţa Unirii. Turn left for the **Muzeul de Istorie al Comunitaţilor Evreieşti din România** ⑬. Next, head west from the Piaţa (it's a long walk, so you may want to use the Metro) to **Palatul Parlamentului** ⑭ and **Palatul Cotroceni** ⑮. Parcul Cişmigiu makes a pleasant rest spot. To get here from Palatul Cotroceni walk east on B-dul Eroii Sanitari. This street merges with B-dul Mihail Kolgălniceanu, which leads to the park.

TIMING

Since it is unlikely you would want to rush past these sites with no photo stops or interior visits, plan a full day for each half of the walking tour. If time is short, choose your stops according to personal interest, and utilize the Metro or taxis for longer stretches such as the trip to Palatul Cotroceni. Ask your hotel about correct taxi fares, and then negotiate.

Sights to See

Due to inflation, entry fees change frequently. The prices below are given in the more stable U.S. dollar equivalents.

⑥ **Arcul de Triumf** (Arch of Triumph). Resembling the Parisian monument, this landmark commemorates the 1877 War for Independence and those who died in World War I. At press time work was under way on opening an interior staircase to the public, which will afford city views. ✉ *At head of Şoseaua Kiseleff.*

★ ② **Ateneul Român** (Romanian Athenaeum). Gorgeous inside and out, this 19th-century concert hall, home of the George Enescu Philharmonic Orchestra, has a Baroque dome and classical columns. In theory, there are tours, but the building is often locked. For a look at the inside, it's best to attend a concert; tickets run $2.15 to $4.95. ✉ *Str. Franklin 1,* ☎ *021/315–6875.*

Bucharest (București)

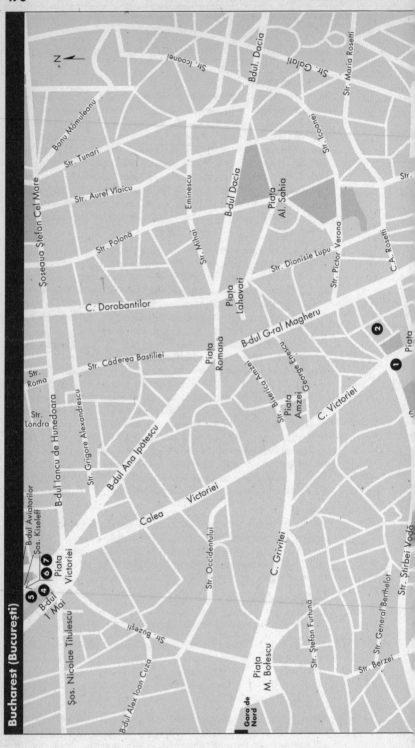

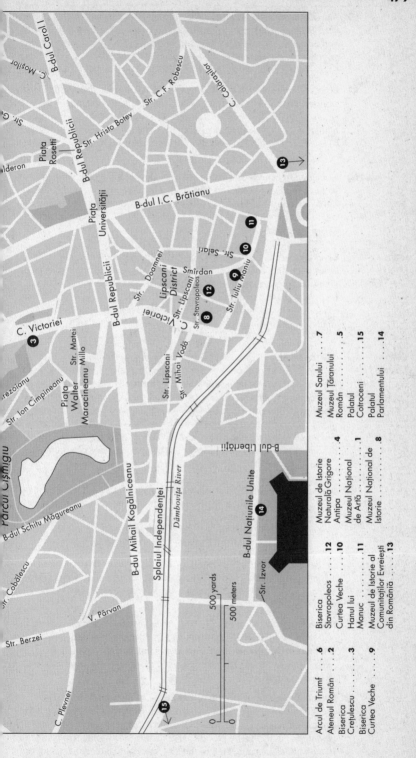

Arcul de Triumf **6**
Ateneul Român **2**
Biserica
Crețulescu **3**
Biserica
Curtea Veche **9**

Biserica
Stavropoleos **12**
Curtea Veche **10**
Hanul lui
Manuc **11**
Muzeul de Istorie al
Comunităților Evreiești
din România **13**

Muzeul de Istorie
Naturală Grigore
Antipa **4**
Muzeul Național
de Artă **1**
Muzeul Național de
Istorie **8**

Muzeul Satului **7**
Muzeul Țăranului
Român **5**
Palatul
Cotroceni **15**
Palatul
Parlamentului **14**

❸ **Biserica Crețulescu** (Crețulescu Church). This 1720s redbrick church next to the former palace has lovely, though faded, interior frescoes and an iconostasis (screen separating the altar from the nave in Eastern churches) depicting religious scenes. ✉ *Piața Revoluției,* ⊙ *Daily 6 AM–7 PM.*

❾ **Biserica Curtea Veche** (Old Court Church). Completed in the mid-16th century, Bucharest's oldest church is an excellent example of that period's Wallachian church architecture, with alternating horizontal bands of brick and plaster moldings. Note the original frescoes next to the altar. The church stands opposite Curtea Veche and is open daily 6 AM–7 PM.

★ ⓬ **Biserica Stavropoleos** (Stravropoleos Church). Lovely wooden and stone carvings and religious paintings adorn the exterior of this church, built between 1724 and 1730. Inside are fresco-covered walls and dome plus an icon-filled gold-leaf iconostasis. ✉ *Str. Stavropoleos.* ⊙ *Daily 6 AM–7 PM.*

NEED A BREAK? **Carul cu Bere** (✉ Str. Stavropoleos 3, ☎ 021/313–7560), Bucharest's oldest surviving beer hall (1880), serves a large selection of beers plus meals (main courses run from $1.20 to $6). Ambience is everything here, with stained glass, painted columns, and a winding staircase leading to balcony seats. The beer hall sits across from Stravropoleos Church.

OFF THE BEATEN PATH **CURTEA DE ARGEȘ** – About 600 years ago this pretty town 150 km (93 mi) northwest of Bucharest was the capital of Wallachia province. Today you can visit on the main street, Strada Basarabilor, the ruins of the 14th-century **Curtea Domnească** (Princely Court) and the intact **Biserica Domnească** (Princely Church), with its lovely interior frescoes. Continuing along Strada Basarabilor, you'll reach the 16th-century **Mănăstirea Curtea de Argeș** (Curtea de Argeș Monastery), an architecturally splendid structure topped by two towers spiraling in opposite directions. Romania's first two kings and queens are buried here.

❿ **Curtea Veche** (Old Court). Dracula buffs can check out the ruins of the palace built by Vlad Țepeș, the 15th-century prince on whom the fictional count was based. There is a small museum. ✉ *Str. Franceză 27–31,* ☎ *021/314–0375.* 🎫 *30¢.* ⊙ *Mon.–Sat. 9–3.*

⓫ **Hanul lui Manuc** (Manuc's Inn). In 1808, a wealthy Armenian built this timbered inn aimed at traveling merchants. Even today, it functions as a hotel (with dingy rooms). The courtyard, however, makes a pleasant stop for a drink. There is also a *cramă* (wine cellar). ✉ *Str. Franceză 62–64,* ☎ *021/313–1415.*

Lipscani. Developed around 1750, the Lipscani district is one of the oldest in Bucharest. Dirty, confusing, and crying for renovation, it's still of interest, especially the charming **Hanul cu Tei,** a rectangular courtyard between Strada Lipscani and Strada Blănari that houses art and antiques shops.

⓭ **Muzeul de Istorie al Comunităților Evreiești din România** (Museum of the History of the Jewish Community in Romania). Housed in a synagogue dating to 1850, this museum traces the history of Romania's Jewish population, the second largest in Europe prior to World War II, with some 750,000. Due to the Holocaust and later emigration, only about 15,000 Jews remain in Romania. ✉ *Str. Mămulari 3,* ☎ *021/311–0870.* 🎫 *Donation.* ⊙ *Mon., Wed., and Sun. 9–1; Thurs. 9–noon and 3–6.*

④ Muzeul de Istorie Naturală Grigore Antipa (Natural History Museum). Wildlife exhibits from around Romania are displayed in realistic settings, as are dioramas of various ethnic cultures. ⊠ *Şos. Kiseleff 1,* ☎ *021/312–8826.* ⊒ *45¢, camera fee $1.85.* ⊙ *Tues.–Sun. 10–5.*

① Muzeul Naţional de Artă (National Art Museum). The former royal palace now houses the country's most important art collection, including 15 rooms of paintings and sculptures by European masters and a large collection of Romanian art dating from medieval times to the present. Among the collection are pieces by the sculptor Brâncuşi and marvelous works from the Brueghel school. Four branch museums are in the vicinity. ⊠ *Calea Victoriei 49–53,* ☎ *021/313–3030.* ⊒ *European and Romanian exhibits $2.15; otherwise, each exhibit $1.25.* ⊙ *Wed.–Sun. 10–6.*

⑧ Muzeul Naţional de Istorie (National History Museum). Don't be discouraged by the initial vast emptiness you encounter upon entering this grand neoclassical building: the museum holds a large collection of objects dating from the Neolithic period to the 1920s. Downstairs, the Treasury section contains a mind-boggling assortment of golden objects spanning from Roman days to the present. ⊠ *Calea Victoriei 12,* ☎ *021/315–8207.* ⊒ *50¢.* ⊙ *Wed.–Sun. 10–5.*

★ **⑦ Muzeul Satului** (Village Museum). This open-air museum in Herăstrău Park provides the best possible introduction to the myriad architectural styles of Romania's traditional houses, workshops, and churches. The structures, some complete with regional furnishings, have been brought here from around the country. ⊠ *Şos. Kiseleff 28–30,* ☎ *021/ 222–9110.* ⊒ *$1.25, camera fee $1.55, video fee $9.25.* ⊙ *Nov.–Mar., daily 9–5; Apr.–Oct., daily 9–8.*

★ **⑤ Muzeul Ţăranului Român** (Romanian Peasant Museum). Some 90,000 items, ranging from traditional costumes and textiles to ceramics and icons, are on view here, at the first museum in Eastern Europe to receive the European Museum of the Year award (1996). Information in English is available in each room. A shop sells traditional crafts. ⊠ *Şos. Kiseleff 3,* ☎ *021/212–9663.* ⊒ *80¢, $4.60 camera or video fee.* ⊙ *Tues.–Sun. 10–6.*

NEED A BREAK?
Just west of Piaţa Victoriei, the cozy Irish-style pub **The Dubliner** (⊠ B-dul. Nicolae Titulescu 18, ☎ 021/222–9473) serves draft beer and tempting dishes, such as "cottage pie" (minced beef and vegetables topped with mashed potatoes, baked in a ceramic bowl). Main courses run $1 to $4.25.

★ **⑮ Palatul Cotroceni** (Cotroceni Palace). The Cotroceni, which incorporates French, Romanian, Art Nouveau, and other styles of architecture, was constructed in the late 19th century as the home of Romania's royal family. After a devastating 1977 earthquake, it was rebuilt and a wing added where the president now has offices. The lavish furnishings, art, and personal effects afford a glimpse into the lives of Romania's former royalty. Guides are required (no extra charge) for the one-hour tour; call ahead to reserve a tour. Taking photographs is prohibited. Since the palace is a bit removed from other sights, you might want to take the Metro to the Politehnica station. ⊠ *B-dul. Geniului 1,* ☎ *021/ 221–1200.* ⊒ *$1.85.* ⊙ *Tues.–Sun. 9:30–4:30.*

★ **⑭ Palatul Parlamentului** (Palace of Parliament). This mammoth modern building, one of the largest in the world, stands witness to the megalomania of the former dictator Ceauşescu. Today, it houses the Romanian parliament. Unlike the royal palaces, every detail is Romanian, from the 24-karat gold on the ceilings to the huge hand-woven carpet on the floor. Forty-five-minute tours of the ground-floor rooms depart from an entrance on the right side of the building. Reservations are required. ⊠ *Calea 13 Septembrie,* ☎ *021/311–3611.* 🎟 *$1.85, camera fee $1.85, video fee $7.70.* ⊙ *Daily 10–4.*

OFF THE BEATEN PATH	**SNAGOV –** On an island in the middle of Snagov Lake stands Snagov Monastery, the reputed burial place of Vlad Țepeș, also known as Vlad Dracula. Boatmen ferry you across for a negotiated price. Just 40 km (25 mi) north of Bucharest, the village of Snagov is a popular retreat for city dwellers.

Dining

New restaurants serving a diversity of cuisines open in Bucharest almost daily, and fast-food chains have invaded the capital. Be sure to sample Romanian cuisine while you're here. Except for at the most upscale places, prices are inexpensive by Western standards. Check your bill for the correct price and number of dishes. No-smoking sections are virtually nonexistent.

$$$$ ✕ **Casa Vernescu.** This elegant French restaurant housed in a magnif-
★   icent 19th-century mansion serves such specialties as beef and goose liver in red wine sauce and lobster with wild rice. A second, smaller menu highlights Romanian dishes. Dine surrounded by gilded moldings, frescoes, and marble columns or, during warm weather, in the garden. ⊠ *Calea Victoriei 133,* ☎ *021/231–0220. AE, DC, MC, V.*

$$$–$$$$ ✕ **Casa Caragiale.** A huge portrait of the 19th-century playwright Ion Luca Caragiale, for whom the restaurant is named (and who briefly lived in this house), watches over you while you nibble on foie gras with gooseberries, shrimp flambéed at your table, and other French delights. Vocalists and a keyboardist entertain with operatic favorites. ⊠ *Str. Ion Luca Caragiale 21–23,* ☎ *021/211–1518. MC, V. Closed Sun.*

$$$–$$$$ ✕ **Casa Doina.** This 19th-century villa turned restaurant houses two dining salons, one of which is open to the outdoors on three sides in warm weather, plus a traditional cramă for more casual dining. Continental cuisine is served in the two dining salons, and the cramă highlights Romanian specialties. A Gypsy band plays each evening. ⊠ *Șos. Kiseleff 4,* ☎ *021/222–6717. AE, DC, MC, V.*

$$–$$$ ✕ **Aquarium.** Glass on two sides and a cream color scheme create a light, airy interior at this Italian restaurant. Choose from meat, fish, and pasta dishes such as tagliatelle with seafood and mushrooms. The servers are not particularly friendly, but the food quality is high and the portions are ample. ⊠ *Str. Alecu Russo 4,* ☎ *021/211–2820. AE, MC, V.*

$$–$$$ ✕ **Silviu's.** An art- and antiques-filled interior, carefully prepared Ital-
★   ian food, and warm, correct service might lead you to expect high prices, but Silviu's is quite reasonable, with main courses costing between $4 and $9. Enjoy pasta, meat dishes, and such specialties as leg of mutton in ginger sauce. Dining is in two salons, two private rooms, and an outdoor pavilion. The restaurant is not far from Cotroceni Palace. ⊠ *Str. Louis Pasteur 44,* ☎ *021/410–9184. MC, V.*

$–$$ ✕ **Bistro Atheneu.** This popular spot may be reminiscent of a Parisian bistro, but the blackboard's daily listings range from a tasty Greek salad to pastas, chicken dishes, and such Romanian favorites as *varza a la Cluj* (layers of chopped meat and cabbage smothered in sour cream). A musical duo entertains in the evenings. ⊠ *Str. Episcopiei 3,* ☎ *021/313–4900. No credit cards.*

$–$$ ✕ **Burebista.** Ceramics, carved wooden spoons, masks, stuffed birds, and animal pelts cover the walls while wooly sheepskins cover the chairs. With a menu as Romanian as the decor, Burebista serves such dishes as *tochitura de pui* (chicken stew with vegetables) and *sarmale* (cabbage stuffed with rice, meat, and herbs). Servers wear traditional dress, and musicians play folk tunes each evening. ⊠ *Calea Moşilor 195,* ☎ *021/201–9704. MC, V.*

$–$$ ✕ **Club Contele Dracula.** At this unique restaurant, each carefully cho-
★ sen item—from service plates to wall decorations—somehow relates to the fictional Dracula or the 15th-century prince Vlad Ţepeş. Several times each week, the count rises from his cellar coffin to wander, candelabrum in hand, among his guests. The menu highlights tasty Transylvanian and wild game dishes. ⊠ *Splaiul Independenţei 8A,* ☎ *021/312–1353. AE, MC, V. No lunch Sun.*

$ ✕ **Brădet.** The name means "Little Fir Tree," so it's not surprising that the interior contains lots of wooden furnishings and paneling. While the menu lists traditional dishes such as tripe soup and tongue with garlic and lemon, you'll also find familiar fish, chicken, beef, and mutton offerings. If cigarette smoke bothers you, you'd best choose another eatery, as Brădet's small size ensures that smoke lingers. ⊠ *Str. Carol Davila 60,* ☎ *021/410–8215. V.*

Lodging

In the last few years, new hotels have opened at a brisk pace in Bucharest and older properties have undergone renovation. Many of the newer hotels are pricey facilities aimed at business travelers, but others have begun to fill a yawning gap in the moderately priced hotel category. At most hotels, reception and at least some restaurant staff speak English. In budget properties, it's wise to check your room before making a commitment.

$$$$ 🏨 **Athenée Palace Hilton.** This historic property on Piaţa Revoluţie
★ continues a tradition of hospitality dating to 1914. The upper lobby's marble columns and the ballroom's stained-glass ceiling recapture this earlier era. Guest rooms are bright and attractive, and the staff is young and enthusiastic. ⊠ *Str. Episcopiei 1–3,* ☎ *021/303–3777,* F̄Ā̄X̄ *021/315–212,* W̄Ē̄B̄ *www.hilton.com. 257 rooms, 15 suites. 3 restaurants, room service, in-room data ports, in-room safes, minibars, cable TV, indoor pool, gym, hair salon, massage, sauna, 2 bars, lobby lounge, casino, shops, laundry service, concierge, business services, meeting rooms, car rental, free parking; no-smoking floors. AE, DC, MC, V.*

$$$$ 🏨 **Inter-Continental.** When this 22-story hotel overlooking Piaţa Uni-
★ versităţii was built in 1971, it became not only Bucharest's first international hotel but also its tallest building. Guest rooms favor gold brocade, cloth wall coverings, and rich woods. Service is punctual and correct. ⊠ *B-dul. Nicolae Bălcescu 4,* ☎ *021/310–2020,* F̄Ā̄X̄ *021/312–0486,* W̄Ē̄B̄ *www.interconti.com. 404 rooms, 19 suites. 3 restaurants, room service, in-room data ports, in-room safes, minibars, cable TV, indoor pool, gym, hair salon, massage, sauna, bar, lobby lounge, casino, shops, baby-sitting, laundry service, concierge, business services, meeting rooms, car rental, travel services, parking (fee); no-smoking rooms. AE, DC, MC, V.*

$$$ 🏨 **Bucureşti.** Guest rooms at this property, part of the Park Plaza chain, are spacious and furnished in light tones. The main restaurant is outstanding, both for its food and service; a band plays each evening. The hotel stands not far from the Piaţa Revoluţiei. ⊠ *Calea Victoriei 63-81,* ☎ *021/312-7070,* F̄Ā̄X̄ *021/312-0927,* W̄Ē̄B̄ *www.hbu.ro. 415 rooms, 31 suites. 2 restaurants, patisserie, room service, in-room safes, minibars, cable TV, indoor-outdoor pool, aerobics, gym, hair salon,* *massage, sauna, lobby lounge, shop, laundry service, concierge, business services, meeting rooms, car rental, travel services, parking (fee); no-smoking rooms. AE, MC, V.*

$$$ 🏨 **Continental.** Constructed in 1828 and now a declared historical monument, this impressive white structure retains the character of its earlier days, with high ceilings, moldings, and antique-style furnishings. Baths appear spartan but have all the necessities. The hotel, part of the first and largest Romanian chain, stands on one of Bucharest's main shopping avenues. ✉ *Calea Victoriei 56,* ☎ *021/312–0133,* FAX *021/312–0134,* WEB *www.continentalhotels.ro. 45 rooms, 9 suites. Restaurant, patisserie, room service, in-room data ports, in-room safes, minibars, cable TV, concierge, meeting rooms, free parking, some pets allowed. AE, DC, MC, V.*

$$$ 🏨 **Helveția.** No two rooms are alike at this white marble structure near
★   Herăstrău Park. Crystal chandeliers, wall sconces, and serene artwork complement light furnishings and fabrics. Each evening, musicians perform in the restaurant. Under the same ownership, the eight-room Savion Villa stands directly behind the hotel. The Metro is across the street, providing a one-station hop to the city center. ✉ *Piața Charles de Gaulle 13,* ☎ *021/223–0566,* FAX *021/223–0567,* WEB *helvetia.netvision.net.il. 24 rooms, 6 suites. Restaurant, room service, cable TV, bar, laundry service, car rental, free parking, some pets allowed. AE, DC, MC, V.*

$$ 🏨 **Central.** This 19th-century property stands two blocks off Calea Victoriei, just a stone's throw from pleasant Cișmigiu Park. Though on the small side, guest rooms are bright and cheery. Baths have a shower but no tub. Don't be deterred by the McDonald's at street level. ✉ *Str. Brezoianu 13,* ☎ FAX *021/315–5637. 58 rooms, 4 suites. Minibars, cable TV, meeting room. MC, V.*

$$ 🏨 **Flanders.** A Belgian-Romanian joint venture converted a private home, in a quiet neighborhood yet close to the city center, into a warm and cozy hotel. Scandinavian-style furniture fills the uncluttered, spotless guest rooms. At the restaurant, jazz musicians entertain diners on Wednesdays, and in summer you can opt to dine on either of two terraces. The room rate for a double drops from more than $100 to just $65 on weekends. Airport transfers are complimentary. ✉ *Str. Ștefan Mihăileanu 20,* ☎ *021/327–6572,* FAX *021/327–6573. 7 rooms, 1 suite. Restaurant, room service, in-room data ports, in-room safes, cable TV, bar, free parking. AE, DC, MC, V.*

$ 🏨 **Batiștei.** Don't let the drab concrete exterior turn you away: the hotel
★   is central at a good price, and guest rooms, while on the small side, have balconies, renovated green-tile baths, and even hair dryers. The four-story building has no elevator, so request a lower floor if stairs are a problem. ✉ *Str. Emanuel Bacaloglu 2,* ☎ *021/314–9022,* FAX *021/314–0887. 29 rooms, 2 suites. Restaurant, in-room data ports, minibars, cable TV, laundry service, meeting rooms, free parking, some pets allowed. AE, DC, MC, V.*

$ 🏨 **Ibis.** The price is hard to beat for what you get here: guest rooms have good work space amid a rust-and-aqua color scheme. Bathrooms have a stall shower but no tub. Right by the main railroad station, the location is great if you're traveling by train, but this is not the best part of town. ✉ *Calea Griviței 143,* ☎ *021/222–2722,* FAX *021/222–2723,* WEB *www.ibishotel.com. 230 rooms, 16 suites. Restaurant, in-room data ports, cable TV, bar, shops, laundry service, meeting rooms, parking (fee); no-smoking rooms. AE, MC, V.*

$ 🏨 **Triumf.** Built in 1935 to house bankers, the excellent-value Triumf has been a hotel since the 1960s. Guest rooms may not be particularly attractive, but they are clean and comfortable and half have balconies.

This brick building stands near the Arch of Triumph, behind a large grassy rectangle. ⊠ *Şos. Kiseleff 12,* ☎ *021/222–3172,* FAX *021/223–2411. 88 rooms, 12 suites. Restaurant, some refrigerators, cable TV, bar, free parking, some pets allowed; no a/c in some rooms. MC, V.*

Nightlife and the Arts

To discover what's playing in cinemas, theaters, and concert halls, check the listings in *Şapte Seri* (Seven Evenings), a free weekly mini-magazine available in most hotels and Western-style bars and restaurants.

The Arts

Bucharest has a great many theaters and concert halls. You can purchase tickets for performances directly at the venue's box office. It's usually easy to get tickets without booking ahead.

FILM

Foreign films are shown in their original language with Romanian subtitles. The Bucureşti Mall's (⊠ Calea Vitan 55–59) 10-screen **Hollywood Multiplex** has the most comfortable seats and best sound and picture quality. Tickets here run $1.65 to $2.75, which though inexpensive is more than you'll pay at most cinemas.

MUSIC

The **Filarmonica George Enescu** (George Enescu Philharmonic Orchestra), based in the Romanian Athenaeum (⊠ Str. Franklin 1, ☎ 021/315–6875), plays classical favorites. The music is top quality, and guest artists often perform. Tickets range from $2.15 to $4.95. Most performances begin at 7 PM.

Sala Radio (Radio Hall; ⊠ Str. Berthelot 60–64, ☎ 021/314–6800), housed in the National Radio Society building, hosts classical concerts by Romanian and international artists. Tickets run from 75¢ to $2.30. Performances begin at 7:15 PM.

OPERA AND BALLET

Opera Română (⊠ B-dul. Kogălniceanu 70–72, ☎ 021/313–1857) hosts productions by many of the opera world's greatest composers. Ballet performances also take place here. Tickets range from 65¢ to $4.55. Most performances start at 7 PM.

Nightlife

Locals and expats alike frequent Bucharest's wealth of bars, clubs, and casinos. Striptease clubs and less reputable bars are part of the scene, so choose your nightspot carefully or it could become an unpleasant, expensive evening. Even in the best places, do not expect a smoke-free environment.

BARS

In Bucharest, as elsewhere, trends change quickly, so check around if your goal is the latest "in" place. The following are likely to maintain their popularity. **Green Hours** (⊠ Calea Victoriei 120, ☎ 021/211–9592) has, appropriately, green loveseats set in little niches, the better to enjoy live jazz or the occasional classical guitar or drama. The interior of **Once Upon a Time** (⊠ Str. Gheorghe Manu 34, ☎ 0722/654–191) replicates a 1930s town, complete with an old street, shops, and a park. But all of this is oddly paired with loud techno music that doesn't really fit the environment. The sometimes outrageous **Planters** (⊠ Str. Mendeleev 10, ☎ 021/659–7606) is dimly lighted and loud and has a small dance floor. There's a disc-jockey Thursday through Saturday nights. Mix with Bucharest's young professionals and TV stars at the **Office** (⊠ Str. Tache Ionescu 2, ☎ 021/659–4518) and sample some of the city's best drinks.

With yellow walls and bright red leather sofas, **Yellow Bar** (✉ Str. Edgar Quinet 10, ☎ 021/310–1351) is a great place to enjoy a drink and pop and dance tunes.

CASINOS

By some counts, Romania claims more casinos than any other European country. At **Casino Palace** (✉ Calea Victoriei 133, ☎ 021/231–0220, WEB www.casinopalace.ro), you can try your luck amid the luxurious surroundings of a 19th-century mansion. All the usual games of chance are available in this Monte Carlo–style casino. Casa Vernescu restaurant is housed in the same building. A photo identification is required for entry, and limo service is available on request.

DISCOS

Locals gyrate and sway on the large, but still crowded, dance floor at **Salsa 2** (✉ Str. Lutherană 9, ☎ 0723/412–267). **Tunnel Club** (✉ Str. Academiei 19–21, ☎ 021/312–6971) has catacomb-like rooms and good dance music.

Shopping

ART AND CRAFTS

For traditional handicrafts, such as embroidery and ceramics, check out *artizanat* stores throughout the city or, better yet, visit the shops connected to the Romanian Peasant Museum and the Village Museum (☞ Exploring Bucharest, *above*).

Galateea (✉ Calea Victoriei 132, ☎ 021/650–4370) carries high-quality paintings, ceramics, glassware, and jewelry. The many galleries and shops at the courtyard at **Hanul cu Tei** (✉ off Str. Lipscani) sell paintings and antiques.

CARPETS

Romania is well known for its handmade carpets; many are woven in monasteries, and each region employs distinct colors and patterns. The shop at the **Romanian Peasant Museum** (✉ Şos. Kiseleff 3, ☎ 021/212–9663) has a good selection of carpets. **Romartizana** (✉ B-dul. Unirii 4, ☎ 021/337–0975) is a good spot for carpet shopping.

CRYSTAL AND PORCELAIN

Fine-quality Romanian crystal and porcelain are relatively inexpensive. **Sticerom** (✉ Str. Şelari 9–11, ☎ 021/315–9699) carries a good selection. Glassmakers ply their trade in the store's courtyard weekdays until 5:30 and Saturday until 2.

SHOPPING CENTERS

The four-story **Bucureşti Mall** (✉ Calea Vitan 55–59, near Piaţa Unirii) houses more than 70 stores, 20 restaurants, a supermarket, a children's play area, an 82-ft fountain, and a 10-screen cinema. The **World Trade Center** (✉ B-dul. Expozitiei 2, next to the Sofitel hotel) has a small shopping mall. The department store–like **Unirea Shopping Center** (✉ Piaţa Unirii 1) can supply all your basic needs.

Bucharest Essentials

AIR TRAVEL

Tarom, the Romanian national airline, operates flights from Bucharest to many Romanian and European cities. The airline also flies from New York to Bucharest, with stops in Timişoara (in western Romania) or Luxembourg. Domestic and international reservations can be made by stopping by any Tarom office or by calling the central reservation number. Many carriers serve Bucharest via European gateways. Austrian Airlines, for example, offers service from New York, Washington, D.C., Montreal, and Toronto to Vienna with two daily connecting flights to Bucharest and Timişoara.

Angel Air serves many Romanian cities from Baneasa Airport.
➤ CARRIERS: **Angel Air** (✉ Str. C. Bălcescu 18, ☎ 021/201–1701). **Austrian Airlines** (☎ 021/312–0545). **Tarom** (✉ Splaiul Independenţei 17, ☎ 021/337–0220; ✉ Str. Brezoianu 10, ☎ 021/314–0524; Str. Buzeşti 59–61, ☎ 021/204–6464; central reservations: ☎ 9361 in Bucharest, 021/337–2037 outside Bucharest; WEB tarom.digiro.net).

AIRPORT
Most international flights land at Bucharest's Otopeni Airport, 16 km' (10 mi) north of the city. Baggage carts are free, and there's an ATM in the baggage claim area. Avoid the currency exchange desk, as rates are not good. Baneasa Airport accepts some domestic flights but is mostly used for charter flights.
➤ AIRPORTS: **Baneasa Airport** (☎ 9371 in Bucharest; 021/232–0020). **Otopeni Airport** (☎ 021/204–1000).

TRANSFERS
Bus 783 runs between the airport and Piată Unirii every 15 minutes between 5:30 AM and 11 PM, stopping at main squares along the way. Buses are crowded and notorious for pickpockets. A better bet is Sky Services, located just as you enter the baggage claim area. A private car costs $25. If you take a taxi, bargain; the fare should be about $10, but count yourself lucky to settle for $20.
➤ CONTACT: **Sky Services** (☎ 021/204–1002).

BUS AND TRAM TRAVEL
RATB surface transit service is extensive, and buses and trams are comfortable. However, both are generally crowded and attract pickpockets, and they can be difficult to navigate if you don't speak Romanian. Purchase tickets at kiosks near bus stops; one trip (*una călătorie*) costs 15¢. Validate your ticket on board. Express bus lines require a special magnetic card.

CAR TRAVEL
Four main access routes lead into and out of the city—E70 west to the Hungarian border, E60 north via Braşov, E70/E85 south to Bulgaria, and E85/60 east to Constanţa and the coast.

Driving within Bucharest itself is not recommended. Poor signposting, numerous one-way streets, huge rotaries from which multiple streets radiate, narrow streets with cars parked on both sides, and a lack of parking spaces are a few of the hazards. Drivers are aggressive and often ignore normal rules and courtesies, and police checks are common. Save the rental car for excursions out of the city.

EMBASSIES
➤ CONTACTS: **Australian Embassy** (✉ B-dul. Unirii 74, ☎ 021/320–9826). **Canadian Embassy** (✉ Str. N. Iorga 36, ☎ 021/307–5000). **U.K. Embassy** (✉ Str. J. Michelet 24, ☎ 021/312–0303). **U.S. Embassy** (✉ Str. Tudor Arghezi 7–9, ☎ 021/210–4042).

EMERGENCIES
Most medical care falls short of Western expectations. Your embassy or hotel can make recommendations. Good facilities include American Medical Center, Bio-Medica International, and Emergency Clinic Hospital.
➤ DENTISTS: **B.B. Clinic** (✉ Str. Ionescu Gion 4, ☎ 021/320–0151). **Biodent** (✉ Piaţa Amzei 10-22, ☎ 021/312–3752). **Dent–A–America** (✉ Str. Varşovia 4, ☎ 021/230–2608).

➤ EMERGENCY CONTACTS: **Ambulance** (☎ 961). **Fire Department** (981). **Police** (☎ 955).

➤ HOSPITALS: **American Medical Center** (✉ Str. Dragoş Vodă 70, ☎ 021/210–2706). **Bio-Medica International** (✉ Str. Eminescu 42, ☎ 021/211–9674; 092/338–383 emergencies). **Emergency Clinic Hospital** (✉ Calea Floreasca 8, ☎ 021/230–0106).

➤ LATE-NIGHT PHARMACIES: **Farmadex** (✉ Calea Moşilor 280, ☎ 021/211–9560). **SensiBlu** (✉ Calea Dorobanţilor 65, ☎ 021/211–1127; ✉ B-dul. Bălcescu 7, ☎ 021/212–4923).

ENGLISH-LANGUAGE BOOKSTORES

For a good selection of English books and videos about Romania and other subjects, visit Libraria Noi. Next door, Sala Dalles sells used books.

➤ BOOKSTORE: **Libraria Noi** (✉ B-dul. Bălcescu 18, ☎ 021/311–0700).

SUBWAY TRAVEL

The *Metrou* (Metro) is the best way to reach the city center from outlying areas or to visit several sights, including the Arch of Triumph, Cotroceni Palace, and Village Museum. The Metro operates between 5 AM and 11:30 PM. Purchase a two-ride card in any station (37¢), place it in the turnstile slot, and retrieve it for the next ride. Day, 10-trip, and monthly tickets cost 45¢, $1.25, and $3.85, respectively.

Stations are marked with a blue-and-white M sign. Metro maps are available in *Bucharest: What, Where, When,* distributed free in most hotels. Within the station you can locate the correct platform by referring to the final stop for your destination's line. Platforms and cars have maps posted, and stops are announced.

TAXIS

Officially, taxis are reasonable—15¢ initial charge, then 15¢ per km (0.6 mi). Many drivers, however, ask outrageously inflated fares or have rigged meters. While the situation has improved, it's best to ask your hotel or restaurant the approximate fare, then negotiate a fixed price before entering the taxi. You can also telephone one of the reputable companies listed below.

➤ TAXI COMPANIES: **Alfa Taxi** (☎ 9488). **Cristaxi** (☎ 9461). **Meridian** (☎ 9444).

TRAIN TRAVEL

Most international and domestic trains operate from Gara de Nord. For tickets and information, go to the Agenţia de Voiaj CFR.

➤ TRAIN INFORMATION: **Agenţia de Voiaj CFR** (✉ Str. Domniţa Anastasia 10–14, ☎ 021/313–2643). **Gara de Nord** (✉ B-dul. Gării de Nord, ☎ 021/223–0880).

TRANSPORTATION AROUND BUCHAREST

Bucharest's historic section and most sights can be explored on foot, though you might prefer the Metro or a taxi for more distant sights. Pick up a tourist map at bookstores, travel agencies, or the Romanian Tourist Office in your home country (☞ Visitor Information *in* Smart Travel Tips).

TRAVEL AGENCIES

Travel agencies have multiplied in Bucharest, so choosing carefully is important. The following are well-established firms that can arrange local sightseeing or trips around the country.

➤ CONTACTS: **Accent Travel & Events** (✉ Str. Episcopiei 5, Suite 2, ☎ 021/314–1980, FAX 021/314–1981, WEB www.accenttravel.ro). **Atlantic Tour** (✉ Calea Victoriei 202, ☎ 021/312–7757, FAX 021/312–6860, WEB www.atlantic.ro). **Romantic Travel** (✉ Str. Prof. Dr. Mihail

Georgescu 24 [Hala Traian], ☎ 021/326–0439, 𝔽𝔸𝕏 021/326–0437, 𝕎𝔼𝔹 www.romantic.ro).

VISITOR INFORMATION

Two English-language publications—*Bucharest: What, Where, When,* available free in hotels and travel agencies, and *Bucharest in Your Pocket,* sold in bookstores for $2.45—are filled with information on sights, restaurants, entertainment, and other useful tidbits. The former is published several times a year, the latter every two months. Also consult travel agencies, hotels, and the Romanian Tourist Office in your home country (☞ Visitor Information *in* Smart Travel Tips).

THE BLACK SEA COAST AND DANUBE DELTA

The Delta Dunării (Danube Delta) is Europe's largest wetlands reserve, covering more than 5,000 square km (about 2,000 square mi) of eastern Romania. As the Danube approaches the end of its 2,860 km (1,773 mi) journey to the Black Sea, it divides into three channels. The northernmost branch forms the border with Ukraine, the middle arm leads to the busy port of Sulina, and the southernmost arm meanders toward the little port of Sfintu Gheorghe. From these channels, countless canals widen into tree-fringed lakes, reed islands, and pools covered with water lilies.

The delta, which is on UNESCO's list of World Heritage Sites, shelters some 300 bird species, including Europe's largest pelican colonies; 160 kinds of fish; 800 plant families; and fishing villages where the Lipoveni, who immigrated centuries ago from Russia, live in traditional reed cottages.

May and September are ideal months for bird-watching. With Tulcea as a starting point, you can travel by boat to villages such as Crişan, Uzlina, Sulina and Sfântu Gheorghe, all deep in the Delta. From these villages, it's possible to explore countless small waterways with local fisherfolk or in boats arranged by your lodging. Accommodation options throughout the region include small hotels and pensions. Facilities are limited and seldom respond to individual inquiries. Let a tour operator in Constanţa or Bucharest advise you and handle arrangements. Operators also run day trips from Constanţa, including a boat excursion in the Delta. Fishing programs can be arranged.

Tulcea

263 km (163 mi) northeast of Bucharest.

Tulcea, the gateway to the Danube Delta, claims some modest Roman remains, a 19th-century mosque, and several museums. **Muzeul Deltei Dunării** (Danube Delta Museum) provides a good introduction to the flora, fauna, and way of life of the communities in the area. ☒ *Str. Progresului 32,* ☎ *0240/515–866.* ☒ *30¢.* ☉ *June–Aug., daily 8–8; Sept.–May, daily 10–6.*

Lodging

$$ 🛏 **Delta.** A large hotel on the bank of the Danube, this property, which is popular with tour groups, is the best in town. Guest rooms have balconies overlooking the river but otherwise are nothing special. ☒ *Str. Isaccei 2,* ☎ *0240/514–720,* 𝔽𝔸𝕏 *0240/516–260. 114 rooms, 3 suites. Restaurant, cable TV, massage, sauna, bar, laundry service, meeting room, parking (fee). MC, V.*

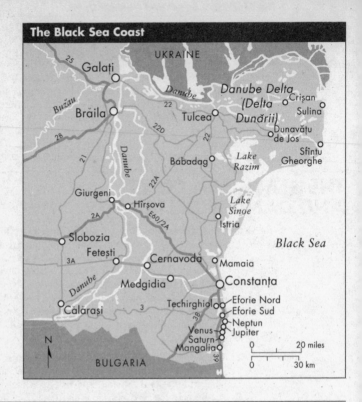

The Black Sea Coast

Constanţa

123 km (76 mi) south of Tulcea, 266 km (165 mi) east of Bucharest.

Known as Tomis in antiquity, Constanţa was founded, it's said, by survivors of a battle with the Argonauts. The Roman poet Ovid was exiled here in AD 8; his statue stands in a main square. Despite being a Black Sea port, Constanţa feels like a small town, and its sights are easily walkable. These range from Roman ruins to churches, mosques, and several museums. Much of ancient Tomis remains unexcavated.

An impressive collection of artifacts from Greek, Roman, and Daco-Roman civilizations is on display at the **Muzeul Naţional de Istorie şi Arheologie** (National History and Archaeological Museum), behind Ovid's statue. ⊠ *Piaţa Ovidiu 12,* ☎ *0241/618–763.* 🎫 *65¢, camera fee $1.10.* ☼ *June–Aug., daily 9–8; Sept.–May, Tues.–Sun. 9–5.*

The **Edificiul Roman cu Mozaic** (Roman Mosaics Building) houses remains of 4th-century Roman warehouses and shops, plus a mosaic floor more than 21,000 square ft in area. The museum stands not far from the National History and Archaeological Museum. ⊠ *Piaţa Ovidiu 12,* ☎ *0241/618–763.* 🎫 *65¢, camera fee $1.10.* ☼ *June–Aug., daily 8–7; Sept.–May, Tues.–Sun. 9–5.*

The **Parcul Arheologic** (Archaeology Park) contains 3rd- and 4th-century columns and fragments and a 6th-century tower. ⊠ *B-dul. Republicii.*

Traditional-culture buffs shouldn't miss the **Muzeul Artă Populară** (Ethnographic Museum), which displays a fine collection of regional handicrafts and costumes. ⊠ *B-dul. Tomis 32,* ☎ *0241/616–133.* 🎫 *55¢; $2.15 includes admission and camera fee.* ☼ *June–Aug., daily 9–7:30; Sept.–May, daily 9–5.*

Dining and Lodging

A string of hotels stretches along the Black Sea just north and south of Constanţa. It won't be mistaken for the Caribbean, but you might enjoy winding up a hectic sightseeing schedule with a few days' relaxation. Let a tour operator match you with a property. Health spas for treatment of medical ills are attached to many hotels. Most properties close from October through May.

$$ ✕ **Cazino.** A turn-of-the-20th-century former casino, this restaurant overlooking the sea has ornate moldings, stained glass, and a terrace open for dining in warm weather. Seafood dishes are the house specialty, and meat and poultry are also served. ✉ *B-dul. Elisabeta 2,* ☎ *0241/617–416. No credit cards.*

$$$$ 🏨 **President.** Perhaps the best of the Black Sea hotels, this year-round property incorporates 2,000-year-old archaeological remains into the decor and has a small museum. Guest rooms favor a light-gray color scheme. Some have balconies overlooking the sea. Rates drop from October through May. ✉ *Str. Teilor 6, Mangalia, 44 km (27 mi) south of Constanţa,* ☎ *0241/755–695,* ☎ FAX *0241/755–861,* WEB *www.hpresident.com. 64 rooms, 1 suite. 2 restaurants, room service, in-room data ports, minibars, cable TV, gym, hair salon, massage, sauna, beach, billiards, bar, shops, baby-sitting, meeting rooms, free parking. AE, MC, V.*

$$$–$$$$ 🏨 **Capri.** White walls, lots of windows, and plant-filled niches lend a
★ Mediterranean air to this property. Pastel colors decorate the guest rooms, and first-floor rooms open onto a terrace. Robes and hair dryers are included. ✉ *Str. Mircea cel Batrân 109,* ☎ *0241/553–090,* ☎ FAX *0241/550–993. 16 rooms, 8 suites. Restaurant, snack bar, room service, in-room data ports, minibars, cable TV, indoor pool, massage, sauna, billiards, bar, laundry service, meeting room, free parking, some pets allowed. AE, DC, MC, V.*

$$–$$$ 🏨 **Guci.** Guest rooms at the warm, welcoming, central Guci have an
★ interesting pale-green-and-black color scheme and include such extras as coffeemakers. The small, cheery restaurant serves Mexican and other international fare. ✉ *Str. Răscoalei 23,* ☎ *0241/695–500,* ☎ FAX *0241/638–426. 10 rooms, 10 suites. Restaurant, room service, in-room data ports, refrigerators, cable TV, massage, sauna, bar, laundry service, free parking, some pets allowed. AE, MC, V.*

The Black Sea Coast and Danube Delta Essentials

AIR TRAVEL

In summer, the Romanian national carrier, Tarom, has daily service between Constanţa and Bucharest. The flight takes 45 minutes.
➤ CARRIER: **Tarom** (☎ 021/337–2037; 9361 in Bucharest; 0241/662–632 in Constanţa).

CAR TRAVEL

The fastest route from Bucharest to Constanţa is east on E60. From Tulcea, follow E87 south.

BOAT TRAVEL

If you're staying in villages you can make arrangements with local fisherfolk for day excursions through the watery highways and byways.

CAR TRAVEL

As public bus service is infrequent, driving can be more convenient. Both Avis and Hertz have offices in Constanţa.
➤ AGENCIES: **Avis** (✉ Ştefan cel Mare 15, ☎ 0241/616–733). **Hertz** (✉ B-dul. Tomis 65, ☎ 0241/661–100).

EMERGENCIES

➤ EMERGENCY CONTACTS: **Fire** (☎ 981). **Medical** (☎ 961). **Police** (☎ 955).

➤ LATE-NIGHT PHARMACIES: **Farmacia 2** (✉ B-dul. Tomis 80, Constanţa, ☎ 0241/611–983). **Marina Santis** (✉ Str. Al. Lăpuşneanu 107, Constanţa, ☎ 0241/638–682).

TOURS

Tourism agencies (☞ Visitor Information, *below*) organize sightseeing bus trips from Black Sea hotels and Constanţa to the Danube Delta, the Murfatlar vineyards, the Grecian ruins of Istria, and the 1st century AD triumphal monument at Adamclisi.

TRAIN TRAVEL

About 10 trains leave Bucharest's Gara de Nord each day for the three-hour trip to Constanţa. Trains in the *Inter-City* class are the newest. In Constanţa, purchase tickets at Agenţia CFR.

➤ TRAIN TICKETS: **Agenţia CFR** (✉ Str. Canarache Vasile 4, ☎ 0241/ 614–960).

TRAVEL AGENCIES

The following Constanţa travel agencies can provide excursions in the Black Sea and Danube Delta regions and throughout the country.

➤ TRAVEL AGENCIES: **Danubius** (✉ B-dul. Ferdinand 36, ☎ 0241/615–686, FAX 0241/618–010). **Latina** (✉ B-dul. Ferdinand 70, ☎ 0241/639–713, FAX 0241/693–107). **Mamaia Tours** (✉ Str. Ştefan cel Mare 55, ☎ FAX 0241/612–511).

VISITOR INFORMATION

The English-language publication, *Constanţa: What, Where, When,* is available free at most Constanţa hotels.

➤ TOURIST INFORMATION: **Centrul de Informare şi Educaţie Ecologică** (Information and Ecological Education Center; ✉ Str. Portului 34A, Tulcea, ☎ 0240/518–945, FAX 0240/518–975, WEB www.ddbra.ro). **Info Litoral: Tourist Information Center** (✉ Str. Traian 36, Bl. C1, Apt. 31, Constanţa, ☎ 0241/555–000, FAX 0241/555–111, WEB www. infolitoral.ro.).

BUCOVINA

Moldavia is Romania's northeastern province. During World War II, portions were annexed by the Soviet Union and remain separate to this day. Moldavia claims some of the country's greatest musicians and writers, including Mihai Eminescu, the national poet, and George Enescu, the national composer.

Bucovina, a region within Moldavia that lies west of Suceava and north of Piatra Neamţ, means "beech-covered land," and indeed the area is heavily forested. Here, Romania's most renowned monasteries stand. Several were constructed by the 15th-century prince Ştefan cel Mare (Stephen the Great) in gratitude for victories against invading Ottoman Turks. The exterior walls of the "Big Five" painted monasteries (Moldoviţa, Suceviţa, Arbore, Humor, and Voroneţ) are covered eave-to-ground with glorious frescoes. Despite the centuries, many paintings retain their vivid colors. All are UNESCO World Heritage monuments.

More than 15 important monasteries dot this region, so it would be difficult to see them all in one trip. The exceptional Voroneţ, Moldoviţa, and Suceviţa monasteries should be at the top of any list. Though lacking exterior frescoes, the monasteries of Văratec, Agapia, and Neamţ,

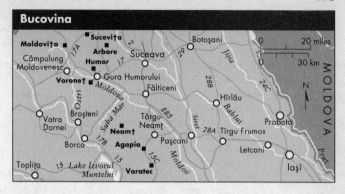

Bucovina

Moldovița · Sucevița · Botoșani · 0 · 20 miles · 0 · 30 km · MOLDOVA
Câmpulung Moldovenesc · Arbore · Suceava · Jijia
Humor · Gura Humorului
Voroneț · Fălticeni
Vatra Dornei · Broșteni · Hîrlău · Probota
Târgu-Neamț · Neamț · Tîrgu Frumos
Borca · Agapia · Pașcani · Letcani
Toplița · Lake Izvorul Muntelui · Varatec · Moldova · Iași

all situated near the town of Târgu Neamț, are also well worth seeing. Văratec's shop sells beautiful carpets made by the nuns. Base yourself in Suceava, Câmpulung Moldovenesc, or a village home. Suceava is a city with museums and a citadel, while Câmpulung is smaller, making it easier to negotiate if you have a car.

Monastery entry fees average 65¢, plus 95¢ for cameras and $1.85 for video. The monasteries are generally open to visitors daily 8 AM–8 PM. If you're lucky, you might chance upon a service where the high voices of nuns sing in response to the chanting of the priest.

Voroneț

★ *41 km (25 mi) west of Suceava.*

Often called the "Sistine Chapel of the East," 15th-century Voroneț is renowned for the quality of its frescoes, with their predominant blue hue so deep and penetrating it has been given a name: Voroneț blue. The frescoes depict angels with the faces of Moldavian women playing the shepherd's musical instrument, the *bucium,* while heaven-bound souls are wrapped in traditional embroidered cloths. To get here from Suceava, travel west on E576 until the turnoff for Voroneț. From there, it is about 5 km (3 mi).

Humor

8 km (5 mi) northeast of Voroneț, 41 km (25 mi) west of Suceava.

From the 15th century, calligraphers and painters of miniatures perfected their craft at this monastery surrounded by wooden ramparts. Humor is the smallest of the Bucovina monasteries and is known for its deep shades of red. Frescoes depict the stories of the *Last Judgment,* the *Return of the Prodigal Son,* and the *Siege of Constantinople.* Some paintings have faded. The turnoff for Humor Monastery is off E576, just east of Voroneț.

Moldovița

★ *32 km (20 mi) northwest of Humor, 103 km (64 mi) northwest of Suceava.*

Enclosed by fortification walls, Moldovița was built in 1532 by Prince Petru Rareș to provide refuge to nearby villagers in case of a Turkish attack. An interior painting shows the prince, along with his wife and sons, presenting the monastery to Jesus. Exterior frescoes include the *Liberation of Constantinople,* the *Last Judgment,* and a *Tree of Jesse,* where multiple human figures are gently entwined in leaves and branches. From Suceava, travel west on E576 through the town of Câmpulung Moldovenesc; then, take 17A north to the monastery.

Sucevița

★ *34 km (21 mi) northeast of Moldovița, 50 km (31 mi) northwest of Suceava.*

The powerful stone fortification walls and towers of this late-16th-century structure suggest a bleak medieval castle within. Instead, you'll find wall after wall of magnificent paintings. Sucevița has the greatest number of images—thousands—of all Bucovina's monasteries. Among the most notable are the *Ladder of Virtue,* depicting the 30 steps from Hell to Paradise, and the *Tree of Jesse,* a symbol of continuity between the Old and New Testaments. From Moldovița Monastery, continue on 17A north to the Sucevița turnoff.

Bucovina Essentials

AIR TRAVEL

Tarom has five flights per week between Bucharest and Suceava; flights take one hour. On arrival, consult a local travel agency or hire a taxi for the day to visit the monasteries.

➤ CARRIER: **Tarom** (☎ 021/337–2037; 9361 in Bucharest; 030/214–686 in Suceava).

CAR TRAVEL

The most direct route from Bucharest to Bucovina takes about eight hours and passes through one of the few unscenic regions of Romania. From Bucharest take E60 northeast toward Urziceni. This road soon becomes E85; follow it north all the way to Suceava. If you are staying in Câmpulung Moldovenesc, take E576 west from Suceava (less than two hours). For a beautiful but longer and partly mountainous drive, follow E60 north through Brașov and Sighișoara to Târgu Mureș, then 15A to Bistrița and 17/E576 northeast to Câmpulung or Suceava.

Driving to the monasteries will allow you to gaze at the frescoes to your heart's content and savor the fir-covered forests of this region in an unrushed manner. The circuit is easy to follow, although sections of road are mountainous and not in the best condition. You might consider ending, rather than starting, at Voroneț simply because this monastery inspires such a sense of perfection.

LODGING

Lodging options include Casa Elena, just 2 km (1 mi) from Voroneț monastery, where doubles cost $40; Continental Hotel Suceava, which runs $49 for a double; and Hotel Zimbrul in Câmpulung Moldovenesc, with doubles for $30.

➤ CONTACTS: **Casa Elena** (✉ Voroneț 8, Voroneț, ☎ 0230/230–651, FAX 0230/230–968, WEB www.casaelena.ro). **Continental Hotel Suceava** (✉ Str. Mihai Viteazul 4–6, Suceava, ☎ 0230/210–944, FAX 0230/227–598, WEB www.continentalhotels.ro). **Hotel Zimbrul** (✉ Calea Bucovinei 1–3, Câmpulung Moldovenesc, ☎ 0230/314–356, FAX 0230/314–358).

TOURS

Due to the limited public transportation between Bucovina's monasteries, you might prefer a packaged tour arranged by an agency in Bucharest. Such tours include an English-speaking guide, lodging, entry fees, and all or some meals, as well as transportation (☞ Travel Agencies *in* Bucharest Essentials, *above*).

TRAIN TRAVEL

Trains to Bucovina depart from Bucharest's Gara de Nord. *Inter-City* and *rapid* trains are fastest, making the trip in six and eight hours, respectively.

TRANSPORTATION AROUND BUCOVINA

The best way to travel around this region, if you aren't visiting on a tour, is by car. Hire a taxi or a rental car, the latter with or without a driver-guide (arrange this in advance with a travel agency in Bucharest). Unless you have endless time and patience, public buses are not a good option for visiting the monasteries.

VISITOR INFORMATION

Consult local travel agencies, hotel staff, agencies in Bucharest, or the Romanian Tourist Office in your home country (☞ Visitor Information *in* Smart Travel Tips) for information on visiting Bucovina.

TRANSYLVANIA

Transylvania, Romania's western province and a favorite with visitors and Romanians alike, is a region of forested mountains, castles, fortified churches, picturesque villages, unspoiled rural landscapes, and cities with historic sections that transport you back to medieval days. And of course, this is the land of the fictional Count Dracula. The architecture of Sibiu, Braşov, and Sighişoara reflects strong Saxon influence. This ethnic group played a major role here from medieval times until the 1980s when many emigrated to Germany. Transylvania was under Austro-Hungarian rule from the end of the 17th century until 1918 and remains home to a large Hungarian minority, as well as to much of Romania's Gypsy population.

Many of the country's most interesting spots are found here. Base yourself in major centers such as Sibiu, Braşov, or Cluj, taking day trips into the countryside, or immerse yourself in village life with occasional overnights in private homes. Look for *camere libere* (rooms available) signs or contact ANTREC (☞ Bed-and-Breakfast Reservation Agencies *in* Romania A to Z, *below*).

Sinaia

127 km (79 mi) northwest of Bucharest.

Prior to World War II and the abdication of the royal family, Sinaia was a summer retreat for Romania's aristocracy. A walk up the mountain road Strada Mănăstirii passes grand homes from this period and leads to **Mănăstirea Sinaia** (Sinaia Monastery), dating to 1695.

★ **Castelul Peleş** (Peleş Palace) is one of the best-preserved royal palaces in Europe. Built in the late 19th century, it was King Carol I's attempt to re-create a Bavarian setting in the mountains of Romania. Its 106 rooms are ornately decorated, with precious woods, stained glass, objets d'art, even scenes from Wagnerian operas. You must join a tour, available in English, to see the palace. Photography is not permitted. The palace lies just beyond the Sinaia Monastery. ⊠ *Str. Peleşului 2, up hill along Str. Mănăstirii,* ☎ *0244/312–184.* ☑ *$1.85.* ⊘ *Wed.–Sun. 9–5.*

Pelişor (Little Peleş) was the summer home of King Ferdinand, Carol's heir. Though less grand than nearby Peleş Palace, Pelişor has a lovely setting amid trees, flowers, and landscaped lawns. ⊠ *Str. Peleşului,* ☎ *0244/312–184.* ☑ *$1.85.* ⊘ *Wed.–Sun. 9:30–4, Thurs. noon–4.*

The **teleferic,** or cable car, takes you up the mountain for panoramic views of the surrounding Carpathian Mountains and the town. Return the same way or hike down the trail, which takes roughly two hours. The cable car is behind Hotel Montana, in the center of town. ✉ *$1.25– $2.45 one-way.* ☉ *Daily 8–4.*

OFF THE
BEATEN PATH

CASTLE BRAN – Looming ominously in the shadow of Mt. Bucegi, Castle Bran is a gloomy though beautifully preserved fortress. Its ramparts, towers, and medieval accoutrements, plus easy accessibility, have led Bran to be hyped as "Dracula's Castle." In reality, Vlad Țepeș had little association with it. His real castle lies in mountaintop ruins in the Argeş Valley. Still, Bran is well worth a visit. Tours in English are available. ✉ *Rte. 73, Bran; go north from Sinaia for about 20 min, taking the turnoff for Râsnov. At the dead-end, make a left.* ✉ *$1.55, camera fee $1.40.* ☉ *Tues.–Sun. 8–4:30.*

Lodging

$$$ 🖾 **Holiday Inn Resort Sinaia.** Guest rooms, which surround an atrium
★   and have balconies, and the restaurant afford marvelous mountain
       views. An on-site spa offers health and beauty treatments, including
       the Gerovital program, said to slow the aging process. This property
       is just off the main road between Bucharest and Braşov. ✉ *Str.
       Toporaşilor 1A,* ☎ *0244/310–440,* FAX *0244/310–551,* WEB *www.
       sixcontinentshotels.com/holiday-inn. 128 rooms, 10 suites. Restaurant, room service, minibars, cable TV, tennis court, indoor-outdoor
       pool, gym, massage, sauna, spa, ski storage, lobby lounge, recreation
       room, shop, baby-sitting, laundry service, business services, meeting
       rooms, travel services, free parking. AE, MC, V.*

Braşo and Poiana Braşov

43 km (27 mi) north of Sinaia, 171 km (106 mi) north of Bucharest.

During the Middle Ages, Braşov was a rich Saxon city devoted to trade, and it is the wonderful old section that draws today's visitors. Braşov's best sights can be found in and around **Piaţa Sfatului,** a large cobblestone square at the heart of the old Germanic town that still bears traces of its original fortress walls. Shops, cafés, and lively restaurants with outdoor terraces line the square and the pedestrian street, **Strada Republicii,** leading off it. Built in 1420 and once the town hall, the large **Muzeul de Istorie Braşov** (Museum of the History of Braşov) stands in the center of the square. ☎ *0268/142–967.* ✉ *20¢.* ☉ *Tues.–Sun. 10–6.*

The Gothic **Biserica Neagră** (Black Church), completed in the 15th century, acquired its name after a 1689 fire left the walls darkened. A superb collection of 119 Turkish carpets, gifts from long-ago merchants, lines the interior. In summer, concerts are presented on a 4,000-pipe organ. The church stands just off Piaţa Sfatului.

Strategically overlooking the city, the **Cetate** (Citadel; ✉ Dealul Cetăţii) was part of Braşov's early defensive fortifications. Within its stone walls, you'll find shops and a restaurant with medieval decor.

For a fine view of the city, ride the **Telecabina Tâmpa,** a cable car, to the top of Mount Tâmpa. ✉ *Aleea T. Brădiceanu,* ☎ *no phone.* ✉ *75¢ one-way, $1.25 round-trip.* ☉ *Tues.–Sun. 9:30–5.*

If time allows, visit the fortified **Saxon churches** in nearby Hărman and Prejmer. Both are UNESCO World Cultural Heritage sites.

A 15-minute drive or bus ride from Braşov leads to **Poiana Braşov,** a mountaintop ski and summer resort area with several excellent restaurants and hotels. In winter, Poiana Braşov has some of the best skiing in Romania. In summer, you can follow hiking trails that wind along the mountainside.

Dining and Lodging

The best hotels and restaurants can be found in the resort area of Poiana Braşov.

$–$$ ✕ **Coliba Haiducilor.** Dried peppers, corn cobs, and animal pelts crowd
★   the walls at the Outlaws' Hut, where dishes such as *friptura haiducu-lui* ("outlaw steak"; six kinds of meat with garnish), sour soups, and vegetables from the eatery's farm tempt diners. Waiters wear traditional outfits, and folk musicians entertain evenings. ⊠ *Poiana Braşov,* ☎ *0268/262–137. No credit cards. Closed Nov.*

$–$$ ✕ **Şura Dacilor.** This popular restaurant near a lake has outdoor pavil-
★   ions, upscale rustic decor, waiters in folk costume, and a Gypsy band evenings. Menu items include game dishes, special cheeses, and freshly baked bread. ⊠ *Poiana Braşov,* ☎ *0268/262–327. No credit cards.*

$$$$ 🏨 **Miruna.** Flower boxes and artwork decorate this attractive prop-erty, where most guest rooms have balconies and several have skylights. Some suites sleep up to five; there also are two villas. The airy restau-rant is done in shades of green. Rates are lower April through December. ⊠ *Poiana Braşov,* ☎ *0268/262–120,* FAX *0268/262–035,* WEB *www. hotelmiruna.ro. 3 rooms, 11 suites, 2 villas. Restaurant, room service, in-room data ports, minibars, cable TV, gym, massage, sauna, bar, play-ground, Internet, meeting room, free parking, some pets allowed. AE, MC, V.*

$$$$ 🏨 **Tirol.** Built in Tyrolean architectural style, this five-story hotel, a Ro-
★   manian-Swiss joint venture, has a cozy lobby with a corner fireplace and a glass-wall restaurant overlooking the mountains. Guest rooms, no two alike, are spacious with light-wood furnishings. Most have bal-conies. The lodging price includes complimentary transfers to the ski slopes. ⊠ *Poiana Braşov,* ☎ *0268/262–453,* FAX *0268/262–439. 54 rooms, 4 suites. Restaurant, room service, in-room data ports, some minibars, cable TV, massage, sauna, ski storage, bar, laundry service, free parking, some pets allowed; no a/c. AE, MC, V.*

$$–$$$ 🏨 **Alpin.** This alpine-style hotel affords marvelous views, and ski lifts and the bus stop for Braşov are within walking distance. Ski packages are available. Guest-room furnishings are dark, but rooms are spacious and many have balconies. The hotel attracts families, so expect chil-dren on the loose. Rates drop in spring and fall. ⊠ *Poiana Braşov,* ☎ *0268/262–343,* ☎ FAX *0268/262–435. 125 rooms, 4 suites. Restaurant, room service, minibars, cable TV, indoor pool, hair salon, massage, sauna, ski storage, bar, travel services, free parking, some pets al-lowed; no a/c. MC, V.*

$–$$ 🏨 **Coroana.** In Braşov, the Coroana, constructed in 1908 in German classic style, is a better option than some of the overpriced competi-tion. It's well located on a pedestrian street just a block from Piaţa Sfat-ului. Though guest rooms could use a renovation, they're clean with full bath facilities. Request one of the larger doubles, at the same price as regular doubles. If you're on a budget consider the Postăvarul, a sep-arate hotel in the same building with rooms for around $20; the rooms have sinks and toilets but share tubs. ⊠ *Str. Republicii 62,* ☎ *0268/ 144–330,* FAX *0268/141–505. 72 rooms, 4 suites. Restaurant, room ser-vice, some refrigerators, cable TV, bar, travel services, some pets al-lowed; no a/c. No credit cards.*

Sighişoara

★   *121 km (75 mi) northwest of Braşov, 248 km (154 mi) northwest of Bucharest.*

As you approach this enchanting place, one of Europe's best-preserved medieval towns, you can see the profile of the towers and spires of

Sighişoara's old section, rising above the modern town. Each July the Medieval Festival, with people in period costume, re-creates Sighişoara's earlier days. Contact the Romanian Tourist Office in your home country for exact dates (☞ Visitor Information *in* Smart Travel Tips).

Plans were under way at press time to construct a major Dracula Land theme park, scheduled to open in 2004, just outside the town. The theme park will include a medieval castle, an Institute of Vampirology, amusement rides, restaurants serving traditional fare, and handicrafts.

High above town is the **citadel,** which you enter through a 14th-century **clock tower** that rises 210 ft. Wooden figures symbolizing the days of the week, peace, justice, and even an executioner adorn the tower. A plaque near the tower identifies the house, now a restaurant, where Vlad Ţepeş, also known as Vlad Dracula, was most likely born. Within the tower, the **Muzeul de Istorie** (History Museum; ☎ 0265/771–108) includes a torture chamber and a medieval arms collection. From the gallery at the top, you can view terra-cotta roofs and the citadel's eight additional remaining towers. The museum is open Monday–Saturday 9–5:30 and Sunday 9 –3:30; admission is 75¢.

A narrow, cobbled street within the citadel leads to **Pasajul Scărilor** (Students' Passage), a 175-step covered staircase that in turn leads to **Biserica din Deal** (Church on the Hill), a 14th-century Gothic structure.

Dining and Lodging

Sighişoara lacks good accommodations, so most people move on to Sibiu for the night.

$–$$ ✕ **Restaurantul Vlad Dracul.** The presumed birthplace of Vlad Ţepeş is a popular spot for a break or a meal. You'll find traditional dishes such as pork escallope with brown sauce, and chocolate-filled pancakes. ✉ *Piaţa Muzeului 6,* ☎ *0265/771–596. No credit cards.*

Sibiu

92 km (57 mi) southwest of Sighişoara, 271 km (168 mi) northwest of Bucharest.

Founded in the 12th century, Sibiu's Old Town retains the grandeur of its earlier days when rich and powerful guilds dominated regional trade. Like Sighişoara and Braşov, it has a distinctly Germanic feel, and was in fact a major Saxon center. Sections of the medieval wall still guard the historic area, where narrow streets pass steep-roofed 17th-century buildings with "eyebrow" windows (windows with gable overhangs) before opening onto vast, church-dominated squares such as Piaţa Mare (Great Square) and Piaţa Mică (Small Square). The mansions of rival Gypsy kings stand on the town's outskirts.

Biserica Romano Catolică (Roman Catholic Church), a splendid high-Baroque structure, stands in Piaţa Mare.

★ The **Muzeul Brukenthal** (Brukenthal Museum) exhibits an impressive collection of silver, paintings, and religious art. Tours are available in English. ✉ *Piaţa Mare,* ☎ *0269/ 211–699, 0269/217–691,* WEB *www. brukenthal.verena.ro.* ✑ *95¢, 2-hr English-language guided tour $18.50.* ☉ *Tues.–Sun. 9–5 (closes at 4 in winter).*

Biserica Evanghelică (Evangelical Church) rises just behind Piaţa Mare in Gothic splendor, its tile-covered spires sparkling in the sun.

Muzeul Civilzaţiei Populare Tradiţionale Astra (Traditional Folk Civilization Museum), a short drive from Sibiu, is a 200-acre outdoor exhibit of original dwellings, workshops, and churches from around the country. ✉ *Calea Rǎşinari*, ☎ *0269/218–195*. 🎞 *90¢, camera fee 80¢, video fee $6.20.* ◷ *May–Aug., Tues.–Sun. 10–6; Sept.–Apr., Tues.–Sun. 9–5.*

In the nearby village of Sibiel, the **Muzeul de Icoane pe Sticlă** (Icons on Glass Museum), in the courtyard of the Orthodox Church, houses some 700 icons. ✉ *Str. Bisericii 326*, ☎ *0269/552–536.* 🎞 *60¢.* ◷ *Daily 8–8.*

Returning to Sibiu on the main road from Sibiel, stop at the village of **Cristian** to see its 14th-century fortified church.

Dining and Lodging

$ ✕ **Crama Sibiul Vechi.** Locals and visitors alike flock to this cellar eatery, where waiters in traditional dress serve such favorites as pork fillet stuffed with ham and mushrooms. Singers render old tunes, embroidered scarves hang from the vaulted brick ceiling, and ceramic plates line the walls. ✉ *Str. Papiu Ilarian 3*, ☎ *0269/431–971. No credit cards.*

$$ 🏨 **Continental.** On the main road into town, this property, part of Romania's biggest chain, is just a 10-minute walk from the historic section. Guest rooms are decorated in blue and white. Geared toward business travelers, the hotel is comfortable and functional. The staff members are helpful, friendly, and professional, and many speak excellent English. ✉ *Calea Dumbrǎvii 2–4*, ☎ *0269/218–100*, 🖷 *0269/ 210–125*, 🌐 *www.continentalhotels.ro. 169 rooms, 13 suites. Restaurant, patisserie, room service, in-room data ports, minibars, cable TV, massage, sauna, bar, laundry service, Internet, meeting rooms, travel services, parking (fee); no a/c in some rooms, no-smoking rooms. AE, DC, MC, V.*

$$ 🏨 **Împǎratul Romanilor.** This 16th-century structure just a block away
★ from Piaţa Mare has been an inn since 1772. Its name translates into "Roman Emperor," and famous guests have included Emperor Josef II and Johannes Brahms. The lobby is elegant in gold and blue, and guest rooms have antique-style white furniture accented by tufted gold cloth headboards. Some rooms have lofts. The restaurant claims a sliding glass ceiling. ✉ *Str. Nicolae Bǎlcescu 4*, ☎ *0269/216–500*, 🖷 *0269/ 213–278. 64 rooms, 32 suites. Restaurant, room service, minibars, cable TV, gym, hair salon, massage, sauna, bar, laundry service, meeting room, travel services, parking (fee); no a/c. MC, V.*

Maramureş

324 km (201 mi) north of Sibiu, 595 km (369 mi) northwest of Bucharest.

Tucked away in the mountains of northwestern Romania, Maramureş County seems a region lost in time. Here, in one of the few parts of the country never conquered by the Romans, people claim descent directly from the Dacians. This is a land of homes hiding behind towering wooden gates attached to fences a fraction of their height. Intricately hand-carved in motifs of twisted rope, acorns, crosses, and the sun, these gates have come to symbolize Maramureş. So have the wooden churches—tiny gems from the 13th through 18th centuries, with multigable shingle roofs and soaring, narrow steeples. Many have fine interior frescoes, and nine are UNESCO World Cultural Heritage monuments. In late afternoon, when women sit on roadside benches, chatting as they coax wool onto spindles, and red-tasseled horses pull wagons overflowing with hay home from the fields, it's easy to fall under the spell of this special place.

Valea Izei (Iza Valley) is ideal for observing the traditional life of Maramureş. Follow Route 186 east from Sighetu Marmaţiei to Sǎcel;

village after village vies for attention. **Onceşti** and **Bârsana** arguably claim the greatest number of impressive gates, and Bârsana's church has a 184-ft steeple. Farther along, admire the wooden churches at **Rozavlea** and **Şieu.** The latter is just off Route 186—take the turn for Botiza. Continue on this side road to a fork: left to **Botiza,** right to **Poienile Izei.** Both have wonderful churches; vivid frescoes depicting ingenious punishments for sinners cover the interior walls of the latter. Back on the main road, turn right to visit the church of **Bogdan Vodă,** which also has good frescoes. Near Bogdan Vodă, take the turn for **Ieud;** this village has fine gates and two **wooden churches.** If the churches are locked, any passerby will help find the person with the *cheie* (pronounced kay-ā), or key. On Sunday most villagers wear traditional dress. In Săcel and Poienile Izei, young people promenade about the village.

The town of **Sighetu Marmaţiei,** though no beauty spot, has some interesting attractions, including the **Muzeul Etnografic al Maramureşului** (Ethnographic Museum of Maramureş), an outdoor collection of homes and farmsteads from around the county. Another ethnographic museum, displaying regional costumes and artifacts, stands in the town's center. Also here are an impressive **synagogue** and the **childhood home of author Elie Wiesel.**

No trip to Maramureş is complete without a visit to **Săpânţa** (a 20-minute drive from Sighetu Marmaţiei) and its **Cimitirul Vesel** (Merry Cemetery). Colorful folk-art paintings and witty words carved into wooden grave markers sum up the deceaseds' lives.

Dining and Lodging
Home stays present a great way to experience Maramureş life. Look for *camere libere* (rooms available) signs. Homes that display the green ANTREC logo (☞ Bed-and-Breakfast Reservation Agencies *in* Romania A to Z, *below*) have been approved by that organization, guaranteeing clean, comfortable accommodations.

$ 🏠 **Mariana and Vasile Bud Home.** This spacious home stay has six guest rooms plus a "traditional room" with a display of regional crafts such as embroidered cloths and pillows, handwoven carpets, and painted ceramic plates. A room and two meals cost $12 per person. ✉ *Str. Principală 335, Onceşti,* ☎ *0262/331–322. 6 rooms share 2 baths. No a/c. No credit cards.*

$ 🏠 **Perla Sigheteană.** Firm mattresses, balconies (some with mountain views), good-quality linens, and hair dryers fill the spotless rooms at this chalet-style hotel. Bathrooms are small but well equipped. The restaurant has good food and service. ✉ *Str. Avram Iancu 65/A, Sighetu Marmaţiei,* ☎ *0262/310–613,* FAX *0262/310–268. 8 rooms. Restaurant, room service, fans, in-room data ports, minibars, cable TV, bar, laundry service, meeting room, free parking, some pets allowed; no a/c. AE, MC, V.*

Transylvania Essentials

AIR TRAVEL
Tarom flies between Bucharest and Sibiu five times a week (50-minute flight), Baie Mare three times a week (1¼-hour flight), and Satu Mare two times a week (1¼-hour flight). The last two are good starting points for Maramureş.
➤ Carrier: **Tarom** (☎ 021/337–2037; 9361 in Bucharest; 0269/211–157 in Sibiu; 0262/221–624 in Baie Mare; 0261/712–795 in Satu Mare).

BUS TRAVEL

Public buses cover the province less extensively and frequently than trains.

CAR RENTAL

Renting a car, with or without a hired driver, provides an appealing, though expensive, option for exploring Transylvania. Avis and Hertz have branches in Braşov, though renting a car from Bucharest and driving through the region will take you past some lovely scenery.

➤ AGENCIES: **Avis** (☎ 0268/413–775). **Hertz** (☎ 0268/471–485).

CAR TRAVEL

From Bucharest, E60 passes some lovely scenery as it stretches north through Sinaia to Braşov and Sighişoara. Figure 2½ hours to Braşov. To reach Sibiu, take Route 14 southwest from Sighişoara or E68 west from Braşov. From Sighişoara to Maramureş, follow Routes 13, 15A, and 17C north to Săcel, where you turn west, traveling through the Iza Valley along Route 186 to Sighetu Marmaţiei.

TOURS

Several travel agencies arrange package bus excursions from Bucharest (☞ Travel Agencies *in* Bucharest Essentials, *above*) and Braşov to Transylvania. In Braşov, try Micomis for tours of Transylvania.

➤ CONTACT: **Micomis** (✉ Str. Republicii 53, Braşov, ☎ 0268/470–472, FAX 0268/410–321).

TRAIN TRAVEL

Trains connect Bucharest to Transylvanian regions mentioned above and also operate between cities in the region. Service to Sinaia and Braşov is frequent. Choose *Inter-City* or *rapid* service to save time. For train information, contact Agenţia de Voiaj CFR in Bucharest.

➤ TRAIN INFORMATION: **Agenţia de Voiaj CFR** (✉ Str. Domniţa Anastasia 10–14, Bucharest, ☎ 021/313–2643).

VISITOR INFORMATION

In Sibiu, visit the helpful Tourist Information Office in Piaţa Mare; it's closed Saturday afternoon and Sunday. The Tourist Information Office in Baie Mare (in Maramureş) can also provide useful information; it's closed weekends. The English-language publication *Brasov: What, Where, When* is available free at most hotels.

➤ TOURIST INFORMATION: **Tourist Information Office** (✉ Str. Nicolae Bălcescu 7, Piaţa Mare, Sibiu, ☎ 0269/211–110, WEB www.primsb.ro; ✉ Str. Gheorghe Sincai 46, Baie Mare, Maramureş, ☎ 0262/215–543).

ROMANIA A TO Z

To research prices, get advice from other travelers, and book travel arrangements, visit www.fodors.com.

ADDRESSES

Knowing basic street sign words can help you find your way around. *Strada,* usually abbreviated as Str., means street; *bulevard* and *bulevardul,* abbreviated as B-dul., translate into boulevard; *Calea* means way; and *piaţa* is a plaza or square.

AIR TRAVEL

See Air Travel *in* Bucharest Essentials, *above.*

BED-AND-BREAKFAST RESERVATION AGENCIES

You can rent rooms in private homes in Bucharest and the countryside. If you make arrangements through local travel agencies or through

ANTREC you can count on a clean, comfortable room and ample meals. Do not expect a private bath or hosts that speak English. Rates run $12–$23 per person including two meals.

➤ CONTACT: **ANTREC** (⊠ Str. Maica Alexandra 7, Bucharest, ☎ FAX 021/223–7024, WEB www.antrec.ro).

BUS TRAVEL

Buses are not the best means of travel within Romania. There are no real bus stations—only pickup points—and bus schedules are not readily available. If you plan on using public transportation, it's better to stick with trains, which are frequent and inexpensive.

BUSINESS HOURS

Banks are open weekdays 9–noon. Exchange office hours vary, but most are open weekdays 9–5 and Saturday 9–1; some are open until 7 on Saturday and 1 on Sunday.

Museums usually are open 10–5, closed on Monday (and sometimes Tuesday). Shops generally are open weekdays 9–6 and Saturday 9–2.

CAR RENTAL

Prices are steep. Major international companies, which have offices in Bucharest and a few other cities in Romania, charge about $100 per day (weekly rates average 20% less) for the least expensive car. Car insurance is mandatory. Local rental agencies charge less but may not be dependable.

➤ AGENCIES: **Avis** (⊠ Otopeni Airport, Bucharest, ☎ 021/201–1957; ⊠ Str. Raphael Sanzio 1, Bucharest, ☎ 021/210–4344, FAX 021/210–6912, WEB www.avis.ro). **Budget** (⊠ Otopeni Airport, Bucharest, ☎ 021/204–1667; ⊠ Str. Polona 35, Bucharest, ☎ 021/210–2867, FAX 021/210–2995, WEB www.budgetro.ro). **Europcar** (⊠ Otopeni Airport, Bucharest, ☎ FAX 021/312–7078; ⊠ B-dul. Magheru 7, Bucharest, ☎ FAX 021/313–1540, WEB www.europcar.com). **Hertz** (⊠ Otopeni Airport, Bucharest, ☎ 021/201–4954; ⊠ Str. Ion Bianu 47, Bucharest, ☎ 021/222–1256, FAX 021/222–1257; WEB www.hertz.com).

CAR TRAVEL

An adequate network of roads covers the country, though the majority only allow for a single lane in each direction. From Hungary, enter at border crossings near the western Romanian cities of Arad, Oradea, Satu Mare, and Timişoara. From Bulgaria, enter through Calafat, Călăraşi, Giurgiu, Negru Vodă, and Vama Veche. Entry is usually fairly quick, but you could run into lines, especially on weekends.

PARKING

There are few parking meters in Romanian cities. Instead, parking attendants in business areas of major cities collect a small fee (about 20¢ per hour) and place a receipt on your windshield. Parking on the sidewalk is not uncommon. Do not park by a blue sign marked with a red cross, or your car will be towed. At the few parking lots around, the fee is about 30¢ per hour.

ROAD CONDITIONS

Although road repair crews are a common sight, potholes remain a serious problem in Romania, and some side roads are not paved at all. Progress may be further impeded by slow-moving trucks and horse-drawn carts. At night, the situation becomes doubly hazardous with poorly lighted or unlighted roads and vehicles.

RULES OF THE ROAD

Foreign visitors staying more than 30 days need an International Driver's Permit (☞ Car Travel *in* Smart Travel Tips).

Driving is on the right. Speed limits are 30 kph (19 mph) in built-up areas, 50 kph (31 mph) within city limits, 80 kph (50 mph) on main roads, and 100 kph (60 mph) on multilane highways. Driving after drinking any amount of alcohol is prohibited. Although the law calls for the issuance of tickets for traffic violations, locals often settle with a negotiated payment on the spot. However, you should avoid this practice and instead accept a ticket. Vehicle spot checks are frequent, but police are generally courteous to foreigners. Road signs are the same as in Western Europe. If asking for directions, refer to major cities or towns along a road rather than the road's official number. At unmarked intersections, traffic coming from the right has priority. For further driving information, contact A.C.R. (Romanian Auto Club).

➤ CONTACT: **A.C.R.** (Romanian Auto Club; ✉ Str. Tache Ionescu 27, Bucharest, ☎ 021/252–7923; 9271 in Bucharest).

CUSTOMS AND DUTIES
ON ARRIVAL
Foreigners' bags are seldom examined. By law, you may bring in a personal computer and printer, two cameras, 10 rolls of film, one video camera and VCR, 10 videocassette tapes, a typewriter, binoculars, a tape recorder, a bicycle, a child's stroller, 200 cigarettes, 2 liters of liquor, and 4 liters of wine or beer. If you declare electronic goods on entry, they must be taken out on departure.

ON DEPARTURE
There is no departure tax. You may be asked to show receipts for artwork or antiques.

EMERGENCIES
➤ CONTACTS: **Ambulance** (☎ 961). **Police** (☎ 955).

HOLIDAYS
January 1–2; Orthodox Easter Sunday and Monday (movable holiday in March or April); May 1 (Labor Day); December 1 (National Day); December 25–26.

LANGUAGE
Romanian is a Latin-based language similar to Italian. If you speak another Latinate language you may be able to understand quite a bit of Romanian. Most Romanians speak at least one foreign language; French is the most common, though young people favor English.

MAIL AND SHIPPING
A letter to the United States or Canada costs around 80¢; a postcard costs 73¢. Within Europe, the postcard rate is 42¢.

Have mail sent to your hotel. Airmail generally takes 7 to 10 days from the United States and Canada. For quicker delivery and tracking of materials, contact DHL International or UPS.

Post offices display a postal horn symbol and the word *Poştă.* Internet cafés are easily found in cities. Rates average 60¢ per hour, but computers are slow. Note that "café" does not always mean beverages are available.

➤ POST OFFICE: **Main Bucharest post office** (✉ Str. Matei Milo 10, ☎ 021/315–9030).

➤ OVERNIGHT SERVICES: **DHL International** (☎ 021/222–1771). **UPS** (☎ 021/410–0604).

MONEY MATTERS
Inflation remains a problem, and prices (in *lei,* not the foreign currency equivalent) rise frequently. Because entry fees change frequently to match

inflation, the prices throughout this chapter are given in the more stable U.S. dollar equivalents.

Although the cost of luxury hotels, top restaurants, gas, and rental cars can be as high as in Western Europe, you can travel both comfortably and inexpensively in Romania. Imported items are seldom a bargain, but well-made handicrafts definitely are.

ATMs are available in major cities.

The following are sample costs: a taxi ride in Bucharest, 15¢ initial fee plus 15¢ per km (½ mi); Bucharest Metro, 18¢ per trip; cup of coffee, 20¢; meal in a nice restaurant, $5; bottle of Romanian beer, 45¢; bottle of Romanian wine in a restaurant, $3, in a store, $1.45; 2-liter bottle of mineral water, 55¢; one-hour Internet use in an Internet café, 60¢; museum entry, 30¢–$1.85; theater ticket, 65¢–$4.95; gallon of gasoline, $2.20.

CREDIT CARDS

Credit cards are accepted in most hotels and better restaurants in cities accustomed to tourists and business travelers, but do not count on their universal acceptance, especially in more rural areas.

CURRENCY

The unit of currency is the *leu* (plural *lei*). It is circulated in denominations of 2,000-, 10,000-, 50,000-, 100,000-, and 500,000-lei notes and 500-, 1,000-, and 5,000-lei coins. At this writing, the official exchange rate was 33,200 lei to the U.S. dollar, 21,000 lei to the Canadian dollar, 51,158 lei to the pound sterling, and 32,318 lei to the euro.

Exchange rates are highest at the *casa de schimb valutar* (exchange bureaus). Rates are posted outside; make sure you're reading *cumpărare* (buying) rates. Most do not charge commission. Keep receipts to change money back on departure. Never change money on the street, as you're likely to be cheated.

Tips in dollars are accepted everywhere. Some hotels and taxi drivers will accept payment in major foreign currencies. Payment must be made in lei for train and bus fares, admission to tourist sites and entertainment, goods in most stores, and bills in many hotels and restaurants.

TRAVELER'S CHECKS

Traveler's checks are accepted only at banks, major hotels in large cities, and selected exchange shops. Banks charge between 1% and 5% commission. The American Express representative in Bucharest is Marshal Turism. This firm can issue checks and replace lost ones, but will not cash checks.

➤ CONTACT: **Marshal Turism** (✉ B-dul. Magheru 43, ☎ 021/223–1204).

PASSPORTS AND VISAS

Citizens of the United States, Canada, and European Union countries need only a valid passport to enter Romania for up to 30 days. Citizens of Australia and New Zealand must obtain visas, but no photos or applications are required. The cost is equivalent to $25 plus a $6 "consular tax." Those on organized tours pay only $1 with proof of prior payment for services.

SAFETY

Violent crime against tourists is virtually unheard of, but in cities and on buses and trains, be alert for pickpockets and scams and do not allow yourself to become distracted. Bucharest has many stray dogs; ignore them and they will ignore you.

Beware of hustlers at the railroad station claiming (falsely) to represent hostels. They will often offer to make a reservation for you at well-known hostels via cell phone, but only on condition that you pay the first night's fee up front. They then send you off on your own to the real hostel, which will turn out to have no affiliation with the hustlers and will have received neither a reservation for you nor the first night's fee.

TELEPHONES
The country code for Romania is 40. Dial "02" before regional area codes when calling from within Romania. It's not necessary to include the area code when dialing within that zone.

DIRECTORY AND OPERATOR ASSISTANCE
Dial 931 for directory assistance. For assistance in a region other than the one from which you are calling, dial 0 + the area code + 931. Not all operators speak English. For international information, dial 971.

INTERNATIONAL CALLS
Direct-dial international calls can be made from most hotels and orange public phones found all over the country; a phone card is necessary for public phones. To place long-distance calls out of Romania, dial "00," then the country code and number. If you have service with AT&T, MCI, or Sprint, you can place a call by dialing the access numbers below.
➤ ACCESS CODES: **AT&T** (☎ 021/800–4288). **MCI** (☎ 021/800–1800). **Sprint** (☎ 021/800–0877).

LOCAL CALLS
To make a long-distance call within the country, simply dial the area code and number.

Orange public phones require a phone card (*cartela telefonică*), which can be purchased at post offices, telephone companies, and many stationery stores. Phone cards come in values of 50,000, 100,000, or 200,000 lei.

MOBILE PHONES
It's possible to rent mobile phones at Otopeni Airport. The mobile phone prefixes—0740, 0744–45, 0721–23, 0766, and 0788—must be used regardless of the calling area.

TIPPING
Tipping has become the norm for many services, although outside cities and tourist areas, it is not always expected. Figure 5%–10% of restaurant bills and the same in bars if you're occupying a table. For airport and train station porters, the equivalent of $2 is appropriate unless you have a lot of bags. Rounding up the taxi fare is adequate. For hotel bellhops, the equivalent of $1 is fine if the bellhop simply escorts you to the room; $2 is better if the bellhop helps with baggage.

TOURS
See Bucharest Essentials and Constanţa Essentials, *above,* for travel agencies that can arrange tours.

TRAIN TRAVEL
International trains connect Bucharest to Budapest, Bratislava, Istanbul, Prague, Sofia, Vienna, and Warsaw.

Romanian Railways (CFR) operates *Inter-City, rapid, accelerat,* and the slow-moving *persoane* trains. Tickets are sold at stations one hour before departure. It's best to reserve a seat in advance; this must be done at a train agency. If your seat is occupied, speak up; the person probably has upgraded himself.

Trains are inexpensive, so opting for first class is a good choice. First-class compartments are clean and reasonably comfortable, but toilets are filthy. For night travel, consider booking a *cuşeta*, with bunk beds, or a roomier *vàgon de dormit* (sleeper car).

CUTTING COSTS

Rail Europe's Balkan Flexipass covers 5, 10, or 15 days of travel within a 15-day period, at a cost of $152, $264, or $317, respectively. Travelers under 26 pay $90, $156, or $190, while those 60 and over pay $121, $210, or $253. The pass is valid in Romania and six nearby countries. The Romanian Pass offers 3 days of unlimited travel within a 15-day period for $80. Keep in mind, however, that Romanian rail prices are quite low, so it may not be worth purchasing these passes if you plan on traveling solely within Romania.

➤ INFORMATION AND PASSES: **Rail Europe** (✉ 500 Mamaroneck Ave., Harrison, NY 10528, ☎ 914/682–5172 or 800/438–7245, FAX 800/432–1329; ✉ 2087 Dundas E, Suite 106, Mississauga, Ontario L4X 1M2, ☎ 800/361–7245, FAX 905/602–4198, WEB www.raileurope.com).

VISITOR INFORMATION

The Romanian Tourist Office in your home country can supply maps, brochures, and good information (☞ Visitor Information *in* Smart Travel Tips). Once you arrive in Romania, local travel agencies can help with excursions, hotels, and restaurants. Your hotel is another good source for dining and entertainment suggestions.

8 SLOVAKIA

More than seven decades of common statehood with the Czechs (which ended in 1992) was just a part of the history of the people living from the Tatra Mountains to the Danube River. Slovensko (Slovakia) differs from the Czech Republic in many aspects. Its folklore and traditions—still evident today—are distinct. Its mountains are higher and more rugged, its pleasures are more grounded in the countryside. Observers of the two regions like to link the Czech Republic geographically and culturally with the Germans, while they put Slovakia with the hospitality-loving Ukrainians, firmly in the east. This is a simplification, yet it contains a bit of truth.

By Mark Baker

Updated by
Lisa Dunford
and Saša
Petriskova

SLOVAKIA BECAME AN INDEPENDENT STATE on January 1, 1993, when Czechoslovakia—what is today Slovakia and the Czech Republic—ceased to exist. Except for a brief period during World War II when Slovakia was an independent state under Nazi control, the Czechs and Slovaks had been politically united since the fall of the Austro-Hungarian Empire in 1918. But when 1989's Velvet Revolution ended Communist rule in Czechoslovakia, politicians were quick to exploit it. Slovak nationalist parties won a bit more than 50% of the vote in the crucial 1992 Czechoslovak elections, and once the results were in, the split was decided. Although they speak a language closely related to Czech, the Slovaks had managed to maintain a strong sense of national identity throughout their common statehood. In the end, it was the Slovaks' very different history that split them from the Czechs, and it's this history that makes Slovakia a unique travel destination.

Part of the Great Moravian Empire in the 9th century, the Slovaks were conquered a century later by the Magyars and remained under Hungarian and Hapsburg rule. Following the Tartar invasions in the 13th century, many Saxons were invited to resettle the land and develop the economy, including the region's rich mineral resources. During the 15th and 16th centuries, Romanian shepherds migrated from Walachia through the Carpathian Mountains into Slovakia, and the merging of these varied groups with the resident Slavs bequeathed to the region a rich folk culture and some unique forms of architecture, especially in the east.

Medieval old towns, neatly renovated and filled with color, still exist in Slovakia today, but Communist-era concrete housing projects tend to dominate the towns. In recent years, some of the old gray panel apartment houses have been given lively new facades and crowned with green shrubs; and a crop of new shopping malls and megamarts has sprung up.

Although there is a growing income disparity, you can't tell it by the people on the streets. The Slovaks have leapt from their Communist central-planning past to the global information age, latching onto mobile communication. The number of mobile phones per capita has nearly caught up with Western levels. Slovaks adore the Internet, too, and cybercafés have popped up across the big cities. A fast-growing network of ATMs has brought a bank machine to every small town.

Slovakia lies to the east of the Czech Republic and is about one-third as large as its neighbor. Most visitors to Slovakia head first for the great peaks of the Vysoké Tatry (High Tatras), where there is an ample tourist infrastructure, catering especially to hikers and skiers. People who come to admire the peaks, however, often overlook the exquisite medieval towns of Spiš in the plains and valleys below the High Tatras, and the beautiful 18th-century country churches farther east. (Removed from main centers, these areas are short on tourist amenities. If creature comforts are important to you, stick to the High Tatras.)

Forty years of Communism left a clear mark on Slovakia's capital, Bratislava, in the form of hulking concrete structures. But though buildings that were torn down cannot be replaced, there's a new life in the old city. Through renovation, the Starý mesto (Old Town) has managed to recapture much of its lost charm.

Pleasures and Pastimes

Bicycling

The flatter areas to the south and east of Bratislava and along the Danube are ideal for biking. A bike trail links Bratislava and Vienna, paralleling the Danube for much of its 40-km (25-mi) length. For the more adventurous bikers, the Nízke Tatry (Low Tatras) have scenic biking trails along the small, secluded rivers surrounding Banská Bystrica. Not many places rent bikes, however. For rental information, inquire at a tourist information center or at your hotel.

Dining

Slovakia's food is an amalgam of its neighbors' cuisines. As in Bohemia and Moravia, the emphasis is on meat, particularly pork and beef. But the Slovaks, revealing their long link to Hungary, prefer to spice things up a bit, usually with paprika and red peppers. Roast potatoes or french fries are often served, although occasionally you'll find a side dish of tasty *halušky* (dumplings similar to Italian gnocchi or German spaetzle) on the menu. *Bryndzové halušky*, the country's unofficial national dish, is a tasty and filling mix of halušky, soft sheep's cheese, and a little bacon crumbled on top for flavor. Vegetarians don't have many options, though vegetable salads are normally available. For dessert, the emphasis comes from Vienna: crepes, poppy-seed tortes, and strudel.

Slovaks don't eat out often, particularly since prices have risen markedly in the past few years. As a result, restaurants often cater to foreigners or a business clientele. *Vináreň* (wine bars) specialize in serving wines along with hearty food. Red wines in particular complement the country's cooking; look for *Frankovka*, which is light and slightly acidic. *Vavrinecké* is dark and semisweet and stands up well to red meats.

Many restaurants put out a special luncheon menu (*ponuka dňa* or *špecialita šéfkuchára*). Dinner is usually served from 5 until 9 or 10, but cooks frequently knock off early on slow nights.

CATEGORY	COST*
$$$$	over 350 Sk
$$$	250 Sk–350 Sk
$$	150 Sk–250 Sk
$	under 150 Sk

per person for an entrée

Fishing

There are hundreds of lakes and rivers suitable for fishing, often amid striking scenery. Demänovská dolina, a valley near Liptovský Mikuláš in central Slovakia, has some excellent places to catch trout. Bring your own tackle or be prepared to buy it locally, because rental equipment is scarce. To cast a line legally, you must have a fishing license (valid for one year) plus a fishing permit (valid for a day, week, month, or year for the particular body of water you plan to fish). Satur (Slovakia's national travel agency) offices sell fishing licenses.

Hiking

Slovakia is great for hiking. More than 20,000 km (12,500 mi) of marked trails thread through the mountainous regions and the agricultural countryside. Colored slashes on trees, fences, walls, rocks, and elsewhere mark trails that correspond to the paths shown on the large-scale Súbor turistických maps, which are available at many bookstores and tobacco shops. The best areas for ambitious mountain walkers are the Low Tatras in the center of the country near Banská Bystrica and the High Tatras to the north. Slovenský raj (Slovak Paradise), in eastern Slovakia, has many waterfalls, caves, and cliffs. An ingenious system of ladders and catwalks makes it possible to see the wild beauty up close.

Lodging

Large hotels outside of Bratislava can be somewhat institutional—gray concrete block buildings with drab furnishings. With a little hunting, it's possible to find accommodation in historic buildings that date as far back as the 16th century; the decor and the conveniences are usually modern. Other options are private rooms in homes and apartments, which provide an up-close cultural experience; these can be booked through a town's information center or at a Satur travel agency branch.

Slovakia is a bargain by Western standards, particularly in the outlying areas. In Bratislava, however, hotel rates often meet or exceed U.S. and Western European averages. And during festivals and holidays, including Christmas and Easter, hotel rates may increase by 15%–25%. Few hotels outside of Bratislava have air-conditioning, but it's not really necessary, especially in the mountains.

CATEGORY	COST*
$$$$	over 4,600 Sk
$$$	2,300 Sk–4,600 Sk
$$	1,100 Sk–2,300 Sk
$	under 1000 Sk

All prices are for a standard double room, including tax and service.

Shopping

The most interesting finds in Slovakia are colorful ceramic pottery (with the colors representing the region of origin), woven textiles, batik-painted Easter eggs, corn-husk dolls, and hand-knit sweaters. These folk-art products are sold from booths in town squares (especially around Christmas), at ÚĽUV shops, and folk-art stores in most major towns. Several Dielo stores sell paintings, wooden toys, great ceramic pieces by Slovak artists, and Slovak folk or classical music at very reasonable prices.

Skiing

Slovakia has some of the region's best downhill skiing, good for both amateurs and experts. The two main skiing areas are the Low Tatras and the High Tatras. The High Tatras have good snow throughout the winter; superior slopes, ski tows, and chairlifts; and places where you can rent equipment. You'll find less rental equipment and fewer ski shops in the Low Tatras. Lifts in both regions generally operate from January through March, though cross-country skiing is a popular alternative.

Exploring Slovakia

Slovakia can best be divided into four regions of interest: Bratislava, central Slovakia, the High Tatras, and eastern Slovakia. Despite being the capital, Bratislava, in the western part of the country, is probably the least alluring destination. The country's true beauty lies among the peaks of the High Tatras in the northern part of central Slovakia.

Great Itineraries

Although Slovakia is relatively small, it's difficult to explore in a short period of time without a car because trains are so slow. Driving from Bratislava to the Tatras will take you a minimum of four hours; the train ride will last at least eight hours, with one connection.

Numbers in the text correspond to numbers in the margin and on the Slovakia and Bratislava maps.

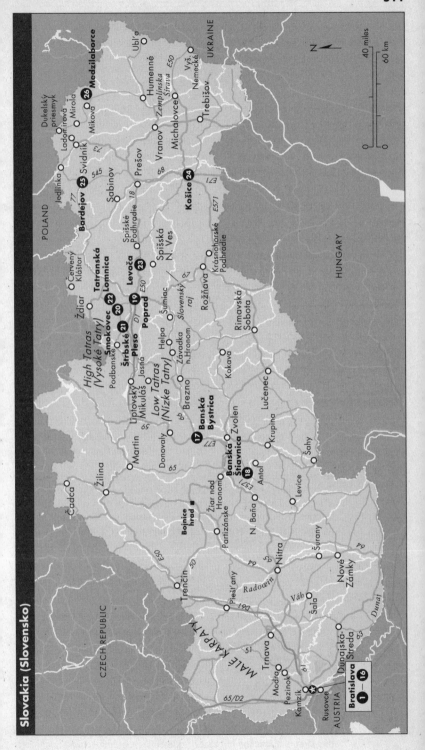

Slovakia (Slovensko)

If you only have a few days to see Slovakia, spend some hours walking through the historic Old Town in ⊡ **Bratislava** ①–⑯ and stop overnight here before heading to the **High Tatras.** Once you get to the mountains, settle down for two nights in a comfortable hotel or a pension in one of the resort towns. ⊡ **Smokovec** ⑳ and ⊡ **Tatranská Lomnica** ㉒ are probably the most convenient places from which to explore the area and go hiking in summer or skiing in winter.

Follow the three-day itinerary above and then take an excursion 45 minutes south of the Tatras to the beautiful old Spiš town of ⊡ **Levoča** ㉓. Spend the night; from here you can also explore the largest castle in Slovakia, Spišský hrad, and the caves and gorges in the area. The following day, head south toward ⊡ **Košice** ㉔, the capital of the Spiš region, to take in some of the historic sights of the Old Town. From Košice, you can fly back to Bratislava or take a direct day or night train to Bratislava or Prague.

When to Tour

The High Tatras are loveliest from January through March. The summer months in the mountains attract mostly hikers. Because of the snow, many hiking trails, especially those that cross the peaks, are open only between June and October. Temperatures are always much cooler in the mountains; even in summer, bring a sweater or jacket.

Bratislava is at its best in the temperate months of spring and autumn. July and August, though not especially crowded, can be unbearably hot, while winter can bring a great deal of snow and rain.

BRATISLAVA

Bratislava's Starý mesto (Old Town), on the bank of the Danube, is sporting a bright new coat of paint these days, and many of its buildings have been renovated to former glory. In the pedestrian zone, whimsical bronze statues are frozen walking arm and arm down the street or popping out of imaginary manholes. But though the Old Town is charming, you may get a bit of a sinking feeling when you first enter Bratislava—or "Blava" as its residents affectionately call it—from Vienna. The Communists' blind faith in modernity is evident in the numerous gray concrete high-rise housing projects on the other bank of the Danube and in the Nový most (New Bridge), which resembles a UFO set on sticks.

The jumble of modern Bratislava, however, masks a long and regal history that rivals Prague's in importance and complexity. Settled by Celts and Romans, the city became part of the Great Moravian Empire around the year 860 under Prince Rastislav. After a short period under the Bohemian Přemysl princes, Bratislava was brought into the Hungarian kingdom by Stephen I at the end of the 10th century and given royal privileges in 1217. Following the Tartar invasion in 1241, when many residents were killed, the Hungarian kings brought in German colonists to repopulate the town and ensure a non-Slovak majority. The Hungarians called the town Pozsony, the German settlers called it Pressburg, and the original Slovaks called it Bratislava.

When Pest and Buda were occupied by the Turks in the first half of the 16th century, the Hungarian kings moved their seat to Bratislava, which remained the Hungarian capital until 1784 and the coronation center until 1835. At this time, with a population of almost 27,000, it was the largest Hungarian city. Only in 1919, when Bratislava became part of the first Czechoslovak republic, did the city regain its Slovak identity. In 1939, with Germany's assistance, Bratislava infamously exerted its yearnings for independence by becoming the capital of the puppet Slovak state, under the controversial Fascist leader Jozef Tiso. In 1945, it became the provincial capital of Slovakia, still straining under the powerful hand of Prague (Slovakia's German and Hungarian minorities were either expelled or repressed). Leading-up to the 1989 revolution, Bratislava was the site of numerous anti-Communist demonstrations; many of these were carried out by supporters of the Catholic Church, long repressed by the regime then in power. Following the Velvet Revolution in 1989, Bratislava gained importance as the capital of the Slovak Republic within the new Czech and Slovak federal state, but rivalries with Prague persisted. It was only following the breakup of Czechoslovakia on January 1, 1993, that the city once again became a capital in its own right.

Exploring Bratislava

To discover Bratislava's charms, travel the city by foot. Imagination is also helpful, as a few of the Old Town's oldest streets are under ongoing reconstruction.

Numbers in the text correspond to numbers in the margin and on the Bratislava map.

A Good Walk

Start your walk at Hurbanovo námestie (Hurbanovo Square), where you can see **Kostol svätej Trojice** ①. Between a shoe store and a café on a passageway leading off Hurbanovo námestie is Michalská ulica, a romantically crumbling entrance to the Old Town. After crossing a statue-lined bridge running through the first archway, you come to the narrow promenade. In front of you is **Michalská brána** ②. Walk through this gate and stroll down Michalská ulica, which is lined with shops and eating and drinking establishments. A few of the buildings along the street are still undergoing ongoing renovations, but notice the eerie blue Kaplnka svätej Kataríny (Chapel of St. Catherine) at No. 6 on the left, built in 1311 but now graced with a sober classical facade. Opposite, at No. 7, is the Renaissance Segnerova kúria (Segner House), built for a wealthy merchant in 1648. Farther down on the right is the Palác Uhorskej kráľovskej komory (Hungarian Royal Chamber), a Baroque palace that housed the Hungarian nobles' parliament from 1802 until 1848 and is now the University Library. Walk through the arched passageway at the back of the building; you'll emerge in a tiny square dominated by the 14th-century **Kostol Klarisiek** ③, which is now the Slovak Pedagogical Library.

Follow Farská ulica southwest to the corner and turn left onto Kapitulská ulica (notice the paving stone depicting two kissing lizards). Ahead of you is the side wall of the **Dóm svätého Martina** ④, one of the more impressive churches in the city.

Next to the church is the freeway leading to the futuristic spaceship bridge, **Nový most** ⑤, formerly called Most SNP (Bridge of the Slovak National Uprising). When the freeway was built, a row of old houses and a synagogue in the former Jewish quarter outside the city walls were destroyed. The only good thing to be said for the road is that its construction led to the discovery of remnants of the city's original walls, which have been partially restored and now line the freeway on the right.

Walk to the right under the freeway (a bus terminus is on your left side) and up a set of stairs on your right. At the top turn left and climb up

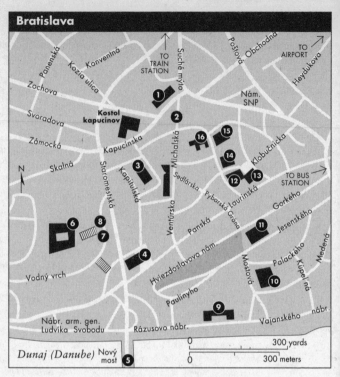

more steps through a Gothic arched gateway built in 1480 to the walled area of **Bratislavsky hrad** ⑥. From the top, on a clear day, you can see over to Austria to the right. After exploring the castle, descend by the same route, but instead of climbing the last stairs by the Arkadia restaurant, continue down Beblavého ulica.

At the bottom of the street on the right stands the **Múzeum umeleckých remesiel** ⑦. Next, go around onto Židovská ulica—the street name (Jews' Street) recalls that this area was the Jewish ghetto—where you can visit the **Múzeum židovskej kultúry** ⑧ in a Renaissance mansion.

Walk south down Starométska and then retrace your steps back under the highway; turn immediately right and continue to Rázusovo nábrežie on the banks of the Danube. To the left are Baroque barracks that were transformed by the Communists to house the modern **Slovenská národná galéria** ⑨, which displays a collection of past and present works by Slovak artists.

Turn left onto Mostová ulica; at the corner of Palackého ulica is the ornate **Reduta** ⑩, home to the Slovak Philharmonic Orchestra. Continue straight (north on Mostová ulica) past Hviezdoslavovo námestie, where to the right and accented by a fountain is the **Slovenské národné divadlo** ⑪, Bratislava's opera house. Cross the square and walk straight (northwest) on Rybárska brana, which leads to the cafés and the artist booths of Hlavné námestie. The square is lined with old houses and palaces representing a spectrum of architectural styles, from Gothic (No. 2), baroque (No. 4), and rococo (No. 7) to a wonderfully decorative example of Art Nouveau at No. 10. To the right as you come into the square from Rybárska brana is the colorful agglomeration of old bits and pieces of structures that make up the **Stará radnica** ⑫. Behind the Stará radnica is Primaciálne námestie, or Primates' Square, dominated by the glorious pale-pink **Primaciálny palác** ⑬. Next to the Stará radnica and museum is the richly decorated **Jezuitský kostol** ⑭.

North past the Jezuitský kostol on Františkánske nám on the right is the **Františkánsky kostol** ⑮. Across from the church is the beautifully detailed rococo **Mirbachov palác** ⑯, which today houses the Municipal Gallery. A quick left on Zámočka and a few more steps will bring you back to your starting point.

TIMING

If you get an early morning start, you can complete a leisurely walking tour of the Old Town in a day. With the exception of the Slovenská národná galéria, which deserves some time, most of the museums are small and won't detain you long. Avoid touring on Monday, as many sights are closed.

Sights to See

❻ **Bratislavsky hrad** (Bratislava castle). Bratislava's castle has been continually rebuilt since its foundations were laid in the 9th century. The Hungarian kings expanded it into a large royal residence, and the Hapsburgs further developed its fortifications, turning it into a very successful defense against the Turks. The existing castle had to be completely rebuilt after a disastrous fire in 1811. Inside is the **Slovenské národné múzeum** (Slovak National Museum), which houses the most precious archaeological finds from across the country in addition to exhibits on furniture, crafts, folklore costumes, and minting. Check out the *fujura*, a shepherd's long horn, in the music exhibit. ✉ *Zámocká ul., Starý mesto,* ☎ *02/5934–1626.* 🎫 *Castle and museum 40 Sk.* ☉ *Tues.–Sun. 9–5.*

Danubiana. Reminiscent of a Roman galley stuck in the shallows, this modern-art museum sits on the tip of a peninsula that juts into the Danube. World-class exhibitions of sculpture and painting, fabulous views of the river from the café, and the interesting wares of the Artshop are all reasons to find this place on the map. Follow highway E75 6 km (4 mi) south toward Hungary or take Bus 91 from under the Nový most. ✉ *Vodné dielo, Čunovo,* ☎ *090/360–5505,* WEB *www.danubiana.sk.* 🎫 *60 Sk.* ☉ *May–Sept., daily 10–8; Oct.–Apr., daily 10–6.*

❹ **Dóm svätého Martina** (St. Martin's Cathedral). This massive Gothic church, consecrated in 1452, hosted the coronations of 17 Hungarian royals between the 16th and 19th centuries. Numerous additions made over the centuries were removed in the 19th century, when the church was re-Gothicized. Nowadays, the three equal-size naves give an impression of space and light. ✉ *Rudnayovo nám., Starý mesto,* ☎ *02/5443–1359.* ☉ *Weekdays 10–11:30 and 2–6, Sat. 10–noon, Sun. 2–4:30.*

⑮ **Františkánsky kostol** (Franciscan Church). In this 13th-century church, only the presbytery is still in early Gothic style. The rest was destroyed in an earthquake in the 17th century and rebuilt in a mixture of Baroque and Gothic. Just around the corner, built onto the church, is another quite different and much more stunning Gothic building, the 14th-century **Kaplnka svätého Jána Evangelistu** (Chapel of St. John the Evangelist). Art historians believe that Peter Parler, architect of Prague's Charles Bridge, may have worked on this gem. You can take a look around before or after services (7 AM and 5 PM daily). ✉ *Františkánske nám. 1, Starý mesto,* ☎ *no phone.*

⑭ **Jezuitský kostol** (Jesuit Church). In 1636 Protestants constructed this church after being granted an imperial concession to build a place of worship on the strict condition that it have no tower. The Jesuits took over the towerless church in 1672 and, to compensate for its external simplicity, went wild with Baroque detailing on the inside. ⊠ *Kostolna 1, Starý mesto,* ☏ *no phone.*

❸ Kostol Klarisiek (Klariský Church). This 14th-century church is simple but inspiring, with a wonderfully peaceful early Gothic interior. The small High Gothic steeple was added in an unusually secondary position at the back of the church during the 15th century. As a mendicant order, the Poor Clares were forbidden to build a steeple atop the church, so they sidestepped the rules and built it against a side wall. The church is now a concert hall—and usually locked, but you may be able to get in for a concert or during rehearsals. ⊠ *Farská ul., Starý mesto,* ☏ *no phone.*

❶ Kostol svätej Trojice (Church of the Holy Trinity). The ceiling of this golden-yellow Baroque church has space-expanding frescoes, the work of Antonio Galli Bibiena from the early 18th century. ⊠ *Hurbanovo nám., Starý mesto,* ☏ *no phone.*

❷ Michalská brána (Michael's Gate). The last remaining of the city's three gates was built in two stages. The bottom section of the gate retains its original Gothic design from the 14th century. The copper, onion-dome *veža* (tower) topped with a statue of St. Michael was added in the 18th century. The tower affords a good view over the Old Town, and inside is a display on ancient weapons and town fortifications. ⊠ *Michalská 24, Starý mesto,* ☏ *02/5443–3044.* ≊ *30 Sk.* ☉ *Wed.–Mon. 10–4:30.*

⓰ Mirbachov palác (Mirbach Palace). This rococo palace with original stucco plasterwork was built in 1770. Today it houses the **Municipal Gallery,** which has a small collection of 18th- and 19th-century Slovak and European art, as well as changing exhibits of modern art. ⊠ *Františkánske nám. 11, Starý mesto,* ☏ *02/5443–1556.* ≊ *40 Sk.* ☉ *Tues.–Sun. 10–5.*

❼ Múzeum umeleckých remesiel (Handicraft Museum). In a Baroque burgher house, this tiny museum displays a few nice works of art and crafts from the 12th to 18th century, including ceramics, silverware, and furniture. ⊠ *Beblavého 1, Starý mesto,* ☏ *02/5441–2784.* ≊ *40 Sk.* ☉ *Mon. and Wed.–Fri. 9:30–4:30, weekends 11–6.*

★ ❽ Múzeum židovskej kultúry (Museum of Jewish Culture in Slovakia). This small but stirring museum celebrates the history and culture of the Jews living in the territory of Slovakia since the Great Moravian Empire. There's a collection of religious objects from around the country, many from synagogues in eastern Slovakia. A section is devoted to Slovakia's 71,000 victims—out of a total Jewish population of 89,000—of the Holocaust. ⊠ *Židovská 17, Starý mesto,* ☏ *02/5441–8507.* ≊ *100 Sk.* ☉ *Sun.–Fri. 11–5.*

Námestie SNP (SNP Square). The square, formerly known as Stalinovo námestie (Stalin Square), was and still remains the center for demonstrations in Slovakia. It's the base from which hundreds of thousands of spectators celebrated independence and the new year on December 31, 1992. SNP stands for Slovenské národné povstanie (Slovak National Uprising), an anti-Nazi resistance movement. In the middle of the square are three larger-than-life statues: a dour partisan and two strong, sad women in peasant clothing.

❺ Nový most (New Bridge). Although it would make a splendid site for an alien flick—it's sometimes called the UFO bridge (pronounced *ooh-fo*)—this modern marvel is a bit of an eyesore for anyone who doesn't appreciate futuristic designs. The bridge is difficult to miss if you're anywhere near the Danube. For a charge of 10 Sk, speedy glass-face elevators take you to the top for views of the city, 262 ft above the Danube River; the elevator runs from 8 AM to 10 PM. Inside the spaceship are a fancy restaurant and a simple café.

NEED A BREAK? Have a coffee at the **Vyhliadková kaviareň** (⊠ Nový most, Petrzalka, ☎ 02/6241–2450) on top of the bridge. Be warned that during stronger winds the café will sway.

★ ⑬ **Primaciálny palác** (Primates' Palace). This pale pink palace is one of the most valuable architectural monuments in Bratislava. Don't miss the dazzling **Hall of Mirrors,** with its six 17th-century English tapestries depicting the legend of the lovers Hero and Leander. In this room, Napoléon and Hapsburg emperor Francis I signed the Bratislava Peace of 1805, following Napoléon's victory at the Battle of Austerlitz. In the revolutionary year of 1848, when the citizens of the Hapsburg lands revolted against the imperial dominance of Vienna, the rebel Hungarians had their headquarters in the palace. Ironically, following the failed uprising, the Hapsburg general Hainau signed the rebels' death sentences in the very same room. ⊠ *Primaciálne nám. 1, Starý mesto,* ☎ *02/5443–5151 or 02/5935–6166.* ☒ *30 Sk.* ☉ *Tues.–Sun. 10–5.*

⑩ **Reduta.** The neo-baroque Reduta, which dates to 1914, hosts the Slovak Philharmonic Orchestra. It's well worth attending a concert just to see the gilt elegance of the theater, which is closed to the public until one hour before a performance. Adjacent is a similarly ornate restaurant. ⊠ *Medená 3, Starý mesto,* ☎ *02/5443–3351 or 02/5443–3352,* WEB *www.filharm.sk.*

⑨ **Slovenská národná galéria** (Slovak National Gallery). A conspicuously modern restoration of old 18th-century barracks houses this gallery. The museum displays an interesting collection of Slovak Gothic, baroque, and contemporary art, along with a small number of European masters and changing exhibits. Guided tours are available in English. ⊠ *Rázusovo nábr. 2, Starý mesto,* ☎ *02/5443–2081.* ☒ *60 Sk.* ☉ *Tues.–Sun. 10–6.*

⑪ **Slovenské národné divadlo** (SND, Slovak National Theater). You can see performances of Bratislava's opera, ballet, and theater in this striking baroque building, which was constructed in the 1880s by the famous Central European architectural duo Hermann Helmer and Ferdinand Fellner. ⊠ *Hviezdoslavovo nám. 1, Starý mesto,* ☎ *02/ 5443–3890 or 02/5443–3764,* WEB *www.snd.sk.*

⑫ **Stará radnica** (Old Town Hall). One of the more interesting buildings in Bratislava, the Old Town Hall developed gradually over the 13th and 14th centuries out of a number of burghers' houses. During the summer brass bands play on a balcony atop the tower; other concerts are given in front of the building on Hlavné námestie in the summer and before Christmas, New Year's, and Easter. At night gentle music plays while a light show illuminates the building's façade. You can stop in the **Mestské múzeum** (City Museum) here and learn about Bratislava's storied past. ⊠ *Primaciálne nám. 3, Starý mesto,* ☎ *02/5443–5800.* ☒ *30 Sk.* ☉ *Tues.–Sun. 10–5.*

Dining

Prague may have its Slovak rival beat when it comes to architecture, but when it's time to eat, you can thank your lucky stars that you're in Bratislava. The long-shared history with Hungary gives Slovak cuisine an extra flavor that Czech cooking lacks. Geographic proximity to Vienna, moreover, has lent some grace and charm to the city's eateries. Prepare for shish kebabs, grilled meats, steaks, and pork dishes.

$$$–$$$$ ✕ **Slovenská restaurácia.** Paprika and cumin are just two of the traditionally Hungarian spices that jazz up the Slovak meals here. Try the Farmer's Specialty: a grilled pork chop and a smoked pork chop in garlic sauce. The attentive waiters dress in rustic rural folk fashion, and the chairs are hand-carved in traditional patterns. Evening meals are accompanied by piano music. ⊠ *Hviezdoslavovo nám. 20, Starý mesto,* ☎ *02/5443–0430. AE, MC, V.*

$$$–$$$$ ✕ **Traja Musketieri.** A swanky cellar restaurant and bar, Three Musketeers is usually overflowing with diplomats, expats, and trendy locals. The menu includes great salmon and trout dishes and a decent house red, all served by period-costume barmaids and stable boys. ⊠ *Sládkocicova 7, Starý mesto,* ☎ *02/5413–1026. AE, MC, V.*

$$–$$$ ✕ **Leberfinger.** Rumor has it that Napoléon stopped at this tavern on the Danube across from Old Town, near the New Bridge. The 50-item menu highlights traditional Slovak cuisine and includes vegetarian dishes, such as the oddly named *hájnikov tanier* (gamekeeper's dish), a potato pancake filled with vegetables, mushrooms, and cheese. Sit indoors beneath murals of old Bratislava, downstairs in a cellar pub, or outside on a patio with a river view. The place is kid-friendly, which is rare in restaurants here. ⊠ *Viedenská cesta 257, Petrzalka,* ☎ *02/6231–7590. MC, V.*

$$–$$$ ✕ **Rybársky cech.** The name means "Fisherman's Guild," and fish is the unchallenged specialty at this refined but comfortable eatery on a quiet street by the Danube. Fresh-water fish is served upstairs, with pricier saltwater varieties available on the ground floor. ⊠ *Žižkova 1, Starý mesto,* ☎ *02/5441–3049. AE, DC, MC, V.*

$$ ✕ **Modrá hviezda.** Candlelight flickers on the barrel-vaulted ceilings of this intimate family-owned wine cellar in the side of the castle hill. Mama's specialty (beef medallions with a cream sauce and lingonberries) is a tasty menu choice that goes well with the *krokety* (fried potato croquettes). ⊠ *Beblavého 14, Starý mesto,* ☎ *02/5443–2747. No credit cards. Closed Sun.*

$$ ✕ **Riviéra.** Locals come here for the Bohemian brews on tap, a leftover from the previous pub on this site, but Riviéra also has an extensive selection of grilled fish and meat dishes. And don't miss the fried onions. In summer you can dine outdoors. The restaurant is a 10-minute drive west of town, along the Danube on the way to Devín castle. ⊠ *Karloveska 132, Karlova ves,* ☎ *02/654–2740. AE, MC, V.*

Lodging

The opening of the Radisson SAS Carlton Hotel in the fall of 2001 raised the lodging standard in Bratislava considerably, challenging other upscale hotels to increase their levels of service and luxury. The room price of hotels in the Old Town is disproportionately higher than the cost of accommodation in the rest of the country. To beat the costs—and have a cultural experience to boot—you can arrange to rent a room in a private house, or a whole apartment through a travel agent. Bratislavská informačná služba (☞ Visitor Information *in* Bratislava Essentials, *below*) can help with hotel reservations.

$$$$ 🏨 **Hotel Danube.** The design of this French-run hotel on the banks of the Danube echoes the river in its flowing shape and blue accents. Pastels decorate the modern rooms, and the gleaming public areas are everything you'd expect from an international hotel chain. ⊠ *Rybné nám. 1, Starý mesto, 81102,* ☎ *02/5934–0000,* ⅎ⅍ *02/5441–4311,* 🕸

www.hoteldanube.com. 264 rooms, 4 apartments, 12 suites. 2 restaurants, minibars, cable TV with movies, pool, health club, sauna, nightclub, business services, convention center; no-smoking rooms. AE, DC, MC, V.

$$$$ 🏨 **Perugia.** This pink postmodern jewel is in a renovated building in the center of the pedestrian zone of the Old Town (taxis can get you here, but it's best not to have a car). The clean, colorful rooms open onto an interior courtyard with a large skylight. This is Bratislava's closest thing to a boutique hotel. ✉ *Zelená 5, Starý mesto, 81101,* ☎ *02/5443–0719,* FAX *02/5443–1821,* WEB *www.perugia.sk. 13 rooms, 1 suite. Restaurant, café, room service, cable TV, minibars, laundry services, business services. AE, DC, MC, V.*

$$$$ 🏨 **Radisson SAS Carlton Hotel.** Millions of dollars went into the renovation of this 1837 landmark property—and it shows. Everything about this place screams luxury, from the bar with gilt mirrors and mahogany furniture to the three-peppercorn fillet in the restaurant, Brasserie at the Opera. Rrooms are traditional, with antique reproductions, plush carpeting, and muted tones, or modern, with blues and reds, and bold furniture. ✉ *Hviezdoslavovo nám. 3, Starý mesto, 81102,* ☎ *02/5939–0000,* FAX *02/5939–0010,* WEB *www. radissonsas.com. 163 rooms, 5 suites. Restaurants, room service, inroom safes, minibars, cable TV with movies and video games, health club, sauna, bar, laundry services, convention center; no-smoking floors. AE, DC, MC, V.*

$$$–$$$$ 🏨 **Hotel Pension No. 16.** This cozy pension in a quiet residential haven ★ a short drive from the castle is a nice alternative to the big chain hotels—it provides all the conveniences, but with character. The rooms are inviting, with wooden floors and ceilings. The apartments, which have kitchenettes, are a good deal for families. Breakfast is included. ✉ *Partizánska 16A, Palisady, 81103,* ☎ *02/5441–1672,* FAX *02/5441– 1298,* WEB *www.internet.sk/hotelno16. 11 rooms, 5 apartments. Some kitchenettes. AE, MC, V.*

$$$ 🏨 **Hotel Kamila.** A family-friendly (and car-necessary) place, Hotel Kamila has numerous outdoor activities away from the hubbub of the central city. Take a golf or a horseback-riding lesson before a dip in the pool or a massage. The Slovak actress Kamila Magálová owns this 18th-century château. Rooms reflect her taste, which runs toward light wood and bold patterns. The restaurant serves French and German dishes. The hotel lies about 14 km (9 mi) from the Old Town, beyond the airport. A shuttle is available to and from the Bratislava or Vienna airport. ✉ *Cierna voda 611, Vajnory, 82108,* ☎ *02/4594–3611,* FAX *02/4594–3631,* WEB *www.kamila.sk. 21 rooms, 4 apartments. Restaurant, room service, tennis court, pool, driving range, gym, massage, sauna, spa, bicycles, archery, horseback riding, wine bar, babysitting, Internet, business services, airport shuttle. MC, V.*

Nightlife and the Arts

Bratislava does not have a roaring bar and nightclub scene, but you can definitely find a place to settle in for a few drinks and even a little music. The pedestrian area of the Old Town is full of cafés and pubs, many with outdoor seating in warm weather. Bratislava hosts an annual jazz festival in October that attracts international talent. In addition, the city has many concerts, dance performances, and operettas to choose from—at reasonable prices (at most 800 Sk).

The English-language *Slovak Spectator* (www.slovakspectator.sk), a Bratislava-based weekly newspaper, is a good place to check for weekly listings on the city's cultural life. *Kam v Bratislave* has a complete list of the month's performances, with the most important information translated into English. The papers are available at many newsstands, chain hotels, and bookstores.

For performance tickets, contact Bratislavská informačná služba or Satur (☞ Visitor Information *in* Bratislava Essentials, *below*) or buy them directly from the venue.

The Arts
CONCERTS

The **Slovenská filharmónia** (Slovak Philharmonic Orchestra; ✉ Medená 3, Starý mesto, ☎ 02/5443–3351 or 02/5443–3352, WEB www.filharm.sk) plays a full program of Slovak and Czech composers as well as European masters at its home in the Reduta. You can purchase tickets at the theater box office, which is open weekdays 1–5 and one hour before performances.

SLUK (✉ Balkanska 31, Rusovce, ☎ 02/6285–9125), a folk ensemble, performs Slovak music and dance. Folk traditions from all over Slovakia are represented in unique arrangements.

FILM

Most new releases are screened in their original language with Slovak subtitles. **Charlie centrum** (✉ Špitálska 4, Starý mesto, ☎ 02/5296–3430) regularly shows American classics, in English, in a friendly, artsy environment with four screens.

OPERA AND BALLET

The **Slovenské národné divadlo** (Slovak National Theater; ✉ Hviezdoslavovo nám. 1, Starý mesto, ☎ 02/5443–3890 or 02/5443–3771, WEB www.snd.sk) is the place for high-quality opera, operettas, and ballet. Buy tickets at the theater office on the corner of Jesenského and Komenského weekdays between noon and 6 or 30 minutes before show time. Tickets may be purchased a month in advance.

THEATER

Traditional theater is usually performed in Slovak. Milan Sladek Mime Theater stages world-class performances at the **Divadlo Arena** (✉ Viedenská cesta 10, Petrzalka, ☎ 02/6225–0013 or 02/6224–6875). You can buy tickets at the theater Tuesday–Friday 3–6 and starting one hour before performances.

Nightlife
JAZZ CLUBS

The tiny **Jazz Cafe** (✉ Ventúrska 5, Starý mesto, ☎ 02/5443–4661) is one of the few jazz clubs in Bratislava.Peter Lipa, a Slovak jazz singer and organizer of the jazz festival, realized a long-time dream when he opened the **Metro Music Club** (✉ Suché myto, Starý mesto, ☎ no phone, WEB www.metroclub.szm.sk). Local and international groups play live music in a former subway tunnel, which actually benefits the acoustics.

ROCK CLUBS

New clubs open and close quickly. Check the *Slovak Spectator* for the lowdown on the latest hot spots. The **Harley-Davidson Club** (✉ Rebarborová 1, Ružinov, ☎ 02/4319–1095) is an American-style hard-rock club. Take Bus 220 from under the New Bridge to the Ružinovský cintorín (Ružinov Cemetery) stop.

Shopping

Bratislava is an excellent place to purchase Slovak arts and crafts of all kinds. Plenty of folk-art and souvenir shops line Obchodná ulica (Shopping Street), and you'll find booths and stores on Hlavné Námestie. Slovak and Czech crystal are also widely available in the Old Town.

Antikvariát Steiner (✉ Ventúrska ul. 20, Starý mesto, ☎ 02/5443–3778) stocks beautiful old books, maps, graphics, and posters. "Unusual" and "fun" are words often used to describe the designer jewelry and clothing, ceramic pieces, and other works of art at the trendy **Dielo** (✉ Nám. SNP 12, Starý mesto, ☎ 02/5296–8648; ✉ Obchodná 27, ☎ 02/5443–4568; ✉ Obchodná 33, ☎ 02/5293–2433).

For Slovak folk art, try **Folk, Folk** (✉ Obchodná 10, Starý mesto, ☎ 02/5443–4292; ✉ Rybárska brána 2, ☎ 02/5443–0176), which carries a wide selection of goods, including pottery, handwoven tablecloths, wooden toys, and dolls with Slovak folk costumes. **Jurista Suveniry** (✉ Razusovo nábr. 6, Starý mesto, ☎ 02/4344–8194) sells Slovak-made crystal and has a small café inside. **ÚĽUV** (✉ Nám. SNP 12, Starý mesto, ☎ 02/5292–3802; ✉ Obchodná 64, Starý mesto, ☎ 02/5273–1343), a national chain, has a nice selection of hand-painted table pottery and vases, wooden figures, and village folk clothing. Small corn-husk figures are dirt cheap and can be very beautiful, though not easy to transport.

Bratislava Essentials

AIR TRAVEL

There are very few international destinations served by Bratislava's airport. The Czech national carrier, ČSA, offers service through Prague to Bratislava from the United States and Great Britain in conjunction with partner airlines. Sky Europe provides service from Zurich and Venice to Bratislava. Slovak Airlines has three flights a week between Bratislava and Moscow.

Vienna's Schwechat Airport is a mere 60 km (37 mi) west of Bratislava. Many international carriers fly into Vienna, and eight buses connect Schwechat Airport to Bratislava; the journey takes just over an hour.

Košice is the only other city in the country to have air service, and it is all domestic. Sky Europe and Slovak Airlines fly between Bratislava and Košice.
➤ CARRIERS: ČSA (✉ Šturova 13, Starý mesto, ☎ 02/5296–1042; 02/5296–1073; 212/765–6545 in the U.S.; 0171/255–1898 in the U.K.; WEB www.czech-airlines.com). Sky Europe (✉ Ivanská cesta 26, Letisko, ☎ 02/4850–4850, WEB www.skyeurope.com). Slovak Airlines (✉ Trnavská cesta 56, Nové Mesto, ☎ 02/4445–0096, WEB www.slovakairlines.sk).

AIRPORTS AND TRANSFERS

Although few airlines provide direct service to Bratislava's M.R. Štefánika Airport, Vienna's Schwechat Airport is only about 60 km (37 mi) to the west and is served by most international carriers.
➤ AIRPORT INFORMATION: Letisko M.R. Štefánika (✉ Ivanská cesta, Letisko, ☎ 02/4857–3353). Flughafen Wien Schwechat (✉ 1300 Wien Flughafen, Postfach 1, Vienna, ☎ 431/70070, WEB english.viennaairport.com).

TRANSFERS

A taxi ride from the Bratislava airport to the town center should cost no more than 700 Sk. Bus No. 61 runs from the airport to the main train station. Eight buses a day make the bus connection between Vienna's airport and Bratislava's main bus station for about 7€. You might try to make an arrangement with a Slovak cab driver, a ride to Vienna's airport could cost as little as 2,300 Sk.
➤ CONTACTS: Bus connection (☎ 02/5557–1312, WEB english.viennaairport.com/bus.html#4).

BOAT TRAVEL

Hydrofoils travel the Danube between Vienna and Bratislava (1 hr, 40 min) and Budapest and Bratislava (4 hr) from May to September. Boats depart in the morning from Bratislava, on the eastern bank of the Danube near the intersection of Mostová and Vajanského nábrežie, and return from Vienna or Budapest in the evening. Tickets cost 29€ to 83€ per person and should be purchased at the dock. Also inquire here about occasional evening cruises with music.

➤ BOAT INFORMATION: **Slovenská plavba a pristavý** (✉ Fajnorovo nábr. 2, Starý mesto, ☎ 02/5293–3518 or 02/5293–2226).

BUS TRAVEL

Three buses a day make the five-hour journey from Prague to Bratislava. From Vienna, there are eight buses a day from Autobusbahnhof Wien Mitte; the trip takes an hour. One bus a day connects Budapest with Bratislava; the ride is a little more than four hours.

Bratislava's main bus terminal is roughly 2 km (1 mi) from the city center. To get downtown from the terminal use a taxi or take Trolley 207 or 208 to Mierové námestie or 202 to the Tesco department store.

➤ BUS INFORMATION: **Autobusová stanica** (✉ Mylinské nivy 31, Nové mesto, WEB www.busy.sk).

BUS AND TRAM TRAVEL WITHIN BRATISLAVA

Bratislava's buses and trams run frequently and connect the city center with outlying sights. Stops are marked with signs that picture a bus or tram and list the transportation lines served from the stop. Tickets cost 12 Sk for a 10-minute ride (roughly five stops) and 70 Sk for a 24-hour ticket. You can buy tickets from large hotels, newsstands, and tobacconists. Buy them ahead of time, since you can't purchase tickets on a bus or tram and the orange vending machines at major stops are often out of order. Validate tickets in the red machine that hangs on a post near the door; a time will be stamped on your ticket. The fine for riding without a validated ticket, or with an expired ticket, is 1,000 Sk—paid on the spot. City maps, available at newsstands and at the visitor center, list bus and tram routes.

CAR TRAVEL

There are good freeways from Prague to Bratislava via Brno (D1 and D2); the 315-km (195-mi) journey takes about 3½ hours. From Vienna, take the A4 and then Route 8 to Bratislava; the 60-km (37-mi) journey takes about an hour. From Budapest, take Route 10 to Komárno, then Route 63 from Komárno to Bratislava; the trip takes roughly 2½ hours.

A car is not really necessary to explore Bratislava, as the Old Town is compact and many sights can be reached on foot. Buses and trams can take you to attractions outside the city center. If you do decide to drive, keep in mind that city roads are narrow. Don't be surprised to see cars parked halfway on a sidewalk.

EMBASSIES

There is no Australian embassy or consulate in Slovakia.

➤ CONTACTS: **Canadian Consulate** (✉ Mišíkova 28D, Palisady, ☎ 02/5244–2175 or 02/5244–2177). **U.S. Embassy** (✉ Hviezdoslavovo nám. 4, Starý mesto, ☎ 02/5443–0861, WEB www.usembassy.sk). **U.K. Embassy** (✉ Panská 16, Starý mesto, ☎ 02/5441–9633, WEB www.britemb.sk).

EMERGENCIES

➤ HOSPITAL: **Fakultna nemonica L. Derera** (✉ Limbova 3, Neigh Kramare, ☎ 02/5954–1111 or 02/5941–4111).

➤ 24-HR PHARMACY: **Pharmacia** (✉ Palackého 10, Starý mesto, ☎ 02/5441–9665).

ENGLISH-LANGUAGE MEDIA

The *Slovak Spectator* (www.slovakspectator.sk), an English daily, is available at major hotels and newsstands. Numerous bookstores have at least tourist books in English; for a larger selection, try Eurobooks.
➤ ENGLISH-LANGUAGE BOOKSTORE: **Eurobooks** (✉ Jesenskeho 9, Starý mesto, ☎ 02/5441–7959, WEB www.eurobooks.sk).

SIGHTSEEING TOURS

Bratislavská informačná služba arranges the best tours of the city, including English-language tours available May through September; call ahead for an appointment. Tours typically take two hours and cost 1,000 Sk for a group of up to 20 (minimum three people). Satur also organizes tours of the capital from May through September for about the same price. As with BIS, you must make an appointment for an English-language tour. *See* Visitor Information, *below*, for more information.

TAXIS

Taxis are easy to hail and are a good option when returning from restaurants or pubs at night. Meters start at 20 Sk–30 Sk and jump 13 Sk–16 Sk per 1 km (½ mi). To avoid being ripped off, watch to see that the driver engages the meter. If the meter is broken, negotiate a price with the driver before even getting in the cab. BP Taxi is reliable.
➤ TAXI COMPANY: **BP Taxi** (02/16333 or 02/16000).

TRAIN TRAVEL

Reasonably efficient train service regularly connects Prague and Bratislava. Trains depart from Prague's Hlavní nádraží (main station) and from Holešovice station; the journey takes five to six hours. The InterCity trains are slightly more expensive but faster. From Vienna Sudbahnhof (south station), four trains daily make the one-hour trek to Bratislava. The trip from Budapest takes from 2½ to 4 hours depending on the train. Bratislava's main train station, Hlavná stanica, is about 2 km (1 mi) from the city center. To travel downtown from the station, take Tram 1 to Poštová ulica or jump in a taxi.
➤ TRAIN INFORMATION: **Hlavná stanica** (✉ Prestaniče nám., Starý mesto, ☎ 02/5058–7565, WEB www.zsr.sk).

TRANSPORTATION WITHIN BRATISLAVA

Bratislava's Old Town is compact, and most sights can be reached easily on foot. Bratislava's buses, electric buses, and trams run frequently and connect the city center with outlying sights.

VISITOR INFORMATION

Bratislavská informačná služba (BIS; Bratislava Information Service) can help you find a hotel or private accommodation. The office is also a good source for maps and basic information. It's open weekdays 8–5, weekends 8–1. There's also a small BIS office in the Hlavná station, open weekdays 9–6, weekends 9–2.

The country's national travel agency, Satur, can help you find accommodations and can book air, rail, and bus tickets. It's open weekdays 9–6 and Saturday 9–noon.
➤ TOURIST INFORMATION: **BIS** (✉ Klobučnícka 2, Starý mesto, ☎ 02/5443–4370; Hlavná stanica, Prestaniče nám., Starý mesto, ☎ 02/5249–5906). **Satur** (✉ Jesenského 5, Starý mesto, ☎ 02/5441–0133 or 02/5441–0129).

CENTRAL SLOVAKIA

Though generally overlooked by tourists, central Slovakia is the country's heart and soul. This is where the nation was born and where Slovak folklore and deep-rooted traditions continue to flourish.

Formerly a medieval mining town, Banská Bystrica lies at the center of the region and is the ideal base from which to explore the towns and villages surrounding it. The region's two other main historical mining towns, Banská Štiavnica and Kremnica, have remained more or less frozen in time since their glory days in the Middle Ages.

The beauty of central Slovakia, however, lies not so much in its architecture as in its inspiring natural landscapes. The region is home to both the High Tatras, the highest range in Slovakia, and the Low Tatras, the second-highest mountain range in Slovakia and the largest by area. In the Low Tatras in winter, ski slopes are mostly free from the hordes of tourists that overrun their higher counterparts. Wonderful hiking trails, caves, and scenic valleys make summer an appealing time to visit as well.

Unfortunately, in central Slovakia you will also find some of the worst crimes against nature. In an effort to enrich the region in the 1950s, the Communist regime built many large steel- and tank-producing factories, which litter some of the most beautiful valleys in the country. Many of the worst can be seen while heading east from Banská Bystrica in the direction of Brezno. To call them eyesores would be an understatement.

Numbers in the margin correspond to numbers on the Slovakia map.

Banská Bystrica

❼ *205 km (127 mi) northeast of Bratislava on Hwys. D61 and E571 and Rte. 66.*

Surrounded by three mountain ranges—the Low Tatras, the Fatras, and the Slovak rudohorie—Banská Bystrica is an ideal starting point for exploring the beauty of the region. Focus on the surrounding woods and hills—the outlying areas are plagued with concrete apartment buildings.

Banská Bystrica has been around since the 13th century, acquiring wealth from the nearby mines. Following the Tartar invasion in 1241, the Hungarian king Béla IV granted special privileges to encourage the immigration of German settlers, who together with the locals developed the prosperous mining of copper and precious metals. During the 19th century, the town was a major focus of Slovak national life, and it was from a school here that the teaching of the Slovak language originated and spread to the rest of the country.

The city is also famous as the center of the Slovak National Uprising (known in Slovak by the initials SNP) during World War II. It was here that the underground Slovak National Council initiated the revolt on August 29, 1944. For some two months, thousands of Slovaks valiantly rose up against the Slovak puppet regime and their Nazi oppressors, forcing the Germans to divert critically needed troops and equipment from the front lines. Though the Germans quashed the uprising on October 27, the costly operation is credited with accelerating the Allied victory and gaining Slovakia the short-lived appellation of ally.

The **Múzeum Slovenského národného povstania** (Museum of the Slovak National Uprising) stands in a large field just outside the center of town, between Horná ulica and Ulica Dukelských hrdinov. It's difficult to miss the tank out front and the monument's massive concrete wings—the effect is particularly striking at night. The museum's focus has been shifting from Communism to more recent national events. ✉ *Kapitulská 23,* ☎ *048/412–3258.* 🖂 *20 Sk.* ☉ *May–Sept., Tues.–Sun. 9–6; Oct.–Apr., Tues.–Sun. 9–4.*

A cheery collection of Renaissance and baroque houses lines Námestie SNP; the most impressive is the **Thurzo dom** (Thurzo House), an amalgamation of two late-Gothic structures built in 1495 by the wealthy Thurzo family. The genuine Renaissance sgraffiti decorations on the outside were added during the 16th century, when the family's wealth was at its height. Today the building houses the **Stredoslovenské múzeum** (Central Slovak Museum), which is more interesting for the chance it affords of seeing the inside of the house than for its artifacts. ✉ *Nám. SNP 4,* ☎ *048/415–5077.* 🖂 *20 Sk.* ☉ *Mid-June–mid-Sept., weekdays 8–noon and 1–5, Sun. 9–noon and 1–5; mid-Sept.–mid-June, weekdays 8–noon and 1–4, Sun. 9–noon and 1–4.*

OFF THE BEATEN PATH
BOJNICE HRAD – Romantic Bojnice Castle, dating from before 1175, has all the necessary elements of a fairy-tale palace: multilevel turrets with decorative spires, ornate parapets, and a sparkling moat. The interior is beautifully restored and furnished in 12th-century style. Costumed guides lead daytime and candlelight tours (by arrangement), which are available in English. Don't miss the Boijnicky *oltar* (altar), a point of contention between newly formed Czech and Slovak republics in 1993—the Czechs wanted to keep it. During the first weeks of May the castle hosts the International Festival of Ghosts and Spirits. ✉ *Off Hwys. E572 and 64, 65 km (40 mi) west of Banská Bystrica,* ☎ *046/543–0633,* 🌐 *www.bojnicecastle.sk.* 🖂 *Day tour 130 Sk, candlelight tour 150 Sk.* ☉ *Tours July–Aug., Sun.–Thurs. 9–5, Fri.–Sat. 9–5 and at 9 PM; June and Sept., Tues.–Sun. 9–5; Oct.–May, Tues.–Sun. 10–3.*

Dining and Lodging

$ ★ ✕ **Starobystrická pivnica.** Grilled food is the house specialty at this classic wine cellar. The delicious *cesnakova polievka* (garlic soup) is served in a bread bowl. For a main course, try the *Starobystica misa*, a mixed plate with different cuts of grilled pork. ✉ *Nám. SNP 9,* ☎ *048/415–4326. MC, V.*

$$$ ★ ✕🏨 **Arcade Hotel.** This 16th-century building on the main square is an ideal place to stay. The rooms and apartments vary in size, comfort, and cost, but each is equipped with the basic creature comforts. The on-site Italian restaurant is set in an old wine cellar with craggy, barrel-vaulted ceilings. ✉ *Nám. SNP 5, 97401,* ☎ *048/430–2111,* 🖷 *048/412–3126,* 🌐 *www.arcade.sk. 9 rooms, 2 suites, 3 apartments. Restaurant, café, in-room safes, minibars, cable TV, bar, meeting room, some pets allowed; no a/c. MC, V.*

Outdoor Activities and Sports

The most attractive hiking trails are to the north and west of Banská Bystrica. A hiking map of the Low Tatras is available at the tourist information center and bookstores.

Banská Štiavnica

🔞 *48 km (30 mi) south of Banská Bystrica on Hwys. E77 and E571, and Rte. 525.*

Since the 11th century, this little town has earned its wealth from mining, and today it's essentially one large mining museum on the UNESCO World Heritage list. German miners arrived here to exploit rich gold and silver deposits, and their success is apparent in some of the town's remaining monuments, such as the golden Trinity column and the impressive Lutheran church.

The **Starý zámok** (Old Castle), built on the rocks above town, dates to the early 13th century, but additions were made in practically every subsequent building style. The castle served as a fortress to protect the wealth of the local bigwigs against the Turkish invaders. ⊠ *Starozámocká 11,* ☎ *045/691–1543.* 🎫 *20 Sk.* ☉ *Tues.–Sun. 9–4.*

The **Nový zámok** (New Castle) was built between 1564 and 1571 as part of an effort to strengthen fortification of the town against invasions of the Turks. The six-story Renaissance building was used as a watchtower and later became the town's live clock—the time was announced every quarter hour by a trumpet. Inside are historical exhibits of the Turkish invasions during the 16th and 17th centuries. ⊠ *Novozámocká 22,* ☎ *045/21543.* 🎫 *20 Sk.* ☉ *May–Sept., Tues.–Sun. 8–4; Oct.–Apr., weekdays 8–3.*

You can view some of the town's original mining buildings and machinery—dating to the early 13th century—and take a trip down into a pit mine at the **Banské múzeum** (Open-Air Mining Museum). The museum is about 2 km (1 mi) from town. ⊠ *Štiavnické bane,* ☎ *045/691–1541.* 🎫 *30 Sk.* ☉ *July–Aug., Tues.–Sun. 9–5; Sept.–June, weekdays 8–3.*

OFF THE BEATEN PATH	**MANSION SAINT ANTON** – Don't miss this charming late-baroque château in the small village of Antol, just outside Banská Štiavnica. The château displays its original furnishings, has an exhibition of hunting arms and game, and is surrounded by French and English gardens. ⊠ *Svätý Anton,* ☎ *045/691–3932.* 🎫 *50 Sk.* ☉ *May–Sept., Tues.–Sun. 8–4; Oct.–Apr., Tues.–Sat. 8–3.*

Dining and Lodging

$ ✕🏨 **Antolský mlyn.** This cheery, family-run pension sits in a tiny village just outside Banská Štiavnica near Mansion Saint Anton. Black lacquer furnishings give the rooms a modern Slovak look. A Continental breakfast is included. The simple whitewashed restaurant has understated dark wood accents and a Slovak menu of pork, beef, poultry, and fish dishes. ⊠ *Svätý Anton, 96972,* ☎ *045/693–1311. 7 rooms, 1 apartment. Restaurant, bicycles; no a/c. No credit cards.*

$$ 🏨 **Hotel Salamander.** Looking at the freshly painted gray-and-white
★ Hotel Salamander sandwiched along the main square, you'd hardly guess the building actually dates from the 16th century. The rooms have high ceilings with decorative plasterwork, and the public areas are filled with antiques. ⊠ *J. Palárika 1, 96901,* ☎ *045/691–3992,* FAX *045/692–1262,* WEB *www.hotelsalamander.sk. 25 rooms, 4 suites. Restaurant, café, ice cream parlor, in-room safes, minibars, cable TV; no a/c. AE, DC, MC, V.*

Central Slovakia Essentials

CAR TRAVEL

The most convenient way to reach Banská Bystrica is by car. From Bratislava, take the D61 and E571 to Zvolen via Nitra, and then follow the 66 to Banská Bystrica; the trip should take roughly 2½ hours. Driving through central Slovakia is relatively quick and hassle-free. Banská Štiavnica lies southwest of Zvolen on Route 525; the road is narrow but well marked.

EMERGENCIES

➤ HOSPITAL: **Nemocnica F.D. Roosevelta** (⊠ Nám. L. Svobodu 1, Banská Bystrica, ☎ 048/413–5240).

TRAIN TRAVEL

Daily trains connect Bratislava to Banská Bystrica; the journey takes almost three hours. The trip from Košice, in eastern Slovakia, to Banská Bystrica lasts about five hours. This is one of the most scenic railway routes in the country (take the northern, not the southern, route). It takes several inconvenient connections to get between Banská Bystrica and Banská Štiavnica by train.

VISITOR INFORMATION

The Satur office in Banská Bystrica can book hotels and arrange English-language tours at a reasonable cost. The tourist information centers in Banská Bystrica and Banská Štiavnica are open weekdays 10–5; from June through August they are open Saturday until noon as well.
➤ TOURIST INFORMATION: **Satur** (⊠ Nám. Slobody 4, ☎ 048/414–2575). **Tourist information centers** (⊠ Nám. Štefana Moyzesa 26, Banská Bystrica, ☎ 048/186; ⊠ Radničné nám. 1, Banská Štiavnica, ☎ 048/691–1859).

THE HIGH TATRAS

A visit to the Vysoké Tatry (High Tatras) alone would make a trip to Slovakia worthwhile. Although the range is relatively compact (just 32 km [20 mi] from end to end), its peaks seem wilder and more starkly beautiful than those of the Alps. The highest is Gerlachovský štít, at 8,710 ft; some 20 others exceed 8,000 ft. The 35 mountain lakes are remote and clear, very cold, and sometimes eerily deep. Swimming is not permitted in the cold glacier lakes of the Tatras. Endemic species of marmot and mountain goat, in addition to the common brown bear, wolf, and lynx, make their home in the mountain range.

The best way to see these beautiful mountains is on foot. A reasonably fit person of any age should have little trouble with any of the walks in the area, which take three to five hours each. Even though the trails are well marked, it is very important to buy a walking map of the area—the detailed *Vysoké Tatry, letná turistická mapa* is available for around 50 Sk at newspaper kiosks. If you plan to take any of the higher-level walks, be sure to wear proper shoes with good ankle support. Exercise extreme caution in early spring, when melting snow can turn the trails into icy rivers and cause avalanches. Check with the Horská služba (Mountain service; ☞ Visitor Information *in* The High Tatras Essentials, *below*) for conditions.

The entire region is crisscrossed with paths ideal for cross-country skiing. You can buy a special ski map at newspaper kiosks. The season lasts from the end of December through April, though the best months are traditionally January and February. Rental equipment is ubiquitous, and you'll get a complete downhill ski set—including skis, boots, and poles—for up to $10 per day. Ždiar, toward the Polish border, has a good ski area for beginners.

Most of the tourist facilities in the High Tatras are concentrated in three neighboring resort towns: Štrbské Pleso, to the west; Smokovec, in the middle; and Tatranská Lomnica, to the east. Each town is fairly similar in terms of convenience and atmosphere, and all provide easy passage to the hills, so it makes little difference where you begin your explorations of the mountains.

Numbers in the margin correspond to numbers on the Slovakia map.

The High Tatras

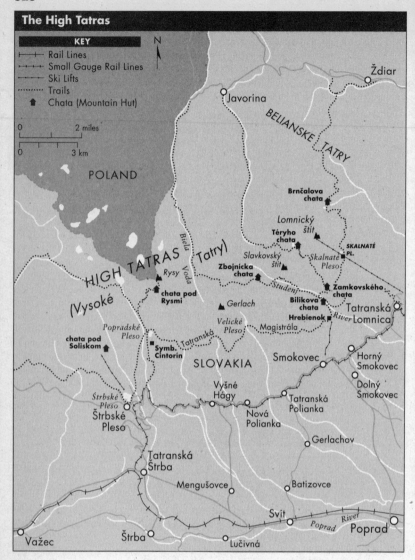

KEY

⊢┼─	Rail Lines
─┼┼─	Small Gauge Rail Lines
────	Ski Lifts
··········	Trails
⛺	Chata (Mountain Hut)

0 ——— 2 miles
0 ——— 3 km

POLAND

Ždiar

Javorina

BELIANSKE TATRY

Brnčalova chata

Biela Voda

Rysy

HIGH TATRAS Tatry

chata pod Rysmi

(Vysoké

Lomnický štít

Téryho chata

SKALNATÉ PL.

Slavkovský štít

Skalnaté Pleso

Zbojnícka chata

Studený

▲ Gerlach

Bilíkova chata

Zamkovského chata

Tatranská Lomnica

Hrebienok

River

Velické Pleso

Magistrála

Popradské Pleso

chata pod Soliskom

Tatranská

Symb. Cintorin

SLOVAKIA

Smokovec

Horný Smokovec

Dolný Smokovec

Štrbské Pleso

Štrbské Pleso

Vyšné Hágy

Nová Polianka

Tatranská Polianka

Gerlachov

Tatranská Štrba

Mengušovce

Batizovce

Svit

Poprad River

Poprad

Važec

Štrba

Lučivná

Poprad

⑲ *329 km (204 mi) east of Bratislava along Hwys. D61 and E50.*

Poprad, the gateway to the Tatras, is a good place to begin exploring the region. But don't expect a beautiful mountain village. Poprad fell victim to some of the most insensitive Communist planning perpetrated in the country after the war. There's no need to linger here. Instead, drive or take the electric railroad to the superior sights and facilities of the more rugged resorts just over 30 km (19 mi) to the north.

Dining and Lodging

$–$$ ✕ **Slovenská Reštaurácia.** If you have to spend a few hours in Poprad,
★ having a meal in this charming rustic restaurant is the best way to do so. Try the bryndzové halušky, *strapačky s kapustou* (homemade noodles with sauerkraut), or *pirohy* (potato-dough dumplings stuffed with meat or cheese). ✉ *Ul. 1. mája 216,* ☎ *052/772–2870. AE, MC, V.*

$ 🏨 **Europa.** This cozy little hotel stands next to the train station. From the reception area to the modest, old-fashioned rooms (with neither private bathrooms nor TVs), the place exudes a faint elegance. ✉ *Wolkerova ul. 1, 05962,* ☎ *052/772–1883. 60 rooms without bath. Bar; no a/c, no room TVs. No credit cards.*

Smokovec

⑳ *12 km (7 mi) north of Poprad on Rte. 534.*

The first town you'll reach by road or rail from Poprad is Smokovec, the undisputed center of the Slovak Tatras resorts and a good starting point for mountain excursions. Smokovec is divided into two principal areas, Starý Smokovec (Old Smokovec) and Nový Smokovec (New Smokovec), which are within a stone's throw of each other.

The Tatras seem tailor-made for hikers of all levels. Starý Smokovec is a great starting point for a trek that parallels a cascading waterfall for much of its three-hour length. From Starý Smokovec, walk out along the main road in the direction of Tatranská Lomnica for roughly 1 km (½ mi). In Tatranská Lesná, follow the yellow-marked path that winds gently uphill through the pines.

Farther along are red markers leading to the funicular at Hrebienok, which brings you back to the relative comforts of Starý Smokovec. However, if you're in good physical shape and there is plenty of daylight left, consider extending your hike by four hours. (The extension is striking, but avoid it during winter, when you may find yourself neck-deep in snow.) Just before the Bilíkova *chata* (a chata is a mountain hut), turn right along the green path and then follow the blue, red, and then green trails in the direction of windswept Téryho chata, a turn-of-the-20th-century chalet perched amid five lonely alpine lakes. The scenery is a few notches above dazzling. Once you reach the chalet after two strenuous hours of hiking, backtrack to Bilíkova chata. A few steps down from the chata is Studenovodske vopady (Cold-water Waterfalls). Follow the signs from Bilíkova to the funicular at Hrebienok and take it down to Starý Smokovec. It runs at 45-minute intervals beginning at 6:30 AM and ending at 7:45 PM; the schedule is posted at the Bilíkova chata.

NEED A BREAK? | Don't pass up the chance to take a break with a warm beverage at the rustic and cozy **Bilíkova chata** (☎ 052/742–2439), in a little clearing just before you reach Hrebienok. It's open 7:30 AM–9 PM from December to March and 7 AM to 10 PM between July and mid-September.

Dining and Lodging

$$-$$$ ✕ **Restaurant Koliba.** This charming restaurant with rustic furnishings ★ and an open-face grill serves tasty local fare. Try the *kapustová polievka* (sauerkraut soup with mushrooms and sausage). ✉ *Starý Smokovec,* ☎ *0952/442–2204. No credit cards. Closed Sun.*

$$-$$$ 🏨 **Grand Hotel.** Along with its sister hotel in Tatranská Lomnica, ★ Grandhotel Praha, this hotel epitomizes Tatra luxury at its turn-of-the-20th-century best. The golden Tudor facade rises majestically over the town, with the peaks of the Tatras looming in the background. In season, skiers and hikers crowd the reception area and hallways (there's ski rental in an adjacent building), but the rooms themselves are quiet. ✉ *Starý Smokovec, 06201,* ☎ *052/442–2154,* FAX *052/442–2157,* WEB *www.hotel.sk/enghot/mpoprad/hgrand/hgrand.htm. 79 rooms, 52 with bath; 5 suites. Restaurant, café, cable TV, pool, gym, massage, sauna, hiking, downhill skiing, bar, dance club, laundry service, meeting rooms; no-smoking rooms. AE, DC, MC, V. BP.*

$$ \quad \boxed{} \text{ **Villa Dr. Szontagh.** Away from the action in Nový Smokovec, this}$$
★   steepled little chalet provides mostly peace and quiet. The darkly furnished rooms and public areas are well maintained, and the courtly
staff goes out of its way to please. The decent restaurant has an extensive wine cellar. ⊠ *Nový Smokovec, 06201,* ☎ *052/442–2061. 9
rooms, 4 apartments, 1 suite. Restaurant, cafeteria. AE, MC, V. Closed
Nov.–mid-Dec.*

Outdoor Activities and Sports

The multipurpose **Tatrasport** (⊠ Starý Smokovec, ☎ 052/442–5241,
WEB www.tatry.net/tatrasport), opposite the bus station, provides numerous sport services—ski lessons, ski rental, sleigh rides, mountain
guides, horseback riding, river rafting, and more. Also available are
spa services, baby-sitting, and a restaurant that serves an excellent salmon
steak for 170 Sk.

Štrbské Pleso

㉑ *18 km (11 mi) west of Smokovec on Rte. 537.*

Štrbské Pleso is the main center in the Tatras for active sports. The best
ski slopes are close by, and many excellent hiking trails are within easy
reach. The town not only has the most modern hotels (and the most
jarringly modern hotel architecture), but it also commands the finest
panoramas in the Tatras.

Lodging

$$–$$$ **Patria.** This modern, slanting pyramid on the shores of a clear
★   mountain lake has two obvious advantages: location and views. Ask
for a room on a higher floor; those overlooking the lake have balconies,
and the other side opens onto the mountains. Rooms consist of modern Swedish furniture and crisp white duvets. The hotel is steps from
the ski jumps and has its own sport shop and ski school. ⊠ *Štrbské
Pleso, 05985,* ☎ *052/449–2591,* FAX *052/449–2590,* WEB *www.
tatry.net/patria. 140 rooms, 10 apartments. 3 restaurants, café, pool,
hair salon, hot tub, massage, sauna, billiards, downhill skiing, ski
shop, bar, children's programs (ages 5–12), convention center. AE, DC,
MC, V.*

Outdoor Activities and Sports

JMG (⊠ Štrbské Pleso, ☎ 052/449–2582, WEB www.jmg.sk), at the Hotel
Patria, can arrange ski lessons and equipment rental as well as sightseeing flights, paragliding, sleigh rides, and mountain guides.

Jur Sport Agency (⊠ Hlavná 260, Závažná Poruba, ☎ 052/554–7279)
arranges two-hour raft trips along the Váh River. The starting point
is 5 km from Liptovský Mikuláš, west of Štrbské Pleso.

Tatranská Lomnica

㉒ *24 km (15 mi) northeast of Štrbské Pleso on Rte. 537.*

Tatranská Lomnica, on the eastern end of the electric rail line, has a
near-perfect combination of peace, convenience, and atmosphere.
Moreover, the lift behind the Grandhotel Praha brings some of the best
walks in the Tatras to within 10 minutes or so of your hotel door.

The Magistrale, a 24-km (15-mi) walking trail that skirts the peaks just
above the tree line, affords some of the best views for the least amount
of exertion. A particularly stunning stretch of the route—marked by
red signposts—begins in Tatranská Lomnica and ends 5 km (3 mi) away
in Starý Smokovec. The total walking time is four hours, plus a taxi
ride back to where you started.

To start the walk, take the small cable car behind the Grandhotel Praha in Tatranská Lomnica to Skalnaté Pleso (400 Sk round-trip). Here you'll find a food court and bar (*varené vino*, hot spiced wine, is especially good in cold weather). From here you can access the trail immediately. But consider a 30-minute detour via cable car (700 Sk round-trip) to the top of Lomnický štít (8,635 ft), the second-highest peak in the range. Because of the harsh temperatures (be sure to dress warmly even in summer), you're permitted to linger on the limited walkways near the observatory at the top for only 30 minutes, after which you take the cable car back down. Reservations are necessary for the cable car to Lomnický štít, and tickets sell out quickly; ask at your hotel for booking assistance.

Dining and Lodging

$$–$$$$ ✕ **Zbojnícka koliba.** This dark-log mountain cottage restaurant specializes in *kurča* (chicken) cooked on a rotisserie over an open pit. You can order a half or a whole, but either way the wait will be about 55 minutes, as the chicken is prepared fresh. To take the edge off your hunger while you wait, munch on the bryndza cheese, with onions and pieces of bacon, and bread and listen to the Gypsy music. ⊠ *Toward Grandhotel Praha, Tatranská Lomnica,* ☎ *052/446–7630. No credit cards. No lunch.*

$$–$$$ 🏨 **Grandhotel Praha.** In the shadow of Lomnický štít rises a cream-color mansion with red-roof-topped turrets. Built in 1905, Grandhotel Praha is one of the wonders of the Tatras. Public rooms retain a historic elegance: the large lower-level lounge, for example, has huge black easy chairs, intricate crystal chandeliers, and golden-yellow walls characteristic of the time when Maria Theresa ruled the Austro-Hungarian Empire. Guest rooms are spacious, and about half have been renovated. Although the new rooms are crisp, the hyper-modern lines and bright teal fabrics seem a bit out of place ⊠ *Tatranská Lomnica, 05960,* ☎ *052/446–7941,* 𝖥𝖠𝖷 *052/446–7891,* 𝖶𝖤𝖡 *www.tanap.sk/grandpraha. 83 rooms, 7 suites. Restaurant, room service, in-room safes, minibars, cable TV, hot tub, massage, sauna, hiking, downhill skiing, ski shop, lounge, nightclub, laundry service, Internet, meeting rooms; no-smoking rooms. AE, DC, MC, V.*

$$–$$$ 🏨 **Villa Beatrice.** Nine apartment suites with at least a bedroom, living room (with pull-out beds), and a kitchen nook make a nice home away from home. Some units have a fireplace, sauna, or whirlpool; No. 9 is spread over two floors. Contemporary wood furnishings and floral upholstery fill the apartments. Ski rental is available. ⊠ *Tatranská Lomnica, 05960,* ☎ *052/446–7313,* 𝖥𝖠𝖷 *052/446–7120,* 𝖶𝖤𝖡 *www.tatry.net/beatrice. 9 suites. Pizzeria, bicycles, ice-skating, ski shop, meeting rooms; no a/c. MC, V.*

Outdoor Activities and Sports

Skalnaté Pleso, above Tatranská Lomnica, has moderately challenging slopes. You can rent skis at the Grandhotel Praha.

Asociácia horských vodcov (Mountain Guides Association; ☎ 052/442–2066, 𝖶𝖤𝖡 www.tatraguide.com) provides guides for the more difficult routes for 2,500 Sk–4,000 Sk per day, per person. Individual rates decrease the larger your group.

The High Tatras Essentials

AIR TRAVEL

The closest airport is Košice's in Eastern Slovakia. From Košice, it's easiest to take a train to Poprad.

BUS TRAVEL

Daily bus service connects Bratislava with Poprad (about 6½ hours) and the smaller towns in the area, but trains tend to be quicker and are much more comfortable.

CAR TRAVEL

Poprad, the gateway to the Tatras, is 328 km (203 mi) from Bratislava, with a four-lane stretch between the capital and Trenčín and a well-marked, two-lane highway thereafter; the drive takes about 4½ hours. If you plan to tour the region's smaller towns and villages or if you are continuing on to eastern Slovakia, a car will prove nearly indispensable.

TOURS

TLS Air offers a biplane flight from Poprad airport over the Tatras region; for details contact the Satur office in Poprad. The Satur office in Starý Smokovec is also helpful in arranging tours of the Tatras and surrounding area.

TRAIN TRAVEL

Regular rail service connects Bratislava with Poprad, but book ahead: the trains are often impossibly crowded in August and during the skiing season. A trip from Bratislava's Hlavná stanica to Poprad's station, Železničná stanica Poprad, takes four hours on an InterCity train, longer on others. You have to switch to the efficient electric railway, which shares the regular train stations but is a smaller gauge, to connect to the High Tatras resort towns. Electric trains run every 30 to 60 minutes. If you're going only to the Tatras, you won't need any other form of transportation.

➤ TRAIN STATION: **Železničná stanica Poprad** (✉ Wolkerova 496, ☎ 052/7166–8484, WEB www.zsr.sk).

VISITOR INFORMATION

Tourist information is available in each resort town. Dom Služieb (House of Services) in Starý Smokovec is open weekdays 8–4, Saturday 8–1. The Tourist Information Centers are open weekdays 11–4, Saturday 8–1. Slovakoturist in Horný Smokovec can arrange accommodations in private homes, including stays in mountain cottages. At the Satur offices in Poprad and Starý Smokovec you can change money, get hiking and driving maps, and book hotel (but not private) rooms. For more in-depth information on trails, mountain chalets, and weather conditions, contact the Horská služba (Mountain Services).

➤ TOURIST INFORMATION: **Dom Služieb** (✉ Starý Smokovec, ☎ 052/442–3440). **Horská služba** (✉ Starý Smokovec, ☎ 052/442–2820). **Satur** (✉ Námestie sv. Egídia 2950, Poprad, ☎ 052/772–1353, FAX 052/776–3619; ✉ Starý Smokovec, ☎ 052/442–2710). **Slovakoturist** (✉ Horný Smokovec, ☎ 052/442–2031). **Tourist Information Center** (✉ Hotel Toliar, Štrbské Pleso, ☎ 052/449–2391; ✉ Múzeum, Tatranská Lomnica, ☎ 052/446–7951).

EASTERN SLOVAKIA

To the east of the High Tatras lies an expanse of Slovakia that seldom appears on tourist itineraries. However, eastern Slovakia is a hiking wonderland. In addition to the offerings at Slovenský raj, trails fan out in all directions in the area known as Spišská Magura, to the north and east of Kežmarok. Good outdoor swimming can be found in the lakes in Slovenský raj and in Michalovce, east of Košice.

For 1,000 years, eastern Slovakia was isolated from the West; much of the region was regarded simply as the hinterland of Greater Hungary. Isolation has its advantages, however, and therein may lie the charm of this area. The baroque and Renaissance facades that dominate the towns of Bohemia and Moravia make an appearance in eastern Slovakia as well, but they're often done in local wood instead of stone. Look especially for the wooden altars in Levoča and other towns.

The relative isolation also fostered the development of an entire civilization in medieval times, the Spiš, with no counterpart in the Czech Republic or elsewhere in Slovakia. The territory of the kingdom, which spreads out to the east and south of the High Tatras, was originally settled by Slavonic and later by German immigrants who came here in medieval times to work the mines and defend the western kingdoms against invasion. Some 24 towns eventually came to join the Spiš group, functioning as a miniprincipality within the Hungarian monarchy. The group had its own hierarchies and laws, which were quite different from those brought in by Magyar or Saxon settlers.

Although the last Spiš town lost its independence 100 years ago, much of the group's architectural legacy remains—another by-product of isolation and economic stagnation. Spiš towns are predominantly Gothic beneath their graceful Renaissance overlays. Their steep shingle roofs, high timber-frame gables, and brick-arch doorways have survived in a remarkable state of preservation. Spiš towns are worth seeking out when you see them on a map—look for the prefix *Spišský* preceding a town name.

Farther to the northeast in the foothills of the Carpathian Mountains, the influences of Byzantium are strongly felt, most noticeably in the form of the typically Rusyn (an ethnic minority that speaks its own language related to Ukrainian and Slovak) Greek Catholic and Orthodox wooden churches with onion domes that dominate the villages along the frontier with Poland and Ukraine. This area marks a border in Europe that has stood for a thousand years: the ancient transitional zone between Rome and Constantinople, between Western Christianity and the Eastern Christianity of the Byzantine Empire.

Numbers in the margin correspond to numbers on the Slovakia map.

Levoča

★ ㉓ *90 km (56 mi) northwest of Košice on Hwy. E50, 358 km (222 mi) northeast of Bratislava on Hwys. D61 and E50.*

Levoča's Old Town is still partially surrounded by walled fortifications, and you most likely will drive through the medieval Košice Gate to enter the square. This medieval capital of the Spiš region was founded around 1245 and flourished between the 14th and 17th centuries, when it was an important trade center for art and crafts.

The main architectural sights in the town are lined along and in the middle of the main square, **Námestie majstra Pavla.** Note the sgraffiti-decorated house at No. 7, **Thurzov dom** (Thurzov House), named for the powerful mining family. The wonderfully ornate gables date from the 17th century, though the sgraffiti decorations were added in the 19th century. At the top of the square at No. 60 is the **Malý župný dom** (Small County House), the former administrative center of the Spiš region, now used as an archive. Above the doorway is the coat of arms of the Spiš alliance. The monumental classical building next door, the **Veľký župný dom** (Large County House), was built in the early 19th century by Anton Povolný, who was also responsible for the Evangelical Church at the bottom of the square.

★ **Kostol svätého Jakuba** (St. Jacob's Church) is a huge Gothic structure begun in the early 14th century but not completed until a century later. The interior is a breathtaking concentration of Gothic religious art. It was here in the early 16th century that the Spiš artist Pavol of Levoča carved his most famous work: the wood high altar, which is said to be the world's largest and incorporates a magnificent limestone relief of the Last Supper. The 12 disciples are in fact portraits of Levoča merchants. A tape recording in an iron post at the back of the church provides detailed information in English. ✉ *Nám. majstra Pavla,* ☎ *no phone.* 🎫 *40 Sk.* ⊙ *June–Aug., daily 9–5:30; Sept.–May, Tues.–Sun. 8:30–4.*

The **Mestská radnica** (town hall), with its fine whitewashed Renaissance arcades, gables, and clock tower, was built in 1551 after the great fire of 1550 destroyed the old Gothic building along with much of the town. The clock tower now houses a museum, with exhibits of guild flags and a collection of paintings and wood carvings. You can also look at the 18th-century Lady in White, painted on a doorway through which, as legend has it, she let in the enemy for a promise of wealth and a title. For this act of treason, the 24-year-old beauty's head was chopped off. ✉ *Nám. majstra Pavla,* ☎ *053/451–2449.* 🎫 *20 Sk.* ⊙ *Tues.–Sun. 9–11:30 and noon–5.*

OFF THE
BEATEN PATH

SLOVENSKÝ RAJ – A wild and romantic area of cliffs and gorges, caves and waterfalls, Slovak Paradise national park is perfect for adventurous hikers. The gorges are accessible by narrow but secure iron ladders, and the main tourist centers are Čingov in the north and Dedinky in the south. To get here from Levoča, head south on Route 533 through Spišská Nová Ves, continuing along the twisting roads to the junction with Route 535. Turn right onto Route 535, following the signs to Mlynky and beyond, through the tiny villages and breathtaking countryside.

SPIŠSKÝ HRAD – This former administrative center of the kingdom is the largest castle in Slovakia—and one of the largest in Europe. Spiš overlords occupied this site starting in 1209. The sprawling fortifications are mostly in ruins, but in the section that has been preserved, the museum houses a collection of torture devices. The hilltop location affords a beautiful view of the surrounding hills and town. From Levoča, it's well worth taking the short 16 km (10 mi) detour east along Route 18 to this striking spot. ✉ *Spišský hrad,* ☎ *053/451–2786.* 🎫 *50 Sk.* ⊙ *June–Aug., daily 9–6; May and Sept.–Oct., Tues.–Sun. 9–6; Nov.–Apr., Tues.–Sun. 9–3; last entry 45 mins before closing.*

Dining and Lodging

$–$$ ✕ **U Janusa.** This family-owned restaurant is the perfect place to get a taste of Slovak culture as well as cuisine. Try one of the local specialties, such as homemade sausage or *zemiakové placky* (potato pancakes). ✉ *Kláštorská 22,* ☎ *053/451–4592. No credit cards.*

$$$ 🏨 **Hotel Satel.** A beautiful 18th-century mansion, flanked by other historic buildings on the town square, Hotel Satel is arranged around a courtyard. The courtyard retains its historic flavor, and in summer a fountain flows here. The decor can be a bit gaudy—particularly the peach lacquer headboards in the bedrooms and the fuchsia tablecloths in the restaurant. ✉ *Nám. majstra Pavla 55, 05401,* ☎ *053/451–2943,* FAX *053/451–4486* WEB *www.satel-slovakia.sk. 21 rooms, 2 suites. Restaurant, cable TV, minibars, wine bar; no a/c. AE, DC, MC, V.*

$$ 🏨 **Arkada Hotel.** An interesting history and reasonable prices make
★ this hotel a standout. In the 17th century this 13th-century building became the first printing shop in the Austro-Hungarian Empire. The large, bright rooms—some with arched ceilings—are mostly done in

⊠ *Nám. majstra Pavla 26, 05401,* ☎ FAX *053/4512255. 23 rooms, 3 apartments. Restaurant, cable TV, bar, shop; no a/c. AE, MC, V.*

Košice

㉔ *100 km (62 mi) southeast of Levoča on Hwy. E50 (through Prešov), 402 km (250 mi) east of Bratislava on Hwys. D61 and E571.*

In Košice you leave rural Slovakia behind. Though rich historically and with an interesting old town square, Košice is a sprawling, modern city, the second largest in Slovakia after Bratislava. Positioned along the main trade route between Hungary and Poland, the city was the second largest in the Hungarian Empire (after Buda) during the Middle Ages. With the Turkish occupation of the Hungarian homeland during the 16th and 17th centuries, the town became a safe haven for the Hungarian nobility.

You won't see many Westerners strolling Košice's enormous, well-preserved medieval square, Hlavná ulica; most of the tourists in this pedestrian zone are Hungarians on a day trip to shop and sightsee. The town square is dominated on its southern flank by the huge tower of

★ the Gothic **Dóm svätej Alžbety** (Cathedral of St. Elizabeth). Begun in the 15th century and finally completed in 1508, the cathedral is the largest in Slovakia. Inside the church is one of Europe's largest Gothic altarpieces, a 35-ft-tall medieval wood carving attributed to the master Erhard of Ulm. Most of the great Hungarian leader Francis Rákoczi II's remains were placed in a crypt under the north transept of the cathedral (he left his heart in Paris). ⊠ *Hlavná ul.,* ☎ *no phone.*

Water from the elaborate **Hudobná fontána** (Music Fountain), which lies between the theater and the cathedral, springs in harmony with music (generally classical), accompanied by colored lights. It's worth a visit in the evening just to see all the pairs of lovers huddled around the fountain. ⊠ *Hlavná ul.*

The **Štátne divadlo** (State Theater), a mishmash of neo-Renaissance and neo-Baroque elements built at the end of the 19th century, dominates the center of the town square. The quality of theater, ballet, and opera productions in Košice is very impressive. ⊠ *Hlavná. 58,* ☎ *055/622–1231.* ⊙ *Weekdays 9–5:30 and 1 hr before performances.*

On the east side of the town square is the **Dom Košického vládneho programu** (House of the Košice Government Program), where the Košice Program was proclaimed on April 5, 1945, announcing the reunion of the Czech lands and Slovakia into one national state after World War II. ⊠ *Hlavná ul. Closed to the public.*

NEED A BREAK? Have cup of coffee and dessert in the Art Nouveau confines of the **Café Slávia** (⊠ Hlavná. 63, ☎ 055/623–3190).

The **Miklušova väznica** (Nicholas Prison), an old Gothic building used as a prison and torture chamber until 1909, now houses a museum with exhibits on Košice's history. You can even visit the underground premises of the former torture chamber to see replicas of the torture instruments. ⊠ *Pri Miklušovej väznici 10,* ☎ *055/622–2856.* ⌑ *20 Sk.* ⊙ *Tues.–Sat. 9–5, Sun. 9–1.*

Dining and Lodging

$–$$ ✕ **Sedliacky dvor.** Decorated as an old country cottage, Sedliacky ★ dvor comes complete with wooden tables, a pitchfork, and a picket fence. Expect an enormous plate piled high with various meats and either rice, mushrooms, and cheese or dumplings and red and white cabbage. ⊠ *Biela 3,* ☎ *055/622–0402. No credit cards.*

$$–$$$ ✕📺 **Hotel Bankov.** Fluffy terry robes and dark-wood reproduction
★ antiques epitomize the luxury of the Bankov—a luxury uncommon
outside of Bratislava. The thick casement windows on the rear ground
level open out onto a summer terrace. The no-smoking restaurant serves
upscale meals such as venison and chateaubriand for two, with an
extensive wine list including Hungarian varieties. Formerly a 19th-
century spa resort, Bankov is now a peaceful respite surrounded by
hiking trails in the cool hills a 10-minute drive outside Košice. ⊠ *Dolný
Bankov 2, 04001,* ☎ *055/632–4522,* 🆁🅰🆇 *055/632–4540,* 🆆🅴🅱 *www.
hotelbankov.sk. 16 rooms, 2 apartments. Restaurant, minibars, cable
TV with movies, pool, massage, sauna, hiking, bar, beer garden,
laundry service, business services, meeting rooms, airport shuttle; no
a/c. AE, MC, V.*

$$ 📺 **Hotel Alessandria.** A few minutes' stroll from Hlavná ulica brings
you to this white-and-green hotel in a residential neighborhood. The
building was originally constructed in the 19th century, which ex-
plains its expansive rooms with antechambers and high ceilings. A lack
of coordinating furniture somehow doesn't detract from the overall pleas-
antness. Breakfast is served in the small restaurant, and in summer a
garden terrace is perfect for drinking a beer. Gated parking is a bonus.
⊠ *Jiskrova 3, 04001,* ☎ *055/622–5903,* 🆁🅰🆇 *055/622–5918. 10 rooms,
3 apartments. Restaurant, minibars, cable TV, bar, beer garden, free
parking; no a/c. AE, DC, MC, V.*

Nightlife and the Arts

Jazz Club (⊠ Kováčska 39, ☎ 055/623–0467), a cozy basement bar,
is a popular local hangout. The name is a bit misleading though, as
the club has not only live and taped jazz music but also disco, coun-
try, and rap music.

The **Štátne divadlo** (State Theater; ⊠ Hlavná. 58, ☎ 055/622–1231)
hosts theater, ballet, and opera productions. Tickets are reasonably priced
and can be bought at the theater box office.

Bardejov

㉕ *80 km (50 mi) north of Košice, 101 km (63 mi) east of Poprad on Rtes.
68 and 77.*

Bardejov is a great surprise, tucked away in this remote corner of Slo-
vakia yet possessing one of the nation's most enchanting squares. In-
deed, Bardejov owes its splendors to its location astride the ancient trade
routes to Poland and Russia. It's hard to put a finger on exactly what
makes the square so captivating—it could be the lack of arcades in front
of the houses, the high pointed roofs, or the colorful pastels and dec-
orative scenes painted on the facades, which have a light, almost comic
effect. Shopping along the pedestrian square is quite pleasant.

The exterior of the Gothic **Kostol svätého Egídia** (St. Egidius Church),
built in stages in the 15th century, is undeniably handsome, but take
a walk inside for the real treasure. The nave is lined with 11 priceless,
purely Gothic side altars, all carved between 1460 and 1510 and per-
fectly preserved. The most famous of the altars is to the left of the main
altar (look for the number 1 on the side). This intricate work of Ste-
fan Tarner depicts the birth of Christ and dates from the 1480s. ⊠
Radničné nám., ☎ *no phone.*

In the center of the town square stands the **radnica** (town hall), a mod-
est building with late-Gothic portals and Renaissance detailing. ⊠
Radničné nám. 17.

★ The **Šariš** (Icon Museum) houses a collection of icons from as early as the 15th century and paintings taken from the area's numerous Greek Catholic and Orthodox churches. Many of the icons depict the story of St. George slaying the dragon (for the key to the princess's chastity belt!). The legend of St. George, which probably originated in pre-Christian mythology, was often used to attract the peasants of the area to the more abstemious stories of Christianity. Pick up the short commentary in English when you buy your ticket; for more detailed information, purchase the Slovak/English book *Ikony* from the reception area. ⊠ *Radničné nám. 13,* ☎ *054/474–6038.* ☜ *25 Sk.* ☉ *May–Sept., Tues.–Sun. 9–noon and 12:30–5:30; Oct.–Apr., Tues.–Sun. 8–noon and 12:30–4.*

Four kilometers (2½ mi) north of Bardejov is the historic spa town of **Bardejovské Kupelé.** The tourist information office in Bardejov can help you arrange treatments, which must be reserved ahead of time. The buildings with elaborate decorations and many porches are dormitories for patients. Don't miss the **Múzeum Ludovej Architektúry,** a *skansen* (open-air village museum). Several 19th- and early 20th-century wooden buildings, including a small wooden church from Zboj, have been relocated here to preserve the folk architecture from the Spiš and Rusyn areas. You can see the way villagers lived and in some cases still live today. No cars are allowed, so to visit the museum you must park for a fee at the town's lot and walk up the hill. ⊠ *Bardejovské Kupelé,* ☎ *054/472–2072.* ☜ *25 Sk.* ☉ *Daily 8:30–noon and 12:30–5.*

This area's great delights are unquestionably the old **Wooden Churches** still in use in their original village settings. For example, in **Jedlinka,** which lies 13 km (8 mi) north of Bardejov, three onion-dome towers from the 18th century rise above the west front of the church. Inside, the north, east, and south walls are painted with biblical scenes; the west wall was reserved for icons, many of which now hang in the Icon Museum in Bardejov. The churches are usually locked, but if you happen across a villager, ask him or her (with appropriate key-turning gestures) to let you in. More often than not, someone will turn up with a key and you'll have your own guided tour. The booklet *Wooden Churches Near Bardejov,* available at hotels and bookstores, provides detailed information, pictures, and a rudimentary map. ⊠ *Off Rte. 545 and Rte. 77.*

Dining and Lodging

$$ ✕🏨 **Hotel Bellevue.** On a hill outside the center of town, Bellevue af-
★ fords splendid views of the countryside. The pool, which juts out to the edge of the hill on which it sits and is enclosed by glass, provides one of the best vantage points. Elegant, contemporary cherrywood furnishings are upholstered in botanical prints with deep greens and earth tones. Heat is provided from below the ceramic-tile floors. Locals often clog up the bar, but the adjoining restaurant menu uses an impressive number of vegetables—uncommon in this area—in dishes such as turkey breast stuffed with asparagus. ⊠ *Mihalov, 08501 (follow signs to Mihalov off Rte. 525, 3 km [2 ½ mi],* ☎ *054/472–6090,* FAX *054/472–8404,* WEB *www.home.sk/www/bellevue. 25 rooms, 3 apartments. Restaurant, cable TV, 2 tennis courts, pool, gym, hot tub, massage, sauna, bar, laundry service; no a/c. No credit cards.*

Medzilaborce

❷⑥ *77 km (48 mi) east of Bardejov on Rtes. 77 and 73.*

The sleepy border town of Medzilaborce holds an unlikely museum.
★ Here, near the birthplace of Andy Warhol's parents, is the **Múzeum moderného umenia rodiny Warholovcov** (Warhol Family Museum of Mod-

ern Art). In all, the museum holds 17 original Warhol silk screens, including two from the famous Campbell's Soup series, and portraits of Lenin and singer Billie Holiday. ⊠ *Ul. Andyho Warhola 749,* ☎ *057/ 748-0072.* 🎟 *100 Sk.* ⊘ *Tues.–Sat. 9:30–4:30, Sun. noon–4:30.*

Eastern Slovakia Essentials

AIR TRAVEL

Sky Europe flies between Bratislava and Košice daily, Slovak Airlines weekdays. Fares start around 1,000 Sk one-way with advance notice.
➤ CARRIERS: **Slovak Airlines** (☎ 02/4445–0096, WEB www. slovakairlines.sk). **Sky Europe** (☎ 02/4850–4850, WEB www. skyeurope.com).

BUS TRAVEL

Daily bus service connects Košice with Bratislava and Poprad, but trains tend to be quicker and more comfortable (InterCity trains have air-conditioning, while buses do not). The ride from Bratislava takes about 5 hours (360 Sk); the trip from Poprad lasts 2½ hours (280 Sk).

Once you arrive in eastern Slovakia you can access most of the towns within the region via the extensive, inexpensive SAD bus network. Plan carefully: many buses run only on weekdays.
➤ TRAIN STATION: **Autobusová stanica** (⊠ Železničná 1, Košice, ☎ 055/ 625–1619, WEB www.busy.sk).

CAR RENTAL

A rental car can run about 2,500 Sk per day, but it provides the best way to see the region. Hertz and Avis have offices at Košice airport. Simocar is a local agency.
➤ AGENCIES: **Avis** (⊠ Letisko Košice-Barca, Košice, ☎ 055/643–3099). **Hertz** (⊠ Letisko Košice-Barca, Košice, ☎ 055/789–6041). **Simocar** (⊠ Maticna 59, Košice, ☎ 055/685–5283).

CAR TRAVEL

The drive from Bratislava to Košice takes about six hours; it's best to take the E571 via Nitra, Zvolen, and Rožňava. Poprad is two hours along E50 from Košice.

A car is essential for reaching the smaller towns and wooden churches in this region. The two-lane roads are generally in good condition; some stretches wind past beautiful panoramas, such as Route 547 between Košice and Levoča.

EMERGENCIES

Lekárne (pharmacies) in larger towns take turns staying open late and on Sunday. Look for the list posted on the front door of each pharmacy. For after-hours service, ring the bell; you will be served through a little hatch door.

TRAIN TRAVEL

Trains regularly connect Košice to Bratislava (5–6 hours, 460 Sk), but book in advance to ensure a seat on these sometimes crowded routes during holidays. The trip from Poprad to Košice takes from 3½ to 4½ hours (380 Sk). You'll have to resort to rental car or bus to reach smaller villages. Train stations, like Košice's Železničná stanica, tend to be in the town center.
➤ TRAIN STATION: **Železničná stanica** (⊠ Železničná 1, Košice, ☎ 095/622–3700, WEB www.zsr.sk).

VISITOR INFORMATION

The travel agency Satur books tours of the region and can reserve you a room at affiliated hotels. Town Information Centers can assist with lodging and sightseeing. Contact the Spirit information office in Bardejov ahead of time to reserve a stay and treatment (you have to reserve both in summer) in the spa town of Bardejovské Kupelé.

➤ TOURIST INFORMATION: **Satur** (✉ Hlavná 1, Košice, ☎ 055/622–3122 or 055/622–3847). **Spirit** (✉ Radničné nám. 21, Bardejov, ☎ 054/472–6273, WEB www.bardejov.sk). **Tourist Information Center** (✉ Nám. majstra Pavla 58, Levoča, ☎ 053/451–3763, www.levoca.sk; ✉ Hlavná 8, Košice, ☎ 055/625–8888, WEB www.kosice.sk).

SLOVAKIA A TO Z

AIR TRAVEL
See Air Travel *in* Bratislava Essentials, *above*.

BIKE TRAVEL
A special bike trail links Bratislava and Vienna, paralleling the Danube for much of its 40-km (25-mi) length. For more strenuous biking, the Low Tatras have scenic trails. Few places, however, rent bikes. For rental information, inquire at a tourist information center or at your hotel.

BOAT TRAVEL
Hydrofoils travel the Danube between Vienna and Bratislava and Budapest and Bratislava from May to September. *See* Boat Travel *in* Bratislava Essentials, *above*, for more information.

BUS TRAVEL
Frequent buses connect Vienna, Prague, and Budapest with Bratislava. However, trains are far more comfortable and the stations are easier to navigate if you don't speak Slovak. You can also take a bus between Prague and Poprad, and from Košice into Hungary or to Uzghorod in the Ukraine.

Slovenská autobusová doprava (SAD), the national bus carrier for Slovakia, maintains a comprehensive network in Slovakia. Buy your tickets (*cestovné lístky*) from the ticket window at the bus station or, in smaller stations, directly from the driver on the bus. Long-distance buses can be full on holidays, so you might want to book a seat in advance; any Satur office can help you do this. A drawback to traveling by bus is figuring out the timetables. Beware of the small letters denoting exceptions to the times given.

➤ BUS INFORMATION: **SAD** (WEB www.busy.sk).

BUSINESS HOURS
Banks are open weekdays 8–4. Museum hours vary, but many are closed on Monday. Shops are generally open weekdays 9–6 and stay open slightly later on Thursday; some close noon–2. Many shops are also open Saturday 9–noon (department stores 9–4) and, in big cities, Sunday. Gas stations along major highways are generally open 24 hours; in smaller towns, gas stations tend to keep the same hours as shops.

CAR RENTAL
Rental cars are readily available in Bratislava and Košice at the airports and in town. There are no special requirements for renting a car in Slovakia, but be sure to shop around, as prices can differ greatly. Hertz offers Western makes for as much as $350 per week. Smaller, local companies may rent cars for as little as $130 per week for a manual transmission, economy car without air-conditioning but with unlimited mileage. You may buy general accident and theft insurance for an additional $25 and $7, respectively. There is a 6% tax on car rentals. Prices are comparable whether or not you arrange for a rental before arriving in Slovakia.

CAR TRAVEL

Highways link Bratislava with Prague (3½ hours) and Budapest (2½ hours). The road to Vienna passes through a few small towns, but the trip is usually still quick (about an hour). From Bratislava to Poprad, about half the journey is over multilane highway, and construction continues to complete the link. As you travel east in Slovakia, roads get narrower but are generally in good condition. Though you might find yourself behind a horse cart on a mountain road, a car is still the best way to get around in the far northeast, where traffic is usually light and train connections scarce.

To report an accident call the police; in the case of car failure call the Autoklub Slovakia Assistance.

➤ CONTACTS: **Ambulance** (☎ 155). **Police** (☎ 158). **24-hr Roadside Assistance** (☎ 124).

PARKING

Downtown parking lots are limited in all major cities, particularly Bratislava; the fees vary. In larger cities, you should get a parking card (*parkovacia karta*) for street parking; place it on your dashboard so it's visible through the windshield. The cards are available from the roaming vendors who wear yellow vests, or at newspaper kiosks, and cost 5 Sk for an hour's parking. A sign with a circle with an "X" in the middle indicates a no-parking zone.

RULES OF THE ROAD

Slovakia follows the usual Continental rules of the road. A right turn on red is permitted only when indicated by a green arrow. On main roads, signposts with yellow diamonds indicate which drivers have the right of way. Signposts with blue circles outlined in red with a single horizontal line in the center indicate a one-way street that you cannot enter. The speed limit is 130 kph (80 mph) on four-lane highways, 90 kph (55 mph) on open roads, 60 kph (37 mph) in built-up areas, and 30 kph (19 mph) in Bratislava's center. The fine for speeding is roughly 1,000 Sk, payable on the spot. To use the highways you need a special label (*diaľničná známka*) displayed on your car window. If you rent a car in Slovakia, the label is provided. Labels cost about 100 Sk for 15 days and are available at border stops. Seat belts are compulsory, and drinking before driving is strictly prohibited. Random Breathalyzer checks are not uncommon.

CUSTOMS AND DUTIES

ON ARRIVAL

You may import duty-free into Slovakia 250 cigarettes or the equivalent in tobacco, 1 liter of spirits, 2 liters of wine, ½ liter of perfume, and up to 1,000 Sk worth of gifts and souvenirs.

ON DEPARTURE

There is no limit on the amount of goods purchased for noncommercial use, but to be on the safe side, hang on to all receipts. You can only export antiques (items more than 50 years old) with approval, based on a court-expert opinion submitted by you to the Sekcia narodneho dedičstva (Department of National Heritage). For a list of court experts, call the department of experts and interpreters at the Krajský súd (Regional Court).

➤ CONTACTS: **Krajský súd** (Regional Court; ⊠ Záhradnícka 10, Starý mesto, Bratislava, ☎ 02/5542–4060 or 02/5542–4042). **Sekcia narodneho dedičstva** (Department of National Heritage; ⊠ Ministerstvo kultury, Nam. SNP 33, Starý mesto, Bratislava, ☎ 02/5441–5629).

EMERGENCIES

➤ CONTACTS: **Ambulance** (☎ 155). **Police** (☎ 158).

HOLIDAYS

January 1 (founding of the Slovak Republic); January 6 (Twelfth Night); Good Friday and Easter Monday (in March, April, or May); May 1 (Labor Day); May 8 (Liberation of the Republic); July 5 (Sts. Cyril and Methodius); August 29 (anniversary of the Slovak National Uprising); September 1 (Constitution Day); September 15 (Our Lady of Sorrows, Assumption); November 1 (All Saints' Day); November 17 (Students' Day, to commemorate the end of Communism); and December 24–26.

LANGUAGE

Slovak, a western-Slavic tongue closely related to both Czech and Polish, is the official language of Slovakia. English is popular today, especially among young people.

MAIL AND SHIPPING

Postcards to the United States and Canada cost 12 Sk; letters cost 18 Sk. Postcards to Great Britain cost 9 Sk; letters cost 14 Sk. If you don't know where you'll be staying, you can have mail held *poste restante* (general delivery) at post offices in major towns, but the letters should be marked Pošta 1 to designate a city's main post office. You will be asked for identification when you collect mail.
➤ CONTACTS: **Bratislava Pošta 1** (✉ Námestie SNP 5, Starý mesto, Bratislava).

MONEY MATTERS

Bratislava is easily the most expensive area in Slovakia. As a rule, small country towns are extremely reasonable. While overcharging foreigners is not a widespread practice, you may find that state-subsidized theaters do charge visitors higher prices.

The following are sample prices: a cup of coffee, 15 Sk; museum entrance, 10 Sk–100 Sk; a good theater seat, 60 Sk–750 Sk; a 2-km (1-mi) taxi ride, 150 Sk; a half liter (pint) of beer, 20 Sk–40 Sk; a glass of wine, 25 Sk–50 Sk; a bottle of Slovak wine in a good restaurant, 100 Sk–250 Sk.

MasterCard and Visa are more widely accepted than American Express, Discover, or Diners Club. ATMs are quite common in towns, and almost every hotel offers exchange services. Though rates might be a bit better at a bank, hotels have more flexible hours.

CURRENCY

The unit of currency in Slovakia is the crown, or koruna, written as Sk, and divided into 100 halierov. There are bills of 20, 50, 100, 200, 500, 1,000, and 5,000 Sk, and coins of 10, 20, and 50 halierov and 1, 2, 5, and 10 Sk. At press time, the rate of exchange was around 43 Sk to the American dollar, 42 Sk to the euro, 27 Sk to the Canadian dollar, and 67 Sk to the pound sterling.

PASSPORTS AND VISAS

American, British, and Canadian citizens do not need a visa to enter Slovakia. A valid passport is sufficient for stays of up to 30 days for a U.S. citizen, up to six months for a U.K. citizen, and up to 90 days for a Canadian citizen.

TELEPHONES

The country code for Slovakia is 421; the area code for Bratislava is 02. When dialing from outside the country, drop the initial "0" from the area code.

DIRECTORY AND OPERATOR ASSISTANCE

Dial "120" for local directory assistance and "121" for assistance on regions in Slovakia outside the city from which you're dialing. Not all operators speak English. International directory assistance is 149.

INTERNATIONAL CALLS

Dial AT&T or MCI to reach an English-speaking operator who can connect your direct, collect, or credit-card call to the United States. You can make a time-consuming and expensive international call from Bratislava's main telecommunications office, Slovenské telekomunikácie. For an even larger fee, you can call from a major hotel.

➤ CONTACTS: **AT&T** (☎ 0800/000–101). **MCI** (☎ 0800/000–112). **Slovenské telekomunikácie** (✉ Kolárska 12, Starý mesto).

PUBLIC PHONES

Public pay phones are easily found in town centers. Most public phones take prepaid phone cards, which are available at post offices and some newsstands. A local call costs at least 2 Sk.

TIPPING

Gratuities are not automatically added to restaurant bills. To reward good service, round up the bill to the nearest multiple of 10 (if the bill comes to 86 Sk, for example, give the waiter 90 Sk). A tip of 10% is considered appropriate in inexpensive restaurants or on group tabs. A 20 Sk tip for porters is usually sufficient. For room service, a 20 Sk tip is sufficient. In taxis, round up the bill to the nearest multiple of 10. Give tour guides and helpful concierges 20 Sk–30 Sk.

TOURS

Tatratour is a large, dependable agency that can help arrange sightseeing tours throughout Slovakia. Limba hosts trips with a focus on rural Slovakia; the guides are excellent.

➤ CONTACT: **Limba** (✉ Medena 13, Starý mesto, Bratislava, ☎ 02/5441–8601, WEB www.limba.sk). **Tatratour** (✉ Bajkalská 25, Starý mesto, Bratislava, ☎ 02/5341–1219 or 02/5341–4828, FAX 02/5341–2781).

TRAIN TRAVEL

Bratislava is the country's international train hub. You can take a direct train from Berlin via Dresden and Prague (en route to Budapest) and from Paris via Frankfurt to Vienna (and connect to another train or bus). One train a day goes to Moscow from Bratislava. Several trains a day link Bratislava with Prague and with Budapest. Vienna has good international connections and numerous trains that make the 70-minute run daily from Vienna's Südbahnhof (South Station) to Bratislava.

Slovakia's state-run rail system, Železnice Slovenskej republiky, is quite extensive. Trains vary in speed, but it's not really worth taking anything other than an "express" train, marked in red on the timetable. Tickets are cheap compared with those in countries farther west. First class is considerably more spacious and comfortable and well worth the cost (50% more than a standard ticket). If you don't specify "express" when you buy your ticket, you may have to pay a supplement on the train. If you haven't bought a ticket in advance at the station, it's easy to buy one from the porter on the train for a small extra charge. On timetables, departures appear on a yellow background, arrivals on white. It's possible to book *couchettes* (sleepers) on most overnight trains, but don't expect much in the way of comfort with four to six bunks per room.

➤ TRAIN INFORMATION: **Železnice Slovenskej republiky** (Railways of the Slovak Republic; WEB www.zsr.sk/english).

CUTTING COSTS

The European East Pass from Rail Europe is good for unlimited first-class travel on the national railroads of Slovakia, Austria, the Czech Republic, Hungary, and Poland. The pass covers five days of unlimited first-class travel within a one-month period for $220. Additional travel days may be purchased. The InterRail Pass, available only to European citizens at Satur offices, is valid for 22 days of unlimited train travel in Slovakia, Croatia, the Czech Republic, Hungary, and Poland. The Eurailpass is not valid in Slovakia.

Keep in mind that because individual train tickets within Slovakia are still quite cheap, a rail pass may not afford significant savings if you plan to travel mainly in Slovakia.

➤ INFORMATION AND PASSES: **InterRail** (WEB www.interrail.com). **Rail Europe** (✉ 500 Mamaroneck Ave., Harrison, NY 10528, ☎ 914/682–5172 or 800/438–7245, FAX 800/432–1329; ✉ 2087 Dundas E, Suite 106, Mississauga, Ontario L4X 1M2, ☎ 800/361–7245, FAX 905/602–4198, WEB www.raileurope.com). **Železnice Slovenskej republiky** (Railways of the Slovak Republic; WEB www.zsr.sk/english).

VISITOR INFORMATION

Satur is the official travel agency for Slovakia. With offices in almost every city throughout the country, it will supply you with hotel and tour information and book air, rail, and bus tickets, as well as change traveler's checks, but do not expect much in the way of general information. Most cities have a tourist information center that can help reserve hotels and private rooms as well as offer city tours. For specific contact information, please see the appropriate city section.

Operators at the government's telephone information center generally speak English and provide details of local events. The Panorama Web site provides good background information—country news in English, descriptions of tourist attractions, and travel services—and the Lodging Slovakia Web site lists many of the country's hotels.

➤ CONTACTS: **Lodging Slovakia** (WEB www.lodging.sk). **Panorama** (WEB www.panorama.sk/en). **Satur** (WEB www.satur.sk/en). **Telephone information center** (☎ 186, preceded by the regional area code).

9 SLOVENIA

Slovenia emerged remarkably unscathed from the breakup of the Yugoslav federation. Today, in contrast to some of its neighbors, Slovenia bears no grudges against anyone. Why should it? A land of magnificent alpine mountains and lakes, undulating farmland and vineyards, plus a tiny strip of emerald blue Adriatic coast, Slovenia seems to have it all. Here, Mediterranean charm and Austrian efficiency blend with a genuine and captivating Slavic friendliness.

BORDERED BY ITALY, AUSTRIA, HUNGARY, AND CROATIA, the territory that is now Slovenia has changed size, shape, and affiliation many times over the course of history. In ancient times the region was inhabited by Illyrian and Celtic tribes. The Romans arrived in the 1st century BC, built villas along the coast, and founded the inland urban centers of Emona (Ljubljana) and Poetovio (Ptuj). The 6th century saw the first influx of Slav migrants, who set up an early Slav state. During the 8th century the region came under the Franks, and in the 9th century it was passed to the dukes of Bavaria.

By Jane Foster

Updated by
Betsy Maury

In 1335 the Hapsburgs took control of inland Slovenia, dividing it into the Austrian crown lands of Carinthia, Carniola, and Styria. Meanwhile, the coastal towns had requested Venetian protection, and they remained under *la serenissima* until 1797, after which they, too, were taken by Austria.

During the 15th and 16th centuries, the Turks, eager to extend the Ottoman Empire right across the Balkans and north to Vienna, made repeated attacks on the region. However, Slovenia remained under the Hapsburgs until 1918, with the exception of a brief period from 1809 to 1813 when it became part of Napoléon's Illyrian Provinces.

In the aftermath of the First World War, Italy seized control of the coastal towns, while inland Slovenia became part of the Kingdom of Serbs, Croats, and Slovenes. In 1929 the name was changed to Yugoslavia (Land of the Southern Slavs).

In 1941 Hitler declared war on Yugoslavia: Axis forces occupied the country, and Slovenia was divided between Germany, Italy, and Hungary. Josip Broz, better known as Tito, set up the anti-Fascist Partisan movement, and many Slovenes took part in resistance activities. When the war ended in 1945 Slovenia became one of the six constituent republics of Yugoslavia, with Tito as president. Slovenes today are proud of their Partisan past, and traveling through the country you see monuments and wall plaques bearing the red star, a symbol of the Partisans and of Communist ideology, and squares and roads still named after Tito.

Half Slovene and half Croat, Tito was undeniably an astute leader. He governed Yugoslavia under Communist ideology, but the system was far more liberal than that of the Soviet-bloc countries: Yugoslavs enjoyed freedom of movement, and foreigners could enter the country without visas. During the Cold War, Tito never took sides but dealt cleverly with both East and West, thus procuring massive loans from both.

However, when Tito died in 1980, the system he left behind began to crumble. The false nature of the economy, based on borrowing, became apparent. During the 1980s economic crisis set in and inflation soared. Slovenia, accounting for only 8% of Yugoslavia's population, was producing one-third of the nation's exports. The hard-earned foreign currency ended up in Belgrade and was used in part to subsidize the poorer republics. It was time for change.

In early 1990 Slovenia introduced a multiparty system and elected a non-Communist government. Demands for increased autonomy were stepped up, with the threat of secession. A referendum was held, and 90% of the electorate voted for independence. Unlike the other Yugoslav republics, Slovenia was made up almost exclusively of a single ethnic group: Slovenes. Thus the potential status of ethnic minorities, should the republic secede, was never an issue. Slovenia proclaimed independence on June 25, 1991, and the so-called 10-Day War followed. Federal troops moved in, but there was relatively little violence. Belgrade had already agreed to let Slovenia go.

In 1992 Slovenia gained recognition, along with Croatia, from the European Community and the United Nations. Since then the economy has stabilized and tourism has flourished. Today Slovenia's focus is turned squarely to the West, with the tiny nation considered to be a leading candidate for EU and NATO membership.

Situated at a geopolitical crossroads, this small Slavic nation has had to redefine its position in the modern world. Visitors will find the culture particularly accessible: a large percentage of the younger generation speaks several foreign languages (English, Italian, and German), and Slovenia is probably the most Internet-friendly country in Central and Eastern Europe.

Pleasures and Pastimes

Bicycling

Slovenia has a number of clearly marked bike trails, with needed services along the routes: bike rentals, maintenance and spare parts, and tourist information. Rental agencies, good hotels, and local tourist information centers can provide detailed information about suitable itineraries. For mountain biking, Triglav National Park is popular. If you prefer less-strenuous riding, try the riverside trails near Maribor. A brochure, *Slovenia by Bicycle,* is available from the Slovenian Tourist Board.

Castles

The earliest castles in Slovenia date back to the Middle Ages and were built as hilltop observation points with views over the surrounding valleys. Several trade-routes traversed the region. Merchandise brought prosperity, but with it the danger of attack. During the 15th and 16th centuries a series of Turkish onslaughts sparked off increased fortification. The castles and manors as we see them today largely reflect the habits of the local aristocracy during the 17th century, with their love of Viennese culture and a propensity for Baroque decoration. A number of castles now house museums and galleries, and several have been converted into first-class hotels and restaurants. A brochure, *Castles and Manors*, is available from the Slovenian Tourist Board.

Dining

When you look at a menu remember two key words: regional and seasonal. This is the way to find the best food in Slovenia. (You'll find menus in English, plus waitstaff who speak English, almost everywhere.) There are no pretensions at the table, and full respect is paid to simple traditional dishes. To really get down to basics, eat in a *gostilna* (country inn). Typical dishes are *krvavice* (black pudding) served with *žganci* (polenta) or Kraški pršùt (air-dried ham). Another favorite is *bograč,* a peppery stew similar to Hungarian goulash, made from either horse meat or beef.

With the Adriatic close at hand, you can also find excellent seafood. Visit a good *restauracija* (restaurant) and try mouthwatering *škampi rižot* (scampi risotto) followed by fresh fish prepared *na žaru* (grilled). Fresh trout with *tržaška* (garlic and parsley) sauce is a staple on any menu near the Soča river. The first-rate fish—usually priced on menus per kilogram (2.2 pounds)—are expensive, so don't be surprised when the bill comes.

For an extra boost stop at a *kavarna* (coffee shop) for a scrumptious, calorie-laden *prekmurska gibanica,* a layered cake combining curd cheese, walnuts, and poppy seeds. Another national favorite is *potica*, a rolled cake filled with either walnuts, chocolate, poppy seeds, or raisins.

CATEGORY	COST*
$$$$	More than SIT 3000
$$$	SIT 2000–SIT 3000
$$	SIT 1000–SIT 2000
$	under SIT 1000

per person for a main course at dinner

Fishing

The River Soča, stocked with rare marble trout, rainbow trout, and grayling, attracts anglers from all over the world with its excellent fly-fishing amid stunning scenery. The season runs from April through October, and daily permits are obligatory. Kobarid makes an ideal base.

Hiking

Slovenes love mountains, and when you reach the northwest of the country you will understand why. The most popular alpine hiking route runs from Maribor near the Austrian border to Ankaran on the Adriatic coast. It crosses Triglav National Park and can be walked in 30 days. For less devoted walkers, a day or two of backpacking from one of the alpine resorts is an invigorating way to explore the landscape. Mountain paths are well marked, and mountain lodges have dormitory-style accommodations. Detailed maps are available at local tourist information centers.

Horseback Riding

The most famous equestrian center is the Lipica Stud Farm, home of the splendid Lipizzaner white horses. Riding lessons are available, and it is also possible to hire horses for gentle hacking.

Visitors to the Krka Valley can ride at the Struga Equestrian Center, at a 12th-century medieval manor near Otočec Castle. In Triglav National Park the best-equipped riding center is Pristava Lepena. A brochure, *Riding in Slovenia, Home of the Lipizzaner,* is available from the Slovenian Tourist Board.

Kayaking, Canoeing, and Rafting

The River Soča has ideal conditions for boating. The best rapids lie between Bovec and Kobarid. Numerous clubs rent out boats and equipment and also offer instruction and guided rafting and kayaking trips.

Lodging

Don't expect Slovenia to be a cheap option: lodging prices are similar to what you'd see in Western Europe. During peak season (July and August), many hotels, particularly on the coast, are fully booked. Hotels are generally clean, smartly furnished, and well run. Establishments built under socialism are equipped with extras such as saunas and sports facilities but tend to be gargantuan structures lacking in soul. Hotels dating from the turn of the 20th century are more romantic, as are the castle hotels. Over the last decade many hotels have been refurbished and upgraded. Many hotels will offer better rates for stays of more than three days.

Private lodgings are a cheap alternative to hotels, and standards are generally excellent. Prices vary depending on region and season. For details contact a local tourist information center.

Between April and October camping is a reasonable alternative. Most campgrounds are small but well equipped. On the coast, campsites are found at Izola and Ankaran. In Triglav National Park and the Soča

Valley there are sites at Bled, Bohinj, Bovec, Kobarid, Soča, and Trenta. It is also possible to camp on the grounds of Otočec Castle in the Krka Valley. Camping outside of organized campsites is not permitted.

To really experience day-to-day life in the countryside you should stay on a working farm. Agrotourism is rapidly growing in popularity, and at most farms you can experience an idyllic rural setting, delicious home cooking, plus a warm family welcome. A brochure, *Tourist Farms in Slovenia,* is available from the Slovenian Tourist Board.

CATEGORY	COST*
$$$$	over €200
$$$	€150–€200
$$	€80–€150
$	under €80

All prices are for a standard double room, including tax and service charge.

Sailing

Slovenia is an ideal starting point for sailing down the Adriatic coast. There are three marinas: Izola (where it is possible to rent yachts), Portorož, and Koper. Portorož Yacht Club organizes a number of annual international regattas.

Shopping

The most interesting gifts to buy in Slovenia are the homemade products you come across in your travels: wine from Ptuj, *rakija* (a potent spirit distilled from fruit) from Pleterje Monastery, herbal teas from Stična Monastery, honey from Radovljica. The Slovenian products best known abroad are connected with outdoor sports. If you'd like some Planika walking boots or Elan skis, you can get a good deal on them here.

Skiing

Skiing is undoubtedly one of the most popular sports in Slovenia. The largest and best-known ski area is Kranjska Gora, on the edge of Triglav National Park. The nearby resorts of Bovec, Bohinj, and Bled provide similar facilities on a smaller scale. To the east, the Pohorje Mountains near Maribor have alpine ski runs and groomed cross-country trails. All centers are well equipped, with rental equipment, ski lifts, and qualified instructors. In a good winter it is possible to ski from December through March (in some places until the beginning of May). Each year Slovenia hosts a number of major World Cup skiing events, the most spectacular being the ski jumping and ski flying at Planica, near Kranjska Gora. A brochure, *Ski Centers in Slovenia,* is available from the Slovenian Tourist Board.

Wine and Spirits

Slovenes enjoy drinking and produce some excellent wines. Most of these they consume themselves, so unfortunately very little reaches the foreign market. You can tour the three main wine regions following a series of established "wine roads." These routes pass through rolling hills, woodlands, and villages and lead directly to vineyards and wine stores. The best white wines, Sivi Pinot (pinot grigio) and Beil Pinot (pinot blanc), are produced in the Podravje region in northeast Slovenia. The best red is Teran, produced in the Karst region to the southwest, close to the Adriatic coast. There has been a recent drive to introduce more sparkling wines: look for the excellent Penina. The favorite national spirit is the potent *rakija.* The base is alcohol distilled from fruit; a variety of wild herbs are added later to give it a more discreet flavor.

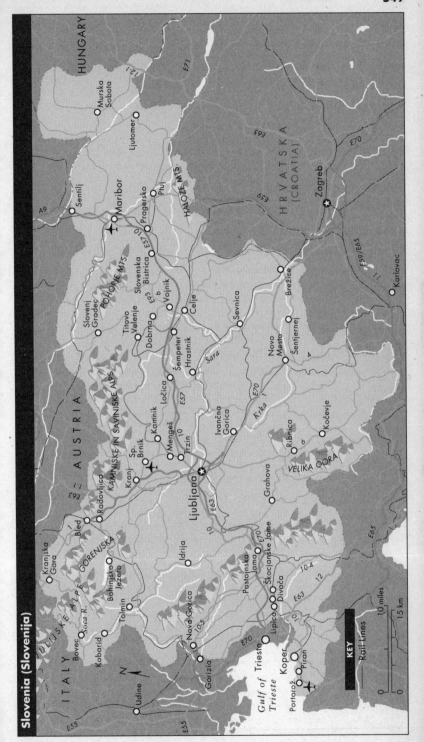

Slovenia (Slovenija)

HUNGARY

Murska Sobota

Ljutomer

Šentilj

A9

Maribor

Ptuj

Pragersko

HALOŽE MTS.

E71

E71

E65

HRVATSKA (CROATIA)

Zagreb

E70

E59

E59/E65

Karlovac

Sloveni Gradec

POHORJE MTS.

Slovenska Bistrica

E57

10

Titovo Velenje

Dobrna

E63

Vojnik

Celje

Sevnica

Brežice

E63

11

Šempeter

Hrastnik

Savra

Šenternej

Novo Mesto

4

Kamnik

Ločica

E57

Ivančna Gorica

Krka

E70

Ribnica

b

Kočevje

AUSTRIA

KAMNIŠKE IN SAVINJSKE ALPS

Sp. Brnik

Mengeš

Trzin

Kranj

Radovljica

E63

11

Ljubljana

E63

Grahova

VELIKA GORA

E65

Kranjska Gora

JULIJSKE ALPE

GORENJSKA

Bled

Bohinjsko Jezero

Idrija

10

E70

Postojnska Jama

Škocjanske Jame

Divača

10.4

12

Bovec

Soča R.

Tolmin

Nova Gorica

10.5

Lipica

E63

10

Kobarid

Gorizia

E70

Gulf of Trieste

Trieste

Koper

Piran

Portorož

ITALY

Udine

N

E55

E55

KEY

Rail Lines

10 miles

15 km

0

0

Exploring Slovenia

Besides the capital, Ljubljana, the principal areas of interest to tourists are Triglav National Park and the Soča Valley to the northwest, and the Adriatic coast and the karst region to the southwest. The Krka Valley, to the east, is notable for its monasteries and castles, while the region to the northeast, centering on Maribor, Ptuj, and the Haloze Hills, has several vineyards and excellent wine cellars.

Great Itineraries

Slovenia's small size (about half the area of Switzerland) can be an advantage. From the centrally located capital, Ljubljana, you can drive to any point in the country in a maximum of three hours.

IF YOU HAVE 3 DAYS

If you have limited time, take one day to discover the Old Town of ☒ **Ljubljana.** The next day, drive out to the alpine mountains and lakes of Triglav National Park and stay the night in ☒ **Bled.** Spend the third day exploring the caves of the karst region, topping it off with a night by the Adriatic in the beautiful Venetian town of ☒ **Piran.**

IF YOU HAVE 5 DAYS

Make Ljubljana your base for the first three days. Explore the capital for a day; then head out to the wine-making area around **Maribor** and **Ptuj.** On day three, visit the monasteries of Stična and Pleterje in the Krka Valley, with the option of a romantic night in a castle hotel. Spend the last two days exploring Triglav National Park and the karst region.

When to Tour

The countryside is at its most beautiful in spring and fall, though the best period to visit depends on what you plan to do during your stay. Ljubljana is vibrant the whole year through. Many visitors want to head straight for the coast. Those in search of sea, sun, and all-night parties will find exactly what they're looking for in peak season (July and August), including cultural events, open-air dancing, busy restaurants, and heaving beaches. If you want to avoid the crowds, hit the Adriatic in June or September, when it should be warm enough to swim and easier to find a space for your beach towel.

In the mountains there are two distinct seasons: winter is dedicated to skiing, summer to hiking and bathing. Some hotels close in November and March, to mark a break between the two periods. Conditions for more-strenuous walking and biking are optimal in April, May, September, and October.

Lovers of fine food and wine should visit Slovenia during fall. The grape harvest concludes with the blessing of the season's young wine on St. Martin's Day, preceded by three weeks of festivities. In rural areas autumn is the time to make provisions for the hard winter ahead: wild mushrooms are gathered, firewood chopped, and *koline* (sausages and other pork products) prepared by hand.

LJUBLJANA

The romantic heart of the Old Town—with a hilltop castle overlooking the winding emerald-green Ljubljanica River, lined with Baroque facades and graceful weeping willows—date back centuries. The earliest settlement was founded by the Romans and called Emona. Much of it was destroyed by the Huns under Attila, though a section of the walls and a complex of foundations—complete with mosaics—can still be seen today. In the 12th century a new settlement, Laibach, was built on the right bank of the river, below Castle Hill, by the dukes of

Carniola. In 1335, the Hapsburgs gained control of the region, and it was they who constructed the existing castle fortification system.

The 17th century saw a period of Baroque building, strongly influenced by currents in Austria and Italy. Walk along the cobblestones of the Town Square and the Old Square to see Ljubljana at its best, from the colored Baroque town houses with their steeply pitched tile roofs to Francesco Robba's delightful Fountain of the Three Carniolan Rivers.

For a brief period, from 1809 to 1813, Ljubljana was the capital of Napoléon's Illyrian Provinces. In 1849, once again under the Hapsburgs, Ljubljana was linked to Vienna and Trieste by rail. The city developed into a major center of commerce, industry, and culture, and the opera house, national theater, national museum, and the first hotels came into existence.

In 1895 much of the city was devastated by an earthquake. The reconstruction work that followed was carried out in florid Viennese Secessionist style. Many of the palatial four-story buildings that line Miklošičeva, such as the Grand Hotel Union, date from this period.

After World War I, with the birth of the Kingdom of Serbs, Croats, and Slovenes, Ljubljana became the administrative center of Slovenia. Various national cultural institutes were founded, and the University of Ljubljana opened in 1919.

If you have been to Prague, you will already have seen some of the work of Jože Plečnik (1872–1957). Born in Ljubljana, Plečnik studied architecture in Vienna under Otto Wagner, then went on to lecture at the Prague School of Arts and Crafts, also playing the role of chief architect for the renovation of Prague Castle. With the opening of Ljubljana University in 1919, he returned to his home town. Here he completed many of his finest projects: the Triple Bridge, the open-air market on Vodnik Square, and the plans for the Križanke Summer Theater.

The Tito years saw increased industrialization. The population of Ljubljana tripled, and vast factory complexes, high-rise apartments, and modern office buildings extended into the suburbs. Ljubljana was considered one of the most alternative and experimental centers in Yugoslavia, especially during the 1980s, when it became the center of the Yugoslav punk movement. The band Laibach, noted for mocking nationalist sentiments, and the absurdist conceptual art group Neue Slowenische Kunst (NSK) both have their roots here.

Exploring Ljubljana

The city center is concentrated within a small area, so you can cover all the sights on foot.

Numbers in the text correspond to numbers in the margin and on the Ljubljana map.

A Good Walk

Begin your walk from Prešernov trg (Prešeren Square), a traffic-free piazza and focal point of public gatherings, overlooked by the Secessionist **Centromerkur** ① department store and the pink Baroque **Franciskanska cerkev** ②. From here cross **Tromostovje** ③, pausing a moment to observe the majestic hilltop castle above the Old Town and the view down the willow-lined River Ljubljanica.

Now on Stritarjeva, take the first left for the colorful open-air market on **Vodnikov trg** ④, noting the tourist information center on the corner. To the left of the fruit and vegetable stalls you can see a row of

Ljubljana

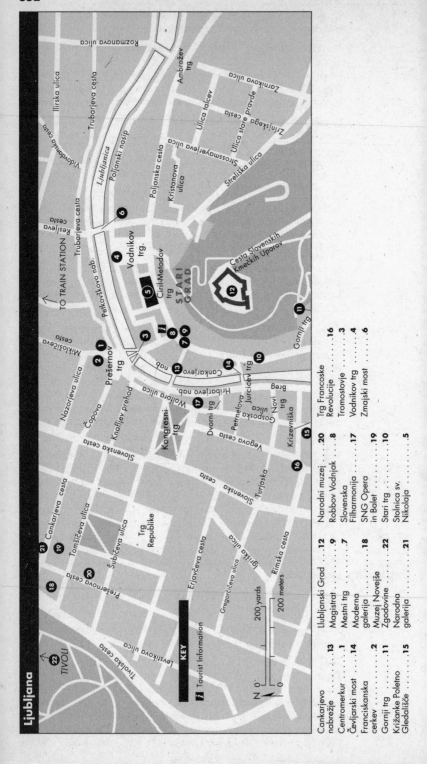

KEY

Ž Tourist Information

Cankarjevo
nabrežje **13**
Centromerkur **1**
Čevljarski most . . . **14**
Franciskanska
cerkev **2**
Gornji trg **11**
Križanke Poletno
Gledališče **15**

Ljubljanski Grad . . .**12**
Magistrat **9**
Mestni trg **7**
Moderna
galerija **18**
Muzej Novejše
Zgodovine **22**
Narodna
galerija **21**

Narodni muzej **20**
Robbov Vodnjak . . .**8**
Slovenska
Filharmonija **17**
SNG Opera
in Balet **19**
Stari trg **10**
Stolnica sv.
Nikolaja **5**

Trg Francoske
Revolucije **16**
Tromostovje **3**
Vodnikov trg **4**
Zmajski most **6**

0   200 yards
0   200 meters

N

bakeries and butchers, with steps leading down to an open-sided arcade that hosts the fish market on the waterfront. To the right—monumental and timeless amid the cries of stallholders and the bustling shoppers—stands **Stolnica sveti Nikolaja** ⑤. At the far end of the market the river is traversed by **Zmajski most** ⑥.

Double back to Stritarjeva, and turn left, then right to arrive on **Mestni trg** ⑦. Here the pace of life slows down to that of years gone by as you enter the heart of the Old Town. See the **Robbov Vodnjak** ⑧ and the **Magistrat** ⑨, and stroll the length of this cobbled square lined with antiques shops and boutiques. Mestni trg runs into **Stari trg** ⑩, animated with bars and cafés frequented by students. Follow the curve of the road left, and you are in **Gornji trg** ⑪, an up-and-coming area with some of the best restaurants in town. Look for a side street to the left called Ulica na Grad; follow this as far as house No. 11, and then take a narrow path up through the woods to arrive at **Ljubljanski grad** ⑫ (Ljubljana castle). From here you have a magnificent panorama of the entire city.

To return to the Old Town, find a narrow path just below the castle tower, which leads you via Studentovska to Ciril-Metodov trg (Cyril-Methodius Square), near the market. Turn left to arrive once more in Mestni trg, and from here take any one of the narrow cobbled passageways between the buildings on your right to reach the riverside promenade of **Cankarjevo nabrežje** ⑬. Follow the river downstream as far as **Čevljarski most** ⑭; then cross over to the other side of town. Turn left, following the river; then take the second right to reach the **Križanke Poletno Gledališče** ⑮ complex and, just above it, **Trg Francoske Revolucije** ⑯.

Walk back a block to Gosposka; then go north all the way to Kongresni trg (Congress Square), site of the **Slovenska Filharmonija** ⑰. Traverse the square to reach the busy Slovenska cesta, cross over and proceed along Šubičeva, turn right on Prešernova cesta, and you reach the main cluster of civic cultural buildings: the **Moderna galerija** ⑱, the **SNG Opera in Balet** ⑲, the **Narodni muzej** ⑳, and the **Narodna galerija** ㉑, all built at the end of the 19th century.

If you are short on time, the one museum you really should see is the **Muzej Novejše Zgodovine** ㉒. To find it, follow Cankarjeva west toward Tivolska cesta, using the underpass to avoid the traffic. This brings you up into the vast green expanse of Tivoli Park. Turn right, and then take a narrow path veering gently uphill to the left. Straight in front of you stands a pink-and-white baroque villa, which houses the museum.

TIMING

If you don't have much time, you should be able to see all the major sights in a day. However, to do the museums and churches justice you need at least two days.

SIGHTS TO SEE

⑬ **Cankarjevo nabrežje.** Numerous cafés line this pretty riverside walkway. When the weather is good, tables are placed outside overlooking the water. ⊠ *Between Tromostovje and Čevljarski most.*

❶ **Centromerkur.** This magnificent Secessionist-style building, dating from 1903, is the oldest department store in town. The entrance, off Prešernov trg, bears a flaring iron butterfly wing and is topped by a statue of Mercury. Inside, graceful wrought-iron stairways lead to upper floors. ⊠ *Trubarjeva 1,* ☎ *01/426–3170.*

⑭ **Čevljarski most** (Shoemaker's Bridge). Linking the old and new sides of town, this romantic pedestrian bridge was built in 1931 according to plans by the architect Jože Plečnik. The name is derived from a wooden structure that once stood here and was lined with cobblers' huts.

❷ Franciskanska cerkev (Franciscan Church). This massive, pink high-Baroque church was built between 1646 and 1660. The main altar, by Francesco Robba (1698–1757), dates from 1736. The three sets of stairs in front are a popular meeting place for students. ⊠ *Prešernov trg 4.* ⊙ *Daily 8–6.*

⓫ Gornji trg (Upper Square). This cobbled street, where you'll find some of the capital's finest restaurants, rises up above the Old Town and leads to the wooded parkland surrounding the castle.

⓯ Križanke Poletno Gledališče (Križanke Summer Theater). In the courtyard of an 18th-century monastery, this open-air theater was constructed according to plans drawn up by Jože Plečnik. It was completed in 1976, nearly two decades after the architect's death. The theater seats 1,400, and there's a movable roof in case it rains. ⊠ *Trg Francoske Revolucije.*

⓬ Ljubljanski grad (Llubljana Castle). Ljubljana's castle sits up on a hill and affords magnificent views over the river and the Old Town's terracotta rooftops, spires, and green cupolas. On a clear day the distant Julian Alps are a dramatic backdrop. The castle walls date from the early 16th century, although the tower was added in the mid-19th century. The surrounding park was landscaped by Plečnik in the 1930s. ⊠ *Studentovska ul., uphill from Vodnikov trg,* ☎ *01/432-7216,* ⊞ *www.ljubljanskigrad.com.* ▨ *Free.* ⊙ *Apr.–Oct., daily 9 AM–11 PM; Nov.–Mar., daily 10–7.*

NEED A BREAK?	The castle ramparts shelter a café and summer terrace. After the steep uphill climb, stop in for a refreshing drink, relax, and capture the essence of this mighty fortress.

OFF THE BEATEN PATH	**PLEČNIK'S HOUSE –** Architecture enthusiasts will enjoy a visit to architect Jože Plečnik's house, still exactly as he left it, to see his studio, home, and garden. From the Križanke Summer Theater, cross Zoisova cesta, and then follow Emonska to Karunova. ⊠ *Karunova 4, Trnovo,* ☎ *01/ 283-5067.* ▨ *SIT 800.* ⊙ *Tues. and Thurs. 10–2.*

❾ Magistrat (town hall). Guarded by an austere 18th-century facade, this building hides delightful secrets within. In the internal courtyard, for example, the walls are animated with murals depicting historic battles for the city, and a statue of Hercules keeps company with a fountain bearing a figure of Narcissus. ⊠ *Mestni trg 1.* ▨ *Free.* ⊙ *Weekdays 9–3, weekends only as part of guided tour of city.*

❼ Mestni trg (Town Square). This cobbled, traffic-free square extends into the oldest part of the city. Baroque town houses, now divided into functional apartments, present marvelously ornate facades: carved oak doors with great brass handles are framed within columns, and upper floors are decorated with balustrades, statuary, and intricate ironwork. Narrow passageways connect with inner courtyards in one direction and run to the riverfront in the other. The street-level floors contain boutiques, antiques shops, and art galleries.

NEED A BREAK?	If you plan to dine in the Old Town, stop first at **Movia** (⊠ Mestni trg 2, ☎ 01/425-5448) for an aperitif. This elegant little wine bar stocks a selection of first-rate Slovenian wines, for consumption both on and off the premises. It is closed weekends.

⑱ **Moderna galerija** (Modern Gallery). The strikingly modern one-story structure contains a selection of paintings, sculpture, and prints by Slovenian 20th-century artists. In odd-number years it also hosts the International Biennial of Graphic Art, an exhibition of prints and installations by artists from around the world. Works by Robert Rauschenberg, Susan Rothenburg, and Max Bill have been shown. ⊠ *Cankarjeva 15,* ☎ *01/251–4106,* WEB *www.mg-lj.si.* 🎟 *SIT 800.* ☉ *Tues.–Sat. 10–6, Sun. 10–1.*

★ ㉒ **Muzej Novejše Zgodovine** (Museum of Modern History). The permanent exhibition on Slovenes in the 20th century takes you from the days of Austria-Hungary, through the Second World War, the victory of the Partisan liberation movement and the ensuing Tito period, and up to the present day. Relics and memorabilia are combined with a dramatic sound-and-video presentation (scenes from World War II are projected on the walls and ceiling, accompanied by thundering gunfire, screams, and singing). You'll find the museum in a pink-and-white baroque villa in Tivoli Park. ⊠ *Celovška 23,* ☎ *01/232–3968,* WEB *www2.arnes.si/ -ljmuzejnz.* 🎟 *SIT 700.* ☉ *Tues.–Sun. 10–6.*

㉑ **Narodna galerija** (National Gallery). This imposing turn-of-the-20th-century building houses a survey of Slovenian art from the 13th through the early 20th century. ⊠ *Cankarjeva 20,* ☎ *01/241–5434,* WEB *www. ng-slo.si.* 🎟 *SIT 1,000.* ☉ *Tues.–Sun. 10–6.*

⑳ **Narodni muzej** (National Museum). The centerpiece here is a bronze urn from the 5th century BC known as the Vace Situle. Discovered in Vace, Slovenia, it is a striking example of Illyrian workmanship. ⊠ *Prešernova 20,* ☎ *01/426–4098,* WEB *www.narmuz-lj.si.* 🎟 *SIT 1,000.* ☉ *Tues.–Wed. and Fri.–Sun. 10–6, Thurs. 10–8.*

❽ **Robbov Vodnjak** (Robba's Fountain). When the Slovene sculptor Francesco Robba saw Bernini's *Fountain of the Four Rivers* on Piazza Navona during a visit to Rome, he was inspired to create this allegorical representation of the three main Kranjska rivers—the Sava, the Krka, and the Ljubljanica—that flow through Slovenia. ⊠ *Mestni trg.*

⑰ **Slovenska Filharmonija** (Slovenian Philharmonic Hall). This hall was built in 1891 for one of the oldest music societies in the world, established in 1701. Haydn, Brahms, Beethoven, and Paganini were honorary members of the orchestra, and Mahler was resident conductor for the 1881–82 season. ⊠ *Kongresni trg 10,* ☎ *01/241–0800.*

NEED A BREAK? From the Philharmonic Hall head to the other side of Kongresni trg to find **Zvezda** (⊠ Wolfova 14, ☎ 01/121–9090). This popular café has comfortable chairs and minimalist lighting, making it a perfect spot for an afternoon *kava smetana* (coffee with whipped cream). The ice cream and cakes are made on the premises and the staff never hurries you.

⑲ **SNG Opera in Balet** (Slovenian National Opera and Ballet Theater). This neo-Renaissance palace, with an ornate facade topped by an allegorical sculpture group, was erected in 1892. When visiting ballet and opera companies come to Ljubljana, they perform here. ⊠ *Županičeva 1,* ☎ *01/425–4840,* WEB *www.sng-mb.si.* ☉ *Weekdays 11–1 and 1 hr before performances.*

⑩ **Stari trg** (Old Square). More a narrow street than a square, the Old Square is lined with cafés and small restaurants. In agreeable weather, tables are set out on the cobblestones.

NEED A BREAK? You can't visit Slovenia without trying the incredibly delicious, hot, sweet and heavy *prekmurska gibanica*. To taste the best in town, stop off at **Nostalgia** (⊠ Stari trg 9), a popular snack bar.

❺ **Stolnica sveti Nikolaja** (Cathedral of St. Nicholas). This proud Baroque cathedral overshadows the daily market on Vodnikov trg. Building took place between 1701 and 1708, and in 1836 the cupola was erected. In 1996, in honor of the pope's visit, new bronze doors were added. The main door tells the story of Christianity in Slovenia, while the side door shows the history of the Ljubljana diocese. ⊠ *Dolničarjeva 1,* ☎ *01/ 231–0684.* 🎫 *Free.* ☉ *Daily 7–noon and 3–7.*

⓰ **Trg Francoske Revolucije** (French Revolution Square). When Napoléon took Slovenia, he made Ljubljana the capital of his Illyrian Provinces. This square is dominated by Plečnik's **Ilirski Steber** (Illyrian Column), erected in 1929 to commemorate that time.

❸ **Tromostovje** (Triple Bridge). This monumental structure spans the River Ljubljanica from Prešernov trg to the Old Town. The three bridges started as a single span, and in 1931 the two graceful outer arched bridges, designed by Plečnik, were added.

❹ **Vodnikov trg** (Vodnik Square). This square hosts a big and bustling flower, fruit, and vegetable market. An elegant riverside colonnade designed by Plečnik runs the length of the market, and a bronze statue of the Slovene poet Valentin Vodnik, after whom the square is named, overlooks the scene. ☉ *Market Mon.–Sat. 7–3.*

❻ **Zmajski most** (Dragon's Bridge). Four fire-breathing winged dragons crown the corners of this spectacular concrete-and-iron structure.

OFF THE   **ŽALE –** To see one of Plečnik's most dramatic structures, ride bus No. 2,
BEATEN PATH 7, or 22 from the post office out to Žale, a cemetery and memorial designed by the architect in the 1930s. The entrance colonnade and adjoining promenades reflect the Secessionist influence, creating a tranquil resting place inside. ⊠ *Tomačevska cesta, Novo Jarse.*

Dining

Central European food is often considered bland and stodgy, but in Ljubljana you can eat exceptionally well. Fresh fish arrives daily from the Adriatic, while the surrounding hills supply the capital with first-class meat and game, dairy produce, and fruit and vegetables. At some of the better restaurants the menu may verge on nouvelle cuisine, featuring imaginative and beautifully presented dishes. Complement your meal with a bottle of good Slovenian wine; the waiter can help you choose an appropriate one. For a lunchtime snack visit the market in Vodnik Square. Choose from tasty fried squid and whitebait in the riverside arcade or freshly baked pies and *kròf* (jelly-filled doughnuts) at the square's bakeries.

$$$–$$$$ ✕ **AS.** This refined restaurant is tucked away in a courtyard near
★   Prešernov trg. AS is the place to try innovative fish dishes (priced by the dekagram) and pasta specialties, all complemented by a first-rate wine list. The ambience is old-fashioned, but the dishes are creative and modern. If you're reluctant to leave, move on to the after-hours bar in the basement. ⊠ *Knafljev prehod,* ☎ *01/425–8822. Reservations essential. AE, DC, MC, V.*

$$$–$$$$ ✕ **Pri sv. Florijanu.** On Gornji trg, on the way to the castle, this pop-
★   ular restaurant serves up a new generation of Slovenian cuisine with a French touch. In every season the chef seems to have the right touch with Slovenia's bounty; porcini mushroom risotto and pumpkin ravioli in the fall, asparagus soup and *motovílec* (lamb's lettuce) salad in the spring. The service is both inviting and discreet. ⊠ *Gornji trg 20,* ☎ *01/251–2214. AE, DC, MC, V.*

$$$ ✕ **Ljubljanski Dvor.** Situated close to Čevljarski most, overlooking the river, this restaurant doubles as a pizzeria (which remains open on Sunday, when the restaurant is closed). The summer terrace makes it an ideal stopping point for lunch. ⊠ *Dvorni trg 1,* ☎ *01/251–6555. AE, DC, MC, V. Closed Sun.*

$$$ ✕ **Rotovž.** This elegant restaurant relaxes in summer, spilling over onto the cobbled square. Order *pastrmka* (trout) with parsley potatoes or a frog-leg specialty, along with a crisp salad and a bottle of *Sivi Pinot* (dry Slovenian white wine). ⊠ *Mestni trg 3,* ☎ *01/251–2839. AE, DC, MC, V. Closed Sun.*

$$$ ✕ **Špajza.** A few doors away from Pri sv. Florijanu, you'll find a restaurant with a series of romantic candlelit rooms and bohemian decor. The menu has local specialties like *Kraši pršut* (Karst air-dried ham) and scampi tails, as well as an inspired selection of salads. They do a great tiramisu. ⊠ *Gornji trg 28,* ☎ *01/425–3094. AE, DC, MC, V. Closed Sun.*

$$ ✕ **Pivnica Kratchowill.** First and foremost a microbrewery, Kratchowill also serves good food. The interior is modern, but the food is classic: beer sausage and sauerkraut, game dishes, tasty pastas, and a salad bar. The beer is brewed according to old Czech recipes. It's near the train and bus stations. ⊠ *Kolodvorska 14,* ☎ *01/433–3114. AE, DC, MC, V.*

$$ ✕ **Zlata Ribica.** An ideal stop after a visit to the Sunday flea market, this popular bar and bistro is frequented by boisterous stallholders and antiques buffs. The fare includes black pudding, squid, and mushroom omelettes. In the spring, tables outside are packed with locals eating fried calamari and drinking white wine spritzers. ⊠ *Cankarjevo nab. 5,* ☎ *01/252–1367. AE, DC, MC, V. No dinner weekends.*

Lodging

Most of the listed hotels are clustered conveniently around Miklošičeva cesta, the main axis running from the train station down to Tromostovje (Triple Bridge). Ljubljana is expensive by Central and Eastern European standards (comparable to those in Western Europe), but hotel standards are high. In summer you can get better deals through private accommodations or university dorms. Ask about these options at the TIC kiosk in the train station.

$$$$ ⊞ **Hotel Lev.** The Hotel Lev makes up for its location—five minutes from the city center—with stunning views of Tivoli Park and the Julian Alps outside of Ljubljana. Parking is free, and you'll find easy access to all major highways; soundproof windows keep traffic from spoiling the comfort. Rooms are decorated in soothing pastel tones. ⊠ *Vošnjakova 1, 1000,* ☎ *01/433–2155,* 𝐅𝐀𝐗 *01/434–3350,* 𝐖𝐄𝐁 *www. hotel-lev.si. 170 rooms. Restaurant, café, hair salon, business services; no-smoking rooms. AE, DC, MC, V. BP.*

$$–$$$ ⊞ **Grand Hotel Union.** The pricier Executive section of this bustling
★ hotel complex in central Ljubljana occupies a magnificent Secessionist-style building; the interior and furnishings remain typically turn-of-the-20th-century Vienna. The Comfort section is in an attached modern building overlooking a pleasant courtyard with fountain. All hotel facilities are shared and have been modernized with great care. ⊠ *Miklošičeva 1–3, 1000,* ☎ *01/308–1270,* 𝐅𝐀𝐗 *01/308–1015,* 𝐖𝐄𝐁 *www.gh-union.si. 297 rooms, 12 suites. 2 restaurants, café, cable TV with movies, some in-room data ports, in-room safes, minibars, indoor pool, gym, shops, Internet, business services; no-smoking rooms. AE, DC, MC, V. BP.*

$$ ⊞ **Best Western Slon Hotel.** Close to the river, this hotel stands on the site of a famous 16th-century inn and maintains an atmosphere of traditional hospitality. The breakfast is among the finest in the city. The run-of-the-mill rooms are comfortable. ⊠ *Slovenska 34, 1000,* ☎ *01/ 470–1100,* FAX *01/251–7164,* WEB *www.hotelslon.com. 185 rooms. 2 restaurants, café, room service, cable TV with movies, in-room data ports, in-room safes, minibars, hot tub, sauna, shops, Internet, meeting rooms, parking (fee); no a/c in some rooms, no-smoking rooms. AE, DC, MC, V. BP.*

$–$$ ☷ **Hotel Turist.** Although the rooms are basic, this hotel has the only budget-priced accommodations within the city center; it's also close to the bus and train stations. In summer breakfast is served in the terrace restaurant. ⊠ *Dalmatinova 15, 1000,* ☎ *01/432–9130,* FAX *01/ 234–9140,* WEB *www.hotelturist.si. 119 rooms. 2 restaurants, cable TV, minibars, meeting rooms. AE, DC, MC, V. BP.*

$$ ☷ **Pension Mrak.** This friendly pension offers good value with simple but comfortable rooms and a decent restaurant. It is situated in a quiet side street, close to the Križanke Summer Theater. ⊠ *Rimska 4, 1000,* ☎ *01/421–9600,* FAX *01/421–9655,* WEB *www.daj-dam.si. 30 rooms. Restaurant, cable TV, Internet. AE, DC, MC, V.*

Nightlife and the Arts

Despite once being considered the workaholics of Yugoslavia, Slovenes do know how to enjoy themselves. One in ten of the capital's inhabitants is a student, hence the proliferation of trendy cafés and small art galleries. Each year the International Summer Festival breathes new life into the Ljubljana cultural scene, sparking off a lively program of concerts and experimental theater. For information about forthcoming cultural events, check *Events in Ljubljana,* a monthly pamphlet published by the Ljubljana Promotion Center, and the English-language magazine *Ljubljana Life* both available in major hotels and tourist offices.

Nightlife

The listed bars and clubs are all situated within walking distance of the center. However, during summer the all-night party scene moves to the Adriatic coast, where open-air dancing and rave parties abound.

BARS AND CLUBS

The most idyllic way to close a summer evening is with a nightcap on the terrace of one of the riverside cafés in the Old Town. These bars all stay open until after midnight. Hip newcomer **Cafe Galerija** (⊠ Mestni trg 5, ☎ 01/241–1770) serves stylish cocktails by candlelight in a North Africa–inspired hideout. With a large terrace and glamorous clientele, **Cafe Maček** (⊠ Krojaška 5, ☎ 01/425–3791) is the place to be seen down by the river. **Caffe Boheme** (⊠ Mestni trg 19, ☎ no phone) in the heart of the Old Town is spacious inside and has a terrace with tables and umbrellas outside. For live jazz visit **Jazz Club Gajo** (⊠ Beethovnova 8, ☎ 01/425–3206), which attracts stars from home and abroad. Clark Terry, Shiela Jordan, and Woody Shaw have all performed here.

For Latino music or a pick-me-up breakfast in the early hours, visit **Casa del Papa** (⊠ Celovška 54A, ☎ 01/434–3158): three floors of exotic food, drinks, and entertainment in tribute to Ernest Hemingway. If you get hunger pangs after a night in the bars in the Old Town, head to **Romeo** (⊠ Stari trg 6, ☎ no phone) for great sandwiches and quesadillas. It's open until midnight.

For all-night dancing, **Club Central** (⊠ Dalmatinova 15, ☎ 01/432– 2093) stays open until sunrise Tuesday through Saturday. The student-run nightclub **K4** (⊠ Kersnikova 4, ☎ 01/431–7010) is something of an institution, attracting a young and alternative crowd; Sunday is gay night. Squatters took over **Metelkova** (⊠ Metelkova, Tabor, ☎ 01/432–3378), a former army barracks in the '80s, creating an organic, ad-hoc club space. Today it retains some of that spirit with a different trendy theme every night.

The Arts

Each year in June, the International Jazz Festival and the Druga Godba (a festival of alternative and ethnic music) are staged at the Križanke Summer Theater. For schedules and tickets contact the box office at Cankarjev dom. Ljubljana's **International Summer Festival** (⊠ Trg Francoske Revolucije 1–2, ☎ 01/426–4340, WEB www.festival-lj.si) is held each July and August in the open-air Križanke Summer Theater. Musical, theatrical, and dance performances attract acclaimed artists from all over the world.

CONCERTS

Ljubljana has plenty of events for classical music lovers. The season, September through June, includes weekly concerts by the Slovenian Philharmonic Orchestra and the RTV Slovenia Orchestra, as well as performances by guest soloists, chamber musicians, and foreign symphony orchestras. **Cankarjev dom** (Cankar House; ⊠ Prešernova 10, ☎ 01/241–7100, WEB www.cd-cc.si), opened in 1980, is a modern, rather characterless venue. As a cultural center it is the driving force behind the city's artistic activities, offering up-to-date general information and tickets. A progressive film festival takes place here every November. The 19th-century **Slovenska Filharmonija** (Slovenian Philharmonic Hall; ⊠ Kongresni trg 10, ☎ 01/241–0804, WEB www.filharmonija.si) is a traditional classical music venue.

FILM

Cinemas generally screen the original versions of films, with Slovenian subtitles. **Kinoteka** (⊠ Miklošičeva 28, ☎ 01/439–6445, WEB www.kinoteka.si) runs some great retrospectives.

THEATER, DANCE, AND OPERA

Ljubljana has a long tradition of experimental and alternative theater. Theater and dance are often mixed. Contemporary dance plays by the internationally recognized choreographers Matjaz Faric and Iztok Kovac and performances by the dance troupes Betontanc and En Knap are ideal for English speakers.

From September through June the **SNG Opera in Balet** (Slovene National Opera and Ballet Theater; ⊠ Župančičeva 1, ☎ 01/425–4840, WEB www2.arnes.si/opera) stages everything from classical to modern and alternative productions.

Shopping

Fashionable shoe stores abound in Ljubljana; for the latest selection head to shops on Stari trg in the Old Town. If you want to do some hiking but have come unprepared, **Anappurna** (⊠ Krakovski Nasip 10, ☎ 01/426–3428) has a good selection of mountaineering equipment. For late-night necessities, there is a 24-hour shop, **Delakatesa Trgovina** (⊠ Kongresni trg 10), right in the center of town. You can pick up antiques and memorabilia at the **Ljubljana Flea Market** (⊠ Cankarjevo nab.), held near Tromostovje (Triple Bridge) each Sunday morning. The most interesting shopping experience is undoubtedly a visit to the **open-air market** (⊠ Vodnikov trg), where besides fresh fruit and vegetables you can find dried herbs and locally produced honey. **Skrina** (⊠ Breg 8, ☎ 01/125–5161) has some unusual local crafts. For a wide selection of quality Slovenian wines try **Vinoteka** (⊠ Dunajska 18, ☎ 01/431–5015), in the Ljubljana trade fair complex.

Side Trip to the Krka Valley

*Numbers in the margins correspond to the Krka Valley map.*A drive through the Krka Valley makes a perfect day-trip from Ljubljana. The monasteries of Stična and Pleterje offer insight into contemporary monastic life, and there are two castles, Otočec and Mokrice, where you can stop for lunch—or a romantic overnight stay in exquisite surroundings.

Take the E70 highway east out of Ljubljana, and then turn right at Ivančna Gorica to follow a secondary road along the Krka Valley. For a fast journey home, return to the E70 just north of Šentjernej. There are also buses from Ljubljana to Ivančna Gorica and Šentjernej, but these are only practical if you don't mind walking the final stretch to the monasteries.

❶ The **Stična Samostan** (Stična Monastery) lies 2 km (1 mi) north of Ivančna Gorica. Founded by the Cistercians in 1135, the monastery was fortified in the 15th century to protect against Turkish invasion. Today there are only 10 monks, plus three nuns who attend to the cooking. The monks produce excellent herbal teas—that work (allegedly) against cellulite, insomnia, poor memory, and practically every other problem you can think of—which are on sale in the monastery shop. The early Gothic cloisters, the Baroque church, and the adjoining **Slovenian Religious Museum** are open to the public. The museum's collections include archives dedicated to the work of Bishop Friderik Baraga, a 19th-century missionary to the United States who compiled the first dictionary of the Native American Otchipwe language. Call first to arrange a visit. ✉ *Stična 17, Ivančna Gorica,* ☎ *01/787-7100.* 🎫 *SIT 700.* 🕐 *Tues.– Sat. 8–11 and 2–5, Sun. 2–5.*

★ ❷ The Carthusian monks of **Pleterje Samostan** (Pleterje Monastery) aim "to find God in silence and solitude." Therefore you can't enter the monastery proper, but you are welcome to view the magnificent 15th-century Gothic church and to watch a fascinating audiovisual presentation (in English) about the way the monks live. The walled monastery is nestled in a lonely valley surrounded by woods. Once a week the monks take a 45-minute walk around the perimeter of the complex. The route is marked with a blue circle and yellow cross, so you can follow the trail independently. A small shop sells rakija, wine, and cheese made by the monks. To reach the monastery from Stična Monastery follow the Krka River through Zagradec, Žužemberk, and Novo Mesto. At Šentjernej, turn south and travel for 6 km (4 mi) to reach Pleterje. ✉ *Drča 1, Šentjernej,* ☎ *07/308-1225.* 🎫 *Free.* 🕐 *Daily 8–5.*

Dining and Lodging

$$$–$$$$ ✕🏨 **Hotel Grad Otočec.** About 8 km (5 mi) west of Šentjernej, on the road to Novo Mesto, you will find the entrance to the medieval Otočec castle, dating from the 13th century. Now a luxury hotel, complete with period furniture, Otočec sits on an island in the Krka River and is accessible by a wooden bridge. You can also camp on the castle grounds. Nonguests are welcome to dine in the restaurant, where the house specialty is locally caught game. Or just stop by for a drink in the courtyard café. Equestrian and tennis centers are close by. ✉ *Grajska 1, Otočec ob Krki, 8222,* ☎ *07/307-5701,* 🆕 *07/307-5420,* 🌐 *www.krka-zdravilisca.si. 16 rooms. Restaurant, cable TV, meeting rooms. AE, DC, MC, V. BP.*

$$–$$$$ ✕🏨 **Hotel Toplice.** With 11 springs supplying thermal water, Terme Čatež is the largest natural spa in Slovenia. Hotel Toplice—the newest of the four hotels connected to the spa—is the ultimate destination for recharging your batteries. It houses expansive indoor thermal baths as well as

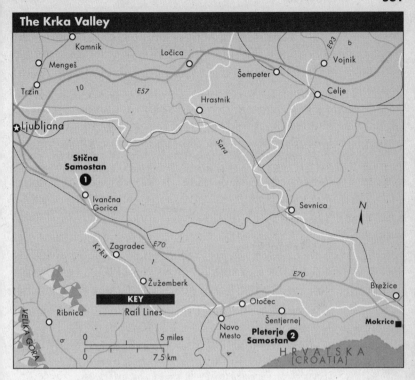

The Krka Valley

a fully loaded sports center. ⊠ *Topliska 35, Čatež ob Savi, 8251,* ☎ *07/493–5000,* FAX *07/493–5900,* WEB *www.terme-catez.si. 140 rooms. Restaurant, 8 tennis courts, 18-hole golf course, indoor pool, gym, aerobics, hot tub, spa, bowling, squash, meeting rooms. AE, DC, MC, V.*

Outdoor Activities and Sports

For horse lovers the **Struga Equestrian Center** (⊠ Otočec, ☎ 07/307–5701), at a 12th-century medieval manor, is a 20-minute walk from Otočec Castle. The center offers riding lessons and horses for hire.

Ljubljana Essentials

AIR TRAVEL

The Slovenian national carrier, Adria Airways flies from many Western European cities to Ljubljana Airport. Adria also has flights to the capitals of other ex-Yugoslav republics from Ljubljana, but no service to former Eastern-bloc countries. In Slovenia, tickets can be purchased by phone and delivered anywhere in the country in 24 hours. Swiss also has daily flights from Zurich.

➤ CARRIERS: **Adria Airways** (⊠ Gosposvetska 6, Ljubljana, ☎ 01/231–3312 or 01/431–3000, WEB www.adria.si). **Swiss** (☎ 04/202–7220, WEB www.swiss.com).

AIRPORTS AND TRANSFERS

The Ljubljana Airport is at Brnik, 22 km (14 mi) north of the city.
➤ AIRPORT INFORMATION: **Ljubljana Airport** (⊠ Brnik, ☎ 04/206–1981, WEB www.lju-airport.si).

TRANSFERS

Shuttle buses run between the airport and Ljubljana's main bus station in the city center. Buses depart every hour on the hour, and tickets cost SIT 1,000. If you're going to the airport, a shuttle service will pick you up at any hotel or address in Ljubljana for SIT 4,000. A taxi costs approximately SIT 6,000.

➤ CONTACTS: **Ljubljana Airport Shuttle** (☎ 040/887–766).

BUS TRAVEL

Bus transportation is available through private coach companies to and from Trieste in Italy and Zagreb in Croatia, as well as Munich, Stuttgart, and Frankfurt in Germany. The Llubljana bus station is opposite the train station, close to the city center.

During the day buses within Ljubljana operate every half hour and cover an extensive network; at night they are less frequent. Tokens (*žetoni*) are sold at kiosks and post offices. As you board the bus, drop your token into the box by the driver. The cost is a little higher if you pay in change (SIT 210).

➤ CONTACTS: **Llubljana Bus Station** (✉ Trg OF 5, Ljubljana, ☎ 01/090–4230).

CAR RENTALS

An international driver's license is required to rent a car in Slovenia. A midsize car costs $112 (SIT 27,440) for 24 hours, with unlimited mileage. You'll need a credit card. Rental agencies can be found in all major towns and at the Ljubljana Airport.

➤ MAJOR AGENCIES: **Avis** (✉ Čufarjeva 2, Ljubljana, ☎ 01/430–8010). **Kompas Hertz** (✉ Miklošičeva 11, Ljubljana, ☎ 01/231–1241). **National Rent a Car** (✉ Baragova 5, Ljubljana, ☎ 01/588–4450).

CAR TRAVEL

Ljubljana is connected to Italy by the E61 highway, Austria by the E57, and Croatia by the E70. It's 249 km (155 mi) to Venice via Trieste, and it's 395 km (245 mi) to Vienna via Maribor. From Austria you can proceed to Prague (609 km [405] mi from Ljubljana) or Budapest (491 km [305 mi] from Ljubljana).

Once in Ljubljana, you'll find that the city center is very compact, and all the sights, restaurants, hotels, and attractions listed can be reached on foot. You won't need a car unless you plan to leave town.

EMBASSIES AND CONSULATES

All embassies and consulates are in Ljubljana. See the A to Z section at the end of this chapter for addresses.

EMERGENCIES

➤ CONTACTS: **Ambulance and Fire** (☎ 112). **Emergency Road Assistance** (☎ 987). **Police** (☎ 113). **Lekarna Miklošič Pharmacy** (✉ Miklošičeva 24, Ljubljana, ☎ 01/231–4558). **Ljubljana Emergency Medical Services** (☎ 01/232–3060).

ENGLISH-LANGUAGE BOOKSTORES

Kod in Kam specializes in maps and travel books. MK Knjigarna Konzorcij has a good selection of English books and magazines on the upper floor.

➤ CONTACTS: **Kod in Kam** (✉ Trg Francoske Revolucije 7, Ljubljana, ☎ 01/251–3537). **MK Knjigarna Konzorcij** (✉ Slovenska 29, Ljubljana, ☎ 01/425–0196).

TAXIS

Private taxis operate 24 hours a day. Phone from your hotel or hail one in the street. Drivers are bound by law to display and run a meter.

➤ CONTACTS: **Airport Taxis** (☎ 01/9700 or 01/9709).

TOURS

Informative and amusing sightseeing walks, organized by the Ljubljana Promotion Center, depart from the Magistrat on Mestni trg daily at 5 PM, June through September. From October through May tours are on Sunday at 11 AM and can be booked through Ljubljana's Turistično Informacijski Center (☞ Visitor Information, *below*).

TRAIN TRAVEL

There are several trains daily to Venice (5 hours), Vienna (6 hours), and Budapest (8 hours). There is an overnight service to Prague (12 hours) and a rapid daytime EuroCity connection to Berlin (15 hours). The train station is just north of the city center.

➤ CONTACTS: **Ljubljana Train station** (✉ Trg OF 6, Ljubljana, ☎ 01/ 291–3332).

VISITOR INFORMATION

Ljubljana's Turistično Informacijski Center (Tourist Information Center) is next to the Triple Bridge on the Old Town side. It's open weekdays 8–7, Saturday 9–5, and Sunday 10–6. If you are arriving by train, the TIC kiosk in the train station can help you find accommodations. It's open daily 8 AM–9 PM June–September and 10–6 October–May.

➤ CONTACTS: **Turistično Informacijski Center** (Tourist Information Center [TIC]; ✉ Stritarjeva, Ljubljana, ☎ 01/306–1215, ₩₩ www. ljubljana.si). **TIC kiosk** (✉ Trg OF 6, Ljubljana, ☎ 01/433–9475).

MARIBOR, PTUJ, AND THE HALOZE HILLS

During the 1st century, Poetovio, now known as Ptuj, was the largest Roman settlement in the area that is now Slovenia. Much later, in the 13th century, Maribor was founded. Originally given the German name Marchburg, the city took its Slavic name in 1836. For centuries the two towns competed for economic and cultural prominence within the region, with Maribor finally gaining the lead in 1846, when a new railway line connected the city to Vienna and Trieste. The area between Maribor and Ptuj is a flat, fertile flood plain formed by the Drava River. South of Ptuj lie the hills of Haloze, famous for quality white wines.

Numbers in the margin correspond to numbers on the Maribor, Ptuj, and the Haloze Hills map.

Maribor

❶ *128 km (79 mi) northeast of Ljubljana on the E57.*

More geared toward business travelers than tourists, Maribor is Slovenia's second-largest city. However, the Old Town has retained a core of ornate 18th- and 19th-century town houses, typical of imperial Austria, and is worth a visit. The heart of the Old Town is **Rotovški trg,** with the **Kužno Znamenje** (Plague Memorial) at its center and overlooked by the proud 16th-century Renaissance **Rotovž** (town hall).

From Rotovški trg, a number of traffic-free streets lead down to a riverside promenade, known as **Lent.** It is lined with bars, terrace cafés, restaurants, and boutiques.

An old vine, **Stara Trta,** carefully trained along the facade of a former inn, is believed to date back to the 16th century and thus to be the oldest continuously producing vine in Europe. The annual harvesting of 100 to 110 pounds of grapes is a special event, and the small quantity of wine produced is highly prized. (It's unavailable to the public.) ✉ *Vojasniska 8.*

Maribor, Ptuj, and the Haloze Hills

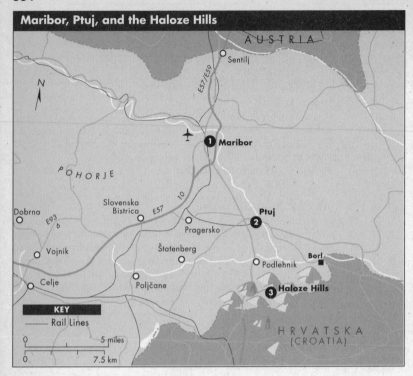

The Vodni Stolp (Water Tower), a former defense tower, houses the **Vinoteka Slovenskih Vin** (Slovenian Wine Shop). Here you can sample and purchase more than 500 different Slovenian vintage wines. ⊠ *Usnjarska 10,* ☎ *02/251–7743.*

Dining and Lodging

In summer Maribor University dorms are open to visitors, providing a cheap alternative to hotels. For details ask at the Maribor tourist information center.

$$$ ✕ **Toti Rotovž.** Close to the town hall, this building has been carefully restored to reveal vaulted brick ceilings and terra-cotta floors. The ground-level restaurant serves typical Slovenian dishes, while the *klet* (wine cellar) in the basement cooks up barbecued steaks. ⊠ *Glavni trg 14,* ☎ *02/228–7650. AE, DC, MC, V.*

$ ☷ **Hotel Orel.** It's nothing special to look at, but Hotel Orel has the best accommodations in the center of town. There is a pleasant restaurant at street level, the rooms are comfortable, and the service is friendly. Hotel guests have free use of the facilities of the town recreation center. ⊠ *Grajski trg 3A, 2000,* ☎ *02/251–6700,* FAX *02/251–8497,* WEB *www.termemb.si. 146 rooms, 7 suites. Restaurant, cable TV, minibars, parking (fee). AE, DC, MC, V. BP.*

Outdoor Activities and Sports

In winter in the Pohorje Mountains, just 6 km (4 mi) southwest of Maribor, you'll find alpine ski runs and cross-country trails. A cable car takes you from the south side of town up to the winter resort.

Two well-established biking paths pass though the region. The 95-km (59-mi) Drava Trail follows the course of the Drava River through the Kozjak Hills to Maribor and then proceeds to Ptuj. The 56-km (35-mi) Jantara Trail runs from Šentilj on the Austrian border to Maribor and continues to Slovenska Bistrica. However, finding a place to rent a bike can be somewhat problematic. Inquire at the Maribor tourist information center for assistance and information.

Ptuj

❷ *25 km (15 mi) southeast of Maribor on the E59.*

Ptuj, built beside the Drava River and crowned by a hilltop castle, hits the national news each year in February with its extraordinary Carnival celebration, known as Kurentovanje. During the 10-day festival the town's boys and men dress in the bizarre Kurent costume: a horned mask decorated with ribbons and flowers, a sheepskin cloak, and a set of heavy bells around the waist. The task of the Kurent is to drive away the winter and welcome in the spring. You can see Kurent figures on 18th-century building facades in the center of Ptuj, on Jadranska ulica No. 4 and No. 6.

Ptujski Grad (Ptuj Castle) stands at the top of a steep hill in the center of town. Planned around a baroque courtyard, the castle houses a museum that exhibits musical instruments, an armory, 15th-century church paintings, and period furniture. ✉ *Grajska Raven,* ☎ *02/771–3081,* WEB *www.pok-muzej-ptuj.si.* ✍ *SIT 600.* ☽ *Mid-Apr.–mid-Oct., daily 9–6; mid-Oct.–mid-Apr., daily 9–4.*

★ **Vinska Klet** (Ptuj Wine Cellars) offers a tasting session with five different wines, bread, and cheese, plus a bottle to take home. You are also given a tour of the underground cellars, and a sound-and-video presentation takes you through the seasons of wine making at the vineyards. The wines stocked here come predominantly from the Haloze Hills. ✉ *Trstenjakova 6,* ☎ *02/787–9810,* WEB *www.slovino.com/ puklavec.* ☽ *Daily 8–6; tasting sessions Fri.–Sun. at 11 AM (daily for groups, but call first).*

Dining

$$ ✕ **Ribič.** This discreet little fish restaurant serves up crab and lobster specialties, as well as river fish such as trout. The interior is simple, and the walls are hung with fishing nets. ✉ *Dravska 9,* ☎ *02/771– 4671. AE, DC, MC, V.*

The Haloze Hills

❸ *Borl Castle is 11 km (7 mi) southeast of Ptuj.*

The Haloze Hills lie south of Ptuj, close to the Croatian border. Grapes are generally planted on the steeper, south-facing slopes, to take full advantage of the sunshine, while the cooler, north-facing slopes are covered with trees and pastures. The best way to explore the region is to pick up the Haloze wine route near Borl Castle, a half-day trip through an undulating landscape of vineyards and woodland. For a map of the route plus a comprehensive list of vineyards and wine stores open to the public, inquire at the Ptuj tourist information center.

On the road between Podlehnik and Poljčane, keep an eye out for the sign for **Štatenberg Castle.** Built between 1720 and 1740, the castle is a typical example of the Baroque style favored by the local aristocracy during the 18th century.

Dining

$$ ✕ **Štatenberg Castle.** This castle houses a restaurant that serves traditional dishes, such as roast meats, accompanied by excellent local wines. Throughout summer you can sit at tables outside in the court-

yard. ⊠ *Štatenberg 86, Makole, 8222,* ☎ *02/803–0216. No credit cards.*
☉ *Closed Mon.*

Maribor, Ptuj, and the Haloze Hills Essentials

BUS TRAVEL

Regular buses link Maribor and Ptuj to Ljubljana. However, the train
is cheaper and more comfortable. An hourly bus service connects
Maribor and Ptuj; the 45-minute journey costs SIT 850.
➤ CONTACTS: **Maribor Bus Station** (⊠ Mlinska 1, Maribor, ☎ 02/251–
1333).

CAR TRAVEL

To reach Maribor from Ljubljana take the E57. For Ptuj turn off at
Slovenska Bistrica. A car is almost essential for exploring the Haloze
Hills wine route. Some of the country roads are narrow and winding.
While there is snow in winter, it is extremely rare to find roads closed.

TRAIN TRAVEL

A regular train service links Ljubljana and Maribor; several international trains continue to Graz and Vienna. It is also possible to reach
Ptuj by train from Ljubljana, though you may have to change at Pragersko. For information contact Ljubljana's train station (☞ Train Travel
in Ljubljana Essentials). Several trains daily connect Maribor and Ptuj,
with a change at Pragersko; the 45-minute journey costs SIT 750.
➤ CONTACTS: **Maribor Train Station** (⊠ Partizanska 50, Maribor, ☎
02/292–2100).

VISITOR INFORMATION

➤ CONTACTS: **Maribor Tourist Information** (⊠ Partizanska 47, Maribor, ☎ 02/234–6611, 🕸 www.maribor.si). **Ptuj Tourist Information**
(⊠ Slovenski trg 14, Ptuj, ☎ 02/771–5691, 🕸 www.ptuj.si).

TRIGLAV NATIONAL PARK
AND THE SOČA VALLEY

Northwest of Ljubljana lies a region of mountain and lakeside resorts,
with ski trails, hiking paths, and thermal springs. The Julijske Alpe (Julian Alps), situated at the junction of the borders of Italy, Austria, and
Slovenia, are contained within Triglavski Narodni Park (Triglav National Park). According to early Slav legend, Triglav, Slovenia's highest peak, is the home of a three-headed deity who rules the sky, the
earth, and the underworld. Triglav Peak is the symbol of Slovenia and
is featured on the national flag.

While Lake Bohinj and the small waterside settlement of Ribčev Laz
sit within the national park, Lake Bled and the town of Bled lie just
outside the park's boundary. The alpine villages of Kranjska Gora and
Bovec are situated on the rim of the park.

The Soča River begins near Trenta, then flows southwest to form the
beautiful Soča Valley. The river passes through Kobarid and snakes down
to Nova Gorica, where it crosses over into Italy (where it's known as
the Isonzo).

En Route   On the road to Bled from Ljubljana you pass a junction for Radovljica.
Turn off here to see the 17th-century town center and visit the intriguing
so **Čebelarski muzej** (Beekeeping Museum). ⊠ *Linhartov trg 1,
Radovljica,* ☎ *04/531–5188.* ☉ *May–Aug., Tues.–Sun. 10–1 and 4–
6; Sept.–Oct., Tues.–Sun. 10–noon and 3–5; Mar.–Apr. and Nov.–
Dec., Wed. and weekends 10–noon and 3–5.*

Triglav National Park and the Soča Valley

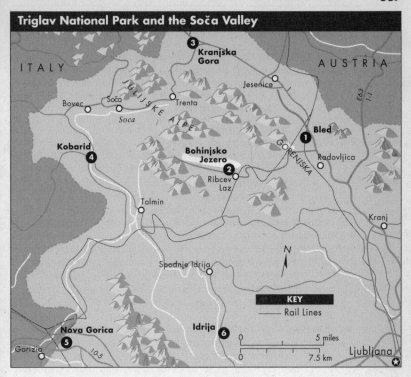

Numbers in the margin correspond to numbers on the Triglav National Park and the Soča Valley map.

Bled

★ ❶ *50 km (31 mi) northwest of Ljubljana on the E61.*

Bled is among the most magnificently situated mountain resorts in Europe. The healing powers of its thermal springs were known during the 17th century. In the early 19th century the aristocracy arrived to bask in Bled's tranquil alpine setting. Since the mid-1970s a spate of new hotels and recreational facilities have sprung up here.

Blejsko Jezero (Lake Bled) is nestled within a rim of mountains and surrounded by forests, with a castle on one side and a promenade beneath stately chestnut trees on the other. Horse-drawn carriages clip-clop along the promenade while swans glide on the water. On a minuscule island in the middle of the lake the lovely **Cerkov svetega Martina** (St. Martin's Pilgrimage Church) stands within a circle of trees. Take a ride over to the island on a *pletna,* an old-fashioned canopied wooden boat similar to a Venetian gondola.

The stately 16th-century **grad** (castle) perches above the lake on the summit of a steep cliff, against a backdrop of the Julian Alps and Triglav Peak. You can climb up to the castle for fine views of the lake, the resort, and the surrounding countryside. An exhibition traces the development of the castle through the centuries, with objects from archaeological finds to period furniture on display. ⊠ Bled, ☎ 04/574-1230. ◷ Mar.–Oct., daily 8–7; Nov.–Feb., daily 9–4.

| NEED A BREAK? | Even if you're not staying at the illustrious Grand Hotel Toplice, you're welcome to use its sauna and soak in the thermal waters (28°C [83°F]) |

of the indoor swimming pool. A small admission fee includes a towel and locker.

··

Ⓒ The **Soteska Vintgar** (Vintgar Gorge) was cut between precipitous cliffs by the clear Radovna River, which flows down numerous waterfalls and through pools and rapids. The marked trail through the gorge leads over bridges and along wooden walkways and galleries. ⊠ *Zgornje Gorje Rd., 5 km (3 mi) northwest of Bled.*

Dining and Lodging

$$$ ✕ **Gostilna Lectar.** This warm country-inn restaurant serves an impressive
★   selection of traditional dishes. For a cross-section of the local cuisine, try the pumpkin soup, the Peasant's Plate (buckwheat dumplings, mixed smoked meats, potatoes, and fresh steamed vegetables), and the apple strudel. The restaurant is 9 km (5½ mi) south of Bled on the E61. ⊠ *Linhartov trg 2, Radovljica,* ☎ *04/531–5642. AE, DC, MC, V.*

$$ ✕ **Gostilna pri Planincu.** This friendly place is busy year-round. Locals meet here for morning coffee or a bargain prix-fixe lunch—or just to drink the cheapest beer in town. While rowdy farmers occupy the front bar, lovers share a candlelit supper in the dining room. Portions are "for people who work all day": roast chicken and chips, steak and mushrooms, black pudding and turnips. For dessert walnut *štrukli* (dumplings) are served with cream. ⊠ *Grajska 8,* ☎ *04/574–1613. AE, DC, MC, V.*

$$ ✕ **Mlino.** Follow the lakeside footpath 20 minutes from the center of Bled to reach this informal family restaurant. Try the Mlino Plate, a mixed platter of barbecued meats served with *djevec* (rice cooked with vegetables). There is a special menu for children, and boats are for hire on the lake. ⊠ *C. Svobode 45,* ☎ *04/574–1404. AE, DC, MC, V.*

$$$ ⌂ **Vila Bled.** Late Yugoslav president Tito was the gracious host to numerous 20th-century statesmen at this former royal residence, amid 15 acres of gardens overlooking the lake. It was converted into a luxurious small-scale hotel in 1984 and became part of the Relais & Châteaux association in 1987. Among the elegant touches are hand-embroidered linen sheets, art deco furnishings, antique rugs, and Asian vases. ⊠ *C. Svobode 26, 4260,* ☎ *04/579–1500,* ℻ *04/574–1320,* 𝚆𝙴𝙱 *www.vila-bled.com. 10 rooms, 20 suites. Restaurant, tennis court, hair salon, beach, boating, bar, shop, meeting rooms. AE, DC, MC, V. BP.*

$$$ ⌂ **Grand Hotel Toplice.** This old-fashioned, ivy-covered resort hotel has
★   been favored by British travelers since the 1920s. Directly on the lake, the main building has balconies and big windows from which you can take in dramatic views of the castle and the Julian Alps. The rooms, the lounges, and the bar are all furnished with antiques and heirloom rugs. ⊠ *C. Svobode 20, 4260,* ☎ *04/579–1000,* ℻ *04/574–1841,* 𝚆𝙴𝙱 *www.hotel-toplice.com. 206 rooms. 3 restaurants, cable TV, indoor pool, gym, hot tub, massage, sauna, bar, conference center. AE, DC, MC, V. BP.*

$ ⌂ **Bledec Youth Hostel.** Just 5 minutes from the lake and 10 minutes from the castle, Bledec is one of the cleanest and most comfortable youth hostels in Europe. Rooms have mostly three or four beds; there are no private double rooms or private baths. ⊠ *Grajska 17, 4260,* ☎ *04/574–5250,* ℻ *04/574–5251,* 𝚆𝙴𝙱 *www.mlino.si. 13 rooms. Restaurant, bar. MC. Closed Nov. BP.*

Outdoor Activities and Sports

During summer, the lake turns into a family playground, with swimming, rowing, sailing, and windsurfing. In winter on Straža Hill, immediately above town, you can ski day and night, thanks to floodlighting. Just 10 km (6 mi) west of Bled, a larger ski area, Zatrnik, has 7 km (4 mi) of alpine trails. For information on winter and summer sports, contact Bled's tourist information center.

Bohinjsko Jezero

❷ *26 km (17 mi) west of Bled.*

Bohinjsko Jezero (Lake Bohinj) lies within Triglav National Park. In a valley surrounded by the steep walls of the Julian Alps, at an altitude of 1,715 ft, this deep-blue lake is even more dramatically situated than Lake Bled and not nearly as developed.

At the east side of Lake Bohinj, you'll find the 15th-century Gothic church of **Sveti Janez** (St. John). The small church has a fine bell tower and contains a number of notable 15th- and 16th-century frescoes. ☉ *Daily 9–noon and 4–7.*

At the west end of Lake Bohinj a cable car leads up **Mt. Vogel** to a height of 5,035 ft. From here you have spectacular views of the Julian Alps massif and the Bohinj valley and lake. From the cable-car base the road continues 5 km (3 mi) beyond the lake to the point where the Savica River makes a tremendous leap over a 195-ft waterfall.

Dining and Lodging

In the Bohinj area several farms cater to agrotourism, offering overnight accommodations and excellent home-cooking—though you should call in advance if you just want to eat. The most authentic dwellings and farm buildings are in the villages of Stara Fužina and Srednja Vas. For information, contact the Bohinj tourist information center. While you are in the Bohinj area, make sure you try the local cheese.

$ 🏨 **Hotel Bellevue.** As the name suggests, the Bellevue affords wonderful views of the lake, so request a room with a view. Agatha Christie fell in love with this old-fashioned hotel and stayed one month here while working on *Murder on the Orient Express.* ✉ *Ribčev Laz 65, Bohinj, 4265,* ☎ *04/572–3331,* ⒻⒶⓍ *04/572–3684,* ⓦⒺⒷ *www.bohinj.si. 76 rooms. 2 restaurants, cable TV, tennis court, volleyball, bar, meeting room. AE, DC, MC, V. BP.*

Outdoor Activities and Sports

In summer Bohinj is an ideal base for walking and biking. In winter you can ski at the ski areas of Vogel and Kobla. **Alpinum** (✉ Ribčev Laz 50, Bohinj, ☎ 04/574–9800) rents mountain bikes and organizes raft, kayak, hydrospeed (a small board for bodysurfing rapids), and canyoning trips.

Kranjska Gora

❸ *39 km (24 mi) northwest of Bled.*

Kranjska Gora, amid Slovenia's highest and most dramatic peaks, is the country's largest skiing resort. In summer the area attracts hiking and mountaineering enthusiasts.

Dining and Lodging

$$ 🏨 **Kompas Hotel.** This chalet-style hotel on the edge of town is an ideal base for skiing, hiking, and biking—and for taking in fine views of the mountains. Besides the main restaurant, there is an outdoor pizzeria open in summer. ✉ *Borovška 100, Kranjska Gora, 4280,* ☎ *04/588–1661,* ⒻⒶⓍ *04/588–1176,* ⓦⒺⒷ *www.hoteli-kompas.si. 156 rooms. Restaurant, pizzeria, cable TV, in-room safes, indoor pool, massage, sauna, tennis court, mountain bikes, bar, nightclub. AE, DC, MC, V. BP.*

Outdoor Activities and Sports

Skiing is the number one sport in Kranjska Gora. There are more than 30 km (20 mi) of downhill runs, 20 ski lifts, and 40 km (25 mi) of groomed cross-country trails. During summer mountain biking is big. Plenty of places rent out bikes, and 12 marked trails totaling 150 km (93 mi) take you through scented pine forests and spectacular alpine scenery. An unused railway track, tracing the south edge of the Karavanke Alps, brings hikers and bikers all the way to the village of Jesenice.

If you're interested in adventure water sports, **Soča Rafting** (⊠ Trg Golobarskih Žrtev 48, Bovec, ☎ 04/389–6200, WEB www.arctur.si/soca rafting) organizes guided descents of the Soča River from its office in Bovec, about 30 km (19 mi) southwest of Kronjska Gora.

En Route   From Kranjska Gora head south over the **Vršič Pass,** 5,252 ft above sea level. You'll then descend into the beautiful Soča Valley, winding through the foothills to the west of Triglav Peak and occasionally plunging through tunnels. From Trenta continue west for about 20 km (13 mi) to reach the rustic mountain resort of Bovec. In Trenta you'll find the Triglav National Park Information Center at **Dom Trenta** (⊠ Na Logu v Trenti, Trenta, ☎ 04/388–9330). Here you can watch a presentation about the history and geography of the region and tour the small museum. The center is open April–October, daily 10–6.

Kobarid

❹ *21 km (13 mi) from Bovec, 80 km (50 mi) from Bled, 115 km (71 mi) from Ljubljana.*

From Bovec the road follows the magnificent turquoise-color Soča River, running parallel with the Italian border, to pass through the pretty mar-
★ ket town of Kobarid. In the center of Kobarid, the **Kobariški muzej** (Kobarid Museum) gives a 20-minute presentation—with projections, sound effects, and narration—of the tragic fighting that took place on the Isonzo Front during World War I, as recorded in Hemingway's *A Farewell to Arms.*

The **Kobarid Historical Walk** takes you on a 5-km (3-mi) hike through lovely countryside, over a hair-raising bridge, and past a spectacular waterfall. You'll follow the former front line and visit various sites related to World War I along the way. The path is clearly marked, and a self-guiding pamphlet and map are available at the Kobarid Museum. ⊠ *Gregorčičeva 10,* ☎ *05/389–0000,* WEB *www.kobariski-muzej.si.* ▨ *SIT 900.* ☉ *Daily 9–7.*

Dining and Lodging

$$ ✕🏨 **Hotel Hvala.** This delightful family-run hotel is possibly one of
★ the most welcoming places you'll ever stay. The hotel restaurant, Restauracija Topli Val, serves local trout and freshwater crayfish, as well as mushrooms and truffles in season. Italians drive over the border just to eat here. ⊠ *Trg Svobode 1, 5222,* ☎ *05/389–9300,* FAX *05/388–5322,* WEB *www.topli-val-sp.si. 28 rooms, 4 suites. Restaurant. AE, DC, MC, V. BP.*

Outdoor Activities and Sports

The Soča is a prime fishing spot. The river is well stocked with marble trout, rainbow trout, and grayling. Bring your own equipment, or be prepared to buy it here, as it is almost impossible to rent. You also need to buy a day permit; for details inquire at Hotel Hvala. The season runs from April through October.

X Point (⊠ Stresova 1, ☎ 05/388–5308) organizes kayaking, rafting, and canyoning trips and also rents out mountain bikes. In Srpenica, 13 km (8 mi) northwest of Kobarid, **Alpine Action** (⊠ Trnovo ob Soči, Srpenica, ☎ 05/388–5022) arranges river trips and rents out bikes.

Nova Gorica

❺ *48 km (30 mi) from Kobarid, 115 km (71 mi) from Kranjska Gora, 100 km (62 mi) from Ljubljana.*

At the south end of the Soča Valley lies Nova Gorica, with a busy border crossing into Italy. The town was constructed after World War II, when the older settlement of Gorizia became Italian. Today Nova Gorica is best known for its casinos: every Sunday afternoon hordes of Italians cross over to try their luck in the gambling halls.

OFF THE BEATEN PATH   **SVETA GORA** – Nova Gorica is overshadowed by Sveta Gora (Holy Mountain), standing 2,250 ft above sea level and affording fantastic views north to Triglav and south to the Adriatic. Pilgrims have visited the site since 1539, when a young shepherd girl claimed to see an apparition of the Virgin Mary. The present church dates back to 1928; an earlier building was destroyed during World War I. You'll need a car to get up here, except on Sunday, when you could be lucky enough to find a minibus taking locals up to the church for mass; ask at the tourist information center for times.

Dining and Lodging

$$–$$$ ✕ **Pri Hrastu.** Despite the general kitsch that prevails in Nova Gorica, this is a genuine old-fashioned restaurant. Traditional local dishes are served up in a wooden-beam dining room with chintz curtains. The house speciality is štrukli. ⊠ C. 25 junija 2, ☎ 05/302–7210. AE, DC, MC, V.

$$ 🏨 **Hotel Casinò Perla.** Too much green landscape and fresh mountain air? Call at Slovenia's largest and newest casino and take a gamble on roulette, blackjack, or poker, or try your hand at one of 400 slot machines. The casino is open nonstop, and the complex has decent accommodations should you wish to stay the night. ⊠ Kidričeva 7, 5000, ☎ 05/336–3000, ✉ 05/302–8886, 🌐 www.hit.si/slo/perla.htm. 94 rooms, 11 suites. Restaurant, indoor pool, sauna, 2 tennis courts, casino, nightclub. AE, DC, MC, V.

Idrija

❻ *50 km (31 mi) from Kobarid, 60 km (37 mi) from Ljubljana.*

To get directly to the Soča Valley from Ljubljana, take the E57 southwest from Ljubljana; then turn off just before Rakek and head northwest, passing through Idrija. The town was founded in the 15th century on the wealth of its mercury mine, no longer used. Idrija is also known for its handmade lace.

Head to **Anthony's Shaft** to see the oldest part of the mine, the miners' chapel dating back to the 18th century, and a video about the way the miners once lived. ⊠ Kosovelova 3, ☎ 05/377–1142. 🕐 Tours weekdays at 10 and 4; weekends at 10, 3, and 4.

Dining and Lodging

$$$ ✕ **Restauracija Barbara.** This refined restaurant serves the local specialty, Idrijski žlikrofi (tortellini filled with potato and smoked ham), as well as other almost forgotten regional dishes. ⊠ Kosovelova 3, ☎ 05/377–1142. AE, DC, MC, V.

$$ 🏠 **Kendov Dvorec.** This beautiful 14th-century manor house is in Spodnje Idrija, 4 km (2½ mi) from Idrija. Each bedroom is individually decorated with 19th-century antique furniture and details such as bed linen edged with local handmade lace. Reserve well in advance. The restaurant is recommendable. ⊠ *Spodnje Idrija, 5280,* ☎ *05/372–5100,* ℻ *05/375–6475. 11 rooms. Restaurant. AE, DC, MC, V. BP.*

Shopping

Numerous boutiques sell *Idrijska čipka* (Idrija lace). For the most original designs try **Studio Irma Vončina** (⊠ Mestni trg 17, ☎ 05/377–1584). It's open weekdays 10–noon and 1– 4, Saturday 10–noon.

Triglav National Park and the Soča Valley Essentials

BUS TRAVEL

Hourly buses link Ljubljana to Bled, Bohinj, and Kranjska Gora. There are also several buses daily from Ljubljana through Idrija to Kobarid. The resorts are linked by local buses; their frequency depends on the season. For schedule and fare information ask at a local tourist information center.

CAR TRAVEL

From Ljubljana a toll road (E61) runs 42 km (26 mi) northwest past Kranj; from there the E651 leads to the resorts of Bled and Kranjska Gora. A local road then follows the Soča Valley south through Kobarid to Nova Gorica. In this region a car gives you more freedom and is preferable to a haphazard local bus. However, in winter snow can make driving treacherous, especially on minor roadways.

TRAIN TRAVEL

In theory it is possible to reach the area from Ljubljana by train, but because Bled Jezero station lies some distance from Lake Bled, and Bohinjska Bistrica station lies even further from Lake Bohinj, it is simpler and quicker to take the bus.

Every Thursday from mid-June to mid-September Slovenijaturist arranges trips on an old-fashioned steam locomotive, following the Bohinj line, through the Soča Valley. The trip begins from Jesenice, stops in Bled and Bohinjska Bistrica, and finally brings you to Most na Soči. The train ride costs SIT 4,600 round-trip.
➤ CONTACTS: **Slovenijaturist** (⊠ Slovenska 58, Ljubljana, ☎ 01/232–5782).

VISITOR INFORMATION

➤ CONTACTS: **Bled Tourist Information** (⊠ C. Svobode 15, Bled, ☎ 04/574–1122, 🖳 www.bled.si). **Bohinj Tourist Information** (⊠ Ribčev Laz 48, Bohinj, ☎ 04/574–6010, 🖳 www.bohinj.si). **Idrija Tourist Information** (⊠ Lapajnetova 7, Idrija, ☎ 05/377–3898, 🖳 www.rzs-idrija.si). **Kobarid Tourist Information** (⊠ trg Svobode 2, Kobarid, ☎ 05/389–9200, 🖳 www.kobarid.si). **Kranjska Gora Tourist Information** (⊠ Tičarjeva 2, Kranjska Gora, ☎ 04/5881–768, 🖳 www.kranjska-gora.si). **Nova Gorica Tourist Information** (⊠ Bergov 4, Nova Gorica, ☎ 05/333–4600, 🖳 www.novagorica.com).

THE KARST REGION AND THE ADRIATIC COAST

The limestone plateau between Ljubljana and the coast is the source of the term *karst*: a geological phenomenon whose typical features are sinkholes, underground caves, and streams. The landscape itself is not all that interesting, but if you like exploring caves, the ones here are visually stunning and well maintained.

Slovenia's tiny piece of the Adriatic coast gives tourists a welcome chance to swim and sunbathe. Backed by hills planted with olive groves and vineyards, the small strip, only 42 km (26 mi) long, is dominated by the towns of Koper, Piran, and Portorož. Following centuries under the Republic of Venice the region remains culturally and spiritually connected to Italy. The best Venetian architecture of the area can still be seen in the delightful medieval town of Piran. Portorož is a more commercial resort, while Koper is Slovenia's largest port.

For beachgoers the best-equipped beach is at Bernadin, between Piran and Portorož. The most unspoiled stretch is at the Strunjan Nature Reserve—which also has an area reserved for nudists—between Piran and Izola.

Along the coast private lodgings are a cheap alternative to hotels. Owners usually live on the ground floor and rent out rooms or apartments upstairs. For help finding private accommodations, contact a local tourist information center.

Numbers in the margin correspond to numbers on the Karst Region and the Adriatic Coast map.

Postojnska Jama

❶ *44 km (27 mi) from Ljubljana.*

Postojnska Jama (Postojna Cave) conceals one of the largest networks of caves in the world, with 23 km (14 mi) of underground passageways. A miniature train takes you through the first 7 km (4½ mi), to reveal a succession of well-lit rock formations. This strange underground world is home of the snakelike "human fish," on view in an aquarium in the Great Hall. Eyeless and colorless because of countless millennia of life in total darkness, these amphibians can live for up to 60 years. Temperatures average 8°C (46°F) year-round, so in summer rent a woolen cloak at the entrance. Tours leave every hour on the hour throughout the year. ✉ *Jamska 30, Postojna,* ☎ *05/700–0100,* WEB *www.postojna-cave.com.* ☞ *SIT 2,400.* ☉ *May–Sept., daily 8:30–6; Apr. and Oct., daily 8:30–5; Nov.–Mar., weekdays 9:30–1:30, weekends 9:30–3.*

Škocjanske Jame

❷ *26 km (16 mi) from Postojna.*

The Škocjanske Jame (Škocjan Caves), near Divača (just off the highway from Ljubljana to Trieste), require walking, but the effort is worthwhile. Here the River Reka thunders along an underground channel, amid a wondrous world of stalactites and stalagmites. ✉ *Matavun 12, Divača,* ☎ *05/763–2840.* ☞ *SIT 1,700.* ☉ *June–Sept., daily at 10, 11:30, and 1–5 (tours leave hourly); Apr.–May and Oct., tours daily at 10, 1, and 3:30; Nov.–Mar., tours weekdays at 10, weekends at 10 and 3.*

Lipica

❸ *5 km (3 mi) west of Divača, 60 km (37 mi) from Ljubljana.*

☙ The **Kobilarna Lipica** (Lipica Stud Farm) near Sežana is the birthplace of the Lipizzaner white horses. Founded in 1580 by the Austrian archduke Karl II, the farm still supplies Lipizzaners to the Spanish Riding School in Vienna. Lipica has developed into a modern sports complex, with two hotels, an indoor riding arena, a swimming pool, and a golf

The Karst Region and the Adriatic Coast

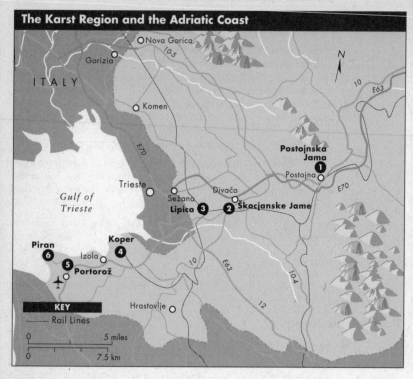

course. The stables are open to the public. Riding classes are available, but you need to book in advance. ⊠ *Lipica 5, Sežana, 6210,* ☎ *05/ 739–1580.* ☉ *Dressage performances June–Oct., Tues., Fri., and Sun. at 3. Stables July–Aug., daily 9–6; Apr.–June and Sept.–Oct., daily 10– 5; Nov.–Mar., daily 11–3.*

Dining

$$ ✕ **Pelicon.** This wonderful farm, now set up as an agrotourism center, serves homemade regional specialties such as *pršut* (cured ham) and salami, roast meats, gnocchi, and štrukli, all served with local Teran red wine. You'll find it near Komen, midway between Sežana and Nova Gorica (from Sežana, take the road north toward Štanjel, then at Dutovlje turn left and follow a narrow country road to Komen). ⊠ *Coljava 5, Coljava, 6223,* ☎ ⅲ *05/766–8061. Reservations essential. No credit cards. Closed weekdays.*

Koper

4 *35 km (22 mi) southwest of Škocjanske Jame.*

Today a port town surrounded by industrial suburbs, Koper nevertheless warrants a visit. The Republic of Venice made Koper the regional capital during the 15th and 16th centuries, and the magnificent architecture of the Old Town bears witness to the spirit of those times.

The most important buildings are clustered around **Titov trg,** the central town square. Here stands the **Cathedral,** which can be visited daily from 7 to noon and 3 to 7, with its fine Venetian Gothic facade and bell tower dating back to 1664. Across the square the splendid **Praetor's Palace,** formerly the seat of the Venetian Grand Council, combines Gothic and Renaissance styles. From the west side of Titov trg, the narrow, cobbled **Kidriceva ulica** brings you down to the seafront.

NEED A BREAK?	Stop for coffee or a glass of wine at **Loggia Cafe,** housed within the 15th-century Venetian Gothic loggia. In summer there are tables out on the terrace overlooking the town square.

OFF THE BEATEN PATH	**HRASTOVLJE** – Hidden behind 16th-century defensive walls of this small town is the tiny Romanesque **Cerkev sveti Trojice** (Church of the Holy Trinity). The interior is decorated with a remarkable series of frescoes, including the bizarre *Dance Macabre,* completed in 1490. The church is locked, but if you ask in the village the locals will be glad to open it for you. From Koper take the main road toward Ljubljana; then follow the signs for Hrastovlje (22 km [14 mi] from Koper).

Dining

$$$ ✕ **Skipper.** Noted for its vast summer terrace overlooking the marina, Skipper is popular with the yachting fraternity. The menu includes pasta dishes, risottos, grilled meats, and fish. ⊠ *Kopališko nab. 3,* ☎ *05/ 627–1750. AE, DC, MC, V.*

Nightlife

During summer the Adriatic coast becomes a haven for all-night parties. **Ambasada Gavioli** (⊠ Izola, ☎ 05/641–8212) specializes in techno and rave. It's one of the largest discos in Central Europe and claims to be Slovenia's "grooviest and sexiest club." Izola is 8 km (5 mi) west of Koper.

Outdoor Activities and Sports

You can rent yachts at the Izola marina from **Jonathon d.o.o.** (⊠ Izola, ☎ 05/677–8930). Prices vary depending on the season and the size of the yacht.

Portorož

❺ *15 km (9 mi) from Koper.*

Portorož, or Port of Roses, takes its name from the lush Mediterranean vegetation that flourishes here, thanks to a warm microclimate created by the surrounding hills. The earliest villas and hotels were built at the end of the 19th century, when Austro-Hungarian aristocrats were attracted by the healing powers of the area's mud baths and saltwater pools. Nowadays the town swarms with summer vacationers in search of sea, sun, invigorating spas, and lively casinos.

Dining and Lodging

$$–$$$ ✕ **Ribič.** Situated 2 km (1 mi) down the coast from Portorož at Seča, ★ Ribič may just be the best fish restaurant in the area. Specialties include baked sea bass with porcini mushrooms, and risotto *Alpe Adria,* which combines wild mushrooms from the Alps and fresh scampi from the Adriatic. In summer you can eat in the garden. ⊠ *Seča,* ☎ *05/677–0790. AE, DC, MC, V. Closed Tues.*

$$ 🏨 **Grand Hotel Palace.** This modern seaside hotel is connected to the thermal-spa recreation center, which offers massages and medicinal treatments. Rooms are comfortable, and the service is professional. Three other hotels are adjacent in the same complex and interconnected, offering a similar level of service. This is the most expensive of the four. ⊠ *Obala 43, 6320,* ☎ *05/696–1025,* FAX *05/696–9003,* WEB *www.hoteli-palace.si. 189 rooms, 7 suites. 2 restaurants, cable TV, minibars, 2 pools (1 indoor), spa, bar, parking (fee). AE, DC, MC, V.*

Piran

❻   *5 km (3 mi) from Portorož, 125 km (78 mi) from Ljubljana.*

The jewel of the Slovenian coast, the medieval walled Venetian town of Piran stands compact on a small peninsula, capped by a neo-Gothic lighthouse and presided over by a hilltop Romanesque cathedral. Narrow, winding, cobbled streets lead to the main square, Trg Tartini, which in turn opens out onto a charming harbor. Historically, Piran's wealth was based on salt-making. Culturally, the town is known as the birthplace of the 17th-century violinist and composer Giuseppe Tartini.

The **Sergej Mašera Pomorski muzej** (Sergej Mašera Maritime Museum) tells the story of Piran's connections with the sea. There is a beautiful collection of model ships, sailors' uniforms, and shipping instruments, as well as museum of the salt-making industry. ⊠ *Cankarjevo nab. 3,* ☎ *05/671–0041,* ⱲⒺⒷ *www2.arnes.si/-kppomm.* ☜ *SIT 500.* ☉ *Maritime Museum Apr.–June and Nov.–Mar., Tues.–Sun. 9–noon and 3–6; July–Aug., Tues.–Sun. 9–noon and 6–9. Museum of Salt-making Apr.–June, Tues.–Sun. 9–1 and 2–6; July–Aug. 9–1 and 2–7.*

Dining and Lodging

$$$ ✕ **Tri Vdove.** House specialties are seafood: the much-sought-after "date mussels" arrive fresh daily, along with shrimp, lobster, and fish. A large terrace overlooks the sea. ⊠ *Trg 1 Maja,* ☎ *05/673–2232. AE, DC, MC, V.*

$–$$ ☖ **Hotel Piran.** Occupying a quiet patch of coastline close to seaside restaurants, Hotel Piran is the place to come if the sea is what you're after. From the hotel lobby the water is less than 50 yards away. Breakfast is served on a rooftop terrace where you can enjoy stunning views of the Adriatic. ⊠ *Kidričevo nab. 4, 6330,* ☎ *05/672–2502,* Ⓕⓐⓧ *05/672–2520,* ⱲⒺⒷ *www.hoteli-piran.si. 80 rooms, 10 suites. Café, cable TV, some refrigerators, bar, some pets allowed. AE, MC, V. BP.*

$$ ☖ **Hotel Tartini.** The old facade hides a modern interior with a spa-
★   cious central atrium. Most rooms have terraces overlooking surrounding red-tiled roofs or the harbor. The location, overlooking the piazza Trg Tartini, is out of this world. ⊠ *Trg Tartini 15, 6330,* ☎ *05/671–1666,* Ⓕⓐⓧ *05/671–1665,* ⱲⒺⒷ *www.hotel-tartini-piran.com. 43 rooms, 2 suites. Restaurant, minibars. AE, DC, MC, V. BP.*

Nightlife and the Arts

Piran Musical Evenings are held in the cloisters of the Minorite Monastery every Friday in July and August. The **Primorski Summer Festival** of open-air theater and dance is staged in Piran, Koper, Portorož, and Izola.

The Karst Region and the Adriatic Coast Essentials

BOAT TRAVEL

During summer, it is possible to reach the Slovenian coast by regularly scheduled boat service from Italy.

BUS TRAVEL

Several buses a day connect Ljubljana to Koper, Piran, and Portorož, passing through Postojna and Divača on the way. In summer a regular service links Nova Gorica to the coast. There is also a daily service connecting the coastal towns to Trieste, Italy.

A network of local buses connects all listed sights, with the exception of Lipica and Hrastovlje. Schedules vary depending on the time of year, so contact a local bus station for information.

CAR TRAVEL

A car is advisable for touring the karst region. However, parking can be a problem along the coast during summer, when town centers are closed to traffic. The E63 highway connects Ljubljana to the coast, passing through the karst region en route.

TOURS

Adriatic Safari arranges boat trips along the coast from the Piran marina.

➤ CONTACTS: **Adriatic Safari** (✉ Kosovelova 8, Piran, ☎ 05/677–1282).

TRAIN

Four trains daily link Ljubljana and Koper, passing through Postojna and Divača en route.

VISITOR INFORMATION

➤ CONTACTS: **Koper Tourist Information** (✉ Ukmarjev trg 7, ☎ 05/663–2010, WEB www.koper.si). **Lipica Tourist Information** (✉ Lipica 5, ☎ 05/739–1580, WEB www.lipica.org). **Piran Tourist Information** (✉ Trg Tartini 2, ☎ 05/673–0220, WEB www.piran.com). **Portorož Tourist Information** (✉ Obala 16, ☎ 05/674–0231, WEB www.portoroz.si). **Postojna Tourist Information** (✉ Jamska 9, ☎ 05/720–1610, WEB www.postojna-cave.com).

SLOVENIA A TO Z

AIR TRAVEL

There are no direct flights between Slovenia and the United States. Adria Airways regularly flies to most major European cities (☞ Air Travel *in* Ljubljana Essentials).

BOAT AND FERRY TRAVEL

From early March to late October the *Prince of Venice* hydrofoil makes regularly scheduled trips between Venice and Portorož. From mid-July to mid-September, the Italian firm Adriatica runs a round-trip service from Trieste, calling at Piran and stopping at several towns on the Croatian Adriatic coast.

➤ CONTACTS: **Adriatica** (Maona; ✉ Cankarjevo nab. 7, Piran, ☎ 05/674–6508). *Prince of Venice* (Kompas Turizem; ✉ Obala 41, Portorož, ☎ 05/617–8000).

BUS TRAVEL

There is daily direct bus service between the capital and cities in Germany, Croatia, and Italy. An extensive bus network also covers the entire country. You can reach even the most outlying villages by bus, though it may take several changes and time lost waiting (☞ Bus Travel *in* Ljubljana Essentials).

BUSINESS HOURS

Most banks are open weekdays 9–noon and 2–4:30, Saturday 9–11. You can also change money at exchange desks in hotels, gas stations, tourist agencies, supermarkets, and small exchange offices. The main museums are open Tuesday–Sunday 10–6. Larger shops are open Monday–Saturday 10–6, while smaller ones may open mornings only 10–2. Most stores are closed Sunday.

CAR RENTALS

An international driver's license is required to rent a car in Slovenia. A midsize car costs $112 (SIT 27,440) for 24 hours, with unlimited mileage. You'll need a credit card. Rental agencies can be found in all major towns and at the Ljubljana Airport. For the names of major rental companies that operate in the country, *see* Car Rentals *in* Llubljana Essentials.

CAR TRAVEL

From Budapest and Vienna the Slovenian border is no more than a two-hour drive; from Prague it's eight hours. A tunnel speeds traffic through the Karavanke Alps between Slovenia and Austria. From Vienna the passage is by way of Maribor to Ljubljana, with a highway from Graz to Celje. Slovenia's roads also connect with Italy's *autostrada.*

Traveling by car undoubtedly gives you the chance to reach remote areas of the country when and as you wish. Main roads between large towns are comparable to those in Western Europe. Highways charge a toll depending on the route and distance traveled.

Gas stations on border crossings and main roads leading to larger towns are open 24 hours a day, while others are open Monday–Saturday 7 AM–8 PM. Unleaded gasoline is available throughout the country.

PARKING

In major towns parking spaces are marked with a blue line and a sign denoting time restrictions. Buy a ticket, obtainable from gas stations and newsstands; write down the time you parked; and attach it to your windshield.

RULES OF THE ROAD

Slovenes drive on the right and are obliged to keep their headlights on at all times. Speed limits are 60 kph (37 mph) in urban areas and 120 kph (74 mph) on highways. Local drivers are courteous by European standards. The permitted blood alcohol level is 0.05%; drivers caught exceeding this level can expect penalties similar to those of other European countries.

CUSTOMS AND DUTIES

ON ARRIVAL

As with most European countries, you can import duty-free 200 cigarettes, 1 liter of spirits, and 2 liters of wine. Foreign citizens can bring personal items into the country without paying customs taxes.

ON DEPARTURE

Any visitor who buys goods worth more than SIT 19,000 ($75) at any one store is entitled to a refund of taxes. When you make a purchase ask for a Request for VAT Refund form, *Zahtevek za vracilo DDV.* A customs officer will certify the form when you leave the country. To obtain the refund, go to the Kompas MTS office at the border crossing point or the airport. Exporting historic artifacts is forbidden.

EMBASSIES AND CONSULATES

➤ CONTACTS: **Australian Consulate** (✉ Trg republike 3/XII, Ljubljana, ☎ 01/425–4252, FAX 01/426–4721). **Canadian Consulate** (✉ Miklošičeva 19, Ljubljana, ☎ 01/430–3570, FAX 01/430–3575). **U.K. Embassy** (✉ Trg republike 3/IV, Ljubljana, ☎ 01/200–3910, FAX 01/425–0174). **U.S. Embassy** (✉ Prešernova 31, Ljubljana, ☎ 01/200–5500, FAX 01/ 200–5555).

EMERGENCIES

➤ CONTACTS: **Ambulance and Fire** (☎ 112). **Automobile Association of Slovenia** (AMZS; ☎ 987 for 24-hour emergency roadside assistance). **Police** (☎ 113).

HOLIDAYS AND LANGUAGE

HOLIDAYS

January 1–2; February 8 (Prešeren Day, Slovene cultural day); Easter Sunday and Monday (usually March or April); April 27 (National Resistance Day); May 1 and 2 (Labor Day); June 25 (Slovenia National Day); August 15 (Assumption); October 31 (Reformation Day); November 1 (All Saints' Day); December 25; December 26 (Independence Day).

LANGUAGE

Slovene is the country's chief language. In the east signs are posted in Slovene and Hungarian; on the Adriatic coast both Slovene and Italian are officially used. English, German, and Italian are spoken in many places.

In Slovene the words for street (*ulica*) and drive (*cesta*) are abbreviated to ul. and c. *Nabrežje* (abbreviated to nab.) means "embankment." The word for square is *trg*.

MAIL AND SHIPPING

POSTAL RATES

Airmail postage to the United States is SIT 190 for a letter, SIT 150 for a postcard. Airmail postage in Europe is SIT 130 for a letter, SIT 120 for a postcard. Post offices are open weekdays 8–6 and Saturday 8–noon. Stamps are also sold at hotels, newsstands, and kiosks.

MONEY MATTERS

Costs for goods and services are on a par with those of Western Europe. Notable exceptions are public transportation, alcohol, and cigarettes, all of which are cheaper here.

CURRENCY

The monetary unit in Slovenia is the Slovenian tolar (SIT). One Slovenian tolar is divided into 100 stotin. There are notes of SIT 10,000, SIT 5,000, SIT 1,000, SIT 500, SIT 200, SIT 100, SIT 50, SIT 20, and SIT 10, and coins of SIT 5, SIT 2, SIT 1, and 50 stotin.

At this writing the exchange rate was about SIT 254 to the U.S. dollar, SIT 162 to the Canadian dollar, and SIT 373 to the pound sterling.

PASSPORTS AND VISAS

No visas are necessary for holders of valid passports from the United States, Canada, the United Kingdom, mainland European countries, Australia, New Zealand, or the Republic of Ireland. South African nationals, however, must have a three-month tourist visa.

TELEPHONES

COUNTRY CODE

The country code for Slovenia is 386. When dialing from outside the country, drop any initial "0" from the area code.

INTERNATIONAL CALLS

To make international calls, dial "00" and then the appropriate country code. International calls can be made from local telephones or post offices. For collect calls dial the operator. For international inquiries, dial international directory assistance.
➤ CONTACTS: **International Directory Assistance** (☎ 989). **Operator** (☎ 901).

LOCAL CALLS

Pay phones take magnetic telephone cards, available from post offices and kiosks. Lower rates apply from 10 PM to 7 AM and all day Sunday.
➤ CONTACTS: **Local Directory Assistance** (☎ 988).

TIPPING
Tax is already included in listed prices. Tips are not included in bills, and a 10% tip is customary. If the service is especially good, tip 15%.

TRAIN TRAVEL
Daily trains link Slovenia with Austria, Italy, Hungary, and Croatia. Many are overnight trains with sleeping compartments (☞ Train Travel *in* Ljubljana Essentials).

The internal rail network is limited, but trains are cheap and efficient (☞ Train Travel *in* regional Essentials sections).

TRAVEL AGENCIES
➤ CONTACTS: **Emona Globtour** (✉ Baragova 5, Llubljana, ☎ 01/588–4400, FAX 01/588–4410, WEB www.emona-globtour.si). **Kompas Turizem Ljubljana** (✉ Pražakova 4, Llubljana, ☎ 01/200–6200, FAX 01/200–6434, WEB www.kompas.si). **Promet T and T** (✉ Celovška 23, Llubljana, ☎ 01/519–3511, FAX 01/519–5345). **Tirtur Ljubljana** (✉ Majorja Lavriča 12, Llubljana, ☎ 01/500–5500, FAX 01/500–5509).

VISITOR INFORMATION
The Slovenian Tourist Board provides information and produces excellent publications on all kinds of tourist activities throughout the country. Each region also has its own tourist information center. For individual centers, *see* Visitor Information *in* regional Essentials sections.
➤ CONTACTS: **Slovenian Tourist Board** (✉ Dunajska 156, Ljubljana, 1000, ☎ 01/189–1840, FAX 01/189–1841, WEB www.slovenia-tourism.si).

10 BACKGROUND AND ESSENTIALS

Further Reading

Vocabulary

FURTHER READING

Since the revolutions of 1989–1990, a number of leading journalists have produced highly acclaimed books detailing the tumultuous changes experienced by Eastern and Central Europeans and the dramatic effects these changes have had on individual lives. Timothy Garten Ash's eyewitness account, *The Magic Lantern: The Revolution of '89 Witnessed in Warsaw, Budapest, Berlin, and Prague,* begins with Václav Havel's ringing words from his 1990 New Year's Address: "People, your government has returned to you!" Winner of both a National Book Award and a Pulitzer Prize, *The Haunted Land* is Tina Rosenberg's wide-ranging, incisive look at how Poland, the Czech Republic, and Slovakia (as well as Germany) are dealing with the memories of 40 years of communism.

Also essential reading is *Balkan Ghosts,* by Robert Kaplan, which traces his journey through the former Yugoslavia, Albania, Romania, Bulgaria, and Greece; it is an often chilling political travelogue that fully deciphers the Balkans' ancient passions and intractable hatred for outsiders. In *Exit into History: A Journey Through the New Eastern Europe,* Eva Hoffman returns to her Polish homeland and five other countries—Hungary, Romania, Bulgaria, the Czech Republic, and Slovakia—and captures the texture of everyday life of a world in the midst of change. Isabel Fonseca's *Bury Me Standing: The Gypsies and Their Journey* is an unprecedented and revelatory look at the Gypsies—or Roma—of Eastern and Central Europe, the large and landless minority whose history and culture have long been obscure.

Travelogues worth reading, though less recent, include Claudio Magris's widely regarded *Danube,* which follows the river as it flows from its source in Germany to its mouth in the Black Sea; Brian Hall's *Stealing from a Deep Place,* a lively account of a solo bicycle trip through Romania and Bulgaria in 1982, followed by a stay in Budapest; Patrick Leigh Fermor's *Between the Woods and the Water,* which relates his 1934 walk through Hungary and Romania and captures life in these lands before their transformation during World War II and under the Soviets. Though its emphasis is on the countries on the eastern side of the Black Sea, Neal Ascherson's widely acclaimed *Black Sea* does touch on Bulgaria and Romania.

Forty-three writers from 16 nations of the former Soviet bloc are included in *Description of a Struggle: The Vintage Book of Contemporary Eastern European Writing,* edited by Michael March. Focusing on novels, poetry, and travel writing, the *Traveller's Literary Companion to Eastern and Central Europe* is a thorough guide to the vast array of literature from this region available in English translation. It includes country-by-country overviews, dozens of excerpts, reading lists, biographical discussions of key writers that highlight their most important works, and guides to literary landmarks. A recent novel about the lure of Eastern Europe for young expatriate Americans is *Prague* by Arthur Phillips.

Bulgaria

Bulgarian writers are less well known than their counterparts in other Eastern and Central European countries. Though their work is not specifically illuminating of Bulgarian life and culture, intellectuals such as Julia Kristeva, Tzvetan Todorov, and Elias Canetti (winner of the 1981 Nobel Prize for Literature, the first Bulgarian to be so honored) are all Bulgarian-born.

Croatia

Although the work of few Croatian writers is well known in the U.S. or available in English, several important authors have been translated. Of contemporary Croatian writers, Dubravka Ugresic is one of the better known. Her novel *In the Jaws of Life* is a warm and funny love story taking place in Zagreb during the 1970s. Another book, *The Museum of Unconditional Surrender,* is a fragmented narrative about contemporary, war-ravaged Eastern Europe. A book of her essays, *A Culture of Lies: Antipolitical Essays,* collects various pieces written after she left Croatia to live in exile in 1993. Slavenka Drakulic, a well-known journalist and feminist in Croatia, has written insightful and sometimes funny essays about the difficulties of post-communist Eastern Europe, particularly her native Croatia. These are collected in *Cafe Europa: Life After Communism.* She is also a novelist; among her novels available in English is *S.: A Novel about the Balkans.* Antun Soljan is another well-known Croatian writer, whose book *A Brief Excursion and Other Stories* has been translated into English. Perhaps the most important contemporary Croatian writer, a contemporary of Tito—not to mention an interesting, politically influential figure—is Miroslav Krieza. His novel *The Return of Philip Latinowicz* is a novel of the inter-war years and an Eastern European classic. Nobel Prize-winner Ivo Adnric, though of Bosnian heritage, is one of the most accomplished and well-known literary figures from the former Yugoslavia. His novel *Bridge on the Drina* depicts the Balkans during the Ottoman rule, which left an important mark on the region as a whole, including Croatia. Finally, the British writer Rebecca West has written a very personal and romantic account of her journey through Yugoslavia in 1937 called *Black Lamb Grey Falcon.*

Several historical works will give insight into the current political situation in Croatia, and indeed to the rest of the former Yugoslav republics. *The Fall of Yugoslavia* by Misha Glenny is an excellent chronicle of the myriad connected, planned, and unplanned events that brought about the war and the dismemberment of Yugoslavia. For a broad overview of the conflict, turn to *The Death of Yugoslavia* by Laura Silber and Alan Little, a book based on their BBC documentary. And for a balanced look at the former Yugoslavian president, turn to *Tito: A Biography* by Jasper Ridley.

Czech Republic

English readers have an excellent range of both fiction and nonfiction about the Czech Republic at their disposal. The most widely read Czech author of fiction in English is probably Milan Kundera, whose well-crafted tales illuminate both the foibles of human nature and the unique tribulations of life in Communist Czechoslovakia. *The Unbearable Lightness of Being* takes a look at the 1968 invasion and its aftermath through the eyes of a strained young couple. *The Book of Laughter and Forgetting* deals in part with the importance of memory and the cruel irony of how it fades over time; Kundera was no doubt coming to terms with his own forgetting as he wrote the book from his Paris exile. *The Joke,* Kundera's earliest work available in English, takes a serious look at the dire consequences of humorlessness among Communists.

Born and raised in the German-Jewish enclave of Prague, Franz Kafka scarcely left the city his entire life. *The Trial* and *The Castle* strongly convey the dread and mystery he detected beneath the 1,000 golden spires of Prague. Kafka worked as a bureaucrat for 14 years, in a job he detested; his books are, at least in part, an indictment of the bizarre bureaucracy of the Austro-Hungarian Empire, though they now seem eerily prophetic of the even crueler and more arbitrary Communist system that was to come.

The most popular Czech authors at the close of the 20th century were those banned by the Communists after the Soviet invasion of 1968. Václav Havel and members of the Charter 77 illegally distributed self-published manuscripts, or *samizdat* as they were called, of these banned authors—among them, Bohumil Hrabel, Josef Škvorecký, and Ivan Klíma. Hrabel, perhaps the most beloved of all Czech writers, never left his homeland; many claim to have shared a table with him at his favorite pub in Prague, U Zlatéyho tygra. His books include *I Served the King of England* and the lyrical *Too Loud a Solitude,* narrated by a lonely man who spends his days in the basement compacting the world's greatest works of literature along with bloodied butcher paper into neat bundles before they get carted off for recycling and disposal. Škvorecký sought refuge and literary freedom in Toronto in the early 1970s. His book *The Engineer of Human Souls* reveals the double censorship of the writer in exile—censored in the country of his birth and unread in his adopted home. Still, Škvorecký did gain a following thanks to his translator, Paul Wilson—who lived in Prague in the 1960s and '70s until he was ousted for his assistance in dissident activities. Wilson also set up 68 Publishers, which is responsible for the bulk of Czech literature translated into English. Novelist, short story writer, and playwright

Ivan Klíma is now one of the most widely read Czech writers in English; his books include the novels *Judge on Trial* and *Love and Garbage*, and *The Spirit of Prague*, a collection of essays about life in the post-Communist Czech Republic.

Václav Havel, onetime dissident playwright turned president of the Czech Republic, is essential nonfiction reading. The best place to start is probably *Living in Truth*, which provides an absorbing overview of his own political philosophy and of Czechoslovak politics and history over the last 30 years. Other recommended books by Havel include *Disturbing the Peace* (a collection of interviews with him) and *Letters to Olga*. Havel's plays explore the absurdities and pressures of life under the former Communist regime; the best example of his absurdist dramas is *The Memorandum*, which depicts a Communist bureaucracy more twisted than the streets of Prague's Old Town.

Among the most prominent of the younger Czech writers is Jáchym Topol, whose *A Visit to the Train Station* documents the creation of a new Prague with a sharp wit that cuts through the false pretenses of American youth occupying the city.

Hungary

Hungarians have played a central role in the intellectual life of the 20th century, although their literary masters are less well known to the West than those who have excelled in other arts, such as Béla Bartok in music and Andre Kertesz and Robert and Cornell Capa in photography.

Novelist and poet Daző Kosztolányi was prominent in European intellectual circles after World War I and was greatly admired by Thomas Mann. His novels, including *Anna Édes* and *Skylark*, are known for their keen psychological insight and social commentary. Also worth discovering is novelist and essayist György Konrád, one of Hungary's leading 20th-century dissidents, whose *The Loser* is a disturbing reflection on intellectual life in a totalitarian state. The English writer Tibor Fischer's novels *Under the Frog* and *The Thought Gang* deal with life in contemporary Hungary. John Lukacs's *Budapest 1900: A Historical Portrait of a City and Its Culture* is an oversize, illustrated study of Hungary's premier city at a particularly important moment in its history. For a more

in-depth look at the city, András Török's *Budapest: A Critical Guide* offers detailed historical and architectural information and is illustrated with excellent drawings.

Poland

For an introduction to Polish history and politics, check out *Heart of Europe: A Short History of Poland*, or the more detailed *God's Playground: A History of Poland*, both by Norman Davies. *The Polish Way* by Adam Zamoyski is another outstanding history of Poland.

Polish classics include the Henryk Sienkiewcz trilogy *With Fire and Sword*, *The Deluge*, and *Fire and the Steppe*, which describes Poland's wars with the Turks, the Sedes, and the Cossacks in the 17th century. *The Doll* by Boleslaw Prus depicts life in 19th century Warsaw.

Bruno Schulz wrote two volumes of stories—*The Street of Crocodiles* and *Sanatorium Under the Sign of the Hourglass*—about life in a Polish *shtetl* before World War II, that, in their fantastical aspect, are not unlike the work of Franz Kafka. Australian Thomas Keneally's *Schindler's List* (originally titled *Schindler's Ark*)—half fiction, half documentary—tells the dramatic, moving story of Oskar Schindler, a German businessman who saved the lives of a thousand Polish Jews. The novel won the Booker Prize; Stephen Spielberg's 1993 Academy Award–winning film based on the book became perhaps the most widely seen movie about the Holocaust. Louis Begley's haunting 1991 *Wartime Lies* is the story of how a young Jewish boy and his aunt manage to stay one step ahead of the Nazis during the war. Tadeusz Borowski's *This Way for the Gas, Ladies and Gentleman* wryly explores the fate of the Jews in Polish concentration camps under the Nazis.

Andrzej Szczypiorski's *The Beautiful Mrs. Seidenman* is a highly praised exploration of the Polish psyche, complex Polish-Jewish history, and notions of East-Central Europe and Polish nationalism. The novelist, essayist, and poet Czesław Miłosz, winner of the Nobel Prize for Literature in 1980, is one of Poland's greatest writers. His major prose works include *Native Realm*, his moral and intellectual autobiography from childhood to the 1950s, and *The Captive Mind*, an exploration of the power of Communist ideology over Polish intellectuals. Another Nobel Prize winner (1996) is poet Wisława Szymborska, and several volumes of her poems have been translated into English. Perhaps the best introduction to her work is *View with a Grain of Sand: Selected Poems*; the first-rate translation is by Stanislaw Baranczak and Clare Cavanagh.

Jerzy Andrzejewski's *Ashes and Diamonds*—the first of a trilogy and the basis for the Andrzej Wajda film of the same name—is a poignant account of Poland in the mid-1940s. Andrzejewski vividly captures this window in Polish history immediately after the war when partisans were still hiding in the fields and before the Soviets and their regime had fully entered the scene. Another excellent book is Eva Hoffman's *Lost in Translation,* an account of her Jewish-Polish childhood and subsequent sense of dislocation when she and her family moved to British Columbia. For lighter reading, Radek Sikorski's *Full Circle* is a personal coming-of-age story set in a small Polish town during the 1970s. Two contemporary coming-of-age novels that beautifully reflect Poland's recent history and the Polish character are *Madame* by Antoni Libera and *Miss Nobody* by Tomek Tryzna.

Romania

Gregor von Rezzori, born in the Bucovina region of Romania to Austrian-German parents, has written two of the most moving memoirs of the 20th century: *Memoirs of an Anti-Semite* and *The Snows of Yesteryear.* Both offer honest and richly detailed recollections of his childhood and young adult life in Romania between the two world wars.

National Public Radio commentator Andrei Codrescu returned to his homeland to witness the December '89 revolution and offers his wry appraisal in *The Hole in the Flag: A Romanian Exile's Story of Return and Revolution.* One of the few Romanian novels available in English is Zaharia Stancu's *Barefoot,* a national classic about a turn-of-the-20th-century peasant uprising. For an outsider's view of the country—one disputed by most Romanians—see Saul Bellow's novel *The Dean's December,* which alternates between Bucharest and Chicago. For profiles of Romania's most famous character, read Radu R. Florescu's *Dracula: Prince of Many Faces* and Raymond T. McNally's *In Search of Dracula,* the first comprehensive histories of the myth and the actual historical figure.

Edward Behr's *Kiss the Hand You Cannot Bite: The Rise and Fall of the Ceauşescus* is a riveting account of the notorious Romanian dictator. *The Land of Green Plums,* by Herta Müller, depicts totalitarianism; it was written in memory of Müller's friends killed during the Ceauşescu regime. Also worth discovering: Norman Manea's *Compulsory Happiness,* an absurdist's view of Romania under Ceauşescu, and his collection of short stories, *October Eight O'clock.*

BULGARIAN VOCABULARY

Bulgarian is written in Cyrillic. The following chart lists only pronunciations written in Roman letters.

English	Pronunciation
Basics	
Yes/no	da/ne
Please	**mol**ya
Thank you (very much)	blago**dar**ya
Excuse me	iz**ven**ete
I'm sorry.	sa**zhal**yavam
Hello, how do you do	**do**bar den
Do you speak English?	go**vor**ite li an**gliy**ski?
I don't speak Bulgarian.	ne go**vor**ya bul**gar**ski
I don't understand.	ne raz**bir**am.
Please speak slowly.	**mol**ya, govo**re**te **bav**no
Please write it down.	**mol**ya vi se, na**pish**ete go
Please show me.	**mol**ya vi se, po**kazh**ete mi
I am American (m/f)	as sum ameri**ka**nets/ameri**kan**ka
I am English (m/f)	as sum angli**chan**in/angli**chan**ka
My name is . . .	**kaz**vam se
Right/left	**dya**sno/**ly**avo
Open/closed	ot**vor**eno/zat**vor**eno
Arrival/departure	**pri**stigane/**za**mina**va**ne
Where is . . . ?	**ka**de e
. . . the station?	. . . **gar**ata
. . . the railroad/train?	. . . zhelez**nits**a/**vla**ku
. . . the bus/tram?	. . . af**to**bus/**tram**vai
. . . the airport?	. . . le**tish**teto
. . . the post office?	. . . **posh**tata?
. . . the bank?	. . . **ban**ka
Stop here	**spre**te tuk
I would like (m/f) . . .	bikh **zhel**al/bikh **zhel**ala
How much does it cost?	**kol**ko **stru**va
Letter/postcard	**pis**mo/**posh**tenska **kart**ichka
By airmail	vaz**dush**na **posh**ta
Help!	**po**mosht
Numbers	
One	**e**din
Two	dva
Three	ri
Four	**che**tiri
Five	pet
Six	shest
Seven	**se**dem
Eight	**os**em
Nine	**de**vet
Ten	**de**set
One hundred	sto
One thousand	**hil**yada

Days of the Week

Sunday	**ned**elya
Monday	po**ned**elnik
Tuesday	**ftor**nik
Wednesday	**sry**ada
Thursday	**chet**vartak
Friday	**pe**tak
Saturday	**sa**bota

Where to Sleep

A room	**sta**ya
The key	**klyu**cha
With bath/shower	sus **ban**ya/dush

Food

A restaurant	restor**ant**
The menu	**kar**tata, **men**yuto
The check, please.	**smet**kata
I'd like to order this	**osh**te **mal**ko
Breakfast	za**kus**ka
Lunch	**o**bed
Dinner	**vech**erya
Bread	hlyab
Butter	**mas**lo
Salt/pepper	sol/**pi**per
Bottle	**but**ika
Red/white wine	**cher**veno/**bya**lo vino
Beer	**bi**ra
(Mineral) Water	(miner**al**na) **vo**da
Milk	mi**ya**ko
Coffee	**ka**fe
Tea (with lemon)	chay (s lim**on**)
Chocolate	za**har**
Plum brandy	**sli**vova

CROATIAN VOCABULARY

	English	Croatian	Pronunciation
Basics			
	Yes/no	Da/ne	dah/neh
	Please	Molim (vas)	**moh**-leem (vahs)
	Thank you (very much)	Hvala (lijepo)	**hvah**-lah (lyeh-poh)
	Excuse me	Oprostite	oh-proh-stee-teh
	Hello	Zdravo	**zdrah**-voh
	I'm sorry.	Žao mi je.	**zhah**-oh mee yeh
	Do you speak English?	Da li govorite engleski?	Dah lee **goh**-voh-ree-teh **ehn**-glehs-kee
	I don't understand.	Ne razumijem.	neh rah-**zoo**-myehm
	Please show me . . .	Molim vas, pokažite mi . . .	moh-leem vahs, **poh**-kah-zhee-teh mee

I am American (m/f).	Ja sam Amerikanac (Amerikanka).	yah sahm **ah**-meh-ree-kah-nahts **ah**-meh-ree-kahn-kah
My name is . . .	Zovem se . . .	**zoh**-vehm seh
Right/left	Desno/Lijevo	**dehs**-noh/**lyeh**-voh
Open/closed	Otvoreno/zatvoreno	**oh**-tvoh-reh-noh/ **zah**-tvoh-reh-noh
Where is . . . ?	Gdje je . . . ?	gdyeh yeh
. . . the train station?	. . . željeznička? stanica/kolodvor	**zheh**-lehz-neech-kah **stah**-neet-sah/**koh**-loh-dvohr
. . . the bus stop?	. . . autobusna stanica?	**ahoo**-toh-boos-nah **stah**-nee-tsah
. . . the airport?	. . . aerodrom?	**ah**-eh-roh-drohm
. . . the post office?	. . . pošta?	**posh**-tah
. . . the bank?	. . . banka?	**bahn**-kah
Here/there	Ovdje/tamo	**ohv**-dyeh/**tah**-moh
I would like. . .	Molim (vas). . . / Htio/htjela bih. . . (m/f)	**moh**-leem (vahs)/ hteeoh/htyeh-lah beeh
How much does it cost?	Koliko košta?	**koh**-lee-koh **kosh**-tah
Postcard	Razglednica	**rahz**-gleh-dnee-tsah
Help!	Upomoć!	**oo**-poh-moch

Numbers

One	Jedan	**yeh**-dahn
Two	Dva	dvah
Three	Tri	tree
Four	Četiri	**cheh**-tee-ree
Five	Pet	peht
Six	Šest	shest
Seven	Sedam	**seh**-dahm
Eight	Osam	**oh**-sahm
Nine	Devet	**deh**-veht
Ten	Deset	**deh**-seht
One hundred	Sto	stoh
One thousand	Tisuća	**tee**-soo-chah

Days of the Week

Sunday	Nedjelja	**neh**-dyeh-lyah
Monday	Ponedjeljak	**poh**-neh-dyeh-lyahk
Tuesday	Utorak	**oo**-toh-rahk
Wednesday	Srijeda	**sryeh**-dah
Thursday	Četvrtak	**cheht**-vruh-tahk
Friday	Petak	**peh**-tahk
Saturday	Subota	**soo**-boh-tah

Where to Sleep

A room	Soba	**soh**-bah
The key	Ključ	klyooch
With bath/shower	S kupaonicom/ tušem	suh koo-pah-**oh**-nee-tsohm/ **too**-shehm

Food

A restaurant	Restoran	rehs-**toh**-rahn
The menu	Jelovnik	yeh-**lohv**-neek
The check, please.	Molim, račun.	**moh**-leem, **rah**-choon
Can I order, please?	Mogu li	**moh**-goo lee
	naručiti,	nah-**roo**-chee-tee,
	molim vas?	moh-leem vahs
Breakfast	Doručak	**doh**-roo-chahk
Lunch	Ručak	**roo**-chahk
Dinner	Večera	**veh**-cheh-rah
Bread	Kruh	krooh
Butter	Putar/maslac	**poo**-tahr/mahs-lahts
Salt/pepper	Sol/papar	sohl/**pah**-pahr
Wine	Vino	**vee**-noh
Beer	Pivo	**pee**-voh
Water/mineral water	Voda/	**voh**-dah/
	mineralna voda	**mee**-neh-rahl-nah **voh**-dah
Milk	Mlijeko	**mlyeh**-koh
Coffee	Kava	**kah**-vah
Tea	Čaj	chay

CZECH VOCABULARY

English	Czech	Pronunciation

Basics

Yes/no	Ano/ne	**ah**-no/neh
Please	Prosím	**pro**-seem
Thank you	Děkuji	**dyek**-oo-yee
Pardon me	Pardon	**par**-don
Hello.	Dobrý den	**dob**-ree den
Do you speak English?	Mluvíte anglicky?	**mloo**-vit-eh ahng-**glit**-ski?
I don't speak Czech.	Nemluvím česky.	nem-**luv**-eem ches-ky
I don't understand.	Nerozumím.	neh-rohz-**oom**-eem
Please speak slowly.	Prosím, mluvte pomalu.	**pro**-seem, **mloov**-teh poh-**mah**-lo
Please write it down.	Prosím napište.	**pro**-seem nah-**peesh**
Show me.	Ukažte mně.	oo-**kazh**-te mnye
I am American (m/f)	Jsem američan/ američanka	sem ah-**mer**-i-chan/ ah-mer-i-**chan**-ka
English (m/f)	Angličan/angličanka	**ahn**-gli-chan/Ahn-gli-**chan**-ka
My name is . . .	Jmenuji se . . .	**ymen** weh-seh
On the right/left	Napravo/nalevo	na-**pra**-vo/na-**leh**-vo
Arrivals	Přílety	**pshee**-leh-tee
Where is . . . ?	Kde je . . . ?	g'deh yeh
. . . the station?	. . . Nádraží?	nah-**drah**-zee
. . . the train?	. . . Vlak?	vlahk
. . . the bus/tram?	. . . Autobus/tramvaj?	**out**-oh-boos/**tram**-vie
. . . the airport?	. . . Letiště?	**leh**-tish-tyeh
. . . the post office?	. . . Pošta?	**po**-shta
. . . the bank?	. . . Banka?	**bahn**-ka
Stop here	Zastavte tady	**zah**-stahv-teh **tah**-dee

I would like (m/f) . . .	Chtěl (chtěla) bych . . .	kh'tyel (**kh'tyel**-ah) bihk
How much does it cost?	Kolik to stoji?	ko-**lik** toh **stoy**-ee
Letter/postcard	Dopis/pohlednice	doh-**pis**-ee/poh-**hled**-nit-seh
By airmail	Letecky	**leh**-tet-skee
Help!	Pomoc!	**po**-motz

Numbers

One	Jeden	ye-**den**
Two	Dva	dvah
Three	Tři	tshree
Four	Čtyři	ch'**ti**-zhee
Five	Pět	pyet
Six	Šest	shest
Seven	Sedm	**sed**-oom
Eight	Osm	**oh**-soom
Nine	Devět	**deh**-vyet
Ten	Deset	**deh**-set
One hundred	Sto	stoh
One thousand	Tisíc	**tee**-seets

Days of the Week

Sunday	Neděle	**neh**-dyeh-leh
Monday	Pondělí	**pon**-dye-lee
Tuesday	Žterý	**oo**-teh-ree
Wednesday	Středa	**stshreh**-da
Thursday	Čtvrtek	ch't'v'**r**-tek
Friday	Pátek	**pah**-tek
Saturday	Sobota	**so**-boh-ta

Where to Sleep

A room	Pokoj	**poh**-koy
The key	Klíč	kleech
With bath/shower	S koupelnou/sprcha	s'**ko**-pel-noh/**sp'r**-kho

Food

The menu	Jídelní lístek	**yee**-dell-nee **lis**-tek
The check, please.	Učet, prosím.	**oo**-chet **pro**-seem
Breakfast	Snídaně	**snyee**-dan-ye
Lunch	Oběd	**ob**-yed
Dinner	Večeře	**ve**-cher-zhe
Bread	Chléb	khleb
Butter	Máslo	**mah**-slo
Salt/pepper	Sůl/pepř	sool/pepsh
Bottle	Láhev	**lah**-hev
Red/white wine	Červené/bílé víno	**cher**-ven-eh/**bee**-leh **vee**-no
Beer	Pivo	**piv**-oh
Mineral water	Minerálka voda	min-eh-**rahl**-ka **vo**-da
Milk	Mléko	**mleh**-koh
Coffee	Káva	**kah**-va
Tea (with lemon)	Čaj (s citrónem)	tchai (se tsi-**tro**-nem)

HUNGARIAN VOCABULARY

English	Hungarian	Pronunciation

Basics

Yes/no	Igen/nem	**ee**-gen/nem
Please	Kérem	**kay**-rem
Thank you (very much)	Köszönöm (szépen)	**kuh**-suh-num (**seh**-pen)
Excuse me	Bocsánat	**boh**-chah-not
I'm sorry.	Sajnálom.	**shahee**-nah-lome
Hello/how do you do	Szervusz	**sair**-voose
Do you speak English?	Beszél angolul?	**bess**-el **on**-goal-ool
I don't speak Hungarian.	Nem tudok magyarul.	nem **too**-dock **muh**-jor-ool
I don't understand.	Nem értem.	nem **air**-tem
Please speak slowly.	Kérem, beszéljen lassan.	**kay**-rem, **bess**-el-yen lush-shun
Please write it down.	Kérem, írja fel.	**kay**-rem, **eer**-yuh fell
Please show me.	Megmutatná nekem.	meg-**moo**-taht-nah **neh**-kem
I am American.	Amerikai vagyok.	uh-**meh**-rick-ka-ee **vud**-yoke
I am English.	Angol vagyok.	**un**-goal **vud**-yoke
My name is . . .	Vagyok . . .	**vud**-yoke
Right/left	Bal/jobb	buhl/yobe
Open/closed	nyitva/zárva	**nit**-va/**zahr**-voh
Arrival/departure	Érkezés/indulás	**er**-keh-zesh/**in**-dool-ahsh
Where is . . . ?	Hol van . . . ?	hole vun
. . . the train station?	. . . a pályaudvar?	uh pah-yo-**oot**-var
. . . the bus station?	. . . a buszállomás?	uh **boose**-ahlo-mahsh
. . . the bus stop?	. . . a megálló?	uh **meg**-all-oh
. . . the airport?	. . . A repülőtér?	uh rep-ewluh-**tair**
. . . the post office?	. . . a pósta?	uh **pohsh**-tuh
. . . the bank?	. . . a bank?	uh bonhk
Stop here	Tlljon meg itt	**all**-yon meg it
I would like . . .	Szeretnék . . .	**sair**-et-neck
How much does it cost?	Mennyibe kerül?	**men**-yibe kair-**ule**
Letter/postcard	levél/képeslap	**lev**-ehl/**kay**-pesh-lup
By airmail	Légi póstaval	**lay**-gee **pohsh**-tuh-vol
Help!	Segítség!	**shay**-geet-shaig

Numbers

One	Egy	edge
Two	Kettő	**ket**-tuh
Three	Három	**hah**-rome
Four	Négy	**nay**-ge
Five	Öt	ut
Six	Hat	huht
Seven	Hét	hate
Eight	Nyolc	nyolts
Nine	Kilenc	**kee**-lents
Ten	Tíz	teez

| One hundred | Száz | sahz |
| One thousand | Ezer | **eh**-zer |

Days of the Week

Sunday	Vasárnap	**vuh**-shar-nup
Monday	Hétfő	**hate**-fuh
Tuesday	Kedd	ked
Wednesday	Szerda	**ser**-duh
Thursday	Csütörtök	**chew**-tur-tuk
Friday	Péntek	**pain**-tek
Saturday	Szombat	**som**-but

Where to Sleep

A room	Egy szobá	edge **soh**-bah
The key	A kulcsot	uh **koolch**-oat
With bath/a shower	Fúrdőszo-bával/ egy zuhany	**fure**-duh-soh-bah-vul/ edge **zoo**-hon

Food

A restaurant	A vendéglő/ az étterem	uh **ven**-deh-gluh/ uz **eht**-teh-rem
The menu	A étlap	uh **ate**-lop
The check, please.	A számlát kérem.	uh **sahm**-lot **kay**-rem
I'd like to order this.	Kéem ezt.	**kay**-rem etz
Breakfast	Reggeli	**reg**-gell-ee
Lunch	Ebéd	**eb**-ehd
Dinner	Vacsora	**votch**-oh-rah
Bread	Kenyér	**ken**-yair
Butter	Vaj	voy
Salt/pepper	Só/bors	show/borsh
Bottle	Üveg	**ew**-veg
Red/white wine	Vörös/fehér bor	**vuh**-ruhsh/**feh**-hehr **bor**
Beer	Sör	shur
Water/mineral water	Víz/kristályvíz	veez/**krish**-tah-ee-veez
Milk	Tej	tay
Coffee (with milk)	Kávé/tejeskávé	**kah**-vay/**tey**-esh-**kah**-vay
Tea (with lemon)	Tea (citrommal)	**tay**-oh **tsit**-rome-mol
Chocolate	Csokoládé	chaw-kaw-**law**-day

POLISH VOCABULARY

English	Polish	Pronunciation

Basics

Yes/no	Tak/nie	tahk/nye
Please	Proszę	**pro**-sheh
Thank you	Dziękuję	dzhen-**koo**-yeh
Excuse me	Przepraszam	psheh-**prah**-shahm
Hello	Dzień dobry	**dzhehn dohb**-ry
Do you (m/f) speak English?	Czy pan (pani) mówi po angielsku?	chee **pahn** (**pahn**-ee) **gyel**-skuu?
I don't speak Polish.	Nie mówi po Polsku.	nyeh **moohv**-yeh po-**pohl**-skoo

I don't understand.	Nie rozumiem.	nyeh rohz-**oo**-myehm
Please speak slowly.	Proszę mówić wolniej.	proh-sheh **moo**-veech **vohl**-nyah
Please write it down.	Proszę napisać.	proh-sheh nah-pee-sahtch
I am American (m/f)	Jestem Amerykani-nem/Amerykanką	**yest**-em ah-mer-i-**kahn**-in-em/ ah-mer-i-**kahn**-ka
English (m/f)	Anglikiem/Angielką	ahn-**gleek**-em/ ahn-**geel**-ka
My name is . . .	Nazywam się . . .	nah-**ziv**-ahm sheh
On the right/left	Na prawo/lewo	nah-**prah**-vo/**lyeh**-vo
Arrivals/departures	Przyloty/odloty	pshee-**loh**-tee/ ohd-**loh**-tee
Where is . . . ?	Gdzie jest . . . ?	gdzhyeh yest
. . . the station?	. . . Dworzec kolejowy?	**dvoh**-zhets koh-lay-oh-vee
. . . the train?	. . . Pociąg?	**poh**-chohnk
. . . the bus?	. . . Autobus?	a'oo-**toh**-boos
. . . the airport?	. . . Lotnisko?	loht-**nees**-koh
. . . the post office?	. . . Poczta?	**poch**-tah
. . . the bank?	. . . Bank?	bahnk
Stop here, please.	Proszę się to zatrzymać.	**proh**-sheh sheh too zah-**tchee**-nahch
I would like (m/f) . . .	Chciałbym . . . / Chciałabym . . .	**kh'chow**-beem/ kh'chow-**ah**-beem
How much?	Ile?	**ee**-leh
Letters/postcards	Listy/kartki	**lees**-tee/**kahrt**-kee
By airmail	Lotniczy	loht-**nee**-chee
Help!	Na pomoc!	na **po**-motz

Numbers

One	Jeden	**yeh**-den
Two	Dwa	dvah
Three	Trzy	tchee
Four	Cztery	**chteh**-ree
Five	Pięć	pyehnch
Six	Sześć	shsyshch
Seven	Siedem	**shyeh**-dem
Eight	Osiem	**oh**-shyem
Nine	Dziewięć	**dzhyeh**-vyehnch
Ten	Dziesięć	**dzhyeh**-shehnch
One hundred	Sto	stoh
One thousand	Tysiąc	**tee**-shonch

Days of the Week

Sunday	Niedziela	nyeh-**dzhy'e**-la
Monday	Poniedsiałek	poh-nyeh-**dzhya**-wek
Tuesday	Wtrorek	**ftohr**-ek
Wednesday	Środa	**shroh**-da
Thursday	Czwartek	**chvahr**-tek
Friday	Piątek	**pyohn**-tek
Saturday	Sobota	soh-**boh**-ta

Where to Sleep

A room	Pokój	**poh**-kooy
The key	Klucz	klyuch
With bath/shower	Złazienką/ prysznicem	zwah-**zhen**-koh/ spree-**shnee**-tsem

Food

The menu	Menu	**men**-yoo
The check, please.	Proszę rachunek	**proh**-sheh rah-**kh'oon**-ehk
Breakfast	Śnidanie	shnya-**dahn**-iyeh
Lunch	Obiad	**oh**-byat
Dinner	Kolacja	koh-**lah**-ts'yah
Beef	Mołowina	voh-woh-**veen**-a
Bread and butter	Chleb i masłło	kh'lyep ee **mahs**-woh
Vegetables	Jarzyny	yah-**zhin**-ee
Salt/pepper	Sół/pieprz	soow/pyehpsh
Bottle of wine	Butelkę wina	boo-**tehl**-keh **vee**-na
Beer	Piwo	**pee**-voh
(Mineral) Water	Wodę (mineralną)	**voh**-deh (**mee-nehr**-ahl-nohn
Coffee with milk	Kawę z mliekem	**kah**-veh **zmleyeh**-kem
Tea with lemon	Herbaté z cytryną	kh'ehr-**bah**-teh **ststrin**-ohn

ROMANIAN VOCABULARY

English	Romanian	Pronunciation

Basics

Yes/no	Da/nu	dah/noo
Please	Vă rog	vuh **rohg**
Thank you	Vă mulţumesc	vuh **mull**-tsoo-mesk
Excuse me	Scuzaţi-mă	skoo-**zatz**-see-muh
I'm sorry.	Îmi pare rău.	uhm pah-ray **ruh**-oo
Hello/how do you do	Bună ziua	boo-nuh **zee**-wah
Do you speak English?	Vorbiţî engleză?	vor-**beetz** ehn-**glehz**-uh
I don't speak Romanian.	Nu vorbesc româ neşte.	noo vor-**besk** roh-muh-**nesh**-tay
I don't understand.	Nu înţeleg.	noo uhn-tseh-**lehgah**
Please speak slowly.	Vorbiţi rar.	vor-**beetz** rahr
Please write it down.	Scrieţi, vă rog.	skree-ets vuh **rohg**
Please show me.	Indicaţi-mi, vă rog.	een-dee-**caht**-zee-mee, vuh **rohg**
I am American (m/f)	Sunt american/ americană	suhnt ah-mehr-ee-**cahn**/ah-mer-ee-**cahn**-nah
I am English (m/f)	Sunt englez/engleză	suhnt ehn-**glehz**/ ehn-**glehz**-uh
My name is . . .	Mă numesc	muh noo-**mesk**
Right/left	Dreapta/stânga	**dryahp**-tah/**stuhn**-gah
Open/closed	Deschis/închis	deh-**skees**/uhn-**kees**
Arrivals/departures	Sosiri/plecări	soh-**seer**-ih/pleh-**cuhr**-ih

Where is . . . ?	Unde este . . . ?	**uhn**-day **ehs**-tay
. . . the station?	. . . gara/stație?	**gah**-ruh/**staht**-zee-ay
. . . the train?	. . . trenul?	**treh**-nul
. . . the bus/tram?	. . . autobuz/tramvai?	ahu-to-**booz**/ trahm-**viy**
. . . the airport?	. . . aeroportul?	air-oh-**por**-tull
. . . the post office?	. . . poștă?	**pahsh**-tah
. . . a bank?	. . . o bancă?	oh **bahn**-kuh
Stop here.	Opriți aici.	oh-**preetz** ah-**eech**
I would like . . .	Aș doresc . . .	ahsh dor-**rehsk**
How much does it cost?	Cît costă?	cuht **cohs**-tuh
a letter/postcard	o scrisoare/carte poștală	oh scree-**swahr**-ray/ **kahr**-tay pohsh-**tah**-luh
By airmail	par avion	par ah-vee-**ohn**
Help!	Ajutor!	ah-**zhoo**-tore

Numbers

One	Unu	**uh**-nuh
Two	Doi	doy
Three	Trei	tray
Four	Patru	**paht**-ruh
Five	Cinci	**cheench**
Six	Șase	**shah**-say
Seven	Șapte	**shahp**-tay
Eight	Opt	**ohpt**
Nine	Nouă	**noh**-oo-uh
Ten	Zece	**zeh**-chay
One hundred	O sută	oh **soo**-tuh
One thousand	O mie	oh **mee**-ay

Days of the Week

Sunday	Duminică	duh-**mih**-nih-kuh
Monday	Luni	**luh**-nih
Tuesday	Marți	**mahrts**
Wednesday	Miercuri	**meer**-kurih
Thursday	Joi	zhoy
Friday	Vineri	**vee**-nehrih
Saturday	Sîmbătă	**suhm**-buh-tuh

Where to Sleep

A room	O cameră	oh **kah**-meh-ruh
The key	Cheia	**kay**-ah
With bath/with shower	Cu baie/duș	koo **bah**-yeh/**doosh**

Food

A restaurant	Un restaurant	uhn rehs-tau-**rahnt**
The menu	Meniul, lista	meh-nee-ool/ **lees**-tah
The check, please.	Plata, vă rog.	**plah**-tah, **vuh** rahg
I'd like to order this.	Aș vrea să comand acesta.	ahsh **vryah** suh coh-**mahnd** ah-**ches**-tah
Breakfast	Micul dejun	**mee**-kuhl deh-**zhoon**
Lunch	Dejun, prînz	deh-**zhoon**/ prunz
Dinner	cina	**chee**-nuh

Bread	pâine	**puhee**-nuh
Butter	Unt	uhnt
Salt/pepper	Sare/piper	**sah**-ray/**pih**-pair
a bottle	O sticlă	oh **steek**-luh
Red/white wine	Vin roşu/alb	veen **roh**-shoo/**ahlb**
Beer	bere	**bare**-ay
(Mineral) Water	Apă (minerală)	**ah**-puh (meen-eh-**rahl**-uh)
Milk	Lapte	**lahp**-tay
coffee (with milk)	cafea (cu lapte)	**cah**-fyah(koo **lahp**-tay)
tea (with lemon)	Ceai (cu lămîie)	**chiy**-ih (koo luh-**muh**-yeh)
Chocolate	Cacao	kah-**cah**-oh
plum brandy	Ţuică	tsooee-kuh

SLOVAK VOCABULARY

English	Slovak	Pronunciation
Basics		
Yes/No	Ano/Nie	ah-no/nee-ay
Please	Prosím	**pro**-seem
Thank you (very much)	Ďakujem	**dyak**-we-em
Pardon me	Pardon	**par**-don
Hello	Dobry deň	**dob**-ree den
Do you speak English?	Hovorite anglicky?	ho-vor-**ee**-teh **an**-glits-kay
I don't speak Slovak.	Nehovorim po slovensky.	**nay**-ho-vor-eem po **sloh**-ven-skee
I don't understand.	Nerozumiem.	**nay**-roz-ooh-me-em
Please, speak slowly.	Hovorte prosím pomaly.	ho-vor-**ee**-teh **pro**-seem po-mal-**ee**
Please, write it down.	Napište mi to prosím.	nah-**peesh**-tay mee toh **pro**-seem
Show me . . .	Ukažte mi . . .	**ooh**-kazh-tay mee
I am American (m/f).	Som Američan/ Američanka.	sum ah-**mer**-ee-chan/ ah-**mer**-ee-chan-ka
My name is . . .	Volam sa ...	vo-**lam** sah
On the right/left	Napravo/nalavo	na-**prah**-vo/ na-**lahv**-oh
Arrivals	Prichody (trains, buses),	**pree**-ho-dee,
	Prilety (planes)	**pree**-let-ee
Where is . . . ?	Kde je . . .	g'deh yeh
. . . the station?	. . . stanica?	**stan**-eet-sa
. . . the train?	. . . vlak?	vlahk
. . . he tram?	. . . električka?	ee-lek-**treech**-ka
. . . the airport?	. . . letisko?	let-**ee**-sko
. . . the post office?	. . . poš	**o**-shta
. . . the bank?	. . . banka?	**bahn**-ka
Stop here.	Zastavte tu.	zah-**stahv**-teh too
I would like (m/f) . . .	Chcel by som/ Chcela by som	huh'cell bee sum/ huh'cel-la bee sum
How much does it cost?	Koľko to stoji?	koal-**koh** toh **stoy**-ee

Letter/postcard	List/pohľadnica	eest/poh-lahd-neet-sa
By airmail	Letecky	**leh**-tet-skee
Help!	Pomoc!	**po**-mots

Numbers

One	Jeden	**ye**-den
Two	Dva	dvah
Three	Tri	tree
Four	Štyri	**shteer**-ee
Five	Peť	pet
Six	Šesť	shest
Seven	Sedem	**sed**-em
Eight	Osem	**oh**-sem
Nine	Deveť	**dehv**-et
Ten	Desať	**deh**-saht
One hundred	Sto	stoh
One thousand	Tisíc	**tee**-seets

Days of the Week

Sunday	Nedeľa	**neyd**-yel-ha
Monday	Pondelok	**pahn**-dyel-ahk
Tuesday	Utorok	**ooh**-tehr-ahk
Wednesday	Streda	**strey**-dah
Thursday	Štvrtok	**sht'ver**-tahk
Friday	Piatok	**pee**-ah-tahk
Saturday	Sobota	**so**-boh-ta

Where to Sleep

A room	Izba	**eez**-bah
The key	Kľuč	klooh'ch
With bath/shower	S kupeľňou	s'kooh-pel-**nyu**

Food

Menu	Jedálny listok	ye-**dahl**-nee **lees**-tahk
The check, please.	Učet, prosím.	**oo**-chet **pro**-seem
Breakfast	Raňajky	rah-**nyike**-ee
Lunch	Obed	oh-bed
Dinner	Večera	**vah**'chair-a
Bread	Chlieb	huh'lee'eb
Butter	Máslo	**mah**-slo
Salt/pepper	Soľ/Korenie	sol/**kor**-en-yee
Bottle	Flaša	**flah**-sha
Red/white wine	Červené/biele vino	**cher**-ven-eh/**bee**-al-ee **vee**-no
Beer	Pivo	**piv**-oh
Mineral water	Minerálka voda	min-eh-**rahl**-ka **vo**-da
Milk	Mlieko	**m'lee'eck**-oh
Coffee	Káva	**kah**-va
Tea (with lemon)	Čaj (s citrónem)	tchai (se tsi-**tro**-nem)

SLOVENIAN VOCABULARY

English	Slovenian	Pronunciation

Basics

English	Slovenian	Pronunciation
Yes/no	Da/ne	dah/nay
Please	Prosim	**proh**-seem
Thank you (very much)	Hvala (lepa)	**hvah**-lah (**lay**-pah)
Excuse me	Oprostite	oh-pros-**tee**-tay
I'm sorry	Žal mi je	zh-**ow** mee yay
Hello/how do you do	Dober dan	**doh**-boo dan
Do you speak English?	Govorite angleško?	goh-vor-**ee**-tay ang-**lay**-shkoh
I don't speak Slovenian.	Ne govorim slovensko.	nay goh-vor-**eem** sloh-**ven**-skoh
I don't understand.	Ne razumem.	nay raz-**oom**-em
Please speak slowly.	Prosim, govorite počasi.	**proh**-seem, goh-vor-**ee**-tay poh-**chah**-see
Please write it down.	Prosim, napišite.	**proh**-seem, nah-**pee**-shee-tay
Please show me.	Prosim, pokažite.	**proh**-seem, poh-**kah**-zhee-tay
I am American	Jaz sem američan	yoo sum ah-mer-ee-**chan**
I am English	Jaz sem anglež	yoo sum ang-**lezh**
My name is . . .	Ime mi je . . .	ee-**may** mee yay . . .
Right/left	Desno/levo	**des**-noh/ **lee**-voh
Open/closed	Odprt/zaprt	**od**-prt/ **za**-prt
Arrival/departure	Prihod/odhod	pree-**hod**/ od-**hod**
Where is . . . ?	Kje je . . . ?	k-**yay** yay . . . ?
. . . the train station?	. . . železniška postaja?	zheh-**lay**-zneesh-kah post-**ay**-ah
. . . the bus stop?	. . . avtobusna postaja?	aw-toh-**boos**-nah post-**ay**-ah
. . . the airport?	. . . letališče?	let-al-**ee**-shuh-cheh
. . . the post office?	. . . pošta?	**poh**-shtah
. . . the bank?	. . . banka?	**ban**-kah
Stop here	Vstavi tukaj	uh-**stah**-vee **took**-ay
I would like . . .	Hotel bi . . .	hot-**ay**-oo bee . . .
How much does it cost?	Koliko stane?	**koh**-lee-koh **stah**-nay
Letter/postcard	Pismo/dopisnica	**pee**-smoh/doh-**pee**-snee-tsah
By airmail	Zračna pošta	**zrah**-chnah **poh**-shtah
Help!	Na pomoč!	nah poh-**moch**

Numbers

English	Slovenian	Pronunciation
One	Ena	enah
Two	Dva	dvah
Three	Tri	tree
Four	Štiri	**shtee**-ree
Five	Pet	pit
Six	Šest	shest
Seven	Sedem	**sed**-em
Eight	Osem	**oh**-sem

Nine	Devet	deh-**vit**
Ten	Deset	deh-**sit**
One hundred	Sto	stoh
Two hundred	Dve sto	dvee stoh

Days of the Week

Monday	Ponedeljek	poh-neh-**dee**-lyek
Tuesday	Torek	**tor**-ek
Wednesday	Sreda	**sree**-dah
Thursday	Četrtek	**chet**-rtek
Friday	Petek	**pee**-tek
Saturday	Sobota	soh-**boh**-tah
Sunday	Nedelja	nay-**dee**-lyah

Where to Sleep

A room	Soba	**soh**-bah
The key	Ključ	kluh-**yooch**
With bath/a shower	s kopanicu/s prho	skoh-pan-**ee**-tsoo/ **spruh**-hoh

Food

Restaurant	Restavracija	rest-aw-**rats**-ee-yah
The menu	Jedilnik	yed-**eel**-nik
The check, please.	Prosim, račun.	**proh**-seem, rach-**oon**
Breakfast	Zajtrk	**zay**-trik
Lunch	Kosilo	kos-**eel**-oh
Dinner	Obed	oh-**bed**
Bread	Kruh	kroo
Butter	Maslo	**mas**-loh
Salt/pepper	Sol/poper	sol/**poh**-per
Bottle	Steklenica	stek-len-**ee**-tsah
Red/white wine	Črno/belo vino	chur-noh/bel-oh **vee**-noh
Beer	Pivo	**pee**-voh
Water/mineral water	Voda/mineralna voda	**voh**-dah/min-er-**al**-nah **voh**-dah
Milk	Mleko	**mlih**-koh
Coffee (with milk)	Kava z mlekom	**kah**-vah **zmlih**-kom
Tea (with lemon)	Čaj z limono	chay zleem-**on**-oh

INDEX

Icons and Symbols

★ Our special recommen-
dations

✕ Restaurant

☒ Lodging establishment

✕☒ Lodging establishment
whose restaurant war-
rants a special trip

☺ Good for kids (rubber
duck)

☞ Sends you to another
section of the guide for
more information

⊠ Address

☎ Telephone number

☉ Opening and closing
times

☒ Admission prices

✍ Sends you to
www.fodors.com/urls
for up-to-date links to
the property's Web site

Numbers in white and black
circles ③ ❸ that appear on
the maps, in the margins, and
within the tours correspond
to one another.

A

Academy of Sciences, 267
Adam Mickiewicz Museum of
Literature, 384, 385
Adio Mare, Korcula ✕, 5
Adriatic Coast. ☞ Karst
Region and the Adriatic
Coast
Aggtelek, 349
Agricultural Museum, 274
Air travel, x
Bulgaria, 29–30, 39–40, 48
Croatia, 71, 96, 109, 111–112
Czech Republic, 178–179,
228, 233
Hungary, 296–297, 366
Poland, 408–409, 425–426,
454, 464, 466
Romania, 486–487, 491, 494,
500, 501
Slovakia, 521, 531, 538, 539,
174
Slovenia, 561, 577
Airports, xii
Aladja Rock Monastery,
36–37
Albena, 37
Alef Café ✕, 420
Aleš Art Gallery, 194
Alexander Nevski Memorial
Cathedral, 8, 21, 22

All Saints' Chapel (Prague),
149
American Embassy
(Budapest), 267
Andrássy Út, 270–274
Angel Pharmacy Museum,
329
Angelika ✕, 260
Anthony's Shaft, 571
Apartment and villa rentals,
xxv
Apollonia Arts Festival, 39
Aquarium, 80
Aquincum, 276, 277
Aranysárkány, Szentendre
✕, 6
Arboretum, 462
Arch of Triumph, 477
Archaeological Museum, 66
Archaeology Park, 490
Archdiocesan Museum
(Kraków), 418
Archdiocesan Museum
(Wrocław), 458
Arkada Hotel, Levoča ☒, 7
Árpád Tóth Promenade, 251,
254
Arsenal Museum, 443
Art galleries. ☞ Also
Museums
Bulgaria, 23,
Croatia, 64, 66, 67, 89, 91
Czech Republic, 135, 142–
143, 158
Hungary, 252, 302, 359
Poland, 390, 408, 440
Slovakia, 515, 517
Slovenia, 555
Artists' Promenade, 262
Arts and Crafts Museum, 66,
67
Artus Mansion, 449
AS, Ljubljana ✕, 6
Astronomical clocks
Prague, 131
Wrocław, 456
At the Red Eagle, 139
At the Three Fiddles, 139
Athenée Palace Hilton,
Bucharest ☒, 7
ATMs, xxvii
Auschwitz and Birkenau, 10,
430–431
Auschwitz and Birkenau State
Museum, 430
Austerlitz, 229
Avas Church, 321

B

Bačvice Bay, 95
Badacsony, 319–321
Balaton Pantheon, 315
Balatonfüred, 314–317
Balatonudvari, 319

Balčik, 37
Balčik Palace, 37
Ballooning, 323
Balkan Range, 3
Ban Jelačić Square, 35
Banská Bystrica, 524–525
Banská Štiavnica, 525–526
Bansko, 46
Banya Bashi Mosque, 21, 22
Baraka, Budapest ✕, 6
Barbakan (Kraków), 413
Barbakan (Warsaw), 384,
385
Bardejov, 12, 536–537
Baroque fountains
(Olomouc), 231
Bârsana, 12
Basilica, 344
Batenberg Palace, 44
Bathhouse (Krynica), 436
Batthyány tér, 260
Beaches
Bulgaria, 37–38
Croatia, 95
Hungary, 243, 316, 321, 323
Bed and breakfasts, xxv
Beekeeping Museum, 566
Beer industry
Czech Republic, 204
Hungary, 246
Belvedere Palace, 393
Belvedere, Warsaw ✕, 6
Bem József tér, 260
Benedictine Abbey (Tyniec),
431
Benedictine Abbey and
Museum (Tihany
Peninsula), 317
Bethlehem Chapel, 127, 128
Bicycling, xii–xiii
Czech Republic, 119
Hungary, 291, 305, 311, 316,
343, 346, 347, 366
Poland, 380, 434
Slovakia, 509, 539
Slovenia, 546, 564, 569, 570
Bilíkova chata, 526
Birkenau, 430–431
Bishop's Palace, 313
Bishop Gregory of Nin, 92
Biserica din Deal, 9
Biserica din Sjes, 9
Biskupin, 462
Black Church, 496
Black Sea Coast and Danube
Delta (Romania), 5, 489–
495
car rental, 491
dining, 491
emergencies, 492
lodging, 489, 491
tours, 492
transportation, 491, 492
travel agencies, 492
visitor information, 492